Encyclopedia of Western Colonialism since 1450

FIRST EDITION

Encyclopedia of Western Colonialism since 1450

FIRST EDITION

VOLUME 1
A-E

Thomas Benjamin
EDITOR IN CHIEF

MACMILLAN REFERENCE USA
An imprint of Thomson Gale, a part of The Thomson Corporation

THOMSON

GALE

Detroit • New York • San Francisco • San Diego • New Haven, Conn. • Waterville, Maine • London • Munich

Encyclopedia of Western Colonialism since 1450

Thomas Benjamin, Editor in Chief

© 2007 Thomson Gale, a part of The Thomson Corporation.

Thomson, Star Logo and Macmillan Reference USA are trademarks and Gale is a registered trademark used herein under license.

For more information, contact
Macmillan Reference USA
An imprint of Thomson Gale
27500 Drake Rd.
Farmington, Hills, MI 48331-3535
Or you can visit our Internet site at
http://www.gale.com

LIBRARY OF CONGRESS CATALOGING-IN-PUBLICATION DATA

Encyclopedia of Western colonialism since 1450 / Thomas Benjamin, editor in chief.
    p. cm.
    Includes bibliographical references and index.
    ISBN 0-02-865843-4 (set hardcover : alk. paper) – ISBN 0-02-865844-2 (vol 1 : alk. paper) – ISBN 0-02-865845-0 (vol 2 : alk. paper) – ISBN 0-02-865846-9 (vol 3 : alk. paper)
    1. Colonies–History–Encyclopedias. 2. Imperialism–History–Encyclopedias. 3. Postcolonialism–Encyclopedias. 4. Europe–Territorial expansion–Encyclopedias. I. Benjamin, Thomas, 1952-
        JV22.E535 2007
        325'.303–dc22   2006010042

This title is also available as an e-book.
ISBN 0-02-866085-4
Contact your Thomson Gale representative for ordering information.

Printed in the United States of America
10 9 8 7 6 5 4 3 2 1

Editorial Board

Editorial and Production Staff

Contents

List of Maps

Preface

The overseas empires of Western Europe shaped the history of all of the continents and peoples of the world during the half millennium from their origins in the mid-fifteenth-century to their final dissolution in the mid-to-late twentieth-century. The colonial empires of the West—Portugal, Spain, France, Great Britain, the Netherlands, Belgium, Germany, Italy and the United States—claimed possession at one time or another all of the Americas and Australia, ninety-nine percent of Polynesia, ninety percent of Africa and nearly fifty percent of Asia. These Western colonial powers, which together constituted less than two percent of the surface of the world, created the first maritime empires that straddled the globe. In so doing Western colonialism dispatched European colonialists to every inhabitable region, implanted and disseminated Christianity throughout the colonial world and exported the languages, laws, institutions, technology and values of the West to nearly all lands, peoples, and cultures worldwide. This political, economic, and cultural expansionism reshaped the non-European societies and cultures with which it came into sustained contact. One can easily understand that the history and very nature of Western colonialism has been a subject of great controversy and conflicting moral claims. This history is not a closed and forgotten chapter without relevance to the problems and promise of today. It remains a fascinating subject open to interpretation and vigorous debate.

The *Encyclopedia of Western Colonialism since 1450* provides the most comprehensive, accessible, and international reference work about the entirety of Western colonialism from the Portuguese voyages of Prince Henry the Navigator in the fifteenth-century to the making of feature films about British colonialism in India in the twenty-first-century. The Encyclopedia presents over four hundred articles in three volumes. These articles are arranged alphabetically to assist readers in finding topics of interest easily and quickly. This work has been designed, first and foremost, as a teaching and learning resource for teachers and students. In the first volume an alphabetical list of articles is followed by the synoptic outline, which organizes all of the articles by topics and subtopics, providing readers with a map of the major subjects within the history, geography, and ideas of Western colonialism. More than three hundred maps, pictures and photographs as well as additional charts and tables appear throughout the volumes to illustrate and support the articles. Each article includes references to related articles in the three volumes and a bibliography of sources as suggested for additional reading. Readers will also find a careful selection of many of the most important documents related to the history of Western colonialism. These primary or historical sources are coordinated with the articles. Readers may explore general themes in the articles and then read the related documents to obtain a more nuanced and in-depth understanding of the issues. There is a glossary of key terms, which provides understandable definitions and explanations of the more specialized, technical and foreign words. A comprehensive index of names, events, places, and key words is found at the end of the third volume.

The Encyclopedia is designed to provide reliable and sophisticated historical knowledge for students, teachers, general readers, and scholars. The articles in this reference work are original works of scholarship and synthesis written explicitly for this project. These articles are written by distinguished scholars and noted specialists— historians, anthropologists, political scientists, geographers, philosophers, sociologists, artists, and economists—and have been carefully reviewed and edited in a common style for easy access by all curious and engaged readers. Particularly important topics are explored in thoughtful synthetic essays of 4,000 to 6,000 words. Some of the subjects of these essays include the separate Western colonial empires such as the Portuguese, French and British Empires; the ideologies that justified expansion, imperialism and colonialism; the impact of Western colonialism on particular non-European peoples and cultures; and the modern theories that attempt to explain the phenomena of colonialism and imperialism. There are more concise articles about significant individuals, events, places, institutions, commodities, and much more related to colonialism. These articles range in size in incremental lengths from 500 to 4,000 words.

The *Encyclopedia of Western Colonialism since 1450* is not only a comprehensive reference work that embraces world history during the past five centuries, it is as well an international intellectual project. The associate editors who organized and compiled this work are a diverse group whose national origins are The Netherlands, Great Britain, Nigeria, and the United States. The more than 240 contributors who wrote articles for this work are scholars who originally came from, or now live and teach in the Americas, Europe, Africa, the Middle East, and Asia. Because this reference work is truly international, it is also diverse in its approach to ideas, interpretations, and intellectual problems related to the history of Western colonialism. The articles provide not simply facts and summaries of facts about the colonial past but current scholarly interpretations. Because scholars disagree about a number of issues, there is no uniformity of opinion in these articles and across these volumes. All is not confusion and chaos, however, in this field of study or in this reference work. Readers will find considerable consensus on a number of important historical developments and topics and they will discover the fewer but more difficult issues where disagreement exists and what those different and sometimes opposing interpretations are.

WESTERN COLONIALISM

As most of the articles in the Encyclopedia point out, such terms and concepts as "colonialism," and "imperialism" are far from simple and self-evident words that all scholars define in the same way. Because the history of Western colonialism and imperialism is politically, economically, and culturally relevant to contemporary issues and, therefore, controversial, these terms themselves are no less contested. Nevertheless, it is possible to provide cautious yet useful definitions. Throughout human history empires have been defined by the political domination of one or more territories by a powerful polity or state, often called an imperial metropole. *Imperial* in the English language was borrowed from the old French term *emperial,* which was derived from the Latin word *imperãre,* meaning to command, to rule and from the word *imperium,* meaning power, mastery, and sovereignty. Imperialism can be defined as the domination and rule by a strong state over a subordinate state, territory and people that exist beyond the boundaries of the imperial metropole. Again throughout history, empires have possessed *colonies*. Once again the English word came directly or indirectly from the Latin verb *colere*, meaning to cultivate and till the land. The Romans established *colonae* as their empire expanded, including Colônia Agrippîna or what is today called the city of Cologne, a beautiful German city on the Rhine. Colonies are dependent territories and populations that are possessed and ruled by an empire. "Colonialism" refers to the processes, policies and ideologies used by metropoles to establish, conquer, settle, govern, and economically exploit colonies. In the age of Western colonization, as well as before, colonization meant not only ruling other peoples but also sending one's own people to settle a foreign territory, or colony.

The history of Western colonialism and imperialism since the fifteenth-century has been organized and classified by historians and scholars in a number of different ways. The political scientist Professor David B. Abernethy provides one of the best or least problematic schemas. By creating a chronology of five periods, Abernethy reminds us that the history of Western colonialism was not a simple "rise and fall" nor the once standard two-stage chronology of "Early" and "Modern" European empires. Abernethy's classification demonstrates some of the complexity that accompanied Western expansion, colonialism and imperialism, contractions, and, finally, decolonization. Abernethy presents the chronology in Table 1.

In the first phase, European oceanic expansion led to the possession of a significant portion of the Americas (and claims to the entire hemisphere) through conquest and colonization, as well as the establishment of coastal enclaves and trading-post settlements on the coasts of West and East Africa, Arabia, India, China, the Spice Islands, and Japan. Western colonialism during these centuries, however, was largely an Atlantic endeavor. In the East, European traders and missionaries integrated themselves into the larger and richer economies of the Indian Ocean and the South China Sea. The European settler societies in the Americas during the fifty-year period from 1775 to 1825, as part of the wider Atlantic Age of Revolution, rebelled against imperial rule and established independent nation-states in the United States, the former colonies of Spanish America and Portuguese Brazil. The descendants of European colonists were not the only revolutionaries in this second phase, a time of imperial contraction. Native Americans, Mestizos, Mulattos, and African slaves rebelled as well during this period. In the French sugar island of Saint Domingue in the Caribbean, a slave rebellion in the 1790s defeated European armies and established the black republic of Haiti in 1804.

Western Colonial and Imperial Phases

Phase	Duration	Direction	Territorial focus
1	1415–1775	Expansion	The Americas
2	1775–1825	Contraction	The Americas
3	1825–1914	Expansion	Africa, Asia, the Pacific
4	1914–1940	Unstable Equilibrium	The Middle East
5	1940–1980	Contraction	Africa, Asia, the Pacific

SOURCE: David B. Abernethy, *The Dynamics of Global Dominance: European Overseas Empires, 1415-1980* (New Haven: Yale University Press, 2000), Table 2.2, p. 24.

Table 1.

The Extent of European Colonialism, 1939

	Great Britain	France	Belgium	The Netherlands
Area of Colonies (Square Miles):	13,100,000	4,300,000	940,000	1,100,000
Population of Colonies:	470,000,000	65,000,000	13,000,000	66,000,000

Colonial Territory of the Four Empires:	19,440,000
Colonial Population of the Four Empires:	614,000,000

SOURCE: Mary Evelyn Townsend, *European Colonial Expansion Since 1871* (Chicago: J.P. Lippincott Company, 1941), p. 19. This table does not include the Portuguese, Spanish, and Italian overseas colonies. Just prior to the Second World War the populations of all of the European colonies constituted somewhat more than one third of the total population of the world.

Table 2.

During the third phase, what is often called the age of "modern imperialism," a new period of European expansion took off in Africa, Asia, and the Pacific. Europeans had long been established in trading "factories" and castles on the coasts of Africa and Asia but in the nineteenth century they used these enclaves as bases to move into the interior of these great continents and seize political control. During this phase of expansion the disparity of power between Europeans and non-Europeans grew as a result of the Industrial Revolution, which provided European empires with steamships and gunboats, repeating rifles and machine guns, railroads, new tropical medicines, as well as attractive and seductive manufactured goods. Between 1824 and 1870 the European empires added approximately five million square miles of new territory in Africa, India, Australia and New Zealand, and Southeast Asia. Between 1878 and 1913 Europeans acquired an additional eight million square miles, or roughly one-sixth of the land surface of the world.

During the fourth phase, World War I (1914–1918) and the Great Depression of the 1930s weakened Western Europe and European colonial power and legitimacy. The World War marked the end of German overseas colonialism and began the process within the British Empire of devolving power to the settlement colonies of Canada, Australia, New Zealand, and South Africa. The war, on the other had, led to the collapse of the Ottoman Empire in the Middle East, which permitted the British and the French, under the League of Nations mandate system, to move into Syria, Lebanon, Palestine, Trans-Jordan, and Iraq. This period of unstable equilibrium saw both an erosion of European colonial power and self-confidence as well as some new imperial expansion. By 1939 the European empires had reached the zenith of their territorial and political control. Table 2 provides an accounting of four of the European empires by that year.

During the late nineteenth-century and the first four decades of the twentieth-century the rise of popular nationalist movements in colonial India, Egypt, Indonesia, Vietnam, and in other European colonies prepared the way for decolonization after World War II. European colonialism was also threatened by the rise of powerful rivals such as Imperial

Japan, Nazi Germany, the Soviet Union and the United States that sought the creation of a new international order.

World War II (1939–1945) abruptly began the last phase of Western colonialism. The war dramatically assaulted the key European imperial powers, France, the Netherlands and Great Britain, at home and overseas. Most of France and all of the Netherlands were occupied by Hitler's Germany in 1940, while Britain's cities were bombed and its once formable financial resources were bled dry. Abroad German armies threatened Egypt and Japanese armies seized French Indochina, Dutch Indonesia, and British Singapore and Malaya (as well as the American colony of the Philippines). Although German and Japanese militarism and imperialism were defeated in the war as a result of the intervention of the United States and the Soviet Union and the French, Dutch and British reestablished colonial rule in their Asian colonies after 1945, Europeans could not longer sustain foreign rule by force or collaboration. Colonial nationalists were determined to attain independence by peaceful negotiation or, if necessary, violent revolution. Thus, between 1940 and 1980 more than eighty colonies achieved their independence and were recognized as sovereign nation-states.

This brief outline of the history of Western colonialism is offered as a starting point in thinking about this vast subject. As readers explore and examine the articles in the Encyclopedia they will find the information, ideas, interpretations, and sources which will give them the tools to craft their own understanding of Western colonialism.

ACKNOWLEDGMENTS

The *Encyclopedia of Western Colonialism since 1450* has taken over three years, and the creativity and hard work of hundreds of women and men, to complete. The title page lists all of the individuals involved in this project but I would like to give special attention and express my gratitude to a few people who were indispensable to the success of this work. Hélène Potter, our publisher at Macmillan Reference, developed the idea for the project, organized the editorial board, and guided and shaped our efforts with her unmatched knowledge of the world of publishing and her great interest in history from the beginning to the end. The first Editor in Chief, B.R. "Tom" Tomlinson, Dean of the School of Oriental and African Studies, University of London, laid the foundation of the Encyclopedia by beginning the selection of the editorial board and identifying the key themes and topics the project needed to cover. When circumstances required Tom to withdraw from this position, he asked me to take over. Jenai Mynatt, our primary editor at Macmillan has worked with the editorial board and the contributors on a daily basis. Jenai has guided and pushed this project to conclusion with amazing patience, good cheer, professionalism, and skill. Judith Culligan, our chief copy editor, fact checked, improved our grammar, and transformed hundreds of different writing styles into one clear and consistent style. Finally, Professor Dennis Hidalgo (Adelphi University and Book Review Editor, *Latin American History, H-Web*) was brought on as a consultant to help us find and recruit scholars to write articles, particularly for the more difficult topics. Dennis enthusiastically used his people and electronic communication skills to search the world for potential contributors.

My colleagues in history, the five associate editors, were indispensable in guiding the project, developing broad themes and specific entries, recommending and vetting contributors, and reading the articles that they commissioned and guiding these pieces through the process of revision and rewriting. Below are very brief bibliographies of the members of the editorial board.

Editor in Chief Thomas Benjamin is professor of history at Central Michigan University. He has published several books in English and Spanish about modern Mexico and the Mexican Revolution including: *A Rich Land, A Poor People: Politics and Society in Modern Chiapas* (1989 and 1996), *Historia regional de la Revolución mexicana: La provincia enter 1910–1929* (1996), *La Revolución: Mexico's Great Revolution as Memory,*

Myth and History (2000), and *La Revolución Mexicana: Memoria, mito e historia,* 2003 and 2005). His primary interest and vision of research and writing in recent years has broadened to embrace the colonial Atlantic World. In 2001 he co-edited *The Atlantic World in the Age of Empire.* His long-awaited history of the Atlantic World, *The Atlantic World: Europeans, Africans and Indians & Their Shared History* will be published by Cambridge University Press in 2007.

Benjamin C. Fortna is Senior Lecturer in the Modern History of the Near and Modern East in the History Department at the School of Oriental and African Studies at the University of London. He is a highly respected scholar of the Ottoman Empire. He has written *Imperial Classroom: Islam, Education and the State in the Late Ottoman Empire* (2002) and has co-edited *The Modern Middle East: A Sourcebook* (2006). Professor Fortna is currently working on a history of reading and the transition from the Ottoman Empire to the Turkish Republic.

Hendrik E. Niemeijer is Project Coordinator for the Research School for Asian, African and American Studies at Leiden University in The Netherlands. As a scholar of the Dutch East Indies Professor Niemeijer helped to create and now leads TANAP ("Towards a New Age of Partnership") which is a Dutch-Asian-South African partnership of scholars and historical archives. Professor Niemeijer is Editor in Chief of *Itinerario,* the official journal of the Forum on European Expansion and Global Interaction. He has written a history of the colonial capital of the Dutch East Indies in *Colonial Dutch Society in Batavia* (2005) and is currently working on a three-volume work on the Protestant church in the Moluccas in 1600–1800.

Chima J. Korieh is Professor of African History at Rowan University in Glassboro, New Jersey. A native of Nigeria, Professor Korieh holds degrees from the University of Nigeria, the University of Helsinki, and the University of Toronto. He has co-edited *Religion, History and Politics in Nigeria* (2005) and *Aftermath of Slavery: Transitions and Transformations in Southeastern Nigeria* (2006). His book *Peasants and Rebels: Socioeconomic Change in Colonial and Early Post Colonial Nigeria, 1900–1980,* will appear in 2007.

Anthony McFarlane is Professor of Latin American History in the History Department and in the School of Comparative American Studies at the University of Warwick, in the United Kingdom. He has published a number of books in English and Spanish about Spanish American history including *Columbia before Independence: Economy, Society and Politics under Bourbon Rule* (1993), *The British in the Americas, 1480–1815* (1994), and as co-editor *Reform and Insurrection in Bourbon New Granada and Peru* (1990). Professor McFarlane is increasingly interested in the comparative history of empires and is currently working on a book on the wars of independence in Spanish America.

Eileen P. Scully is professor of history at Bennington College, Bennington, Vermont. Professor Scully has lived and studied in Russia and Hong Kong as well as at the Harvard Law School and the Henry Dunant Institute in Geneva. She is a scholar of American and international history and has written *Bargaining with the State from Afar: American Citizenship in Treaty Port China, 1844–1942* (2001). In 2005, she was the recipient of the American Historical Association's Eugene Asher "Distinguished Teaching" prize.

On behalf of Hélène, Jenai, Benjamin, Hendrik, Chima, Anthony and Eileen, and the more than 240 colleagues who contributed articles to this work, I invite readers to explore the fascinating and troubling issues and topics of exploration and expansion, colonization, resistance, slavery, evangelization, and much more in the *Encyclopedia of Western Colonialism since 1450.*

Thomas Benjamin
Editor in Chief

List of Articles

XIX

Thematic Outline

This systematic outline provides a general overview of the conceptual scheme of the *Encyclopedia of Western Colonialism since 1450, listing the titles of each entry. The outline is divided into nineteen parts.*

1. Commodities and Trade
2. Concepts and Ideas (Economic)
3. Concepts and Ideas (General)
4. Corporations/Businesses
5. Empires
6. Explorations and Migrations
7. Foreign Policy
8. Geographical Regions (Cities, Countries, and Regions)
9. Ideologies
10. Industries
11. Infrastructure
12. Laws, Treaties, and Declarations
13. Organizations and Institutions
14. People and Peoples
15. Politics and Political Movements
16. Religion and Religious Concepts
17. Rivalries
18. Scientific and Cultural Practices
19. Wars, Battles, and Incidents

1. COMMODITIES AND TRADE

Alcohol
American Crops, Africa
Atlantic Colonial Commerce
Bengal, Maritime Trade of
Blackbird Labor Trade
Bullion Trade, South and Southeast Asia
Cacao
China, Foreign Trade
Cinnamon
Coffee Cultivation
Coffee in the Americas
Colonization and Companies
Commodity Trade, Africa
Compradorial System
Copper Trade, Asia
Coromandel, Europeans and Maritime Trade
Cotton
Diamonds
Export Commodities
Fur and Skin Trades in the Americas
Indian Ocean Trade
Malabar, Europeans and the Maritime Trade of
Money in the Colonial Americas
Rubber, Africa
Shipping, East Asia and Pacific
Shipping, the Pacific
Silk
Slave Trade, Atlantic
Slave Trade, Indian Ocean
Sugar Cultivation and Trade
Tea
Tobacco Cultivation and Trade
Tribute

2. CONCEPTS AND IDEAS (ECONOMIC)

African Slavery in the Americas
Arabia, Western Economic Expansion in
Atlantic Colonial Commerce
Bengal, Maritime Trade of
Colonization and Companies
Commonwealth System
Compradorial System
Enlightenment and Empire
Enlightenment Thought
Financing, Debt, and Financial Crises
Imperialism, Free Trade
Independence and Decolonization, Middle East
Indigenous Economies, Middle East
International Trade in the pre-Modern Period, Middle East
Java, Cultivation System
Mercantilism
Modern World-System Analysis
Oceania
Opium

3. CONCEPTS AND IDEAS (GENERAL)

Anti-Americanism
Anticolonialism
Assimilation, Africa
Assimilation, East Asia and the Pacific
Association, Africa
Censorship
Creole Nationalism
Crown Colony
Dual Mandate, Africa
Enlightenment and Empire
Enlightenment Thought
Eurocentrism
French Colonialism, Middle East
Hegemon and Hegemony
Human Rights
Imperialism, Cultural
Imperialism, Gender and
Imperialism, Liberal Theories of

Warrant Chiefs, Africa
Xavier, Francis

15. POLITICS AND POLITICAL MOVEMENTS

Abolition of Colonial Slavery
Afrikaner
Anti-colonial Movements, Africa
Anticolonialism, East Asia and the Pacific
Anticolonialism, Middle East and North Africa
Apartheid
Assimilation, Africa
Assimilation, East Asia and the Pacific
Association, Africa
Brazilian Independence
Crown Colony
Independence and Decolonization, Middle East
Indian National Movement
Indonesian Independence, Struggle for
Irish Nationalist Movement since 1800
Minas Gerais, Conspiracy of
New Spain, the Viceroyalty of
Segregation, Racial, Africa
Slavery and Abolition, Middle East

16. RELIGION AND RELIGIOUS CONCEPTS

Catholic Church in Iberian America
Christianity and Colonial Expansion in the Americas
Islam, Colonial Rule, Sub-Saharan Africa
Islamic Modernism
Mission, Civilizing
Missionaries, Christian, Africa
Missions, China
Missions, in the Pacific
Muslim Brotherhood

Netherlands Missionary Society
Papal Donations and Colonization
Religion, Roman Catholic Church
Religion, Western Perceptions of Traditional Religions
Religion, Western Perceptions of World Religions
Religion, Western Presence in Africa
Religion, Western Presence in East Asia
Religion, Western Presence in Southeast Asia
Religion, Western Presence in the Pacific

17. RIVALRIES

Anglo-Russian Rivalry in the Middle East
British Colonialism, Middle East
British India and the Middle East
Central Asia, European Presence in
Irish Nationalist Movement since 1800
Sudan, Egyptian and British Rivalry in

18. SCIENTIFIC AND CULTURAL PRACTICES

African Slavery in the Americas
Art, European
Cartography
Cartography in the Colonial Americas
Clothing and Fashion, Middle East
Colonialism at the Movies
Human Rights
Language, European
Literature, Middle Eastern
Medical Practices, Middle East
Negritude
Race and Racism
Science and Technology
Segregation, Racial, Africa
Sex and Sexuality

Slavery and Abolition, Middle East
Sugar and Labor: Tracking Empires
Travelogues

19. WARS, BATTLES, AND INCIDENTS

Aceh War
Afghan Wars
American Revolution
Anglo-Burmese Wars
Anglo-Russian Rivalry in the Middle East
Asante Wars
Boer Wars
Boxer Uprising
Chinese Revolutions
Dinshaway Incident
Dutch-Indonesian Wars
Haitian Revolution
Igbo Women's War
Indian Revolt of 1857
Java War (1825-1830)
Maji Maji Revolt, Africa
Mau Mau, Africa
Opium Wars
Russo-Japanese War
Scramble for Concessions
Southeast Asia, Japanese Occupation of
Spanish American Independence
Suez Canal and Suez Crisis
Taiping Rebellion
Tobacco Protest, Iran
Túpac Amaru, Rebellion of
United States Interventions in Postindependence Latin America
Urabi Rebellion
War and Empires
World War I, Africa
World War II, Africa
World War I, Middle East
Zulu Wars, Africa

Contributors

Edmund Abaka
Associate Professor
University of Miami
History
 AMERICAN COLONIZATION SOCIETY
 ASANTE WARS
 NORTH AFRICA, EUROPEAN
  PRESENCE IN
 SLAVE TRADE, ATLANTIC

Christopher Abel
Senior Lecturer
University College, London
Latin American History
 MONROE DOCTRINE
 NEOCOLONIALISM IN LATIN AMERICA

Tomoko Akami
Lecturer
The Australian National University
Asian Studies
 JAPAN, COLONIZED

Kwabena Akurang-Parry
Professor
Shippensburg University
History
 ABORIGINES' RIGHTS PROTECTION
  SOCIETY
 ANTI-COLONIAL MOVEMENTS, AFRICA
 NKRUMAH, KWAME

Maysam J. al Faruqi
Professor
Georgetown University
 INDIGENOUS ECONOMIES, MIDDLE
  EAST

Seema Alavi
Associate Professor
Jamia Millia University, New Delhi
History
 INDIAN REVOLT OF 1857

Robert Aldrich
Professor
University of Sydney
History
 PACIFIC, EUROPEAN PRESENCE IN
 SELF-DETERMINATION, EAST ASIA
  AND THE

Carmen Alveal
Ph.D. Candidate
The Johns Hopkins University
History
 LAW, COLONIAL SYSTEMS OF,
  PORTUGUESE
 MINAS GERAIS, CONSPIRACY OF

Camron Michael Amin
Associate Professor
University of Michigan-Dearborn
Social Sciences-History
 IRAN
 PAHLAVI DYNASTY

Barbara Watson Andaya
Professor
University of Hawaii
Asian Studies Program
 MALAYSIA, BRITISH, 1874-1957

Anthony Anghie
Professor

University of Utah
S.J. Quinney School of Law
 LAW, CONCEPTS OF INTERNATIONAL

Ogechi Emmanuel Anyanwu
Ph.D. Fellow and Instructor
Bowling Green State University
History
 ORGANIZATION OF AFRICAN
  UNITY (OAU)

Catherine Armstrong
Tutor
University of Warwick
History
 TOBACCO CULTIVATION
  AND TRADE

Ralph A. Austen
Professor
University of Chicago
History
 HUMAN RIGHTS

R. Jovita Baber
Assistant Professor of Iberian World
Texas A&M University
History Department
 LAW, COLONIAL SYSTEMS OF, SPANISH
  EMPIRE

Tracey Banivanua Mar
Lecturer
University of Melbourne
History
 SUGAR AND LABOR: TRACKING
  EMPIRES

Kristi Barnwell
Ph.D. Candidate
University of Texas at Austin
ARABIA, WESTERN ECONOMIC
EXPANSION IN

Alison Bashford
Associate Professor
The University of Sydney
History
AUSTRALIA, ABORIGINES
SCIENCE AND TECHNOLOGY

Thomas Benjamin
Professor
Central Michigan University
History
ANTICOLONIALISM
BUCCANEERS
COLONIALISM AT THE MOVIES
LIMA
MAGELLAN, FERDINAND
NEOCOLONIALISM
POSTCOLONIALISM

Bhaswati Bhattacharya
Professor
International Institute of
Asian Studies
CALCUTTA

Cristina Blanco Sío-López
Researcher
European University Institute of
History and Civilization
INCA EMPIRE
MITA

Michael Brett
Professor
SOAS, University of London
History
NORTH AFRICA

Gavin Brockett
Assistant Professor
Wilfrid Laurier University
History
ATATÜRK, MUSTAFA KEMAL

Matthew Brown
Lecturer in Latin American Studies
University of Bristol
Department of Hispanic,
Portuguese and Latin American
Studies
EUROPEAN EXPLORATIONS IN SOUTH
AMERICA
GAMA, VASCO DA
SPANISH AMERICAN INDEPENDENCE

William Harris Brown
Editor
North Carolina Office of Archives and
Historical Publications
ROYAL DUTCH-INDISCH ARMY

Elizabeth Brownson
Ph.D. Candidate
University of California, Santa Barbara
History
CURZON, LORD
HUDA SHA'RAWI
KHOMEINI, AYATOLLAH RUHOLLAH

Deborah Bryceson
Research Associate
Oxford University
African Studies
ALCOHOL

David Cahill
Professor
University of New South Wales
School of History
CREOLE NATIONALISM

Giampaolo Calchi-Novati
Professor
University of Pavia, Italy
Political and Social Studies
AFRIKANER
LUGARD, FREDERICK JOHN DEALTRY

Laura M. Calkins
Oral Historian, Assistant Archivist
Texas Tech University
Vietnam Archive
ANTICOLONIALISM, EAST ASIA AND
THE PACIFIC
CHINESE REVOLUTIONS
DECOLONIZATION, EAST ASIA AND
PACIFIC
LAW, COLONIAL SYSTEMS OF,
JAPANESE EMPIRE

Alicia J. Campi
President, U.S.-Mongolia
Advisory
U.S.-Mongolia Advisory Group
INDIGENOUS RESPONSES, EAST ASIA
MONGOLIA

Mark E. Caprio
Professor
Rikkyo University
Law and Politics
ASSIMILATION, EAST ASIA AND
THE PACIFIC
KOREA, TO WORLD WAR II
OCCUPATIONS, EAST ASIA

David Carletta
Teaching Assistant
Michigan State University
History
UNITED STATES INTERVENTIONS IN

John M. Carroll
Assistant Professor
Saint Louis University
Department of History
COMPRADORIAL SYSTEM

James Carson
Associate Professor
Queen's University
History
EMPIRE IN THE AMERICAS, FRENCH
NATIVE AMERICANS AND EUROPEANS

Adrian Carton
Lecturer
Macquarie University, Sydney
Modern History
FRENCH EAST INDIA COMPANY

Pär Cassel
Ph.D Candidate
Harvard University
History
EXTRATERRITORIALITY

Gokhan Cetinsaya
Professor
Istanbul Teknik University
Department of Humanities and Social
ABDÜLHAMID II

Choon-Lee Chai
Ph.D. Candidate
University of Saskatchewan
Sociology
STRAITS SETTLEMENTS

Martha Chaiklin
Associate Professor
University of Wisconsin-Milwaukee
SILK

John Chalcraft
Lecturer in History and Politics
London School of Economics and
Political Science
Department of Government
BARING, EVELYN

Abdin Chande
Assistant Professor
Adelphi University
History
WORLD WAR I, AFRICA
WORLD WAR II, AFRICA

David Chandler
Emeritus Professor
Monash University
History
    FRENCH INDOCHINA
    MEKONG RIVER, EXPLORATION
      OF THE

Matt Childs
Assistant Professor
Florida State University
History
    RACE AND RACISM

Youssef M. Choueiri
Reader in Islamic Studies
University of Manchester
Religions and Theology
    IDEOLOGY, POLITICAL, MIDDLE EAST

Parks Coble
Professor
University of Nebraska
History
    EMPIRE, JAPANESE

John Connell
Professor
University of Sydney
School of Geosciences
    BLACKBIRD LABOR TRADE

Edward Countryman
University Distinguished Professor
Southern Methodist University
Clements Department of History
    AMERICAN REVOLUTION

Kenneth Cuno
Director
University of Illinois at Urbana-
Champaign
Program in South Asian and Middle
Eastern Studies
    UNITED STATES POLICY TOWARDS THE
      MIDDLE

Antoon De Baets
Doctor
University of Groningen, The
Netherlands
History
    CENSORSHIP
    EUROCENTRISM

Susan Deeds
Professor
Northern Arizona University
History
    NEW SPAIN, THE VICEROYALTY OF

Henk den Heijer
Professor
University of Leiden
Department of History
    DUTCH WEST INDIA COMPANY

Nirmal Ranjith Dewasiri
Senior Lecturer
University of Colombo
History and International Relations
    KANDY, COLONIAL POWERS'
      RELATIONS WITH THE
      KINGDOM OF

Charles Dobbs
Professor
Iowa State University
History
    ATLANTIC COLONIAL COMMERCE
    EAST ASIA, AMERICAN PRESENCE IN
    EUROPEAN EXPLORATIONS IN NORTH
      AMERICA
    OPEN DOOR POLICY
    PERRY, MATTHEW CALBRAITH
    RACIAL EQUALITY AMENDMENT,
      JAPAN
    SCRAMBLE FOR CONCESSIONS
    WAR AND EMPIRES

Michel René Doortmont
Associate Professor
University of Groningen
International Relations and African
Studies
    ACEH WAR
    ETHICAL POLICY, NETHERLANDS
      INDIES
    RHODES, CECIL
    SNOUCK HURGRONJE, CHRISTIAAN

Lane R. Earns
Professor, Provost and Vice Chancellor
University of Wisconsin-Oshkosh
History
    NAGASAKI

Cord Eberspaecher
Research Fellow
Secret Prussian State Archive
    CHINA, TO THE FIRST OPIUM WAR
    RUSSO-JAPANESE WAR

Bruce Elleman
Associate Professor
U.S. Naval War College
Maritime History Department
    EXPLORATION, THE PACIFIC
    NORTHWEST PASSAGE TO ASIA
    SHANDONG PROVINCE

Robert Eric Entenmann
Professor
St. Olaf College
History and Asian Studies
    TIBET

Sibel Erol
Senior Lecturer
New York University
Middle Eastern and Islamic Studies
    EDIB, HALIDE

Khaled Fahmy
Associate Professor
New York University
Middle Eastern and Islamic Stdudies
    MUHAMMAD ALI

Andrew B. Fisher
Assistant Professor
Carleton College
Department of History
    AFRICAN SLAVERY IN THE AMERICAS

John Fisher
Professor
University of Liverpool
Institute of Latin American Studies
    EMPIRE IN THE AMERICAS, SPANISH
    MINING, THE AMERICAS
    MONEY IN THE COLONIAL AMERICAS
    POTOSÍ

Eep Francken
Lecturer
Leiden University
    MULTATULI (EDUARD DOUWES
      DEKKER)

William Gallois
Lecturer
Roehampton University
History
    MEDICAL PRACTICES, MIDDLE EAST

Indira Falk Gesink
Assistant Instructor
Baldwin-Wallace College
History
    DINSHAWAY INCIDENT
    MUSLIM BROTHERHOOD
    URABI REBELLION

Donato Gómez Díaz
Professor
Almeria University, Spain
Economics
    GOVERNMENT, COLONIAL, IN SPANISH
      AMERICA

Anthony Gorman
Research Fellow
School of Oriental and African
Studies,
History
  EGYPT
  NASIR, GAMAL ABD AL
  SUEZ CANAL AND SUEZ CRISIS

Allan Greer
Professor
University of Toronto
History
  CARTIER, JACQUES
  COMPANY OF NEW FRANCE
  NEW FRANCE
  QUEBEC CITY

Jyoti Grewal
Associate Professor of History
Zayed University
Social and Behavioral Sciences
  INDEPENDENCE AND
    DECOLONIZATION, MIDDLE
  RAILROADS, EAST ASIA AND THE
    PACIFIC

William Guéraiche
Researcher, Dubai
  LAW, COLONIAL SYSTEMS OF, FRENCH
    EMPIRE

Lynne Guitar
Resident Director
Pontificia Universidad Católica Madre
CIEE program for Spanish Language &
  COLUMBUS, CHRISTOPHER

Martin Haas
Professor
Adelphi University
History
  MODERN WORLD-SYSTEM ANALYSIS

R.F.F. Habiboe
Freelance Publicist
Leiden University
  VALENTIJN, FRANÇOIS

Chris Hagerman
Assistant Professor
Albion College
European History
  RAFFLES, SIR THOMAS STAMFORD
  SEPOY
  WORLD WAR I, MIDDLE EAST

Stefan Halikowski Smith
Lecturer
Brown University

History
  CARTOGRAPHY
  COROMANDEL, EUROPEANS AND
    MARITIME

Doina Pasca
Assistant Professor
Central Michigan University
History
  ANTI-AMERICANISM
  HARKIS
  IMPERIALISM, LIBERAL THEORIES OF

Jonathan Hart
Professor
University of Alberta
English and Comparative Literature
  LANGUAGE, EUROPEAN
  PAPAL DONATIONS AND COLONIZATION

Aline Helg
Professor
University of Geneva
History
  CARTAGENA DE INDIAS

Peter Hempenstall
Professor of History
University of Canterbury, New
Zealand
History
  BISMARCK ARCHIPELAGO

Christian Henriot
Professor
Lumière-Lyon University
Institut d'Asie Orientale (CNRS)
  SHANGHAI

Francis X. Hezel
Director
Micronesian Seminar, Pohnpei, FSM
  MARSHALL ISLANDS

Dennis Hidalgo
Assistant Professor
Adelphi University
History
  ANTICOLONIALISM
  BUCCANEERS

David Hilliard
Associate Professor
Flinders University, Adelaide, Australia
History
  MISSIONS, IN THE PACIFIC

Mason C. Hoadley
Professor
Lund University, Sweden
Department of East Asian Languages

  COFFEE CULTIVATION
  LAW, COLONIAL SYSTEMS OF, DUTCH
    EMPIRE

Jacqueline Holler
Assistant Professor
University of Northern British
History and Women's Studies
  ACAPULCO
  AMERICAN CROPS, AFRICA
  MEXICO CITY

Thomas Holloway
Director
Hemispheric Institute on the Americas
Professor
University of California, Davis
History
  COFFEE IN THE AMERICAS

James Horn
Director of Research
The Colonial Williamsburg Foundation
  ENGLISH INDENTURED SERVANTS
  EUROPEAN MIGRATIONS TO
    AMERICAN

Sharon House
Associate Professor
Central Michigan University
Art
  ART, EUROPEAN

Timothy Howe
Assistant Professor
St. Olaf College
History
  DIVIDE AND RULE: THE LEGACY OF
    ROMAN

G. Douglas Inglis
Research Professor
Texas Tech University
History
  HAVANA
  SUGAR CULTIVATION AND TRADE

Wiebke Ipsen
Visiting Scholar
University of Illinois,
Latin American Studies
  BRAZILIAN INDEPENDENCE

Robert H. Jackson
Historian
U.S. Office of Federal
Acknowledgements Department
of the Interior
  CHRISTIANITY AND COLONIAL
    EXPANSION IN THE AMERICAS

Jon Jacobs
Adjunct Professor
Barry University, Johnson and Wales
University, Miami Dade College
History
　MISSION, CIVILIZING

Ogbu Kalu
Henry Winters Luce Professor of
World Christianity and Missions
McCormick Theological Seminary
　ISLAM, COLONIAL RULE, SUB-SAHARAN
　　AFRICA
　MISSIONARIES, CHRISTIAN, AFRICA
　RELIGION, WESTERN PRESENCE IN
　　AFRICA
　SIERRA LEONE

Marianne Kamp
Associate Professor of History
University of Wyoming
Department of History
　CENTRAL ASIA, EUROPEAN PRESENCE IN

Daniel C. Kane
Ph.D. Candidate
University of Hawaii, Manoa
History
　KOREA, FROM WORLD WAR II

Vicki Karaminas
Lecturer
University of Technology Sydney
School of Design
　CLOTHING AND FASHION, MIDDLE EAST

Nikki Keddie
Professor Emerita
University of California, Los Angeles
History
　AFGHĀNĪ, JAMAL AD-DĪN AL-
　TOBACCO PROTEST, IRAN

Sean P. Kelly
Ph.D. Candidate
Texas A&M University
Department of History
　CAPITULATIONS, MIDDLE EAST

Peter Keppy
Researcher
Netherlands Institute for War
　DUTCH-INDONESIAN WARS

Martin Kich
Professor
Wright State University-Lake Campus
　EMPIRE, ITALIAN
　FEDERATED STATES OF MICRONESIA
　INDIGENOUS RESPONSES, THE PACIFIC
　PORTUGAL'S AFRICAN COLONIES

Diane Kirkby
Reader
La Trobe University
History
　LAW, COLONIAL SYSTEMS OF

Martin Klein
Professor Emeritus
University of Toronto
History
　COMMODITY TRADE, AFRICA
　DIAGNE, BLAISE
　FRANCE'S AFRICAN COLONIES
　MANUMISSION
　SUB-SAHARAN AFRICA, EUROPEAN
　　PRESENCE IN

Wim Klooster
Professor
Clark University
History
　EMPIRE IN THE AMERICAS, DUTCH

Keng We Koh
University of Hawaii at Manoa
Department of History
　COLONIAL PORT CITIES AND TOWNS,
　　SOUTH AND

Chima J. Korieh
Assistant Professor
Rowan University
History
　AFRICAN NATIONAL CONGRESS
　BERLIN CONFERENCE
　CABRAL, AMILCAR
　DIAMONDS
　MAJI MAJI REVOLT, AFRICA
　MANDELA, NELSON
　WARRANT CHIEFS, AFRICA
　ZULU WARS, AFRICA

Paul A. Kramer
Associate Professor
The Johns Hopkins University
History
　UNITED STATES COLONIAL RULE
　　IN THE

Michelle Ladd
Ph.D. Candidate
Claremont Graduate University
Cultural Studies
　BRITISH AMERICAN TOBACCO
　　COMPANY

Tom Lansford
Associate Professor
University of Southern Mississippi
Political Science

　EMPIRE IN THE AMERICAS,
　　PORTUGUESE
　EMPIRE, UNITED STATES
　GOVERNMENT, COLONIAL, IN
　　PORTUGUESE
　HEGEMON AND HEGEMONY
　IMPERIALISM, CULTURAL
　IMPERIALISM, FREE TRADE

Monika Lehner
Lecturer
University of Vienna
East Asian Studies / Chinese Studies
　ANGLO-RUSSIAN RIVALRY IN THE
　　MIDDLE EAST
　LI HONGZHANG

Virginia Leonard
Professor
Western Illinois University
History
　HAITIAN REVOLUTION

Lamont Lindstrom
Professor
University of Tulsa
Anthropology
　OCCUPATIONS, THE PACIFIC

Tim Lockley
Senior Lecturer
University of Warwick
History
　DRAKE, SIR FRANCIS
　EMPIRE IN THE AMERICAS, BRITISH
　GOVERNMENT, COLONIAL, IN BRITISH
　　AMERICA
　THIRTEEN COLONIES, BRITISH NORTH
　　AMERICA
　VIRGINIA COMPANY

Roger D. Long
Professor
Eastern Michigan University
History and Philosophy
　EMPIRE, BRITISH, IN ASIA AND PACIFIC

Tai-Lok Lui
Professor
Chinese University of Hong Kong
Sociology
　HONG KONG, FROM WORLD WAR II

Murdo J. MacLeod
Graduate Research Professor, Emeritus
University of Florida
History
　CACAO
　EXPORT COMMODITIES

Pius Malekandathil
Reader
Sri Shankaracharya University of
Sanskrit, Kalady
History
GOA, COLONIAL CITY OF

Ruby Maloni
Professor
University of Mumbai, India
Department of History
BOMBAY

A.M. Mannion
Honorary Fellow
University of Reading
Geography
RIO DE JANEIRO
VESPUCCI, AMERIGO

Iik Arifin Mansurnoor
Associate Professor
University of Brunei Darussalam
History
KARTINI, RADEN AJENG
RELIGION, WESTERN PRESENCE IN
SOUTHEAST

Eric Martone
Teacher
John F. Kennedy High School,
Waterbury, Connecticut
Social Studies
FINANCING, DEBT, AND FINANCIAL
CRISES

Derek Massarella
Professor
Chuo University
Economics
ENGLISH EAST INDIA COMPANY, IN
CHINA

Eugenio Matibag
Associate Professor of Spanish
Iowa State University
World Languages and Cultures
SOUTHEAST ASIA, JAPANESE
OCCUPATION OF

Weldon C. Matthews
Associate Professor
Oakland University
History
SECULAR NATIONALISMS, MIDDLE
EAST

James McDougall
Assistant Professor
Princeton University

History
ALGERIA
FRENCH COLONIALISM, MIDDLE EAST

Charles Ivar McGrath
Doctor
Trinity College Dublin
School of Histories and Humanities
IRELAND, ENGLISH COLONIZATION

Jeffrey Lee Meriwether
Assistant Professor
Roger Williams University
History
APARTHEID
GREAT TREK
KRUGER, PAUL
PAN-AFRICAN CONGRESS

Richard Middleton
Professor
Queens University Belfast
History
BOSTON
MASSACHUSETTS BAY COMPANY
NEW YORK

Edith Miguda
Assistant Professor
Saint Mary's College
Centre for Women's Intercultural
Leadership
KENYATTA, JOMO
MAU MAU, AFRICA
NYERERE, JULIUS

William F.S. Miles
Professor
Northeastern University
Political Science
VANUATU

Monique Milia-Marie-Luce
Assistant Professor
University of the French West Indies
History
FRENCH POLYNESIA

Paul Moon
Principal Lecturer
Auckland University of Technology
Faculty of Maori Development
WAITANGI, DECLARATION OF
INDEPENDENCE

John Morello
Senior Professor of History
DeVry University
Department of General Education
PIZARRO, FRANCISCO

Andrew Muldoon
Assistant Professor
Metropolitan State College of
Denver
History
COMMONWEALTH SYSTEM

David Mungello
Professor
Baylor University
History
MISSIONS, CHINA
RELIGION, WESTERN PRESENCE IN
EAST ASIA

Todd Munson
Assistant Professor
Randolph-Macon College
Asian Studies and History
JAPAN, OPENING OF
TREATY PORT SYSTEM

Dhiravat na Pombejra
Lecturer
Chulalongkorn University
History
SIAM AND THE WEST, KINGDOM OF

Jürgen G. Nagel
Assistant Professor
Open University Hagen
History
EAST ASIA, EUROPEAN PRESENCE IN
FACTORIES, SOUTH AND SOUTHEAST
ASIA
FREEBURGHERS, SOUTH AND
SOUTHEAST ASIA

George O. Ndege
Professor
Saint Louis University
History
BRITAIN'S AFRICAN COLONIES
GERMANY'S AFRICAN COLONIES

Caryn E. Neumann
Lecturer
Ohio State University - Newark
History
TEA

Linda Newson
Professor
King's College London
Geography
BIOLOGICAL IMPACTS OF EUROPEAN
EXPANSION
ECOLOGICAL IMPACTS OF
EUROPEAN

Tak-Wing Ngo
Lecturer
Leiden University
HONG KONG, TO WORLD WAR II

Hendrik E Niemeijer
Scientific Project Coordinator
Leiden University
Research School for Asian, African and
Amerindian Studies
DUTCH UNITED EAST INDIA
COMPANY
EMPIRE, DUTCH

Raphael Njoku
Assistant Professor
University of Louisville
History, and Pan African Studies
ASSIMILATION, AFRICA
ASSOCIATION, AFRICA
AZIKIWE, NNAMDI
MACHEL, SAMORE

Obioma Nnaemeka
Professor
Indiana University
Foreign Languages & Cultures/
Women's Studies Program
ACHEBE, CHINUA
NEGRITUDE
SENGHOR, LÉOPOLD SÉDAR

Apollos O. Nwauwa
Associate Professor
Bowling Green State University
History/Ethnic Studies
DECOLONIZATION, SUB-SAHARAN
AFRICA
EDUCATION, WESTERN AFRICA

Timothy O'Neil
Assistant Professor
Central Michigan University
History
IRISH NATIONALIST MOVEMENT SINCE
1800

John N. Oriji
Professor
California Polytechnic State
University
History
IGBO WOMEN'S WAR

Esin Örücü
Professor Emeritus
University of Glasgow, Erasmus
Comparative Law
LAW, COLONIAL SYSTEMS OF,
OTTOMAN EMPIRE

Thomas Otte
Lecturer in Diplomatic History
University of East Anglia
History
TREATIES, EAST ASIA AND THE PACIFIC

Adebayo Oyebade
Associate Professor
Tennessee State University
History
DUAL MANDATE, AFRICA
LIBERIA

Azmi Özcan
Professor
University of Sakarya, Turkey
History
EMPIRE, OTTOMAN

Gabriel B. Paquette
Visiting Instructor
Wesleyan University
History
JUSTIFICATION FOR EMPIRE,
EUROPEAN
MERCANTILISM
SOCIAL DARWINISM

Michael Pasquier
Ph.D. Candidate
Florida State University
Religion
RELIGION, WESTERN PERCEPTIONS OF
TRADITIONAL

Christer Petley
Senior Lecturer
Leeds Metropolitan University
School of Cultural Studies
CARIBBEAN

Alasdair Pettinger
Visiting Research Fellow
Nottingham Trent University
English Studies
TRAVELOGUES

Vincent Kelly
Lecturer
University of Hawai'i at Manoa
Asian Studies Program
HAWAI'I

David Pong
Professor and Director of East Asian
Studies
University of Delaware
History
CHINESE, IMPERIAL MARITIME
CUSTOMS

Jonathan Porter
Professor
University of New Mexico
History
MACAO

Michael Pretes
Assistant Professor
University of North Alabama
Geography
AUSTRALIA
BOER WARS
CAPE COLONY AND CAPE TOWN
COTTON
DEE, JOHN
ETHIOPIA
HAKLUYT, RICHARD
MELANESIA
MICRONESIA
NEW ZEALAND
POLYNESIA

Patrick Provost-Smith
Assistant Professor
Harvard Divinity School
History of Christianity
ACOSTA, JOSÉ DE
PERU UNDER SPANISH RULE
RELIGION, ROMAN CATHOLIC
CHURCH
RELIGION, WESTERN PERCEPTIONS OF
WORLD

Bambang Purwanto
Professor and Director, Center for
Korean Studies
Gadjah Mada University
History
JAVA WAR (1825-1830)

Matthew Quest
Assistant Professor
Lewis University
History
PAN-AFRICANISM

Remco Raben
Researcher
Netherlands Institute for War
BATAVIA

Mohanalakshmi Rajakumar
Ph.D. Candidate
University of Florida
INDIA, IMPERIAL
INDIAN NATIONAL MOVEMENT

Susan Elizabeth Ramirez
Neville G. Penrose Chair of History
and Latin American Studies

Texas Christian University
History
ENCOMIENDA
HACIENDAS IN SPANISH AMERICA
TRIBUTE

Andrew Redden
Lecturer
University of Bristol
Department of Historical Studies
CATHOLIC CHURCH IN IBERIAN
AMERICA

Anne Reinhardt
Assistant Professor
Williams College
History
CHINA MERCHANTS' STEAM
NAVIGATION
JARDINE, MATHESON & COMPANY
SHIPPING, EAST ASIA AND PACIFIC

Dennis Reinhartz
Professor of History and Russian
University of Texas at Arlington
History
CARTOGRAPHY IN THE COLONIAL
AMERICAS

Thomas Reins
Lecturer
California State University, Fullerton
History
CHINA, FIRST OPIUM WAR TO 1945
OPIUM

Matthew Restall
Professor
Pennsylvania State University
History
AZTEC EMPIRE

Jeremy Rich
Assistant Professor
Middle Tennessee State University
History
COLONIAL CITIES AND TOWNS,
AFRICA
SCRAMBLE FOR AFRICA

Kevin Roberts
Assistant Professor
New Mexico State University
History
RACE AND COLONIALISM IN THE
AMERICAS

Jane Samson
Associate Professor
University of Alberta

History and Classics
FIJI
OCEANIA
PAPUA NEW GUINEA
RELIGION, WESTERN PRESENCE IN
THE PACIFIC

Rhonda A. Semple
Assistant Professor
University of Northern British
History and Women's Studies
IMPERIALISM, GENDER AND
LONDON MISSIONARY SOCIETY

Heather J. Sharkey
Assistant Professor
University of Pennsylvania
Near Eastern Languages and
Civilizations
BRITISH COLONIALISM, MIDDLE EAST
SUDAN, EGYPTIAN AND BRITISH
RIVALRY IN

Ryuto Shimada
Researcher
Leiden University
BULLION TRADE, SOUTH AND
SOUTHEAST ASIA
COPPER TRADE, ASIA

Peter Sluglett
Professor of Middle Eastern History
University of Utah
History
ANTICOLONIALISM, MIDDLE EAST AND
NORTH
INTERNATIONAL TRADE IN THE
PRE-MODERN

Tony Smith
Cornelia M. Jackson Professor
Tufts University
Political Science
WILSONIANISM

Selçuk Aksin Somel
Assistant Professor
Sabanci University
EDUCATION, MIDDLE EAST

George Bryan Souza
Associate Professor
University of Texas, San Antonio
History
CINNAMON

Mark G. Spencer
Assistant Professor
Brock University
History
ENLIGHTENMENT THOUGHT

Andrea L. Stanton
Ph.D. Candidate
Columbia University
History, Middle East
LITERATURE, MIDDLE EASTERN

Paul Starkey
Professor
Durham University
School of Modern Languages and
WESTERN THOUGHT, MIDDLE EAST

Ward Stavig
Professor
University of South Florida
Latin American and Caribbean Studies
TÚPAC AMARU, REBELLION OF

Mark Stein
Assistant Professor
Muhlenberg College
History
OTTOMAN EMPIRE: FRANCE AND

Philip J. Stern
Assistant Professor
American University
History
BRITISH INDIA AND THE MIDDLE EAST
COLONIZATION AND COMPANIES
ENGLISH EAST INDIA COMPANY (EIC)
ENLIGHTENMENT AND EMPIRE

Brian Stokes
Adjunct Professor
Camden County College
History
CITIES AND TOWNS IN THE AMERICAS
JAPAN, FROM WORLD WAR II

Lakshmi Subramanian
Senior Fellow
Centre for Studies in Social Sciences,
Calcutta
History
BENGAL, MARITIME TRADE OF
INDIAN ARMY
MALABAR, EUROPEANS AND THE
MARITIME
SINGAPORE

Robert C.H. Sweeny
Professor
Memorial University of
Newfoundland
History
IMPERIALISM, MARXIST THEORIES OF

Eric Tagliacozzo
Assistant Professor
Cornell University

History
INDIAN OCEAN TRADE

Dan Taulapapa McMullin
Independent Writer
AMERICAN SAMOA
PACIFIC, AMERICAN PRESENCE IN
SHIPPING, THE PACIFIC

John G. Taylor
Professor of Politics
London South Bank University
EAST TIMOR

Karen Taylor
Associate Professor
College of Wooster
History
EMPIRE, FRENCH
SEX AND SEXUALITY

Gerard P.A. Termorshuizen
Researcher
Royal Netherlands Institute of
Southeast Asian and Caribbean
Studies, Leiden
DAUM, PAULUS ADRIANUS

Ehud R. Toledano
Professor
Tel Aviv University
History of the Middle East
SLAVERY AND ABOLITION, MIDDLE EAST

Dale W Tomich
Professor
Binghamtom University
Sociology and History
PLANTATIONS, THE AMERICAS

Stephen A. Toth
Assistant Professor
Arizona State University West
Language, Cultures and History
NEW CALEDONIA
TRUSTEESHIP

Blanca Tovías
University of New South Wales
History
FUR AND SKIN TRADES IN THE
AMERICAS

Lisa Tran
Assistant Professor
California State University, Fullerton
History
BOXER UPRISING
SELF-STRENGTHENING MOVEMENTS,
EAST ASIA
ZONGLI YAMEN (TSUNGLI YAMEN)

Carl Trocki
Professor of Asian Studies
Queensland University of Technology
School of Humanities and Human
Services
CHINESE DIASPORA

Ernest Tucker
Associate Professor
U.S. Naval Academy
History
EMPIRE, RUSSIAN AND THE MIDDLE
EAST

Laurier Turgeon
Professor
Laval University
History and Ethnology
ATLANTIC FISHERIES

G.N. Uzoigwe
Professor and Head
Mississippi State University
History
INDIRECT RULE, AFRICA
NATIONALISM, AFRICA

Wim van den Doel
Professor of Contemporary History
Leiden University
History
INDONESIAN INDEPENDENCE,
STRUGGLE FOR
LINGGADJATI AGREEMENT

Thomas van den End
Missionary and Translator in
Indonesia
NETHERLANDS MISSIONARY SOCIETY

Chris F. van Fraassen
Leiden University
MOLUCCAS

S.E.A. van Galen
Researcher
Leiden University
ANGLO-BURMESE WARS
BURMA, BRITISH

Robert van Niel
Professor Emeritus
University of Hawaii
History
JAVA, CULTIVATION SYSTEM

E. van Veen
Researcher
Leiden University
EMPIRE, PORTUGUESE

Arnold van Wickeren
Director
Alkmaar University, The Netherlands
Economics
ALBUQUERQUE, AFONSO DE

Elizabeth Van Wie Davis
Professor
Asia-Pacific Center
Regional Studies
CHINA, AFTER 1945

Guy Vanthemsche
Professor
Free University Brussels
History
BELGIUM'S AFRICAN COLONIES
LUMUMBA, PATRICE
STANLEY, HENRY MORTON

Markus Vink
Associate Professor
State University of New York at
Fredonia
Department of History
COEN, JAN PIETERSZ
HEEREN XVII
SLAVE TRADE, INDIAN OCEAN

Willem Vogelsang
Curator and Researcher
National Museum of Ethnology
(Leiden), and Leiden University
Southwest and Central Asia (National
Museum of Ethnology), and Research
School of Asian, African, and
Amerindian Studies (CNWS), Leiden
University
AFGHAN WARS

Charles F. Walker
Professor
University of California, Davis
History
LIMA

John Walsh
Assistant Professor of Marketing and
Communications
Shinawatra International University
CHINA, FOREIGN TRADE

James Walvin
Professor
University of York
History
ABOLITION OF COLONIAL SLAVERY

Dong Wang
Associate Professor of History
Gordon College

East-West Institute of International
Studies
   GUANGZHOU
   MAO ZEDONG
   QING DYNASTY

Andrew J. Waskey
Associate Professor
Dalton State College
Social Science
   OIL

Itzchak Weismann
Senior Lecturer
University of Haifa
History of the Middle East
   ISLAMIC MODERNISM

Roland
Lecturer
Humboldt-Universitaet, Berlin
Centre for British Studies
   CROWN COLONY
   EMPIRE, BRITISH
   LAW, COLONIAL SYSTEMS OF, BRITISH
     EMPIRE

NiraItzchak Wickramasinghe
Professor
University of Colombo, Sri Lanka
Department of History and
International Relations
   CEYLON

Peter Wien
Assistant Professor
University of Maryland, College Park
History
   IRAQ

Ken Wilburn
Director, Undergraduate Studies
East Carolina University
History
   RAILROADS, IMPERIALISM

Caroline A. Williams
Senior Lecturer in Latin American Studies
University of Bristol
Hispanic, Portuguese, and Latin
American Studies
   CONQUESTS AND COLONIZATION
   CORTÉS, HERNÁN

Mary Wilson
Professor
University of Massachusetts Amherst
History
   MANDATE RULE

Donald Richard Wright
Distinguished Teaching Professor
State University of New York-
Cortland
History
   HENRY THE NAVIGATOR, PRINCE

Jonathan Wright
Independent Scholar
   XAVIER, FRANCIS

Liu Yong
Ph.D. Candidate
Leiden University
Institute for the History of European
Expansion
   OPIUM WARS

Maochun Yu
Associate Professor
U.S. Naval Academy
History
   MERCENARIES, EAST ASIA AND THE
     PACIFIC
   TAIPING REBELLION

Alexander M. Zukas
Professor
National University
Social Sciences
   CHARTERED COMPANIES, AFRICA
   GERMANY AND THE MIDDLE EAST
   TREATY OF TORDESILLAS

Lorna Lueker Zukas
Associate Professor and Director of
National University's Center for
Cultural and Ethnic Studies
National University
   RUBBER, AFRICA
   SEGREGATION, RACIAL, AFRICA

A

ABDÜLHAMID II
1842–1918

Ottoman sultan (r. 1876–1909). The reign of Sultan Abdülhamid II began on August 31, 1876, during a period of profound crisis for the Ottoman Empire. In 1878 the sultan inaugurated a new course in domestic and foreign policies that had a lasting impact on the history of modern Turkey and the Middle East.

Abdülhamid's prime foreign policy objective was to defend the empire's independence and territorial integrity. He was preoccupied with the empire's vulnerability to the influence of the European Great Powers. He feared not only military attack from without but also the Powers' "peaceful penetration" of the empire's independence and integrity from within, such as through the establishment of "zones of influence" leading ultimately to partition, as in Egypt and India. Abdülhamid's success in preserving the empire's integrity and independence for thirty years must be attributed primarily to his diplomacy. He avoided peacetime alliances with the Great Powers, maintaining an overall diplomatic stance of "neutrality" or "noncommitment." He distanced the empire from its former protector, Great Britain. He harmonized relations with the empire's traditional enemy, Russia, and initiated the longest period of peace in Russo-Ottoman relations for more than a century. He also inaugurated a close relationship with Germany in order to restrain Britain and Russia.

Abdülhamid was a staunch authoritarian. He dissolved the parliament in 1878, establishing his own absolute control over the executive organs of government. Abdülhamid was determined to control in detail the initiation and implementation of policy. He ignored the rules of bureaucratic hierarchy, exerting personal authority over provincial as well as central officials. Abdülhamid was a strong centralizer, determined to curb all tendencies toward provincial autonomy.

Abdülhamid saw Islam and Muslim solidarity, expressed in a common loyalty to the caliphate, as crucial to the empire's efforts to resist European penetration and the separatist aspirations of his non-Turkish Muslim subjects. This policy was expressed in much official deference to Islam and to religious leaders, and in an officially sponsored religious propaganda that at times assumed a "pan-Islamic" form by appealing to Muslim solidarity outside the Ottoman Empire. Abdülhamid emphasized Islam domestically in order to invoke the loyalty of his Muslim subjects—in particular non-Turkish Muslims like the Albanians and the Arabs.

The reign of Abdülhamid was one of considerable achievements in the field of social and economic reform. He continued the beneficial aspects of the Tanzimat reforms and encouraged construction of schools, railways, harbors, irrigation works, telegraph lines, and other infrastructural projects. He also encouraged improvement in finance, trade, mining, and agricultural export, as well as in education, civil administration, security, and military affairs. However, his financial caution did significantly limit the extent of his civil and economic reforms.

Opposition to his rule was led by the so-called Young Turks, a group consisting of intellectuals, students, and officers. Their chief organization, the Committee of Union and Progress (CUP), demanded the restoration of the parliament as a means to curb autocracy and

1

Yasamee, F. A. K. *Ottoman Diplomacy: Abdülhamid II and the Great Powers, 1878–1888*. Istanbul: ISIS, 1996.

Gökhan Çetinsaya

Sultan Abdülhamid II. *The reign of Abdülhamid II began in 1876 when the Ottoman Empire was at war with Serbia and Montenegro and facing a threat from Russia.* **THE ART ARCHIVE/ TOPKAPI MUSEUM ISTANBUL/DAGLI ORTI. REPRODUCED BY PERMISSION.**

preserve the integrity of the empire. CUP military officers staged an uprising in Macedonia in the summer of 1908. Fearing internal chaos, the sultan proclaimed the restoration of the parliament on July 24, 1908. A counter-revolution broke out in Istanbul in April 1909 against the policies of the CUP. The CUP crushed this rebellion and also dethroned Abdülhamid on April 27, 1909, falsely accusing him of having instigated the rebellion. He was placed under house arrest, which he remained under until his death on February 10, 1918.

SEE ALSO *Empire, Ottoman.*

BIBLIOGRAPHY

Akarli, Engin D. "The Tangled Ends of an Empire and Its Sultan." In *Modernity and Culture: From the Mediterranean to the Indian Ocean*, edited by Leila Tarazi Fawaz and C. A. Bayly, 261–284. New York: Columbia University Press, 2002.

Shaw, Stanford J., and Ezel K. Shaw. *History of the Ottoman Empire and Modern Turkey*, Vol. 2: *Reform, Revolution, and Republic: The Rise of Modern Turkey, 1808–1975*. Cambridge, U.K.: Cambridge University Press, 1977.

ABOLITION OF COLONIAL SLAVERY

From its beginnings, black slavery in the Americas proved remarkably durable. There were early religious protests against the pioneering use of slaves in the Americas, most notably by Bartolomé de las Casas (1474–1566), but the economic benefits that soon flowed from the work of African slaves, especially after the formation of plantation societies, overcame most moral or theological complaints. Though slavery was most dominant in key areas of staple production (sugar, tobacco, rice, and later cotton), it also seeped into most corners of the colonial Americas. Domestic and urban slavery, maritime slavery, artisanal slavery, and slavery on the rural frontiers all existed, though all were economically marginal compared to plantation slavery. In Brazil, the Caribbean, the Chesapeake, and later in the U.S. South black slavery held sway, its economic centrality apparently impervious to complaints about its ethical or religious problems. Moreover, the economic benefits of slavery seemed indispensable. Although the precise accountancy of the major slave systems was unusually complex, few contemporaries doubted that here was a form of labor that defied its critics via the manifest prosperity it yielded (to everyone except the slaves of course). But all that began to change in the mid-eighteenth century.

Although early complaints were directed at the use of slave labor in the Spanish Americas, the major starting point for the antislavery movement was the Atlantic slave trade. The enforced movement of millions of Africans across the Atlantic was vast and prolonged. Over four centuries, some twelve million Africans were loaded onto ships, and more than ten million were landed in the Americas. In addition, millions of Africans were also transported north, overland, and east into an Indian Ocean slave trade. But it was the Atlantic trade that caught the eye. It lasted from the late fifteenth century until the 1860s. The huge numbers involved, and the squalid inhumanity of the prolonged oceanic crossings, inevitably attracted attention. Tens of thousands of Europeans and Americans were involved in the trade— on the ships and in European and American ports—and the grim facts of the slave ships and their human cargoes were widely known. But the commonplace horrors on the ships, which were periodically given wide publicity by news of the latest outrage or disaster, tended not to make

The legal abolition of the slave trade

Country	Date
Denmark	1804
Great Britain	1808
The United States	1808
Sweden	1813
The Netherlands	1814
France	1818
Spain	1820
Chile	1823
Mexico	1824
Brazil	1831
Paraguay	1842

THE GALE GROUP.

much political or social impact until the mid-eighteenth century onward. By then there was a growing body of opposition, in North America and Britain, against the trade.

Opposition effectively began among American and British Quakers. Though George Fox had taken a fundamental stand against slavery as early as the 1670s, it was not until the 1770s that Quaker outrage, expressed at meetings and in print, began to register. Quaker influence in the English-speaking world was out of all proportion to their numbers. They ran efficient, nation-wide campaigns, aided by their own publishers and by Quaker distribution systems. But they were also able to tap into a more broadly based theological unease about slavery, which was grounded in the newly emergent nonconformist churches, notably the Methodists and Baptists. By the last years of the eighteenth century, they were joined by a small band of Evangelicals, led most famously by William Wilberforce, within the established Anglican Church. By the late 1780s there was a broad religious dislike of slavery in Britain and North America. But in Britain it focused on (and campaigned against) the Atlantic slave trade, largely from a belief that this was the most practical of tactics. Ending the slave trade seemed more manageable than ending slavery itself.

This dissenting attack merged with a more inchoate, but no less influential body of thought that slowly emerged from the writings of Enlightenment thinkers in both France and Scotland. Montesquieu's *L'ésprit des lois* (1748) proved most influential, with its deeply ironic attack on slavery, which he considered contrary both to natural law and the public good. Though the debate about slavery was continued by the Encyclopedists, Montesquieu's writing remained the major influence on subsequent English-language abolitionists, notably Granville Sharpe (1735–1813), William Blackstone (1723–1780), William Paley (1743–1805), and Edmund

Burke (1729–1797). But theoretical discussions about slavery were overshadowed by Adam Smith's *Wealth of Nations* (1776), which, for the first time, challenged the universally held belief that slavery was the most economically productive form of labor. Thereafter, the intellectual foundations of antislavery were secure. It was possible to attack slavery on both ethical and economic grounds. At the same time, a growing band of activists attacked slavery on religious grounds. Slavery (via the slave trade) was, by 1789, under attack from all angles.

The revolution in France in 1789 transformed everything. Firstly, it instantly sowed ideas of equality—belief in "the Rights of Man"—that utterly recast the whole debate. It also created the seismic waves that inspired the successful slave revolt in Saint Domingue, and the creation of an independent black republic in Haiti. Slavery throughout the Americas was threatened by events in Haiti, as thousands, black and white, fled to neighboring islands and to North America. Slaves themselves had, of course, been a critical element throughout the abolition debates. Slave cases in British courts, slave unrest in the islands, and the latent threat of slave unrest everywhere (confirmed by events in Haiti) was the backdrop against which abolitionist debates were played out. To add to the confusion, more and more slaves were being converted to Christianity, mainly by dissenting missionaries. Thus, by the early nineteenth century both black and white Christians had raised their voices against slavery.

The slave trade itself was ended by both Americans and the British in 1807, thereby cutting off supplies of fresh Africans flowing to the Americas. Despite this abolition, some three million Africans were shipped into the Americas after 1807, mainly to Brazil and Cuba (to man their expanding tobacco and coffee plantations). The British and the Americans, however, no longer needed the Atlantic slave trade. And when, after 1800, slaves began to be moved to the new cotton plantations in the U.S. South, they came not across the Atlantic from Africa, but from the buoyant black populations of the old slave societies in the United States. Here was an irony: at the very time slavery had come under fierce attack, and when the slave trade had been abolished, black slavery experienced a revival (in the United States, Brazil, and Cuba).

The British maintained their own Caribbean slave system after 1807. Because they wanted to understand what effect the abolition of the slave trade was having on that system, they introduced slave "registration" (a census) to check for illegal slave importations. Abolitionists, for their part, hoped that stemming the flow of new slaves would force planters to treat their existing slaves better. Despite this attempt to regulate it, slavery in the Caribbean was to be characterized by successive, and ever

British Abolitionist Emblem. *This image of a kneeling slave in shackles became the familiar emblem of the abolitionist movement in England. The first versions of the design appeared in the 1780s.* LIBRARY OF CONGRESS.

more violent slave revolts (Barbados, 1816; Demerara, 182; and, most violent of all, Jamaica, 1831–1832). The revolts clearly showed that slavery would not die of its own accord. Indeed, its problems seemed to get worse. Hence, from the mid-1820s abolitionists began to press for full emancipation. Using the old, tested methods of widespread public lectures, tract-publishing, and massive petitions to Parliament, abolitionists won over more and more Members of Parliament (MPs) and Ministers. The British campaign for full black freedom also thrived on the broader domestic campaign for reform, especially for parliamentary reform. When Parliament was reformed in 1832, slavery was doomed, for many of its former supporters had lost their seats to newly elected MPs.

Thereafter, the British transmuted themselves into a fiercely abolitionist nation, demanding an end of slavery and slave trading worldwide. Using the growing power of the Royal Navy, and the influence of the Foreign Office, the British tried to win over the world to abolition. Many other nations, however, were not attracted to the idea, not least because slave trading and slavery continued to offer scope for profitable trade and business. Sweden, Denmark, and Holland had ended their slave trades by 1815. France, however, persisted until 1830, the Brazilians/Portuguese until 1850, and Spain until as late

as 1867. As with Britain, slavery in the Europeans' colonies survived longer than their Atlantic slave trades. Although revolutionary France had abolished slavery in 1794, France actually reintroduced slavery in 1802, and then did not finally emancipate its slaves until 1848.

Sweden emancipated its slaves in 1848, Denmark a year later, and the Netherlands as late as 1863. Spain, wrestling with the independence movements in its various American settlements, clung to slavery until between 1870 and 1873 in Puerto Rico and until 1886 in Cuba. Brazil finally ended slavery in 1888, although it had been long in decline there, and most slaves had been freed long before then. Of course slavery was not equally important throughout the Americas. Where it had been marginal, it was quickly ended (Chile, 1823; Mexico, 1829). In the short period between 1842 and 1855, slaves were emancipated in Uruguay, Bolivia, Colombia, Ecuador, Argentina, Venezuela, and Peru.

Slavery in the United States survived (thrived, really) until destroyed in the violence of the Civil War. The rise of Northern abolition, the pressure from abroad (notably from Britain), and the remarkable Underground Railroad did little to deflate the success of Southern slavery, which was buoyed by the global demand for cotton (channeled mainly through the mills of industrial Lancashire). There is little reason to doubt that without the Civil War, U.S. slavery would have continued.

It took a relatively short time for British and American abolitionists to end their respective slave trades, which they both did in 1807. Yet it was to take another century before slavery itself was finally ended throughout the Americas. And even then, slavery lived on, if not in the Americas, then in many other regions of the world. For their part, the British turned from slavery to a revival of indentured labor (from India) to fill the demand for labor throughout the far-flung British Empire. By 1914 the British had shipped almost 1.5 million Indians into indentured servitude.

Throughout much of the Americas, slavery was undermined by a complex mix of cultural and political forces. A transformation in cultural values was set in motion by Enlightenment thinkers, the seismic impact of the French Revolution, and above all by the Haitian revolt—and, of course, by slaves everywhere, who added their voices and actions to demands for freedom. British abolitionists, as well, exerted a remarkable and persistent pressure. Another wider, less easily defined influence was the modernizing of Western society, notably the impact of industrialization, with its emphasis on economic freedom. The precepts of Adam Smith converged with the examples of British industrial power to prove that wage labor was more efficient than slavery and unfree labor. It seemed indisputable, by the mid-nineteenth century, that

Proclamation of the Abolition of Slavery in the French Colonies, 23rd April 1848. (1849), by the French painter François-Auguste Biard. ROGER VIOLLET/GETTY IMAGES. REPRODUCED BY PERMISSION.

free labor was more profitable (and ethically more acceptable) than slavery. Yet this did *not* seem true in the U.S. South. Moreover the cotton grown by American slaves in the first half of the nineteenth century made possible the rise and power of Britain's major industry—the cotton industry of the northwest. Thus, even in this, its last phase, black slavery continued to make economic sense in certain regions and under certain circumstances. Though U.S. slavery was Southern, it lay at the heart of American economic power. Slave-grown cotton provided the nation with its largest export by far; it steered profits, investment, and business back to Northern cities and institutions. U.S. slavery held within its powerful gravitational pull a host of other major industries and economic institutions. On the eve of the Civil War, there was little reason to feel that U.S. slavery had had its day.

In the half-century between British and Brazilian emancipation, the Americas were purged of colonial slavery. Britain, the major slave power of the eighteenth century, had become the major abolitionist power of the nineteenth century. Yet slavery had proved a really durable system (though in truth it was a series of slave

systems—it varied greatly), simply because it yielded such material benefits. Moreover, once slavery took root, it could not easily be displaced, even under changed economic circumstances. Slavery tended to take on a life of its own, and slave owners became attached to the broader culture of slave-ownership and could not imagine life without slavery. Slaves, on the other hand, derived little from the system and struggled, throughout, to escape from it, alleviate it, or bring it to an end. Across the Americas slavery had started slowly and unpredictably. It was finally brought to an end in an equally piecemeal fashion.

SEE ALSO *Haitian Revolution; Slave Trade, Atlantic; Sugar Cultivation and Trade.*

BIBLIOGRAPHY

Berlin, Ira. *Many Thousands Gone: The First Two Centuries of Slavery in North America.* Cambridge, MA: Belknap/Harvard University Press, 1998.

Craton, Michael. *Empire, Enslavement, and Freedom in the Caribbean.* Kingston, Jamaica: Randle, 1997.

Eltis, David. *The Rise of African Slavery in the Americas.* Cambridge, U.K.: Cambridge University Press, 2000.

Engerman, Stanley, Seymour Drescher, and Robert Paquette, eds. *Slavery.* Oxford: Oxford University Press, 2001.

Inikori, Joseph E. *Africans and the Industrial Revolution in England.* Cambridge, U.K.: Cambridge University Press, 2002.

Kolchin, Peter. *American Slavery, 1619–1877.* London: Penguin, 1993.

Morgan, Philip D. *Slave Counterpoint: Black Culture in the Eighteenth Century Chesapeake and Lowcountry.* Chapel Hill: University of North Carolina Press, 1998.

Walvin, James. *Black Ivory: A History of British Slavery*, 2nd ed. Oxford: Blackwell, 2001.

James Walvin

ABORIGINES' RIGHTS PROTECTION SOCIETY

The Gold Coast Aborigines' Rights Protection Society (ARPS) was formed in 1897 in the port city of Cape Coast, a hub of intellectual and political activism in colonial Ghana. The ARPS remained the voice of colonized Africans until its demise in the 1930s. The idea of forming the society had been incubated as early as 1895, but was shelved until May 17, 1897, when a meeting organized by the African intelligentsia in Cape Coast to protest the proposed Lands Bill of 1894 to 1897 culminated in the formation of the society. Thus, the main catalyst for the formation of the ARPS was the African intelligentsia's protest against the Lands Bill. Had the Lands Bill been passed, it would have allowed the colonial government to take over so-called waste or public lands.

Several developments in the preceding decades, including the lack of African representation on the Gold Coast Legislative Council, the problem of direct taxation, and the implementation of the Native Jurisdiction Ordinance of 1883, contributed to the formation of the ARPS. The ARPS had been preceded by the activities of the Mfantsi Amanbuhu Fekuw (Fante National Association), led by members of the African intelligentsia, including John Mensah Sarbah, J. W. de Graft Johnson, Chief J. D. Abraham, and J. P. Brown. The Mfantsi Amanbuhu Fekuw had been founded in 1889 to promote African cultural values that were being undermined by the corrosive effects of the European presence.

Although the ARPS was an alliance between the African intelligentsia and the chiefs or the indigenous rulers, its leadership was mostly made up of educated Africans who were able to use their literacy to negotiate with the colonial government. The African intelligentsia had the full support of the chiefs, especially from the inception of the ARPS to about 1912, when Governor Hugh Clifford effectively implemented indirect rule, which used the chiefs as the main agents of local administration. Thereafter, smarting under overt criticism from African intellectuals, the colonial government systematically marginalized them while it preoccupied itself with the promotion of the illegitimate power of the chiefs. This divide-and-rule tactic created antagonism between these educated Africans and the local chiefs.

The ARPS was led by elected officers; during its first years, its president was Jacob W. Sey, while the vice president was J. P. Brown. The society also had a secretary and a treasurer. ARPS activities were not restricted to Cape Coast; as early as 1897, the society had local branches in cities along the Gold Coast littoral regions, including Elmina, Saltpond, Winneba, and Axim. Its overall influence was felt throughout the Gold Coast, especially in districts where there was a sizeable number of African intellectuals, such as Krobo and Akuapem in the Eastern Province.

Indeed, by the first two decades of the twentieth century, the influence of the ARPS was being felt colonywide as it extended its concerns to cover problems of colonial rule, including forced labor and taxation in Asante and the Northern Territories. For much of the southern regions of the Gold Coast, the ARPS gained political ascendancy because of its ability to capitalize on publicity in the local newspapers.

Although the Lands Bill was its immediate preoccupation, the aims of the ARPS were broad and encompassing. Among other things, the ARPS hoped to make sure that various bills and colonial policies involving taxation, labor, and constitutional changes would not burden the Africans. During the early twentieth century, the ARPS occupied itself with colonial policies on education, sanitation, health, the provision of infrastructure, and imperial labor and military recruitment in the Gold Coast during World War I. The society also sought to modify or prevent the passing of several bills, including the Town Councils Ordinance of 1894 that came into force in 1904, and the Forest Bill (1907–1911). The Forest Bill can be traced to the Native Jurisdiction Ordinance of 1883. It empowered chiefs to pass local bylaws for forest preservation. This was vigorously implemented in 1907 with the passing of the Timber Protection Ordinance which sought to prevent the cutting of saplings. Eventually, the Forest Bill led to the establishment of forest reserves. The Town Councils Ordinance dealt with the levying of municipal house rates.

Some of the methods used by the ARPS included campaigns in local newspapers, namely the *Gold Coast Methodist Times* and the *Gold Coast Aborigines* in the late nineteenth century and the *Gold Coast Nation* and the *Gold Coast Leader* during the first two decades of the twentieth century. These newspapers, read by the African intelligentsia and Europeans, including government officials, in the Gold Coast, were used as political platforms to call attention to African demands.

Additionally, the ARPS, through the instrumentality of a few Africans serving on the Gold Coast Legislative Council, was able to address the council directly. For example, on June 4 and 5, 1897, J. H. Cheetham, an African unofficial member of the council (unofficial members had no voting rights), arranged for John Mensah Sarbah and P. Awooner Renner, members of the African intelligentsia, to address the council. The ARPS also held public meetings, not only in Cape Coast but in various places where it had branch offices. Aimed at discussing national issues and strategies, the meetings were attended not only by the ARPS echelons but by ordinary ARPS members and the public at large.

Apart from various petitions issued by the ARPS, the society also sent delegations to meet with the colonial government. Most significantly, in 1898 it sent a delegation, including President Sey and other prominent members, such as T. F. E. Jones and George Hughes, to England to meet directly with British officials to discuss problems of colonial rule, especially the Lands Bill. The ARPS delegation met with Joseph Chamberlain (1836–1914), the colonial secretary, with whom they discussed the questions of land, taxation, and constitutional reform. The delegation was successful because the Colonial Office later asked the colonial government to abandon the Lands Bill and the hut tax. In 1906 another delegation led by Reverend K. Egyir-Assam was sent to England under the auspices of the ARPS to demand the repeal of the Town Councils Ordinance, though this time the Colonial Office did not grant the wishes of the ARPS.

The activities of the ARPS were not always an all-male affair. Although colonial society was dominated by men, throughout the period of colonial rule several women's groups teamed up with men or supported men in anticolonial protest politics. For example, in 1906, following the campaigns against the Town Councils Ordinance championed by the ARPS, Cape Coast market women unleashed a large-scale, well-organized protest against the ordinance when Governor John Rodger visited Cape Coast to open an agricultural show.

The ARPS has been described as a protonationalist organization because it sought not to overthrow colonial rule, but to reform it. Overall, however, the protest politics of the ARPS went beyond mere reformism. From the late nineteenth century to the immediate post–World War I period, the society gradually sowed the seeds of revolutionary nationalism not only in the Gold Coast but in the West African region as a whole as its members contributed to the formation of the National Congress of British West Africa (NCBWA) in 1919. More importantly, the ARPS demanded radical constitutional reforms to enable the African intelligentsia to participate in the administration of the colony.

By the mid-1930s, the ARPS was in a state of decline. In the first place, it never gained strong roots beyond Cape Coast in the Central Province. For example, the society never developed in the adjoining Eastern Province. The society also remained elitist, and its decisions were made by a few individuals at the helm of the organization. Above all, the Cape Coast elite, in spite of the rapid economic transformation and social change as well as the vigorous consolidation of colonial rule, had called for radicalization of African protests and could not disengage from the old reformist protests of the nineteenth century. Thus, by the 1930s the ARPS, having lost popular support, existed as a ghost of its former self. Indeed, in the 1920s it had been taken over by the equally elitist but broader-based and more radical NCBWA, which sought to bring about fundamental change in colonial rule.

Overall, deprived of an effective voice in the administration of the colony and its dependencies, the ARPS served as the main representative of colonized Africans. The society was able to mediate between Africans and the colonial government, thereby moderating colonial rule. Although the formation of the ARPS was due to the cumulative effects of colonial rule in the late nineteenth century, the immediate reason for its formation was the Lands Bill. Having successfully forced the colonial government to abort the implementation of the Lands Bill, the ARPS tackled other objectionable colonial policies, including forced labor, taxation, indirect rule, and the lack of African representation on the Legislative Council. It also vigorously campaigned for improvements in education, sanitation, health, and the provision of infrastructure. Above all, it served as a precursor to revolutionary nationalism not only in the Gold Coast, but in the entire West African region in the 1930s.

SEE ALSO *Nationalism, Africa.*

BIBLIOGRAPHY

Agbodeka, Francis. *African Politics and British Policy in the Gold Coast.* London: Longman, 1971.

Agbodeka, Francis. *Ghana in the Twentieth Century.* Accra: Ghana Universities Press, 1972.

Boahen, Adu. *Ghana: Evolution and Change in the Nineteenth and Twentieth Centuries.* London: Longman, 1975.

Gocking, Roger. *Facing Two Ways: Ghana's Coastal Communities Under Colonial Rule.* Lanham, MD: University Press of America.

Kimble, David. *A Political History of Ghana*. Oxford: At the Clarendon Press, 1963.

Korang, Larbi, K. *Writing Ghana, Imagining Africa: Nation and African Modernity*. Rochester, NY: University of Rochester Press, 2003.

Okyere Vincent. *Ghana: A Historical Survey*. Accra: Vinojab Publications, 2000.

Kwabena Akurang-Parry

BIBLIOGRAPHY
Bakewell, Peter. *A History of Latin America: Empires and Sequels, 1450–1930*. Oxford: Blackwell, 1997.

Gerhard, Peter. *Pirates of the Pacific, 1575–1742*. Lincoln: University of Nebraska Press, 1990.

Lynch, John. *The Hispanic World in Crisis and Change, 1598–1700*. Oxford: Blackwell, 1992.

Jacqueline Holler

ACAPULCO

Acapulco was the only true seaport on the western coast of Mexico throughout the colonial period. Situated only 400 kilometers (about 250 miles) from Mexico City and blessed with a good harbor, Acapulco was settled between 1530 and 1550 as a base for Pacific exploration. The small port's fortunes changed in 1564 when an Asian expedition sponsored by King Philip II (1527–1598) of Spain recommended the use of Acapulco as the American port for trade with the Philippines.

In 1573 the first galleon laden with Asian goods arrived in the harbor. This inaugurated the Manila trade, or "China fleet," which carried Asian wares across the ocean to Acapulco, where they were exchanged for American silver. The arrival of each fleet saw Mexico City merchants flood Acapulco to bargain for silk, spices, and other luxury goods, which traded at favorable prices as a result of chronic bullion shortages in Asia.

Increasingly after 1575, Asian merchandise arriving at Acapulco was shipped not only inland to Mexico City but to Peru, where Asian goods commanded higher prices than they did in New Spain. Indeed, by the early seventeenth century, the amount of Potosí silver flowing through Acapulco to Asia was a serious concern to the Spanish Crown, leading to the outright if ineffective banning of trade between Peru and New Spain in 1631.

A tempting target for pirates as the Manila trade grew, Acapulco was fortified in the early seventeenth century and thus escaped sacking, though the galleons themselves were vulnerable. Because the fleet arrived only once a year, Acapulco never grew to a size reflecting its importance as an entrepôt in such a valuable trade. Moreover, it went into a precipitous decline with the waning of the Manila trade in the eighteenth century, a manifestation of a generalized loss of Spanish dominance. In 1774 there were only eight Spanish *vecinos* (propertied residents) left in Acapulco. The last galleon from Manila arrived in Acapulco in 1815, signaling the end of Acapulco's prominence in transpacific trade.

SEE ALSO *Cities and Towns in the Americas; Exploration, the Pacific; Mexico City.*

ACEH WAR

The sultanate of Aceh developed as an independent state in the fifteenth century. In the beginning of the seventeenth century, the sultanate of Aceh reached the summit of its political and economic power, and was one of the largest states in the region. At this time, it had control over large parts of both the island of Sumatra in present-day Indonesia and the peninsula of Malacca in Malaysia.

In the eighteenth century, Aceh sided repeatedly with the British colonial powers in the region against the Dutch. With the Treaty of London of 1824—between the United Kingdom and the Netherlands—Aceh's independence was guaranteed against further Dutch expansion in the archipelago. However, with the growth of colonial intervention in the region, and the growing intensity of shipping through the Strait of Malacca, incidents of Acehnese piracy became more and more of a nuisance for both Dutch and British colonial authorities. This led to a change in Dutch colonial policy, in which the annexation of Aceh became an option.

The Sumatra Treaty of 1871 between the United Kingdom and the Netherlands facilitated this shift in policy. With the treaty, the Netherlands got a free hand in northern Sumatra, while the British retained economic access to Aceh. This treaty was part of a package deal—although never acknowledged officially as such—that also involved the transfer of the Dutch possessions on the Gold Coast (West Africa) and a treaty for the recruitment of coolie labor in India for the Dutch colony of Surinam in the West Indies. With a free hand in Aceh, a prestigious colonial prize as well as a rich agricultural area and a repository of mineral oil, the annexation of Aceh became a priority for the Netherlands. The military struggles that took place in Aceh for forty years, from 1873 to 1913, were to be of central importance in shaping the Netherlands Indies colonial state and, eventually, the Republic of Indonesia.

The Aceh War can be divided into three phases: 1873 to 1893, 1894 to 1903, and 1904 to 1913. The first phase heralded several Dutch efforts at conquering and pacifying Aceh. In March 1873 the Netherlands Indies Army under the command of Major-General

J. H. R. Köhler attacked the capital of Aceh, Banda Aceh or Kutaraja. The idea behind the attack was to seize the sultan's fortified palace, the Kraton, perceived by the Dutch as the administrative center of the sultanate. The expedition, comprising a force of three thousand well-equipped infantrymen and artillery, was beaten back from the Kraton. Sultan Mahmud Syah (r. 1870–1874) had organized such a well-armed and determined resistance to the Dutch that the conquest of a mosque turned sour when Major General Köhler was killed there. The expeditionary force had to retreat with 56 dead and 438 wounded.

Late in 1873 a second expedition was organized with the same objectives, but also to save face. The Dutch army was even better armed this time and was put under the command of the highly experienced Lieutenant General Jan van Swieten. The force consisted of more than 8,500 men, and an additional 1,500 troops in reserve, as well as several thousand servants and bearers. Banda Aceh was captured, and the sultan was chased from the town. Sultan Mahmud Syah did not give up resistance, but rather retreated into the hills. After his death from cholera, he was succeeded by Sultan Ibrahim Mansur Syah (r. 1875–1907), who, although a figurehead, was instrumental in unifying the opposition against the Dutch.

In the early phase of the war, the Dutch grossly overestimated the power of the sultan. Aceh was not a unified state ruled by the sultan's court. Therefore, the Dutch efforts at subduing Aceh were not only militarily problematic, but also politically unsuccessful. This meant that even when the local representatives of the Acehnese state and gentry, the *uleebelang*, gave up after the death of the sultan in 1874, military resistance continued. Armed bands of peasants, connected through a common Islamic identity as well as kinship and village ties, fought a series of very successful guerrilla battles against the Dutch occupation.

Despite a precarious military situation, the Dutch government declared the war in Aceh ended in 1880. The Dutch army set up a system of sixteen forts (*benteng*) to encircle the remaining guerrilla fighters, and developed a road and tramway system to connect the forts and establish controlled zones. Within this so-called concentrated front, a specially established elite force (the Korps Marechaussee) executed counterinsurgency operations, making use of guerrilla tactics themselves. After 1893 the Dutch abandoned the strategy of a concentrated front as an unsuccessful tactic, but the elite troops continued their operations, now patrolling hotspot areas on a smaller scale with mobile columns.

Dutch efforts to establish alliances with local leaders through supplies of weapons and opium, as well as payments in money, characterized the first half of the second phase of the Aceh War (1894–1903). The best-known ally of the Dutch was the local leader Teuku Umar (1854–1899), who established an army of his own with the assistance and approval of the Dutch in 1894. However, two years later, he switched sides and turned on the Netherlands Indies Army with his force, which was armed with modern weaponry supplied by the Dutch. After a protracted campaign to neutralize Teuku Umar and his force, the Dutch army eventually chased him down and killed him in 1899.

The military officer J. B. van Heutsz (1851–1924) and government advisor and scholar of Islam Christiaan Snouck Hurgronje (1857–1936) dominated government policy in Aceh in the late 1890s. On the basis of field research in Aceh from 1891 to 1893, Snouck Hurgronje advised strongly that the Dutch depart from a wait-and-see policy and break Acehnese resistance with force. Snouck Hurgronje promoted the view that resistance in Aceh was religious in character, led by fanatic Islamic leaders (*ulema*) who were intent on waging a holy war or jihad against the infidel Dutch. The government was hesitant, however, and only adopted Snouck Hurgronje's proposal in 1896 after several incidents.

The implementation of the new policy was in the hands of Major (later General) van Heutsz. Snouck Hurgronje pushed for van Heutsz's appointment as civil and military governor of Aceh, which appointment came about in 1898. Snouck Hurgronje was appointed as advisor for indigenous and Arabic affairs in the same year, and in this position he served as van Heutsz's second in command from 1898 to 1903.

The pacification of Aceh became a show of brute force. Exemplary in this respect is the Gayo Expedition of 1900 to 1903 under Lieutenant-Colonel G. C. E. van Daalen (1863–1930), which resulted in the deaths of about three thousand people, more than a third of whom were women and children. These terror tactics were an advanced form of the antiguerrilla tactics developed by special Dutch troops more than a decade earlier.

After 1900 the ideas of Snouck Hurgronje and van Heutsz about pacification started to diverge, with the result that the former left Aceh in 1901, although he formally kept his position until 1903. Despite their disagreements about policy, Snouck remained loyal to van Heutsz in the sense that he recommended his appointment as governor-general of the Netherlands Indies in 1904 and refused to head a commission of inquiry into the Gayo massacre.

On February 10, 1903, the sultan of Aceh surrendered to the Dutch government. Hostilities between the Dutch and the Acehnese forces had turned into a war of attrition. Van Heutsz's commandos hunted the sultan down for years, making life impossible. The arrests of other political leaders of noble background along with their families broke the back of the official and organized opposition. Besides, van Heutsz saw a role for the sultan in a colonial Aceh.

Nevertheless, the war was not over. The last phase of the war, between 1904 and 1913, involved the continuation of guerrilla tactics against local leaders, but these were rearguard actions by the remainder of the once broad military resistance. Due to years of Dutch military presence, terror, oppression, destruction of villages and communities, and repeated forced relocation of village populations, the country was destroyed and the population psychologically broken. What Snouck Hurgronje had overlooked in his original analysis of the early 1890s was that Aceh had come under the influence of nationalism and the resistance against the Dutch was as much a social movement of ordinary people fighting for emancipation from their feudal bonds as it was a religious movement. Destroying the resistance through brute force also meant mental decay, apathy, and eventually the destruction of society. These circumstances would plague Dutch efforts to develop the area into a viable colonial province until the Japanese forced them out in 1942, as did the Indonesian authorities after independence.

SEE ALSO *Snouck Hurgronje, Christiaan.*

BIBLIOGRAPHY

Reid, Anthony. *The Contest for North Sumatra: Atjeh, the Netherlands, and Britain, 1858–1898.* Kuala Lumpur, Malaysia: Oxford University Press, 1969.

Schulten, C. M. "Tactics of the Dutch Colonial Army in the Netherlands East Politics." *Revue internationale d'histoire militaire* 70 (1988): 59–67.

Siegel, James T. *The Rope of God.* Berkeley: University of California Press, 1969.

Veer, Paul van 't. *De Atjeh-oorlog.* Amsterdam: De Arbeiderspers, 1969.

Michel R. Doortmont

ACHEBE, CHINUA
1930–

Born on November 16, 1930, in Ogidi (southeastern Nigeria), Albert Chinualumogu (Chinua) Achebe is one of Africa's best-known writers. Isaiah Okafor Achebe, a Church Missionary Society catechist, and his wife, Janet, named their fifth child Albert, after Prince Albert, the husband of Queen Victoria. In college, Albert dropped his "Christian name" for his Igbo name, Chinualumogu ("may God fight for me")—Chinua, for short. He

Chinua Achebe. *One of Nigeria's best-known authors, Achebe established an international reputation with his 1958 novel* Things Fall Apart, *which explores Nigeria's response to British colonialism during the late 1800s.* AP/IMAGES. REPRODUCED BY PERMISSION.

became a fighter himself through his writings—fighting to rectify the distortions in colonial narratives of Africa and her peoples in the works of writers such as Joyce Cary and Joseph Conrad; and fighting to expose and challenge what is wrong with postcolonial Nigeria—specifically, the failure of leadership.

Chinua Achebe's long, brilliant career includes many years in broadcasting, teaching, publishing, and creative writing. Rejecting the art for art's sake school of thought, Achebe insists that art has social value and function and the artist has a role to play in social change. He sees the writer as a teacher, moral voice, truth-teller, and social critic (*Morning Yet on Creation Day, Hopes and Impediments*, and *The Trouble with Nigeria*), and as a storyteller and a guardian of the word and memory (*Anthills of the Savannah*).

A versatile writer who has published short stories, essays, and poetry, Achebe is best known for his novels, which are written with a simplicity that is both elegant and poetic. Achebe's first and best-known novel, *Things*

Fall Apart (1958)—which takes its title from W. B. Yeats's "The Second Coming"—is set in an Igbo village of the late 1800s and captures the violence, disruption, and humiliation of colonialism. It posits the inevitability of change in cultural encounters, and argues for the necessity to negotiate and reconcile with change. His second novel, *No Longer at Ease* (1960), continues to probe the consequences of cultural collision and conflict, particularly the dilemma, ambiguity, and contradictions faced by those at the crossroads of cultures.

Achebe is a wordsmith for whom the use and abuse of language is a central concern. Not surprisingly, he joined the language question debates that exploded in African literary circles four decades ago. Disagreeing with those who insist that African writers write in indigenous languages, Achebe advocated the use of colonial languages, but in such a way that they are able to carry the weight and force of the African landscape, worldview, and imagination.

At seventy-four, Chinua Achebe speaks with the same moral clarity and writes with the same force and consistency as he did over four decades ago, when his first novel contributed to set the stage for what we know today as postcolonial literature. In 2004 Achebe was awarded Nigeria's second-highest honor, but in an open letter to the Nigerian president, Achebe turned down the honor in protest: "I write this letter with a heavy heart. . . . Nigeria's condition today under your watch is, however, too dangerous for silence. I must register my disappointment and protest by declining to accept the high honor awarded me."

SEE ALSO *Indirect Rule, Africa; Postcolonialism.*

BIBLIOGRAPHY

Achebe, Chinua. *Things Fall Apart*. London: Heinemann, 1958.

Achebe, Chinua. *No Longer at Ease*. London: Heinemann, 1960.

Achebe, Chinua. *Arrow of God*. London: Heinemann, 1964.

Achebe, Chinua. *A Man of the People*. London: Heinemann, 1966.

Achebe, Chinua. *Girls at War and Other Stories*. London: Heinemann, 1972.

Achebe, Chinua. *Morning Yet on Creation Day: Essays*. London: Heinemann, 1975.

Achebe, Chinua. *The Trouble with Nigeria*. Enugu, Nigeria: Fourth Dimension, 1983.

Achebe, Chinua. *Anthills of the Savannah*. London: Heinemann, 1987.

Achebe, Chinua. *Hopes and Impediments: Selected Essays, 1965–1987*. London: Heinemann, 1988.

Achebe, Chinua. *Home and Exile*. Oxford: Oxford University Press, 2000.

Achebe, Chinua. *Collected Poems*. New York: Anchor Books, 2004.

Booker, Keith M., ed. *The Chinua Achebe Encyclopedia*. Wesport, CT: Greenwood Press, 2003.

Egejuru, Phanuel Akubueze. *Chinua Achebe: Pure and Simple, An Oral Biography*. Lagos, Nigeria: Malthouse Press, 2002.

Emenyonu, Ernest N, ed. *Emerging Perspectives on Chinua Achebe*. Trenton, NJ: Africa World Press, 2003.

Ezenwa-Ohaeto. *Chinua Achebe: A Biography*. Bloomington, IN: Indiana University Press, 1997.

Innes, Catherine Lynette. *Chinua Achebe*. Cambridge, MA: Cambridge University Press, 1990.

Lindfors, Bernth, ed. *Conversations with Chinua Achebe*. Jackson: University Press of Mississippi, 1997.

Ogbaa, Kalu. *Gods, Oracles and Divination: Folkways in Chinua Achebe's Novels*. Trenton, NJ: Africa World Press, 1992.

Petersen, Kirsten Holst and Anna Rutherford, eds. *Chinua Achebe: A Celebration*. Portsmouth, NH: Heinemann, 1991.

Sallah, Tijan and Ngozi Okonjo-Iweala. *Chinua Achebe, Teacher of Light: A Biography*. Trenton, NJ: Africa World Press, 2003.

Wren, Robert M. *Achebe's World: The Historical and Cultural Context of the Novels of Chinua Achebe*. Washington, DC: Three Continents Press, 1980.

Obioma Nnaemeka

ACOSTA, JOSÉ DE
1540–1600

There is perhaps no more potent expression of the tense and complex relationship between the European colonial enterprise and the work of Christian missionaries than the life and writings of the Spanish Jesuit José de Acosta. By the time of his death in 1600 large portions of his work were known on four continents, and in at least eight languages. Famous for writing his era's most influential treatise on the conversion of indigenous peoples of the Americas to Christianity, Acosta is also credited with forming the first of the "reductions" that laid the basis for Jesuit missions in Paraguay, for writing the first indigenous-language Catholic catechism in the Andes, and for being a forceful critic of the violent Spanish conquests of Mexico, Peru, and the Philippine Islands.

Born in 1540 to a merchant family in the town of Medina del Campo in central Spain, Acosta left home at the age of twelve to join the newly formed Society of Jesus. The Jesuits were part of a new initiative for the revitalization of European religious life begun in Italy by the Basque Ignatius of Loyola. With fewer than fifty members in the first couple of years, the Jesuits numbered in the thousands by the end of the sixteenth century and were to be found on every continent save Antarctica. At the Jesuit schools Acosta studied Latin and Greek grammar and rhetoric, classical history, and geography—all of which would deeply inform his writings on the Indies—and at the universities of Alcalá and Salamanca, Acosta pursued studies in philosophy and theology. The Spanish universities of the time were hotbeds of controversy between *humanists* (advocates of classical learning) and *scholastics* (heirs of the medieval philosophical and theological schools)—a tension also reflected in Acosta's work.

Through his studies, Acosta became enamored with the religious revitalization work of the Jesuits. He sought to apply his humanistic education to the challenge of converting to Christianity peoples with histories, customs, and languages entirely different than those of Europe. Eager for intellectual debate, Acosta originally requested to be sent to China—the land most enigmatic to Europeans, yet known for its highly developed civilization and its rich philosophical and religious traditions. Acosta wrote to his superiors that he would willingly go where needed, but preferred to go where the people "were not too thick" and where his intellectual skills might be the most useful. Yet Acosta was not sent to mine the philosophical riches of China, but assigned to manage the troublesome Jesuit province of Peru—a Peru torn by controversies between religious and colonial administrators, and faced with the tense aftermath of the Spanish conquest led by Francisco Pizarro nearly a generation earlier.

Acosta arrived in Peru in 1569 amidst some anticipation: he was a highly respected orator and theologian, and it was also hoped that he would bring some clarity to the troubled world of newly colonized Peru. Acosta gained the first chair in theology at the new University of San Marcos in Lima, and in 1576 was elected Provincial of the Society of Jesus for the Province of Peru. He also acted as official theologian to the Third Council of Lima, which proposed reforms in religious practice and in colonial administration. As a result of these positions, he was able to travel widely throughout the Andean region and gain firsthand knowledge of the many difficulties faced by an indigenous population continually confronted with ambitious colonial administrators and often ignorant and unsympathetic priests and missionaries. Those experiences led Acosta to write what would become his three primary works: *De natura novi orbis* (on the geography of the New World and the customs and habits of its indigenous peoples), *De procuranda indorum salute* (on the evangelization of the indigenous peoples of the Americas), and *The Natural and Moral History of the Indies* (an expanded Spanish edition of *De natura novi orbis*).

Acosta considered his works on natural and moral history to be a preface to the more theological work on the question of conversion and its historical, political, and social preconditions. Acosta wrote that his task was to combine his experience in Peru with a rigorous study of the Holy Scriptures and Fathers of the Church—a project he fulfills in part by taking to task the early Church Fathers for their errors in understanding the natural world and their too hasty rejection of Aristotle. And yet Acosta was no Aristotelian: the great philosopher also comes in for rebuke when Acosta finds that he too was mistaken in matters ranging from geography to human customs and habits to moral philosophy. Only firsthand experience of the New World, coupled with classical knowledge, could guide proper enquiry into its natural and human diversity, Acosta argued. Combining his anthropological and theological interests, Acosta also worked to apply the thought of the Church Fathers, especially Augustine and Chrystosom, to the religious world of the Andes. The range of erudition that Acosta exhibited in these works was enormous, and his writings are replete with arguments from and allusions to the works of the Greek philosophers, Greek and Latin historians and poets, the Greek and Latin Fathers of the Church, and medieval historians, theologians, and jurists. Stylistically, his writing combined "erudition" with "eloquence" along models advanced by earlier European humanists.

In the heightened and conflicted colonial context in which he worked, Acosta's attitudes toward indigenous religions in the Americas range from moments of subtle understanding to the harsh rejection of practices he thought—following the Church Fathers—to be demonically inspired. He thus found himself perpetually engaged in debates ranging from the meaning of human sacrifice in Mexico to how to extirpate idolatry in Peru. Yet his most evocative arguments were with his fellow Spaniards. Acosta spared few harsh words and argued that the Spanish conquests were not "just wars," and that the "greatest sin" perpetuated in the Americas was the horrific violence of a conquest that enriched the Spaniards while robbing the indigenous peoples of their lives and liberty. He further argued that indigenous hostility to Christianity was not a result of their incapacity to understand it, but was a direct result of Spanish violence and the scandalous behavior of priests, missionaries, and colonial administrators who were supposed to be examples of the love of Christ.

In 1587 Acosta returned to Spain, and he published his primary works there in 1589. He continued to engage in controversies over the Spanish colonial project, and even worked to block a proposal for the conquest of China launched by Jesuits in the Philippines. For the remainder of his life he worked to train Jesuits to apply the lessons learned in the Americas to the "other Indies" of Spain itself. He was even called to investigate how missionary methods derived from Peru might be applied to the formerly Muslim population of southern Spain, in order to stave off renewed pressure for their expulsion from an increasingly homogenous religious landscape. Hence Acosta ended his career continuing full circle the program of religious revitalization with which he began, only with the difficult experience of Peru and Mexico behind him. The argument made centuries later by post-colonial theorists that the colonial experience deeply shaped and transformed the colonizer as well as the colonized was certainly true for José de Acosta.

SEE ALSO *Peru under Spanish Rule.*

BIBLIOGRAPHY

Acosta, José de. *Obras del P. José de Acosta.* Biblioteca de Autores Españoles 73. Edited by Francisco Mateos. Madrid: Atlas, 1954.

Acosta, José de. *De procuranda Indorum salute.* Edited by Luciano Pereña. Madrid: Consejo Superior de Investigaciones Científicas, 1984–1987.

Acosta, José de. *The Natural and Moral History of the Indies.* Edited by Jane Mangan; translated by Frances Lopez-Morillas. Durham, NC: Duke University Press, 2002.

Álvarez López, Enrique. "La filosofia natural en Padre José de Acosta." *Revista de Indias* (1943): 305–322.

Ares Queija, Berta, et al. eds. *Humanismo y visión del otro en la España moderna: Cuatro estudios.* Madrid: Consejo Superior de Investigaciones Científicas, 1992.

Baciero, Claudio. "Acosta y el Catecismo Limense: Una nueva pedagogia." In *Inculturación del Indio,* edited by Luciano Pereña et al. Salamanca, Spain: Universidad Pontifica de Salamanca, 1988.

Burgaleta, Claudio M. *José de Acosta (1540–1600): His Life and Thought.* Chicago: Loyola University Press, 1999.

Carducci, Luigi Guarnieri Calò. *Nuovo mondo e ordine politico: La Compagnia di Gesù in Perù e l'attività di José de Acosta.* Rimini, Italy: Il Cerchio, 1997.

Echánove, Alfonso. "Origen y evolución de la idea jesuítica de 'reducciones' en las misiones del Virreinato del Perú." *Missionalia Hispanica* 12 (1955): 95–144; 13 (1956): 497–540.

Lopetegui, Léon. *El padre José de Acosta, S. I., y las misiones.* Madrid: Consejo Superior de Investigaciones Científicas, 1942.

MacCormack, Sabine. *Religion in the Andes: Vision and Imagination in Early Colonial Peru.* Princeton, NJ: Princeton University Press, 1991.

Pagden, Anthony. *The Fall of Natural Man: The American Indian and the Origins of Comparative Ethnology.* New York: Cambridge University Press, 1982.

Pagden, Anthony. *European Encounters with the New World: From Renaissance to Romanticism.* New Haven, CT: Yale University Press, 1993.

Pinta Llorente, Miguel de la. *Actividades diplomáticas del P. José de Acosta: En torno a una política, y a un sentimiento religioso.* Madrid: Consejo Superior de Investigaciones Científicas, 1952.

Rivara de Tuesta, María Luisa. *José de Acosta, un humanista reformista.* Lima: Gráf. de Editorial Universo, 1970.

Shepherd, Gregory. *An Exposition of Jose de Acosta's* Historia natural y moral de las Indias, *1590: The Emergence of an Anthropological Vision of Colonial Latin America.* Lewiston, NY: Mellen Press, 2002.

Patrick Provost-Smith

AFGHANI, JAMAL AD-DIN AL-
1838–1897

Jamal ad-Din al-Afghani is one of the best-known political thinkers and agitators of the nineteenth-century Muslim world. He is known for his calls for modernization and pan-Islamic solidarity, which he saw as the means by which the Muslim world could strengthen itself in its struggle against European aggression. Although he usually claimed to be an Afghan, making possible a Sunni identity in the majority Sunni Islamic world, overwhelming primary evidence shows that he was born and raised as a Shi'i in Iran. In adolescence he went to the Shi'i shrine cities of Iraq for further education and then to India, where he was during the 1857 revolt, which probably contributed to his lifelong anti-British stance.

Afghani went to Afghanistan for the only time in 1866; there he tried to convince the emir to fight the British, but in 1868 he was expelled by a new emir. He then went to Istanbul and was again expelled after giving a talk comparing prophets with philosophers. His most fruitful years, 1871 to 1879, were spent in Egypt, where he gathered a group of young disciples, several of whom became important, especially Muhammad 'Abduh (1849–1905). He preached a rationalist and modernist Islam that adapted the teachings of various Greek-influenced medieval Islamic philosophers. After being expelled from Egypt he went to Hyderabad, India, where he wrote several articles and a treatise known as the "Refutation of the Materialists." From there he joined Muhammad 'Abduh in Paris, where they edited the newspaper *al-'Urwa al Wuthqa,* distributed throughout the Muslim world. Afghani also published in French his answer to Ernest Renan's "Islam and Science," in which Afghani was portrayed as an unorthodox rationalist.

From France Afghani went to England and then Iran, where he made two stays in 1886 to 1891, during which he agitated against the state's granting of numerous concessions to foreigners. Between the two stays in Iran he went to Russia to agitate against the British. Afghani's activities in Iran brought about his forcible expulsion to Iraq, where he played a part in getting the leading Shi'i cleric to support a major, successful Iranian mass movement against the concession of all tobacco transactions to a British subject. After a trip to London, Afghani accepted Sultan

Abdülhamid's invitation to Istanbul, where at Abdülhamid's behest he wrote Shi'i clerics to urge them to recognize the sultan as the leader of Islam. The sultan kept Afghani in a "gilded cage," as Afghani was not allowed to publish or leave Istanbul. In 1896 an Iranian disciple, saying he was inspired by a visit to Afghani, assassinated Naser al-Din Shah. Afghani died of cancer in 1897.

Afghani was impressive as a teacher and fiery speaker. He was one of the first to provide popular arguments for modernizing and unifying the Muslim world and against capitulation to foreigners, especially the British. Though he was not especially orthodox, his combination of religious language with activist politics has made him attractive to many in the Muslim world who reject the more gradualist and compromising approach of intellectuals like 'Abduh. The ambiguity and variety of his record have made him appealing to many different schools of Muslim thought up until the present day. His ideas were often similar to those of the earlier Young Ottomans, but his travels, activities, and writing in Arabic and Persian, not Turkish, made him much better known in the Muslim world.

SEE ALSO *Abdülhamid II.*

BIBLIOGRAPHY

Keddie, Nikki R. *An Islamic Response to Imperialism: Political and Religious Writings of Sayyid Jamal ad-Din al-Afghani: With a New Introduction: From Afghani to Khomeini.* Berkeley: University of California Press, 1983.

Keddie, Nikki R. *Sayyid Jamal ad-Din "al-Afghani:" A Political Biography.* Berkeley: University of California Press, 1972.

Pakdaman, Homa. *Djemal-ed Din Assad Abadj, dit Afghani.* Paris: G.P. Maisonneuve et Larose, 1969.

Nikki Keddie

AFGHAN WARS

When the British Indian army invaded Afghanistan during the First Anglo-Afghan War (1838–1842), the country was a mere shadow of the mighty and feared Kingdom of Afghanistan of the eighteenth century. The demise of the Afghan state resulted partly from internal reasons, but it was mainly due to the loss of its traditional source of income—namely, raiding the wealthy neighboring lands of India and Iran. Both the Sikhs of the Panjab in the east and the Qajars of Persia in the west had managed to repel the Afghan assaults. As a result, the Afghan king, whose position among the Afghan tribes had never been strong, lacked the means to pay and bribe his subjects, and central authority virtually disappeared. The weak Afghan state was consequently perceived as vulnerable to outside influence.

FIRST ANGLO-AFGHAN WAR

The First Anglo-Afghan War resulted from British fear of growing Russian influence in Central Asia and the subsequent threat to Great Britain's Indian possessions. Since the eighteenth century, Russia had pushed its domain southward into the Caucasus and South Central Asia. This marked the start of the so-called Great Game, the struggle between the British and the Russians for control of the Indo-Afghan mountains.

The strife between Britain and Russia came to a head in November 1837 when the Russians supported their ally, the Iranian king, in his attempt to take the city of Herat from a local Afghan leader. The British regarded the Russian presence in the area as a serious threat and tried to force the Iranians and their Russian advisors to withdraw. The British succeeded in doing so in September 1838 following their naval attack on the island of Kharq in the Persian Gulf.

Before the Iranian withdrawal the British tried to convince the Afghan leader in Kabul, Amir Dust Muhammad Khan (1793–1863), not to side with the Iranians and Russians. Instead, they wanted him to conclude a treaty with their allies, the Sikhs. The Afghans could never accept such a demand, since they were still sensitive about the Sikh occupation of parts of the former Kingdom of Afghanistan, including Peshawar (1818) and Kashmir (1819). Although Dust Muhammad Khan had no intention of siding with the Russians, the British authorities decided he was a liability and needed to be replaced by another Afghan leader more amenable to British interests.

In the summer of 1838 the British asked the Sikhs and the former Afghan king, Shah Shuja (ca.1792–1842), to confirm their earlier agreements concerning the return of Shah Shuja to Kabul. On October 1, 1838, Lord Auckland (George Eden, 1784–1849) issued the *Simla Manifesto,* which called for the removal of Dust Muhammad Khan and the reinstatement of Shah Shuja. British troops, supported by Sikh units, occupied much of Afghanistan, including Kabul, during the spring and summer of 1839 and put Shah Shuja on the Afghan throne. The British were initially successful, but later were confronted by local resistance throughout the country. Eventually the British were forced to evacuate their cantonment in Kabul and start their famous "retreat from Kabul" in January 1842.

Most of the sixteen thousand troops were either killed or taken prisoner. Shah Shuja was killed by his own subjects in Kabul. The British quickly reoccupied Kabul in the summer of 1842, but it was clear that they could never hold Afghanistan without heavy costs. The British now wanted a relatively strong Afghanistan that was friendly to them and that would resist the Russians. The decision was made to withdraw permanently and to allow Dust Muhammad Khan, whom the British now

Afghan Highlanders, 1879. *During the Second Anglo-Afghan War, Afghan soldiers wore kilts in imitation of British Highlander troops from Scotland, whose skills the Afghans admired.* © **HULTON-DEUTSCH COLLECTION/CORBIS. REPRODUCED BY PERMISSION.**

regarded as the only Afghan leader with enough influence to build up central control and pacify the country, to return from exile and regain the Afghan throne.

In the ensuing years the British maintained a policy of "masterly inactivity," without any interference in the affairs of the Afghans. However, during this time British dominion spread to the foot of the Afghan mountain passes, including the town of Peshawar. Simultaneously, Russian influence in South Central Asia also spread. Tashkent was occupied in 1865, Samarqand in 1868, and the emirate of Bukhara was made into a Russian protectorate in 1869, while Khiva fell in 1873 and Kokand in 1876. The weakened state of Afghanistan seemed destined to fall, either to the British or the Russians.

SECOND ANGLO-AFGHAN WAR

In 1874 a new government in London, led by Benjamin Disraeli (1804–1881), adopted a more aggressive stance in India and appointed a strong-minded governor general. In an atmosphere of growing tension, a Russian delegation, apparently uninvited, visited Kabul in July 1878. The British issued an ultimatum asking for equal rights of access to Kabul. When this ultimatum was rejected, the British crossed the border and thereby started the Second Anglo-Afghan War (1878–1879).

The Afghans were quickly defeated, and the war was concluded with the Treaty of Gandamak (May 29, 1879). The treaty included the stipulation that Afghanistan would remain an independent nation, but would conduct its foreign policy via the British rulers in India in lieu of regular subsidies and a British guarantee regarding the security of the country.

In the summer of 1879 a British embassy under Major Pierre Louis Cavagnari (1841–1879) was sent to Kabul, but shortly afterwards (September 1879), it was wiped out by an angry Afghan mob. The British felt compelled to occupy Kabul, but again realized that a

Khyber Pass Border Crossing. *British soldiers stand guard at the Khyber Pass, which connects present-day Pakistan with Afghanistan, during the third Anglo-Afghan War in 1919.* **HULTON ARCHIVE/GETTY IMAGES. REPRODUCED BY PERMISSION.**

permanent occupation of the country was too costly. British troops eventually withdrew from Afghanistan in 1881, leaving behind a young and ruthless ruler, Abdur Rakhman Khan (ca. 1844–1901). Under the protection of the British and under the stipulations of the Treaty of Gandamak, Abdur Rakhman Khan quickly modernized the country and built up central authority.

The relationship between the Afghans, British, and Russians was initially precarious. In 1885 the Russians defeated an Afghan garrison in Panjdeh, in the northwest of the country. This led to considerable tension. Eventually the British refused to help the Afghans, although they were obligated to do so. The relations with the Russians slowly improved after a treaty was signed that demarcated the northwestern borders of the country. In later years the complete borderline of Afghanistan was chartered by British officers; often in full cooperation with the Russians. Afghanistan was made into a buffer state separating British India from Russia.

THIRD ANGLO-AFGHAN WAR

The Great Game came to an end in 1907 when the Russians and British signed the Anglo-Russian Convention, thereby dividing their respective political and commercial spheres of interest in Iran and Afghanistan. Complete independence only came to Afghanistan in 1919 with the Third Anglo-Afghan War.

Following the collapse of Russia and World War I, the Afghans wanted their full independence, which the British were reluctant to grant. Although the Afghans proved no match to the British, the latter did not want to fight another war. After about one month and the bombing of the emir's palace in Kabul, the British agreed to the Peace Treaty of Rawalpindi (August 8, 1919), which was followed by the Anglo-Afghan Treaty of November 22, 1921. This treaty stipulated the complete independence of Afghanistan.

SEE ALSO *Anglo-Russian Rivalry in the Middle East; British India and the Middle East.*

BIBLIOGRAPHY

Adamec, Ludwig W. *Historical Dictionary of Afghanistan,* 3rd ed. Lanham, MD: Scarecrow Press, 2003.

Hopkirk, Peter. *The Great Game: On Secret Service in High Asia.* London: Murray, 1990.

Vogelsang, Willem. *The Afghans*. Oxford and Malden, MA: Blackwell, 2002.

Willem Vogelsang

AFRICAN NATIONAL CONGRESS

The African National Congress (ANC), the oldest black political organization in South Africa until it became multiracial in the 1990s, was founded on January 8, 1912, in Bloemfontein by chiefs, representatives of African peoples and church organizations, and other prominent individuals. The aim of the ANC was to bring all Africans together and to defend their rights and freedoms in a then racially divided South Africa.

The ANC was formed at a time of rapid change in South Africa. The organization began as a nonviolent civil rights group, but its tactics and strategy changed over time. The discovery of diamonds in 1867 and gold in 1886 transformed not only the social, political, and economic structure of South Africa, but the racial attitude of whites towards blacks. The contestations over mining rights, land, and labor gave rise to new laws that discriminated against the black population. Laws were designed to force Africans to leave their land and provide labor for the expanding mining and commercial agriculture industry. The most severe law was the 1913 Land Act, which prevented Africans from buying, renting, or using land except in the so-called reserves. Many communities or families lost their land because of the Land Act. Millions of blacks could not meet their subsistence needs off the land. The Land Act caused overcrowding, land hunger, poverty, and starvation.

The political activism of the ANC dates back to the Land Act of 1913. The Land Act and other laws, including the pass laws, controlled the movements of African people and ensured that they worked either in mines or on farms. The pass laws also stopped Africans from leaving their jobs or striking. In 1919 the ANC in Transvaal led a campaign against the passes. The ANC also supported a militant strike by African mineworkers in 1920. However, there was disagreement over the strategies to be adopted in achieving the goals set by the ANC. Some ANC leaders disagreed with militant actions such as strikes and protests in preference for persuasion, negotiation, and appeals to Britain. But appeals to British authorities in 1914 to protest the Land Act, and in 1919 to ask Britain to recognize African rights, did not achieve these goals.

In the 1920s, government policies became harsher and more racist. A color bar was established to stop blacks from holding semiskilled jobs in some industries. The ANC did not achieve much in this era. J. T. Gumede (1870–1947) was elected president of the ANC in 1927.

He tried to revitalize the organization in order to fight these racist policies. Gumede thought that communists could make a contribution to this struggle and he wanted the ANC to cooperate with them. However, in 1930, Gumede was voted out of office, and the ANC became inactive in the 1930s under conservative leadership.

The ANC was very prominent in its opposition to apartheid in the 1940s. The formation of the ANC Youth League in 1944 gave the organization new life and energy, and transformed it into the mass movement it was to become in the 1950s. The leaders of the Youth League, including Nelson Mandela (b. 1918), Walter Sisulu (1912–2003), and Oliver Tambo (1917–1993), aimed to involve the masses in militant struggles. They believed that the past strategy of the ANC could not lead to the liberation of black South Africans.

The militant ideas of the Youth League found support among the emerging urban black workforce. The Youth League drew up a Programme of Action calling for strikes, boycotts, and defiance. The Programme of Action was adopted by the ANC in 1949, the year after the National Party came to power on a pro-apartheid platform. The Programme of Action led to the Defiance Campaign in the 1950s as the ANC joined with other groups in promoting strikes and civil disobedience. The Defiance Campaign was the beginning of a mass movement of resistance to such apartheid laws as the Population Registration Act, the Group Areas Act and Bantu Education Act, and the pass laws.

The government tried to stop the Defiance Campaign by banning its leaders and passing new laws to prevent public disobedience. But the campaign had already made huge gains, including closer cooperation between the ANC and the South African Indian Congress, and the formation of a new South Africa Colored Peoples' Organization (SACPO) and the Congress of Democrats (COD), an organization of white democrats. These organizations, together with the South African Congress of Trade Unions (SACTU), formed the Congress Alliance.

The Congress Alliance called for the people to govern and for the land to be shared by those who work it. The alliance called for houses, work, security, and free and equal education. These demands were drawn together into the Freedom Charter, which was adopted at the Congress of the People at Kliptown on June 26, 1955. The government claimed that the Freedom Charter was a communist document and arrested ANC and Congress Alliance leaders and brought them to trial in the famous Treason Trial. The government tried to prove that the ANC and its allies had a policy of violence and planned to overthrow the state.

Nelson Mandela and Thabo Mbeki, February 28, 1999. *South African president Nelson Mandela (left) stands with Deputy President Thabo Mbeki at a campaign rally in Soweto, South Africa. Mbeki succeeded Mandela as head of the ANC in 1997 and as president of South Africa in 1999.* **PER-ANDERS PETTERSON/GETTY IMAGES. REPRODUCED BY PERMISSION.**

The struggles of the 1950s brought blacks and whites together on a larger scale in the fight for justice and democracy. The Congress Alliance was an expression of the ANC's policy of nonracialism. This was expressed in the Freedom Charter, which declared that South Africa belongs to all who live in it. But not everyone in the ANC agreed with the policy of nonracialism. A small minority of members, who called themselves Africanists, opposed the Freedom Charter. They objected to the ANC's growing cooperation with whites and Indians, whom they described as foreigners. They were also suspicious of communists who, they felt, brought a foreign ideology into the struggle. The differences between the Africanists and those in the ANC who supported nonracialism could not be overcome. In 1959 the Africanists broke away and formed the Pan Africanist Congress (PAC).

Anti–pass law campaigns were taken up by both the ANC and the PAC in 1960. The massacre on March 21, 1960, of sixty-nine peaceful protestors at Sharpeville, near Johannesburg, brought a decade of peaceful protest to an end. The ANC was banned in 1960, and the government declared a state of emergency and arrested thousands of ANC and PAC activists. The following year, the ANC initiated guerrilla attacks. In 1964 its leader, Nelson Mandela, was sentenced to life in prison and the ANC leadership was forced into exile.

The ANC went underground and continued to organize secretly. An underground military wing of the ANC, Umkhonto we Sizwe or Spear of the Nation, was formed in December 1961 to "hit back by all means within our power in defense of our people, our future and our freedom." The ANC continued to be popularly acknowledged as the vehicle of mass resistance to apartheid in the late 1970s and the 1980s. In spite of detentions and bans, the mass movement took to the city streets defiantly. In February 1990, the government was forced to lift the ban on the ANC and other organizations and signaled a desire to negotiate a peaceful settlement of the South African problem.

At the 1991 National Conference of the ANC, Nelson Mandela, who was released from prison in 1990, was elected ANC president. Oliver Tambo, who served as president of the ANC from 1969 to 1991, was elected national chairperson. The negotiations initiated by the ANC resulted in the holding of South Africa's first democratic elections in April 1994. The ANC won these historic elections with over 62 percent of the votes. On May 10, 1994, Nelson Mandela was inaugurated as the president of South Africa. Thabo Mbeki (b. 1942) succeeded Mandela as head of the ANC in 1997 and as president of South Africa in 1999.

SEE ALSO *Apartheid; Mandela, Nelson.*

BIBLIOGRAPHY

African National Congress: South Africa's National Liberation Movement. Available from http://www.anc.org.za/.

Manifesto of Umkhonto we Sizewe. Command of Umkhonto we Sizwe leaflet, December 16, 1961.

Thompson, Leonard. *A History of South Africa*, 3rd ed. New Haven, CT: Yale University Press, 2001.

Chima J. Korieh

AFRICAN SLAVERY IN THE AMERICAS

Slavery, a fairly universal development across many of the world's ancient and early modern societies, took myriad forms reflecting a number of variables within a given historical setting. The enslavement of both Native American and African peoples in the Americas was no different, in this respect, from previous developments. Yet slavery in the Americas was exceptional as the transatlantic slave trade developed concurrently with a nascent capitalist system that touched much of the Western world. During this transformation, older forms of slavery—where enslavement was often a temporary status mediated by tribal customs or protective legal codes—were transformed into an institution in which the enslaved were marked as chattel, that is, personal property, and of inferior racial status.

THE INTRODUCTION OF AFRICAN SLAVERY

Spain and Portugal led Europe's initial efforts to colonize the Americas and first introduced African slavery to the hemisphere. Given their late medieval history, both powers were uniquely suited for experimenting with African slavery in the Americas. While the institution of slavery declined in importance throughout much of Europe following the collapse of the western half of the Roman Empire during the fifth century CE the institution was revitalized in Iberia (the peninsula now occupied by Spain and Portugal) with the invasion of the Moors in 711 and the intermittent Christian campaign to retake

lost territory over the subsequent seven centuries. As Christian and Muslim kingdoms collided and competed with one another, raids and warfare led to the occasional enslavement of captives and subjugated populations.

The Portuguese Crown completed its campaign of reconquest by the mid-thirteenth century, which led within a few decades to a shift of commercial aspirations and the crusade impulse into the Atlantic. Portuguese maritime activity involved the exploration of the western coast of sub-Saharan Africa and various uninhabited Atlantic islands (e.g., Madeira, the Azores, and the Cape Verdes). The Portuguese sought to tap into the lucrative, preexisting trade network of the West African coast, bringing to Lisbon cargoes of ivory, peppers, gold, and some African slaves.

European demand for enslaved Africans during the fifteenth century was relatively small compared to later developments and probably exerted a negligible influence on sub-Saharan slave markets. The impact of the slave trade was soon noticeable in Iberia, however; by the start of the sixteenth century, several thousand enslaved and freed people of African descent resided in such Iberian cities as Lisbon and Seville. The expulsion of the Moors from the Christian kingdoms of Spain took longer, but Spanish ships soon joined their Portuguese counterparts in plying the Atlantic. Spanish efforts concentrated on the conquest of the Guanches, the original inhabitants of the Canary Islands, at the close of the fifteenth century.

Following earlier Portuguese precedent, particularly on Madeira, plantations were established to cultivate sugar for the insatiable European market. Throughout these Atlantic islands, and eventually São Tomé off the African coast, various enslaved groups were shipped to the plantations, including conquered Moors from Spain, the Guanches of the Canaries, and finally Africans purchased along the western coast of Africa. These initial experiments with sugar plantations and imported African slaves served as a harbinger for later developments in the Americas.

THE CARIBBEAN

While the Portuguese developed trade relations along the western and central African coast, Spain benefited from the fortuitous discovery of the American hemisphere through its support of the Genoese navigator Cristóbal Colón (Christopher Columbus, 1451–1506). Columbus made landfall in late 1492 in the Lesser Antilles and eventually Hispaniola (the island comprising the modern nations of Haiti and the Dominican Republic). While he famously searched for the "Great Khan" of China, Columbus also sought potential commercial opportunities for his royal sponsors, including the traffic of Indian slaves. He noted the servile and peaceful nature

Slave arrivals in the Americas, 1451–1870	
1451–1600	274,000
1601–1700	1,341,100
1701–1800	5,729,100
1801–1870	2,902,400
Total	10,247,500

SOURCE: For the period 1451 to 1700, Philip D. Curtin, *The Atlantic Slave Trade: A Census* (Madison: The University of Wisconsin Press, 1969), p. 268; for the period 1701–1870, David Eltis' revision of Curtin's figures, Eltis, *Economic Growth and the Ending of the Transatlantic Slave Trade* (New York, 1989).

THE GALE GROUP.

of the Arawak inhabitants of the Caribbean, who might be coerced into laboring in the gold mines that he rightly guessed would be discovered on Hispaniola.

Spanish colonization of the Caribbean began in earnest with Columbus's second voyage in 1493. Discipline and work were concepts difficult to instill in a colonist population seeking fortune and a quick return home. Spanish-Indian relations thus turned sour as colonists demanded greater access to native labor and provisions. A version of the Iberian *encomienda*, through which non-Christians were placed under the vassalage of a Christian lord, was adapted to the Caribbean context to satisfy these demands. In its various guises, the *encomienda* would serve as the initial instrument for tapping indigenous labor and goods as the Spanish expanded their control over new lands and peoples.

Old World diseases and exploitation decimated Hispaniola's native population, spurring colonists to begin raiding much of the Caribbean basin for substitute labor. Such actions were commonly justified by the Spanish perception of the existence of hostile, man-eating Caribs (from which the term *cannibalism* originates). Slave raiding emptied out the Bahamas by 1513, while the military conquest of Puerto Rico in 1508 and Cuba in 1511 supplied even larger numbers of war captives.

This initial experimental phase raised profound questions for Spanish jurists concerning the nature of the colonial enterprise, Spanish obligations to autochthonous groups, and eventually a rationale for importing African slaves. Spain's initial claim to sovereignty over the Americas rested largely on a series of papal bulls (decrees) and treaties promulgated after the return of Columbus's first voyage to the New World. Pope Alexander VI (1431–1503) had effectively divided the world into two spheres of influence, providing Spain a monopoly over most of what would become the American continents while setting aside Africa and the Far East for rival Portugal. This decision, however, rested upon the moral obligation of the crown to evangelize newly discovered pagan peoples and to establish a protective tutelage over them.

These early ideological underpinnings of the colonial enterprise brought significant consequences for how the Spanish monarchy approached its indigenous subjects and the topic of slavery. Facing a demographic catastrophe in its Caribbean colonies by the second decade of the sixteenth century, the crown responded with decrees that restricted conditions for waging "just war" against hostile Indians and limited enslavement to known cannibals. Enforcement proved difficult, however. The invasion of Central America in 1500, for example, led to a half century of Indian slaving that resulted in the export of tens of thousands of captives out of the region. In response to the precipitous decline of indigenous groups throughout the mainland, the so-called New Laws of 1542 banned definitively Indian slavery, although the practice persisted well into the eighteenth century in precariously held frontier zones in northern Mexico, Chile, and Argentina. As the legality of Indian slavery became more nebulous and their numbers dwindled, the demand for compliant labor took a different direction.

The introduction of slaves of African descent to the Americas took place within this larger juridical conversation regarding the crown's obligations to the indigenous population. Small numbers of black slaves had been present since the earliest stages of the colonization of the Caribbean. Originating from Iberia, many of these individuals were considered *ladino*, a term indicating they had assimilated elements of Hispanic culture and spoke Spanish. Concerns regarding the presumed fragility of the New World's population, coupled with a desire to maintain the economic viability of the Caribbean colonies, led to an escalation of African slavery as a replacement for various forms of coerced indigenous labor. Simultaneously, with the opening of the transatlantic slave trade in the 1530s through the Portuguese-held trade factory of São Tomé off the African coast, a growing number of Africans were shipped to the New World who had very little or no Hispanic acculturation. They were called *bozales*.

MESOAMERICA AND SOUTH AMERICA

Spanish colonization and African slavery took an enormous step forward with the conquest of mainland indigenous societies, beginning in 1521 with the fall of the Aztec state in central Mexico and that of the Inca in the Andes in 1532. While success is often attributed solely to Spanish conquistadors, slaves and freedmen of African

Slave Populations in the Americas, ca. 1770

Region	Slave Population	Total Population
Spanish America	290,000	12,144,000
Brazil	700,000	2,000,000
British Caribbean	428,000	500,000
British North America	450,000	2,100,000
French Caribbean	379,000	430,000
Dutch Caribbean	75,000	90,000

SOURCE: Adapted from Robin Blackburn, *The Overthrow of Colonial Slavery, 1776–1848* (London: Verso, 1988), p. 5.

THE GALE GROUP.

descent played a crucial role as auxiliaries and porters. Despite their contributions to these campaigns, few "black conquistadors" received significant compensation for their efforts, spurring many to participate in further conquests in more marginal zones of Central and South America, or to accept minor positions in newly established cities.

Colonial exploitation in these core areas rested on coerced but nominally free Indian labor. As they had in the Caribbean, Spanish settlers turned to the *encomienda* as the principal motor of enrichment and economic development. Preexisting tribute and labor levies inherited from the conquered native polities enabled a fairly rapid transition to a new colonial regime. Indian tributaries were to provide the Spanish elite with marketable goods and new urban zones with foodstuffs. While some forms of indigenous slavery existed prior to the arrival of Europeans and carried over into the early colonial era, most Indian labor was organized and channeled through indigenous lords and their subject communities via the *encomienda*.

State labor drafts of indigenous tributaries began to overshadow the private *encomienda* by the second half of the sixteenth century. This was particularly the case once significant deposits of silver were discovered starting in the 1540s in sparsely populated zones (northern Mexico and the high Andes of Bolivia).

African slavery complemented Indian labor from the very inception of these mainland viceroyalties. Slaves were particularly important in urban economies, filling various labor niches as skilled artisans, truck gardeners, and household servants. Early colonists also considered slaves effective foremen of their Indian tributaries, which helped give rise to a reputation of blacks as abusive and threatening to native people, an image that only recently has been challenged and at least partly debunked.

African slavery in Spanish America accelerated after the mid-sixteenth century due to two principal factors. First, the indigenous population of newly conquered areas suffered a demographic catastrophe similar to that which had befallen the Caribbean. As the tributary population declined due to disease and exploitation, and the demands of the Spanish sector expanded due to its own demographic growth, colonial entrepreneurs and the state again looked to replace the Indian laborers with African slaves. The fortuitous union of the Spanish and Portuguese crowns (1580–1640) provided the colonies a more reliable source of slaves that coincided with the nadir of indigenous population levels.

African slavery reverted to a more supplemental role in Mesoamerica and the Andes during the second half of the seventeenth century as Spain and Portugal split politically and the native population began to recover. The Spanish maintained the so-called *asiento* (monopoly contract), however, which licensed select European powers with access to the coast of Africa to transport and market slaves in Spain's American ports of entry.

Meanwhile, the Portuguese discovery of Brazil in 1500 opened up additional possibilities for colonization and African slavery. Unlike the populous societies Spain conquered in Mesoamerica and the Andes, the Portuguese encountered stateless, semi-sedentary groups living along the coast in a near incessant state of tribal warfare. Brazil was considered a less promising opportunity than the lucrative trade networks the Portuguese were tapping into along the coast of Africa and later in the Indian Ocean and Far East. The colonization impulse was therefore dampened for several decades in Brazil, while early Portuguese-Indian relations centered on the relatively peaceful Brazil wood trade.

Efforts by the French to initiate their own colonies in Brazil (between 1555 and 1615) compelled the Portuguese Crown to sponsor a more serious colonization effort that eventually centered on sugar cultivation in the northeast. Planters tried to gather Indian men, either voluntarily or not, to supply the necessary labor, but encountered serious difficulties. Decimated by disease and facing a harsher labor regime than they were accustomed to, native laborers fled the plantations in droves. Further complicating matters were indigenous attitudes that associated agricultural work with women. Planter demands for labor led to a deterioration in tribal relations and an escalation in frontier violence.

The relative proximity of Brazil to advanced agricultural societies in Africa made feasible the decision to seek alternative labor. During the early seventeenth century, African slaves replaced Indian workers as the principal motor of plantation production throughout the Brazilian northeast. Nevertheless, raids into the Brazilian interior for Indian slaves continued. Of these efforts, the most famous were the *bandeirantes* of the southern city of São Paulo, themselves a multiethnic and polyglot group, who opened up territory deep in the continent for later settlement by the Portuguese.

Over the course of the seventeenth century, northern Europeans began encroaching on territories claimed by Spain and Portugal and experimenting with African slavery. Of particular significance were the Dutch, who revolted against Spanish rule in 1572 in a protracted conflict that eventually embroiled the Portuguese. Founded in 1621, the Dutch West Indies Company sought over the next two decades to wrest away from Portugal its sugar zones in Brazil and slaving ports along the African coast.

Although the Dutch were ousted from Brazil in 1654, the interim period proved decisive in the subsequent development of American slavery. Dutch planters who had gained expertise in the production of sugar and its mill technology began colonizing Caribbean islands (Barbados, Martinique, and Guadeloupe) as early as the 1640s. Like Brazil, much of the Caribbean remained vulnerable to colonization efforts by Iberia's imperial rivals. Joining the Dutch were increasing numbers of British and French planters who benefited from their nations' own efforts to gain a foothold on the African slave trade. By the eighteenth century, this multinational experiment ended Brazil's dominance of the international sugar market while also drawing significant numbers of African slaves to the region.

NORTH AMERICA

Labor demands in British North America also fostered the growth of an African slave population. Until the late seventeenth century, however, labor demands throughout much of the American eastern seaboard were met through a combination of family members, indentured servants, and only a scattering of African slaves. This initial "charter" generation of slaves tended to be drawn from those already living in this emerging Atlantic world, and like the early *ladinos* of the Spanish colonial world, these individuals benefited from a familiarity with diverse European languages, cultures, and institutions. Often working in small numbers and alongside white servants and even their masters, the social distance between enslaved and free was smaller than that which would develop under the plantation regime. While brutality and coercion were not absent, the possibility existed for manumission and some degree of social mobility through market participation, the purchase of land, and affiliation with Christian churches.

Similar to developments in the Hispanic world, the transition to a plantation system throughout much of the North American colonies (e.g., tobacco in the Chesapeake and rice and indigo in South Carolina) by the early eighteenth century led to a predominance of African-born slaves and fewer opportunities for manumission or social mobility for those already freed. For half a century, the slave population in these zones was characterized by the retention of African languages, culture, and religion before being outpaced by the gradual development of an African-American generation with its own culture, informed by both its ancestral roots and that of the European colonists.

LATER DEVELOPMENTS

Slavery also continued to evolve in much of Latin America. New commercial opportunities, such as cacao in Venezuela, produced variations in the plantation model. Despite its decline relative to the Caribbean plantation systems, Brazil remained the single largest destination for African slaves. As the sugar industry suffered from international competition, new demands for African slaves emerged.

Indian slave raiding by the *bandeirantes* led to the discovery of gold and diamond mines in the interior of central Brazil in 1693 to 1695 and in 1729 respectively. Miners, slaves, and royal tax collectors followed in the wake of these bonanzas, stimulating the creation of new urban zones and market demands. Extraction took two principal forms. In some areas, large gangs of supervised slaves worked in placer mines created through elaborate and costly hydraulic works and sluices. Those with less capital established agreements whereby largely unsupervised slaves prospected in return for a share of the findings.

Within decades, a substantial freed population emerged as slaves were able to purchase their freedom from the surpluses they retained. Similar developments occurred in areas of Spanish America, such as the gold mines of the Chocó (the Pacific coastal lowlands of modern Colombia). African slaves were preferred over intransigent Indian groups, leading to an increasingly African and freed population by the end of the eighteenth century.

As these examples suggest, the impact of the slave trade varied widely across space and time given the diverse conditions of different regions of the New World. Despite an early prominence in the traffic of bondsmen, the viceroyalties of New Spain and Peru, for example, remained heavily indigenous due to the vast size of the pre-Hispanic population, even after the sixteenth- and seventeenth-century collapse. While slavery persisted as an institution, over time it played a diminishing role in the lives of most individuals of African descent. High rates of manumission and interracial sexual unions led to an African-based population creolized in culture and with free people outnumbering the enslaved.

Where the indigenous population was initially much thinner, the demographic results varied. In what became the viceroyalty of the Río de la Plata in 1776 (comprising mostly modern Argentina), both the European and African presence was sparse. Nevertheless, the port of Buenos Aires continued to contain a discernible black population well into the nineteenth century. In the Spanish Caribbean, in contrast, Puerto Rico and Cuba witnessed a dramatic rise in slavery during the eighteenth century, which left a pronounced African presence that persists to the present day. Much of Brazil and parts of British North America, which contained lower population densities than Mesoamerica and the Andes, also developed discernible African-based (and creolized) populations by the end of the eighteenth century.

CONDITIONS FOR SLAVES IN THE AMERICAS

The relative numerical strength of African populations throughout the Americas was in turn shaped by each region's relationship to the Atlantic slave trade. Estimating the volume of the trade remains a difficult and contentious exercise. Philip Curtin (1969) offered the first systematic scholarly effort to measure the slave trade, concluding that as many as 11.8 million Africans were shipped to the Americas and approximately 9.4 million reached its shores.

Since Curtin, other scholars have tested his analysis, suggesting various revisions. The tentative consensus today is that some 11 million slaves left Africa over the course of three and a half centuries. Of this number, about 15 percent (over 1.5 million) may not have survived the infamous Middle Passage, a horrific experience marked by inhuman conditions of transport, insufficient food, and disease. Mortality rates incurred from the point of capture in the African interior to transfer to a slave ship along the coast may have been even higher, suggesting the tremendous toll on human lives that slave trafficking exacted.

The vast majority of slaves (around 10 million) were shipped after 1660 following the expansion of the sugar plantation complex, with regions most associated with this regime receiving the largest number of slaves. Thus, between 1662 and 1867 Brazil obtained some 40 percent of all slaves shipped to the Americas, while the British, French, and Spanish Caribbean combined received over 47 percent of the total.

A better understanding of the historical contours of the Atlantic slave trade has allowed scholars to examine more closely what happened to African cultural practices, languages, and beliefs under American slavery. To summarize a complex discussion, historians dispute the extent to which African culture carried over and persisted in the Western Hemisphere. Stanley Elkins (1959), building on the work of Frank Tannenbaum (1947) and others, posited that slavery was so extreme and brutal an experience in the capitalistic regimes of British America that those held in bondage were essentially stripped of their previous identities.

This position has fallen out of favor. The debate today revolves more around the issue of cultural survival versus creolization. On the one hand, some scholars have pointed to the experience of the Middle Passage and bondage as leading to a blurring of African cultural divisions and the creation of a unique African-American culture that borrows from a diverse set of origins. Others have countered that various regions of America tended to draw slaves from distinct zones of Africa, which resulted in a concentration of individuals from similar cultural backgrounds for generations, reinforcing African rather than creolized cultures.

Scholars who emphasize the continuities of African culture in the Americas often point to the profound demographic impact of slavery to support their position. Slave populations throughout the Americas tended to depend upon continued imports from Africa since slave mortality rates usually outpaced birth rates. Indeed, it has long been noted that the only significant exception to this rule was the antebellum United States, although the reasons for this fact are complex and still only partially understood. Part of the problem involves the skewed gender ratios of the slave trade itself, which favored young adult males. Scholars are divided whether this was due more to the market demands of American planters or a refusal of African merchants to sell female slaves, who were highly coveted in domestic slave markets.

Clearly, though, a separate issue involved the appalling conditions under which most slaves lived. While disease did not spare owners, slaves were much more vulnerable due to the poor nutrition, abysmal living conditions, and extreme work hours that characterized their daily existence. Critics within the Brazilian Catholic Church, for instance, often berated planters who would rather pay for a new African slave than assume the costs involved in the proper care of those already owned. Unproductive infants and young children likewise required years of maintenance before they could begin to compete with the productivity levels of newly acquired adults shipped directly from Africa.

The issue of rising enslaved birth rates in the United States, and the reasons for why it seems to have been so exceptional, relates to another point of contention in the comparative history of American slavery. In the 1940s Tannenbaum argued the treatment of African slaves in Latin America was better than in British America. He suggested that centuries of contact with Moors and

Africans had provided Spain and Portugal with a relatively humane system of laws and attitudes concerning the treatment of slaves and racial difference, arising from legal and cultural sensibilities that northern Protestant countries lacked given their more isolated historical development. Iberian law, based on Roman precedent, recognized the human personality of the slave, placed constraints on the owner's ability to dole out punishment, and offered the possibility for manumission through self-purchase or the release from service upon the owner's death. The regulatory power of the Catholic Church, which likewise recognized the humanity of the enslaved, made for a decidedly different slave system than that of Protestant colonies.

While it is true that Iberian colonial law and institutions offered a modicum of concern for African slaves, the reality was more problematic, as the absence of American-born slave populations throughout much of Latin America might attest. Legal protection, for one matter, was rarely proactive and always inconsistently enforced. In contrast to Tannenbaum's effort to distinguish systems of slavery across broad cultural divides, more recent scholarship tends instead to emphasize other determinant factors related to the particular economic roles slavery fulfilled in a given colony or region. Throughout most slave societies, for example, treatment and living conditions declined in situations where slavery became the dominant institution and economic pressures for profit were most severe. In contrast, where slavery played a less important economic role, levels of coercion and abuse might be less extreme.

The evolution of slavery in Cuba is a good example of this phenomenon. Long a backwater of the Spanish empire, Cuban agriculture (tobacco, sugar, coffee, and livestock) rested on a mix of free and slave labor. In 1763 the island was seized by England and underwent a rapid transformation as a result of an opening up of international trade. The Spanish continued these efforts after retaking the island, and as a result Cuba was transformed into a major plantation-based economy with a typically oppressive labor regime based on the use of slave gangs. What had changed in Cuba, in other words, was the economic regime rather than the cultural or legal framework theoretically guiding slave-owner relations.

While slavery was undoubtedly an oppressive system, those held in bondage often sought to resist or minimize its pernicious influence on their lives. Resistance began during the Middle Passage itself, which witnessed numerous revolts on slave ships. Bondage in the Americas also offered its own range of opportunities for slaves to oppose the will of owners and overseers. Acts of passive resistance, such as work slowdowns, the destruction of

property, or theft, are common throughout the historical record.

Escape was also an early and persistent tactic that slaves employed to resist oppression. Plantations located along frontier zones or inaccessible terrain offered potential safety for those who could reach it. The phenomenon of flight could take on an individual or temporary dimension, or become a permanent and collective act of resistance. The famed community of Palmares in Brazil, for example, endured for decades (1630–1697) despite repeated efforts by the Portuguese to crush it militarily. Elsewhere, imperial frontiers offered the possibility of freedom. Runaway slaves from South Carolina and Georgia, for example, found sanctuary in Spanish Florida, where they formed free communities and militias that supported the defense of St. Augustine.

Less frequent were slave rebellions in which violent resistance to the regime took a collective dimension. The potential for such an outbreak was never far from the minds of owners and state authorities alike, although actual instances are probably outnumbered by alleged discovered conspiracies. Whether instances of the latter were actual plots or simply the paranoid fantasies of slave-owners remains uncertain and no doubt depended on the individual case. Armed resistance at a collective level did occur, however. The 1835 revolt in Bahia, Brazil, by Muslim slaves is one notable example, as is the more famous and ultimately successful slave revolt that culminated in Haitian independence (1791–1804).

Finally, slave resistance contributed significantly to the eventual abolition of slavery over the course of the nineteenth century in various American republics. The activities of abolition societies, the Underground Railroad, and regiments of freedmen who fought in the American Civil War (1861–1865) are perhaps the best known examples. Like their brethren to the north, slaves participated in the wars of independence in mainland Spanish America (1808–1821), often in response to the promise of freedom. The abolition of slavery in much of Spanish America during the 1840s and 1850s was encouraged not only by the enforcement of the British ban of the slave trade and the transformation of domestic economies, but also by the actions of slaves and freed people alike, who fought and clamored for the rights promulgated in the republican constitutions of the era.

But legal freedom, although a tremendous achievement, did not ensure parity or full citizenship despite the efforts and political mobilization of freed people in the fledgling American republics. Indeed, the legacy of slavery and the racism it had fostered remained pressing concerns in postabolition societies, as it does in today's continuing struggle for equality and civil rights across the American hemisphere.

SEE ALSO *Abolition of Colonial Slavery; Export Commodities; Haitian Revolution; Mining, the Americas.*

BIBLIOGRAPHY

Andrews, George Reid. *The Afro-Argentines of Buenos Aires, 1800–1900.* Madison: University of Wisconsin Press, 1980.

Andrews, George Reid. *Afro-Latin America, 1800–2000.* Oxford: Oxford University Press, 2004.

Bastide, Roger. *African Civilisations in the New World.* Translated by Peter Green. New York: Harper, 1971.

Berlin, Ira. *Many Thousands Gone: The First Two Centuries of Slavery in North America.* Cambridge, MA: Belknap. 1998.

Bowser, Frederick P. *The African Slave in Colonial Peru, 1524–1650.* Stanford, CA: Stanford University Press, 1974.

Curtin, Philip. *The Atlantic Slave Trade: A Census.* Madison: University of Wisconsin Press, 1969.

Elkins, Stanley. *Slavery: A Problem in American Institutional and Intellectual Life.* Chicago: University of Chicago Press, 1959.

Eltis, David. *The Rise of African Slavery in the Americas.* Cambridge, U.K.: Cambridge University Press, 2000.

Eltis, David, and David Richardson. "The 'Numbers Game' and Routes to Slavery." In *Routes to Slavery: Direction, Ethnicity, and Mortality in the Transatlantic Slave Trade*, edited by David Eltis and David Richardson, 1–15. Portland, OR: Frank Cass, 1997.

Hemming, John. *Red Gold: The Conquest of the Brazilian Indians.* Cambridge, MA: Harvard University Press, 1978.

Herskovits, Melville J. *The Myth of the Negro Past.* New York and London: Harper, 1941.

Heuman, Gad, ed. *Out of the House of Bondage: Runaways, Resistance, and Marronage in Africa and the New World.* London: Frank Cass, 1985.

Klein, Herbert S. *African Slavery in Latin America and the Caribbean.* Oxford: Oxford University Press, 1986.

Mintz, Sidney W., and Richard Price. *The Birth of African-American Culture: An Anthropological Perspective.* Boston: Beacon, 1992.

Moreno Fraginals, Manuel. *The Sugar Mill: The Socioeconomic Complex of Sugar in Cuba, 1760–1860.* Translated by Cedric Belfrage. New York: Monthly Review Press, 1976.

Palmer, Colin. *Slaves of the White God: Blacks in Mexico, 1570–1650.* Cambridge, U.K.: Cambridge University Press, 1976.

Price, Richard, ed. *Maroon Societies: Rebel Slave Communities in the Americas.* Baltimore, MD: Johns Hopkins University Press, 1973.

Reis, João José. *Slave Rebellion in Brazil: The Muslim Uprising of 1835 in Bahia.* Translated by Arthur Brakel. Baltimore, MD: Johns Hopkins University Press, 1993.

Restall, Matthew. "Black Conquistadors: Armed Africans in Early Spanish America." *The Americas* 57, (2) (2000): 171–205.

Restall, Matthew, ed. *Beyond Black and Red: African-Native Relations in Colonial Latin America.* Albuquerque: University of New Mexico Press, 2005.

Schwartz, Stuart B. *Sugar Plantations in the Formation of Brazilian Society: Bahia, 1550–1835.* Cambridge, U.K.: Cambridge University Press, 1985.

Schwartz, Stuart B. *Slaves, Peasants, and Rebels: Reconsidering Brazilian Slavery.* Urbana: University of Illinois Press, 1992.

Sharp, William F. *Slavery on the Spanish Frontier: The Colombian Chocó, 1680–1810.* Norman: University of Oklahoma Press, 1976.

Sweet, James H. *Recreating Africa: Culture, Kinship, and Religion in the African-Portuguese World, 1441–1770.* Chapel Hill: University of North Carolina Press, 2003.

Tannenbaum, Frank. *Slave and Citizen: The Negro in the Americas.* New York: Knopf, 1947.

Thornton, John. *Africa and Africans in the Making of the Atlantic World, 1400–1800*, 2nd ed. Cambridge, U.K.: Cambridge University Press, 1998.

Andrew B. Fisher

AFRIKANER

The first Afrikaner(s) were settlers, mainly of Dutch origin, who established themselves in the Cape of Good Hope region. Their descendants controlled South Africa for a long time and were the architects of the racist system that prevailed there until the 1990s. Initially, the Afrikaner were known as *Boers*, a word that means "farmer," "peasant." The Afrikaner speak Afrikaans, a language derived from Dutch with some contributions from German and French, the latter a legacy of the Huguenots who sailed to Africa in the seventeenth century to escape Europe's religious wars. Traditionally, the great majority of Afrikaner have been members of the Dutch Reformed Church, one of the pillars of Afrikanerdom. Afrikaner identity was formed through a gradual indigenization that dissolved connections with the former motherland: hence the choice to use terms for themselves and their language that signaled that their destiny as individuals and a nation was rooted in Africa.

BEGINNINGS

The first Dutch community in the Cape was set up by the Dutch East India Company in 1652 under the command of Jan van Riebeeck, who was instructed to build a fort and a resupply station for ships traveling to and from Batavia (present-day Indonesia), the headquarters of Dutch possessions in Asia. In principle there was no intention to establish a colony, but increasing food needs and the favorable climate pushed settlers to farm and occupy more land. While extending settlements and spreading farther afield, the Boers encountered the communities of Bantu-speaking farmers. Much more developed and intimidating than the Khoikhoi and San—cattle-breeders and hunter-gatherers living in the region around the Cape, whom the Afrikaner had easily outnumbered—the Bantu formed a barrier to further Afrikaner expansion. The eighteenth century saw warfare on the border of Afrikaner-controlled territory that precariously divided whites and blacks. The Afrikaner expanded their possessions across the Fish River at the expense of the southern Nguni (Xhosa). Because the metropolitan power was far away and its representatives almost absent, the Boers developed a unique culture centered on independence, patriarchal authority, and firm hierarchization (the agricultural economy was based on slave labor and most of the servants, artisans, and laborers were slaves). They believed themselves to have been charged with a semi-divine duty to civilize Africa. The turning point in the history of the Afrikaner was the occupation of the Cape by the British during the Napoleonic Wars. In 1806 Britain replaced Holland as the colonial power and nine years later the occupation of the Cape was ratified at the Congress of Vienna.

THE GREAT TREK

Despite their common European background, rural Dutch and urban English settlers were separated by a cultural divide. This was bound to have great political significance. The British were not willing to let the Afrikaner manage their affairs autonomously and shaped the institutions of the country in a way that the Afrikaner found odious and untenable. The abolition of slavery was the final affront to Afrikaner habits. In order to escape obtrusive British administration, the Boers decided to resettle outside the colonial boundaries. The massive emigration northeastward that resulted, carried out in organized groups with ox-driven wagons, is known in Boer mythology as the Great Trek. It is conventionally dated to 1838. The Boers' aim was to establish a new motherland. After battling and expropriating resources from the black tribes they encountered, the Voortrekkers founded two republics: the Transvaal or South African Republic (with Pretoria as the capital city) and the Orange Free State (with its capital in Bloemfontein). In the iconology of the civil religion constructed by Afrikaner, the Great Trek was the *revolution*: the liberation from British imperialism and the advent of a new nation.

However, Cape authorities and arch-colonial lobbies both in Britain and in Africa were determined to wipe out the Boer republics, daringly founded in a region under the paramount influence of the British. The conventions British emissaries signed with the Transvaal Voortrekkers in 1852 and with the representatives of the Free State in 1854—the latter a formal recognition of Afrikaner independence—were just a postponement of the unavoidable collision, ultimately precipitated by the discovery of the diamonds of Kimberley and of the immense gold fields in the Witwatersrand (Transvaal). In 1870 the European population of the territories occupied by the Voortrekkers numbered about 45,000. The republics' autocratic regime was soon seriously challenged by an industrial and urban boom and by the flood of cosmopolitan Europeans in search of fortune. The British backed the claims of foreigners (Uitlanders) over the franchise and other rights of Afrikaners and thus caused a dispute with President Paul Kruger of Transvaal, champion of Afrikaner nationalism and inflexible warden of an anachronistic regime reserved for a pure elite of "founders." The outcome was full-fledged war.

Hostilities erupted in 1899 after Kruger, wanting to act before the arrival of fresh troops from India and Europe, delivered an ultimatum to the British government. In spite of the resolute heroism of the Boer army and the Boer people in general (women and children were amassed in camps by the British in order to separate fighters from their family and social environment), British military forces succeeded in defeating the Boers. The Boer republics ceased to exist with the Treaty of Vereeniging, signed in 1902; Transvaal and Orange merged with the Cape Colony and Natal was absorbed into the South African Union under British control. The Anglo-Boer (or South African) War marked the end of the petty Boer nationalism personified by Kruger. It signaled the birth of a new Boer consciousness, one better suited to coping with development and modernity. The blacks, not the British, were now the enemy of the Afrikaner; for their part, the British accepted the revision or abrogation of the few rights enjoyed by black Africans as the price of ending the devastating war.

FROM APARTHEID TO DEMOCRATIC SOUTH AFRICA

The *volk* (the Afrikaner nation) survived the military catastrophe: in their self-conception, if the British were the colonial officials and owners of the mines, the Afrikaner were the authentic representatives of the soul of unified South Africa. The sophisticated and multifaceted apartheid regime—the system of racial segregation and discrimination imposed by the Afrikaner's Nationalist Party after its victory in the 1948 elections—was a sort of apotheosis in the story of a people supposedly elected by God to carry out a very special mission in Africa. D. F. Malan was the first of a series of Afrikaner leaders (including H. F. Verwoerd, B. J. Vorster, P. W. Botha, and others) committed to creating Afrikanerdom by crushing or subduing black

Voortrekker Monument in Pretoria, South Africa. *Pretoria's Voortrekker Monument, designed by Gerard Moerdijk and inaugurated in 1949, honors the original Afrikaner settlers of the Transvaal and the Orange Free State.* © JOSE FUSTE RAGA/CORBIS. REPRODUCED BY PERMISSION.

African aspirations to liberty, equality, and power. The British segment of South Africa's white population never fully endorsed the rationale for this extreme form of racism (though racism as a system was significant to the growth of South African capitalism), but they were unable to or did not really want to combat apartheid. All the heads of government and state in South Africa were Afrikaner from 1910, when independence was proclaimed, up to Nelson Mandela in 1994, when apartheid was formally abolished. The year 1994 also saw the country's first universal elections and the triumph of the African National Congress (ANC), the party that had built the antiracist movement by mobilizing black Africans and people of any race who rejected racism. After 350 years of colonialism, the ANC's victory established majority rule for the first time in South Africa's history.

SEE ALSO *African National Congress; Apartheid.*

BIBLIOGRAPHY

Thompson, Leonard. *The Political Mythology of Apartheid.* New Haven, CT: Yale University Press, 1985.

Troup, Freda. *South Africa: An Historical Introduction.* Harmondsworth, U.K.: Penguin, 1972.

Van Jaarsveld, F. A. *From Van Riebeeck to Vorster, 1652–1974.* Pretoria, South Africa: Perskor, 1975.

Giampaolo Calchi Novati

ALBUQUERQUE, AFONSO DE
1453–1515

Afonso d'Albuquerque, known as "the Great," was born in Alhandra, near Lisbon, Portugal, and died at sea off Goa, India. He was the second governor of India, who laid the foundations of the Portuguese Empire in the Orient.

Albuquerque was the second son of the senhor of Vila Verde. His ancestors and those of his wife, Dona Leonor de Meneses, served the Portuguese kings John I (1357–1433) and Edward (1391–1438) in high and confidential offices, and he himself served ten years in Morocco under Afonso V (1432–1381), John II (1455–1495), and Manuel I (1469–1521), where he gained early military experience crusading against Muslims. Albuquerque was most prominent under John II, but his reputation rests on his service in the East.

When Vasco da Gama (ca. 1469–1524) returned to Portugal in 1499 from his pioneering voyage to India, King Manuel straightaway sent a second fleet under Pedro Álvares Cabral (ca. 1467–1520) to open relations and trade with the Indian rulers. The Muslim traders who had monopolized the distribution of spices asked the *zamorin*, or Hindu prince of Calicut, for assistance against the Portuguese. His dependency, the raja of Cochin, on the Malabar Coast, however, welcomed the Iberians. In 1503 Albuquerque arrived with his cousin Francisco to protect the ruler of Cochin, where he built the first Portuguese fortress in Asia and placed a garrison. After setting up a trading post at Quilon, he returned to Lisbon in July 1504, where he was well received by Manuel and could participate in the formulation of the Portuguese policy toward Asia.

In 1505 Manuel appointed Dom Francisco de Almeida (ca. 1450–1510) the first governor in India, with the rank of viceroy. Almeida's main aim was to develop trade and aid the allies of the Portuguese. Albuquerque left Lisbon with Tristão da Cunha (1460–1540) in April 1506 to explore the east coast of Africa. In August 1507 he build a fortress on the island of Socotra to block the mouth of the Red Sea and cut off Arabic trade with India. After that, Albuquerque captured Hormuz (Ormuz), an island in the channel between the Persian Gulf and the Gulf of Oman, to open the European-Persian trade. The fortification at Hormuz had to be abandoned because of differences with his captains, who departed for India. Albuquerque, left with only two ships to Socotra, continued to raid the Arabic coasts.

King Manuel appointed Albuquerque to succeed Almeida at the end of his term, though without the rank of viceroy. When Albuquerque reached India in December 1508, Almeida had crushed the improvised sea force of Calicut, but a navy from Egypt had defeated and killed his son. Almeida insisted on remaining in power until he had avenged his son's death; to prevent any interference, Almeida decided to imprison his successor, Albuquerque. Almeida succeeded in defeating the Muslims off Diu in February 1509, and in November, with the arrival of marshal Fernando Coutinho from Portugal, he finally turned his office over to Albuquerque.

Albuquerque's plan was to assume active control over all the main maritime trade routes of the East and to establish permanent fortresses with settled populations. He realized that it was better to try to supplant the Muslims. With the assistance of a powerful corsair named Timoja, he took twenty-three ships to attack Goa, long ruled by Muslim princes. Albuquerque occupied this city in March 1510, but was forced out of the citadel by a Muslim army in May. In November he took Goa

again after a final assault. The Muslim defenders were put to the sword.

After this victory over the Muslims, the Hindu rulers accepted the Portuguese presence in India. Albuquerque used Goa as a naval base against the Muslims. He also diverted the spice trade to Goa, and used the city as a base for supplying Persian horses to Hindu princes. By marrying his men to the widows of his victims he would give Goa its own population. The village's communities, under a special regime, would assure an abundance of supplies and merchandise.

After providing for the government of Goa, Albuquerque embarked on the conquest of Malacca, on the Malay Peninsula, the immediate point of distribution for spices in the East. He took this port town in July 1511, garrisoned it, and sent an ambassador to the king of Siam to open trade. He also sent ships in search of spices to the Banda Islands and the Moluccas.

In the meantime, Goa was again under heavy attack. Albuquerque left Malacca in January 1512 and came to Goa's relief. Having resecured the city, and after establishing a licensing system to control the movement of goods, Albuquerque set off for the Red Sea with a force of Portuguese and Indian soldiers. Because Socotra was inadequate as a base, he attempted to take Aden, but his forces proved insufficient. He thereupon explored the Arabian and Abyssinian (Ethiopian) coasts. Returning to India, he finally subdued Calicut, hitherto the main seat of opposition to the Portuguese.

In February 1515 Albuquerque again left Goa with twenty-six ships bound for Hormuz, gaining control of part of the island. He fell ill in September and returned to Goa. On the way he learned that he had been superseded by his personal enemy, Lope Soares de Albergaria. Albuquerque died embittered onboard the ship before reaching his destination.

Albuquerque's plans derived from the crusading spirit of John II and others. He did not allow himself to be diverted from his schemes by considerations of mercantile gain. His boldest concepts, such as turning the Persians against the Turks or ruining Egypt by diverting the course of the Nile, may have been superhuman, but perhaps his achievements were as well.

SEE ALSO *Empire, Portuguese; Goa, Colonial City of.*

BIBLIOGRAPHY

Albuquerque, Braz de. *Commentarios do grande Afonso Dalboquerque.* Lisbon: Na Regia Officina Typografica, 1774. Available in English as *The Commentaries of the Great Afonso Dalboquerque, Second Viceroy of India.* Translated from the 1774 edition by Walter de Gray Birch. New York: Burt Franklin, 1964.

Cortesão, Jaime. *História dos Descobrimentos Portugueses*. Lisbon: Círculo de Leitores, 1979.

Danvers, Frederick Charles: *The Portuguese in India*. London: W. H. Allen, 1894.

Diffie, Bailey W., and George D. Winius. *Foundations of the Portuguese Empire, 1415–1580*. Minneapolis: University of Minnesota Press, 1977.

Marques, António Henrique R. de Oliveira. *History of Portugal*, 2nd ed. New York: Columbia University Press, 1976.

Panikkar, K. M. *Malabar and the Portuguese: Being a History of the Relations of the Portuguese with Malabar from 1500 to 1663*. Bombay: D. B. Taraporevala Sons, 1929.

Arnold van Wickeren

ALCOHOL

Alcohol has a long history predating European colonialism in sub-Saharan Africa. African traditional drinks include first and foremost the thick, cloudy grain beers of the savannah areas of East Africa and southern Africa and the Sahelian zone, and the palm and banana wines of the higher rainfall areas, especially in Central and West Africa.

TRADITIONAL PATTERNS OF PRODUCTION AND CONSUMPTION IN AFRICA

The indigenous alcoholic drinks of Africa were fermented and usually of low ethanol content—between 2 and 4 percent. The grain-based beer production and consumption in rural areas was highly seasonal, whereas the supply of palm wine would have been continuous throughout the year. Traditionally, the pattern of ceremonial festivities and drinking occasions rotated around the agricultural cycle. Many family and community celebrations, such as weddings and puberty rites, would have been deliberately scheduled to take place in the postharvest period when the availability of ingredients for alcohol production was assured. A successful grain harvest was a cause for celebration and the giving of thanks to the ancestors. Alcohol could appear out of season at other occasions, such as funerals. Given alcohol's close association with ancestors, it was not surprisingly a feature of wakes.

Traditionally, alcohol drinking to the point of intoxication was considered primarily the privilege of male elders, who held the highest status in Africa's rural communities. The drinking of low-ethanol alcohol, which was woven into special community-wide ceremonies and occasions marking life-cycle passages, constituted an intensely social event.

Fermented alcoholic beverages also provided basic food and drink. Men were more likely to consume their grain intake in the form of beer than women and children. However, traditional forms of thick, cloudy sorghum and millet beers veer toward the boundary between alcohol and nutritional gruel. Women and children drank the nutritious gruel. Furthermore, these beverages provided liquid refreshment in places where the water supply was unsafe.

ALCOHOL USE IN AFRICA DURING THE COLONIAL ERA

Onto this localized pattern of community-based alcohol production and consumption, Portuguese, Dutch, British, French, and German, as well as Danish and Swedish, slave-trade activities in Africa expanded the world trade in distilled liquor. Distilled liquor was an ideal long-distance trading good, capable of being stored for exceptionally long periods, little damaged by climatic fluctuation, and eagerly demanded in a wide range of foreign lands. In effect, alcohol served as a currency in early European trading, conquest, and labor recruitment.

The slave trade and European alcohol importation were intricately entwined. European mercantile interests introduced parts of the African continent to strong distilled alcohol and recreational drinking habits that were divorced from community ritual contexts. Alcohol was traded primarily with chiefs and merchant elites, and the drinking of imported spirits was generally restricted to coastal areas or navigable river routes. Thus, at a very early stage, these parts of Africa became part of the global market for alcohol under an economic regime of unfettered free trade.

Along the Gold Coast, imported spirits became prevalent during the seventeenth century and, according to foreign travelers, were incorporated into rituals by the eighteenth century. Hair, Jones, and Law's 1992 study of the letters of a French slave trader, Jean Barbot, reveal the multiple utilities of spirits. Besides trading French brandy for slaves, the brandy served as a tribute payment and a lubricant for trade negotiations, helping European traders gain bargaining advantage. The ship's crew drank it liberally as well, so its inclusion in the hold was never in vain, even when, as on one unexpected occasion, Barbot found that the English traders who preceded him had swayed local demand in favor of Barbados rum.

Beyond West Africa, seventeenth-century records of the Dutch East Indies Company at the Cape of Good Hope reveal that their African slaves were issued a daily glass of brandy in the belief that it would increase their alertness. After the abolition of slavery, tots of spirits and, later, wine were used as a method of payment for manual labor. Attitudes of the day embraced the notion that

South African Sorghum Beer. *Traditional forms of thick grain beers provided basic nourishment and refreshment throughout the savannah areas of East Africa and southern Africa, even after Europeans began importing distilled spirits. In this photograph, a Zulu cook in South Africa ladles a sorghum mixture into a calabash to make beer.* © ROGER DE LA HARPE; GALLO IMAGES/CORBIS. REPRODUCED BY PERMISSION.

alcohol had medicinal benefits. European traders and employers complained about the market sale of alcohol, fearing that public drunkenness and disorder could threaten social stability, but the desire for public regulation of alcohol did not coalesce into any systematic legal control.

The end of the nineteenth century saw a glut of so-called trade spirits on the world market. These consisted primarily of cheaply produced potato schnapps that had been the staple drink of peasants throughout much of continental Europe. As the Industrial Revolution absorbed Europe's rural populations, their drinking tastes gravitated toward smoother grain schnapps and beer. New markets were sought just as Africa was being colonized. Traders based in Hamburg and Rotterdam acted with alacrity, finding a receptive market in West Africa. They even managed to circumvent import duties to penetrate the booming South African market by shipping their schnapps via Portugal.

Alcohol played a significant role in mobilizing wage labor on a continent with no legacy of wage labor and where acute labor scarcity prevailed. In effect, alcohol provided the lever for labor recruiters to pry self-sufficient agrarian societies open, and it served as an expedient means for employers to attract and hold their workforce, given their limited need for cash. By the 1880s Portuguese wine and spirit imports in Mozambique had helped mold a proletarianized workforce whose dependence on alcohol was readily recognized as an asset across the border in South Africa. The Transvaal gold mines, rapidly expanding their labor force, eagerly recruited such workers.

TEMPERANCE AND PROHIBITION

Khama III (d. 1923) of Bechuanaland (later Botswana) was notable as a traditional leader who took a firm stand against the trade in bottled spirits. The mining concession he granted in 1887 stipulated the ban of such imports. Temperance concerns began to be expressed, bolstered by local merchants interested in diverting some of the cash spent on drinks at mining canteens to the purchase of their commodities.

However, it was mine owners themselves who decisively threw their weight behind tighter controls. The poor productivity and high absentee rates of a drunken labor force were expensive, as well as posing a threat to civil order in frontier mining settlements where effective police control was lacking. At the turn of the twentieth century, heavy investment in deep-level mining necessitated a more disciplined and productive labor force. Mine owners radically altered their position, forsaking their financial interests in canteen alcohol sales. Bigger financial stakes beckoned, and they began pressing for total alcohol prohibition.

They did so in an atmosphere of increasing British imperial sympathy for the temperance cause. British empire builders Cecil Rhodes (1853–1902) and Frederick Lugard (1858–1945) joined ranks with Christian missionaries to advocate tighter alcohol controls, despite the inevitable loss of alcohol import duties that such a position would entail. Colonial economies had the onus of being financially self-sustaining, and many West African colonies relied heavily on the fiscal flow of alcohol import duties.

At the Berlin Conference of 1884, the dominant European powers of the day had mutually agreed to partition sub-Saharan Africa amongst themselves, but the issue of the lucrative alcohol trade that had been fostered during the preceding three centuries was left as unfinished business. As palm oil and other agricultural commodities replaced slaves as the region's major exports, more Africans gained access to cash, facilitating the expansion of alcohol imports into West Africa.

Prohibition groups felt that the "white man's burden" was to prevent Africans' alcoholic overindulgence and moral degeneration. They successfully pressured the European powers attending the Brussels Conference of 1890 into establishing an alcohol prohibition zone between the latitudes 20° north and 22° south across the continent. In this zone, the signatory governments agreed to ban the importation and distillation of liquors where their use did not already exist.

The significance of an international treaty was more symbolic than real in curbing African access to alcohol. South Africans and most West Africans accustomed to imported alcohol were not included in the ban. Prohibition did not extend to the non-African population anywhere on the continent, so imports per se did not cease, making leakages of supply common, especially in northern Nigeria, where the ban was implemented to accommodate the predominately Muslim population.

Minimum duty rates were set, and a secretariat in Brussels was established to monitor the controls without powers of enforcement. Following World War I, the international moral crusade of alcohol prohibition gave way to political pragmatism. Alcohol control represented an overconcentration of too many conflicting emotions and economic interests to be tackled by the League of Nations' prudent international civil service cadre.

International intervention had given colonial governments scope to institute policies that rewarded or punished segments of the population with differential alcohol access according to their attainment of "civilized" behavior in the eyes of colonial officialdom. Alcohol control served as a signposting on the rungs of the colonial social hierarchy based on race and class; it amounted to a "division of leisure," the reverse side of the colonial division of labor.

Broadly, the policies of the higher-latitude beer-drinking and spirit-drinking European colonial nations like Britain and Germany differed from those of the more southern wine-drinking French and Portuguese, who were far less influenced by the temperance movement. France and Portugal accommodated the possibility of cultural assimilation and class advancement by making wine and beer available to Africans who could afford to purchase it. Alcohol access in British and German colonies was more punitive in nature, pivoting on a stark racial distinction between Europeans and Africans. Africans in the British colonies of East Africa and southern Africa were not allowed European drinks, defined as wine, clear beer, and bottled spirits. In southern and South Africa, the racial content of alcohol policy was reinforced by the presence of a large white settler population. The rural/urban divide among Africans was ignored: urban Africans were assumed to have "unrefined" rural tastes.

NEW PATTERNS OF PRODUCTION AND CONSUMPTION IN AFRICA

Generally, most rural agricultural production consisted of low-alcohol beers and wines. Limitations on brewing to conserve staple food crops and prevent famine were commonly incorporated into native authority bylaws. Home brewing was left to the jurisdiction of local native authorities.

Local brewing recipes were changing as new crops and foods were adopted. Throughout much of East and southern Africa, higher-yielding maize edged out lower-yielding indigenous sorghums and millets, nudging the importance of maize forward in alcohol production and encouraging the discovery of faster brewing techniques. Brewing became more commercialized with women producers at the center of the growth of alcohol as a cottage industry, first in urban areas and later throughout rural Africa. Women's illegal brewing was often highly beneficial to family provisioning at the microlevel.

Evidence suggests that alcohol consumption increased during colonial rule with a proliferating array of alcoholic drinks, widening availability, and increasing alcoholic strength, while the proportion of the population drinking and the amount they drank on an annual per capita basis rose. In the process, the purpose of drinking gradually transformed from public ceremonial celebration at which relatively few imbibed, to a communally-shared leisure pastime in which broader sections of the community participated. Drinking took on new temporal dimensions. Previously alcohol had been limited by seasonal supply. Now the market offered year-round availability.

At the turn of the twentieth century, sugar became readily available in towns, and its ethanol-enhancing properties were quickly exploited, spreading to rural areas as well. Fermented sugar drinks boosted alcohol contents to between 6 and 8 percent, offering value for the money for those desiring intoxication. It was these new experimental drinks, concentrated in the urban areas, rather than the traditional rural brews, that colonial officialdom endeavored to curb.

At the same time, distillation techniques were expanding, fanned in West Africa by the attempts of colonial governments to curtail or ban importation of European distilled drinks like gin and whiskey that had been a feature of the area since the transatlantic slave trade. In East and southern Africa, distillation techniques were often introduced by worldly-wise returning soldiers or contract laborers who appreciated the get-drunk-quickly quality of the beverages produced. This occurred despite the dangers of producing alcohol with sometimes suspect ingredients and relatively primitive equipment that, under the pressurized conditions of the distilling process, was liable to explode. The production of distilled drinks was generally banned in rural and urban areas on health and safety grounds.

The colonial state had a strong fiscal interest in alcohol, dating back to early colonial penetration. In Nigeria, import duties on alcohol provided about half of the state's fiscal revenue. Gradually, domestic alcohol production displaced imports, and other forms of liquor taxation had to be devised. The difficulty of licensing and collecting taxes from alcohol producers in the ubiquitous informal sector led some governments to embark on state production. Interventionist states, notably those of southern Africa, favored the erection of production and distribution monopolies. The South African beer hall became a model for urban beer distribution in the region during the first half of the twentieth century. Revenues were used by the state to finance the building of the apartheid urban infrastructure in the name of African welfare.

In connection with this move, governments embarked on production of officially authorized brews. To ensure the market for their product, the state outlawed local cottage alcohol production, subjecting women brewers and distillers to campaigns of harassment. The aim was to produce a beer that African drinkers, particularly male laborers in urban areas and mining compounds, would be willing to drink, but that had a relatively low alcohol content and was nutritious like home brews. South Africa pioneered this effort, and other southern African colonies followed. By contrast, in Francophone Africa the manufacture of beer by private enterprises was more pronounced.

Over time, the heavy drinking patterns of southern African waged laborers, first cultivated then repressed by state and market forces, coalesced into a drinking subculture with its own momentum. In South Africa, a strong temperance movement supported by an emerging class of Christianized, educated Africans emerged in the early twentieth century in reaction to it. Middle-class black township women in Johannesburg voiced concern about the association between male drinking and the role of "lower-class" women brewers and prostitutes.

In the twilight years of colonial rule, the racist basis of the colonial divisions of labor and leisure were increasingly challenged. Resistance to state regulatory control of alcohol surfaced. In northern Rhodesia, the beer hall boycotts of the 1950s made alcohol an overt political issue. As nationalist pressures mounted, bans on Africans drinking "European liquor" were lifted in one colony after another.

A political victory for African nationalism, the consumption of nontraditional manufactured drinks was also an economic victory for the embryonic African elite, catalyzing conspicuous consumption, which marked the line between the rapidly rising affluence of the civil service cadre and the rest of the population. National independence had arrived with alcohol production and consumption patterns taking on new contours of African self-determination.

SEE ALSO *North Africa; Slave Trade, Atlantic; Sub-Saharan Africa, European Presence in; Sugar Cultivation and Trade.*

BIBLIOGRAPHY

Akyeampong, Emmanuel K. *Drink, Power, and Cultural Change: A Social History of Alcohol in Ghana, c. 1800 to Recent Times.* Oxford: James Currey, 1996.

Ambler, Charles. "Alcohol, Racial Segregation, and Popular Politics in Northern Rhodesia." *Journal of African History* 31 (1990): 295–313.

Ambler, Charles, and Jonathan Crush, eds. "Alcohol in Southern African Labor History." In *Liquor and Labor in Southern Africa*, 1–55. Athens: Ohio University Press, 1992.

Bryceson, Deborah F. *Food Insecurity and the Social Division of Labour*. London: Macmillan, 1990.

Bryceson, Deborah F. "Changing Modalities of Alcohol Usage." In *Alcohol in Africa: Mixing Business, Pleasure, and Politics*, edited by Deborah F. Bryceson, 23–52. Portsmouth, NH: Heinemann, 2002.

Dumett, R. E. "The Social Impact of the European Liquor Trade on the Akan of Ghana (Gold Coast and Asante), 1875–1910." *Journal of Interdisciplinary History* 5 (1) (1974): 69–101.

Gewald, Jan-Bart. "Diluting Drinks and Deepening Discontent: Colonial Liquor Controls and Public Resistance in Windhoek, Namibia." In *Alcohol in Africa: Mixing Business, Pleasure, and Politics*, edited by Deborah F. Bryceson, 117–138. Portsmouth, NH: Heinemann, 2002.

Hair, P. E. H., Adam Jones, Robin Law, eds. *Barbot on Guinea: The Writings of Jean Barbot on West Africa, 1678–1712*. London: Hakluyt Society, 1992.

Heap, Simon. "'We Think Prohibition is a Farce': Drinking in the Alcohol-Prohibited Zone of Colonial Northern Nigeria." *International Journal of African Historical Studies* 31 (1) (1998): 23–51.

Heap, Simon. "Living on the Proceeds of a Grog Shop: Liquor Revenue in Nigeria." In *Alcohol in Africa: Mixing Business, Pleasure, and Politics*, edited by Deborah F. Bryceson, 139–159. Portsmouth, NH: Heinemann, 2002.

Karp, Ivan. "Beer Drinking and Social Experience in an African Society: An Essay in Formal Sociology." In *Explorations in African Systems of Thought*, edited by Ivan Karp and Charles S. Bird, 83–119. Bloomington: Indiana University Press, 1980.

La Hausse, Paul. *Brewers, Beerhalls, and Boycotts: A History of Liquor in South Africa*. Johannesburg, South Africa: Ravan Press, 1988.

Molamu, Louis, and Winnie G. Manyeneng. *Alcohol Use and Abuse in Botswana: Report of a Study*. Gaborone, Botswana: Health Education Unit, 1988.

Pan, Lynn. *Alcohol in Colonial Africa*. Helsinki, Finland: Finnish Foundation for Alcohol Studies, 1975.

van Onselen, Charles. "Randlords and Rotgut, 1886–1905: An Essay on the Role of Alcohol in the Development of European Imperialism and South African Capitalism." *History Workshop Journal* 2 (1976): 32–89.

Willis, Justin. *Potent Brews: A Social History of Alcohol in East Africa, 1850–1999*. Oxford: James Currey, 2002.

Deborah Fahy Bryceson

ALGERIA

Algeria's significance in the history of Western colonialism can be seen in four stages. In Algeria the transition from medieval and early modern (in the fifteenth to eighteenth centuries) to modern and contemporary interactions (in the nineteenth and twentieth centuries) between Europe and the southern Mediterranean is particularly visible. Algeria was the scene of both the beginning (1830) and the end (1962) of the second French colonial empire. Algerians experienced both a more far-reaching colonial rule than was imposed elsewhere in the Middle East and North Africa, and a more protracted and bitter struggle for decolonization. From the 1950s into the 1970s Algeria was a model of national liberation and third-world self-assertion, and then a striking example of the disintegration of these projects since the 1980s.

THE OTTOMAN REGENCY

Algeria was politically unified within its principal modern boundaries as a province of the Ottoman Empire. Declining North African dynasties and the expansion of Spanish and Portuguese power in the early sixteenth century produced regional instability in which conflicts between European and Muslim powers in the Mediterranean were still thought of as continuations of medieval holy wars. An adventurer from the Aegean, Khayr ad-Dīn (d. 1546), known to Europeans as Barbarossa, received support from the Ottoman sultan Selim I (1467–1520) to fight the Spanish and their local allies in North Africa, and established himself at Algiers as governor general of North Africa in 1517. He removed local dynasties in eastern and western Algeria and defeated Charles V (1500–1558), the Holy Roman emperor, before Algiers in 1541. The Ottomans exercised a nominal sovereignty over the province.

After 1587 governors from Istanbul were named to three-year postings, but they became dependent on the military garrison (*ocak*) of Algiers and the ruling council of notables. From the 1670s the *ocak* combined with the guild of privateer captains (*ta'ifat al-ra'is*), who controlled the major part of the city's income, to appoint the ruler with the Turkish title of *bey*, effectively an autonomous sovereign. Although troops still came from Turkey in exchange for tribute every three years, the regency was beyond effective Ottoman control. The economy was based on agriculture and arboriculture by the peasantry (approximately half of the population), livestock raised by nomadic and seminomadic groups, as well as maritime and overland trade and privateering.

Algerian piracy, the main theme of colonial European depictions of the regency, was most successful in the sixteenth and seventeenth centuries and declined in the eighteenth. From the sixteenth century onward, trading relations with the Netherlands, Britain, and France increased, with European companies establishing commercial presences under capitulation agreements, which accorded special privileges to European consuls and their protégés. In the eighteenth century Algeria was an exporter of grain to Europe—the 1827 diplomatic incident that provided the pretext for the later French invasion originated in a dispute over payments due to Algiers for grain shipped to supply French armies in the 1790s.

CONQUEST AND COLONIZATION

The French expedition of 1830, conceived as a foreign adventure to relieve domestic political pressure, quickly decapitated the Ottoman regime in Algiers and installed a military government. Hesitation over policy in Algeria remained, however, into the 1840s. Treaties concluded with the Algerian leader, the Emir 'Abd al-Qadir (1808–1883), in 1834 and 1837, limiting the territory under French occupation, but hostilities resumed in 1839, lasting until 'Abd al-Qadir's surrender in 1847. In 1848 Algeria was declared an integral part of French territory. Civilian colonization expanded; from around 56,000 in 1850, the European population reached some 130,000 in 1870, owning 765,000 hectares of land, up from some 115,000 hectares in 1850.

Over the same period, the Algerian population declined from an estimated 3 million in 1830 to an official total of some 2.3 million in 1856, and 2.1 million by the end of the wars of conquest and armed resistance in 1872. The Algerian population grew again, however, in the 1870s, and by the 1920s had reached around 5 million, against a European population of around 800,000. By the mid-1950s just fewer than 1 million Europeans dominated the country and Muslim Algerians numbered almost 9 million. The political regime that developed from 1871 onward reflected the tension between the belief in a French Algeria and the demographic insecurity of the colonial settlers; Algerians were considered French nationals, but not full-fledged citizens, and Muslims' electoral rights were consistently limited to preserve minority rule.

A series of attempts at reform began after World War I (1914–1918), in which some 200,000 Muslim Algerians served in French uniform, and of whom some 98,000 became casualties. The Algerian electorate was expanded, and from 1919 to 1936, politics in the colony revolved primarily around reform proposals by a series of Algerian leaders. At the same time as the development of this liberal and professionally based loyal opposition, which argued for Algerians' emancipation within the framework of a reformed French state, there also emerged, among the community of migrant workers established since World War I in France, a radical nationalism aimed at separation and independence.

In 1926 the first nationalist organization with a program demanding Algerian independence, the Étoile Nord-Africaine (ENA), or North African Star, was formed in Paris. At the same time as the most significant of the liberal reform projects, advanced by the antifascist Popular Front government in 1936, became stalled in the national assembly, the ENA leader, Messali Hadj Hajd (1898–1974), began to organize the radical nationalist movement in Algeria. The reform programs ultimately failed to restructure the guiding logic of the colonial system. Until 1944 special repressive legislation—the native code (*régime de l'indigénat*)—criminalized various activities not otherwise illegal under French law, if committed by Algerians.

When parity of parliamentary representation was eventually granted after 1944, Algerians elected the same number of representatives as the European community one-eighth their numbers, and elections up until 1951 were rigged by the administration. The persistence of this repressive system, and massive reprisals against the Algerian population by settler militia and the military after an abortive insurrection at Sétif and Guelma in eastern Algeria on May 8, 1945, prepared the ground for the resort to arms by militant nationalists.

THE WAR OF INDEPENDENCE

The nationalist movement created in France in the 1920s gained in popularity through the 1940s. The political organization, the *Parti du people algérien* (PPA), or Algerian People's Party, created a paramilitary wing, the *Organisation spéciale* (OS), in 1947, to prepare an armed insurrection. On November 1, 1954, former OS members launched a coordinated series of attacks across Algeria and announced the creation of the *Front de libération nationale* (FLN), or National Liberation Front. Denounced as bandits and terrorists by the French authorities, the FLN set about creating a generalized insecurity among Algeria's Europeans and simultaneously began to construct a counter state to assume power in the name of the Algerian nation. By persuasion and coercion, the FLN gained the upper hand in Algerian opinion, shown by the massive popular demonstrations of December 1960. No mass insurrection occurred, however, after the orchestrated violence of August 20, 1955, when the local peasantry and FLN guerillas killed 71 Europeans in Philippeville (now known as Skikda).

The repression after Philippeville killed over 1,000 Algerians according to official estimates (the FLN claimed 12,000 dead); the cycle of violence thus marginalized remaining moderate forces. The counterinsurgency war eventually involved collective reprisals against civilians, and the systematic use of internment, torture, and summary executions. By the war's end, some 300,000 Algerians had become refugees, 400,000 were in prison or detention camps, 8,000 villages had been destroyed, and some 3 million people forcibly relocated from the countryside into regroupment centers. Some 300,000

An Algerian Cafe. *A French colonist receives a shoeshine at a small cafe in Oran, Algeria, during the 1890s.* **ROGER VIOLLET/GETTY IMAGES. REPRODUCED BY PERMISSION.**

Algerians were killed (the official Algerian figure would be 1 million or 1.5 million). The FLN's most spectacular offensives, at Philippeville and in the Battle of Algiers (1956–1957), were also military defeats, and by late 1959, the French army had largely regained control of Algerian territory.

The political situation created by the war and the FLN's successful international diplomacy, however, made a negotiated solution inevitable. Brought to power by the army in May 1958, as the savior of the empire after the Algerian crisis precipitated the collapse of the government, Charles de Gaulle (1890–1970) insisted that France would win the war, but, by late 1961, ultimately recognized the need to disengage from Algeria. De Gaulle's negotiations were opposed by French Algerian ultras, who formed the paramilitary *Organisation armée secrète* (OAS) to resist decolonization by force of arms. The end of the war was marked by violence between the Gaullist authorities, the OAS, and the FLN. In the Évian accords of March 1962, a cease-fire was agreed, and Algeria became independent later that same year on July 5.

ALGERIA AND THIRD WORLD REVOLUTION

Fighting continued in the first months of independence between rival FLN factions struggling for power. The revolutionary provisional government was ousted by Ahmed Ben Bella (b. 1918), who became Algeria's first president in September 1962 with the support of the army. Ben Bella's presidency saw the establishment of a bureaucratic single-party state against which other founding nationalist leaders became dissidents. A spontaneous workers' self-management movement, though adopted as policy, was bureaucratized and power effectively centralized. In response to purges of the regime, however, the army under Defense Minister Houari Boumédienne (1927–1978) overthrew Ben Bella in a coup d'état on June 19, 1965. Already an icon of third-world self-assertion through its revolutionary war and under the charismatic

Ahmed Ben Bella. *Ahmed Ben Bella, shown here in the early 1960s, fought against colonial France as a leader of the Algerian National Liberation Front. In 1963 he became the first president of independent Algeria.* AP IMAGES. REPRODUCED BY PERMISSION.

Ben Bella, Algeria under Boumédienne became the standard-bearer of the third worldism of the 1960s and 1970s.

A statist development program based on hydrocarbon revenues (first tapped in 1958) established an economic infrastructure whose basic industries achieved an average annual growth rate of 13 percent from 1967 to 1978. Foreign holdings were progressively nationalized, culminating in the takeover of 51 percent of French oil interests in 1971. At the nonaligned states' Algiers summit in 1974, Boumédienne called for a new international economic order in which developing nations should control the extraction, processing, and pricing of their own natural resources. In the Organization of Petroleum Exporting Countries (OPEC) and a member of the Arab steadfastness front opposed to the separate Egyptian peace with Israel in 1978, Algeria maintained a revolutionary and anti-imperialist foreign policy stance. Domestically, dissidence was curbed and the military-security apparatus remained the regime's backbone, with

the FLN party reduced to a powerless administrative instrument. An official nationalist unanimity articulated around Arab-Islamic cultural identity and the mythologizing of the armed struggle as the foundation of the state dominated the public sphere in education and the media.

At the death of Boumédienne in 1978, Chadli Benjedid (b. 1929) became president, and the socialist economic project was precipitately abandoned. State-managed enterprises were dismantled and the ambitious hydrocarbon-led development plan initiated in 1976, and projected to 2005, was cancelled. The growth of middle-class consumption and retreat of state management did not, however, lessen dependence either on oil exports or on food imports, which grew to crisis proportions with the collapse of world oil prices in 1985 and 1986. Annual average gross domestic product (GDP) growth declined from 15 percent between 1978 and 1984 to 3 percent in 1986. Factional struggle between Benjedid and an old guard opposed to market-led reform intensified. In October 1988 riots broke out in Algiers and other cities, signaling the onset of a generalized political crisis.

CIVIL VIOLENCE SINCE 1988

Benjedid hoped to maintain power and push through economic reforms while pluralizing political competition. Constitutional amendments in 1989 allowed for the creation of political parties; municipal elections were held in 1990 and legislative elections in 1991. This sudden opening of politics was most effectively capitalized upon by the Islamist movement, tapping into popular frustration as well as piety and articulating a utopian Islamic solution presented as having been the true aim of the war of independence. When the *Front islamique du salut* (FIS), or Islamic Salvation Front, swept the first round of parliamentary elections in December 1991 with 81 percent of contested seats (but only 24.6 percent of the registered electorate), the military intervened, forcing Benjedid's resignation and the suspension of the electoral process. The repression of the Islamists was met by the radicalization of the fringes of the movement and the emergence of extremist armed groups between 1992 and 1994. Through 2000 between 100,000 to 200,000 Algerians are thought to have been killed in the resulting violence.

SEE ALSO *Anticolonialism.*

BIBLIOGRAPHY

Ageron, Charles-Robert. *Modern Algeria. A History from 1830 to the Present.* Translated and edited by Michael Brett. London: Hurst, 1991.

A Meeting of the American Colonization Society. *This nineteenth-century engraving depicts a meeting in Washington, D.C., of the American Colonization Society, formed in 1817 by prominent Americans to promote the repatriation and settlement of free blacks in Africa.* © BETTMANN/CORBIS. REPRODUCED BY PERMISSION.

Bennoune, Mahfoud. *The Making of Contemporary Algeria: Colonial Upheavals and Post-Independence Development, 1830–1987.* Cambridge U.K.: Cambridge University Press, 1988.

Horne, Alistair. *A Savage War of Peace: Algeria, 1954–62.* London: Macmillan, 1977.

Roberts, Hugh. *The Battlefield: Algeria, 1988–2002. Studies in a Broken Polity.* London: Verso, 2003.

Ruedy, John. *Modern Algeria: The Origins and Development of a Nation.* Bloomington: Indiana University Press, 1992.

Schatz, Adam. "Algeria's Ashes," *New York Review of Books,* 18 July 2003.

Stora, Benjamin. *Algeria, 1830–2000. A Short History.* Ithaca, NY: Cornell University Press, 2001.

James McDougall

AMBOINA

SEE *Moluccas*

AMERICAN COLONIZATION SOCIETY

The American Colonization Society (ACS), formed in 1817, actualized aspirations of some African American leaders who supported repatriation and settlement of free blacks in Africa

African American participation in the American Revolutionary War did not yield anticipated results—emancipation and justice. Two main schools of thought, migration and integration, competed as solutions to the conditions of blacks in America. Black leaders like James Forten (1766–1842) and Paul Cuffe (1759–1817) supported migration to Africa, and in 1815 Cuffe transported thirty-eight African Americans to Sierra Leone.

The ACS was formed in 1817 by prominent Americans whose ranks included Supreme Court justice Bushrod Washington (1762–1829), Presbyterian clergyman and educator Robert Finley (1772–1817),

Congressman Charles Marsh (1765–1849), and lawyer and writer Francis Scott Key (1779–1843). It was also supported by President James Madison (1751–1836), Henry Clay (1777–1852), and others. In 1820 the ACS acquired a parcel of land from a local chief on Sherbro Island near Sierra Leone, and in 1821 sent the first batch of eighty-six freed slaves on the ship *Elizabeth* to the new settlement. Sherbro Island and its swampy surroundings exacted a high mortality rate on the African American settlers.

To save the colonization project from collapse, the ACS sent Eli Ayres to look for a healthier site for the settlers. With the help of naval Lieutenant Robert F. Stockton (1795–1866) and the armed schooner *Alligator*, Ayres navigated the coast of Sierra Leone and Liberia in November 1821. The two men selected territory around Cape Mesurado in Liberia as the site for the new settlement. Through persuasion and threat of force, they obtained land from the Bassa people. Ayres and the remnant of the colonists at Sherbro moved to Cape Mesurado. However, fever and conflicts with the local people made life difficult for the settlers, and Ayres and some of the colonists returned to Sierra Leone.

In August 1822, a ship carrying immigrants from Baltimore (including recaptured Africans) arrived at Cape Mesurado under the leadership of Jehudi Ashmun (1794–1828), a Methodist missionary, as the new ACS representative and colony leader. Disease and problems with the local people continued to plague the settlement. On November 11 and November 30, 1822, the colonists fought against the local people, but a peace treaty later ushered in peace and stability.

In 1823 to 1824 some of the colonists rebelled against Ashmun, accusing him of unfair allocation of town lots and rations. The conflict forced him to flee. The following year, Eli Ayres took over from Ashmun. Ayres surveyed the land around Monrovia, Liberia, and distributed some of it to the colonists. Ill with fever, Ayres returned to the United States, to be replaced by Ashmun, who restored order in the new settlements. Stricken with disease himself, Ashmun left for the Cape Verde Islands to recuperate, leaving Elijah Johnson (1780–1849) in charge.

At Cape Verde, Ashmun met Reverend Ralph Gurley (1797–1872), who "with full power from the United States Government" was to look into the conditions of the new settlement and help set up a system of government. Ashmun returned to the colony with Gurley, and the two men worked on a constitution for the colony, which was later adopted. Gurley returned to the United States in August 1822, leaving Ashmun in charge of the colony. Ashmun continued to work in the colony for five years, until his departure for the United States on March 25, 1828. He died later that year.

By 1830, the ACS had settled 1,420 African Americans in the new colony. In 1838 colonies established by United States slave states in Liberia (the Virginia Colonization Society, the Colonization Society of Pennsylvania, and the Maryland State Colonization Society had all established colonies) merged with the colony of the ACS to become the Commonwealth of Liberia. In 1839, it adopted a new constitution and named Virginian merchant and successful military commander, Joseph Jenkins Roberts (1809–1876), lieutenant governor. He became the first African-American governor of the colony in 1841. In 1847, the colony of Liberia declared its independence.

The ACS itself struggled along for several years and became moribund in the decade before the civil war, but not before many auxiliary societies had seceded from the parent organization. In 1964 the ACS was formally dissolved due partly to the objections of African Americans and abolitionists, partly to the scale of repatriation and the expense involved, and partly to the difficulty of finding new settlements for the large African American population.

SEE ALSO *Liberia; Sierra Leone.*

BIBLIOGRAPHY

Foster, Charles I. "The Colonization of Free Negroes, in Liberia, 1816–1835." *The Journal of Negro History* 38 (1) (1953): 41–66.

Franklin, Vincent P. "Education for Colonization: Attempts to Educate Free Blacks in the United States for Emigration to Africa, 1822–1833." *The Journal of Negro Education* 43 (1) (1974): 91–103.

McDaniel, Antonio. *Swing Low, Sweet Chariot: The Mortality Cost of Colonizing Liberia in the Nineteenth Century.* Chicago: University of Chicago Press, 1995.

Miller, Floyd J. *The Search for a Black Nationality: Black Emigration and Colonization, 1787–1863.* Urbana: University of Illinois Press, 1975.

Rosen, Bruce. "Abolition and Colonization, the Years of Conflict: 1829–1834." *Phylon* 33 (2) (1972): 177–192.

Streifford, David M. "The American Colonization Society: An Application of Republican Ideology to Early Antebellum Reform." *The Journal of Southern History* 45 (2) (1979): 201–220.

Edmund Abaka

AMERICAN CROPS, AFRICA

The Columbian Exchange left significant marks on African history and society, arguably nowhere more than in the introduction of American food crops, which occurred within the context of Portuguese trade in slaves and commodities and the development of a broader Atlantic economy. Subsequent increase in the cultivation of these crops is inseparable from population growth and the development of commercial agriculture. Today, though pre-Columbian African crops such as rice, sorghum, and millet continue to be important on the continent, American crops have eclipsed them.

MAIZE

Claims have been made for the pre-Columbian origin of maize, either as an indigenous crop or as evidence of earlier contact between Africa and the Americas. However, despite lack of precise evidence for the dating of maize's introduction, most scholars concur that maize was introduced in the sixteenth century either by the Portuguese or by trans-Saharan Arab traders. The Portuguese required cheap, storable, and local food sources to support the slave trade, and maize served this need, becoming the principal food of slave ships. The crop's spread in the sixteenth century is poorly mapped, though contemporary reports suggest a fairly wide diffusion and growing adoption by Africans. African horticulture was amenable to experimentation, allowing intercropping and therefore the dedication of part of a garden plot to new crops. The advantages of maize over African crops such as sorghum and millet were soon recognized by African agriculturalists; maize can be eaten immature, gives higher yields, renders more calories per acre, and is less prone to bird damage. By the seventeenth century the crop had spread to interior sites including the Congo Basin and Senegal River Valley, and there are also reports of its cultivation in East Africa. Maize is generally reckoned to have enabled population expansion; certainly it enabled the slave trade, both by providing a cheap food source to feed slaves and, possibly, because crop failures produced displaced and saleable populations. Maize also had political implications; for example, it furthered the hegemony of groups such as the Asante of Ghana. Travelers' reports from the eighteenth century confirm the spread of maize deep into the interior of western Africa. By the end of the 1800s maize was found virtually everywhere in sub-Saharan Africa with the exception of Uganda. Its current status as the core dietary staple in much of eastern and central Africa, however, was a later development enabled by the growth of large-scale commercial farming. The history of maize in Africa is thus a narrative of growth from its origins as a cheap food linked to the slave trade to its current status as (perhaps fragile) mainstay of many African diets.

MANIOC (CASSAVA)

Manioc or cassava is another American crop whose importance continued to grow from the sixteenth century to the twentieth. Like maize, manioc was originally introduced by Portuguese traders as a food suitable for feeding slaves and spread quickly with the growth of the trade in human beings. Native to tropical America, manioc is well suited to tropical African conditions, as it tolerates poor soils, resists drought and locust attack, and stores well. Its superiority to maize in these regards led to its supplanting that crop in tropical regions where maize gained early acceptance, such as the south-central Congo Basin. However, manioc spread more slowly; despite cultivation in Angola in the sixteenth century, there is no contemporary evidence for manioc planting on the Guinea Coast. Nonetheless, by the seventeenth century manioc was spreading through west central Africa. Adoption was slower elsewhere; anecdotal reports of manioc poisonings in East Africa may suggest good reason for greater caution. Indeed, despite widespread Amerindian development of toxin-eliminating processing techniques, in Africa manioc was sometimes fed to slaves in a minimally processed form. Overall, however, manioc produced declines in infant mortality in African communities and increased the possibility of survival during times of drought. Like maize, manioc thus furthered population increase but did not completely end the cycles of drought and crop loss that often led to the sale of individuals into slavery. Thus this "agricultural revolution" enjoyed an ironic symbiosis with the slave system. Manioc's spread continued after the eighteenth century and into the modern era. Though manioc has not experienced a recent dramatic growth in cultivation as seen in the case of maize, manioc is the most widely planted crop in tropical Africa, the continent's second most important food crop, and a cherished cultural tradition despite its foreign provenance. Tropical Africa is the world's leading producer of manioc, which remains at the core of Africa's hopes for food self-sufficiency and economic growth.

OTHER CROPS

Other American crops were introduced during the period of Portuguese trade, though the exact circumstances of their introduction are even more clouded than those surrounding the introduction of maize and manioc. American groundnuts or peanuts were introduced and became an important source of protein as well as an important cash crop for small producers; tomatoes, avocados, squash, beans, papayas, pineapples, guavas, and chilies had varying impacts on the diet of different regions, and were all enthusiastically adopted in the cuisines of West Africa. Sweet potatoes, however, have had greater impact than any of these crops, in some places attaining the status of a staple crop and contributing significantly to total caloric intake.

The introduction of American crops continued into the modern period in the context of global market competition in the agricultural sector. In the nineteenth century, vanilla was introduced to Madagascar, which is

Cassava Processing in Madagascar. *A man dries cassava in a village near Betioky in Madagascar in 2000. The cassava plant, which is native to South America, was brought to Africa by Portuguese traders.* © **JEREMY HORNER/CORBIS. REPRODUCED BY PERMISSION.**

today a much more significant producer than vanilla's Mesoamerican homeland, though it is facing vulnerability to new sources of competition. Cacao was introduced to West Africa at the end of the nineteenth century to compete with American production; though the region is now the largest producer of cacao, its cultivation has brought deforestation and vulnerability to fluctuations in the world market. Cacao production has also revived the association of American crops with slavery, as child slavery has recently been reported in Ivory Coast cacao plantations. American crops have thus had an ambivalent history in Africa; they have been central to the sustenance of the African population, but have also often been associated with a more general history of domination.

SEE ALSO *Cacao; Commodity Trade, Africa.*

BIBLIOGRAPHY

Crosby, Alfred W. *The Columbian Exchange: Biological and Cultural Consequences of 1492.* Westport, CT: Greenwood, 1972.

Jones, William O. *Manioc in Africa.* Stanford, CA: Stanford University Press, 1959.

McCann, James C. *Maize and Grace: Africa's Encounter with a New World Crop. 1500–2000.* Cambridge, MA: Harvard University Press, 2005.

McNeill, William H. "American Food Crops in the Old World." In *Seeds of Change,* edited by Herman J. Viola and Carolyn Margolis. Washington, DC: Smithsonian Institution Press, 1991.

Miller, Joseph C. *Way of Death: Merchant Capitalism and the Angolan Slave Trade, 1730–1830.* Madison: University of Wisconsin Press, 1988.

Miracle, Marvin P. *Maize in Tropical Africa*. Madison: University of Wisconsin Press, 1966.

Newman, James L. "Africa South from the Sahara." In *The Cambridge World History of Food, Vol. 2, Part 5, Section E: The History and Culture of Food and Drink in Sub-Saharan Africa and Oceania*, edited by Kenneth F. Kiple and Kriemhild Coneè Ornelas. Cambridge, U.K.: Cambridge University Press, 2000.

Thornton, John. *Africa and Africans in the Making of the Atlantic World, 1400–1680*. Cambridge, U.K.: Cambridge University Press, 1992.

Jacqueline Holler

AMERICAN REVOLUTION

All real revolutions, from England in the 1640s to Iran in the 1970s, destroy one set of human arrangements and create another. Such revolutionary leaders as Oliver Cromwell (1599–1658) in England, Thomas Jefferson (1743–1826) in America, Maximilien Robespierre (1758–1794) in France, Simón Bolívar (1783–1830) in South America, V. I. Lenin (1870–1924) in Russia, Mao Zedong (1893–1976) in China, Fidel Castro (b. 1926) in Cuba, and the Ayatollah Khomeini (1900–1989) in Iran would have understood one another, whatever their differences. All these men's revolutions transformed their societies. None created heaven on earth.

Yet the American Revolution seems problematic. Was it about equality, liberty, and the pursuit of happiness? How, then, to explain the "drivers of Negroes" among its leaders and the spread of slavery across their American republic? Was it radically transforming, even though it started from an urge to conserve? Was the transformation it wrought within Americans' minds, or in how they lived with one another? Was the revolution a national liberation, "one people" separating "the political bonds that have connected them with another," as Jefferson wrote in the Declaration of Independence? Until independence, most white Americans regarded themselves as British and the driving issue had been no more than the terms on which they were to be treated as British subjects. Even war did not change that question at first.

Unquestionably the revolution was anticolonial. Alexander Hamilton (1755/57–1804) caught that dimension perfectly in the eleventh *Federalist* paper (1787). "Europe," he wrote, "by force and by fraud" had "extended her dominion over.... Africa, Asia, and America" and "consider[ed] the rest of mankind as created for her benefit." But even this dimension is problematic. Hamilton's prescription was not general liberation. It was that his own people should "aim at an ascendant in the system of American affairs."

George Washington (1732–1799) already had congratulated those people on having made themselves "lords" of their own "mighty empire." He and his successors declined to assist Francisco de Miranda (1750–1816), Simón Bolívar, and José de San Martín (1778–1850) in their efforts to liberate Spanish America from colonial rule. These early American leaders also shunned independent Haiti. The Monroe Doctrine (1823) asserted United States primacy in Western Hemisphere affairs, and the United States went on to seize one-third of Mexico.

What difference did the American Revolution make to the colonial world? That question is best approached around two dimensions. One dimension is space, the whole territory that one Treaty of Paris defined as British in 1763 and another Treaty of Paris redefined as American two decades later. That territory stretched from the Atlantic to the Mississippi River and from the Great Lakes–Saint Lawrence Basin to Florida. Native people, the progeny of white settlers, and slaves all dwelled within it. The second dimension is the terms on which those people "belonged," first to Britain and then to America.

Two themes, liberty and subjection, had underpinned the American sense of British belonging. British liberty had meant not equal rights but rather an uneven tissue of privileges and immunities that went with the kind of person one was, and with the community to which one belonged. Some Britons had the suffrage in parliamentary or colonial elections. Some communities, including counties, boroughs, manors, the universities of Oxford and Cambridge, and the College of William and Mary, had their own representatives in Parliament or the local assembly. Britons in America also had the privilege, or liberty, of owning slaves. Britons at home did not. All were subject to the king-in-Parliament. George III (1738–1820) was not an absolute ruler. But together with the House of Lords and the House of Commons he could make laws to bind all Britons, including colonials, "in all cases whatsoever." So said Parliament in 1766. Moreover, the king's protection and laws covered all, from the Prince of Wales to the meanest person, at least in theory.

White colonials had accepted that London could run their external affairs. Parliament set the terms of their commerce with Britain, with one another, and with the non-British world. The king appointed colonial officials and could veto colonial laws, all for the sake of fostering British wealth and keeping that wealth within British boundaries. The colonies prospered. By 1770 one-third of the British merchant fleet had been built in colonial shipyards, and one-seventh of the world's iron came from American smelters. White colonials believed

Bostonians Paying the Excise-Man. *This copy of a 1774 mezzotint attributed to Philip Dawe illustrated what the British saw as the unruly behavior of American colonists. It depicts Bostonians forcing tea down the throat of John Malcolm, a customs official who has been tarred and feathered, with the liberty tree and the Boston tea party in the background.* **ROGER VIOLLET/GETTY IMAGES. REPRODUCED BY PERMISSION.**

they were fully British, without much questioning or doubt.

Yet inequalities abounded. North American colonials could not, for example, refine their iron beyond its crudest stage, so that British metallurgy could flourish. The needs of West Indies sugar planters counted more than those of North American refiners and distillers, so there were severe taxes on non-British sugar and molasses. The king wanted revenue without worrying about Parliament; taxes on Chesapeake tobacco provided it. By the mid-eighteenth century, some colonials, such as Benjamin Franklin (1706–1790), were praising North America's rising glory, seeing no contrast with British glory as a whole. But London officials were beginning to see a rival, particularly in the mostly free-labor, non-plantation colonies of the North.

Native Americans gave London more worry. White colonials wanted Indian land, but the Indians were strong enough to resist, both by playing the imperial game and, if necessary, by outright war. Indians were important in defeating France during the long struggle for North American mastery. But when the French withdrew in 1763, native people set out to drive Europeans back from the Great Lakes country. The brief war called Pontiac's Rebellion failed, and British posts remained at Niagara, Fort Pitt, and Detroit. But Britain did proclaim that colonial expansion had to stop, which infuriated colonial speculators. In 1774 Britain decreed that its appointed government in conquered Quebec would have jurisdiction over the Ohio Country. In effect, the Indians had forced their own terms of belonging on the British.

Underpinning all disputes were issues about the very nature of the British Empire. Metropolitan Britons were moving toward the idea of a unitary state, in which colonials were subordinate and their institutions were mere conveniences, like local councils "at home." But to colonials, their assemblies were local parliaments, existing by right and beyond the British Parliament's control. Pressed on the matter, they would have seen the monarchy not as unitary but rather as composite, with the monarch ruling each province on its own terms, much as James I (of England, r. 1603–1625) and VI (of Scotland, r. 1567–1603) and his successors had ruled over two separate kingdoms until the Act of Union in 1707. Indians would have agreed. They were allies, not subjects at all.

But London was determined to rule. Its attempts between 1764 and 1773 to tax the colonists for the sake of their own defense and administration provoked massive protest. Britain's attempts to regulate Indian affairs for the sake of frontier peace provoked resentment all around. The problem of slavery was emerging too, in no simple way. Certain that their slaves could reproduce themselves, Virginia planters tried to cut off the obnoxious trade to Africa, only to meet a royal veto. Jefferson made that a grievance in his draft of the Declaration of Independence.

Yet "Somerset's Case" (1771–1772) seemed to put the highest British authorities on the side of liberty, at least within Britain, as slaves in America learned. In his decision, Lord Chief Justice Mansfield described slavery as "so odius" that only a positive law could enact it. Britain had no such positive law of slavery. Mansfield's decision acquired an exaggerated reputation as having abolished slavery within England. It did not actually do so, but it did mean that slave owners could not forcibly export the slaves elsewhere, as James Somerset's owner had tried to do. When the Earl of Dunmore (John Murray, 1730–1809), governor of colonial Virginia, and British general Henry Clinton (1730–1795) offered the king's freedom to slaves "pertaining to rebels," they rallied. But others found their freedom on the American side. The issue of slavery was thus brought alive, but it did not fit with the principal concerns of those who led the rebellion against Britain, nor with their notions of liberty.

By July 1776, enough white colonials agreed on independence to make it politically necessary and militarily possible. Severing the tie to Britain raised the problem of organizing a new order. Americans would be republican; that was clear. Whether they would be a single nation or fourteen linked republics (counting Vermont, which broke free of New York) was less certain.

Not the least of their problems was the complex overlay of lines that rendered colonial-era maps exercises in confusion. Virginia went a long way toward resolving that problem in 1781, by ceding a claim that had included most of what now is the Midwest. Two years later, the peace treaty ceded all British claims south of the Great Lakes and east of the Mississippi River. As a result, the emerging United States was rich with land, if it actually could establish control over the land.

Decolonization meant a transfer of sovereignty, and one aspect of sovereignty was the exclusive right to deal with aboriginal people. Even before independence, the Continental Congress and the separate states were jockeying for the right to acquire Indian land. As a consequence, both Congress and the states established colonial relations of their own with Indians who supposedly belonged to them. Not until the implementation of the Constitution of the United States in March 1789 was the matter resolved in Congress's favor. In each case, the goal was to acquire as much Indian land as possible and transform its meaning and use.

Congress established a lasting pattern with its three "Northwest Ordinances." Two, in 1784 and 1787, worked out a new system of white colonies, to be called *territories* and having the right to advance to full statehood and membership in the Union. In that way Congress solved the problem of inequality between the thirteen colonies and their distant metropolis on which the British Empire had foundered. The Ordinance of 1785 established the land grid that is visible on any flight over the Midwest. What had been Indian country would be divided into perfect squares. Sales of the land would bring revenue. Grants would pay off former soldiers. Separate ownership would foster civic individualism. Easy sale would allow owners to cash in capital gains. Indians would be forced to retreat, and retreat again.

In large terms that is precisely what happened, and in large terms the political and economic transformation of western land underpinned the emergence of the United States as a capitalist society. In the long run, the change pointed toward the breakup of family patriarchy and stable communities. The final result was the Homestead Act of 1862, which made public land available for free, to women and men alike. But until the Civil War (1861–1865), land south of the Ohio River was available to slave owners.

The attempt of the Cherokees to establish a quasi-independent republic failed in the face of determination by the state of Georgia and President Andrew Jackson (1829–1837) that all Indians had to go and all Indian land had to be open for development. North of the Ohio River, Jefferson's vision of an "empire of [white] freedom" did approach reality. But below the river the "Cotton Kingdom" took shape. To the extent that the fusion of slavery, racist thought, and plantation economics was a legacy of the colonial era, the South remained colonial. Yet both developments were direct consequences of the Revolution. Resolving that contradiction would require a second revolution, far more bloody than the first. But the destruction of slavery was no greater a transformation than the changes that the earlier revolution had set in motion.

At the point of independence the new states were half-formed, ill-defined societies hugging the seaboard. Fifty years later, the United States claimed sovereign rights as far as the Pacific Ocean and exercised real control well beyond the Mississippi. There had not been a single bank in America at independence; by 1826 a full if ramshackle financial system existed, able to control the disposition of both foreign and domestic capital. New York State's Erie Canal crossed what had been the land of the Six Iroquois Nations, linking the Great Lakes directly and easily to New York City. Other states were planning to emulate the Erie's success, not only with canals but with good highways and railroads. After a shaky start, a factory system was flourishing between Maine and Delaware, creating two new social classes, industrialists and workers. In a very real way, the United States had succeeded at forming a metropolitan society in its own right. Its white male political society was reaching the stage that the contemporary French observer Alexis de Tocqueville (1805–1859) would describe and analyze as "Democracy in America."

Yet as with all revolutions, independence had produced as many problems as it had resolved. A blanket American liberty, supposedly evenly spread, had replaced the patchwork of British liberties. Equal citizenship had replaced uneven subjection as the dominant political metaphor, but the citizenship of slaves was nil and that of free black people and white women remained unequal. Chief Justice John Marshall (1755–1835) would shortly define tribal Indians as "domestic dependent nations," possessed of rights, but not of the right to seek redress in the federal courts, with consequences that still remain unresolved. The revolution had been real, as Washington Irving's (1783–1859) fictional Rip Van Winkle found when he awoke from his long sleep into a world that he did not recognize. But no more than any other had the American Revolution succeeding in creating a perfect society.

SEE ALSO *Empire in the Americas, British.*

BIBLIOGRAPHY

Countryman, Edward. *The American Revolution*, rev. ed. New York: Hill & Wang, 2003.

Davis, David Brion. *Revolutions: Reflections on American Equality and Foreign Liberations.* Cambridge, MA: Harvard University Press, 1990.

Draper, Theodore. *A Struggle for Power: The American Revolution.* New York: Times Books, 1996.

Egnal, Marc. *A Mighty Empire: The Origins of the American Revolution.* Ithaca, NY: Cornell University Press, 1988.

"Forum: Rethinking the American Revolution." *The William and Mary Quarterly* 53 (2) (1996): 341–386.

Frey, Sylvia. *Water from the Rock: Black Resistance in a Revolutionary Age.* Princeton, NJ: Princeton University Press, 1991.

Hoffman, Ronald, and Peter J. Albert, eds. *The Economy of Early America: The Revolutionary Period, 1763–1790.* Charlottesville: University Press of Virginia, 1988.

Hoffman, Ronald, and Peter J. Albert, eds. *The Transforming Hand of Revolution: Reconsidering the American Revolution as a Social Movement.* Charlottesville: University Press of Virginia, 1996.

Hoxie, Frederick E., Ronald Hoffman, and Peter J. Albert, eds. *Native Americans and the Early Republic.* Charlottesville: University Press of Virginia, 1999.

Morris, Richard B. *The Emerging Nations and the American Revolution.* New York: Harper, 1970.

Norton, Mary Beth. *Liberty's Daughters: The Revolutionary Experience of American Women, 1750–1800,* rev. ed. Ithaca, NY: Cornell University Press, 1996.

Onuf, Peter S. *Statehood and Union: A History of the Northwest Ordinance.* Bloomington: Indiana University Press, 1988.

Wood, Gordon S. *The Radicalism of the American Revolution.* New York: Knopf, 1993.

Young, Alfred F., ed. *Beyond the American Revolution: Explorations in the History of American Radicalism.* DeKalb, IL: Northern Illinois University Press, 1993.

Edward Countryman

AMERICAN SAMOA

Samoa is an archipelago of islands situated in the South Pacific. The western islands of the archipelago, including Upolu and Savai'i, comprise the present-day independent nation of Samoa. The eastern islands comprise the present-day U.S. Territory of American Samoa since the 1899 Treaty of Berlin division of Samoa, at which time Germany and the United States divided Samoa, while giving up interest in Fiji to Great Britain. During World War II, American soldiers in Samoa outnumbered Samoans, and greatly influenced their relations with the outside world. Pago Pago Airport accommodates U.S. military aircraft daily and at its U.S. Army Reserve Base Samoan soldiers are trained for the Middle East and other American military endeavors.

The chiefs of the islands of American Samoa, under influence of the U.S. Navy commandant of the Pacific based in Pago Pago, signed documents of cession as unincorporated territory of the United States in 1900 when Tutuila and Aunu'u Islands were ceded, and in 1904 when the Manu'a group of islands, or Ofu, Olosega, and Ta'u islands, were ceded, including Rose Atoll and Swain's Island. The U.S. Navy leveraged its takeover of the copra industry, with promises of protection from land speculation, and the support of the Congregationalist Church, against the sustainability and sovereignty interests of local chiefs, especially the Tui Manu'a Elisala, the former sovereign of Manu'a. In the 1950s Chief Tuiasosopo urged the establishment of a legislature, the Fono of American Samoa, and helped stop a U.S. Department of Interior attempt to incorporate the territory. In the 2001 and 2003, the United States attempted to have the U.S. Territory of American Samoa removed from the United Nations' list of nations to be decolonized, stating that American Samoa is "not a colony" (Governor Tauese, *Samoa News,* 2001).

In the distant past, Samoa was ruled by a group of women paramount chiefs, including Nafanua and her niece Salamasina. These women and their talking chiefs helped formalize growing Samoan protocols of governance called the *fa'amatai,* and courtesies of language and relationships called the *fa'asamoa.* These protocols govern the way families relate, especially within the *fono* or council, maintaining localization and decentralization of governance in the Samoa Islands, in times of sovereignty or colonization. Although the United States has claimed that territorialization of American Samoa protects the *fa'asamoa,* the *fa'asamoa* is as well maintained or even stronger in independent Samoa, while the practice of *fa'asamoa* often dissolves colonial borders between Samoans.

SEE ALSO *Missions, in the Pacific; Pacific, American Presence in; Pacific, European Presence in.*

BIBLIOGRAPHY

Ellison, Joseph. *Opening and Penetration of Foreign Influence in Samoa to 1880.* Corvallis: Oregon State College, 1938.

Meti, Lauofo. *Samoa: The Making of the Constitution.* Apia: Government of Samoa, 2002.

Sunia, Fofo I. F. *The Story of the Legislature of American Samoa (In Commemoration of the Golden Jubilee 1948–1998)*. [New Zealand]: Legislature of American Samoa, 1998.

Turner, George. *Samoa: A Hundred Years Ago and Long Before (1884)*. New York: AMS Press, 1979.

United Nations. UN Working Paper on American Samoa. A/AC.109/2002/12. New York: United Nations, 2002.

Vaai, Salaimoa. *Samoa Faamatai and the Rule of Law*. Apia: The National University of Samoa Le Papa-I-Galagala, 1999.

Dan Taulapapa McMullin

ANGLO-BURMESE WARS

Three wars were fought between Burma and the British colonial empire during the nineteenth century.

THE FIRST ANGLO-BURMESE WAR OF 1824–1826

From the end of the eighteenth century the Burmese king Bodawpaya (r. 1782–1817), steadily expanded his realm westward. At the same time the British gained territorial control over Bengal and elsewhere in India. In 1784 Bodawpaya attacked and annexed the kingdom of Arakan on the coast of the Bay of Bengal and brought his frontier to what would become British India. Arakanese rebels operating from within British territory created a tense situation on the Anglo-Burmese border, resulting in frequent border clashes. The Burmese threatened invasion if the British failed to stop rebel incursions from their territory.

From the late eighteenth century the kingdom of Assam to the North of British Bengal was in decline. The kingdom covered the Brahmaputra valley from the Himalayas to the entry of the river into the plains of Bengal. Rival groups at the Assamese court turned both to the British and the Burmese for assistance, leading to a British expedition in 1792. In 1817 turmoil at the Assamese court led to another request for assistance and this time Bodawpaya sent an invading army. The Assamese were defeated and a pro-Burmese premier was installed.

Two decades earlier Bodawpaya had invaded Manipur, a kingdom set in a small valley to the west of the Chindwin River, and installed a puppet prince. In 1819 the Manipur Prince asserted his autonomy from the Burmese court by not attending the coronation of Bagyidaw, Bodawpaya's successor. The Burmese invaded again and stationed a permanent garrison in Manipur. Manipur would now form a base from which further Burmese military expeditions into Assam would be conducted. In 1821, following years of local unrest, Bagyidaw sent general Mahabanula with a 20,000-person-strong army across the mountains to consolidate Burmese rule in Assam. In 1823, with Assamese resistance largely broken, Mahabandula set up his base at Rangpur and began his attacks on Cachar and Jaintia. The British in turn declared Cachar and Jaintia a protectorate. British Bengal was now hemmed in on its northern and eastern borders by the Burmese Empire.

In January 1824 Mahabandula assumed command in Arakan and started on a campaign against Chittagong with the ultimate goal to capture Bengal. In response, on March 5, 1824, the British declared war on Burma from their headquarters at Fort William in Calcutta. The British plan was to draw away Mahabandula's forces from the Bengal frontier by performing a large-scale sea-borne invasion of Lower Burma. The attack on Rangoon, lead by Sir Archibald Campbell, completely surprised the Burmese and the city was taken on May 10, 1824 without any loss to the invaders. The news of the fall of Rangoon forced Mahabandula to a quick retreat. The British force in Rangoon had meanwhile been unable to proceed upcountry because it did not have adequate river transports. After having been resupplied after the monsoon Campbell continued the operations and in 1825 at the battle of Danubyu Mahabandula was killed and the same year Arakan, Lower Burma, and Tenasserim were conquered.

After a second battle the way to the Burmese capital, Amarapura, lay wide open. Campbell now possessed adequate river transport and rapid progress was made up the Irrawaddy. British peace terms were so staggering that not until the British army arrived at Yandabo, a few days' march from the Burmese capital, did the Burmese accept the terms. After the peace of Yandabo the Burmese had ceded to the British Arakan, Tenasserim, Assam, and Manipur. An indemnity in rupees, equal to 1 million pound sterling, was paid to guarantee removal of British troops from Lower Burma.

THE SECOND ANGLO-BURMESE WAR OF 1852

The inglorious defeat of the Burmese in the first war did not provoke a change in attitude toward the British. Successive Burmese kings went so far as to revoke the treaty of Yandabo and treated representatives of the governor-general with contempt. After quelling rebellions in Lower Burma in 1838 and 1840, King Tharrawaddy staged on a visit to Rangoon in 1841 a military demonstration that caused great alarm with the British in Arakan and Tenasserim. King Pagan, who had succeeded Tharrawaddy in 1846, concentrated his energy on his religious obligations and left the day-to-day government to his ministers. In Rangoon this meant that an unbending Burmese administration combined with profit-hungry British traders created a volatile atmosphere. In 1851 tension erupted and a minor incident between the

King Thibaw and Queen Supayalat of Burma. *The king and queen of Burma are pictured along with the queen's sister at their palace in Mandalay, Burma, in the 1800s. Thibaw reigned from 1878 to 1885, when the British forced him from the throne.*
© HULTON-DEUTSCH COLLECTION/CORBIS. REPRODUCED BY PERMISSION.

governor of Rangoon and two British traders resulted in the Governor-General Dalhousie sending three warships with a request for reparations to Rangoon.

Although the Burmese complied with Dalhousie's demands, the situation in Rangoon spiraled out of control when the British commodore leading the naval squadron felt the new governor of Rangoon had treated him unjustly. The commodore blockaded the port, destroyed all warships in the vicinity of Rangoon, and took a ship belonging to the Burmese Crown. War was now imminent. Dalhousie sent the Burmese a further ultimatum demanding compensation for the preparations for war. When the ultimatum expired on April 1, 1852, the British had already landed in Lower Burma.

This time the British arrived well prepared, with adequate supplies and sufficient river transports. In a few days 'time Rangoon and Martaban were taken. When the Burmese offered no further resistance

Dalhousie decided to occupy large areas of Lower Burma, mainly comprised of the former province of Pegu, in an effort to link up Arakan and Tenasserim and create a stable and viable new colony. Without waiting for a formal treaty with the Burmese, Dalhousie proclaimed the annexation of Lower Burma on December 20, 1852. At the Burmese court a peace party overthrew King Pagan, and a few months following the annexation of Lower Burma a new king, Mindon, was crowned. In peace talks King Mindon tried in vain to recover the rich teak forests that had been taken by the British.

THE THIRD ANGLO-BURMESE WAR OF 1885

During the late 1870s, at a time when France was consolidating its hold over Vietnam, Laos, and Cambodia, politicians and officials in Britain and India began considering intervention in what was left of the Burmese kingdom. They feared French influence in Burma and viewed with suspicion Burmese missions to European capitals. At the same time the British became increasingly interested in the possibility of trading with China via Burma. Some officials even viewed Burma as a "highway to China." The Burmese economy, once jealously guarded by mercantilist kings, was laid open to British trade.

The unbridled expansion of British commerce meant, however, that Burmese concessions to British merchants never went fast and far enough. British traders developed great interests in the trade of rubies, teak, and oil from northern Burma. In commercial treaties of 1862 and 1867 an informal empire was imposed in Burma. The Burmese Crown, in the last years before the start of the third war, adopted a policy aimed at developing friendly relations with Britain's European rivals, including France and Italy. In 1878, following the death of King Mindon, his son Thibaw succeeded to the throne. After another commercial dispute in 1885 and amidst fears of growing French influence in Burma, Lord Randolph Churchill, secretary of state for India, decided to invade Upper Burma and depose Thibaw. The war began on November 14, 1885, and a fortnight later, after an almost bloodless campaign, the capital Mandalay was surrounded and the king surrendered. Thibaw was sent into exile in India and the British took control of Burma.

SEE ALSO *Burma, British; Empire, British.*

BIBLIOGRAPHY

Hall, D.G.E. *A History of South-east Asia*, 4th rev. ed. London: Macmillan, 1981.

Pollak, Oliver B. *Empires in Collision: Anglo-Burmese Relations in the Mid-Nineteenth Century.* Westport, CT: Greenwood Press, 1979.

Wilson, Horace Hayman. *Narrative of the Burmese War, in 1824-25.* London: W.H. Allen and Co., 1852.

Stephan van Galen

ANGLO-RUSSIAN RIVALRY IN THE MIDDLE EAST

For centuries, the rivalry between Russia and Great Britain in the Middle East was a major factor in geopolitics. The decline of the Ottoman Empire beginning in the 1700s had brought up what became known as the *eastern question*: The term does not refer to a single question but to a variety of issues, including the instability of European territories that were part of the Ottoman Empire. The term *great game*, known in Russia as the *tournament of shadows*, refers to the Anglo-Russian rivalry

with regard to Iran (Persia), Afghanistan, and northern India. Both Russia and Great Britain took measures to gain influence in southeastern Europe, in the Middle East, and in Central Asia.

THE EASTERN QUESTION

The Ottoman Empire was at the height of its power during the seventeenth century, annexing wide parts of central Europe. The Ottoman defeat at Vienna by Austria and Poland in 1683 brought expansion toward the west to a sudden halt, and the Treaty of Karlowitz (1699) forced Ottoman rulers to cede most of the empire's central European possessions, including Hungary. Although the Ottoman Empire was thereafter no longer a threat to Austria, tensions with Russia were growing.

The introduction of the eastern question is commonly dated to 1774, when the Russo-Turkish War (1768–1774) ended in defeat for the Ottoman Empire. The Treaty of Kuçuk Kainarji (July 21, 1774) established Russia as the major power in the Black Sea region. Furthermore, the treaty was interpreted by Russia as permission to act as the protector of Orthodox Christians living under the sovereignty of the Ottoman sultan.

During the Russo-Turkish War of 1787 to 1792, Empress Catherine II (1729–1796) of Russia sought an alliance with the Holy Roman emperor, Joseph II (1741–1790). The two powers agreed to partition the Ottoman Empire, thereby alarming other European powers, especially the United Kingdom, Prussia, and France. The Treaty of Jassy (January 9, 1792) ended the war with and confirmed Russia's increasing dominance in the Black Sea region.

The positions of the European powers relative to the Ottoman Empire became clearer during the early nineteenth century. The power most directly involved was of course Russia, whose major concerns were control of the Black Sea and access to the Mediterranean. Russia was eager to acquire exclusive navigation rights for its merchant fleet and warships while denying these privileges to other European powers. Less important was Russia's role as the protector of Orthodox Christians in the Balkans.

Russia's plans with regard to the Ottoman Empire were strongly opposed by Austria, which had once been the major European opponent of the Ottoman Empire. However, Austria considered Russia's advance along the Danube River in central and southeastern Europe to be a major threat and feared that a disintegration of the Ottoman Empire into individual nation-states would foment nationalism among ethnic groups within the empire. Austria therefore worked to maintain the unity of the Ottoman Empire. This position was similar to that of the British, who regarded the rise of the Russian

Empire to be a threat to the security of British colonial possessions in India. Britain was also concerned that Russian control of the Bosporus Strait could threaten British domination of the eastern Mediterranean. Furthermore, the fall of the Ottoman Empire would undermine the traditional balance of power in Europe.

The Treaty of Tilsit (1807) established an alliance between France and Russia: When Russia agreed to aid the French emperor Napoléon Bonaparte (1769–1821) in a war against Britain, the Russian czar was to receive in return the Ottoman territories of Moldavia and Wallachia, known as the Danubian Principalities. If the Ottoman sultan refused to surrender these territories, France would join a Russian attack against Turkey and both powers would divide the Ottoman possessions among themselves.

This alliance, which would have left Britain, Austria, and Prussia almost powerless, was dissolved by Napoléon's invasion of Russia in 1812. After Napoléon's defeat, the representatives of the victorious powers met at the Congress of Vienna, but failed to take action relating to the integrity of the decaying Ottoman Empire. Thereafter, the eastern question became a Russian domestic issue that was of less importance to the other European powers.

The eastern question again became a major issue when the Greeks declared independence from the Ottoman Empire in 1821, a development that made a Russian invasion of the Ottoman territory more likely. Viscount Castlereagh (Robert Stewart, 1769–1822), the British foreign minister, and Count Klemens von Metternich (1773–1859), the Austrian chancellor, convinced Czar Alexander I (1777–1825) to maintain the "Concert of Europe," a spirit of collaboration that had arisen after Napoléon's defeat. The Holy Alliance, which had brought together Russia, Austria and Prussia in an effort to continue peaceful cooperation after the Vienna Congress did not take decisive action in Greece.

Alexander's successor, Czar Nicholas I (1796–1855), choose to intervene in Greece. In order to prevent Greece from becoming a Russian vassal state, the United Kingdom and France became involved, while Austria did not. Ottoman sultan Mahmud II (1785–1839) was outraged by the interference of the European powers and denounced Russia as an enemy of Islam. Russia declared war against the Ottoman Empire in 1828, but was unable to resolve the eastern question because the other European powers did not intervene. The Treaty of Adrianople (1829) allowed Russian commercial vessels access to the Dardanelles, a strait in northwest Turkey, and enhanced Russian commercial rights in the Ottoman Empire.

The Greek war ended when Greece was granted independence by the Treaty of Constantinople (1832). Shortly after the war, a new conflict emerged in the Ottoman Empire. The Ottoman governor in Egypt, Mehmed Ali (1769–1849), had consolidated power in Egypt and set out to gain independence from the sultan. His well-trained *nizami* army overran Syria, captured the port of Acre (now part of Israel) after a six-month siege, and advanced into Anatolia in Turkey. By this point, it had become obvious that Mehmed Ali might overthrow the reigning Osmanli dynasty and seize control of the Ottoman Empire.

Czar Nicholas offered the Ottoman sultan military aid, which was accepted. The Treaty of Unkiar Skelessi (July 8, 1833) promised mutual assistance, but a secret clause exempted the Ottoman Empire from sending military forces. Instead, the Ottoman leaders would close the Dardanelles to all non-Russian ships when Russia was at war. The treaty was met with suspicion in Britain and France, for both powers feared that Russia had gained freedom of action to send warships through the Dardanelles.

Russian intervention led to a peace agreement between the sultan and Mehmed Ali. In the peace of Kutahya (1833), the Egyptian viceroy agreed to withdraw from Anatolia; in compensation, he received the territories of the Hijaz and Crete. In 1839, however, war broke out again. When Sultan Mahmud II died that year, his son and successor, Abdülmecid I (1823–1861), ascended to the throne in difficult times. The forces of Mehmed Ali had defeated the Ottoman armies, and the Ottoman fleet had been seized by Egyptian insurgents. Although France continued to support Mehmed Ali, Russia, France, and Great Britain intervened in the conflict to prevent the collapse of the Ottoman Empire. In 1840 the European powers settled on a compromise in which Mehmed Ali agreed to make a (nominal) act of submission and was granted hereditary control of Egypt.

Although the collapse of the Ottoman Empire had been prevented, control of the Dardanelles remained at issue. In 1841 Austria, France, Prussia, Russia, and the United Kingdom agreed on the reestablishment of the "ancient rule," according to which the strait would be closed to all warships with the sole exception of the sultan's allies during times of war. With the acceptance of the Strait Convention, Czar Nicholas I abandoned his effort to reduce the Ottoman sultan to a state of dependence on Russia. Instead, Russia returned to plans to partition Ottoman territories in Europe.

Although the Ottoman Empire was no longer dependent on Russia, it continued to rely on the European powers for protection. Despite many attempts at internal reform, the decline of the Ottoman Empire continued, rendering Turkey the "sick man of Europe," as it came to be known. Its dissolution was considered inevitable.

The Plight of Turkey. *This cartoon, printed around 1900, shows the position of Turkey relative to Europe and its colonies in the Middle East at the turn of the century. Turkey is surrounded by Austria, depicted as an eagle with two heads; Russia, seen as a crowned bear; and Britain, shown as a rotund man straddling Corfu and Malta and restraining Egypt, a lion, with a leash.* © BETTMANN/CORBIS. REPRODUCED BY PERMISSION.

The Revolutions of 1848 in Europe moved the eastern question from the center of attention. Russia could have taken the opportunity to attack the Ottoman Empire, while France and Austria were occupied with internal affairs. Russia did not take this action, however; instead, Nicholas committed his forces to the defense of Austria. Nicholas deemed that the goodwill established in 1848 would allow him to seize Ottoman possessions at a later date.

After the suppression of the revolution in Austria, a joint Austro-Russian war against the Ottoman Empire seemed imminent. The sultan had refused to repatriate Austrian rebels who had found asylum in Turkey. When Austria and Russia withdrew their ambassadors, France and the United Kingdom dispatched their fleets to protect the Ottoman Empire. To avoid military confrontation, Austria withdrew its demand for the surrender of fugitives.

During the 1840s, British leaders expressed growing fears of Russian encroachment on Afghanistan and India, and they tried to find opportunities to obstruct the Russian advance. Britain found a pretext in the protection of Christian holy places sites in Palestine, then part of the Ottoman Empire. Eighteenth-century treaties had

given France the responsibility of protecting Roman-Catholics in the Ottoman Empire, while Orthodox Christians were to be protected by Russia. Roman Catholic and Orthodox Christian monks had disputed possession of the Church of the Holy Sepulchre in Jerusalem and the Church of the Nativity in Bethlehem, and Sultan Abdülmecid was unable to satisfy the demands of both sides. In 1853 he adjudicated in favor of the French and the Catholics.

The sultan had been committed to protecting the Christian religion and holy sites, but after the decision in favor of the French, Czar Nicholas I sent an emissary, Prince Aleksandr Sergeyevich Menshikov (1787–1869), to negotiate a new treaty. Menshikov was to negotiate a treaty that allowed Russia to interfere whenever it considered the protection of Christians inadequate. At the same time, the British government sent its own emissary, Lord Stratford Canning (1786–1880), who managed to convince the sultan to reject the Russian treaty by pointing out that it would compromise the independence of the Porte (the Ottoman government). Benjamin Disraeli (1804–1881), the British prime minister during part of the 1860s and 1870s, later blamed the outbreak of war on actions taken by British premier Lord Aberdeen (George Hamilton Gordon, 1784–1860) and Lord Stratford, which led to Aberdeen's forced resignation shortly thereafter.

When Nicholas learned of the failure of Menshikov's negotiations, he seized the pretext of the sultan's failure to protect Christian holy places, and sent armies into Wallachia and Moldavia, where Russia was acknowledged as the guardian of Orthodox Christianity. Given Russian involvement in suppressing the 1848 revolution, the czar was convinced that the European powers would not object strongly to his annexation of two neighboring provinces.

To maintain the security of the Ottoman Empire, both the United Kingdom and France sent fleets to the Dardanelles. Despite attempts at diplomacy by Austria, France, Prussia, and the United Kingdom, a diplomatic solution proved impossible. While Austria and Prussia tried to continue negotiations, Ottoman armies attacked the Russian army near the Danube. In response, Russian warships attacked and destroyed the Ottoman fleet at the Battle of Sinop on November 30, 1853, thereby opening way for Russian troops to land and supply their forces easily. This alarmed Britain and France, causing them to step forth in defense of the Ottoman Empire. After Russia ignored an Anglo-French ultimatum to withdraw, Britain and France declared war.

Czar Nicholas had presumed that, in return for support in 1848 Austria would side with Russia, or at least remain neutral in the Crimean War (1853–1856). However, Austria regarded the presence of Russian troops in the Danubian Principalities to be a major threat, and supported British and French demands for Russian withdrawal from the region. Furthermore, Austria refused to guarantee neutrality. The original cause for the war was eliminated when Russia withdrew from Moldavia and Wallachia, but France and the Untied Kingdom were determined to use this opportunity to finally address the eastern question.

Therefore, the European allies proposed the following conditions for the cessation of hostilities: Russia should give up its protectorate over the Danubian Principalities, and abandon all claims granting Russia the right to interfere in Ottoman affairs on behalf of Orthodox Christians. Furthermore, Russia must agree to a revision of the 1841 Strait Convention and guarantee free access to the Danube. The czar rejected these conditions, and the Crimean War proceeded.

Nicholas's successor, Alexander II (1818–1881), began peace negotiations in 1856. In the Treaty of Paris, he agreed to four points: Russian privileges relating to Moldavia and Wallachia were transferred to the European allies as a group, and warships were to be barred from the Black Sea. Russia and the Ottoman Empire further agreed not to establish military or naval arsenals along the Black Sea coast. On these grounds, all the European powers agreed to respect the territorial integrity and the independence of the Ottoman Empire.

The eastern question was thus temporarily settled—until France was defeated in the Franco-Prussian War in 1870. The French emperor Napoléon III (1808–1873), eager for British support, opposed Russia over the eastern question, although Russian interference in the Ottoman Empire did not threaten French interests. After the establishment of the Third French Republic in 1870, France abandoned its opposition. Russia now denounced the Black Sea clauses of the 1856 treaty, and reestablished a fleet in the Black Sea.

When in 1875 Herzegovina, Bosnia, and Bulgaria rebelled against the Ottoman sultan, Europe's great powers considered an intervention necessary to prevent war in the Balkans. The "League of the Three Emperors" (Austria-Hungary, Germany, and Russia) stated their mutual stance toward the eastern question in the Andrássy Note (named after the Hungarian statesman Count Gyula Andrássy [1823–1890]), which stipulated the following: To avoid widespread conflict in southwestern Europe, the sultan must institute a number of reforms, including the granting of religious liberty to Christians in Ottoman territories; to ensure appropriate reforms, a joint commission was to be formed. The Andrássy Note, which was approved by the United Kingdom and France, was submitted to the Porte. Sultan Abdülaziz (1830–1876) agreed to the proposal on January 31, 1876, but Herzegovinian leaders rejected it.

Before representatives of Austria-Hungary, Germany, and Russia could take further action, the Ottoman Empire faced major internal struggles that led to the deposition of the sultan. His successor, Murad V (1840–1904), was deposed after only three months because of mental instability. He was followed by Sultan Abdülhamid II (1842–1918).

The Ottoman treasury was empty by this time, and the sultan faced insurrections not only in Bosnia and Herzegovina, but also in Serbia and Montenegro. In August 1876 the Ottoman armies crushed the insurgents, but widespread rumors of atrocities against the civilian populations shocked the public. While Russia considered entering the war on the side of the rebels, delegates of six European powers (Austria, France, Germany, Italy, Russia, and the United Kingdom) held a conference in Constantinople (now Istanbul, Turkey). Their proposals were repeatedly rejected by the Ottoman sultan.

Russia secured Austro-Hungarian neutrality with the Reichstadt Agreement of July 1876, which stated that territories captured during the war would be partitioned between Russia and Austria-Hungary, with control of Bosnia and Herzegovina going to Austria-Hungary. On April 24, 1877, Russia declared war on the Ottoman Empire.

Although the United Kingdom feared Russian threats to British dominance in Central Asia, Britain did not intervene. After the defeat of the Ottoman forces in February 1878, peace was established with the Treaty of San Stefano, which greatly increased Russian influence in southeastern Europe. After large-scale British intervention, revisions of the peace treaty were negotiated at the 1878 Congress of Berlin. The new treaty adjusted the boundaries of the newly independent states (Romania, Serbia, and Montenegro) and divided Bulgaria into two separate states (Bulgaria and Eastern Rumelia). Bosnia and Herzegovina nominally stayed within the Ottoman Empire, but control was transferred to Austria-Hungary.

In 1908 the so-called Young Turks, a broad-based political organization that opposed the absolute rule of the Ottoman sultan, led a rebellion against Abdülhamid II and deposed him a year later. Under his successor, Mehmed V (1844–1918), political and constitutional reforms were instituted; the decay of the Ottoman Empire, however, continued.

Austria-Hungary took advantage of Ottoman weakness by annexing Bosnia and Herzegovina. Austria-Hungary secured Russian approval for the annexation by declaring support for a treaty that granted Russian warships the right to pass through the Dardanelles and the Bosporus straits. Serbia sought Russian assistance against Austro-Hungarian plans, but Russia could not comply because it had not recovered from the devastating effects of the Russo-Japanese War (1904–1905). After Austria-Hungary announced its annexation on October 6, 1908, Russia declared that it would seek access to the Dardanelles. This move was strongly opposed by France and the United Kingdom, who were not directly concerned with the annexation in itself.

During the Balkan Wars (1909–1912), the Ottoman Empire finally lost most of its European territories. In an effort to keep power in Ottoman hands, regain some of the lost territories, and challenge British authority over the Suez Canal, the Ottoman Empire allied itself with the Central Powers, led by Austria-Hungary and Germany, during World War I (1914–1918).

In the early years of the war, the Ottoman Empire had successes: The Allies were defeated in the Battle of Gallipoli in Turkey in 1915, and in Iraq and the Balkans, and British landing attempts were repulsed. In the Caucasus, however, the Ottoman Empire lost several battles. Russian forces proceeded in a line from Lake Van in eastern Turkey to the cities of Erzurum and Trabzon in the north. During the 1917 Russian Revolution, the Ottomans took back control of these areas, but the empire was ultimately defeated by the Allies by the end of World War I, the Ottoman Empire was defeated by the Allies. The Armistice of Mudros (1918) and the Treaty of Sèvres (1920) formally established the partition of the Ottoman Empire, and led to the establishment of the Republic of Turkey on October 29, 1923.

PERSIA AND THE ANGLO-RUSSIAN RIVALRY

In 1722 Peter I ("the Great," 1672–1725) of Russia invaded Persian territory as part of his attempt to gain domination of Central Asia. At the same time, Ottoman forces successfully besieged the Persian city of Isfahan. Persia was able to weather the invasions, but the Safavid rulers were severely weakened, and the last Safavid shah was executed in 1722.

During the 1730s and 1740s, Nadir Shah (1688–1747) consolidated the Persian Empire, drove out the Russians, and launched campaigns against the Central Asian khanates. Shortly after his death, however, the empire fell into decline. Persia was not prepared for the expansion of European empires in the late eighteenth century. The country was sandwiched between the growing Russian Empire in Central Asia and the expanding British Empire in India. Because of the growing importance of India, Great Britain regarded Persia as an important region in the defense against Russia, first against France and later against the Russians. When the French failed to support the shah in Persia's war against Russia, the shah ousted the French from their advisory position and replaced them with the British. The British, however, tried to appease the Russians rather than support their ally. Facing quick Russian advances in Central Asia, British attitudes were changing.

Although Persia was never invaded, it became more and more economically dependent on Europe. The Anglo-Russian Convention of 1907 formalized British and Russian spheres of interest and dominance over economic development in the area.

During World War I, Persia was drawn into the periphery of the war because of its geographically strategic position. To prevent the Ottomans from taking control of Persian oilfields, Britain sent military forces to Mesopotamia. In 1916 fights between Russian and Ottoman forces reached Persian territory, where Russia had gained more and more influence. In the wake of the Russian Revolution, however, most of the Russian armies collapsed. In addition, Persian civilians were starving after years of deprivation and war. After the war, Persia became a tool in the political battles of other empires. Although Reza Shah Pahlavi (1878–1944) seized power and established a new dynasty in Iran, Britain and the Soviet Union remained influential in the region well into the early years of the Cold War.

AFGHANISTAN

In the early nineteenth century, British India and the frontiers of Russia were separated by about 2,000 miles (about 3,220 kilometers). There were no trade routes, and the great cities along the old Silk Road, such as Bukhara, Khiva, Merv, Tashkent, and Chimkent, were forgotten. The territory was unmapped, even though both czarist Russia and Qing-dynasty China promoted surveying and cartographic projects in Central Asia during the eighteenth century in projects intended to secure state boundaries and control nomadic populations. Russian maps of that time gave yet another image—they reflected knowledge about Central Asia, but they were not based on detailed surveys.

Russian efforts to gain control over major portions of Central Asia were reinforced in the early eighteenth century. In 1717 Czar Peter I sent a Russian expedition to Khiva, but the Russians were slaughtered there. Shortly after the death of Peter, a story arose that he had commissioned his heirs to take possession of Constantinople and India as the keys to world domination. To subdue and control the Kazakh tribes, the Russians built the fortress of Orenburg (north of the Caspian Sea). At the same time, Persians and Afghans invaded India, where British influence was growing steadily. Czarina Catherine considered a plan to impede this growing influence, but it was never implemented.

When Russian attempts to consolidate the southern frontier began to collide with the increasing British dominance of the Indian Subcontinent and adjacent territories, the two powers engaged in a subtle "game" of imperialistic diplomacy, exploration, and espionage throughout Central Asia. However, the conflict never broke out into open warfare.

In May 1798, Napoléon's invading fleet set out for Egypt and India. The French fleet was defeated by Admiral

Horatio Nelson (1758–1805) of Britain, and the threat to British India was thus eliminated. To deal with growing British influence along the southern border, Czar Paul I (1754–1801) proposed a Russian-French invasion of India. The Russian forces were sent to India in 1801, but they were recalled after the death of the czar.

At the same time, a British diplomatic mission approached the Persian shah and signed two treaties. However, when Russian troops besieged Yerevan in Armenia (then part of Persia) in 1804, Britain did not take action.

The Russian position in the "game" was further strengthened by a peace treaty with the Ottoman Empire. In the Treaty of Adrianople (1829), Russia gained free passage through the Dardanelles and trading privileges. The Russians gained further privileges when the sultan gave Russia exclusive access to the Dardanelles after Russian forces protected the Ottomans against an attacking Egyptian army in 1833. Furthermore, the reconciliation with the Ottoman Empire gave Russia greater flexibility in Central Asia.

Meanwhile, the Circassians from the Caucasus region found British support for their cause of independence from Russia. In addition, Dost Mohammad (1793–1863), the leader of Afghanistan, approached Russia in 1835 for help in recapturing Peshawar from Ranjit Singh (1780–1839), the Sikh ruler of Punjab and an ally of Britain.

From the British perspective, Russian plans for territorial expansion toward the south threatened to destroy the "Pearl of the Empire," India. When Russian troops set out to subdue khanate after khanate, British observers expressed concern that Afghanistan might become the base for a Russian advance into India. The British therefore initiated the First Anglo-Afghan War (1838–1842), in which Britain tried to impose a puppet regime in Afghanistan. Both sides suffered heavy losses, and the attempt to annex Afghanistan to British India failed. Instead, rival Afghan tribes join forces to fight the British, and Dost Mohammad returned to the throne in 1843.

Dost Muhammad expanded Afghan territory by adding Balkh and Baldakhshan in 1855 and Heart in 1863. Nevertheless, Russia continued to advance steadily toward Afghanistan, formally annexing Tashkent in 1865 and Samarkand in 1868. Although the British government enforced a policy of "masterly inactivity," Afghanistan increasingly became the focus of Anglo-Russian tensions.

Tensions were renewed in 1878, when Russia sent an uninvited diplomatic mission to the Afghan ruler Sher Ali (1825–1879), the son of Dost Mohammad. Britain responded by immediately demanding acceptance of a British diplomatic mission in Kabul. When Sher Ali rejected Britain's appeal, British troops crossed the

border, thereby launching the Second Anglo-Afghan War (1878–1879). British operations, however, were nearly as disastrous as in the First Anglo-Afghan War forty years earlier, and Britain was forced to pull out of Kabul in 1881. Abdur Rahman Khan (ca. 1844–1901) remained on the Afghan throne. He agreed to let Britain maintain its foreign policy, but managed to consolidate his position by suppressing all internal rebellions, thereby bringing much of Afghanistan under central control.

In 1884 the Russian seizure of Merv brought about the next crisis, the Panjdeh Incident. Russia claimed all the territory of the former ruler of Merv and fought Afghan troops over the oasis of Panjdeh. When direct military conflict between Russia and Britain seemed inevitable, the British accepted Russia's capture of Merv. Without consulting with the Afghans, the Joint Anglo-Russian Boundary Commission agreed that the Russians would also retain Panjdeh. The agreement designated a northern frontier for Afghanistan along the Amu Dar'ya River.

While Russia concentrated on the Far East and the completion of the Trans-Siberian Railway and the naval base of Port Arthur (Lüshun, China), Britain focused its efforts on Tibet, with mixed results. On August 31, 1907, the Anglo-Russian Convention fixed the boundaries of Persia, Afghanistan, and Tibet. Persia was divided into spheres of Russian interest in the North and British interest in the southeast, keeping the Russians away from the Persian Gulf and the Indian border. The 1907 convention finally brought the so-called classic period of the "great game" to an end: Russia accepted British control over Afghan politics as long as Britain did not change the regime. Britain, for its part, agreed to maintain the current borders and discourage any Afghan attempts to encroach on Russian territory.

When the 1917 revolution nullified all of Russia's existing treaties, the second phase of the "great game" ensued. After the assassination of Afghan emir Habibullah Khan (1872–1919), his successor, Amanullah Khan (1892–1960), declared full independence for Afghanistan and attacked the northern frontier of British India. In the Third Anglo-Afghan War (1919), there was little room for military gains, and the Rawalpindi Agreement of 1919 resolved the stalemate: Britain granted Afghanistan self-determination in all foreign affairs.

The Soviet Union and Afghanistan signed a treaty of friendship in 1921, according to which the Russians provided aid in form of technology, military equipment, and money. Nevertheless, relations between Russia and Afghanistan were tense because many Afghans wished to regain the oases of Merv and Panjdeh, while Russia wanted to extract more concessions from the treaty arrangement. By this time, British influence in Afghanistan was waning, and Britain feared that Amanullah was slipping out of their sphere of influence.

As a response to the Afghan-Russian treaty of 1921, Britain imposed sanctions because British leaders realized that Afghanistan aimed to control all the Pashtun-speaking groups on both sides of the Durand Line (the border between Afghanistan and British India, which had been settled in an agreement signed on November 12, 1893 by the Afghan representative Amir Abdurrahman Khan and the British representative Sir Henry Mortimer Durand). Amanullah responded to British sanctions by taking the title of king *(padshah)*. He also offered refuge for Indian nationalists in exile and for Muslims fleeing the Soviet Union. The Afghan ruler's reforms proved insufficient, however. Amanullah was not able to strengthen his military power quickly enough, and he was forced to abdicate. His brother, who succeeded him, was also forced to abdicate shortly thereafter. A new leader emerged, Muhammad Nadir Shah (1883–1933), who ruled Afghanistan from 1929 until he was assassinated in 1933.

Both Russia and Britain turned the situation to their advantage, the British by helping Afghanistan create a professional army, the Soviets by securing aid against a Uzbek rebellion. World War II (1939–1945) brought a temporary alignment of British and Soviet interests. During the war, the Allied Powers pressured Afghanistan into removing a large German nondiplomatic contingent. Afghanistan initially resisted, but the period of cooperation brought the second phase of the "great game" to an end.

In the early stages of the Cold War, when the United States displaced Britain as a global power, a new phase of the "great game" evolved. The United States took measures to secure access to oil and other resources in the Middle East, and to contain the Soviet Union. In the military, in security, and in diplomatic communities, the term *great game* continues to be used to frame events in India, Pakistan, Afghanistan, and the Central Asian states. American diplomat Zbigniew Brzezinski's *The Grand Chessboard* (1997), for example, explored this new version of the "great game."

SEE ALSO *Abdülhamid II; Afghan Wars.*

BIBLIOGRAPHY

Allison, Roy A., and Edmund Herzig. *Subregionalism and Foreign Policy Transformation: Russia and Iran in Central Asia.* Swindon, U.K.: Economic and Social Research Council, 2004.

Brzezinski, Zbigniew. *The Grand Chessboard: American Primacy and its Geostrategic Imperatives.* New York: BasicBooks, 1997.

Duggan, Stephen P. *The Eastern Question: A Study in Diplomacy.* London: King & Son, 1902.

Edwardes, Michael. *Playing the Great Game: A Victorian Cold War.* London: Hamilton, 1975.

Ehteshami, Anoushiravan, ed. *From the Gulf to Central Asia: Players in the New Great Game.* Exeter, U.K.: University of Exeter Press, 1994.

Ewans, Martin, ed. *The Great Game: Britain and Russia in Central Asia.* 8 vols. London: Routledge, 2004.

Hopkirk, Peter. *The Great Game: The Struggle for Empire in Central Asia.* New York: Kodansha International, 1992.

Hopkirk, Peter. *Quest for Kim: In Search of Kipling's Great Game.* Ann Arbor: University of Michigan Press, 1997.

Jenkinson, Anthony. *Early Voyages and Travels to Russia and Persia by A. Jenkinson and Other Englishmen.* Edited by E. D. Morgan and C. H. Coote. London: Hakluyt Society, 1886.

Khan, Aftab Ahmad. *Central Asia: Political Ascendancy and Diplomatic Pulls: An Imperial Era.* New Delhi: Dilpreet, 2002.

Lyons, James Gervais. *Afghanistan: The Buffer State.* Madras, India: Higginbotham; London: Luzac, 1910.

Martens, Fedor Fedorovich. *Russland und England in Central-Asien.* Saint Petersburg, Russia: Kaiserliche Hofbuchhandlung H. Schmitzdorff, 1880.

Meyer, Karl Ernest, and Shareen Blair Brysac. *Tournament of Shadows: The Great Game and the Race for Empire in Central Asia.* Washington, DC: Counterpoint, 1999.

Mojtahed-Zadeh, Pirouz. *Small Players of the Great Game: The Settlement of Iran's Eastern Borderlands and the Creation of Afghanistan.* London: RoutledgeCurzon, 2004.

Moran, Neil K. *Kipling and Afghanistan: A Study of the Young Author as Journalist Writing on the Afghan Border Crisis of 1884–1885.* Jefferson, NC: McFarland, 2005.

Morgan, Gerald. *Anglo-Russian Rivalry in Central Asia: 1810–1895.* London: Cass, 1981.

Orr, M. J. *The Russian Garrison in Tajikistan: 201st Gatchina Twice Red Banner Motor Rifle Division.* Camberley, U.K.: Conflict Studies Research Centre, 2001

Perdue, Peter C. *China Marches West: The Qing Conquest of Central Eurasia.* Cambridge, MA: Belknap Press of Harvard University Press, 2005.

Pikulina, Marina. *Russia in Central Asia: Third Invasion, An Uzbek View.* Camberley, U.K.: Conflict Studies Research Centre, 2003.

Saumjan, Tatiana L. *Tibet: The Great Game and Tsarist Russia.* New Delhi: Oxford University Press, 2000.

Siegel, Jennifer. *Endgame: Britain, Russia, and the Final Struggle for Central Asia.* London: Tauris, 2002.

Smith, Mark. *Russia, the USA, and Central Asia.* Camberley, U.K.: Conflict Studies Research Centre, 2002.

Taylor, Alan John Percivale. *Struggle for Mastery in Europe, 1848–1918.* Oxford: Clarendon, 1954.

Vambery, Armin. *Rivalry Between Russia and England in Central Asia.* London: Allen, 1868.

Verrier, Anthony. *Francis Younghusband and the Great Game.* London: Cape, 1991.

Monika Lehner

ANTI-AMERICANISM

Anti-Americanism, understood as habitual aversion to all things American as opposed to impartial criticism, started in the eighteenth century with the gloomy narratives of natural scientists.

THE THEME OF DEGENERATION

The Dutch scholar Cornelius de Pauw (1739–1799) sounded the alarm in 1768: America's unhealthy climate produced poisonous plants and degenerated animal species. As for the indigenous inhabitants, de Pauw's harsh description of them as lazy, dim-witted, and cowardly calls to mind the philosopher Thomas Hobbes's (1588–1679) "nasty, brutish and short" existence in the state of nature rather than the lofty image of the noble savage.

With the successful outcome of the American Revolutionary War, however, concerns about nature or indigenous peoples faded in favor of the exciting image of a society modeled upon European enlightened ideas. In 1777 the French philosopher Condorcet (1743–1794) merged de Pauw's gloom with enthusiasm for the American experiment and declared that the discovery of America had been a disaster to which the 1776 revolution brought the remedy. Thenceforth, anti-Americanism became a discourse aimed exclusively at social and political developments in the United States. Throughout the nineteenth century, it cast the theme of decay into the frame of disappointment and found the Americans guilty of lowering the potentially uplifting pursuit of happiness to the vulgar level of the vacuous pursuit of profits. Disillusionment, like familiarity, breeds contempt; disdain for the "Yankee" prompted large sections of the European public to back a presumably polished and debonair Confederate South in the American Civil War, despite "the peculiar institution" of slavery. After the victory of the Union, a disturbing appetite for domination came to complement vulgarity and greed as distinctive features of the American character, now entirely assimilated to the Yankee. Derision turned to fear.

SOCIALIST DISINTEGRATION AND MONSTROUS CAPITALISM

The somehow snobbish disparagement of American lowbrow pursuits merged with a new brand of left-wing anti-Americanism born out of frustration with the downward spiral of socialism in America. Countering pervasive anti-Yankee prejudices, philosophers Karl Marx (1818–1883) and Friedrich Engels (1820–1895) insisted that, as the most advanced capitalist country in the world, the United States had to be seen as a laboratory for socialism, the next stage of social development. Consequently, that American socialism evolved in "prodigious zigzags" (Engels) rather than in a neat upward progression paralleling capitalist development mystified all European socialists.

Many made the journey to the United States to decipher the riddle formulated in 1906 by the German sociologist Werner Sombart (1863–1941): "Why is there no socialism in America?" The answers combined disinterest in abstract thinking, an intellectual deficiency deemed characteristic of the American mind, with the narrow policies of bread and butter pursued by trade unions at the expense of the loftier goal of defeating capitalism. As in the case of Enlightenment ideals, America's failure to live up to its role of successful laboratory for a new social order bred disappointment and contempt. The American worker, the French writer Urbain Gohier (1862–1951) concluded, grew fat, a bourgeois in all but name ("well fed, well clothed and...even clean") while the robust tactics of the American unions illustrated obtuse materialism, not revolutionary foresight.

On the other hand, European readers were entertained with rags-to-riches sagas of American robber-barons uninhibited by the traditional norms of European patriarchal capitalism. The rapid soar from obscurity to dizzying heights and of individuals like the Vanderbilts and the Hearsts, the worrisome reports on the merciless nature of American capitalism, of risky financial speculations, and cut-throat competition, led to the image of the American capitalist as evil incarnate. Writers of all stripes excoriated the "trust system," run by coarse-mannered billionaires who managed to corrupt even capitalism itself. Turning Marx's theory of progress on its head, American capitalism dragged society backwards into a grotesque form of technologized feudalism instead of pushing it forward. In short, everything in the United States grew into a monstrous aberration, and that included American idealism.

After the decisive American intervention in World War I, the United States became the senior partner among the diplomatic delegations who gathered at Versailles to decide the fate of post war Europe. Woodrow Wilson (1856–1924) presented a program for reshaping European geography and political arrangements on the basis of democratic reform and the right of each people to self-determination. Wilson's blueprint, the famous fourteen points, as well as his conviction that Europe's best hope for the future was to follow America's lead, inspired anxiety and contempt, the opposite of the reaction he expected. At best, European leaders and opinion makers marveled at Wilson's naiveté and self-assurance. At worst, his forceful idealism seemed just another example of the American aptitude for distortion, this time applied to European politics. Furthermore, Sigmund Freud (1856–1939) curtly diagnosed the American president with paranoia. By extension, the entire American society came into focus as a huge madhouse, for the famed analyst declared that in any other country such an individual would have been institutionalized. Echoing Freud, the French nationalist writer Charles Maurras (1868–1952) warned Europeans against a superpower where money talks and lunatics become presidents. At stake was again degeneration but in its modern form, psychopathology. "America went from barbarism to degeneration without the usual interval of civilization" quipped France's president Georges

An Anti-American Protestor in Korea. *South Korean riot police block a protester holding a poster of U.S. Secretary of State Condoleezza Rice during a rally in Seoul on March 20, 2005. Rice was meeting with South Korean officials to discuss nuclear armament in North Korea.* © YOU SUNG-HO/REUTERS/CORBIS. REPRODUCED BY PERMISSION.

Clemenceau (1841–1929) in a one-liner that captured perfectly the tone of anti-American sentiments.

In the 1930s cupidity, authoritarianism, and degeneration combined seamlessly to add an anti-Semitic note, whereby Uncle Sam morphed into Uncle Shylock, Shakespeare's eponymous Jewish usurer, and the United States an "abomination" where Jews and Yankees reigned together.

EVIL DIVERSIFIED

The ugly American and the ugly American state, as the most glaring examples of the misdeeds of capitalism, naturally took their place in the Soviet anticapitalist discourse. The Soviet Union also portrayed the United States as the sole aggressor during the Cold War, in view of its well-established reputation for "Yankee" belligerence and domineering impulses.

Soviet propaganda resonated with the soaring unofficial anti-Americanism in Western Europe, where governments were closely allied with the United States. Communist, socialist, and fellow-traveler organizations in the West shared the ideological beliefs of the Soviet government, and therefore propagated the same images of the United States as a desolate land ravaged by capitalism. Considering the postwar political alignments, the Western European Left also had the task of eliminating American influence on the continent. The American presence was felt especially through the Marshall Plan, a comprehensive program of targeted investments, run by American economic advisers, aimed at rebuilding the European economies on the basis of free market policies. Such policies, coupled with the requirement that countries who accepted the program implement multiparty democracy, made the Soviet Union and its satellites reject this and any American aid. Self-righteous campaigns against the Marshall Plan, especially in France, claimed to unmask the evils hidden behind the benign facade of friendly assistance. According to these critics, the main program of American aid only sugarcoated the wholesale takeover of Europe by American moguls and had to be regarded as nothing but a Trojan horse of the worst kind of capitalism.

The Marshall Plan also came under attack from the Right for stifling national creativity, market forces included, in favor of American models of development. At stake was the very soul of Europe, from authentically civilized lifestyles to intellectual sophistication, all of which risked succumbing to the mind-numbing onslaught of American mass culture. Writers of all persuasions relished sharing with their readers nightmarish images of the artificial and dull world created by technology and productivity, incidentally the chief issues raised by the Marshall Plan. The novelist Georges Bernanos (1888–1948) proposed, only half-jokingly, that "the civilization of machines" be put on trial at Nuremberg. Imprisoned in an industrialized universe obsessed with efficiency, comfort, and high-tech gadgets, the United States presented the sad spectacle of technologically altered humanity. This particular form of degeneration affected all aspects of American life, from the acquiescent conformism that passed for democracy to the characterless art amassed in large but uninspiring museums, as French author Simone de Beauvoir (1908–1986) suggested. This train of thought culminated with the call issued by famed French philosopher Jean-Paul Sartre (1905–1980) to cut all ties with Europe after the execution of convicted spies Ethel and Julius Rosenberg: "Beware, America has the rabies! Let's cut all ties which attach us to her, lest we shall be in turn bitten and infected ourselves" (*Libération*, June 22 1953).

Even when acknowledged, American prosperity with its corollary, American optimism, was to be dreaded as an indication of intellectual degradation. From all perspectives the United States came across as an "abomination" and a menace to the civilized world. This agreement of principle, often expressed in the media, gave anti-Americanism a mass audience and created the popular images of Americans as rich, naive, but authoritarian and violence-prone ignoramuses who were now largely taken for granted. On the academic side, the philosopher Jean Baudrillard furthered the analysis of degenerated humanity steeped in technological efficiency by arguing that the United States had achieved the supreme act of distortion: it had counterfeited reality itself and had itself become a "simulacrum."

America's status as supreme imperialist power is another outcome of the ideological battles of the Cold War. Having practiced its greedy, self-interested policies on the defenseless countries of Latin America, with the known results of economic backwardness and political tyranny, the United States felt ready to take on the rest of the world after emerging victorious from World War II.

The next victim was Europe, as explained by the left-wing discourse, fortified by antimaterialistic and nationalistic brands of anti-Americanism coming from other ideological quarters. By the 1950s it became a cliché that, under the guise of liberation, the "Yankees" had reduced the entire segment of Europe in the American zone of influence to the humiliating status of colony.

Coming in the midst of anticolonial movements, this reading of the postwar settlement turned the United States into a common universal foe. That the imperial powers in the third world were in fact various European countries mattered less than the urgency of resisting, together, American imperial designs. In this view, what it could not conquer militarily the United States was poised to control deviously by flooding the entire world with various American gadgets, foodstuffs, or movies.

Interestingly, accusations of imperialism grew stronger when the United States took resolute anti-imperialist positions, as it did during the Suez Canal crisis in 1956. The United States was then suspected of lording over both Europe and the third world through the system, perfected in the aftermath of World War II, of disguising instruments of dependence into the appearance of support. The Vietnam War brought additional arguments to this line of thinking and made anti-Americanism and anti-imperialism interchangeable concepts all over the world.

The end of the Cold War left the United States the sole superpower. The familiar themes of degeneration, greed, aggressiveness, and, more recently, imperialism combined with fear of the nations's unmatched military power put an American face on globalization. Well-publicized attacks against McDonald's outlets in France, similar to the anti-Coca-Cola campaigns of the 1950s, merely adapt the themes of the anti-American discourse of the Cold War to contemporary concerns.

It is not just that American-dominated multinational companies, reminiscent of the prewar "trust system," control the economy and corrupt the politics of the entire planet; American consumer goods suffocate other cultures, distort natural lifestyles, and pervert local tastes, going as far as endangering the health of hapless consumers everywhere. In short, American movies make people stupid and American foods make people sick; consequently, Americanization does not mean just American domination, it means regressing to the dismal level of American cultural degeneration and social absurdity.

Such anxieties are only exacerbated by the exceptional diversity and de facto multiculturalism of contemporary American society, which appears to many as the reality for the future. Aggressive, aloof, and self-assertive in spite of being "a world in itself" as many worried observers note, the United States is failing once more in its role as laboratory for the future order of things.

The belief that with the attacks of September 11, 2001, the United States only got its comeuppance was expressed in most parts of the world, from Arab countries, where large segments of the public received the news with unconcealed glee, to university halls in Western Europe, where somber conferences on the roots of terrorism invariably found these roots in America. The conspiracy theory blaming the whole event on secret American and Israeli machinations found sympathetic audiences in France, Germany, and the Arab world.

The 2003 American invasion of Iraq raised the anti-American discourse to yet unattained heights. Publishers churned out work after work updating the essential American characteristics of greed, violence, obtuseness, and, less damning but no less dangerous, dimwitted naiveté, while vast popular demonstrations across all continents designated the United States as a danger to all humanity.

André Glucksman, a rare opponent, distilled this pervasive mindset into an axiomatic formula: "there is no evil but the evil caused by America," a conviction, it should be added, more or less openly linked with America's support for Israel. Glucksman and a few other writers (Jean-François Revel from the French Academy, for instance) detect a psychological factor in the gleeful diabolization of the United States. With the collapse of the balance of fear established by the Cold War, in the face of the perplexing threat of terrorism and imminent destabilization, it is reassuring to draw all anxieties back to the superpower of the times. The well-rehearsed patterns of anticapitalism and anti-imperialism, reinforced by time-honored cultural stereotypes, provide a certain level of comfort every time they help to rationalize the current global angst as a function of that familiar evil, America.

Judging by these developments, anti-Americanism will continue to be part of both the intellectual and the popular discourse for many years to come, although not at the same level of intensity everywhere. Unlike criticism leveled at given American policies, anti-Americanism is an emotional discourse, activated by American policies, but disinclined to discern fact from stereotype. As such, anti-Americanism is more reflective of the societies that produce it than of American realities. That France is one of the main producers of anti-American literature while such literature is quite rare in Italy and practically absent in Poland, for instance, reflects certain particularities of these countries' political and cultural identity.

Anti-Americanism relies and will most likely continue to rely on the recurrent themes of degeneration, greed, and aggressiveness, sometimes with surprising results. Thus French author Emmanuel Todd argued in *After the Empire* (2003) that the United States has in fact collapsed already and is waging wars out of fear that its impotence might come to light. Put into perspective, this argument brings the theme of degeneration to its logical conclusion. Degeneration, the ill that de Pauw had already detected in America's natural environment, has successively consumed the American character, humanity, and very reality, and will ultimately destroy its self-aggrandizing power. Despondency in the face of America's panoply of evils can thus be alleviated by the knowledge that the United States will in the end succumb to the very poison with which it has infected the whole world.

SEE ALSO *Anticolonialism; Empire, United States.*

BIBLIOGRAPHY

Berman, Russell A. *Anti-Americanism in Europe: A Cultural Problem.* Stanford, CA: Hoover Institution Press, 2004.

Revel, Jean-François. *L'obsession anti-américaine: Son fonctionnement, ses causes, ses inconséquences.* Paris: Plon, 2003. Translated by Diarmid Cammell as *Anti-Americanism* (San Francisco: Encounter, 2003).

Roger, Philippe. *L'ennemi américain: Généalogie de l'antiaméricanisme français.* Paris: Seuil, 2002.

Todd, Emmanuel. *After the Empire: The Breakdown of the American Order.* Translated by C. Jon Delogu. New York: Columbia University Press, 2003.

Doina Pasca Harsanyi

ANTICOLONIALISM

Western colonialism has engendered anticolonialism from the beginning of the age of European expansion. All empires, in fact, have provoked local and indigenous defiance, backlashes, and resistance throughout human history. The conquest, domination, exploitation, and rule of neighboring and distant peoples and their lands by a powerful and often alien polity, by their very nature, has time and again produced many different kinds of challenges, opposition, and violence.

Beginning in the fifteenth and sixteenth centuries the overseas colonies of western Europe met resistance, and created resistance, by the native peoples in the Americas, Africa, the Middle East, Asia, and the Pacific. Indigenous opposition and resistance, however, were rarely a simple matter of non-Europeans rejecting European governance, order, or culture. Overseas imperialism and colonialism also produced a tradition of

A Protest Against Globalization, Colonialism, and the United States. *An antiglobalization protestor marches in Paris in November 2003 during the annual European Social Forum.* © ANTOINE SERRA/IN VISU/CORBIS. REPRODUCED BY PERMISSION.

intellectual critique, criticism, and condemnation within the West itself. Western anticolonialism was based upon various and evolving objections, stemming from moral, religious, humanitarian, economic, and political concerns and interests.

The immigrant settlers of Europe's overseas colonies in time developed their own anticolonial critiques that led, in the Americas most particularly, to resistance, rebellion, and revolutions creating independent states. Anticolonialism contributed to, and was a product of, nationalism and the struggles to create new identities for the peoples of Europe's overseas colonies. Indeed, true anticolonialism—that is, the theoretical and active resistance to colonial rule with the objective of overthrowing imperial control and establishing independent, national states—became nearly indistinguishable from nationalism in Africa, the Middle East, and Asia by the late nineteenth and twentieth centuries.

There are a number of entries devoted to anticolonialism and indigenous and settler nationalist and independence movements in the Americas, Africa, the Middle East, South Asia, East Asia, and the Pacific in this encyclopedia. There are, as well, several entries that describe

and analyze Western thought regarding colonialism. This entry, as a result, does not retrace all of these historical developments, nor does it reconsider the history or historiography of anticolonial thought. Although this entry presents no all-embracing theory to explain anticolonialism, it does identify, describe, and classify the broad patterns of anti-Western anticolonialism of the past five hundred years in an effort to translate an extraordinarily complex historical phenomenon into an understandable and useful analysis.

Although anticolonial thought and action has existed for many centuries, indeed, for millennia, the concept "anticolonialism" is quite recent. The word *colonialism* did not appear in an English dictionary until the mid-nineteenth century. Although theorists in the past have emphasized the difference between colonialism and imperialism, writers and even historians today often use these concepts interchangeably. Following the lead of political scientist David Abernethy, *empire* is defined as a state (metropole) that dominates and legally possesses one or more territories beyond its boundaries (colonies). *Imperialism* refers to the process of expansion and conquest necessary in the construction of an empire. The territories seized, dominated, and possessed by the imperial state are *colonies*. "Colonialism," writes Abernethy, "is the set of formal policies, informal practices, and ideologies employed by a metropole to retain control of a colony and to benefit from control" (2000, p. 22). Anticolonialism is a broad concept that includes every kind of opposition—from political thought to popular violence—against imperialism and colonialism.

Defiance, opposition, and resistance to European expansion, conquest, and colonization by indigenous communities, organized groups, disparate "mobs," states and empires, and slaves took different forms and sought different outcomes. The most significant and widespread kinds of indigenous resistance over the five centuries of Western colonialism were the following:

1. Preexisting indigenous polities, states, and empires used violence to defend their people, land, autonomy, and power against Western expansion.

2. Popular nativist uprisings were often violent reactions to the interference by, or imposition of, Western colonists, institutions, and customs, which often came in the form of militant or missionary Christianity.

3. African and Creole slaves revolted against, primarily, the plantation and the master class.

4. In all colonies, protest uprisings and movements appeared to highlight colonial injustice, and often specific abuses and impositions, in order to provoke concessions, reform, and improvements. These ameliorative protest uprisings and movements challenged colonial regimes but did not attempt to destroy or defeat them.

5. State builders, often nationalists or nationalist movements, organized violence against colonial regimes to defeat them and create new states governed by leaders from the majority indigenous population.

When historians examine specific uprisings, revolts, rebellions, and insurrections, the artificial boundaries of these categories begin to bend and collapse. The Hidalgo Revolt (1810–1811) in central Mexico was a popular nativist uprising against "whites" and the wealthy, but it was also a genuinely anticolonial—that is, anti-Spanish—rebellion intended to establish Spanish-American and popular self-government in Mexico, if not an independent nation-state in time. There were, of course, many more kinds of indigenous resistance to Western colonialism, both violent and nonviolent, than the five described above. These five forms of resistance, however, represent the basic models that dominated the non-Western responses to Western colonialism.

In most parts of the world, the expansion of European empires came into direct conflict with existing indigenous states and empires. The Spanish defeat of the armies of the Inca Empire and the occupation of the imperial capital of Cuzco in 1536 was the beginning, not the end, of serious organized resistance to Spanish encroachment in the central Andes. Less than a year later, a massive Inca rebellion besieged the Spaniards in Cuzco and attacked them in Lima. Although the siege was broken, in 1538 the defiant Inca leader Manco Inca had two armies in the field and had organized local rebellions across the Andes. The Inca army in the northern Sierra fought the Spaniards for eight years. Manco Inca and his successors retreated to the remote eastern Andean site of Vilcabamba and defended the restored neo-Inca state until 1572.

In southern Africa, the expansionist Zulu kingdom and empire came into conflict with Dutch colonists (Boers), and then the British colonial state, in the nineteenth century. For more than fifty years the Zulu fought the Boers and the British until their defeat and "conquest" in 1879. The Zulu, nevertheless, rose in rebellion in 1906.

A quite distinct and more widespread form of resistance was nativist uprisings, popular indigenous reactions against colonial exploitation and the imposition of Western culture, religion, and governance. The Tzeltal Revolt of 1712, a Maya uprising against the Spanish in southern Mexico, aimed to kill or drive out of the province all Spaniards, mestizos, and mulattos and establish a new Indian Catholic society and kingdom. The Indian Revolt of 1857 in India and the Boxer Rebellion in China in 1900 were popular explosions of violence against Christian missionaries, local converts and collaborators, and "foreign devils" in general.

Slave revolts in the Atlantic world from the sixteenth to the nineteenth century—violent uprisings by enslaved Africans for many centuries and, later, by Creole African-Americans—attacked one of the most important economic institutions and social systems erected by Western colonialism. In the numerous assaults against the plantation system and its masters, and against the degrading, exploitive, and violent slave system itself, African and Creole slaves attacked colonialism or colonial rule indirectly and inadvertently. Rebel slaves used violence to respond to violence and injustice. Rebels sought revenge, escape, return to Africa, the creation of a new society, and, occasionally, the extermination of the slave-owners and their like.

Wolof slaves revolted against the Spanish in Hispaniola in 1521. Across the Atlantic, a slave revolt beginning around 1544 in the Portuguese island colony of São Tomé in the Gulf of Guinea produced a settlement of free Africans who continued to fight the Portuguese. These Angolares (originally, slaves exported from Angola) raided plantations and burned fields and sugar mills, and in 1574 attacked and largely destroyed the city of São Tomé. In 1595 a leader named Amador led a slave army of five thousand men and women that burned or destroyed some seventy sugar plantations on the island.

Over the next four hundred years, there were many hundreds of major slave revolts and insurrections in the Americas. The massive slave insurrection that began in 1791 in France's richest colony, Saint-Domingue (now Haiti) became transformed into an organized military campaign led by the ex-slave Toussaint L'Ouverture (1743–1803) that defeated Spanish, British, and French armies. In 1804 the black generals established the independent nation-state of Haiti, the second new state in the Americas and the first modern state ever created by a slave insurrection.

Ameliorative protest uprisings and movements employed violence against the colonial regime or its officials, but also nonviolent methods of protest and resistance, such as demonstrations, riots, strikes, petitions, and more. Many, if not most, of the village uprisings in colonial Mexico were provoked by specific abuses or perceived threats and ended when colonial officials promised to act upon the grievances of villagers. As William B. Taylor, a historian of colonial Mexico, notes, community outrage was directed against local officials, the tax collector, or the parish priest. "Villagers in revolt generally did not make the connection between their grievances and the colonial system as a whole" (1979, p. 134).

In the Gold Coast, the British colony in West Africa, the Aborigines' Rights Protective Society (ARPS) was formed in the 1890s to appeal to, and it was hoped to influence, British public opinion against the colonial authorities on the spot. The colonial government began a program to transform property rights and relations. The ARPS, formed by traditional chiefs working with African lawyers educated in Britain, organized the first colonywide protest and sent a delegation to London that succeeded in getting legislation that protected their land rights.

In the wake of the French conquest of Algeria in the 1830s, the Muslim Sufi order of the Qadiriyya in western Algeria provided the religious and political legitimacy for a resistance movement. In 1834 'Abd al-Qadir (1808–1883) became the head of the order and fought tribal authorities and the French to expand his authority. Within three years, the French recognized 'Abd al-Qadir's authority and the sovereignty of the Qadiriyya state over two-thirds of Algeria. In the 1840s conflict with the French—that is, with the more technologically advanced French army—led to the defeat and surrender of 'Abd al-Qadir in 1847.

In the Egyptian colony of Sudan, the *Mahdi* (a messianic Muslim leader) Muhammad ibn-Abdallah began a campaign in the 1880s to create an independent theocratic state. The campaign took advantage of Egypt's turmoil and weakness in the face of French and then British intermeddling. In 1883 the forces of the Mahdi destroyed the ten-thousand–strong Egyptian army. General George Gordon (1833–1885) went to Khartoum, Sudan, to evacuate Egyptians, but was besieged and killed in 1885. The middle Nile Valley was controlled by the Mahdist state, thereafter, it seemed, for more than a decade. In 1898 an Anglo-Egyptian army invaded the Sudan and met the Mahdist army at Omdurman on the banks of the Nile River. The British forces, armed with Maxim (machine) guns, repeating rifles, and gunboats, killed and wounded tens of thousands of Mahdist dervishes. After the five-hour battle, only forty-eight British soldiers were killed. The Mahdist state was overthrown as the British Empire took control of Sudan.

Anticolonialist nationalist revolts of the twentieth century were remarkably successful. A nationalist Egyptian uprising in 1919, followed by mass demonstrations, prodded the British to grant independence in 1922. Within three months of the assignment of the mandate of Iraq by the League of Nations to Britain 1919, the "Great Arab" insurrection in the new country began. The Arabs of Iraq had reasons of their own to oppose British colonialism, but the Communist International (or Comintern, a Soviet-led revolutionary organization), trying out its anticolonial legs, employed propaganda in an attempt to add fuel to the fire: "In your country there are eighty-thousand English soldiers who plunder and rob, who kill you and violate your wives!" (quoted in Kiernan 1998, p. 191). Over the next seven years, the British occupation faced not only Arab resistance but also Kurdish insurrection, which began in 1922. At the end of 1927, Britain recognized the independence of Iraq under the sovereignty of King Faisal (1885–1933) and in 1932 Iraq was admitted to the League of Nations.

Indochina (today Vietnam, Laos, and Cambodia) was not brought under effective French colonial rule until the 1880s and 1890s. However, at the Paris Peace Conference (1919–1920), which established the terms of peace after World War I ended in 1918, Ho Chi Minh (1890–1969) and other Vietnamese nationalists were attracted by U.S. president Woodrow Wilson's (1856–1924) call for national self-determination and the possibility they might negotiate some degree of self-government and autonomy with the Great Powers. The Vietnamese spokesmen, like those from India, Egypt, Senegal, and other colonies, were ignored.

Back in Vietnam, Ho Chi Minh and other nationalists formed the Communist Party in 1925; the party organized an uprising in 1930. The repression that followed kept order until a revolt erupted in 1940. After this uprising was crushed, Ho Chi Minh and other nationalists in 1941 established a united front of various parties and resistance groups called the Vietminh. At the conclusion of World War II (1939–1945), following the Japanese surrender in Hanoi, the Vietminh declared the independence of Vietnam. The French, however, unwilling to give up control of the colony, sent an army to Vietnam and fought the Vietminh from 1946 until 1954, when a garrison of sixteen thousand French and African soldiers at Dien Bien Phu surrendered to a superior Vietminh force. In that same year, a French-Chinese agreement, accepted by the Geneva Conference on the Far East (1954), divided Vietnam at the seventeenth parallel. The Communist Vietminh government took control of the northern section and established the Democratic Republic of Vietnam. France then granted independence to South Vietnam, Laos, and Cambodia.

These five distinct kinds of indigenous resistance to Western colonialism disguise a social complexity that characterized the establishment and maintenance of colonialism itself. Colonialism was not something that was imposed from outside or that operated with the collusion of forces inside; it was a combination of both developments. Anticolonialism, in a similar way, was resistance to the outside imposition, as well as a contestation of political authority, among indigenous leaders, groups, regions, and classes within a colony.

The Indian Revolt, or Great Rebellion, of 1857 to 1859 began as a mutiny of Indian soldiers or *sepoys* who served the British East India Company. The sepoys of the Bengal Army protested their pay and conditions. Once British rule began to waver in the north, towns, artisans, and peasants rose up in rebellion to restore, at least symbolically, the Mughal Empire. The British defeated the rebellion in large measure because large sections of the Indian army, the Ghurkas and Sikhs in particular, remained loyal. When Delhi fell to "British" forces, most of those forces were Indian.

The Boxer Rebellion in China in 1900 was both an anti-Manchu and an anti-Western rebellion. "Boxers," a secret society, were Han Chinese nationalists who opposed the "Manchu" Qing regime and foreigners, particularly missionaries and businessmen, who supported the regime.

Table 1 provides a list of important anticolonial rebellions and slave revolts of the past five hundred years.

It suggests the great geographical diversity and temporal persistence of anticolonial struggles around the world. This list, however, is far from definitive and complete. Scholars of colonized peoples, furthermore, have emphasized that peasants, slaves, women, and other relatively powerless groups have employed "weapons of the weak"—that is, everyday forms of resistance, such as shirking, theft, sabotage, arson, and flight—to resist, recoup, or survive colonialism. While these "quiet" and often clandestine forms of resistance have rarely entered the history books, they have, according to James C. Scott (1985), constituted the greatest part of peasant politics.

The long and bloody history of resistance to Western colonialism that is suggested by the names and dates in Table 1 influenced Western political and social thought from the sixteenth century to the present. Prior to the mid-eighteenth century, European encounters with other peoples and lands prompted philosophical debates about the nature of humans and the moral responsibility of Christian monarchs and colonizers to the "barbarians" and "savages" they encountered, conquered, and ruled. A number of sixteenth-century Europeans, such as Antonio de Montesinos, Thomas More (1478–1535), Desiderius Erasmus (ca. 1466–1536), Bartolomé de las Casas (1474–1566), Alonzo de Zorita (1512-1585), Michel de Montaigne (1533–1592), Philippe de Mornay (1549–1623), and José de Acosta (1539–1600), opposed war and violent expansion, and in particular criticized Spanish colonial excesses and abusive policies, but they never rejected the imperial project. Some French Protestants, and more English and Dutch Protestant critics, seized upon the discourse of the Spanish critics and created the "Black Legend," an exaggerated reprimand of Spanish colonialism.

Not all western European writers in the seventeenth century, however, were anti-Spanish, and very few criticized, let alone opposed, their own nation's imperial projects. A number of French Catholic philosophers and missionaries in the seventeenth century praised Spanish attempts to legislate protections on behalf of Native Americans in their New World kingdoms. By the 1660s, the English dramatist John Dryden (1631–1700) romanticized the Spanish conquest of Mexico in his play *The Indian Emperor* (1665).

By the mid to late eighteenth century, a number of prominent European and American thinkers and politicians not only criticized the abuses and excesses of Western colonialism, but for the first time challenged "the idea that Europeans had any right to subjugate, colonize, and 'civilize' the rest of the world" (Muthu, 2003, p. 1). Such Enlightenment philosophers and writers as François-Marie Arouet, known as Voltaire (1694–1778), Jean-Jacques Rousseau (1712–1778), Denis

Non-European rebellions, resistance movements and slave revolts

Date	Leadership/People	Event
Phase 1: Expansion, 1415-1773		
1490s	Hispaniola (Sp.)	Taino Chieftain's Revolts
1521	Hispaniola (Sp.) Mexico (Sp.)	Wolofs: Slave Revolt
1540s	Mexico (Sp.)	The Mixtón War
1520s–1540s	Yucatan (Sp.)	Yucatec Maya Resistance
1540s–1550s	Brail (Por.)	Potiguar, Caeté & Tupinambá: Resistance and Wars
1550s–1600	Northern Mexico (Sp.)	The Chichimeca War
1567	Bahia, Brazil (Por.)	Indian Slave Revolt
1595	São Tomé (Por.)	Amador: Slave Revolt
1622	Virginia (Br.)	Powhatan Confederation Attack
1637	Connecticut (Br.)	Pequot War
1673	Jamaica (Br.)	Slave Revolt
1680–1692	New Mexico (Sp.)	Pope: Pueblo Rebellion
1712	Chiapas (Sp.)	Tzeltal Rebellion: Maya Revolt
1731	Louisiana (Fr.)	Samba: Slave Revolt
1733	St. Johns (Dm.)	Slave Revolt
1734–1738	Jamaica (Br.)	Cudjoe: Chief of Trelawny Town: First Maroon War
1739	South Carolina (Br.)	Stono Rebellion: Slave Revolt
1742–1750s	Peru (Sp.)	Juan Santos Atahualpa
1760	Jamaica (Br.)	Tacky's Revolt: Slave Revolt
1761	Yucatan (Sp.)	Canek: Maya Uprising
1763–1766	North America (Br.)	Pontiac's Rebellion
Phase 2: Contraction, 1775-1824		
1777	Upper Peru (Sp.)	Tomás Katari: Aymaras
1780–1783	Peru-Upper Peru (Sp.)	José Gabriel Condorcanqui (Tupac Amaru II Rebellion)
1791–1804	Saint Domingue (Fr.)	Toussaint L'Ouverture: Slave Rebellion
1795	New Granada (Sp.)	Slave Revolt
1795	Demerara (Da.)	Slave Revolt
1795–1796	Jamaica (Br.)	Second Maroon War
1810–1811	Central Mexico (Sp.)	Miguel Hidalgo: Popular Uprising
1811–1815	Mexico (Sp.)	José María Morelos: Continuation of the Hidalgo Uprising
1816	Barbados (Br.)	Slave Revolt
1823	Demerara (Br.)	Slave Revolt
Phase 3: Expansion, 1824-1912		
1825–1830	East Indies (Dt.)	Prince Dipangara: Java War
1831	Jamaica (Br.)	Slave Revolt
1831	Virginia (US.)	Nat Turner: Slave Revolt
1832–1847	Algeria (Fr.)	Abd el Kader: War of Resistance
1835	Brazil (Por.)	African Muslim Slave Revolt
1838	South Africa (Br.)	First Zulu War
1843–1847	New Zealand (Br.)	First Maori War
1857–1859	India (Br.)	The Indian Mutiny
1865–1872	New Zealand (Br.)	Second Maori War
1860–1890	North America (US.)	Sitting Bull & Crazy Horse: Sioux Wars
1862–1872	North America (US.)	Cochise: Apache War
1865	Jamaica (Br.)	Morant Bay Rebellion
1871	Algeria (Fr.)	Kabyle Revolt
1879	South Africa (Br.)	Second Zulu War
1882–1885	Sudan (Egpt/Br.)	The Mahdi: Islamic Revolt and War for Independence
1891–1894	German East Africa	Mkwawa Rebellion
1895	Madagascar (Por.)	Red Shawl Uprising
1896	Ethopia (Ind.)	Italian Defeat at Adowa
1896–1897	Southern Rhodesia (Br.)	Shona and Ndebele Rebellion
1899–1900	India (Br.)	Birsa Rising
1900	China (Ind.)	The Boxer Rebellion
1899–1902	Philippines (US.)	Emilio Aguinaldo: Philippine Insurgency
1899–1920	Somaliland (Br.)	Muhammad Abullah Hassad: Resistance Movement
1899–1905	Somaliland (It.)	Muhammad Abullah Hassad
1904–1907	South-West Africa (Gr.) (Nambia)	Nama & Herro Revolt: resistance to German settlers
1905–1906	East Africa (Ger.) (Tanganyika)	Maji Maji: Popular Uprising
1906	South Africa (Br.) (Natal)	Zulu Revolt
1908, 1912, 1918, 1925	Panama (Pro.)	Social and Political "Unrest": US. Military Intervention
1912–1918	Libya (Fr.)	Sanussi Sheikhs
[continued]		

Table 1. THE GALE GROUP.

Non-European rebellions, resistance movements and slave revolts [CONT]		
Date	Leadership/People	Event
Phase 4: Unstabe Equilibrium, 1914–1939		
1915	Nysaland	John Chilembwe
1920	Mesopotamia (Br.)	'The Great Iraqi Revolt'
1921-26	Morocco (Sp.)	Abd el-Krim: Berbers' Rif War
1925-26	Morocco (Fr.)	Rif War against the French
1922-31	Libya (Fr.)	Sanussi Sheikhs
1930-31	Vietnam (Fr.)	VNQDD: Yen Bay Uprising
1930-32	Burma (Br.)	Saya San
1930s-48	Palestine (Br.)	Arab and Jewish Revolts
Phase 5: Contraction, 1940–Present		
1945-49	East Indies (Dt.)	Independence War
1946-54	Vietnam (Fr.)	Ho Chi Minh: Independence War
1947-60	Madagascar (Por.)	Independence Rebellion
1948-56	Kenya (Br.)	Mau Mau Rebellion: Kikuyu People
1954-61	Algeria (Fr.)	FLN: War for Independence
1961-75	Angola (Por.)	Independence War
1962-75	Mozambique (Por.)	War for Independence led by FRELIMO
1963-75	Guinea-Bissau (Por.)	Amilcar Cabral: Independence War
1972-79	Rhodesia (Ind.)	Robert Mugabe: Civil War
1979-1989	Afghanistan (Ind.)	Anti-USSR Insurgency
1994-Present	Chechnya (Ru.)	Anti-Russian War
2003-Present	Iraq (Ind.)	Anti-United States & Coalition Insurgency

Abbreviations: Br. British Colony, Dn. Danish, Dt. Dutch, Fr. French, Ger. German, Ind. Independent, Por. Portuguese, Pro. Protectorate, Ru. Russia, Sp. Spanish, US. United States, USSR. Union of Socialist Soviet Republics.

SOURCES: This table is based on Table 13.1, "Colonial Rebellions by Indigenous or Slave Populations," in David B. Abernethy, *The Dynamics of Global Dominance: European Overseas Empires, 1415–1980* (New Haven: Yale University Press, 2000), 308–309. Using Abernethy's template, data from other sources have been added to this table: See C.A. Bayly, *The Birth of the Modern World, 1780–1914* (Oxford: Blackwell Publishing, 2004); Jeremy Black, *Europe and the World, 1650–1840* (London: Routledge, 2002); *Chambers Dictionary of World History* (Edinburgh: Chambers, 2005); Seymour Drescher and Stanley L. Engerman, eds., *A Historical Guide to World Slavery* (Oxford: Oxford University Press, 1998); Susan Schroeder, ed., *Native Resistance and the Pax Colonial in Colonial New Spain* (Lincoln: University of Nebraska Press, 1998).

Table 1. [CONT]. THE GALE GROUP.

Diderot (1713–1784), Abbé Guillaume-Thomas Raynal (1713–1796), Richard Price (1723–1791), Immanuel Kant (1724–1804), Joseph Priestly (1733–1804), Thomas Paine (1737–1809), Marquis de Condorcet (1743–1794), Thomas Jefferson (1743–1826), Johann Gottfried Herder (1744–1803), and others rejected imperialism and colonialism for a number of different reasons. For Diderot, European imperialism had been a disaster for non-European peoples in terms of war, oppression, and slavery and had, in addition, corrupted Europe itself. Many of these anti-imperialist Enlightenment writers opposed European imperialism and colonialism on the basis of the idea that all the world's different peoples were human and therefore deserved respect and fair treatment. Not only did these thinkers accept the concept of shared humanity, they shared the idea that non-Europeans were peoples of culture (as were Europeans), not savages or "natural" humans, and that their cultures were not necessarily

better or worse than the oppressive, corrupt, and violent societies of Europe.

Thomas Jefferson, the American philosophe, wrote in the Declaration of Independence in 1776 "that all men are created equal," and as a consequence governments derive "their just powers from the consent of the governed." Jefferson's shattering of the moral underpinning of colonialism was complemented by Alexander Hamilton's (1755/57–1804) American anticolonialism expressed in *The Federalist* over a decade later:

The world may politically, as well as geographically, be divided into four parts, each having a distinct set of interests. Unhappily for the other three, Europe, by her arms and by her negotiations, by force and by fraud, has, in different degrees, extended her dominion over them all. Africa, Asia, and America, have successively felt her domination. The superiority she has long maintained has tempted her to plume herself as the Mistress of the World, and to consider the rest of mankind as created for her benefit. (Hamilton, 1787)

This state of affairs, according to Hamilton, will no longer be tolerated. "Let Americans disdain to be the instruments of European greatness!"

Not all, or even most, Enlightenment philosophers and writers, of course, opposed imperialism and colonialism. Eighteenth-century political thought was complex and even contradictory regarding certain issues. Anti-imperial and anticolonial writings, like the antislavery tracts of the eighteenth century, were profoundly novel and uniquely Western. Both intellectual critiques were founded upon centuries of Western thought and, in particular, nearly three centuries of observing, listening to, and writing about non-Europeans. Antislavery arguments, political campaigns, and diplomatic and military actions in the eighteenth and nineteenth centuries led to the abolition of the transatlantic slave trade and the emancipation of all bondsmen in the Americas. The anti-imperial and anticolonial discourse of the eighteenth century, on the other hand, while undoubtedly significant over the long term, was followed by a new wave of European imperial expansion and annexation in the nineteenth century. The great political thinkers of the nineteenth century—conservatives, liberals, and radicals—generally accepted the arguments on behalf of imperialism.

Even Karl Marx (1818–1883), who argued that Western colonies were often set up in rich and well-populated countries for the specific purposes of plunder, thus providing Europe with "primitive" or "original" accumulation of wealth and capital, could not deny the historical necessity and advantage of colonialism. "In actual history," Marx wrote in 1867, "it is a notorious fact that conquest, enslavement, robbery, murder, in short, force, play the greatest part" in this accumulation (1867/1990, p. 874). As was true for many of his contemporaries, however, Marx viewed European colonialism as an indispensable element of world progress. Colonialism was an important modernizing force, noted Marx, part of "the process of transformation of the feudal mode of production into the capitalist mode" (1867/ 1990, pp. 915-916).

Marx's twentieth-century intellectual heirs— Marxists, communists, neo-Marxists, dependency and world-systems analysts, postcolonialists, and others— had little difficulty condemning imperialism and colonialism. Karl Kautsky (1854–1938), Rosa Luxemburg (1870–1919), and V. I. Lenin (1870–1924) in the early twentieth century redirected "Marxist" thought against capitalist imperialism and colonialism. In 1920 Lenin's Comintern in Moscow offered a systematic program for global decolonization.

Liberal anticolonial principles were as influential during the twentieth century as Marxist ones. In 1918 President Woodrow Wilson proclaimed his "Fourteen Points" in a message to the U.S. Congress as a plan to end World War I. In his fourteenth point, Wilson suggested the creation of an association of nations to facilitate the sovereignty and independence of all nations based upon self-determination. The Fourteen Points encouraged a number of colonial leaders, including Ho Chi Minh, to attend the Paris Peace Conference and present petitions for autonomy and independence. The Atlantic Charter, a declaration of principles issued by U.S. president Franklin D. Roosevelt (1882–1945) and British prime minister Winston Churchill (1874–1965) in 1941, echoed Wilson's Fourteen Points and called for the rights of self-determination, self-government, and free speech for all peoples.

Anticolonial leaders and movements in Asia, Africa, the Middle East, and elsewhere during the twentieth century drew upon elements of both liberal and Marxist anticolonial thought. Anticolonial movements generally spoke the rhetoric of liberalism (freedom, self-determination, self-government, individual rights, and so on) when discussing politics, and the rhetoric of Marxism (equality, economic development, social rights, and so on) when discussing social and economic problems. Twentieth-century anticolonial thought was also saturated by the development of nationalism and the use of history to help create or invent national identities. The great anticolonial movements of the century, it is not surprising to note, were nationalist movements: the African National Congress, the Indian National Congress, the Conference of Nationalist Organizations of the Portuguese Colonies, the National Congress of British West Africa, and others.

In the past, historians have argued that the anticolonial movements of Asia, Africa, and the Middle East—of the so-called third world—adopted the liberal and Marxist anticolonial critiques, the ideas and forms of nationalism, and even rational, narrative history from the West. There is little doubt that there was substantial borrowing. As more and more non-Western historians are exploring their national histories, however, they are learning that their form of anticolonialism was not simply a "derivative discourse." Indian historian Partha Chatterjee argues that as colonized, Anglicized, Bengali intellectuals were schooled in Western statecraft and economics, they also worked to create through schools, art, novels, and theater an Indian aesthetic sphere that was distinctively Indian. "The bilingual intelligentsia," writes Chatterjee, "came to think of its own language as belonging to that inner domain of cultural identity, from which the colonial intruder had to be kept out" (1993, p. 7).

Other historians have charged that anticolonialism, or at least the history of anticolonialist struggles, has focused too much on elites and intellectuals. Amílcar Cabral (1924–1973), leader of the independence movement of Guinea-Bissau and the Cape Verde Islands, in the late 1960s and the early 1970s realized that genuine anticolonialism is the "cultural resistance of the people, who when they are subjected to political domination and economic exploitation find that their own culture acts as a bulwark in preserving their *identity*" (1973, p.61).

Anticolonialism, in violent actions and in formal thought, and in the hands, pens, and movements of non-Europeans as well as Europeans and Americans, has a history that is long, complex, and still being debated and written. There are many interesting questions but few easy answers.

SEE ALSO *American Revolution; Anticolonial Movements, Africa; Anticolonialism, East and North Africa, Asia and the Pacific; Anticolonialism, Middle East; Creole Nationalism; Enlightenment and Empire; Enlightenment Thought; Imperialism, Free Trade; Imperialism, Liberal Theories of; Imperialism, Marxist Theories of; Modern World-System Analysis; Spanish American Independence.*

BIBLIOGRAPHY

Abernethy, David B. *The Dynamics of Global Dominance: European Overseas Empires, 1415–1980.* New Haven, CT: Yale University Press, 2000.

Barshay, Andrew E. "The Sciences of Modernity in a Disparate World." In *The Cambridge History of Science; Vol. 7: The Modern Social Sciences,* edited by Theodore M. Porter and Dorothy Ross, 407–412. Cambridge, U.K.: Cambridge University Press, 2003.

Bayly, C. A. *The Birth of the Modern World, 1870–1914: Global Connections and Comparisons.* Oxford: Blackwell, 2004.

Black, Jeremy. *Europe and the World, 1650–1830.* London: Routledge, 2002.

Cabral, Amílcar. *Return to the Source: Selected Speeches By Amílcar Cabral.* New York: Monthly Review Press and Africa Information Service, 1973.

Chatterjee, Partha. *The Nation and its Fragments: Colonial and Postcolonial Histories.* Princeton, NJ: Princeton University Press, 1993.

Curtin, Philip D. *The World and the West: The European Challenge and the Overseas Response in the Age of Empire.* New York: Cambridge University Press, 2000.

Genovese, Eugene D. *From Rebellion to Revolution: Afro-American Slave Revolts in the Making of the Modern World.* Baton Rouge: Louisiana State University, 1979.

Hamilton, Alexander. *The Federalist* No. 11: "The Utility of the Union in Respect to Commercial Relations and a Navy." 1787. Available from the Library of Congress at http://thomas.loc.gov/home/histdox/fed_11.html.

Hart, Jonathan. *Comparing Empires: European Colonialism from Portuguese Expansion to the Spanish-American War.* New York: Palgrave Macmillan, 2003.

Hart, Jonathan. *Contesting Empires: Opposition, Promotion, and Slavery.* New York: Palgrave Macmillan, 2005.

Kiernan, V. G. *Colonial Empires and Armies, 1815–1960.* Montreal: McGill-Queen's University Press, 1998.

Marx, Karl. *Capital: A Critique of Political Economy,* Vol. 1 (1867). Translated by Ben Fowkes. London: Penguin, 1990.

Muthu, Sankar. *Enlightenment Against Empire.* Princeton, NJ: Princeton University Press, 2003.

Schroeder, Susan, ed. *Native Resistance and the Pax Colonial in New Spain.* Lincoln: University of Nebraska Press, 1998.

Scott, James C. *Weapons of the Weak: Everyday Forms of Peasant Resistance.* New Haven, CT: Yale University Press, 1985.

Scott, James C. *Domination and the Arts of Resistance: Hidden Transcripts.* New Haven, CT: Yale University Press, 1990.

Taylor, William B. *Drinking, Homicide, and Rebellion in Colonial Mexican Villages.* Stanford, CA: Stanford University Press, 1979.

Wesseling, H. L. *The European Colonial Empires, 1815–1919.* Translated by Diane Webb. Harlow, U.K.: Pearson Longman, 2004.

Thomas Benjamin
Dennis Hidalgo

ANTICOLONIALISM, EAST ASIA AND THE PACIFIC

European colonialism in East Asia developed in a piecemeal fashion, launched as it was against the centralized hereditary dynasties of China, Japan, and Korea. Likewise, there were discontinuities in the West's colonization of the Pacific, where vast stretches of ocean, rather than dense populations and ingrained traditions, complicated the task of projecting and consolidating Western military and administrative authority.

Japan's colonial history is unique in East Asia. Initially an object of Western colonial aspirations, Japan became a major colonial power in its own right. Its strong central government and martial ruling class resisted Western encroachments in the 1860s, and in response to the Western threat undertook a massive program of industrial and scientific modernization. Its key national goal was the creation of a modern military. This project soon sparked Japan's own colonial expansion in both East Asia and the Pacific. Beginning with neighboring islands, including Ryukyu and the Kurile chain in the 1880s, Japan's fledgling empire grew following its naval victories over China in 1895 and Russia in 1905 to 1906. Japan acquired first special rights and then full colonial authority over Taiwan, Korea, and the Pescadore Islands, as well as the profitable trading advantages already enjoyed by the Western Powers at China's "treaty ports." After Germany's defeat in World War I, Japan acquired virtually all German territories in the Far East and the Pacific.

Japan portrayed its expansion as Pan-Asianism, a development that would limit Western imperialism, but anticolonialism developed in all of Japan's possessions. The most extensive opposition developed in Korea, where Japan established a military protectorate in 1905. In the following years urban Korean nationalists organized strikes and street demonstrations, which were forcibly broken up by Japanese police and military forces; some 12,000 Korean were killed. Despite Japan's complete domination of civil affairs and communications, small pockets of resistance persisted. After World War I, continuing Japanese oppression and the influence of Wilsonian ideals of political self-determination provoked the "March First Movement," an explosion of anti-Japanese resentment and Korean nationalism culminating in strikes, protests, and boycotts involving over two million Koreans. Japan's military reacted, crushing its unarmed opponents. Modest reforms were introduced, however, including improved access to education for Koreans, tolerance of moderate Korean newspapers, and the development of a small Korean film industry. In the 1920s Japan intensified its demands on Korean farmers, exporting all rice surpluses to Japan. During the 1930s, Korean industries were reorganized to supply Japan's expanding military. World War II brought continued political oppression and greater deprivation: Grievances over food shortages and inflation were exacerbated by Japan's policy of kidnapping Korean women, sending them overseas with Japanese military forces, and maintaining them as sexual slaves, known as *comfort women*, for Japan's soldiers. Underground anti-Japanese movements, particularly the Korean Workers' Party, a Communist group, gradually gained adherents during the war, but only Japan's final surrender in September 1945 allowed Korean nationalists, both Communists and democrats, to make plans for postcolonial Korea.

Anticolonialism in Taiwan was less widespread. A rural-based resistance movement briefly developed immediately following Japan's seizure of the island in 1895. During a brutal campaign that cost thousands of lives on both sides, Japanese troops occupied most of the island by the end of the year. A small guerrilla force survived in Taiwan's mountainous interior for another thirty years, occasionally launching harassing attacks on Japanese properties. Most of Taiwan's population passively accepted Tokyo's authority. A short-lived "home rule" movement emerged in 1914, as war broke out in Europe, but colonial officials ignored its demands, focusing instead on manipulating Taiwan's agricultural

economy to supply Japan's requirements, especially for sugar. However, during the 1930s a small aboriginal mountain tribe, angered by the seizure of its ancestral lands, launched the "Musha Rebellion," which was quickly overcome when Japanese aircraft and artillery slaughtered the tribe. Taiwan reverted to China after Japan's defeat in World War II, but after the Chinese civil war of the late 1940s it was ruled by a pro-Western government, once again politically isolated from the mainland.

Among Germany's territories lost to Japan in World War I were several possessions in China, including the strategically valuable Liaodong Peninsula on the Yellow Sea. Rich in mineral resources, with China's second-busiest port at Dalian (Dairen), the territory controlled water-borne traffic to northeastern China. Sparked by fury at the Chinese government's capitulation to Japan's demand for the peninsula, a vehement anticolonial protest campaign soon enveloped all of China's major cities and many of its eastern provinces. This "May Fourth movement," which coincided with the 1919 anti-Japanese upheaval in Korea, involved mass demonstrations, strikes, anti-Japanese boycotts, and attacks on Japanese businesses and property. Launched by radical students, it sparked a new awakening of Chinese nationalism, and drew on anticolonial sentiments stoked by decades of foreign intrusion into China. Not only Japanese, but also British, French, and American assets were threatened or attacked. Anti-Japanese agitation was particularly strong, and continued into the early 1930s. The May Fourth movement spawned new political parties that called for China to "stand up" to foreign imperialism, including the Chinese Communist Party, which was founded in 1921 and eventually seized power in China in 1949.

In 1914 to 1915 Japan seized Germany's territorial possessions in the Pacific, meeting little native resistance. A military government was established at Truk for all of Japan's new island territories, and after the war the Japanese language and Japanese education systems were introduced. The docile population of Micronesia, for example, readily accepted Japan's construction of sugar plantations and mining industries. Tokyo initially placated local chieftains and respected traditional landholding patterns, but during the 1930s tens of thousands of Japanese laborers migrated to Micronesia. Native clans' common lands were seized, and anticolonial sentiments intensified. During World War II anti-Japanese natives aided American forces, acting as aircraft spotters and laborers, and building affinities with America that lasted into the postwar era.

In the late nineteenth century the widely scattered archipelagoes of the Pacific had been the objects of intense competition among the Western powers, which needed coaling stations for their Pacific naval fleets. Britain, France, Germany, and the United States all seized islands throughout the Pacific, becoming more aggressive as profitable new industries took shape, including cash crop plantations, commercial fishing, and mining. For example, the United States recognized the commercial and strategic value of the sovereign nation of Hawaii and moved to wrest informal control of the islands from the British. Hawaii's monarchy and its population accepted America's growing influence and then American rule with resentment, but only minimal resistance. Most native populations in the Pacific followed the Hawaiian model of accommodating rather than fighting colonial authority. However, the combination of military occupation, foreign laws, and economic manipulation occasionally provoked resistance. In New Caledonia, for example, France encountered stiff opposition. Armed clashes in 1878 to 1879 between French troops and native Melanesians resulted in hundreds of deaths, as local people disputed the imposition of French law, land seizures, the desecration of sacred sites, and the arrival of thousands of convicts at a newly created penal colony.

In the 1920s a wave of anticolonial resistance developed across the western Pacific. Militant Indian immigrant laborers in Fiji were silenced by Australian naval vessels and troops from New Zealand. In Western Samoa, then administered by New Zealand under a mandate from the League of Nations, local chieftains organized the Ola Mau a Samoa (the Firm Opinion of Samoa) movement, known as *Mau*, which pressed for Samoan self-determination; its leaders were arrested and interned in prison camps. In December 1929 colonial police fired into a crowd of Samoans, killing Mau leader Tupua Tamasese Lelofi and eleven others. The Mau movement also influenced the population of American Samoa, but violence was forestalled by allowing local chieftains more autonomy over land and property disputes.

Nonviolent anticolonialism characterized most of the Pacific. In British Nauru in the early 1920s, low-wage phosphate miners threatened to strike, citing environmental damage and monopoly prices charged by the company store. Strike leaders were arrested and police were called out. However the British "resident," London's official on the scene, ordered the release of the dissident leader, Timothy Detudamo, and allowed workers to organize their own cooperative store; he also arranged for the mining company to enlarge the trust fund that would pay for land reclamation. A similar strike threatened by agricultural workers on Tonga in 1921 was also resolved without violence when British

officials provided slight wage increases. The Americans' "island-hopping" strategy during the Pacific war brought many Pacific islands under United Nations or American authority, allowing paths to peaceful decolonization to develop in many island nations.

SEE ALSO *Decolonization, East Asia and the Pacific; East Asia, American Presence in; East Asia, European Presence in; Empire, British, in Asia and Pacific; Occupations, the Pacific; Pacific, American Presence in; Pacific, European Presence in; Self-Determination, East Asia and the Pacific.*

BIBLIOGRAPHY

Allen, Helena G. *The Betrayal of Liliuokalani: Last Queen of Hawaii, 1838–1917.* Honolulu, HI: Mutual Publishing, 1982.

Connell, John. *New Caledonia or Kanaky? The Political History of a French Colony.* Canberra: National Center for Development Studies, Australian National University, 1987.

Douglas, Bronwen. "Conflict and Alliance in a Colonial Context: Case Studies in New Caledonia, 1853–1870." *Journal of Pacific History* 15, no. 1 (1980): 21–51.

Duus, Peter, Ramon H. Myers, and Mark R. Peattie, eds. *The Japanese Informal Empire in China, 1895–1937.* Princeton, NJ: Princeton University Press, 1989.

Duus, Peter, Ramon H. Myers, and Mark R. Peattie, eds. *The Japanese Wartime Empire, 1931–1945.* Princeton, NJ: Princeton University Press, 1996.

Lee, Chong-Sik. *Korean Workers' Party: A Short History.* Stanford, CA: Hoover Institution Press, 1978.

Lowe, Peter. *Britain in the Far East: A Survey from 1819 to the Present.* London: Longman, 1981.

Meleisea, Malama. *The Making of Modern Samoa: Traditional Authority and Colonial Administration in the Modern History of Western Samoa.* Suva, Fiji: Institute of Pacific Studies, University of the South Pacific, 1987.

Peattie, Mark R. "The Japanese Colonial Empire, 1895–1945." In *The Cambridge History of Japan,* Vol. 6: *The Twentieth Century,* edited by Peter Duus. Cambridge, U.K.: Cambridge University Press, 1988.

Laura M. Calkins

ANTICOLONIALISM, MIDDLE EAST AND NORTH AFRICA

In many parts of the Middle East and North Africa, resistance to the imposition of colonial rule appeared almost immediately after the first attempts to establish colonial regimes. Examples include the revolt led by ʻAbd al-Qadir in Algeria in the 1840s, the Mahdist revolt in the Sudan, the rebellion of ʻUmar Mukhtar in Libya, more than two decades of tribal resistance to French rule in Morocco, the Iraqi rebellion of 1920, the Syrian revolt of 1926 to 1927, and the Palestine rebellion of 1936 to 1939. In Egypt, a nationalist uprising in protest against the stringent fiscal provisions laid down by Britain and France was the pretext for British military intervention in 1882.

Between the early nineteenth century and the outbreak of World War I (1914-18), much of the area along the southern shore of the Mediterranean between Morocco and what is now Turkey came under different forms of European colonial rule. Thus France began the conquest of Algeria in 1830, took over Tunisia in 1881, and (in partnership with Spain) took over Morocco in 1912. Britain occupied Egypt in 1882, formalizing the occupation by the declaration of a protectorate in 1914, and Italy began its conquest of Libya in 1911.

With the exception of Morocco, the entire region either had been, or still was in the nineteenth and early twentieth centuries, at least nominally part of the Ottoman Empire, a multiethnic entity that had been in existence since the late thirteenth century and that collapsed at the end of World War I. While the Ottomans cannot be accurately regarded as an "imperial power," it is nevertheless the case that in spite of the Tanzimat reforms (ca. 1839–1876), one of whose principal purposes was to extend full citizenship to all Ottoman subjects, all the empire's Christian provinces in southeastern Europe became independent states in the course of the nineteenth century as a result of more or less bitter struggles to assert their individual ethnolinguistic identities. In contrast, regardless of their ethnicity, the overwhelmingly Muslim population of the Arab provinces continued to regard the (Turkish) Ottomans as the "natural defenders of Islam," with the result that, contrary to most earlier received wisdom, most of the Middle East was little affected by the ideology of Arab nationalism until World War I.

On the coasts of the Arabian Peninsula, Britain's concern to keep the route to India safe and open led to the signing of a series of treaties with various local rulers between the 1820s and 1916, under which the rulers generally agreed not to grant or dispose of any part of their territories to any power except Britain. In return, British recognition confirmed the ruling families of the Gulf emirates in the positions they have continued to hold until today. In 1839 Britain annexed Aden and turned it into a naval base. "Exclusive" treaties were signed with the tribal rulers of the interior, and in 1937 the area was divided into the port and its immediate hinterland (Aden Colony) and the more remote rural/tribal areas (Aden Protectorate). Principally because of their remoteness and their apparent lack of strategic importance, central Arabia and northern Yemen were never colonized.

After the collapse of the Ottoman Empire at the end of World War I, the empire's remaining Arab provinces were assigned to Britain and France as mandates from the newly created League of Nations, with Britain taking responsibility for Iraq, Palestine, and Transjordan, and France taking responsibility for Lebanon and Syria. The guiding principle of the mandate system was that the states concerned should remain under the tutelage of the mandatory power until they were able to "stand alone," a period that, although not specified, was viewed as not being of indefinite length. The mandate period was relatively short-lived; Britain left Iraq in 1932, France left Lebanon and Syria in 1945 to 1946, and Israel was created from the former Palestine mandate in 1948.

A number of factors are crucial to understanding the various manifestations of anti-colonialism in the Arab world in the nineteenth and twentieth centuries. In the first place, the colonial period in the Middle East coincided with movements of "renewal" throughout much of the wider Islamic world; similar phenomena can be observed in the Indian subcontinent, West Africa, Central Asia, and Southeast Asia. Some movements clearly were, or became, "reactions to colonialism," but one of the most influential, that of the Wahhabis in the center of the Arabian Peninsula, both predated colonialism in the region and originated in an area relatively distant from any direct colonial activity. In the late eighteenth and nineteenth centuries, such renewal or reform movements spread out over a wide geographical area. Some, like the Sanusi jihad, based in Saharan Libya, later the backbone of resistance to Italian colonization, exhibited an organizational form similar to that of the Sufi orders, based on a far-flung network of *zawiyas,* or lodges; others were urban-based, and often grouped around traditional centers of Islamic learning, while yet others were millenarian. Thus in the 1880s the Sudanese Mahdi (ca. 1844–1885) preached that he was the divinely appointed regenerator of Islam, and consciously imitated the life and career of the Prophet. The renewal movements were by no means always sympathetic to, or even tolerant of, one another; thus Muhammad al-Mahdi al-Sanusi (1844–1902) was at pains to point out that the Sudanese Mahdi was not entitled to claim either the leadership of the universal Islamic community or a transcendental relationship with the Prophet Muhammad, and Wahhabism (when not checked by more prudent political considerations) has tended to exhibit considerable intolerance toward other manifestations of Islam.

The Islamic reform movements contributed to the growth of anti-colonialism in a number of different ways. One of their effects was to draw a battle line between those rulers and elites in the Islamic world who were prepared to make forms of accommodation with European colonizers and those sections of the community who were not. Thus 'Abd al-Qadir (1808–1883), the leader of the tribal jihad against the French in Algeria, sought and made use of a *fatwa* (legal opinion) from the *mufti* of Fez, which stated that those Muslims who cooperated with non-Muslims (i.e., the French) against other Muslims could be considered apostate or having abandoned one's religion, and could be treated as such if defeated. In contrast, later in the nineteenth century, Ba Ahmad, the influential chamberlain for the first few years of the reign of the Moroccan sultan 'Abd al-'Aziz (1894–1908), believed his only recourse was to buy off or otherwise accommodate the French, who were making incursions into southern Morocco from both Algeria and Senegal. This policy alienated many influential religious and tribal leaders, who were bitterly opposed to the Commander of the Faithful giving up "the lands of Islam" to foreign invaders; some of them considered that this made him illegitimate, and in consequence transferred their allegiance to a more combative, and, it must be said, quixotic, leader, Ma'al-Aynayn.

An important effect of colonialism was to hasten the disintegration of long-established social and economic relations based (generally, though not exclusively) on a subsistence economy that was superseded by the often far harsher dictates of the market. The precolonial world was no egalitarian paradise, but, for example, the confiscation or purchase of land by colonists in North Africa and by Zionists in mandatory Palestine, and the formation of large landed estates in Syria and Iraq as a result of the establishment—generally with the encouragement of the colonial authorities—of regimes of private property under the mandates, often resulted in cultivators either being driven off the land or their status being reduced from "free peasants" to serfs. Incorporation into the world market to a far more all-embracing extent than before, and the simultaneous pressure to cultivate cash rather than subsistence crops, often forced peasant households to migrate to an uncertain and generally near destitute existence in slum settlements on the edges of the major cities.

Finally, as far as twentieth-century resistance to colonialism is concerned, such movements as arose inevitably partook of the general experience of modernity in their day. This included assertions of national or ethnic identity, often easier to promote and maintain in the face of an alien colonizing "other," as well as new forms of communication and organization. Thus the press, the radio, political parties, professional associations, and labor unions all provided a variety of opportunities for disseminating ideologies of anticolonialism. To these must be added the example of Germany in the 1930s, as a previously fragmented state that had turned its recent unification into a means of challenging the old colonizers, Britain and France, as well as, for much of the 1940s, 1950s, and 1960s, the example of the Soviet Union as the home of a new form of social and economic organization, under which a previously archaic feudal regime was being transformed into an egalitarian welfare state. Of course, such visions were especially attractive to those who had not experienced the realities of daily life under these regimes.

Provided certain flexibility is adopted, it is possible to identify the major templates of anticolonial resistance, which varied according to the nature of the colonizing process. The Algerian case is probably the most extreme, because of the extent of the devastation caused by the colonization process over a period of some 130 years. In the months after the conquest of the city of Algiers in July 1830, the French military began to encourage the settlement of French *colons* (settlers) in the city's rural hinterland. At the time, Algeria was, if only nominally, an Ottoman province, and had no developed indigenous political structures. Local leaders in the west of the country turned first to the Moroccan sultan, but the French warned him not to interfere. The leaders then turned to the Sufi orders, the only bodies with an organizational structure, and Muhi al-Din, the leader of the Qadiriyya order, and his shrewd and energetic son, 'Abd al-Qadir, were asked to lead a tribal jihad against the French.

Between 1832 and 1844 'Abd al-Qadir managed to keep the French at bay with an army of about ten thousand. Initially, he achieved this by making agreements with the French that recognized his authority over certain parts of the country, but by the 1840s the French had decided on a policy of total subjugation, and 'Abd al-Qadir, defeated at Isly in 1844, eventually surrendered in 1847. By this time the European population, which was mostly concentrated in the larger towns, had reached over one hundred thousand. In the 1840s the French had begun a policy of wholesale land confiscation and appropriation, and there were a number of local uprisings in protest. The settlers had influential allies in Paris, and throughout the nineteenth century the indigenous population faced the gradual erosion of most of their rights. The last major act of resistance until the war of 1954 to 1962 was the rebellion in Kabylia in 1870 to 1871, led by Muhammad al-Muqrani. For a while, al-Muqrani's army controlled much of eastern Algeria, but they were no match for the better-equipped French troops. After the defeat of al-Muqrani's rebellion (he was killed in battle in May 1871) the local communities involved were fined heavily and lost most of their tribal lands.

The Algerian national movement was slow to develop in the twentieth century, because the tribal aristocracy had been defeated and there was no former indigenous governing class or emerging business bourgeoisie (as in, say, Morocco or Tunisia, not to mention Syria and Lebanon). A significant and fairly vocal minority of Algerians felt that France had brought them into the modern world, and they thus wanted to become "more French," that is, to enjoy the same rights as the French in Algeria without having to give up their Islamic identity. This tendency, generally called *assimilation*, was represented by Ferhat Abbas (1899–1985), a pharmacist from Sétif, who sought to become a member of the French Chamber of Deputies. The first strictly nationalist movement, the Étoile Nord-Africaine (later the Parti du Peuple Algérien), initially connected with the French Communist Party, was founded by Messali Hadj (1898–1974) in 1926, and recruited among Algerian workers in France. Yet another tendency was represented by Ahmad Ibn Badis (1889–1940), who asserted the Muslim nature of Algeria and sought to reform Algerian popular Islam through the Association of Ulama.

From the 1930s onward, rapid urbanization fueled Algerian resistance to France. By the end of World War II (1939-45) it was hoped that compromises could be worked out that might deflect violent nationalism, but the European community in Algeria's dogged insistence on hanging on to its privileges meant that these hopes soon evaporated. Ferhat Abbas's movement soon became insignificant, and ibn Badis's death in 1940 meant that the Association of Ulama lacked influence, which left Messali Hadj dominating the field, with supporters among Algerian workers in France as well as in Algeria. However, his organization was regarded as too moderate, and a splinter group, the Organisation Secrète, seceded from it in the mid-1940s. Its members included such major revolutionary figures as Ahmed Ben Bella, Ait Ahmad, Didouche Mourad, Mohammed Boudiaf, and Belkacem Krim. This group subsequently launched the "Algerian revolution," or war of national liberation, on November 1, 1954; it lasted until 1962, when Algeria became independent. Over the eight years, between 1 and 1.5 million Algerians, and 27,000 French were killed. The struggle proved intensely divisive, especially as more Algerian Muslims fought on the French side than in the Algerian army.

In the cases of Tunisia, Egypt, and Morocco, the decision of Britain and France to take over the reins of government (in 1881, 1882, and 1912, respectively) was at least partly precipitated by local opposition to the draconian financial measures that the European powers had insisted local governments impose in order to repay debts contracted on the various European money markets. The ruler of Tunisia, Ahmad Bey (r. 1837–1855), made strenuous efforts both to modernize Tunisia and to assert its independence from Istanbul, and he had been aided substantially by France in the latter objective.

By the time of his death Tunisia had a modern army and navy, largely thanks to the efforts of his treasurer, Mustafa Khaznadar (1817–1878). In 1861, much to the discomfort of Tunisia's new ruler, Muhammad al-Sadiq Bey (r. 1859–1882), and under great pressure from Khayr al-Din (ca. 1823–1890)—the reform-minded finance minister and prime minister who was also Khaznadar's son-in-law—Tunisia adopted a constitution and a modern (that is, generally secular) legal system under which the *bey's* prerogatives were considerably limited.

These "reforms" were better received in the outside world and among the sizeable local European community than within Tunisia, where a rural uprising (against the new legal system and the new taxes) was put down with considerable brutality in 1864. As happened in Egypt at much the same time, the contracting of substantial foreign debts (generally incurred from the building of infrastructure and the use of European consultants—officers, engineers, and so forth) and the general mismanagement and corruption associated with the loans, meant that the country found itself increasingly at the mercy of its foreign creditors. Tunisia declared bankruptcy in 1869, Egypt in 1876. The efforts of the Tunisian prime minister Khayr al-Din to balance the budget were no match for French colonial ambitions, which were eventually realized when in May of 1881 the *bey* was forced to accept a protectorate under the terms of the Treaty of Bardo. By 1892 four-fifths of cultivated lands were in French hands.

The situation in Egypt was very similar; the additional taxes imposed as a result of British and French administration of the public debt, initiated in 1876 essentially to ensure that the bondholders got their money back, eventually gave rise to a nationalist movement. Many nationalists had the additional grievance that the government of Egypt was conducted by a clique widely perceived as "foreigners," that is, a Turco-Circassian aristocracy consisting of the descendants of Muhammad Ali and their courtiers. Another interesting component of the rebellion led by Ahmad Urabi between 1879 and 1882 was the emphasis on restoring Egypt fully to the bosom of the Ottoman Empire. One of the peculiarities of the colonial situation in Egypt was that although relatively large numbers of foreigners resided in the country, they could not be described as *colons* in the French North African sense, because they lived mostly in the cities and engaged in commerce or in other service occupations. In addition, most of them were not citizens of the occupying power; only 11 percent of the foreign population of Alexandria was British in 1917.

In spite of a succession of strong rulers for much of the nineteenth century, Morocco was also unable to avoid colonial penetration, first economic (imports of tea, sugar, candles, and cotton cloth; and exports of wool, cereals, and ostrich feathers) and then military. The first major confrontation between locals and Europeans occurred between 1859 and 1860, when Spain besieged Tetouan. A month later, Spain demanded an indemnity as the price of withdrawal, and although the terms were punitive, half the indemnity was paid within two years. This was not done without great hardship, particularly from the imposition of additional nontraditional agricultural taxation, which caused considerable unrest. There was also a massive devaluation of the currency and a near universal switch to foreign coinage. Like Tunisia and Egypt, Morocco gradually moved from a state of general economic self-sufficiency to dependence on the world market. In addition, Morocco became dependent on foreign loans and declared bankruptcy in 1903. Largely to preempt German colonial efforts, France and Britain signed the *Entente Cordiale* in 1904, under which Britain recognized France's preeminence in Morocco and France formally accepted the British occupation of Egypt. Franco-Spanish occupation of Morocco was formalized in 1912.

In November 1914, partly as a result of public pressure and partly as a result of miscalculations by those responsible for the decision, the Ottoman Empire entered the war on the side of the Central Powers (Austria-Hungary and Germany), fighting France, Great Britain, Italy, and Russia. Iraq was invaded immediately by British Indian troops, who eventually took Baghdad in 1917 and were in control of almost all the territory of the modern state by the end of the war. Palestine and Syria were invaded from Egypt at the end of 1917 with similar results. The long-term consequence was the end of the empire and the foundation of the independent Turkish Republic in 1923, and the division of the former Arab provinces of the empire into separate nation states. Two of these, Yemen and what became Saudi Arabia in 1932, were more or less independent; in the Fertile Crescent, five new states—Iraq, Lebanon, Syria, Palestine, and Transjordan—were established as mandated territories of the newly created League of Nations.

A great deal of ink has been spilt throughout the better part of the twentieth century in fruitless, and largely pointless, attempts to assess what the political ambitions and aspirations of the inhabitants of the eastern Arab world might have been had they somehow been left to their own devices. The major factor muddying the waters has been the claim of the Hashemite family, represented by themselves and their admirers as the standard bearers of Arab independence, to have been cheated out of their just due by British perfidy. While the charge of British perfidy is not without merit, the Hashemites's claims somehow to represent "the Arabs" cannot stand

up to serious scrutiny. In all probability, given that it was only in early 1918 that the prospect of an Allied victory came to look increasingly ambiguous, the more politically conscious inhabitants of the Fertile Crescent gradually came to the conclusion that if the Ottoman Empire was to disappear, they would favor an arrangement under which they would rule themselves; only a very few saw advantages in accepting the rule of minor potentates from the Hijaz. Even fewer were enthusiastic at the prospect of European, especially French, colonial rule, given what was known about French rule in North Africa.

For a variety of reasons, therefore, British and French mandatory rule in the Levant and in Iraq faced a fair degree of resistance. Substantial numbers of Syrians had tried to persuade the Turks to return to Syria after the establishment of Faysal's Arab kingdom in October 1918, and were not to be reconciled to Faysal for several months. In Iraq, parts of which had been under British occupation and administration since the end of 1914, a major uprising broke out against British rule in the summer of 1920, organized by some former members of Faysal's entourage in Syria (the French would send Faysal into exile in July 1920), prominent Baghdadi notables, some senior *mujtahids* (religious scholars) from the Shiite holy cities of Karbala and Najaf, and, at the latter's instigation, tribal leaders and tribesmen from lower Iraq. British administration ceased to function outside the towns throughout most of the summer and early autumn, and there were moments when it seemed at least possible that British forces would be obliged to leave, especially when the scale of expenditure and the commitment of manpower became the subject of serious criticisms in the British press. Tribal revolts, partly against British semicolonial rule and partly against the British-sponsored Iraq government, occurred regularly in southern Iraq (the last major uprising there was in 1935, three years after the end of the mandate), and of course the Kurds of northern Iraq, who had originally been promised autonomy, remained in a state of more or less constant rebellion against Britain's, and later Baghdad's, refusal to grant it.

In Syria/Lebanon, the French faced similar opposition: although Faysal (1883–1933; king of Syria, 1918–1920, king of Iraq, 1921–1933) had by no means been universally popular, the provocative and often brutal nature of French rule was acutely opposed for much of the mandate. In the first place, Lebanon, considerably enlarged by the addition of areas traditionally considered parts of Syria, was constituted by the French as a separate state. What remained of "Syria" was then further divided into three administrative units: One included the four main cities of Aleppo, Hama, Homs, and Damascus; one was for the minority groups the Druzes and the Alawites; and the third was the *sanjak* (district) of Alexandretta,

Algerian Independence Campaign. *Men in Algiers drink coffee on June 17, 1962, in front of a wall painted with a command to vote for independence in the upcoming referendum.* **AFP/GETTY IMAGES. REPRODUCED BY PERMISSION.**

which the French eventually ceded to Turkey (in violation of the terms of the mandate) in 1939. The thinking behind the divisions was that the religious minorities living mostly in the rural areas would become bound to France by "ties of loyalty and gratitude" for having "saved" them from the domination of the Sunni majority, who were considered to be infected by the virus of Arab nationalism. The extent to which this plan failed can be gauged by the fact that the Druze area in particular was the source of some of the most vigorous opposition to the French, and that the rural minorities frequently made common cause with the people of the cities against their colonizers and occupiers.

The major revolt of the mandate period began in the Druze area, under the leadership of the Druze notable Sultan al-Atrash, in 1925. Starting off as a tribal uprising against the French administration of the Jabal Druze, it became a national revolt when al-Atrash was joined

by a number of Damascene notables, particularly 'Abd al-Rahman al-Shahbandar (1880–1940) and his People's Party, who called for national independence. Although the uprising was defeated in 1926, it eventually led to some relaxation in French policy, in that the French showed themselves prepared to countenance a constitution and the gradual withdrawal of French troops. Negotiations continued well into 1928, and the nationalists were successful to the extent that a national assembly was elected and asked to draw up a constitution for Syria.

In time, most of the anticolonial movements of the twentieth century developed into urban-based mass movements. They were often led by charismatic leaders, perhaps most notably Habib Bourguiba (1903–2000), who led the Tunisian Neo-Destour Party between 1934 and the country's independence in 1956, and remained president until 1987. Allal al-Fassi (1910–1974), leader of the Istiqlal Independence Party, might have played a similar role in the history of Morocco, but in 1953 the French exiled the sultan, Muhammad V (r. 1927–1961), to Madagascar. As a result, the rallying cry of the national movement became the return of the sultan from exile, which led in turn to the sultan/king retaining his position as ruler after Morocco's independence in October 1956 and the virtual eclipse of the "secular" political parties.

In Egypt, a kind of independence was achieved in 1936, but, as in Iraq and Syria, the national movement went through two stages. In the first stage, some limited powers (in fact all powers in the case of Syria) were handed over to local elites. In Egypt and Iraq this arrangement involved a degree of power-sharing with the former colonial rulers, which gradually became increasingly intolerable to wide sections of the population. However, given the balance of forces, it was not possible to break these links by democratic means, that is, by voting in a political party or coalition that would thus have a mandate to end the relationship. Thus a second stage was necessary, in which a determined group within the military seized power, destroying, in the process, the admittedly fairly rudimentary institutions of parliamentary government that the colonial powers had put in place. In this way, first Mohammad Naguib (1901–1984) and then Gamal Abdel Nasser (1918–1970) took power in Egypt in 1952, and ʿAbd al-Karim Qasim (1914–1963) in Iraq in 1958. A similar but more complex process took place in Syria, although the "old social classes" still ruling in 1961 had long severed any links they may have had with France.

The final and highly anomalous instance of anticolonialism in the Middle East is Palestine, unique among its immediate neighbors in that it was a settler state. The text of the Palestine mandate included the terms of the Balfour Declaration (1917), in which Britain as mandatory power undertook to facilitate the setting up of a "national home for the Jewish people." In 1922 there were 93,000 Jews in Palestine and about 700,000 Arabs; in 1936 there were 380,000 Jews and 983,000 Arabs, and in 1946 there were about 600,000 Jews and 1.3 million Arabs; thus the Jewish population increased from 13 to 31 percent over a period of twenty-four years. Anticolonialism took different forms, principally opposition by both Arabs and Zionists to British policy, which they tried to combat in different ways, and Arab opposition to Zionism. The Palestine rebellion of 1936 to 1939 was mostly a peasant insurrection against colonial rule and the Zionist settlers; by February 1947 a war-weary Britain no longer felt able to sustain the mandate and submitted the problem to the United Nations. In November the United Nations recommended that Palestine should be partitioned into an Arab state and a Jewish state. By December fighting had already begun between the two

states. By May 1948 some 300,000 Palestinians had fled, and on May 14 David Ben-Gurion (1886–1973) proclaimed the state of Israel, after which a ragbag of Arab armies and the poorly organized Palestinian resistance forces tried to deflect the Zionists, to little effect.

Opposition to colonial rule and colonial settlement was fairly widespread throughout the Middle East and North Africa in the nineteenth and twentieth centuries, and it took a variety of forms, both rural and urban, organized and spontaneous, religious and political, with greater or lesser degrees of coherence. In addition, as in any colonial situation, reaction to colonial rule covered a wide spectrum, with resistance at one end, acquiescence in the middle, and collaboration at the other end. Some members of the colonized population rebelled, some collaborated, but the majority acquiesced, at least for most of the time. In the nationalist historiography of the colonial period, the struggle for colonial freedom or national independence is often characterized in a fairly monochrome manner, with the brave freedom fighters ranged against the brutal colonial authorities. The "achievements" of colonialism have long been open to question, and the divisions and chaos of the postcolonial world make the value of the colonial legacy more questionable as time passes. Nevertheless, it is also important to understand the complexity and multifaceted nature of anticolonialism, and the venality and corruption of so many of the competing, often warring, factions. It is also important for national maturity, and increasingly for national reconciliation, that such uncomfortable truths should be boldly confronted rather than willfully ignored.

SEE ALSO *Independence and Decolonization, Middle East; Secular Nationalisms, Middle East.*

BIBLIOGRAPHY

Anderson, Lisa. *The State and Social Transformation in Tunisia and Libya, 1830–1980.* Princeton, NJ: Princeton University Press, 1986.

Batatu, Hanna. *The Old Social Classes and the Revolutionary Movements of Iraq: A Study of Iraq's Old Landed Classes and of Its Communists, Ba'thists, and Free Officers.* Princeton, NJ: Princeton University Press, 1978.

Botman, Selma. *Egypt from Independence to Revolution, 1919–1952.* Syracuse, NY: Syracuse University Press, 1991.

Gelvin, James. *Divided Loyalties: Nationalism and Mass Politics in Syria at the Close of Empire.* Berkeley: University of California Press, 1998.

Horne, Alistair. *A Savage War of Peace: Algeria, 1954–1962.* London: Macmillan, 1977.

Khoury, Philip S. *Syria and the French Mandate: The Politics of Arab Nationalism, 1920–1945.* Princeton, NJ: Princeton University Press, 1987.

Morris, Benny. *Righteous Victims: A History of the Zionist-Arab Conflict, 1881–2001.* New York: Vintage Books, 2001.

Morsy, Magali. *North Africa, 1800–1900: A Survey from the Nile Valley to the Atlantic.* London: Longman, 1984.

Prochaska, David. *Making Algeria French: Colonialism in Bône, 1870–1920.* Cambridge, U.K.: Cambridge University Press, 1990.

Sluglett, Peter. *Britain in Iraq, 1914–1932.* London: Ithaca Press, 1976.

Sluglett, Peter. "Formal and Informal Empire in the Middle East." In *The Oxford History of the British Empire*, Vol. 5: *Historiography*, edited by Robin W. Winks, 416–436. Oxford: Oxford University Press, 1999.

Thompson, Elizabeth. *Colonial Citizens: Republican Rights, Paternal Privilege, and Gender in French Syria and Lebanon.* New York: Columbia University Press, 2000.

Peter Sluglett

ANTICOLONIAL MOVEMENTS, AFRICA

Anticolonial movements in Africa were responses to European imperialism on the continent in the late nineteenth century and the greater part of the twentieth century. African responses to colonial rule varied from place to place and over time. Several forms of both armed and nonviolent resistance to colonialism occurred. Nonviolent forms of anticolonialism included the use of the indigenous press, trade unionism, organized religion, associations, literary and art forms, and mass migrations. Various African states used one or several of these nonviolent forms of anticolonialism at one time or another, but what is significant is that most of them resorted to armed resistance or cataclysmic actions to safeguard their way of life and sovereignty.

African resistance to colonial rule may be divided into four phases. The first was African responses to the colonial conquest itself. This occurred from about 1880 to 1910. The second phase spanned 1914 to 1939, the period of the consolidation of colonial rule. The third phase ran from the end of World War II (1939–1945) to the attainment of independence between the early 1950s and the 1980s. The final phase may be broadly categorized as African responses to neocolonialism—that is, their bid to redefine not only their relationships with the former colonizers, but also their efforts to deconstruct negative images associated with the continent.

Apart from its tendency to fall into these phases, anticolonialism in Africa differed from place to place and over time. The littoral states that had longer contact with Europeans, usually since the fifteenth century (e.g., the Fante of Ghana), and in some cases had experienced acculturation and social change, tended to initially accommodate colonial rule. But this changed dramatically when they realized that colonial rule was not as beneficent as they had assumed. Conversely, the interior peoples, largely non-Christians whose contacts with Europe were comparatively evanescent, resisted the colonial conquest by deploying vigorously militant forms of anticolonialism.

The Islamic areas in Africa—for example, French West Africa and the North African states—resisted colonial rule more than areas where indigenous African religions were the norm. The Islamic areas were influenced by the Muslim doctrine that recognized Euro-Christianity as an infidel entity, indeed, the antithesis of Islam. Hence, compared to non-Islamic Africa, anticolonial efforts in the Islamic regions were more vigorous, militant, and prolonged

Additionally, the nature of African anticolonialism depended on whether the colony was a settler or nonsettler one. Settler colonies were colonies with a large number of resident migrant Europeans. These developed, for example, in Kenya and Algeria. In such colonies, the European settlers were directly involved in the administration of the colony. In contrast, nonsettler colonies were colonies that lacked large numbers of permanent European settlers, such as Nigeria and the Cameroon. Overall, anticolonialism efforts in the settler colonies tended to be more violent and prolonged than those in nonsettler areas because the European settlers were not willing to allow Africans to regain their independence. In Algeria, for example, about one million Africans perished because of the tenacity of resistance adopted by the French settlers.

ARMED RESISTANCE

The first phase of African resistance to colonial rule from about 1880 to 1910 was broadly characterized by several forms of militant anticolonialism in which military resistance was the norm. Most African states took up arms to safeguard their independence during this period. The idea that it was only centralized states that took up arms against the European aggressors, as some researchers have argued, is no longer tenable. Even kin-based, noncentralized societies, such as the Tiv of Nigeria and the Tallensi of Ghana, resorted to militant forms of resistance. In southern Africa, the Chikunda, Chokwe, and Nguni, all noncentralized societies, also resorted to military resistance.

Numerous other African states and societies resorted to armed resistance: for example, in West Africa, Lat Dior, the ruler of Cayor (in present-day Senegal), confronted the French from 1864 to 1886; the Baule of the Ivory Coast put up spirited resistance against the French from 1891 to 1902; the Asante of Ghana engaged the British in several wars during the nineteenth century and went to war against them again in 1900 to 1901; and the Fon of Dahomey (now Benin) fought against the French from 1891 to 1902. In addition, the Yoruba state of Ijebu fought against the British in 1892, while the Sokoto Empire in Northern Nigeria confronted the British from 1899 to 1903. The most celebrated military resistance to colonialism in West Africa is credited to Samori Ture (ca. 1830–1900), a Muslim leader in the Madinka Empire, who engaged the French in protracted armed resistance from 1882 to 1898.

East Africa was also a theater of armed resistance to colonial rule. The Swahili coast of Tanzania under the Muslim leader Abushiri engaged the Germans from August 1888 to December 1899. The Hehe people of Tanzania fought against the Germans from 1891 to 1894; when the Hehe leader, Nkwana, realized the futility of resistance, he committed suicide. Similarly, armed resistance broke out in northern and northeastern Africa. Egyptians rose up against the British in 1882, while the Sudanese confronted the British from 1881 to 1889. Somalis confronted the multiple forces of the British, Italians, and the French between 1884 and 1887. In the northern arc of the continent, the Libyans, Tunisians, and Moroccans fought against the French, the Italians, and the Spanish.

In sum, overwhelming numbers of African states and societies resorted to military resistance in an effort to safeguard their independence. In the end, the European-led armies carried the day. This is not to say that Africans did not put up spirited resistance. Indeed, if one considers the duration of individual resistance, there is evidence to suggest that African armies, in spite of their limited military technology, fought bravely and were able to prolong their resistance to the dismay of the European aggressors. This was especially true in cases where Africans possessed comparatively unlimited military resources, martial prowess, and unbridled determination. The resistance of Samori Ture of the Madinka Empire, who fought the French in West Africa in the late 1800s, illustrates this point best.

Ture had a well-organized, professional infantry and cavalry that were further divided into battalions, each of which played different roles in battle. Additionally, Ture, unlike some other African leaders, was able to equip his armies with modern weapons. For example, by 1893, he had amassed about six thousand Gras repeater rifles. He equipped his troops by selling gold and ivory, which were abundant in his empire. He also benefited from his region's vast population, which enabled him to recruit large numbers of soldiers for his armed forces. Compared to most African armies, Ture had larger military forces. By 1887 the size of his infantry ranged from 30,000 to 35,000 troops, while the cavalry was about 3,000 strong.

In addition, Ture's army had skilled workers who repaired and even improved European-made guns.

Above all, Ture was a capable leader and a skilled general. His scorched-earth strategy and his tactic of initiating intermittent military skirmishes allowed Ture to determine when he wanted to fight instead of when the French were ready to fight. This approach enabled him to prolong his resistance against the French. In order to make his policies more effective throughout the seventeen years of military campaigns against the French, he moved the base of his empire and army from region to region. He covered several thousand miles from French West Africa to the northern reaches of Ghana. This process of migration enabled Ture to expand his empire by conquering some African states along the way. For example, between 1895 and 1896, he conquered the Abron and Gyaaman kingdoms, as well as parts of Gonja, all in northern Ghana. Such military conquests significantly added to Ture's ability to replenish his resources. Eventually, he was captured by the French in 1898 and exiled to Gabon, where he died in 1900. Ture's French adversaries wrote that to the end he was a man of honor.

If Samori Ture is remembered for his prolonged resistance to the French, Emperor Menelik II (1844–1913) of Ethiopia is celebrated for having decisively humiliated Italy in 1896 at the Battle of Adwa. There are several similarities in the way that Ture was able to prolong his resistance against the French and how Menelik was able to defeat the Italians. First, both had well-trained, disciplined, and well-equipped professional armies. Menelik also imported large quantities of guns from France and Russia. By 1893 the Ethiopian forces had 82,000 rifles and twenty-eight canons. At the decisive Battle of Adwa, Menelik's forces numbered over 100,000 compared to Italy's approximately 17,000 men. Geography also played to the advantage of Menelik and Ture because they knew the terrain of battle better than their European adversaries. In contrast, while the French assiduously pursued Ture and his mobile army, the Italians blundered by assuming that the Ethiopian armies, like those of other African states, could be easily defeated.

In the end, it was only Ethiopia that was able to decisively defeat a European power, Italy, to maintain its independence. However, from 1935 to 1936 the Italian fascist leader Benito Mussolini (1883–1945) occupied Ethiopia in revenge for the humiliating defeat that Italy suffered in 1896. The Italian occupation stimulated African nationalism and Pan-Africanism because many Africans, including diasporic Africans, believed that Ethiopia was a symbol of African resilience and independence. Some historians have even suggested that had it not been for the outbreak of World War II, the seething disenchantment unleashed by the Italian occupation could have served as a watershed for decolonization in Africa.

Several factors explain the success of the European-led armies in Africa. The paramount reason was the superiority of European military technology. As the famous lines of English author Hilaire Belloc (1870–1953) attest, "Whatever happens, we have got / the Maxim gun, and they have not" (*The Modern Traveller*, 1898). By the later part of the nineteenth century, military technology in Europe had developed considerably. It was this technological advantage that accounted for the ability of the Europeans to conquer not only Africa, but other parts of the world. Those African societies, such as Ture's, that could muster large forces and equip their armies to a level comparable to the Europeans, were able to put up the greatest degree of anticolonial resistance.

Another reason for the success of European armies in Africa is that most African armies were not professional, but were mobilized in the event of war. Thus they lacked systematic training, military discipline, and the martial prowess to withstand the well-equipped, disciplined European-led armies. Most African armies were mobilized when events dictated that colonialism was imminent, but African enthusiasm and dedication could not withstand the technological superiority of the European forces.

Few African states and societies engaged in mutual assistance to fight the forces of colonialism. One exception involves the cooperation of Ture and King Prempeh I (1872–1931) of Ashanti in the late 1890s during the final stages of Ture's resistance to the French. In general, however, Africans failed to unite against the European aggressors. Some commentators refer to this fact as evidence of the extent of local crisis and the contending political polarities in Africa on the eve of the colonial conquest. The evidence does not support this contention, however. It is based on the erroneous view that precolonial Africa was a monolithic state, and therefore all of Africa could have united in anticolonialism. Rather, precolonial Africa was made up of a multiplicity of states with different political systems. Not surprisingly, some African states, such as the Fante of Ghana, even assisted the British against Ashanti because throughout the nineteenth century, the Fante had struggled against the forces of Ashanti hegemony. The idea of Pan-Africanism had not yet developed among African states on the eve of the colonial conquest, which helps explain the lack of political unity among African states at the time.

The first two decades of the twentieth century also witnessed militant forms of anticolonialism against forced labor, forced cultivation of crops, land alienation, and taxation. In Tanganyika (now part of Tanzania), for example, the German colonial authorities' harsh demands for cotton cultivation, forced labor, and taxation unleashed the Maji Maji Rebellion in 1905. The rebellion, led by Kinjikitile Ngwale (d. 1905), an indigenous prophet, was organized across ethnic lines and involved over twenty different ethnic groups inhabiting an area of 10,000 square miles (about 25,900 square kilometers). Other such rebellions included the peasant revolts in Madagascar in 1904 to 1905 and 1915; the Mahdi revolts in Sudan from 1900 to 1904; a vigorous protracted rebellion in Somaliland from 1895 to 1920; and the Egba revolt in southeastern Nigeria in 1918. Armed uprisings during this phase were not only responses to the political economy of colonial rule, they were also efforts to overthrow colonial rule. The latter rationale explains why colonial regimes brutally suppressed such anticolonialism, as exemplified by the brutal response of the Germans to the Maji Maji Rebellion, in which more than 75,000 Africans were killed.

NONVIOLENT ANTICOLONIAL STRATEGIES

Realizing the futility of armed resistance in the face of the European possession of superior military technology, Africans adopted new strategies, one of which was mass migration. This involved communities, groups, and individuals migrating from theaters of objectionable colonial politics to areas where their independence could be safeguarded. It has been suggested that this strategy of anticolonialism was common in the French, Belgian, German, and Portuguese colonies because of arbitrary exploitation based on forced labor, taxation, forced cultivation of certain crops, and military recruitment, among other things.

Mass migrations could be seasonal, occurring, for example, during periods of forced labor recruitment in the dry season. Such migrations could also be episodic, occurring during periods of taxation, as when fifty thousand Africans fled from the Zambezi Valley to Southern Rhodesia (Zimbabwe) and Nyasaland (Malawi) between 1895 and 1907. Colonial forced labor and military recruitment during both world wars also stimulated mass migrations; for example, in 1916 and 1917, more than two thousand people migrated from the French Ivory Coast to neighboring Ghana.

Permanent mass migrations occurred in situations where European settlers seized African lands and then forced the Africans to become laborers and landless peasants. In Kenya, for example, the Kikuyu, who lost their ancestral territory in the so-called white highlands to European settlers, migrated en masse to burgeoning urban centers like Nairobi in search of employment. In the Belgian Congo, Africans suffering from the predatory policies of European companies, whose main aim was profit by any means, migrated to neighboring districts. The importance of mass migration as a vehicle of anti-colonialism is that it freed Africans from the claws of colonialism and at the same time rendered certain colonial policies ineffective.

Although armed resistance was the norm, other forms of confrontation, which have been compositely described as peaceful or diplomatic, occurred. Diplomacy was employed, for example, by King Jaja (d. 1891) of Opobo in the Niger Delta and King Prempeh of Ashanti. Prempeh, convinced that negotiations with the colonial government in the Gold Coast (Ghana) would remain fruitless, sent an embassy to the British government in London. The delegation left on April 3, 1895, arrived in England on April 24, 1895, and remained in London until December of that year. But the British government failed to meet with the Ashanti delegation, and instead British forces in the Gold Coast attacked and subjugated Ashanti in 1896. This action culminated in a final military showdown in 1900, when Yaa Asantewaa (d. 1921), the Queen of Edweso in Ashanti, decided that in order to redeem their independence, the Ashanti had to go to war against the British. Eventually, the British efforts to subdue Ashanti materialized in 1901 when the British-led armies emerged victorious.

Independent Christian churches and variants of syncretic Christianity generically termed *millennial* movements or *Ethiopianism* also served the anticolonial agenda of Africans. Christianity was seen as a pathfinder for colonial rule and European hegemony, both of which undermined the African way of life. This way of life included, for example, the spectrum of African rites of passage, namely, indigenous ceremonial rites that underscored birth, naming, puberty, marriage, and death and funerals. The European attack and denigration of African culture through the ideological artery of Christianity forced Africans to distill Christianity in order to render it more amenable to their way of life.

The millennial movements and other anticolonial religious movements thrived in an environment of apocalyptic vision, divine intervention, divination, and healing espoused by leaders such as Nehemiah Tile, who founded the Tembu Church in South Africa in 1884; Willie J. Mokalapa, who founded the South African Ethiopian Church in 1892; Reverend John Chilembwe and his Providence Industrial Mission in Malawi in 1900; and Wade Harris, who lead the millennial movement in the Ivory Coast in 1915. These religious movements involved a synthesis of European Christianity and indigenous African religions. For example, members practiced Christian liturgies along with spirit possession derived from indigenous African religions. Moreover, Old Testament prophetism became synonymous with African forms of divination. These millennial and other movements exemplify the way that Africans grappled with objectionable aspects of Christianity and succeeded in grafting the useful aspects of it onto their indigenous worldview and ontology.

Overall, these religious movements empowered Africans by restoring faith in African religions and cultures, which had been placed in the vortex of colonial rule. More significantly, some of these movements became powerful anticolonial movements as well. Chilembwe, for example, used his Providence Industrial Mission to spread his views that colonialism was an anathema to the Bible and Christianity. Consequently, in January 1915 he organized a revolt against the colonial system, and was eventually persecuted by the colonial authorities.

Another form of peaceful anticolonialism that began in the nineteenth century and continued throughout the colonial period, was the use of indigenous and foreign-based newspapers to promote anticolonial views. The London-based Pan-Africanist newspaper *African Times,* for example, became an anticolonial platform. In the Gold Coast, James Hutton Brew founded the anticolonialist *Gold Coast Times* in 1874. Black South Africans presented their views in *Imvozaba Ntsundu* or *Native Opinion,* established in 1884 by J. T. Jabavu and published in both English and Xhosa. Others periodicals with an anticolonialist bent included *The Lagos Weekly Record,* founded in Nigeria in 1891, and the *Nigerian Chronicle,* established in 1908.

The life spans of these newspapers differed: Some lasted several years, while others survived for only a few months. The Gold Coast, for example, had about twelve newspapers from 1874 to 1919. The African intelligentsia used the press to question objectionable colonial policies. This occurred more in West Africa, North Africa, and southern Africa than in Central Africa and East Africa. Barred from serving on the legislative councils and from participating in colonial administration because of their anticolonial views, the African intelligentsia used the press to articulate anticolonialism.

The use of the indigenous press as a political platform can be divided into phases. The first period, from about the 1870s to the 1920s, can be conveniently described as reformist anticolonialism because the objective of the African intelligentsia was not to overthrow colonialism but to better it. They attacked colonialism for the following reasons: the lack of African representation on legislative councils, brutalization of Africans, forced labor, taxation, lack of educational opportunities, and indirect rule that allowed illiterate indigenous rulers to govern educated African intellectuals.

In the aftermath of World War I (1914–1918), African intellectuals intensified their anticolonialist activities through the medium of the press. Several conditions help explain the revolutionary change in the African intelligentsia's attitude toward colonialism at this time. First, after the war the colonial powers, especially France and Britain, systematically implemented vigorous colonial policies aimed at maximizing exploitation to make up for losses incurred during the war. Second, the forceful winds of the Pan-African movement reshaped the anticolonial perspective of intellectuals in Africa. Finally, social changes, especially in urban centers, fueled the anticolonial movement: Rapid population growth and urbanization provided mass support for the evolving anticolonial constituencies.

The African intelligentsia also used societies, clubs, and associations as vehicles for the dissemination of anticolonialism. In 1912 South African blacks formed the South African Native National Congress. The congress became instrumental in challenging the Native Land Act of 1913, which had dispossessed Africans of their lands. In addition, the formation of the Gold Coast Aborigines' Rights Protection Society (ARPS) in 1888 was directly associated with the colonial government's effort to take over what it considered to be public lands. The ARPS campaigned in local newspapers, in particular the *Gold Coast Methodist Times* and the *Gold Coast Aborigines*, both in the late nineteenth century, and the *Gold Coast Nation* and the *Gold Coast Leader* during the first two decades of the twentieth century.

Apart from various petitions issued by the ARPS, in 1898 the organization sent a delegation to England to meet directly with British officials. The delegates wanted the British government to address various problems of colonial rule, especially the Lands Bill. The delegation was successful because the British government's Colonial Office asked the colonial government to abandon both the Lands Bill and the hut tax. In 1906 another delegation was sent to England under the auspices of the ARPS to demand the repeal of the Town Council Ordinance, though this time the Colonial Office did not grant the wishes of the ARPS.

Apart from the questions relating to land that led to the formation of anticolonial associations, other exigencies of the colonial situation also resulted in the founding of clubs and associations. In Senegal, the Young Senegalese Club fought for better working conditions. In Malawi, the North Nyasa Native Association, founded in 1912, and the West Nyasa Native Association, established in 1914, agitated for better working conditions and educational reforms. The Egyptian pan-Islamist writer

Shiekh Ali Yusuf founded the Hizb al-Islah al Dusturi (Constitutional Reformers) in 1907, while the intellectual Mustafa Kamil founded the Nationalist Party, also in 1907. Both organizations campaigned for the independence of Egypt. These political organizations, formed during the late nineteenth century and the first two decades of the twentieth century, paved the way for the revolutionary nationalism that would emerge in the 1920s and would crystallize in the 1930s and 1940s into vigorous independence movements.

Some of the political associations of the early decades of the twentieth century cut across colonial frontiers. The National Congress of British West Africa (NCBWA), for example, was founded in the Gold Coast by J. E. Casely Hayford in 1919 to 1920. Its membership was elitist, constituting mostly African intellectuals. The NCBWA, unlike earlier associations, had a regional base: it represented four English-speaking colonies—Nigeria, the Gold Coast, Sierra Leone, and Gambia. Thus, by embracing several colonies, the organization combined the idea of national unions based on specific colonies with Pan-Africanism. The NCBWA worked for political representation, the establishment of municipal corporations, and the promotion of higher education, among other things.

The achievements of the NCBWA were long term rather than immediate. The NCBWA gained political concessions from colonial governments, including the Clifford Constitution of Nigeria (1922) and revised constitutions in Sierra Leone (1924) and Ghana (1925). The NCBWA also contributed to the formation of radical political parties: NCBWA leader Herbert McCauley formed the Nigerian National Democratic Party in 1923, while Wallace Johnson is credited with founding the West African Youth League in 1938. In the long term, the activities of the NCBWA radicalized the African intelligentsia's stand against colonial rule.

Pan-Africanism also served as an agency of anticolonialism. It was a global movement, championed by various organizations and individuals who believed that all people of African descent shared a common identity and shared their struggles against the vestiges of slavery, racism, and colonialism. The proponents of the Pan-African movement included Liberian Edward Wilmot Blyden (1832–1912), W. E. B. DuBois (1868–1963) of the United States, the Jamaican-born Marcus Garvey (1887–1940), and J. E. Casely Hayford of the Gold Coast (1866–1903). The aim was to bring all peoples of African descent together to discuss the inequalities facing Africans worldwide.

A series of Pan-African congresses were held during the interwar years. The last conference, held in Manchester, England, in 1945, was attended by several future leaders of independent Africa, including Kwame

Nkrumah (1909–1972) of Ghana. From the Pan-African movement grew a nationalist idea that empowered Africans to address colonialism. For example, in the course of the independence struggles in Africa, especially in the 1950s and 1960s, Nkrumah organized a series of Pan-African congresses in Accra, Ghana, aimed at empowering other African nationalist leaders to overthrow the colonial yoke.

The changing landscape of colonial economies also provided opportunities for African anticolonialism. During the 1920s and 1930s, the import-export trade in Africa was dominated by expatriate firms. Due to the monopoly these firms exercised, they were able to dictate not only the prices of African cash crops, but also those of goods imported from Europe. The monopolization of commerce by expatriate traders and firms not only had an impact on local farmers, it also had adverse effects on the fortunes of African merchants, in particular, the great tradition of African merchant families, which had been crucial in the import-export trade since the precolonial period.

This situation resulted in new forms of anticolonialism. Some African societies boycotted European goods and also refused to sell their cash crops to expatriate traders. For instance, in response to price-fixing by Europeans in 1921, rural Transkei women in South Africa boycotted European goods. Similarly, in Ghana a spate of boycotts of European goods and refusals to sell cash crops to expatriate firms occurred periodically from 1920 to 1937. This form of anticolonialism intensified during the worldwide Great Depression of the 1930s, when prices of cash crops fell sharply while those of imported goods increased astronomically.

Indeed, the economic downturn in the 1920s and 1930s provided opportunities for rural peoples who had used armed resistance in the nineteenth century to stage boycotts and holdups in opposition to colonialism. During the same period, rural peoples increasingly teamed up with residents of urban areas to seek redress for injustices in the colonial economic systems. They objected to policies that resulted in rural communities receiving poor prices for their crops, while those living in urban areas experienced escalating costs of living due in part to increasing prices for imported goods.

Trade unionism or organized labor formed another area of economic anticolonialism when African workers, both men and women, joined forces to demand better working conditions from their European employers. African laborers staged strikes and boycotts to support their demands. In 1890 workers on the Dakar–Saint Louis railway lines went on strike in Senegal. In 1891 Dahomian women working in the Cameroon also resorted to a strike. In Mozambique, a series of strikes

organized by African employees of the Merchants Association in 1913, train workers in 1917, and railroad technicians in 1918 rocked the local economy. In South Africa, sewage and garbage collectors staged a strike in Johannesburg in 1917. In fact, throughout the 1920s, 1930s, and the postwar period, trade union activities formed a vital part of African anticolonialism. For example, railway workers' strikes occurred in French West Africa in 1946 and 1947, and in Tunisia the colonial police killed thirty-two and wounded about two hundred Tunisian trade unionists who were agitating for labor reforms.

Trade union activism was instrumental in the eventual decolonization of Africa. By resorting to demonstrations, boycotts, and strikes, trade unions were able to bring the injustices associated with the colonial system to the attention of a larger anticolonial audience. Additionally, their organizational abilities, which cut across class, religious, and ethnic lines, benefited the anticolonial movements. Most significantly, some of the leaders of the labor unions also assumed the leadership of revolutionary anticolonial movements. Both Siaka Stevens (1905–1988) of Sierra Leone and Sékou Touré (1922–1984) of Guinea were labor leaders who became leaders of their liberated countries.

From about the 1930s forward, new kinds of political organizations emerged that were more forceful and revolutionary than those that existed in earlier decades. The new political parties were no longer interested in reforming the colonial system, but aimed to overthrow it. The New-Destour Party in Tunisia, founded by Habib Bourghiba in 1934; the *Istiqlal* (Independence) Party, founded in Morocco in the late 1930s; the National Council of Nigeria and the Cameroons, launched in 1944; and Kwame Nkrumah's Convention People's Party, founded in Ghana in 1949, all championed anticolonialism.

A rapid population growth beginning in about the 1930s provided mass support for the new political parties. In addition, the well-educated African middle class played an important role by rallying others to the cause of the independence movements. There was a considerable number of primary- and middle-school dropouts who had besieged urban centers in search of employment. Because of the inherent hardships and deprivations of urban settings, they latched on to the grand promises of anticolonial campaigners and offered their support for decolonization.

Rapid urbanization during the colonial period created opportunities for interaction among different ethnic groups. Unlike the early period of resistance to colonial conquest, Africans on the eve of decolonization presented a formidable united front in their quest for decolonization. Furthermore, the return of African soldiers who participated in World War II brought new political insights to the decolonization movements. For example, in Ghana it was the revolutionary actions of the former servicemen in 1948 that contributed to popular discontent against the British colonial government. Overall, local anticolonial trends, which had developed in different forms in various places, reached fruition in the 1950s, enabling Africans to overthrow colonial rule.

TOWARD INDEPENDENCE: POSTWAR ANTICOLONIALISM

Several global developments in the aftermath of World War II paved the way for decolonization. In 1941 Winston Churchill (1874–1965), the British prime minister, and American president Franklin D. Roosevelt (1882–1945) signed an agreement that became known as the Atlantic Charter. The agreement stipulated that at the end of the war, the Allied nations could determine their own political destinies. Roosevelt insisted that the agreement should be applied universally. As a result, African and Asian nationalists capitalized on the promise of the Atlantic Charter to argue for political independence.

Additionally, the two major colonial powers in Africa, France and Britain, had been weakened considerably by the war. Indeed, had it not been for assistance from the United States, their fortunes at the end of the war would have been worse. However, the United States and the Soviet Union, the two superpowers that emerged after the war, were determined to dismantle colonialism in Africa. This development was enhanced during the ensuing Cold War, when the Soviet Union gave material and ideological support to African nationalists in their effort to gain independence.

Furthermore, the creation of the United Nations in 1945 benefited anticolonialism. The human rights doctrine of the United Nations challenged the inequalities inherent in the colonial situation. More importantly, African and Asian countries used the forum of the General Assembly of the United Nations to articulate and internationalize their anticolonialism campaigns. Finally, the independence of Asian countries in the late 1940s and early 1950s served as a precedent for Africans. Thus, in the postwar period, a mixture of local and international events unleashed the powerful winds of anticolonialism in Africa that culminated in decolonization.

In the first decade of the twenty-first century, neocolonialism exists in myriad forms in Africa. These are exacerbated by the Western media's propagation of negative images of the African continent that are undoubtedly vestiges of the colonial system itself. For this reason, various African states have adopted policies to reconstruct

the image of the continent. These strategies include changes in school curricula, the establishment of institutes of African studies, artistic production, and literary and populist movements, all wrapped in powerful ideologies.

Finally, actual decolonization took several forms. Nonsettler colonies like the Gold Coast (Ghana) and Nigeria used constitutional methods, sometimes marked by occasions of militancy and violence, to achieve decolonization. Ghana, for example, pursued decolonization through a constitutional process involving political parties, but there can be no doubt that the revolutionary actions of soldiers on February 28, 1948—the so-called 1948 Riots—constituted a major turning point in the country's relentless march for independence. The "riots" started in Accra, the colonial capital, and were occasioned by two incidents. The first occurred when a British senior police officer ordered his men to open fire on unarmed former servicemen who were intent on marching to Osu Castle, the seat of the colonial government, to present a petition to the governor. The second event was a reaction to an anticipated nationwide drop in the prices of European goods that failed to materialize. The disturbances, which lasted seventeen days, resulted in the deaths of twenty-nine people, left 237 injured, and destroyed property estimated at two million British pounds. In this case, popular agitation forced the hand of the colonial government to grant political concessions. More significantly, the riots energized political parties to campaign for decolonization. This occurred on March 6, 1957, when Nkrumah's Convention People's Party won the day.

The decolonization period also witnessed armed resistance, which occurred in such settler colonies as Kenya, Algeria, Zimbabwe, and Mozambique. In all cases, Africans took up arms against stubborn colonial regimes that were bent on staying put. Unlike Ghana and other nonsettler colonies, the main issue of contention in the settler colonies was land. For this reason, much of the revolutionary fervor that underscored the movement for independence came from landless peasants, such as the Mau Mau in Kenya, who rebelled in the 1950s. The cost was enormous because the Europeans in Africa—for example, the Portuguese in Mozambique and Guinea Bissau, the British in Kenya, and the French in Algeria—resorted to extreme measures, such as aerial warfare, to suppress African resistance. In Algeria, about one million Africans were killed. Although the futility of resistance loomed, Africa's settler colonies eventually won independence, but only after protracted, costly wars with the European colonizers.

CONCLUSION

African anticolonialism began with efforts to safeguard African independence and ways of life. By the early

1900s, armed resistance had failed, but Africans continued their anticolonial efforts by using other methods. Indeed, by the early 1900s the indigenous press had become an invaluable tool for anticolonialists. The trend was fueled by the political changes ushered in by the Pan-African movement. The African intelligentsia thus moved their stake from reform activism to revolutionary anticolonialism.

From about the second decade of the twentieth century, the colonial powers vigorously implemented administrative policies that had an impact on Africans. Economic exploitation nursed an alliance between the African intelligentsia and the native chiefs, as well as between rural and urban Africans. During the interwar years, the activities of Pan-Africanists and the formation of viable political parties served to question the essence of colonialism. In addition, rapid population growth, urbanization, and educational attainments before World War II engendered mass support for nationalist parties. Finally, the effects of World War II propelled the forces of African anticolonialism and nationalism to greater heights by placing Africans on the pathways of eventual decolonization.

SEE ALSO *Ashanti Wars; Decolonization, Sub-Saharan Africa; Maji Maji Revolt, Africa; Mau Mau, Africa; Nationalism, Africa; Nkrumah, Kwame; Pan-Africanism.*

BIBLIOGRAPHY

Boahen, A. Adu, ed. *UNESCO General History of Africa*, Vol. 7: *Africa Under Colonial Domination, 1880–1935*. London: Heinemann, 1985.

Boahen, A. Adu. *African Perspectives on Colonialism*. Baltimore, MD: John Hopkins University Press, 1987.

Cooper, Frederick. *Africa Since 1940: The Past of the Present*. New York: Cambridge University Press, 2002.

Crowder, Michael. *West Africa Under Colonial Rule*. Evanston, IL: Northwestern University Press, 1968.

Falola, Toyin. *Nationalism and African Intellectuals*. Rochester, NY: University of Rochester Press, 2001.

Falola, Toyin. *The Dark Webs: Perspectives on Colonialism in Africa*. Durham, NC: Carolina Academic Press, 2005.

Fanon, Frantz. *A Dying Colonialism*. Translated by Haakon Chevalier. New York: Grove, 1965.

Gann, L. H., and Peter Duignan, eds. *Colonialism in Africa, 1870–1960*, 5 vols. London: Cambridge University Press, 1969–1975.

Hargreaves, John D. *Decolonization in Africa*, 2nd ed. New York: Longman, 1996.

Kwabena Akurang-Parry

APARTHEID

Apartheid (ap-ar-taed) is an Afrikaans word meaning "separation" or literally "apartness." It was the system of laws and policy implemented and enforced by the "white" minority governments in South Africa from 1948 until it was repealed in the 1990s. As the idea of apartheid developed in South Africa, it grew into a tool for racial, cultural, and national survival.

While apartheid became official state policy only in 1948, its social and ideological foundations were laid by the predominantly Dutch settlers in the seventeenth century. Apartheid's body of laws, arising from legislation passed in the years following the 1910 unification, helped define it as a legal institution enforcing separate existence for South Africa's races. Not until the late 1980s did it crumble under pressure from international condemnation and Nelson Mandela's appeal to freedom and democracy in South Africa. Nevertheless, the ultimately failed system was one many Afrikaners *and* Europeans in southern Africa believed in, and it is important to appreciate how this racial and cultural policy developed.

The arrival of the Dutch East India Company (Verenigde Oost-Indische Compagnie, or VOC) at the Cape of Good Hope in 1652 ushered in the first wave of colonial change for the region. As the relationship between Europeans and Africans developed, the VOC came to expect cooperation and subjugation from its Khoikhoi and Khoisan neighbors. Relations had been fairly equal at first, but a growing European population, as well as the requirements of foreign trade, increased demand upon the native Africans for resources, including the Khoikhoi's prized cattle. This demand could not be met, and native ranchers who formerly held contracts with the company were forced into its service. In addition to cattle trading, cattle rustling also occurred on both sides, and the company began fencing off VOC property, physically separating itself from African neighbors and thereby introducing the first racial divisions. Africans were still allowed within company boundaries, but only if they were slaves or there to conduct business.

This process continued to intensify, and over time Africans found themselves increasingly dependent upon the VOC for survival. They adopted European customs and came to be dominated by European ideas and culture. Regardless of these changes and the fact that many settlers intermarried with the Khoikhoi, the Europeans did not consider the Africans to be equal. Moreover, these developing notions of apartheid were not limited to Euro-African relationships. The VOC could be a stern taskmaster. It expected its workers to labor strictly in the interest of company venture. Over time, however, some of the more entrepreneurial employees yearned for a life apart from their service to the VOC. They felt the urge to

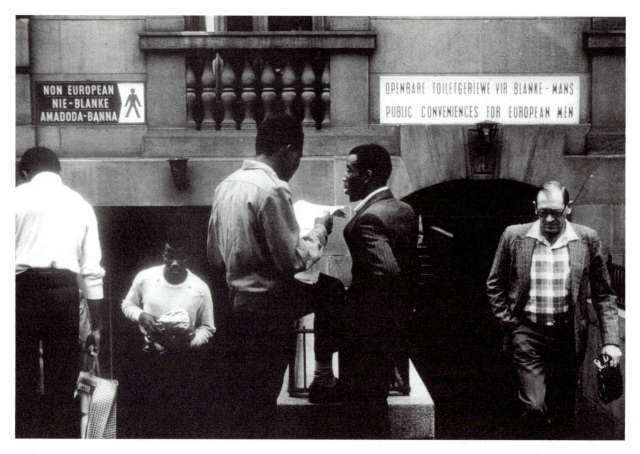

A Segregated Lavatory in South Africa. A group of men stand in front of a lavatory in apartheid-era South Africa with separate entrances for "European" and "non-European" men. © IAN BERRY/MAGNUM PHOTOS. REPRODUCED BY PERMISSION.

settle down and raise families, and while the company allowed them to develop plots of land beyond the company boundaries, the VOC vigorously sought to contract with them for agricultural products. The wealthier *freeburghers*, as these independent farmers were called, managed to win the choicest contracts, leaving their poorer neighbors distrustful of the VOC's methods. Corruption among company officials, and the need to tax and administer the freeburghers, further inflamed tensions already growing between the two camps.

Added to this were the cultural ramifications of the presence of a developing freeburgher community. As more employees and settlers arrived at the Cape, neo-Calvinism took root, enabling the VOC-recognized Dutch Reformed Church to build a local following. Cape Town had developed into a frontier community, with a varied population and myriad ideas. The more devout Calvinists were offended by a culture not aligned with the teachings of the church, and sought an existence separate from the debauchery of the growing town.

This moral conflict, combined with the Calvinist belief in a pure, divinely selected society, influenced

many to leave. Administrative corruption also drove settlers out, and so the Cape settlement spun off new communities. One cannot understate the importance of this need to exist apart from the larger society. People were driven to create lives free from outside oppression in any form. Religion certainly played an important role, but so did this frontier mentality that space and opportunities were unlimited.

Britain's arrival to the region only enhanced this dynamic culture of separateness. After revolutionary France aided Dutch liberals with the creation of the Batavian Republic, Britain moved to protect the Cape from republican Dutch and French annexation. The Cape was an ideal refueling stop on the way to India, and France's acquisition of it would have been a strategic blow to Britain's naval supremacy. Britain's presence was only temporary, however, and the new administrators found it more efficient to maintain the established VOC methods of control. Britain quit the Cape in 1803 after making peace with France, but returned again in 1806 and established itself as the de facto power in the region. A formal assumption of control followed in 1814.

With its reappearance in 1806, Britain introduced its own administrative system, one that proved much more efficient than the VOC's. Tax revenues increased, and as a result more settlers, or *Boers* (farmers), considered themselves to be at the mercy of an oppressive power. The British also introduced a circuit court system (the Black Circuit) that brought justice to the outlying regions, specifically to those settlers who had removed themselves from the confines of Cape Town. It also brought justice to the Africans, who began to bring suit against their employers for wrongdoing.

For many settlers, the circuit court was a violation of their rights. This violation was reaffirmed in 1815 when a farmer, Frederick Bezuidenhout, was charged with assaulting his servant. He resisted arrest and was shot. When his brother attempted to raise a rebellion, the British hanged him and four accomplices. For the Boers this British response was clear proof that they could not be trusted, especially as they had sided with the Africans. Such an act was impossible to fathom for a people who believed in racial purity and superiority. Already the British had aided the Xhosa in their ongoing wars with the Cape settlers. Now it appeared that the authorities were dispensing African justice.

It was in this way that the relationship between the Boers and the British developed throughout the rest of the nineteenth century. Although many Boers left the Cape during the period of the Great Trek (1835–1843), Britain's reach extended into settlements in Natal and north of the Orange River. In the 1850s Britain recognized the establishment of the two Boer republics of the Orange Free State and Transvaal. This did not stop the British from meddling in Boer affairs, however, and by 1902 the opponents had fought two wars, the second of which (1899–1902) cost Britain over £200 million and opened a seemingly permanent rift between the two cultures.

The Boers, by then known also as the Afrikaners, began to refer to a "century of wrong," citing ongoing British oppression, as well as the fresh wounds caused by the war and the British concentration camps. Once again, Afrikaner culture was threatened. However, the British government in Westminster recognized the danger in imposing harsh peace terms upon the Boers. The government wanted a peaceful empire. In addition to paying for the damage caused in the war, therefore, the British put off any discussion of African suffrage and civil rights until self-government was established. At that time, South Africans themselves could decide the suffrage question.

While the Cape maintained its theoretically color-blind franchise law, the Afrikaner territories opted for racial domination. Upon establishing the Union of South Africa in 1910 (a sovereign imperial dominion),

Afrikaners finally were in control of their own destiny. In the coming decades apartheid would become increasingly formalized. Its future depended upon the path that Afrikaner politics and culture would follow, and the 1920s and 1930s witnessed the battle between the moderates and the conservatives for state control.

Jan Smuts, a one-time Transvaal state attorney and commando leader, had become a great friend of Britain. As prime minister, Smuts favored a pragmatic state administration, choosing to work with the empire for the benefit of South Africa. More conservative Afrikaners believed a complete separation from Britain was essential, but the moderates held sway, and South Africa supported Britain in the two World Wars. Many of the conservatives, if not openly hostile to Britain, assumed a position of neutrality, although there were those who identified with National Socialism's racial theories.

The moderation disappeared in 1948 when Daniel Malan's Reunited National Party defeated Smuts's government. Malan appealed to those Afrikaners who believed it was time that South Africa concentrated on its own development. Moreover, Smuts had loosened controls upon the flow of African labor to aid the war effort, and Malan now focused upon the evils of race mixing and the threat to a stable Afrikaner labor force. The new government formally enacted apartheid as state policy in 1948, and there followed a series of legislation targeting the non-white community.

Legislators envisioned a pure society, and drew on notions of unity and racial exclusivity when drafting new apartheid legislation. Laws promoting these principles were not new, for the 1913 Land Act stipulated who could and could not own certain lands. After the 1948 election, however, such legislation provided the new infrastructure of the Afrikaner state. The population was recategorized under the Population Registration Act of 1950, which spawned the issue of a new list of documents, and the creation of official, nationally recognized racial groups (*White, Coloured, Asian, Bantu,* and *Others*). With racial separation came physical separation as well, culminating in the Group Areas Act in 1950. The Group Areas Board identified zones based on race, clearing specific areas of families and entire communities for use by other groups. No longer would different races live in the same neighborhoods.

Movement between towns and cities had been required prior to the Abolition of Passes and Co-ordination of Documents Act (1952), but the new legislation mandated birth, residency, employment, marriage, and travel permits for all Africans. In 1953 the Reservation of Separate Amenities Act ensured that all services available to Afrikaners were also available to the other races. Although "separate but equal" was the theory, the reality was a

TIME

THE WEEKLY NEWSMAGAZINE

SOUTH AFRICA'S MALAN
Does white make right?

Daniel François Malan (1874–1959). *Malan, the prime minister of South Africa from 1948 to 1954 and one of the primary architects of the apartheid system, appeared on the cover of the May 5, 1952, issue of* Time *magazine.* **TIME LIFE PICTURES/GETTY IMAGES. REPRODUCED BY PERMISSION.**

marked difference in the quality and cleanliness of amenities. This reality was made painfully obvious in the Bantu Education Act (1953). The government provided race-specific educational institutions, along with curricula designed to meet racial needs. In the Afrikaner state, necessary topics of study included Afrikaans and Christianity.

Apartheid reached the epitome of its influence under H. F. Verwoerd's leadership (1958–1966). As prime minister, Verwoerd pulled South Africa out of the Commonwealth, declaring the state a republic in 1961. He introduced the Homeland or "Bantustan" system, whereby the South African government recognized self-governing, and eventually fully independent, African states within the nation's borders. Verwoerd took to heart the notion of separateness, and he preached a message of two streams of development, with the Afrikaner and African societies existing equally (in theory) and independently of each other. Often it was the less desirable land that comprised the newly independent African states. In 1971 the government completed the process with the

Black Homeland Citizenship Act, which rescinded homeland residents' South African citizenship.

Although Verwoerd hoped that delegation of civil authority would free Afrikaners from managing millions of Africans, thereby helping to bring about that elusive, purely Afrikaner society, the Bantustans would serve to undercut the government's power in the years to come. Moreover, Verwoerd's death in 1966 signaled the beginning of apartheid's slow decline. While the system still had another two decades of life, it was increasingly undercut by an emerging progressivism.

Apartheid's peak in the 1960s coincided with the dissolution of European empires. The 1960s was the "decade of independence," and apartheid appeared increasingly as a tired, discredited system. Even as African colonies elsewhere in Africa prepared for sovereignty, the white South African government was arresting African nationalists, including Nelson Mandela, and trying them for treason. Nationalist organizations, such as the African National Congress (ANC) and the Pan-Africanist Congress (PAC), espoused socialism, reinforcing the National Party's argument that it was defending the state against militant revolutionary elements. This was an effective argument in a society traditionally concerned with white domination of the labor market. That African nationalism had become an increasingly divided movement in the 1950s and 1960s only made the National Party's job easier. The division, however, also forced a conversation among African nationalists, who began to hone their message in the 1970s.

Apartheid's last hurrah came in the mid-1980s under P. W. Botha (prime minister, 1978–1984; president, 1984–1989). He wavered between a reluctant acceptance that the white-dominated state could not last in its current form, and a last-ditch battle to resurrect apartheid's exclusive culture. Botha faced Afrikaner liberals, African nationalists, and foreign governments on the left, and disenchanted reactionaries on the right. The latter were leaving the National Party to join the Conservatives. Botha held the advantage in the mid-1980s, however, for African nationalists continued to face internal divisions over their movement's direction. Moreover, homeland leaders wanted nothing to do with African nationalism, because it threatened their sovereignty within apartheid South Africa. As the ANC attempted to undercut its opposition, Botha imposed a state of emergency in 1985 to contain a growing African insurgency. Boycotts and work stoppages had the desired effect, however, and, combined with the power of foreign sanctions, began to bring about the collapse of the apartheid government.

President F. W. de Klerk (president, 1989–1994) replaced Botha in 1989 and attempted to introduce limited reforms to improve conditions for minorities without removing Afrikaners from positions of power. Negotiations with the ANC proved that approach to be unrealistic, and de Klerk found himself forced by internal and external pressure to release Nelson Mandela from prison in 1990. As Paul Kruger symbolized the Boers' steadfastness, so did Mandela personify the African struggle. It was Mandela and the ANC, and not de Klerk, who had the political momentum. The last vestiges of apartheid crumbled as the ANC guided the terms of the negotiations. Mandela was both adept and reasonable, seeking not to punish the Afrikaners, but rather to enable Africans to assume their rights as the majority population. Mandela's election to presidency in April 1994 sealed the fate of apartheid.

Although it is identified with white oppression in South Africa, apartheid also defined the Afrikaner struggle to maintain racial and cultural purity in a harsh land. The Boers competed with everyone, even themselves, to live the life in which they believed.

SEE ALSO *Afrikaner; Boer Wars.*

BIBLIOGRAPHY

Beinart, William. *Twentieth-Century South Africa.* Oxford: Oxford University Press, 1994.

De Villiers, Marq. *White Tribe Dreaming: Apartheid's Bitter Roots as Witnessed by Eight Generations of an Afrikaner Family.* New York: Viking Penguin, 1987.

Harvey, Robert. *The Fall of Apartheid: The Inside Story from Smuts to Mbeki,* 2nd ed. New York: Palgrave Macmillan, 2001.

Kruger, Paul. *The Memoirs of Paul Kruger: Four Times President of the South African Republic.* London: T. F. Unwin, 1902; reprint, New York: Negro Universities Press, 1969.

Pakenham, Thomas. *The Boer War.* New York: Avon, 1979.

Shillington, Kevin. *History of Southern Africa.* Harlow, U.K.: Longman, 1992.

Thompson, Leonard. *A History of South Africa,* 3rd ed. New Haven, CT: Yale University Press, 2000.

Jeffrey Lee Meriwether

ARABIA, WESTERN ECONOMIC EXPANSION IN

From the fifteenth century onward, the Arabian Peninsula has attracted significant foreign interest. Its location between large empires first made it a strategic trade route; later, in the twentieth century, the discovery of oil also made the region an important source of wealth. The significance of oil to industrialized countries in the early- and mid-twentieth century turned the Arabian Peninsula, and even the states surrounding it,

into an area of vital importance and thus subjected the region to a great deal of foreign influence. Early on, industrial companies in the West were the only available sources of the technical and mechanical expertise necessary to tap the immense oil reserves; agreements with Western companies, however, led to the companies' increased political influence, to economic ties to Western governments, and to dependence on Western military support. Oil and the connections it brought to Western states have proven to be both a blessing and a curse for the states of the Arabian Peninsula. Oil revenues have allowed countries to develop basic state infrastructure, improve educational opportunities for citizens, and provide healthcare and other services to their populations. At the same time, disagreements over the question of how much Western influence should be allowed in the region have increased tensions within the populations of the Arabian Peninsula.

THE RISE OF EUROPEAN INFLUENCE

The Arabian Peninsula, a landmass situated between Europe, Africa, and Asia, has served as an important commercial hub from as early as the sixth century. Since that time, Arabia acted as a principal center for trade between the Middle East, Africa, China, and Europe. Many of the most luxurious goods in the world passed through the hands of Gulf merchants before reaching their final destinations. The regions within the peninsula produced valuable products as well: Coffee traveled outward from what is now Yemen, and from the eastern coast of Arabia came valuable pearls of the highest quality. Transit trade generated some of the largest revenues in the Arabian Peninsula. Arabian merchants and tribal leaders collected taxes in exchange for safe travel and provided economic services to those traveling through.

In 1498, however, Vasco da Gama discovered the water route around Africa, which subsequently allowed European businessmen to circumvent the expense of traveling through the Ottoman and Persian empires, thus diminishing the Arabian Peninsula's significance as trade center. This development coincided with a commercial revolution in Europe, which gave rise to a mercantilist system and brought European merchants to the forefront of the world economy. The combination of improved travel and increased wealth aided in Europe's expanding economic influence outside of Europe, most notably in India. From the sixteenth century onward, the primary value of Arabia in the eyes of European merchants became its proximity to Indian trading routes.

Beginning in the early sixteenth century, the Portuguese, Dutch, and French each made forays into the Arabian Peninsula. The Portuguese came first, conquering the south and east coasts of the peninsula in order to monopolize trade routes from India. They were quickly forced out by the Safavid Empire in 1602 with the help of the British, who then chartered their East India Company and established a stake in securing the region for themselves. The French and Dutch India Companies soon followed. The subsequent two hundred years were characterized by struggles between the Safavids, Europeans, and local Arab rulers for control over the Arabian coastlands and seas.

The most important contest between the Arabs and Europeans arose out of competition for trade between the British and the Qasimi tribes located in what is now the United Arab Emirates (UAE). The Qawasim (the plural of Qasimi) maintained an extensive fleet of approximately nine hundred ships, which they used for trade and warfare. Throughout the eighteenth century, they maintained important trade connections in the Persian Gulf. As the British East India Company expanded into the north and west of the subcontinent, however, it attempted to extend British power into the Gulf region, bringing it into direct contact with Qasimi traders. War broke out between the two naval powers and continued to rage until 1809, when the British succeeded in occupying Ras al-Khaimeh and severely damaged the Qasimi's maritime strength. This was followed by a similar British expedition to Ras al-Khaimeh in 1820 that obliterated what remained of the Qasimi navy.

As a result of their defeat, the tribes of the southern and eastern Arabian coasts became inextricably linked to the British, both politically and economically. The tribal leaders along the Gulf Coast of Arabia signed a series of treaties with the British in 1820 and 1861. The first treaties were General Treaties of Peace, which established peace between the leading sheikhs of Ras al-Khaimeh, Sharjah, Ajman, Umm al-Qaiwain, Abu Dhabi, Dubai, and Bahrain. Between 1835 and 1853 some of these Gulf States signed peace treaties under British auspices to prevent disruptive warring amongst themselves; after 1853 this peace was made permanent by the Perpetual Maritime Treaty. Bahrain joined the trucial agreement in 1861. From the mid-nineteenth century until the final British withdrawal from the region in 1971, these tribal kingdoms came to be known collectively as the Trucial States.

The port city of Aden, located on the southwestern tip of the peninsula, also came under an indirect form of British rule after the British captured it in 1839. Aden's significance to British security and trade in India increased when the Suez Canal opened thirty years later. In 1937 Aden became the only crown colony on the peninsula, and its status as such lasted until 1944.

Striking Oil in Masjed Soleyman in Persia, circa 1900. *Iran's first oil wells were drilled in the early 1900s in fields near Masjed Soleyman.* © **HULTON-DEUTSCH COLLECTION/CORBIS. REPRODUCED BY PERMISSION.**

Over the course of the second half of the nineteenth century, the British further involved themselves in Gulf affairs. They helped settle a family dispute in Zanzibar that resulted in Oman's separation from that state and made Oman almost entirely dependent upon Great Britain for economic survival. In order to avoid coming under Ottoman domination at the end of the nineteenth and early twentieth centuries, Kuwait and Qatar joined the British Trucial System as well; the British, then, had gained significant influence over the eastern Arabian Peninsula.

The western and interior regions of the Arabian Peninsula, however, remained outside of Western purview until the British supported Sharif Husayn of the Hijaz in his Arab Revolt against the Ottomans in 1915. Husayn failed to garner widespread Arab support following the war and proved incapable of defending his position on the west coast of Arabia against the rising power of the Wahhabi movement led by Abd al-Aziz ibn Sa'ud in the peninsula's interior. In 1924 Sa'ud and the Wahhabis defeated Husayn. Three years later, the newest government in Arabia signed the Treaty of Jiddah with the British, which recognized the Sa'ud family as the

Microsoft Executive Steve Ballmer in Dubai, April 25, 2005. *Ballmer (right), the chief executive of the American software company Microsoft, chats in Dubai with Sheik Mohammad bin Rashid Al Maktoum, the crown prince of Dubai and defense minister of the United Arab Emirates. Microsoft and the Dubai government signed an agreement to develop software applications.* **AP IMAGES. REPRODUCED BY PERMISSION.**

ruler of the Hijaz and the expansive Nejd plateau and affirmed Great Britain's sovereignty in the Gulf.

OIL AND ARABIA

Prior to the discovery of oil in the region, the Arabian economy was quite diversified. Coastal towns and oases that received enough rainfall produced a variety of fruits, vegetables, and cereals; tribes along caravan routes continued to provide goods and services to traveling merchants, or dealt in animal husbandry. The Saudi government also continued to collect substantial revenue from pilgrims traveling to the Hijaz, while fishing, trade, and the pearling industry sustained the states along the Persian Gulf and Indian Ocean.

The collapse of the world economy after 1929, however, had a heavy impact on Arabian economies. Saudi Arabia's currency, which was linked to the British pound in 1931, suffered as a result of the devaluation of the pound. The depression also limited the demand for luxury goods, which nearly devastated the pearling industry in the Gulf; this was further compounded by a concurrent shift in world preference to Japanese cultured pearls. By the early 1930s the only economy not enduring the full effects of the world economic crisis was that of Aden, which managed to buoy its economy through considerable sales of sea salt to the British Empire. The economic historians Roger Owen and Sevket Pamuk noted that in 1937 Aden supplied half of the Empire's demand for that product.

British, American, and Japanese companies mitigated some of the economic pressure in the region, however, when they began expressing interest in oil exploration in several of the Gulf States and Saudi Arabia. With the exception of Kuwait, oil concessions were signed between the individual rulers of the states and one of two companies: Standard Oil Company of California (SOCAL) and the Iraq Petroleum Company (IPC). The Anglo-Persian Oil Company and Gulf Oil made arrangements with the ruling family in Kuwait.

These larger companies then each established regional companies within each of the Arab states. SOCAL in Bahrain formed the Bahrain Petrol Company, for example, and SOCAL's branch in Saudi Arabia became the Arabian American Oil Company (ARAMCO). The IPC formed Petroleum Development Qatar and Petroleum Development Trucial Coast on the Gulf Coast.

The first concessions to oil companies were made in Bahrain in 1930, followed by concessions in Saudi Arabia in 1933, Kuwait in 1934, Qatar in 1935, and Oman in 1937, as well as in four of the smaller Trucial States in 1938 and 1939. Oil concessions took the same general form throughout the region. They provided the ruler with an immediate sum of money as prepayment of initial royalties, an annual fee until oil was discovered, and subsequent royalty payments for the duration of the concessionary agreement; in exchange, the company received exclusive exploratory and extraction-related rights. These arrangements were intended to remain in effect for lengthy periods of time, sometimes up to seventy-five years, as was the case in Kuwait and Qatar.

The bulk of the large oil discoveries in the region came at the end of the 1930s, just on the verge of World War II. As a result, Saudi Arabia was the only country to develop oil extraction facilities before the war, and it was able to collect large revenues by 1939. Kuwait began to reap the benefits of its oil deposits in the late 1940s and early 1950s, and Qatar began exporting oil in 1949; Abu Dhabi, Dubai, Ras al-Khaimeh, and Oman had a later start, only beginning to export oil in the 1960s. The presence of oil raised the level of the Arabian Peninsula's significance in Western eyes, particularly for the United States. In the 1940s the U.S. government began providing Saudi Arabia with economic subsidies, which continued to grow throughout the decade. By 1945 the United States had applied pressure upon Great Britain to reduce their subsidies to Saudi Arabia by half. When the British government withdrew from its last bases in the Trucial States in 1971, the United States became a hegemonic political influence, which it remains at the start of the twenty-first century.

Even with the rapid influx of wealth, however, the Arab states were not yet capable of providing the necessary infrastructure to support the large engineering projects and great number of employees that oil extraction projects required. In the case of Saudi Arabia, ARAMCO undertook the building of roads, hospitals, schools, and other basic public services as well as irrigation projects to provide food. These activities bound some of the most basic elements of everyday life to the oil companies.

Control over oil production and oil prices remained in the hands of Western oil companies throughout the 1930s and well into the 1960s. In the 1950s the British,

American, and Anglo-Dutch oil companies produced around 90 percent of the world's oil outside of the Soviet Bloc. The predominance of Western oil companies in the region elicited criticism from other Arab states in the Middle East that was inspired by the radical anti-Western ideologies of the 1960s. In response to this pressure, several of the states in the Gulf established national oil companies, such as the Kuwait National Petroleum Company and the Saudi General Petroleum and Mineral Organization. These new companies loosened some of the hold that American and British companies in particular maintained over oil production, but Western-based companies maintained firm holds on the majority of the oil production.

They also regulated oil prices internally rather than by following market forces. From 1951 through 1971 these companies paid a fixed price, between $1.75 and $1.80 per barrel, to the rulers in Saudi Arabia and the Gulf. In the 1970s, however, the oil-producing companies were able to gain some control over oil prices through their membership in the Organization of Petroleum Exporting Companies (OPEC). OPEC had been established in 1960 as a multinational organization designed to coordinate oil production and prices especially through the setting of production quotas, though it did not become an important player in the oil market until the 1970s. Kuwait, Saudi Arabia, Qatar, and the United Arab Emirates (formed in 1971 from the lesser Trucial States) all joined the organization. Arab membership in the organization had some extreme consequences for the world oil market in the 1970s. The Arab-Israeli War in 1973 led Arab oil-producing companies to boycott sales to Western countries that had supported Israel during the war, causing oil prices to rise to more than $11 per barrel. The revolution in Iran produced similar consequences, and oil prices rose to $32 per barrel. Since that time oil prices have remained relatively stable, with the exception of price increases caused by the two American wars against Iraq in 1990 and 2003.

WESTERN INFLUENCE AND ITS CONSEQUENCES

In spite of its oil wealth, the Arabian Peninsula remains heavily dependent on Western powers for its economic and defense needs. The states in the Gulf and Saudi Arabia have been unable to institute effective defenses alone, forcing them to rely on British, and later, American governments for their military needs. The states in the Arabian Peninsula have, at times, spent more than 10 percent of their GDP (Gross Domestic Product) on military equipment and bases. Their attempts to build up defenses have also been supplemented with an increasing number of permanently stationed foreign troops numbering between the thousands and tens of thousands. American troops used military facilities in Bahrain following the Iran-Iraq war, and maintained air bases in Qatar, Oman, and the UAE. American military presence in Saudi Arabia and Kuwait has grown exponentially following the Desert Storm action in 1990 and the 2003 American invasion of Iraq. U.S. military involvement in the region has led to domestic instability in many of the states on the peninsula. Some of this can be attributed to resentment over American support for Israel. The two American wars in Iraq were also immensely unpopular and contributed to strained relations between some regional governments and the United States.

The states of the Arabian Peninsula are similarly reliant upon economic investment both in and from the West. Some experts have noted that 60 percent of Saudi Arabia's investments abroad are tied up in U.S. ventures. International economic development agencies, such as the United Nations Development Programme and the World Bank Organization, have also pushed the countries in the Arabian Peninsula to improve their governmental and business climates to bring in more foreign investments.

Attracting diverse foreign investments has been especially important for countries like the United Arab Emirates (UAE), which is due to run out of oil in the early part of the twenty-first century. Many of the new development projects in the region have remained linked to U.S. and Western businesses. Dubai, the second-largest emirate in the UAE has begun to develop economic strategies in technology-related fields in order to maintain economic growth following the depletion of its reserves. In 2000 the ruler launched the Dubai Internet City, a free-trade zone and e-commerce center that provides office buildings and inexpensive employees, as well as medical and education facilities. The project has succeeded in attracting large business clients, such as Microsoft, IBM, CISCO, and Canon, among others. Most of these companies are based out of the United States and Europe.

As economic and political relations between the West and the states in the Arabian Peninsula have increased, so has Western scrutiny of the region via the media. American movies and news coverage have raised questions in the West about the legitimacy of Arab governments in the Gulf region and about women's rights, among other topics, and have often presented skewed or exaggerated images of the Arab societies. Such representations, combined with the visible presence of Western economic, military, and even popular culture in the Arabian Peninsula, have generated resentment and frustration among Arab governments, which continue to balance their economic interests and social and cultural values with the West's increasing demands for reform.

SEE ALSO *British Colonialism, Middle East; Oil.*

BIBLIOGRAPHY

"Dubai Internet City." Dubai Internet City. Available from http://www.dubaiinternetcity.com.

Gelvin, James L. *The Modern Middle East: A History*. New York: Oxford University Press, 2005.

Kelly, J. B. *Britain and the Persian Gulf, 1795–1880*. Oxford: Clarendon, 1968.

Kelly, J. B. *Arabia, the Gulf, and the West: A Critical View of the Arabs and Their Oil Policy*. New York: Basic Books, 1980.

Owen, Roger. *The Middle East in the World Economy, 1800–1914*, 2nd ed. New York: I. B. Tauris, 1993.

Owen, Roger, and Sevket Pamuk. *A History of Middle East Economies in the Twentieth Century*. Cambridge, MA: Harvard University Press, 1999.

Qasimi, Sultan Muhammad al-. *The Myth of Arab Piracy in the Gulf*, 2nd ed. New York: Routledge, 1988.

Richards, Alan, and John Waterbury. *A Political Economy of the Middle East: State, Class, and Economic Development*. Boulder, CO: Westview, 1998.

Rodenbeck, Max. "Time Travellers: A Survey of the Gulf." *The Economist* 362 (March 21, 2002): 3–18.

Yergin, Daniel. *The Prize: The Epic Quest for Oil, Money, and Power*. New York: Simon and Schuster, 1991.

Zahlan, Rosemarie Said. *The Making of the Modern Gulf States: Kuwait, Bahrain, Qatar, the United Arab Emirates, and Oman*. Lebanon: Ithaca Press, 1998.

Kristi N. Barnwell

ART, EUROPEAN

All empires in human history have glorified their victories and triumphs in the visual arts—painting, sculpture, and architecture. The Egyptians, Persians, Greeks, Romans, and others have raised monuments to their imperial cities and states. Republican and imperial Rome, the great exemplar of the later European empires, raised statues, arches, and columned monuments to glorify military victories, conquering emperors, and the city and empire itself. Romans also created triumphal paintings to depict historical events and celebrate victories, conquests, and the cult of the emperors. In their imperial expansion, the Romans came to appreciate, expropriate, and copy the art of peoples and cultures they conquered. The Romans were particularly influenced by Greek sculpture and architecture. Relief sculpture carved into triumphal arches, victory columns, and statues of emperors glorified both the imperial throne and the empire. The Arch of Titus, dedicated in 81 CE in Rome, immortalized the successful conquest of Jerusalem in the year 70. The relief panel, *Spoils from the Temple of Jerusalem*, showing Roman troops carrying trumpets, the menorah, and the golden table from the temple, dramatizes one of the most important motivations of all empires.

One of the characteristics of premodern empires around the world was their tendency to assimilate the more advanced cultures of peoples and civilizations they conquered. The European empires of the early modern and modern ages, on the other hand, showed little interest in or appreciation of the cultures and arts of their subject peoples and, indeed, the rest of the world. In time this would change. By the late nineteenth and throughout the twentieth century, many artists in the Western world would become captivated by the vernacular and formal arts of the Americas, Africa, the Middle East, and Asia, and would, as a result, transform the visual arts of the West.

European imperialism and colonialism influenced Western art in three fundamental ways. First, the imperial powers, monarchs, and patrons created paintings, sculpture, and architecture to glorify their expansionist, imperialist, and idealistic objectives. Second, the expansion of European power and settlement around the world spread European traditions of painting, sculpture, and architecture to colonies in the Americas, Africa, and Asia. Finally, European trade and contact with the rest of the world brought non-European luxury goods, aesthetic values, and arts to the West—as well as Western artists to the colonies—which gradually came to influence, in various ways, the course of Western art.

Portuguese architecture began to reflect its overseas expansion in the reign of King Manuel I, "the Fortunate" (1469–1521), creating what has come to be called the Manueline style of architectural ornamentation. This *estylo manuelina* incorporated nautical and maritime motifs, such as sea monsters, shells, nautical rope, and much else. One of the monuments of the Manueline style is the Jerónimos Monastery in Lisbon, which was built to glorify and commemorate the voyage of Vasco da Gama (ca. 1469–1524) to India. The sumptuous main entrance features several carved figures, including one of Henry the Navigator (1392–1460), the royal prince who promoted the African voyages of discovery and trade in the fifteenth century. The Jerónimos Monastery came to hold the tomb of Gama, as well as that of Luís de Camões (ca. 1524–1570), the great national poet of Portugal's age of discovery.

The Spanish Empire began its self-glorification with a painting by Ajejo Fernañdez (1475–1545), *The Virgin of the Navigators* (ca. 1535), a work designed for the altarpiece of the chapel of the Casa de Contratación (the House of Trade) in Seville. The painting depicts a devotional image of the Virgin Mary in which the Madonna shelters Spain's Indies fleet and its great navigators—Christopher Columbus (1451–1506), Ferdinand Magellan (1480–1521), and one of the Pinzón brothers, as well as King Ferdinand (1452–1516) and indistinct Indians and Africans. The Virgin of the Navigators is standing astride the new Iberian Atlantic world. It is a painting that indicates the success of Spain's imperial mission and the glory of Spain's Holy Faith, *La Santa Fé*, with the substantial enlargement of Christendom.

During Spain's great age of imperial glory in the sixteenth century, there were few civic monuments and little statuary sponsored by royal patronage. The portal of the University of Salamanca (completed in 1529) raised the imperial arms of Charles V (1500–1558) beside those of Ferdinand and Isabella (1451–1504). The Royal Monastery of San Lorenzo de El Escorial of King Philip II (1527–1598), a religious retreat and royal palace, the greatest architectural project of the age, demonstrated the grandeur and power of the Spanish Habsburgs. Philip had his throne room decorated with the beautiful Renaissance maps of the Spanish realms in Europe and the Americas taken from Abraham Ortelius's (1527–1598) *Theatrum orbis terrarum* (Theater of the World, 1588), an atlas of hand-colored engravings.

Two centuries later, the Royal Palace in Madrid was used as one of the best stages to glorify the monarchy and empire. In the throne room, the ceiling fresco, *The Wealth and Benefits of the Spanish Monarchy under Charles III* by the Venetian artist Giovanni Battista Tiepolo (1696–1770), presented one of the great allegorical works of European art. This room was the center of the palace and the symbolic center of the empire: the various Spanish imperial possessions were visible from the throne. This fresco shows the loading of a ship with the treasures of the American continent, and in the foreground two Native Americans are shown throwing themselves in front of the ship, symbolizing the conquest of the Americas by Spain. On the exterior façade of the Royal Palace stand sculptures of the Inca and Aztec emperors—Atahualpa and Moctezuma—captured by Spanish conquerors in the early sixteenth century as a prelude to the conquest and destruction of their realms. Philip V (1683–1746) commanded the erection of these large statues of the vanquished to stand as symbols not only of the power of Spain but also of the new Age of Enlightenment. These sculptures presented these Native American emperors as great and honorable kings, worthy to stand alongside the statues of Spanish kings.

In the mid-seventeenth century, the Dutch Republic expressed its rising power and wealth in the Amsterdam Town Hall (Het Stadhuis), one of the largest architectural undertakings of the early modern era. The exterior statuary on the roof pediments showed, on one side, the Dutch Atlas bearing the weight of the globe and, on the other, Amsterdam receiving the tribute of the four continents. This latter allegory, one of the classic images of the age of European colonialism, represented the non-European world naturally subordinate to Europe, and the world's wealth and resources the inevitable fruit of European commerce and empire. In the greatest room in the greatest building of the Dutch Republic, the Burgerzaal (the "town hall" or public gallery), the Dutch Republic was placed in the center of a marble-inlaid world map that covered the entire floor. Not unlike the other expansionist European empires, even the modest and mercantile Dutch were moved to "acts of elaborate self-congratulation" (1997, p. 223), as the historian Simon Schama put it, in ceremonies, architecture, sculpture, and—indeed—most of the visual arts.

During the Dutch "golden age," the seventeenth century, Dutch painters created a substantial body of marine art, sea paintings, that depicted naval battles, great fleets, specific ships, and everyday shipping and commerce. Ludolf Backhuysen's *The "Eendracht" and a Dutch Fleet of Men-of-War Before the Wind* (early 1670s) gives a heroic representation of the Dutch fleet with its flagship, the *Eendracht* (Unity). Historical paintings of the sea battles with the Spanish and the English, returning fleets from the East Indies, and great ships of battle were extremely popular among patrons and public institutions in the Netherlands and reflected and promoted Dutch pride in naval and commercial preeminence.

The British similarly glorified their empire in murals, history paintings, sculpture, architecture, and even royal coaches. In the Commissioner's House of the Royal Navy at Chatham Dockyard is a large painting on the ceiling of the main staircase. Completed around 1705, this painting shows Mars receiving a crown of shells from Neptune, while in the foreground stand figures that symbolize Peace, Plenty, Justice, and Charity. The figure of a majestic Neptune was significant to onlookers of the age because it was a symbol of the Royal Navy's mastery of the sea. More than a century later, Queen Victoria's (1819–1901) residence on the Isle of Wight, Osborne House, also had an allegorical fresco above the main staircase. William Dyce's *Neptune Resigning the Empire of the Seas to Britannia* (1847) reveals the figure of "Britannia" receiving the crown of the sea from Neptune. Britannia, and Britain's seaborne empire, is also accompanied by three figures that both produced and were benefits of global empire: Industry, Commerce, and Navigation.

Beginning in the mid-eighteenth century, the British created imperial history painting, a tradition that portrayed and glorified the great and symbolic events in the creation of the British Empire. From Benjamin West's *The Death of General Wolf* (1770), to Arthur William Devis's *Death of Nelson* (1805), and *The Death of (1844–1925) General Gordon, Khartoum, 26 January*

1885 by G. W. Joy, artists created a cult of heroism that glorified and promoted patriotic imperialism. Empires and their rulers found myriad and varied ways to glorify empire. King George III (1738–1820), for example, had England's best artisans make one of the most remarkable royal coaches in the age of horse-drawn vehicles. This colossal four-ton coach topped by three gilded cherubs symbolized the British kingdoms of English, Scotland, and Ireland. Over the four wheels were gilded sea gods that suggested that Britannia ruled the four oceans of the world. "It was as though the very grandeur, wealth, and weight of the British Empire," wrote historian David McCullough, referring to this great golden coast pulled by eight horses and accompanied by six footmen, "were rolling past" (2005, p. 4).

During the first three centuries of European empire and colonialism, the imperial monarchies, metropoles, and elite patrons employed the visual arts to justify and glorify empire. Imperial themes, particularly nonclassical and nonmythological imperial themes, or references to oversea colonies, however, were relatively few and unimportant. France's Louis XIV (1638–1715), the "Sun King"—Le Roi Soleil—perhaps the greatest patron of art in European history, collected Renaissance sculpture and paintings of classical legends and history, sponsored frescos of the glories of the king himself, ordered statuary of the ancient gods and Roman emperors, and so much more. Very little of this enormous artistic patronage and creation had to do directly with French overseas imperialism and colonialism.

Louis XIV's commission and construction beginning in 1678 of the Palais de Versailles, an enormous complex of palaces and gardens, was Bourbon France's statement of grandeur much like El Escorial was the symbol of the power and glory of Philip II's Spain. The king's chief minister warned that such construction, which by the mid-1680s required 36,000 laborers and some 6,000 horses, would bankrupt the treasury. Louis continued to build, however, and filled the palace with the finest tapestries of France; hundreds of specially commissioned paintings; dozens and dozens of statues, busts, great vases, and other kinds of sculpture; and thousands of articles made of silver and gold, many of these inscribed and struck with the symbols of the king. The peerless Hall of Mirrors (the Grand Galerie, also called the Galerie des Glaces due to the seventeen windows and seventeen arched mirrors) was 73 meters (239.5 feet long), and on the ceiling Charles Le Brun (1619–1690) painted the mythological symbols of the triumphs of France over Spain, the Netherlands, and Germany. By the early eighteenth century, Versailles and its gardens became the model for royal and noble palaces from Moravia to England. "Not since the extension of ancient Latin culture through Western Europe," wrote Will and Ariel

PHILHELLENISM

Philhellenism, literally, the "love of Greek culture," is an intellectual movement rooted in a growing interest in classical art and architecture that developed in Europe and England during the late 1700s. This Neoclassicism, fueled by the discovery of the ruins at Pompeii and the arrival of the Parthenon's Elgin Marbles in London, was also influenced by Jean Jacques Barthelemy's 1788 *Travels of Anacharsis the Younger in Greece*, a fictional account of an ancient traveler that captured the popular imagination and spread philhellenism from France to Great Britain and greater Europe.

To its adherents, philhellenism embodied the egalitarian ideologies of the failed French revolution. It was inspired by an idealized vision of the Ancient Greeks as the founders of Western civilization. Ignoring the historical record, philhellenists transformed the ancients into a free people who espoused equality. This ideal, while not substantiated by fact, melded with Enlightenment philosophies and the political and social goals of both the French and American revolutions. As a political force, it was pushed underground as the restoration of the French monarchy following the Battle of Waterloo crushed liberal zeal in France, and elsewhere. It reemerged, however, as the suppression of other newly radicalized populations throughout the Old World fomented rebellion. The uprising of the Greek people against their Ottoman rulers was particularly inspiring to Napoléon's defeated followers throughout France, as well as to that country's student population. Meanwhile, as a romanticized ideal, philhellenism entered the culture of the prosperous merchant class via literature, clothing styles, and the clean, classically influenced lines of Empire furniture.

The culmination of the philhellenic ideal, and the vision that most inspired philhellenism's artistic and intellectual adherents, was the goal of establishing a Greek state on the same land where stood the ruins of the Parthenon. Though the Greeks' unsuccessful uprising against the Ottoman Turks in 1770 had sparked some creative passion, their 1821 revolt prompted intellectuals such as British writer Lord Byron to call for governments to support the Greek independence movement. In his writings, Byron depicted Greece as a "sad relic" of an ancient culture and the Greek revolutionaries as "primitive savages" in need of help from Western society to overthrow the tyrannical Turks. Viewed in hindsight, the philhellenic movement also reflected the patronizing racism of the age; the Greeks, viewed as early Europeans, were thought of as fighting off the despotism of a non-white oppressor; their victory could only come through the aid of white Europeans.

In Great Britain, Byron so strongly influenced public sentiment that the British government overlooked its longstanding support for Ottoman claims and sided with the rebel forces in Greece. European public opinion also sided heavily with the rebels, particularly in larger cities. The British government contributed financial aid, as well as volunteers from among philhellenism's more zealous followers, and influenced continental European powers to do likewise. Ironically, Byron, who joined the Greek insurgents in 1923, succumbed to marsh fever and died at Missolonghi, in central Greece, a year later.

Durant, "had history seen a cultural conquest so rapid and complete" (1963, p. 103).

Western Europeans, of course, did not visually ignore their overseas colonies. Princes, merchants, and ordinary readers expressed a great interest about the "New Worlds" that mariners, conquerors, traders, and settlers were finding, colonizing, and writing about. The first books about the Americas, Africa, and Asia were often illustrated with woodcuts and then engravings. The sixteenth-century engraver Theodor de Bry (1528–1598) became one of the most important popularizers of the European discoveries and conquests of the Americas. He shaped, to a considerable extent, how Europeans first viewed and understood the New World of America. De Bry, however, who never traveled to the Americas, used classical and Renaissance models to create his American landscapes, buildings, and native body types. In 1590 de Bry published twenty-eight engravings of North America taken from the drawings and watercolors of the English artist and governor John White, who was one of the settlers of the Roanoke colony. White's original watercolors, unquestionably the most skilled and sensitive renderings of Native Americans to that time, were not discovered until the early eighteenth century. White's artistry, however, helped de Bry produce the best engravings of his career.

In Dutch Brazil in the 1630s and 1640s, Governor Count Johan Maurits van Nassau-Siegen (1604–1679) brought two exceedingly talented painters from the Netherlands. Frans Post (1612–1680) painted Brazilian landscapes that pictured plantations, native villages, and the lushness of American tropical nature. The paintings of Albert Eckhout (ca. 1610–1665), following those of John White, provided the most detailed and realistic representations of Native Americans. Eckhout's *Dance of the Tapuya Indians* (ca. 1640), one of twenty-four paintings of Native Americans and Africans that have resided in Copenhagen since 1654, contributed to the European concept of the exotic savage. Eckhout's three portraits of an African ambassador, on the other hand, show a dignified, if somewhat sad, black African dressed in the finest clothing available to European noblemen of the age.

The paintings of Post and Eckhout began a European tradition of natural history drawing and painting by artist-scientists. Hans Sloane (1660–1753), "Fellow of the College of Physicians and Secretary of the Royal-Society [for promoting natural knowledge]," made a voyage to Jamaica in the late seventeenth century and employed a local artist to illustrate specimens of plants, fishes, birds, and insects. Paul Hermann (ca. 1646–1695), a doctor for the Dutch East Indies Company in Ceylon in the 1670s, drew detailed pictures of native plants, some animals, and illustrations of a Dutch toddy palm plantation (an enterprise that produced the alcoholic "toddy" made from the sap of a palm tree). A German artist and naturalist, Maria Merian (1647–1717), spent two years (1699–1701) in Surinam observing nature, which allowed her, when she returned to Amsterdam, to create sixty colored engravings of butterflies and moths and a few frogs, snakes, and one incredible caiman, shown biting a large coral snake.

The voyages in the Pacific in the late eighteenth century by the English explorer Captain James Cook (1728–1779) produced thousands of drawings and paintings by the artists and draftsmen who accompanied these expeditions. The three principal artists produced landscapes, coastal profiles, depictions of plants and animals, and "'ethnographic" (that is, realistic) and sympathetic portraits of the indigenous peoples of the Pacific. There were, of course, many more examples of Europeans drawing and painting what was to them the new, the exotic, and the previously unknown nature and peoples of their overseas colonies and trading posts. This extended and extensive intrusion into other parts of the world gave Europeans images not only of different peoples and cultures, but also images of different kinds of adornment, design, beauty, and aesthetic values. But neither indigenous arts nor any European representation of them, from the sixteenth to the nineteenth century, appeared to have the slightest influence on the evolution of the visual arts in Western Europe during these centuries.

When Europeans established overseas trading enclaves and territorial colonies they carried their broader Western and specific regional and national cultures with them. An important part of this cultural transmission included the visual arts, as seen, perhaps most significantly, in religious architecture, sculpture, painting, and decoration; secular architecture in governmental and private palaces; and historical painting, among many other activities.

The Portuguese and the Spanish built chapels, churches, and cathedrals in the Americas, Africa, and Asia. By the early seventeenth century, estimated one cleric, the Spanish had built some seventy thousand chapels and churches throughout their territories in the Americas. This enormous building campaign, which also included many thousands of impressive secular public buildings in the new and well-ordered towns and cities of Spanish America, constituted one of the great imperial projects in human history. The rapid and widespread imposition of Spanish architecture of very large, dramatically positioned, and impressively ornamented buildings signified and broadcast to the colonized natives, as well as to colonial settlers, the religious, cultural, and technological superiority and power of Spain and Europe.

Although the designs were European, the lack of sufficient numbers of European craftsmen required the missionaries to train and employ Native American, African, and Asian craftsmen, sculptors, gilders, painters, and other skilled workmen to do almost all of the work. The Portuguese carried the Manueline style of architecture to Angola, Mozambique, and India. In the Portuguese Indian port of Goa, Hindu artists and artisans for several decades painted and sculpted Christian images for the chapels and churches of the city. Their likenesses of Christ, Mary, and the saints, however, had too much Indian "flavor" for the Portuguese. By 1546, the king ordered the viceroy to end the practice of using Hindu craftsmen to make Christian art. The archbishop of Goa, equally unhappy, forbade Christians in his province to commission or purchase religious art from Hindu artists. In the interior of Brazil, however, ivory crucifixes from Goa made by Hindu craftsmen found their way into the cathedral of São Luís do Maranhão.

In Spanish America, native craftsmen—in fact, native artists—injected pre-Columbian motifs, symbols, and stylistic conventions in the murals they painted, the altar screens they gilded, and the church façades they sculpted. In the Augustinian convent in Tlayacapan, Morelos (Mexico), for example, the mural painting is decorated here and there with scenes of Aztec warriors and other preconquest images. The façades of early missionary churches and monasteries often had pre-Columbian motifs as part of the overall decoration. In New Spain, this artistic syncretism did not survive the sixteenth century. In Spanish South America, on the other hand, it flourished in the seventeenth and eighteenth centuries.

Anonymous pupils of the Indian painter Quispe Tito (1611–1681), an influential native artist who adopted European fresco painting, produced paintings in colonial Peru in the second half of the seventeenth century that fused Spanish and Inca artistic styles, symbols, and motifs. The fresco *Corpus Christi Procession with the Parishioners of Santa Ana* (ca. 1660) in Cuzco, Peru, shows a Corpus Christi procession led by an Indian leader dressed in royal Inca costume. A little more than half a century later, the Indian architect José Kondori constructed churches in the great silver mining boom city of Potosí. In the façade of his baroque San Lorenzo Church (ca. 1728), one finds an Inca princess and Andean half-moons.

In Portuguese Brazil, Antônio Francisco Lisboa (1738–1814), known as O Aleijadinho, "the Little Cripple," became the most influential sculptor and architect of the Brazilian baroque. This mulatto artist, the son of a Portuguese architect and an African slave, designed, built, and decorated a number of chapels, churches, and convents in the gold-rich province of Minas Gerais in the second half of the eighteenth century. Some of his significant commissions include the Church of São Francisco de Assis in Ouro Preto (1776), the church of the Ordem Terceira do Carmo de Sabará, and sculptures on the façade of the church of the Ordem Terceira de São Francisco in Ouro Prèto. Beginning in the 1770s, this skilled artist and artisan began to suffer from a debilitating disease that increasingly left him crippled. In spite of this disability, Aleijadinho produced life-size, cedarwood sculptures of scenes of the passion and death of Christ during the 1790s. Undoubtedly the most extraordinary works of art created by this remarkable colonial artist are the soapstone statues of the twelve prophets of the Old Testament that lead up to the Sanctuary of Bon Jesus do Matozinho in Congonhas do Campo (1800–1803). With a chisel bound to his nearly-paralyzed fingers, Aleijadinho produced figures that have a gothic, expressionistic appeal and appearance. "These impressive works," wrote the art historian Edward J. Sullivan, "are among the most significant sculptures of the Western Baroque-Rococo tradition" (2001, p. 238).

The West had always desired some of the decorative arts of specific other civilizations, although this interest was often a craving for rare and exotic "crafts" rather than a true appreciation of such work as genuine art. Western markets had long demanded Chinese porcelain (porcelaneous ceramics), lacquer wares (with a varnish made from the sap of the lac tree), and cloisonné enamel (fired enamel designs on copper cups, vases, and boxes), as well as works of jade, glass, and silk. Aristocratic, wealthy, and eventually even gentry households throughout Europe and the Americas were considered bereft if they did not possess at least one set of "chinaware" for serving meals and decorating the house.

By the early eighteenth century, a great many Chinese, Korean, and Vietnamese craftsmen were manufacturing *chinoiserie*—all things Chinese—for the European market. Europeans also came to demand all manner of Indian textiles—chintz, calicoes, muslins, silks, madras, and many others—as well as richly carved ivories, inlaid chests, cupboards, tables, and other kinds of Oriental furniture. From the Middle East, Europeans exported carpets made in Turkey and Cairo, as well as Central Asia.

In the mid and late eighteenth century, European artists began, more than ever before, to travel to the many and often quite distant outposts of their overseas colonies to record, represent, and interpret the landscapes, architecture, peoples, and customs of the non-European world and bring these images before the connoisseurs and public at home. The French artist Anne-Louis Girodet (1767–1824) wrote in 1817: "Painting and navigation in changing the face of the world necessarily had a powerful influence on the destiny of the arts. The first did so in ceaselessly extending the sphere of ideas; the second, in drawing further and further back the limits of the horizon." He noted that the restless artist sought foreign encounters: "The artist's restless curiosity compelled him courageously to sail from one pole to another in order to observe the foreign faces, extraordinary countries, and singular costumes of the most savage peoples" (quoted in Grigsby 2002, p. 3).

The European images of Surinam, India, Greece, Egypt and North Africa, Sudan, South Africa, and elsewhere created in the late eighteenth century and throughout the nineteenth century presented no single imperialist discourse about the triumph of the West and the inferiority or even barbarism of non-Europeans. Many works of art, of course, were both condescending and triumphalist. Taken as a whole, however, European artistic representations of Native Americans, Africans, East Indians, and other "others" were ambivalent and complex. Many artists, indeed, many of the best artists, depicted slaves and chieftains as dignified and noble individuals. The historian C. A. Bayly suggests one motive for artists: "They seemed to long for a past which had now sadly become 'the other'" (2004, p. 378). Appreciation of "the other" as a subject for art, for whatever reason, however, did not lead to any serious appreciation of non-European arts, at least not for many decades.

As Europe, and the European world of settler colonies and independent states, increasingly came into contact

Corpus Christi Procession, Eighteenth Century, Peru. This painting is an example of colonial art in the Americas. THE ART ARCHIVE/MUSEO PEDRO DE OSMA LIMA/MIREILLE VAUTIER. REPRODUCED BY PERMISSION.

with the colors, motifs, and styles of African, Asian, and Polynesian art, particularly after 1880, artists and the avant-garde among them first began to be influenced by, and incorporate elements of, non-European arts. During the last and most intense period of decolonization in the 1950s and 1960s, art museums in the cities of the West all had important collections of African, Middle Eastern, Chinese, Japanese, Native American, and other non-European arts. Western art itself, furthermore, was extremely eclectic, giving little more respect to classical or Renaissance traditions than to Maori, Bushman, Aztec, Inuit, Japanese, or other non-Western artistic traditions.

The late eighteenth century saw a new and serious European interest in the Orient and all things Oriental. By this time, Europeans were becoming fascinated, if not obsessed in some circles, with Oriental despotism, Oriental eroticism, Oriental exoticism, and other "isms" that seemed so alien yet interesting and appealing to the rising bourgeois culture. British artists had begun to draw, etch, and paint the scenery, peoples, and customs of India. One of these customs, the infamous sati (the Hindu practice by which a widow incinerated herself with the corpse of her husband), became a popular subject of artists in India. Johann Zoffany's *Sacrifice of a Hindoo Widow on the Funeral Pile of Her Husband* (ca. 1780), and many similar such pictures, suggested the barbarism of non-European traditions and "superstitions."

Thomas Daniell (1749–1840) and William Daniell (1769–1837) traveled through India between 1785 and 1794 and, upon their return, produced 140 rich color aquatints. Between 1795 and 1808 the Daniells published six volumes of *Oriental Scenery*, with pictures of Indians antiquities, exotic architecture, and spellbinding landscapes that enchanted and fascinated Britons.

The organized and popular campaigns in Britain and France to abolish the Atlantic slave trade, and plantation slavery itself, inspired artists to reveal and portray this terrible and violent outgrowth of Western colonialism. The English radical, poet, and artist William Blake (1757–1827) illustrated the raw nature of American slavery in the Dutch plantation colony of Surinam in John Gabriel Stedman's *Narrative of a Five Years Expedition against the Revolted Negroes of Surinam* (1796, 1st ed.). Using Stedman's drawings and narration, Blake engraved sixteen plates for this book. He did not flinch in portraying the torture of African men and women in various and cruel ways. His engraving of the sadistic *Flagellation of a Female Samboe Slave* shows a naked young black woman tied by both arms above her head to a tree. She had received two hundred lashes for the "crime," according to Stedman, of refusing her master's "romantic embraces."

Anne-Louis Girodet in 1797 exhibited *C Jean-Baptiste Bellêy, Ex-Representative of the Colonies*, a portrait of the African deputy, the first representative from Saint-Domingue (now Haiti) to the French National Assembly. Citizen Belly, unlike most abolitionist images of the 1790s, is presented standing, not kneeling, impeccably dressed, a dignified French gentleman. To enhance the power of the image, the artist had Belly lean against the bust of the *philosophe* Guillaume-Thomas Raynal (1713–1796), one of the most vociferous critics in Enlightenment Europe of racial slavery and European colonialism.

Napoléon Bonaparte's (1769–1821) invasion of Egypt (1798–1799) with his "Army of the Orient" initiated a new wave, indeed the "high age of European imperialism," in the nineteenth century. Although the military campaign ultimately was a failure, the cultural, scientific, and artistic reverberation of the expedition continued for decades. Napoléon took more than 160 scientists, linguists, naturalists, architects, artists, and other experts to study, record, collect, and understand ancient and modern Egypt. The Army of the Orient produced victories against the ruling Ottomans but ended up surrendering to the British. Nevertheless, the Egyptian campaign became an integral part of the myth of the rise of the emperor. Antoine-François Callet (1741–1823) in *Allegory of the Eighteenth of Brumaire* (1801) includes a symbolic Egyptian among the images that chart the rising glory of Napoléon.

Antoine-Jean Gros (1771–1835), an official artist in an earlier military campaign, became one of the most important mythmakers of early nineteenth-century France. His *Battle of Nazareth* (1801) shows an outnumbered French army fighting, and eventually defeating, the Turks in Syria in 1799. In this painting, as is true for most of the paintings of the Egyptian campaign, the viewer is presented with a genuine clash of civilizations. The outnumbered yet orderly and courageous French soldiers are confronted with wild, murderous Muslim Turks who decapitated their wounded enemies. Both Gros in *Battle of Aboukir* (1806) and Louis-François Lejeune (1775–1848) in *Battle of the Pyramids* (1806) present images of enlightened valor contrasted with unthinking ferocity, the classic definition of civilization against barbarism.

Europe's rediscovery of the East in the last part of the eighteenth century, what art historian Raymond Schwab (1984) calls the "Oriental Renaissance," was one of the inspirations, if not the most important one, he argues, for the emergence of Romanticism. Romantic artists of the first half of the nineteenth century were interested in passion and drama, and sought to create unique and sometimes eccentric works of art, and many were fascinated with the exotic world of the Orient.

One such artist was Eugène Delacroix (1798–1863). Like many artists, poets, and intellectuals of his generation, the Greek war of independence against the Ottoman Turkish Empire in the 1820s became the *cause célèbre* of the their generation. During the war, the Turks massacred approximately twenty thousand Greeks on the island of Chios, an action that outraged the liberals and Romantics of Western Europe. This event was memorialized by Delacroix in *Scenes from the Massacres at Chios* (1822–1824). The picture focuses on defenseless Greek men, women, and children in the foreground waiting to be slaughtered by a determined and ruthless Turk on horseback. A few years later, Delacroix took a theme from ancient history for *The Death of Sardanapalus* (1827). This painting presents the Assyrian king, just prior to his own capture and execution, ordering and calmly watching the murder of his concubines, slaves, and animals in his harem. For European audiences, no better image could depict or symbolize the nature of Oriental despotism and cruelty.

The British, fighting colonial wars in Africa and Asia throughout the nineteenth century, had many battles, some great victories, and a few heroic defeats, which artists made into popular romantic and mythic spectacles. Frederick Goodall (1822–1904) condensed the great Indian Revolt of 1857 in *The Relief of Lucknow 1857: Jessie's Dream* (1858). In this intimate scene on the ramparts of the fort at Lucknow, brave British soldiers, and one unflappable officer in particular, defend their white women, who had been at the mercy of the dark Indian rebels. What this painting only hints at, with the inclusion of one Indian soldier among the ranks of the British, was that during the siege of Lucknow about half of the seven thousand people who sought refuge in the garrison were loyal Indian soldiers and their families.

In the Indian Revolt, as in most colonial wars, the battles were not simply between Europeans and non-Europeans. Nineteenth-century paintings, however, rarely tried to illustrate this reality. Lady Elizabeth Butler's (1846–1933) *The Defence of Rorke's Drift* (1880) is an unrivaled example of this tendency. In this battle scene of the Zulu War, a small, all-white band of British soldiers fight off vast, indistinct, and darkened African warriors on the horizon. The artist was praised in Britain for not including images of Africans. As one critic noted, she omitted "such an unsavory adjunct" (Honour, 1988, p. 288).

Not all Romantic artists or nineteenth-century painters portrayed non-Europeans in a condescending manner that "explained" European superiority or justified European imperialism and dominance (a tendency that much later came to be called *Orientalism*). Théodore Géricault (1791–1824) in his masterpiece *Raft of the Medusa* (1819) depicts the survival and deaths of a small group of shipwrecked passengers seemingly abandoned on a raft. Géricault froze the moment when the survivors first sighted the ship that would rescue them. The dead and hopeless victims of the tragedy were placed at the bottom of the composition. The central and strongest figure in the painting, a black man, rises up to signal the ship. The usual symbol of oppression and hopelessness, a black body, in this painting reverses expected roles and becomes a striking representation of hope and salvation.

In 1832 Géricault's younger friend, Delacroix, journeyed to Morocco as part of a diplomatic mission. France's near-Orient captivated Delacroix. "I am quite overwhelmed by what I have seen," wrote Delacroix from Tangier. "I am like a man dreaming, who sees things he is afraid to see escape him." The women of Morocco, he continued, "are pearls of Eden" (quoted in Benton and DiYanni, 1998, vol. 2, p. 263). Two years later, the artist unveiled *The Women of Algiers* (1834), which contemporaries and later critics praised for its authenticity and scrupulous attention to North African living conditions, dress, customs, and physiognomy. Of course, no work of art, not even photographs, are truly transparent, objective, or "true." Although Delacroix was sympathetic to his Algerian subjects, contemporaries often brought their own judgments of Muslim cultures to this painting. These women of a harem, it was repeated time and again, were lazy, arrogant, ignorant, insipid, unclean, and, noted Alexandre Decamps (1803–1860), "fattened for pleasure" (quoted in Porterfield, 1998, p. 135).

Delacroix's painting *Arab Cavalry Practicing a Charge* (1832) reversed the usual image Europeans were given of non-European warriors. In this picture the artist shows a line of orderly and magnificent Arab horsemen shooting rifles at a gallop. This painting is Romanticism at its best: Delacroix offered the viewer an opportunity to share with him an intensely exciting, unrestrained, and romantic moment.

In the nineteenth century, the noted English art critic John Ruskin (1819–1900) opined that Indians could "not produce any noble art, only a savage or grotesque form of it" (quoted in MacKenzie 1996, p. 311). More than a century earlier, one of court painters of the Chinese emperor Kangxi (1662–1722) noted that he admired European craftsmanship but concluded, "foreign painting cannot be called art." For Europeans, this standoff began to change in the last decades of the nineteenth century. Japanese art, particularly landscape painting and woodblock printing, became recognized and admired by the 1860s. The artist-printer Hokusai Katsushika (1760–1849) created *The Great Wave off Kanagawa* (ca. 1831), a print that became one of the most popular and well-known images representing Japan and the Japanese aesthetic. His popular series of prints called *Thirty-Six Views of Mount Fuji* (1858) was part of the impetus that started the Western craze for *japanoiserie* in the last part of the century.

Some of the paintings of Edgar Degas (1834–1917), such as *Ballet Rehearsal (Adagio)* (1876) and *The Morning Bath* (1883), reflect his interest in eighteenth-century Japanese prints. The American painter Mary Cassatt (1845–1926), who joined the European impressionists and also studied Japanese prints, assimilated both of these influences. Her painting *The Bath* (1891), with its simplified form and flat composition, clearly reflects more than a flirtation with Japanese aesthetics. Japanese prints "were the first definitive non-European influence on European pictorial design" (Gardner et al. 1996, p. 988).

Also near the end of the century, the French painter Paul Gauguin (1848–1903) abandoned the corruption of European civilization and the illusion (as he saw it) of reproducing the world in art. "Civilization," he once famously pronounced, "is what makes you sick" (quoted in Gardner et al. 1991, p. 939). In the French South Pacific colony of Tahiti, Gauguin produced sixty-six paintings during his first two years. One of these, *Manao Tupapao* (The Spirit Watches Over Her) (1892), depicts his Tahitian lover terrified one night by the spirits of the dead ("the Tupapao"). Although he drew upon the European tradition of the reclining nude in this picture, this and other paintings from Tahiti reflect

Tahiti's brilliant colors, native motifs, and "primitive" life. The renewal of Western art and civilization, he argued, had to come from "the Primitives."

One artist who followed this advice was Pablo Picasso (1881–1974). Inspired by the ancient Iberian sculpture and African masks he had seen at a Paris exhibition, his famous *Les Demoiselles d'Avignon* (1907), a group portrait of five nudes, introduced Europeans to cubism and a strong dose of primitivism. The curvy bodies of the women in this painting are distorted and disjointed and broken into angular pieces in a way that came to define cubism. The faces of the three figures on the left were influenced by the ancient sculptures Picasso found in the Louvre in Paris. More interesting and shocking are the two faces on the right, which are elongated, almond-shaped grotesqueries, unmistakably primitive and suggestive of masks.

In sculpture, Henry Moore (1898–1986) also came to reveal his appreciation and embrace of the non-Western and "primitive" art he discovered in the British Museum in London. His *Reclining Figure* (1929) departed from a long Western tradition by presenting a figure that looked more like an ancient native "Earth Mother" than a well-proportioned classical or Renaissance marble.

As the century proceeded, Western artists in the former colonies of Europe increasingly drew upon the forms, concepts, motifs, colors, and more of non-Western art. In the 1920s, the Algonquin School of Canadian landscape painters broke away from the nineteenth-century Canadian landscape tradition that produced large and impressive paintings emphasizing the grandeur of the North American mountains, lakes, and forests. *October on the North Shore, Lake Superior* (1927), a painting by Arthur Lismer (1885–1969), translates this corner of Canadian wilderness into a more impressionist jumble that also reflects the gradations and tones, as well as the cool abstractionism, of Japanese prints.

Mexican painters, many of whom studied in Spain, France, and Italy, assimilated the styles and traditions of the grand masters, the impressionists, the expressionists, and the cubists, as well as that of the ancient and contemporary native cultures of Mexico. The internationally admired muralists of the 1920s and 1930s, particularly Diego Rivera (1886–1957), José Clemente Orozco (1883–1949), and David Alfaro Siqueiros (1896–1974), produced a "revolutionary" public art that was populist and didactic. These artists, known as the Tres Grandes (the Three Greats), and others of this generation were inspired and influenced by the ancient murals and sculptures of Teotihuacán, the Maya, the Aztecs, and others. Rivera's fresco *Carnival in Huexotzingo* (1936) presented a contemporary Mexican carnival in the way ancient painters pictured kings, priests, and warriors. "The

Manao Tupapau, Paul Gauguin, 1892. *In this picture, Gauguin depicts his Tahitian lover terrified one night by the spirits of the dead. Although the artist drew upon the European tradition of the reclining nude, Manao Tupapau also reflects Tahiti's brilliant colors, native motifs, and "primitive" life.* © CORBIS. REPRODUCED BY PERMISSION.

composition, the harmony of this developing art recapture something of the spatial definitions of ancient Mexican sculpture," wrote Agustín Velázquez Chávez in 1937, "together with the baroque of the Churrigueresque altars" (p. 167). (The Churrigueresque style of the Spanish Baroque refers to particular architectural elements in late seventeenth-century Mexican churches and, more generally, to riotous decorations of all spaces with all manner of ornamental forms.)

As in Mexico, artists in the former British colonies around the world, the dominions, sought to create unique national arts that promoted national identity by connecting with the past, both colonial and native, and with the different peoples and cultures of the present. "The artists of the Dominions," writes MacKenzie, "began to draw upon the motifs, pigments, and spiritual concepts of indigenous art. By the middle of the twentieth century, this fusing of local symbols with European techniques had become standard throughout the territories of white settlement" (1996, p. 315).

In 1989 an exhibition in Paris called *Magiciens de la terre* (Magicians of the Earth), opened as "the first worldwide exhibition of contemporary art." This show presented works by one hundred artists, fifty from Europe and America, and fifty from Native America, Australia, Africa, and Asia. One of the most interesting and revealing commonalities revealed in the contemporary "Western" and "indigenous" artworks in this exhibition is the practice of abstraction. In one room, Aboriginal artists from the community of Yuendumu in Australia created a sand painting that represents the "dreams" or marks of ancestral beings upon the places and landscapes they visited or inhabited. Above the abstract sand-painted circles, waves, and lines is a work by the English artist Richard Long (b. 1945), *Red Earth Circle.* Long's large "messy" circle on a black background was made of mud collected on a visit to the community that created the sand painting. Who has most influenced whom? "Successful and dominant countries impose their laws and styles on other countries," writes Jean-Hubert Martin, "but they also borrow from them and so become permeated by other ways of life" (Benton and DiYanni, 1998, vol. 2, p. 487).

SEE ALSO *Divide and Rule: The Legacy of Roman Imperialism; Empire, British; Empire, Dutch; Empire, French; Empire, Italian; Empire, Japanese; Empire, Ottoman; Empire, Portuguese.*

BIBLIOGRAPHY

Archer, Mildred, and Ronald Lightbown. *India Observed: India as Viewed by British Artists, 1760–1860, An Exhibition Organised by the Library of the Victoria and Albert Museum as Part of the Festival of India, 26 April–5 July 1982.* Exhibition catalog. London: Victoria and Albert Museum and Trefoil Books, 1982.

Auerback, Jeffrey. "Art and Empire." In *The Oxford History of the British Empire;* Vol. 5: *Historiography,* edited by Robin W. Winks, 571–583. Oxford: Oxford University Press, 1999.

Bayly, C. A. *The Birth of the Modern World, 1780–1914: Global Connections and Comparisons.* Oxford: Blackwell, 2004.

Benton, Janetta Rebold, and Robert DiYanni. *Arts and Culture: An Introduction to the Humanities,* 2 vols. Upper Saddle River, NJ: Prentice Hall, 1998; 2nd ed., 2005.

Brown, Jonathan. "Another Image of the World: Spanish Art, 1500–1920." In *The Spanish World: Civilization and Empire, Europe and the Americas, Past and Present,* edited by J. H. Elliott, 149–184. New York: Harry N. Abrams, 1991.

Brown, Jonathan. *Painting in Spain, 1500–1700.* New Haven, CT: Yale University Press, 1998.

Davies, Kristian. *The Orientalists: Western Artists in Arabia, the Sahara, Persia, and India.* New York: Laynfaroh, 2005.

Doggett, Rachel, ed. *New World of Wonders: European Images of the Americas, 1492–1700.* Washington, DC: Folger Shakespeare Library, 1992.

Durant, Will, and Ariel Durant. *The Age of Louis XIV: A History of European Civilization in the Period of Pascal, Molière, Cromwell, Milton, Peter the Great, Newton, and Spinoza: 1648–1715.* New York: Simon and Schuster, 1963.

Elsner, Jaś. *Imperial Rome and Christian Triumph: The Art of the Roman Empire, A.D. 100–450.* Oxford: Oxford University Press, 1998.

Ferguson, Niall. *Empire: The Rise and Demise of the British World Order and the Lessons for Global Power.* New York: Basic Books, 2003.

Fraser, Valerie. *The Architecture of Conquest: Building in the Viceroyalty of Peru, 1535–1635.* Cambridge, U.K.: Cambridge University Press, 1990.

Gardner, Helen, Horst de la Croix, Richard G. Tansey, and Diane Kirkpatrick. *Gardner's Art Through the Ages,* 9th ed. San Diego, CA: Harcourt Brace Jovanovich, 1991.

Gardner, Helen, Richard G. Tansey, and Fred S. Kleiner. *Gardner's Art Through the Ages,* 10th ed. Fort Worth, TX: Harcourt Brace College, 1996.

Grigsby, Darcy Grimaldo. *Extremities: Painting Empire in Post-Revolutionary France.* New Haven, CT: Yale University Press, 2002.

Hobsbawm, Eric. *The Age of Empire, 1875–1914.* New York: Pantheon, 1987.

Holliday, Peter James. "'Ad Triumphum Excolendum': The Political Significance of Roman Historical Painting." *Oxford Art Journal* 3 (2) (1980): 3–8.

Holmes, C. J. "The Uses of Japanese Art to Europe." *The Burlington Magazine for Connoisseurs* 8 (31) (1905): 3–10.

Honour, Hugh. *The Image of the Black in Western Art,* Vol. 4: *From the American Revolution to World War I: Slaves and Liberators,* Pt. 2: *Black Models and White Myths.* Cambridge, MA: Harvard University Press, 1988.

Ishikawa Chiyo, ed. *Spain in the Age of Exploration, 1492–1819.* Seattle, WA: Seattle Art Museum, 2004.

Keyes, George S. *Mirror of Empire: Dutch Marine Art of the Seventeenth Century.* Cambridge, U.K.: Cambridge University Press; Minneapolis, MN: Minneapolis Institute of Arts, 1990.

Levenson, Jay A., ed. *Circa 1492: Art in the Age of Exploration.* Washington, DC: National Gallery of Art; New Haven, CT: Yale University Press, 1991.

MacKenzie, John A. "Art and the Empire." In *Cambridge Illustrated History of the British Empire,* edited by P. J. Marshall, 296–315. Cambridge, U.K.: Cambridge University Press, 1996.

Makdisi, Saree. *William Blake and the Impossible History of the 1790s.* Chicago: University of Chicago Press, 2003.

McCullough, David. *1776.* New York: Simon & Schuster, 2005.

Nochlin, Linda. "The Imaginary Orient." *Art in America* 71 (1983): 118–131.

Pierce, Donna, Rogelio Ruiz Gomar, and Clara Bargellini. *Painting a New World: Mexican Art and Life, 1521–1821.* Denver, CO: Denver Art Museum, 2004.

Porterfield, Todd. *The Allure of Empire: Art in the Service of French Imperialism, 1798–1836.* Princeton, NJ: Princeton University Press, 1998.

Rice, Tony. *Voyages of Discovery: Three Centuries of Natural History Exploration.* London: Natural History Museum, 2000.

Schama, Simon. *The Embarrassment of Riches: An Interpretation of Dutch Culture in the Golden Age.* New York: Knopf, 1987; Vintage, 1997.

Schwab, Raymond. *Oriental Renaissance: Europe's Rediscovery of India and the East, 1680–1880.* Translated by Gene Patterson-Black and Victor Reinking. New York: Columbia University Press, 1984.

Stedman, John Gabriel. *Stedman's Surinam: Life in an Eighteenth-Century Slave Society,* edited by Richard Price and Sally Price. Baltimore, MD: Johns Hopkins University Press, 1992.

Stevens, Mary Anne, ed. *The Orientalists, Delacroix to Matisse: European Painters in North Africa and the Near East.* Exhibition catalog. London: Royal Academy, 1984.

Sullivan, Edward J., ed. *Brazil: Body and Soul.* New York: Guggenheim Museum, 2001.

Velázquez Chávez, Agustín. *Contemporary Mexican Artists.* New York: Covici-Friede, 1937.

Sharon Lee House

ASANTE WARS

European influence in West Africa was negligible in the eighteenth century. However, this situation underwent a dramatic change in the nineteenth century as a result of the abolition of the slave trade and the adoption of so-called legitimate trade, which would only thrive in the wake of peace and stability. Under these circumstances, ongoing wars between the Asante (Ashanti) and Fante, two indigenous Gold Coast peoples, during the eighteenth century led to instability and impeded trade. Consequently, the British became involved in the Asante-Fante wars in the early nineteenth century to restore peace and stability and promote "legitimate" trade. This economic interpretation of British colonial policy is one of the multifaceted aspects of British-Asante relations, which resulted in a series of wars between 1824 and 1901.

The desire to drive the Asante people from the coastal Gold Coast so as to gain access to markets beyond Asante, coupled with misunderstandings between Asante and British perspectives, and a desire by the British to humble the Asante, underlie the Anglo-Asante wars of 1824 (Nsamankow), 1826 (Katamansu), 1863 (Dodowa), 1874 (Sagrenti), and 1900 to 1901 (Yaa Asantewaa). After Asante's annexation to the British Colony of the Gold Coast, the term Ashanti, as in Ashanti region, was often used to refer to both the Asante people and the core of what used to be the Asante empire.

From the third decade of the nineteenth century, the relationship of Britain vis-à-vis the Asante underwent a dramatic change. Instead of their old position as mediators of conflicts, the British assumed a more aggressive role on the Gold Coast. The period of informal control gradually gave way to invasion and occupation as the European scramble for African colonies intensified. Fear of Asante control of the entire coastline of the Gold Coast, thereby negating years of informal British control, fuelled British hostility towards the Asante.

J. K. Fynn (1971) gives three main reasons for this apprehension. First, British merchants believed that their Dutch counterparts would be the beneficiaries in the event of an Asante occupation of the coast. Second, the British regarded the Asante king as an absolute monarch, much like his counterpart in Dahomey (present-day Benin), and they therefore dreaded a situation whereby European traders on the coast would be dependent on this absolute monarch. Finally, British traders felt morally bound to help the Fante, whose assistance had been crucial to them during periods of commercial rivalry among the Europeans.

The desire to stop the slave trade and promote "legitimate" trade was a major British concern in the Gold Coast in the nineteenth century. The British were desirous to promote what they deemed legitimate products, such as palm oil, rubber, and cotton. This occurred at a time, by 1820, when Asante was a major source of slaves on the Gold Coast. Furthermore, in the context of the European civilizing mission, the British wanted to ensure peace and order as prerequisites for the introduction of "civilization," western education, and evangelization. British officials and merchants believed that only Asante defeat would make this possible and this led eventually to the assumption of crown responsibility for the administration of the Gold Coast forts and castles.

In the economic sphere, the British merchants on the coast were convinced by the third decade of the nineteenth century that if Asante power were broken, the interior of the Gold Coast would be open to them, making trade possible as far as Bonduku (in present-day Ivory Coast), Kong (Ghana), Timbuktu (Mali), and Hausaland (Nigeria). Thus, the policy of cooperation with Asante pursued by the British governor from 1807 was terminated by the new governor, John Hope Smith. Smith, who served as governor from 1817 to 1822, also rejected the treaty of amity and peace negotiated between the British and the Asante by Joseph Dupuis (resident from 1819–1820) in 1820.

The next governor of Sierra Leone, who had oversight over the Gold Coast, Charles MacCarthy (1822–1824), discarded Dupuis's advice to remain on friendly terms with the Asante. Rather, he organized an anti-Asante coalition between December 1822 and May 1823. MacCarthy's contempt for the Asante was exemplified in his failure to send a message to Kumasi, the Ashanti capital, on his arrival in the Gold Coast, as demanded by custom. He also rejected the overtures of accommodation from the *Asantehene* (ruler) Osei Bonsu (r. ca. 1801–1824).

Furthermore, MacCarthy used the trial and execution of an Anomabo man as the occasion to wage war against the Asante but he lost his life in the ensuing battle. Fear of Asante reaction after the defeat of 1824 led to the dissolution of crown rule, and control devolved on the British Company of Merchants. Company rule under George Maclean (1801–1847) from 1830 to 1841 witnessed a transformation in Anglo-Asante relations. Maclean worked for peace and encouraged the revival of agriculture and trade. In April 1831, he concluded a tripartite treaty by which the *Asantehene* recognized the independence of the coastal states and agreed to submit all disputes to the Cape Coast castle. In addition, the coastal states agreed to open the trade routes, thus ending the hostilities of 1824 and 1826. But Maclean's successors did not possess his tact and prudence, and Anglo-Asante relations soured.

The Defeat of Kumasi by the British. *In 1874 British forces commanded by Major General Garnet Wolseley decisively defeated Asante burnt Kumasi, and later arrested Prempe I, the Asante ruler.* © HULTON-DEUTSCH COLLECTION/CORBIS. REPRODUCED BY PERMISSION.

The period of Governor H. W. Hill (1844–46) saw the resumption of crown rule on the Gold Coast. Following Maclean, Hill convinced the Fante chiefs to sign the celebrated Bond of 1844. The bond did not involve abdication of sovereignty, and the chiefs were to continue holding their courts. According to historian Thomas Lewin (1978), progressive deterioration in diplomatic contacts between Asante and Britain in the 1840s and 1850s reached a midpoint during Richard Pine's governorship (1862–1865). His refusal to recognize Asante laws and customs led to the Anglo-Asante war of 1863. Asante forces secured the release of hostages in 1863, and a British counteroffensive against Asante ended disastrously.

In 1873 the ministry of British prime minister William Gladstone (1809–1898) faced a crisis on the frontiers of British influence in West Africa, Malaya, and the South Pacific. Urged by Edward Knatchbull-Hugessen (1829–1893), Lord Kimberley (John Wodehouse, 1826–1902), the colonial secretary, attempted a firmer administration in the Gold Coast and intervened in force against Asante. W. David McIntyre (1967) argues that this "new imperialism" was the culmination of a period of tentative innovation rather than the beginning of a forward movement. By 1873, it was felt that the internal conditions of the adjacent states posed serious threats to the security of the Fante colony.

In 1874 British forces (and West Indian troops) commanded by Major General Garnet Wolseley (1833–1913) decisively defeated Asante, burnt Kumasi, and by the Fomena Treaty (1874) compelled the Asante to recognize the independence of all states south of the River Pra. This defeat led to secessionist wars by states that had been under Asante rule. However, a disintegrating Asante empire was gradually revived by Mensa Bonsu (r. 1874–83), Kwaku Dua II (r. 1884–1884), and Agyeman Prempe I (1888–1896).

Alarmed at the steady Franco-German encroachment from the Ivory Coast and Togo, and afraid of Asante revival, British prejudice against intervention gave way to a new determination in 1895 under Joseph Chamberlain (1836–1914) as colonial secretary. To protect the Gold Coast hinterland and stave off French encroachment, the British invited Prempe I to place his country under British protection. Prempe's rejection in 1894 of British protection culminated in a British expedition of 1896. Together with family members, Prempe was arrested and deported first to Sierra Leone, and later, to Seychelles. However, when Governor Frederick Hodgson (1897–1900) demanded the surrender of the Golden Stool in 1900 (The Golden Stool, according to Asante founding tradition, contained the "soul" of the Asante nation and only the Asantehene sat on the stool, usually at the time of enstoolment. Hodgson asked for the stool to sit on in his capacity as the representative of the victorious Queen of England.) Anglo-Asante hostilities were resumed. In response to his request, the Asante under the queen mother of Edweso, Yaa Asantewaa (ca. 1850–1921), fought a final battle (1900–1901) against the British, after which Asante was annexed to the British protectorate.

SEE ALSO *Britain's African Colonies.*

BIBLIOGRAPHY

Agbodeka, Francis. *African Politics and British Policy in the Gold Coast, 1868–1900: A Study in the Forms and Force of Protest.* Evanston, IL: Northwestern University Press, 1971.

Boahen, A. Adu. "Asante, Fante, and the British, 1800–1880." In *A Thousand Years of West African History: A Handbook for Teachers and Students,* edited by J. F. Ade Ajayi and Ian Espie, rev. ed., Ibadan, Nigeria: Ibadan University Press; London: Nelson, 1969, pp. 121-136. Boahen, Adu. *Ghana: Evolution and Change in the Nineteenth and Twentieth Centuries.* London: Longman, 1975.

Fynn, John Kofi. *Asante and its Neighbours, 1700–1807.* Harlow, U.K.: Longman; Evanston, IL: Northwestern University Press, 1971.

Lewin, Thomas. *Asante Before the British: The Prempean Years, 1875-1900.* Lawrence: Regents Press of Kansas, 1978.

McCarthy, Mary. *Social Change and the Growth of British Power in the Gold Coast: The Fante States, 1807–1874.* Lanham, MD: University Press of America, 1983.

McIntyre, W. David. *The Imperial Frontier in the Tropics, 1865–75: A Study of British Colonial Policy in West Africa, Malaya, and the South Pacific in the Age of Gladstone and Disraeli.* London: Macmillan; New York: St. Martin's Press, 1967.

Wilks, Ivor. *Asante in the Nineteenth Century: The Structure and Evolution of a Political Order.* London: Cambridge University Press, 1975.

Wilks, Ivor. "Asante: Human Sacrifice or Capital Punishment? A Rejoinder." *International Journal of African Historical Studies* 21 (3) (1988): 443–451.

Edmund Abaka

ASSIMILATION, AFRICA

The word "assimilation" comes from the Latin term *assimilatio,* which means, "to render similar," or "cause to be similar." The import of this idea in French colonial politics may be linked to the ideals of fraternity, equality, and freedom emerging from the 1789 revolution there. Although colonial subjugation mitigated these core radical values, late-eighteenth-century France considered it appropriate to extend rights of citizenship and political rights to the African residents of Dakar, Gorée, Rafisque, Saint Louis, and Senegal. This foremost French colonial enclave in West Africa became the experimental laboratory for assimilation practice.

As an imperial policy, assimilation tried to affirm the assumed superiority of French culture to those of its non-European colonies. Generally, the various European imperial powers—Britain, Germany, France, Holland, Spain, and Portugal—had claimed the obligation to civilize the "barbaric" peoples of the world as the major motive behind colonial exertion. In other words, "civilization" for the peoples of French Africa involved the imposing of French values on African culture. This implied, unquestioned acceptance of French language, dress, food, education, mannerisms, and ways of life distinguished France from its colonial peers. Instead of an indirect approach, France treated African political institutions and culture as if they were irrelevant.

However, a big dilemma confronted the implementation of assimilation policy. Theoretically, assimilation expounded the potential equality for people of all races. This implied political, economic, and social equality among the French and the inhabitants of their overseas extensions, including Africans. But the consequences of this understanding and the attempt by the French to evade them drew indignation of the colonized people, while provoking a nationwide debate among politicians, academics, and colonial officials in France. The conservative monarchists and their Catholic allies confronted the more liberal-minded republicans. Consequently, the intention to assimilate was restricted to Senegal, while being subjected to closer scrutiny, revisions, and changes—especially between 1815 and 1945.

These changes underpinned the dilemma facing an imperial France that tried, with limited success, to clothe its colonial interests in a liberal and progressive garb. France's intentions became more obvious in the 1860s when Louis Léon César Faidherbe (1818–1889), the governor of French West African territory, received orders to embark on a more aggressive and ambitious territorial acquisition. While Faidherbe strengthened French possessions in Senegal from one to four communes, now comprising Dakar, Gorée, Saint Louis, and Rafisque, the privileges of the four communes were denied to the vast population of Africans that eventually came under French control. The great majority of Africans were denied assimilation and French citizenship. Only the African citizens of the French communes in Senegal were granted the right to elect deputies to the National Assembly in France. Prior to 1914, the African deputies to Parliament had come from a small class of elite, mainly people of European descent or of mixed race. But by 1914 a new African educated elite had emerged. Among them was Blaise Daigne, whose election in 1916 marked the first appearance of an African deputy in the French Parliament.

Meanwhile, as the French expanded its African empire in the late nineteenth century more voices joined the rank of conservatives in the debate over the appropriateness of assimilation in colonial administration. Some held the view that Africans were unfit for complete assimilation. Others opposed the huge costs of educational programs needed in making assimilation a success, arguing that only rudimentary education was more proper for the Africans. There also were groups who desired that colonial development focus more on Algeria with its huge and influential French population.

These relentless attacks on the policy resulted in restricting full citizenship rights and privileges to very few Africans in the colonies. In 1912, for instance, a law established that no one except those in West Africa could gain French citizenship. Additionally, those hoping to acquire citizenship were to meet a certain level of Western education, speak French, and accept both Christianity and European mannerisms. For the Africans, these conditions entailed a total rejection of their indigenous roots and African personality. In effect, between 1914 and 1937, the total number of assimilated Africans in Senegal was roughly 50,000.

In the late 1930s, the French eventually began to acquiesce to the reality that Africans had a very different culture. The logic was then accepted that a different policy was required to make colonial administration attuned to African needs. This understanding led to the adoption of "association" as a new policy for building a better colonial order.

SEE ALSO *Association, Africa; France's African Colonies.*

BIBLIOGRAPHY

Chafer, Tony. *The End of Empire in French West Africa: France's Successful Decolonization?* Oxford; New York: Berg, 2002.

Conklin, Alice L. *A Mission to Civilize: the Republican Idea of Empire in France and West Africa, 1895–1930.* Stanford, CA: Stanford University Press, 1998.

Crowder, Michael. *Senegal: A Study of French Assimilation Policy.* London: Oxford University Press, 1962.

Crowder, Michael. *West Africa Under Colonial Rule.* Evanston, IL: Northwestern University Press, 1968.

Genova, James E. *Colonial Ambivalence, Cultural Authenticity, and the Limitations of Mimicry in French-Ruled West Africa 1914–1956.* New York: Peter Lang, 2004.

Gosnell, Jonathan K. *The Politics of Frenchness in Colonial Algeria, 1930–1954.* Rochester, NY: University of Rochester Press, 2002.

Lugard, Frederick. *The Dual Mandate in British Tropical Africa,* 5th ed. Hamden, CT: Archon Books, 1965.

McNamara, Francis Terry. *France in Black Africa.* Washington, DC: National Defense University, 1989.

Mendonsa, Eugene L. *West Africa: An Introduction to its History, Civilization, and Contemporary Situation.* Durham, NC: Carolina Academic Press, 2002.

Raphael Chijioke Njoku

ASSIMILATION, EAST ASIA AND THE PACIFIC

Assimilation as a colonial policy sought the integration of colonized peoples into the colonizer's cultural, social, and political institutions. The philosophy that drove this practice emphasized the Enlightenment ideas of such thinkers as the French philosopher Jean-Jacques Rousseau (1712–1778), who wrote in his *The Social Contract and Discourses* that men "who may be unequal in strength and intelligence, become every one equal by convention and equal right."

The idea of assimilating colonized peoples is most associated with the French. The image of multiracial French national assemblies elicits the belief that this colonial power welcomed representatives from throughout its empire to the colonial homeland as a people equal in stature to their own citizens. The French policy of assimilation, which involved the practice of direct rule over the peoples to which it was applied, stood in contrast to the English, whose colonial practices involved indirect rule and the maintaining of native political, social, and cultural institutions.

These characterizations are somewhat misleading. Recent research suggests that the French assimilated few of their colonial subjects, and when they did it was often as "native," rather than French, citizens. French standards prevented many colonial subjects from inclusion in French society, for they required that the subject must speak French, convert to Catholicism, and reject traditional ("barbarian") customs. In contrast, the English introduced a successful policy of political, rather than cultural, assimilation for colonized peoples residing in neighboring territories. Following the passage of Britain's acts of union, the Welsh, Scots, and Irish all closed their local parliaments and sent representatives to the British Parliament.

Beginning in the late nineteenth century, social Darwinists began to attack the practice of assimilating colonized peoples. In France, the social scientist and physician Gustave Le Bon (1841–1931) led a movement that criticized the policy's primary tenet: that "inferior" peoples could be civilized to join the ranks of the enlightened. Assimilation as an institution, he argued, was "one of the most harmful illusions that the theories of pure reason have ever engendered" (Betts 2005 [1961], pp. 64–69).

German advocates of "scientific colonialism" offered similar arguments after their country began expanding into Africa. However, in neighboring Alsace and Lorraine, the German government did employ assimilation as an administrative approach. These examples suggest that the success of assimilation policies was contingent on form (political over cultural) and familiarity (geographic and ethnic proximity).

Early Japanese examples of an administration practicing assimilation predate many of the above examples. One of the first Japanese attempts at assimilation began in the late eighteenth century when encroaching Russian traders and explorers encouraged the Tokugawa government (1603–1868) to assimilate the indigenous Ezo (Ainu) peoples of present-day Hokkaido.

This experiment was aborted soon after the Russian threat abated, but it was revived following the 1868 Meiji restoration. On both occasions the Japanese government trained the people of Hokkaido in the Japanese language and encouraged them to adopt Japanese attire and cuisine. Beginning in the late nineteenth century, the Japanese government herded the people of Hokkaido into schools to instruct them in the Japanese language and farming techniques. The aim was to encourage their settlement into communities that would replace their traditional nomadic hunting-and-gathering way of life. The Japanese government employed similar practices in the Ryukyu kingdom (present-day Okinawa) after gaining control of this archipelago in the 1870s.

Whereas the Japanese could claim (albeit weakly) of having held suzerain relations over Hokkaido and Okinawa during the Tokugawa period, its later colonial acquisitions included territory that had either been part of another empire (Taiwan) or had held outright sovereignty (Korea). This situation, and the backlash that assimilation faced at the time, encouraged the Japanese to choose their policy of colonial administration with caution after it acquired Taiwan following its victory in the Sino-Japanese War (1894–1895).

Prime Minister Ito Hirobumi (1841–1909), requesting opinion papers from top foreign advisors, was advised by the French representative to assimilate peoples in colonized areas. The British advised Japan to introduce an indirect policy that maintained the colonized people's traditional customs. Deputy Foreign Minister Hara Takashi (1856–1921) advised in his opinion paper that Japan follow the practices used by the English in Scotland, Wales, and Ireland, the French in Algeria, and the Germans in Alsace and Lorraine: assimilation.

By 1910, when Japan annexed the Korean Peninsula, assimilation had been designated as the state's colonial policy by imperial decree. The Japanese government even declared this policy as its administrative strategy in the South Pacific islands that it acquired from Germany during World War I (1914-18).

Differing from the French rhetoric of assimilation's universal applicability, the Japanese justified their adoption of this policy in bilateral terms relating to the cultural and historical similarities that the colonizers shared with the peoples they colonized. Japan's leaders argued that ethnic similarities would bring them success in implementing this assimilation policy in places where European colonizers had failed. These arguments referred to ancient times, when the Japanese, Korean, and Chinese peoples resided as a single people on the Asian continent. Through migration and physical separation, they developed their separate identities.

These arguments also pointed to other similarities in, for example, religion and language, which the Japanese shared with the subjugated peoples. By the time the Japanese had incorporated the South Pacific islands into the empire, assimilation was regarded as Japan's official colonial policy, even if the people to be colonized shared little in common with the colonizers. Nor should it have mattered, for whether the colonized people were Korean, Taiwanese, or Micronesian, the Japanese regarded them as imperial subjects, rather than Japanese citizens.

Despite Japan's rhetoric of assimilation, the colonial policies that the country implemented advanced segregation. Education presents a representative example of this result. Japan probably built more schools in its empire than any other colonial power, yet most of these schools consistently segregated the colonized from the colonizer. Mark Peattie's description (1988) of the education system in Japan's Nan'yo (South Seas) territories demonstrates continuity with practices in Japan's other colonial possessions—a widespread system in which students were kept segregated from those attending Japanese expatriate schools.

The Korean example reflects the situation found in Japan's other colonies. Here Japanese schools limited Korean enrollment to around 10 percent; the Japanese enrollment in Korean schools was less than 5 percent. The schools established for the colonizers were better endowed financially and offered the students better conditions in which to study. Gaining entrance to Japanese schools did not necessarily advance assimilation, however. Koreans and Japanese who studied together frequently formed separate clubs and lived in different residence halls.

This segregation reflected the ethnic zones of the Korean capital, Seoul. Koreans and Japanese tended to reside in separate parts of the city. Groups of colonized peoples who organized to promote assimilation in Japan's colonies did not achieve much success. The Japanese ordered one such association in Taiwan to disband.

Neither the European nor Japanese assimilation practices managed to successfully integrate colonized peoples into the colonizer's society. Resistance by those to be assimilated only partly explains this; resistance by expatriate colonizers to accept the colonized as equals also prevented the success of assimilation policies.

SEE ALSO *Anticolonialism, East Asia and the Pacific; Chinese Diaspora.*

BIBLIOGRAPHY

Betts, Raymond F. *Assimilation and Association in French Colonial Theory, 1890–1914.* New York: Columbia University Press, 1961. New ed., Lincoln: University of Nebraska Press, 2005.

Caprio, Mark E. "Koreans into Japanese: Japan's Assimilation Policy." Ph.D. diss., University of Washington, Seattle, 2001.

Dong Wonmo, "Japanese Colonial Policy and Practice in Korea, 1905–1945: A Study in Assimilation." Ph.D. diss., Georgetown University, Washington, D.C., 1965.

Myers, Ramon H., and Mark R. Peattie, eds. *The Japanese Colonial Empire, 1895–1945.* Princeton, NJ: Princeton University Press, 1984.

Peattie, Mark R. *Nan'yo: The Rise and Fall of the Japanese in Micronesia, 1885–1945.* Honolulu: University of Hawaii Press, 1988.

Rousseau, Jean-Jacques. *The Social Contract and Discourses.* Trans. G.D.H. Cole. London: Everyman's Library, 1973.

Shin, Gi-Wook, and Michael Robinson, eds. *Colonial Modernity in Korea.* Cambridge, MA: Harvard University Press, 1999.

Mark E. Caprio

ASSOCIATION, AFRICA

The French policy of association in Africa was adopted to resolve the problems connected with the implementation of its assimilation policy. Rather than causing Africans to be black Frenchmen, the association acknowledged that the Euro-African relationship should be one of mutual cooperation for the overall profit of the colony and metropolis. In theory, the new policy was supposed to respect African culture and institutions. The association also was considered more cost-effective, and less prone to local resistance.

In practice, however, the association was nothing remarkably different from assimilation. In fact, many scholars agree that, from the start, the French had practiced a combination of assimilation and association. Once the colonies were subdued, the various colonizing powers tried many strategies. While the British adopted the system of indirect rule, the Portuguese used assimilation, the Dutch used racial segregation, and the Germans used colonialism. Whatever it was called, the systems were broadly the same. They were forms of exploitation, oppression, and a way of selling colonizers abroad, while inferiorizing the colonized.

Under association, the French created auxiliary instruments for entrenching authority in the hands of French officials. The Africans were hardly allowed to offer any input in policy decisions. Under the new policy, the French divided African societies into thousands of cantons or districts placed under chiefs who were, in reality, collaborators in the colonial system. Indigenous rulers who understood the culture and customs of their people, but remained hostile to colonial control, were alienated from the system. In this way, the French systematically eliminated African customary law, and created advisory councils to provide knowledge of African law and customs at each level of the bureaucracy.

Determined to maintain the distinction between citizens and subjects, the French legal code was set aside for whites and other assimilated Africans, whereas the millions of unassimilated Africans were subjected to a system called *indigène*. On paper, *indigène* was established to implement African law in civil and criminal justice administration, but it actually operated according to the whims and caprices of the French officials and their African collaborators. Additionally, this policy empowered colonial officers to incarcerate their African subjects without trial. The policy also mandated Africans to volunteer twelve days of unpaid labor for civic services.

Forced labor, harsh penal codes, heavy taxation, and poor living conditions put the African subjects of French West Africa through intense sufferings. The people were denied freedom of speech and association while being exploited through heavy taxation that undermined local food production as the people struggled to cultivate more cash crops to meet their tax obligations. To avoid this hardship, large numbers of Africans emigrated in droves. Some of the migrants left the French colonial territories. New diseases and other health hazards accompanied the mass movement of people. However, African population increased in many areas of colonial Africa, as a consequence of a decline in death rates and the introduction of Western medical services.

With the exception of Senegal, educational development evolved slowly in French West Africa. This was partly because the predominantly Muslim hinterland people of

West Africa demonstrated little interest in Christian mission schools. Also, the colonial education system was elitist, and French was the language of instruction. The curriculum, completely modeled after that in France, neglected African needs. In other words, assimilation was sustained as before despite the adoption of association.

Suddenly, things began to improve for the better after World War II (1939–1945). The defeat of the French by Germany had so hurt French colonial pride that it would have amounted to criminal shortsightedness not to reward the contributions of Africans to the Allied victory. Accordingly, the colonial officials began to treat their African colonies more as an integral part of France. In addition to the rights to elective deputation in the French parliament, a free press, trade unions, and political parties were allowed to grow in the colonies.

By and large, nationalist movements developed slowly in French West Africa, in contrast with the British colonies. This was because the openings of the post–World War II era brought the African political elite into a close-knit relationship with France. A handful of them served in French cabinets in the period of decolonization. Except for Guinea, where the emergent political leaders demanded immediate independence, and in Algeria, where nationalists engaged France in a bloody independence struggle in the 1950s, French West Africa demonstrated an attitude of complacency to colonial rule.

SEE ALSO *Assimilation, Africa; France's African Colonies.*

BIBLIOGRAPHY

Chafer, Tony. *The End of Empire in French West Africa: France's Successful Decolonization?* Oxford; New York: Berg, 2002.

Conklin, Alice L. *A Mission to Civilize: the Republican Idea of Empire in France and West Africa, 1895–1930.* Stanford, CA: Stanford University Press, 1998.

Crowder, Michael. *Senegal: A Study of French Assimilation Policy.* London: Oxford University Press, 1962.

Crowder, Michael. *West Africa Under Colonial Rule.* Evanston, IL: Northwestern University Press, 1968.

Genova, James E. *Colonial Ambivalence, Cultural Authenticity and the Limitations of Mimicry in French-Ruled West Africa 1914–1956.* New York: Peter Lang, 2004.

Gosnell, Jonathan K. *The Politics of Frenchness in Colonial Algeria, 1930–1954.* Rochester, NY: University of Rochester Press, 2002.

Lugard, Frederick. *The Dual Mandate in British Tropical Africa*, 5th ed. Hamden, CT: Archon Books, 1965.

McNamara, Francis Terry. *France in Black Africa.* Washington, DC. National Defense University, 1989.

Mendonsa, Eugene L. *West Africa: An Introduction to its History, Civilization, and Contemporary Situation.* Durham, NC: Carolina Academic Press, 2002.

Raphael Chijioke Njoku

ATATÜRK, MUSTAFA KEMAL
1880–1938

Born Mustafa in 1880 or 1881 in Salonica, a prosperous city in the late Ottoman Empire. Later known as Mustafa Kemal, he assumed the surname Atatürk—"Father of the Turks"—in 1934. Son of Ali Rıza, a civil servant, and Zübeyde, Mustafa Kemal became a prominent officer in the Ottoman army during World War I, the leader of the Turkish struggle for independence (1919–1922), and then founding president (1923–1938) of the Republic of Turkey. Atatürk died from cirrhosis of the liver in Istanbul on November 10, 1938.

Mustafa Kemal grew up under the authoritarian Ottoman sultan, Abdülhamid II (r. 1876–1909). He attended military high school in the town of Manastır before studying at the War College in Istanbul between 1899 and 1904. At a time when a growing number of Ottoman intellectuals and officers—collectively known as the Young Turks—were becomingly increasingly disillusioned with the state of the empire under Abdülhamid II, Mustafa Kemal found himself involved in revolutionary plots to overthrow the sultan. Appointed to serve in Syria in 1905, he returned to Salonica in 1907, where he was active in the Ottoman Freedom Society and the Committee of Union and Progress (CUP). Mustafa Kemal played only a minor role in the Young Turk Revolution of July 1908, but as a junior officer he was an active member of the Operational Army that marched on Istanbul in April 1909 to suppress a counterrevolution that aimed to restore power to Abdülhamid II.

Between 1909 and 1914 Mustafa Kemal held various posts in the Ottoman army and participated in campaigns against Italy in Tripoli in 1911 and after that in the Balkans. An opinionated and strong-willed young man, Mustafa Kemal developed a rivalry with the leadership of the CUP—Enver Paşa in particular—that prevented him from rising quickly within the ranks of the military and from having much influence over Ottoman politics. In late 1914 Enver Paşa committed the Ottoman Empire to World War I on the side of Germany and Austria-Hungary, and throughout the war Mustafa Kemal served as an officer on numerous fronts. His most important campaign—for which he was to gain considerable fame after the fact—was at Gallipoli, where he played a critical role helping to defend the Dardanelles. There he gained a reputation for personal bravery and effective leadership, but also for challenging the authority of allied German commanders and of Enver Paşa. Thereafter Mustafa Kemal commanded forces in Eastern Anatolia and in Syria/Palestine, where he commanded the Seventh Army when the Ottoman government concluded an armistice at Mudros on October 30, 1918.

Atatürk as a Young Man. *As the first president of the Republic of Turkey, Atatürk modernized the country by instituting numerous political, economic, and social reforms.* © HULTON-DEUTSCH COLLECTION/CORBIS. REPRODUCED BY PERMISSION.

With the conclusion of the war, the Allies set out to divide up Ottoman territory and to incorporate much of it into their own spheres of influence, while also permitting Greek and Armenian occupation of parts of Anatolia and Thrace. In Istanbul, Ottoman politicians and officers debated how to respond to these developments: the sultan advocated acquiescing to Allied demands, while nationalists—including Mustafa Kemal—discussed ways to resist the terms of the armistice. Meanwhile, across Anatolia and Thrace local Turkish groups dedicated to "the defense of national rights" had emerged by May 1919 to oppose the presence of British, French, Italian, Greek, and Armenian occupying forces. Unable to exercise much influence in Istanbul, Mustafa Kemal secured an appointment as inspector of the Ninth Army and was dispatched to Anatolia by the sultan to oversee Ottoman compliance with the armistice. Mustafa Kemal, however, had very different ideas and following his arrival in

Samsun on May 19, 1919, he began to assume leadership of the nationalist opposition and to unite it into a cohesive political and military movement. He devoted the next three years to leading the Turkish War of Independence, and against considerable odds Turkish forces succeeded at driving out all occupying forces, while Mustafa Kemal adroitly isolated the sultan's influence in Istanbul. The Ottoman parliament had reconstituted itself as the Grand National Assembly of Turkey in Ankara, and, increasingly under Mustafa Kemal's influence, it then declared an end to the sultanate on November 1, 1922; it subsequently proclaimed the Republic of Turkey with Mustafa Kemal as its first president on October 29, 1923.

Mustafa Kemal served as president for fifteen years, during which time he strove to ensure Turkey's independence at a time of ongoing Western colonial activity throughout Asia and Africa. Contrary to Western predictions that "Eastern" or "Oriental" peoples would prove too backward to be capable of self-governance, Mustafa Kemal pursued a cautious foreign policy that did not invite foreign interference and looked to Soviet Russia for support; moreover, he was determined to modernize the Turkish nation so that it might take its rightful place in the "civilized" world. Convinced that his vision alone was best for Turkey's future, Mustafa Kemal tolerated neither political nor popular opposition and ruled the country in an increasingly authoritarian manner. His vision for the country gradually developed into an ideology known as *Kemalism*, which denigrated the Ottoman-Islamic past and stressed the importance of a united modern nation rooted in an ancient Turkish history. Mustafa Kemal is frequently associated with efforts to reform and "secularize" Turkish culture and society, but while these efforts had an undeniable impact, his policies did not eliminate popular commitment to Muslim beliefs and practices. In fact, developments in the nearly seven decades since his death demonstrate that while Turks did indeed come to identify with Mustafa Kemal's Turkish nation-state, they also maintained a strong identity as Muslims.

After Atatürk's death in 1938, the Republican People's Party, which he had established, declared Atatürk the nation's "eternal leader." In many ways he lives on today: His portrait, statues, and excerpts from famous speeches are displayed prominently throughout the country. Since the late 1940s there has been some debate as to the efficacy of Atatürk's reforms and the nature of his leadership, in reaction to which the Grand National Assembly passed legislation in 1951 prohibiting his public defamation. Yet Atatürk today still remains deeply revered and respected and is mythologized for the role he played in leading what Turks consider to have been the first successful struggle of an Eastern nation against Western imperialism. Indeed, Atatürk provided important inspiration for subsequent nationalist movements from

North Africa to South Asia, although his commitment to secularization won him many critics in the Arab world especially. Few other nationalist leaders of the twentieth century continue to be as popular and prominent as does Atatürk in Turkey. He must be considered one of the great statesmen of the twentieth century.

SEE ALSO *Abdülhamid II.*

BIBLIOGRAPHY

Lord Kinross [Baron Patrick Balfour Kinross]. *Atatürk: A Biography of Mustafa Kemal, Father of Modern Turkey.* New York: Morrow, 1965. Reprint, New York: Quill, 1992.

Mango, Andrew. *Atatürk: The Biography of the Founder of Modern Turkey.* Bergenfield, NJ: Overlook Press, 2000.

Zürcher, Erik J. *Turkey: A Modern History,* rev. ed. London and New York: I. B. Tauris, 1997.

Gavin D. Brockett

ATLANTIC COLONIAL COMMERCE

In the aftermath of the voyages of Christopher Columbus (1451–1506) to the Caribbean and Central America, there arose by the eighteenth century a complex system of trade and commerce between the Americas, the Caribbean, West Africa, and Europe, a truly Atlantic colonial commerce. Moreover, this Atlantic colonial commerce was a significant part of a larger system of trade and commerce that increasingly tied South and East Asia into this European-dominated system of trade.

There were common elements in these emerging and competing systems that the great European naval and mercantile powers established. Colonies in the New World produced raw products that they traded to the Old World for manufactured goods and slaves captured in West Africa. European imperial powers all sought to control trade with their colonies, drawing on *mercantilist* ideas, which suggested that states could best build their power by channeling all colonial trade through metropolitan ports and merchants.

In many ways, colonial economies and transatlantic commerce were dependent upon the great cities of Atlantic Europe. And, despite harsh laws designed to protect these competing trading systems, the colonial powers often did not, or could not, strictly enforce the laws, and colonial merchants and others violated them for their own economic benefit. Thus, there existed an official system in law, not always followed, and an unofficial system in practice, not always recognized.

SPAIN AND PORTUGAL

Hernando Cortés (1484–1547) in Mexico and Francisco Pizarro (ca. 1475–1541) in Peru discovered vast wealth, and looted it for the benefit of Spain. In the case of Pizarro, the Inca king, Atahualpa (d. 1533), paid a ransom that consisted of a room, 6.7 meters (22 feet) long by 5.1 meters (17 feet) wide, piled some 2.1 meters (7 feet) deep with gold and silver in various shapes and arrangements—a vast fortune. Pizarro took the ransom, killed Atahualpa, decimated the Incas, and established the Spanish colonial empire in western South America.

Cortés, aided by more than twenty thousand Indians who wanted to break Aztec control of central Mexico, destroyed the capital, and Mexico City arose on the ruins of Tenochtitlán. Other conquistadores sought wealth elsewhere, and, as in the cases of Francisco Vásquez de Coronado (ca. 1510–1554), Juan Ponce de León (ca. 1460–1521), and Hernando de Soto (ca. 1500–1542), were not successful. Still this great wealth filled Spanish treasure ships, and whether they safely returned to Spain, or British and other freebooters operating in the Caribbean captured and looted them, the wealth of the New World helped spur the economy of Atlantic Europe. This influx of precious metals contributed to economic growth and, although unevenly spread, increased prosperity. The influx of gold and silver combined with an increase in the production of goods, and a fall in relative prices, especially for luxury goods, ushered in a long period of generally good economic times for Atlantic European countries.

Mines in Mexico, Peru, and Bolivia continued to produce great wealth, but, in time, production declined, and the Spanish economic empire weakened. Despite Spanish efforts, silver production declined, and attacks by Dutch, French, and English pirates on the great treasure fleets increased. This resulted in a decline of the so-called Carrera de Indias (the system of armed convoys that connected Spain to Mexico, via Veracruz, and to South America via Cartagena de Indias and the Isthmus of Panama), and the costs—ships, crews, weather challenges, and piracy—remained high.

Spain had problems in developing a viable colonial economic system that strengthened both the mother country and the colonies. Spain did try to convert Native Americans to Christianity and to have them work in agriculture, raising animals and crops to feed the miners and populations in coastal cities. But diseases inadvertently imported from Europe decimated Native American populations, and the remainder resisted the Spanish.

Landholdings in the Americas were complex, including villages, ranchos, haciendas, and estancias, which made it difficult to exploit the land to produce a valuable crop for export. In theory, Spanish settlers tried to recreate the great estates that characterized the Castilian nobility, but practice varied widely. Farmers found it more profitable to produce grains, livestock, textiles, and hides for local and sometimes regional but not transnational markets. While individual colonies may have prospered, the mother country and the closed trading system it sought to establish gradually declined.

Eventually, Spain would find more profitable crops—first sugar, and later tobacco, cotton, and coffee—that its colonies in the West Indies would produce. Indeed, in 1503, Spain bought African slaves that had been brought to its Caribbean islands, introducing of a system of African slavery that was gradually to become widespread throughout Spanish America. Although the Spanish did not capture or transport African slaves, Spanish farms used many slaves because comparatively few Spanish middle-class or lower-class families emigrated to the New World. But Spain wasted the great mineral wealth it gained in the Americas in its involvement in the religious wars in Europe, and, along with Portugal, Spain became subservient to the other European Atlantic countries.

Portugal was not as systematic in occupying Brazil. Despite the Treaty of Tordesillas in 1494, Portugal looked around Africa, towards India, for wealth and its future. There was some value in the wood of the Brazil wood tree and the red dye it created. Still, the king would divide Brazil into fifteen captaincies, and although many of these great landholdings failed, two of them, Pernambuco and São Vicente, did succeed based on sugar cane farming. Raising cane was difficult and labor intensive, and in time these Portuguese plantations would rely on African slave labor. These vast plantations required a great deal of labor, and given the relatively short distance from Brazil to West Africa, Brazil became the greatest importer of West African slaves.

While Spanish explorers found precious metals in the New World, French, English, and Dutch sailors found the great fisheries near the Newfoundland coast. This also proved to be a great source of wealth. John Cabot (ca. 1450–1499) returned to England in 1496 having failed to find a Northwest Passage but with quantities of salt cod. Fish fed Europeans in winter and was important in the Catholic calendar, and the vast reserves of fish in North American waters helped create wealth for the merchants backing these fleets.

GREAT BRITAIN, FRANCE, AND THE NETHERLANDS

Weaknesses in the Spanish colonial system encouraged British and also Dutch and French merchants and adventurers to fill gaps left by Spanish merchants. Such British

ship captains as John Hawkins (1532–1595) recognized that Spain needed a workforce for the sugar plantations and the mines, and he helped start the English trade in West African slaves. The initial profits were so great that Queen Elizabeth I (1533–1603) secretly invested in his voyages. Despite Spanish protests and the harsh measures used against captured foreign sailors, these English privateers continued to raid Spanish treasure ships and also supply the needs of Spain's New World colonies. Dutch and French captains soon joined the English.

At this time, the Dutch were the great traders of the world, for they possessed ships that were faster and safer—more likely to reach their planned destinations—than their competitors. In Southeast Asia, Dutch traders became wealthy shipping goods within that region, which led to Holland's empire in the East Indies. The Dutch also dominated trade from north to southwest Europe and along the Baltic Sea. But, after losing New Amsterdam (New York) to the British, Holland was not a great player in the Atlantic economy of the seventeenth and eighteenth centuries. Nonetheless, one reason for the English Navigation Laws starting in the 1660s was to strengthen British merchants and break the power of the Dutch, a development taking place in the eighteenth century.

France established an empire in North America based on agriculture, fishing, lumbering, commerce, and fur trading. The French had strategic locations, controlling the Bay of Saint Lawrence, the Saint Lawrence River, the Ohio River, and the upper and lower Mississippi River. But France never had the population movement—not of French people and not of African slaves—to rival the population of its English colonial neighbors. In the West Indies, France held Martinique and Guadeloupe, useful for sugar, tobacco, and indigo (a blue dye used for naval uniforms), as well as for trade with the richer Spanish possessions. Still, defeat in the French and Indian War (known in Europe as the Seven Years War) ended France's North American empire in 1763, save for two small islands, Saint Pierre and Miquelon, which permitted the French to salt and dry cod captured off Newfoundland prior to the long journey back to Europe.

Although the French empire in the Americas was never as great or powerful as that of Spain or Britain, France also had its mercantilist policies. The French minister, Jean Baptiste Colbert (1619–1683), promulgated such rules as requiring French manufacturers to purchase raw materials only from French or French colonial sources, to control trade to the colonies through French ports, and to encourage French emigration to the colonies to help populate them, but France was not

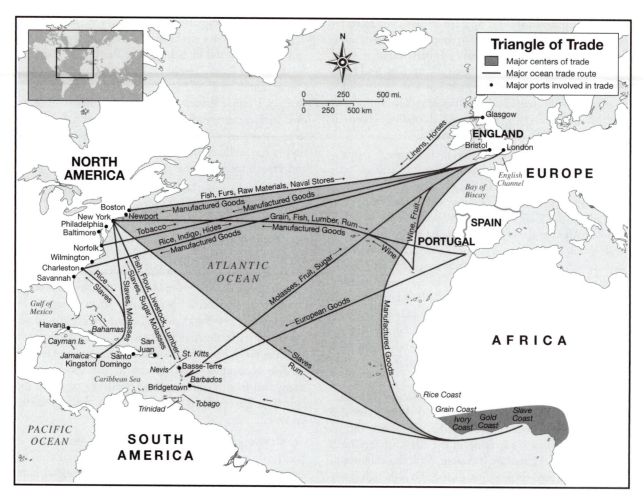

MAP BY XNR PRODUCTIONS. THE GALE GROUP.

as successful as its major opponent in the seventeenth and eighteenth centuries, Great Britain.

Then there was Great Britain. Britons settled along the Atlantic seaboard, and after some fits and starts a series of flourishing colonies in Virginia and Massachusetts, Pennsylvania, and in other regions of the eastern seaboard arose. The British Hudson's Bay Company secured furs and other precious items through bases north of French-held Quebec. And British colonies in the Caribbean provided sugar, tobacco, and coffee, all commodities highly valued in Europe.

It is interesting that Britain built such a successful first empire in the Americas, since British colonists discovered little gold or precious metals; they also were unable to use or exploit the native workforce to any profitable extent. British success in competing with the other European colonial powers owed much to the greater openness of its colonial system to commerce and immigration, and to the development of an extraordinary

maritime power that it could use both for peaceful trade and for fighting wars.

MERCANTILISM AND THE TRIANGULAR TRADING SYSTEM

When historians talk of the so-called triangular trading system, they usually refer to Great Britain and its colonies in the Americas and slave colonies in West Africa. By the late seventeenth century, the countries of Atlantic Europe and their colonies to the west were connected by a relatively elaborate network of trade and commerce. It is important to note that most ships followed one route, and while the system is frequently called the triangular trade system, it was a series of separate routes that fit together into a whole.

For example, ships designed to transport slaves on the so-called Middle Passage from ports in West Africa to the Caribbean could not easily and profitably convert to transport other kinds of cargo. Manufactured products from Europe and rum from North America, a byproduct of sugar production, were traded for slaves in West Africa. West African slaves, more than ten million, were forcibly shipped to the Caribbean, Jamaica being the chief trading center, and then transshipped to Brazil, British North America, and other Caribbean islands. New England and the Carolinas produced naval stores; Boston also shipped furs and fish. The Middle Colonies consumed manufactured goods, for which they exchanged tobacco, and the southern colonies added rice, indigo, and furs. It was a complex system that most benefited Great Britain, providing goods for reexport to Europe, markets for British manufactures, and a carrying trade that strengthened the growth of its navy.

Colonial trading systems were underpinned by the theory of *mercantilism*, which determined the ways in which European states organized commerce with their colonies. The goal was to develop a closed trading system, where colonies provided the mother country with needed raw materials and also absorbed surplus production; colonies should not compete with the mother country in producing manufactured and finished goods. Ideally, the system would produce a surplus of a valuable good that other, competing European nations would be forced to purchase using their precious metals, thereby enriching one mercantilist empire at the cost of the others. Thus some economic historians refer to mercantilism as *bullionism*. To enforce this theory of mercantilism, a mother country needed a powerful navy and the capacity to force its colonies to sell valuable raw materials only to merchants of the mother country and, likewise, to purchase finished products only from the same merchants, even if a competing nation was willing to pay more or to sell finished goods for less.

Such regulations inevitably created tensions. In the Americas, colonists wanted to sell their goods for the highest possible price, purchase at the lowest, and have a navy safeguard goods to market. While they were not disloyal to their respective mother countries, they were not particularly loyal either. The British colonists in North America were probably the most guilty of this practice, favoring the Dutch through the port of Saint Eustacious in the Caribbean or the French in nearby Quebec, thereby seeking the benefits of the British trading empire without its attendant costs.

Britain, as with other imperial powers, sought to control the economies of its colonies for its own benefit. The British Parliament passed a series of so-called Navigation Acts beginning in 1651 and continuing until they were revoked in the mid-nineteenth century, long after Britain's original North American colonies had successfully revolted and established the United States. The acts required the shipping of goods to England or English colonial ports unless such goods were transshipped through a major port in Great Britain. The original acts in 1651 and again in the 1660s were clearly aimed at the Dutch, whose ships regularly visited colonial ports, and who thus profited from a system that the British Royal Navy protected but who avoided paying appropriate taxes and charges.

In the 1660s Britain produced a list of "enumerated goods," including tobacco, sugar, cotton, wool, and dyeing woods, which colonies could only trade among themselves or with Great Britain. Other European countries would have to pay marked-up prices, and thus their precious metals would flow into British ports, strengthening Britain. Later acts suppressed colonial manufactures, which would strike New York and the New England colonies especially hard had the colonists followed the law, and had British colonial agents and the Royal Navy enforced them.

DECLINE OF THE ATLANTIC COLONIAL COMMERCIAL SYSTEM

About the time this Atlantic colonial commercial system was relatively firmly in place, great changes occurred. France and England fought four great wars for empire. In each case, a conflict in Europe led to a war between French Quebec and British North America. In the fourth and final war, the Seven Years (1756–1763) or French and Indian War (1754–1763), England hired German and other mercenaries to contain France on the European continent while seizing control of France's holdings in North America and elsewhere. France lost Canada and was left with only two islands off the Newfoundland coast, together with its islands in the Caribbean and its foothold on the Caribbean coast of South America.

Britain's victory over France led to the American Revolution. Britain had spent a vast fortune to defeat France, and, since one of the main beneficiaries of this overwhelming victory was Britain's colonies in North America, King George III (1738–1820) and Parliament not unnaturally wanted the colonists to help pay the cost. The colonists demurred, citing a lack of appropriate representation in the British Parliament, and eventually the situation devolved into war. When the Revolutionary War ended with the Treaty of Paris in 1783, Britain's largest holdings in the Americas were now independent, and outside of any of the imperial trading blocs.

Soon thereafter Europe plunged into the French revolutionary and Napoleonic wars. Beginning with the French Revolution in the 1790s, various combinations of European countries fought for more than two decades until, in the aftermath of the defeat of Napoléon Bonaparte (1769–1821) at Waterloo in central Belgium in 1815, a peace of sorts seemed to descend on Europe. Thereafter, the scene of colonial exploitation and hence trade would move to Asia; to the British takeover of India; to the competition in Southeast Asia between the Portuguese, the Dutch, and other late arrivers; and finally to the great prize of China, which had reached its peak and was beginning to descend in power, prestige, and control.

SEE ALSO *Company of New France; Export Commodities; Massachusetts Bay Company; Mercantilism; Virginia Company.*

BIBLIOGRAPHY

Alderman, Clifford L. *Rum, Slaves, and Molasses: The Story of New England's Triangular Trade.* New York: Crowell Collier, 1972.

Armitage, David, and Michael J. Braddick, eds. *The British-Atlantic World, 1500–1800.* New York: Palgrave Macmillan, 2002.

Crouse, Nellis M. *The French Struggle for the West Indies, 1665–1713.* New York: Columbia University Press, 1943

Davies, David W. *A Primer of Dutch Seventeenth Century Overseas Trade.* The Hague, Netherlands: Nijhoff, 1961.

Dunn, Richard S. *Sugar and Slaves: The Rise of the Planter Class in the English West Indies, 1624–1713.* Chapel Hill: University of North Carolina Press, 1972.

Emmer, P.C. *The Dutch in the Atlantic Economy, 1580–1880: Trade, Slavery, and Emancipation.* Brookfield, VT: Ashgate, 1998.

Knight, Franklin W., and Peggy K. Liss, eds. *Atlantic Port Cities: Economy, Culture, and Society in the Atlantic World, 1650–1850.* Knoxville: University of Tennessee Press, 1999

Liss, Peggy K. *Atlantic Empires: The Network of Trade and Revolution, 1713–1826.* Baltimore, MD: Johns Hopkins University Press, 1983.

McCusker, John J., and Kenneth Morgan, eds. *The Early Modern Atlantic Economy.* New York: Cambridge University Press, 1993.

Ormrod, David. *The Rise of Commercial Empires: England and the Netherlands in the Age of Mercantilism, 1650–1770.* New York: Cambridge University Press, 2003.

Parry, John H. *Trade and Dominion: The European Overseas Empires in the Eighteenth Century.* New York: Praeger, 1971.

Pritchard, James. *In Search of Empire: The French in the Americas, 1670–1730.* New York: Cambridge University Press, 2004.

Solow, Barbara L., ed. *Slavery and the Rise of the Atlantic System.* New York: Cambridge University Press, 1993.

Charles M. Dobbs

ATLANTIC FISHERIES

Codfish was the first New World product consumed on a large scale in Europe. It has seldom been considered a colonial product because the cod fishery began long before the establishment of colonies in northeastern North America. The acquisition of codfish did not require trade or even contact with the continent's indigenous peoples, since fishermen took cod out at sea, either out on the banks or along the coasts of what is now known as Newfoundland, Labrador, the Gaspé Peninsula, the Canadian maritime provinces, and the American state of Maine.

Europeans did not compete with indigenous peoples for codfish because this stretch of the North American coast was one of the least populated areas of the entire continent, the fishermen themselves only frequented it for a short period each year, and codfish was not a resource exploited by the Amerindians, who relied almost exclusively on intertidal and river species for their livelihood. European fishermen salted and preserved codfish directly onboard their ships or on uninhabited islands or shores during the summer months, but even the latter operation did not necessitate the installation of permanent settlements, since the codfish were loaded onto the ships and the drying stations were abandoned at the end of the season.

Nonetheless, the cod fishery allowed the European fishermen, particularly the French and the English, to "occupy" the coast, to symbolically consume this space, and progressively construct a colonial territory. The fishery was a "protocolonial" activity that helped to initiate the process of colonization through mass consumption.

The New World cod fishery developed early in the sixteenth century and at a rapid pace in a large number of Atlantic ports in southern England, western France, northwestern Spain, and northwestern Portugal. Cod fishing in the "New-Found-Land" is mentioned as early as 1502 in English records, 1510 in Norman archives, and 1512 in French Basque archives. Already substantial by the 1520s and 1530s, this fishery grew at a remarkable rate in the middle of the century. Wherever they have been preserved, the notarial archives reveal a rapid increase in voyages to Newfoundland, especially from France. For example, in Bordeaux the departures registered by notaries grow from approximately ten per year in the 1540s to more than fifty per year beginning in 1560. The same increase took place in La Rochelle and Rouen.

The tally made by the sixteenth-century English navigator Anthony Parkhurst in the course of a reconnaissance mission in 1578 set the number of European ships involved in the fishery at approximately 380: 150 French cod-fishing vessels, 100 Spanish, 50 Portuguese, and 30 to 50 English, along with 20 to 30 Basque whalers. Parkhurst probably underestimated the size of the fleet, since the incomplete notarial records of Bordeaux, La Rochelle, and Rouen indicate that there were more than 150 vessels at midcentury at these three French ports alone. More plausible are the figures of Robert Hitchcock, author of, *A Political Platt for the Honour of the Prince* (London, 1580), based on intelligence reports sent from French ports, setting the French fleet at approximately 500 ships in about 1580, to which one must add the less substantial, but nevertheless sizable, Spanish, Portuguese, and English fishing fleets.

These figures point to an immense fishing enterprise that has been largely overlooked in the maritime history of the North Atlantic.. In light of these figures, it would appear legitimate to estimate the European cod fishing fleet in the early 1580s at 700 or 800 ships, which would have had a combined loading capacity of some 60,000 tons burden, and they mobilized more than 16,000 fishermen each year.

The Newfoundland fleet surpassed by far the prestigious Spanish fleet that traded with the Americas, which had only one quarter the loading capacity and crewmembers. According to Pierre and Huguette Chaunu (1953), the fleet engaged in Hispano-American commerce comprised between fifty and one hundred large vessels, which loaded an annual average of 16,000 tons and were crewed annually by four to five thousand men during the 1570s. These figures demonstrate that the Gulf of the Saint Lawrence represented a site of European activity fully comparable to the Gulf of Mexico or the Caribbean. While North American codfish obviously did not possess the value of silver and gold, it demanded large numbers of vessels and men—at least three to four times what was needed for the routes that led to the South American trades—and thus had unexpected implications for the development of the North Atlantic maritime economy.

Little known in the Middle Ages, in the sixteenth century codfish became the most widely consumed fish in western Europe, surpassing hake and even herring, the king of medieval fish. The French naturalist Pierre Belon (1517–1564) devotes a long article to codfish in *La nature et diversité des poissons* (The Nature and Diversity of Fish, 1555)—the first natural history on fish written in French—and states that "there is no place where it is not sold." Codfish penetrated far into the interior of France, Spain, and Portugal, reaching even small country towns. Cod was not only found everywhere, almost everyone consumed it. It turned up on the tables of princes as well as those of villagers and peasants.

In all of the large port cities, professional sorters (who were incorporated) carefully graded the fish so that they would meet the demands of consumers from different social classes. The top-quality cod reached the best aristocratic tables of both Protestant and Catholic families, and it was featured in the most refined French cookbooks. The most renowned cookbook in seventeenth-century France, the *Cuisinier françois* by François Pierre de La Varenne (1618–1678), the cook for the bishop of Châlons near Troyes—a location well inland—offers five recipes for codfish and another for codfish pâté. Cod figured in the privileged diet of both religious and secular institutions, and it often appeared on tables in the refectories of ecclesiastical institutions, establishments that served as models in matters of food, perhaps even more than aristocratic tables. The French navy also ordered large quantities of cod to feed ships' crews during military campaigns at sea. And account books for hospitals or convents show regular purchases of codfish. Cod also graced servants' tables in large houses, hostels, and inns.

Codfish was sought after and widely consumed because it satisfied a European longing for space and a desire to consume the "New Land," especially in France and England. Exotic foods are directly linked to space. As Sidney Mintz (1985) and others such as David Bell and Gill Valentine (1997) have demonstrated, to eat a foreign food is to bring its place of origin to one's own place and even into oneself, to domesticate it and make it familiar. Consuming an exotic food requires a symbolic appropriation of the place of origin and at the same time an occupation of that territory, in order to make appropriation possible. It is because of this double affiliation with territories, that consumption and colonization are so intimately linked and the production of food so central to colonization. Notably, most colonial products brought from the Americas in the early modern period were foods: codfish, sugar, coffee, and cocoa.

Codfish was considered an exotic product in the sixteenth century because the name of its place of origin, the New Land, is regularly paired with the name of the fish in the documents of the period. The earliest English and French records that mention cod-fishing expeditions to the New World specify that the product comes from the New Land. In Bordeaux, long before wine had acquired this privilege, the contracts for sales of cod drawn up by notaries indicated "codfish from the New Land"; the same is true of the provisioning contracts of the great aristocratic houses of Paris. And La Varenne, in his celebrated *Cuisinier françois*, titles one of his recipes "Codfish from the New Land"; of the ninety-three recipes he provides for fish, this is the only one to which he attributes a place name.

As its name suggests, the New Land evoked the mythic origins of a virgin territory, exempt from original sin, a paradise that sheltered the fountain of eternal youth. The term expressed the hope of attainment of the terrestrial paradise promised in the New Testament *Apocalypse* (the *Book of Revelation*)—a world dating from before the Fall described in *Genesis*, in which Christians could live in harmony with the elements and establish a direct and peaceful relation with their creator.

During the sixteenth century, the French, English, Spanish, and Portuguese began to actively include North American codfish in their everyday lives. The consumption and domestication of codfish was a means of symbolically appropriating the geography of the New Land and of making it financially feasible for colonization, at the same time that it immediately changed the daily lives of those future colonizers. North America was being incorporated into the European diet, domesticated as it were, whereas on the other side of the Atlantic, fishermen transmitted European diseases, which decimated native populations and cleared the land for European settlement. This first protocolonial phase of colonization set the stage for the establishment of permanent French and English settlements and a colonial administration in New France, Newfoundland, and New England at the beginning of the seventeenth century.

SEE ALSO *Atlantic Colonial Commerce; European Explorations in North America; New France.*

BIBLIOGRAPHY

Bell, David, and Gill Valentine. *Consuming Geographies: We Are Where We Eat.* London: Routledge, 1997.

Chaunu, Pierre, and Huguette Chaunu. "À la recherche des fluctuations cycliques dans l'économie des XVIe et XVIIe siècles." In *Éventail de l'histoire vivante: Hommage à Lucien Febvre,* edited by Fernand Braudel, 392–407. Paris: Armand Colin, 1953.

Innis, Harold A. *The Cod Fisheries: The History of an International Economy,* rev. ed. Toronto, ON: University of Toronto Press, 1978.

La Morandière, Charles de. *Histoire de la pêche française à la morue dans l'Amérique septentrionale,* 3 vols. Paris: Maisonneuve and Larose, 1962.

Mintz, Sidney. *Sweetness and Power: The Place of Sugar in Modern History.* New York: Viking, 1985.

Quinn, David B., ed. *New American World: A Documentary History of North America to 1612,* Vol. 4: *Newfoundland from Fishery to Colony, Northwest Passage Searches.* New York: Arno, 1979.

Turgeon, Laurier. "Bordeaux and the Newfoundland Trade During the Sixteenth Century." *International Journal of Maritime History* 9 (2) (1997): 1–28.

Turgeon, Laurier. "Le temps des pêches lointaines: Permanences et transformations (vers 1500–vers 1850)." In *Histoire des pêches maritimes en France,* edited by Michel Mollat, 133–181. Toulouse, France: Privat, 1987.

Laurier Turgeon

AUSTRALIA

Australia is a country in the Southern Hemisphere, lying between the Indian and Pacific oceans. The only country to occupy an entire continent, Australia is about the same size as the United States, not including Alaska. Australia is relatively flat and, with the exception of outlying tropical and temperate regions, has a dry climate. The capital is Canberra and the largest cities are Sydney, Melbourne, and Brisbane. Australia includes the large island of Tasmania as well as smaller offshore territories such as the Coral Sea Islands, Norfolk Island, Macquarie Island, Christmas Island, and the Cocos Islands; it also claims part of Antarctica. Australia is rich in mineral wealth and is ranked among the world's top five producers of such minerals as bauxite, lead, zinc, gold, iron, cobalt, uranium, coal, copper, nickel, and silver. The country's agricultural sector is also considerable, with wheat, wool, and beef cattle especially important.

Australia's indigenous inhabitants are known as Aboriginal people (the preferred term) and also as Aborigines. Aboriginal people settled in Australia at least forty thousand years ago and possibly as early as seventy thousand years ago; they settled the entire continent, as well as Tasmania, and developed hunting, fishing, and gathering cultures appropriate to various environments. About six hundred different Aboriginal societies, or tribes, most with their own distinctive languages, flourished in Australia prior to European arrival. Though their technology was relatively simple, Aboriginal people developed complex religions and legal systems and were able to survive and prosper in extremely harsh environments.

The first European to visit Australia was the Dutch explorer Willem Jansz, who sighted the northern coast in 1606 and named it New Holland; some scholars, however, believe that Spanish and Portuguese explorers may have made earlier sightings. Later Dutch and British expeditions provided Europeans with greater knowledge of this "new" continent. In 1770 Captain James Cook landed at Botany Bay, near present-day Sydney, and explored the eastern coast of Australia, claiming it for Great Britain and naming it New South Wales. By the beginning of the nineteenth century Australia had been circumnavigated and its coastline mapped; much of the interior, however, remained unknown to Europeans until the nineteenth and twentieth centuries.

British settlement in Australia began in 1788 with the founding of Sydney (then known as Port Jackson) as a penal colony. Prisoners from Great Britain, many of them charged with minor offenses, were settled in the Sydney area. The British believed that transporting convicts to Australia would help reduce prison overcrowding in England, would remove "undesirable" people from the mother country, and would help populate Australia. Penal colonies were also established elsewhere, notably in Tasmania and in Western Australia. About 160,000 convicts were sent to Australia between the 1780s and the 1860s. Convict life varied, but punishments for infractions could be severe, and included beatings, solitary confinement, and even death. When freed, convicts were often given land.

The Founding of Australia. *In January 1788 Captain Arthur Phillip established an English settlement at Sydney Cove on the southeast coast of Australia. In this illustration based on a 1937 painting by Algernon Talmadge, Phillip and his crew hoist a flag on the site, an event that is considered the beginning of European settlement in Australia.* HULTON ARCHIVE/GETTY IMAGES. REPRODUCED BY PERMISSION.

Australia remained something of an economic backwater until the discovery of gold north of Melbourne in 1851. As in California, the Australian gold rush resulted in many new settlers and the further exploration of the continent's interior. The gold rush stimulated other economic sectors, such as agriculture, and Australia in the 1860s was transformed from a penal colony into six flourishing colonies of free settlers. At intercolonial conferences beginning in 1863 the separate colonies of New South Wales, Victoria, Tasmania, Queensland, South Australia, and Western Australia debated joining together. They did so in 1901, forming the Commonwealth of Australia, with a federal system consisting of a national government and state governments.

Until the 1960s, Australia's economy was closely tied to Great Britain through a system of imperial preference that gave trade advantages to British dominions. When Britain joined the forerunner of the European Union, Australia's trade began to shift to Asia and the United States. Though Australia is independent, the British monarch remains the country's formal head of state. An antimonarchy movement is gaining influence, but a referendum on creating a republic was defeated in 1999.

Australia sent troops to support the British in both World Wars. Australia's participation in the failed campaign to win the Gallipoli Peninsula in Turkey in 1915 and its loss of over eight thousand soldiers created a strong sense of Australian, as opposed to British, national identity. In the 1940s, when Japan posed a threat to the country's northern coast, Australia requested assistance from the United States, which led to a strong new alliance and a shift in the country's military ties away from Britain.

From federation in 1901 until 1973, Australia had a restrictive immigration policy, known as the "White Australia" policy, which limited immigration mainly to emigrants from the British Isles, though some exceptions

AUSTRALIA

0   200   400   600 Miles

0   200   400   600 Kilometers

INDONESIA

NEW GUINEA PAPUA NEW GUINEA

Port Moresby ✪

Arafura Sea

Torres Strait

Coral Sea

Timor Sea

Melville I.

Bamaga ● Cape York

Van Diemen Gulf

INDIAN OCEAN

Joseph Bonaparte Gulf

Darwin *Arnhem Land*

Cape Arnhem

Gulf of Carpentaria

Cape York Peninsula

Pine Creek ●
Katherine ●

Groot Eylandt I.

Edward River ●

BONAPARTE ARCHIPELAGO

Kimberley Plateau

Bullo River ●
Lake Argyle

Borroloola ●

Mornington I.

Cairns ●

GREAT DIVIDING RANGE

Great Barrier Reef

Beagle Bay ● ● Derby

Dampier Land

NORTHERN TERRITORY

Barkley Tableland

Burketown ●

Townsville ●

Eighty Mile Beach

● Port Hedland

GREAT SANDY DESERT

Balgo ●

Tanami Desert

Mount Isa ●

QUEENSLAND

Mackay ●

Barrow I. ●

HAMERSLEY RANGE

MACDONNELL RANGES

Rockhampton

North West Cape

Exmouth ●

Alice Springs ●

Great Artesian Basin

Bundaberg ●

Red Bluff

▲ Mt. Newman 3,451 ft. 1053 m.

Gibson Desert

▲ Ayers Rock 2,844 ft. 867 m.

Simpson Desert

Gympie ●

Carnarvon ●

WESTERN AUSTRALIA

▲ Mt. Sir Thomas 2,536 ft. 773 m.

Channel Country

Toowoomba ● **Brisbane** ●

Dirk Hartog I. ● Denham

Lake Eyre

Gold Coast

Geraldton ●

GREAT VICTORIA DESERT

SOUTH AUSTRALIA

Lake Torrens

Hungerford ●

DARLING RANGE

Kalgoorlie ●

Nullarbor Plain

Yalata ●

Darling

Tamworth ●

GREAT DIVIDING RANGE

John Eyre Motel ●

Scorpion Bight

Point Brown

Broken Hill ●

NEW SOUTH WALES

Newcastle ●

Perth ●

Point Culver

Whyalla ●

Orange ●

Sydney ●

Fremantle
Bunbury ●

Esperance ●

Cape Pasley

Great Australian Bight

Port Lincoln ●

Spencer Gulf

Adelaide ●

Murrumbidgee

Albury ●

Murray

✪ **Canberra**

Wollongong ●

Cape Naturaliste

Hood Point

Meningie ●

Kangaroo I.

Bendigo ●

Mt. Kosciusko 7,310 ft. 2228 m.

Flinders Bay

Walpole ● Albany

Cape Jaffa

Ballarat ● **VICTORIA**

Geelong ●

Melbourne ●

Tasman Sea

King I.

Bass Strait

Flinders I.

Devonport ● **Launceston** ●

Tasmania

Hobart ●

South West Cape   Cape Pillar

Christmas I.

Ashmore & Cartier Is.

Cocos Is.

Coral Sea Islands Territory

Islands administered by Australia

AUSTRALIA

Norfolk I.

Heard & McDonald Is.

Macquarie I.

N W E S

© MARYLAND CARTOGRAPHICS. REPRODUCED BY PERMISSION.

were made for southern and eastern Europeans, especially after World War II. In the 1970s the country began to admit Asian immigrants and today Australia has a large Asian and Pacific Islander community.

Australia became a colonial power in its own right when it acquired formerly British as well as formerly German territories in New Guinea; Australia administered these as colonies from the end of World War I until the independence of Papua New Guinea in 1975. Australia also acquired the phosphate-rich Pacific island of Nauru after World War I and administered it until Nauruan independence in 1968. Australia is still involved in the economic and political affairs of these countries.

Australia has increasingly come to terms with its Aboriginal population and the consequences of colonialism.

Aboriginal people were finally granted Australian citizenship and the right to vote in 1967. In 1992 the country's High Court, in the *Mabo* case, overturned the legal doctrine of *terra nullius*, which had stated that Australia was "unoccupied" at the time of British settlement and that therefore Aboriginal people had no legal title to lands. The *Mabo* decision, along with subsequent court cases, initiated a process of land claims, in which Aboriginal communities that could demonstrate continued association with their traditional lands would receive land titles as well as compensation. Australians at the start of the twenty-first century are also addressing the historical treatment of Aboriginal people, as the process of reconciliation continues.

SEE ALSO *Commonwealth System; Pacific, European Presence in.*

BIBLIOGRAPHY

Denoon, Donald, et al. *A History of Australia, New Zealand, and the Pacific*. Oxford: Blackwell, 2000.

Flannery, Tim F., ed. *The Explorers: Stories of Discovery and Adventure from the Australian Frontier*. New York: Grove, 2000.

Hughes, Robert. *The Fatal Shore: The Epic of Australia's Founding*. New York: Vintage, 1988.

Macintyre, Stuart. *A Concise History of Australia*. Cambridge, U.K.: Cambridge University Press, 1999.

Moorehead, Alan. *The Fatal Impact: An Account of the Invasion of the South Pacific, 1767–1840*. New York: Harper and Row, 1966.

Powell, J. M. *An Historical Geography of Modern Australia: The Restive Fringe*. Cambridge, U.K.: Cambridge University Press, 1988.

Ward, Russel. *The Australian Legend*, 2nd ed. Melbourne: Oxford University Press, 1978.

Michael Pretes

AUSTRALIA, ABORIGINES

Aboriginal people understand their ancestors to have always been on the Australian continent, and archaeologists have dated their remains at over forty-thousand years old. Contact between Europeans and Aborigines was sporadic from the Dutch, Portuguese, and British expeditions across the Indian Ocean in the seventeenth century, to the British and French explorations of the Pacific Ocean in the eighteenth century. Explorer James Cook (1728–1779) navigated the eastern coast of Australia in 1770, claiming it for Britain, and in 1788 Cameragal, Gayimai, and Cadigal people around what is now Sydney, witnessed the arrival of hundreds of convicts and soldiers. Unlike previous Europeans who came and went, this group stayed to establish a new penal colony.

Wherever the British established pastoral, penal, and shipping communities—inland from Sydney, in Tasmania, around the bay of what is now Melbourne—Aboriginal people were displaced from traditional lands, were sometimes killed by settlers, became ill, and often died from exotic diseases, especially smallpox. Occasionally, in this early period, encounters across cultures resulted in ongoing familial, sexual, or companionate relationships: Tasmanian Aboriginal women lived and had families with British sealers and whalers; escaped British convicts sometimes incorporated into Aboriginal communities; and indigenous men known to the historical record, like Bennelong (1764–1813), or Baneelon, formed friendships with British officials, albeit initially unwillingly, and occasionally traveled to England.

From the 1830s, Aboriginal people in the British colonies in the south and east (New South Wales, Tasmania, Victoria) were increasingly managed by governments through various 'protection' acts. Land was set aside for them, and 'reserves' and 'missions' were headed by British officials or religious bodies. The system of missions and reserves became more rigid in the early twentieth century, with the Aborigines Protection Acts strictly limiting movement beyond the reserves.

In the early twentieth century, Aboriginal families were increasingly subject to policies of child removal. This was driven by concern about interracial sex, and so-called 'mixed-race' children, whom the government sought to assimilate. Many Aboriginal and non-Aboriginal historians consider that the state practice of child removal was genocide, as defined by the UN Convention. There is a long history of indigenous protest against this removal, the limitation of movement, exploitive working conditions, and the active exclusion of Aboriginal people from the civic body. Aboriginal people always link this protest to the original dispossession of land. Resistance has ranged from formal petitions (to King George V [1865–1936] in 1934, for example), to mothers hiding their children from welfare agents, to successful labor strikes on cattle stations, as well as long-standing campaigns for the restoration of land, and recognition of native title. A major campaign in 1967 successfully changed the Australian constitution by referendum, transferring power over Aboriginal affairs from state governments to the federal government. More civic rights gradually ensued. Currently, Aboriginal and Torres Strait Islander people deal with many social, political, and health problems that are a direct legacy of the colonial past. The meaning of this history forms a major aspect of political and cultural debate in Australia.

SEE ALSO *Australia.*

BIBLIOGRAPHY

Australia. Human Rights and Equal Opportunity Commission. *Bringing Them Home: Report of the National Inquiry into the Separation of Aboriginal and Torres Strait Islander Children from their Families*. Sydney: Human Rights and Equal Opportunity Commision, 1997.

Goodall, Heather. *Invasion to Embassy: Land in Aboriginal Politics in New South Wales, 1770–1972*. St. Edwards, Australia: Allen & Unwin, 1996.

Alison Bashford

AZIKIWE, NNAMDI
1904–1996

Born of Igbo parents on November 16, 1904, in Zungeru, Nigeria, soothsayers had foretold a great future for Nnamdi Azikiwe. In a traditional African society where the gods saw all and knew all, one fortune-teller named the new babe Ibrahim after a local ruler who stoutly resisted British colonialism in northern Nigeria. Indeed, by his death in May 1996, the "Great Zik of Africa" had left an enviable legacy of accomplishments.

Early in life, Azikiwe clearly understood the importance of Western education in the neocolonial world order. His formal education began at the mission schools in Nitsha in 1912. Afterward, he attended the Wesleyan Boys High School in Lagos, and later transferred to the Hope Waddell Training Institute in Calabar. With this education, Azikiwe acquired proficiency in Hausa, Igbo, Yoruba, and Efik languages, while also being attuned to their various indigenous cultures and customs. In 1925 Azikiwe traveled to the United States in search of an American education. By 1931, Azikiwe had earned degrees in journalism, law, political science, and anthropology from different American institutions. American education exposed Azikiwe to the thoughts of black intellectuals like Marcus Garvey (1887–1940), W. E. B. DuBois (1868–1963), and James Emmanuel Aggrey (1875–1927). Prolific in words and writing, Azikiwe authored many articles that were published in scholarly journals. His essays addressed the African experiences with European colonialism and the hope for a renascent Africa. Overall, Azikiwe published over fifty-six books, articles, poems, and monographs, including *Liberia in World Politics* (1934), *Renascent Africa* (1937), and his autobiography, *My Odyssey* (1970).

After he left the United States in 1934, Azikiwe spent three years on the Gold Coast editing the *African Morning Post*, 1937, Azikiwe established a group of newspapers based in Nigeria, dedicated to the nationalist struggle. That same year he joined the Nigerian Youth Movement (NYM) and acquainted himself with Sir Herbert Macaulay (1864–1946), the father of Nigerian nationalism. Their friendship blossomed while creating the National Council for Nigeria and Cameroon (NCNC) in 1944, to accelerate the political development of the country. While Macaulay served as council president, Azikiwe was the secretary general.

In 1945, when the leader of labor, Michael Imoudu (b. 1902), called for a general strike, Azikiwe quickly mobilized his NCNC and chain of newspapers—the *West African Pilot, The Eastern Nigerian Guardian, the Daily Comet, The Nigerian Spokesman* and *the Southern Nigerian Defender*—to make the strike a stunning success. For his role, the colonial authorities hated Azikiwe, and there were rumors about an assassination plan as his popularity rose dramatically among the working class. The tragic demise of Macaulay during a nationwide tour organized in protest to the Richards Constitution of 1945—which was packaged without input from Nigerians—left Azikiwe as the undisputed inheritor of national politics.

Azikiwe's charisma and ideas inspired many youths who came together to form the "Zikist Movement." At the same time, his stature and political rhetoric provoked fear and envy among his peers. This would result in a far-reaching political realignment in the early 1950s that polarized Nigerian politics into three major ethnic-based political parties—the Action Group (AG) in the West, the Northern People Congress (NPC) and the NCNC in the East. This formation determined the course of Nigeria's postcolonial politics. On the eve of Nigeria's independence in October 1960, Azikiwe's NCNC forged a coalition with the victorious party, the NPC. This move guaranteed his appointment as senate leader. In 1963, Azikiwe became the first indigenous governor-general of the country.

On January 15, 1966, Nigeria took a rapid plunge into military coups, anarchy, and a civil war that lasted from 1967 to 1970. Nigeria was ruled by various military regimes until 1979 when the Second Republic elections were held. Twice, Azikiwe unsuccessfully vied for the presidency under his new political party, the Nigerian People's Party. In 1983 Azikiwe announced his retirement from active politics. He died on May 11, 1996.

SEE ALSO *Nationalism, Africa.*

BIBLIOGRAPHY

Azikiwe, Nnamdi. *Economic Reconstruction of Nigeria*. London: African Books, 1943.

Azikiwe, Nnamdi. *Liberia in World Politics*. Westport, CT: Negro Universities Press, 1970.

Azikiwe, Nnamdi. *My Odyssey: An Autobiography*. New York: Praeger, 1970.

Igwe, Agbafor. *Nnamdi Azikiwe: The Philosopher of Our Time.* Enugu, Nigeria: Fourth Dimension Publisher, 1992.

Jones-Quartey, K.A.B. *A Life of Azikiwe.* Baltimore, MD: Penguin, 1965.

Olisa, Michael S. O. and M. Ikejiani-Clark, eds. *Azikiwe and the African Revolution.* Onitsha, Nigeria: Africana-FEP, 1989.

Ugowe, C. O. O. *Eminent Nigerians of the Twentieth Century.* Lagos: Hugo Books, 2000.

Raphael Chijioke Njoku

AZTEC EMPIRE

In 1790, laborers paving the streets in downtown Mexico City came across an extraordinary piece of stone. The workers were descendents of the Aztecs (or *Mexica*, as they called themselves; pronounced Me-sheeka) who had built the city upon which Mexico City stood, the Aztec imperial capital of Tenochtitlán. The piece of stone, nearly twelve feet in diameter, had been buried in rubble when the city was destroyed in 1521. The date on the stone indicates that it was placed in the city's center in 1427. Called the Sun Stone or Calendar Stone, the carving depicted a face at its center, probably that of Tlaltecuhtli, the monstrous Earth god.

Just as Tlaltecuhtli was presented in the stone as the monstrous center of the Earth, so was Tenochtitlán hereby conceived as the fearsome center of its world. Tlaltecuhtli's tongue was carved as a flint knife, the symbol for war in the Aztec writing system, and extending from his ears were claws grasping human hearts. The concentric circles that surround this image represent the five creations of the world, extending back in time, as well as the twenty day signs making up a month, and a set of icons depicting the unceasing and all-important motion of the sun. Thus Tenochtitlán's position in time and space was more than significant; it was sacred, it sanctioned and even required warfare and sacrifice, and it indicated an awesome destiny.

What happened before 1427 that led to the carving of this stone and the development of this ideology? And in what ways did the *Mexica* of Tenochtitlán realize this destiny in the century that followed?

Like many cultures, the *Mexica* had turned the history of their ancient semisedentary lifestyle and migration into an origin myth. According to that myth, the original nomadic *Mexica* lived on the shores of a mythical Lake Aztlán (hence the modern name Aztec, which first came into vogue in the eighteenth century). Here they wandered until their patron god Huitzilopochtli told them to migrate south and to settle where they saw an eagle with a snake in its mouth alight on a prickly pear cactus (an image preserved today on the Mexican national flag). According to *Mexica* legend, this omen was sighted in 1325 on an island in Lake Texcoco, where the twin cities of Tlatelolco and Tenochtitlán were then founded.

This lake was in the center of the Valley of Mexico (the lake is now covered by Mexico City), where the *Mexica* had been living as mercenaries on marginal marshlands for about a century, according to their own history. After 1325 they continued to sell their military services and to pay tribute to the dominant city-state in the valley, Azcapotzalco, while also slowly building their own network of tribute-paying subject towns and pursuing an aggressive policy of marrying *Mexica* nobles into the ruling families of the valley.

The turning point in *Mexica* history came in 1427, the year Itzcoatl (1360–1440), the fourth *Mexica* king, took the throne and set the Calendar Stone in Tenochtitlán's plaza. The following year Itzcoatl formed an alliance with two lakeside cities, Texcoco and Tlacopan, and led a successful war against Azcapotzalco. This was not just the rise to regional dominance of the *Mexica*, but the birth of the Aztec Empire. For the next century, until stopped by the Spanish invasion, the *Mexica* engaged in an aggressive imperial expansion across Central Mexico and to its southeast. The Aztec method of imperial rule was not direct; local elites were confirmed in office, providing they were willing to accept client status within the empire. But the *Mexica* did require significant tribute payments in the form of labor and a wide variety of goods—from bulk food products to luxury items.

Thus the empire was not built upon territorial acquisition and colonization (unlike the Spanish Empire). But it was augmented through a stepping-stone method, with each conquered town providing resources (even warriors) for the next conquest, and with local rivalries exploited and intimidation tactics employed wherever possible (all methods subsequently imitated by the Spaniards). The Aztec Empire's control of trade routes and local resources through the tribute system allowed Tenochtitlán to grow into a populous, prosperous, and powerful capital city. The first Europeans to set eyes on the Aztec capital were amazed at its size, setting, and beauty. The twin island cities of Tlatelolco and Tenochtitlán—with their grid of canals, busy streets, and two plazas bounded by pyramids and plazas—seemed to float on shimmering Lake Texcoco.

Divided by a great dike to keep salt water from the city and prevent flooding, the lake was covered in canoes, its shores were studded with more cities, each with their own plazas and pyramids. There were about a quarter of a million people living in Tenochtitlán, and several million in the whole valley (with the Central Mexican

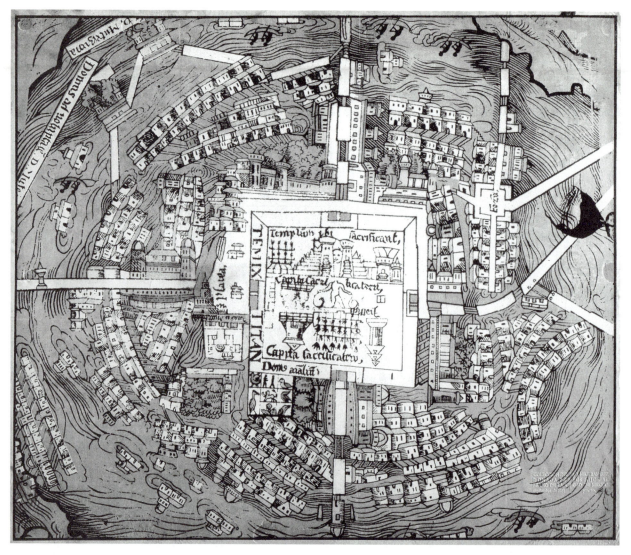

Tenochtitlán. *This plan of Tenochtitlán (Mexico City) is a sixteenth-century engraving based on a drawing attributed to Hernando Cortés. Cortés included this picture in a letter to Charles V, the Holy Roman emperor.* **THE ART ARCHIVE/MUSEO CIUDAD MEXICO/ DAGLI ORTI. REPRODUCED BY PERMISSION.**

population at an estimated 15 million or more). Visitors to the city approached it either by canoe or along one of the three great causeways that connected it to the lakeshore and held the aqueducts that brought in fresh water. One first passed some of the small elevated corn fields that bordered the lake and city, passing through the outer neighborhoods (*calpulli*) before reaching the center, where the royal family lived in palaces and where imperial administrators worked; one of the palatial compounds included a large zoo. At the heart of the city was the great plaza, dominated by twin pyramids devoted to Huitzilopochtli and Tlaloc.

In 1428, Itzcoatl and his chief minister and general, a nephew named Tlacaelel, collected and burned all

hieroglyphic books that recorded the history of the region. That history was then rewritten with the *Mexica* at its center, as the heirs to the cultural and imperial legacy of the Toltecs (whose city of Tula had dominated the valley four centuries earlier), and as the divinely sanctioned rulers of the known world. More political and economic authority was now concentrated in the hands of *Mexica* royalty, as a relatively weak monarchy was transformed into an imperial dynasty. The power that emperors would exercise for 100 years over the *Mexica* themselves and their neighbors was justified by the claim of privileged access both to the regional great tradition of the Toltecs and to the will of the gods, especially Huitzilopochtli and Tlaloc.

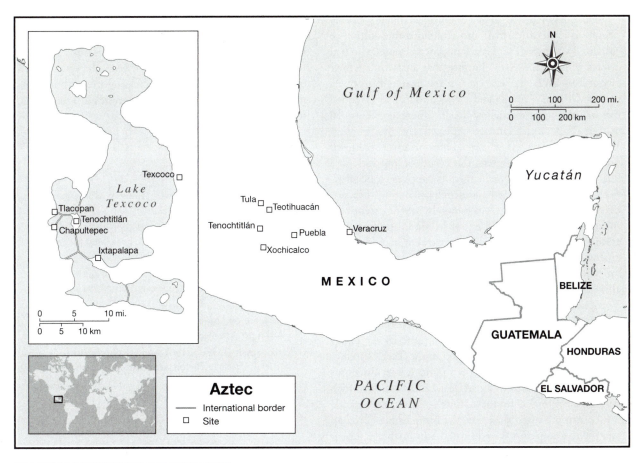

Lake Texcoco (inset)
- Texcoco
- Tlacopan
- Tenochtitlán
- Chapultepec
- Ixtapalapa

Main map:
- Tula
- Teotihuacán
- Tenochtitlán
- Puebla
- Veracruz
- Xochicalco

Gulf of Mexico

Yucatán

MEXICO

BELIZE

GUATEMALA

HONDURAS

EL SALVADOR

PACIFIC OCEAN

Aztec
— International border
□ Site

MAP BY XNR PRODUCTIONS. THE GALE GROUP.

A century after Itzcoatl became emperor, the Aztec rulers that had either survived the Spanish invasion or assumed office in its wake, met "the Twelve," the first Franciscan friars to reach Mexico. An exchange of speeches took place, and the words of the Aztec lords (written down sixty years later by Bernardino de Sahagún in his *Coloquios y doctrina cristiana*) give us some sense of a division of responsibility among religious and civil leaders in the Aztec Empire:

> We have priests who guide us and prepare us in the culture and service of our gods. There are also many others with distinct nameswho serve in the temples day and night, who are wise and knowledgeable about the movement of the heavenly bodies as well as about our ancient customs. They have the books of our forebears which they study and peruse day and night. These guide us and prepare us in counting the years, days, months, and feasts of our gods, which are celebrated every twenty days. These same priests are in charge of the histories of our gods and the rules about serving them, because we are in charge only of warfare, collection of tribute, and justice.

This is not to say that the division of responsibility between those governing religious and calendrical matters, and those managing the empire through military campaigns and tribute collection, did not amount to anything like a separation of church and state. On the contrary, the Aztec ideology of empire was profoundly interwoven with religious ideas and beliefs. The ritual execution of war captives and other carefully chosen victims had been practiced in Mesoamerican societies for thousands of years, but in the fifteenth century the *Mexica* appear to have taken human sacrifice to new levels, both in terms of meaning and scale. Huitzilopochtli, the patron god of war and of the imperial capital, was the divine audience for the killing of war captives, who typically had their hearts removed and their heads placed on the skull rack in the plaza of Tenochtitlán. Children were sacrificed to Tlaloc, the rain god, who needed their tears. The annual sacrifice to Tezcatlipoca was a specially chosen young man, who led a life of luxury and privilege for a year before his execution. At some festivals, there was a single victim; at others, there may have been thousands.

To a lesser extent, other Nahuas (Nahuatl-speaking people of Central Mexico) also embraced this culture of ritualized violence. The Tlaxcalans, for example, who had always resisted the Aztec Empire that surrounded their city and its lands, likewise cut out the hearts of prisoners of war. In fact, Tlaxcala and Tenochtitlán had extended this ritual to the battlefield itself, where conventional warfare had been partially replaced by the Flowery Wars (*xochiyaoyotl*), in which red blossoms were scattered on the ground to represent the blood of warriors, and selected warriors then exchanged as captives to be sacrificed. Tlaxcala remained independent, but its life was overshadowed in numerous ways by the existence of *Mexica* hegemony across Central Mexico, breeding generations of resentment. This resentment would prove crucial to the outcome of the Spanish invasion in 1519, for without Tlaxcalan assistance the Spaniards would almost certainly have been defeated in 1520 and Tenochtitlán would not have fallen the following year.

Tlaxcala was not the only city-state to resist *Mexica* expansion. To the west of the *Mexica* imperial capital lay the city of Tzintzuntzan, the center of the Tarascan kingdom, a modest empire in its own right. Lesser kingdoms and cities also resisted the Aztecs, a couple of which became surrounded by the empire's clients, as Tlaxcala was. But more often than not, the campaigns of Itzcoatl and the five emperors who followed him further augmented Aztec control—from Moctezuma Ilhuicamina (1390–1464), who succeeded his uncle Itzcoatl in 1440, through three of the first Moctezuma's sons, Axayácatl (r. 1469–1481), Tizoc (r. 1481–1486), and Ahuitzotl (ruled from 1486–1502). According to the early colonial account compiled by Diego Durán, the rulers of tributary cities from throughout the empire, who attended Ahuitzotl's coronation in 1486, "saw that the Aztecs were masters of the world, their empire so wide and abundant that they had conquered all the nations and that all were their vassals. The guests, seeing such wealth and opulence and such authority and power, were filled with terror" (Duran 1994, p. 336).

After the reigns of his three sons, the first Moctezuma's grandson and namesake, Moctezuma Xocoyotl (1466–1520), became emperor. From 1502, until his murder by Spanish invaders in 1520, he aggressively consolidated his authority and extended the empire of his ancestors. Long after his death, both Spaniards and natives unfairly blamed the second Moctezuma for the destruction of his empire. In fact, the arrival of Spaniards set loose a chain of events beyond Moctezuma's control, whereas for the previous eighteen years the emperor had been very much in control, increasing the authority and influence of Tenochtitlán and the *Mexica* as much, if not more, than any of his predecessors.

SEE ALSO *Mexico City.*

BIBLIOGRAPHY

Berdan, Frances F. *Aztec Imperial Strategies.* Washington DC: Dumbarton Oaks Research Library and Collection, 1996.

Carrasco, Pedro. *The Tenochca Empire of Ancient Mexico: The Triple Alliance of Tenochtitlan, Tetzcoco, and Tlacopan.* Norman: University of Oklahoma Press, 1999.

Clendinnen, Inga. *Aztecs: an Interpretation.* Cambridge, MA; New York: Cambridge University Press, 1991.

Duran, Fray Diego. *The History of the Indies of New Spain.* Translated by Doris Heyden. Norman: University of Oklahoma Press, 1994.

Gillespie, Susan D. *The Aztec Kings: The Construction of Rulership in Mexica History.* Tucson: University of Arizona Press, 1989.

Gruzinski, Serge. *The Aztecs: The Rise and Fall of an Empire.* New York: Harry N. Abrams, 1992.

Hassig, Ross. *Aztec Warfare; Imperial Expansion and Political Control.* Norman: University of Oklahoma Press, 1988.

Lanyon, Anna. *Malinche's Conquest.* Melbourne, Australia: Allen & Unwin, 1999.

Moctezuma, Eduardo Matos and Felipe Solis Olguin, eds. *Aztecs.* London: Royal Academy Books, 2002.

Oudijk, Michel R., and Matthew Restall. "Mesoamerican Conquistadors in the Sixteenth Century." In *Native Militaries in the Conquest of Mesoamerica*, edited by Michel R. Oudijk and Laura Matthew. Norman: University of Oklahoma Press, forthcoming.

Restall, Matthew. *Seven Myths of the Spanish Conquest.* New York: Oxford University Press, 2003.

Sahagun, Bernardino de. *Coloquios y doctrina cristiana.* Mexico City: UNAM, 1986.

Solis, Felipe. *The Aztecs: Catalogue of the Exhibition.* New York: Solomon R. Guggenheim Foundation, 2004.

Thomas, Hugh. *Conquest: Montezuma, Cortes, and the Fall of Old Mexico.* New York: Simon and Schuster, 1993.

Matthew Restall

B

BARING, EVELYN
1841–1917

Sir Evelyn Baring, who became Lord Cromer after the name of his Norfolk birthplace in 1892, was the de facto ruler of Egypt between 1883 and 1907, bearing the title HM's (Her/His Majesty's) Agent and Consul General. He was the sixth son of Henry Baring of Cromer Hall and a member of the well-known banking family, the Baring Brothers.

Evelyn Baring attended a vicarage school in Norfolk before being sent away at age eleven to Carshalton Ordnance School in Surrey. Baring entered the Royal Military Academy in Woolwich as a cadet at the age of fourteen, and was commissioned as a lieutenant in the Royal Artillery in 1858. After taking various administrative posts in Corfu, Malta, and England, he became private secretary to Lord Northbrook (Thomas George Baring, 1826–1904), viceroy of India, from 1872 to 1876.

Baring married Ethel Errington on his return to England in 1876, shortly thereafter departing to Egypt to act as British commissioner for the Public Debt Commission (1876–1880). Baring served as finance minister under Lord Ripon (George Robinson, 1827–1909) in India (1880–1883) before moving straight to Cairo in 1883. After the death of Ethel in 1898, he married Lady Katherine Thynne in 1901. Lord Cromer took up his seat in the House of Lords in 1908 after returning from Egypt, and he remained active in politics in spite of failing health. He died in 1917 and was buried alongside his first wife in Bournemouth.

Cromer's commanding presence seemed to personify the assurance of British imperialism at its height in late Victorian times. He believed that British rule brought "numberless blessings" on the "subject races" of the Empire, and was only ever half-hearted about self-government. He considered "dark-skinned" Orientals excitable, illogical, incompetent, and corrupt—and in need of the benign but firm hand of British tutelage.

Cromer's rule in Egypt began with "sound finance" over debt repayment and gradually came to encompass a number of administrative, legal, civil, and other "reforms," cautiously pursued. Egypt, he believed, was by nature an agricultural country, and Cromer's government plowed money into irrigation and extended the railway, while neglecting education and industrialization. Cromer opposed early attempts to build up an Egyptian textile industry with an unfavorable excise tariff. His rule thus presided over the entrenchment of labor-repressive agriculture based on large estates and village headmen, and he failed to accommodate or comprehend the aspirations of new, increasingly nationalist social groups comprised of the urban middle and working classes. Cromer's unbending stance and heavy-handed tactics eventually brought growing nationalist opposition, as well as calls from London for his recall. He resigned and left Egypt in 1907.

Imperial changes accompanying World War I, Wilsonian self-determination, and the mandate system made Cromer's high-handed approach appear outdated, even from London. In Egypt, opposition to Cromer only intensified after his departure, with the financial crash of 1907, problems with Egypt's cotton monoculture, and the growth of Egyptian nationalism. Cromer had undoubtedly managed the affairs of Egypt with diplomatic and administrative skill for decades, but the very

Evenly Baring. *The British statesmans, colonial administrator. and consul general of Egypt from 1883 to 1907, in an 1985 photograph.* HULTON ARCHIVE/GETTY IMAGES. REPRODUCED BY PERMISSION.

centralization of power that this process involved turned a hard-working, relatively colorless administrator into a remote, even authoritarian figure who came to blur the distinction between his own interests and those of Egypt, and who was incapable of changing with the times.

SEE ALSO *British Colonialism, Middle East; Cotton; Egypt; Sudan, Egyptian and British Rivalry in.*

BIBLIOGRAPHY

Cromer, Evelyn Baring, Earl of. *Modern Egypt, by the Earl of Cromer.* New York, The Macmillan Company: 1908.

Owen, Roger. *Lord Cromer. Victorian Imperialist, Edwardian Proconsul.* Oxford: Oxford University Press, 2004.

John Chalcraft

BATAVIA

Batavia was the headquarters of the Dutch East India Company (VOC). As such, it was the most powerful center of trade and power in Southeast Asia, and dominated the region until the founding of Singapore in 1819.

Batavia was built near the site of the Sundanese principality of Jayakerta. The Dutch East India Company had established relations with the prince in 1610, but it was only in 1619, after a local conflict, that Governor-General Jan Pieterszoon Coen took full possession, destroyed the old town and palace, and chose the site as VOC's permanent headquarters. Initially the city was dominated by Company personnel, above all military, a small but thriving Chinese business community, and slaves. After mid-century, the nature of Batavian society changed rapidly. Ambitions to turn Batavia in a European settlement colony were cast aside.

Behind the façade of a European town, much admired by visiting Europeans, was an Asian city of truly cosmopolitan dimensions. At its highest point in the 1720s, the city harbored almost 30,000 inhabitants and Company personnel within its walls and more than 80,000 in its vicinity. It became a magnet for Chinese, Malay, Indian and Arab traders, Javanese labor migrants, and military auxiliaries from the archipelago. But above all it was the slave trade that dominated the demography of Batavia. The cultural boil of slaves and migrants gave rise to the typical Betawi (Batavia) culture, combining traits of the many immigrant groups into its own idiosyncratic blend.

In the eighteenth century two disasters befell Batavia. First were the malaria epidemics that held the city in its grip since 1732, taking an immense human toll of all newcomers to the city. Only the shift of the city several kilometers inland around 1810 took away the most glaring effects of the endemic malaria.

Second was the massacre inflicted upon the Batavian Chinese in October 1740. In only a few days, around ten thousand Chinese were murdered in a frenzied panic by Europeans as retaliation of a revolt of desperate Chinese laborers in the countryside. Chinese migrants soon returned to Batavia, but were concentrated more intensively than before in their own quarter in the area called Glodok—still a predominantly Chinese neighborhood in present-day Jakarta.

Batavia's growth was reversed by epidemics and by the official ban on slave trade in 1812. Besides, the colonial state after 1799 was manned much more sparsely than its Company predecessor. After the Napoleonic wars and the British occupation of Java (1811–1816), Batavia developed as the capital of a expanding exploitation colony. More than anything else, the city was the seat of colonial administration and heavily bore the imprint of in the form of a strictly hierarchical society, dominated by European officials. But a truly imperial city it never

Batavia's Governmental Palace. *Now called Jakarta, Batavia was the headquarters of the Dutch East India Company and the most powerful commercial center in Southeast Asia during much of the seventeenth and eighteenth centuries. Batavia's governmental palace is shown here in an eighteenth-century engraving.* **ROGER VIOLLET/GETTY IMAGES. REPRODUCED BY PERMISSION.**

became. Architectural pomp never was a characteristic of the Dutch "empire."

Batavia remained a commercial center. Until about 1870, trade was primarily geared towards channelling the fruits of the infamous Cultivation System, with its forced delivery system of agricultural produce to the Dutch government, to be sold at the world markets. Industry was hardly an asset of Batavian economy and would be developed to the full only after independence. By 1880, harbor functions were concentrated in the new facilities at Tanjung Priok, eight kilometers east of the old town, offering a deep harbor where ships could load and at quays. The old concentric town of VOC days had evolved into a tripartite structure of administrative and residential area at Weltevreden (nowadays around Medan Merdeka), services and trade offices in the old town (Kota), and shipping and industry in Tanjung Priok.

After 1900, new technologies, modern lifestyles and education left their marks on Batavia, first mainly among the European classes. Gas lamps lighted the streets, cars took over the streets from after 1900, movie theatres became wildly popular, and shops offered an increasing range of international fashion clothing and technical novelties. These products became increasingly available to Indonesians and Chinese, as was western education. Batavia harbored many institutions of higher education, such as a medical school, law school and school of arts. These curricula brought together Indonesians from around the archipelago and became the hotbed of Indonesian political activities.

In March 1942, Japanese forces occupied the city without as much as a gunshot fired, changed its name into Djakarta, and made it into the headquarters of the 16th Army, the new authorities over Java. Now it was the

Europeans who were evicted from the city and imprisoned in guarded city quarters and camps.

The centrality of Batavia in nationalist visions of an independent Indonesia became clear by on 17 August 1945, when Sukarno and Hatta proclaimed the independent Indonesian Republic in the city. For some months the city was the theater of revolutionary and counterrevolutionary violence. Under pressure of the returning Dutch, the seat of the Republic was moved to Yogyakarta, only to return after the formal handing over of sovereignty on December 27, 1949. Jakarta retained its dual character as center of the political establishment as well as of intellectual dissent until the present day.

SEE ALSO *Coen, Jan Pietersz; Dutch United East India Company.*

BIBLIOGRAPHY

Abeyasekere, Susan. *Jakarta: A History.* New York: Oxford University Press, 1987. Rev. ed., 1989.

Remco Raben

BELGIUM'S AFRICAN COLONIES

When Belgium became a nation in 1830, it had almost no tradition of long-distance trade or colonial activity. Even in the first decades of its existence, it showed little inclination toward overseas expansion. Although a few attempts were made by the first king, Leopold I (1790–1865), these were not successful. If this small European country nevertheless succeeded in ruling a vast colony in Central Africa, this was due only to the tenacity of its second king, Leopold II (1835–1909).

THE CONGO FREE STATE (1885–1908)

Leopold II, an ambitious and enterprising monarch, was fascinated by the Dutch colonial "model" in Java and wanted to enhance his country's grandeur by exploiting a vast colonial domain, destined to enrich the mother country. After several unsuccessful attempts in different parts of Asia and Africa, Leopold developed a keen interest in Central Africa. The king took several personal initiatives, without the formal backing of his country's government and even without the support of Belgium's leading economic players.

In 1876 Leopold convoked an International Geographic Conference in Brussels, where prominent geographers and explorers were invited. Under the cloak of humanitarian and scientific interests, he then created successive private organizations, the most important of which was the Association Internationale du Congo (AIC). These organizations, controlled by the king himself, had in fact a commercial purpose. When France, in the early 1880s, started to develop a political hold along the banks of the lower Congo, the AIC (which, in the meantime, had hired the British explorer Henry Morton Stanley (1841–1904) as its local manager) also began to conclude treaties whereby African chiefs recognized the association's sovereignty. Because the United Kingdom, France, and Portugal had conflicting interests in this region, Leopold's skillful personal diplomacy succeeded in playing the contradictory ambitions of these countries against each other.

In the margins of the 1884–1885 Berlin Conference, the world's main powers recognized the AIC as the legal authority over a vast territory in the heart of Africa, a new "state" called the Congo Free State. The main contenders in this region, particularly France and the United Kingdom, hoped to reap the benefits of Leopold's "whim," which, in their opinion, would not last long.

Indeed, in the beginning, the Congo Free State seemed to be an unviable enterprise. The Free State's expenses outstripped its incomes. Setting up an administration and waging exhausting military campaigns in order to secure the Free State's grip on a territory more than eighty times as large as Belgium turned out to be very expensive. The Congo survived mainly through the king's personal funds. But from 1895 on, the Congo Free State, which Leopold ruled as an absolute monarch, was saved from bankruptcy by the growing demand for rubber.

The king imposed a harsh labor regime on the Congolese populations in order to extort ever-growing amounts of wild rubber. On the Congo Free State's own domains, as well as on the vast tracks of land that had been conceded to private companies, brutal and repressive practices took the lives of large numbers of Africans—though exact figures are impossible to establish. The Congo Free State, officially presented to the world as a humanitarian and civilizing enterprise destined to abolish slavery and introduce Christianity, became the target of an international protest campaign, led by the British activist Edmund Dene Morel (1873–1924) and his Congo Reform Association.

In the first years of the twentieth century, the Congo question became an important international issue, since the British government took this matter to heart, especially after an official enquiry commission, appointed by king Leopold, had confirmed the existence of excesses (1904). Belgium itself could not stay aloof, because of its growing involvement in the Congo Free State. An increasing number of volunteers had joined the public service and the military in the Congo; Belgian Catholic missions had been protected and promoted by the Free State's authorities; the Belgian Parliament had granted loans to the Congo; and important private groups had started investing in colonial enterprises, particularly in 1906. Consequently, the Belgian Parliament agreed in 1908 to accept the Congo as its own colony, in order to avoid international intervention or a takeover by a foreign power.

THE CONGO AS A BELGIAN COLONY (1908–1960)

The so-called Colonial Charter of 1908 set out the main lines of the Belgian colonial system: a rigorous separation between the budgets of the colony and the mother country; a strict parliamentary control of executive power (in order to avoid the excesses of the former Leopoldian despotism); the appointment of a governor-general in Congo, whose powers were strictly limited by the metropolitan authorities; and a tight centralism in the colony itself, where provincial authorities were granted little autonomy.

In reality, Belgium's political parties and public opinion showed little interest in Congolese matters. Consequently, colonial policy was determined by a small group of persons, in particular the minister of colonies, a handful of top civil servants in the Ministry of Colonies, some prominent Catholic ecclesiastics, and the leaders of the private companies that were investing increasing amounts of capital in the colony. A classic image depicts the Belgian Congo as being run by the "Trinity" of administration, capital, and the (Catholic) Church. These three protagonists had an enormous influence in the colony, and assisted each other in their respective ventures, even if their interests did not always coincide and, indeed, sometimes openly conflicted.

The Belgian administration of the Congo was run by a relatively modest corps of civil servants (in 1947 only about 44,000 whites, 3,200 of whom were public employees, were present in this vast country, inhabited by some 11 million Africans). The lowest level of administration consisted of the indigenous authorities, the more or less "authentic" traditional African chiefs, who were strictly controlled by Belgian officials. On the local level, in close contact with the African population, the missionaries played an important role in evangelization, in (primary) education, and in health services. Protestant missions were present in the Congo next to Catholic ones, but the latter enjoyed, during most of Belgian rule, a privileged position.

As in most colonies, the Congolese economy consisted of a heterogeneous mix of different sectors. The rural masses were primarily engaged in a neglected and stagnating indigenous agriculture, aimed at self-subsistence but facing growing difficulties feeding the increasing population, particularly from the 1950s. The colonial authorities also obliged these agriculturalists to produce export crops (e.g., cotton), which made them vulnerable to the ups and downs of world markets. A third economic sector consisted of large-scale plantations (e.g., palm oil production by the enterprise founded by the British businessman William Lever [1851–1925]), also oriented toward export.

The Congo was also characterized by the extraordinary development of huge mining industries (particularly in the province of Katanga, well known for its copper, and in the Kasai region, famous for its industrial diamonds). From the 1920s on, heavy investments in the exploitation of the colony's rich mineral resources transformed the Congo into a major actor in the world economy. During both world wars, the Belgian Congo played a great role as purveyor of raw materials for the Allies, while the Congolese troops also engaged in warfare against the German and Italian forces.

In order to wipe out the stain of Leopoldian ill treatment of the African population and gain international respectability, the Belgian authorities tried to turn the Congo into a "model colony." Although forced labor, repression, and a "color bar" (a form of racial segregation) persisted till the very end of their domination, the Belgians made serious efforts to promote indigenous wellbeing, particularly during the 1950s, by developing a network of health services and primary schools. From the late 1920s, some important mining companies had also developed a paternalistic policy aimed at stabilizing and controlling their labor force (Congo had one of the largest wage labor contingents in Africa). The final decade of the Belgian presence in the Congo was characterized by a notable improvement of the living standard of the growing black urban population.

However, one of the main failures of Belgian colonial policy was the choice not to develop an indigenous elite. Secondary and university education were seriously neglected. The Congolese petty bourgeoisie remained embryonic: local entrepreneurs or proprietors were almost nonexistent. Only a tiny fraction of the Congolese population, the so-called *évolués*, succeeded more or less in assimilating the European way of life, but their Belgian masters kept them at the bottom levels of the public service or private companies, without any short-term prospects of exercising responsible tasks.

Anticolonialism and nationalism found their way into the Congolese population comparatively late—indeed, not until the second half of the 1950s. Belgian authorities were caught practically unprepared by the sudden wave of black political activism, and subsequently engaged in a process of "precipitous decolonization." In just a few months' time (from early 1959 to the beginning of 1960), the political prospects for the colony evolved from a long-term

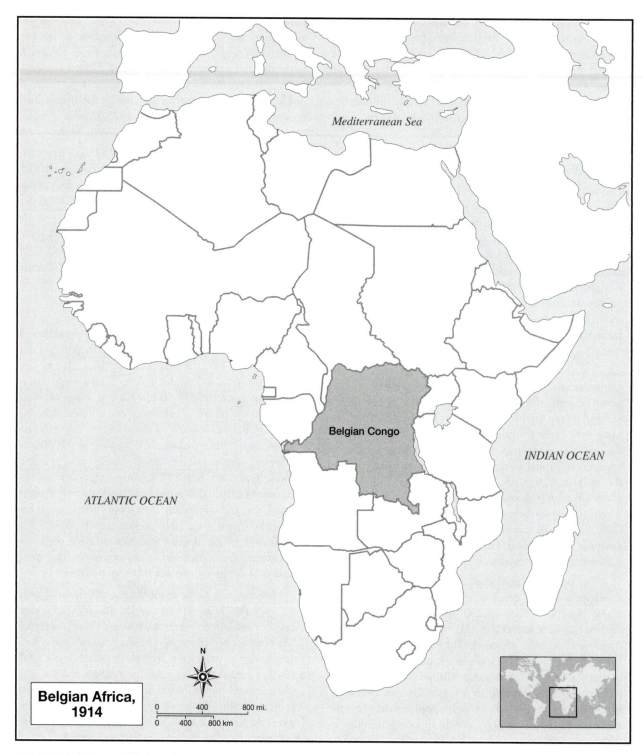

MAP BY XNR PRODUCTIONS. THE GALE GROUP.

loosening of the ties between Belgium and the Congo, to the immediate independence of the African country.

When Congo became a sovereign nation on June 30, 1960, this new state was utterly unprepared to handle the enormous problems that it had to face, and it slid into years of chaos, internal disruption (e.g., regional secessions, such as Katanga's), and civil war—only to emerge in 1965 under the Mobutu Sese Seko (1930–1997)

THE CONGO FREE STATE

In 1876 Belgium's King Leopold II convened the Brussels Geographical Conference, which led to the formation of the African International Association. Though its goals were purportedly humanitarian and scientific, Leopold used the association to fund expeditions and establish posts along the Congo River.

With the promise of open trade, Leopold convinced world powers to recognize what eventually became the Association Internationale du Congo (AIC) as the legal authority over a vast territory in the heart of Africa. In April of 1885 Belgium's parliament made Leopold the sovereign ruler of this new "state," called the Congo Free State, incorporating all lands not directly occupied by Africans. European traders came to the new country, which was not a colony in the normal sense, but essentially the personal possession of King Leopold, to obtain beeswax, coffee, fruits, ivory, minerals, palm oil, and especially rubber.

While some Africans initially welcomed European rule, others opposed it from the start. Natives eventually faced dire conditions, characterized by displacement, forced labor, and taxation. The rubber trade, which was of critical economic importance to sustaining Leopold's enterprise, was marked by especially inhumane conditions.

Uprisings, revolts, assassinations, and other acts of resistance were common during King Leopold's rule. According to one estimate, casualties were as high as 66 percent of the local population. Such conditions led to opposition from other European powers, and the Congo Free State ceased to exist in 1908 when it was annexed by Belgium.

dictatorship, which was to last more than thirty years and thoroughly pillaged the country's enormous riches.

BELGIAN MANDATE TERRITORIES IN AFRICA

During World War I, Belgian colonial troops participated in the military campaigns against the Germans in East Africa. They occupied a large part of this German colony. After the end of the war, the Belgian government tried to exchange these territories against the left bank of the Congo River mouth, which was in Portuguese hands. This plan failed to materialize, and finally, on May 30, 1919, according to the Orts-Milner Agreement (named after its Belgian and British negotiators), Belgium's spoils of war only consisted of two small territories in the Great Lakes region bordering the immense Belgian Congo, namely Rwanda and Burundi (their ancient names being Ruanda and Urundi).

As was the case with the other former German colonies, the League of Nations entrusted both of these territories to the victorious power as "mandates." Belgium administered these mandates through a system of indirect rule. The pre-colonial social and political authorities, consisting of a Tutsi king (*mwami*) and a tiny aristocracy (predominantly of Tutsi origin), ruling over a vast majority of mainly Hutu agriculturalists, were kept in place—even if the Belgians reshaped the traditional structures by constantly intervening in them. Until almost the end of the mandate period, the Belgian administrators, with the help of the Catholic Church and its schools, did their best to turn the Tutsi elite into docile auxiliaries of their own rule. Only in the final phase of their presence in Rwanda and Burundi at the end of the 1950s did the Belgians change their attitude toward the Hutu majority. They favored the takeover of political power by the latter, a policy that succeeded in Rwanda but failed in Burundi.

When both countries became independent on July 1, 1962, Rwanda was governed by a Hutu president, Burundi by a Tutsi king. Belgian native policy, which had rigidified the ethnic boundaries between Tutsi and Hutu and consequently had exacerbated the ethnic identity of these groups, was largely responsible for the intensification of ethnic rivalry between these groups after the end of foreign rule. This antagonism, coupled with the high population density in these overwhelmingly agricultural countries, was to form a volatile environment in the following decades, causing several interethnic massacres, of which the Rwandan genocide of 1994 was the most terrifying example.

SEE ALSO *Mandate System.*

BIBLIOGRAPHY

Anstey, Roger. *King Leopold's Legacy. The Congo under Belgian Rule 1908-1960.* Oxford: Oxford University Press, 1966.

"Archives Africaines" of the Ministry of Foreign Affairs, Brussels (Archives of the former Belgian Ministry of Colonies). In French. Available at: http://www.diplomatie.be/fr/archives/archives.asp.

Maurel, Auguste. *Le Congo: De la colonisation Belge à l'indépendance,* 2nd ed. Paris: Harmattan, 1992.

N'Daywel è Nziem, Isidore. *Histoire générale du Congo: De l'héritage ancien à la République Démocratique,* 2nd ed. Brussels: De Boeck & Larcier, 1998.

Nzongola-Ntalaja, Georges. *The Congo From Leopold to Kabila. A People's History.* London: Zed Books, 2002.

Stengers, Jean. *Congo, mythes et réalités: 100 ans d'histoire.* Paris: Duculot, 1989.

Vellut, Jean-Luc, Florence Loriaux, and Françoise Morimont, eds. *Bibliographie historique du Zaïre à l'époque coloniale (1880–1960): Travaux publiés en 1960–1996.* Louvain-la-Neuve, Belgium: Centre d'histoire de l'Afrique de l'université catholique de Louvain, 1996.

Guy Vanthemsche

BENGAL, MARITIME TRADE OF

The province of Bengal comprises both a section of the Indo-Gangetic plain and a delta region. Its position on the eastern coast of the Indian subcontinent make it a key region for Indian Ocean trade.

The maritime trade of Bengal centered on the eastern half of the Bay of Bengal. For the greater part of the sixteenth and seventeenth centuries, Bengal's principal ports, Satgaon and Chittagong and subsequently Hugli, maintained significant trading connections with Burma, Malacca, and Acheh. A second set of trade routes connected Bengal with Sri Lanka, Maldives, and the Malabar Coast, while a third, subsidiary route connected Bengal with Gujarat and West Asia. Equally significant was Bengal's coastal trade with the Coromandel, which relied on annual imports of Bengal grain.

The principal exports in the coastal and overseas traffic of Bengal were a range of manufactured goods and agricultural products—textiles, rice, wheat, gram, sugar, opium, clarified butter, and saltpeter. In return, Bengal imported spices, camphor, porcelain, silk, sandalwood, ivory, metals, conch shells, and cowries, the last of which circulated as an important medium in Bengal's monetary transactions. It was with the advent of the Portuguese in the sixteenth century that Bengal entered the web of Euro-Asian exchanges that were to become central to the region's economy. Portuguese involvement in the trade of the Bay of Bengal began after the capture of Malacca in 1511, although it was only in the 1560s that private Portuguese initiative made an appreciable impact on the region's maritime profile. The Portuguese operated from Chittagong and Hugli, the latter of which was taken over by the Mughals in 1642.

The context for Bengal's expanding maritime trade in the seventeenth century was provided on the one hand by the political stability of Mughal rule (1575–1717) and on the other by the operations of the North European trading companies in the Indian Ocean. The integration of Bengal within the larger trading system of Mughal India, the acceleration of commercial contacts between Bengal and West Asia, and the increasing participation of Mughal officials in Bengal's overseas and coastal trade meant that the Bengal merchants (local as well as domiciled) were able to take a larger share in the trade of the western Indian Ocean.

The importance of Bengal's textiles and silk in the markets of Southeast Asia and Japan encouraged the English and Dutch East India Companies to enter into the commercial economy of Bengal. By the middle decades of the century, the Dutch and English, largely in response to the pressures of the spice trade in Southeast Asia, were participating in the intra-Asian trade of the Indian Ocean in a big way and had established a number of factories and settlements in Hugli, Balasore, and Pipli. The result was an expanding demand for Bengal textiles, silk, opium, sugar, and rice in the markets of Southeast Asia, Sri Lanka, and the Coromandel. In return, Bengal imported huge volumes of metal and bullion, which helped service the monetary system of the region.

The volume of Bengal's trade handled by the Europeans increased very substantially from the second quarter of the seventeenth century, with the Dutch enjoying a decided advantage over their rivals until the second quarter of the eighteenth century. Quantitative estimates available for the value and volume of European exports from Bengal suggest that these increased from an average of 100,000 rupees in the 1640s to 3 million at the end of the century. The historian Om Prakash estimates that Dutch exports from Bengal went up from 100,000 ruprees in the 1640s to 3 million in 1720. We do not have corresponding figures for the trade carried on by Asian and Indian merchants, whose operations we know were extensive. We do have some figures for Indian shipping directed from the Bengal ports of Hugli and Balasore, and these suggest that the strength of Bengal shipping was around eighty–to a hundred–odd ships of 200-ton capacity.

By the latter decades of the seventeenth century, there was a qualitative change in the Euro-Asian trade, which had important implications for Bengal's maritime economy. The increasing popularity of Bengal's textiles and raw silk in the European market meant that Bengal became by far the most important region for the trade of the European Companies. Bengal's textiles accounted for the majority of the European Companies' exports into Europe. At the same time, the increasing importance of the private trade of the English Company's agents in Bengal indicated quite clearly that Bengal was a region where the struggle for control would be fierce.

The early colonial policies of the European East India Companies had important effects on the maritime trade of Bengal. The enforcement of the pass system that the Portuguese had initiated meant that Indian merchants were compelled to take passes and call at specified ports and pay custom duties before proceeding to the

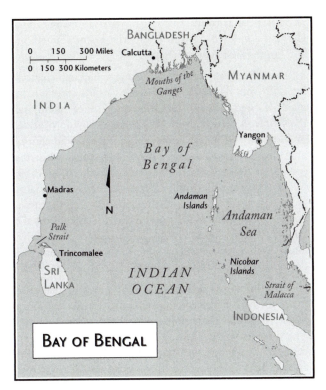

BANGLADESH
Calcutta
MYANMAR
INDIA
Mouths of the Ganges
0 150 300 Miles
0 150 300 Kilometers
Bay of Bengal
Yangon
Madras
Andaman Islands
Andaman Sea
N
Palk Strait
Trincomalee
SRI LANKA
INDIAN OCEAN
Nicobar Islands
Strait of Malacca
INDONESIA
BAY OF BENGAL

MAP BY XNR PRODUCTIONS. THE GALE GROUP.

destinations enumerated in their documents. The pass system was intended to both generate revenues and restrict Indian shipping to certain routes. Thus, while the opening up of new markets for Bengal goods in Asia by the European Companies represented a net addition to the volume of total exports from Bengal, monopoly restriction imposed on certain routes like the Bengal–Sri Lanka sector and the Bengal–Malay/Indonesian archipelago routes had a baneful effect.

It was, however, only in the eighteenth century that the European Companies and European markets began to assume a critical role in the workings of Bengal's maritime economy. Until then, Indian merchant shipping appears to have survived the European intrusion. What set the stage for the decline of Bengal's eastward trade was the Mughal state officials' withdrawal from overseas trade. Following this, the first half of the eighteenth century witnessed a huge expansion in the value of Indo-European trade carried out by the English and French East India Companies (at the expense of the Dutch, who began losing momentum). What underscored the English and French ventures was the expansion and ramifications of private trading activity by Company agents, who traded extensively in the country trade of Asia and who, in pursuit of their private ventures, articulated an aggressive political strategy against local merchants and rulers. Between 1707 and 1740,

Calcutta emerged as the premier port of Bengal and the seat of English shipping and trade. The unprecedented expansion of English private trade had two important consequences. On the one hand, it displaced Hugli and the Asian merchants from the Indian Ocean trade, and on the other, it cut into the operations of the Dutch trading company. The private merchants' trade embraced both the westward and eastward segments of Bengal's maritime traffic. European shipping, and in particular English shipping, absorbed virtually the bulk of the freight trade and it became common for private traders to carry Indian merchants' goods in addition to their own. Among the reasons for English success were the relative security of English shipping against piracy and the greater seaworthiness of English vessels. The Calcutta fleet, numbering about twenty ships around 1715 doubled in the 1720s and 1730s and displaced the Dutch, as well as local merchants, from the Persian Gulf and Red Sea routes. The decline of Hugli followed inevitably, as the traditional trading structure with its node in Surat went under in the aftermath of Mughal decline and the unrestrained expansion of English private trade.

Between 1740 and 1757, the English Company steadily expanded its trade and political agenda and engineered the infamous Plassey conspiracy (1757), which gave them vital control over the political system. Plassey brought in its wake an unprecedented expansion of English private trade. Company agents abused the newly acquired political privileges to make deep inroads into the internal trade of Bengal. Simultaneously, there was a perceptible shift in Bengal's trading orientation; the decline of markets in West Asia combined with the increasing popularity of Indian raw cotton and opium in Chinese and Southeast Asian markets encouraged English private traders to look east once more. The shift to the east embodied a new era in Bengal's maritime trade as it became increasingly subordinated to the imperatives of new, multilateral trading arrangements that accompanied the formalization of British colonial power in India.

SEE ALSO *Coromandel, Europeans and Maritime Trade; Indian Ocean Trade; Malabar, Europeans and the Maritime Trade of; Slave Trade, Indian Ocean.*

BIBLIOGRAPHY

Chaudhuri, K. N. *The Trading World of Asia and the English East India Company, 1660–1760.* Cambridge, U.K.: Cambridge University Press, 1978.

Chaudhury, Sushil. *From Prosperity to Decline: Eighteenth Century Bengal.* New Delhi: Manohar, 1995.

Marshall, Peter. *East Indian Fortunes: The British in Bengal in the Eighteenth Century.* Oxford: Clarendon, 1976.

Prakash, Om. *The Dutch East India Company and the Economy of Bengal, 1630–1720.* Princeton, NJ: Princeton University Press, 1985.

Prakash, Om. *The New Cambridge Economic History of India,* Vol. 2, No. 5: *European Commercial Enterprise in Pre-Colonial India.* Cambridge, U.K.: Cambridge University Press, 1998.

Lakshmi Subramanian

BERLIN CONFERENCE

The Berlin Conference, an international meeting held from November 1884 to February 1885, was convened to settle the issues connected with European colonization of Africa. Although many European nations had established commercial relations with parts of Africa beginning in the fifteenth century, the majority of African societies remained under local control by the mid-nineteenth century. However, European economic and political interest in Africa increased considerably from the 1880s. European missionaries, adventurers, and fortune hunters began to open a new chapter in African-European relations, and their aim went beyond the commercial interests that had drawn Europeans to Africa in earlier centuries. Political and diplomatic problems in Europe were played out in Africa during this period. The new sense of nationalism that followed the unification of Germany and Italy, along with the national pride of other European nations, called for expansion overseas.

The discovery in the mid-1870s by Welsh-born journalist and explorer Henry Morton Stanley of the Congo River Basin (1874–1877) opened vast unexplored parts of the continent to Europeans. Belgian King Leopold II (1835–1909) invited Stanley in 1878 to assist him in studying and "civilizing" the African continent. While Leopold's intentions were purportedly philanthropic and scientific, the International Association of the Congo that he formed in 1878 had the economic goal of exploiting the resources of the vast Congo region. Leopold's imperialist agenda was not lost on other European powers.

Meanwhile, the French naval officer Pierre Savorgnan de Brazza (1852–1905) was colonizing the western Congo Basin. In 1881 he founded city of Brazzaville for France. Portugal also claimed the region based on old treaties with the native Congolese. This contestation was complicated when Portugal entered into a treaty with Great Britain on February 26, 1884, to block the International Association of the Congo's access to the Atlantic Ocean. The scramble for African territories continued when the French occupied Tunisia in 1881 and Guinea three years later. Great Britain gained control of Ottoman Egypt, as well as Sudan and parts of Somalia, while Italy took

possession of parts of Eritrea in 1870 and 1882, and Germany declared protectorates over Togo, Cameroon, and South-West Africa in 1884.

In 1884, at the request of Portugal, German chancellor Otto von Bismarck (1815–1898) called together the major Western powers, including the United States and the Ottoman Empire, to negotiate questions and consider problems arising out of European penetration and control of Africa. Fourteen countries were represented when the conference opened in Berlin on November 15, 1884: Austria-Hungary, Belgium, Denmark, France, Germany, Great Britain, Italy, the Netherlands, Portugal, Russia, Spain, Sweden-Norway (then unified), Turkey, and the United States. However, Belgium, France, Germany, Great Britain, and Portugal were the major players, and they eventually controlled most of colonial Africa.

The initial purpose of the meeting was to guarantee free trade and navigation in the Congo, while the lower Niger River and its basins would be considered neutral and open to trade. The Berlin Conference ended on February 26, 1885, with the signing of the General Act of the Berlin Conference, also called the Congo Act. Among other provisions, the act guaranteed free trade throughout the Congo Basin and the Lake Nyasa (Lake Malawi) region, and proclaimed the Niger and Congo rivers open for ship traffic. The Congo Act also implemented an international prohibition on the slave trade. In addition, the Berlin Conference Act of February 1885 established the "principle of effective occupation" for colonial powers claiming territory in Africa. Article XXXV of the Act required the European powers signatory to the Act to insure the establishment of sufficient authority in the regions they occupied to protect existing rights and freedom of trade and transit. Furthermore, new possession by any country of any portion of the African coast would have to be formally declared to the other signatories of the Congo Act.

The Berlin Conference had several implications for Africa. Without any African representation at the conference, the colonial powers imposed their domains on the African continent. Before the conference, only the coastal areas of Africa were under European control; the conference inaugurated the European scrambled to gain control over the interior of the continent. The territorial adjustments made among the colonial powers and the fragmentation of the continent, without due regard to ethnic and linguistic boundaries, remains a lasting consequence of the Berlin Conference.

Despite its purported neutrality, part of the Congo Basin became the personal estate of Leopold II. Under Leopold's rule, more than half of the region's population died from atrocities committed by Belgians. Prior to the conference, Britain dominated much of the trade in the

340   FRANK LESLIE'S ILLUSTRATED NEWSPAPER.   [JANUARY 10, 1885.

The Pictorial Spirit of the Illustrated Foreign Press.—SEE PAGE 343.

GERMANY.— THE CONGO CONFERENCE IN SESSION AT BERLIN.

The Congo Conference in Session at Berlin. *The meeting to resolve issues surrounding the European colonization of Africa that became known as the Berlin Conference is shown here in an engraving published in January 1885 in* Frank Leslie's Illustrated Newspaper. *The conference was held from November 1884 to February 1885.* © **CORBIS. REPRODUCED BY PERMISSION.**

Bight of Biafra and had concluded several treaties of "protection" with several chiefs in the Niger delta. The United African Company, an amalgamation of all major British firm trading along the Niger Coast and Delta, was also busy signing treaties with the chiefs along the banks of Rivers Niger and Benue. Armed with such treaties, Britain convinced other European countries of its interest in the region. The sovereignty of Great Britain over what became Southern Nigeria was recognized at the Berlin Conference by European powers. Britain established control of the important territories of Nigeria and Ghana, in addition to most parts of eastern Africa. Sudan came under effective British-Egyptian control after the British suppressed the Mahdi Rebellion during the 1880s and resolved the 1898 Fashoda crisis, a tense territorial dispute between Britain and France.

Britain continued its domination of southern Africa after the second Anglo-Boer War (1899–1902). France claimed large territories in sub-Saharan Africa but French claims to parts of the Congo and to Nigeria and the historical claim of Portugal to the mouth of the Congo were ignored by other European powers at the Berlin Conference. The French and Spanish divided Morocco in 1911, and Libya came under Italian domination in 1912. The scramble for Africa came to an end with the annexation of Egypt by the British in 1914. By this time,

all of Africa except Liberia and Ethiopia was under European control.

SEE ALSO *Scramble for Africa; Sub-Saharan Africa, European Presence in.*

BIBLIOGRAPHY

Chamberlain, Muriel E. *The Scramble for Africa.* London: Longman, 1974, 2nd ed., 1999.

Crowe, Sybil E. *The Berlin West African Conference, 1884–1985.* New York: Longmans, Green, 1942.

Förster, Stig, Wolfgang J Mommsen, and Ronald Edward Robinson. *Bismarck, Europe, and Africa: The Berlin Africa Conference 1884–1885 and the Onset of Partition.* Oxford: Oxford University Press, 1988.

Chima J. Korieh

BIOLOGICAL IMPACTS OF EUROPEAN EXPANSION IN THE AMERICAS

The arrival of Europeans in the Americas in 1492 precipitated a demographic catastrophe. Although some controversy exists over the size of the pre-Columbian population, it is not unreasonable to suggest that it may have fallen from about 50 to 60 million in 1492 to 6.5 million in 1650, a decline of about 90 percent.

Many factors contributed to this decline, but most researchers agree that a major cause was the introduction of Old World diseases. Because of the isolation of the American continent from the rest of the world, Native Americans had not been exposed to diseases that ravaged the Old World and therefore had not acquired any immunity to them. The most notable killers were smallpox, measles, and influenza, which are spread by face-to-face contact. Smallpox is associated with mortality rates of between 30 and 50 percent. The impact of recent measles epidemics among nonimmune populations in Amazonia and isolated regions, such as in Polynesia and Iceland, indicates that measles might result in equally high levels of mortality. In the fifteenth century, most Europeans would have possessed some immunity to smallpox and measles, having been exposed to them in childhood. Other devastating diseases were plague, typhus, malaria, and yellow fever. These diseases are spread by insects, such as lice, fleas, or mosquitoes, and their incidence is strongly influenced by climatic conditions.

THE FIRST IMPACT

The Caribbean was the first region to experience the devastating impact of Old World diseases. The population of the island of Hispaniola, which today is shared by the Dominican Republic and Haiti, declined from at least one million in 1492 to about eighteen thousand in 1518; by the mid-sixteenth century, only a few hundred were left. Prior to the 1980s scholars thought that the smallpox epidemic of 1518 was the first to hit the region, but even accepting that the ill treatment and sometimes the enslavement of indigenous peoples contributed significantly to the decline, the scale of the demographic catastrophe was difficult to explain. However, it is now thought that the island was struck by influenza contracted from pigs suffering from swine fever that were carried by the second expedition of Christopher Columbus (1451–1506) in 1493. A number of other unspecified diseases might also have taken their toll of Caribbean populations before 1518.

The first known epidemic to afflict the American mainland was probably associated with the arrival of smallpox in the Caribbean in 1518, but it is possible that earlier expeditions, such as that of Francisco Hernández de Córdoba (?–1517) in 1517, introduced smallpox at an earlier date to the Maya of Yucatán. What is known is that in 1520 smallpox was carried from Cuba to the Gulf Coast by a sick African slave on the expedition of Pánfilo

de Narváez (ca. 1480–1528). It spread rapidly through the native population, devastating the Aztec capital, Tenochtitlán. This weakened its inhabitants physically and psychologically, and shifted the military advantage the Aztecs had possessed to Hernán Cortés (1484–1547) and his troops, who took control of the city in 1521.

One contemporary observer, Toribio de Motolinia (d. 1569), claimed that in most provinces of Mexico, more than half the population died. Further south, smallpox spread through Guatemala and then through native population chains, often arriving ahead of the invaders. In the mid-1520s it struck the Andes in western South America, where it not only caused high morality but also resulted in the death of the Inca emperor, Huayna Capac sometime between 1524 and 1527. His death precipitated a dynastic war between his two sons, Huascar (d. 1532) and Atahualpa (d. 1533), raising mortality to even higher levels and weakening Inca resistance to the Spanish invaders. The Incas claimed that if it had not been for the epidemic, they would not have been conquered so easily.

CONTINUING IMPACTS: VARIATIONS IN TIMING AND GEOGRAPHY

The initial impact of epidemics was devastating, but native societies were hit by Old World diseases not once but several times during the sixteenth century. For example, in the Andes the smallpox epidemic of the mid-1520s was followed by an outbreak of measles from 1531 to 1533 and by plague or typhus in the 1545 to 1546 period; from 1557 to 1562 the region was struck by measles, along with influenza and smallpox, and finally from 1585 to 1591 by smallpox, measles, and typhus. Since each epidemic carried off a significant proportion of the survivors, a population could be easily hammered down to a fraction of its preconquest size.

This chronology was repeated in many parts of the Americas, but even those societies that did not come into direct contact with conquistadors, explorers, or missionaries may not have been spared the ravages of disease. Infections might spread equally easily through native contacts and systems of exchange. As a result, there is considerable debate over the extent of depopulation that might have occurred in relatively remote areas, such as Amazonia and much of North America, prior to the arrival of Europeans.

During the early colonial period, population losses were higher in the lowlands than the highlands. Many people have explained the greater depopulation in the lowlands by reference to the introduction of malaria and yellow fever, which only thrive in warm climates where the average temperature exceeds 20 degrees centigrade (68 degrees Fahrenheit). Both diseases are spread by

Estimated Native American populations, 1492–1996

1492	53,904,000
1570	13,507,000
1650–1700	9,359,000
1820	8,470,000
1996	40,000,000

SOURCES: The estimates for 1570 and 1650–1700 are from Angel Rosenblat, *La población indígena y el mestizaje en América, 1492–1950,* 2 tomos (Buenos Aires: Editorial Nova, 1954), I, p. 59 and Peter C. Mancall, "Native Americans and Europeans in English America, 1500–1700," Table 15.1, *"Indian and colonist demography, 1500–1700,"* in Nicolas Canney, Ed. *The Oxford History of the British Empire.* Volume I: *The Origins of Empire: British Overseas Enterprise to the Close of the Seventeenth Century* (Oxford: Oxford University Press, 1998), p. 331. The estimate for 1820 is from Angus Maddison, *The World Economy: Historical Statistics* (Paris: OECD, Development Centre, 2003), Table 4.2, "Ethnic Composition of the Americas in 1820," p. 115. The estimate for 1996 is Emma Pearce, "Appendix 1: Indigenous Population Figures." In Phillip Wearne, *Return of the Indian: Conquest and Revival in the Americas* (Philadelphia: Temple University Press, 1996), pp. 204-215.

THE GALE GROUP.

mosquitoes, but in the case of yellow fever the particular mosquito that acts as a carrier for the parasite would also need to have been introduced. It is generally thought that it arrived in the New World as the African slave trade expanded and that the first definitely identifiable epidemic of yellow fever occurred in the Caribbean in 1647 to 1648.

Yellow fever came to be associated with port cities, even extending to temperate zones in the summer, where it occasionally afflicted such cities as Boston, Philadelphia, and New York. Malaria may have spread more rapidly because many Europeans already suffered from a mild form of the disease *(Plasmodium vivax)* and the mosquitoes required for its spread were already present in the New World. However, apparently healthy slaves from Africa probably introduced the more deadly form, *Plasmodium falciparum.*

RESISTANCE AND RECOVERY

The initial impact of Old World diseases was disastrous, but over time native populations began to develop resistance to some infections. Some individuals have innate immunity to infections because of their genetic, biochemical, or physiological makeup, but most acquire it through constant exposure to infections. A community acquires immunity as those people who are resistant survive and reproduce, while those who are not resistant die in childhood.

Historical experience suggests that at least a century of constant exposure is required for an infection to become an endemic and a more benign disease of childhood. There is evidence that smallpox was becoming a childhood disease in parts of the Andes in the early seventeenth century. However, this type of immunity can only be acquired where communities are sufficiently large to sustain infections indefinitely, so that the population is constantly exposed to them. It has been suggested that a population of between one hundred thousand and two hundred thousand is needed to sustain smallpox.

In areas of low population density, diseases tend to "fade out" because they can find no new susceptible people to infect. In such circumstances, populations are not constantly exposed to diseases and do not therefore acquire immunity to them, with the result that when diseases are reintroduced from the outside these communities continue to experience high mortality.

Following the initial impact of Old World diseases in the sixteenth century, therefore, populations in densely settled areas experienced a degree of recovery, though its timing varied. The native population began to increase in Mexico in the 1620s and 1630s, whereas this did not occur in Central America until the end of the seventeenth century, and in Peru not until the mid-eighteenth century.

Despite this gradual recovery, highland populations were still afflicted by occasional outbreaks and in the eighteenth century there appears to have been a more general resurgence of epidemics that inflicted heavy losses. In Mexico, for example, severe smallpox epidemics occurred in 1711, 1734, 1748, 1761 to 1762, 1779 to 1780, and 1797. Meanwhile, the sparse native populations in the lowlands did not participate in the recovery experienced in the highlands. Here Old World diseases continued to take an elevated toll, so that populations in these regions continued to decline throughout the colonial period.

PRE-COLUMBIAN DISEASES

There is no doubt that the introduction of Old World diseases had a devastating impact on Native American peoples. However, this does not mean that in pre-Columbian times they had lived in a disease-free environment. They suffered from intestinal and respiratory infections, such as diarrhea, dysentery, and tuberculosis, as well as leishmaniasis, Chagas' disease, bartonellosis, and nonvenereal syphilis. What were absent in pre-Columbian times were acute infections that are spread by face-to-face contact and are associated with high mortality.

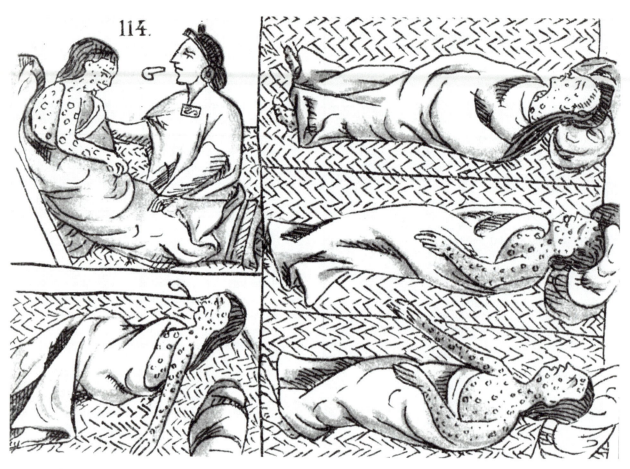

Victims of Smallpox in New Spain. *This illustration from* Historia general de las cosas de Nueva España *(General History of the Things of New Spain, 1569–1575) by Bernardino de Sahagún depicts the suffering experienced by those infected with smallpox.* **AKG LONDON. REPRODUCED BY PERMISSION.**

Sufficiently large populations existed in pre-Columbian times to sustain such diseases if they had existed. However, most human diseases originate in animals and jump the species barrier to become human diseases. It is suggested that the relative absence of domesticated animals in pre-Columbian times and the lack of close contact between humans and the few species that existed would have discouraged their emergence. It seems likely, however, that a form of typhus was present in pre-Columbian times, being carried by lice found on guinea pigs, which were kept in many Andean households.

SEE ALSO *European Explorations in North America; European Explorations in South America; European Migrations to American Colonies, 1492–1820.*

BIBLIOGRAPHY

Alchon, Suzanne A. *Native Society and Disease in Colonial Ecuador.* Cambridge, U.K.: Cambridge University Press, 1991.

Cook, Noble David. *Demographic Collapse: Indian Peru, 1520–1620.* Cambridge, U.K.: Cambridge University Press, 1981.

Cook, Noble David. *Born to Die: Disease and New World Conquests, 1492–1650.* Cambridge, U.K.: Cambridge University Press, 1998.

Cook, Noble David, and W. George Lovell. *"Secret Judgments of God": Old World Disease in Colonial Spanish America.* Norman: University of Oklahoma Press, 1991.

Crosby, Alfred W. *The Columbian Exchange: Biological and Cultural Consequences of 1492.* Westport, CT: Greenwood, 1972.

Crosby, Alfred W. "Virgin Soil Epidemics as a Factor in the Aboriginal Depopulation in America." *William and Mary Quarterly* 33 (1976): 289–299.

Dobyns, Henry F. "An Outline of Andean Epidemic History to 1720." *Bulletin of the History of Medicine* 37 (1963): 493–515.

Guerra, Francisco. "The Earliest American Epidemic: The Influenza of 1493." *Social Science History* 12 (1988): 305–325.

Lovell, W. George. "'Heavy Shadows and Black Night': Diseases and Depopulation in Colonial Spanish America. *Annals of the Association of American Geographers* 82 (1992): 426–443.

Newson, Linda A. *Life and Death in Early Colonial Ecuador.* Norman: University of Oklahoma Press, 1995.

Linda A. Newson

BISMARCK ARCHIPELAGO

The Bismarck Archipelago stretches in a counterclockwise arc northeast of the New Guinea mainland. Comprising the large islands of New Britain and New Ireland, the Admiralty group containing Manus, and many smaller islands, this island sphere is one of the most fertile of the northern Melanesian region. It may also be the "homeland" of the Lapita ceramic culture around 1500 BCE, whose migration south and east began the formation of the proto-Polynesian populations.

The colonial history of the Bismarck Archipelago properly begins with the Germans who started copra plantations in the fertile Gazelle Peninsula of New Britain among the Tolai people in the 1870s. In 1884 the German flag was raised in Blanche Bay where Rabaul lies, and the Neu-Guinea Kompagnie, followed by the imperial German government in 1899, began the administration of the region. The Bismarck Archipelago became part of what was known as the "island sphere," which together with the northeastern mainland of New Guinea, the islands of Micronesia, and Western Samoa further south comprised Germany's Pacific empire.

The Germans fought wars of pacification with the Tolai people in the 1890s and appropriated and purchased 40 percent of the arable land. They also fought with the Manus people and groups on New Ireland to establish their rule. Governor Albert Hahl (1868–1945) established the foundations of an orderly administration with local leaders as officials, but relations with regional groups of New Guinea peoples remained haphazard and punitive expeditions were relatively frequent.

In 1914 an Australian naval force occupied German New Guinea, and Rabaul was the center of fighting. A military administration then ruled over the area until the League of Nations awarded Australia a mandate over the former German colony. The islands were then administered in a more commercial manner by Australian planting and trading interests, provoking the first major industrial strike in Rabaul in 1929, until the Japanese invaded in 1942. Australian planters and missionaries were executed or imprisoned, and the local New Guineans were made to work supplying Japan's forces. Many also died in the continual bombings.

After 1945 Australia resumed control of the Bismarck Archipelago and the mainland as a trustee of the United Nations. Not until the 1960s was any radical move made towards independence for the people of New Guinea, and the Tolai people of New Britain played a major role in pressuring Australia, organizing an anticolonial movement, the Mataungan Association, in the 1960s. The people of the Bismarck Archipelago shared with their mainland cousins ninety years of formal colonial rule under three different colonial regimes, the Tolai bearing the brunt of commercial development during that time. They were able to turn economic growth to their advantage and entered independence as the most prosperous and influential group vying for power in the newly independent country of Papua New Guinea.

SEE ALSO *Pacific, European Presence in.*

BIBLIOGRAPHY
Firth, Stewart. *New Guinea Under the Germans.* Carlton, Australia: Melbourne University Press, 1982.

Howe, K. R., Robert C. Kiste, Brij J. Lal, eds. *Tides of History: The Pacific Islands in the Twentieth Century.* Honolulu: University of Hawaii Press, 1994.

King, David, and Stephen Ranck, eds. *Papua New Guinea Atlas: A Nation in Transition.* Bathurst, Australia: R. Brown and the University of Papua New Guinea, 1982.

Moore, Clive. *New Guinea: Crossing Boundaries and History.* Honolulu: University of Hawaii Press, 2003.

Ryan, Peter, ed. *Encyclopedia of Papua New Guinea*, 2 vols. Carlton, Australia: Melbourne University Press, 1972.

Peter Hempenstall

BLACKBIRD LABOR TRADE

Blackbirding was the colloquial term for the earliest forms of labor trade, initiated as illegal recruitment and effective slavery long after such practices had ended in Europe and Africa.

In the 1860s Polynesians and Micronesians were forcibly taken from such contemporary Pacific states as Kiribati, Tuvalu, Tokelau, and French Polynesia (Tahiti) to work in Chilean and Peruvian plantations and mines. Some never arrived and few ever returned home; hence, several islands, including Easter Island (Rapa Nui) and Nukulaelae (Tuvalu), lost more than half their population in just three years.

From 1847 to 1872 a more extended labor trade took Melanesians from many islands, mainly to Queensland sugarcane plantations, but also to plantations in Fiji and Samoa and mines in New Caledonia.

Most came from the Loyalty Islands (New Caledonia), the New Hebrides (especially Tanna), and the Solomon Islands. Particularly in the New Hebrides this practice led to population declines in the southern islands. Initially laborers were kidnapped or promised great wealth, until the growth of widespread opposition in various Western countries, often resulting from the protests of missionaries, who themselves followed local pressure. Retaliation was often considerable and the murder of Bishop John Patteson (1827–1871) in the New Hebrides (Vanuatu) was one measure of the strength of local opposition.

Eventually the British government passed the Pacific Islanders Protection Act in 1872 and blackbirding ended. It was replaced by legal recruitment until the end of the century; most of these migrants returned home, but one outcome was a small descendant population of South Sea Islanders (Kanakas) living in Australia.

In the twentieth century there was a diversity of forms of labor migration in the Pacific islands, including the movement of Wallisians and Tahitians to New Caledonia, Indians to the cane fields of Fiji, and Filipinos to Micronesia, but none of these migrations involved the violence, deception, and mortality rates that marked nineteenth-century blackbirding. In a sense the South Sea Islanders represent the first phase of a diasporic population of Pacific islanders that has parallels with Indians within the Pacific.

SEE ALSO *Chinese Diaspora.*

BIBLIOGRAPHY

Corris, P. *Passage, Port and Plantation: A History of Solomon Islands Labour Migration.* Melbourne University Press, 1973.

Graves, A. Graves. *Cane and Labour: The Political Economy of the Queensland Sugar Industry.* Edinburgh University Press, 1993.

John Connell

BOER WARS

The Boer Wars were a series of conflicts fought between the descendants of Dutch settlers and British troops in South Africa in the late nineteenth and early twentieth centuries. The conflicts stemmed from Britain's attempts to expand its South African colonial empire.

Dutch colonists had settled the Cape region of South Africa since the seventeenth century, where they became known as *Boers*, meaning "farmers" in Dutch. After Great Britain acquired control of the Cape in 1806, many Boers felt harassed by British colonial policies, especially the abolition of African slavery, and they began migrating inland to escape British rule. The Boers eventually established two landlocked independent republics: the South African Republic (also known as the Transvaal Republic) and the Orange Free State. The Boers were conservative, deeply religious, and practiced an agricultural way of life; they spoke a form of Dutch later called *Afrikaans*, and called themselves *Afrikaners*, meaning "Africans" in their language.

By the 1870s the British had annexed most of southern Africa with the exception of the two Boer republics, and they now hoped to incorporate the two republics into a larger South African federation. The discovery of diamonds at Kimberley in 1867, and British annexation of the diamond region near the border with the Orange Free State, also brought the British into conflict with the Boers.

FIRST BOER WAR (1880–1881)

The first war between the British and Boers was short and resulted in little loss of life. In 1877 the British annexed the Transvaal, claiming the territory as their own. In 1880 the Boers revolted, and the Transvaal declared its independence from Great Britain. The Boers attacked British army garrisons in the Transvaal and defeated the British at the Battle of Laing's Nek on January 28, 1881; this was followed by other Boer victories. On February 27, 1881, the Boers defeated the British in the decisive Battle of Majuba Hill.

At this point the British government under Prime Minister William Gladstone (1809–1898) decided to recognize Boer independence, and the Convention of Pretoria was signed on April 5, 1881, confirming the sovereignty of the Orange Free State and the South African Republic (Transvaal). To the Boers, the war became known as the First War for Freedom; it is also known to historians as the First South African War and the First Anglo-Boer War.

SECOND BOER WAR (1899–1902)

The Second Boer War is also known to Afrikaners as the Second War for Freedom, and as the Second South African War and the Second Anglo-Boer War. Though the end of the First Boer War restored peace in the Transvaal, it did not end the disputes between the British and the Boers. The discovery of gold on the Witwatersrand in the Transvaal resulted in a huge influx of new settlers, most of them British or from British colonies. Gold mining began apace and the city of Johannesburg became the center of the gold mining region.

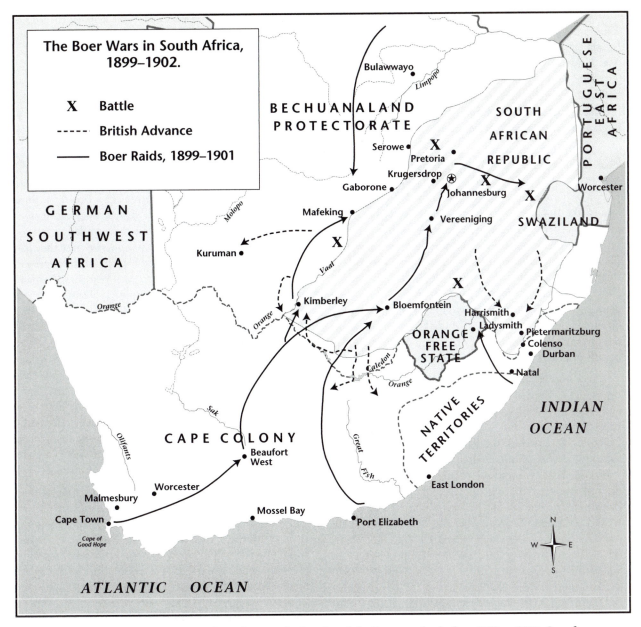

The Second Anglo-Boer War. *The second war between the British and the Boers was fought from 1899 to 1902. Boer forces won early victories at Ladysmith, Mafeking, Colenso, and Kimberley. By 1900, however, the tide had shifted toward the British.*
© EPD PHOTOS.

The rise in new settlers, known in Afrikaans as *Uitlanders*, or "foreigners," disturbed the Boers; the Uitlanders appeared to have little respect for Boer culture and were instead focused on profiting from the Transvaal's resources. The Boers therefore required a long period of residency—fourteen years—in order to acquire Transvaal citizenship and voting rights in the republic, but Uitlanders were still taxed. These conditions angered the Uitlanders, most of whom supported British colonial expansion into the Transvaal.

In 1895 Dr. Leander Starr Jameson (1853–1917), with the backing of the Cape Colony's prime minister, Cecil Rhodes (1853–1902, who had his own commercial interests in the region later to be called Rhodesia), staged a raid on the city of Johannesburg, a nearly farcical event that was a dramatic failure. The failed raid embarrassed the British government, as it made Britain appear to be engaged in aggression against a republic whose independence it had guaranteed. Rhodes was forced to resign as prime minister of the Cape. To the Boers, the event revealed British imperial designs. Paul Kruger (1825–1904), the Transvaal president, was especially effective in rallying his people against the British, as was President Marthinus Steyn (1857–1916) in the Orange Free State. The Transvaal and Orange Free State formed an alliance, and both republics began importing arms from Germany. Germany had given verbal support to the Boer cause, but never intervened when war began.

The British continued their scheming to acquire the Boer republics. The Cape high commissioner, Sir Alfred Milner (1854–1925), as well as the colonial secretary, Joseph Chamberlain (1836–1914), both wanted war against the Boer republics on the grounds of poor treatment against the Uitlanders, but really as part of their imperialist design for the expansion of empire, as well as the desire for gold. At a conference between British and Boer leaders in 1899, the British demanded citizenship and voting rights for Uitlanders, while the Boers demanded that British troops withdraw from the borders of the Transvaal. When the British failed to withdraw their troops, President Kruger ordered the Boers to attack British positions in the Cape Colony and Natal.

War was declared on October 12, 1899. Initially, the Boers had the advantage, besieging the cities of Ladysmith, Mafeking, and Kimberley, and defeating British troops at the battles of Magersfontein and Colenso. Nevertheless, the British prime minister, Lord Salisbury (Robert Arthur Talbot Gascoyne-Cecil, 1830–1903), of the Conservative-Unionist Party, was optimistic and expected the war to last only a few months. British troops led by Sir Redvers Buller (1839–1908) arrived in Cape Town at the end of October, with reinforcements under Lord Frederick Sleigh Roberts (1832–1914) arriving in February 1900, helping to relieve the besieged cities. Robert Baden-Powell (1857–1941, founder of the Boy Scouts) also led a raid against the Transvaal. The British captured the Orange Free State's capital of Bloemfontein in March 1900 and the Transvaal capital of Pretoria in June 1900. The fall of the two capitals led the British to believe that the war would now be over.

At this point, however, the war entered into a guerilla stage as the Boers continued to resist the British onslaught. Unlike the British, who wore uniforms and were organized into hierarchical and highly structured military units, the Boers wore civilian clothes, and were organized into self-governing commandos led by such generals as Jacobus Hercules (Koos) De la Rey (1847–1914), Christiaan de Wet (1854–1922), Louis Botha (1862–1919), and Jan Smuts (1870–1950). Boer commandos continued their attacks on British garrisons and communications lines. The British replaced their earlier command with more able leaders, including Lord

Roberts and Lord Horatio Herbert Kitchener (1850–1916), both military heroes. About 80,000 Boers fought against about 450,000 British troops, including colonial troops from Australia, New Zealand, and Canada. Africans fought for both sides, though most fought for the British, believing that a British victory would bring them greater rights.

The continuance of war in South Africa prompted an antiwar movement in Great Britain, supported by parliamentary opposition parties, including most of the Liberals (such as David Lloyd George [1863–1945]) and the various smaller Labor parties. The British antiwar movement was also motivated by British treatment of Boer prisoners. The Boers themselves tended to release captured British soldiers after a few days because they had no place to imprison them. The British sent their prisoners of war out of the country to such places as Bermuda and Ceylon. The British also employed a scorched earth policy, burning crops and farmhouses (about 30,000 homes were burned), and evicting Boer families, placing women and children in concentration camps. Over 116,000 Boers were imprisoned in about forty-five concentration camps, where 27,000 of them, mainly children, died. Over 120,000 Africans were also imprisoned in concentration camps. Though Africans were important participants in the war and were substantially affected by it, there is relatively little documentation about their experiences and most historians have focused on the British-Boer conflict, rather than on the African role.

Faced with overwhelming force as well as the destruction of their farms, the Boers considered surrendering. Boer generals disagreed among themselves; some, such as Botha, argued for surrender with better terms, while others, such as de Wet, wanted to hold out until the bitter end. Eventually the Boers came to an agreement and surrendered. The Treaty of Vereeniging was signed on May 31, 1902, with the Boers recognizing British annexation of the Transvaal and the Orange Free State, which now became British colonies. These colonies would be merged into the new Union of South Africa in 1910, with Louis Botha becoming the first prime minister of a united South Africa.

The British were active in reconstructing the former republics in an attempt to gain Boer confidence. Africans gained little from the Second Boer War. Many had supported the British in the belief that they would obtain voting rights with a British victory. With the exception of the recognition of some preexisting rights for Africans in the Cape Province, the war did little to help them.

The Boer Wars were significant in defining modern South Africa. The peace treaty in 1902 brought the British and Boers together in an uneasy alliance, allowing the formation of a unified South Africa. Afrikaner

AU TRANSVAAL
SIGNATURE DU TRAITÉ DE PAIX

Boer Peace Treaty. *The Treaty of Vereeniging, which ended the Second Anglo-Boer War, was signed in Pretoria in 1902 by British military commander Horatio Kitchener and Boer leader Christiaan De Wet.* © MARY EVANS PICTURE LIBRARY/THE IMAGE WORKS. REPRODUCED BY PERMISSION.

feelings about the war are still strong, helping to define Afrikaner nationalism in a way similar to how the American Civil War defines southern political culture. The Boer Wars have been compared by some historians to both the Vietnam and Gulf Wars, in which smaller independent nations were attacked by imperial forces.

SEE ALSO *Afrikaner; Cape Colony and Cape Town; Kruger, Paul; Rhodes, Cecil.*

BIBLIOGRAPHY

Beck, Roger B. *The History of South Africa.* Westport, CT: Greenwood, 2000.

Davenport, T. R. H., and Christopher Saunders. *South Africa: A Modern History,* 5th ed. New York: St. Martin's Press, 2000.

Jackson, Tabitha. *The Boer War.* Basingstoke, U.K.: Channel 4 Books/Macmillan, 1999.

Judd, Denis, and Keith Surridge. *The Boer War.* Basingstoke, U.K.: Palgrave Macmillan, 2003.

Pakenham, Thomas. *The Boer War.* New York: Random House, 1979.

Plaatje, Sol T. *Mafeking Diary: A Black Man's View of a White Man's War.* Cambridge, U.K.: Meridor, 1990.

Reitz, Deneys. *Commando: A Boer Journal of the Boer War.* London: Faber and Faber, 1929.

van Hartesveldt, Fred R. *The Boer War.* Stroud, U.K.: Sutton, 2000.

Michael Pretes

BOMBAY

It is only in the context of the history of India that the history of Bombay (Mumbai) can be properly understood. For the British, the establishment of a fortified trading post on Salsette Island—the origins of the city of Bombay—rapidly evolved into a bid to penetrate and gain hegemony over the hinterland. Bombay was for them above all a gateway, an entry point to the whole of the Indian peninsula. For the rising Indian educated class, Bombay was to become a window to the West. Unlike many other Indian cities, Bombay did not develop around a pilgrimage shrine or a royal court.

In the seventeenth century, Bombay consisted of seven islands, its original inhabitants being the Koli community of fisherfolk. In 1665, on the marriage of Catherine of Braganza to Charles II of England, it was given by the Portuguese to the British Crown as part of the future queen's dowry. The commercially unproductive islands were transferred within three years to the East India Company (EIC), leased at the paltry sum of nine pounds sterling per annum. The English factors would soon realize the value of their new acquisition. By 1687 the directors of the EIC had transferred the seat of administration from Surat to Bombay. Its deepwater natural harbor offset the demerits of what Samuel Pepys called "a poor little island." It was believed that Bombay would become as beneficial to the English as Batavia was to the Dutch. Bombay lived up to expectations, and in the nineteenth century became the most important city in India.

By the beginning of the eighteenth century, Bombay had become a metropolitan city, as special religious and economic privileges were offered to people to entice them to come and settle there. Eminent merchants and skilled Parsi shipwrights such as the Wadias were among those who migrated to Bombay from Surat. Expert weavers were induced to come from the hinterland areas of Chaul, Thana, and Bhivandi. Early governors of Bombay, like Sir George Oxinden (1668–1669) and Sir Gerald Aungier (1669–1677), can be described as the true architects of the city. Administrative, judicial, and commercial systems were initiated, shaped on the British model. Bombay's historical identity undoubtedly rests on its image as a colonial city.

The original British settlement was a walled town, with both British and Indian inhabitants, the former in the south and the latter in the north. James Forbes in his *Memoirs* of 1780 records that the town of Bombay was about two miles in circumference, and surrounded by fortifications. Bombay's urban nucleus was Bombay Castle, the administrative, commercial, and military stronghold of the British, adjoining the harbor. Around it was built the semi-circular Esplanade. Landmarks included St. Thomas Church and the Mint. An old resident, Sir Edward Arnold, returning in the 1880s after a twenty-year absence was inspired to remark, in the style of Augustus describing Rome, "I left Bombay a town of warehouses and offices; I find her a city of parks and palaces." (S.M.Edwardes, *The Rise of Bombay, A Retrospect,* Times of India Press, 1902, p. 327).

As the English historian Pamela Nightingale stresses, nineteenth-century Bombay's political hinterland was expanded for the purely commercial reason of gaining control over areas of cotton production. It stretched in a broad arc from Kathiawad and Gujarat in the north to Malabar in the south. As the Industrial Revolution gathered momentum, Bombay started to export raw cotton to the new cotton mills of Manchester and Liverpool. This trade was also supplemented by the opium trade, mainly with China.

During the latter half of the nineteenth century, Bombay's economy experienced a boom due to the American Civil War, which cut the raw cotton supply to England, making Bombay the major exporter. This newfound prosperity stimulated prolific construction of various symbols of British imperial grandeur. Edifices that survive today include Bombay University and Elpinstone College (founded in 1857 and 1860 respectively), the Municipality, the General Post Office, and the High Court buildings. The railway station, named Victoria Terminus and designed after St. Pancras station in London, is today a World Heritage site.

The Bombay, Baroda, and Central India Railway and the Great Indian Peninsular Railway, the very first railways in India, made their appearance in Bombay, starting from Victoria Terminus. Marshy lands were reclaimed, and causeways were built at Mahim, and between Cumballa Hill and Worli, to drain the "Great Breach," the area then known as Breach Candy. Wharves and docks were constructed on a large scale. In the mid-nineteenth century, after the opening of the Suez Canal, Bombay port became a focus of steamship navigation. Companies such as the famed Peninsular and Oriental

Steam Navigation Company, the Messageries Maritimes Company, the Bombay Steam Navigation Company, the Austrian Lloyd Company of Trieste, and the Rubattini Company of Genoa set up offices in Bombay. Sailing clippers were also engaged in the tea and opium trade. Agency houses of the British became a common feature of Bombay city. Modern milling technology was introduced through the construction of cotton mills, the first one being started in 1854. A supply of cheap labor from the neighboring areas (mostly the Konkan and Deccan) led to a massive influx of population. Over the course of the nineteenth century, the population grew from an estimated 200,000 to almost a million.

The culture of the city has been and continues to be pan-Indian rather than provincial. From the beginning, ethnic multiplicity was reflected in the population, which included Parsis, Gujarati "Baniyas," and the Muslim trading communities of Bohras and Khojas. Contributions to the development of Bombay were made by affluent members of the indigenous entrepreneurial class, such as Jagannath Shankarseth and Sir Jamsetjee Jeejeebhoy. With the formulation of his famous Drain Theory, Bombay's Dadabhai Naoroji took his place as India's leading economic nationalist. In 1885 Bombay played host to the founding session of the Indian National Congress. During World War II, the industrialists of the city brought forth detailed proposals for the economic development of the country in their "Bombay Plan." By the end of the war, Bombay was well established as the industrial hub of India: it had 477 metal industries, 210 printing presses, 75 chemical plants, and 94 other industries, while 184 textile mills were still in operation (David 1998, p.249). Bombay strongly supported the Civil Disobedience Movement and Mahatma Gandhi, and was the site of heroic working class struggles, as it had a large labor force, mainly cotton mill workers. In the immediate postwar period, the Bombay Naval Mutiny, strongly supported by the organized trade unionists and Left parties, sent a clear signal that Britain's hold on India could not much longer be maintained. Once India gained independence, Bombay overtook Calcutta to become the unquestioned economic capital of independent India.

In the nineteenth century the city of Bombay was once described as "the connecting link between Europe and Asia," the point where two civilizations meet and mingle. This description might also be appropriately applied to the contemporary cosmopolitan social structure of the city, as well as to its internationally focused economy. It could also characterize the physical image of Bombay. Like other British colonial ports of India, Bombay has been an architectural hybrid, presenting an evolving juxtaposition of Indian and European concepts of environment. Bombay has in common with Madras (Chennai) and Calcutta (Kolkata) that it grew from a small fortified trading settlement into a sprawling commercial metropolis. Because of its physical setting, however, Bombay has been in many ways unique. Bombay began as seven small islands, and through gradual reclamation, was a single land mass by the end of the eighteenth century. The physical formation of Bombay has thus necessitated extensive reclamation and land-filling activities. There have been two twentieth-century landfill projects, the Backbay Reclamation (creating the seaside Marine Drive) and Ballard Estate. In the post-Independence years, two additions were made to Bombay's land surface, Nariman Point and Cuffe Parade. Land has thus been scarce and expensive, a factor that has continued to promote dense building patterns and a predominant use of multistoried structures. Industrial prosperity has been accompanied by environmental deterioration and traffic congestion.

Bombay remains a city of immigrants and a commercial metropolis. It continues to be known as a seaport, railhead, air traffic hub, and center of finance, as well as a textile mill city and a high technology pole. It is also dubbed "Bollywood," as it is the center of the world's premier cinema industry.

SEE ALSO *English East India Company (EIC).*

BIBLIOGRAPHY

Albuquerque, Teresa. *Bombay: A History.* New Delhi: Rashna/Promilla, 1992.

David, M. D. *Bombay: The City of Dreams.* Bombay: Himalaya, 1998.

Dossal, Mariam. *Imperial Designs and Indian Realities: The Planning of Bombay City, 1845–1875.* Bombay: Oxford University Press, 1991.

Gupchup, Vijaya. *Bombay: Social Change, 1813–1857.* Bombay: Popular Book Depot, 1993.

Kosambi, Meera. *Bombay in Transition: The Growth and Social Ecology of a Colonial City, 1880–1980.* Stockholm: Almqvist and Wiksell, 1986.

Maloni, Ruby. "Surat to Bombay: Transfer of Commercial Power." *Itinerario* 26, no. 1 (2002): 61–74.

Nightingale, Pamela. *Trade and Empire in Western India, 1784–1806.* Cambridge, U.K.: Cambridge University Press, 1970.

Patel, Sujata, and Alice Thorner, eds. *Bombay: Mosaic of Modern Culture.* Bombay: Oxford University Press, 1996.

Tindall, Gillian. *City of Gold: The Biography of Bombay.* Calcutta: Penguin, 1982.

Ruby Maloni

BOSTON

Boston was the site chosen in 1630 by the English Puritans for their political, administrative, and religious capital. Located on a promontory, it offered both a defensive position and a central location for the other settlements of Massachusetts Bay. Under the leadership of John Winthrop (1588–1649) the town grew rapidly, sustained by a stream of immigrants from England and the presence of a good harbor. For the first ten years, Boston's commerce was largely with the mother country. The outbreak of the English Civil War (1642–1651), however, prompted its merchants to open new markets in the Chesapeake and West Indies. Despite the Navigation Acts of 1660 and 1663, Boston continued to prosper, as witnessed by its expanding fleet and numerous wharfs and warehouses. By the end of the seventeenth century its population had reached almost 8,000, making it the largest overseas English town. Unsurprisingly its inhabitants played a leading role in the overthrow of the Dominion of New England in 1689.

During the first half of the eighteenth century, Boston did not enjoy such unremitting growth. One reason for this was the emergence of New York and Philadelphia as rivals for the carrying trade. In addition, Boston lacked a dynamic internal market, because the region's rocky soils limited its agricultural potential. During the wars of the eighteenth century, Boston did profit from military contracting and the equipping of privateers. But the coming of peace invariably led to economic dislocation and unemployment, though the population continued to grow, reaching 16,000 by 1760. Boston, as a result, was the first American town to experience urban poverty. However, it remained a center of politics, culture, and ideas because of the presence of nearby Harvard College. It also was the most democratically governed town in British North America, having a franchise that effectively included all white males. Boston had a heady mixture of an educated elite and working-class majority citizens that Samuel Adams (1722–1803) and his patriot colleagues exploited against Britain during the Stamp Act riots, the Boston Massacre, and final separation from Britain in 1776.

SEE ALSO *American Revolution; Atlantic Colonial Commerce.*

BIBLIOGRAPHY

Nash, Garry B. *The Urban Crucible: Social Change, Political Consciousness, and the Origins of the American Revolution.* Cambridge, MA: Harvard University Press, 1979.

Rutman, Darett B. *Winthrop's Boston, Portrait of a Puritan Town, 1630–1649.* Williamsburg, VA: University of North Carolina Press, 1965.

Whitehill, Walter Muir, and Lawrence W. Kennedy. *Boston: A Topographical History,* 3rd ed. Cambridge, MA: Belknap Press of Harvard University Press, 2000.

Richard Middleton

BOXER UPRISING

As the nineteenth century drew to a close, China found itself reduced to semicolonial status: The Qing state remained intact, but most of China was divided into spheres of influence under the control of foreign powers, a process that had begun with the first Opium War (1839–1842) and concluded with the first Sino-Japanese War (1894–1895). Although the Qing continued to stumble along for another decade, what accelerated the process of dynastic collapse was the Boxer Uprising. Known collectively as the Boxers United in Righteousness (*Yihequan*) and sharing the belief that spirit possession and invulnerability rituals would protect them from bullets, a motley crew of peasants, laborers, and drifters launched the movement in 1898. From their origins in northwestern Shandong, the Boxers spread across the North China Plain, extending as far as Manchuria and Inner Mongolia.

A combination of deteriorating conditions in the countryside and increasing Chinese resentment of the missionary presence in Shandong fueled the Boxer movement. The North China Plain had been hard hit by a series of natural disasters; banditry, smuggling, and corruption also were rife in the area. The devastation caused by flood and drought coupled with the government's failure to effectively address the crisis made the impoverished peasants easy recruits for the Boxer movement. Furthermore, missionary activity in the area and the special privileges accorded to Chinese converts exacerbated relations between the Chinese on the one hand, and the Christian missionaries and their converts on the other. The physical assault of missionaries and Christian Chinese as well as the destruction of railroad and telegraph lines—symbols of the Western presence in China—defined the Boxer Uprising as an antiforeign, anti-Christian, and anti-missionary movement.

However, the Boxers were not anti-Qing as is sometimes thought; after all, their slogan was "Revive the Qing; destroy the foreigner." And despite later representations portraying the Boxers as rebels, the Qing court did support the Boxers. Although the rumor that the Empress Dowager Cixi (1835–1908) had ordered the expulsion of all foreigners and Chinese Christians proved to be false, she did declare war on all eight foreign powers on June 21, 1900. Early interpretations maintain that the Boxers were initially against the Qing, being an outgrowth of secret societies with a tradition of rebellion against the state. However, later studies indicate that the Boxers were pro-Qing from the outset, based as they were on local militia loyal to and under the supervision of the Qing. In his study of the origins of the Boxer Uprising, historian Joseph Esherick agrees with the latter

Chinese Rebel During the Boxer Uprising, 1900. *A Chinese rebel waves a banner in support of the Boxer Uprising, a violent rebellion against foreign interests in China.* © CORBIS. **REPRODUCED BY PERMISSION.**

interpretation, but dismisses the Boxers' sectarian and loyalist origins, emphasizing instead their genesis in popular culture.

The Boxer Uprising peaked in the summer of 1900 with the siege of the foreign legation quarters in Beijing and the Qing court's declaration of war against the foreign powers. It took an eight-nation alliance to end the siege. The Boxer Protocol in 1901 demanded that China pay a huge indemnity in the amount of 450 million taels (equivalent to about $333 million at the time); by some estimates, that amount would total a billion taels in 1940 when the indemnity was to be paid in full. In 1908, the United States allocated its portion of the indemnity to fund scholarships for Chinese students. Through its "open door notes," the primary objective of which was to protect American commercial interests in China, the United States also sought to slow down if not thwart the scramble for concessions. The Qing state emerged from the Boxer Uprising a weaker, if not fatally crippled, country unable to hold onto the reins of power without foreign assistance. To restore peace and order, American troops occupied Beijing; historian Michael Hunt attributes the smoothness of the American occupation to Chinese collaborators.

For the mainland Chinese, the Boxer event has held different meanings at different times. During the New Culture Movement (1915–1925), the Chinese viewed the Boxers as ignorant peasants blinded by xenophobia and bound by superstition; later, the rising tide of nativism and nationalism reconfigured the Boxers' antiforeign sentiment as patriotic fervor. During the Cultural Revolution (1966–1976), the Chinese Communist Party mythologized the Boxers as revolutionary vanguards.

SEE ALSO *China, First Opium War to 1945; Chinese Revolutions; East Asia, American Presence in; East Asia, European Presence in; Missions, China.*

BIBLIOGRAPHY

Cohen, Paul A. "The Contested Past: The Boxers as History and Myth." *The Journal of Asian Studies* 51 (1) (Feb. 1992): 82–113.

Esherick, Joseph. *The Origins of the Boxer Uprising.* Berkeley: University of California Press, 1987.

Hunt, Michael H. "The Forgotten Occupation: Peking, 1900–1901." *Pacific Historical Review* 48 (4) (Nov. 1979): 501–529.

Lisa Tran

BRAZIL

SEE *Empire, Portuguese, in America*

BRAZILIAN INDEPENDENCE

When Brazil declared its independence on September 7, 1822, it had traversed a truly unusual path. Once a conventional colony, it had evolved into the seat of the Portuguese empire by 1808, only to be declared a kingdom, equal in status with Portugal, in 1815. The Portuguese royal family, fleeing before the Napoleonic troops that had entered Portugal in late 1807, were the only European monarchs to ever see their American colony, and they were the only ones to rule their empire from the colonies. Last but not least, for much of the nineteenth century Brazil was the only American colony to have become an independent monarchy. Yet independence, declared in 1822, did not fully signify Brazilian sovereignty. The Portuguese crown had needed help in order to relocate before the advancing French troops and later to recover their throne in Portugal, help that Great Britain had agreed to provide—in return for generous commercial advantages in Brazil. Nor did independence mean freedom for slaves, the mainstay of the Brazilian labor force.

As Napoleon's troops closed in on Lisbon in late 1807, João VI, the Portuguese king, after much hesitation decided against joining France's continental blockade of Great Britain, and instead availed himself of the British offer to protect the Portuguese monarchy. Hurriedly, the entire court, including part of the army and navy, along with the royal treasury and several libraries, relocated to the most important Portuguese colony at the time, Brazil. All in all, an estimated ten to twenty thousand people moved to Brazil. Once the royal family arrived in Rio de Janeiro, it set up its court in the colonial capital, and began expanding the existing institutions to develop a functioning state in the place of a formerly dependent colony.

The royal family and particularly the prince regent (soon to become king João VI) quickly came to consider Rio de Janeiro as more than a temporary place of exile. In 1815 João VI raised Brazil to the status of a kingdom on equal footing with its former mother country, which was governed at the time by the Council of Regency and protected by the British army. The new kingdom carefully kept its distance from the turbulence of European warfare. For Brazilians, the presence of the Portuguese court in Rio meant a growing identification of royal policies with Brazilian interests. At the same time, however, it meant that Portuguese took up some of the political offices previously open to Brazilians while relying almost entirely on the Brazilian economy for government revenues. Thus the relocation of the Portuguese court produced mixed responses among the Brazilian elites. It did, however, provide the country with a recognizable and generally accepted center of power that fostered stability and thus helped Brazil maintain its territorial integrity while other Latin American nations fragmented.

Brazil's political independence was hastened by the political events in Portugal after 1820. Liberal-nationalist revolts in the cities of Oporto and Lisbon led to the establishment of a *junta provisória* (provisional assembly) in Portugal, replacing the Council of Regency that had been presided over by Field Marshal Beresford, an Englishman. The Junta demanded the king's return to Portugal, and began to put together a *cortes* (constituent congress) with the purpose of writing a constitution. When João VI and the royal court returned to Portugal

A Government Employee in Brazil Leaves Home. *A government employee with his family and servants leaves home shortly before Brazil gained independence, in a lithograph printed in* Voyage pittoresque et historique au Brésil *(1839) by Jean-Baptiste Debret.*
BIBLIOTHEQUE NATIONALE, PARIS, FRANCE/ARCHIVES CHARMET/THE BRIDGEMAN ART LIBRARY. REPRODUCED BY PERMISSION.

in 1821 due to increasing pressure by the Cortes, João left his son, Pedro I, as prince regent in Rio de Janeiro.

Initially, Brazilians seized on the opportunity of sending delegates to the Cortes, which they assumed would recognize Brazil's status as equal to that of Portugal, and which they hoped would incorporate Brazilian interests into Portuguese policy to a heretofore-unprecedented degree. Instead, the Cortes's policy toward Brazil revealed itself as an attempt to return the country to its former status as a colony. It limited the jurisdiction of Pedro I to southern Brazil, and dispatched governors to other provinces. Furthermore, in 1821, the Cortes demanded the return of prince Pedro I to Lisbon, where he was to finish his education.

By now, Brazilian nationalists had transferred their allegiance from João VI to Pedro I, and exercised pressure on the prince to remain in Brazil. On January 9, 1822, the prince officially declared his intentions of staying

in Brazil. From May 1822 onwards, no decision from the Cortes was implemented in Brazil without the explicit approval of the prince regent. Following the receipt of correspondence from the Cortes reaffirming its demands, Pedro I, on the advice of Brazilian nationalists, such as José Bonifácio de Andrada e Silva, and his wife Leopoldina, declared Brazil's independence on September 7, 1822. At the banks of the river Ipiranga, he exclaimed the famous words, "Independence or Death," which, together with British navy and commercial backing, sealed Brazil's separation from Portugal. On December 1 of the same year, Pedro I was crowned "Constitutional Emperor and Perpetual Defender of Brazil." Not all provinces recognized Brazil's independence, and in northeastern and southern Brazil Pedro I had to use military force to quell several regional revolts against his rule following the declaration of independence.

Political independence for Brazil was not tantamount to economic independence. Prior to 1822, the

Portuguese court in Brazil had continued the country's economic dependence on the export of primary goods to generate revenue (and thus in fact finance the royal government). This pattern continued after 1822. Moreover, in return for Britain's speedy assistance in relocating the court and protecting Portugal, King João VI, upon his arrival in Brazil, declared all Brazilian ports open to trade with friendly nations—which in reality meant Great Britain—effective January 28, 1808. While the declaration ended Portugal's colonial monopoly on trade with Brazil, it transferred, rather than ended, the former colony's commercial dependence. Great Britain quickly became the main recipient of Brazil's primary exports, at the same time that Brazil's importation of manufactured goods from England increased. In many ways, the declaration simply eliminated Portugal's role as the commercial entrepôt between Brazilian planters and British manufacturers.

In 1810 a treaty between Brazil and Great Britain cemented this shift in economic dependence. British merchants received special trading privileges, including a maximum tariff of 15 percent on their merchandise, in comparison to the 24 percent tariff levied on imports from all other nations. Moreover, the treaty granted England jurisdiction over British merchants living in Brazil. As a consequence of the favorable economic treaty and Great Britain's exclusion from the European market due to the Continental Blockade, Brazil by the 1820s had become Great Britain's third-largest export recipient. In fact, the growth of commerce between the two nations became so important that Great Britain applied diplomatic pressure on Portugal in 1825 to recognize Brazil's political independence, despite the fact that this might jeopardize British trading interests in Portugal itself. It was only in 1844, when the 1810 treaty expired and the Alves Branco Tariff more than doubled the duties on British goods, that Brazil regained a greater degree of economic independence from Great Britain.

Nor did political independence produce any fundamental changes in the structure of the Brazilian economy and society. Although manufacturing, previously forbidden in the colony, was encouraged once the royal court arrived in Brazil, the mainstay of the Brazilian economy remained the export of primary goods. Indeed, the Brazilian elite that had come to support independence by no means endorsed a more profound restructuring of the social and economic foundations of the newly independent nation. Thus slavery remained in place, and large estates focused on growing export crops such as sugar and increasingly coffee continued to dominate the economy. This left Brazil at the mercy of often unstable world market prices for its exports and dependent on the

import of manufactured goods from Europe and, increasingly, from the United States.

SEE ALSO *Minas Gerais, Conspiracy of.*

BIBLIOGRAPHY
Bethell, Leslie. "The Independence of Brazil." In *Brazil: Empire and Republic, 1822–1930*, edited by Leslie Bethell. Cambridge, U.K.: Cambridge University Press, 1989.

Boxer, C. R. *The Portuguese Seaborne Empire, 1415–1825*. New York: Knopf, 1969.

Burns, E. Bradford. *A History of Brazil*, 3rd ed. New York: Columbia University Press, 1993.

Cavaliero, Roderick. *The Independence of Brazil*. London: Tauris, 1993.

Graham, Richard. *Independence in Latin America: A Comparative Approach*. New York: Knopf, 1972.

Russell-Wood, A. J. R., ed. *From Colony to Nation: Essays on the Independence of Brazil*. Baltimore, MD: Johns Hopkins University Press, 1975.

Viotti da Costa, Emília. *The Brazilian Empire: Myths and Histories*. Chicago: University of Chicago Press, 1985.

Wiebke Ipsen

BRITAIN'S AFRICAN COLONIES

British imperial interests in Africa predate the Berlin Conference of 1884 to 1885, which is usually considered the defining event in the scramble and partition of Africa. By 1871 Britain had established crown colonies in Gambia, Sierra Leone, Lagos, and at the Cape and Natal provinces in South Africa. England built Fort James at the current site of Banjul on the Gambia River in 1618. Sierra Leone became a colony in 1801, and Britain brought the Cape and Natal provinces under its control in the early nineteenth century. These territorial acquisitions that occurred before the dawn of "new imperialism" provided the British with a foundation they built on during the second half of the nineteenth century.

Besides Gambia and Sierra Leone, the other British colonies in western Africa included the Gold Coast (Ghana) and Nigeria. The West African coast was part of the elaborate network of transatlantic slave trade and hence was not immune from the commercial interests of various European nations. In 1844 British officials signed treaties with Fante chiefs as equals. The British economic interests were subsequently enhanced and by the 1870s they monopolized trade in the region. In 1874 the British colonized the coastal Fante states. However, it was not until 1901 that the British conquered Ashanti (Asante). This followed a series of wars between the British and the Ashanti in which the latter lost. This was a significant step in bringing the coast and hinterland regions under British colonial rule.

In the context of Nigeria, the British declared Lagos its protectorate in 1851. The Royal Niger Company was granted a charter to help advance the political and economic interests of the British in the Niger Delta region. It was not until 1900 that the northern part of Nigeria was brought under control, thereby bringing the entire country under formal British colonial rule.

In 1875 Britain increased its influence in Egypt when it bought a substantial share in the Suez Canal. Safeguarding the canal became a major preoccupation of the British government. When the Egyptian economy went into recession and defaulted on its debts, the British government increased its military involvement in Egypt, suppressed the Ahmed Urabi revolt, and occupied the country in 1882. Egypt thus came under British rule as a protectorate. Once Britain occupied Egypt in 1882, it made its way to the Egyptian colony of Sudan. The Anglo-Egyptian forces met stiff resistance from the Mahdi forces in Sudan, and it was not until the 1890s that the country was formally brought under control.

In eastern Africa, the Imperial British East Africa Company was instrumental in establishing Kenya and Uganda as British spheres of influence before the two countries were formally brought under the direct control of the British government: Uganda in 1894 and the British East Africa Protectorate (Kenya) in 1895. In eastern Africa, some communities, including the Giriama, Kikuyu, and the Nandi in Kenya, fiercely contested the imposition of British imperial control, while in Uganda the British sent military expeditions against the Bunyoro.

In contrast, some communities supported the imposition of British rule because they wanted to maintain their preexisting political and economic situation by working closely with the British. The Baganda had an elaborate governance infrastructure, which the British wished to preserve with a view to using Baganda agents in establishing colonial rule. The Masai in Kenya sought assistance from the British because of emergent humanitarian needs brought about by drought and famine. Britain's control of British Somaliland, which is the territory at the mouth of the Red Sea, was concluded in 1884 when it was declared a protectorate.

The British colonization of the Cape Colony between 1802 and 1806 was significant in the context of its imperial interests in India. Having conquered the Cape from the Dutch, the British made it a port of call for their ships en route to India. It was the discovery of gold and diamonds eight decades later that forced Britain to get directly involved in southern Africa with a view to controlling the economic and political destiny of the region. British colonists went to South Africa in large numbers, a development that provoked resentment from the Afrikaners who fiercely resisted the British expansion into the interior as well as their permanent presence. Their stay was bound to undermine the Afrikaner dominance in South Africa.

The arrival of one of the great British empire-builders in Africa, Cecil Rhodes (1853–1902), drastically changed the hitherto existing territorial situation in southern Africa by pressing inland and winning for the British the territories of Bechuanaland (Botswana), Northern Rhodesia and Southern Rhodesia (Zambia and Zimbabwe, respectively), and Nyasaland (Malawi). The African communities, especially the Shona and Ndebele, fiercely resisted the conquest of these lands in Central Africa. In what is today the Republic of South Africa, the provinces of Cape Colony, Natal, Orange Free State, and the Transvaal were united to form the Union of South Africa, which was granted autonomy and thus began to be self-governed in 1910. The whites dominated the political system until 1994, when the country attained majority rule under the leadership of Nelson Mandela (b. 1918).

The British method of colonial administration was dependent on the prevailing local situation. The British retained governmental structures in preexisting centralized polities. The examples of the kingdom of Buganda in Uganda and the Sokoto caliphate in Nigeria are instructive of the British determination to maintain the status quo so long as the leadership accepted its status as subject to the British Crown.

In situations of decentralized polities, the British appointed chiefs through whom orders and directives were communicated to the local population. This method of rule in which the British officials were appointed as governors as well as provincial and district commissioners, while Africans served as chiefs under the designated European officials, is called *indirect rule*. The system was cost-effective because the British needed only a few European officials to govern the colony. The governor was the most powerful person in the colony and was assisted by executive and legislative councils in carrying out the duties of governance. For most of the colonial period these councils were the preserve of European colonial officials. It was the European missionaries who often represented African interests in these councils.

The construction of physical and social infrastructure was a major undertaking of the British colonial state. Roads and railways were built, as were social facilities such as schools and hospitals. English and vernacular languages were promoted in primary schools, but as students proceeded to higher levels, English became the

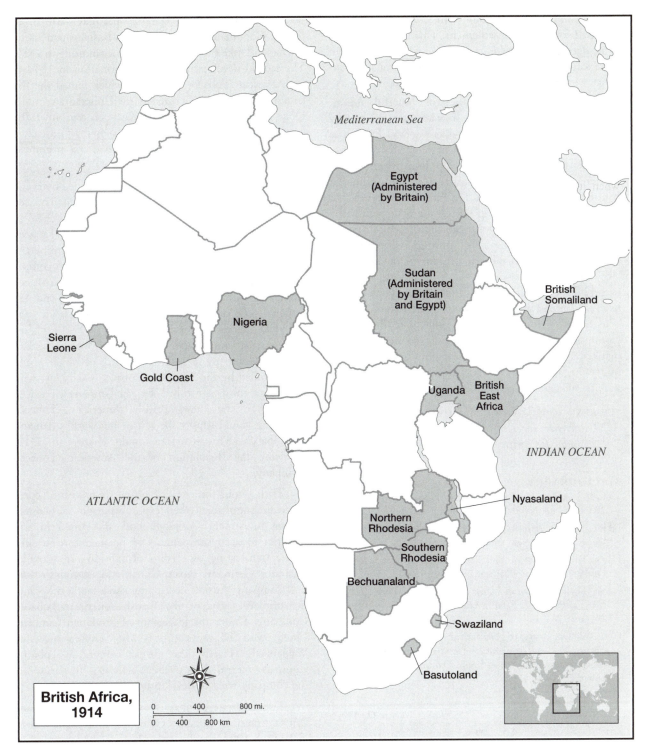

Mediterranean Sea

Egypt
(Administered
by Britain)

Sudan
(Administered
by Britain
and Egypt)

British
Somaliland

Nigeria

Sierra
Leone

Gold Coast

Uganda

British
East
Africa

ATLANTIC OCEAN

INDIAN OCEAN

Nyasaland

Northern
Rhodesia

Southern
Rhodesia

Bechuanaland

Swaziland

Basutoland

N

**British Africa,
1914**

0   400   800 mi.
0   400   800 km

MAP BY XNR PRODUCTIONS. THE GALE GROUP.

only language of instruction. Education served to produce elite that would serve in the administration.

The British imposed their law, but also encouraged customary law in the colonies. In the context of the economy, there were few attempts at industrializing the colonies. Besides South Africa, most British colonies were dependent on agriculture as the mainstay of their economy. In the predominantly settler colonies, such as

Kenya, Zimbabwe, and South Africa, African land was alienated for European settlement. This became a major issue during the decolonization era, when Africans in these settler colonies took up arms to fight for independence with a view to getting back their land.

Whether through resistance or peaceful means, Britain managed to negotiate its way out of Africa by leaving a legacy that is still evident today. English is either the official language or one of the official languages in the former British colonies. The legal system in the former colonies is, in its basic structure and outlines, a continuing legacy of colonialism. Also, the governmental system and bureaucracy still reflects the basic parameters of what was bequeathed to African countries by Britain at independence. The inequality institutionalized during colonialism is still manifested in some of the countries. The explosive land issue in the former settler colonies exemplifies the challenges that independent governments have to contend with in confronting their colonial past. The former colonies are still members of the British Commonwealth and meet regularly to deliberate on matters of education, health, economy and trade, and human rights. Finally, Britain still retains strong links with its former colonies through diplomatic missions.

SEE ALSO *Urabi Rebellion; Asante Wars; Berlin Conference; Indirect Rule, Africa; Rhodes, Cecil; Scramble for Africa; Warrant Chiefs, Africa.*

BIBLIOGRAPHY

Cain, P. J., and A. G. Hopkins. *British Imperialism, 1688–2000,* 2nd ed. London and New York: Longman, 2001.

Elkins, Caroline. *Imperial Reckoning: The Untold Story of Britain's Gulag in Kenya.* New York: Henry Holt, 2005.

Falola, Toyin, ed. *Africa;* Vol. 3: *Colonial Africa, 1885–1939.* Durham, NC: Carolina Academic Press, 2001.

Falola, Toyin, ed. *African Politics in Postimperial Times: The Essays of Richard L. Sklar.* Trenton, NJ: Africa World Press, 2001.

Louis, William Roger, ed. *The Oxford History of the British Empire;* Vol. 4: *The Twentieth Century,* edited by Judith M. Brown and William Roger Louis. Oxford, U.K.: Oxford University Press, 1999.

George O. Ndege

BRITISH AMERICAN TOBACCO COMPANY

As the nineteenth century drew to a close, three significant developments in the tobacco industry led to the formation of the British American Tobacco Company. The first was James Bonsack's invention in 1881 of a machine capable of rapid cigarette production—between 100,000 and 120,000 cigarettes per day—which, as Jordan Goodman reports, American businessman James Buchanan Duke's tobacco company began using in 1885. The second development was the formation in 1890 of the American Tobacco Company, which joined the five largest cigarette manufacturers in the United States under Duke's leadership. The final event occurred in 1901, when the American Tobacco Company purchased Ogden Ltd., a British tobacco firm that was beginning to achieve prominence.

In response, thirteen British companies, led by H. D. and H. O. Wills Ltd., formed the Imperial Tobacco Company within a few months of Duke's purchase of Ogden. Three more firms joined the Imperial Tobacco Company the next year. After a period of commercial warfare, the American and the Imperial tobacco companies reached an agreement: the American Tobacco Company withdrew from the British market and the Imperial Tobacco Company withdrew from the American market. As Jordan Goodman (1994) explains, the two companies then formed the British American Tobacco Company in 1902, two-thirds of which would be controlled by the American Tobacco Company, with the other third controlled by the Imperial Tobacco Company. The new British American Tobacco Company would supply the rest of the world's demand for tobacco. This structure would change in 1912, following the dissolution of the American Tobacco Company.

Throughout the world, high tariffs prompted companies to supplement their export strategies with direct foreign investment. Although both the American and Imperial tobacco companies had pursued foreign subsidies, transferring ownership of subsidies in Canada, Australia, Germany, Japan, China, and Australia to the new company, further developing these markets became the primary focus of the British American Tobacco Company. Under the leadership of Sir Hugo Cunliffe-Owen, who led the company after Duke's successor William R. Harris, the British American Tobacco Company increased its overseas activities. In particular, the company tried to develop its market in China.

Two cigarette companies existed in China, and the British American Tobacco Company consolidated them in 1902 to 1903; the company then sought to expand its sales in China. According to Sherman Cochran (1980), the company's success in China resulted from its decision not to dump surplus goods, but to invest in the creation of an efficient and vertically-integrated company. To do so, it relied on two competitive methods of distribution. The head of British American Tobacco Company's China branch, James Thomas, hired a combination of Western salaried employees—Wu Ting-sheng chief among them—and Chinese middlemen, who guided the managers to the best sites for growing tobacco and to sources of labor. At the same time, the company also developed a complex network of local commission agents, led by Zheng Bozhao. Although these two types of networks competed against each other, the Chinese sales network played a key role in the company's success in China.

The British American Tobacco Company employed a similar strategy of combining Western-style management with local distribution networks in its ventures in India and throughout Africa. In India, Howard Cox reports, the company also focused on growing leaf tobacco locally, setting up a subsidiary that even grew Virginia leaf. Eventually, in these business arrangements, the Western sales staff's job became one of managing the local distribution networks.

Through its cooperation with local competitors and investment in the tobacco industry where it sought market share, the British American Tobacco Company achieved a unique status among early multinational corporations. Indeed, its business practices became models for other companies seeking to expand access to foreign markets.

SEE ALSO *Plantations, the Americas; Tobacco Cultivation and Trade.*

BIBLIOGRAPHY

Cochran, Sherman. *Big Business in China: Sino-Foreign Rivalry in the Cigarette Industry, 1890–1930.* Cambridge, MA: Harvard University Press, 1980.

Cochran, Sherman. *Encountering Chinese Networks: Western, Japanese, and Chinese Corporations in China, 1880–1937.* Berkeley: University of California Press, 2000.

Cox, Howard. *The Global Cigarette: Origins and Evolution of British American Tobacco, 1880–1945.* London: Oxford University Press, 2000.

Goodman, Jordan. *Tobacco in History: The Cultures of Dependence.* London: Routledge, 1994.

Michelle Ladd

BRITISH COLONIALISM, MIDDLE EAST

Historians date the beginning of British imperialism in the Middle East to 1798, the year Napoléon invaded Egypt. Concerned that France would block British access to the eastern Mediterranean and thereby threaten critical trade routes to India, the British navy collaborated with Ottoman authorities to evict French troops from Egypt. From this episode until decolonization in the mid-

twentieth century, British policies in the region reflected the interplay of Great Power rivalries and the balancing of strategic and economic interests.

This essay surveys the history of British imperialism in the Middle East by examining four major periods of interaction: (1) the period of political and economic consolidation that occurred in the decades after the Napoleonic conquest of Egypt; (2) the period of formal entrenchment that began in 1882 with the British Occupation of Egypt and that included the World War I years of open warfare and behind-the-scenes scheming; (3) the post–World War I period when Britain dismantled the Ottoman Empire, redrew the region's political map, and claimed new territories under the guise of mandates; and (4) the post–World War II period of global decolonization. For Britain's empire in the Middle East, this last period began with a jolt in 1948 when Israel emerged from the Palestine mandate, giving rise to the Arab-Israeli conflict and the Palestinian refugee problem.

For the purposes of this essay, the Middle East is defined as the region ranging from Egypt to Iran and from Turkey to Yemen. With the notable exception of Iran, which remained a center of independent Islamic government for centuries, this region in the nineteenth century fell largely within the orbit of the Ottoman Empire, an Islamic sultanate that was based after 1453 in Istanbul. At its peak in the seventeenth century, and before the onset of the economic and territorial contraction that accompanied the rise of Western imperialism in the Middle East, the Ottoman Empire ruled over a vast multicultural domain in southeastern Europe, western Asia, and northern Africa as far west as Algeria.

BRITISH IMPERIALISM IN THE OTTOMAN EMPIRE AND IRAN: THE CONTEXT

Before tracing the rise of British prominence in the Middle East after 1798, it is important to note the historical antecedents of Britain's involvement in the region as well as the political and economic condition of the Ottoman Empire and Iran on the eve of Britain's ascendance.

As early as 1580, English merchants (like their Venetian, French, and other European counterparts) secured formal commercial privileges for trading in the Ottoman Empire (and later gained comparable rights in Iran). Called *capitulations* in English, from the Latin term *capitulas* referring to the chapters or clauses of the agreements, these privileges were renegotiated several times over the next two centuries. They proved significant as the basis for a series of extrajudicial and fiscal rights that Britons continued to enjoy in the Middle East until the early twentieth century.

From the late sixteenth century, commercial contacts with the Ottoman Empire provided not only economic, but also cultural foundations for Britain's imperialism in the region, insofar as they inspired a popular English literature about Turks and Muslims that flourished in the form of travel accounts, plays, and histories. These representations constituted the early matter of what the literary critic Edward Said called *Orientalism*—that is, the body of stereotyped portrayals of the Islamic "Orient" that Western powers later used to justify their expansion in the Middle East. Accumulated literary and artistic representations of the exotic, despotic East, retrograde and debauched, also provided the foil against which late nineteenth-century British writers constructed an image of the British national and imperial character as rational, modern, moral, and strong.

By the end of the eighteenth century, when Britain stood poised to expand its influence in the Middle East, the Ottoman Empire had already begun to suffer military losses to Austria, Russia, and France and to lose territories along its fringes, for example, in Hungary and the Crimea. At the same time, Iran, newly consolidated under the Qajar dynasty (r. 1796–1925), was proving vulnerable to Russian expansion. In short, the same forces in the global economy that had been working to Europe's advantage since the sixteenth century now began to work to the detriment of both the Ottoman Empire and Qajar Iran, which lacked the wherewithal and internal coherence to stave off military, territorial, and economic challenges to their sovereignty. Along with Russia and France especially, Britain was one of the new "Great Powers" that began to assert itself in the Middle East as the nineteenth century began. In the long run, Britain was arguably the most important of these powers in shaping the region's political destiny.

POLITICAL AND ECONOMIC CONSOLIDATION, 1798–1882

In the period from 1798 to 1882, Britain pursued three major objectives in the Middle East: protecting access to trade routes in the eastern Mediterranean, maintaining stability in Iran and the Persian Gulf, and guaranteeing the integrity of the Ottoman Empire. The ultimate goal behind the first two objectives was to secure and protect sea and land routes to India, which was becoming increasingly vital both to Britain's economy and to its imperial psyche. The third objective was related to what nineteenth-century observers called the *Eastern Question*—that is, the challenge of preserving the Ottoman Empire in order to avoid inflaming both competition between the Great Powers and the generally contentious atmosphere created by Western imperial expansion.

At the end of the eighteenth century, British trade in the eastern Mediterranean lands of the Ottoman Empire (the Levant region) accounted for a mere 1 percent of total British foreign trade. In the aftermath of the Napoleonic conquest of Egypt, Britain significantly improved its economic status in the region by using its good favor with Ottoman authorities to secure advantageous trading agreements. As a result, Britain became the Middle East's biggest trading partner in the early nineteenth century, outstripping France, Austria, and Russia. It retained this role as late as World War I, notwithstanding the growing prominence of Germany and Italy in the region's economy during the late nineteenth century. Britain was a major supplier of cheap colored cotton textiles (which constituted more than half of its exports to the Middle East until the 1870s) and also supplied what some economic historians call *colonial goods*—commodities such as Caribbean sugar and Indian tea that came from the larger British empire. In return Britain secured long-staple cotton from Egypt and other food and animal products such as dates, barley, and leather. Economic historians note that Britain's provision of industrial manufactured goods contributed to the long-term decline of local handicrafts industries.

By the 1830s British transport from the eastern Mediterranean to the Indian Ocean occurred along two main routes: the first stretched from the Syrian Desert, down the Euphrates River, and into the Persian Gulf; the second, which became increasingly important as the nineteenth century progressed, crossed the isthmus of Suez into the Red Sea. A desire to protect the Suez route influenced Britain's decision to annex Aden (now part of Yemen), at the southern tip of the Arabian Peninsula, in 1839. The vital importance of the Suez route was confirmed after 1869, when a French engineering firm cut a waterway through the 116-kilometer-wide (72-mile-wide) isthmus, creating the Suez Canal. Together with new technologies—above all, the steamship, the railway, and the telegraph—the Suez Canal transformed Britain's contacts with India by dramatically reducing travel time.

After 1798 the protection of India's northwest frontier became a dominant factor in Britain's policy in Iran. Britain was initially concerned about the prospect of a French invasion of India through Iran and Afghanistan, but this threat had dissipated by the time the Napoleonic wars ended in 1815. Britain's attention in Iran shifted increasingly to Russia, which had been expanding its empire by encroaching on Iran's northern domains in the Caucasus (in what is now Georgia, Armenia, and Azerbaijan) and by asserting its hold over the Caspian Sea and Central Asia. Neither Britain nor Russia wanted the other power to seize control over Iran because the region was strategically valuable to both. This Anglo-Russian competition over Iran, which endured into the

Edward, Prince of Wales, Visits Aden. *Edward, prince of Wales, is greeted with a banner proclaiming support for his father, King George V, during a 1921 state visit to Aden, a British protectorate in what is now Yemen.* © **HULTON-DEUTSCH COLLECTION/CORBIS. REPRODUCED BY PERMISSION.**

twentieth century, preserved the weak central government of the Qajar shahs from formal colonial takeover. Instead, Britain and Russia vied to exert their influence in Iran politically, by supplying military and foreign policy advisors, and economically, by securing trade privileges and concessions pertaining to commodities and services. Britain negotiated an advantageous commercial treaty with Iran in 1857, while in the late nineteenth century British concerns won concessions to develop a telegraph system and a modern central bank in Tehran. British businesses accounted for at least half of Iran's foreign trade by the mid-nineteenth century, exchanging manufactured goods and textiles for Iranian carpets, silk, and other raw agricultural materials.

Competition with the other growing European imperial powers also prompted Britain's closer involvement in the Ottoman Empire, which British sources of the time portrayed as a "Sick Man of Europe" that needed to be propped up. As mentioned above, British

strategists worried about maintaining Ottoman territorial integrity in order to avert wars and contests for influence among the Great Powers themselves. Of particular concern for British policy-setters were Ottoman territories in the Balkans, where fledgling local nationalist movements together with Russian and Austrian imperial ambitions threatened the region's stability. On two major occasions, during the Crimean War (1854–1856) and the Russo-Turkish War (1877–1878), Britain formed alliances with the Ottomans to counteract Russian expansion. Britain used both occasions to extract advantages for itself. In 1856, for example, Britain helped to persuade the Ottoman sultan to issue the famous Humayun decree (one of the landmark measures of the mid-nineteenth-century Ottoman Tanzimat, or reformist, period), which proclaimed religious equality among Muslims, Christians, and Jews. In theory if not in practice, this decree reversed the traditional Islamic imperial assumption of Muslim hegemony over non-Muslim subjects (*dhimmis*). In 1878, meanwhile, Britain persuaded the Ottoman authorities to grant it the island of Cyprus as a naval base, leading to a form of British control over Cyprus that persisted until 1960 and that outlasted the Ottoman Empire itself by forty years.

Britain's vested interests in the Ottoman Empire also influenced its policies toward Egypt in the early twentieth century. Muhammad Ali, the Ottoman army officer who established, consolidated, and expanded his hold over Egypt after the Anglo-Ottoman expulsion of the French army in 1801, had already conquered parts of the Sudan when he sent his son, Ibrahim Pasha, to take Ottoman Syria in 1831. (In other words, Muhammad Ali, the Ottoman underling, was trying to take over the empire from within, for the sake of building his own empire centered in Egypt.) Concerned that Muhammad Ali, as an emerging local power, was complicating the Eastern Question by upsetting the regional status quo, Britain helped to arrange a deal between the Sublime Porte (i.e., the Ottoman sultan and central authorities in Istanbul) and Muhammad Ali in 1841: In return for evacuating his forces from Syria, Muhammad Ali gained the right to pass his governorship in Egypt to his heirs. This policy led to the creation of the Muhammad Ali Dynasty, which endured in Egypt until 1952.

It is worth noting that Britain's protection of Ottoman territorial integrity did not apply to Greece, where an anti-Ottoman nationalist revolt broke out in 1821. Along with Russia and France, Britain supported the Greek Revolt and helped to broker the agreement that led in 1832 to Greek independence from the Ottomans—that is, to liberty from what Greek nationalist historians have often called *Turkocracy*. Influencing Britain's policy was *philhellenism*, a romantic fascination with ancient Greece that inspired the English poet Lord Byron, among other intellectuals, to join the Greek Revolt.

In the 1870s Ottoman policymakers in Istanbul, and their counterparts under the leadership of Khedive Ismail (the grandson of Muhammad Ali) in Egypt, began to take out loans from French and British businesses for the sake of pursuing westernizing, modernizing reforms. When the loans came due in 1875, the Ottoman and Egyptian governments found themselves unable to pay. Hoping to raise the needed funds, the Egyptian government sold its 44 percent stake in the Suez Canal Company to the British government, to no avail. When both the Ottoman and Egyptian treasuries declared bankruptcy, Britain and France installed joint public debt commissions to supervise and guarantee repayments from Istanbul and Cairo; in effect, these measures meant a loss of Ottoman and Egyptian economic sovereignty.

In Egypt in 1881, a nationalist uprising broke out against a backdrop of widespread economic distress and growing anti-European sentiment. Known as the 'Urabi Rebellion—after the military officer, Ahmed 'Urabi, who emerged to lead it—this uprising prompted deep concern among Britons, who feared that instability in Egypt could threaten the Suez Canal—the British imperial life-line to India—as well as local British investments. Much to the dismay of France, which had only recently occupied Tunisia, Britain took action in 1882 by bombarding the coast of Alexandria and occupying Egypt. British authorities maintained that the occupation would be a short-term affair, pending the restoration of political stability. But in fact Britain kept a hold over Egypt for the next seventy years and only withdrew its last troops from the Suez Canal in 1956.

COLONIAL OCCUPATION AND REGIONAL ENTRENCHMENT, 1882–1918

In 1961 the historians Ronald Robinson and John Gallagher famously argued that the British occupation of Egypt in 1882 was the trigger for the "Scramble for Africa." That is, fears over a possible Ottoman collapse and over the Egyptian nationalist threat to the Suez Canal (as manifest in the 'Urabi Revolt) prompted the British occupation. This event, in turn, had a domino effect, and set off the headlong rush for territory that brought nine-tenths of the African continent under European control by 1898 (the year when Britain, working jointly with Egyptian forces, conquered the Sudan). Robinson and Gallagher's narrative emphasized the interconnectedness of Britain's imperial holdings in the Middle East, sub-Saharan Africa, and Asia, as well as the importance of river and ocean access routes in determining Britain's strategic priorities.

In this maritime scheme of British imperialism, the Persian Gulf was also vitally important. Hence the British government forged treaties with local Arab Gulf leaders in Bahrain (1880), Muscat (1891), and Kuwait (1899). Britain agreed to recognize and if necessary protect the signatories and their heirs, in return for gaining exclusive control over their foreign policy.

The outbreak of World War I in 1914 prompted Britain to reconfigure its Middle East presence. Bristling against a long record of British, French, and Russian interference in its affairs, Ottoman authorities in Istanbul joined forces with Germany and the Central Powers, lining up against Britain and the Allies. Britain responded by unilaterally severing Egypt from the Ottoman Empire and by declaring Egypt to be a British protectorate; Egypt then became an important base for military planning and coordination on the Middle East front. British troops (including many soldiers recruited from the far corners of the empire) went on to fight important engagements in the Dardanelles (the ill-fated Gallipoli campaign), Mesopotamia (in the region corresponding to what is now southern and central Iraq), and the Suez Canal zone and Greater Syria (culminating in the British entry into Jerusalem in December 1917).

During World War I, oil made its debut as a major political factor in the region. In Iran in 1901, a British businessman named William Knox D'Arcy had secured a concession over local oil extraction; in 1909 D'Arcy founded the Anglo-Iranian Oil Company (AIOC). The British navy switched from coal to oil fuel in 1912; in 1914, as the war began, the British government bought most of the AIOC shares. This situation meant that Iran's strategic value now lay not only in its proximity to India and its position along the Persian Gulf, but also in its importance as an oil supplier and naval refueling site. Although Iran's government declared official neutrality during World War I, British and Russian fears over German propagandizing in the country prompted a de facto joint occupation in which Britain occupied central and southern Iran (including the oil zones), while Russia consolidated its hold over the north. Iran suffered under the burdens of wartime requisitioning and in 1918–1919 faced a massive famine that killed as much as one quarter of the population.

During World War I, British authorities engaged in a series of behind-the-scenes negotiations that ultimately transformed the political destinies of Middle Eastern people. Three deals or sets of promises, enshrined in the Husayn-McMahon Correspondence, the Sykes-Picot Agreement, and the Balfour Declaration, proved to be most practically and symbolically important in both the short term and the long run. Understanding what each of these deals entailed and how they were later applied is critical to understanding the impact of British imperialism on the twentieth-century Middle East.

The Husayn-McMahon Correspondence. Deeply concerned by the Ottoman discourses that portrayed the war as a jihad, and fearful lest Muslims throughout the wider British Empire rise up to support the Ottoman cause (and thereby the Central Powers), British leaders made extra efforts to cultivate wartime alliances with Muslim dignitaries who could offset the Ottoman bid for Muslim support. They identified a possible ally in Husayn ibn Ali, also known as Sharif Husayn of Mecca. A person of influence in the Hijaz (the western region of the Arabian Peninsula that includes the holy Muslim cities of Mecca and Medina), and a man of political ambitions, Sharif Husayn traced descent from the Prophet Muhammad and was therefore known as a *Hashimite* (from the name of Muhammad's clan of Hashim). The Husayn-McMahon Correspondence consisted of a series of ten

letters exchanged between Sir Henry McMahon, the British High Commissioner in Egypt, and Sharif Husayn in 1915 and 1916. In these letters, Sharif Husayn promised to stage an anti-Ottoman revolt if Britain promised, in return, to recognize an Arab state that would be led by Sharif Husayn and his family after the war. This Arab state would include the Fertile Crescent (including the general region that today includes Syria, Lebanon, Israel and the Palestinian territories, Jordan, and Iraq) and the Arabian Peninsula. While McMahon expressed some reservations about parts of coastal Syria and while the two men never confirmed the final details on this point, McMahon nevertheless assured Sharif Husayn that "Great Britain is prepared to recognize and uphold the independence of the Arabs in all the regions lying within the frontiers proposed by the Sherif [Sharif] of Mecca." Acting on this agreement, and bolstered by British funds, weapons, and military advising, Sharif Husayn built up an army to attack the Ottomans. His efforts led to the Arab Revolt, headed by his son, Faisal, which began in 1916 and culminated with the capture of Damascus from the Ottomans in 1918.

The Sykes-Picot Agreement. The Sykes-Picot Agreement was a secret wartime treaty signed in 1916 between Britain and France; it was named after its chief negotiators, Sir Mark Sykes of Britain and Georges Picot of France. (It was signed one year after a comparable treaty between Britain and Russia, the Constantinople Agreement of 1915, which Russia's postrevolutionary Bolshevik government later waived.) Based on the premise that the Allied Powers would win the war, the Sykes-Picot Agreement reflected France and Britain's effort to divide the Arab Middle East amicably, into spheres of influence that would come into effect after the war. The treaty recognized the region now corresponding to Syria and Lebanon, where France had longstanding economic and cultural interests, as part of a future French sphere, and the region of Mesopotamia (now Iraq) as part of a future British sphere. Plans for Palestine were left somewhat vague with the treaty suggesting some kind of international administration. In fact, Britain had its eye on Palestine and was toying with the idea of building a railway from Haifa to Basra—a plan that would have yielded a direct route from the eastern Mediterranean to the Persian Gulf, and at the same time secure yet another route to India.

The Balfour Declaration. The Balfour Declaration of November 1917 was a letter from the British Foreign Secretary, Arthur Balfour, to Lord Rothschild, a prominent British member of the Zionist movement (a Jewish response to modern European anti-Semitism). On behalf of the British government, Balfour declared that "His Majesty's Government view with favour the establishment in Palestine of a National Home for the Jewish people, and will use their best endeavours to facilitate the achievement of this object, it being clearly understood that nothing shall be done which may prejudice the civil and religious rights of existing non-Jewish communities in Palestine, or the rights and political status enjoyed by Jews in any other country." While the Balfour Declaration reflected a degree of British official sympathy with Zionist aspirations, it also may have served British strategic interests: first, by building wartime support among the Jews in Europe and North America, and second, by bolstering postwar British claims to influence over the territory to the northeast of the Suez Canal.

When the war ended in 1918, Britain faced the impossible task of implementing and reconciling the three, mutually contradictory agendas of the Husayn-McMahon Correspondence, the Sykes-Picot Agreement, and the Balfour Declaration.

COLONIAL MANDATES AND THE LAST BURST OF IMPERIAL EXPANSION

According to the historian Elizabeth Monroe, the post–World War I period was "Britain's moment in the Middle East." She argued that from the British capture of Jerusalem and Baghdad in 1917 until the Suez Crisis of 1956, Britain was the paramount power in most of the Middle East and the shaper of political destinies.

Along with France, Britain played the leading role in dismantling the Ottoman Empire after World War I and in creating new government entities in the Fertile Crescent, that is, future nation-states. At the San Remo Conference in 1920, Britain and France ensured the essential implementation of the wartime Sykes-Picot Agreement. The San Remo Conference separated the Arab provinces from the Ottoman Empire and allocated spheres of influence to France and Britain, drawing the outlines for the country borders that we see today on the Middle East map. The San Remo Conference formalized these spheres of influence by defining them as *mandates*, a term that served as a euphemism for colonial control. The League of Nations, which was the post–World War I antecedent of the United Nations, clarified this term by stating that mandates were territories "inhabited by peoples not yet able to stand by themselves under the strenuous conditions of the modern world." In what amounted to a last burst of imperial expansion, France gained mandates over Syria and Lebanon; Britain gained Palestine and Iraq and ensured that the boundaries of the new Iraq included the oil-rich region around Mosul. France and Britain agreed up front that in running these so-called mandates they should try to prepare these regions for eventual self-rule—that is, independence on some distant horizon.

Another highly significant post–World War I settlement was the Treaty of Sèvres, signed by the Ottoman government in August 1920. The Treaty of Sèvres delivered the final blow to the Ottoman Empire. It awarded the Ottoman region of Thrace to Greece and provided for French and Italian interests in railways and coal mining; it also reasserted British and French control over the region's finances (because the empire's late nineteenth-century debts were still on the books). However, Turkish-speaking nationalists led by an Ottoman war veteran named Mustafa Kemal (later called Atatürk, or "Father of the Turks") rallied to prevent the implementation of this treaty and to set up a counter-government in the central Anatolian village of Ankara. These resisters, who went on to declare the birth of a Turkish republic in 1920 and the end of the Ottoman order, succeeded in winning international recognition for the new country of Turkey and in preventing the full implementation of the Treaty of Sèvres.

Britain never fulfilled its wartime promises to Sharif Husayn of Mecca in their entirety but made three gestures toward the Hashimites. First, Britain invited Faisal (Sharif Husayn's son, who had been ousted from the leadership of a nascent Arab Kingdom in Damascus by the French) to become king of British-mandated Iraq in 1921—thus creating the Hashimite Kingdom of Iraq, which lasted until a violent leftist coup in 1958. (In 1932 Britain granted Iraq a form of official, yet nominal independence: it was nominal because Britain reserved control over Iraq's military and communications and retained a major share in Iraq's burgeoning oil industry.) Second, and also in 1921, Britain invited Abdallah, another son of Sharif Husayn, to become emir of Transjordan, an arid and thinly populated region that Britain had gained with the Palestine mandate—but an area that was excluded from the sphere of Zionist settlement. Operating under close British watch and dependent on annual British subventions, Transjordan enjoyed quasi-autonomy until 1946 when it gained independence as the Hashimite Kingdom of Jordan. Third, Britain recognized Sharif Husayn himself as ruler of a Hashimite kingdom of the Hijaz (western Arabia). Husayn did not retain power for long, however, as in 1924 the Wahhabist forces of 'Abd al'Aziz Ibn Sa'ud overran the region and seized control, forcing him to flee into exile. By the Treaty of Jidda in 1927, Britain agreed to recognize the family of Ibn Sa'ud as rulers over most of the Arabian peninsula (i.e., Britain recognized the kingdom of Saudi Arabia) in return for extracting a promise from the Saudis to respect the integrity of Transjordan and of Hashimite rule in that vicinity.

Meanwhile, with Russia internally distracted after its 1917 communist revolution, Britain moved to confirm its postwar position in Iran, which remained subject to quasi-colonial control. In 1919 Britain extracted a new Anglo-Persian treaty that made Britain the sole provider of advice to Iran's military and central government and the sole source of transportation and communications development. Britain's heavy-handed intervention in Iranian affairs and its control over Iranian oil resources increasingly rankled educated elites, and contributed, by the late 1930s, to a degree of pro-German sentiment in the country. Though Iran's Pahlavi monarch, Reza Shah, declared Iran to be neutral when World War II broke out, British suspicions regarding his wartime sympathies prompted the shah in 1941 to abdicate in favor of his son, Mohammed Reza, as a way of safeguarding the monarchy. Years later, the Islamic Revolution of 1978–1979 unseated Mohammed Reza Shah and brought to power the Ayatollah Khomeini, whose anti-Western message was a response to Iran's modern history of Western imperialism.

In Egypt, British colonialism after 1882 had not only provoked but had indirectly aided the development of local nationalism. It helped in the long run that Lord Cromer, architect of British policy in the 1883 to 1907 period, had believed in the value of the press as a safety valve for local grievances, because under British colonialism, Egypt's Arabic periodical press flourished and brought Egyptian nationalism into greater focus. By the end of World War I, nationalism was arguably a stronger and more coherent force in Egypt than in any other Arabic-speaking country. In 1919 Egyptian nationalists demanded the right to Egyptian self-determination (reflecting an ideal that U.S. president Woodrow Wilson had so famously articulated during the war) and called for an end to the British protectorate. When Britain tried to prevent Egyptian nationalist leaders from airing their views at the Paris Peace Conference, a popular nationalist revolt broke out. Yielding partly to these pressures, Britain went on to declare unilateral independence for Egypt three years later in 1922. This independence was "unilateral" because it was one-sided in Britain's favor, and enabled Britain to retain significant influence in and power over the country—for example, it allowed Britain to control Egypt's foreign policy and to keep British troops on Egyptian soil. After 1922 Egypt gained a parliament, while its dynastic ruler, a descendant of the Ottoman governor Muhammad Ali, was declared king. In 1936 the Anglo-Egyptian Treaty gave Egypt a greater degree of autonomy—for example, by providing for a phased abolition of the capitulatory privileges that foreigners had enjoyed in Egypt. Arguably, the informality of the British influence in Egypt made British colonialism especially tenacious there, with the result that Egypt gained independence only incrementally.

The most controversial history of post–World War I British imperialism in the region pertains to Palestine. Unlike the other Middle East mandates, the League of Nations–approved agreement for Palestine did not cite self-determination as a long-term goal for the territory's indigenous inhabitants, who were overwhelmingly Muslim and Christian Arabs. On the contrary, the mandate for Palestine laid out a framework for Zionist administration and settlement, according to which Britain would facilitate Jewish immigration. Opposition to the Zionist agenda grew slowly among members of Palestine's non-Jewish majority (i.e., those who later became known as the Palestinians) and escalated into a series of clashes in the years after 1929, when the non-Jewish population was still estimated at 85 percent and when the landless Arab peasant population was growing, particularly as wealthy Arab landowners sold their property to Zionist settlers who extolled ideals of Jewish labor. In the next decade, Britain responded to the increasingly tense situation on the ground by issuing *white papers*, or policy statements, that affirmed the need to address the concerns of both Palestine's Arab and Jewish inhabitants and that suggested possible limits on Zionist immigration. By 1939 two trends were evident: first, that Arab resistance to Zionist immigration had reached the boiling point, and second, that Hitler's virulent anti-Semitism was proving the desperate need for a Jewish haven. The Holocaust-in-progress steeled the resolve of Zionists in Palestine, who had long supported a program to create not only a Jewish homeland (as the Balfour Declaration had intimated in 1918), but also a full-fledged Jewish state. Yet even by the outbreak of World War II, Arabs still formed a clear majority of Palestine's population.

The situation in Palestine was reaching an impasse just as World War II broke out. With Mussolini's Italy in control of Libya, on Egypt's western flank, Britain faced up to the possibility of a German and Italian invasion within North Africa. British troops managed to stave off an Axis invasion of Egypt in 1942, and Britain and the other Allied powers went on to win the war. As historians later acknowledged, however, Britain's victory in war also entailed a defeat, in a sense, for its empire.

THE END OF THE EMPIRE IN THE MIDDLE EAST

To explain the rapid contraction of the British Empire in the middle of the twentieth century in the aftermath of World War II, historians often note that postwar Britain lacked the economic strength and willpower to maintain its far-flung colonies, particularly in the face of mounting anticolonial nationalism. While several key events stand out in the global history of decolonization, India's independence in 1947 represented the critical watershed. The Middle East followed quickly behind South Asia, with Palestine's decolonization occurring in 1948.

Having come under increased attacks from armed Zionist groups whose members regarded Britain's presence as an obstacle to Jewish statehood, and realizing the intractability of the situation that the mandate had created for local Arabs, British authorities hoisted down the Union Jack on May 14, 1948, and beat a hasty retreat. A few hours later the Jewish community proclaimed the independence of the new state of Israel. Army units from Egypt, Syria, Lebanon, Jordan, and Iraq invaded the next day, but fared poorly. By the time the fighting stopped and the dust settled, an estimated 700,000 Arabs, or 60 percent of Palestine's Arab population, had fled from their homes and were barred by Israelis from returning. British decolonization in Palestine thereby gave rise to both the Arab-Israeli conflict and the Palestinian refugee problem.

The most symbolically important event in Britain's Middle East decolonization was the Suez Crisis, which occurred in Egypt in 1956, four years after a leftist revolution that had overturned Egypt's parliamentary monarchy and only a few months after the negotiated withdrawal of Britain's last troops from the Suez Canal Zone. Determined to secure revenues to fund the extension of the Aswan Dam, Egypt's president, Gamal Abdel Nasser, declared the nationalization—that is, the Egyptian government seizure—of the Suez Canal, which a British-French consortium had long owned and operated for the sake of the tolls that ships paid to go through it. In nationalizing the canal, Nasser drew some inspiration from the Iranian Prime Minister, Mohammed Mossadegh, who had tried to nationalize the Anglo-Iranian Oil Company in 1953 (until a CIA-backed coup in Iran had thwarted his efforts). Responding to Nasser's maneuver, Britain and France, in alliance with Israel, declared war on Egypt. However, the United States and the Soviet Union interceded to call off the Anglo-French-Israeli invasion out of a concern that the conflict could escalate in the Cold War milieu. More than any other event, the Suez Crisis showed that the United States and the Soviet Union were displacing Britain and France as the Great Powers in the region.

The last enclaves of British colonial influence in the Middle East were in the Gulf region. As oil revenues began to transform this poor region into the Middle East's wealthiest corner, Britain began to withdraw. Kuwait, for example, gained independence in 1961, while Bahrain, Qatar, and the Trucial States (later called the United Arab Emirates) gained independence in 1971.

This survey of British imperialism in the Middle East has emphasized political and diplomatic history and the decisions of government policymakers. Yet it is important to note that Britons in the Middle East not only included government officials but also missionaries, travelers, soldiers, merchants, archaeologists, and many others—that is, a diverse group of historical actors who exerted cultural, political, and economic influences in their own right. Furthermore, as historians increasingly acknowledge, cultural and social influence was reciprocal. British government representatives in the age of empire may have had the power to dictate or otherwise transform Middle Eastern political destinies, but colonial encounters with the Middle East and other parts of the empire had a substantial impact on British society, culture, and national identity as well. Colonialism, in other words, was a two-way street.

SEE ALSO *Baring, Evelyn; British India and the Middle East; Mandate Rule.*

BIBLIOGRAPHY

Bidwell, Robin, ed. *British Documents on Foreign Affairs: Reports and Papers from the Foreign Office Confidential Print*, Part 2: *From the First to the Second World War.* Series B, *Turkey, Iran, and the Middle East, 1918–1939.* 35 vols. Frederick, MD: University Publications of America, 1985–1997.

Cleveland, William L. *A History of the Modern Middle East.* 3rd ed. Boulder, CO: Westview, 2004.

Codell, Julie F., and Dianne Sachko Macleod. *Orientalism Transposed: The Impact of the Colonies on British Culture.* Brookfield, VT: Ashgate, 1998.

Crinson, Mark. *Empire Building: Orientalism and Victorian Architecture.* New York: Routledge, 1996.

Daly, M. W., gen. ed. *The Cambridge History of Egypt*, Vol. 2: *Modern Egypt.* Cambridge, U.K.: Cambridge University Press, 1999.

Darling, Linda T. "Capitulations." In *The Oxford Encyclopedia of the Modern Islamic World*, Vol. 1, edited by John L. Esposito, 257–260. New York: Oxford University Press, 1995.

Gershoni, Israel, and James Jankowski. *Egypt, Islam, and the Arabs: The Search for Egyptian Nationhood, 1900–1930.* New York: Oxford University Press, 1986.

Gillard, David, ed. *British Documents on Foreign Affairs: Reports and Papers from the Foreign Office Confidential Print*, Part I: *From the Mid-Nineteenth Century to the First World War*, Series B: *The Near and Middle East, 1856–1914.* 20 vols. Frederick, MD: University Publications of America, 1984–1985.

Issawi, Charles. *An Economic History of the Middle East and North Africa.* New York: Columbia University Press, 1982.

Keddie, Nikki R. *Modern Iran: Roots and Results of Revolution.* New Haven, CT: Yale University Press, 2003.

Kennedy, Dane. *Britain and Empire, 1880–1945.* London: Longman, 2002.

Kent, Marian. *Moguls and Mandarins: Oil, Imperialism, and the Middle East in British Foreign Policy, 1900–1940.* London: Frank Cass, 1993.

Kolinsky, Martin. *Britain's War in the Middle East: Strategy and Diplomacy, 1936–1942.* New York: St. Martin's, 1999.

Lewis, Bernard. *The Emergence of Modern Turkey.* 3rd ed. New York: Oxford University Press, 2002.

Louis, Wm. Roger, and Roger Owen, eds. *A Revolutionary Year: The Middle East in 1958.* London: Tauris, 2002.

Massad, Joseph A. *Colonial Effects: The Making of National Identity in Jordan.* New York: Columbia University Press, 2001.

Matar, N. I. *Turks, Moors, and Englishmen in the Age of Discovery.* New York: Columbia University Press, 1999.

Méouchy, Nadine, and Peter Sluglett, eds. *The British and French Mandates in Comparative Perspectives.* Leiden, Netherlands; Boston: Brill, 2004.

Monroe, Elizabeth. *Britain's Moment in the Middle East, 1914–1971.* 2nd rev. ed. Baltimore, MD: Johns Hopkins University Press, 1981.

Owen, Roger. *The Middle East in the World Economy, 1800–1914.* London: Methuen, 1981.

Paris, Timothy J. *Britain, the Hashemites, and Arab Rule, 1920–1925.* London: Frank Cass, 2003.

Porter, Andrew. *Religion versus Empire? British Protestant Missionaries and Overseas Expansion, 1700–1914.* Manchester, U.K.: Manchester University Press, 2004.

Quataert, Donald. *The Ottoman Empire, 1700–1922.* New York: Cambridge University Press, 2000.

Robinson, Ronald, and John Gallagher. *Africa and the Victorians: The Climax of Imperialism in the Dark Continent.* New York: St. Martin's, 1961.

Said, Edward W. *Orientalism.* New York: Pantheon, 1978.

Sluglett, Peter. *Britain in Iraq, 1914–1932.* London: Ithaca, 1976.

Smith, Charles D. *Palestine and the Arab-Israeli Conflict.* 5th ed. Boston: Bedford/St. Martin's, 2004.

Smith, Simon C. *Britain's Revival and Fall in the Gulf: Kuwait, Bahrain, Qatar, and the Trucial States, 1950–71.* London: Routledge/Curzon, 2004.

Teitelbaum, Joshua. *The Rise and Fall of the Hashemite Kingdom of Arabia.* New York: New York University Press, 2001.

Tignor, Robert L. *Modernization and British Colonial Rule in Egypt, 1882–1914.* Princeton, NJ: Princeton University Press, 1966.

Tignor, Robert L. *Egyptian Textiles and British Capital, 1930–1956.* Cairo: American University in Cairo Press, 1989.

Turhan, Filiz. *The Other Empire: British Romantic Writings about the Ottoman Empire.* New York: Routledge, 2003.

Wilson, Mary C. *King Abdullah, Britain, and the Making of Jordan.* Cambridge, U.K.: Cambridge University Press, 1987.

Yapp, Malcolm. *The Making of the Modern Near East, 1792–1923.* London: Longman, 1987.

Yapp, Malcolm. *The Near East since the First World War: A History to 1995.* 2nd ed. London: Longman, 1996.

Yapp, Malcolm, ed. *British Documents on Foreign Affairs: Reports and Papers from the Foreign Office Confidential Print, Part 3: From 1940 through 1945,* Series B: *Near and Middle East.* 10 vols. Bethesda, MD: University Publications of America, 1997.

Heather J. Sharkey

BRITISH INDIA AND THE MIDDLE EAST

India and the Middle East share a history that far predates the coming of the British Empire. Commercially, for over a millennium, the two had been linked by the overland caravan trade in silks, spices, and other commodities and by an Indian Ocean maritime trade in calicoes (a type of cotton cloth), coffee, specie (money in the form of coins), and slaves. Information traveled quickly around the Indian Ocean world, particularly from Arab merchants and explorers, such as the fourteenth-century Moroccan traveler Ibn Battuta (ca. 1304–1368).

By the thirteenth century, a great portion of North India was ruled by Muslim dynasties of Central Asian and Turkish origins: the Delhi Sultanate from 1210, followed by the Mughal Empire in 1526. The Mughal military relied heavily on irregulars and mercenaries, particularly horsemen, from Central Asia, and by the reign of the Emperor Akbar (r. 1556–1605), the Mughal officers corps and nobility were dominated by Persian *mansabdars* (ranked nobles) and *jagirdars* (holders of revenue assignments). The Persian Empire could also be a threat to Mughal India, perhaps no more strikingly than when Nadir Shah (1688–1747) sacked Delhi in 1739, taking with him the Koh-i-noor diamond and the famed Peacock Throne.

Islam also bound South Asia, Arabia, and the Ottoman Empire through common laws, languages, scholarship, and, in theory, the spiritual leadership of the caliph, the head of the universal community of Islam. Though most commonly recognized to reside in the Ottoman sultan, the caliphate was also claimed by Mughal rulers after Akbar. Furthermore, the annual hajj, the Muslim pilgrimage to the holy city of Mecca in present-day Saudi Arabia, provided for a direct and constant exchange between western India and the Arabian Peninsula.

THE SEVENTEENTH AND EIGHTEENTH CENTURIES: COMMERCE, WAR, AND PIRACY IN THE INDIAN OCEAN

Thus, when Britons first arrived in Asia in the later sixteenth century, they imagined southern and western Asia as encompassing a connected and unified commercial, if not political, system. The English East India Company, chartered by Queen Elizabeth I (1533–1603) in 1600, had a monopoly on all English trade and politics east of the Cape of Good Hope, and was therefore concerned with affairs in Asia broadly. Much of its early leadership and financing came from members and directors of the English Levant (or Turkey) Company, who envisioned the East India Company as an opportunity to circumvent the overland caravan route and to more directly access the raw silk markets in the eastern reaches of the Ottoman Empire and Persia.

The first factory (residence and trading post) the East India Company sought in India was in the western Gujarati town of Surat (1616), the most important overseas commercial port in Mughal India and its most direct connection to the Persian Gulf and Red Sea. The trade from Surat to Mokha and Jedda on the Arabian Peninsula became a principal part of company business, and the next factory the company established after Surat was at Isfahan in Persia (1617).

As it had been for the Portuguese in the sixteenth century, maritime strength in the Indian Ocean soon became central to English East India Company strategy and was a key component to its regional power. The company's first and perhaps most significant early aggressive move came in 1622, when it allied with the Persian shah to expel the Portuguese from Hormuz. As a term of the alliance, the company was given a share of the customs revenue and trading privileges at the port of Gombroon (Bandar 'Abbas), which became a base of its operations through the century. It also solidified the company's permanent presence in Persia.

The relationship between British activities in India and the Middle East intensified with the East India Company's acquisition of Bombay in 1668. The former Portuguese island off the West Indian coast was home to a cosmopolitan and maritime community of traders, sailors, and soldiers with deep connections to western Asia. By the 1680s, it had become the center of the company's Asian government, and the factories in western India and Persia, as well as all its commercial and military affairs in the Indian Ocean region, fell under the jurisdiction of Bombay's governor and council. As Bombay grew in importance to the company, so too did the correlation between company strategic and commercial interests in India and its affairs in western Asia.

Crises in one part of Asia could also have vast ramifications in other parts of Asia. In the late 1680s, for example, when a spate of pirates from Europe and America seized a number of Indian ships in the Red Sea, many important Surat merchants lost a great deal of money and blamed the English East India Company at Surat for the assaults. In 1696 a ship belonging to the

Mughal emperor Aurangzeb (1618–1707), carrying both a rich cargo as well as hajjis (Muslim pilgrims), fell to an assault from an English pirate, Henry Avery (d. 1728). The appearance on the western Indian coast a couple of years later of the New York privateer-turned-pirate, the infamous Captain William Kidd (ca. 1645–1701), only made matters worse. In both instances, company officials in Surat were arrested and all European trade stopped from the port. The crisis only abated when the English East India Company, along with the Dutch, agreed to various demands, including providing convoys for Mughal shipping to Arabia.

This late seventeenth-century crisis was important in reinforcing to the English East India Company the great interdependence between its affairs in the Middle East and India. It also profoundly affected the growth of the company's maritime power in the eighteenth century. The company had now become politically and martially committed to the eradication of piracy, which most directly led to the development of its western Indian naval force known as the Bombay Marine.

By the 1720s, American violence in the Indian Ocean had all but vanished. East India Company officials at Bombay then turned their attention to Indian "piracy," aiming most specifically at their greatest western Indian rival: the Maratha Confederacy and its maritime power, a coastal tributary state led by Kanhoji Angre (1669–1729). Whether Khanoji, or his successor, Tulaji, were pirates or commanders of a navy is a matter of perception. Still, under the banner of suppressing piracy, the English East India Company defeated the Angres by the 1750s, rendering British maritime supremacy in the eastern Indian Ocean unrivaled.

After defeating the Angres, Bombay again turned its attention back to the Red Sea and Persian Gulf. The new "piratical threat" came from the so-called Muscat Arabs of the Persian Gulf coastal sultanates. In fact, the British even dubbed the region the "Pirate Coast." After more than a half-century of assault, the Bombay Marine and the British Royal Navy succeeded in forcing these coastal polities into submission. In 1820 a series of treaties imposed upon them transformed the Pirate Coast into the so-called Trucial Coast. The treaties declared the "cessation of plunder and piracy by land and sea on the part of the Arabs," ended the Eastern African slave trade to Arabia, and firmly established British India's sphere of influence in the Gulf sultanates. Soon after, company trade in the region began to flourish.

Meanwhile, as the English East India Company's role as a territorial power in India grew, the company also began to design stronger commercial and financial ties with the Ottoman Empire. Its first governor-general in Bengal, Warren Hastings (1732–1818), attempted to

The Defeat of Tipu Sultan. *British forces lead by Charles Cornwallis are shown in this engraving attacking Seringapatam during the Third Mysore War in India in 1792. The British were successful, and Tipu, Sultan of Mysore, was forced to surrender.*
© BETTMANN/CORBIS. REPRODUCED BY PERMISSION.

encourage trade with Egypt in the early 1770s, primarily as a way to bolster the company's financial affairs at Calcutta. The volatility of Egyptian politics and the hostility of rulers in the Hejaz (a region along the Red Sea in present-day Saudi Arabia), particularly that of the sharif of Mecca towards Europeans traveling as far north as Suez, meant that these plans never came to fruition. The company's lucrative trade elsewhere in western Asia, particularly with Baghdad, was also on the wane.

Though still valuable to the Eurasian trade, Arabia and Mesopotamia were no longer commercial priorities for British India by the close of the eighteenth century. Nonetheless, British officials wanted very much to preclude other Europeans, particularly the French, from gaining a foothold there. Even worse than the commercial threat was the possibility that France could use these ties directly or indirectly to involve itself in British affairs in India, from which it had been largely expelled after the Seven Years' War (1756–1763).

THE NINETEENTH CENTURY: NORTH AFRICA, THE WESTERN LEVANT, AND THE SUEZ CANAL

Active French diplomacy and pressure in Egypt, Baghdad, Oman, Persia, and Sind (part of modern Pakistan) in the 1780s seemed threatening enough, but the rise of Napoléon Bonaparte (1769–1821) and expansion of the French Empire brought these issues to the fore. Napoléon's alliance with Tipu Sultan (1750–1799), the sultan of Mysore, the English East India Company's South Indian rival, seemed evidence of France's renewed South Asian ambition. More importantly, Napoléon's invasion of Egypt in 1798 and Syria in 1799, though eventually repelled, made palpable the prospect of the French danger to India. The invasion was a watershed. For the nineteenth century, Britain's overriding concern in the Middle East would be to exclude European rivals and to buttress its influence in the region, all to protect India.

The English East India Company's defeat of the *nawabs* (provincial governors) of Bengal in eastern India (at the Battle of Plassey in 1757 and the Battle of Buxar in 1764), Tipu Sultan (1799), the Maratha Confederacy in western India (1818), and the coastal Arabian sultanates after 1820 confirmed the company as an expanding territorial sovereign power in India, led from Calcutta, with maritime power emanating from Bombay and radiating around the Indian Ocean littoral. Still, the British Indian government could never feel entirely secure, particularly at its borders. Under the governor-generalship of Marquis Wellesley (1798–1805), British India pursued a particularly aggressive policy for expanding and protecting its frontiers.

This was a crucial moment in the development of the British Indian government's own foreign and imperial policies. British policy, especially after the 1820s, was designed not necessarily to control formal colonies in western and Central Asia, but to keep other European powers out and to exert such influence as to create a buffer between Europe and British India, particularly in Turkey and Persia. The Middle East, particularly the three points of the northwestern Afghani town of Herat, the Red Sea port of Aden, and the island of Kishm in the Strait of Hormuz, was to become a buffer and frontier for the British Indian Empire. This so-called subimperialism—or what at least one historian has dubbed an "empire of the Raj"—consisted both in formal expansion as well as in the use of military, financial, and political influence to maintain "informal" or "subsidiary" alliances with key strategic polities and princes. Diplomacy in Persia, the Ottoman Empire, and Arabia was considered an Indian problem to be conducted from Calcutta, not London.

While power in the Persian Gulf was important, it was the base at Aden that more or less secured British dominance of maritime western Asia. It became even more critical in 1869 with the opening of the Suez Canal. The canal cut in half the journey to India. Yet, what Britain gained in convenience and efficiency it lost in security. The English East India Company and the British Royal Navy had dominated the centuries-old maritime route around the southern tip of Africa since its acquisition of the Cape Colony from the Dutch in 1815. The Suez Canal undercut this monopoly by giving both Britain and its European rivals access to the Red Sea from the Mediterranean. This route was also much more volatile. Political or military rivals in Europe, such as France or Russia, or instability in the Ottoman Empire could much more easily threaten British access to the Suez Canal, and thus to India.

Despite these concerns, the first actual crisis for British interests in the Suez Canal came from within Egypt itself. The efforts of Ismail Pasha (1830–1895), the Ottoman tributary ruler *(khedive)* of Egypt from 1863, through the 1870s to modernize Egypt left the country significantly indebted to European investors. Furthermore, in 1875 the British state became directly interested when it bought Ismail's 44 percent share in the Suez Canal Company. Nonetheless, Egypt went bankrupt the next year. Its Western creditors essentially foreclosed on the Egyptian government, replacing Ismail with a new khedive, his son Tewfik Pasha (1852–1892).

In 1881, dissatisfaction with Western intervention growing, Tewfik was overthrown by a nationalist rebellion led by the Egyptian military officer and nationalist Ahmad 'Urabi Pasha (1839–1911). France, concerned for its financiers as well as its other colonial interests in North Africa, designed an invasion. The liberal British government, headed by William Gladstone (1809–1898), was more reluctant, but agreed to a joint expedition. The French Parliament refused to sanction the plan, withdrawing from the arrangement. By then, however, the revolt had grown in size and strength. In July 1882 the British Royal Navy began bombarding Alexandria, and soon after British forces occupied Egypt.

NINETEENTH CENTURY: CENTRAL ASIA, ARABIA, AND "THE GREAT GAME"

Perhaps an even greater concern for nineteenth-century British India than threats to the Suez Canal route was the perceived continental ambition in Central Asia of Britain's other great European rival: imperial Russia. The landlocked Herat proved much more difficult to control than the more southern maritime frontiers in the Indian Ocean. War, diplomatic intrigue, and political posturing with Russia over this region ensued through most of the nineteenth century.

Known as the "Great Game," perhaps exemplified most famously in British author Rudyard Kipling's novel *Kim* (1900), this century of conflict centered to a great extent on British efforts to unite and secure Afghanistan against rival Persian and Russian claims. Its first attempt came in the mid-1830s when the British Indian government moved to install Shah Shuja-ul-Mulk (1780–1842), who had been living in exile in India, as ruler of Afghanistan. In 1838 the British Indian army attempted to seize Kabul, leading to the First Anglo-Afghan War. This attempt to make Afghanistan into a British imperial puppet state ended in disaster and a humiliating retreat by 1842.

By the 1860s and 1870s, further Russian expansion and its rebounding from the Crimean War (1853–1856) again made an Afghan buffer seem to be an imperative. In 1878 the British Conservative prime minister Benjamin Disraeli (1804–1881) declared war. Though Gladstone's newly elected Liberal (and anti-imperial) government in 1880 withdrew from the war, this

Second Anglo-Afghan War concluded with the establishment of a de facto protectorate over Afghanistan marked by British control over its foreign policy and defense.

Nonetheless, the Afghan issue remained unsettled until the Anglo-Russian Convention of 1907. In the wake of defeat at the hands of the Japanese (1905), Russia was forced to accept Britain's dominance in Afghanistan and a division of spheres of influence in Persia.

British India's Middle Eastern strategy by the beginning of the twentieth century still depended largely on "informal empire," particularly by buttressing the rule of its unstable and weakening allies in the Ottoman Empire, Persia, and the so-called Trucial states. Nonetheless, this impulse to jockey over the Middle East in defense of British India also led to the formal expansion of British India's borders. Often against orders from London, local military and civil officials in British India saw expansion as the only solution for instability at the frontier. The annexation of Sind (1843) and the Punjab (1849) directly resulted from the perceived need on the ground for security at the empire's western front. (The conflict between the "man on the spot" and the India and Foreign Offices in London was perhaps most infamously encapsulated in a cartoon in the British magazine *Punch*, which satirized Sir Charles Napier's [1782–1853] seizure of Sind with a single-word double-entendre for a caption: *peccavi*, Latin for "I have sinned.")

Russian attempts in the 1870s and 1880s at extending its railways to ports on the northern Persian Gulf only exacerbated the problem. The virtual annexation of Baluchistan, in present-day Pakistan, in the 1870s was designed primarily to buttress British India's position in the Arabian seas as well as to exert diplomatic pressure on Persia to repel Russian overtures.

The viceroyalty of George Curzon (1899–1905) marked perhaps the apogee of this aggressive independence on the part of the government of India. Though increasingly opposed by officials in the British Foreign Office (which he would later head), Curzon argued fervently—and mostly unsuccessfully—that the defense of India should continue to be the cornerstone for British policy in the Middle East, best achieved by expansion on India's northern, eastern, and western borders.

THE TWENTIETH CENTURY: NATIONALISM AND THE WORLD WARS

By the beginning of the twentieth century, the British had occupied Egypt, expanded its territory in Central Asia, and become financially and politically entangled in bolstering allied regimes in Persia, the Ottoman Empire, and the Arabian Peninsula. Much of this was done defensively and with the preservation of the British imperial system, with India at its center, always foremost in mind.

However, the "informal" empire in the Middle East became much more complex and volatile with the onset of World War I in 1914. While the Great War intensified the need to defend India's borders, it also drew the Middle East squarely to the center of the European conflict. The players in the game had also changed sides. Old British allies were now its rivals in the Middle East: a Prussian-led Germany, which had for a decade been provoking the British and French with an attempt to build a railway across Turkey to Basra, and the Ottoman Empire, which joined the Central Powers in 1914.

The war realigned India's relationship with the Middle East. Britain's declaration of war on the Ottomans, the occupation of Basra, and the subsequent campaign under the British Mesopotamian Expeditionary Force in the fall of 1914 animated British India's interests in the region. Indian troops were used extensively in campaigns around the world, including Turkey, Egypt, German East Africa, and Mesopotamia. Where the Middle East had once been envisioned as protection for India, now India found itself charged with defending British interests in the Middle East.

Furthermore, though officially agnostic on the future fate of the dismembered Ottoman Empire, the British government had been engaging in secret negotiations with France and Russia to carve out a vision for the postwar Middle East. The result was the secret Sykes-Picot Agreement (1916), made public by the Bolsheviks after the Russian Revolution, which endorsed the creation of an Arab confederated state that would be independent but divided into "spheres of influence" between Britain and France. Both the British and the French believed that the promise of an independent state would inspire Arab revolts against the Ottoman Empire, a keystone to Middle Eastern strategy during the war. Importantly, this master plan for a pan-Arab revolt was orchestrated not from India but Egypt, where Britain had established a protectorate in 1914 under the diplomatic stewardship of Sir Henry McMahon (1862–1949), the high commissioner, and later the strategic designs of Gilbert Clayton (1875–1929), director of military intelligence at Cairo and head of the Arab Bureau (established in 1916), perhaps best known for its connections to T. E. Lawrence ("Lawrence of Arabia," 1888–1935) and his mission in the Hejaz.

The government of India continued to insist on the centrality of the Middle East in protecting its borders, but for Britain victory in Europe far outweighed the importance of Asia. The war also made clear the importance of the Middle East as a source for strategic resources, particularly oil. The very idea of the "Middle East" was created in this period; that the term itself is an early twentieth-century neologism stands as further evidence that Europe was beginning to consider its interests in the region as important in themselves.

While India agreed on the importance of protecting oil supplies and the much-needed alliances with the Gulf sultanates, British Indian officials thought the only way to accomplish this was to establish a formal empire in the region. Only a protectorate or colonial settlement, particularly in Iraq and its environs, under British guidance and control could prevent the emergence of an independent Arab state. After all, British India was home to eighty million Muslims, vastly more than the number in the Middle East and slightly less than one-third of India's population. The possibility of a large and powerful state emerging on its borders, with religious, historical, and political ties to India seemed even more menacing than the nineteenth-century threats of France and Russia.

Therefore, the coming of the war highlighted the growing divergence between the interests of British India and the British Empire as a whole. The resurgence of anticolonial nationalism in India after World War I only amplified this problem, making British Middle Eastern politics not just a foreign policy concern, but also bringing it firmly to the center of British Indian domestic politics.

The service of vast numbers of Indian troops in the war effort, amongst other places in the Middle East and North Africa, was rewarded not, as expected, with gestures towards home rule for India, but with an extension of wartime restrictions on assembly, speech, and print and a move away from prewar measures towards conciliation. Many Muslim nationalists responded hostilely to the perceived assault on Islam during the war, particularly in the toppling of the caliph and the Ottoman Empire. Indian Muslims had not heeded the sultan's call to wage a *jihad* (holy war) against the British, but postwar British expansion in the Middle East not controlled by Delhi threatened to exacerbate the perception that the British Empire was unconcerned with the protection of Muslim minorities in India.

This perception had its strongest articulation in the caliphate movement (1919–1924), a pan-Islamic Indian nationalism that rallied around the assault on Islam perceived in the toppling of the Ottoman Empire. The Indian nationalist leader Mohandas Gandhi (1869–1948) soon allied his noncooperation and *swaraj* (self-rule) movements with the caliphate movement, making a pan-Indian, nationwide home-rule movement seem possible. These efforts were short-lived, however, undercut by a number of circumstances, including the related

hijra, a protest and mass-exodus of almost thirty thousand Muslims from British India to Afghanistan.

World War II again put a good deal of focus on the key place the Middle East held in British geopolitical imperial strategy. Italy's entry into the war in 1940 put new pressures on protecting access to the Suez Canal, while German ambitions in Iraq and Iran, long the prevailing territorial Middle Eastern concerns of British India, again revealed the deep connections between British policies in both imperial theaters.

THE TWENTIETH CENTURY: DECOLONIZATION

The rising power of Indian nationalism in the 1920s and 1930s and reforms in the British Indian government were making a greater degree of home rule in India an impending reality. This only further inspired officials in London to wrest the remaining control of Middle Eastern policy from the government of India and relocate it to London and Cairo. When independence did come to India in August 1947, it struck a blow to the material strength of British influence in the Middle East.

Even earlier, the Labour government that had come to power in Britain in 1945 seemed to be committed to development of its interests in the Middle East as an economic replacement for its desired withdrawal from formal empire, particularly in India. What was more, overshadowed by the loss of India, the anti-imperial Labour government was unlikely to endure great costs, both human and financial, in holding onto its interests in the Middle East, particularly in Palestine. Many commentators and statesmen, including Winston Churchill (1874–1965), warned that even the appearance that the British Empire was remaining tenacious in their hold on Palestine, in the face both of Jewish and Arab violence, would be taken as evidence of a Machiavellian attempt to hold on to its last vestige of power in the region. Ironically, the abandonment of Palestine and the birth of the state of Israel in 1948 only fueled the appearance that the British Empire was on the eve of its dissolution.

Thus, by the end of World War II, British imperial policy in the Middle East had been completely reoriented from where it stood just a half-century earlier. A policy that had been primarily a means for protecting India, and for much of its history conducted from India, had been dismantled. So, while Indian independence did not signal an immediate withdrawal of British concerns in the Middle East, it did perhaps imply its final fate.

Despite eleventh-hour attempts to strengthen its influence through the 1950s, the British Empire faced stiff opposition from nationalists across the region, as well as the new superpowers in the region: the United States and the Soviet Union. Soon, the old passageways to India were lost to the British, bookended perhaps by

Egyptian president Gamal Abdel Nasser's (1918–1970) nationalization of, the Suez Canal Company and the failed joint British-French-Israeli invasion to topple him in 1956, and culminating in the final and formal abandonment of the Trucial system in the Persian Gulf states with the creation of the United Arab Emirates in 1971.

SEE ALSO *'Urabi Rebellion; Afghan Wars; British Colonialism, Middle East; World War I, Middle East.*

BIBLIOGRAPHY

Balfour-Paul, Glen. "Britain's Informal Empire in the Middle East." *The Oxford History of the British Empire,* Vol. 4: *The Twentieth Century,* edited by Judith M. Brown and William Roger Louis. Oxford: Oxford University Press, 1999.

Blyth, Robert J. *The Empire of the Raj: India, Eastern Africa, and the Middle East, 1858–1947.* Houndmills, U.K.: Palgrave Macmillan, 2003.

Chaudhuri, K. N. *The Trading World of Asia and the English East India Company, 1660–1760.* Cambridge, U.K.: Cambridge University Press, 1978.

Darwin, John. *Britain, Egypt, and the Middle East: Imperial Policy in the Aftermath of War, 1918–1922.* London: Macmillan, 1981.

Davies, Charles E. *The Blood-Red Arab Flag: An Investigation into Qasimi Piracy, 1797–1820.* Exeter, U.K.: University of Exeter Press, 1997.

Fisher, John. *Curzon and British Imperialism in the Middle East, 1916–19.* London: Frank Cass, 1999.

Gallagher, John, and Ronald Robinson with Alice Denny. *Africa and the Victorians: The Official Mind of Imperialism.* London: Macmillan and St. Martin's Press, 1961.

Ingram, Edward. *In Defence of British India: Great Britain and the Middle East, 1775–1842.* London: Frank Cass, 1984.

Jackson, William. *The Pomp of Yesterday: The Defence of India and the Suez Canal, 1798–1918.* London: Brassey's, 1995.

Kumar, Ravinder. *India and the Persian Gulf Region, 1858–1907: A Study in British Imperial Policy.* New York: Asia Publishing House, 1965.

Louis, William Roger. *The British Empire in the Middle East, 1945–1951: Arab Nationalism, the United States, and Postwar Imperialism.* Oxford: Clarendon Press, 1984.

Porter, Bernard. *The Lion's Share: A Short History of British Imperialism, 1850–2004,* 4th ed. New York: Longman, 2004.

Risso, Patricia. "Cross-Cultural Perceptions of Piracy: Maritime Violence in the Western Indian Ocean and Persian Gulf Region during a Long Eighteenth Century." *Journal of World History* 12 (2) (2001): 293–319.

Ritchie, Robert C. *Captain Kidd and the War Against the Pirates.* Cambridge, MA: Harvard University Press, 1986.

Robinson, Francis. "The British Empire and the Muslim World." In *The Oxford History of the British Empire,* Vol. 4: *The Twentieth Century,* edited by Judith M. Brown and William Roger Louis. Oxford: Oxford University Press, 1999.

Subrahmanyam, Sanjay. "*Un Grand Dérangement*: Dreaming an Indo-Persian Empire in South Asia, 1740–1800." *Journal of Early Modern History* 4 (3–4) (2000): 337–378.

Yapp, M. E. *Strategies of British India: Britain, Iran, and Afghanistan, 1798–1850.* Oxford: Clarendon, 1980.

Philip J. Stern

BUCCANEERS

Commerce raiders called *privateers, pirates, buccaneers,* and other such names roamed the Caribbean Sea, as well as the Atlantic and Indian oceans, in the sixteenth, seventeenth, and eighteenth centuries as the detritus of the first Western colonies. During the sixteenth and first half of the seventeenth centuries, French, English, and Dutch raiders of Spanish and Portuguese shipping and ports generally acted under the authorization of their governments. The English Crown, for example, granted merchants and captains "letters of marque and reprisal," which authorized attacks on Spanish shipping and ports. This legal document required that the privateer captains deliver to an admiralty court their captured ships, whereupon everyone would legally carve up a share of the spoils.

These privateers became invaluable military forces in times of war in an age when permanent navies did not exist. Until the late seventeenth century, the powers of Europe generally did not recognize truces and peace agreements outside of Europe. Privateers, therefore, were tolerated and often encouraged, even in peacetime. In the second half of the seventeenth century, there was often little meaningful difference between a privateer and an independent sea raider, that is, a pirate. Letters of marque and reprisal were widely granted.

When the French, English, and Dutch were becoming established in the Caribbean in the early to mid-seventeenth century, privateers were important naval forces in their own right. Perhaps the first commerce-raiding outpost to appear in the Caribbean arose around French Tortuga, lying just northwest of Hispaniola. These raiders became widely known as *boucaniers* or *buccaneers,* after a Tupi Indian word for a smoking frame *(boucan)* used to roast wild cattle. These raiders were also called *freebooters* in the sense they that soldiered without pay for booty. To the Dutch, a commerce raider was a *vrijbuiter,* which the French translated to *flibustier.* The English and French word *pirate* derived from centuries-old Latin and Greek words.

In 1630, the same year the Puritan colony of Massachusetts Bay was founded, a second Puritan colony was founded on Providence Island off the Caribbean coast of Nicaragua. The colony had little success as an agricultural settlement, but a change in foreign policy and the issuance of letters of marque and reprisal to the

Providence Island Company in 1626 turned the island into a privateering base and a new source of profit. In 1641 the Spanish retook the island. Thereafter, however, the Spanish and the buccaneers fought over the island and its harbors and inlets for decades.

After the English seized Jamaica in 1655, that island, in the center of the Spanish Caribbean, became the center of privateering and privacy. To maintain possession of the island, England issued letters of marque to French, Dutch, Danish, Italian, Swedish, Portuguese, and English captains. One of Jamaica's first historians, Bryan Edwards (1743–1800), noted that "nothing contributed so much to the settlement and opulence of this island in early times, as the resort to it of those men called Bucaniers; the wealth which they acquired having been speedily transferred to people whose industry was employed in cultivation or commerce." But, he continued, these men were not "piratical plunderers and public robbers which they are commonly represented." Because of the Spanish War, he noted, these buccaneers "were furnished with regular letters of marque and reprisal" (Edwards 1793, vol. 1, p. 160).

The first royal governors of Jamaica established the seaport of Port Royal, which attracted privateers and pirates, as well as merchants, tavern-keepers, runaway servants, prostitutes, and others. This town, encouraged by the governor, sent fleets of privateers under Henry Morgan (1635–1688) between 1665 and 1671 to plunder Spanish seaports on the coasts of Cuba, Panama, Venezuela, and Nicaragua. Despite England's promise to Spain to end privateering and suppress piracy in the Treaty of Madrid in 1670 and the Jamaica Act of 1683, buccaneers continued to freely operate from Port Royal until the end of the century. Over time, however, the "scum of the Indies drifted away from Jamaica," writes Violet Barbour, "to Hispaniola and Tortuga where aliens of any nation or reputation were received with obliging catholicity" (1911, p. 567). Port Royal was hit by a great earthquake in 1692 that utterly destroyed the port. The government of Jamaica rebuilt a new port, Kingston, on firmer ground across the harbor, and the buccaneers moved to new haunts in the Bahamas, North America, and West Africa.

During the second half of the seventeenth century, buccaneers not only attacked Spanish and Portuguese shipping and ports but also English, French, and Dutch shipping and American and African ports and posts. When wars erupted between the northern European powers, governments and their colonial authorities began issuing letters of marque to captains of just about any nationality, so long as the holder was clear who the "enemy" was.

A Buccaneer. *Buccaneers, also known as privateers and pirates, roamed the Caribbean Sea, as well as the Atlantic and Indian oceans, in the sixteenth, seventeenth, and eighteenth centuries as the detritus of the first Western colonies. This buccaneer guards his booty with a flintlock rifle and a pistol.* © BETTMANN/ CORBIS. REPRODUCED BY PERMISSION.

During the Anglo-Dutch Wars and the Franco-Dutch Wars of the second half of the seventeenth century, the English in Jamaica and the French in Tortuga enlisted buccaneers to cruise against the Dutch. In 1666 when France entered the war on the side of the Netherlands, the Dutch in Curaçao and the French in Tortuga directed buccaneers against English islands and trade. In 1673 the Dutch launched a serious effort to seize the French West Indies, and Dutch privateers, assisting the effort, brought more than twenty-five French prizes into Curaçao that year.

During the next several years of the war, aggressive Dutch privateers eliminated a few hundred French buccaneers and brought about the decline of commercial traffic from France. The buccaneers themselves, while no friend of any government, generally preferred in the seventeenth century to enrich themselves from the Spanish and stay away from English, French, and Dutch prizes. The Spanish had more hard money, and the buccaneers had more reasons to take vengeance on them. The French buccaneer Sieur de Grammont in 1683 mounted a raid on Vera Cruz, the principal port of New Spain, which yielded four days of uninterrupted looting. The Dutch buccaneers Nicholas van Hoorn and Laurens de Graaf two years later attacked the city of Campeche on the eastern coast of the Yucatán Peninsula, and left the city in ashes after looting the government treasury, churches, and private houses.

A Dutch buccaneer known as Roche Brasiliano provides an example of the buccaneer's basic animosity to the Spanish. A fellow buccaneer described Brasiliano's particularly infamous modus operandi: "Unto the Spaniards he always showed himself very barbarous and cruel, only out of an inveterate hatred he had against that nation. Of these he commanded several to be roasted alive upon wooden spits, for no other crime than that they would not show him the places, or hog-yards, where he might steal swine" (Exquemelin 1678/2000, p. 73).

French buccaneers in Tortuga were also active during the last three decades of the seventeenth century. One buccaneer captain was so successful in his looting as to invest his wealth in Martinique and become the owner of the largest sugar plantation in the French West Indies. Buccaneers who found a hostile reception in their nation's different entrepôts in the Caribbean, or were welcome nowhere else, eventually made their way to Tortuga.

It was from Tortuga in the seventeenth century that the French and other buccaneers began to colonize the western end of Hispaniola. In 1669 the governor of French Saint-Domingue (now Haiti) claimed there were 1,600 freebooters, hunters, settlers, and indentured servants on Tortuga and the coast of Saint-Domingue. Two years later, a navy captain estimated that about 500 or 600 freebooters and about 100 *boucaniers* lived in the Cul-de-Sac or western district of Saint-Domingue alone. The successful privateers and petty noblemen established tobacco and later sugar plantations. The Spanish officially recognized French possession of its new colony in the Treaty of Ryswick in 1697. During the next fifty years, Saint-Domingue would become the most valuable European colony in the Atlantic.

By the late seventeenth century, the English, French, and Dutch had achieved the recognition they had long sought from the Spanish of their New World colonies. The buccaneers that they themselves had commissioned were increasingly not only interfering with but also seriously ravaging Atlantic commerce. The early eighteenth century would see the golden age of piracy and its brutal suppression.

The most famous buccaneers of the period were Anglo-Americans based largely in New Providence in the Bahamas. Men like Edward Teach (Blackbeard), Bartolomew "Black Bart" Roberts, William Kidd, and John "Calico Jack" Rackman operated on a much smaller scale than Henry Morgan. They led only one or two heavily-armed ships and sought prizes isolated from convoys. The governor of Bermuda in 1718 reported the deeds of "Tatch [Blackbeard] with whom is Major Bonnett of Barbados in a ship of 36 guns and 300 men, also in company with them a sloop of 12 guns and 115 men and two other ships" (Cordingly 1996, p. 111). Some, like Black Bart, were extraordinarily successful. In the 1710s and 1720s he captured some four hundred ships of all nationalities. Some buccaneers, such as William Kidd, found the Caribbean too confining when the English and French navies were fighting piracy, and employed their skills in the Indian Ocean.

Some buccaneers in the seventeenth and eighteenth centuries saw themselves as social bandits, agents of the poor and oppressed against rich and powerful merchants and tyrannical captains. One pirate captain named Bellamy described the enemies of piracy among the ruling class thus: "They vilify us, the Scoundrels do, when there is only this Difference, they rob the Poor under the Cover of Law, forsooth, and we plunder the Rich under the protection of our own Courage" (Bolster 1997, p. 14). Captain Thomas Checkley in 1718 told of the capture of his ship by pirates who "pretended to be Robbin Hoods Men" (Rediker 1993, pp. 267–269).

English suppression of piracy became serious at the end of the seventeenth and the beginning of the eighteenth century. The British Parliament's 1699 Act of Piracy established vice-admiralty courts in the American colonies that permitted local authorities to hang pirates. From 1716 to 1726, some four hundred to five hundred pirates were executed in Anglo-American ports. The British Crown also began to replace governors and other officials who were accomplices of buccaneers. The new governors seized buccaneer ships docked in their ports, as well as their cargos.

The War of the Spanish Succession (1701–1714) brought many pirates into official service and their decommission led to a last flurry of piracy in the Atlantic. After the war the British and French governments deployed more and more naval power in the Caribbean to protect their own commerce from each other and from the buccaneers. Authorities and colonial governors offered bounties for captured pirates, and in 1717 and 1718 King George I (1660–1727) granted general pardons for piracy—about 450 pirates turned themselves in. Any and all contact with pirates thereafter was criminalized.

The Bahamas was brought under control by a special expedition led by Woodes Rogers (ca. 1679–1732) with four Royal Navy men-of-war. Examples were made of pirates who fell into the hands of authorities: corpses were hung in British ports all around the Atlantic. By 1730 pirate attacks were becoming isolated and rare events and only a handful of buccaneers remained in business. Many of these pirates, still free and unreformed, moved on to Madagascar in the Indian Ocean.

SEE ALSO *War and Empires.*

BIBLIOGRAPHY

Andrews, Kenneth R. *English Privateering Voyages to the West Indies, 1588–1595: Documents Relating to English Voyages to the West Indies from the Defeat of the Armada to the Last Voyage of Sir Francis Drake.* Cambridge, U.K.: Hakluyt Society, 1959.

Barbour, Violet. "Privateers and Pirates of the West Indies." *The American Historical Review* 16 (3) (1911).

Bolster, W. Jeffrey. *Black Jacks: African American Seamen in the Age of Sail.* Cambridge, MA: Harvard University Press, 1997.

Burney, James. *History of the Buccaneers of America* (1816). New York: Norton, 1950.

Cordingly, David. *Under the Black Flag: The Romance and the Reality of Life Among the Pirates.* New York: Random House, 1996.

Defoe, Daniel. *A General History of the Robberies and Murders of the Most Notorious Pirates* (1724). New York: Carroll & Graf, 1999.

Edwards, Bryan. *The History, Civil and Commercial, of the British Colonies in the West Indies.* Dublin: Luke White, 1793. Reprint, New York: Arno, 1978.

Exquemelin, Alexander O. *The Buccaneers of America* (1678). Translated by Alexis Brown. Mineola, NY: Dover, 2000.

Gage, Thomas. *The English-American, His Travail by Sea and Land, or, A New Survey of the West-Indies.* London: Cates, 1648.

Kupperman, Karen Ordahl. *Providence Island, 1630–1641: The Other Puritan Colony* Cambridge, U.K.: Cambridge University Press, 1993.

Lane, Kris E. *Pillaging the Empire: Piracy in the Americas, 1500–1750.* Armonk, NY: Sharpe, 1998.

Rediker, Marcus. *Between the Devil and the Deep Blue Sea: Merchant Seamen, Pirates, and the Anglo-American Maritime World, 1700–1750.* Cambridge, U.K.: Cambridge University Press, 1993.

Swanson, Carl E. *Predators and Prizes: American Privateering and Imperial Warfare, 1739–1748.* Columbia: University of South Carolina Press, 1991.

Williams, Eric. *From Columbus to Castro: The History of the Caribbean, 1492–1969.* London: Deutsch, 1970.

Williams, Neville. *The Sea Dogs: Privateers, Plunder, and Piracy in the Elizabethan Age.* London: Weidenfeld and Nicolson, 1975.

Thomas Benjamin
Dennis Hidalgo

BULLION TRADE, SOUTH AND SOUTHEAST ASIA

In the early modern period, bullion (uncoined silver or gold in the form of ingots or bars), silver in particular, was the most essential commodity of European-Asian trade. From the early years of European expansion during the sixteenth century, European traders had to bring gold and silver coins to Asia to participate in Asian trade, since Europe did not provide other commodities to Asia in exchange for the Asian commodities in demand in Europe, such as spices, pepper, and cotton textiles. These European coins were usually sold is Asia as bullion.

The main area of silver production was Latin America, with mines operating in Potosí (Bolivia) and Zacatecas (Mexico). This American silver, including its currency, Spanish (and Mexican) dollars, was exported to Asia by two routes, with the first being via Europe. Silver was imported to Europe and then reexported to Asia via the Cape of Good Hope or Levant (the countries bordering the eastern Mediterranean). The second route was through direct trade across the Pacific Ocean by galleon ships from Acapulco to Manila.

The exact volumes of the bullion influx have been subject to controversy, but in a rough estimate 32,000 metric tons (about 35,275 short tons) of silver was sent via Europe and 3,000 metric tons (about 3,307 short tons) via Manila in total between 1600 and 1800. From 1710 to 1720, the Dutch East India Company sent precious metal, composed of silver (87%) and gold (13%), to Asia through the Cape route amounting to 38,827,000 guilders in value. Besides Latin America, Japan was also a substantial silver exporter in the sixteenth and seventeenth centuries. China and India absorbed most of this bullion, with China importing roughly one-third of the total silver inflows to Asia.

In the mid-eighteenth century, the structure of global silver circulation drastically changed. British exports of silver declined substantially around 1760, and the British colonial government was required to pay home charges (for the colonial administration costs in the home country) to Britain from the late eighteenth century. Moreover, Japan began to import gold and silver in 1763.

It is unclear whether large volumes of bullion inflows contributed to Asian economic growth or not. Based on the elementary Fisher equation of the quantity theory of money, a rise in the quantity of money should have caused an increase in prices. But available contemporary records do not offer evidence of price increases according to the bullion influx. Some historians assume that economic growth, in reference to the volume of transactions, should have increased, but others believe that bullion was hoarded, an assumption based on the decrease in the velocity of circulation.

Imported silver was mostly smelted into various forms of traditional currency. However, over the centuries Asian traders, especially in East and Southeast Asia, accepted dollar coins for payment from foreigners. In the nineteenth century, silver currency was practically standardized to the Mexican dollar for the purpose of international trade. The adaptation of the gold standard in Western countries caused the silver value to increase against gold after 1873. Apart from the Dutch Indies adapting the gold standard in 1877, Asian countries sustained the silver standard. Although it was more burdensome to pay the Indian home charge fixed in gold, Asian countries generally enjoyed the benefits of European-Asian trade until their adaptation of the gold standard, for example, in 1893 (India) and in 1902 (Siam).

SEE ALSO *Acapulco; Mining, the Americas; Potosí.*

BIBLIOGRAPHY

De Vries, Jan. "Connecting Europe and Asia: A Quantitative Analysis of the Cape-route Trade, 1497–1795." In *Global Connections and Monetary History, 1470–1800*, edited by Dennis O. Flynn, Arturo Giráldez, and Richard von Glahn. Aldershot, U.K.: Ashgate, 2003.

Frank, Andre Gunder. *ReOrient: Global Economy in the Asian Age.* Berkeley: University of California Press, 1998.

Latham, A. J. H. *The International Economy and the Undeveloped World, 1865–1914.* London: Croom Helm, 1978.

Ryuto Shimada

BURMA, BRITISH

After the first Anglo-Burmese war in 1826 two former provinces of the Burmese Empire, Arakan and Tenasserim, were governed by British commissioners. The two provinces developed distinctly different forms of government. In Arakan colonial policy paid little deference to traditional Arakanese or Burmese institutions; rather, it reflected more strongly the influence of neighboring Bengal. In Tenasserim the British built on existing forms of government, using indigenous leadership and codifying local law. In 1862 Arakan and Tenasserim were united with the rest of Lower Burma to form the province of British Burma. The administrative layout in theory conformed to the Indian model, but in practice tended to conform to Burmese traditional methods. The mode of government used by the British during this period was not unlike the Dutch system in Java, in which indirect rule prevailed.

In Upper Burma, which remained under Burmese rule until the third Anglo-Burmese war of 1885, the economy became dangerously dependent on the export of mainly cotton and teak. In the teak industry elaborate contracts and concessions were developed over time and honored to such a degree as to warrant substantial investments on the part of British-Indian trading houses. At the same time, in other fields royal monopolies often excluded independent merchants. Rice however had to be imported in ever-larger quantities, which drained Upper Burma of cash. The world depression of the 1870s led to a dramatic decline in prices and plunged the Burmese state into economic hardship and fiscal collapse.

Under British rule Lower Burma developed into an export-oriented economy depending almost totally on rice production. Lower Burma's rice exports helped make up for food shortages in other parts of the empire. In this sense the colonial state in Burma developed within the context of a larger set of imperial, economic, political, and strategic interests.

Immediately at the end of the third Anglo-Burmese war, with the last Burmese king in exile, several important decisions were taken by the colonial power, which would dramatically change the way Burma was governed. A first attempt to govern through the old royal council, the Hlutdaw, failed. The reforms the British subsequently introduced meant nothing less than a complete dismantling of existing institutions of political authority. They resulted in the undermining of many established structures of social organization. In contrast to India the British decided that Burma would be governed directly, without making use of local elites. The monarchy, the nobility, and the army all disappeared. In the countryside local ruling families lost their positions. The existing political framework vanished. Only in outlying areas like the Shan states did the British use local intermediaries in government. In the heartland of the old Burmese empire, the Irrawaddy Valley, the colonial rulers imposed bureaucratic control right down to the village level. A wholly new framework of government rapidly supplanted existing institutions.

From the late nineteenth century onward village headmen were frequent targets of peasant uprisings, indicating how much they were perceived as tools of the colonial administration. At the same time the colonial power failed to adopt the symbols and roles that had legitimized precolonial rulers. The precolonial state had relied for the maintenance of order and security on its intimate involvement with the symbolic and spiritual life of society. The colonial state viewed its role very differently. The British administrators were not only foreigners, their idea of government presumed a marked distinction between the public and private spheres of life. British rule in effect destroyed the Burmese cosmological order and signified for the Burmese the end of a Buddhist World Age. This produced armed resistance in which Buddhist monks played a significant part. Burmese monks fanned rural rebellion, notably during the economic depression of the 1930s. The main causes of rural unrest and rebellions in the 1930s were taxes, usury, and depressed rice prices.

At the end of World War II, Burma was equipped with social and political institutions established only at the beginning of the twentieth century and without roots in local society. Apart from Buddhism, it would be difficult to define a supra-local institution that survived from precolonial times. As for the colonial administration, it had been shattered by the Japanese during the war years. Burma thus faced at independence in 1948 a weak institutional legacy, a vacuum that would be soon filled by the army.

SEE ALSO *Anglo-Burmese Wars.*

BIBLIOGRAPHY

Desai, Walter Sadgun. *History of the British Residency in Burma.* London: Gregg International, 1968.

Harvey, Godfrey. *British Rule in Burma 1824–1942.* London: Ams Pr., 1992.

S. E. A. van Galen

C

CABRAL, AMÍLCAR LOPES

1924–1973

Born on September 12, 1924, in Bafatá, Guinea-Bissau, Amílcar Lopes Cabral was one of Africa's greatest revolutionary leaders and political thinkers. Born of a Cape Verdean father, Juvenal Cabral, and Guinean mother, Iva Pinhel Evora, his father's concerns for the environment and the conditions of Africans in Portuguese Guinea had an early influence on him.

A brilliant student, Cabral completed secondary school in Mindelo on the island of São Vicente in Cape Verde in 1943. After working with the National Printing Office from 1944, Cabral was awarded a scholarship to study at the Agronomy Institute in Lisbon, Portugal, in 1945. He graduated from the institute in 1950 as an agricultural engineer.

Like other emerging African elites during the colonial period, Cabral felt the urge to return to Africa where he felt that people needed his contribution in struggle against colonialism and nature itself. Cabral returned to Guinea-Bissau in 1952 to work for the Agricultural and Forestry Services of Portuguese Guinea after a period of apprenticeship at the Agronomy Center in Santarém, Portugal. Between 1952 and 1954, Cabral worked as an agronomist traveling throughout Guinea.

But Cabral was deeply troubled by the political condition of Portuguese Guinea, where the increasing Portuguese military contingent on the island gave rise to several conflicts with the local population. Drought and famine complicated the situation. This was the atmosphere in which Amílcar Cabral spent his early days and which may have been reflected in his decision to become an agricultural engineer.

The twenty-eight-year-old agricultural engineer did not limit his goals to his profession; he was concerned with creating awareness among the Guinean people. His work as an agronomist which gave him the opportunity to travel also helped him to obtain detailed knowledge of the Guinean land and people and in turn helped him develop a strategy for national liberation. He left a more prestigious job as a researcher at the Agronomy Center to take a job as an engineer in Guinea, from which base he aspired to the higher goal of fighting Portuguese imperialism. He used his position as the manger of the agricultural station at Pessube to interact with rural workers, including Cape Verdeans. Cabral did not distinguish between his work as a political activist and as an agricultural engineer. He raised anticolonial sentiments and consciousness among both intellectuals and rural peasants through what he called the *reafricanization* of the spirit. He tried to use a radio program to make Cape Verdeans aware of their conditions, but the Portuguese forbade his broadcasts.

In 1955 Cabral moved to Angola after Diogo António José Leite Pereira de Melo e Alvim, who was governor from 1954 to 1956, ordered him out of the colony. He was allowed to return once a year for family reasons. This was a period of increasing anticolonial activity in Africa. Cabral came into direct contact with the founders of the Popular Movement for the Liberation of Angola, and he became a member. In 1957 he attended a meeting in Paris to discuss strategies for the anticolonial struggle against the Portuguese. The meeting provided him the opportunity to meet with other anticolonialists.

He also attended a Pan-African meeting in Ghana, among other international anticolonial conferences.

In 1959 Cabral and Aristides Pereira (b. 1923), Luís Cabral (b. 1931), Julio de Almeira, Fernando Fortes, and Elisee Turpin founded a new political party called the African Party for Independence and Union of Guinea and Cape Verde (PAIGC). This underground organization acquired legal status four years later.

Between 1960 and 1962, the PAIGC operated out of the Republic of Guinea with the objective of preparing armed militants and obtaining international support. War broke out against the Portuguese in 1962 with the aim of attaining independence for both Portuguese Guinea and Cape Verde. Cabral adopted guerrilla tactics and led one of the most profound revolutionary movements in Africa. Over the course of the conflict, the PAIGC gained land.

In 1972 Cabral began to form a people's assembly in preparation for independence, but a disgruntled former associate, Inocêncio Kani, and other members of the All Guineans Party assassinated him in January 1973. Cabral provided the military and intellectual leadership for the anticolonial movement for over a decade before his assassination. When Guinea-Bissau became independent in 1974, Cabral's brother, Luís, became president (1974–1980).

SEE ALSO *Anticolonialism; Portugal's African Colonies.*

BIBLIOGRAPHY

Bienen, Henry. "State and Revolution: The Work of Amilcar Cabral." *Journal of Modern African Studies* 15 (4) (1977): 555–568.

Chabal, Patrick. *Amilcar Cabral: Revolutionary Leadership and People's War.* New York and Cambridge, U.K.: Cambridge University Press, 1983.

Chailand, Gérard. *Armed Struggle in Africa: With the Guerrillas in "Portuguese" Guinea.* New York: Monthly Review Press, 1969.

McCollester, Charles. "The Political Thought of Amilcar Cabral." *Monthly Review* 24 (March 1973): 10–21.

Chima J. Korieh

CACAO

Cacao (*Theobroma cacao*), known as "the food of the gods," and its main byproduct, chocolate, come from the seeds, or nibs, of a pod, the fruit of a tree native to tropical America. The cacao tree usually requires shade trees, often the so-called *madre de cacao* (mother of cacao), also an American native. Experts disagree about the number of cacao types.

The *criollo* or native cacaos are often held to be the best. They are more delicate and low-yielding, and grow traditionally in Mesoamerica and the Caribbean. *Forastero* cacaos are more robust and prolific, but of lower quality. Cultivated in colonial Ecuador and Venezuela, this variety was also carried from Brazil to West Africa by the Portuguese, and is now a leading crop in several countries there, including the Ivory Coast and Ghana. *Forastero* is also cultivated in Southeast Asia. The third variety, *trinitario*, so named because it was apparently first cultivated commercially in Trinidad, is probably a crossbreed of the original varieties and is now grown worldwide.

Cacao trees are slow growing, sensitive to cold and drought, and require constant water from rain or irrigation. The nibs are extracted from the shell and the pulp, then fermented and dried. The beans are then bagged and shipped to markets, where they are manufactured into hard chocolate, cacao powder or cocoa, cacao butterfat, and other products.

Cacao is generally considered Amazonian in its "wild" state, although some dispute this. The nibs have a short fertility after being picked, and so transplantation was difficult before the availability of rapid modern transportation, causing wide distances between areas of cultivation and the emergence of different varieties. Cacao has obviously been modified by human intervention for many centuries.

It is in Mesoamerica that the first recorded histories of the plant and its fruit are found. Cacao was part of very ancient mythologies. The word itself may be Olmec, possibly dating to before 1000 BCE. Cacao was also of great importance to the Maya and other Mesoamerican cultures, including the city-centered states of the Valley of Mexico. Chocolate drinks are mentioned frequently in Mayan hieroglyphics, and elite tombs often hold pottery containing the residue of liquid chocolate. Some scholars have claimed that in some parts of Mesoamerica, chocolate drinks were a privilege limited to the nobility, but others find this unlikely because the widespread cultivation of the tree in the lowlands suggests general consumption by all classes. Certainly the drink was very much part of public ceremony and ritual.

The beans or nibs were an important trade and tribute item for centuries before the Spanish invasions. The plants' strict climatic requirements, and the elaborate, long-distance trade and taxation networks that developed, encouraged regional specialization. In coastal Guerrero, Colima, Veracruz, and Tabasco in Mexico, as well as the Gulf of Honduras—to use modern geographical nomenclature—cacao was grown intensively for export to population centers before the arrival of Europeans. Christopher Columbus (1451–1506), on his

Ramus arboris Cacao

Siliqua fructus Cacao

Fructus Cacao

The Cacao Plant. *Cocoa and its main byproduct, chocolate, come from the nibs of a pod, the fruit of a tree native to tropical America. Cocoa beans were an important trade and tribute item among indigenous Americans for centuries before the Spanish invasion.* © BETTMANN/CORBIS. REPRODUCED BY PERMISSION.

fourth voyage in 1502, seized a large seagoing canoe in the Gulf of Honduras carrying cacao beans as part of its cargo.

The great centers of cacao cultivation around the time of the first European invasions of America were Soconusco (today the Pacific coast of Chiapas in Mexico) and the coast running all the way from Chiapas to present-day El Salvador. From these plantations, beans found their way to the highland centers. Soconusco, a Culhua-Mexica outlying colony, sent cacao as tribute to the Aztec emperor Montezuma (ca. 1466–1520) in Tenochtitlán (now Mexico City). The beans were stored in great warehouses in the cities of the central valley.

In pre-Columbian Mexico, cacao beans served as coinage; it might be said, then, that money "grew on trees." Cacao beans were used as a rudimentary means of exchange from ancient times, and at least as far south as highland Costa Rica during the colonial period, especially when there were shortages of official metal coinage. What we know of pre-invasion cacao coinage is scanty, but in western Nicaragua, a Mesoamerican periphery, there may well have been standard equivalencies recognized by officialdom. Certainly such tables relating cacao beans to other coinages can be found sporadically during the three Spanish colonial centuries. Cacao beans also entered the numerical systems of measures based on serial numbers of beans. In the same way, there is some evidence of the counterfeiting of beans, certainly a sign of their monetary and symbolic value.

As far as we know, hard chocolate was not consumed. Still, the people of Mesoamerica had many recipes for cacao. The ground beans were mixed with hot or cold water and with maize, ground chilies, annatto, and vanilla, as well as seeds, roots, and flowers of a great variety. A favorite method was to beat these mixtures to a froth. Many of the dishes were soups, and the liquid chocolate, poured over other ingredients, may be the ancestor of modern *mole* sauces. The aristocracy and the *pochteca*, a kind of official merchant class, drank huge quantities of these libations at festivals and public banquets. The first Europeans to taste these native recipes, however, found them to be unpalatable. One early Italian visitor described them as "fit only for pigs."

The conquistadors of central Mexico captured warehouses of cacao, which they used as money. Other invading bands found groves in Soconusco and Izalcos in today's El Salvador. Soon these groves were exploited by powerful Central American *encomenderos*. These Spaniards usually did not seize ownership of the groves, because cultivation was a specialized business and required hard work in a humid subtropical climate. Instead, they coerced labor and tried to extract surpluses and taxes for trading. Large cargoes of cacao were carried by mule trains and small ships to central Mexico.

Within a few years, avaricious *encomenderos* and their governmental allies forced native growers to intensify planting and harvesting, which appears to have been counterproductive. The native population was in severe decline because of the Old World epidemiological shock, and overwork and exploitation made the demographic catastrophe worse. Imported labor from the highlands did not solve the resulting labor shortage, and overplanting, along with the cutting down of shade trees, destroyed the understory needs of the cacao trees.

All this occurred at a time when market demand was increasing. Apparently, consumption among the native peoples of central Mexico and highland Guatemala grew rapidly, and observers described the quaffing of almost unbelievable quantities of chocolate drinks. Demand was such that cacao from more distant plantations could pay expensive freight charges and still show a profit. By the seventeenth century, coastal Venezuela and Guayaquil in Ecuador had begun to replace Central America, Tabasco, and Guerrero as the main suppliers, and Mexico started to import large cargoes of the hardier and more plentiful *forastero* crops. Venezuelan growers dominated at first using African slave labor, and eventually sent much of their crop to Spain and to Dutch smugglers in Curaçao as the taste for chocolate developed in western Europe and markets organized in Amsterdam and elsewhere.

Guayaquil began to export beans at about the same time as Venezuela and was able to produce considerable quantities of inexpensive cacaos. Guayaquil prices, despite long and inefficient trade routes, undercut those of Central America and even Venezuela. Central American growers obtained a royal ban on Guayaquil and other South American imports but contraband flourished. By 1700 or so, Guayaquil chocolate began to reach even Spain and other European centers, as well as to supply some three-quarters of Mexican demand. New producers such as Trinidad, Caribbean Costa Rica, Martinique, and Saint-Domingue (Haiti) also took minor places as suppliers to the transatlantic markets.

Europeans developed a taste for chocolate slowly, compared to Americans of all ethnic groups. The addition of Old World sugar and New World vanilla helped with its acceptance. Cacao beans probably reached Europe by the 1520s, and its use as a drink spread from Spain, first to France, where chocolate houses were fashionable by mid-seventeenth century, and then to London, Holland, and elsewhere. The Dutch, who captured Curaçao from the Spanish in 1634, soon sent large cargoes of Venezuelan contraband cacao to Amsterdam, the great chocolate mart of Europe. The chocolate mart in Amsterdam became so monopolistic, in fact, that even Spanish merchants had to buy there.

By the eighteenth century, American chocolate was being drunk throughout Europe and its colonies with varying degrees of enthusiasm. In the late century, some people began to add milk, wine, and cloves. Recipes stipulated the best ways to prepare chocolate, with emphasis on ways of heating and whipping to provide the ideal frothy frappé. Chocolate, however, remained quite expensive.

Gradually, intensification of production and new technologies turned chocolate into the solid, inexpensive bars and hard candies of today. The popularity of chocolate as a drink was surpassed by coffee and tea in most places, and the product went its separate way as a confectionary. The Swiss followed the Dutch and English pioneers. The Nestlé brothers and Rodolphe Lindt (1855–1909) developed the first milk chocolates, and in the United States Milton Hershey (1857–1945) took advantage of economies of scale, vertical integration of needed products, and mass marketing to capture a giant share of the confectionary market. The "food of the gods," produced mainly in West Africa since about 1900, had become the candy of the masses.

SEE ALSO *Aztec Empire; Commodity Trade, Africa; Empire in the Americas, Spanish.*

BIBLIOGRAPHY

Alden, Dauril. *The Significance of Cacao Production in the Amazon Region During the Late Colonial Period: An Essay in Comparative Economic History.* Philadelphia: American Philosophical Society, 1976.

Bergman, James L. "The Distribution of Cacao Cultivation in Pre-Columbian America." *Annals of the Association of American Geographers* 59 (1969): 85–96.

Coe, Sophie D., and Michael D. Coe. *The True History of Chocolate.* New York: Thames and Hudson, 1996.

Piñero, Eugenio. *The Town of San Felipe and Colonial Cacao Economies.* Philadelphia: American Philosophical Society, 1994.

Young, Allen M. *The Chocolate Tree: A Natural History of Cacao.* Washington, DC: Smithsonian Institution Press, 1994.

Murdo J. MacLeod

CALCUTTA

Situated on the east bank of the River Hugli about 129 kilometers (80 miles) from the Bay of Bengal, Calcutta lies close to the mouth of the two great river systems of the Ganga (Ganges) and the Brahmaputra. Consequently, the port possesses the advantage of excellent inland navigation for transporting foreign imports upstream and sending down the products of the fertile interior by the same channel.

Already prior to the arrival of the English merchant Job Charnock (d. 1693) in 1690, the settlements on the east bank of the river had attracted a number of high-caste Hindu families with literary traditions. The foundation of a British settlement raised the potential of the site, but the political events in the eighteenth century that changed the course of history were not to be predicted in the 1690s.

The right of fortification, obtained by the British in 1696, allowed the construction of Fort William. In 1698 the English East India Company purchased the right of revenue and tax collection for the three villages of Kalikata, Sutanuti, and Govindapur. In 1700 the settlement received the status of a presidency. This put the

English technically on an equal footing with the Mughal *nawabs* (local rulers) of Bengal, who were now confronted with the unrestrained extracommercial ambitions of East India Company officials.

Bengal *subah* (province) in the early eighteenth century had obtained autonomy and economic stability under the *nawab* Murshid Quli Khan, and Bengal was known as the granary of India. Muslin, silk, saltpeter, indigo, and opium attracted the European trading companies, and the arrival of private merchants from different parts of the world made Calcutta the home of Abyssinians, Afghans, Armenians, Burmese, Chinese, and Persians, as well as English, Dutch, French, and other Europeans.

The grant of a *firman* (imperial permit) by the Mughal emperor to the English in 1717 led to the growth of Calcutta as a center of English private trade. Extensive fortifications and the ambition of East India Company officials, however, led to a rupture with the *nawab* Alivardi Khan. Alivardi's successor, Siraj ud daula, attacked and overran Calcutta and renamed it Alinagar (1756). Robert Clive (1725–1774) and Admiral Charles Watson (1714–1757) recaptured Calcutta in February 1757. In June 1757 Clive won the Battle of Plassey, a triumph more of intrigue than of military action, and laid the foundation for British paramountcy in India. From 1773 to 1911, Calcutta was the capital of British India and the second city in the British Empire.

There was a cleavage in the pattern of Calcutta's urban growth. The European Town around the Tank Square and Chowringhee areas witnessed a high level of real-estate development, especially under the governors-general Warren Hastings (1774–1785) and Marquis Wellesley (1798–1805). The massive buildings of New Fort William, the Supreme Court, the Writers' Building, and Saint John's Church established marks of colonial rule. The British-built Town Hall, Metcalf Hall, and the Senate House were a few of the public buildings that lent Calcutta the epithet "city of palaces." The Indian Town in the north, and the intermediate zone were, however, overcrowded and lacked adequate municipal amenities.

These deficiencies did not stand in the way of the growth of the city. Between 1742 and 1901 the area of the settlement grew from about 1,307 to 5,357 hectares (3,229 to 13,237 acres), while the population rose from 179,917 to 542,686 during the same period. Calcutta was the most important port in India for shipping cotton, coal, jute, opium, and indigo. The large concentration of jute mills within a radius of 64 kilometers (40 miles) from Calcutta by 1911 resulted in a large-scale migration of laborers from up-country provinces to the city. Another important migrant group was the Marwaris, who came to dominate trade and industry in the region.

The phenomenal growth of the metropolis led to a demand for municipal services. Statutory civic services began in 1794. Calcutta received a municipal government in 1852, which became the Calcutta Corporation in 1899. The city's public sewerage system was completed in 1859, and filtered water became available from 1860. Railway services began in the city in 1854. Telegraph lines were installed in 1851, and the telephone exchange was opened in 1883. Horse-drawn trams were introduced in 1873, and following the introduction of electricity in 1899, electric trams started running in the city in 1902. Regular bus service began in 1924.

Warren Hastings's interest in the revival of Oriental learning and arts led to the foundation of the Calcutta Madrasa (1781) and the Asiatic Society (1784). The establishment of the printing press (1777) stimulated the growth of public opinion. Fort William College, founded in 1800, was designed to impart the knowledge of Indian languages and culture among East India Company civilians. The spread of English education was facilitated through the foundation of Hindu College in 1817 and Bethune School, the first public school for girls, in 1850. Calcutta Medical College and Calcutta University were established in 1835 and 1857 respectively.

The interaction of the Bengali intelligentsia with Western education, British Orientalism, and Christianity brought about an awakening commonly known as the Bengal Renaissance. Its earliest spokesman was Raja Rammohun Roy (1772–1833), the founder of the Brahmo Samaj, a monotheistic Hindu reform movement based on the Upanishads, ancient Hindu texts of wisdom. The British Indian Association, established in 1851, reflected a growing political consciousness in the region. Calcutta's Muslim community had the Mohammedan Literary Society (1863) and the Central National Mohammedan Association (1877) as their platform. Surendranath Banerjea (1848–1925), the founder of the Indian Association (1876), was the main force behind the National Conference held in Calcutta in 1883. Between 1885 and 1905, Calcutta was the nerve center of Indian politics and of the Indian National Congress, the forum of Indian public opinion on political issues.

During the Swadeshi movement (a movement pledging the use of indigenous products) that followed the partition of Bengal (1905), the demand for complete *swaraj* (self-rule) became a pan-Indian issue. A widespread boycott and the rise of extremist revolutionary groups in Bengal seriously threatened British rule. Consequently, the British moved the capital to Delhi. In August 1946 the city was shaken by the Hindu-Muslim riots, which resulted in the killing of large numbers of people on both sides, known as the "great Calcutta killings," following the direct action demanding a separate electorate for the Muslims. Riots broke out again in August 1947, just before and after India gained independence. Due to the partition of India, Calcutta lost much of its hinterland, which became part of East Pakistan.

SEE ALSO *Colonial Port Cities and Towns, South and Southeast Asia; Indian National Movement.*

BIBLIOGRAPHY

Bhattacharya, Sukumar. *The East India Company and the Economy of Bengal from 1704 to 1740*, 2nd ed. Calcutta, India: Firma KLM, 1969.

Broomfield, J. H. *Elite Conflict in a Plural Society: Twentieth-Century Bengal.* Berkeley: University of California Press, 1968.

Chaudhuri, Sukanta, ed. *Calcutta: The Living City*, Vol. 1: *The Past.* Calcutta, India: Oxford University Press, 1990.

Chaudhuri, Sushil. *Trade and Commercial Organization in Bengal, 1650–1720, with Special Reference to the English East India Company.* Calcutta, India: Firma KLM, 1975.

Chaudhuri, Sushil. *The Prelude to Empire: Plassey Revolution of 1757.* New Delhi, India: Manohar, 2000.

Gordon, Leonard. *Bengal: The Nationalist Movement, 1876–1940.* New Delhi, India: Manohar; New York: Columbia University Press, 1974.

Gupta, Brijen K. *Sirajuddaullah and the East India Company, 1756–1757: Background to the Foundation of British Power in India.* Leiden, Netherlands: Brill, 1966.

Kopf, David. *British Orientalism and the Bengal Renaissance: The Dynamics of Indian Modernization, 1773–1835.* Berkeley: University of California Press, 1969.

Kopf, David. *The Brahmo Samaj and the Shaping of the Indian Mind.* Princeton, NJ: Princeton University Press, 1979.

Marshall, Peter James. *East Indian Fortunes: The British in Bengal in the Eighteenth Century.* Oxford: Clarendon: 1976.

Marshall, Peter James. *Bengal—the British Bridgehead: Eastern India, 1740–1828.* Cambridge, U.K.: Cambridge University Press, 1987.

Moorhouse, Geoffrey. *Calcutta.* London: Weidenfeld, 1971.

Prakash, Om. *The Dutch East India Company and the Economy of Bengal, 1630–1720.* Princeton, NJ: Princeton University Press, 1985.

Sarkar, Sumit. *The Swadeshi Movement in Bengal, 1903–1908.* New Delhi, India: People's Publishing House, 1973.

Sinha, Narendra Krishna. *The Economic History of Bengal*, 3 vols. Calcutta, India: Firma KLM, 1956–1970.

Tripathi, Amales. *Trade and Finance in the Bengal Presidency, 1793–1833*, rev. ed. Calcutta, India: Oxford University Press, 1979.

Bhaswati Bhattacharya

CANTON

SEE *Guangzhou*

CAPE COLONY AND CAPE TOWN

The Cape Colony was a Dutch and later British colony at the southern tip of Africa, with Cape Town as its capital and largest city. The region was originally inhabited by the San and Khoikhoi peoples (known together as Khoisan), who were nomadic hunters and pastoralists, and by Bantu-speaking Africans. Europeans first reached the Cape region in 1488, when the Portuguese navigator Bartolomeu Dias (ca. 1450–1500, also spelled Diaz) rounded what he named the Cape of Good Hope. The Portuguese did not establish any permanent settlement, but used the Cape as a stopping place on their way to India and East Africa.

European settlement began in 1652, when Jan van Riebeeck (1619–1677), in the employ of the Dutch East India Company, founded Cape Town as a permanent supply station linking the Netherlands with its colonies in Southeast Asia. Khoisan were recruited as laborers for the settlement, but the Dutch also imported slaves from Indonesia and other parts of Asia. Intermingling among these peoples and the European settlers created a population of mixed race, known in South Africa as "colored" people, in addition to the European and African populations.

Dutch, as well as French Huguenot, settlement increased and the European population at the Cape reached one thousand by 1745. By this time many settlers began moving away from Cape Town, and established farms further into the interior of Africa. These early pioneers, known as *trekboers*, lived independently but often came into conflict with the indigenous African population. Some of the French Huguenot settlers were instrumental in establishing a wine industry near Cape Town, which still flourishes.

Events in Europe had a significant effect on the later colonization of the Cape region. As a result of the French Revolutionary and Napoleonic Wars, Britain occupied the Cape Colony in 1795 and acquired it from the Dutch in 1806, renaming it the Cape of Good Hope Colony. British settlers brought a different language and legal system to the Cape and abolished slavery, to the dissatisfaction of the original Dutch settlers. In 1835 another group of Dutch Boers (meaning "farmers") left the Cape on a long migration, or trek, into the interior of Africa, much as the earlier *trekboers* had done. This movement, known as the Great Trek, resulted in the formation of independent Boer republics in interior South Africa. British settlers also expanded their territory eastward, which brought them into a series of wars with the indigenous Xhosa people.

British development of the colony and of Cape Town continued, especially after the annexation of the important diamond-producing region of Kimberley in 1880. The colony had expanded in size to encompass over half the area of present-day South Africa, had become self-governing in 1872, and was one of the most important British colonies in Africa. In 1910, after the defeat of the Boer republics in the Boer War, the Cape became one of the original provinces in the Union of South Africa. Since 1994 the former Cape Province has been divided into several smaller provinces, but Cape Town remains one of the most important cities in Africa.

SEE ALSO *Colonial Cities and Towns, Africa.*

BIBLIOGRAPHY

Beck, Roger B. *The History of South Africa.* Westport, CT: Greenwood, 2000.

Davenport, T. R. H., and Christopher Saunders. *South Africa: A Modern History,* 5th ed. New York: St. Martin's Press, 2000.

Worden, Nigel, Elizabeth van Heyningen, and Vivian Bickford-Smith. *Cape Town: The Making of a City.* Cape Town: David Philip, 1998.

Michael Pretes

CAPITULATIONS, MIDDLE EAST

The term *capitulations* (from the Turkish word *imtiyazat*) has come to be associated with the preferential commercial privileges and extraterritorial rights European merchants enjoyed during the Ottoman period. Muslim rulers throughout the Middle East, including the Mamluk sultans of Egypt, issued capitulations. The precise impact of the capitulatory system on the development of Ottoman social, economic, and political institutions remains a contentious issue among scholars; particularly vexing is the issue of whether or not the Ottoman Empire could have maintained parity with western Europe had the capitulations never been granted. The capitulatory system that developed within the Middle East, historian Carter Findley suggests, bears a striking resemblance to the methods used by Europeans to establish their economic dominance throughout the world during the free-trade era.

EARLY HISTORY

The capitulatory system arose out of the notion that only Ottoman subjects were worthy of the sultan's law. As such, any foreigner whose state had not been granted a capitulation had no legal protection when traveling through or residing in the Ottoman Empire. Although a few scholars trace the granting of capitulations back to the mid-fourteenth century, Suleyman the Magnificent (r. 1520–1566) is normally considered to have granted the first capitulation in 1536 to King Francis I (r. 1515–1547).

In placing French merchants under the legal jurisdiction of their consul at Constantinople, thereby rendering them immune from Ottoman and Islamic law, and allowing them to import/export goods at greatly reduced tariff rates, the Ottoman government or Sublime Porte hoped to promote commercial exchange with the West.

With capitulatory privileges lapsing upon the death of the sultan who granted them, giving Europeans special privileges seemed harmless enough during a period characterized by Ottoman military preeminence. In the fifteenth century, the Ottoman Empire was one of, if not the most, powerful states in the world and affected the development of Europe as a whole; arguably only England was remote enough to dismiss the Porte as irrelevant. Even the English, however, could not ignore the rapid spread of French commerce in the Near East. In addition to their presence in Constantinople, the French were permitted to establish trading posts and consular missions in Syria and Egypt. Between the late 1530s and early 1570s, when Ottoman maritime strength was at its height, English trade with the eastern Mediterranean had virtually collapsed.

Following the renewal of hostilities with Persia in 1578, the Sublime Porte was in desperate need of steel, lead, and especially tin for the production of bronze guns. A papal ban, however, forbid the export of munitions from Christendom to the Ottoman Empire, but as they were already drifting toward war with Spain the English ultimately decided to ignore the ban. In May 1580, in a unilateral gesture, Sultan Murad III (r. 1574–1595) formally placed the English on an equal footing with the French. Not long after the Levant Company had been formed, English consuls were despatched to Cairo, Alexandria, Aleppo, Damascus, Algiers, Tunis, Tripoli in Barbary and Tripoli in Syria. Although it was not recognized at the time, the European (commercial) penetration of the Ottoman Empire had begun in earnest.

Foreign trade initially contributed, whether directly or indirectly, to the provisioning of both the Ottoman court and armed forces. In addition to the shipment of metals for Ottoman foundries, Europeans were a significant source of the sinews of war gold and silver. As Ottoman military power began to decline, the nature and meaning of the capitulatory system slowly changed to the ever increasing detriment of the Porte. Prior to the eighteenth century, sultans believed that the privileges they bestowed upon foreigners could be revoked at any time during their reign. After 1683, when second siege of Vienna failed, the Porte was increasingly forced to offer permanent capitulations in exchange for diplomatic assistance. Nevertheless, as late as 1740, Ottoman officials could still search the residence of foreigners, who had capitulatory privileges, if they believed the house contained fugitives or smuggled goods.

Under the terms of the capitulation granted to the French in 1536, which formed the basis for all subsequent treaties, consular courts had sole jurisdiction over cases involving only foreigners but were essentially powerless in disputes between foreigners and Ottoman subjects. The Treaty of Kuçuk Kainarji negotiated with Czarist Russia in 1774 ended this jurisdictional division. The Russian embassy began employing Ottoman subjects, the so-called dragomans, who in time became virtual intermediaries between the embassy and the Sublime Porte, to interpret the terms of the treaty. Eventually any non-Muslim Ottoman subject could obtain such an appointment (*berat*) from a European consul in exchange for a "modest" fee, thereby acquiring all the benefits of that country's capitulatory agreement. Although the selling of *berats* obviously undermined Ottoman revenue collection, and would lead Sultan Selim III (r. 1789–1807) to grant all Ottoman merchants the same privileges as their European competitors, it was the need to secure the consent of the Western powers to any alteration in the empire's tariff rates that ultimately proved far more destructive.

THE TRANSFORMATION OF THE CAPITULATORY SYSTEM

By the later half of the eighteenth century, the Renaissance, the military revolution, and the discovery of the New World had all combined to give western Europe a distinct military and commercial advantage over the Ottoman Empire. It was not until the late eighteenth century, however, that the Ottomans fully realized the gravity of the challenge facing them. Napoléon's invasion of Egypt in 1798 completely shattered the illusion of Ottoman invulnerability. Prior to this event, Europe's military advance into the Islamic world had largely been confined to the Ottoman Empire's northern border; Austria and Russia were steadily advancing into the Balkans and along the eastern shore of the Black Sea. The increasing commercial and industrial strength of Europe, and in particular, Britain, ultimately led to the almost total domination of Ottoman commerce by the European powers. Until the early nineteenth century, the Porte still believed it could modify the capitulations to prevent gross abuses; in 1809, for example, Britain accepted that its consuls had abused the *berat* system.

Reforming the capitulatory system paled in importance to the quelling the internal crises that beset the Ottoman Empire throughout the first quarter of the nineteenth century; the rise of Mehmed Ali Pasha and the Greek revolt being the most striking examples. In fact, as Ottoman bureaucrats began to view Western-styled reforms as the key to preserving the independence and integrity of the empire, efforts designed to limit the

integration of the Ottoman economy into the ever expanding European market were abandoned. In repealing the privileges Selim III had given indigenous merchants, Mahmud II (r. 1808–1839) made it all but impossible for them to compete with Europeans. Viewed in this light, the signing of the 1838 Anglo-Turkish Commercial Convention at Balta Liman arguably becomes the logical conclusion to Ottoman policy over the preceding ten to fifteen years and not simply the price that had to be paid for British assistance in halting the aggrandizement of Mehmed Ali Pasha's Egypt. Whatever its origins, the results of the Convention were unmistakable.

THE CAPITULATORY YOKE

The treaty of Balta Liman marked the end of the traditional system of capitulations, which had been becoming increasingly detrimental to Ottoman interests. Henceforth, trade between the Ottoman Empire and Europe was governed by bilaterally negotiated commercial treaties. The 1838 convention confirmed all existing capitulatory privileges, set tariff rates for European goods at 3 percent and, most importantly, abolished all state monopolies within the Ottoman Empire. In forcing the Porte to accept the principle of free trade, the British effectively delivered the coup de grâce to Ottoman manufacturing and helped bring an end to the industrial and economic development of Mehmed Ali Pasha's Egypt. Combined with the ill-fated Ottoman attempt to centralize its tax collection system that same year, the Anglo-Turkish Commercial Convention initiated a downward spiral from which the Ottoman Empire never recovered.

By the second half of the nineteenth century, the capitulatory system had come to be seen as the symbol of Ottoman inferiority vis-à-vis Europe. Whereas capitulations had originally been bestowed upon the Great Powers of Europe, between 1838 and 1856 minor states like Sardinia, Sweden, Spain, Portugal, the Netherlands, Belgium, Denmark, Tuscany, the Hanseatic Towns, Greece, the two Sicilies, Prussia, and the other signatories of the Zollverein all signed similar treaties. The Ottomans also signed commercial treaties with non-Europeans countries; the United States in 1830, Brazil in 1858, and Mexico in 1864.

Throughout the Tanzimat era, which refers to the attempted administrative reorganization of the Ottoman Empire between 1839 and 1876, Ottoman statesmen believed that as long as the European powers respected their country's sovereignty there was little or no danger in allowing Europeans ever greater access to their country's economy. In 1869, in yet another attempt to curb the selling of berats, the Porte granted citizenship to all Ottoman subjects thereby making it both unnecessary and in fact illegal for people to seek or accept the protection of a foreign power. Both foreign embassies and the vast majority of Ottoman subjects, who continued to identify with their religious community (*millet*) and not the state, largely ignored the new law.

The disregard displayed by the European powers toward Ottoman efforts to limit their influence eventually gave way to outright contempt as social Darwinism and other aspects of mid- to late-nineteenth-century imperialism led Europeans to view the Turks as corrupt and racially and morally inferior. The promise of reformers that westernization would eventually lead to parity with Europe rang increasingly hollow as the Tanzimat era drew to a close. Beginning in the 1860s, the social strata most affected by westernization became increasingly critical of (further) reform. The Balkan revolt of 1875 and the Ottoman defeat in the Russo-Turkish War of 1877–1878 only strengthened the position of the so-called Young Ottomans.

It was not until Abdülhamid II came to the throne in 1876 that the Porte turned away from its almost total reliance on Britain. Turning to Imperial Germany, however, offered little practical benefits. The kaiser agreed to abolish the capitulations but only if the other great powers did so as well. The Western penetration of the Ottoman Empire increased during the course of the nineteenth century. Consuls were being despatched throughout Ottoman lands to defend the commercial and legal interests of European merchants and the increasing number of missionaries. The spread of persons endowed with capitulatory powers significantly undermined Ottoman administrative structures. By the early twentieth century, for example, an Ottoman policeman could not even enter the home of a foreign national without the permission of the latter's consul/embassy. Abdülhamid II's reign, not surprisingly, marked a decisive turning point in Ottoman attitudes toward the capitulatory system.

No longer perceived to be mere violations of imperial sovereignty, the capitulations came to be seen as the foremost barrier to the future (economic) development of the Ottoman Empire. The ever-increasing prosperity of Germany, whose economy was protected by high tariffs, seemed to offer the Porte a new approach. Raising Ottoman tariffs would not only provide badly needed revenues but could also stimulate the growth of domestic industry. It was only after twenty-six years of negotiations that the capitulatory signatories consented in 1907 to raising Ottoman tariffs from 4 to 7 percent as long as the increased revenues came under the purvey of the Ottoman Public Debt Administration. The Western powers dictated that one-quarter of said revenues should be used to service the massive Ottoman debt, while the remainder would be used to finance reforms in Macedonia. So far as Europe was concerned, the Ottoman Empire had for all instance and purposes become another colony to be administered for their (economic) benefit.

THE DOWNFALL OF THE CAPITULATORY SYSTEM

In 1908 the Young Turks deposed Abdülhamid II in a coup designed to bring about the transformation of the empire into the "Japan of the Near East." The success of the Japanese in achieving near equality with the Western powers inspired the disparate collection of exiles, disgruntled civil servants and students, and disaffected army officers stationed in the empire's European provinces that made up the Young Turk movement. Although they could restore the 1876 constitution, until the capitulations were abolished there was little else the Young Turks could do. The gulf between the Ottoman Empire and Europe was made abundantly clear when, after declaring its independence in 1908, Bulgaria was immediately freed from its capitulatory yoke. Large sections of Ottoman society correctly perceived that Europe was using the capitulations as the means by which to exclude their Empire from the "civilized" world. In the years before the outbreak of World War I (1914–1918), the European powers repeatedly sought to undermine all efforts to weaken the capitulatory system. It was widely recognized within the chancelleries of Europe that keeping the Porte starved for money offered the surest way of keeping it in line.

The outbreak of World War I offered the Committee of Union and Progress (CUP), which emerged from the power struggle that took place after the fall of Abdülhamid II, the best chance to date to weaken the capitulatory system. In exchange for a defensive alliance between the Ottoman Empire and the Entente powers, the CUP demanded among other things the outright abolition of the capitulations. The British ambassador at Constantinople likened the Ottoman offer to terms normally imposed upon a defeated enemy.

The Germans, however, proved more accommodating. In exchange for allowing their warships, the *Goeben* and *Breslau*, to enter the straits, in violation of international law, they had to agree to a number of conditions, one of which was the abolition of the capitulations. Although the Germans found the provisions outrageous, with the British Mediterranean squadron lurking just beyond the entrance to the straits, they had little choice. Only a few weeks later, and over the objections of their German ally, the Porte announced the unilateral abrogation of the capitulations, effective October 1, 1914. For the duration of World War I, the Ottoman Empire exercised unrestricted sovereignty for the first time in centuries.

Following the defeat of the Central Powers, the Western powers believed the capitulatory system should be reintroduced. In 1919 the U.S. State Department made clear its belief that American's rights in occupied Ottoman territories included those outlined in the prewar capitulation agreements. The Treaty of Sèvres, which was signed in August 1920, reintroduced the capitulations as part of the larger Anglo-French effort to severely curtail Ottoman sovereignty. The government in Constantinople, desperate not to lose everything, signed the treaty but the nationalist uprising(s) in Anatolia, which would eventually come to be led by Mustafa Kemal, ensured the treaty was never ratified.

The Treaty of Lausanne formally abolished capitulations in Turkey. The situation in former Ottoman provinces, however, was more complicated. In Iraq the capitulations were abolished in 1922; it was not until the 1937 Montreux Convention that they were abolished in Egypt. The League of Nations' mandates for Syria, Lebanon, Palestine, and Transjordan never included extraterritorial privileges for foreigners.

SEE ALSO *Abdülhamid II; Empire, Ottoman.*

BIBLIOGRAPHY

Ahmad, Feroz. "Ottoman Perceptions of the Capitulations 1800–1914." *Journal of Islamic Studies* 11 (1) (2000): 1–20.

Cleveland, William. *A History of the Modern Middle East*, 2nd ed. Boulder, CO: Westview Press, 2000.

Faroqhi, Suraiya. "Before 1600: Ottoman Attitudes Towards Merchants from Latin Christendom." *Turcica* 34 (2002): 69–104.

Findley, Carter. *Bureaucratic Reform in the Ottoman Empire: The Sublime Porte, 1789–1922*. Princeton, NJ: Princeton University Press, 1980.

Findley, Carter. *Ottoman Civil Officialdom: A Social History.* Princeton, NJ: Princeton University Press, 1989.

Fromkin, David. *A Peace to End All Peace: The Fall of the Ottoman Empire and the Creation of the Modern Middle East.* New York: Avon Books, 1989.

Inalcik, Halil. *The Ottoman Empire: The Classical Age, 1300–1600.* Translated by Norman Itzkowitz and Colin Imber. London: Weidenfeld & Nicolson, 1973.

Quataert, Donald. *The Ottoman Empire, 1700–1922.* Cambridge, U.K.: Cambridge University Press, 2000.

Sousa, Nasim. *The Capitulatory Regime of Turkey: Its History, Origin and Nature.* Baltimore, MD: Johns Hopkins University Press, 1933.

Sean Kelly

CARIBBEAN

The Caribbean islands lie on the northern and eastern sides of the Caribbean Sea, stretching in an elongated S shape from the Bahamas and Cuba in the north and west to Trinidad in the south. The islands are divided into two main groups: the large islands of the Greater Antilles and the smaller islands of the Lesser Antilles. Strong historical connections with the islands mean that the mainland territories of Guyana and Belize are frequently categorized as part of the Caribbean.

THE FIRST INHABITANTS

The Caribbean islands were probably first settled from the South American mainland. When Europeans arrived in the region there were three main groups of people living there. The Ciboney people were found in parts of Hispaniola and Cuba. The Arawak people occupied most of the Greater Antilles, while the Caribs lived throughout the Lesser Antilles. The Caribs were the latest to arrive in the region, migrating northward. As a result of this movement, the peoples of the Caribbean were experiencing change before the arrival of Europeans. However, the arrival of people from the Old World set in motion transformations on a previously unimaginable scale.

THE ARRIVAL OF EUROPEANS

In 1492 the three ships of Christopher Columbus's Spanish expedition made landfall in the Bahamas, before heading south to Cuba and Hispaniola. Columbus famously thought that he had reached the East Indies and clung to this belief until his death in 1506. On his second voyage to the New World, Columbus brought seventeen ships, over a thousand soldiers, and European plants, horses, and livestock. This expedition explored and named many of the Caribbean islands, landing on Dominica, Guadeloupe, Montserrat, Antigua, Puerto Rico, and Jamaica.

The first Spanish settlements were in the Greater Antilles, the largest being on Hispaniola. The principal aim of Spanish colonization was to find and extract silver and gold, and Spanish settlers established mines as well as breeding horses and livestock. By the early sixteenth century, large deposits of gold and silver had been discovered in the mainland areas of Mexico and Peru. Thereafter, Spanish Caribbean settlements operated as staging posts and recruitment areas for expeditions to these regions.

The Spanish sought to convert the original inhabitants of the region to Christianity, but these efforts met with little success, and relations between the two groups were generally violent and exploitative. The Spaniards conquered the islands by force and gave no quarter when

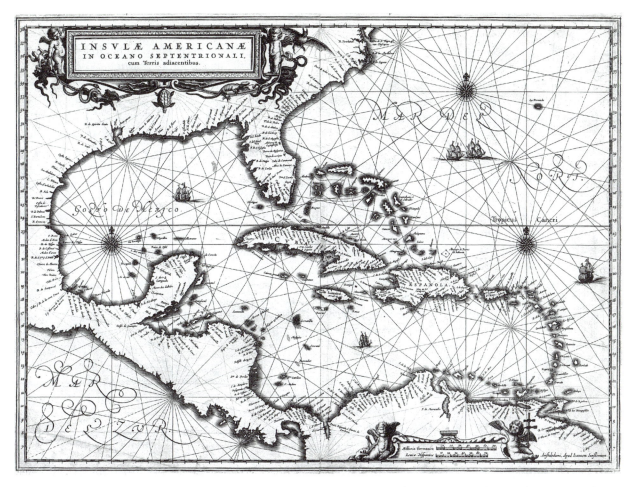

Map of the Caribbean, circa 1630s. *The Caribbean islands lie on the northern and eastern sides of the Caribbean Sea, stretching in an elongated S shape from the Bahamas and Cuba in the north and west to Trinidad in the south.* **REPRODUCED COURTESY OF MAP COLLECTION, YALE UNIVERSITY LIBRARY.**

faced with resistance. They coerced native people into working in the mines, and disturbed local patterns of food production, causing many to starve. Furthermore, natives of the islands lacked immunities to European diseases. It is unclear exactly what proportion of them died as a result of illnesses imported from the Old World, but the arrival of Europeans in the region was certainly a social and demographic disaster, and native people were either destroyed or integrated into the Spanish society. The vast majority were wiped out within a few generations, certainly on the larger islands.

THE END OF SPANISH HEGEMONY

Prior to the end of the sixteenth century, Spain was the only colonial power in the Caribbean. However, Spain's power and influence was declining in Europe and it was increasingly difficult to exclude the English, Dutch, and French from the Caribbean. Initially, the only challenge to Spanish hegemony came from the increasingly

common raids on ships and ports by pirates, such as John Hawkins and Francis Drake, who came in search of Spanish gold and silver. Buccaneers (raiders operating from bases in the Caribbean) continued to harass and plunder ships and ports in the region until the eighteenth century.

By the seventeenth century the period of Spanish hegemony was over, and the English, French, and Dutch began to trade and form colonies in the Caribbean. European powers fought to expand their empires and gain dominance of the sea, and because the financial value of Caribbean products and trade was high, competition between the main powers was particularly fierce in the region. The Caribbean became a focal point in the increasingly globalized conflicts between Britain and France during the eighteenth century. At times of war, sea battles were fought and islands were captured and recaptured. Between 1762 and 1814 control of the island of St. Lucia alternated between Britain and France seven times.

SUGAR AND SLAVERY

The expansion of sugar production and slavery helped to ensure that Caribbean colonies were economically and strategically vital to European governments. During the seventeenth century, having experimented with other crops, notably tobacco, northern European settlers began planting sugar, which grew well in tropical conditions and fetched a high price in Europe. Until the mid-eighteenth century, the wealthiest English plantation colony was Barbados, which was then superseded by the larger island of Jamaica, conquered from the Spanish in 1655. The most lucrative sugar colony in the Caribbean was French Saint-Domingue, in the western third of Hispaniola.

Effective sugar production required large holdings of land. This resulted in the creation of plantations that often covered thousands of acres. The cultivation and processing of this crop was also extremely labor-intensive, and, having experimented with indigenous slaves and indentured European labor, Caribbean planters turned to African slaves to meet their labor needs. Slaves imported from the west coast of Africa proved hardier than the indigenous islanders and a more reliable source of labor than European workers. Existing slaving networks in Africa ensured that there was a steady supply of slaves to meet European demand, and because they were treated as items of personal property, enslaved people could be easily bought and sold. The transatlantic slave trade therefore solved the planters' labor problems and permanently altered all aspects of life in the Caribbean colonies. Over five million Africans arrived in the Caribbean, having endured the horrors of the Middle Passage across the Atlantic.

Sugar plantations and the institution of slavery expanded together and had reached the height of their growth and profitability by the end of the eighteenth century. The precise demographic structure of slave societies differed from place to place, but everywhere in the Caribbean they were characterized by large black majorities, as slaves came to heavily outnumber the white inhabitants of the islands. For example, in 1800 there were about twenty slaves to every white person on the island of Jamaica. Across the region, a class of free colored people also emerged, occupying a social and legal position in between the islands' enslaved majorities and privileged white minorities.

Several factors discouraged whites from permanently settling in the region. A plethora of highly contagious diseases and the threat of slave uprisings rendered life in the Caribbean uncomfortable and dangerous. Many larger proprietors lived in Europe as absentees, and those whites who remained in the region did not consider the islands to be a permanent home and maintained a close affinity with the colonial metropole. Caribbean slaveholders also relied upon European military support to control their slaves. Such ties of dependency helped to ensure that Caribbean colonists did not follow their mainland Spanish and North American counterparts in demanding independence from European colonial systems.

In all colonies, slaves were worked hard and faced harsh treatment. In spite of this, enslaved people across the region created viable cultures that allowed them to resist the effects of slavery. Afro-Caribbean cultures emerged that reconfigured African beliefs, practices, and traditions in a New World setting. These cultures often merged with European traditions, especially because many slaves were converted to Christianity and most were forced to learn the language of their masters.

Resistance to slavery was a constant feature of life in the colonies. This ranged from day-to-day forms of resistance, such as working slowly, all the way to large-scale rebellions. Many slaves attempted to run away, and on larger islands, such as Jamaica and Hispaniola, some formed semiautonomous "Maroon" communities. While slave rebellions were common in the Caribbean, most ended in failure. In Saint-Domingue, however, unrest caused by the French Revolution resulted in a successful slave uprising—led by Toussaint L'Ouverture, a former slave—which culminated in the creation of the independent state of Haiti in 1804.

THE ENDING OF CARIBBEAN SLAVERY

In 1807 the British abolished the transatlantic slave trade after a popular campaign led mainly by wealthy evangelicals. This came at a time when slave-produced sugar was still profitable. In the British Caribbean, an economic slump followed the ending of the trade, partly as a result of the demographic impact of abolition. In the British Caribbean, slaves eventually gained emancipation in 1838 as the result of continued pressure in Britain and ongoing slave resistance in the Caribbean. In the remaining French territories of Martinique and Guadeloupe, slavery ended in 1848, while slaves in the Dutch Caribbean were freed in 1863.

The abolition of slavery did not end the tensions that characterized societies long based on racialized social and economic divisions. Emancipated slaves sought independence from the sugar estates. Former slaveholders used a range of tactics to try to retain the freed people's labor, limit their access to land, and prevent their involvement in political life, causing tensions that resulted in protests and riots in British Caribbean territories throughout the postemancipation period. Some planters, especially those in Trinidad and Guyana, responded to their labor problems by importing South and East Asian indentured workers. Many of these laborers settled permanently,

Seventeenth–Century Tilework in the Casa de Obrapia, Havana, Cuba. *Tilework depicts of a visit to the Plaza Vieja in Havana, Cuba.* © FRANCESCO VENTURI/CORBIS. REPRODUCED BY PERMISSION.

contributing to the social and cultural composition of those colonies.

Even as the sugar industry in the British and French Caribbean declined during the nineteenth century, Cuban production rose rapidly. Abundant fertile land, the removal of Spanish trade restrictions, and technological advances meant that the island experienced an economic boom that lasted until the late nineteenth century. Black slaves were used on Cuban plantations along with free workers from Europe, Asia, and Mexico, making the social structure and labor relations in the colony distinct from those in the British and French islands. Slavery survived in Cuba until the 1880s, when the institution was gradually phased out before a complete abolition in 1886.

SEE ALSO *Plantations, the Americas; Sugar Cultivation and Trade*

BIBLIOGRAPHY

Beckles, Hilary, and Verene Shepherd, eds. *Caribbean Freedom: Society and Economy from Emancipation to the Present.* Kingston, Jamaica: Ian Randle, 1993.

Knight, Franklin W. *The Caribbean: The Genesis of a Fragmented Nationalism*, 2nd ed. Oxford and New York: Oxford University Press, 1990.

Rogoziński, Jan. *A Brief History of the Caribbean: From the Arawak and the Carib to the Present*, rev. ed. London: Penguin, 2000.

Shepherd, Verene, and Hilary Beckles, eds. *Caribbean Slavery in the Atlantic World.* Kingston, Jamaica: Ian Randle, 2000.

Christer Petley

CARTAGENA DE INDIAS

Located on a magnificent bay on the northern coast of present-day Colombia and originally inhabited by Caribs, Cartagena de Indias was founded by the Spaniard Pedro de Heredia in 1533. From there, expeditions were launched to explore the interior of what became the kingdom of New Granada. By 1574 Cartagena had attracted sixteen *encomenderos* (those granted the right to extract tribute and labor from the native population) and hundreds of adventurers. Progressively eclipsing Santa Marta (founded in 1526), it became the port that monopolized the legal trade of northern South America, through the system of galleons importing Spanish goods and exporting gold and silver. Cartagena also had the monopoly of the slave trade to

Spanish South America. Between the sixteenth and the eighteenth centuries, some 120,000 African slaves arrived there to be "seasoned" before reaching further destinations. The capital of New Granada's Cartagena province, it had its own governor (appointed by the Spanish king) and bishop, and was home to one of the three Spanish-American headquarters of the Inquisition.

After falling prey to various pirates and buccaneers, Cartagena lastingly attracted English and Dutch contrabandists. In 1697, following a successful attack by Admiral Pointis, it was temporarily occupied by the French, and in 1741 it was besieged by the British. In response, Spain extended Cartagena's system of walls and fortifications and reformed its defense forces (which consisted of a regular army and white, mulatto, and black militia).

By 1778 Cartagena had 13,396 inhabitants: 27 percent were white, 57 percent were free people of color, and 16 percent were slaves (with women outnumbering men except among whites). In 1809 white creoles and free people of color united against Spanish domination, leading to the declaration of independence of November 11, 1811. Internal divisions and war against the royalist Santa Marta weakened Cartagena, however, and it was retaken by the Spaniards after a deadly siege in December 1815—only to be liberated anew by the patriot army in 1821. In the nineteenth and twentieth centuries, Cartagena lost its economic and political preeminence to Barranquilla, another Colombian port city.

SEE ALSO *Buccaneers; Empire in the Americas, Spanish; Slave Trade, Atlantic*

BIBLIOGRAPHY

Helg, Aline. *Liberty and Equality in Caribbean Colombia, 1770–1835.* Chapel Hill: University of North Carolina Press, 2004.

Lemaître, Eduardo. *Historia general de Cartagena,* 4 vols. Bogotá, Colombia: Banco de la República, 1983.

Aline Helg

CARTIER, JACQUES
1491–1557

A mariner from Saint-Malo in Brittany, France, Jacques Cartier had probably visited Brazil and Newfoundland before receiving a commission from King François I (1494–1547) in 1534 to undertake a voyage in search of treasure and a sea route to Asia. Following the established routes of French fishermen, Cartier sailed west to Newfoundland and then entered the Gulf of Saint Lawrence. He was consistently suspicious of the natives he encountered, referring to them as "wild and savage folk" and firing on them when they approached to trade.

Cartier's most important encounter occurred at Gaspé, where some Iroquoians from the Saint Lawrence River, led by Donnacona (d. ca. 1539), had established a summer fishing camp. Cartier's men erected a cross there with the king's coat of arms and gave presents to the Indians. The latter appeared to object strenuously to the captain's attempt to claim their land. Cartier attempted to assure them that his aims were friendly and then kidnapped two of Donnacona's sons before setting sail for France with them on board.

A new expedition set out in 1535 with the two Iroquoian boys pressed into service as interpreters and guides. They showed Cartier the entrance to the great river and led him up to their village, Stadacona, on the site of present-day Quebec City. Donnacona's people seemed intent on cementing an alliance and trade connection with the French; they actively discouraged them from further explorations that might undermine their own exclusive access to European goods. Brushing aside objections, Cartier took his men upstream in small boats to visit the large town of Hochelaga on the site of Montreal. Returning to Stadacona, the French built a fort and prepared to wait until spring.

The winter of 1535 to 1536 turned out to be cold beyond anything they could imagine; scurvy set in, and one by one the crew succumbed to the disease until Donnacona's son showed them how to brew an effective remedy from white cedar. Through this time of hunger and disease, Cartier remained suspicious of the Indians, ordering his men to go armed at all times, much to the consternation of his hosts. On leaving Stadacona in the spring, he took the precaution of seizing the two boys once again, along with Donnacona and a handful of others; hostages, guides, and living museum exhibits, the captive Iroquoians might have been useful to a future expedition had any of them survived.

Cartier did not return to Canada until 1541, when a third voyage was launched, much more ambitious than the others. Five ships carrying fifteen hundred men took part, and they came equipped to establish a French settlement colony. For obvious reasons, Cartier chose a site some distance to the west of Stadacona and ordered his men to fortify their settlement against the increasingly hostile natives of the country. The next spring, Jean-François de la Roque de Roberval (ca. 1500–1560), arrived to take charge of the colony and Cartier hastily deserted, carrying to France a cargo of worthless stones he thought were diamonds. The subsequent history of the colony, obscurely documented, appears to have been short and disastrous. The French would only return sixty years later to the country on which Cartier had bestowed the name Canada.

SEE ALSO *Empire, French; European Explorations in North America*

BIBLIOGRAPHY

Braudel, Fernand, ed. *Le monde de Jacques Cartier: L'aventure au XVIe siècle.* Montreal: Libre-expression, 1984.

Cook, Ramsay, ed. *The Voyages of Jacques Cartier.* Toronto: University of Toronto Press, 1993.

Gagnon, François Marc. *Jacques Cartier et la découverte du Nouveau Monde.* Quebec: Musée du Québec 1984.

Trudel, Marcel. "Cartier, Jacques." *Dictionary of Canadian Biography,* Vol. 1, 154–172. Toronto: University of Toronto Press, 1966.

Trudel, Marcel. *The Beginnings of New France, 1524–1663.* Toronto: McClelland and Stewart, 1973.

Allan Greer

CARTOGRAPHY

In the Middle Ages, few people in Christendom could ever have seen a map. Only those concerned with navigation or scholarship were in a position to come across one. Then, what they cast their eyes over were what historians have suggested were essentially two very different kinds of maps: area maps known as portolan charts, especially of southern European waters, as attempts to illustrate an itinerary or sailing instructions in diagrammatic form; secondly, and until the thirteenth century, European world maps, which had been devotional objects, intended to evoke God's harmonious design in a schematic form, appropriate, for instance, for an altarpiece.

These would appear very strange objects to today's public, encyclopedias of Christian lore and legend that were primarily symbolic reflections of the world and that tried to tailor what was genuinely known about the world to what could be gleaned from biblical scripture. The European cartographic revolution of the Renaissance took on many forms, embodied by great technological strides both in dissemination (printing) and production (the nautical revolution, mathematical innovations in how the world could be measured). But it was primarily a change in the way the world was pictured in people's minds, and here the cool, measured rationality of Euclidean geometry slowly came to replace the colorful mental projections of inherited belief.

The arrival of printing in the fifteenth century de-professionalized and democratized geographical knowledge. It did not fully supplant manuscript charts, which flourished in the cultures of secrecy in Iberian absolutist regimes, or the decorative maps that decked Florence's Palazzo Vecchio or the Vatican's Hall of Maps. The greater possibilities for divulgence, as well as the accompanying steps forward in literacy among European populations, meant that cartography could keep better pace with the geographical discoveries as they were being unveiled and break men of learning's enduring reluctance to accept that knowledge could be outdated.

Mapmaking capitalized on the nautical revolution of the thirteenth and fourteenth centuries, which saw the widespread adoption of the magnetic lodestone from the late twelfth century; the invention of Jacob's staff from 1300 for checking the heavens; and innovations in ship design, of which the most important was perhaps the sternpost rudder. Maritime navigation was given the tools to move on from coast-hugging to sailing boldly the open seas though, as the Seville pilot Pedro de Medina (1493–1567) expressed in print as late as 1555, it remained a mystery that "a man with a compass and rhumb lines can encompass and navigate the entire world." Maps, then, were an integral part of the nautical revolution.

It would be wrong, however, to see cartographic science as a set of progressive steps toward enlightenment. The illuminated medieval Arab worldview of geographers like ash-Sharif al-Idrisi (1100–1165), for example, as shown on a silver plate presented to King Roger II (1095–1154) of Sicily, was not necessarily passed on to mainland Europe. Secondly, second-century geographer Ptolemy's mistaken legacy of the impossibility to circumnavigate the southern tip of Africa—a corollary of the antique belief in the *orbis terrarum,* a planet constituted primarily of land in which the seas were little more than giant lakes—was only strengthened with the wave of Latin language editions following the reintroduction into Europe of Ptolemy's *Geography* from Constantinople. It was a mistake only gradually set right with the Portuguese voyages around the African shoreline from 1418 and which culminated with Bartolomeu Dias's (ca. 1450–1500) rounding of the Cape of Good Hope in 1496, faithfully reproduced in the world map of Henricus Martellus.

At the same time, it is easy to understand why Ptolemy's map, and particularly the geometric projection printed from 1477, served as the world map of Renaissance times, against all contemporary maps. The crucial concept is that of ordered space. Even the latest and most sophisticated of the circular *mappae mundi,* the Fra Mauro world map of 1459, appears to have an element of chance, guesswork, almost disorder in its structure. The circular framework was known to be illogical, the sources for its place-names were literary and anecdotal, even legendary, and their location was often arbitrary. Other maps, such as the Genoese map of 1457 drew from a store of graphic images, which by the late fifteenth century were largely rhetorical.

Waldseemüller's 1507 Map of the World. *This map by the German cartographer Martin Waldseemüller (ca. 1470–ca. 1522) is accompanied by text explaining the use of the term* America *to describe the New World. Waldseemüller named the continent after the Italian-born explorer Amerigo Vespucci, whose geography identified the Americas as separate from Asia.* © THE BRITISH LIBRARY/HIP/THE IMAGE WORKS. REPRODUCED BY PERMISSION.

By contrast Ptolemy appeared to have cast a transparent net over the earth's surface, every strand of which was precisely measured and placed. Moreover, Ptolemy's work was a map not a visual encyclopedia, so that a dispassionate sense of geographic reality prevails. This sense of ordered space was precisely the ideal toward what the artists of fifteenth-century Italy were striving, and where one can read Renaissance paintings like one reads a map, with a new emphasis on the spatial dimension.

The historian Felipe Fernández-Armesto has suggested that the undoing of the mythical Atlantic was perhaps cartography's greatest triumph in the fifteenth century. Islands named Brendan, St. Ursula, and Brazil had previously littered depictions and accounts of the medieval Atlantic, reflecting classical and early Christian legend. Over the course of the fifteenth century, Atlantic space was increasingly discovered and appreciated as a body of water in its own right and not just a section of the "all-encircling ocean," and the real mid-Atlantic archipelagos were plotted into it, initially using rhumb lines, but increasingly according to the grid-line geometrics of longitude and latitude. It took a long time, however, both before the full dimensions of the Atlantic were appreciated and before all fictitious islands were

removed from the Atlantic. As late as the nineteenth century, concessions were being made to presupposed rocks and islets.

To what degree Christopher Columbus's (1451–1506) landfall of October 12, 1492, on an island in the Bahamas was predicted by Western cartographic science is a lively point of discussion between historians. It is well known how the Florentine cosmographer Paolo Toscanelli dal Pozzo (1397–1482) suggested in a famous letter of June 1474 addressed to the Portuguese king that the distance from the Canaries to Cathay might be around 5,000 nautical miles, a journey possibly broken at Antilla and Japan—a chronic misguidance then. Columbus himself is thought to have had some doubts as to the Aristotelian model of the earth, as contested in 1483 and 1484 before Spanish royal cosmographers, natural philosophers who specialized in the relation of cosmic and terrestrial spheres and who based their claims on celestial observations. The fact that Ptolemy reduced the earth's circumference probably encouraged Columbus to "sail the parallel" to cross the Atlantic in 1492. In any case, only after some years of doubts and confusions was Columbus's discovery recognized by cosmographers and mapmakers for its novelty, rewarded with the epithet *Mundus Novus,* the title of a tract based on a letter of Amerigo Vespucci (1454–1512). It fell to the German geographer Martin Waldseemüller (1470–1518 or 1521) to put the suggestion into action on the large woodcut world map, printed in 1507 in one thousand copies, in which he showed North and South America as continents, designated by name. The implications of this New World scheme for shibboleths, such as the idea that all men were descended from Adam and that the apostles had preached throughout the world, was profound. Columbus, then, created the problem of the Western Hemisphere, though right down to his death he refused to admit to his delusion and only at the beginning of the eighteenth century was it shown conclusively through the expeditions of the Danish navigator, Vitus Jonassen Bering (1681–1741), that Asia was not connected to North America.

If the discovery of the Western Hemisphere was one problem Western mapmaking was confronted with, then the acknowledgement of the Antipodes was another. The ideas of the Greek cosmographer Strabo (64 or 63 BCE–23 CE)—in print in translation by Guarino da Verona (1370 or 1374–1460) from 1469—had fomented this idea, though he probably envisaged the Antipodes as lying to the west in the temperate sphere, rather than underneath, and an impediment to Eratosthenes's (276–194 BCE) view that sailing from Iberia directly to India was theoretically possible if the immensity of the Atlantic did not prevent it. The notion of a southern continent nevertheless persisted until Captain James Cook's (1728–1779) successive voyages in the 1760s and 1770s across the South Pacific explicitly sought to engage this last of the great classical cosmographical conundrums.

How maps reflected people's assumptions and beliefs is an engaging and fruitful line of recent scholarship. Maps in medieval times had been chiefly symbolic constructs reflecting the Holy Trinity in the three *pars* of which the world was constituted (Europe, Asia, Africa), suitably depicted around the form of a cross, Christ's cross. These have been called by historians T-O maps, where the "T" within the "O" is formed by the rivers Don and Nile flowing into the Mediterranean, these waters forming the boundaries of the three continents known to the ancient world. In deference to the Holy Land, not only churches but also maps were commonly oriented toward the east, at the head of which Christ was often depicted enthroned at the Last Judgment, as is the case in the Hereford *mappamundi* of circa 1300. Also at the top, but located within the bounds of this world, is the Garden of Eden. Jerusalem had previously been considered the center of the world; this is a reflection of Christian belief and the enduring concept of Christendom.

T-O maps continued to be produced well into Renaissance times, as in the *Rudimentum Novitiorum*

published in Lübeck in 1475. However, the first printed editions of Ptolemy to be published north of the Alps launched a profound onslaught on the last T-O maps, whereas the decline of the Christian commonwealth and the corresponding emergence of notions of Europe saw to it that Europe as a whole, rather than Jerusalem, came to be placed in the center of maps of the world. There were other changes, perhaps deeper motivational changes, casting aside the traditional T-O schema. By the fifteenth century, mapmakers were motivated by geographic realism, most probably because they wanted to emphasize the practical utility of their work as navigational aids, but they may also have been influenced by the same current of thought as the naturalism that influenced Renaissance artists. It no longer became perfunctory to see empty cartographic space as space to fill with all kinds of flourishes and emblems, as if fearing the emptiness of white sections of parchment. In any case, maps were no longer simply devotional objects, but came to record the progress in that European project which has become known as the Discoveries.

Maps had other strategic uses. The crusading propaganda of Marino Sanudo (1466–1536), for example, was illustrated with maps of uncanny accuracy, drawn by Pietro Vesconte, while the territorial rivalries of European states saw to it that from 1482 the first maps made with explicit attention to national boundaries started to be produced. Maps were of crucial importance in the protracted negotiations for the series of international treaties (Alcaçovas-Toledo, 1479; Tordesillas, 1494; Saragossa, 1529) that decided upon meridian lines establishing spheres of colonial influence between Portuguese and Spanish crowns. But at the same time we have to be aware that these strategic functions could impinge upon the mapmaker's task of reflecting reality as faithfully as possible. The French royal mathematician Oronce Fine (1494–1555), for example, devised a cordiform (heart-shaped) projection on a central meridian around 1536 in order to emphasize France's proximity to the new world and her colonial possibilities there. J. B. Harley has unearthed the coded relations of power in outwardly realistic Renaissance maps, showing how they concealed information for political or economic reasons, and used allegorical decoration to further hidden agendas. For example, blank spaces in early maps of the Americas presented those territories as available for European conquest. In some cases, what was reality was entirely relative. Matteo Ricci (1552–1610), the Italian Jesuit missionary to China, presented a world map to the governor of Chao-K'ing in 1584 titled "Great Map of Ten Thousand Countries," but had to spend the next nineteen years redesigning it, primarily to accommodate his host's desire for China to appear as the center of the world and not Europe.

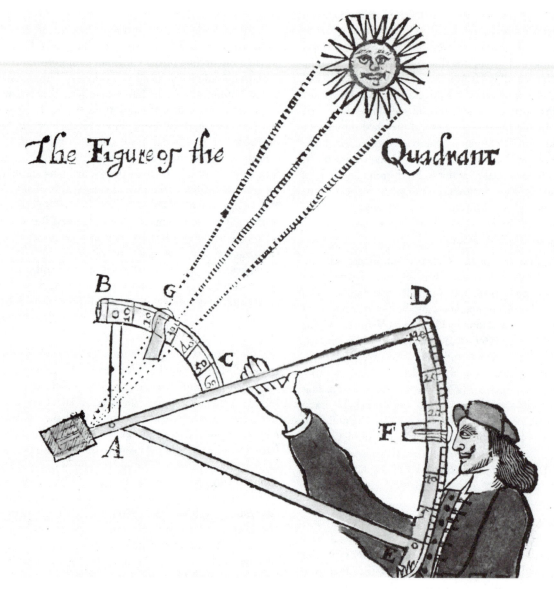

The Figure of the Quadrant

Quadrant. *Simple quadrants allowed early cartographers, as well as sailors and explorers, to accurately measure altitude and determine latitude.* **THE GRANGER COLLECTION, NEW YORK. REPRODUCED BY PERMISSION.**

That the world was a sphere was known throughout the Middle Ages and there is even some evidence that the question of map projection had been perceived as a theoretical problem, by Roger Bacon (1220–1292) for example in the Opus Major of circa 1270. But it had little practical importance, since the known world scarcely exceeded the bounds of Europe. It was only when new knowledge enlarged the world that cartography began to acknowledge the sphericity of the world in the elements of rough spectroscopy implicit in the Catalan Atlas of 1375 and the final settlement for the oval world map as we find in Francesco Rosselli's (1448–1513) world map

of 1508, or from the early seventeenth century spate of twin-hemisphere maps issuing from England and the Netherlands.

Globe-making, however, only really came into being following Nicholas de Oresma's (1320 or 1325–1382) *De sphaera*. Part of the project sought to illustrate the cosmographic scheme implicit in Ptolemy's *Geography*, which as we have suggested was widely disseminated once it had been translated into Latin in the fifteenth century. No medieval globe of the world has, however, survived from before Martin Behaim's (1436–1507) of 1492, now in the National Museum of Nuremberg.

Cartography, of course, specialized into many other branches. Some of the earliest maps we possess are medieval road maps, often for helping pilgrims find their way. The maritime variant was the rutter, which was of great service to pilots. The mid-sixteenth century governor of Portuguese possessions in the East, João de Castro (1500–1548), has left us some of the finest exemplars of this genre. One of the great cartographic particularities of the Age of Discovery, however, was the *isolario*, an atlas exclusively given over to charting the islands of the world, and for which the prototype was provided by Christopher Buondelmonti at the beginning of the fifteenth century, to be followed up by Benedetto Bordone (1460–1531) and Tommaso Porcacchi da Castiglione (1530–1585), as well as the French geographer André Thevet (1502–1590). It corresponded, as the Florentine scholar Leo Olschki has tried to show, to what he came to label *insulamania,* a passing social craze for islands.

Increasingly, maps catered to a variety of different professions. Landowners, particularly in England and the Low Countries, began commissioning estate plans to help them manage their holdings. It was not by chance, so historian David Buisseret argues, that it was precisely in these regions that the first signs of the Agricultural Revolution began to appear.

Governments were another patron of an increased outpouring of printed maps from the sixteenth century; they were typically required for the task of fortifying the frontiers, planning campaigns, acquainting heads of state with ill-known parts of their lands, and mounting overseas expeditions. Both in the lagoon and hinterland of the Venetian Republic, water management showed itself to be an important state activity delegated to the Rural Land Office and the Water Management Board for the Lagoon. Some monarchs, such as Philip II (1527–1598), who commissioned the *Relaciones Geográficas*, or Henry IV (1553–1610) of France, had access to maps that showed even small villages in the whole of their lands, while others such as the Habsburg Maximilian I (1493–1519), rather than commissioning maps of the empire as a whole, preferred to delineate only such separate constituents as Tyrol or Lower Austria. In the territories of eastern Europe, such as Poland, where magnates enjoyed "golden freedoms" and vast powers, particularly after the Law of Entail (1589), it was they, rather than the state, that commissioned maps.

Perhaps the most thorough of the state-sponsored exercises was the 1791 completion of the Ordinance Survey of Great Britain, as its name suggests, for military ends. Even before then, surveyors like James Rennell (1742–1830) had undertaken extensive surveys of British colonial possessions such as Bengal (culminating in his "Bengal Atlas" of 1779) on sophisticated graticules

of meridians and parallels, and which illustrated the progression in imperial thinking toward large-scale territorial domination in the East issuant from a period of intense rivalry between French and British interests for control of the lands of the Mughal empire. Rennell's maps of India produced between 1783 and 1788 illustrated the limits of British dominion and depicted the subcontinent as a coherent geographic entity for the first time. Other European imperial powers, such as France, rapidly followed suit. Napoléon Bonaparte's (1769–1821) survey of Egypt following invasion in 1798 was an explicit emulation, motivated by a desire to gain territorial compensation for France's loss of overseas colonies.

Cartography was also deployed as an accompaniment to the mania for travel guides and illustrated gazetteers of cities that engulfed Europe from the middle of the sixteenth century. Originally inspired by the ancients like Strabo and moderns like Flavio Biondo (1392–1463), early antiquarian *compendia* such as Leandro Alberti's (1479–1553) 1550 *Descrittione di tutta Italia* or Hartmann Schedel's (1440–1514) *Liber cronicarum* of 1492 commissioned bird's-eye views of towns, circular area maps, and illustrated maps to aid travelers.

It was in this manner that the uses of cartography, and also the readership of Renaissance maps, spread rapidly. Although maps still tended to be the preserve of the literate upper classes, they were not the preserve of kings only. Merchants, government officials, churchmen, and even sailors and artisans could obtain at least the simpler printed editions, though the maps of state-owned concerns such as the Dutch East India Company (from 1602), the Dutch West India Company (founded 1621), and the Hudson's Bay Company (1670) were still jealously protected as economic and state secrets. In this way, the cartographic way of seeing the world spread through the same sectors of early modern European society that purchased books and became literate. Maps became indispensable to Europeans' sense of space, and thus, Buisseret hints, to the process of modernization that began in the West in the Renaissance.

But as cartography catered to the needs of early modern society, with its specializations reflecting this, the mapping of the world went on at very different paces. The search for El Dorado and the Northwest Passage were reflected in an intense cartographic interest in these regions of the globe, whereas others waned. Desert regions were ignored, so that Sir Walter Raleigh (1554–1618), believing in and searching for a suitably empty spot on the map where to locate the terrestrial paradise, chose Mesopotamia. Although the external shape of the African continent was, as has been discussed, largely resolved by Bartholomeu Dias and subsequent Portuguese voyages at

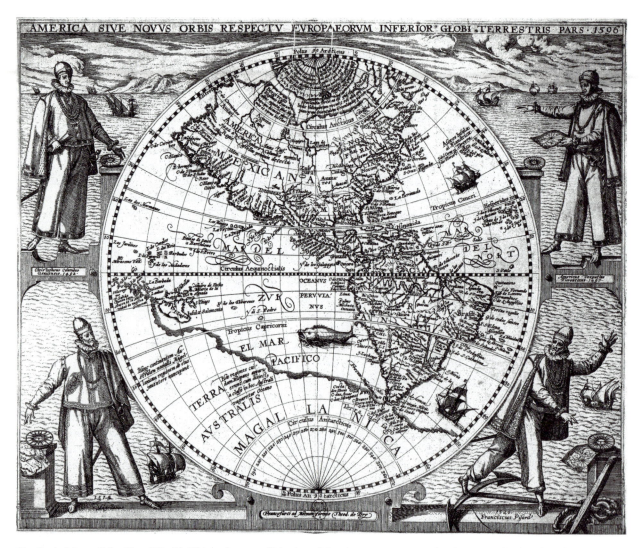

De Bry's Map of the New World. *This early map of North and South America was rendered in 1596 by the Flemish engraver Theodor de Bry (ca. 1527–1598).* **ROGER VIOLLET/GETTY IMAGES. REPRODUCED BY PERMISSION.**

the end of the fifteenth century, the African interior remained very much a blank space until the late eighteenth century, and cosmographers were forced to fall back on classical schemes as an aid, for example, in resolving questions such as the true sources of the Nile. It is probably for this reason that mythical constructs such as the Kingdom of Prester John were so slow to disappear from European maps as, for example, we find from Abraham Ortelius's (1527–1598) map of 1573. The vast spaces of the Pacific, as understood from Ferdinand Magellan's (1480–1521) epic circumnavigation of the world (1519–1521), were also only gradually revealed in the second half of the eighteenth century and, as historians like Alan Frost have pointed out, functioned as a second New World at the time of the European Enlightenment.

The next great cartographic leap is the work of the Flemish geographer Gerhardus Mercator (1512–1594), who tried in 1568 to solve a very practical problem, that of representing the globe as a flat surface on which courses could be logged and plotted. Basically he turned the globe into a cylinder. Cut down one side and unrolled, this produced a grid of lines of longitude and latitude that would always tell you where you were with reference to the poles. What it could not do was provide accurate comparisons of surface area because, of course, the ends of the cylinders are lines; the poles, though, should be points. Mercator's picture of the world therefore becomes very distorted as one sails a long way away from the equator. Although not universally approved, Mercator's projection provided a good scientific basis for the calculation of position and direction on the high seas. Subsequent work, such as Edward Wright's (1561–1615) correction for magnetic variations in the North Sea, was able to build on Mercator's legacy rather than require an entirely new platform.

Other problems remained for later generations to resolve. The inability to calculate longitude accurately, for example, which resulted in the east-west extensions of the Mediterranean and of North and South America, was initially approached nationally through the establishment of meridian lines running through the national observatory (founded in London 1675; Paris in 1699). This functioned as a basis for the first large-scale general maps of the nation. But as a more widely international and theoretical problem, the solution, as Dava Sobel has shown, was hit upon by five revolutionary timekeepers constructed between 1730 and 1770 by Yorkshireman John Harrison (1693–1776) in his single-minded pursuit of the £20,000 longitude prize offered by parliament.

While mapmakers struggled with the mathematical challenges of depicting the world in two dimensions, a number of scientific steps forward were made in the task of gathering information about the shape of the earth at a local level and transforming that information onto local maps, and then by way of coordinates on to a continuous projection. The mathematician Gemma Frisius (1508–1555) explained the construction of surveying techniques by means of triangulation in 1533, and what followed was a rapid rise in triangulated surveys serving primarily the practical task of defining boundaries, lines of property, and military fortifications, and from which certain conventions of descriptive geography emerged as well as a technical discussion as to the measuring and depiction of land in small scale. These were known as chorographic maps, and the discipline as chorography.

It is, however, one of the paradoxes of the Renaissance that it was not principally a scientific movement. Even the Ptolemaic revival was more of a literary event, a rediscovery of classical theory, whose content, as we have seen, was ultimately irrelevant to the fifteenth century. The most popular works on geography of the age, such as Sebastian Münster's (1489–1552) *Cosmographia* of 1544, were still essentially traditional topographic catalogues, rich with cultural features such as costumes and illustrations, and, as the French historian Frank Lestringeant has shown, by the end of the Renaissance was a genre in crisis. In cosmology, the classical, geometric model of the heavens with its interlocking spheres was still dominant. The experiment and discovery that were taking place in the projections of the maps, on the other hand, and the treatises from 1590 that dealt with this theme hardly mirrored the conservative world of the seafarers. Seafarers stuck to their unscientific plane-chart model, which was not built on a mathematical projection at all, but simply divided space evenly into squares or rectangles of one latitude degree by one longitude degree. In effect, these charts ignored the fact that the earth was a sphere.

In conclusion, the cartographic revolution of the Renaissance was a revolution that only went so far. Experience and reason were values and approaches much trumpeted, but did not completely outweigh inherited authority as a source of knowledge. Iconoclastic refusals to sanction the past that we find in the French cosmographer André Thevet, for example, were isolated voices. Secularization of the map as an object had certainly occurred and determined both its new form and its new social context. But even mathematicians like Mercator consciously presented traditional geographical thought and legend alongside the recent discoveries of his contemporaries.

SEE ALSO *Art, European; Dutch United East India Company; Dutch West India Company; Treaty of Tordesillas.*

BIBLIOGRAPHY

Brown, L.A. *The Story of Maps.* New York: Dover Publications, 1979.

Buisseret, David, ed. *Monarchs, Ministers, and Maps: the Emergence of Cartography as a Tool of Government in Early Modern Europe.* Chicago: University of Chicago Press, 1992.

Buisseret, Davis. *The Mapmaker's Quest: Depicting New Worlds in Renaissance Europe.* Oxford: Oxford University Press, 2003.

Fernández-Armesto, Felipe. *Before Columbus: Exploration and Colonisation from the Mediterranean to the Atlantic, 1229–1492.* Basingstoke, England: Macmillan Education, 1987.

Lestringeant, Frank. *André Thevet. Cosmographe des derniers Valois.* Genève: Droz, 1991.

Sobel, Dava. *The Illustrated Longitude.* New York: Walker, 1998.

Whitfield, Peter. *The Image of the World. Twenty Centuries of World Maps.* San Francisco: Pomegranate Artbooks, 1994.

Stefan Halikowski Smith

CARTOGRAPHY IN THE COLONIAL AMERICAS

Although Norse voyagers such as Leif Eriksson, who first crossed the North Atlantic to the Americas around 1000 CE, did not use other than mental maps, physical cartography has been an important part of European transatlantic discovery, exploration, and colonialism since at least the fifteenth century. Over the centuries, better maps contributed significantly to the European and eventual American outreach to, and competition for, empire in the Atlantic world and beyond. The center of the map trade followed these imperial developments from Lisbon and Seville to Antwerp and Amsterdam, Paris, London, and Philadelphia, Washington, DC, and Chicago.

In the fifteenth century, three important cartographic practices came together in Europe to lay the foundation for modern mapmaking. Aspects of the medieval traditions of the *mappamundi* (Christian diagrammatic world maps) and the *portolans* (amazingly accurate coastal charts, primarily for commerce) merged and were profoundly influenced by the reappearance of the *Geographia* by the second-century Roman geographer Claudius Ptolemy.

The *Geographia* not only described the known world, but it also provided instructions on how to make maps with projections and locational grid systems of longitude and latitude. During the Middle Ages, the *Geographia* had been lost to Europe but not to the Islamic world, where it was preserved, studied, and expanded. In the early 1400s it reappeared in Arabic and was translated into Latin and various vernacular languages, then disseminated across Europe via the new technology of mechanical printing on rag paper. In the last quarter of the fifteenth century, various editions contained new "Ptolemaic maps" of the world and its parts printed from woodblocks (200 to 300 copies) and hand colored.

The 1500 manuscript chart of the New World by Juan de la Cosa (d. 1510), pilot to Columbus on the *Santa Maria* in 1492, is the oldest surviving map to show a part of North America. But "America" was first named on a large Ptolemaic map of the world published in 1507 by the German mapmaker Martin Waldseemüller (ca. 1470–1518) in Saint Dié, Lorraine, along the French-German border. Apparently ignorant of the discovery of Christopher Columbus (1451–1506), Waldseemüller named the New World after the Italian explorer-geographer Amerigo Vespucci (1454–1512), whose geography of it actually identified the Americas as separate from Asia. Once informed about Columbus, Waldseemüller apologized and removed the name *America* from the later editions of his maps, but other cartographers, including Gerardus Mercator (1512–1594), had begun to use the name and it soon became accepted.

Waldseemüller also published an edition of Ptolemy in 1513 that included the first printed map of the Atlantic Basin. In 1569 Mercator, who was the author of many important maps, created the Mercator projection, a method of showing the three-dimensional world on a two-dimensional map that satisfied many of the requirements of explorers and other mariners.

From the first Portuguese expeditions down the West African coast and Columbus's great voyage of discovery, the European nations considered cartographic information to be critical to the maintenance and expansion of their empires. Until the eighteenth century, the data on the now-lost *Padrón real*—the constantly updated master map of the growing Spanish American and Asian empires in the *Casa de la contratación de la Indias* (House of the Indies) in Seville—was closely, albeit not always successfully, guarded as a state secret. Cartographic espionage for American particulars was common between the European powers. The now quite rare 1534 woodcut map of the New World by the Venetian geographer and historian Giovanni Battista Ramusio (1485–1557) is in part based on these Spanish secrets and gives some indication of the state of Spanish knowledge of the Americas at that time.

In their early maps of the Americas, the Spanish and other Europeans also relied on Native American maps and knowledge of the interior, but as they explored more extensively, the Indian information and place names gradually disappeared from American maps. Cartography greatly helped Spain preserve its near monopoly over much of the New World in the sixteenth and seventeenth centuries, for to map a place was not only to better know and explain it, but also to claim it.

The first wide public distribution of American cartographic imagery across Europe came in the first modern atlas, *Theatrum orbis terrarum* (Theater of the World), published in Antwerp by the Flemish cartographer Abraham Ortelius (1527–1598) in multiple editions in various languages from 1570 to 1644. The maps were struck from engraved copperplates, which had come to replace woodblocks and provided finer but still hand-colored images, as well as more copies (500 to 600) per plate. In the eighteenth and nineteenth centuries, zinc and steel plates were also employed for similar reasons.

Each successive edition of the *Theatrum orbis terrarum* was an immediate best-seller. The American maps in the atlas showed the discoveries of Spanish, Portuguese, French, and English explorers, the conquests in Mexico and Peru, and the information gathered by the remarkable *entradas* (Spanish exploratory expeditions) into North America led by Álvar Núñez Cabeza de Vaca (ca. 1490–1560), Francisco Vásquez de Coronado (ca. 1510–1554), and Hernando de Soto (ca. 1500–1542). The *Theatrum orbis terrarum* contained the first regional maps (Mexico and the Caribbean) of the Americas, and each new updated edition revealed more and more to its readers about the New World and the growth of Europe's empires there. Ortelius inaugurated the great age of Dutch cartography, which spanned late into the seventeenth century.

Ortelius's Map of the New World. *This early map of North and South America, by the Flemish mapmaker Abraham Ortelius, was first published in the atlas Theatrum orbis terrarum* (Theater of the World) *in 1570.* © **FINE ART PHOTOGRAPHIC LIBRARY/CORBIS. REPRODUCED BY PERMISSION.**

In the seventeenth and eighteenth centuries, the Europeans explored deeper into the Americas, and their maps correspondingly reflected additional knowledge of the New World. These same maps also began to show the demarcations of the European empires in the Americas more clearly, although not necessarily more accurately. The borders between the Russian, Spanish, and British territories in the Pacific Northwest were precisely drawn lines on maps, but in reality they were much more vague; so too were those between the Portuguese and Spanish domains in Amazonia, for example.

There was no more blatant a situation of "cartographic imperialism" than between Spain and France in the heartland of North America. The age of the *entradas* had extended the boundaries of New Spain northward from Hernando Cortés's (1484–1547) Mexico to present-day California, New Mexico, Texas, and beyond. The French based their claims to New France and Louisiana on the explorations of the Belgium missionary Louis

Hennepin (ca. 1626–1705), French explorer Sieur de La Salle (1643–1687), and others in the Mississippi Valley and Gulf of Mexico.

In the absence of reliable published Spanish maps, French royal cartographers such as Marco Vincenzo Coronelli (1650–1718), Nicolas Sanson (1600–1667), and Guillaume Delisle (1675–1726) took the opportunity to move the boundary of Louisiana westward from the Sabine and Red Rivers to the Rio Grande, thereby claiming much of Spanish Texas. Other popular mapmakers whose countries were not directly involved in the area, such as the British geographers Herman Moll (d. 1732) and Thomas Jefferys (ca. 1710–1771), readily accepted and copied the highly respected French maps, while at the same time disputing the French maps over the border between Canada and New England and Spanish maps over the border between the Carolinas and Florida.

Somewhat later, the new United States under President Thomas Jefferson (1743–1826) employed similar cartographic tactics in defining the border with Spanish Florida and the extent of the Louisiana Purchase at the expense of Spain and Britain. Consequently, in the late eighteenth century, Spain was forced at considerable cost to further explore, evaluate, map, and fortify the northern and eastern frontiers of New Spain and other parts of its New World empire.

Additionally, in the period between the end of the Thirty Years' War in 1648 and the start of the American Revolution in 1776, a series of conflicts between shifting coalitions of powers, such as the Seven Years' War (1756–1763), took place in Europe, all of which had counterparts, such as the French and Indian War (1754–1763), in the Americas. Thus, military mapping in the Americas gained importance and increased substantially. Contemporary printed maps, on the other hand, served as a major source of information about these distant colonial wars for a still largely illiterate European public.

In the second half of the eighteenth century, maps became more scientific and otherwise reflective of the Enlightenment. The use of triangulation and of advanced mathematics, such as trigonometry and calculus, in surveying made maps more accurate and authoritative. Similarly, the introduction in the 1770s of English inventor John Harrison's (1693–1776) chronometer for the correct determination of longitude at sea, which was dependent on real time measurement, substantially influenced not only navigation but also more precise place location. Adhering to the principle of simplicity through fine engraving and the abandonment of ornate decorations, excess color, and other distractions that had been especially prevalent in Dutch and French cartography, Enlightenment maps emphasized content over appearance.

Furthermore, lithography was introduced and gradually replaced metal plate printing to emerge as the major method of map reproduction of the nineteenth century. With this new technology and the growing use of pulp paper, many more color images could be produced per lithographic stone at far less cost. Lithography was readily compatible with the national political, economic, social, and military cartographic demands of the expanding, democratic, new United States and other countries that developed out of and broke up the European empires in the Americas in the nineteenth century.

SEE ALSO *Cartography; Columbus, Christopher.*

BIBLIOGRAPHY

Buisseret, David. *The Mapmakers' Quest: Depicting New Worlds in Renaissance Europe.* Oxford and New York: Oxford University Press, 2003.

Merás, Luisa Martín. *Cartografía marítima hispana: La imagen de América.* Barcelona, Spain: Lunwerg, 2000.

Reinhartz, Dennis, and Gerald D. Saxon. *The Mapping of the Entradas into the Greater Southwest.* Norman: University of Oklahoma Press, 1998.

Schwartz, Seymour I., and Ralph E. Ehrenberg. *The Mapping of America.* New York: H. N. Abrams, 1980.

Dennis Reinhartz

CATHOLIC CHURCH IN IBERIAN AMERICA

By the time Christopher Columbus (1451–1506) first reached the Caribbean on October 12, 1492, the kingdoms of Spain had been united under the Catholic monarchs Ferdinand (1452–1516) and Isabella (1451–1504). The last Muslim kingdom, Granada, had surrendered in January of that same year. The move towards unification had been encouraged by the marriage of Ferdinand and Isabella in 1469, but it was above all the Catholic religion that conferred a universal character on the monarchy.

The campaign against Granada coincided with an internal campaign against heresy, specifically directed against lapsed converts from Judaism to Christianity, known as *conversos.* The apparent threat they posed to the faith led to the establishment of the Inquisition in 1478. In March 1492, only two months after the fall of Granada, the Spanish Crown issued an edict that gave the Jewish community the stark choice of conversion or exile. While many thousands did convert—many of them, most probably, out of expediency—great numbers also chose exile.

After the Christian occupation of Granada, the monarchs appointed Fray Hernando de Talavera (1428–1507) as the first archbishop of Granada. His respect for the terms of "capitulation," which gave Muslims the right to continue to practice their religion, even allowing for the protection of Christian converts to Islam, earned him both the admiration of the newly assimilated population and the harsh criticism of members of the hierarchy, such as the archbishop of Toledo, Francisco Jiménez de Cisneros (1436–1517). In 1499 Cisneros sidelined Talavera and began a much more forceful policy of conversion involving the persecution of apostates, burnings of the Koran, and mass baptism. His contravention of the capitulations caused riots in Granada and a revolt in the Alpujarras that swiftly spread throughout the region. Once Ferdinand had put down the rebellion, the capitulations were dissolved and the Muslim population was given the same choice that had been given to the Jews in 1492.

Meanwhile, in the newly discovered lands across the Atlantic, Columbus seemed impressed by the suitability of the native peoples for conversion to Christianity. As a result, in 1493 Pope Alexander VI (1431–1503) issued a bull in favor of the rights of the Spanish monarchs over all the lands already discovered by Columbus and any more as yet unknown beyond a line 100 leagues (about 555 kilometers, or 345 miles) west of the Azores in the North Atlantic and the Cape Verde Islands off the western coast of Africa, on the condition that the indigenous peoples were evangelized. That same year, a number of priests and friars under the leadership of Bernal Boyl (ca.1440–1507) accompanied Columbus on his second voyage, but it was not until the beginning of the sixteenth century that formal missionary activity began to have an impact. Meanwhile, in 1494, with papal agreement, the Treaty of Tordesillas redrew the line of demarcation between Spain and Portugal to 370 leagues (about 2,055 kilometers, or 1,277 miles) west of the Cape Verde Islands, unwittingly including the yet-to-be-discovered Brazil within Portuguese jurisdiction.

Papal bulls in 1501 and 1504 establishing new dioceses and granting the Spanish Crown the right to tithes from the new territories were followed by Pope Julius II's (1443–1513) bull of 1508, the *Patronato Real* (Right of Patronage), granting the Spanish monarchs full control over the Catholic Church in the Americas, including the appointment of bishops. In 1574 King Philip II (1527–1598) redefined the Right of Patronage as perpetual and inviolable, effectively excluding the papacy from interference with royal authority over ecclesiastical institutions in the Americas. The Portuguese Crown received its Right of Patronage in 1522, and the first bishop in Brazil was appointed to the newly created diocese of Bahia in 1551. Both Spain and Portugal directed church appointments and policy in the Americas through the use of councils: in Spain, the Royal Council for the Indies; in Portugal, the Ultramarine Council, together with the Table (literally, *Mesa*) of Conscience and Orders.

Given the speed with which vast territories were incorporated and the difficulty of maintaining lines of communication between the Iberian Peninsula and the Americas, it was no mean task to establish an entirely new ecclesiastical structure that functioned alongside secular institutions. As a result of the Portuguese pre-occupation with the African spice route to the Indies, the colonization of Brazil and the subsequent expansion of the Catholic Church were much slower than those of Spanish America and were also hindered by the Dutch occupation of Bahia between 1630 and 1654.

In 1511 the local Hispanic population of Santo Domingo was scandalized when the Dominican friar,

Antonio de Montesinos, preached a sermon that accused them of being in a state of mortal sin for their cruel treatment of the indigenous population. His sermon addressed a pressing issue in the Caribbean, where disease, slavery, and exploitation had practically depopulated the archipelago. Queen Isabella had already taken exception to Columbus enslaving Indians (her vassals) and distributing them among the Spanish settlers. However, the capture and Christianization of indigenous peoples was encouraged and even institutionalized under the *encomienda*, an institution that allowed Spaniards to be granted the labor of a number of Indians on the condition that they were well treated and given catechesis.

Montesinos's sermon marked the beginning of a long campaign against the *encomienda* system and the enslavement of Indian populations. The polemic led to the issuing of the Laws of Burgos in 1512, which regulated the treatment of native peoples in an attempt to prevent abuse. Largely due to the efforts of the Dominican friar Bartolomé de las Casas (1474–1566), the phasing out of *encomiendas* was formally initiated with the promulgation of the New Laws in 1542. The controversy continued throughout the colonial period, sometimes even turning into armed conflict, as between the Jesuit-Guaraní missions of Paraguay and the *bandeirantes* (armed groups of slavers) from São Paulo, Brazil, in the seventeenth century. During the eighteenth century this fed into a wider antagonism between church and state.

With the conquest of Mexico in 1519, the optimism that had accompanied the conquest of Granada resurfaced. Initially, responsibility for the spiritual welfare of the population lay with the regular orders, especially the Franciscans, the Dominicans, and the Augustinians, all of whom showed a genuine concern for the protection of the indigenous peoples from the more devastating effects of colonial exploitation. Nevertheless, this did not prevent disputes arising over methods of evangelization and jurisdiction over parishes. The Franciscan approach favored mass baptisms to confer God's grace on the people alongside the establishment of schools and catechesis in indigenous languages. The Dominicans, however, contested that mass baptisms without previous and thorough catechesis would lead inevitably to apostasy and idolatry.

As the conquest continued, and dioceses were founded across Spanish America (for example, Panama in 1511, Mexico in 1530, Oaxaca in 1535, and Quito in 1546—the same year that Mexico, Lima, Bogotá, and Santo Domingo were made into archdioceses), seminaries and universities were instituted to train new priests in theology, philosophy, canon law, and classical and

Church of Saint Michael Archangel, Mexico. *Catholic dioceses were founded across Spanish America during the mid-1500s, and numerous churches were constructed in the years that followed.* © DANNY LEHMAN/CORBIS. REPRODUCED BY PERMISSION.

indigenous languages. As the numbers of the secular clergy increased, bishops were able to establish cathedral chapters and appoint clergy as parish priests (*doctrineros*) to outlying towns. Gradually, secular clergy replaced the regular orders as priests to indigenous parishes. Subsequent disputes over regular and secular parish boundaries and the numbers of indigenous parishioners were not uncommon. Alongside the *corregidor* (crown judicial representative) and the *cacique* (official indigenous leader), the local parish priest was one of the most powerful figures in the town.

The relationship between church and state was not always felicitous. Notwithstanding the *Patronato Real*, the clergy were not above voicing criticisms. In the 1570s, for example, Viceroy Francisco de Toledo (1515–1584) of Peru came under severe criticism for ordering the execution of the last Inca, Túpac Amaru. During the Hapsburg period (1516–1700), therefore, church and state were mutually interdependent but separate enough to act as a check on each other's power: Both, in their own way, represented the monarch. With the onset of regalist

reforms during the Bourbon period (1700–ca.1812), the delicate balance between church and state was overturned as the state attempted to weaken the power of religious orders, take control of education and social welfare, and appropriate collective wealth.

The most significant attack was directed against the Society of Jesus (the Jesuits), whose influence in the field of education was second to none and whose collective wealth and powerful semiautonomous missions flew in the face of Bourbon ideas about the defense of private property under the direct control of the state. The expulsion of the Society of Jesus (in 1759 from Portuguese lands and in 1767 from Spanish ones) caused much ill-feeling among the general populace. Moreover, since the majority of Jesuits were Creoles, the expulsion encouraged the growth of an identification with a land that was not Spain and which should not be subject to Spanish rule.

Conflict between peninsular Spaniards and Creoles had increased over the years with growing frustration at the tendency to place Spaniards in positions of authority over equally (and perhaps more) capable Creoles. As rebellions and independence movements gained momentum, lesser clergy were often able to act as a bridge between the ideals of the Creole elite and the social aspirations of their campesino, and often largely indigenous, parishioners. Numerous clergy participated in the Túpac Amaru rebellions of the 1780s across the central and southern Andes, and, in fact, two heroes of the 1810 precursor to Mexican independence, Miguel Hidalgo (1753–1811) and José María Morelos (1765–1815), were priests.

After independence, social groups vied for positions of influence in the new regimes. Governments attempted to assume the continuation of the *Patronato Real*, but soon the Catholic Church found itself out of alignment with the Liberal thought of the ruling elites, who increasingly undermined the church as an archaic and anti-modern institution.

SEE ALSO *Christianity and Colonial Expansion in the Americas.*

BIBLIOGRAPHY

Barnadas, Josep M. "The Catholic Church in Colonial Spanish America." In *The Cambridge History of Latin America*, Vol. 1, edited by Leslie Bethell, 511–540. Cambridge, U.K.: Cambridge University Press, 1984.

Brading, D. A. "Bourbon Spain and its American Empire." In *The Cambridge History of Latin America*, Vol. 1, edited by Leslie Bethell, 389–439. Cambridge, U.K.: Cambridge University Press, 1984.

Dussel, Enrique, ed. *The Church in Latin America, 1492–1992.* Tunbridge Wells, U.K.: Burns & Oates; Maryknoll, NY: Orbis, 1992.

Elliot, J. H. "Spain and America in the Sixteenth and Seventeenth Centuries." In *The Cambridge History of Latin America*, Vol. 1, edited by Leslie Bethell, 287–339. Cambridge, U.K.: Cambridge University Press, 1984.

Elliot, J. H. "The Spanish Conquest and Settlement of America." In *The Cambridge History of Latin America*, Vol. 1, edited by Leslie Bethell, 149–206. Cambridge, U.K.: Cambridge University Press, 1984.

Harvey, Leonard Patrick. *Islamic Spain, 1250–1500.* Chicago: University of Chicago Press, 1990.

Hoornaert, Eduardo. "The Catholic Church in Colonial Brazil." In *The Cambridge History of Latin America*, Vol. 1, edited by Leslie Bethell, 541–556. Cambridge, U.K.: Cambridge University Press, 1984.

Kamen, Henry. *The Spanish Inquisition: An Historical Revision.* London: Weidenfield and Nicolson, 1997.

Schwaller, John F., ed. *The Church in Colonial Latin America.* Wilmington, DE: Scholarly Resources, 2000.

Andrew Redden

CENSORSHIP

Dissident historical views on Western colonialism were regularly censored, and historians and others holding such views were often persecuted. In the following entry, a representative sample of these dissident views is discussed. The examples are taken from a continuously updated worldwide database of the censorship of history covering views produced between 1945 and 2005. To demarcate this survey more precisely, it is worth noting that it is *not* on censorship of views prior to 1945; *nor* on Eastern colonialism; *nor* on precolonial history; *nor* on powers that annexed other territories; *nor* on minorities or majorities whose past is labeled (semi)colonial by some of their members; *nor* on independent states whose past is labeled (semi)colonial by opposition members or as subject to imperialist influences by the government; *nor* on independence as a result of partition instead of colonialism; *nor* on occupation during a war.

After a look at the evidence for archival destruction, cases of censorship of professional and popular history will be reviewed. Three groups of censors are considered: colonial powers, former colonial powers, and former colonies. Discussion of these groups is centered around three themes: colonialism in general, its start (the conquest and accompanying crimes), and its end (anticolonial resistance and nationalism).

DESTRUCTION, REMOVAL, AND SECRECY OF COLONIAL ARCHIVES

Archives form the infrastructure of historical research. There is a long—by its very nature poorly documented—history of archival destruction by colonial powers. Although they fall outside the chronological scope of this entry, it is tempting to recall first two early examples from Mexico and Congo.

In the fifteenth century the Aztecs of Mexico destroyed documents not in line with their view of the past, which endorsed continuation of the revered Toltec civilization. One century later, Spanish conquistadores burned the pagan Aztec and Mayan archives.

In the mid-nineteenth century Portuguese colonists set fire to the archive of the kings of Congo, built up since the sixteenth century. When this territory (together with other regions) became the Congo Free State (1885–1908) and the private possession of the Belgian king, Leopold II (1835–1909), the possible transfer to Belgium of sovereignty over Congo was discussed twice, in 1895 and in 1906 to 1907. Leopold II gave detailed instructions to destroy or transfer to the royal palace the archives of the Congo. "Je leur donnerai mon Congo, mais ils n'ont pas le droit de savoir ce que j'y ai fait" ("I shall give them my Congo, but they have no right to know what I have done there"), he said. It is estimated that probably half of the population died in Leopold's Congo. The surviving archives were examined by German forces occupying Belgium during World War I, but the archives were subsequently treated carelessly until the late 1940s.

Within the survey period of this entry, cases of colonial mismanagement of archives are documented for Africa and the Caribbean. In Kenya, many official records on the Mau Mau rebellion (1952–1956) were destroyed by the British before independence. When in 1962 Algeria became independent, the French government exported all the official documents they could to France, thus taking with them vital sources of Algerian history. In what was to become Zimbabwe, much material relating to African history and to the activities of Africans was removed from the files open to the public at the national archives after the emergence of the Rhodesia Front government in 1962, an act glossed over by recataloguing. From 1979 to 1980 the Rhodesian government destroyed documents produced by its security and intelligence services.

Switching to the Caribbean, a recent case was the postponement in late 2000 of the publication of an official history of Dutch decolonization policy in the Caribbean between 1940 and 2000, written by Gert Oostindie and Inge Klinkers. Quoting too abundantly from the post–1975 Dutch Council of Ministers minutes and other top-level documents, the authors had to delete certain data, particularly data concerning the personal policy views of politicians and civil servants, before the volumes could be published in mid–2001.

Evidence that former colonies destroyed colonial archives is sporadic. Under Equatorial Guinea's first president, Francisco Macías Nguema (1924–1979), for example, school textbooks of the colonial period and large parts of the national archive were condemned as "imperialist" and publicly burned.

CENSORSHIP BY COLONIAL POWERS

Colonial powers did not welcome unfavorable interpretations of their rule, as the following examples about the British and Portuguese show.

In India, the British banned Marxist-inspired "economic-nationalist" interpretations of Indian history, such as pleas for economic independence based on historical arguments and criticism of "landlordism" and nineteenth-century deindustrialization, at schools and universities. The 1946 edition of W. C. Smith's *Modern Islam in India: A Social Analysis*, published in London and describing the transformation of the traditional Muslim community into a modern society during the preceding seventy-five years, was not allowed into India because of its alleged communist approach, despite the fact that an

earlier edition had been published in Lahore in 1943. A pirated version appeared without the author's consent in 1954, after Pakistan's independence, again in Lahore.

Interestingly, two of India's leaders wrote histories while staying in British prisons: Future prime minister Jawaharlal Nehru (1889–1964) wrote *The Discovery of India,* and future president Rajendra Prasad (1884–1963) authored *India Divided.* Both works were published in 1946. The latter book, arguing from an Indian nationalist viewpoint but emphasizing unity between the historical traditions and political ideals of Hindus and Muslims, went through three editions before India's partition in 1947. Before his *Discovery,* Nehru had also written a world history in prison.

In 1962 Portugal declared British historian Charles Boxer persona non grata for drawing attention to Portugal's record of control in its colonies in a series of lectures in the United States. Boxer denied the frequent assertion of Prime Minister António Salazar (1889–1970) that the Portuguese had always had good relations with black Africans and that the latter were themselves Portuguese; Boxer showed that most colonizers believed in white superiority and that race prejudice prevailed. In an earlier paper, he described seventeenth-century Portugal as a "disintegrating power." Portuguese historian Armando Cortesão suggested that Boxer return his (many) Portuguese honors. The Portuguese press labeled Boxer dishonest, and his books were no longer sold. His 1969 classic, *The Portuguese Seaborne Empire, 1415–1925,* was not translated into Portuguese until 1977. In 1954 British journalist and historian of Africa Basil Davidson experienced an episode similar to Boxer's.

Colonial conquests were very sensitive events, especially when accompanied by atrocities, as demonstrated by examples from the United States and Belgium. As a student, the future dissident and revisionist Philippine historian Renato Constantino was briefly arrested in 1939 and interrogated by the American colonial authorities at Fort Santiago in Manila because he had written an article exposing American atrocities perpetrated against the Filipino population during the "pacification campaign" of 1899 to 1902. Constantino was released after he declared that his source was *The Conquest of the Philippines by the United States, 1898–1925* (1926), a book published uncensored in New York by Moorfield Storey and Marcial Lichauco in 1926. This incident made Constantino determined to reexamine Philippine history.

In 1959 (a year before the independence of the Belgian Congo) the Belgian Royal Academy of Colonial Sciences refused twice to publish papers of its member, historian and missionary Edmond Boelaert, because they contained evidence of abuses committed in the early phases of Congo's colonization. The papers were eventually published long after Congo's independence—and the author's death—in 1988 and 1995 respectively.

Research into anticolonial resistance and nationalism had the power to demonstrate that the colonized possessed historical agency, and such research therefore demolished part of the ethnocentric legitimation upon which colonial power rested. In Australia, a dissertation by Allan Healy critically approaching the history of Australian colonial control over Papua New Guinea (which lasted until 1975) and presenting the case for more rapid political devolution of power was put under lock and key in the library of the Australian National University between 1959 and 1962. In the French Maghreb, a region in northwestern Africa, research in contemporary history was ignored for being too sensitive. In 1952 the sale of French historian Charles-André Julien's new book, *North Africa on the March: Muslim Nationalism and French Sovereignty,* was blocked by the colonial administration after it aroused controversy for its anticolonialist stance. Julien's first book, *History of North Africa: From the Arab Conquest to 1830* (1931), which supported demands of North African nationalists for colonial reform, had already earned him the hostility of many French in the Maghreb.

In 1967 Terence Ranger, a British historian deported from Rhodesia in 1963, published *Revolt in Southern Rhodesia 1896–97: A Study in African Resistance.* It became a classic history of the Chimurenga revolt—the Shona name for the 1896 to 1897 uprisings of the Ndebele and Shona people against the imposition of British colonial rule—and inspired blacks to compare the revolt with their own uprising against the Rhodesian regime after its 1965 Unilateral Declaration of Independence from Britain. Ranger's book was banned until independence in 1980. Ironically, the Rhodesian army reportedly used it as a textbook in counterinsurgency.

CENSORSHIP BY FORMER COLONIAL POWERS

After independence was granted to their colonies, Western countries remained sensitive to statements about their former colonial role. For example, *Years of the Century,* a 1979 Portuguese television series that included a personal view of the Estado Novo (New State; the Portuguese dictatorial regime from 1932 to 1974) by a left-wing historian, was canceled after complaints from the Catholic Church about the first episode. The film explicitly attacked the Catholic hierarchy's support of the Estado Novo repression of black nationalists.

The first stages of colonization proved to be problematic in Australia, Germany, and Belgium. In June 1992, in *Mabo and Others v. State of Queensland,* the Australian High Court recognized that the concept of *terra nullius* (Australia as "a land of no one" before European settlement began in 1788) was a fiction, thereby strengthening Aboriginal claims to ancestral lands. This "Mabo judgment" (after Aboriginal leader Eddie Mabo [1936–1992]), called historic, reversed a historical view of Australia's past in which the role of Aboriginals was downplayed. The ruling led to protracted debates—known as the "History Wars" and yet unfinished—about British colonialism in Australia and the fate of the Aboriginals.

In Germany, a journalist who in 1965 attacked the *Koloniallegende* (the emphasis on Germany's achievements in its pre-1918 colonies without mentioning the violence) on television received death threats. Another person living abroad had to cope with censorship threats by the German foreign office after pointing out parallels between the genocide of the native Herero in German South-West Africa (present-day Namibia) in 1904 and that of the Jews and the Poles in Europe during World War II.

For the Belgians, the crimes against humanity committed in the Congo Free State remained a sensitive subject until well into the 1980s. Beginning in 1975 diplomat Jules Marchal published several books in Dutch and French on those crimes under a pseudonym. For eight years he could not gain access to the archives of the Belgian Ministry of Foreign Affairs.

In another case, retired Lieutenant-General Émile Janssens, chief of staff of the Force Publique (the army in the Belgian Congo) until 1960 and president of the patriotic committee Pro Belgica (established in 1980 to commemorate the 1830 foundation of Belgium) wrote a letter in 1986 to the minister of national education about historian and anthropologist Daniel Vangroenweghe. Janssens accused Vangroenweghe of libeling King Leopold II in his 1985 Dutch-language book *Red Rubber: Leopold II and His Congo* by writing about the crimes committed in the Congo Free State. Janssens also questioned Vangroenweghe's position as a secondary-school history teacher. When members of parliament supporting Pro Belgica asked questions about the affair, the minister established a commission of school inspectors, which concluded that the charges were unfounded.

Janssens also wrote to the publisher who translated Vangroenweghe's book into French, as a result of which a publisher's note was printed in the 1986 French-language edition to warn readers of its controversial nature. Vangroenweghe was asked to sign a statement that he would take all responsibility in the eventuality of a lawsuit. Although the French-language edition sold out in a few months, it was not reprinted. Pro Belgica also published rebuttals of Vangroenweghe's "lies." In the course of the affair, Vangroenweghe was threatened in anonymous letters, and his public lectures on the subject were interrupted by former colonials and attended by the secret police.

The final stages of colonialism proved to be delicate subjects in the Netherlands and France. In the Netherlands, the 1984 publication of a volume in the official war history, *Kingdom of the Netherlands in World War II,* dealing with the Dutch East Indies and the later Indonesia, led to a protracted lawsuit. The suit was finally decided against the petitioners (representatives of part of the community of those who formerly lived in the East Indies, organized as the Committee for the Historical Rehabilitation of the Dutch East Indies) in April 1990. They had accused the author, historian Loe De Jong, of portraying too negatively the role of the colonial administration. They also objected to passages about war crimes committed by Dutch troops against Indonesian nationalists from 1945 to 1949, and they asked the state to commission "a less prejudiced historian" to rewrite the history of colonial relations.

The 1987 manuscript of De Jong's next volume, also about Dutch-Indonesian relations from 1945 to 1949, was leaked to the press by two military reviewers and evoked strong protests from veterans because it contained a forty-six-page section entitled "War Crimes." Some veterans demanded nonpublication of that part, sued De Jong for libel, or published denials of his claims. The defamation case, including the demand for nonpublication, was dismissed in 1988, chiefly because the controversial statements were made in a manuscript, not a published book. When the volume was finally published, the title of the provocative section was changed to "Excesses." A few years later Dutch war veterans sued novelist Graa Boomsma on similar charges; the case was dismissed.

In France, the violent Algerian independence struggle (1954–1962) proved traumatic. Gillo Pontecorvo's 1966 film *The Battle of Algiers* treated the theme and was banned. Shot on location in Algiers in 1965 with the assistance of the Algerian government, the film gave a sympathetic account of the Algerian fight and criticized the use of torture by colonial authorities. The French ban lasted five years; the film's eventual release was delayed because cinema managers were intimidated. *The Battle of Algiers* was also banned in Uruguay in 1968 because it was seen as indirectly condoning the Tupamaro *guerrilla,* a National Liberation Movement very active at the time.

A 1996 issue of the Algerian daily *Liberté* was seized by the French police because it included an article commemorating the anniversary of a pro-independence demonstration by Algerians in Paris on October 17, 1962. The demonstration had ended in a bloodbath. The article mentioned a death toll and the disappearance of as many as two hundred people instead of the official

tally of three deaths and sixty-four injured. In 1998 Maurice Papon, the chief of the Paris police at the time, sued historian Jean-Luc Einaudi for libel because the latter had written in the newspaper *Le Monde* that the 1962 events constituted a "massacre perpetrated by the police on Papon's orders." In addition, Einaudi denounced the removal or destruction of several relevant archives. In 1999 the court ruled that the statement had been defamatory; damages were not awarded, however, because the court also ruled that Einaudi's method had been careful. Only in the same year did the French National Assembly officially acknowledge that France had fought a "war," rather than "an operation for keeping order," against Algerian nationalists from 1954 to 1962.

CENSORSHIP BY FORMER COLONIES

In former colonies, colonialism was widely condemned, with little reason for substantial differences of opinion. One example reveals, however, that the role of locals could be thorny. In 1977 the Indonesian Film Censorship Board banned *Saija dan Adinda,* a Dutch-Indonesian film directed by Fons Rademakers. The 1976 film, an adaptation of the nineteenth-century novel *Max Havelaar,* told the story of the corrupt and exploitative practices of the local gentry under Dutch colonial rule. The board declared that the ban was imposed because the film created the impression that colonialism was good and that the people were exploited by the local gentry rather than the Dutch.

If evidence for censorship of colonialism in general was understandably scarce, the reverse was true for its beginning and end. In some cases, episodes of colonial conquest were extremely difficult to interpret, as examples from Mexico and South Africa prove.

From 1950 to 1951 a Mexican scientific commission devoted thirty-seven sessions to verifying the authenticity of the bones of Cuauhtémoc (the last Aztec emperor and a national symbol of resistance to European imperialism), which had been "discovered" shortly before. When the commission found no proof of the bones' authenticity, and thus was unable to satisfy national pride, it was confronted with extreme hostility in the press. In 1975 a new commission came to the same conclusion as the 1951 group.

In the run-up to the 1992 quincentenary marking the arrival of Christopher Columbus (1451–1506) in the Americas, an intense debate raged in Mexico about whether it was legitimate to describe this "discovery" as the start of an encounter between the Old and the New World. In South Africa, two books published in 1952 criticized the celebration of three hundred years of white settlement and looked at South Africa's history as a struggle between oppressors and oppressed. The books,

Three Hundred Years: A History of South Africa by Mnguni (Hosea Jaffe) and *The Role of the Missionaries in Conquest* by Nosipho Majeke (Dora Taylor), had to appear under pseudonyms and were banned. Both books anticipated the work of radical historians in the 1970s.

The early stages of colonialism were sometimes problematic. In February 2005, a 6-meter (19.5-foot) statue of the Leopold II was reerected in Congo after it had been removed on the orders of President Mobutu Sese Seko (1930–1997) in 1967. It was taken down again just hours later, reportedly because several ministers opposed having a memorial to a man who had caused so much exploitation and death.

The last stages of colonialism, however, were by far the most sensitive in the former colonies.

Latin America. There are many examples in Latin America, where independence from Spain and Portugal came in the early nineteenth century for most colonies. In 1976, during the military dictatorship, Uruguayan historian Alfonso Fernández Cabrelli was arrested and held without trial. He was accused of "an attempt to subconsciously influence the reader of his book *The Uruguayans*" (*Boletín informativo* 1979, p. 6) by drawing parallels between Uruguay's hero of independence, General José Artigas (1764–1850), and the revolutionaries Camilo Torres (1929–1967) and Che Guevara (1928–1967). The book was called excessively critical of "the measures taken by the authorities to preserve the values of our nationality against the penetration of Marxism" (*Boletín informativo* 1979, p. 6) .

In the 1980s the Colombian Academy of History directed comparable criticism to some authors of history textbooks. The author Rodolfo Ramón de Roux was accused of omitting or ridiculing the most important figures of the independence period and of overemphasizing contemporary history. His New History approach was labeled Marxist and unpatriotic. A similar approach used in a textbook by Silvia Duzzan and Salomón Kalmanovitz was equally condemned. An academy member declared in a newspaper that the textbook depicted Spaniards and Creoles unfavorably, thus inciting hatred against them. Despite the academy's attitude, the textbooks continued to be used in schools.

Elsewhere, analogous cases were noted. In Peru, historian Heraclio Bonilla was criticized in the 1970s for his revisionist interpretation of the Peruvian independence movement. Bonilla's work was attacked for unpatriotically debunking the nation's traditional heroes and overemphasizing socioeconomic factors.

Under the Argentinean dictatorship (1976–1983) of General Jorge Videla and others a historical study, *From Montoneros to Caudillos,* was banned because its title contained the forbidden word *Montonero* (adopted by left-wing Peronists in memory of the irregular armies of gauchos who fought against Spanish troops during Argentina's independence wars of 1810 to 1816).

In 1983 in Mexico, the National Autonomous University of Mexico planned a production of *Martyrdom of Morelos* (1981), a play by Vicente Leñero. Leñero's portrayal of Mexican independence hero José María Morelos (1765–1815) as someone who under torture betrayed the names, strategies, and troop strengths of other rebel commanders caused a great stir, especially because President Miguel de la Madrid (b. 1934) had "adopted" Morelos as his spiritual mentor from the past. Some rehearsals were reportedly interrupted, a controversial actor playing the part of Morelos was replaced, and precautions against violent protests were taken on opening night.

In Cuba, finally, prominent independence leaders such as José Martí (1853–1895), Máximo Gómez (1836–1905), and Antonio Maceo (1845–1896) formed part of the pantheon inspiring and legitimizing the government of Fidel Castro (b. 1927) and were, as such, sensitive subjects.

Asia. In Asia, problems were comparable. In 1952 the Indian Ministry of Education appointed an editorial board to compile an official history of the Indian freedom movement, to be published in conjunction with the centenary celebration of the 1857 revolt of Indian soldiers (sepoys). In 1954 board director and historian Romesh Chandra Majumdar presented a draft of the first volume to the other editorial board members; after a delay he learned from the minister of education that some board members had criticized his draft as exaggerating the role of Bengal in the freedom movement.

Equally controversial was the starting date of the freedom movement in India, situated by Majumdar in 1870. Others preferred to designate the 1857 revolt itself as the beginning of the movement, or even the thirteenth century—implying that Muslims were foreigners in India, an assumption undermining the Congress Party's ideal of India as a secular democracy.

A third point of conflict was the nature of the 1857 revolt (was it a national war of independence or not?). Majumdar resigned and the editorial board was dissolved in 1955. The government entrusted the work to National Archives director Surendra Nath Sen, whose book *Eighteen Fifty-Seven* appeared in 1957. The same year Majumdar published his own findings as *The Sepoy Mutiny and the Revolt of 1857.*

In Indonesia, Pramoedya Ananta Toer, a nominee for the Nobel Prize for Literature, wrote persuasive anticolonial novels. Imprisoned at Buru Island, Pramoedya was

ANANTA TOER PRAMOEDYA

The son of a school headmaster, Ananta Toer Pramoedya was born February 6, 1925, in Blora, East Java, Indonesia. Imprisoned by each of Indonesia's three twentieth-century governments for alleged subversive political activities and writings, he is widely considered Indonesia's most estimable writer.

In his fictional works, Pramoedya has created insightful and forward-looking characters who challenge traditional political doctrines through thought and action. The complex political history of the Indonesian islands serves as the context for many of Pramoedya's works, which are also marked by his experiences during World War II.

After Japan's surrender at the end of World War II, the Dutch tried to regain the islands of the East Indies. However, Indonesian nationalist sentiment led several paramilitary rebel groups to engage the Dutch in a four-year struggle for control of the country. While serving as a soldier in this nationalist movement, Pramoedya was captured and jailed in 1947.

While serving in a Dutch forced labor camp, Pramoedya wrote *The Fugitive*, which was published several months after his release in 1949. The book, which earned him an Indonesian literary prize, marked Pramoedya's emergence as a politically influential author. In 1990, some forty years after it was originally published, *The Fugitive* became Pramoedya's first novel widely available to English-speaking audiences.

Once out of prison, Pramoedya developed several leftist affiliations, though he never became a communist. He served as a leading figure in *Lekra*, a socialist literary group, and visited Beijing in 1956, expressing support for that country's communist revolution. Among his significant publications of the period was a defense of Java's Chinese minority community. In 1965, after the failure of a coup aimed at overthrowing the by-then independent Indonesian government, Pramoedya was deemed an enemy of the state on account of his earlier leftist associations. The author's library, notes, and manuscripts were burned, and he was held without trial for fourteen years on the prison island of Buru in eastern Indonesia.

For the first seven years of his incarceration, Pramoedya was denied access to paper and pencil. Lacking these rudimentary tools of his trade, he composed stories in his head. Upon his release in 1979, Pramoedya turned those prison stories into a historical tetralogy, based loosely on the life of Tirto Adisoerjo, an early Indonesian nationalist.

The Indonesian government has suppressed Pramoedya's works, citing alleged Marxist-Leninist leanings and elements of class conflict that pose a potential threat to society. Some observers have viewed these bans as an attempt to quell liberalism and debate among Indonesians.

Pramoedya's work has been circulated in the form of "illegal" photocopies, at great personal risk to Indonesian readers, and has remained largely inaccessible to foreigners. In addition, journalists have often been denied permission to interview him and the Australian translator of the Buruquartet was expelled from Java. When asked to describe his feelings about his works being banned, Pramoedya told the *Washington Post*: "I consider it an honor. . . . To do creative work you must be prepared to pay, and this is one of the costs" (North, p. D5, April 1988).

not allowed to write in the 1970s. In the evenings, he told his fellow inmates stories about the incipient nationalist movement in the early twentieth-century Dutch East Indies entirely from memory. When Pramoedya was finally allowed to write in 1975, the other inmates gave him paper and did his duties while he transformed the stories into a set of four historical novels.

When the quartet was published after Pramoedya's release in 1979 and proved immensely popular, each of the volumes was banned. Susandi, the head of the investigation team at the office of the Indonesian attorney general, claimed that the books represented a threat to security and order and that the author "had been able by means of historical data to smuggle in Marxist-Leninist teachings." The ban was also partially inspired by fear that analogies would be drawn between the abuses committed by the Dutch colonial power and those of the regime of President Suharto (b. 1921), who ruled Indonesia from 1967 to 1998.

Africa. In Africa also, independence struggles left their uncertain legacies. In Kenya, the interpretation of the independence movement, and especially of one part of it, the Mau Mau rebellion (1952–1956), was a predominant subject of debate among historians because the conclusions of the debate had direct implications for the legitimacy of the authoritarian leadership. Mau Mau was an uprising of members of the Gikuyu, Kenya's largest ethnic group, against British colonial rule to obtain land and freedom. Writers with a Marxist-inspired interpretation of the rebellion risked persecution.

Kenyan novelist Ngugi wa Thiongo, who wrote fiction on the Mau Mau, spent the last year (1978) of the presidency of Jomo Kenyatta (1891–1978) in prison because one of his recent plays had dealt with Kenyans who collaborated with the colonial administration by serving in the Home Guard during the Mau Mau rebellion. Ngugi's play also treated the struggle over land between a peasant farmer and a rich landowner. In the words of Eliud Njenga, the Kiambu district commissioner, "it promoted the class struggle." The play was "too provocative, would make some people bitter and was opening up old graves." After his release and much further harassment, Ngugi eventually went into exile until his temporary return to Kenya in 2004.

Another Kenyan victim, this time under the government (1978–2002) of President Daniel arap Moi (b. 1924), was Marxist historian Maina wa Kinyatti, known for his controversial work on Mau Mau. It cost him six years of imprisonment under severe duress (1982–1988), an eye disease, and exile afterwards.

At the other side of the interpretation spectrum, neoconservative historian William Ochieng, who viewed Mau Mau as an internecine struggle among the Gikuyu, stayed relatively aloof from criticism until a group of Mau Mau veterans in 1986 demanded that his writings be banned from the schools. The veterans also decided to commission the "correct" historiography of the Mau Mau rebellion. In an official reaction, President Moi declared that he could not allow history to be written in a way that might divide the Kenyans and that any history of the Mau Mau rebellion should provide a correct account of independence. As late as October 2001, dozens of members of the Kenyan nongovernmental group Release Political Prisoners were detained for several days on charges of holding an illegal meeting because they had commemorated Mau Mau day.

Elsewhere in Africa, books about left-wing leaders who were assassinated during or as a result of decolonization, like Ruben Um Nyobè (1913–1958) in Cameroon or Patrice Lumumba (1925–1961) in Congo, were confiscated and banned, partly because the books implicated their country's rulers. Such was the fate of *Patrice Lumumba: The Fifty Last Days of His Life* (1966), a book written under a pseudonym by Belgian scholars Jules

Gérard-Libois and Jacques Brassinne, and *Cameroon's National Problem* (1985), edited by historian Achille Mbembe.

In Namibia, the crimes committed by the South West Africa People's Organization (SWAPO), a black African nationalist liberation movement, before the 1990 independence caused controversy. In 1996 president and former SWAPO leader Sam Nujoma (b. 1929) attacked German Lutheran Church pastor Siegfried Groth, who for many years had actively supported SWAPO's antiapartheid struggle, in a television broadcast to the nation. The reason was Groth's *Namibia— The Wall of Silence: The Dark Days of the Liberation Struggle,* a 1995 book that included eyewitness accounts of the torture and disappearance of detainees in the SWAPO preindependence exile camps in Zambia and Angola. The detainees had been accused of internal dissent or of spying for South Africa. Although the book sold out quickly, some two thousand people called for its banning and for public burning at a rally celebrating the sixth anniversary of Namibia's independence.

FIVE CONCLUSIONS

From this survey, five conclusions can be drawn. First, popular history channels were watched as closely as academic history. Second, reasons for archival destruction, removal, and secrecy by colonial powers can be subsumed under three factors: political (legitimation of abusive power), military (erasure of traces of crimes and rebellions), and cultural (ethnocentric depreciation of the historical sources of subjected peoples).

Third, colonial powers censored historical works about colonial violence written by both national and "indigenous" scholars; those works were banned at home and in the colony. More surprisingly, colonial powers also attempted quite often to attack criticism by foreign scholars.

Fourth, for former colonial powers, precarious subjects that were liable to censorship or taboo status mainly related to wars in the earliest and last stages of colonialism. Unofficial interest groups were players as important as governments. Frequently, conflicts had to be decided in court. In the long run, violent conquest and violent decolonization came to be seen as adversely affecting the democratic legitimation of power and the construction of a national identity—in short, they came to be seen as sources of shame.

Finally, in former colonies, the last stage of colonialism was the most explosive period. Remarkably, censorship attempts were often not directed at representations of the role of the former colonial power, but at portrayals of former anticolonial resistance leaders. Left-wing explanations for this crucial period were seldom cherished.

Historians had to portray the country's heroes of independence very carefully: praising them could powerfully suggest comparison with, and criticism of, present leadership, and blaming them could provoke retaliation by veterans and the establishment.

SEE ALSO *Anticolonialism; Lumumba, Patrice; Portugal's African Colonies.*

BIBLIOGRAPHY
Boletín informativo (Newsletter of Amnesty International) (February 1979): 6.

De Baets, Antoon. "Censorship and Historical Writing." In *A Global Encyclopedia of Historical Writing*, edited by D. R. Woolf, 149–150. New York and London: Garland, 1998.

De Baets, Antoon. "History: Rewriting History." In *Censorship: A World Encyclopedia*, Vol. 2, edited by Derek Jones, 1062–1067. London and Chicago: Fitzroy Dearborn, 2001.

De Baets, Antoon. "History: School Curricula and Textbooks." In *Censorship: A World Encyclopedia*, Vol. 2, edited by Derek Jones, 1067–1073. London and Chicago: Fitzroy Dearborn, 2001.

De Baets, Antoon. *Censorship of Historical Thought: A World Guide, 1945–2000*. London and Westport, CT: Greenwood, 2002.

De Baets, Antoon. "Defamation Cases against Historians." *History and Theory: Studies in the Philosophy of History* 41 (2002): 346–366.

Jones, Derek, ed. *Censorship: A World Encyclopedia*. 4 vols. London and Chicago: Fitzroy Dearborn, 2001.

Simpson, J., and J. Bennett. *The Disappeared: Voices from a Secret War*. London: 1985.

Antoon De Baets

CENTRAL ASIA, EUROPEAN PRESENCE IN

In 1450 Central Asia from west of Mongolia and the Hindu Kush to the eastern Caspian Sea was dominated by nomadic and sedentary peoples, speakers of Turkic and Persian. The remnants of the Mongol "Golden Horde," Turkic-speaking nomads, claimed tribute from Muscovy, a principality that preceded the Russian Empire. After 1552, when the Russian Czar Ivan IV (1530–1584) conquered the Kazan khanate, Russians began to move into the steppe zone, taking control from nomadic peoples. Cossack conquest was followed by Russian peasant settlement.

In the seventeenth century, Russia established Orenburg as a frontier post, to separate the nomadic Bashkords, who paid tribute to Russia, from the nomadic Kazakhs, whom the Russian government viewed as dangerous raiders and slave traders. In the eighteenth century, the Jungars, a western Mongolian (Oirat) people, expanded into Kazakh lands. This led one Kazakh tribal leader, Bukei Khan, (d. 1823) to seek protection from the Russian government. His followers were granted land in the steppe on the west bank of the Volga River, and were named the Inner Horde, to denote their status within Russian lands.

Between the early eighteenth century and the mid-nineteenth century, Russia came to control all of the other Kazakh hordes as well by expanding into the steppe lands with Cossack forward posts, by establishing treaties of protection when various Kazakh tribal leaders faced conflict, and by negotiating leases of steppe land to be granted to Russian (and other European) settlers.

Until the late eighteenth century, Russian colonial expansion was based on the concept of tribute relationships. As Cossacks in service to Russia expanded Russian control beyond Kazan, across Siberia to the Pacific coast (by the late 1600s), the Russian government accepted the obeisance of conquered peoples, established the amount of annual tribute (*iasak*) they would pay to the government, and took representatives from the ruling or leading households to live in Moscow. These representatives were used as hostages when the Russian government faced problems in its relationship with tribute-paying peoples, but they were also integrated into the Russian nobility, granted titles, and assimilated (at least to some extent) to elite Russian culture.

The Russian state viewed these treaty relationships as permanent, but the Kazakh hordes saw them as negotiations between individual leaders, ending with the death of the leader who made the commitment. Thus, leadership changes among Kazakhs led to conflict; if the new leader did not recognize treaty obligations with Russia, Russia sent forces to reestablish its conditions.

In the late eighteenth century, under the rule of Catherine I (1729–1796), Russia's elite explored Enlightenment ideas, and these turned its colonial project from a haphazard expansion into a purposeful spread of Russian power and culture. By the nineteenth century, Russian colonialism imitated aspects of British and French colonialism.

After conquering Kazakh nomads and demanding tribute and hostages, the Russian government began to "civilize" the Kazakhs. The Steppe Governate was organized, turning conquered nomad lands into a Russian province that had special colonial administration. The government levied taxes that pressured nomads to settle and farm, and to lease land to settlers. Eventually the government assessed land use, determined a norm for the amount of land that each nomad family needed, and seized what it deemed unused or underused lands for distribution to Russian farmers.

The conquered peoples of Central Asia who did not belong to a few noble families were deemed inferior and were not granted citizenship in the empire. They were given separate courts of law, lived under their own laws (as codified and revised by Russian administrators), were not allowed to serve in the military, were not given passports, paid different taxes than Russian citizens did, and were allowed only limited representation in Russia's first elected body of government, the Duma.

Until the mid-nineteenth century, Russia's relations with the Central Asian khanate of Kokand, the khanate of Khiva, and the emirate of Bukhara were both profitable and contentious. Central Asian merchants brought cotton and luxury goods to Orenburg's market, and they purchased sugar, matches, and other Russian manufactures. In the 1840s and 1850s Russia accused the Central Asian states of inciting rebellion among Kazakhs, and of enslaving Russians. The Russian army established advance positions, building forts at Verny (Almaty), Ak Mechet, and Shymkent in the 1850s.

In 1865 the Russian army took Tashkent from Kokand, and by 1876 Russia had defeated Khiva, Bukhara, and Kokand. Kokand's land became a new Russian colonial territory, Turkestan Territory, under the special regime of a Russian military governor. Bukhara and Khiva became protectorates, autonomous internally but controlled by Russia in foreign affairs. While the Russians deposed the khan of Kokand, they recognized the emir of Bukhara and the khan of Khiva, bestowing Russian noble status on them and inviting symbolic interaction with the Russian court.

Russia expanded its territorial control in Central Asia in competition with two other aspirants, China and Britain. Russian diplomatic missions and scientific expeditions reconnoitered Central Asia when British agents were doing the same in Afghanistan, with both sides working toward the Pamirs, the Amu Dar'ya (the Oxus River of Greek geography), and the Turkmen (Turcoman) territories. After the Jungar threat vanished in the late eighteenth century (due largely to an epidemic), Russian expansion eastward in Central Asia met little resistance until the 1850s.

China asserted its authority over Xinjiang (the New Territories, or Eastern Turkistan) but was faced with challenges from local forces, especially those of the Uighur military and political leader Yakub Beg (1820–1877). Russia held Kuldja (Yining), as an extension of its steppe territory, from 1871 to 1881, but then returned it to China. Russia continued to compete with China for influence in Eastern Turkistan until the 1940s.

Throughout the nineteenth century, the British tried to extend control of Afghanistan from their imperial territory of India. After the Afghans thoroughly defeated the British army and drove them from Kabul twice, Britain held strong influence over Afghanistan, but did not make it a colony. Afghanistan remained an independent state under the Durrani shahs.

Competing with Britain for dominance in Central Asia, in what English poet Rudyard Kipling (1865–1936) dubbed the Great Game, Russia defeated Turkmen tribes in the region that Russia named "Transcaspia," and in the 1890s Russia took control of the Pamir region. Russian control over these distant regions of Central Asia was secured in part by improved transportation. The Russian government established steamship navigation on the Aral Sea and the Syr Dar'ya, and transported troops from the Transcaucasus to the Turkmen coast by ship across the Caspian Sea.

In 1879 the Tekke Turkmen defeated the advancing Russian army. However, a quickly constructed railroad from the coast to Merv allowed the Russian army to move larger numbers of troops, and to defeat the Tekke in 1881. Russia consolidated its control of the region by defeating the Merv (Mari) Turkmen in 1884. In the 1880s and 1890s, Russia and Britain negotiated the boundary between Russian-controlled territory and Afghanistan.

Russia sent agricultural colonists to nomad lands. By 1917 more than one million Russians were farming in the Steppe Governate and Turkestan Territory. They were concentrated in Jetti-Su (Seven Rivers), the region around present-day Almaty, Kazakhstan, and the Chu Valley, near Bishkek, Kyrgyzstan. By contrast, in the sedentary farming zones of Central Asia, Russia promoted cotton cultivation but sent few agricultural colonists; most Russian colonists in the rest of Central Asia settled in cities. Russians founded or expanded cities throughout Central Asia, and established the Tashkent-Orenburg rail line, which linked the Central Asian colony to Moscow. Oil was found on the eastern Caspian, increasing Russian settlement in Krasnovodsk (Turkmenbashi), Turkmenistan.

With encouragement from the imperial government, a diaspora of Tatar Muslims from Russia expanded in the Steppe Governate and Turkestan Territory. Many who had facility in Russian as well as their native Turkic language acted as interlocutors for the colonial administration. Tatar missionaries preached traditional and modernist (Jadid) Islam. They also opened traditional Koran schools and reformed Islamic schools in these regions. Russia sent Orthodox missionaries and established Russian-Native schools, modern schools that taught subjects in Russian and in the native languages.

As the colonial economy expanded wealth in Turkestan's cotton-growing regions, Central Asians responded to these new cultural trends in a variety of ways. The ancient *madrasas* (institutions of higher Islamic learning) in Bukhara expanded, as did the amount of land put into *waqf* (Islamic charitable foundations).

Fledgling movements for cultural reform or defense emerged among the colonized peoples, who became divided between those seeking greater accommodation with and advantage from Russia, and those striving to protect their land and culture from encroachment. After Russia's 1905 revolution and the ensuing relaxation of press censorship, Central Asians began publishing their own newspapers, opening more reformed schools, experimenting with theater, and organizing political movements.

In 1916, although the Russian government feared that "pan-Turkist" Central Asians would fight on behalf of the Ottoman Empire, there was instead a Central Asian uprising against conscription into the Russian army and against Russian colonial settlement. The uprising was most violent in areas where nomad lands had recently been given to colonists; there the uprising continued until the February 1917 revolution brought down the Czar's imperial government. Following the February Revolution, Russians in Central Asian cities maintained the crumbling empire. The Communist leadership did not allow Central Asians to claim independence.

Kazakhs formed several political parties that called for freedom and fought against the Bolsheviks until 1920. Several hundred Turkestani political activists established an autonomous Turkestan government at Kokand in January 1918, but the Soviet Red Army destroyed much of Kokand and dispersed the leaders. Many of them continued to fight against Bolshevik control in Central Asia into the 1920s; the Communists called them Basmachis.

Central Asians sought support from outsiders in their struggle against the Bolshevik government. The Turkish soldier and politician Enver Paşa (1881–1922), in flight from the Ottoman Empire after its demise at the end of World War I and from occupation by the British, joined the Basmachis. The British launched part of their anti-Bolshevik intervention from Afghanistan's territory into Turkmen lands and Bukhara. However, some Kazakhs and Turkestanis joined the Communist Party in its early years, and their numbers expanded rapidly after the Bolsheviks fully reconquered Central Asia and eliminated political alternatives.

The Bolshevik government ended the protectorates of Khiva and Bukhara, fomenting uprisings against the traditional rulers and creating in their place short-lived People's Republics. In 1924 the Nationalities Commission of the Soviet Union's government drew boundaries to create the Soviet republics of Kazakhstan, Kyrgyzstan, Tajikistan, Turkmenistan, and Uzbekistan. Turkestani exiles saw this as a typically imperial "divide and rule" strategy, one that ended any possibility for united Central Asian opposition to Moscow's authority. The Nationalities Commission presented its justification for boundary making through its understanding of the idea of "nation." Groups that shared language, history, culture, and territory needed to have political units within the Soviet Union in order to develop, and the planners in Moscow applied this concept to the five groups that they saw as the main "nationalities" of Central Asia: Kazakhs, Kyrgyz, Tajiks, Turkmen, and Uzbeks.

The Soviet government tried to secure its hold on Central Asia not only through force, but also through incentives. Establishing national republics opened positions in government, in Communist Party membership, and in many sectors of development, to members of the "titular" nationalities. Policies designed to attract support from the poor, such as land reform, made Soviet rule more secure, although in the 1920s many thousands of Central Asians fled from famine, hardship, and Soviet rule to Xinjiang or to Afghanistan.

Throughout the Soviet period, while the Soviet government regarded its own policies as anti-imperialist and anticolonial, exiles and outsiders condemned the Soviet Union's control of Central Asia as imperialistic and colonial. Many elements of Soviet rule in Central Asia were similar to twentieth-century colonialism elsewhere, but many aspects were strikingly different, so that arguments over whether the Soviet Union was a colonial empire are complex.

From the 1920s until the 1960s the Soviet government encouraged immigration of skilled workers, Communist Party members, and peasants from the rest of the Soviet Union to Central Asia. In the 1930s many Russians immigrated in the hope of improving their quality of life. In the 1940s refugees from the European regions of Russia under attack in World War II moved to Central Asia, as did unwilling exiles from nationality groups that the Soviet government dubbed *enemies*, including Volga Germans, Koreans, Crimean Tatars, Chechens, and others. In the 1950s and 1960s, as heavy industry grew in Central Asia, immigrants from other parts of the Soviet Union moved there as expert workers and for improved work opportunities.

But in the 1970s this trend ended; emigration of Russians and other nonnative nationality groups from Central Asia to other parts of the Soviet Union exceeded immigration. Throughout this period, every Central Asian republic experienced a rapid natural increase in population, and Uzbekistan, Turkmenistan, and Tajikistan's populations remained overwhelmingly dominated by their titular nationalities.

In Kazakhstan, due to famine-related starvation of nomads in the 1930s and to heavy Russian immigration, Kazakhs formed less than half of the population during most of the Soviet period. But out-migration of Russians in the 1980s and 1990s, plus Kazakh natural increase, made Kazakhs the absolution majority of the population in independent Kazakhstan. In Kyrgyzstan, the situation was similar, though Kyrgyz always maintained a scant majority.

The Soviet state encouraged immigration from other regions to Central Asia largely to support economic and political development. In the 1970s, when other regions of the Soviet Union began to face labor shortages, and when Central Asia, with its rapid population growth, had an excess of young workers, the Soviet Union's central planners tried unsuccessfully to attract Central Asians as labor emigrants to other regions. In spite of high birth rates, a third world population structure, underemployment, and lower living standards, Central Asians very rarely chose to move to other parts of the Soviet Union. However, in the tenuous economic conditions following 1991, many Central Asians began to seek a living through temporary labor migration.

During the 1920s and 1930s, Soviet economic planning treated Central Asia as a source of agricultural products. The state collectivized agriculture between 1929 and the mid-1930s, forcing nomads to settle and small farmers to turn their land over to large collective farms. The policy was disastrous in its initial stages. Nomads slaughtered their livestock rather than turn it over to the collective farms, and then starved under famine conditions in the early 1930s, due to reduced herds, drought, and government neglect. Perhaps a quarter to a third of the Kazakh population died.

Collective farms in sedentary areas were required to plant cotton rather than grain crops, and with drought this led to severe hardship, though not to mass starvation. Nationalization of land and the formation of collective farms was intended to give the government control of farm production and to facilitate mechanization. In the 1940s and 1950s some of these plans started to be fulfilled, with tractors and other farm machinery becoming increasingly available in Central Asia.

Turkmenistan, Uzbekistan, and Tajikistan produced the vast majority of the Soviet Union's cotton. In each of these regions, the government invested heavily in the extension of irrigation canal systems. The largest, the Kara-Kum Canal, built between the 1950s and the 1980s, diverted half of the flow of the Amu Dar'ya River into a new channel that eventually crossed Turkmenistan. The project raised Turkmenistan's cotton output and standard of living, but also led to the demise of the Aral Sea, as each year the water flowing in was reduced.

Kyrgyzstan and Kazakhstan produced primarily grain and livestock, with Kazakhstan's output expanding rapidly after Soviet prime minister Nikita Khrushchev (1894–1971) initiated the "Virgin Lands scheme," opening grazing lands in northern Kazakhstan to tilled agriculture. Although the Virgin Lands were not reliable in producing grain, farm output expanded until the 1970s, when it began to stagnate.

In the 1920s and 1930s the state did little to invest in industry in Central Asia. Mines were developed in Kazakhstan to feed the growing industrial complex in Russia. The state invested in some textile mills in Central Asia, mainly for processing silk. Until the 1940s, the Soviet Union seemed to treat Central Asia much as any empire treated its colonies, as a source of raw materials. But during World War II, the policy changed, as Soviet economic planners decided that industry should be placed in areas of the Soviet Union less vulnerable to invasion.

In addition, the postwar boom necessitated finding new sources of energy. Uzbekistan became home to part of the Soviet Union's airplane manufacturing industry, and its gas supplies were rapidly exploited. Kazakhstan gained diverse metallurgical industries and became a large producer of oil. Kazakhstan also became home to part of the Soviet space program at Baikonur and to aboveground nuclear-weapons testing at Semipalatinsk (Semay). Turkmenistan's gas output outstripped Uzbekistan's by the 1960s, and pipelines exported that gas to Ukraine and Russia. The Soviet state built hydroelectric dams and factory complexes in Turkmenistan, Kyrgyzstan, and Uzbekistan.

In the early twentieth century, there was almost no industrialization in Central Asia; this changed rapidly after 1940. However, throughout the Soviet period, agriculture remained the dominant economic sector in each of the Central Asian republics except Kazakhstan, and none of the Central Asian republics approached the level of industrial development found in central Russia, Ukraine, or the Baltic republics.

The Communist Party of the Soviet Union considered education to be the key to social change, to economic development, and to the creation of a Communist society. In the 1920s in Central Asia, the state took control of all schools, closed Islamic schools, and promoted modern, socialist education by founding teacher training programs and passing laws making basic education mandatory. In the 1930s collective farms built schools that made education widely available in rural regions for the first time. Literacy grew through a program of "end illiteracy" courses that taught adults to read and write. By the 1960s almost all Central Asian children attended school, and the government claimed literacy rates of more than 90 percent in the under-fifty population in all of the Central Asian republics.

Large numbers of Central Asians entered specialized institutions of secondary education and higher education. Although Russian was the language of the Soviet government, most educational institutions in Central Asia taught in the native languages, and included Russian as a second language. In every Central Asian republic, Russian language schools were available in cities and larger towns, but statistics show that for primary and secondary education, the percentage of children who attended schools in which instruction occurred in the titular nationality's language was equal to or greater than the percentage of the titular nationality within the population.

Although many parents saw benefit in having their children learn Russian for future career advancement, the real possibility that children would learn to speak Russian was related to the presence of native Russian speakers in the population. In Kazakhstan, Russians and other Russian-speaking immigrants were as numerous as Kazakhs and were present in most rural regions as well as in the cities. By 1989, 60 percent of Kazakhs claimed fluency in Russian. The percentages were much lower in the other republics, where Russians were significantly fewer and were concentrated in cities: Fluency in Russian was claimed by 35 percent of Kyrgyz, 27 percent of Turkmen, 28 percent of Tajiks, and 23 percent of Uzbeks.

Throughout the Soviet period, the state supported both Russian-language and native-language media and cultural institutions in all of the Central Asian republics. As a whole, the Soviet state's policies on cultural assimilation were ambiguous. Although in the 1950s and 1960s, government policy proclaimed that nationalities would "draw close" and "merge," the state provided the resources both for Russification, and for full use of native languages in government, education, cultural institutions, and many branches of service and industry. Many Central Asians believed that mastering Russian would lead to advancement, while many also resented Russia's "big brother" attitude toward Central Asians, and the refusal of Russian immigrants to learn Central Asian languages. In the realm of education and culture, the Soviet Union's policies could be seen as colonial and Russifying, but they were dramatically unlike those of

any other empire in promoting the rapid expansion of modern education and universal literacy.

Russians dominated political decision making for Central Asia, but native people moved up in Communist Party ranks to positions of authority. As each republic was established, titular-nationality Communists were given the most public roles as leaders, with Russian advisors standing in secondary positions. Before World War II, Russians outnumbered titular nationals in the republic-level Communist Parties. But after World War II, the Communist Party came to mirror the relative numbers of each nationality group in each republic more closely, so that in republics where titular nationals predominated, they also comprised the party majority.

The republic-level Communist Party had limited scope for decision making. Economically and politically, the Soviet Union was centralized, and decisions were handed down from Moscow. But having a titular national at the head of the republic's state and party structures became an important symbol, significant enough that when Prime Minister Mikhail Gorbachev (b. 1931) replaced the Kazakh Party leader Dinmukhamed Kunaev (1911–1993) with a Russian late in 1986, Kazakhs in Almaty rioted, and the replacement came several years later.

World War II was an important turning point in Central Asia. Central Asians were equal citizens of the Soviet Union along with all other nationality groups, and Central Asian men were conscripted into the Soviet army at the same high rate as men from other parts of the Soviet Union. Central Asians who had not previously met Russians learned at least limited Russian, enough to understand commands, and they fought far from their homes beside other Soviet soldiers.

Germany attempted to appeal to anti-Communist nationalism among Central Asians, forming exiled Central Asians into the Turkistan Brigade, which fought on the German side and tried to attract deserters from Central Asia. However, despite many reasons for discontent, the vast majority of Central Asian soldiers fought loyally for the Soviet Union, and the experience transformed them. Following World War II, Central Asia was far more deeply Soviet than it had been before.

From the 1950s until the 1980s, the Soviet Union used Central Asia to promote to third-world countries the advantages of socialism and alignment with the Soviet bloc. The factors that made Soviet Central Asia unlike most colonial territories, including heavy government investment in education, increasing industrial development, and the full presence of Central Asians in the Communist Party and in government, were the factors that made Central Asia a showplace for the third world.

However, although Central Asians had equality, and sensed themselves to be Soviet citizens, their standard of living, levels of income, rates of participation in the most prestigious positions in politics and the economy, and their ability to influence general policies in the Soviet Union, never reached the levels of the country's European territories. Central Asia lagged behind much of the Soviet Union in almost every development measure.

Central Asian republics declared their independence late in 1991, as the Soviet government fell. Each had republic-level government institutions that formed the base for a new state, but Soviet economic integration meant that each had difficulty establishing a viable independent economy. Tajikistan suffered civil war and extreme impoverishment. Outside states vied for influence in Central Asia. Turkey invested in schools, factories, and the media. Iran emphasized relations with Tajikistan. Pakistan expanded trade, as did China.

Many missionaries came, Muslim and Christian. Russia tried to maintain influence by forming the Commonwealth of Independent States and later by drawing up economic and security agreements with Central Asian states. United States oil, gas, and minerals companies invested in Kazakhstan, Turkmenistan, and Uzbekistan. The Great Game for external dominance of Central Asia was not an extension of the Russian or Soviet colonial projects; it was neocolonial economic control of a region where states refused to be dominated politically by outsiders.

Uighurs in the Xinjiang Province of China had been the target of programs hatched in the Soviet Union to enhance the nationalist movement and separatism from China. From the 1920s to 1940s, several Uighur nationalist parties formed, and some of their leaders received support and training from the Soviet Union. In addition, the Soviets had invested in oil development in Xinjiang. However, during and after World War II, the Soviets abandoned this policy. The East Turkistani political leadership was decimated in the late 1940s (partly due to a plane crash), and the Chinese Communist Party asserted control over the province in the 1950s.

The Chinese Communist Party's policy was more overtly colonial in Xinjiang than was Soviet policy in Central Asia. China encouraged massive Han Chinese immigration to Xinjiang, treated Xinjiang as a raw-material–producing periphery, carried out nuclear testing at Lop Nor, and has not aggressively pursued raising the educational level of Uighurs or promoting their presence in the party. In most development indicators and measures of living standards, Uighurs lag behind Han Chinese in Xinjiang Province. They also lag behind most of China's more developed provinces. After the demise of the Soviet Union and the de facto independence of the five Central Asian states, the Uighur nationalist movement became more active, with exiles operating in Kazakhstan and Kyrgyzstan. The Chinese government repeatedly cracked down on any signs of nationalist activity, which it termed *separatism*.

SEE ALSO *China, after 1945; China, First Opium War to 1945; Empire, British; Oil.*

BIBLIOGRAPHY
Benson, Linda. *The Ili Rebellion: The Moslem Challenge to Chinese Authority in Xinjiang, 1944–1949.* Armonk, NY: Sharpe, 1990.
Howe, G. Melvyn. *The Soviet Union: A Geographical Survey,* 2nd ed. Estover, U.K.: Macdonald and Evans, 1983.
Kappeler, Andreas. *The Russian Empire: A Multiethnic History.* Translated by Alfred Clayton. Harlow, U.K.: Longman, 2001.
Olcott, Martha Brill. *The Kazakhs,* 2nd ed. Stanford, CA: Hoover Institution Press, 1995.
Ryan, Michael. *Contemporary Soviet Society: A Statistical Handbook.* Brookfield, VT: Edwin Elgar, 1990.

Marianne Kamp

CEYLON

For 450 years the island of Ceylon (now called Sri Lanka) was the prey of successive naval powers. Colonial conquest of the island was predicated on superior sea power and arms, military organization, political strength, and economic wealth. Popular history has generally differentiated between Portuguese rule (1505–1658), Dutch rule (1658–1796), and British rule (1796–1948) in the guise of first the East India Company and then the British Crown. The "rule" in Ceylon of these three powers was sometimes nothing more than a presence that grew, spread, or declined in space and time.

CONQUEST AND CONTROL

In the early sixteenth century, there were three native centers of political power in Ceylon: two Sinhalese kingdoms in Kotte and Kandy and a Tamil kingdom in Jaffna. When the king of Kotte died in 1597, he bequeathed his territories to the king of Portugal, and the Portuguese became de jure sovereigns over the lowlands of Ceylon. The Portuguese annexed the north of the island in 1619. Their attempts to invade the kingdom in the mountains in the center of the island met with resounding defeat in 1592 to 1594 and on many subsequent occasions.

brought the Kandyan provinces under British sovereignty.

AN EXPORT-BASED ECONOMY

In the colonial system, the economy was tied to the export of tropical goods and the import of food products such as rice. In the sixteenth century, the Portuguese were intent on building a system of trading and military outposts connected by sea lanes and on gaining control of spice production. In Ceylon they found cinnamon, which they developed by relying on the Salagama people, who were relatively recent migrants from South India, to provide their counters with supplies. The Dutch continued this practice in a more systematic way with the creation of the first cinnamon plantations. The canals they built permitted spices to be transported efficiently and shipped overseas.

Under the British, export trade turned successively to coffee (ca. 1840), tea and coconut (ca. 1880), and rubber (ca. 1900). The island became one of the principal plantation colonies of the British Empire with the main areas of production and extraction increasingly located within the territories of the Kandyan kingdom. British production techniques were modeled on those of the plantations in the Caribbean. The demands of the plantation industry required a network of roads linking the interior of the island with the coasts, thus marking the beginning of a modern transportation system. Another ethnic element was added with the arrival of immigrant plantation labor from South India.

There was little interest on the part of the European colonizers for peasant agriculture, although some reservoirs in the dry zone were repaired in the late nineteenth century. On the whole, state policy was inimical to peasant agriculture in two specific areas: the levying of taxes and colonial policy in relation to shifting agriculture, a system in which farmers move from site to site. Under this system, forest land is brought into cultivation by the slash and burn method and farmed until its productivity falls. Peasant agriculture in Ceylon failed to achieve the dynamic growth of the plantation sector during this same period, while methods of cultivation remained unchanged.

CONDITIONS OF DIFFERENTIATION

Portuguese colonialism did not lead to substantial changes in the native administrative system. When the Catholic Church arrived in Sri Lanka, however, it functioned as the ideological apparatus of the Portuguese colonialists. The arrival of the church therefore marked the beginning of a dark age for the Buddhists and Hindus of the island. Many converted to Catholicism or intermarried with the colonizers, spawning new social formations, such as

Ceylonese Chief from Kandy. *An 1815 treaty known as the Kandyan Convention brought Ceylon's Kandyan provinces under British sovereignty. Ceylon is now called Sri Lanka.* © HULTON-DEUTSCH COLLECTION/CORBIS. REPRODUCED BY PERMISSION.

The Dutch commercial company, the Verenigde Oost-Indische Compagnie (VOC, or Dutch United East India Company), entered the Sri Lankan scene at the beginning of the seventeenth century under the pretext of helping the king of Kandy wage war against the Portuguese. When the Dutch took possession of the island's Low Country, King Rajasinghe II (1635–1687) of Kandy organized a resistance that combined guerilla warfare, negotiation, and attempts at alliances with France and England. After his death, the VOC resorted to force against the Kandyans when they did not cease from inciting the Low Country Sinhalese to revolt against colonial rule.

In 1766 colonial rule in Ceylon was given written sanction when the Kandyan king was obliged to sign a treaty that gave the Dutch sovereignty over the entire coastline of the island up to a depth of one Sinhalese mile (5.6 kilometers; 3.5 miles). From then on, the kingdom of Kandy was a landlocked entity. The British took over the Dutch-controlled territory of Ceylon in 1796, and with an 1815 treaty known as the Kandyan Convention,

A Tea Plantation in Ceylon. *Laborers on a tea plantation in Ceylon (modern-day Sri Lanka) in the early twentieth century hang sacks of tea on ropes to move them to the drying house.* © HULTON-DEUTSCH COLLECTION/CORBIS. REPRODUCED BY PERMISSION.

Catholic Sinhalese or Tamils, as well as people of mixed descent. Converts were exempted from various taxes and generally given preferential treatment.

Portuguese rule also created conditions of differentiation between Kandyans and Low Country Sinhalese—the latter bearing the mark of the foreign presence in their legislation, land structures, and customs. Another significant change came with the upward mobility of certain castes associated with colonial power, especially the Salagamas (cinnamon peelers).

During Dutch rule, a number of natives converted to Protestantism, while interracial marriages created the Burgher community. The Dutch contributed to the evolution of the judicial system of the island as indigenous laws and customs that did not conflict with Dutch-Roman jurisprudence were codified. This was the case of the Tamil legal code of Jaffna (the Thesavalamai) and Muslim law. In the Low Country, courts applied Roman Dutch law, thus modifying traditional notions of property and affecting family structures.

The rapid expansion of plantation agriculture in the mid-nineteenth century was the major catalyst of social change in Sri Lanka. The growth of services to support the needs of the plantations and their workers stimulated the development of the Kandyan highlands and the city of Colombo. A class of local capitalists emerged, especially in the mining and export of graphite and in the coconut plantations. The island's traditional elite landowners, the Mudaliyars, were soon challenged by a new English-educated elite derived from all ethnic groups and castes.

THE TRANSFER OF POWER

The British transferred power in 1948 to a conservative multiethnic elite that had spearheaded a mild nationalist movement. The British felt that this group would offer the best resistance to the forces of cultural nationalism and Marxism then gaining momentum in the country. The westernized elites had on the whole been willing partners of the British. What resistance there had been occurred in the first two decades of the century when the temperance movement rallied Sinhalese Buddhists against the imposition of Christian values. Paradoxically, it was only in 1956 that a powerful nationalist movement would emerge to shake off the remnants of the colonial state.

SEE ALSO *Empire, Dutch.*

BIBLIOGRAPHY

Abeyasinghe, Tikiri. *Portuguese Rule in Ceylon, 1594–1612.* Colombo, Sri Lanka: Lake House Investments, 1966.

Abeyasinghe, Tikiri. "Princes and Merchants: Relations between the Kings and the Dutch East India Company in Sri Lanka, 1688–1740." *Journal of the Sri Lanka National Archives* 2 (1984): 35–60.

Arasaratnam, Sinnappah. Dutch *Power in Ceylon. 1658–1687.* Amsterdam: Djambatan, 1958.

De Silva, Kingsley M., ed. *A History of Ceylon*, Vol. 3. Peradeniya, Sri Lanka: University of Ceylon, 1973.

De Silva, Kingsley M., ed. *A History of Sri Lanka*, Vol. 2. Peradeniya, Sri Lanka: University of Peradeniya, 1995.

Dewaraja, Lorna. *The Kandyan Kingdom of Sri Lanka, 1707–1782.* Colombo, Sri Lanka: Lake House Investment, 1988.

Gombrich, Richard, and Obeysekere Gananath. *Buddhism Transformed: Religious Change in Sri Lanka.* Princeton, NJ: Princeton University Press: 1988.

Gunawardana, Leslie. "The People of the Lion: The Sinhala Identity and Ideology in History and Historiography." *Sri Lanka Journal of the Humanities* 5 (1979): 1–36.

Jayawardena, Kumari. *Nobodies to Somebodies: The Rise of the Colonial Bourgeoisie in Sri Lanka.* Colombo, Sri Lanka: Social Scientists Association, 2000.

Malalgoda, Kithsiri. *Buddhism in Sinhalese Society, 1750–1900: A Study of Religious Revival and Change.* Berkeley: University of California Press, 1976.

Wickramasinghe, Nira. "Divide and Rule in Ceylon (Sri Lanka) During the Period of Transfer of Power." Special Issue: Tikiri Abeyasinghe Commemoration. *University of Colombo Review* 10 (1991): 75–92.

Wickramasinghe, Nira. *Sri Lanka in the Modern Age: A History of Contested Identities.* London: C. Hurst, 2006.

Nira Wickramasinghe

CHARTERED COMPANIES, AFRICA

Chartered companies were companies that received certain rights and privileges under a special charter issued by the sovereign of a European state. This charter usually gave the company a nationally recognized trading monopoly for a specific geographic area and for specific trade items, and the right to use force to open and maintain trade. Dominant in the seventeenth and eighteenth centuries and from 1880 to 1900—the eras of mercantilism and of the "scramble for Africa," respectively—royally chartered companies proved to be indispensable tools for the opening of Africa to European commercial and imperial ambition.

As a way to defray government costs, European exploits in Africa from 1340 until 1900 were usually funded by high-risk venture capital in the form of royally chartered companies, the forerunners of the modern corporation. The crown provided political support and authorization for overseas business but the economic risks and military expenses were borne by private individuals and corporations. After 1600 large chartered companies like the Dutch West India Company, the Royal African Company, and the Portuguese Guinea Company created permanent strongholds on the coasts of Africa, though they had to form alliances with local African states in order to prosper. After 1870 the imperial ambitions of chartered companies like the British South Africa Company and the Royal Niger Company paved the way for Europe's formal colonization of most of the African continent.

CHARTERED COMPANIES IN THE AGE OF MERCANTILISM AND THE SLAVE TRADE, CA. 1450–1830

The European discovery of the Canary Islands off the west coast of Africa in the early 1330s prompted impoverished Spanish nobles, with financial backing from investors and royal charters from various monarchs, to organize repeated invasions of the islands until the final conquest of the native inhabitants in 1496 under a charter granted by the sovereign of Castile. The charter provided royal authorization for the invasion without costing the monarch any money. The invaders assumed governmental powers and were authorized to collect rent and taxes for themselves, their investors, and the monarch. Throughout their history chartered companies demonstrated that the relationship between entrepreneurship and violence was ever-present in the European engagement with Africa. While trade and profit were dominant elements in the exchanges between the two continents, state-sanctioned violence achieved far more than entrepreneurial activity could do alone.

Leaving the Canary Islands to the Spanish, the Portuguese established a fort at Elmina near the deltas of the Volta and Niger rivers in 1482 and became involved in the inter-African slave trade. Italian and Portuguese investors, excited by the strong European market for sugar, obtained charters from the Portuguese crown to develop sugar plantations on the islands of São Tomé, Principe, and Fernando Po, which lay off the coast of tropical Africa. Unable to attract Europeans as a workforce, they relied on Portuguese connections with African commerce to supply African slave labor. In the year 1500, these islands became the first true plantation societies in the Atlantic.

By the mid-1500s Dutch, Flemish, and German capitalists had entered the sugar boom that had shifted to the Portuguese colony of Brazil. The famous Triangle Trade had begun: Africa imported European capital, manufactured goods, and weapons and exported labor in the form of slaves, while the plantation colonies in the Americas specialized in the mass production of a few tropical products (sugar, tobacco, cacao, coffee, and indigo) for the European market and imported capital, labor, and supplies. Chartered companies like the Portuguese Guinea Company and the Dutch West India Company became the main suppliers of African slaves to the New World in the sixteenth and seventeenth centuries respectively, whereas the English dominated the slave trade in the eighteenth century.

England and the Netherlands underwrote their colonial expansion between 1600 and 1800 by creating chartered joint-stock companies. These new types of chartered companies allowed larger amounts of capital to be raised; they separated stock ownership from management, and investors could sell stock instead of liquidating the firm periodically to retrieve assets and profits. In a hallmark of an emerging capitalist economy, the new chartered companies built up and reinvested their capital rather than redistributing all the invested capital and profits back to their owners after each voyage. In the tradition of earlier chartered companies, these new chartered companies were licensed to trade and to make war to promote trade. The Dutch and English chartered companies, following earlier Portuguese practice, tapped into indigenous trade networks and maintained relations with African states in Benin, Oyo, and Kongo. Their presence created a growing African market for European hardware, textiles, and weapons, for which Africans traded gold, ivory, and slaves.

These new chartered companies, like the Dutch West India Company (WIC; founded 1621), had a legal monopoly on imports from Africa back to the home country and a license to seek monopolies in other markets, using armed force if necessary. They maintained standing armies and forts in addition to carrying out routine business transactions. The Dutch state chartered the WIC to conduct economic warfare against Spain and Portugal by striking at their colonies in the Americas and on the west coast of Africa. The state granted the company a monopoly on Dutch trade in the Atlantic region between the Americas and Africa and empowered it to negotiate treaties and make war and peace with native rulers, appoint governors, and legislate in its territories. With military and financial support from the government, the WIC acquired ports on the west coast of

Africa to supply slaves for plantations in the Americas. Because of intense Portuguese, English, and French competition, the WIC was never able to monopolize the supply of slaves from Africa. No chartered company ever was.

Most chartered companies lasted no more than a generation or two. The longest-lived in Africa was the Dutch East India Company, which founded a restocking station for its East India ships at the Cape of Good Hope in 1652. When the company dissolved in 1799, Cape Town formed the nucleus of European (Boer) settlement of the Cape Colony in South Africa. The second-longest-lived chartered company in Africa was the WIC (1621–1674), which folded due to debts incurred by long wars with the Portuguese and other European powers and the loss of key trading posts destroyed or captured by rival European nations. Parliament chartered the Royal African Company (RAC) in 1672 as the English slave-trading monopoly after a similar venture in the 1660s failed due to war with Holland. The monopoly was limited to London merchants, but merchants from Bristol and Liverpool lobbied successfully to have the monopoly charter ended by 1713—even though supporters of the monopoly argued that it ensured profits needed to build ships, maintain African trading settlements, and pay attractive dividends to shareholders, and that the highly advantageous trade between England and its colonies relied on the military protection of RAC forts on the coast of Africa. The RAC continued to engage in the slave trade, however, until 1731.

Europe and Africa were changed by the activities of chartered companies. The slave trade provided the kingdoms of coastal Africa with foreign exchange that soon exceeded their earnings from traditional exports like gold, pepper, ivory, and cotton cloth. As the Atlantic slave trade expanded from a few dozen slaves a year in the 1520s to ninety thousand a year in the 1780s, it allowed African elites on the Atlantic coast to buy European ironware, luxury goods, textiles, and weapons (to the tune of thousands of muskets a year in the 1780s). This trade, facilitated by European chartered companies, did not undermine African independence so much as it changed the balance of power between African states. The great empires of the interior grasslands like Mali and Songhay lost revenue and began to disintegrate when trade was diverted to the Atlantic kingdoms of Benin, Oyo, and Kongo, which became richer and acquired new military technology. The economies of interior states weakened as families and work were disrupted by massive forced abductions of people. Initially Africa's Atlantic trade was a reciprocal exchange of commodities, but soon that exchange was overshadowed by the slave trade. An estimated ten to eleven million Africans were sent to the

Americas as slaves between 1443 and 1870 by chartered companies and millions more died on the forced marches to the coastal ports.

Europe was also caught up in the transformations wrought by chartered companies. Europeans controlled each leg of the Triangle Trade and enormous wealth was consolidated by European investors as a result. That control was fostered by chartered companies and the economic ideas of mercantilism they embodied. Mercantilism held that there was a fixed amount of wealth in the world, measured by possession of gold and silver, and that each country had to fight to obtain as large a share of this wealth as possible, aided by government policies that limited imports and promoted exports to create a favorable balance of payments. Economics was war by other means: Colonies and fortified trading stations existed to provide revenue for the mother country and to ensure that the trade was as monopolistic as possible, in order to keep gold and silver at home. Competing and aggressive chartered companies could not maintain secure monopolies, but the transfer of credit and profits around the world that they facilitated was a major step in the rise of a modern capitalist world economy. As the costs of war making soared in the eighteenth century, however, British and Dutch chartered companies staggered under the burden and they were all bankrupted by the 1830s: they did not outlast Britain's abolition of the Atlantic slave trade in 1807 and of slavery in 1833.

CHARTERED COMPANIES AND THE NEW IMPERIALISM, 1880–1924

After a brief hiatus, chartered companies were once again the vanguard and spur of imperial ambition when Europeans took direct control of Africa after 1880. Europeans colonized Africa under the impetus of the Long Depression (1873–1896), a world economic crisis that sparked the creation of monopolies and cartels and new colonial empires and monopoly trading relations in Africa as ways to stabilize the profitability of the new industrial capitalism. Chartered companies played a vital role in these territorial annexations and in the securing of sources of raw materials and valuable minerals for European nations.

The rise of Germany, Belgium, and Italy as industrial powers after 1870 accelerated the tempo of colonial growth as these nations sought protected markets and sources of raw materials for their industries in a depressed world economy. Britain, fearing these new colonial challengers, joined the colonial scramble in Africa. Belgium's claim to the Congo River basin and Germany's annexationist activities on the west and east coasts of Africa prompted a conference in Berlin in 1884 to lay out ground rules for annexations. Article 35 of the Berlin Act stated that a mere claim to territory was not enough for international recognition of a colony. Under the doctrine of "effective occupation" the colonizer had to prove that it had authority over a colony, and thus European monarchs turned to chartered companies to ensure effective economic and political occupation. This new political climate induced the Portuguese to set up chartered companies like the Companhia de Boror to secure their four-hundred-year-old claim to Mozambique.

After the Berlin Conference, Britain concentrated its colonizing efforts on the Niger and southern African regions (the centers of its commercial activity in Africa) and on Kenya, France focused on the area between Senegal and Lake Chad, and Germany sent chartered companies to Togo, Cameroon, South-West Africa, and Tanganyika. The most effective and successful chartered companies were British, such as the Royal Niger Company and the British South Africa Company. They secured Britain's empire in Africa.

Building on the commercial ideas of George Goldie (1846–1925), the Royal Niger Company (RNC), chartered in 1886, amalgamated British business interests in the lower Niger region. Its charter of incorporation authorized it to administer the Niger delta and the country along the banks of the Niger and Benue Rivers. Palm oil was a major export and the main imports were cloth and alcoholic beverages. The company secured its monopoly of trade in the area of present-day Nigeria against French and German competitors by concluding treaties, some of doubtful legality, with local rulers. In negotiations with the French and German governments Goldie set the boundaries of the British sphere of influence. The establishment of trading stations in the interior, contrary to earlier agreements, resulted in African uprisings against the RNC in 1886 and 1895, which were put down with gunboats, the company's police force, and ships of the Royal Navy. The continuation of the RNC's commercial and territorial disputes with France and the continuing complaints of local peoples against the company caused the British government to revoke the company's charter in 1899, but by then Britain had effectively occupied the lower Niger region.

Another British commercial adventurer, Cecil Rhodes (1853–1902), received a charter for the South Africa Company (SAC) in 1889 with the object of acquiring and exercising commercial and administrative rights in south central Africa. The charter, initially granted for twenty-five years, gave the company rights to make treaties, promulgate laws, acquire economic concessions, establish a police force, and provide, at the company's expense, the infrastructure of a new colony initially in Matabeleland (now part of Zimbabwe) but extending as far as current-day Zambia, Malawi, and Botswana. Mineral wealth (gold and diamonds), communications (a Cape-to-Cairo railroad), and white settlement were Rhodes's objectives. Gold and diamond mining was the company's main business and by 1900 SAC was administering Southern and Northern Rhodesia. Company rule ended in Southern Rhodesia (now Zimbabwe) in 1923, when partial self-rule for whites was implemented; in Northern Rhodesia (now Zambia) it ended in 1924, when the Colonial Office assumed control. By then, the activities of the SAC had secured British control and claims on this area of southern Africa.

In the final analysis, the development of the chartered joint-stock company, forerunner of the modern corporation, was instrumental in European commercial and colonial incursions into Africa. Chartered companies in Africa aided the emergence of a European-centered global capitalism that required African labor, commerce, and colonies to thrive, but which took more from Africa than it gave in return.

SEE ALSO *Cape Colony and Cape Town; Dutch United East India Company; Dutch West India Company; English East India Company (EIC).*

BIBLIOGRAPHY

Hobsbawm, E. J. *The Age of Empire, 1875–1914.* New York: Vintage, 1989.

Pomeranz, Kenneth, and Steven Topik. *The World That Trade Created: Society, Culture, and the World Economy, 1400 to the Present.* Armonk, NY: M. E. Sharpe, 1999.

Ringrose, David R. *Expansion and Global Interaction, 1200–1700.* New York: Longman, 2001.

Alexander M. Zukas

CHINA, TO THE FIRST OPIUM WAR

China was first confronted with European colonialism in the course of the Portuguese expansion in Asia during the early sixteenth century. In 1511 Malacca (Melaka), on the west coast of the Malay Peninsula, was occupied by a force under the command of the Portuguese viceroy of India, Afonso de'Albuquerque (d. 1515). Malacca became an important base for Portuguese trade contacts with China. Malacca had been a Chinese vassal state and the sultan called for assistance, but the Chinese emperor only issued an edict to Siam (Thailand) to send help, which never arrived.

The Portuguese arrived on China's southern coast in 1514 to 1516 and reached Canton (Guangzhou) in 1517. China granted the Portuguese permission to trade, but after several confrontations the Portuguese were driven out in 1522 to 1523. Nevertheless, some Portuguese traders, mainly involved in smuggling, remained in China. In 1557 they achieved permission to settle in Macao on the southern coast of China, which became the region's main base for Western trade for over a century.

Spain began colonizing the Philippine archipelago in 1565. Shortly thereafter, galleon trade between Acapulco in Mexico and the Philippine port city of Manila was established, bringing goods, mainly silver, from the New World into the Asian trade system. This development caused the emergence of a silver money economy in China and stimulated Chinese commerce.

Spain soon challenged the Portuguese position in the China trade and in 1598 even tried to establish a trading post near Canton. Even after Portugal fell under Spanish rule in 1581, the Portuguese in Macao remained eager to keep their monopoly, and they repeatedly attacked Spanish shipping.

In 1601 the first Dutch ship entered Chinese waters near Macao. The Dutch quickly became a serious rival for Portuguese trade. They attacked Macao and established a base on Taiwan. However, the Dutch were besieged and driven out of Taiwan in 1662 by the army of Koxinga (Zheng Chenggong, 1624–1662), which was retreating from the increasing power of the upcoming Qing dynasty.

One important factor of European influence in China were Christian missionaries. The Jesuit Matteo Ricci (1552–1610) arrived in southern China in 1582 and went on to Beijing in 1601. Ricci not only attempted to convert the Chinese to Christendom, he also introduced such Western knowledge as the solar calendar. Ricci's most prominent successors were the Jesuits Johann Adam Schall von Bell (1591–1666), who reached Macao in 1619, and Ferdinand Verbiest (1623–1688). The Jesuits also brought knowledge of China to Europe, which led to a "China fashion" in philosophy and art. Most missionaries were expelled from China by the Kangxi emperor in 1721 after Pope Clement XI (1649–1721) decided in the "Chinese rites controversy" that the adoption of Chinese customs was incompatible with Catholic principles.

China's contact with the outside world had been repeatedly limited. Ming dynasty (1368–1644) rulers prohibited private trade completely and limited foreign trade contacts to tribute missions. China still participated in the Southeast Asian trade system, but this participation expanded considerably only after the Ming officially lifted their ban in 1567. Chinese communities developed in growing colonial ports, such as Batavia (Jakarta) and Manila, and became important agents for contacts between the European colonies and mainland China.

China was itself an empire, and maintained considerable interests in and colonial relations with its neighbours. Ming China regarded itself as the center of the world, foreign relations being only possible as tribute relationships. Although the early Qing dynasty (1644–1911) originated as foreign rulers over China, the Qing emperors soon adopted the Ming view of the Chinese world order. The Qing quickly moved from consolidation to expansion. In the course of exterminating the last Ming forces, they occupied territories in southern China and the island of Taiwan. In the eighteenth century, the high Qing period, China conquered Tibet and parts of Central Asia and gained control over Mongolia.

Soon after the Qing came to power, they banned most contacts with the outside world to prevent any foreign support for the remaining Ming armies. But in 1684, when the Qing dynasty established its hold on power, the Kangxi emperor relaxed the earlier ban and permitted limited trade along China's southeast coast.

The first British ship called at Xiamen (Amoy) in 1685. Other nations, such as Denmark, France, the Netherlands, and Sweden, were quick to follow. The first American traders arrived in 1784 after their war of independence. The British, however, dominated this renewed trade with China from the start, and around 1800 British trading vessels to China amounted to twice as many as all other nations combined.

The Western trade concentrated at the southern Chinese port of Canton, and in 1760 the Qianlong emperor restricted trade to this port. The so-called Canton system developed at this time, according to which Western traders were only allowed to trade during the winter season and had to remain in Macao for the rest of the year. Trade was confined to a small area outside the city walls, and transactions with Chinese were limited to a group of licensed merchants called *cohong* (after the Chinese *gonghang*, meaning "official company").

Russia was the only Western power to trade with China via her inland borders. After minor conflicts, China and Russia resolved their border conflicts and regulated trade in the treaties of Nerchinsk (1689) and Kyakhta (1727).

The most important goods exported from China were porcelain, silk, and tea. The English East India Company enjoyed the monopoly of direct trade between China and England and thus profited enormously, as did the British government through import taxes. The main problem in this exchange was the inability of the West to bring products of equivalent value to China. Chinese exports were mainly paid for in silver.

Great Britain hoped to change the restrictive Canton system in 1793 by sending Lord George Macartney (1737–1806) to request the opening of additional ports, but China's Qianlong emperor refused to alter the terms of trade. To compensate for the trade deficit, the East India Company began growing opium in India and exporting the drug to China. As the opium disrupted the trade balance and silver began to flow out of China, the Qing rulers reacted by banning opium imports. In response, British and other Western traders smuggled the opium into China. With the growing popularity of the concept of free trade, however, the East India Company's monopoly was abolished in 1834. When the Chinese government resolved to implement harsher measures against the opium trade in 1839, the British government came under severe pressure from the free trade lobby to bring down the restrictive Canton system, leading to the first Opium War (1839–1842).

SEE ALSO *China, First Opium War to 1945; China, Foreign Trade; Guangzhou; Hong Kong, to World War II; Religion, Western Presence in East Asia; Shanghai; Taiping Rebellion; Treaties, East Asia and the Pacific.*

BIBLIOGRAPHY

Fairbank, John King, ed. *The Chinese World Order: Traditional China's Foreign Relations.* Cambridge, MA: Harvard University Press, 1968.

Fairbank, John King, ed. *The Missionary Enterprise in China and America.* Cambridge, MA: Harvard University Press, 1974.

Gernet, Jacques. *A History of Chinese Civilization,* 2nd ed. Translated by J. R. Foster and Charles Hartman. Cambridge, U.K.: Cambridge University Press, 1996.

Osterhammel, Jürgen. *China und die Weltgesellschaft: Vom 18, Jahrhundert bis in unsere Zeit.* Munich: Verlag C. H. Beck, 1989.

Perdue, Peter C. *China Marches West: The Qing Conquest of Central Eurasia.* Cambridge, MA: Harvard University Press, 2005.

Twitchett, Denis, and Frederick W. Mote. *The Cambridge History of China;* Vol. 8: *The Ming Dynasty, 1368–1644,* Pt. 2. Cambridge, U.K.: Cambridge University Press, 1998.

Cord Eberspaecher

CHINA, FIRST OPIUM WAR TO 1945

China, the world's oldest continuous civilization, possessed a heritage of greatness that a rapidly changing industrial world began to dispute by the early nineteenth century. The culture that gave the world printing, paper, the compass, gunpowder, and provided its people a reasonably stable social and economic environment over the centuries, now confronted foreign and domestic challenges to the Confucian world order that had guided China for nearly two millennia. From that time until the end of World War II (1939–1945), China suffered incessant military attacks from homegrown rebels and foreign assailants, producing colossal social and economic dislocation, massive death and destruction, as well as traumatic intellectual and cultural crises of confidence. China's rulers, intellectuals, and eventually the common people have since searched for the means by which to unify the nation, expel the foreigners, embrace a successful model of development, and thus restore China to its former greatness.

CHALLENGE TO THE OLD ORDER, 1800–1860

Without the benefit of hindsight, the White Lotus Rebellion of 1796–1804 could reasonably be considered a harbinger of dynastic decline that would eventually result in the removal of the Mandate of Heaven from the ruling foreign Manchu Qing dynasty (1644–1911) and bring about the establishment of another dynasty promising to govern by appropriate Confucian principles. Instead of being yet another example of China's dynastic cycle in operation, it proved to be the event that exposed a weak and corrupt dynasty to a modernizing West determined to finance its China trade with illegal opium and to substitute its structure of international relations—this assumed equality among nations for China's tributary system of international interaction, which presumed a hierarchical arrangement, with China at the top.

The opium trade grew out of the West's unfavorable balance of trade with China, which bought very little from abroad but sold very much to foreigners. Illegal opium sales to willing Chinese customers provided the necessary currency to fund the purchase of Chinese goods, such as tea, silk, and porcelain. Illegal opium trafficking led to an outflow of silver, which upset the bimetallic silver and copper coinage structure. Opium smoking hurt the poor, who were the largest consumers, and it involved government and military officials. The opium trade was further complicated by the emergence of free trade in England. The Chinese tributary system allowed only Chinese and foreign monopoly merchants to conduct trade, and only at Guangzhou (Canton), a protocol agreed to by foreign governments until the growing pressure of free traders and Beijing's evident inability to enforce the system led to its collapse. In 1836, the high Qing officials debated the opium problem and decided to continue the policy of prohibition and committed it to enforcing prohibition. Beijing sent

Commissioner Lin Zexu (ca. 1785–1850) to Guangzhou to carry out the policy, and when he confiscated British opium it served as a pretext for war, which the Chinese label the first Opium War (1839–1842) and the British call the first Anglo-Chinese War.

China's defeat resulted in a century of "unequal treaties" that gave foreign powers special rights in China, including extraterritoriality in treaty ports (five in 1842 and more than two hundred by the turn of the twentieth century), a favoring of nation status, and control over China's tariffs. The 1842 Treaty of Nanjing, which ended the war, officially terminated the tribute system, provided foreigners extraterritorial rights, ceded Hong Kong to Britain, and required a Chinese monetary indemnity. China resisted the terms of this and subsequent treaties with the West, especially the opening of the city of Guangzhou to foreign residence, which created a second Opium War (1856–1860). With China's defeat, resulting in a new set of treaties, loss of territory, and new indemnities, both the court and bureaucracy realized that some modification of Confucian ways needed to be made.

That realization was made all the more evident with the outbreak of the Taiping Rebellion (1851–1864), a native challenge to the Confucian order. Taipings or God worshippers led by "God's Chinese son" Hong Xiuquan (1814–1864) proclaimed the Heavenly Kingdom of Great Peace, which called for communal land use, a common treasury to be filled by surplus products and to be drawn from by those in need, an examination system that tested candidates' knowledge of the Bible, equality of the sexes, the elimination of ancestor worship, as well as other far-reaching transformations. Only fundamental Qing government reform (the Tongzhi Restoration), foreign neutrality, and inherent Taiping leadership weaknesses saved the Confucian order.

ATTEMPTS TO SALVAGE THE OLD ORDER, 1860–1900

A quarter century of potentially fatal foreign and domestic assaults on traditional government, thought, and behavior led the Manchu Qing dynasty and its Chinese Confucian bureaucracy to consider basic changes. Generally labeled *self-strengthening*, this new Chinese reform program sought to begin a program of modernization that embraced foreign techniques (*yong*), but maintained an essential Confucian foundation (*ti/t'i*). This reform program included the creation of a foreign office (Zongli Yamen), a foreign-language school, an interpreters college, factories and arsenals, as well as the sending overseas of Chinese students and the hiring of Anson Burlingame (1820–1870) to represent China's interests in Europe and America.

But self-strengthening reform moved at a snail's pace owing to several factors. First, the urgency to change China declined as the court in Beijing realized that the industrial powers were tied to the treaty benefits agreed to by the Qing government, benefits that might not be honored by a new Chinese regime. Further, a heated debate arose within the Confucian bureaucracy over reform, the more conservative-minded arguing that using foreign techniques would in fact change the essence of China.

Indeed the Confucian elite could well be displaced by some new industrial elite. The foreign Manchu court under the Empress Dowager Cixi (1835–1908) chose to balance conservative and reform interests as the best means of maintaining power.

The result was a timid move toward modernization, the limitations of which became apparent in the first Sino-Japanese War of 1894–1895, fought to determine whether China or Japan would protect Korea against the outside world. China was soundly defeated militarily, and the Treaty of Shimonoseki (1895) ended the conflict provided that Japan would receive Taiwan, a large monetary indemnity, the right to open factories in China, and other benefits. The humiliating loss launched a wave of protest and in 1898 a brief reform movement, which the empress dowager quickly crushed. Desperate for a means of dealing with domestic dissidents determined to transform China and foreign aggressors eager to divide up the country, the court turned to the Boxers, who had originally been anti-Qing but by the late nineteenth century had become pro-Qing and antiforeign. The Righteous and Harmonious Fists, thus Boxers, soon became the Righteous and Harmonious Militia that promised to drive the foreigners from China and destroy Christian missions, as well as besieging the foreign legations in Beijing. This immediately brought eight foreign armies to Beijing to crush the "rebellion" and impose on China the Boxer Protocol, yet another embarrassing agreement signed under military duress. From this point on, China's elite generally conceded at the very least the need for fundamental reform. But even revolution did not sound intolerably extreme at this moment.

SEARCHING FOR A NEW ORDER, 1900–1945

The first half of the twentieth century in China was a time of searching for the best means of reorganizing itself so it could survive in a terribly dangerous world. The dynasty's post-Boxer reforms indicated the extent to which even the most conservative thinkers were willing to go in saving China from the perils of partition and perpetual weakness. These restructurings included the elimination of many government positions deemed unnecessary, especially those that were purchased. New

offices were created to deal with what were becoming universal Western ways of business, diplomacy, law, national defense, education, and social intercourse. Thus a ministry of foreign affairs emerged, as did the rudiments of a modern army; universities replaced Confucian academies, and the civil service examination system was abolished in 1905; social reform included the end of footbinding and a serious anti-opium campaign; and political reform was launched in 1905—the court's thinking being that a constitutional monarchy would suit China (and the dynasty) much better than a revolution advanced by Sun Yat-Sen (1866–1925).

Although one could argue that this reform program did amount to something, most historians believe it came too late. Less than a decade into reform, the emperor and the empress dowager died within a month of each other (December 1908 and January 1909) and no Manchu leadership emerged to deal with the nation's problems. Increasingly, native Chinese also began to view the Manchu leadership as the principle cause for China's weakness and perceive these rulers as foreign occupiers.

In October 1911 a revolution broke out, and by the end of the year the dynasty abdicated and the Republic of China proclaimed independence. Inspired by Sun Yat-Sen, but controlled by former high Qing official Yuan Shi-kai (1859–1916), the new government, which had promised to operate on democratic principles, functioned instead by dictatorial means. With Yuan's death in 1916 the nation descended into warlordism, which resulted in the common people's oppression, divided China into military satrapies, and thus increased the country's susceptibility to foreign encroachment. Even before Yuan's passing, Japan had attempted to impose its control over China with the so-called Twenty-one Demands in 1915.

Chinese nationalism had clearly emerged at this point, best evidenced by the forming of the New Culture Movement beginning in 1915, the outbreak of the May Fourth Movement in 1919, the early 1920s reorganization of Sun Yat-Sen Nationalist Party (Guomindang), as well as the creation of the Communist Party. The New Culture Movement sought to bring literacy to the common people, the foundation of a modern nation, by supporting the introduction of vernacular Chinese as the written language. The May Fourth Movement erupted when the victorious allies at Versailles gave Qingdao, a German leasehold, to Japan instead of returning it to China. Chinese nationalists, mainly urbanites, produced massive protest movements in Tiananmen Square and elsewhere in China, which served as launching platforms for organizations dedicated to destroying the warlords, unifying the country, and driving out the foreigners.

Both the Nationalist and Communist parties sought these goals, the significant difference between them being

TWENTY-ONE DEMANDS

■

The Twenty-one Demands were issued on January 18, 1915, by Japanese prime minister Okuma Shigenobu in an opportunistic attempt to dominate Manchuria's natural resources. Taking advantage of the opportunity provided by World War I, which had been ongoing against Germany since August of 1914, Shigenobu hoped to achieve supremacy in the Pacific region and ignored the fact that China was, like Japan, allied with the Triple Entente that included Great Britain, France, and Russia. After Japanese troops invaded the German-controlled Jiaozhou region in China's southern Shandong Province, Shigenobu presented Chinese president Yuan Shi-kai with a five-part ultimatum, demanding that:

- Japan formally be given control of Jiaozhou;
- the coal-rich regions of south Manchuria and eastern Inner Mongolia's Shandong Province be made open to Japanese commercial exploitation and colonization by right of Japan's historic geographical and commercial interests there;
- China discontinue allowing other governments to lease or otherwise take control of any territory within its borders;
- Japanese nationals be allowed religious freedom and the right to own land within China; and
- that Japanese advisors have the final word on China's military, economic, and commercial policies, as well as positions of authority in urban law enforcement throughout China.

When news of the Twenty-one Demands was made public, worldwide opinion demanded their withdrawal.

Through the intervention of British and U.S. diplomats, Japan dropped its demand for control of China's military, commercial, and financial affairs, as well as certain specific demands regarding schools and hospitals, supplying arms and ammunition to Japanese law enforcement within Chinese borders, and the establishment of arsenals and railway concessions in South China. With several demands still on the table, months of negotiations between China and Japan ensued, only ending when Japan threatened to make further military inroads into China. Recognizing that his military was no match for that of Japan, President Yuan accepted Shigenobu's revised terms. Although two treaties were signed on May 25, 1915, officially transferring German interests in Qingdao to Japan and extending Japan's lease of Manchuria's coal-rich Liao-d-ung Peninsula and railroad system, they were never ratified by the Chinese legislature. Public protest over Yuan's acceptance of Japan's claims resulted in a wide-scale boycott of Japanese goods throughout China.

Two years later, the Japanese reinforced these claims in secret treaties, and a second agreement was coerced from the Chinese government in 1918. At the Versailles Conference held at the close of World War I, Japan was awarded Qingdao on the strength of its coerced and clandestine treaties with Yuan, despite China's protest. Consequently, China refused to sign the Treaty of Versailles. Japan continued to station troops in Shandong Province and to control Qingdao until their claims were rendered void in the Washington Naval Conference of 1921–1922.

the need for social revolution. The emergence of the Soviet Union in 1917 and its desire to protect itself and promote world revolution resulted in the formation of the First United Front (1923–1927) between Nationalists and Communists, brokered by Moscow with the expectation of weakening those capitalist nations politically and economically active in China. The two parties formed an army and launched a Northern Expedition in 1926 and 1927 to drive out the warlords, but by the spring of 1927 had a falling out as the new leader of the Nationalists, Jiang Jieshi (1887–1975),

broke with the Communists over the need for social revolution, while drawing closer to the United States and England, abandoning the Soviets, and isolating Japan. Tokyo had substantial political and economic interests in China, especially in Manchuria, and ultimately protected them by gradually annexing Manchuria between 1931and 1933 and invading parts of northern and coastal China.

Meanwhile the domestic battle between the Nationalists and the Communists continued. After Jiang purged the Communists from the alliance against the warlords, he established a national government at

Nanjing in 1927 and ruled China until defeated by the Communists in 1949. The Nanjing or Nationalist government had three major tasks on its agenda: defeating the Communists; keeping the Japanese at bay until the Communists were defeated and the country unified; and modernizing the country. The campaign against the Communists looked promising, especially so long as the Communists sought to overthrow the Nationalists by attacking the cities where the proletariat resided. Such attempts utterly failed.

When by the mid-1930s Mao Zedong (1893–1976) emerged to challenge the urban approach to revolution and instead sought to mobilize the peasants, the Communists got a new breath of life. Even though driven from its rural Jiangxi Soviet base in 1934 and forced on the Long March to Yan'an, the Communists seemed stronger. When Jiang ordered one of his generals to attack the Yan'an Communist base area, Zhang Xueliang (1898–2001) refused, instead insisting that all Chinese unite to resist Japanese encroachment. Jiang flew to Xian to confront Zhang just before Christmas 1936, but instead was taken prisoner himself. The Communists sent an emissary to Xian to seek Jiang's release, arguing that he was the only person capable of rallying the people of China against Japan. This Xian Incident provided the basis for the Second United Front between Nationalists and Communists that nominally lasted until the end of World War II.

On July 7, 1937, Japan launched yet another attack on China, but on this occasion the Chinese responded militarily. The war went badly for the Nationalists, who lost their urban, modern, coastal base to the Japanese and ended up in backwater Chongqing. The Communists, on the other hand, fared well as they were able to mobilize the peasants and expand throughout much of rural North China. As war erupted in Europe in 1939, Adolf Hitler (1889–1945) and his Japanese allies seemed increasingly dangerous and thus worthy of confronting after two decades of nations attempting to avoid any action that might provoke another world war. With the Japanese attack on Pearl Harbor in December 1941, the fate of Japan now rested in American hands. Accordingly, Nationalists and Communists jockeyed for position in China after Japan's defeat.

By 1945 the Nationalist government was exhausted and would eventually succumb to Communist energy and efficiency. Yet the Nationalist Party did move China closer to regaining its lost prestige, even though its tenure was marked by chronic civil and international conflict. It began a program of modernization in the cities, brought about an end to the "unequal treaties" in 1943, and established China as one of the five great powers on the security council of the newly formed

United Nations. And though it proved incapable of creating a system of government to replace the old Confucian political arrangements, neither did the successor Communist Party, as the Marxist model of development has been substantially abandoned. By the early twenty-first century, China still searches for a consensus about where it is heading and how it should get there.

SEE ALSO *British American Tobacco Company; China, after 1945; China, Foreign Trade; China, to the First Opium War; Chinese Revolutions; Compradorial System; Extraterritoriality; Guangzhou; Hong Kong, from World War II; Hong Kong, to World War II; Mao Zedong; Opium; Opium Wars; Self-Strengthening Movements, East Asia and the Pacific; Treaties, East Asia and the Pacific.*

BIBLIOGRAPHY

Hsü, Immanuel C. Y. *The Rise of Modern China*, 6th ed. New York: Oxford University Press, 2000.

Levenson, Joseph R. *Confucian China and Its Modern Fate; A Trilogy.* Berkeley, CA: University of California Press, 1968.

Sheridan, James E. *China in Disintegration: The Republican Era in Chinese History, 1912–1949.* New York: Free Press, 1975.

Spence, Jonathan D. *The Search for Modern China.* New York: Norton, 1990.

Tu, Wei-ming, ed. *China in Transformation.* Cambridge, MA: Harvard University Press, 1994.

Wakeman, Frederic, Jr. *The Fall of Imperial China.* New York: Free Press, 1975.

Thomas Reins

CHINA, AFTER 1945

Tattered and torn from decades of Western colonial extraterritoriality and Japanese military occupation, China emerged from the ashes of World War II only to plunge full force back into civil war that had begun in the late 1920s but had been put on hold while the country struggled with the Japanese occupiers. Ferociously resumed between the Nationalists and the Chinese Communist Party, the civil war raged until October 1949 when the communists, lead by Mao Zedong, declared victory with a speech from the Forbidden City. The Nationalists retreated to the island of Taiwan by December 1949. With the establishment of the communist government, all of the extraterritorialities—a system by which the colonial powers were not bound by Chinese laws and de facto ruled portions of the country—were disbanded and virtually all westerners were expelled from China as the government began the long, and often tumultuous, task of transforming the once great, but now shattered, country.

China set on the task of rebuilding. Throughout the 1950s, the country was reorganized, with major social reforms such as the banning of multiple wives and reordering villages into communes. By the end of that decade, however, there was a major split between China and the Soviet Union, one of China's few supporters in this early phase of the Cold War, due to differences over their efforts in the Korean War (1950–1953), over ideological interpretations of communism, and over the Soviet refusal to share atomic bomb technology.

With continued boycott by all the Western powers now supplemented with hostile relations with the Soviet Union, China launched into the 1960s with a disastrous approach called the Great Leap Forward, which was an attempt to rapidly push the still the underdeveloped country into industrialization and resulted in one of the largest famines in the world history. The decade ended no more smoothly than it began with yet another devastating movement called the Cultural Revolution, from approximately 1966 to 1976. Remnants of the Cultural Revolution, a massive social and political movement meant to destroy Chinese traditions and society, lasted until the death of Mao in 1976. After a brief struggle with the Maoist faction, the notorious Gang of Four, China ushered in a more prosperous and less turbulent era.

The faction that opposed Mao's policies, initially called the "pragmatists," rose to power in 1979 through the leadership of Deng Xiaoping. Deng initiated a policy of domestic reform, both politically and economically, and began opening to the West and the world. Deng not only changed the Chinese economy from a centrally controlled communist economy to a market-based economy, but also revamped the political system so that just one tyrant would no longer rule the country. The impact throughout the 1980s was a booming Chinese economy and growing political pluralism in China, which welcomed Western and Japanese investment for the first time since 1949.

The country's 1980s growth was chilled by the Tiananmen Square incident, a two-month-long demonstration in the Chinese capital city of Beijing, by student and worker protesters desiring social and political change to accompany the economic change and protesting the economic ills of inflation and unemployment as a result of these same economic changes. The government ultimately responded with force against the protesters in the early morning hours of June 4, 1989. Western governments reacted with bans on certain trade with China.

As a result of the Tiananmen Square incident, a new president, Jiang Zemin, came to power in the 1990s. Jiang continued the policies of economic growth and reform without political reform. China prospered in the 1990s, accelerating exports to the world. Although tensions with the government on Taiwan continued, China's relations with the rest of the world advanced as China became a responsible member in global organizations, such as the World Trade Organization, and took on a leadership role in Asia.

A new page in Chinese history dawned in the twenty-first century. Not only has China reemerged as a powerful global economy, but also subtle political changes were revealed in 2003 with the rise of the president, Hu Jintao, a candidate not backed by the outgoing President Jiang. China began the twenty-first century on a more level playing field with the Western powers and began building new relationships. While some scholars and politicians in the West talk about the "China threat" from this reemerging power, others believe that a stronger, more stabile China will not only help the one-quarter of the world's population that lives within its borders, but also will contribute to a more balanced world.

SEE ALSO *British American Tobacco Company; China, First Opium War to 1945; China, Foreign Trade; China to the First Opium War; Chinese Revolutions; Compradorial System; Extraterritoriality; Guangzhou; Hong Kong; Mao Zedong; Opium; Opium Wars; Shanghai; Taiping Rebellion; Treaties, East Asia and the Pacific.*

BIBLIOGRAPHY

Davis, Elizabeth Van Wie. *Chinese Perceptions on Sino-American Relations, 1950–2000.* Lewiston, NY: Edwin Mellen Press, 2000.

Fairbank, John King. *East Asia: Tradition and Transformation.* Boston: Houghton Mifflin, 1978.

Hsu, Immanuel Chung-yueh. *The Rise of Modern China*, 6th ed. New York: Oxford University Press, 1999.

Spence, Jonathan D. *The Search for Modern China.* New York: Norton, 1999.

Elizabeth Van Wie Davis

CHINESE REVOLUTIONS

China's Five-thousand-year-old imperial government entered the twentieth century under the traditionalist Qing dynasty (1644–1911) at a time when China faced challenges from industrialized European powers anxious to expand their Asian empires, and from Japan, which followed the Western example of modernizing its civil society and its military. Beginning in 1842, with China's defeat by Britain in the First Opium War, Qing officials had allowed Britain, Germany, France, and the United

States to set up miniature colonies, known as settlements, in scores of China's major cities. Japan, with a new modern navy, defeated China in the war of 1894 to 1895, and claimed favorable trading and legal concessions similar to those already accorded to Western governments. Confined by tradition and unwilling to alter its policies, the Qing dynasty's weaknesses provoked widespread domestic political discontent. In southern China, where Western penetration was greatest and Qing domination was weakest, a twenty-year peasant-led utopian uprising, known as the Taiping Rebellion, had its roots in popular distrust of the central government and its tolerance of opium smoking, footbinding, and slavery. The Taiping Rebellion demonstrated the Qing's military weakness even within China's borders.

THE NATIONALIST PERIOD

Sun Yat-Sen (Sun Zhongshan, 1866–1925) emerged as the nationalist leader around whom the Chinese people rallied as the Qing leadership's deficiencies became increasingly evident in the early 1900s. Sun was a born organizer who had spent much of his youth in the largely westernized kingdom of Hawaii. He received a Western education, earned a medical degree, and returned to China to promote radical changes there. Sun's popular Three Principles program included a call for democracy in China, freedom from foreign powers, and governmental attention to the people's welfare.

In 1895 Sun led an attempt to overthrow the Qing dynasty, but the coup's collapse forced him into exile in Japan and Europe. In 1911 a military uprising by reform-minded politicians and military commanders in central China provided a pretext for Sun's return, and in late December the Qing rulers were deposed. Sun, backed by the political network known as the Guomindong (Kuomintang [KMT]) or Nationalist Party, became president of the new Republic of China. The KMT publicly endorsed Sun's Three Principles, but corrupt officials enacted policies that benefited China's wealthy business and landowning classes, often at the expense of the poor.

Although Sun was popular with China's general population, he had few advocates within China's military. Sun sought support from China's most powerful general, Yuan Shi-kai (1859–1916), whose army was based in the north. Unfamiliar with military politics, Sun was ousted by Yuan and exiled to Japan. From there Sun reorganized his KMT supporters, and in 1921, once again in southern China, he was proclaimed president of the National Government based at Guangzhou (Canton).

Meanwhile, Yuan had imposed military rule from his headquarters in the north, even proclaiming himself "emperor" of China in 1915. This decision alienated most of his generals, and when Yuan died in 1916 his administration fractured into several competing regions led by warlords who used brutal methods to retain power. Sun recognized that the warlords' competition presented an opportunity for the KMT to establish its power throughout China. Guided by his Three Principles of nationalism, democracy, and socialism (which Sun understood to mean equal distribution of land among China's peasant farmers), the KMT recruited new members and trained troops. In 1926 KMT forces marched northwards against the warlords, but Sun did not live to see the KMT's victories, having died in Beijing in 1925.

Sun was succeeded by KMT military commander Jiang Jieshi (Chang Kai-Shek, 1887–1975). Jiang had overseen the growth of the KMT military and approved its policy of cooperating with the small but vibrant Chinese Communist Party (CCP). The CCP had been founded by a group of intellectuals, writers, and students, many of whom were radicalized during China's May Fourth Movement, a period of nationalist fervor and intellectual ferment that grew out of mass protests against the 1919 Treaty of Versailles, which settled the immediate aftermath of World War I. Students, workers, and civil servants had been appalled to learn that China, having joined the Allies in 1917, was not represented at Versailles, and that instead Japan had been awarded special concessions at China's expense by the Western powers.

The resulting shock and shame soon developed into renewed interest in China's modernization and reform. University students in many of China's major cities formed coalitions with merchants and industrialists, and organized a mass boycott of Japanese imports. Nonetheless, the examination of Western ideas that characterized the May Fourth Movement was limited to small groups of students and writers who began to form nationalist, prodemocracy, and communist study circles. In 1921 one of these groups formed the CCP.

The CCP helped the KMT capitalize upon anti-Japanese sentiment of the kind that erupted in Shanghai after the shooting on May 30, 1925, of a Chinese laborer by his Japanese foreman. The nationwide wave of antiforeign strikes that followed this May 30 Incident strengthened urban CCP networks, including those in Guangzhou, the center of KMT influence. Jiang, the new KMT leader, invited the much smaller CCP to cooperate in a "united front," but the cooperative relationship only lasted until April 1927, when KMT forces turned on CCP organizers, destroying much of the Communists' organization.

The KMT then established its capital at Nanjing (Nanking), marking the beginning of the Nationalist Decade (1927–1937). The KMT ruled most of southern and central China, while the north came under the control of a series of warlords, who claimed to be the lawful successors to the Qing dynasty, which had finally been overthrown in 1911. The KMT introduced banking, legal, and other reforms. Film and literature flourished, and the new Chinese elite produced lavish entertainments for Western visitors. However, Jiang's supporters indulged in corrupt business practices and employed paramilitary organizations to keep order and to crack down on the resurgent CCP.

THE RISE OF THE COMMUNIST PARTY AND THE CIVIL WAR

In August 1927 CCP operatives had formed a fledgling military wing of their own, but harassment by Nationalist troops hobbled its development. In 1934 KMT troops pursued the nucleus of CCP forces on a zigzag route through west-central China. During this Long March, as it came to be known, the CCP selected a new leader, Mao Zedong (1893–1976), who emphasized the revolutionary potential of China's vast agricultural peasantry and who prescribed peasant-based guerrilla warfare as the means to seize power in China. Mao saw the potential to reap a political windfall by harnessing the ancient grievances of peasants against landowners. The CCP began recruiting peasants as political cadres, teachers, and soldiers, initiating land redistribution programs, and building a huge army trained in hit-and-run warfare techniques.

World War II began for China in 1931 when Japanese troops invaded Manchuria. The KMT, always weakest in the north, did not contest Japan's aggression. In 1937 Japan invaded central China, seizing Beijing, Shanghai, and Nanjing in succession. The attack on Nanjing was especially brutal, with over 400,000 civilians reported to have been terrorized, raped, and murdered. The attack forced the KMT to move its capital to Chongqing (Chungking) in remote southwestern China.

Japan's defeat in 1945 allowed KMT and CCP forces, which had largely avoided direct confrontations with Japanese troops, to reoccupy huge sections of China's mainland. Civil war between the two sides ensued. Communist troops, recruited from the peasantry, enjoyed the cooperation of rural farmers who resented the KMT's failure to fight the Japanese. Following Mao's "mass line," which proclaimed that the interests of the masses, rather than those of elites, must guide China's future, the CCP also gained adherents in China's cities, where the Japanese occupation had given way to the KMT's political suppression, corrupt practices, and hyperinflation.

Employing both conventional and mobile guerrilla tactics, CCP forces pushed KMT armies out of northern and central China. American mediation efforts failed, and the KMT was finally driven from the mainland altogether, exiled to the island of Taiwan, in 1949. Mao declared the founding of a new Communist government, the People's Republic of China (PRC), on October 1, 1949.

THE CHANGING CHINESE CONTEXT

The breadth of the revolutions that occurred in China between 1911 and 1949—in international relations, government, civil society, education, political expression, and the arts—was virtually without modern parallel. The half-baked modernization efforts permitted by the Qing dynasty were replaced by a self-confident, ideologically driven government backed by an enormous, albeit technologically backward, military organization.

KMT officials, who lacked political cohesion and tenacity in combating Japanese aggression, were replaced by a highly organized Communist Party whose cadres followed Mao's doctrines to make China "stand up." Under Mao's leadership the CCP unleashed China's greatest asset, its enormous manpower, to modernize its economy. Communist China quickly emerged as a regional military power, as the Korean War (1950–1953) demonstrated, while also addressing such tradition-bound social injustices as usurious interest rates, predatory taxes, and the notorious practice of female footbinding.

In the early years of the twenty-first century, the Chinese Communist government founded by Mao still governed mainland China, but its orientation toward its past reflected political accommodations with Mao's revolutionary legacy. After Mao's death in 1976, reformer Deng Xiaoping (1904–1997) took power, setting aside Mao's "mass line" in favor of "socialism with Chinese characteristics," in which the role of ideology was subordinated to the demands of economic efficiency. Mao's use of propaganda and mass mobilization campaigns gave way to macroeconomic planning and free-market mechanisms. Material incentives replaced political appeals, marking a trend that continued into the early years of the twenty-first century.

Several controversies about China's revolutionary period persist into the early twenty-first century. These include questions about Japanese atrocities committed during the "rape of Nanjing" in 1937, about the CCP's use of intimidation and brutality in land-reform campaigns, and about the silencing of CCP members who criticized Mao. Scholars in the West have also engaged in interpretive debates on whether the ouster of the Qing dynasty was in any real sense a "revolution," how far Western powers manipulated the KMT-CCP struggle, and whether Mao himself was a visionary social theorist or a ruthless political operator.

SEE ALSO *Extraterritoriality; Hong Kong, from World War II; Hong Kong, to World War II; Mao Zedong; Opium Wars; Self-Strengthening Movements, East Asia and the Pacific; Shanghai; Treaties, East Asia and the Pacific.*

BIBLIOGRAPHY

Chi, Hsi-sheng. *Nationalist China at War: Military Defeats and Political Collapse, 1937–45.* Ann Arbor: University of Michigan Press, 1982.

Fenby, Jonathan. *Chiang Kai-shek: China's Generalissimo and the Nation He Lost.* New York: Carroll and Graf, 2004.

North, Robert C. *Moscow and Chinese Communists,* 2nd ed. Stanford, CA: Stanford University Press, 1963.

Selden, Mark. *The Yenan Way in Revolutionary China.* Cambridge, MA: Harvard University Press, 1971.

Snow, Edgar. *The Long Revolution.* New York: Random House, 1971.

Solomon, Richard. *Mao's Revolution and the Chinese Political Culture.* Berkeley: University of California Press, 1971.

Teng, Ssu-yü, and John K. Fairbank. *China's Response to the West: A Documentary Survey, 1839–1923.* Cambridge, MA: Harvard University Press, 1954.

Laura M. Calkins

CHINA, FOREIGN TRADE

China undertook extensive forms of foreign trade from the creation of a unified state under the Han dynasty until the fifteenth century, when a change in direction saw the country increasingly isolated from its neighbors and a continual downgrading of the importance and value of trade. Much of the early forms of trade were conducted under the guise of collecting tribute from vassal, or nominally vassal, states. At sea, foreign trade became dominated by Chinese junks, which were of a size and scope that greatly exceeded any international competition, including Arabian and Javanese rivals. Chinese maritime domination reached its apogee under Admiral Zheng He's (1371–1433) journeys, by which time Chinese trade reached from Madagascar to perhaps as far as the Americas. Chinese porcelain was then unparalleled and represented the dominant export good.

By land, the various routes that together constituted the Silk Road further linked the Chinese market with the Arab, Indian, and Mediterranean markets to the west. This led to the presence of extensive communities of foreigners in cities and towns in prominent positions along the Silk Road and to sophisticated methods of regulating trade. However, periodic outbreaks of xenophobia by some of the Chinese and perennial complaints

by foreigners of having to provide economic rents to local officials were the causes of tension and occasional conflict.

However, Confucianist thought, which has been influential in China throughout history, considered trade to be the province of inferior people and the ability of local officials (or mandarins) to squeeze taxes on foreign imported goods further brought the names and reputations of merchants into disrepute. Nevertheless, overseas goods continued to move in and out of fashion throughout history, even if the central government saw little of value in Western merchandise and preferred exotic goods from Southeast Asia and elsewhere.

OPIUM WARS AND UNEQUAL TREATIES

The closing of China's markets roughly coincided with the arrival of Europeans wishing to trade and ultimately to colonize Asia. While the Europeans recognized the Chinese achievements in building and technology, as expressed by the wonderment of the author Marco Polo (ca. 1254–1324), they resented being told what to do and how to conduct their trade. The emperor permitted only one legal outlet for international trade with the Europeans, and their traders were obliged to remain within their enclave, which was a place forbidden to women and generally a much less pleasant posting than Southeast Asian markets. Further, all trade was to be conducted with a court-appointed monopoly known as the *cohong* system.

The opening of trade routes between the Philippines and Spain and between Spain and the New World enabled almost all the global distribution of products. The silks produced in China were cheaper than those of Spain and the Spanish found themselves being priced out of their own markets in Mexico and Central America. This led to a ban on sales of Chinese products in the New World, which was enforced after 1604. Control of the Chinese market, it was felt in Europe, was essential for stability and imperial development. However, the Chinese state was not prepared to make any compromises with Europeans, who were considered to be essentially unimportant. It was a different situation where Russia was concerned, as its eastward expansion collided with Chinese territory and represented a definite threat. This led to a treaty demarcating borders and the installation of a Russian ambassador to Beijing, the only foreigner to be given this privilege.

Nevertheless, the pressure for increased trade led inevitably to open confrontation. The British took position as the most important mercantile presence in the region from the Portuguese and Dutch and found their home market increasingly dependent on a Chinese commodity, tea, not the silks and porcelains that had been of so much demand elsewhere. The demand for tea in Britain grew at an enormous rate, but there was little that the China market wanted from Britain in return, which led to a steady transfer of silver from west to east. Considering this to be destabilizing, the British cast around for a suitable export to China and eventually decided upon opium.

When the British colonized India, a three-way trade was established in which British-grown opium was exported from India to China in exchange for tea. The demand for opium grew very rapidly and led to considerable social disorder in China, whereas previously it had been of very limited impact. However, when the Chinese authorities banned the trade, the British were quite prepared to continue on an illegal basis by smuggling. Nevertheless, determined efforts by some Chinese officials to end the trade by destroying stocks of opium led to inevitable confrontation. In the two resulting so-called Opium Wars (1839–1842 and 1856–1860), European technology and organization defeated outmatched Chinese methods, and British naval vessels dominated both rivers and seas. The Chinese were obliged to sign a series of unequal treaties with not just Britain but also France, the United States, and other powers. These treaties ceded the treaty ports, including Hong Kong and Shanghai, where foreign trade was to be permitted and enabled the Western merchants to benefit from extraterritoriality, which meant they would no longer be subject to Chinese law or justice in their enclaves.

COLONIZATION AND ITS END

Beijing was thoroughly looted during the Opium Wars and its government was forced to stand by while the population was introduced to the dubious pleasures of a debilitating and addictive narcotic on an industrial scale. Capital now flowed from East to West as a result of this trade and the extraordinarily heavy reparations regularly laid upon the Chinese state were intensified with every outbreak of antiforeigner unrest. Free traders, glorified pirates, traveled up and down the coast and rivers to spread trade further through China, while central authority broke down in many provincial areas. While not formally colonized by Europeans, most of China's significant decisions were made by cabals of external powers, whose primary interest was in extracting resources at as great a rate as possible.

The final phase of colonization involved the physical conquest by the Japanese, whose brutal assaults remain an open wound in diplomatic relations decades later. Once again, the Chinese economy was subjected to the needs of conquerors rather than being allowed to develop itself and industrialize. The victory of the Nationalists of Jiang Jieshi (1887–1975) and the Communists led by Mao Zedong (1893–1976) restored independence but forced the country into a new period of comparative economic isolation in which Chinese society and industry was deprived of useful imports. As such, their technology remained far below international standards.

OVERSEAS CHINESE

For approximately fifteen hundred years the Chinese have been traveling overseas to make their homes there. Although few countries these days do not have a Chinese community of some sort, most of this migration has involved Southeast Asian countries. Overseas Chinese have historically felt a strong loyalty to their original home and continued to conduct many economic transactions with it. This ranged from exporting unmarried women for overseas workers, to remittances to complex social organizations linking home villages with expatriates. Much of this trade and investment took place informally, or at least without official records. It continued at a high level between Taiwan and the mainland during years of tension between the two states, whereas much of the high level of trade registered in Hong Kong has been a form of round-tripping that saw money invested in the mainland with some incentives actually having originated there.

WORLD TRADE ORGANIZATION AND FUTURE PROSPECTS

Intense negotiations preceded China's entry into the World Trade Organization (WTO), which will require more open markets for trade and investment and will lead to considerable structural change in the Chinese economy as workers are moved out of noncompetitive industries into others that are competitive. The low wage cost of manufacturing goods that has played such an important part of China's economic growth at the end of the twentieth century will increasingly be supplemented by advanced electronics and telecommunications products and services.

SEE ALSO *China, after 1945; China, First Opium War to 1945; China, to the First Opium War; Compradorial System; Guangzhou; Opium; Opium Wars; Treaties, East Asia and the Pacific.*

BIBLIOGRAPHY

Brook, Timothy. *The Confusions of Pleasure: Commerce and Culture in Ming China.* Berkeley, CA: University of California Press, 1998.

Curtin, Philip D. *Cross-Cultural Trade in World History.* Cambridge, U.K.: Cambridge University Press, 1984.

Hodder, Rupert A. *Merchant Princes of the East: Cultural Delusions, Economic Success, and the Overseas Chinese in Southeast Asia.* Chichester, U.K.: John Wiley and Sons, 1996.

Pomeranz, Kenneth. *The Great Divergence: China, Europe, and the Making of the Modern World Economy.* Princeton, NJ: Princeton University Press, 2000.

Zhaojin, Ji. *A History of Modern Shanghai Banking: the Rise and Decline of China's Finance Capitalism.* Armonk, NY: M. E. Sharpe, 2003.

John Walsh

CHINA MERCHANTS STEAM NAVIGATION COMPANY

Qing dynasty official Li Hongzhang (1823–1901) established the China Merchants Steam Navigation Company (*Lunchuan zhaoshang ju*) in 1872 in order to reclaim for China a share of the profits from steam shipping in Chinese waters that had been enjoyed by foreign shipping firms since the early 1860s.

The China Merchants Steam Navigation Company was the first of several "officially supervised, merchant managed" (*guandu shangban*) industrial enterprises set up by Chinese officials in the late nineteenth century (e.g., Kaiping Mines, Shanghai Cotton Cloth Mill, and Hanyeping Coal and Iron Corporation, among others). The company was supervised by Li Hongzhang (as governor-general of Zhili Province and commissioner of the northern ports), and managed by former compradors with experience in steamship operations. Government support of the company consisted of an exclusive contract to carry the tribute grain (a yearly tax in kind) from the Yangzi Valley to the capital, as well as loans from government sources and monopoly rights that precluded the founding of rival Chinese steamship companies.

In its first decade, the China Merchants Steam Navigation Company competed successfully with foreign companies, extended routes to Japan and Southeast Asia, and purchased the fleet of the failing American Shanghai Steam Navigation Company. Although it remained one of the four most prominent shipping companies in China between the 1880s and World War II, the China Merchants Steam Navigation Company did not grow at the same rate as rival British and Japanese firms. After government official Sheng Xuanhuai (1844–1916) became China Merchants director-general in 1885, the merchant managers lost much of their autonomy and the company became increasingly subject to official exactions in the form of both routine corruption and the diversion of funds to other *guandu shangban* enterprises.

In 1911 the company's board of directors voted to sever its official connection, and it operated as a private concern until the Nanjing regime of Chiang Kai-shek (Jiang Jieshi, 1887–1975) nationalized it in 1935, renaming it the National China Merchants Company (*Guoying lunchuan zhaoshang ju*). After 1949, the China Merchants' mainland branches were incorporated into the state shipping company of the People's Republic of China. The Hong Kong branch remained in business, becoming an important investor in mainland China's special economic zones in the 1980s and 1990s.

SEE ALSO *Chinese Diaspora; Compradors; Hong Kong, to World War II; Self-Strengthening Movements, East Asia and the Pacific; Shanghai.*

BIBLIOGRAPHY

Feuerwerker, Albert. *China's Early Industrialization: Sheng Hsuan-huai (1844-1914) and Mandarin Enterprise.* Cambridge, MA: Harvard University Press, 1958.

Lai, Chi-kong. "Li Hung-chang and Modern Enterprise: The China Merchants' Company, 1872-1885." In *Li Hung-chang and China's Early Modernization,* edited by Samuel C. Chu and Kwang-ching Liu. Armonk, NY: M. E. Sharpe, 1994.

Liu, Kwang-ching. "British-Chinese Steamship Rivalry in China, 1873-85." In *The Economic Development of China and Japan,* edited by C.D. Cowan. New York: Frederick A. Praeger, 1964.

Anne Reinhardt

CHINESE DIASPORA

The Chinese diaspora was initially directed toward the countries around the South China Sea. Chinese mariners or "junk" traders from the southern provinces of Fujian and Guangdong had been frequenting the "Nanyang" (i.e., the South China Sea and the countries surrounding it) since the Song dynasty (960–1279), and some individuals had settled in the port cities of the region. Most were wealthy traders who dominated commerce with China, some serving as tax farmers.

Following the Qing takeover during the 1600s and the rising Chinese demand for pepper and tin, Chinese laborers were sent to the region to produce them. By the 1780s, there were important settlements of Chinese miners and planters scattered throughout the region. They numbered about 100,000 and came mainly from parts of Fujian near Xiamen and Guangdong near Shantou. The settlers included speakers of Kejiahua, Chaozhouhua, and Minanhua.

This emigration of coolie labor was the distinctive mark of the Chinese diaspora for the next century. Their labor drove the emerging economy of colonial Southeast

Asia. After 1819, the British colony of Singapore became the major center for the coolie trade. From there, Chinese traders, brokers, and crimps managed the dispatch of this important resource to the mines and plantations of Southeast Asia. At the same time, cities, such as Bangkok, Saigon (Ho Chi Minh City), Manila, Batavia (Jakarta), and hundreds of smaller towns in the region grew as they filled with thousands of Chinese workers, hawkers, craftsmen, and traders. By the mid-nineteenth century, the population of laborers continued to increase, but the products began to flow increasingly to the West.

In 1848, with the discovery of gold in California, and later in Australia, Chinese labor, both Cantonese and Hakka, primarily from the Guangzhou area, began to move across the Pacific. This migration flourished until the 1880s, when both the United States and Australia enacted Asian exclusion policies. Nonetheless, significant settlement nodes had developed along the west coast of both North and South America and in Australia.

Before the twentieth century, very few Chinese women had emigrated, and those that did were often kidnapped and fated to lives of prostitution. During the 1920s, however, significant numbers of Chinese women began to emigrate, following their menfolk to the large Chinese settlements throughout Southeast Asia and the United States. This migration saw the establishment of family life among the Chinese working classes of the diaspora, as well as the stabilization of communities, the growth of schools and newspapers, and a rise of political and social awareness and activity. For the first time, new migrants were from China's intellectual classes. Fleeing political persecution in China, they worked as teachers and writers and revolutionary activists. Indigenous Southeast Asians and colonial governments both came to view this growth of Chinese nationalism as a threat.

With the economic depression in the 1930s, Chinese migration slowed dramatically and was even reversed in many areas. World War II and the subsequent disorder of the Chinese civil war brought waves of refugees out of China. Some went to Hong Kong, others to Taiwan, with many others fleeing to already established communities in the Nanyang and the United States. Following the establishment of the People's Republic of China in 1949, however, legal emigration from China completely stopped, except for a small flow of refugees through Hong Kong.

SEE ALSO *China, after 1945; China, First Opium War to 1945; China, to the First Opium War.*

BIBLIOGRAPHY

Mackie, Jamie. "Thinking about the Chinese Overseas." *American Asian Review* 21 (4) (2003): 1–44.

Purcell, Victor. *The Chinese in Southeast Asia*, 2nd ed. London: Oxford University Press, 1965.

Trocki, Carl A. "Boundaries and Transgressions: Chinese Enterprise in Eighteenth- and Nineteenth-Century Southeast Asia." In *Ungrounded Empires: The Cultural Politics of Modern Chinese Transnationalism*, edited by Aihwa Ong and Donald Nonini, 61–88. London: Routledge, 1997.

Wang, Gungwu. *Community and Nation: China, Southeast Asia, and Australia.* Saint Leonards, Australia: Allen & Unwin, 1992.

Carl A. Trocki

CHINESE, IMPERIAL MARITIME CUSTOMS

This foreign-managed customs collection agency evolved from the Shanghai Foreign Inspectorate of Customs, an improvisation by Rutherford Alcock, British consul at Shanghai, for collecting customs duties on behalf of the Chinese government, after it temporarily lost control of the city to rebels in 1853. It began operation in mid-1854 under inspectors nominated by British, American, and French consuls. Its success, coupled with China's weakness, led to its continuation and, after the second Opium War (1856–1860), its extension to all treaty ports. Its name was duly changed to the Chinese Imperial Maritime Customs Service (the prefix *Imperial* was dropped after the fall of the Qing dynasty in 1912). Having lost control of tariff autonomy in 1842, the Chinese now suffered another erosion of their sovereignty.

The early development of this institution owed much to Robert Hart, an Ulsterman, who served as inspector-general for forty-five years (1863–1908). His insistence on honesty and efficiency turned the Customs Service into an important revenue collector for the Qing government. Customs duties, which increased with trade, rose from 7 million taels (US$11,200,000) in the 1860s, to 22 million (US$17,600,000) in the early 1890s, and 35 million (US$22,800,000) in the early 1900s. Though the revenue financed modernizing projects for China, such as government shipyards and arsenals, it was increasingly pledged to paying China's war indemnities and foreign loans. Foreign management also made it impossible for the Chinese to shield the revenue from disbursements that favored foreign interests. After the Sino-Japanese War (1894–1895) and the Boxer uprising (1900) practically all its revenues were pledged to meeting China's loans and indemnities.

The Customs Service's activities went beyond customs collection, however. It completed the charting of the China coast and the Yangzi River, a task begun by the British Navy, erected lighthouses as well as other navigational aids and harbor facilities. It also founded the Imperial Post Office in 1896, which became independent in 1911. These facilities were first instituted to benefit the foreigners and their penetration into China. Nevertheless, the Customs Service also represented China in twenty-eight international trade exhibitions. Its commercial reports remained the only accurate account of China's foreign trade.

Foreign personnel dominated the Customs Service. In 1875 it employed 400 Westerners and 1,400 Chinese. The numbers increased to 700 and 3,500 respectively in 1895. Higher-level offices were reserved for foreigners; the Chinese held lower-level jobs, often with outdoor duties. More than half of the westerners were British. Control of the Customs Service reverted to the Chinese in 1933.

SEE ALSO *China, after 1945; China, First Opium War to 1945; Extraterritoriality; Opium; Shanghai.*

BIBLIOGRAPHY

Wright, Stanley F. *Hart and the Chinese Customs.* Belfast: William Mullan and Son Publishers, 1950.

David Pong

CHRISTIANITY AND COLONIAL EXPANSION IN THE AMERICAS

Spain was the first European country to colonize what today is North and South America, and the Spanish approach to the region came from several directions. One was from the Caribbean area, primarily Cuba and Puerto Rico, into Florida. At its height of development, Spanish Florida included the coastal regions of Georgia and southern South Carolina. A second was into central Mexico and then northward to what today is the northern tier of the Mexican states and California, Arizona, New Mexico, and Texas in the United States. From Mexico and the Caribbean, the Spanish moved into Central America, which in turn served as a base of operations for the conquest of Peru. Other points of entry were through the Río de la Plata region and *tierra firme* (firm land, mainland), the coast of Colombia and Venezuela.

Several elements framed the Spanish colonization of the Americas. The first was the *reconquista,* the seven-century-long process of reconquest of much of Iberia (the peninsula now occupied by Spain and Portugal) from Muslims who first invaded the region in 711. The protracted *reconquista* often proceeded in fits and starts, and the frontier between Muslim and Christian territories was permeable, with sides not always clearly defined. There are numerous instances of alliances between Christians

and Muslims, as well as figures such as El Cid (Ruy Díaz, count of Bivar, ca. 1043–1099), a Spanish soldier who joined the other side.

However, the conflict had a profound influence on the development of Iberian Catholicism and Iberian society. Iberian Catholicism became highly chauvinistic, exclusivistic, and militant. Iberian Catholicism also had a strong thread of mysticism and Marianism (devotion to the Virgin Mary), and championed the acceptance by the Catholic Church of the concept of the Immaculate Conception, which held that Mary was born free from original sin. Finally, the reform of the church, and particularly of the mendicant and monastic orders in the late fifteenth century, created a pool of missionaries to be sent to the newly conquered lands to convert the natives.

As the *reconquista* drew to a close in 1492 with the conquest of Grenada, the last Muslim state in the southern part of Iberia, Queen Isabella (1451–1504), "the Catholic" ordered the expulsion of Jews who refused to convert to Christianity. Castile became increasingly intolerant in the fourteenth and fifteenth centuries, and Jews in particular faced persecution. They already resided in separate ghettos in the major cities, and they experienced periodic pogroms, such as occurred in 1398.

About a century later in 1609, the crown ordered the expulsion of the remaining Muslim population in southern Iberia. Castile was also the first country to initiate a national inquisition independent of the papacy in 1478, and the court used the Holy Office (a Roman Catholic body charged with protecting the faith) to enforce the Catholic orthodoxy and insure that the *converses* (Jews forcibly converted to Catholicism) did not secretly practice their old beliefs. Iberia was Europe's only multiethnic and multicultural frontier during most of the medieval period, but as the Christians gained the advantage over the Muslims they initiated colonial policies designed to control the Muslim majority in the southern part of the peninsula and to transform the region into a Christian land.

The *reconquista* was also viewed as a crusade to liberate formerly Christian lands from the hands of the infidels, and the papacy recognized the reconquest as such. Crusader military orders, such as Santiago and Calatrava, evolved and were given extensive privileges and feudal jurisdictions in southern Iberia. The Iberian monarchs, the nobility, and the crusader orders were standard bearers for the "true faith," and they waged war to defeat the infidels, as well as for profit.

This crusader mentality was carried with the first overseas expansion into the Canary Islands in the fifteenth century and later into the Americas. Moreover, the crusade to carry the true faith to non-Christians provided a justification for conquest, and the religion of conquest formed the basis for the ideology of Iberian expansion into the Americas. Christopher Columbus (1451–1506) and the other Iberian explorers and *conquistadores* carried the banner of the crusader faith, and also sought profit while saving the souls of the infidels and pagans.

Following the encounter with the New World after 1492, the papacy theoretically assumed responsibility for the organization of missions to evangelize the newly encountered peoples. However, the papacy in the late fifteenth and early sixteenth century was embroiled in convoluted Italian politics, wars, and massive building projects that left the popes with insufficient resources to undertake such a major enterprise.

The 1494 Treaty of Tordesillas between Portugal and Spain, negotiated by the Spanish-born Pope Alexander VI (r. 1492–1503), ratified the donation and division of the non-Christian world between the two countries. The papacy later made a number of concessions to the Crown of Castile known as the *real patronato* (royal patronage). In exchange for organizing and financing the evangelization of the large native populations in its newly acquired territories, the crown gained considerable authority over the Catholic Church in its American territories. This authority included the right to nominate bishops and archbishops, to create new church jurisdictions, and to fill most positions in the church. The crown also collected and retained a part of the tithes paid to the church.

The Spanish and other Europeans believed that their faith was the only true faith, and that it was their obligation to bring their faith to pagans. The experience of the *reconquista* in Iberia was not unique in European history. Christians had faced non-Christians for centuries, and these contacts were often confrontational and violent. In the Mediterranean area, and this included Iberia, the threat came from Muslims, and war raged for centuries. Expansion by the Ottoman Turks brought the conflict to Central Europe in the fifteenth and sixteenth centuries.

During the early modern period in Europe (fifteenth century on), nation-state and national identities emerged, and Christianity was a key element of those identities. As the Spanish and other Europeans invaded and colonized Europe, it would have been inconceivable for them to have not brought their faith with them and plant it in the New World.

The evangelization of the native peoples of the Americas first occurred within the context of private colonization. The first expansion overseas to the Canary Islands was organized by private individuals given grants of jurisdiction. Similarly, private individuals or consortiums of individuals organized most expeditions of exploration and conquest. The crown attempted to establish basic ground rules to insure that the native peoples were not subject to an unjust war of conquest, and that

the *conquistadores* made provisions to evangelize the natives in the true faith. Spaniards could initiate a just war against peoples who rejected the authority of the king and had known and rejected Christianity. For example, Christians could wage war against and enslave Muslims, who had known Christianity for centuries and persisted in their own beliefs.

The crown stipulated the reading of the *Requerimiento* (Requirement) to native peoples before initiating war. The document, written in 1510 by the jurist Juan López de Palacios Rubios (1450–1524), gave the natives an opportunity to embrace the true faith and the authority of the king. The Laws of Burgos, legislated in 1512 and 1513, attempted to limit the exploitation and abuse of the native populations of the island of Hispaniola (now Haiti and the Dominican Republic) under *encomienda* grants of jurisdiction. The laws stipulated that the holders of the *encomiendas* provide priests to convert the natives, although this provision was not always observed. The laws proved to be too little too late for the island's population, which was rapidly declining as a result of mistreatment and disease.

The conquests of Mexico (1519–1521) and other regions on the American mainland were followed by a more concerted effort at the evangelization of the native peoples. In 1524 the first group of twelve Franciscans arrived in Mexico. The "twelve apostles," as they were called, were only the first of a growing number of missionaries from orders including the Franciscans, Mercedarians, Augustinians, and Dominicans. The missionaries first engaged in mass baptisms and campaigns to extirpate the old gods and religion. This included efforts to destroy the images of the pre-Hispanic gods, which did not always prove successful. The statue of Huitzilopochtli from the Templo Mayor in Tenochtitlán evaded the Spanish, this despite a high-profile Inquisition trial in the mid-1530s. The ancestor religion persisted in the Andean region well into the colonial period

The mood of the early evangelization campaigns in Mexico, the Andean region, and other parts of mainland America was one of triumphalism. The missionaries reported thousands of baptisms that they equated to conversion, and native workers erected new and increasingly imposing churches designed to replace the sacred precincts of the pre-Hispanic religions. The missionaries also believed that they were bolstering Spanish rule in the Americas by converting the natives. However, the majority of the missionaries chose to ignore the old religious practices and beliefs of the new converts beyond the minimal knowledge necessary to extirpate the gods they equated to the devil. The Franciscan Bernardino de Sahagún (1499–1590) was one of the few to record the culture of the natives.

Disillusionment came in some instances within a generation or two of the arrival of the missionaries, as it became evident that pre-Hispanic religions, such as the Andean practices of ancestor worship, persisted underground. The organization of anti-idolatry campaigns confirmed the superficiality of the mass baptisms in the early phase of evangelization. Moreover, there were revitalization movements, such as Taki Onqoy in Peru in the 1560s, centered on the belief that the old gods would vanquish the new Christian gods. Royal policy also worked against the members of the missionary orders working in the Americas. There was a series of conflicts between the missionary orders and local bishops concerning episcopal authority over the missionaries or the lack thereof. In the 1570s in Mexico, for example, the crown ordered the missionary orders to hand over the native towns to the bishops, and to transfer personnel to work on missions on the northern frontier.

In such core areas as central Mexico and the Andean Highlands, the Spanish encountered sedentary agriculturalists living under highly stratified hierarchical state systems. On the fringes of the American territories, however, were native peoples who were nomadic hunters and gatherers or sedentary farmers living under tribal or clan polities. The crown initiated mission programs on these frontier regions, with the goal of creating a new colonial order based on autonomous communities on the model of those in central Mexico or the Andean region. Missions, also known as *reducciones* in some areas, became the most important frontier institution. Missions operated on all Spanish frontiers in the Americas. Well known examples include the Jesuit missions of Paraguay and the Franciscan missions of California.

Religion and the church also played an important role in the social control of Spanish America and in solidifying Spanish authority. Until the late eighteenth century, Spain did not have armies in Spanish America. Therefore, Spanish rule depended on the consensus of the colonized, and particularly of the Creole elites who presided over a society where peoples of color (natives, peoples defined as being of mixed ancestry) formed the majority. Priests preached obedience and compliance with the social rules that governed colonial society. Moreover, they stressed the rewards of an afterlife attained by not challenging the status quo.

The attitude of the Spanish government towards the role of the church changed in the mid to late eighteenth century with the growing influence of Enlightenment ideas and the initiation of reform of the colonial system in the Americas following a serious defeat at the hands of the British during the Seven Years' War (1756–1763). The so-called Bourbon reforms stressed the strengthening

Archangel, Peru, circa 1700. This eighteenth-century oil painting from Peru depicts a Christian archangel dressed as a colonist and shouldering a musket. THE GRANGER COLLECTION, NEW YORK. REPRODUCED BY PERMISSION.

of royal authority in the Americas and the reining in of the Catholic Church.

One example of the growing anticlericalism was the order to expel the Jesuits in 1767 from the Spanish empire. Significantly, of the different missionary orders, only the Jesuits had a truly international organization. Other orders, such as the Franciscans, had separate organizations in each European country.

Bourbon anticlericalism also had a pragmatic side. A common belief was that the church controlled significant resources held in a form of entail that retarded economic development, which was a Bourbon goal. More economic activity generated more tax revenues. There was also considerable debate over the continued reliance on missions on the frontier, but a pragmatic decision was made to continue supporting them.

CHURCH AND CHRISTIANITY IN OTHER EUROPEAN COLONIES

Both Portugal and France brought missionaries to the Americas to evangelize the native populations. Moreover, both countries established Catholicism as the official state religion in the American colonies. Beyond this, there were significant differences in Portuguese and French policies towards the native peoples.

The Portuguese introduced commercial plantation agriculture into Brazil, and in the early stages of economic development relied heavily on Indian slave laborers. The colonists of São Paulo engaged heavily in the trade in Indian slaves, and in the late sixteenth and early seventeenth centuries Paulistas (colonists from São Paulo), also known as *bandeirantes,* ranged through the interior of South American enslaving Indians. In the 1630s the Paulistas attacked the Jesuit missions in the Río de la Plata region.

African slaves gradually replaced Indian slaves on the plantations. Jesuit missionaries came to Brazil and organized communities of natives called *aldeias* that were in some ways similar to Spanish frontier missions. However, the *aldeias* were generally located close to Portuguese settlements and served as labor reserves for the settlers.

The French in Canada, on the other hand, sought profit from the fur trade, and they relied on Indians for trade. Agriculture was developed at only a subsistence level and did not rely on Indian labor. Jesuits and other missionaries established missions for natives in Canada, the Great Lakes region, also known as the Terre Haut, and Louisiana. The Jesuit missions among the Hurons in the 1620s to late 1640s were the most successful, and the Black Robes, as native peoples called the Jesuits, converted about a third of the total Huron population. Sainte Marie des Hurons, located in Ontario, Canada, is a reconstruction of one of the missions. However, conflict between the Huron and the Iroquois led to the destruction of the Jesuit missions.

The state religion of England in the seventeenth century was the Church of England, and by law all residents of England were required to adhere to the doctrine of the church contained in the *Book of Common Prayer*, which was a compromise between Catholicism and the beliefs of the different Protestant sects. The colonies in North America offered "dissenters" (groups that rejected the doctrine of the Church of England) an opportunity to practice their beliefs free of persecution.

The Calvinists, commonly known as the Puritans, were one group that migrated to North America to practice their religious beliefs without interference. They created a theocracy that endured for some fifty years. The Catholic nobleman Lord Baltimore (Cecil Calvert, ca. 1605–1675) established Maryland in the 1630s as a haven for persecuted Catholics. William Penn (1644–1718), whose father had been an admiral and had connections at court, established Pennsylvania in 1682 for members of the Society of Friends, also known

as Quakers, a radical Protestant sect founded by George Fox (1624–1691). Pennsylvania during the colonial period was a haven for persecuted religious minorities. The German Pietists, better known as the Amish, was one such group that migrated to Pennsylvania to escape persecution in Europe.

Unlike the Spanish, the English did not initiate a systematic campaign to evangelize the native peoples they encountered in North America, and they generally viewed the natives as an obstacle to creating European communities in America. One exception was the effort by Puritan John Eliot (1604–1690) to establish what he called "praying towns" in New England. Eliot first preached to the Nipmuc Indians in 1646 at the site of modern Newton, Massachusetts. In 1650 Eliot organized the first praying town at Natick, also in Massachusetts. By 1675, there were fourteen praying towns, eleven in Massachusetts and three in Connecticut, mostly among the Nipmuc. Eliot also translated the Bible into the native language and published the translation between 1661 and 1663. The outbreak of the conflict between the English and native peoples known as King Philip's War (1675–1677) led to the collapse of the praying towns.

Protestant missions to native peoples continued in the eighteenth, nineteenth, and even into the twentieth centuries. In the second half of the nineteenth and the twentieth centuries, the missions often operated on reservations created by the United States government. Protestant missionaries often ran the schools for native children that attempted to obliterate most aspects of their native culture, which identified the missions with the assimilationist policies of the Bureau of Indian Affairs.

Why did Catholic missions achieve a higher degree of success than did Protestant missions? Three possible explanations have been suggested. The first has to do with the very nature of colonization by the Spanish, French, and English. The Spanish developed a colonial system based on their contacts with advanced sedentary native societies in central Mexico and the Andean region. Their colonial system relied on the exploitation of the native populations, and, as noted above, they gained legitimacy for their conquests from the papal donation that required the evangelization of the native peoples. This, taken with the experience of the *reconquista,* the drive towards orthodoxy within Iberia in the fifteenth century, and the longstanding crusader ethic, gave rise to the impulse to bring the true faith to the native peoples.

The vision of Europe's Hapsburg monarchs in the sixteenth century only reinforced these tendencies. The Hapsburgs viewed themselves as the defenders of the true faith, and led crusades against the Turkish threat in the

Mediterranean world and the growing number of Protestants in central Europe.

The government-supported missionaries and the evangelization of French and English colonies in North America were quite different from that of the Spanish. The French established settlements in the Saint Lawrence River valley, but also engaged in trade with native groups for furs. The French also believed their faith to be superior and to be the only true faith, and felt the responsibility to take that faith to the native peoples. At the same time the presence of missionaries, particularly Jesuits among the Huron, also facilitated the fur trade.

The English colonies were different from the French and Spanish. The English came to America to firmly implant Europe there. They came to establish towns and farms, and arrived in large numbers and wanted the land that was occupied by the natives. Whereas the Spanish and French had reasons to establish relations with native peoples, the English did not. The American natives occupied lands the English wanted, and the native inhabitants were generally viewed as a threat to the English settlements. Thus the colonial governments did not support missions in the same way that the Spanish and French did.

The nexus of relations between the English and native peoples can be see in the example of the New England Puritan colonies, as well as early Virginia. The Puritans believed that God had given them the land in New England to exploit, and Puritan leaders were inclined to push native communities aside. The relationship was often violent, as evidenced by the Pequot War in 1636 and 1637 and King Philip's War. The latter conflict was a desperate attempt by native peoples to preserve their society and culture in the face of aggressive English occupation and creation of new communities that forced natives off of their lands.

In Virginia, the colonization of Jamestown and other new communities was met by resistance from native groups almost from the beginning, resulting in two major conflicts in the 1620s and again in the 1640s. These conflicts, and the general attitude of the English towards native peoples, did not create a climate conducive to the launching of missionary campaigns. Moreover, the English colonists developed generally autonomous local governments that tended to be unsympathetic to evangelization of native peoples.

A second factor was theological. Catholicism was and is a religion with mass appeal, because it offers salvation to those who repent. Moreover, doctrine dictates the baptism of children as soon as possible after birth, because of the belief that unbaptized children will go to purgatory after they die. Furthermore, a degree of syncretism occurred in Catholic missions established on native communities in central Mexico, the Andean region, and the fringes of Spanish territory, such as the north Mexican frontier. Syncretism, such as the association by native peoples of old gods with Catholic saints, was a key factor in what the missionaries believed to be the conversion of native peoples to the true faith.

The sixteenth-century Protestant Reformation, on the other hand, introduced new beliefs that did not lend themselves to the conversion of native peoples with cultures that did not have a foundation in Christianity. The Anabaptists, for example, rejected the baptism of newborn children, and instead believed that the acceptance of God's covenant should be a decision made when people could fully understand the decision being made. The Calvinist belief in predestination, the idea that God had already chosen those who would gain salvation and those who would not, also did not lend itself to mass conversion.

Moreover, the seventeenth-century Puritan theocracy in New England, which afforded full church membership only to the "elect" (those who could show that they had God's grace and would gain salvation), was a cause of friction between native peoples in the region and the colonists. The Puritan leadership expected native peoples to live by an alien set of moral and social rules, even if the natives had chosen not to embrace the new faith. This policy contributed to the outbreak of King Philip's War, and it certainly did not make the new religion attractive to native peoples. Puritan leaders did not tolerate any deviation from their teachings, and they did not tolerate the syncretism that facilitated "conversion" in Spanish America.

Finally, demographic patterns undermined evangelization, particularly in Protestant English colonies. In the centuries following the first European incursions into the Americas, native populations declined in numbers because of disease and other factors. Mortality rates were particularly high among children, the segment of the native population in which missionaries placed their greatest hopes for indoctrination.

In the California missions, for example, the Franciscans continued to relocate pagans on the missions while indoctrinating the children and adults already living there. This meant that there were always large numbers of pagans interacting with new converts already exposed to varying levels of Catholic indoctrination. These conditions created a climate conducive to the covert survival of traditional religious beliefs. Moreover, infant and child mortality rates were high, and most children died before reaching their tenth birthday. This limited the ability of the missionaries to create a core of indoctrinated children in the mission populations.

The United States today is a Christian country because of the imprint of European colonists and their descendants and not because of the conversion of native peoples to the new religion. The trajectory of Spanish colonization established a strong Catholic tradition in much of Latin America.

SEE ALSO *Catholic Church in Iberian America; Mission, Civilizing; Religion, Roman Catholic Church.*

BIBLIOGRAPHY

Axtell, James. *The Invasion Within: The Contest of Cultures in Colonial North America.* New York: Oxford University Press, 1985.

Deeds, Susan. *Defiance and Deference in Mexico's Colonial North: Indians Under Spanish Rule in Nueva Vizcaya.* Austin: University of Texas Press, 2003.

Gibson, Charles. *The Aztecs Under Spanish Rule: A History of the Indians of the Valley of Mexico, 1519–1810.* Stanford, CA: Stanford University Press, 1964.

Gould, Rae. "In Search of the Wabbaquasset Praying Village." New Directions in American Indian Research: A Gathering of Emerging Scholars. The Graduate School, University of North Carolina at Chapel Hill. Available from http://gradschool.unc.edu/natam/panels/gould.html/.

Jackson, Robert H., ed. *New Views of Borderlands History.* Albuquerque: University of New Mexico Press, 1998.

Jackson, Robert H. *Missions and the Frontiers of Spanish America: A Comparative Study of the Impact of Environmental, Economic, Political, and Socio-Cultural Variations on the Missions in the Rio de la Plata Region and on the Northern Frontier of New Spain.* Scottsdale, AZ: Pentacle, 2005.

Jackson, Robert H., and Edward Castillo. *Indians, Franciscans, and Spanish Colonization: The Impact of the Mission System on California Indians.* Albuquerque: University of New Mexico Press, 1995.

Lockhart, James, and Stuart Schwartz. *Early Latin America: A History of Colonial Spanish America and Brazil.* Cambridge, U.K.: Cambridge University Press, 1983.

Milanich, Jerald. *Laboring in the Fields of the Lord: Spanish Missions and Southeastern Indians.* Washington, DC: Smithsonian Institution Press, 1999.

Trigger, Bruce, ed. *The Handbook of North American Indians,* edited by William C. Sturtevant, Vol. 15: *Northeast.* Washington, DC: Smithsonian Institute Press, 1978.

Trigger, Bruce. *The Children of Aataentsic: A History of the Huron People to 1660.* Reprint, Toronto: McGill-Queen's University Press, 1987.

Wade, Maria. *The Native Americans of the Texas Edwards Plateau, 1582–1799.* Austin: University of Texas Press, 2003.

Worth, John E. *The Timucuan Chiefdoms of Spanish Florida,* 2 vols. Gainesville: University of Florida Press, 1998.

Robert H. Jackson

CINNAMON

Cinnamon is the dried bark from several varieties of small evergreen trees or bushes of the laurel family that provide similar flavors. Early cinnamons—such as *Cinnamomum burmanni,* which originated in Burma (Myanmar) and grows in southern China, South Asia, and Southeast Asia—were actually harvested from other varieties of evergreen laurel trees, known as cassia. Cassia bark is peeled into strips that curl into a "quill" shape when dried. Because the exterior bark is left on, the strip is thick, coarse, and dark brown.

True cinnamon, or *Cinnamomum zeylanicum,* is native only to Sri Lanka. It possesses a more delicate flavor and aroma than cassia. It is handled in the same manner, with an important exception—the coarse, first bark is removed by scraping, leaving a thinner, paler, light red-brown quill. The variation in handling cassia and true cinnamon sounds slight, but consumers perceived a difference and were prepared to pay for it.

Cinnamon was found in the wild and was not exploited on plantations in Sri Lanka until the later half of the eighteenth century. Multiple efforts were made in the seventeenth through the nineteenth centuries by different colonial powers (the Portuguese in Brazil; the Spanish on Mindanao in the Philippines; the Dutch on Sumatra; and the French on Mauritius and Réunion and in Guyana) to transplant true cinnamon. They were less successful than with other spices, in part because of the extra semiartisanal handling required in its peeling. Some colonial powers and others, such as the Chinese, chose to increase deliveries of false cinnamon, which found market acceptance on the basis of price. Their efforts to break the Dutch and subsequent British monopoly of true cinnamon met with success in the nineteenth century.

The Portuguese, from 1506 until 1658, actively commercialized the commodity in Europe and Asia, but they did not establish an effective monopoly. The Dutch East India Company from 1658 to 1796, and later the English East India Company, did establish a monopoly over cinnamon.

The Dutch controlled deliveries and prices. From 1658 to 1760, the total volume of cinnamon delivered to them on Sri Lanka approximated 27,670 metric tons (about 30,500 short tons). Three-quarters of this volume was exported to Europe. The other quarter was ostensibly meant for sale in Asia, but most of it was sold to intermediaries or directly to the Spanish in the Philippines for transshipment to markets in the New World; only a small fraction was sold and consumed in Asia. Approximately one-half of the cinnamon sold in Europe was destined for Spain and its empire. Other major markets were France, the Netherlands, and the early political configurations of modern Italy and Germany.

From 1650 to 1700 the Dutch doubled the price of cinnamon in Europe from 1.50 to 3 guilders per pound. By 1750 they had doubled it again, to 6 guilders. In the 1780s it neared 9 guilders. It returned to an average of 6 or 7 guilders in the 1790s. The profits were considerable. A precise calculation is not possible because colonial administrative expenditures were kept separate from cinnamon income.

SEE ALSO *Ceylon; Dutch United East India Company.*

BIBLIOGRAPHY

Dalby, Andrew. *Dangerous Tastes: The Story of Spices.* Berkeley: University of California Press, 2000.

Glamann, Kristof. *Dutch-Asiatic Trade, 1620–1740.* Copenhagen: Danish Science Press, 1958.

Stobart, Tom. *Herbs, Spices, and Flavorings.* Woodstock, NY: Overlook Press, 1982.

George Bryan Souza

CITIES AND TOWNS IN THE AMERICAS

Spanish towns in America were generally based on an unvarying plan, laid down as early as 1523 and finalized in what is known as the Laws of the Indies. The plan, first used in the town of Santo Domingo on the island of Hispaniola (now occupied by Haiti and the Dominican Republic), is commonly referred to as a *gridiron* and may have its origin in many sources. The design called for a central square with a series of perfectly straight streets extending out in all directions and forming blocks with four-building lots. The gridiron form was not seen at that time in Spain or the rest of Europe, and its adoption in the New World is one of the legacies left by the Spanish.

In Santo Domingo, the soldiers who laid out the town were not concerned with creating a well-proportioned city, and instead possibly copied a military design with which they were familiar—that of the base of Santa Fe used by Isabella (1451–1504) and Ferdinand (1452–1516) during the siege of the Moorish stronghold of Granada in southern Spain. The design also had precursors in the ancient Greco-Roman world, and Spain may have been especially influenced by the layout of Roman cities that had been built on Spanish land. The gridiron design was also in line with the theories of Italian humanists whose work was becoming popular in Spain. Along with the gridiron design, the Laws of the Indies specified criteria in terms of terrain and climate to be observed when founding towns.

Government in Spanish America was in theory very centralized, and its major centers were towns and cities. All Spanish holdings in America were considered to be extensions of Spain itself, and most who were involved in colonial government were sent from Spain specifically for that purpose.

In Europe, the king of Spain created the Council of the Indies, which was to run all governmental affairs in the Americas. On the other side of the Atlantic, Spanish territories were divided between two viceroys—one in Mexico City (1535) and the other in Lima (1544). The viceroys were assisted by the main courts or *audiencias,* as well as the prelates of the Catholic Church. Below the viceroys were the governors and captain-generals, while towns and cities were run by municipal councils.

On the local level, this system was similar to Europe, with the difference that these were essentially islands of Spanish urban settlement in a countryside largely populated by Indian peasants living in a subsistence economy and supplying forced labor through the system known as the *encomienda.* Spanish towns were thus centers for government and for the domination of native rural populations, and with their European architecture, churches, and government buildings, they were the symbols and headquarters of Spanish culture and control. Urban growth in Spanish America was greatly stimulated by the discovery of rich resources of precious metals during the sixteenth century, and towns also became centers for international and regional trade.

All Spanish trade to the new world was monopolized by a few ports. Trade from Spain to America was channeled through the port of Seville and later Cadiz on the European side of the Atlantic. Trade was received at the ports of Veracruz for Mexico, and Cartagena in present-day Columbia and Portobelo in Panama for South America. All trading was heavily taxed, and though goods landed at certain ports, they would then be distributed to other parts of the colonies. Local merchants in Mexico City and Lima would play a significant role in this aspect of the trading process. Mining towns were also established throughout Mexico and South America, many of them to be abandoned when the mines ran dry.

The English method of establishing towns, cities, and a colonial economy was different from that of Spain. Though based on tradition and experiences in England, the construction of English-American towns and cities did not follow any predetermined plan. Furthermore, the failure to discover precious metals, along with the more decentralized English system of government, allowed England's colonial towns and cities to develop differently from those of Spanish America.

The English monarchs backed the founding of English colonies, but the colonies were much more autonomous than their Spanish counterparts. English settlers did not have large native cities, such as Cuzco or Mexico City, to occupy or rebuild, and the character of their towns varied with the nature of the colonies in which they were founded. New England towns provided for clusters of small farmers, while cities in the tobacco-growing lands of Virginia and Maryland were more oriented to trading.

Most English American cities were on or close to the coast, and the major ports were built around excellent natural harbors. The city of Boston, for example, was established by the Massachusetts Bay Company, a Puritan chartered company, in 1630 with a view to acting as the point of contact for trade and communication with the exterior. Built on a peninsula in a harbor, Boston became the capital and merchant center of a quickly growing colony; within fifteen years approximately twenty thousand colonists lived in and around Boston.

To the south, the Dutch colony of New Netherlands was captured by the British in 1664. The acquisition also brought with it the port of New Amsterdam, which was soon to be renamed New York and would continue under the English as one of the major trading locations in North America. In the American South, the best English port was Charlestown, now called Charleston. The city was established by the proprietors of the Carolina colony in 1690 and flourished as a port for agricultural products produced in what later became South Carolina.

By the eighteenth century, British America was home to some of the great cities of the Americas—Boston, New York, and Philadelphia—and they had began to compete in size and beauty with the leading cities of Spanish America. One notable difference remained, however. The cities of North America were much more likely to be lively centers of trade and artisanal industry than most of those in Spanish America. British American cities also enjoyed greater cultural and political freedom, and were better positioned to become dynamic centers for new patterns of trade and industry in the future.

SEE ALSO *Acapulco; Boston; Cartagena de Indias; Encomienda; Havana; Lima; Mexico City; New York; Potosí; Rio de Janeiro.*

BIBLIOGRAPHY

Croach, D., Garr, D. and Mundigo, A. *Spanish City Planning in North America.* Cambridge, MA: MIT Press, 1982.

Harboy, J. Urban. "Cartography in Latin America during the Colonial Period." *Latin American Research Review* 18(3) (1983): 127–134.

Lockhart, J. and Swartz, S. *Early Latin America: A History of Colonial Spanish America and Brazil Cambridge.* New York: Cambridge University Press, 1983.

Markman, S. "Santa Cruz, Antigua, and the Spanish Colonial Architecture of Central America." *Journal of the Society of Architectural Historians* 15(1) (1956): 12–19.

Smith, R. "Colonial Towns of Spanish and Portugese America." *Town Planning Issue, Journal of the Society of Architectural Historians* 14(47) (1955): 3–12.

Brian Stokes

CLOTHING AND FASHION, MIDDLE EAST

The fashion and clothing of the Middle East represents an evolution of historical and political change and a mixture of influences that has enriched and modernized its diverse cultures and produced a custom of dress both progressive and yet true to its traditional design identities. Although distinct fashions can be traced back to particular regions, the overall effect is a vast collection of clothing traditions adapted and adjusted to new social orders, local climates, and activities. These geographical and cultural variations reflect a complex set of relations between historical change and clothing practices as markers of changing identity over time, including differences relating to gender, age, wealth, and religious status.

Women's dress marks gendered differences in certain settings, differing from that of men of the same age, social "level," and marital status. Men's attire generally differs within the gender more than women's, whose modes of dress have been traditionally dictated by patriarchal taste and political reform. Similarly, the structure and meaning of clothing varies across regions in design, fabric, shape, and ornament.

The Ottoman Empire (1299–1923) is widely acknowledged as the Middle East's greatest influencing force in terms of fashion. The Ottoman period established a tradition of antiquity enforcing national modes of dress via national military uniforms, as well as practical and fashionable trends from the region's existing clothing styles. As the Ottoman Empire evolved and expanded throughout the eighteenth and nineteenth centuries, clothing styles were evaluated, developed, and enforced, mirroring the many levels of society and the cosmopolitan nature of Ottoman cultural tastes. Whether parodied or satirized by the rebellious populace of the time and subsequent generations, what is described as Middle Eastern clothing continues to represent the traditional views of the culture. Yet, within the national and political economy, Middle Eastern clothing also exhibits cyclical fashion trends influenced by European and Western tastes and modernity.

Saudi Arabian history is significant to the tradition of dress in the Middle East because the kingdom comprises 80 percent of the Arabian Peninsula as opposed to Yemen, Oman, Iran, Iraq, Jordan, Syria and Sudan, and its tradition of dress is highly representative of the significance of the land, history, and to religion. Its unification in 1932 was marked by a rising national identity and homogeneity of dress, as well as a growing interaction and trade with Egypt and Lebanon from 1945 to about 1970, the impact of oil wealth from 1970 to 1980, and beginning in 1980 the exploration of combinations of cosmopolitan fashion and various local, regional, Arab, and Islamic styles.

For Saudi Arabian men, dress was an important aspect of Arab identity and was employed to distinguish the wearer's profession and social status. Prior to unification, the *tujjar* merchants of Hejaz in Saudi Arabia, for instance, dressed in contrast to the *ulema* (religious teachers) and the *mutawwifin* who served as guides to pilgrims. The *tujjar* merchants wore long floor-length, loose-flowing coats of plain or printed light fabric with bright turbans or caps, the *ulema*, whose role was to elect the king along with members of the royal family, wore ample gowns and the *mutawwifin,* who guided the pilgrims both in prayer and in direction, usually wore less-elaborate local dress. Also differing in dress style was the *ashrāf,* who were descendants from the lineage of the Prophet Muhammad.

The rest of the male population, mostly in the Arabian Peninsula region, were traditionally seen in mid-calf-length tunics that were belted at the waist. The sleeves tended to be long and consisted of several variations, including straight then tapering at the wrists or flaring down towards the wrist to form a wing effect of differing lengths. Pants were generally full at the top and narrow at the ankle, with large gussets in the crotch. The top of the pant was overturned to the outside and stitched down to form the casing for a drawstring.

Turban headdresses were made up of a continuous strip of narrow fabric, usually 30 or 40 centimeters (about 12 or 16 inches) wide, that was wound around the head over a felt, truncated conical cap. Turban sizes varied from small to large, depending on social class. At times the cloth ends would be made of a decorated silk fabric in meticulous weaves that often incorporated repeated floral motifs or embroidered designs.

The traditional head cloth commonly worn by Saudi Arabian men today was called a *kaffiyeh.* The plain head cloths worn over felt caps, which were secured with pins or held in place by a headband consisting of a strip of cloth or rope was known as an *agal.* In the central Arab region of Najd and its hinterlands, the *agal* was simply a camel hobble (from the Arabic root *agal,* meaning "to

hobble"), which was carried on the head when not in use. Gradually this rope came to distinguish the Bedouins of north and central Arabia and the descendants of ruling families from other Bedouins.

At the same time, male sartorial style included *tiraz* bands that were intricately woven, embroidered, or painted and then sewn over one or both shoulders of a garment. Although commonly seen on men, the *tiraz* was also a feature of women's dress. *Tirazes* were adorned with Arabic script that either named the owner of the garment (in the case of royalty) or quoted a religious phrase.

In winter, men generally wore a cloak, or *bisht*, which featured piping that ran from the cuff up the seams of the sleeve and ended in a wider band down the front lapel. The winter *bisht* was made of a rough sacklike fabric, usually dyed in bright colors. In summer, men's cloaks were made of a light, fine material and tended to be black, brown, or beige, with piping made of gold thread on the cloak's sleeves. This garment was worn primarily during ceremonial occasions.

Prior to unification in 1932, Saudi Arabian women favored a long tunic or robe worn over light trousers, cut similarly to men's garments. The sleeves were close-fitting at the wrists, and bands of trim were added to the sleeves as an embellishment. The more urbanized Hejazi women wore a long, fitted dress called a *zabun.* Under this was a blouse or bodice (*sidriyya*), which was designed to be seen through the opening of the *zabun.* The blouse was fastened with buttons of silver, gold, or diamonds, depending on the wearer's wealth. The typical garment of the desert-dwelling women of the Arabian Peninsula was known as a *thobe.* These were boxlike in construction and narrowed at the hem. Either worn with a belt or loose, the *thobe* was also decorated with bands of embroidery at the hems and sleeves.

The *hijab* veil and the *burka* facemask continue to be worn by women in parts of central and eastern Arabia, as well as Iran. These have variations in meaning and use between regions, as well as between rural and urban settings. The veil and the garments that accompany it (*milaya* in Egypt, *abbayah* in Iraq, *chador* in Iran, *yashmak* in turkey, *burka* in Afghanistan, and *djellabah* and *haik* in North Africa) are manifestations of cultural practices and meanings that are firmly embedded in Middle Eastern traditions and centered around religious morality, sexuality, gender, and honor.

Although the veil has often been treated as a symbol of class identity, social mobility, and resistance or opposition to the West, it is important to note that it has since become central in the popular Western press as an indicator of colonialism and patriarchy. The fact that large groups of women in the Middle East continue to embrace it as part of contemporary everyday fashion and clothing is indicative of the complex level of nationalism and entrenched cultural and religious codes that have always dictated the traditional clothing of the Middle East.

SIGNIFICANT DRESS REFORMS THAT CHANGED THE MIDDLE EAST

The intersection between dress, gender, and state control are important in understanding how men and women (and veiled women in particular) are felt to embody the identities of a religion or a nation. By the early twentieth century, a number of Middle Eastern countries, including Turkey and Iran, embarked on programs instigated by Turkey's Mustafa Kemal Atatürk (1881–1938) and Iran's Reza Shah (1878–1944) in the 1920s and 1930s to reform their social and political infrastructures. In these countries, the wearing of various types of traditional headdresses, such as the veil for women and the fez (a cylindrical cap) for men, was considered symbolic of the country's backwardness and, to some extent, its oppressiveness, and they were subsequently outlawed.

What was known as "folkloric" or "traditional" dress was closely associated with particular ethnicities and was relegated to rural areas, while fashionable indicators of social status and Western and European influences were revived. Various Arab governments decreed that regional or ethnic dress was "backward" or "primitive." As a result, the Middle East began to adopt modes of Western dress, including bowler hats, Western pants, and jackets.

Political dissidents in the Middle East denounced the wearing of such Western fashions, a sentiment that culminated in acts of defiance, a show of pride and local integrity, and physical signs of commitment to regional or ethnic autonomy. Though Reza Shah had outlawed ethnic dress in 1928, various items of men's and women's clothing, such as *dogushi* (two-eared Qashqai men's hats) were worn by dissidents in that region as statements of revived Qashqai power, autonomy, and identity, and ultimately as a physical satire of the shah's own sense of prevailing power.

Turkey and Dress Reform. The fez, which remains a global symbol of Middle Eastern fashion, is an important marker of clothing tradition. The fez was not of Turkish but of North African origin, and it bears the name of the city of Fez, the cultural and spiritual capital of Morocco. The fez is a cylindrical cap of scarlet or purple felt, ornamented with a tassel on the end of a long black cord. The earliest varieties were in the form of a bonnet with a long red, white, or black turban wound around it.

After eliminating the Janissaries (an Ottoman army corps) in 1826, Turkey's sultan Mahmud II (r. 1808–1839), established a new army, the Asakir-i Mansur-i Muhammediye. The soldiers at first retained the *kavuk*, a padded or quilted cap around which the sash of a turban could be wound, and the *şalvar* (full trousers). Later, each man was issued a *setre* (an old-fashioned form of European frock coat) and trousers, to resemble Turkey's European contemporaries.

In order to standardize dress customs, Mahmud II introduced the fez to the Ottoman court, and further decreed the reform to civilians in 1829. Gradually the fez was accepted for general civilian use, with exception of the *ulema,* who retained the robe and turban. Civilians also adopted the European frock coat and cape, preferring trousers instead of robes and black leather boots instead of slippers. It is interesting to note that the image of this mix of Middle Eastern and European fashion was very much part of popular colonial cultural stereotypes of Middle Eastern dress. The turban and Turkish pants are also, with the fez and frock coat, part of the grand narratives of Orientalists and have widely influenced the way the West constructs its visions of the Middle East in both dress and custom.

By 1868 there were ten groups of fez makers in Istanbul. As demand for production accelerated, fez makers were brought from Tunisia, and a factory was established in the Eyüp area of Istanbul. Over time, a variety of fez styles appeared, ranging in shape, length, material, and molds. Fez making soon became a recognized national craft.

Since the discovery of synthetic dyes at the turn of the nineteenth century, Austria had become the chief centre of the fez industry. In 1908, during the Young Turk Revolution, Austrian goods were boycotted for two months by the Committee of Union and Progress in protest against the Austro-Hungarian annexation of Bosnia-Herzegovina. At the time, fezzes were mainly supplied to Turkey by the Austrians (because they had the only fez manufacturing plant) and during what was dubbed the "Fez Boycott" men wore instead either an *arakiye* (a form of skull cap) or a *kalpak* (a brimless sheepskin or *astrakhan* cap). By 1909, beyond the boycott, the *kalpak* had become an accepted item of dress. Nevertheless, the fez remained an integral part of male sartorial style until 1925, when Atatürk began his modernization campaign by banning the fez in favor of the wide-brimmed Western-style hat.

The tradition of veiling in Turkey can be traced from the Hittite period (1400–1200 BCE), where images of women wearing long mantles over their heads that reached to their ankles were depicted at the sites of Carchemish and Yazilikaya. The tradition continued well into the medieval period. During the Ottoman rule in the 1800s, reformers and liberals began denouncing the idea of women's protective clothing. New interpretations of the

Koran were argued in 1899, and the gradual impact of nationalism and independence meant that women were encouraged to be symbols of the new state, so much so that various Turkish elites mocked those women who resisted ideas of social progress, calling them "beetles."

In 1915 an imperial decree was issued that permitted women to discard the veil during office hours. Although initially there were numerous protests in opposition, more and more women eventually left their veils at home, opting for a Western-style hat and long coat. Although Atatürk banned the fez and advocated the wearing of it as a criminal offence, there was no action taken by the legislature against veiling. Nevertheless, as he began to build a secular nation-state in 1923, he denounced the veil, calling it demeaning and a hindrance to a civilized nation, without actually outlawing it. Educated women in Turkey began to leave the house unveiled, but still wore the *hijab*.

Soon a small veil called a *litham* became the fashion, with all the nationalists' wives adopting it as part of their clothing. Gradually, unveiling became common among women of the wealthier, educated upper classes in large towns or cities. Veiling continued in more conservative rural areas in the form of a *peçe* (veil) and a *çharshaf*, commonly made of silk or wool and usually black in color, or the more fashionable *ferece*, which also concealed the whole body and had straight sleeves extending to the length of the fingers. A type of veil (*yashmak*) was also worn over the face, and boots or decorative clogs were worn on the feet.

Iran and Dress Reform. Before 1873, the *kolah-i pahlavi*, a tall black lambskin headdress of the Qajar regime (1796–1925), was worn by Iranian men to replace the four-pointed cap of the former Afsharids regime (1736–1749). A fezlike headdress were also introduced as required dress for government officials.

Official modernization and reform programs were accompanied by dress regulations decreed by Persian ruler Reza Shah (r. 1925–1941). Reza Shah initiated a process of "westernization," which included the abolition of the chador for women and the introduction of Western-style dress for men. In 1928 the cabinet announced the correct dress for men to be a Western coat, jacket, trousers with a leather belt, and leather shoes in European styling. All government workers and school boys were required to wear the brimless *kolah-i pahlavi* hat as devised by the shah. The stipulation to wear the European-style garments was extended to all Iranian males, except Shi'i and Sunni *ulema*, non-Muslim dignitaries, and male children under the age of six.

The 1928 Uniform Dress Law came into effect in urban centers and within the year was introduced into rural regions. Noncompliance by townsmen was punishable by a fine of one to five *tomans* (later increased to thirty *tomans*) and a jail sentence of one to seven days. By 1929 a major redrafting of Iranian legal codes relating to commercial, civil, family, and penal matters involved moving away from Islamic *shari'a* law in the direction of a European legal system. The legal reform was also accompanied by an official requirement that all judges and lawyers wear secular dress instead of the long robes and turbans associated with *ulema* jurists. After returning from a visit to Turkey in the spring of 1934, Reza Shah ordered the brimmed hat (the trilby or fedora) to be worn by all Iranian men, and he required that Western lounge suits be worn by court officials. In 1935 he abolished the *kolah-i pahlavi* headdress.

In early 1936, the shah appeared at the new Normal School in Tehran to address the female students. All of the women of the royal Iranian Party were unveiled and wore Western-style clothing. By February of the same year, regulations designed to encourage the abandonment of the chador came into effect. The chador is a large semicircular piece of fabric that covers the head, hair, and body, but leaves the face uncovered. In the thirteenth century, the chador was worn with a burka, and by the fifteenth century, a black face veil made of horsehair called a *picheh* appeared as a second form of veiling. This type of veil was fastened to the head with two ties and was classified as a burka.

After the official announcement banning the chador and *picheh*, women wearing the chador were not permitted in public places. Bus and taxi drivers who accepted veiled women as passengers were subject to fines or dismissal. Doctors were forbidden to treat and admit veiled women into hospitals. Police and the armed forces were also instructed to forcibly remove any veil worn in public and to enter homes to enforce the law.

One of the unexpected effects of outlawing the chador was that the garments worn underneath became public, which exposed the poverty of many women. This resulted in the Iranian government sending its trade commission to Germany and France in 1936 to purchase 500,000 rials worth of women's ready-to-wear clothes for distribution. The ban on chadors was strictly enforced from 1936 to 1941, after which the law was eased following the Allied occupation and consequent abdication and exile of Reza Shah. Today, many Iranian women continue to wear the chador as a matter of religious and cultural principle. Once again, some in the West have come to regard this dress code as oppressive.

CONCLUSION

The clothing of the Middle East has often been used as a symbol of political and religious affiliations and represents a sartorial history that is equally complex and controversial. Garments and fabric styles have evolved from traditional lines to the introduction of European styles, accessories, and fabrics. Similarly, the fashions of Turkey and Iran have been influenced by secularization, modernization. and legislation. Beyond this, the clothing and fashions of the Middle East communicate a set of social and political relations that are connected with notions of gender and class, as well as with the cultural construction of identity and the "modern" nation.

SEE ALSO *Education, Middle East; Ideology, Political, Middle East; Literature, Middle East.*

BIBLIOGRAPHY

Abu-Lughod, Lila, ed. *Remaking Women: Feminism and Modernity in the Middle East.* Princeton, NJ: Princeton University Press, 1998.

Bailey, David A., and Gilane Tawadros, eds. *Veil: Veiling, Representation, and Contemporary Art.* Cambridge, MA: MIT Press, 2003.

Baker, Patricia L. "The Fez in Turkey: A Symbol of Modernization." *Costume* 20 (1986). 72–85.

El Guindi, Fadwa. *Veil: Modesty, Privacy, and Resistance.* New York: Berg, 1990.

El Guindi, Fadwa. "Veiling Resistance". *Fashion Theory. Vol. 3. Issue 1.* 51–80.

Fernea, Elizabeth. W. and Robert A. Fernea. "Symbolizing Roles: Behind the Veil." In *Dress and Identity*, edited by Mary Ellen Roach-Higgens, Joanne B. Eicher, and Kim K. P. Johnson. New York: Fairchild, 1995.

Göçek, Fatma M., and Shiva Balaghi, eds. *Reconstructing Gender in the Middle East: Tradition, Identity, and Power.* New York: Columbia University Press, 1994.

Goldschmidth, Arthur, Jr. *A Concise History of the Middle East,* 7th ed. Boulder, CO: Westview, 2002.

Grace, Daphne. *The Woman in the Muslin Mask: Veiling and Identity in Postcolonial Literature.* London: Pluto, 2004.

Gürtuna, Sevgi. "The Clothing of Ottoman Women." In *The Great Ottoman-Turkish Civilization*, edited by Kemal Çiçek. Ankara, Turkey: Yenì Türkíye, 2000. 78–92.

Hoodfar, Homa. "The Veil in Their Minds and on Our Heads: The Persistence of Colonial Images of Muslim Women." In *The Politics of Culture in the Shadow of Capital*, edited by David Lloyd and Lisa Lowe. Durham, NC: Duke University Press, 1997. 248–279

Kamrava, Mehran. *The Political History of Modern Iran: From Tribalism to Theocracy.* Westport, CT: Praeger, 1992.

Kandiyoti, Deniz, ed. *Gendering the Middle East: Emerging Perspectives.* New York: Syracuse University Press, 1996.

Lewis, Raphaela. *Everyday Life in Ottoman Turkey.* London: Batsford, 1971.

Mackenzie, John M. *Orientalism: History, Theory, and the Arts.* Manchester, U.K.: Manchester University Press, 1995.

Moghadam, Valentine M. *Modernizing Women: Gender and Social Change in the Middle East,* 2nd ed. Boulder, CO: Reinner, 2003.

Olson, E. A. "Muslim Identity and Secularism in Contemporary Turkey: The Headscarf Dispute." *Anthropological Quarterly* 58 (4) (1985): 161–171.

Reese, Lyn. *Women in the Muslim World: Personalities and Perspectives from the Past.* Berkeley, CA: Women in World History Curriculum, 1998.

Roach-Higgins, Mary Ellen, Joanne B. Eicher, and Kim K. P. Johnson, eds. *Dress and Identity.* New York: Fairchild, 1995.

Scarce, Jennifer. *Middle Eastern Costume from the Tribes and the Cities of Iran and Turkey.* Edinburgh: Royal Scottish Museum, 1981.

Scarce, Jennifer. *Women's Costume of the Near and Middle East.* London: Unwin Hyman, 1987.

Shaw, Stanford J., and Ezel K. Shaw. *History of the Ottoman Empire and Modern Turkey;* Vol. 2: *Reform, Revolution, and Republic: The Rise of Modern Turkey, 1808–1975.* Cambridge, U.K.: Cambridge University Press, 1977.

Wilcox, R. Turner. *The Dictionary of Costume.* New York: Scribner's, 1969. Reprint, London: Batsford, 1992.

Vicki Karaminas

COCHIN
SEE *Colonial Port Cities and Towns, South and Southeast Asia*

COEN, JAN PIETERSZ
1587–1629

Jan Pietersz Coen, twice governor-general of the Dutch East Indies, was born in the city of Hoorn, in the province of Holland, on January 8, 1587. Raised in a strict Calvinist environment, he received a commercial training in the firm of the Flemish merchant Justus Pescatore (Joost de Visscher) at Rome. In 1607 he entered the service of the Dutch United East India Company (VOC). Rising quickly through the ranks, in 1613 Coen was appointed bookkeeper-general of all company settlements in Asia and president of the VOC establishments at Banten and Jakarta in West Java. In 1614 he became director-general, the highest company official in Asia next to the governor-general. In April 1618 Coen was appointed governor-general by the board of directors, called the *Heeren XVII* or Gentlemen Seventeen.

In 1614, even before he became governor-general, Coen had submitted a series of recommendations to the board of directors in his *Discoers toucherende den Nederlantsche Indischen Staet* (Discourse on the State of the Dutch East Indies). First, he advocated aggressive action against European competitors and indigenous rulers. Whereas his precursor, Governor-General Laurens Reael (1616–1619), had been cautious in the

Jan Pietersz Coen. *The governor-general of the Dutch East India Company during the early seventeenth century, shown here in an eighteenth-century portrait.* **HULTON ARCHIVE/GETTY IMAGES. REPRODUCED BY PERMISSION.**

establishment of the spice monopoly as desired by the Gentlemen Seventeen, Coen had little consideration for the interests of the indigenous population. Second, Coen called for the settlement of Dutch colonists as "freeburghers" in certain parts of company territory. These European settlers could subsist on agriculture, manufacturing, and trade (though only in less lucrative commodities not monopolized by the company). In case of emergency, the "freeburghers" could also support the company militarily. Third, Coen urged the company to participate in the intra-Asiatic trade, and claimed that its profits could completely finance the purchase of commodities destined for Europe. Coen was particularly interested in the Chinese overseas trade. To achieve these goals, Coen called on the Gentlemen Seventeen to dispatch more capital and ships than they had done so far in order "to prime the pumps."

During his first term as governor-general (1619–1623), Coen's primary goal was to realize the company's wish to establish a central administrative and commercial headquarters in Asia. At the time, Banten was the main commercial center on the island of Java. Relations with the local ruler of Banten, however, were tense, and competition with English and Chinese rivals fierce. Coen gradually moved more company goods to the warehouses at nearby Jakarta, where the VOC had had an establishment since 1610. In 1618 the English founded a trading post opposite the Dutch settlement. Coen responded to this "affront" by fortifying the VOC establishment without the consent of the local ruler. Learning that the English had captured a Dutch ship, Coen had the English settlement razed to the ground. In the ensuing hostilities, the small Dutch garrison was able to maintain itself due to divisions amongst its Jakatran, English, and Bantenese rivals. Returning with a large relief fleet, Coen put the city of Jakarta to the torch. On its ruins rose like a phoenix the VOC capital of Batavia, soon known as the "Queen of the East."

The second item on Coen's agenda was to attain a nutmeg and mace monopoly for the VOC. The Banda Islands in eastern Indonesia were the world's sole production area. Exclusive agreements with the Bandanese, however, were not observed, partly because the company was unable to provide the inhabitants with sufficient food and clothing. Coen opted for the iron fist approach and in 1621 appeared with a large force in the Banda Sea. Following the capture of the islands, the entire population, an estimated 15,000 Bandanese, either perished—at the hands of the Dutch or through starvation—or were enslaved. The depopulated islands were divided into spice gardens, worked by European freeburgher "gardeners" and slaves imported from elsewhere across the Indian Ocean basin.

Finally, Coen also had a shot at the China trade. By attacking Portuguese Macao and Spanish Manila, Coen hoped to redirect Chinese shipping to Batavia. Several blockades of Manila proved fruitless. An attack on Macao in 1622 ended in disaster, though a fort was established on the Pescadores off the Chinese mainland. The Chinese authorities, however, ignored Dutch demands concerning the junk trade. Company attacks against Chinese ships and coastal settlement proved counterproductive, and the VOC was forced to withdraw from the Pescadores to Taiwan.

At his own request, Coen returned to the Dutch Republic in 1623. He was feted and appointed company director of the Hoorn chamber. In a *Memorie* (Memorandum), Coen drew up regulations for trade by the Dutch "freeburghers" in Asia, largely corresponding with the ideas he had first expressed in 1614. The Gentlemen Seventeen approved the memorandum and, duly impressed, successfully requested Coen to accept a second term as governor-general.

Coen's second term as governor-general (1627–1629) was dominated by the two sieges of Batavia in 1628 and 1629 by the ruler of Mataram in the interior of Java. Having conquered the bulk of the island, Sultan Agung (r. 1619–1646) demanded Dutch assistance against or free passage of his forces across company territory en route to Banten. Coen rejected the demand, which led to two abortive sieges of Batavia. During the second siege, however, Coen suddenly died, probably due to cholera, on September 21, 1629.

Jan Pietersz Coen, initially admired as the founder of the Dutch colonial empire in the East, has more recently been vilified as "the butcher of Banda." Admittedly, the harsh policies of "Iron Jan" were condemned even by some of his contemporaries. Coen's "grand design," however, was largely in accordance with prevalent mercantilist thought. In general, the company's board of directors, influenced by like-minded empire-builders such as the Rotterdam director Cornelis Matelieff, shared Coen's oft-quoted maxim "do not despair, and do not spare your enemies" (*Dispereert niet, ontsiet uwe vyanden niet*).

SEE ALSO *Batavia; Dutch United East India Company; Freeburghers, South and Southeast Asia; Moluccas.*

BIBLIOGRAPHY

Colenbrander, H. T., and W. Ph. Coolhaas, eds. *Jan Pietersz Coen: Bescheiden Omtrent zijn Bedrijf in Indië.* 7 vols. The Hague, Netherlands: M. Nijhoff, 1919–1953.

Fuchs, Johannes Marius. *Jan Pieterszoon Coen in Uitspraken van Hemzelf en Anderen.* Baarn, Netherlands: Bosch and Keuning, 1937.

Gerretson, F. C. *Coens Eerherstel.* Amsterdam, Netherlands: P. N. van Kampen, 1944.

Huijbers, H. F. M. *Jan Pieterszoon Coen.* Utrecht, Netherlands: A. W. Bruna, 1914.

Kiers, Lucas. *Coen op Banda.* Utrecht, Netherlands: A. Oosthoek, 1943.

Kohlenberg, Karl F. *IJzeren Jan: Jan Pieterszoon Coen, Grondlegger van de Koloniale Macht van Nederland.* Baarn, Netherlands: Uitgave Hollandia, 1979.

Milton, Giles. *Nathaniel's Nutmeg, or, the True and Incredible Adventures of the Spice Trader Who Changed the Course of History.* New York: Penguin, 2000.

Romein, Jan, and Annie Romein. "J. P. Coen: Couste que Couste." In their *Erflaters van onze Beschaving*, 70–107. 13th ed. Amsterdam, Netherlands: Querido, 1979

Spruit, Ruud. *J. P. Coen: Dagen en Daden in Dienst van de VOC.* Houten, Netherlands: De Haan, 1987.

Woude, Johan van der. *Coen, Koopman van Heeren Zeventien: Geschiedenis van den Hollandschen Handel in Indie (1598–1614).* Amsterdam, Netherlands: C. de Boer Jr., 1948.

Markus Vink

COFFEE CULTIVATION

Coffee (from the Arabic *qahwa*, "that which prevents sleep") is second only to oil as a legally traded commodity, with annual global retail sales at roughly seventy billion dollars.

The Rubiaceae (a large family of plants) *Coffea arabica*, *Coffea canephora* (robusta), and *Coffea liberica* require moderate temperatures, which are found in the tropics between 650 and 1,600 meters (2,133 and 5,249 feet) elevation; rainfall in the neighborhood of 1,500 millimeters (59 inches) per year; and shelter from wind, sun, and tropical downpours. Virgin jungle soils are optimal. Coffee is sensitive to drainage; too steep a slope results in fast runoff of nutrients, too little the danger of drowning. While these conditions are reasonably common in the tropics, they seldom are found together with the labor resources necessary to make coffee cultivation commercially profitable.

Coffea arabica probably originated on the plateaus of central Ethiopia. Originally cooked from green beans, by the late thirteenth century it was brewed from roasted and ground coffee beans. Coffee was used as a stimulant or aphrodisiac. Although the export of fertile coffee seeds was forbidden by the Arabian ruler, by the mid-seventeenth century the seeds had been brought to southern India.

It was the Dutch East India Company (1602–1799), however, which pioneered large-scale exploitation. Smuggling of plants to Java (an island in present-day Indonesia) in the late seventeenth century made possible a thriving agro-industry so indelibly associated with the island that Java became synonymous with coffee. This first flowering of the coffee industry was an amalgam of a mercantile system atop a feudal one.

The Dutch East India Company sold coffee on the open market in Europe, but obtained its goods by dictating price, quality, and quantity to Javanese potentates. The latter came increasingly to resemble feudal lords, complete with ownership of land, hereditary rights, and absolute control over their subjects. At the end of the nineteenth century the leaf disease *Hemileia vastratrix* harried Java and destroyed coffee cultivation in Ceylon (Sri Lanka) as well.

In 1723 a French naval officer, Gabriel Mathieu de Clieu, brought a seedling to Martinique, an island in the West Indies, from which much of the world's coffee derives. A few years later, in 1727, coffee spread to Brazil, where it thrived. At the end of the eighteenth century, Brazil's largest customer had become the newly independent United States of America, which was destined to remain the world's largest and most consistent coffee market. Although overshadowed by the combined consumption of the various European nations, Europe's not infrequent upheavals caused sharp swings in consumption.

By 1810 Brazil was exporting some 40 percent of the world's coffee, a figure that remained at 70 percent throughout much of the late nineteenth century. However, with the abolition of slavery, the Brazilian coffee industry was threatened by a scarcity of labor. The coffee barons of São Paulo made concerted efforts to obtain free labor through recruiting southern Europeans on short-term wage contracts. The drive to assure sufficient labor, coupled with the need for scarce capital, led the plantation owners to cooperate in improving transportation, finance, and export activities.

Brazil's coffee cultivation remains extensive. Scarce resources of labor are applied to seemingly unlimited virgin forest lands, which are abandoned after exhausting their soils. The situation with regard to both land and the spin-off to other areas of development was similar in the second largest coffee-producing nation, Colombia, where manpower requirements differed sharply. There, access to land, temporarily or permanently, was granted as part of wages. This in turn led to the establishment of smallholder production, eventually resulting in conflicts between landlords and tenants. The situation is roughly similar to developments in Central America, although with an ethnic twist.

African production of robusta (*Coffea canephora*) returned to the world scene only in the twentieth century. Begun in the English colonies of East Africa (Kenya) in the 1890s, it subsequently spread to Central Africa (Congo, Cameroon, and Angola) and finally to Liberia and the Ivory Coast. Robusta is disease resistant and thus has replaced *Coffea arabica* in South and Southeast Asia. It is also more tolerant in that it can be grown at lower elevations without shade trees. Moreover, robusta is a cheaper coffee that is used to blend with better-tasting arabica, as well as for instant coffee, both characteristic of the U.S. market in the wake of World War I.

Common to most coffee-growing nations is the extent to which basic socioeconomic features—ownership of production, access to land, class conflict, and racial differentiation—were shaped by the coffee industry. Despite the fact that production systems have ranged from plantation slavery (West Indies and Brazil) through quasifeudal modes of production (Java, Ceylon) and rural proletariat (Colombia, Central America) to authoritarian regimes (Uganda, Angola), the majority of the world's coffee is now produced on smallholder plots. Thus, some 70 percent of the world's total coffee production derives from plots of fewer than twenty-five acres, which gives employment to as many as twenty million individuals.

SEE ALSO *Java, Cultivation System.*

BIBLIOGRAPHY

de Graf, J. *The Economics of Coffee.* Wageningen, Netherlands: Pudoc, 1986.

Dekker, Edward Drewes (Multituli). *Max Havelaar: Or the Coffee Auctions of the Dutch Trading Company* (1860). New Harmondsworth, U.K.: Penguin, 1987.

Hoadley, Mason C. *Towards a Feudal Mode of Production: West Java, 1680–1800.* Singapore: Institute of Southeast Asian Studies, 1994.

Pendergrast, Mark. *Uncommon Grounds: The History of Coffee and How it Transformed our World.* New York: Basic Books, 1999.

Thurber, Francis B. *Coffee, from Plantation to Cup: A Brief History of Coffee Production and Consumption with an Appendix Containing Letters Written During a Trip to the Coffee Plantations of the East, and through the Coffee Consuming Countries of Europe.* New York: American Grocer Publishing Association, 1881.

Mason C. Hoadley

COFFEE IN THE AMERICAS

The coffee plant, native to Ethiopia and adjacent areas or to the Arabian Peninsula, was well known in the Muslim world from ancient times. The coffeehouses that emerged as centers of social and intellectual interaction in the port cities of Europe in the seventeenth century were supplied from Red Sea sources, particularly Yemen. The plant was introduced into the Caribbean islands, the Guianas, and Brazil in the early 1700s, and was produced primarily for local consumption for some time thereafter. Large-scale commercial cultivation of coffee in the tropical regions of the Americas emerged only in the nineteenth century, as demand grew in Europe and North America and transportation technology connected remote producing areas to seaports. Thus coffee as a major international commodity is specific to the era of neocolonialism or economic dependency, notwithstanding the participation of colonial Cuba and Puerto Rico in the coffee trade in the nineteenth century.

Coffee requires a frost-free climate with well-distributed rainfall and rich soils. While cultivation is possible at sea level, the cooler climate of tropical highlands is better suited to large-scale production of a high-quality product. These conditions are met in the interior uplands of southeast Brazil, as well as in the highland areas closer to the equator in Colombia, Central America, southern Mexico, and the larger Caribbean Islands. Cultivation is relatively labor intensive through much of the annual cycle, and the spread of coffee in the Americas has been accompanied by the occupation of frontier zones by either plantations, nearly all in the hands of local landowners, or small-scale peasant holdings. It has historically involved little foreign investment in producing areas except in transportation infrastructure, especially railroads after the mid-nineteenth century. Large firms in the European and North American areas of high consumption, however, have dominated international transportation, processing (roasting), distribution, and marketing. These areas included continental Europe and the United States, where industrialization and the general expansion of wage labor and increases in the purchasing power of working people accompanied the growth of commercial coffee production in tropical America.

As an international commodity, coffee first expanded into the Paraíba river valley north and west from the port city of Rio de Janeiro, Brazil, in the first decades of the nineteenth century. By 1830 coffee had supplanted sugar as Brazil's most important export crop, and it held that position until surpassed by soybean exports around 1980. Slavery had been the mainstay of the plantation system introduced into the sugar areas of northeast Brazil in the 1530s, and the spread of coffee three centuries later gave slavery and the African slave trade to Brazil a new lease on life, just at the time when the antislavery movement was gaining force in Europe and some former colonial areas. In 1827, under pressure from the British government, Brazil agreed to halt the importation of slaves from Africa by 1831. Primarily spurred by labor demand in the Paraíba valley coffee sector (sugar was by then in decline), the (illegal) importation of slaves to Brazil actually increased in the two decades after 1831. Before and, increasingly, after the end of the international slave trade to Brazil in 1851, the internal transfer of slaves from elsewhere in the country, particularly the depressed sugar areas of the northeast, fed labor demand in the coffee zone, which by the middle of the century had expanded into the western plateau of the adjacent province of São Paulo.

Coffee production under slavery was as ruthless and regimented as in other slave plantation regimes. Clearing virgin forests was rough and dangerous work, after which seedlings were planted that had to be tended for three to four years before the first harvest. Gangs of workers driven by whip-wielding *feitores* (slave drivers) weeded the groves several times a year, a routine punctuated by intense labor during the harvest from September to December. The harvested beans were milled to remove the cherry-like hull, dried on brick-paved platforms, and bagged for shipment to the port. Perhaps half of the slaves on the plantation worked in activities other than coffee production, as all manual labor—construction, transportation, tending livestock, household maintenance and service, and food production, processing, and preparation—was done by slaves. Slave diets consisted primarily of locally produced maize mush, rice, beans, and manioc flour, with the occasional addition of pork, and some salted beef imported from the cattle-producing regions of southern Brazil.

Transportation of coffee to ports was by slow and expensive mule train until the railroad was built into the Paraíba valley beginning in 1855, using British and U.S. technology, capital, and rolling stock. In the following decade a railroad was built, by an English firm, over the steep escarpment separating the port of Santos and the interior plateau of São Paulo. This facilitated the spread of coffee into the rolling tablelands to the west, into

which several locally financed railroads were built in subsequent decades. Just as the available land in the Paraíba valley was exhausted in the 1880s and slavery entered the decline that culminated in final abolition in 1888, western São Paulo surpassed Rio de Janeiro as the center of the Brazilian coffee industry.

A coffee blight in the colonial Dutch East Indies (Java and Sumatra) in the 1870s eliminated a major alternative source of supply, and from the mid-1880s to the mid-1890s high world prices led to rapid expansion of coffee in Brazil and elsewhere in the Americas. During the first two decades of the twentieth century Brazil supplied some three-fourths of the coffee in the world market, with São Paulo alone accounting for fully half.

From the mid-1880s to the onset of the Great Depression, São Paulo was the destination of some two million European immigrants, primarily from Italy, Spain, and Portugal, who replaced the slaves in the coffee labor force and toiled in the various industries that developed during the subsequent era of expansion. Immigrants worked as *colonos* under a complex system of compensation known as the *colonato*. Families contracted their labor as a unit, for the yearly cycle of weeding and pruning the groves, for which they received an annual wage calculated in blocks of 1,000 trees; for the harvest, for which they received a stipulated wage per basket picked; and for occasional daily labor around the *fazenda*, or plantation. In addition, they were given the use of a modest house in the *colonia* and access to land on which to plant food crops and pasture livestock, the proceeds of which were for the *colono* family's consumption or sale in regional markets. By using the extensive frontier lands of the São Paulo plateau in this way, this system solved the perennial problem of provisioning the plantation labor force. It also provided the *colono* family with a remuneration package that in good times was potentially lucrative, especially in comparison to the situation of workers in many other colonial and neocolonial plantation complexes. A significant number of *colono* families were able to use their savings from plantation work to acquire land and become coffee farmers themselves, if usually on a modest scale. By the early 1930s more than one-third of the coffee farms in São Paulo, accounting for one quarter of the state's production, were owned by first-generation immigrants.

Colombia first exported small quantities of coffee in 1835, and by the early twentieth century was exporting about half a million 132-kilogram bags per year (at a time when annual Brazilian exports averaged some 12 million bags). While most Colombian production has come from small and medium-sized farms, the formation of the National Federation of Coffee Growers in 1927 institutionalized a system whereby most Colombian coffee was marketed through what became a powerful

Shoveling Coffee Beans, El Salvador, 1955. *Workers on a coffee plantation in El Salvador collect dried and sifted coffee beans from the* beneficio, *or drying area.* **HULTON ARCHIVE/GETTY IMAGES. REPRODUCED BY PERMISSION.**

organization controlling the country's main export. As a result of astute marketing and specialization in higher-quality arabica varieties (much Brazilian production was of the *robusta* variety), Colombia's production expanded during the 1920s and especially after World War II. By the 1980s the aggregate value of Colombia's coffee exports rivaled that of Brazil (whose large internal market absorbs about half its total production).

In the nineteenth century cultivation began in the highland areas of Central America, and also in southern Mexico, as consolidating national elites encroached on indigenous lands through laws limiting corporate village ownership, and through usurpation. Many formerly autonomous peasants were coerced or drawn into the labor force of the new export activity. German planters and coffee traders were important in some areas of Guatemala and neighboring Chiapas, Mexico, from the 1870s to World War I. Costa Rica's coffee production, like that of Colombia and adjacent western Venezuela, involved a greater proportion of smaller farms, in contrast to Guatemala and El Salvador, where larger plantations were the norm.

Coffee in tropical America has been produced under a wide variety of ecological conditions, agrarian structures, and labor regimes, and it has at times been an important export commodity in most countries from Mexico to Brazil, to the larger Caribbean islands. In the late twentieth and early twenty-first centuries, movements were launched in consuming areas to ensure that peasant growers received fair prices for their product, even as the expansion of coffee cultivation in Vietnam and Africa brought lowered prices due to excess supply. Coffee continues to suffer the boom and bust cycles that have characterized its price on the international market for nearly two centuries.

SEE ALSO *African Slavery in the Americas; Export Commodities.*

BIBLIOGRAPHY

Bergad, Laird. *Coffee and the Growth of Agrarian Capitalism in Nineteenth-Century Puerto Rico.* Princeton, NJ: Princeton University Press, 1983.

Bergquist, Charles. *Coffee and Conflict in Colombia, 1886–1910.* Durham, NC: Duke University Press, 1978.

Bethell, Leslie. *The Abolition of the Brazilian Slave Trade: Britain, Brazil, and the Slave Trade Question, 1807–1869.* Cambridge, U.K.: Cambridge University Press, 1970.

Holloway, Thomas. *Immigrants on the Land: Coffee and Society in São Paulo, 1886–1934.* Chapel Hill: University of North Carolina Press, 1980.

Palacios, Marco. *Coffee in Colombia, 1850–1970: An Economic, Social, and Political History.* Cambridge, U.K.: Cambridge University Press, 1980.

Roseberry, William, Lowell Gudmundson, and Mario Samper Kutschbach, eds. *Coffee, Society, and Power in Latin America.* Baltimore, MD: Johns Hopkins University Press, 1995.

Stein, Stanley. *Vassouras, a Brazilian Coffee County, 1850–1900.* Cambridge, MA: Harvard University Press, 1957.

Wickizer, Vernon D. *The World Coffee Economy, with Special Reference to Control Schemes.* Stanford, CA: Stanford University Press, 1943.

Winson, Anthony. *Coffee and Democracy in Modern Costa Rica.* New York: St. Martin's, 1989.

Thomas Holloway

COLOMBO

SEE *Colonial Port Cities and Towns, South and Southeast Asia*

COLONIAL CITIES AND TOWNS, AFRICA

Colonial rule helped pave the way for the rapid expansion of many African cities after 1960. Some older towns remained important centers of commerce and cultural life, while others were completely transformed by changing economic and political developments. Still other cities, from Bangui in the Central African Republic to Nairobi, Kenya, and Windhoek, Namibia, began as small colonial administrative centers that eventually became gigantic settlements. The evolution of cities in colonial Africa varied a great deal, especially between settler colonies in southern and eastern Africa in comparison to other regions. The motivations of migrants, city planners, and urban communities also differed considerably from one locale to the next. However, the formation of cities reflected a series of challenges and innovations in African everyday life throughout the continent, especially from roughly 1880 to 1960.

Europeans established settlements in colonial coastal enclaves before the late nineteenth century. During the heyday of Atlantic slavery, a range of European countries established small forts on the East and West African coasts. These fortifications usually were built on the site of already existing towns, and thus local communities played a key role in providing these fledging municipalities with supplies. From Cape Coast in modern Ghana to Luanda in Angola, founded in 1579 by the Portuguese, Atlantic port towns nominally under European control helped to foster a cosmopolitan society where European and African bloodlines and influences merged. Historian Ira Berlin has called members of these communities *Atlantic creoles* because of their connections to different African and European social and political networks.

The export of slaves and natural resources served as the main business of these towns. Urban inhabitants often went by both European and African names, celebrated indigenous religious ceremonies and attended Christian services, and adopted elements of European clothing. *Signares,* female traders who formed intimate and social alliances with visiting Europeans in the Senegalese port of Saint Louis, became themselves important leaders in the town's social life. European governments did not try to radically reshape these settlements. Even in the Swahili town of Mombasa (Kenya), which the Portuguese controlled from the early sixteenth century to 1694 and the site of the enormous Portuguese Fort Jesus, indigenous people rather than Europeans controlled how the city was organized.

On the coast of East Africa, the eighteenth century brought a new innovation in colonial cities that was unique in African history. Rulers of the Omani sultanate established control over Zanzibar Island (now part of Tanzania) in 1698 by driving out the Portuguese. Zanzibar became a major trading center for ivory and slaves from the East African interior during the eighteenth and early nineteenth century, as well as a major producer of cloves through local slave plantations.

Omani rulers, Indian merchants, local Swahili elites, visiting European traders, and the burgeoning numbers of slaves living on Zanzibar helped to create a fluid and multicultural town identity. Slaves sought to demonstrate their equality with free Zanzibaris through adopting Islam and the dress of free townspeople.

By 1800, a stone town had been built with a blend of local and Middle Eastern architectural styles. Sultan Sayyid Said bin Sultan Al-Busaid (1790–1856), ruler of Oman, even moved his capital to Zanzibar from the Arabian Peninsula in 1840. Omani rulers in the nineteenth century brought in mirrors, plates, and even mechanical clocks featuring wind-up Austrian soldiers to show off their wealth and their prestige. Although Zanzibari leaders eventually surrendered their independence to England in 1890, the struggles for rights and shifting identities brought on in Zanzibar town in the nineteenth century continued well into the following century. Through songs, public dance performances, dress, and the formation of soccer clubs, descendants of slaves claimed their rights and challenged the power of well-off aristocratic families backed by the British.

Another regional urban heritage developed in southern Africa in the late seventeenth and early eighteenth century. Dutch colonialists established a small colony run by the Dutch East India Company in 1652. Like Zanzibar, this small colony's towns developed an international flavor early in their history. Cape Town, the capital of the colony, housed a mix of sailors from around the world, as well as slaves brought from India and Indonesia by the Dutch, French Huguenots, and members of Khoi and San African communities who lived either as free people or as dependent clients of Boer families.

Dutch settlers to Cape Town drew from their homeland for architectural styles, but these went through local alterations. Fires, often set by slaves, influenced the building patterns of Dutch residents of the town. Afrikaans, the Dutch dialect that developed in Cape Town and other South African cities, owed much of its vocabulary to the slaves who spoke it. Once the English occupied the colony in 1814, British adventurers and missionaries also moved to the city. Although some mission-educated Africans managed to claim some political rights in Cape Town in the nineteenth century, racial tensions and struggles between Dutch and English groups provoked conflict within the city as well.

The late eighteenth and early nineteenth centuries brought on the creation of new colonial coastal settlements. The British government, increasingly opposed to the international slave trade, established a small port named Freetown in Sierra Leone in 1787. Former slaves who had fled American masters during the American Revolution moved to Freetown, as did captives rescued from slave vessels by the British navy in later decades. Yoruba, Kru, and other ethnic communities formed in the town, and the pidgin form of English spoken in the town became the lingua franca of much of Sierra Leone. Female traders from nearby African communities as well as of foreign descent ran businesses and became leaders in town life.

In the early 1840s, French naval officers established a fort on the Gabon Estuary that briefly became a refuge for slaves rescued from Spanish vessels. The fort, Libreville, remained a small port for over a century, but it housed West African artisans, Vietnamese convicts, and Senegalese soldiers, and it attracted Africans from all over Gabon.

The decision of European governments to support invasions of much of Africa affected cities after the 1860s. Such towns as Accra (Ghana), Saint Louis, Lagos (a Nigerian port city annexed by the English in 1860), and Dar es Salaam (Tanzania) became administrative centers of imperialist expansion. In some cities, European governments moved very slowly in trying to remake the laws and spatial organization of cities. For example, British officials only gradually tried to ban slavery and engage in disputes over local leadership in Accra.

Although leaders in many coastal cities lost their previous ability to act as middlemen between Europeans and interior trade networks, townspeople in older colonial cities could also find work through their privileged access to education and their familiarity with colonial administrations. Urban settlement also altered in locales taken over by colonial governments. The defeat of the Sokoto caliphate by British forces between 1900 and 1903 left English administrators in charge of Hausa cities like Kano in Nigeria. Clerks, railroad workers, and other migrants from southern Nigeria moved to Kano. However, for decades British officials did little to disturb the institutions of slave officials or push for emancipation in Kano and other Northern Nigerian cities. Likewise, British officials in Zanzibar tried to favor slave-owning merchant families over slaves well after colonial conquest.

However, the growth of colonial authority also led to dramatic changes in some cities. European authorities pushed for segregated European and African neighborhoods in cities like Conakry (Guinea) and Freetown. Officials, strongly influenced by the growth of biological racist doctrines and associations between disease, poor hygiene, and Africans, promoted segregation on health grounds. This "sanitation syndrome," as Maynard Swanson has called this conjuncture of racial prejudice and public health, also became a means of justifying the destruction of African neighborhoods and the strict

Cape Town, South Africa. *The coastal city of Cape Town, founded by the Dutch in 1652, is now home to South Africa's legislature. The parliament building appears in the foreground of this photograph.* TERRENCE SPENCE/TIME LIFE PICTURES/GETTY IMAGES. REPRODUCED BY PERMISSION.

separation of neighborhoods by racial categories in South African cities.

Concerns about bubonic plague inspired turn-of-the-century South African city planners to promote segregation, while their counterparts in the Belgian Congo after 1908 argued that the creation of separate neighborhoods based on race was needed to protect Europeans from malaria. These ideas also fit with changing notions of city management in European cities that administrators sought to apply in African colonies. However, this push for segregation based on health issues did not occur everywhere. In Libreville, for example, efforts to segregate the small city into African and European sections never came to pass, thanks largely to protests launched by mission-educated Gabonese living in the city.

From the late nineteenth century through the 1950s, the greatest move toward urbanization on the entire continent took place in South Africa. The discovery of gold and diamonds in the 1860s and 1870s led to the creation of cities, most notably Johannesburg. These cities attracted a range of Europeans, Africans, and South Asians. After British forces defeated the independent Dutch settler republics in the second Anglo-Boer War between 1900 and 1902, officials struggled to maintain order and racial hierarchies in South Africa. Between the formation of the Union of South Africa in 1910 and the Nationalist Party's 1948 electoral victory, city planners helped to prepare the way for the apartheid era. African farmers and herders migrated to cities by the thousands, often motivated to the massive appropriation of land by white settlers, as well as the close proximity of giant mines always in need of African labor. City officials promoted the use of passes for African men and women, and the creation of separate African-only townships, and they banned the making of beer by Africans so that customers would patronize municipally-owned bars.

Many of these policies were designed to limit the ability of women to support themselves independently in cities. City governments and some rural African leaders formed an alliance to keep women in rural areas away from cities. Economic opportunities deteriorated in overcrowded African reserves in the countryside, and often rural women found that their husbands and relatives who had left to find work in cities did not send enough support home. Many women chose to brave government opposition and police persecution by working in cities, whether as prostitutes or bar owners, or by selling food at the markets. Some men who moved to cities formed evangelical prayer groups, while others formed gangs that battled police and robbed other Africans.

At the same time, Boer farmers hit hard by agricultural recessions in the 1920s and 1930s also moved to cities, often seeking government help to limit competition for jobs from Africans. A lively urban culture of music, cinema, and sports like football and cricket emerged from this strife. However, the willingness of many to support apartheid policies by 1948 came from European fears of African migration as well.

Historians have long taken South African urbanization as the model by which to understand the growth of African cities as a whole, although there are many differences as well as similarities. Cities in settler colonies like Rhodesia (Zimbabwe) and Kenya did resemble South African cities in certain respects. Much like in South Africa, city planners often tried to block the permanent resettlement of women and families to Nairobi and Salisbury (now Harare, Zimbabwe). Administrators were convinced that Africans ultimately belonged in rural locations and feared the supposedly destabilizing effects that city life had on indigenous people. Coercing Africans back to rural areas also, not coincidentally, pushed the cost of health-care and social services onto African families rather than city governments.

Many women, however, moved to these cities. Some sold produce at market. Others sought to escape restrictive marriage practices in their home communities by resettling in cities. Luise White (1990) has demonstrated how prostitutes could use their earnings to buy homes and live independently of men in cities like Nairobi. Still other women developed careers as domestic help, even while many European families preferred to hire men as cooks and domestics. The uneven growth of state, missionary, and independently run African schools in cities by the 1920s also created some job opportunities for educated Africans of both sexes. Many officials throughout settler colonies feared the formation of urban African communities that could challenge institutionalized discrimination against Africans through violent and nonviolent protest.

Outside of settler colonies, urbanization varied greatly. East African cities like Kampala (Uganda) and Dar es Salaam remained fairly small. Many cities in thinly populated parts of Central Africa were centered around administrative posts or economic centers. Officials in the German colony of Kamerun, French

Equatorial Africa, and the Congo Free State (later the Belgian Congo) of King Leopold II (1835–1909) set up posts such as Brazzaville, Yaoundé, Léopoldville (Kinshasa), Stanleyville (Kisangani), and Elisabethville (Lubumbashi) that emerged as cities in Central Africa. These settlements gradually attracted men and women for a range of reasons. They provided economic opportunities for skilled workers, a sanctuary for women trying to leave family difficulties, and better educational and health-care facilities than most rural locations.

These cities became cultural centers as well. Soccer clubs, new musical and dress styles, and independent African-run religious movements flourished. Especially in larger cities, officials often had trouble monitoring and controlling the activities of urban residents. Given that many residents of rural Central Africa faced forced-labor obligations and limited chances for social advancement between the 1890s and the 1950s, urban growth was not surprising. In some areas where the rural economy did offer profits for some Africans (in, for example, the timber industry in Gabon), the speed of urbanization lagged behind other places.

The growth rate and organization of cities in West Africa also differed from city to city. Lagos and Accra blossomed into booming cities by the 1920s and 1930s. They served as the foundation for new understandings of community as older ties based on village and clan merged into larger constructions of ethnic identity. Descendants of early African settlers often struggled through petitions, recourse to land claims, and control over ceremonies associated with the supernatural to assert their primacy despite the fact that they often were greatly outnumbered by newcomers.

These cities also became centers of political action. Africans in such cities as Abidjan in Côte d'Ivoire (Ivory Coast), Porto-Novo in Dahomey (now Benin), and other French cities joined French human rights groups and pushed for reforms in the 1920s and 1930s. Saint Louis and Dakar (Senegal) had actually been given representation in France during the mid-nineteenth century, and Senegalese politicians like Blaise Diagne (1872–1934) and Lamine Guèye (1891–1968) pushed for African political rights.

Women's protest movements also became a feature of such cities as Lagos and Onitsha (Nigeria), where market women often took to the streets to protest taxes and state interference from African state-appointed chiefs. Unlike in Central Africa, where most cities did not have a large popular press, newspapers, plays, and popular fiction were widely read in West African cities by the early twentieth century. However, large West African cities shared with their Central African counterparts a vigorous music scene. Highlife, a popular style of music that blended local percussion with horns, flourished in Anglophone cities in the Gold Coast (Ghana) and Nigeria.

Major international conflicts in the twentieth century had a great impact on African cities. World War I (1914–1918) brought a sharp rise in food prices in many West African cities as German submarines and the disruption of international trade greatly reduced shipping traffic. Between 1939 and 1945, urban life again was again transformed; World War II brought on an economic boom in many cities in southern Africa as Allied forces needed a tremendous amount of natural resources, which usually left Africa through port cities. In Dakar, the capital of French West Africa, pro-Nazi followers of Vichy France successfully battled an Allied raid in 1940. Portuguese Africa, though officially neutral in World War II, exported tea and cash crops to England and other countries.

Urbanization thus grew in Lourenço Marques (now Maputo, Mozambique) and Luanda. British and French officials became more concerned with urban development during and after the war, especially in efforts to create a stable and docile urban workforce. Efforts by colonial governments to build closer ties between metropole and empire after 1945 also remade urban space. French development money paid for the construction of apartment complexes, canals, and port facilities at Abidjan, Libreville, and elsewhere. Strikes in Mombasa, Lagos, Dar es Salaam, and other cities between 1945 and 1950 led colonial municipal governments to push for more social benefits for African city residents. Belgian officials promoted European notions of hygiene, health services, childcare, and household management through welfare programs, while British and French authorities considered providing limited social welfare for some city dwellers in the 1950s. Municipal bureaucratic structures backed by increased budgets after 1945 became the foundation for postcolonial city governments after independence.

Although most African cities became independent by the early 1960s, southern African cities remained under colonial rule for several more decades. Portuguese officials and military leaders employed the use of the secret police and security forces to maintain control over cities in their African colonies, which largely remained under their control until Portugal's withdrawal from Africa in 1975. The apartheid regime's decision to purge South African cities of most of their African urban population through forced removals in the 1960s brought widespread misery to city residents. Many African neighborhoods were bulldozed to make way for all-white housing complexes. City inhabitants played a key role in pushing for African rights from the cooperative movements of the 1940s through the nonviolent "defiance campaigns" of the following decade.

The Soweto neighborhood of Johannesburg, entirely made up of Africans, became the center of antiapartheid resistance from 1976 through the early 1990s. Street gangs, youth groups, police, and migrant workers' associations all used violence against one another, which left many Africans living in a state of endemic insecurity. In many cases, South African security forces allowed organized criminal organizations, like the Marashea gangs, to operate unchecked in many African neighborhoods. The legacy of lawlessness and brutality of the apartheid era explains much behind the extremely high crime rates of South African cities in the early twenty-first century. Just as the flourishing popular culture in African cities marks a positive development extending to the colonial period, the stark legacy of brutality in South African urban settlements also shows the impact of the colonial past today.

SEE ALSO *Apartheid; Segregation, Racial, Africa.*

BIBLIOGRAPHY

Anderson, David, and Richard Rathbone, eds. *Africa's Urban Past.* Portsmouth, NH: Heinemann, 1999.

Berlin, Ira. *Many Thousands Gone: The First Two Centuries of Slavery in North America.* Cambridge, MA: Harvard University Press, 2000.

Cooper, Frederick. *On the African Waterfront: Urban Disorder and the Transformation of Work in Colonial Mombasa.* New Haven, CT: Yale University Press, 1987.

Coquery-Vidrovitch, Catherine. *The History of African Cities South of the Sahara: From the Origins to Colonization.* Translated by Mary Baker. Princeton, NJ: Lynne Reiner, 2005.

Fair, Laura. *Pastimes and Politics: Culture, Community, and Identity in Post-Abolition Urban Zanzibar, 1890–1945.* Athens: Ohio University Press, 2001.

Guyer, Jane, ed. *Feeding African Cities: Studies in Regional Social History.* Bloomington: Indiana University Press, 1987.

Kynoch, Gary. *We Are Fighting the World: A History of the Marashea Gangs in South Africa, 1947–1999.* Athens: Ohio University Press, 2005.

Lemon, Anthony, ed. *Homes Apart: South Africa's Segregated Cities.* Bloomington: Indiana University Press, 1991.

Martin, Phyllis. *Leisure and Society in Colonial Brazzaville.* Cambridge, U.K.: Cambridge University Press, 1995.

Parker, John. *Making the Town: Ga State and Society in Early Colonial Accra.* Portsmouth, NH: Heinemann, 2000.

Swanson, Maynard. "The Sanitation Syndrome: Bubonic Plague and Urban Native Policy in the Cape Colony, 1900–1908." *Journal of African History* 18(3) (1979): 387–410.

White, Luise. *The Comforts of Home: Prostitution in Colonial Nairobi.* Chicago: University of Chicago Press, 1990.

Jeremy Rich

COLONIALISM AT THE MOVIES

Since the beginning of the motion picture industry, Western colonialism has been one of the themes, and at times one of the popular themes, of European and American movies. Cinema continued the nineteenth-century western European and American trend of telling romantic, exotic, and patriotic stories of expansion, conquest, and—increasingly—mission, or bringing the benefits of "civilization" to the "inferior races." Such stories had earlier been told in paintings, popular books, museums, illustrated journals, juvenile literature, and comics. Over the decades of the twentieth century, films with "imperial" and "colonial" themes celebrated and glorified imperial adventures and colonial triumphs and crises. Popular movies projected more myth than reality regarding the nature of colonialism, particularly as experienced from the indigenous African and Asian perspectives.

After World War II (1939–1945), and particularly by the 1970s and 1980s, Western filmmakers began to portray colonial encounters in more complex and nuanced ways. In the first decade of the twenty-first century, cinema around the world, from the perspective of both filmmakers and audiences, remained drawn to the themes of Western colonialism and, particularly, the difficult issues and problems created by the colonial encounters between Europeans and non-Europeans.

Colonialism at the movies began at the dawn of the motion picture industry in the late 1900s. A fifty-second reel about the French colony of Annam (central Vietnam) in Indochina was made by Gabriel Veyre (1871–1936), a collaborator of the Lumière Brothers (Auguste [1862–1954] and Louis Jean [1864–1948] Lumière, the inventors of cinema in Europe) in 1897. This short, entitled *Enfants annamites ramassant des sapèques devant la pagode des dames,* shows two French women giving money to a group of Vietnamese children who scramble and fight for every coin.

Only a small fraction of French films made in the 1920s and 1930s were colonial in subject or made in exotic locations. The Franco-Moroccan films of the 1920s respected local Berber customs, and the best "colonial" French films of the era, *Le Sang d'Allah* (The Blood of Allah, dir. Luitz Morat, 1922), *Itto* (dir. Jean Benoît-Lévy, 1934), and *Pépé le Moko* (dir. Julien Duvivier, 1937) provided realistic and ethnographically informed representations of North Africans. *Pépé le Moko* was popular in the United States. It was remade by Hollywood as *Algiers* (dir. John Cromwell, 1938). These films helped establish the exotic casbah in the imagination of Americans and contributed to the success of Michael Curtiz's *Casablanca* (1942). The American cartoonist Chuck Jones (1912–2002), who joined Warner Brothers in

1938, apparently was inspired by *Pépé le Moko* when he created his character Pepe Le Pew, who was debonair in a skunklike way.

French film critics constantly praised French filmmakers for their attention to *actualités*—not unlike nineteenth-century art critics who praised the North African paintings of French artist Eugène Delacroix (1798–1863) for their authenticity and transparency. French film critics, of course, reacted against the American and British "French Foreign Legion" films of the era, such as *The Sheik* (dir. George Melford, 1921), *Son of the Sheik* (dir. George Fitzmaurice, 1926), *The Spahi* (1928), and *Beau Geste* (dir. Herbert Brenon, 1926; and William Wellman's 1939 remake). French filmmakers, however, made their share of colonial adventure stories that shored up the idea of empire and idealized the Foreign Legion as the "thin white line" defending civilization from the Arabs. David Henry Slavin counts fifty such films set in North Africa in the 1920s and 1930s that "legitimated the racial privileges of European workers, diverted attention from their own exploitation, and disabled impulses to solidarity with women and colonial peoples" (2001, p. 3).

The British, with an empire upon which the sun never set, had uncounted colonial topics and stories that provided themes for popular feature films from before World War I (1914–1918) to the 1950s. The British and Colonial Kinematograph Company began the production of films in 1908 and produced a number of movies in colonial locales. The British Board of Film Censors, beginning in 1912, insured that "controversial" issues were avoided and only "wholesome imperial sentiments"—as the dominion premiers agreed in 1926—would be disseminated in the three thousand cinemas operating in Britain in the late 1920s (MacKenzie 1999, p. 226).

In the mid-1930s the Hungarian-born British producer Alexander Korda (1893–1956) produced his "Empire Trilogy," three popular films directed by his brother Zoltan Korda (1895–1961) that glorified the British Empire: *Sanders of the River* (1935), *The Drum* (1938), and *The Four Feathers* (1939). *Sanders of the River,* about a British district commander allied with an African chief played by the American actor Paul Robeson, so offended Robeson's sense of racial stereotyping that he attempted unsuccessfully to buy the rights to the film and all prints to prevent its distribution. *The Drum,* about a native Indian prince who gave assistance to a Scottish army regiment to overcome a rebel tyrant, triggered Hindu-Muslim riots in Bombay in 1938.

One of the favorite colonial stories, a 1902 novel by the British author A. E. W. Mason (1865–1948) about the courage of a former British soldier during the Sudan campaign of 1898, *The Four Feathers* was first made into a film during World War I and was remade by Zoltan Korda in 1939. The 1939 film presented the Sudanese enemy, the Arab dervishes, and the African "Fuzzy Wuzzies" as mindless warriors in the service of a madman. These and other British films with colonial themes of the 1930s offered little justification for empire other than, writes Jeffrey Richards, "the apparent moral superiority of the British, demonstrated by their adherence to the code of gentlemanly conduct and the maintenance of a disinterested system of law and justice" (quoted in Nowell-Smith 1996, p. 364). (Mason's 1902 novel has appeared on film seven times, including a 2002 version by the Indian director Shekhar Kapur. Kapur's film, unlike the previous ones, injected a dose of anti-imperialism in its double perspective of how British imperialism affected the subordinate native people and the British and native soldiers who enforce foreign rule.)

Italy's film industry during the fascist regime of Benito Mussolini (1883–1945) in the 1920s and 1930s was intended to create statist, nationalist, and imperialist propaganda, as Mussolini noted when he paraphrased Russian Communist leader V. I. Lenin (1870–1924): "For us cinema is the strongest weapon" (quoted in Nowell-Smith 1996, p. 354). In fact, however, official, "fascist" films constituted only a small percentage of Italian productions between 1930 and 1943. Fascist filmmakers, however, did produce movies about Italy's "African mission" with *Squadrone bianco* (White Squadron, dir. Augusto Genina, 1936) and *Sentinelle di bronzo* (Bronze Sentries, dir. Romolo Marcellini, 1937). The great costume drama and epic *Scipione l'Africano* (Scipio the African, dir. Carmine Gallone, 1937) reminded Italian audiences that Italian (Roman) soldiers had conquered Africa before and would do so again.

The Nazi state in Germany through the Ministry of Propaganda made many more films than the Italian fascist state, but there was little interest in overseas imperialism. Of the more than one thousand feature films produced in Germany between 1933 and 1945, few dealt with subjects other than Germany. *La Habanera* (dir. Douglas Sirk, 1937) and *Germanin* (dir. Max Kimmich, 1943), about Latin America and Africa respectively, focused on fever, sickness, and premature death.

The Soviet Union, officially anti-imperialist, made internationally recognized avant-garde films in the 1920s, but under Joseph Stalin (1879–1953) in the 1930s and 1940s production declined, as did quality. During World War II and the buildup to the war, Soviet cinema fell back on Russian imperial themes to promote nationalism and support for the state. *Kutuzov* (dir. Vladimir Petrov, 1944) presented Mikhail Kutuzov (1745–1813), the general who saved Russia from the Napoleonic invasion, as a loyal Russian and brilliant strategist. The great Soviet filmmaker Sergei Eisenstein (1898–1948) in *Ivan grozny* (Ivan the Terrible, part 1, 1945) depicted the sixteenth-century czar as a troubled character but great national hero. The film was begun on Stalin's request, but the dictator viewed it as a critique as his own autocracy and banned it. During the Stalin years, the Soviet republics were permitted to make their own film epics about national heroes (*Bogdan Khmelnitsky* [dir. Igor Savchenko, 1941] in Ukraine, for example), but the Soviet censors made sure that these were heroes who had never fought against Russian oppressors.

By 1929 over 80 percent of the world's feature films came from the United States, and most of those from Hollywood, California. The United States had long viewed itself as an anti-imperialist nation, despite its expansion across the transcontinental West, its seizure of Native American lands and Mexican provinces, and its late nineteenth- and early twentieth-century adventures in overseas acquisitions of Hawaii, Cuba, Puerto Rico, the Philippines, and the Panama Canal Zone. American filmmakers, and apparently American audiences, were not interested in any American "empire" other than the "Wild West" and cowboys and Indians.

The *western* dominated American cinema from the silent period through the 1950s. Not unlike French and British colonial films, American westerns contrasted white civilization and Indian "savagery," as well as the conflicts within newly settled colonial societies. Many American western films, beginning with *The Battle at Elderbush Gulch* (1913) directed by D. W. Griffith (1875–1948), present the advance of the frontier as a triumph of character and heroism. Not all westerns before the 1960s and 1970s, however, were vehicles for anti-Indian propaganda. Hundreds of early silent films were based on the popular Wild West shows of Buffalo Bill, Broncho Billy, Tom Mix, and others that had genuine Indian performers who provided the attraction of an exotic and clichéd past. A number of feature films, from Griffith's *The Squaw's Love* (1911) to Howard Hawks's *Broken Arrow* (1950) and John Ford's *The Searchers* (1956), presented sympathetic portraits of Indian life and relations with whites, and complex observations on the nature of American racism. The famed "Cavalry Trilogy" directed by John Ford (1895–1973)—*Fort Apache* (1948), *She Wore a Yellow Ribbon* (1949), and *Rio Grande* (1950)—was scathing in its portrayal of U.S. Indian agents, cavalry officers, and other whites who took advantage of the Apaches or misunderstood them.

Americans were as interested in the adventure and romance of the British and French overseas empires as the British and French were themselves, although American films set in the French and British empires

BOLLYWOOD

The roots of India's Mumbai-based cinema industry, informally known as Bollywood, stretch back to July 7, 1896, when the Lumière Brothers showed six silent short films at a Bombay hotel. However, Dhundiraj Govind Phalke (Dada Saheb Phalke) has been recognized as setting the industry in motion with the production of *Raja Harishchandra*. Introduced in Bombay on May 3, 1913, this film was the country's first totally indigenous silent feature. Silent films soon proved popular, in part because they provided entertainment that transcended the barriers to communication created by India's great diversity of languages.

A formal film industry structure emerged in Bollywood during the 1920s, and by the 1930s the organization of India's cinema industry very much resembled the manner in which Hollywood was organized in the United States, with studios directly employing actors and directors. This structure eventually changed due to the influence of independent producers.

Silent films quickly gave way to pictures with sound during the early 1930s. The Imperial film company released *Alam Ara*, India's first "talkie," on March 14, 1931. In addition to creating indigenous language barriers, talkies also isolated India from Western films, allowing Indian films to flourish. A number of productions that addressed social injustice were produced during the 1930s, and the industry continued to create significant films during the 1940s.

The 1950s marked the so-called "golden age" of Bollywood. As the *Economist* noted in its September 15, 2001, issue, in a review of Nasreen Munni Kabir's book, *Bollywood: The Indian Cinema Story*: "Back in the 1950s

film makers such as Mehboob Khan, Raj Kapoor, and Guru Dutt rode on a wave of intellectual dynamism that had been whipped up by the raising of the Indian flag at independence. These directors were happy to take on realistic themes, such as caste, morality and the place of women in a fast-changing world."

During the 1960s color films emerged, and Bollywood began to concentrate heavily on the production of escapist, romantic pictures. Some have characterized the Indian films of this decade as being produced mainly with box office receipts and distributors in mind. Directors like Ritwik Ghatak, Satyajit Ray, and Mrinal Sen pioneered the New Indian Cinema in reaction to such films, by focusing on the production of more artistic pictures with social significance.

During the 1970s big-budget Bollywood productions tended to focus on the themes of action and revenge, even as New Cinema productions continued to be released. Some have argued that Bollywood reached an all-time low during the 1980s, which they see as an era marked by films of poor quality. After declining in number during the 1970s, roles for female actresses virtually disappeared. The 1990s saw a trend toward "glamorous realism," which brought a return to romantic films and the reemergence of strong roles for female actresses. In addition, the introduction of satellite and cable television created new entertainment options and new venues for music drawn from Indian films.

By the early twenty-first century, Bollywood had produced, since its humble origins, roughly 27,000 feature films and many more short films. Bollywood continues to produce more than 100 films per year.

were often more attuned to non-European sensibilities. In 1916 Hollywood made Anatole France's novel *Thaïs* (1890) into *The Garden of Allah* (dir. Colin Campbell). This story about very little, a man and a women abandoning their religion and seeking their selves in the North African desert, was remade in 1927 (by Rex Ingram) and in 1936 (by Richard Boleslawski) in the United States, apparently because of the popularity of the exoticism and romance of the desert.

The Sheik (1921), the film that made the Italian-born actor Rudolph Valentino (1895–1926) a star,

involves a London socialite traveling across the Sahara, where she is attacked by bandits. She is rescued by Sheik Ahmed Ben Hassan (Valentino), and the English lady and the Arab sheik fall in love. North Africa also served as the setting for *Beau Geste*, an adaptation of a British story about three English Geste brothers and the French Foreign Legion. This story, set in French North Africa, highlighted the virtues of English and French manliness and brotherhood in the context of relentless Arab attacks.

The 1930s became the golden age of British colonialism in Hollywood and the classic action-adventure

***Gunga Din* Poster, 1939.** Gunga Din, *director George Stevens's take on Rudyard Kipling's smug commemoration of a loyal Indian water-bearer, portrays British soldiers as brave and heroic.* **EVERETT COLLECTION. REPRODUCED BY PERMISSION.**

spectacular. Henry Hathaway's *The Lives of a Bengal Lancer* (1934), a blockbuster success in America and Britain, is a melodrama about three British officers stationed in northwest India. This film set the civilized British soldiers against the ruthless and treacherous Afghan rebel Mohammed Khan, who tortured well-bred Englishmen. The success of *Bengal Lancer* brought more films like it: *Clive of India* (dir. Richard Boleslawski, 1935), *Storm over Bengal* (dir. Sidney Salkow, 1938), *The Sun Never Sets* (dir. Rowland Lee, 1939), *Gunga Din* (dir. George Stevens, 1939), and *Stanley and Livingston* (dir. Henry King, 1939).

Gunga Din, George Stevens's (1904–1875) take on the British author Rudyard Kipling's (1865–1936) smug commemoration of a loyal Indian water-bearer, naturally portrays the British soldiers as brave and heroic. However, the anti-British enemy is noted to be lovers of "Mother India" and therefore not mindless fanatics

but believers in a worthy cause. Kipling's multicultural theme, and the one often pushed by liberal American filmmakers, was found in the story of Gunga Din, who was a nobody and who in the end sounded his bugle, warned the troops, rescued his friends, and saved the day.

Prior to World War II, French, British, and American films rarely deviated from the accepted values and norms of their times regarding the framework of colonialism. Filmmakers took the dichotomy of civilized settlers and primitive natives for granted. However, not all films on colonial subjects followed these rules. The disintegration and liberation of the European colonial empires in the decades following 1945 transformed the way the West understood colonialism and therefore changed cinema's view of colonialism. This change did not happen immediately. *King Solomon's Mines* (dirs. Compton Bennett and Andrew Marton, 1950, a remake of the 1937 British film), *Storm over Africa* (dir. Lesley

Selander, 1953), *West of Zanzibar* (dir. Harry Watt, 1954), *Zulu* (dir. Cy Endfield, 1963), and *Khartoum* (dirs. Basil Dearden and Eliot Elisofon, 1966) continued to portray the British colonial soldier or adventurer as the noble agent of "civilization." The story of how Muhammad Ahmad, the Mahdi, an Islamic mystic, organized an army and drove the British out of the Sudan in 1885 is told in *Khartoum*. British General George Gordon (1833–1885), martyred in the campaign, was played by the handsome and heroic American actor Charlton Heston. The British actor Laurence Olivier, as the Mahdi, on the other hand, presented a lunatic religious fanatic, an Islamic stereotype that was reinforced in later movies from time to time.

By the 1960s, with the demise of most of the European empires, Western filmmakers had begun their passage into cinematic collective guilt, cultural self-condemnation, and moral instruction. *La bataille d'Alger* (The Battle of Algiers, 1966), an Italian film directed by Gillo Pontecorvo (b. 1919) about the anticolonial uprising against French colonialism in the capital of Algeria from 1955 to 1957, brought the bitter history of colonialism and anticolonialism to life in French cinemas and everywhere else. This documentary-style film won awards in Venice, London, and Acapulco largely because of its obvious political perspective, a defense and justification of the National Liberal Front (FLN), the Algerian insurrectionary organization. Bosley Crowther, writing the review for the *New York Times*, observed that Pontecorvo's film was essentially about valor, "the valor of people who fight for liberation from economic and political oppression. And this being so, one may sense a relation in what goes on in this picture to what has happened in the Negro ghettos of some of our American cities more recently" (Crowther 1967/2004, p. 82).

French audiences, along with other Europeans and Americans, were outraged by the provocations, torture, and killings that *The Battle of Algiers* attributed solely to the colonial police and the French army. The terrorism of the FLN is explained by the planting of a bomb by the police in a crowded apartment building. Although the police and the army committed many abuses and crimes in the war, this particular event was a fabrication of the filmmaker. The insurrection began in August 1955 when the FLN launched a campaign to murder every French civilian and official in the country. FLN death squads killed men, women, and children, and immediate French reprisals led to mass arrests and more murders. This war, a bloodbath of atrocity and reprisal that began in 1955 and continued until the cease-fire of 1962, killed more than eighty thousand French settlers and soldiers and many hundreds of thousands of Muslim Algerians. Neither *The Battle of Algiers* nor the more commercial American film *Lost Command* (dir. Mark Robson, 1966)

provided any kind of nuanced or even historically reliable and complete picture of this tragic war.

By the 1960s and 1970s, the sins of European colonialism were being compounded with those of the American war in Vietnam in British and American films. Tony Richardson's *The Charge of the Light Brigade* (1968), a film about the British war against Russia in the Crimean Peninsula in the 1850s, abandoned the heroics of both the 1854 poem by Alfred Lord Tennyson (1809–1892) and Michael Curtiz's 1936 American film on the same subject. In Richardson's version, the doomed Light Brigade is a symbol of everything wrong with Victorian England: jingoism, elitism, ideological blindness, and strategic bungling.

Zulu Dawn (dir. Douglas Hickox, 1979), the prequel to 1964's *Zulu*, depicted the Battle of Isandhlwana of 1879, which was the worst defeat of the British army in Africa. This anti-British epic contrasted the peaceful yet heroic Zulu (as suggested by the title) with the arrogant and stupid British. Director Hickox (1929–1988) and screenwriter Cy Endfield (1914–1995) compared the British in Africa to the Nazis. Prior to the British invasion of Zululand, the colonial governor is made to say, "Let us hope that this will be the final solution to the Zulu problem" (quoted in Roquemore 2000, p. 373).

American westerns by the 1970s presented the white man as the savage antihero and the Indian as the respectable and courteous husband, brother, citizen, and leader. *Little Big Man* (1970), directed by Arthur Penn (b. 1922), tells the story of Jack Crabb, the sole survivor (perhaps) of George Armstrong Custer's "Last Stand" in the 1876 Battle of the Little Bighorn in Montana Territory. Penn demystifies a vain and neurotic Custer and sadly allows the audience to see the extinction of the Cheyenne (who call themselves "human beings") through the story and eyes of Jack.

The propagandistic *Soldier Blue* (dir. Ralph Nelson, 1970) focused on the U.S. Cavalry's 1864 Sand Creek massacre in Colorado. The murderous glee of most of the racist soldiers was reflected in the outrage of the one appalled hero. This film, like *Little Big Man*, made visual references to the Vietnam War and American "atrocities," such as the infamous My Lai massacre of March 1968. The ultimate triumph of this cinematic revisionism was Kevin Costner's *Dances with Wolves* (1990), a three-hour epic about the Lakota Sioux that portrayed the Indians as peaceful, sophisticated, and above all civilized people in contrast to the violent, incompetent, and barbaric white soldiers. This beautiful atonement for Hollywood's too many "Injun" insults won seven Academy Awards, including Best Picture. The "evils of civilization" and the "conquest of paradise" themes continued to be explored through fabulous cinematography *1492: Conquest of Paradise* (dir. Ridley Scott, 1992) and *The New World* (dir. Terrence Malick, 2005).

One of the most important themes in colonial studies, as well as in colonial films, is the allure of the "other" or the exotic, that is, the attraction or enticement of colonial culture and the temptation of "going native." The usual or "normal" assumption that the *other* culture is offensive, savage, unsophisticated, and generally uncivilized is reversed when a hero or heroine adopts not only the outward signs and customs of the foreign and colonial culture, but in the most personal, physical, and emotional manner "becomes" the other. We see this with Costner's Lieutenant John Dunbar, who easily abandons his soldierly, white, and American identity in order to become "Dances with Wolves," the husband of "Stands with a Fist" and a member in good standing of one band of the Lakota Sioux.

One of the classic films of British colonialism, indeed one of the classic films of all time, David Lean's *Lawrence of Arabia* (1962), is the story of an eccentric British officer, T. E. Lawrence (1888–1935), who joined forces with Arab tribesmen during World War I and became a legendary man of the desert. Peter O'Toole's Lawrence was, like his Arab allies, a magnificent warrior, both courageous and enigmatic. Lean also shows Lawrence as the fallible westerner, whose good intentions for Arab independence allowed his confidence to turn into arrogance and bloodlust. Although Lean and scriptwriter Robert Bolt had no difficulty presenting the Turks as vicious enemies, their portraits of the Arabs were as attractive yet indistinct as the desert cinematography. The vain and weak Prince Feisal who led the tribes of the peninsula was played by Alex Guinness as cagey, educated, and wise.

The 1980s and 1990s witnessed a new wave of what would generally be called rich and complex colonial stories in the movies. Not since the 1930s had English-speaking movie houses seen so many colonial stories about India and Africa. *Staying On* (dir. Silvio Narrizzano, 1981), *Heat and* Dust (dir. James Ivory, 1982), *Gandhi* (dir. Richard Attenborough, 1982), *A Passage to India* (dir. David Lean, 1985), *Out of Africa* (dir. Sydney Pollack, 1985), *The Mission* (dir. Roland Joffé, 1986), *Dien Bien Phu* (dir. Pierre Schoendoerffer, 1991), *Indochine* (dir. Régis Wargnier, 1992), *L'Amant* (The Lover, dir. Jean-Jacques Annaud, 1992), and the 1984 British television series *The Jewel in the Crown* were beautiful, passionate, and popular films about colonial relationships. In most of these films, the nature of colonialism and the colonial relationship is viewed from the perspective of a European. In *Indochine*, for example, French colonialism in Vietnam from the 1930s to the

Lawrence of Arabia **Poster, 1962.** *One of the classic films of British colonialism,* Lawrence of Arabia *depicts T. E. Lawrence as the fallible westerner, whose good intentions for Arab independence allowed his confidence to turn into arrogance and bloodlust.* EVERETT COLLECTION. REPRODUCED BY PERMISSION.

1950s is seen through the eyes and experience of a privileged daughter of a rubber plantation owner, Eliane de Vries (played by the French actress Catherine Deneuve). When Eliane adopts a Vietnamese orphan and is radicalized by the Communist revolution, the audience is taken on the journey of anti-French sentiment that pushed the Vietnamese into rebellion, revolution, and the war against the French.

The rest of the world—North Africans, Arabs, Latin Americans, Africans, Indians, Asians, and others—have been making films since the beginning of filmmaking. French-Moroccan filmmakers in the 1920s and 1930s made dozens of quality films about contemporary life and history. In many parts of the world, and not simply in colonies, early filmmaking was the result of joint productions between Europeans and locals. States created national studios to support local directors and screenwriters and to finance national productions. In Algeria, for example, the newly independent revolutionary state set up Casbah Films in 1962, led by Yacef Saadi, which coproduced *The Battle of Algiers*. By the 1950s and 1960s, films from the so-called third world, such as *Bharat Mata* (Mother India, dir. Mehboob Khan, 1957) from India and *Bab El Hadid* (Cairo Station, dir. Youssef Chahine, 1958) from Egypt, were becoming recognized around the world.

Colonial themes have appeared in many films from the third world, although, perhaps surprisingly, this topic has never been dominant. In the non-Western cinema, as in the West, filmmakers and audiences are drawn to a wide variety of stories. Films on colonialism from the third world, like those from the West, can be divided into two groups: the many films that feature nationalist and politicized lectures on the evils of colonialism, and the fewer eloquent stories that reveal the weakness of the seemingly strong empires and the strength of the apparently oppressed people. Satyajit Ray (1921–1992), India's best-known director, took the second approach in *Shatranj Ke Khiladi* (The Chess Player, 1977). The French-Egyptian production *Al-Wida'a ya Bonaparte* (Adieu Bonaparte, dir. Youssef Chahine, 1985) is an intimate focus on Napoléon Bonaparte's 1798 Egyptian campaign; the film translates colonial relations into the homosexual love affairs of a Frenchman and two Arab brothers. Private dramas acquire political dimensions that, given the context of colonialism, alter even the best intentioned of human contacts.

The movie *Lagaan: Once Upon a Time in India* (dir. Ashutosh Gowariker, 2001), a nearly four-hour period film set in 1893, is a masterpiece from Bollywood (the Bombay-based Indian film industry) by Bombay's hottest movie producer and actor, Aamir Khan. Set in the little village of Champaner near a British cantonment, the villagers discover that they must pay twice the amount of *lagaan* (land tax) because the local Indian prince does not eat meat. The arrogant British officer in charge demands complete obedience but is willing to make a bet: The soldiers will play a game of cricket with the villagers (who have never played the game). If the villagers lose, they must pay triple the tax. Khan, playing a young farmer, organizes the village and obtains the support and instruction of the British officer's sister. What starts out as a gesture of pity evolves into an exotic love story. In the end, naturally, the simple villagers triumph over the sophisticated British at their own game, the weak beat the strong, and the oppressed obtain justice.

Although they had many opportunities, Khan and Gowariker did not paint the Indian villagers and the British soldiers with the broad ideological brush strokes that even the best filmmakers have been known to use, as

can be seen in *The Mission, Dances with Wolves, 1492: Conquest of Paradise,* and *The New World.* In *Lagaan*, both villagers and British soldiers are portrayed as people, people with their particular problems and flaws. The audience is inspired by the villagers' spirited efforts to build a cricket team, but also grateful to the filmmakers for refusing to slip into the easy path of portraying the ordinary British soldiers as racist and violent monsters.

As is true with many Bollywood pictures, *Lagaan* is a musical filled with singing and dancing and is perhaps one of the best movies yet made about Western colonialism. It is mostly in Hindi, with subtitles in English. Other films may be more important—*Lawrence of Arabia, Gandhi, The Rising* (dir. Ketan Metha, 2005)— but *Lagaan* blends the serious and humorous, a love story and the love of sports, the imperial colossus and the peasant village in the middle of nowhere, and interesting stories of individual characters.

Perhaps the greatest historical epic film ever produced in India is Metha's *The Rising*, a telling of the Sepoy Revolt of 1857 (called the "First War for Independence" by Indians) against the British East India Company. This film concentrates on the life of Mangal Pandey, the sepoy who started the rebellion, who is played by Aamir Khan.

For students and teachers, scholars and readers, and movie fans and history buffs, the world's filmmakers have offered many movies about colonialism, far more than can be touched upon in this short entry. The adaptation of this relatively new art form to the historic events, classic stories, great personalities, moral dilemmas, and personal relationships of Western colonialism has produced great film epics, exciting dramas, exotic romances, good and bad propaganda, and much more. In the early twenty-first century, filmmakers have new technologies and special effects, as well as more money, to produce epics, and they have barely touched many of the great stories of modern colonialism and empire.

The desire to see colonial cinema, from the filmmakers of Hollywood and Bollywood, from the studios of France, Britain, and Mexico, as well as Senegal, China, and Egypt, is a continuing and widening challenge, like finding and reading good and interesting colonial history and historiography. Cinephiles search video and DVD shops and now the Internet, looking for both the classic colonial movies and the lesser-known Western and non-Western films that have explored colonial themes. Scholars are researching how "empire cinema constructed the colonial world" (Chowdhry 2001), and professors are teaching courses in colonial cinema. Nearly every university in the United States offers courses in film studies, and courses on films about Western colonialism are not uncommon. It is a great time to be watching colonialism at the movies.

BIBLIOGRAPHY

Chowdhry, Prem. *Colonial India and the Making of Empire Cinema: Image, Ideology, and Identity*. New Delhi: Vistaar, 2001.

Crowther, Bosley. Review of *The Battle of Algiers. The New York Times*, September 21, 1967. In *The New York Times Guide the Best 1,000 Movies Ever Made,* updated and rev. ed., edited by Peter M. Nichols. New York: St. Martin's Griffin, 2004.

Hill, John, and Pamela Church Gibson, eds. *The Oxford Guide to Film Studies*. Oxford: Oxford University Press, 1998.

MacKenzie, John M., ed. *Imperialism and Popular Culture*. Manchester, U.K.: University of Manchester Press, 1986.

MacKenzie, John M. "The Popular Culture of Empire in Britain." In *The Oxford History of the British Empire; Vol. 4: The Twentieth Century,* edited by Judith M. Brown and Wm. Roger Louis, 212–231. Oxford: Oxford University Press, 1999.

Murray, Alison. "Teaching Colonial History through Film." *French Historical Studies* 25 (1) (2002): 41–52.

Nichols, Peter M., ed. *The New York Times Guide to the Best 1,000 Movies Ever Made,* updated and rev. ed. New York: St. Martin's Griffin, 2004.

Nowell-Smith, Geoffrey, ed. *The Oxford History of World Cinema*. Oxford: Oxford University Press, 1996.

Pontecorvo, Gillo, dir. *The Battle of Algiers (La bataille d'Alger)* (1966). Special edition, three-disc set. Irvington, NY: The Criterion Collection, 2004.

Pym, John, ed. *Time Out Film Guide*, 14th ed. London: Time Out Guides, 2005.

Richards, Jeffrey. *The Age of the Dream Palace: Cinema and Society in Britain, 1930–1939*. London, 1984.

Richards, Jeffrey. "'Boy's Own Empire': Feature Films and Imperialism in the 1930s." In *Imperialism and Popular Culture,* edited by John M. MacKenzie. Manchester, U.K.: University of Manchester Press, 1986.

Roquemore, Joseph. *History Goes to the Movies: A Viewer's Guide to the Best (and Some of the Worst) Historical Films Ever Made*. New York: Main Street Books, 1999.

Schneider, Steven Jay, ed. *1001 Movies You Must See Before You Die,* rev. ed. London: Quintet, 2005.

Slavin, David H. "French Cinema's Other First Wave: Political and Racial Economies of *Cinéma Colonial*, 1918 to 1934." *Cinema Journal* 37 (1) (1997): 23–46.

Slavin, David H. "French Colonial Film Before and After *Itto*: From Berber Myth to Race War." *French Historical Studies* 21 (1) (1998): 125–155.

Slavin, David H. *Colonial Cinema and Imperial France, 1919–1939: White Blind Spots, Male Fantasies, Settler Myths*. Baltimore: Johns Hopkins University Press, 2001.

Stevens, Donald F., ed. *Based on a True Story: Latin American History at the Movies*. Wilmington, DE: SR Books, 1997.

Vann, Michael G. "The Colonial Casbah on the Silver Screen: Using *Pépé le Moko* and *The Battle of Algiers* to Teach Colonialism, Race, and Globalization in French History." *Radical History Review* 83 (2002): 186–192.

Voytilla, Stuart. *Myth and the Movies: Discovering the Mythic Structure of 50 Unforgettable Films*. Studio City, CA: Michael Wiese Productions, 1999.

Thomas Benjamin
Doina Harsayni

COLONIAL PORT CITIES AND TOWNS, SOUTH AND SOUTHEAST ASIA

The term *colonial port city* evokes, in a Southeast and South Asian context, images of sprawling cosmopolitan urban centers, with their polyglot trading communities, linking long-distance maritime trading and shipping networks with regional movements of people, commodities, and ideas. Such cities are also seen as foreign enclaves, socially, morphologically, and culturally distinct from their hinterlands, but exercising economic and political control over them, tying these areas into imperial and global economic modes of production and consumption. Historically, they often served as regional or imperial capitals for the various European empires of the region.

In nineteenth- and twentieth-century South and Southeast Asia, such cities included Aden, Karachi, Bombay, Madras, Colombo, and Calcutta along the littorals of the Indian Ocean; Penang, Melaka and Singapore along the Straits of Melaka; Batavia, Semarang, Surabaya, and Makassar around the Java Sea; and Saigon, Hong Kong, and Manila on the South China Sea.

While the origins of these cities can be traced to the fortified Asian and European-controlled port towns established in these regions between the sixteenth and early nineteenth centuries, the colonial port city can easily be distinguished from their predecessors out of which they developed. They differ not only in terms of size and morphology, but also in terms of the extent of control colonial cities exercised over their hinterlands, the scale and scope of the commercial, financial, administrative, and socio-cultural functions they handled, and their role in integrating their respective hinterlands into broader structures of the colonial economy.

THE EUROPEAN PORT TOWNS

The commercial functions of the European port towns, including Manila, and their political and economic environments shaped the towns' social and physical morphology and their roles between the sixteenth and eighteenth centuries. Foremost among the factors that defined these port towns was their cosmopolitanism. Rhoads Murphey (1989) has argued that this cosmopolitanism was inextricably linked with the commercial functions of such towns. It was an outgrowth of the European trading companies' desire to gain access to preexisting structures and networks of trade in Asia, and was reinforced in the early modern period by the social structuring of trade and occupations in the region along ethnic, religious, and, in the case of the Indian subcontinent, caste lines.

Attracting particular ethnic trading communities and artisan groups to the new European port towns was often seen as crucial to the towns' success. In Southeast Asia, these port towns were usually polyglot centers with Chinese, Arab, Malay, Bugis-Makassarese, Balinese, and Javanese communities. However, it was the Chinese who were the most important migrant community in the development of port towns in Southeast Asia, from the Dutch-controlled Batavia, Semarang, Surabaya, and Makassar, to the Spanish port town of Manila and the British port towns of Penang and Singapore. This was because of their connections with China and Chinese trading networks (especially maritime trade), and their relative amenability to control, despite several major revolts and massacres in Batavia and Manila respectively. Chinese based in the port towns not only mediated regional and transregional trade with China, but also brokered the movement to these port towns of Chinese laborers and artisans, many of whom were ultimately responsible for the construction of new towns and the expansion of old ones into the hinterland. They were usually part of established networks of *peranakan* or localized Chinese, many of whom had converted to Islam. This pattern of urban development was replicated in the northern Javanese port towns of Semarang, Surabaya, Jepara, and Tegal.

In South Asia, too, diasporic trading communities, both regional and trans-regional in origin, were crucial in the establishment and functioning of the European port towns, especially Bombay, Madras, Calcutta, and Pondicherry—although the Dutch ports, Paleacat and Negatpatnam, because of their monopolistic policies aimed at protecting Dutch East India Company (EIC) trade, tended to view such communities as competitors. The founding of Bombay and the establishment of Madras by the English East India Company were followed by attempts to attract Hindu, Jain, Muslim, Parsi, Jewish, and Armenian Christian merchants from neighboring ports, through offers of trading privileges, customs exemptions, freedom of religion, and corporate privileges. Families and networks from other regions of South Asia, such as the Gujaratis, Rajasthanis, Telegus, and Marwaris, were also active in the trade between these port towns and their hinterlands. Prominent Jews in Cochin were central in transactions between the local ruler and the Dutch EIC, and even established contacts with Dutch Jews in the Netherlands.

Religious freedom and religious tolerance were both important dimensions of the port towns' cosmopolitanism. Except in the Philippines—where Catholicization was one of the main colonial objectives, notwithstanding the presence of Chinese and other non-Catholic traders—the promotion of religious tolerance as a way of attracting and holding different merchant groups was a key European trading company policy. The Dutch, after defeating the Portuguese in the port town of Cochin, granted religious privileges and liberties to the Jewish merchant community. Religious differences remained important as a marker of communal distinction, however, although this did not prevent people from marrying out of their religion. While there was a general tolerance of religious diversity in the Dutch port towns, there was also a drive to "Europeanize" local forms of Christianity. The Dutch Reformed Church attempted to socialize local Christians, either Catholics or new converts through marriage, into what was considered to be proper Christian society in the Indies. The churches in the port towns were seen by trading company officials as important bastions of European society and ideals.

The administrative organization of European port-town society along ethnic, religious, and in the case of India, caste lines was reinforced by the segregated residential patterns of the different communities. As with their Asian counterparts, such as Surat, Masulipatnam, Melaka, Ayutthaya, and Makassar, the South and Southeast Asian port towns were organized in a manner that reflected the limited ability of Europeans to fully administer them, due to the European's lack of social and cultural capital, and the costs of any such attempt at direct control. A policy of semi-autonomous governance, with more important matters handled through consultation between the trading company councils and community leaders, was the usual practice.

In the Dutch port towns of Batavia, Semarang, Surabaya, Tegal, and Makassar, hierarchies of ranked leaders (from lieutenant to major) were set up for each ethnic community, while in some instances, as with the Chinese in Batavia and Semarang, communal bodies like the *kongkoan* were established to administer cases involving the local Chinese community. Where this *kapitan* system was not used, as in the Straits Settlement ports of Penang and Singapore, informal structures involving different communal organizations (based on shared place of origin, language, and family clan names) and secret societies were used by the Chinese communities for organizing themselves and by the state for maintaining order.

In Bombay, Calcutta, Madras, Pondicherry, and Cochin too, each of the religious, ethnic, and caste communities were allowed to set up their own *panchayats* or councils for the governance of affairs related to their

Boats on the Pasig River, Manila. *The Pasig River runs through the center of Manila, a colonial Spanish port that grew to become the largest city in the Philippines.* JOHN WANG/PHOTODISC GREEN/GETTY IMAGES. REPRODUCED BY PERMISSION.

respective communities. They also tended to congregate around symbolic centers, especially shrines, temples, mosques, or churches, associated not only with their religious affiliation as a whole, but also with their places of origin and with other ethnic or caste markers.

Despite this segregation along ethnic, religious, and caste lines, the growth of *mestizo* (mixed-marriage or hybrid) populations was also an important feature of these European port towns. In Batavia and other Dutch EIC port towns in the archipelago, intermarriages between trading company officials and local women, often Indo-Portuguese mestizos or slaves, were common and seen as inevitable. So was the practice of concubinage, because of the disproportionate gender ratio in migrant populations. The Portuguese, and later, the Dutch, saw this group of mestizos as crucial to the establishment of a community with links and loyalty to the Europeans.

The emergence of *peranakan* society in Java and other parts of the East Indies through the marriage of local women to Chinese men—who chose to retain their "Chineseness," albeit in rather hybrid cultural forms—paralleled the growth of the Chinese mestizo populations in Manila and its environs. In the *ommelanden* or suburbs

of Batavia, intermarriage between different ethnic communities from the Indies, and the residential patterns of these groups, often frustrated the attempts of the Dutch to segregate them, leading to groups with mixed ethnicities, even among groups commonly labeled as *native*.

Such hybridizations often presented problems for the Europeans in the port towns in their efforts at classification and taxation, and in the administration of legal cases. It also led to rivalries between the different communal hierarchies and structures established in these towns with the blessing of the European rulers. In Makassar, for example, there were disputes between the Captains of the Malay and Chinese communities over the relative status of men and women who married across the ethnic divide, especially for Chinese *peranakan* who chose to remain Muslim. The control over people was crucial to the power and authority of ethnic community leaders. In certain cases, like the Malay community, the leader was obliged to render and coordinate labor services for the colonial administration.

These European port towns, perhaps with the exception of Manila, never came to dominate the trade or the populations of their respective regions or subregions, nor attain the scale and scope of their Asian counterparts, or of the later colonial port city. Despite their morphological differences from Asian port towns or other settlements in parts of South and Southeast Asia, they had only a limited impact on their hinterlands and political environment.

Their claims to commercial monopoly, even in the area of spices like cloves and nutmeg, was continually undermined by the various Asian and private trading networks, even where they managed to control the "hinterland" producing these items. The European trading companies depended on local rulers and local merchant networks in the hinterland for access to various products—as in Cochin, where they were forced to deal with the raja and other local rulers in order to obtain commodities such as textiles and peppers.

Even in regions where Europeans had port towns, such as Bombay and Calcutta in the case of the British, they maintained factories in Asian port towns controlled by petty rulers or inland empires—such as the towns Surat and Masulipatnam, at various times under the sway of the Mughals and Marathas—or their respective representatives or tributaries. In Calcutta, and Bengal as a whole, the English EIC had to operate through a network of local rulers—like the Nawab of Bengal and other local princes—purporting to act for inland empires (such as the Mughals), and with a host of trading communities organized along ethnic as well as kinship lines.

While European port towns did influence the politics and trading patterns of the hinterlands by their presence in regional markets, and sometimes through violent means, their direct impact in terms of restructuring relations and trade was mild compared to the colonial port cities of the nineteenth and twentieth centuries. Their aims were fundamentally different, and in the case of the European trading companies, commercial and limited.

NINETEENTH-CENTURY TRANSFORMATIONS AND THE RISE OF THE COLONIAL PORT CITY

The emergence of the colonial port city was predicated on changes in imperial vision that became more evident by the middle of the nineteenth century. These were not sudden or momentous changes, but the culmination of a series of overlapping processes. Their beginnings can be found in the eighteenth century and in the convergence of several factors that reinforced the position of certain European port towns and transformed them into rapidly expanding port cities operating within new political, economic, and technological frameworks. The military, political, and administrative incorporation of the hinterlands of the port towns into their respective imperial frameworks meant, in different places, varying degrees of transformation of the relationships between the colonial state, local rulers and elites, and society-at-large

in the hinterlands, leading, in turn, to changes in the relationships of land-ownership, production, and trade.

The eighteenth century saw the extension of British and Dutch control in the hinterlands of strategic parts of South Asia and Southeast Asia, namely on the east coast of the Indian Subcontinent and the west coast of Java, respectively. The context and pretext was the decline of inland empires, namely the Mughal in India and the Mataram in Java, and the subsequent political instability created by aspiring powers (like the Marathas in India) and contesting claimants in imperial, regional, and local contexts. Nevertheless, the aims of the British and Dutch remained conservative. In both these regions, they claimed, at least in principle, to be the representatives or *diwan* for the declining Mughal Empire and the Kartasura court, respectively, and continued to operate through established local rulers or "political entrepreneur" princes.

The integration of these hinterlands into new political and administrative structures was a long-term process, accelerated by the taking over of the British and Dutch trading companies' interests and territories in South and Southeast Asia in the late eighteenth and nineteenth centuries by their respective national governments in Europe, after the collapse of the Dutch EIC in 1799 and the Indian Mutiny of 1857. This process saw the incorporation of local elites and rulers into a new system of governance, in which their executive powers were much diminished or restricted to cultural or religious spheres, alongside an expanding European bureaucracy. Many local rulers lost their previous sources of income, which were mainly derived from tribute and other forms of direct fiscal exactions, and received instead a fixed income from the state, which they thus became dependent upon. This process was paralleled by a codification of laws concerning land, settlement, and movement of people that was based on European legal notions and understandings of local customs, and put the relationship between the colonial state and local elites on a new footing.

These changes paved the way for the economic transformation of the hinterland, first through trading company and state-sponsored enterprises, such as the cultivation system in Java and West Sumatra, and subsequently through the influx of western capital into the new extractive industries and plantation economy of east Sumatra, Java, Malaya, and the islands of Riau, Bangka, Belitung, and Borneo. The industrial and agricultural revolutions in late-eighteenth- and nineteenth-century Europe, especially in Britain, changed the patterns of Eurasian trade, in terms of mass production capability and by creating the affluence that increased demand for tropical foods, beverages, and other consumption items, as well as raw materials.

These revolutions reinforced the importance of colonial port cities by making them gateways into the new hinterlands for investment capital, labor, and technology. This was evident in the mass migration of Chinese and later Indian and Javanese labor to Malaya, and of Chinese and Javanese labor to Sumatra. It was also reflected in the creation of new satellite towns linked to the port cities of Singapore and Penang and Kuala Lumpur-Klang in northwest Malaya, which became the main collecting, distributing, and processing centers.

Technological changes in maritime and land transport and communications strengthened the positions of the colonial port cities in their regional contexts. The advent of the steamship and the growing traffic of cargo and shipping resulted in a rapid increase in the draught, tonnage, and sophistication of the ocean carriers, which were well beyond the capabilities of the existing ports. The costs of building specialized port facilities, whether through state enterprise or through private corporations, or both, often meant that such facilities were concentrated in areas of highest traffic.

Port cities also became important regional centers for industrial production and for the distribution of manufactured products from the metropoles. This led to the expansion of the cities beyond their old physical confines, namely the town walls and forts. Their architectural appearance also achieved a certain uniformity, as part of a colonial style. This was a very drawn-out process, which in the case of primary colonial cities like Batavia and Manila had begun much earlier. As cities developed industrial economies, distinctions in terms of class became as important as the divisions of ethnicity and religion.

The effects on the hinterland were evident in the increasing migration into the cities in search of opportunity. The port cities also began to take on cultural, social, and economic roles vis-à-vis the hinterland to a much greater extent, especially through their monopoly of print media and through becoming the site of new secondary and tertiary educational institutions. New patterns of migration also created new divisions within and changing attitudes toward existing migrant communities. The growing number of women migrants resulted in changing attitudes toward the mestizo and *peranakan* communities.

Marriage between European men and local women became increasingly frowned upon, as was concubinage, due to a growing ethnic divide based on racial (rather than cultural) conceptions and associations of Asia with weakness and moral debasement. The *peranakan* Chinese communities in Indonesia and in British Malaya were also coming to terms with the sociopolitical implications, in some quarters, of the cultural differences between an English-educated *peranakan* elite and the Chinese-educated business and intellectual elite.

Thus, just as these port cities became sites of ethnic and cultural mixing, like the older colonial European port towns, which made them socially and morphologically distinct from their environs and hinterland regions, they also became sites of ethnic competition and conflict. The growing scale of foreign migration (European, Chinese or Indian depending on the region in question) after the 1870s, and the increasingly apparent class and economic divisions along ethnic lines in these cities, provided the seeds for ethnically charged politics during the nationalist period.

It was in the colonial port cities that important branches of emergent nationalist and political organizations were formed. These cities were important sites and nexuses of movement, first for commerce, work, and administration, but later, also religious, educational and in terms of print and media. They gradually encapsulated both "foreign" diasporic networks, as well as local and regional systems. Thus, they became important channels for the movement of ideas, technology, and people between the region and the world, especially the colonial metropoles, and other Asian capital port cities (colonial or otherwise). They became the sites in which these "new" tools were harnessed to ideologies and movements that challenged the colonial order.

They provided the contexts for the creation of new elites whose educational background and professional or commercial dealings allowed them to straddle different worlds—the local-regional environments and the different European and Asian diasporas. This was as evident in Colombo and Calcutta in the Indian Ocean rim as in Singapore, Batavia, and Semarang east of the Bay of Bengal. In colonial Java, the port city of Semarang hosted the first meeting of the socialist Indische Partij in the Dutch East Indies and was also the base of one of the radical branches of Sarekat Islam influenced by the communists. Bombay, Calcutta, and Madras, to different degrees, were also sites of such cultural dialogues and debates, with important consequences for emerging nationalist movements in India.

Port cities also came to play important roles as gateways for new ideas and new types of political and social consciousness, from Europe as well as from other Asian centers, such as Mecca, India (for Indonesia and British Malaya), China, and Japan. Circles and movements associated with socialism, nationalism, modernism, and religious reformism often emerged in these port cities due to the cities' population size and economic and social characteristics.

CONCLUSION

The colonial port city can be distinguished from the European port town in terms of its dominance over the hinterland, the scale and scope of economic, administrative, and port functions arrogated to it, and its function in linking the hinterland to a global and regional colonial political economy oriented toward a metropole in Europe. This concentration of functions was a reflection of the earlier strategic importance of the towns and of the relative success of the European trading companies and their successor colonial states, as well as of various technological developments, which began in the eighteenth century but accelerated after the mid-nineteenth century.

Parallel to these processes, new port hierarchies developed. Malacca, the old maritime stalwart of the Straits bearing its name, came to be displaced by the new British ports of Penang and Singapore, due to a combination of factors in the late eighteenth century. These included Anglo-Dutch rivalry and diplomacy, the nexus between English and European country trade networks and Asian shipping networks, and the regional politics in the Straits and Java Sea region in this period. Penang became the center of the northern Straits region in the late eighteenth and early nineteenth century, while the founding of the other free port of Singapore, further challenged the position of Dutch-controlled Malacca. The Anglo-Dutch Treaty led to British control of these three ports on the peninsular side of the Straits of Malacca.

In the course of the nineteenth century, Singapore, due to its free trade environment, its strategic location in terms of maritime routes with China and with the eastern archipelago, and the operations of the European country trade (especially with respect to opium, became the primary port in the Straits region. The gradual concentration of administrative, technological, and other functions in the settlement further augmented its importance in the peninsular economy. Penang, in the context of Singapore's rise as the main entrepôt for Malaya and the western archipelago, was able to maintain its position due to the extension of colonial rule over its economic development of its hinterland under colonial auspices, by predominantly Chinese labor, capital and enterprise, of first tin mining in the northern Malayan hinterland in the late nineteenth century. It was followed by the influx of European capital and technology, first in the tin fields, and subsequently in the rubber industry after the late 1890s.

In Java, the establishment of Batavia as the main stapling port for the Dutch East India Company in its Asian trade, and the gradual territorial expansion of the Company after the 1670s, both along the north coast of Java and in the hinterland, led to the subordination, through force and then policy, of the other major maritime centers on the northern coast. This included Semarang, Surabaya, Japara, and Cirebon, among others.

It restructured the hierarchy of polity and trade in the region. Nevertheless, these ports remained important in the regional trade, namely within the Java Sea, and with the Straits of Malacca.

Furthermore, Company policy and development of the hinterlands into centers of production for the European market changed the relationship between coast and hinterland yet again, as Mataram, the major inland power in central Java was gradually fragmented and subordinated to Dutch rule and sovereignty from the coast by the mid-nineteenth century. The gradual creation of the colonial state in Java with Batavia as the administrative, communications and transport capital, first under the East India Company and state-sponsored enterprises, and subsequently private European corporate ventures, saw the reinforcement of its position within the coastal port network.

Nevertheless, policy and economic changes after the 1870s, which saw the influx of European capital and technology into the Dutch possessions in the east, saw the further transformation of the regional ports into major players in the regional market. The development of the plantation economies, especially sugar, and tobacco, led not only to the resurgence of ports like Cirebon, Semarang and Surabaya, but also to the development of new port centers like Deli (now Medan) on the northeast coast of Sumatra.

In South Asia, Colombo outstripped Galle (with its better harbor) because of its access to the commercial agricultural areas in the southwest of the island, and the construction by the British of port facilities and a road and rail network oriented toward it. British imperial success no doubt led to the growth of Britain's colonial port towns on the subcontinent—namely Calcutta, Madras, and Bombay—relative to other European port towns like Pondicherry, Cochin, Paleacat, and Negatpatnam, as well as Indian ones like Surat and Masulipatnam.

In the Philippines, the continued importance of Manila was based on similar processes of colonial expansion, concomitant with infrastructural, commercial, and economic transformations, as seen in Java, Malaya and Ceylon. It reflected the geopolitical patterns of territorial expansion by the Spanish, as well as the ways in which the Spanish (and Chinese) commercial systems based on Manila connected with regional trading networks. The development of the hinterland and expansion to the other islands outside Luzon expanded the networks of ports, but Manila nonetheless retained its importance as the commercial, administrative, religious, and cultural center for the colonial Philippines.

The convergence of various political, administrative, economic, and technological forces in the nineteenth century determined the fortunes of earlier European port towns, and bound the selected ones that made the transition to colonial port city status more closely to the hinterland than their predecessors ever had been. The new port cities were also able to dominate their hinterlands to a hitherto unprecedented extent, and to play a leading role in shaping the economic and even sociopolitical landscape.

They played leading roles in mediating the flow of capital, people, ideas, and technology between Europe and Asia, as well as across colonial (and often linguistic) boundaries in Asia. Ironically, these cities also provided the contexts and nexuses for political and ideological movements that challenged the colonial order, often with concepts, methods, organizations, and technologies, derived from the metropole and Europe.

Nevertheless, the continued importance of these colonial port cities in the postcolonial period underlies the deep foundations of the hinterland/port city relationship and its centrality to the new nation-states, which despite their supposed antithesis to the colonial state and colonialism, retained many of its functions, structures and attitudes. The position of many of these port cities, especially the capital cities, have been strengthened rather than weakened in the post-colonial period.

SEE ALSO *Batavia; Bombay; Calcutta; Freeburghers, South and Southeast Asia; Singapore.*

BIBLIOGRAPHY

Arasaratnam, S. *Merchants, Companies, and Commerce on the Coromandel Coast, 1650–1740.* Delhi: Oxford University Press, 1986.

Arasaratnam, S. "European Port-Settlements in the Coromandel Commercial System, 1650–1740." In *Brides of the Sea: Port Cities of Asia from the 16th–20th Centuries*, edited by Frank Broeze, 75–96. Honolulu: University of Hawaii Press, 1989.

Atiya, Habeeb Kidwai. "Port Cities in a National System of Ports and Cities: A Geographical Analysis of India in the Twentieth Century." In *Brides of the Sea: Port Cities of Asia from the 16th–20th Centuries*, edited by Frank Broeze, 207–222. Honolulu: University of Hawaii Press, 1989.

Basu, Dilip K., ed. *The Rise and Growth of the Colonial Port Cities in Asia.* Santa Cruz: Center for South Pacific Studies, University of California, 1985.

Bayly, C. A. "Inland Port Cities in North India: Calcutta and the Gangetic Plains, 1780-1900." In *The Rise and Growth of the Colonial Port Cities in Asia*, edited by Dilip K. Basu, 97–104. Santa Cruz: Center for South Pacific Studies, University of California, 1985.

Bayly, C. A. *Indian Society and the Making of the British Empire.* New Cambridge History of India series, vol. 2, no. 1. Cambridge, U.K.: Cambridge University Press, 1988.

Blackburn, Susan. "Political Relations among Women in a Multi-Racial City: Colonial Batavia in the Twentieth Century." In *Jakarta-Batavia: Socio-Cultural Essays*, edited by

Kees Grijns and Peter J. M. Nas, pp. 175–198. Leiden, Netherlands: KITLV Press, 2000.

Blussé, Léonard. *Strange Company: Chinese Settlers, Mestizo Women, and the Dutch in VOC Batavia.* Dordrecht, Holland; Riverton, NJ: Foris, 1986.

Blussé, Léonard, and Chen Menghong. *The Archives of the Kong Koan of Batavia.* Leiden, Netherlands; Boston: Brill, 2003.

Broeze, Frank, ed. *Brides of the Sea: Port Cities of Asia from the 16th–20th Centuries.* Honolulu: University of Hawaii Press, 1989.

Broeze, Frank, ed. *Gateways of Asia: Port Cities of Asia in the 13th–20th Centuries.* London and New York: Kegan Paul, 1997.

Conlon, Frank. "Functions of Ethnicity in a Colonial Port City: British Initiatives in Early Bombay." In *The Rise and Growth of the Colonial Port Cities in Asia*, edited by Dilip K. Basu, 47–54. Santa Cruz: Center for South Pacific Studies, University of California, 1985.

Das Gupta, Uma, ed. *The World of the Indian Ocean Merchant, 1500–1800: Collected Essays of Ashin Das Gupta.* New Delhi and New York: Oxford University Press, 2001.

Dharmasena, K. "Colombo: Gateway and Oceanic Hub of Shipping." In *Brides of the Sea: Port Cities of Asia from the 16th–20th Centuries*, edited by Frank Broeze, 152–172. Honolulu: University of Hawaii Press, 1989.

Dossal, Mariam. "Bombay and the Famine of 1803–6: The Food Supply and Public Order of a Colonial Port City." In *Gateways of Asia: Port Cities of Asia in the 13th–20th Centuries*, edited by Frank Broeze. London and New York: Kegan Paul, 1997.

Faber, G. H. von. *Oud Soerabaia: De geschiedenis van Indië's eerste koopstad van de oudste tijden tot de instelling van den Gemeenteraad (1906).* Surabaya, Indonesia: Gemeente Soerabaja, 1931.

Grijns, Kees, and Peter J. M. Nas, eds. *Jakarta-Batavia: Socio-Cultural Essays.* Leiden, Netherlands: KITLV Press, 2000.

Ham, J. G. van. *Eerste boekjaar der Indische Partij (1912): samengesteld in gevolge art. 12, al 1, der statuten, voor het Eerste Indiers-congres (21-23 Maart 1913) te Semarang gehouden.* Bandeong: Eerste Bandoengsche Stoomdrukkerij, 1913.

Jonge, Huub de. "A Divided Minority: The Arabs of Batavia." In *Jakarta-Batavia: Socio-Cultural Essays*, edited by Kees Grijns and Peter J. M. Nas, 143–156. Leiden, Netherlands: KITLV Press, 2000.

Lewandowski, Susan. "Urban Growth and Municipal Development in the Colonial City of Madras, 1860–1900." *Journal of Asian Studies* 34 (1975): 342–360.

Lewandowski, Susan. "Merchants, Temples, and Power in the Colonial Port City of Madras." In *The Rise and Growth of the Colonial Port Cities in Asia*, edited by Dilip K. Basu, 97–104. Santa Cruz: Center for South Pacific Studies, University of California, 1985.

Lohanda, Mona. "The Inlandsche Kommandant of Batavia." In *Jakarta-Batavia: Socio-Cultural Essays*, edited by Kees Grijns and Peter J. M. Nas, 115–124. Leiden, Netherlands: KITLV Press, 2000.

Marshall, P. J. *East Indian Fortunes: The British in Bengal in the Eighteenth Century.* Oxford. Clarendon, 1976.

Marshall, P. J. *Bengal: The British Bridgehead: Eastern India, 1740–1828.* New Cambridge History of India series, vol. 2, no. 2. Cambridge, U.K.: Cambridge University Press, 1987.

Mathew, K. S. *French in India and Indian Nationalism (1700 A.D.–1963 A.D.).* Delhi: B. R. Publishing, 1999.

McPherson, Kenneth. "Penang 1786–1832: A Promise Unfulfilled." In *Gateways of Asia: Port Cities of Asia in the 13th–20th Centuries,* edited by Frank Broeze. London and New York: Kegan Paul, 1997.

Murphey, Rhoads. "On the Evolution of the Port City." In *Brides of the Sea: Port Cities of Asia from the 16th–20th Centuries,* edited by Frank Broeze, 223–245. Honolulu: University of Hawaii Press, 1989.

Murphey, Rhoads. "Colombo and the Re-Making of Ceylon: A Prototype of Colonial Asian Port Cities." In *Gateways of Asia: Port Cities of Asia in the 13th–20th Centuries,* edited by Frank Broeze. London and New York: Kegan Paul, 1997.

Nagtegaal, Luc. *Riding the Dutch Tiger: The Dutch East Indies Company and the Northeast Coat of Java, 1680–1743.* Leiden, Netherlands: KITLV Press, 1996.

Nas, Peter J. M., and Kees Grijns. "Jakarta-Batavia: A Sample of Current Socio-Historical Research." In *Jakarta-Batavia: Socio-Cultural Essays,* edited by Kees Grijns and Peter J. M. Nas, 1–24. Leiden, Netherlands: KITLV Press, 2000.

Niemeijer, Hendrik E. "The Free Asian Christian Community and Poverty in Pre-Modern Batavia." In *Jakarta-Batavia: Socio-Cultural Essays,* edited by Kees Grijns and Peter J. M. Nas, 75–92. Leiden, Netherlands: KITLV Press, 2000.

Poelinggomang, Edward L. *Makassar Abad XIX: Studi tentang Kebijakan Perdagangan Maritim.* Jakarta, Indonesia: KPG and Ford Foundation, 2002.

Raben, Remco. "Round about Batavia: Ethnicity and Authority in the Ommelanden, 1650–1800." In *Jakarta-Batavia: Socio-Cultural Essays,* edited by Kees Grijns and Peter J. M. Nas, 95–114. Leiden, Netherlands: KITLV Press, 2000.

Reed, Robert R. *Colonial Manila: The Context of Hispanic Urbanism and Process of Morphogenesis.* University of California Publications in Geography no. 22. Berkeley: University of California Press, 1978.

Reed, Robert. "The Foundation and Morphology of Hispanic Manila: Colonial Images and Philippine Realities." In *The Rise and Growth of the Colonial Port Cities in Asia,* edited by Dilip K. Basu, 197–206. Santa Cruz: Center for South Pacific Studies, University of California, 1985.

Reeves, Peter, Frank Broeze, and Kenneth McPherson. "Studying the Asian Port City." In *Brides of the Sea: Port Cities of Asia from the 16th–20th Centuries,* edited by Frank Broeze, 29–53. Honolulu: University of Hawaii Press, 1989.

Roberts, Michael. "The Two Faces of the Port City: Colombo in Modern Times." In *Brides of the Sea: Port Cities of Asia from the 16th–20th Centuries,* edited by Frank Broeze, 173–187. Honolulu: University of Hawaii Press, 1989.

Sandhu, Kernial Singh, and Paul Wheatley, eds. *Melaka: The Transformation of a Malay Capital, c. 1400–1980,* 2 vols. Kuala Lumpur and New York: Oxford University Press, 1983.

Segal, J. B. *A History of the Jews of Cochin.* London: Vallentine Mitchell, 1993.

Jacob, Hugo K. *The Rajas of Cochin, 1663–1720: Kings, Chiefs, and the Dutch East India Company.* New Delhi: Munshiram Manoharlal, 2000.

Soe, Hok Gie. *Di bawah lentera merah: Riwayat Sarekat Islam Semarang, 1917–1920.* Yogyakarta, Indonesia: Yayasan Bentang Budaya, 1999.

Stoler, Ann Laura. *Race and the Education of Desire: Foucault's History of Sexuality and the Colonial Order of Things.* Durham, NC: Duke University Press, 1995.

Subrahmanyam, Sanjay. "Masulipatnam Revisited, 1550–1750: A Survey and Some Speculations." In *Gateways of Asia: Port Cities of Asia in the 13th–20th Centuries,* edited by Frank Broeze. London and New York: Kegan Paul, 1997.

Subramanian, Lakshmi. *Indigenous Capital and Imperial Expansion: Bombay, Surat, and the West Coast.* Delhi and Oxford: Oxford University Press, 1996.

Sutherland, Heather. "Eastern Emporium and Company Town: Trade and Society in Eighteenth-Century Makassar." In *Brides of the Sea: Port Cities of Asia from the 16th–20th Centuries,* edited by Frank Broeze, 97–128. Honolulu: University of Hawaii Press, 1989.

Taylor, Jean Gelman. *The Social World of Batavia: European and Eurasian in Dutch Asia.* Madison: University of Wisconsin Press, 1983.

Wickberg, Edgar. *The Chinese in Philippine Life, 1850–1898.* Quezon City, Phillipines: Ateneo de Manila University Press, 2000.

Yasmine, Shahab. "Aristocratic Betawi: A Challenge to Outsiders' Perceptions." In *Jakarta-Batavia: Socio-Cultural Essays,* edited by Kees Grijns and Peter J. M. Nas, 199–210. Leiden, Netherlands: KITLV Press, 2000.

Keng We Koh

COLONIZATION AND COMPANIES

In the sixteenth, seventeenth, and eighteenth centuries, a great deal of Europe's long-distance trade, cross-cultural contact, and colonial enterprise was designed, engineered, and managed not by monarchies or the state, but by companies. These companies, whether primarily designed for plantation or long-distance trade, generally possessed royal charters that detailed rights to wage war, conduct diplomacy, control commerce, and administer settlements in the known and undiscovered world. While their propriety and viability has been a matter of debate since their creation, such bodies were a crucial feature of early modern European empires.

EARLY EXPERIENCES

The ideas of corporate partnership with both public and private rights had intellectual and legal roots in the late medieval financial associations of the Mediterranean, northern European guilds, and other kinds of corporate bodies, such as towns, universities, and ecclesiastical establishments. Perhaps the most famous early experiment with such an arrangement was the Hanseatic League, an association of traders from various northern German cities and states. The Hanseatic League dominated the late medieval Baltic and Russian trades, maintaining its own enclaved settlements, legislative assemblies, and military.

The Hanseatic League and other such efforts to protect intra-European trade ultimately gave way to the rising power of European national states by the sixteenth century. However, European monarchies and republics often lacked the resources or will to protect directly extra-European overseas commerce and colonization. Such efforts demanded much more capital, sustained over much vaster distances and longer periods of time, than these states could or would muster. It also necessitated an even more elaborate organization, not just for commerce but also for diplomacy, defense, and governance abroad than was within reach of any individual merchant.

Though the Spanish and Portuguese empires, the pioneers of European expansion, were for the most part the business of the monarchy and state, companies did emerge as crucial to this project. Companies for trade or associations of *conquistadores* were usually more or less uncharted partnerships, coordinated or theoretically sanctioned by state institutions like the Spanish Council of the Indies and its subordinate, La Casa de Contratacion, (House of Trade) or the slightly more independent Portuguese Estado da India (State of India).

The Consulado de Sevilla, which began as guild for the Spanish American traders, soon had a de facto monopoly on legal Atlantic commerce. Spanish officials and political economists also began to entertain the idea of chartered monopoly companies as a solution to smuggling, piracy, and attacks from European rivals. Portugal's Brazil Company (1649–1720) was responsible for organizing the Atlantic trade into fleets and armed convoys, and became even closer to a monopoly after individuals' voyages were outlawed in 1660. Still, other Portuguese attempts to form companies in the seventeenth century were less successful, including the Companhia do Comércio da India Oriental (East Indies, 1628–1633), and the Companhia de Cachéu e Rios de Guiné and Companhia do Cabo Verde e Cachéu (West Africa, 1676 and 1696 respectively).

Since other European leaders were largely reluctant or unable to challenge the Iberian empires directly, such efforts were left primarily to private "adventurers" with either tacit or explicit state endorsement. Though the exploits of privateers, explorers, and merchants like Francis Drake (ca. 1543–1596), Walter Raleigh (ca.

1554–1618), and John Hawkins (1532–1595) are perhaps the most famous, important challenges to Portuguese and Spanish maritime and colonial dominion were organized collectively in "regulated" companies, like the English Russia (or Muscovy) Company (1553) and the Levant (or Turkey) Company (1581). These were guildlike conglomerates in which merchants funded and prosecuted their own trade but shared chartered rights, some infrastructure, and diplomatic representation.

THE JOINT-STOCK COMPANY

This model did not, however, prove adequate for the political and commercial risks of trading in areas of the world that were more distant, dangerous, and uncertain. For this, northern European traders, particularly in England and the United Provinces of the Netherlands, turned to the joint-stock company. This kind of company was much more novel, though increasingly in use in the sixteenth and seventeenth centuries for local trades and industries, such as mining, fisheries, manufacturing, public works, and financial services. The joint-stock company solved a range of political and entrepreneurial problems specific to long-distance trade and colonization. Unlike in the regulated company, capital stock was raised through investment, not the trade itself. This allowed companies to accumulate much more money, which would be more permanent, liquid, and able to absorb much greater risks.

The joint-stock system also involved new constituencies in overseas activities, including the gentry and nobility, which had little place in a regulated or unincorporated trade. Politically, these bodies were corporate singularities, legal "persons" with an expectation of institutional permanence and "perpetual succession." They also had the rights and duties of self-governance and did so through an often sophisticated hierarchical internal and external political organization. Neither public nor private, these companies were bodies politic in themselves.

From the mid-sixteenth through the seventeenth century, there was an explosion in the number of joint-stock companies, particularly in the English Atlantic: the Guinea Company (1618) and later the Royal African Company (1672) in West Africa; the Somers Island (Bermuda) Company (1615) and the Providence Island Company (1630) in the West Indies; and the Newfoundland Company (1610), the Virginia Company (1606), and the Plymouth (1606) and later Massachusetts Bay Company (1629) in North America. A good number of these companies lasted only decades, but they laid the foundations for the English slave trade, Atlantic commerce, and "foreign plantations" in the Americas.

The Massachusetts Bay Company, though never having much of a trade, continued to govern its colony

Jamestown, Virginia. *Situated on the banks of the James River in present-day Virginia, Jamestown was established by the Virginia Company in 1607 and became the first permanent English settlement in America. Jamestown is depicted here as it may have looked in the early seventeenth century.* **HULTON ARCHIVE/GETTY IMAGES. REPRODUCED BY PERMISSION.**

almost to the end of the seventeenth century. In fact, much of the literature and propaganda behind these companies, like Richard Hakluyt's (ca. 1552–1616) *Discourse on Western Planting* (1584), insisted that commerce was only one goal of such expansion, which also promoted Protestantism, could rival Spain, and add to the national "fame." Furthermore, settlement and exploration had the potential to open a new path to Asia through a much-pursued "Northwest Passage." The Hudson's Bay Company (1670), which commanded the English fur trade and settlements in Canada, was founded with this initial goal in mind.

Unlike the English, early Dutch expansion in the Atlantic was prosecuted under the auspices of one all-encompassing company. The Dutch West India Company (West-Indische Compagnie, 1621) was given a monopoly on all Dutch trade in the Atlantic basin. It established slave-trading forts in West Africa and settlements in the West Indies and North America, most notably the New Netherlands (later lost to the English and restyled New York). Though it was ultimately unprofitable, the Dutch West India Company took a leading role in establishing colonies, regional monopolies, and well-armed fleets and garrisons against the Iberian powers. Though some contemporaries saw such efforts as unsuccessful, raids on Spanish and Portuguese shipping in the company's first decade yielded over five hundred prize ships. In 1624 its forces briefly seized the Brazilian town of Bahia, and the company soon had established itself in parts of Brazil, Venezuela, and the Caribbean. The Dutch West India Company's only real source of profit, though, was its monopoly on the gold trade, which also led to a more permanent Dutch presence in West Africa as well.

Ultimately, perhaps the most profitable and powerful of these new joint-stock companies were the English and Dutch efforts to rival the Portuguese in Asia. As early as the seventeenth century, the English East India Company (1600) and the Dutch East India Company (Verenigde Oost-Indische Compagnie, 1602) began to dominate the Eurasian trade in spices and other Asian goods; they also established and governed colonial cities, maintained military forces, fought wars, and conducted diplomacy. They set the stage for future European expansion in Asia, and served as models for a number of other European efforts at prosecuting a trade in the East.

France, Sweden, Denmark, the Holy Roman Empire (Austrian Netherlands/Ostend), and Scotland all established their own East India companies in the seventeenth or eighteenth centuries, with varying success. The Company of Scotland (1695–1707) even planted a short-lived colony in Panama with the twin goals of strategically disrupting Spanish American power and using the isthmus as a bridge between the West and East Indies—an idea only realized two centuries later in the Panama Canal.

COMPANY, STATE, AND EMPIRE

The independence from their respective states marked the crucial difference between these Dutch and English companies and their Iberian rivals. Still, as European national and dynastic rivalries spread across the globe, these companies assumed powerful roles in actively defining the future of European empire more generally. Controversies over such companies were at the heart of seventeenth-century political economy debates that shaped contemporary and future imperial policies. The East India companies in particular also contributed to empire as critical players in the seventeenth-century "financial revolution," underpinning state expansion as a source of revenue, through customs, excise, and state debt.

The most explicit use of companies for state building was found in late seventeenth-century France. There were French attempts in the early seventeenth century to rival Dutch and English expansion, under the stewardship of Cardinal Richelieu (1585–1642, chief minister of France from 1624 to 1642), but the Compagnie du Corail (Barbary Coast), Compagnie de la Nouvelle-France (Americas), and the Compagnie des Indes orientales were almost immediately failures. More dramatically, Jean-Baptiste Colbert (1619–1683, intendant and comptroller-general under King Louis XIV [1638–1715] from 1661 to 1683), used his Compagnie des Indes orientales and Compagnie des Indes occidentals as part of a broader scheme of state imperial expansion, commerce, finance, and even as farmers of colonial revenue, such as tobacco. Unlike in England or the Netherlands, the French state was the largest investor in these projects and had a greater hand in their administration.

This power of colonial companies did have its limits. Interlopers, pirates, and smugglers were difficult and costly to contain, and profits were hard to sustain. The French companies in particular were notoriously unsuccessful as business enterprises. Furthermore, early eighteenth-century crises in stock markets that emerged alongside these companies sent shocks through this system.

In 1720 the "bubbles" burst on two notorious overseas colonial schemes. A frenzied run and crash in the stock of the French Mississippi Company, which was initially chartered to trade in and govern Louisiana but was soon quixotically given control of all French Asian trade, caused a financial crisis in France that some historians list among the long-term causes for the French Revolution (1789–1799). In 1719, the British South Sea Company (1711), which had been vested with a monopoly on the South Sea trade and the Atlantic slave trade, attempted to assume the entire British state debt. Although the stock had no real assets behind it, speculation drove up its price from about £100 (British pounds) to over £1000 in six months. When the bubble of speculation burst, the ensuing panic led in 1720 to a crash in the company, the inchoate British stock market, and the political system that had so wholeheartedly backed it.

Meanwhile, as modern European national states continued to grow, they began to assume a much more direct role in their colonial empires. By the end of the seventeenth century, the English Crown and Parliament had created a Board of Trade (1696) to govern the Atlantic trade, put the Royal African Company and Newfoundland fisheries under increasing scrutiny, and attempted to absorb American colonies previously held under proprietary charters. In the next century, emerging liberal economic ideologies, most notably those detailed in Scottish economist Adam Smith's (1723–1790) *Wealth of Nations* (1776), argued that monopolies and colonial companies were detrimental to trade and national wealth. The Compagnie des Indes had its exclusive privileges withdrawn in 1764, and the Dutch West India Company was absorbed by the state in 1791 and abolished in 1794. The English East India Company, which had acquired its own territorial empire in South Asia by midcentury, fell under increasing state scrutiny and was progressively shorn of its monopoly (1813), trade (1833), and governance (1858) and was eventually abolished entirely (1873).

As the northern Europeans were abandoning the system of colonial companies, the Spanish Crown began to entertain numerous proposals for monopoly companies in an attempt to keep its American empire afloat. The Havana Company (1740) was given a monopoly on the tobacco trade of Cuba (1740), and the Barcelona (Catalan) Company (1755) was chartered for trade to Santo Domingo (in present-day Dominican Republic), Puerto Rico, and Margarita (in Venezuela).

The most famous and successful of these eighteenth-century efforts was the Real Compañía Guipuzcoana de Caracas (1728), or the Caracas Company. This company set about developing Venezuela's economy and defending it from the Dutch. The Caracas Company was soon granted an indefinite monopoly, but under the pressure of wars with Britain and abuses within the company, Spain began to favor free trade as a means for rescuing its declining empire. The Caracas Company was absorbed into the newly chartered Philippines Company in 1785, which turned out to be the last holdout among these Spanish monopoly companies. It endured, if only in name, until 1834. Though free trade and liberal political philosophy on the one hand, and imperialism as a political ideology on the other, reached their apotheosis in the nineteenth century, European powers increasingly turned back to private companies as agents for colonization. Indeed, joint-stock companies became the vanguard of certain European colonial efforts, particularly in Africa. Corporations like George Goldie's (1846–1925) Royal Niger Company, Cecil Rhodes's (1853–1902) DeBeers Consolidated Mining Company and British South Africa Company, the British and German East Africa companies, and, perhaps most famously, Belgian King Leopold II's (1835–1909) International African Association, which acquired the Congo under the "Partition of Africa" in 1885, among many others, were critical in administering and defining modern European colonial empires.

SEE ALSO *Cacao; Coffee Cultivation; Company of New France; Conquests and Colonization; Massachusetts Bay Company; Virginia Company.*

BIBLIOGRAPHY

Ames, Glenn J. *Colbert, Mercantilism, and the French Quest for Asian Trade.* DeKalb, IL: Northern Illinois Press, 1996.

Andrews, Kenneth R. *Trade, Plunder, and Settlement: Maritime Enterprise and the Genesis of the British Empire, 1480–1630.* Cambridge, U.K.: Cambridge University Press, 1984.

Armitage, David, and Michael Braddick, eds. *British Atlantic World, 1500–1800.* Houndmills, U.K., and New York: Palgrave Macmillan, 2002.

Blussé, Leonard, and Femme Gaastra, eds. *Companies and Trade: Essays on Overseas Trading Companies During the Ancien Régime.* The Hague, Netherlands: Leiden University Press, 1981.

Brenner, Robert. *Merchants and Revolution: Commercial Change, Political Conflict, and London's Overseas Traders, 1550–1653.* Princeton, NJ: Princeton University Press, 1993.

Carlos, Ann M. "Giants of an Earlier Capitalism: The Chartered Companies as Modern Multinationals." *Business History Review* 62 (1988): 398–419.

Cawston, George, and A. H. Keane. *The Early Chartered Companies (A.D. 1296–1858).* London and New York: Edward Arnold, 1896.

Craven, Wesley Frank. *The Virginia Company of London, 1606–1624.* Charlottesville: University of Virginia, 1957.

Fitzmaurice, Andrew. *Humanism and America: An Intellectual History of English Colonisation, 1500–1625.* Cambridge, U.K., and New York: Cambridge University Press, 2003.

Hussey, Roland Dennis. *The Caracas Company, 1728–1784: A Study in the History of Spanish Monopolistic Trade.* Cambridge, MA: Harvard University Press, 1934.

Israel, Jonathan I. *Dutch Primacy in World Trade, 1585–1740.* Oxford: Clarendon, 1989.

Rabb, Theodore K. *Enterprise and Empire: Merchant and Gentry Investment in the Expansion of England, 1575–1630.* Cambridge, MA: Harvard University Press, 1967.

Russell-Wood, A. J. R. *A World on the Move: The Portuguese in Africa, Asia, and America, 1415–1808.* New York: St. Martin's Press, 1992.

Scott, William Robert. *The Constitution and Finance of English, Scottish, and Irish Joint-Stock Companies to 1720,* 3 vols. London: Cambridge University Press, 1912. Reprint, Gloucester, MA: Peter Smith, 1968.

Steensgaard, Niels. *The Asian Trade Revolution of the Seventeenth Century: The East India Companies and the Decline of the Caravan Trade.* Chicago and London: University of Chicago Press, 1974.

Subrahmanyam, Sanjay. *The Portuguese Empire in Asia, 1500–1700: A Political and Economic History.* London and New York: Longman, 1993.

Philip J. Stern

COLUMBUS, CHRISTOPHER
1451–1506

Christopher Columbus was an Italian navigator and explorer whose four voyages to the Americas "opened the gates" for western Europe's overseas expansion.

Columbus was born in Genoa, a thriving commercial port on the Mediterranean Sea, in 1451—the same year as Queen Isabella (1451–1504). Two years later, Ottoman Turks took control of Constantinople (present-day Istanbul, Turkey), the last Christian foothold in Asia. Columbus thus grew up among merchants seeking new routes to the silks, spices, and gold of the "Indies" to circumvent the routes that the Turks had restricted.

By age twenty, Columbus was a full-time trader with the Spinola family, sailing the Mediterranean and the Ocean Sea (the Atlantic) north to England. Shipwrecked off the coast of Portugal in 1476, he swam ashore near Prince Henry the Navigator's (1394–1460) school for mariners in Sagres. Columbus then moved to Lisbon, where he took up mapmaking. Lured by the sea, he sailed south to Portuguese trading forts along the African coast and far north of England, improving along the way his knowledge of commerce, navigation, and sea and wind currents. In 1479 he married Felipa Moniz Perestrello, an impoverished Portuguese noblewoman whose father had been raised by Henry the Navigator and was now governor of Porto Santo in the Canary

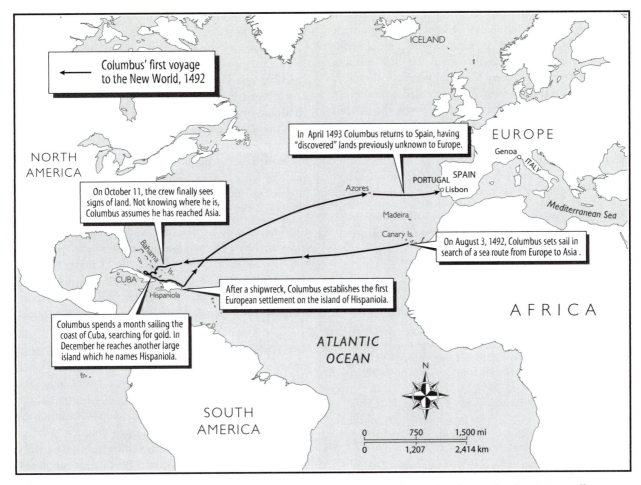

Columbus' first voyage to the New World, 1492

In April 1493 Columbus returns to Spain, having "discovered" lands previously unknown to Europe.

On October 11, the crew finally sees signs of land. Not knowing where he is, Columbus assumes he has reached Asia.

On August 3, 1492, Columbus sets sail in search of a sea route from Europe to Asia .

After a shipwreck, Columbus establishes the first European settlement on the island of Hispaniola.

Columbus spends a month sailing the coast of Cuba, searching for gold. In December he reaches another large island which he names Hispaniola.

The Voyages of Columbus. Christopher Columbus's four voyages to the Americas during the 1490s and early 1500s set off a new era of European competition, exploration, and expansion. **MAP BY XNR PRODUCTIONS. THE GALE GROUP.**

Islands. Perestrello gave his son-in-law all his papers and nautical instruments.

It may have been while residing on Porto Santo, watching the sun set to the west and thinking about his future and that of his newborn son Diego (Felipa died shortly after giving birth), that Columbus came up with the idea for his Great Enterprise of the Indies—an enterprise that would take him west across the Ocean Sea to the riches of the East faster than the circum-African route the Portuguese were seeking. After Paolo Toscanelli (1397–1482), a scholar in Florence, confirmed that such an enterprise was feasible, Columbus approached King John II (1455–1495) of Portugal for backing. King John turned him down.

Columbus spent eight frustrating years seeking backing from the Spanish monarchs. In 1492, triumphant but broke after finally reconquering Granada, the last Moorish stronghold on the Iberian Peninsula, Queen Isabella agreed to support Columbus and his enterprise. She needed money, and she admired Columbus's religious fervor.

Leaving Palos, Spain, on August 3, 1492, and stopping in the Canary Islands for fresh food and water, Columbus and his men sailed west in three ships, the *Niña*, *Pinta*, and *Santa María*. They sighted land on October 12, an island that was part of a continent previously unknown to Europeans, later called America, though Columbus believed he had reached islands off the Asian continent.

Columbus returned to Spain in 1493 as viceroy and governor of the Indies, a title granted to him along with "admiral of the Ocean Seas" and a percentage of the Spanish Crown's profits through the legal agreement (capitulations) he had signed with the crown. He was quickly granted permission to return and colonize the island of Hispaniola, which Columbus said was rich with gold—1,200 Spaniards accompanied him in 17 ships. Although Columbus was an excellent navigator, he was not a good governor. So many complaints were made against him and his two brothers that the crown permanently replaced him as governor in 1502.

Columbus made two more exploratory voyages in 1498 and 1502. On his last voyage, he explored the eastern coast of Central America, seeking a strait to the Indian Ocean. Many scholars think he died without knowing he had discovered a new continent. Columbus's notes indicate that he realized it, but could not admit it, for that would nullify the capitulations and the benefits that were to be passed on to his heirs.

Columbus's discoveries of new lands, mineral wealth, and new people and animals, and the idea of a strait through the American continent to Asia, set off a new era of European competition, exploration, and expansion.

SEE ALSO *Empire in the Americas, Spanish; European Explorations in South America; Vespucci, Amerigo.*

BIBLIOGRAPHY

Colón, Ferdinand. *The Life of the Admiral Christopher Columbus by his Son, Ferdinand.* Translated by Benjamin Keen. New Brunswick, N.J.: Rutgers University Press, 1959.

Columbus, Christopher. *The Diario of Christopher Columbus's First Voyage to America, 1492–1493, Abstracted by Fray Bartolomé de las Casas.* Edited and translated by Oliver Dunn and James E. Kelley Jr. Norman: University of Oklahoma Press, 1989.

Dor-Ner, Zvi. *Columbus and the Age of Discovery.* New York: Morrow, 1991.

Fernández-Armesto, Felipe. *Columbus.* Oxford: Oxford University Press, 1991.

Morison, Samuel Eliot. *Admiral of the Ocean Sea: A Life of Christopher Columbus.* Boston: Little, Brown, 1942.

Lynne Guitar

COMMODITY TRADE, AFRICA

The first Portuguese navigators to cruise along the African coast in the fifteenth century were particularly interested in gold, but they also bought slaves, pepper, gum arabic, ivory, hides, beeswax, and dye-woods. Slaves soon became the most important commerce between Europeans and Africans, but in the late seventeenth century, two-fifths of the trade of the British Royal Africa Company was still in commodities. Gold was the most important export from the Gold Coast until the late seventeenth century. Gum dominated exports from the Senegal River. The major limitation to development of trade was the cost of shipping, which limited exchange to commodities that had a high value for their weight. European ships also carried African cloth and food products between different African ports.

By the late eighteenth century, European shipping had become more efficient. The Industrial Revolution was creating new needs. Machinery needed lubrication, which was provided by vegetable oils. Nineteenth-century Europe also saw an increasing concern with personal cleanliness, particularly in Britain. Soap was made from vegetable oil. Palm oil exports to Britain from West Africa began in the 1790s, rose to 1,000 tons a year in 1810 and over 40,000 tons in 1855. French consumers were not interested in the soft yellow soap the British industry produced from palm oil, but French industrialists learned to produce an attractive soap from peanut oil. Starting with a small purchase in Gambia in 1833, peanut exports rose to over 200 tons in 1845 and over 5,500 in 1854.

The growth in vegetable oil production was also stimulated by a dramatic shift in the terms of trade, that is to say, what producers received in exchange for what they produced. The Industrial Revolution meant that cotton cloth, by far the most important African import, was produced at prices as low as 5 percent of earlier prices.

In the years that followed British abolition of the slave trade in 1807, Britain used diplomatic and naval pressure to shut it down. The new commerce is often called "legitimate trade" by comparison to the slave trade. The slave trade was, however, illegitimate only in the eyes of Europeans. The slave trade persisted into the 1860s, but West Africans increasingly found it wiser to focus on producing commodities, often using slave labor to do so. The slave trade within Africa thus continued. Slaves were used not only as agricultural labor, but also for mining gold and in extracting gum from acacia trees, which grew in desert-side areas. The best measure of the demand for slaves is that prices of slaves within Africa dropped slightly after 1807, but by 1830 they were higher than they had ever been.

The emphasis on commodity production in West Africa often contributed to a radical change in social and political structures. Income from the slave trade went primarily to kings, chiefs, and military leaders, that is to say, to those who commanded military forces. Peanuts and palm oil were produced by peasants, and though the traditional state tried to extract revenue from them, peasants received much of the profit and were often able to purchase weapons. During the course of the nineteenth century, much of the West African population was pulled into the market economy as producers of palm oil and peanuts.

The development of steamboats dramatically reduced the cost of shipping. From the middle of the nineteenth century, steamship companies began calling regularly at African ports, making it possible for both European and African merchants with limited capital to buy space and participate in the export economy.

Late Nineteenth-Century Ivory Traders in Zanzibar. *Next to the slave trade, trade in ivory was the most profitable enterprise in Zanzibar during the nineteenth century.* © **BOJAN BRECELJ/CORBIS. REPRODUCED BY PERMISSION.**

The early growth of a peasantry was more characteristic of West Africa than of other parts of the continent. Palm oil exports were important in parts of Equatorial Africa, but in most of the rest of the continent, the pattern was different. The Cape Colony lived primarily off shipping to Asia. Though Cape entrepreneurs developed a trade in wool, South Africa remained an economic backwater until the discovery of diamonds in 1867 and of gold in 1884 began the transformation of South Africa into a modern industrial state.

In East and Central Africa, people were less numerous and elephants more so. The Industrial Revolution stimulated demand for ivory products by rapidly increasing the size and wealth of the European upper classes. Carvers competed for scarce ivory with industrialists, who used it for piano keys and billiard balls. Well-armed hunters fanned out across the region, often decimating elephant herds in a short period of time. Hunters often also engaged in slaving, and the caravans that moved toward the coast included both slaves and elephant tusks. As elephant herds were reduced, slaves became more important.

The largest market for slaves was the clove plantations of Zanzibar (in present-day Tanzania). From 1818,

Sayyid Said (r. 1806–1856), sultan of Oman and Zanzibar, had encouraged his Arab countrymen to develop clove plantations. He also encouraged Indian financiers to settle in the port cites of the coast and provide funding for traders going into the interior. Zanzibar thus became the hub of a vast commercial empire and an important port of call for European and American shipping

Slave exports were largely a byproduct of the demand in Zanzibar. Zanzibari clove production expanded so dramatically that by the mid-1840s, it surpassed demand and the price began to drop. During the second half of the century, slaves flowed increasingly into coastal plantations that produced sesame, copra, and grain directed toward both local and international markets. Concentrations of slaves also produced food crops around the major trade hubs and port cities.

After the middle of the nineteenth century, the terms of trade changed. Prices were no longer improving for the African producer. In spite of this, the demand for new products increased. The European textile industry found a new source of cotton in Egypt, but was less successful south of Sahara, partly because of problems of quality control, partly because local weavers were often willing to pay higher prices than European importers. Coffee, a crop first domesticated and traded from southern Ethiopia, was developed as a plantation crop on the island of São Tomé from about 1850. It was also introduced in Angola, Liberia, and Madagascar. Cocoa was introduced as a plantation crop to São Tomé in 1822 and to the island of Fernando Póo (now Bioko, Equatorial Guinea) in 1836. Cocoa pods were taken to the Gold Coast in 1879, where cocoa spread rapidly as a smallholder crop. By 1911, the Gold Coast was the world's largest cocoa producer, exporting almost 45,000 tons a year.

The development of industrial processes capable of converting latex into rubber and the use of rubber for bicycle and, later, automobile tires created a rapidly increasing demand from about 1870. In the Congo, brutal methods were used to force rural dwellers to work as tappers of latex trees. In areas with a more developed market economy like Guinea, African traders fanned out in forest regions to buy latex. For a number of years, rubber replaced peanuts as the most important export of France's African colonies. Then, in 1908, the same year that a scandal over the methods used to gather rubber forced Belgium's King Leopold II (1835–1909) to yield control of the Congo, plantation rubber from Malaya came onto the market. The price for wild rubber declined rapidly. The only major plantation rubber operation in twentieth-century Africa was the Firestone concession in Liberia.

Colonization stepped up the level of commodity production. Railroads were built into potentially productive areas. Steamboats were placed on navigable rivers and lakes. During the period between the two world wars, roads were built. The imposition of taxation forced Africans to either produce cash crops or, if they lived in areas distant from markets, to sell their labor in areas that were better suited for cash-crop production.

A mineral economy was developed in southern Africa, centered around gold in South Africa and Southern Rhodesia, copper in the Congo and Northern Rhodesia. Uganda became a major producer of cotton and coffee. Tanganyika (German East Africa) produced sisal. In real terms, the value of West Africa's exports multiplied fifteen times over a fifty-year period. In 1951 the Gold Coast was the world's largest cocoa producer with 300,000 tons of exports.

Africans were coerced by the colonial regime in many ways. Forced labor was used to build roads and often to harvest settler crops. High taxes were used to force people into the market economy. In the Congo, peasants were often assigned quotas of certain crops they had to produce. In spite of this, African innovation and enterprise was crucial to much of what happened. Men migrated to seek work without being coerced. In Ghana,

peasants devised ways to generate capital, spread risk, and acquire land. Knowledge of how to grow cocoa was spread in Ghana by peasants and by the Swiss Basle mission. In Nigeria, it was spread by African independent churches. In Northern Nigeria, the government wanted peasants to grow cotton, but the price paid for peanuts was higher. In Senegambia, peasants with land devised ways to attract migrant laborers. Truck and taxi transport was developed largely by African entrepreneurs.

SEE ALSO *Sub-Saharan Africa, European Presence in.*

BIBLIOGRAPHY

Alpers, Edward. *Ivory and Slaves in East Central Africa: Changing Patterns of International Trade to the Later Nineteenth Century.* London: Heinemann, 1975.

Austen, Ralph. *African Economic History: Internal Development and External Dependency.* Portsmouth, NH: Heinemann, 1987.

Dike, K. O. *Trade and Politics in the Niger Delta, 1830–1885: An Introduction to the Economic and Political History of Nigeria.* Oxford: Clarendon, 1956.

Goerg, Odile. *Commerce et colonisation en Guinée, 1850–1913.* Paris: Harmattan, 1986.

Hopkins, Anthony G. *An Economic History of West Africa.* New York: Columbia University Press, 1973.

Isaacman, Allen, and Richard Roberts, eds. *Cotton, Colonialism, and Social History in Sub-Saharan Africa.* Portsmouth, NH: Heinemann, 1995.

Law, Robin. *From Slave Trade to "Legitimate" Commerce: The Commercial Transition in Nineteenth-Century West Africa.* Cambridge, U.K.: Cambridge University Press, 1995.

Sherriff, Abdul. *Slaves, Spices, and Ivory in Zanzibar: Integration of an East African Commercial Empire into the World Economy, 1770–1873.* London: James Currey, 1987.

Martin Klein

COMMONWEALTH SYSTEM

The evolution of the Commonwealth paralleled the deconstruction of the British Empire through the twentieth century, and the changing meaning and purpose of the Commonwealth reflected British efforts to maintain some influence as formal empire declined. Originally a small group of self-governing white dominions within the empire, the Commonwealth is now a voluntary association of over fifty nations, independent of British control, but linked by the culture of a common colonial heritage.

By the early twentieth century, the settler colonies of the British Empire had achieved self-rule as dominions, although they were still largely dependent on Britain for defense and financial assistance. Following their participation in the First World War (1914–1918), these dominions, especially Canada, South Africa, and the new Irish Free State, moved for clarification of this status. The 1926 Imperial Conference declared the dominions to be autonomous communities within the British Empire, equal in status, and freely associated as members of the British Commonwealth of Nations. The ambiguity of this definition led to pressure to translate Arthur James Balfour's (1848–1930) sentiments into constitutional law. The result was the 1931 Statute of Westminster, which formally declared the autonomy of dominion governments and their complete freedom from any dictates of the Westminster Parliament.

The rapid decolonization that followed 1945 brought significant change to the Commonwealth. Ireland declared itself a republic and left the body in 1948. Independent India wished to remain in the Commonwealth, but as a republic with no allegiance to the Crown. Determined to maintain the Commonwealth as a means of exercising informal influence, Britain moved to alter the association's nature to keep India within the fold. In 1948 the word "British" was dropped, creating a Commonwealth of Nations, and in 1949 the London Declaration stated that the monarch was only the symbolic head of a Commonwealth of freely associated states. India thus stayed in, and the precedent allowed later postcolonial states like Ghana and Nigeria to participate in the group as well.

In this incarnation, the Commonwealth since the 1960s has sought both meaning and relevance. The Singapore Declaration (1971) and the Harare Declaration (1991) reaffirmed the Commonwealth as committed to democracy, human rights, and economic development. Contradictions appeared though, as member states pursued their own economic interests (Britain in Europe, for example) and as states moved from democracy to dictatorship.

Relations between Britain and its former colonies were strained during the 1980s over issues like immigration, foreign policy, and sanctions on the apartheid-state of South Africa. However, there were also examples of successful cooperation. Various Commonwealth-sponsored trusts and organizations have provided funding and economic and technical advice to developing nations within the body. The Commonwealth has acted politically, too, providing a forum in the late 1970s for negotiations to end white rule in Rhodesia, and imposing sanctions on states like Nigeria and Zimbabwe for undemocratic and violent actions.

The 1990s saw a few notable events as well. In 1995 Bermuda voted against autonomy and to remain a Crown Colony. Moreover, a British desire to forge new economic relationships in Asia, after the loss of Hong Kong especially, led to a renewed interest in the association, and the proclamation that 1997 was "The Year of the Commonwealth."

SEE ALSO *Australia; Pacific, European Presence in.*

BIBLIOGRAPHY

Darwin, John. *Britain and Decolonization: the Retreat from Empire in the Post-War World.* New York: St. Martin's Press, 1988.

Gallagher, John. *The Decline, Revival, and Fall of the British Empire: the Ford Lectures and other essays.* Cambridge, U.K.; New York: Cambridge University Press, 1982.

McIntyre, W. D. *The Significance of the Commonwealth, 1965– 90.* Basingtoke, Hampshire: Macmillan, 1991.

Moore, R. J. *Making the New Commonwealth.* Oxford: Clarendon Press; New York: Oxford University Press, 1987.

Andrew Muldoon

COMPAGNIE DES INDES ORIENTALES

SEE *French East India Company*

COMPANY OF NEW FRANCE

Founded in 1627 by Cardinal Richelieu (1585–1642), the chief minister of France, the Company of New France was designed as a vehicle for advancing French colonial claims in North America. Since the late sixteenth century, the French monarchy had granted monopoly rights over the Canadian fur trade to a succession of consortiums. Each was required to promote settlement, but none found it profitable to comply; consequently, there were only about one hundred colonists on the ground by 1625, some at Quebec and others far away in Acadia on the Atlantic Coast. With the establishment of the new company, the Bourbon state signaled a willingness to involve itself much more directly in colonization than heretofore and to channel considerable resources into New France.

Like the Dutch East India Company and the Virginia Company, the Company of New France was designed to mobilize private fortunes in the service of state projects overseas. However, rather than opening the enterprise to all profit-seeking investors, Richelieu exercised tighter control on behalf of King Louis XIII (1601–1643), appealing to a small circle of one hundred shareholders, mainly courtiers, officials, and ecclesiastics; the enterprise became known as the "Company of the Hundred Associates." Shareholders sought not only monetary return on their investments, but also royal approval and the prospect of receiving titles of nobility.

Its charter awarded the company feudal title to all of North America from Florida to the Arctic Circle, with rights of property, jurisdiction, and government; there was no mention of English claims or of existing indigenous possession of this almost limitless domain. The company later granted large territories along the Saint Lawrence as fiefs to favored individuals and ecclesiastical bodies. These latter, known as *seigneurs*, could then award farm-size portions of their estates to rent-paying settlers. Thus was seigneurial tenure established in Canada, an arrangement that would survive long after the Company of New France was defunct.

Additionally, the company was to enjoy a fifteen-year monopoly over all import/export trade, with an exemption from commercial duties; after 1643 the monopoly would cover only furs and skins; and colonists could trade freely with the Indians, but they had to sell their furs to the Company of New France at a specified price. In return, the company was required to bring to New France four thousand settlers—every one of them French and Catholic (Louis XIII signed the charter during the siege of Huguenot La Rochelle)—and to bear the expenses of the civil and ecclesiastical administration.

Rather more than the contemporaneous colonial charters granted by the British Crown, that of the Company of New France expressed a religious purpose. Colonization, it stated, was "for the purpose, with divine assistance, of introducing to the people who inhabit [Canada] the knowledge of the Only God, cause them to be civilized and instructed in the Catholic, Apostolic and Roman Religion." Protestants were not welcome, it implied.

A second distinctive quality of the charter is the aspiration expressed to encompass native nations within the colonial project. While granting no recognition to Indian sovereignty or property, this document looks forward to a time when natives and settlers would unite under the cross and the crown. Indigenous converts to Christianity would henceforth "be considered and reckoned natural born subjects of France," with full legal rights. Many of the legal provisions of the charter, as well as the ideals of Catholic purity and native-French partnership, would remain powerful forces throughout the history of New France.

The new company's history began on a disastrous note. War broke out with England just as it was getting organized and a company of privateers led by the Kirke brothers rushed to take possession of the post at Quebec and then captured the company's first fleet, together with all the supplies and settlers on board, in 1628. Four years later, New France was restored to France and the company began its work anew under the leadership of the governor of New France, Samuel de Champlain (ca. 1570–1635).

Settlers did arrive in both Saint Lawrence (Canada) and Acadia, the majority of men enlisted in France as *engagés* (indentured servants) on three-year contracts, but their numbers fell short of the four thousand required by the company's charter.

The company did take its religious mandate seriously and, to that end, shipped along with the earliest settlers a small contingent of Jesuits charged with evangelizing the indigenous nations and bringing them into the Christian fold. With their base at Quebec and missionaries ministering to the Hurons and other inland tribes, the Jesuits were a dominant presence, not only in the emergent colonial church, but also in the civil politics of Canada under the Company of New France.

A group of idealistic lay Catholics arrived from France in 1641 with the aim of furthering the same cause of converting the "savages." They pushed up the Saint Lawrence to establish what they hoped would be a Christian utopia of Indians and French on the island of Montreal. Though only partially successful in their missionary objectives, the founders of Montreal did succeed in extending the French presence westward. Their frontier settlement controlled a strategic crossroads of waterways linking the Great Lakes, the north, and the Saint Lawrence estuary, and as a result, it quickly emerged as the thriving center of the fur trade.

Meanwhile, the separately administered Acadian colony received an initial injection of supplies and settlers under the leadership of Isaac de Razilly, a leading member of the Company of New France. After Razilly's death in 1635, however, the neglected colony lapsed into a period of chaos and civil strife until it was captured by New England forces in 1654.

In 1663 the crown, in the person of Louis XIV's (1638–1715) minister, Jean-Baptiste Colbert (1619–1683), intervened once again in the affairs of New France, proclaiming that the company had neglected its duty to establish the colony on a solid footing. At this point, there were only about 2,500 French settlers on the Saint Lawrence, their livelihood excessively dependent on the fur trade, and they were very much on the defensive in the face of Iroquois attacks. The government blamed the company, which it promptly dissolved, and took charge of New France as a crown colony.

SEE ALSO *Colonization and Companies; Conquests and Colonization; Massachusetts Bay Company; Mercantilism; New France.*

BIBLIOGRAPHY

Levi, Anthony. *Cardinal Richelieu: And the Making of France.* New York: Carroll & Graf Publishers, 2001.

Allan Greer

COMPRADORIAL SYSTEM

An arrangement whereby a local intermediary helped foreigners conduct trade, the compradorial system was used in various parts of East Asia. It was most prevalent in China, where it originated in the late Ming dynasty (1368–1644), but came to prominence in the early 1800s during the Qing dynasty (1644–1911). The term "comprador" derives from the Portuguese word for "buyer" (*compradore*). When the monopolistic *cohong* (or Canton) system was abolished in 1842 after the first Opium War (1839–1842), compradors replaced the traditional Hong merchants as the main commercial intermediaries between Chinese and Western traders.

Even after the abolition of the *cohong* monopoly, many obstacles hindered free trade: linguistic and cultural barriers, currency differences and complexities, different weights and measures, and varying commercial and social customs. The compradorial system became more prevalent after the second Opium War (1856–1860), which opened more Chinese ports to foreign trade. Western firms also used Chinese compradors in Japan, mainly at Nagasaki (the only place Chinese merchants had been allowed during the Tokugawa period [1603–1867]) and Yokohama. When Japanese firms started to trade in China at the end of the nineteenth century, they also relied on Chinese compradors.

The compradorial system was indispensable for the rise of Sino-foreign commerce. Hired for their honesty and reliability but mainly for their ability to provide customers, compradors were critical links between Chinese commerce and foreign firms. Because foreign firms owed much of their success to their compradors, they competed for the best compradors. The incentive for hiring a comprador for even a short period was great because a foreign firm generally kept in close touch with its comprador after he eventually became an independent merchant, thereby further widening the firm's range of potential customers. Some Western company officials were so dependent on their compradors that they were hardly aware of how their businesses in China functioned below the highest levels of operation.

By the end of the nineteenth century, compradors were among the richest men in China. Famous compradors include Zheng Guanying (1842–1922), who after working for Butterfield and Swire became a prominent merchant in his own right and in the late 1800s called for China to use commercial warfare to strengthen its modern economy; Zhu Dachun, the comprador for Jardine and Matheson in Shanghai from the 1890s to 1900, and one of the wealthiest men in China; and Robert Ho Tung (He Dong) (1862–1956), the Eurasian comprador for Jardine and Matheson in Hong Kong from 1883 to 1900 and the richest man in the colony.

The terms "comprador" and "compradorial" have also been used pejoratively to describe any type of economic or political collaboration with colonial or neocolonial exploiters—not only in Asia, but also in Africa and Latin America. This usage derives from criticism in the 1920s of the compradors as the running dogs of imperialism. Chinese Marxist scholars have generally viewed the compradors as a result of China's unique semicolonial, semifeudal state and as spearheads of the economic imperialism that drained China's wealth, stifled Chinese-owned enterprises, and upset China's traditionally self-sufficient economy. They argue that the comprador system was not simply an economic arrangement, but a tool for suppressing Chinese nationalism and weakening China's sovereign rights.

The system eventually fostered a giant class of merchants and officials who ultimately helped foreign firms influence China's economy and government in the late 1800s and early 1900s. According to this argument, through their compradors the foreigners were able not only to open Chinese markets, but also to penetrate traditional guilds, hongs, and other commercial organizations, force the Qing government to implement Western-style enterprises, and ultimately to control most of China's largest industries, exports and imports, and shipping.

For scholars who believe that international trade and investment was beneficial to China's economic development, however, the compradors are heroes rather than villains. As the first Chinese to invest in modern enterprises, they were crucial to China's industrialization and economic modernization. They created external economies, promoted a national market, stimulated mercantile nationalism, and channeled Chinese savings into modern investments. Furthermore, because the compradors eventually became the rivals of the Western firms, they ended up curbing foreign economic intrusion.

The compradorial system began to decline in the early 1900s, mainly because foreign merchants became more knowledgeable about China while Chinese merchants became more experienced in foreign trade, but also because the development of modern banking and credit services made the system less necessary. Still, most foreign companies in China continued to rely on Chinese managers or Chinese agents, whereas the compradorial system survived in Hong Kong until after World War II (1939–1945).

SEE ALSO *China to the First Opium War; China, First Opium War to 1945; Imperialism, Marxist Theories of.*

BIBLIOGRAPHY
Allen, G. C. and Audrey G. Donnithorne. *Western Enterprise in Far Eastern Economic Development: China and Japan.* London: Allen & Unwin, 1954.

Bergère, Marie-Claire. *The Golden Age of the Chinese Bourgeoisie, 1911–1937*. Translated by Janet Lloyd. Cambridge, U.K.; New York: Cambridge University Press, 1989.

Cochran, Sherman. *Big Business in China: Sino-Foreign Rivalry in the Cigarette Industry, 1890–1930*. Cambridge, MA: Harvard University Press, 1980.

Hao, Yen-p'ing Hao. *The Comprador in Nineteenth Century China: Bridge between East and West*. Cambridge, MA: Harvard University Press, 1970.

Huang Yifeng, et al. *Jiu zhongguo di mai ban jie ji* [The Comprador Class in Old China]. Shanghai: Renmin chubanshe, 1982.

Nie Baozhang. *Zhongguo maiban zichanjieji de fasheng* [The Emergence of the Chinese Comprador Class]. Beijing: Zhongguo shehui kexue chubanshe, 1979.

Smith, Carl T. "Compradores of The Hongkong Bank." In *Eastern Banking: Essays in the History of the Hongkong and Shanghai Banking Corporation*, edited by Frank H. King, 93–111. London: Athlone Press, 1983.

John Carroll

COMPRADORS

SEE *Compradorial System*

CONQUESTS AND COLONIZATION

The voyages of exploration that began in 1492 provided the Crown of Castile with a unique opportunity to take the lead role in the process of westward expansion and the creation of New World empires. No such intentions, of course, were in evidence when, in August 1492, Genoese mariner Christopher Columbus (1451–1506) sailed out of the port of Palos in southwestern Spain in search of a sea passage to the Orient.

There being no reason to believe that Columbus would reach lands other than the fringes of Asia, he and his sponsors, the Catholic monarchs Isabella (1451–1504) and Ferdinand (1452–1516), envisaged no more than the establishment of a chain of fortified trading posts similar to the *feitorias* pioneered by the Portuguese in Africa. Staffed by salaried crown employees, the Spanish *factoría* was to serve as the means through which to obtain high value goods (principally, it was hoped, gold and spices) without the need to settle the land and exploit it directly.

However, early reports of the potential of the Indies, the name by which Spain's New World possessions came to be known, and especially of the large island of Hispaniola (now occupied by Haiti and the Dominican Republic), with its large population as yet to be exposed to Christian teachings, were sufficient to persuade Isabella and Ferdinand to redefine their objectives, and abandon the trading-post model in favor of that which was more familiar to Castilians, namely, occupation and settlement.

Columbus's second expedition, undertaken in 1493, consisted of more than one thousand men of varied trades and occupations, supplied with all the necessities, including agricultural stock, to found a colony capable of providing the resources for continued exploration of the surrounding area. Most of this first wave of emigrants either died or returned to Spain broken and disillusioned by the harsh reality of life on Hispaniola. But as news of the discoveries spread from Seville through Andalusia, Extremadura, and eventually throughout Castile, thousands of men, motivated in part by a spirit of adventure, but attracted above all by the prospect of untold wealth, made their way across the Atlantic, steadily increasing the Spanish presence and providing a pool from which future expeditionary leaders would draw to man further voyages of exploration within the Caribbean and beyond.

Hispaniola was soon to be overshadowed by Cuba and especially by the mainland territories of the Aztecs and Incas. But the occupation and settlement of this, the first permanent European colony in the Western Hemisphere, was crucial in enabling Spain to formulate the policies and practices that were to make possible the acquisition of an empire and to develop the institutions through which it was to be governed for the following three centuries.

One such practice was that whereby the Spanish Crown, unwilling to take direct control of, or invest heavily in, the incorporation of new territories, relied on entrepreneurial individuals to organize, finance, and undertake the exploration, conquest, and settlement of unexplored regions, in exchange for wide-ranging political and economic privileges, or *mercedes*. These agreements took the form of a contract or license called a *capitulación*, which stipulated the duties and responsibilities of the expeditionary leader, as well as the privileges he could expect to enjoy in the newly subjugated area.

Principal among these duties and privileges were the military title of *adelantado*, the governorship of the territory concerned, and preferential rights over its economic resources so as to enable him to pay off his investors, reward his followers, and derive a handsome profit for himself. To this end, the crown also sanctioned the introduction in the Indies of another key institution—that of *repartimiento*, later to become the *encomienda*. Literally a distribution to selected individuals of designated groups of Indians for the purpose of labor and tribute, *repartimiento* served as the means whereby new territory was secured, its economic potential developed, and its most "deserving" conquerors and early settlers appropriately rewarded.

The notion of reward for services originated in the *reconquista* (reconquest), the centuries-long advance against the Muslims within the Iberian Peninsula, and was successfully extended to the colonization of the Canary Islands beginning in 1479. In the New World, it proved a crucial method for promoting, at minimal cost to the crown, the speedy occupation of the vast territories that were to comprise Spain's empire in America.

Over the decades that followed Columbus's first landing in the Bahamas in October 1492, dozens of *conquistadores*, many but not all of whom were minor nobles or hidalgos who saw military service on behalf of the crown and the Christian religion as the most promising route to social advancement, led bands of followers of lesser social status (soldiers, sailors, blacksmiths, bakers, tailors, and scribes, among others) into the waters surrounding Hispaniola and onto the mainland beyond. The lure of wealth and control of Indians being the principal incentives for participation in expeditions of conquest, new areas that failed to yield sufficient resources to satisfy the high expectations of its conquerors and first settlers, the arrival of large numbers of emigrants ambitious for wealth and status of their own, or even rumors of the existence of richer and more densely populated lands elsewhere, invariably stimulated further exploration. In this way, each territorial gain served as a launching pad for another advance into the surrounding area: Those who endured the hardships of the Atlantic crossing and the discomforts and dangers of an unfamiliar and hostile environment did so not in the expectation of new opportunities for work, but to live on the fruits of the labor of others. Over time, as Spaniards consolidated control over the most rewarding and densely populated parts of the hemisphere, *capitulaciones* declined in utility, but they continued to be employed late into the colonial period as a method for extending Spanish domination over the peripheries of empire.

Critical to the Spaniards' fortunes were the responses of local indigenous populations. Thus, the early occupation and settlement of Hispaniola were facilitated by the initially amicable reaction of the Taíno peoples. Surprised by the unexpected arrival of men so different from themselves, and unaware of the long-term implications of a development for which nothing in their prior experience had prepared them, those Taíno *caciques* (chiefs) with whom Spaniards first made contact were sufficiently curious about, and impressed by, the newcomers and their glass and metal objects not only to engage in trade but to offer hospitality and protection.

Resistance mounted as the real objectives of the Spaniards were gradually revealed and as the Taíno began to experience the consequences of colonization—enslavement, forced labor, the destruction of crops by European livestock, and the impact of European diseases to which the indigenous peoples of the Americas, having developed in isolation from the rest of the world, had no acquired immunity. For the peoples of Hispaniola and neighboring islands, disease was to be the most devastating effect of conquest: Within a few decades of contact, their populations had been virtually wiped out by repeated outbreaks, the most damaging of which were smallpox, measles, and influenza. Sporadic resistance notwithstanding, the initial welcome offered by Hispaniola's *caciques*, combined with the continuing assistance of at least some among their number, permitted the Spaniards to establish a firm and permanent foothold on the island without a full-scale conquest of the kind that would subsequently be necessary almost everywhere the Spaniards went on the mainland.

The conquest of mainland peoples proved considerably more costly. Nevertheless, within just a few years of landing on the coasts of Mexico (1519) and Peru (1532), Spanish *conquistadores* under the leadership of Hernán Cortés (ca. 1484–1547) and Francisco Pizarro (ca. 1475–1541) respectively, had taken possession on behalf of the Spanish Crown of the large, rich, and densely populated empires of the Aztecs and the Incas. A number of factors came together in the early sixteenth century to deliver the Spaniards quick and decisive victories.

First, Cortés and Pizarro, though they began their conquests more than a decade apart, were immeasurably advantaged by the political situation prevailing in the Aztec and Inca empires at the time of the arrival of the Spanish. Both empires had come into being over a period of approximately a century prior to contact through the incorporation by conquest or intimidation of weaker neighboring groups. By the beginning of the sixteenth century, both empires were driven by internal discontent, attributable in large part to the resentment of subject peoples deprived of their former autonomy and required to pay tribute to their imperial overlords.

For those under the dominion of the Aztecs, tribute could include the provision of sacrificial victims to the god Huitzilopochtli, upon whom the survival of the universe was thought to depend. Among the Incas, such tensions were further complicated by division within their own ranks arising from a bitter war of succession between the half-brothers Atahualpa (d. 1533) and Huascar (d. 1532), caused by the death of their father and Sapa Inca (emperor), Huayna Capac, in the mid-1520s. The emperor was an early victim of a smallpox epidemic that spread through native trade routes years before Europeans penetrated Inca-controlled territory.

Internal divisions within the Aztec and Inca empires proved absolutely critical to the Spaniards. Some native groups, clearly aware of the ways in which the numerically insignificant but militarily powerful Europeans could aid their struggle against imperial domination, made the decision to ally with the newcomers in the belief that a combined Spanish-Indian force offered them the best chance of regaining their independence.

Such alliances between Spaniards and resentful subject peoples within Aztec and Inca domains were made possible by the initial vacillation of the emperors Motecuhzoma (Montezuma, ca. 1466–1520) and Atahualpa—a second factor that was to have a decisive effect on the course of the conquests. Motecuhzoma, though fully informed of the activities of the Spaniards who had disembarked on the Mexican coast, made the decision to await developments before responding to a threat he did not yet fully understand. Why he hesitated remains a matter of debate, but the consequences of his inaction are well known. The delay in confronting a Spanish force comprising fewer than six hundred men enabled Cortés to make contact with the Totonacs of Cempoallan and, even more importantly, the independent kingdom of Tlaxcala, from whose peoples Cortés obtained intelligence, as well as the manpower and material resources that would make possible the conquest of the Aztec Empire.

In Peru, Atahualpa made a similar error of judgment. Having recently emerged victorious from civil war, the new emperor was sufficiently curious about the identity of the Spaniards, and confident of his ability speedily to dispatch a mere 168 men, to allow Pizarro to enter Inca territory in safety. The Inca failure to react quickly enough proved their undoing. Taking advantage of the surprise caused by horses and firearms, Cortés and Pizarro seized the emperors by force, in both cases provoking confusion, destabilizing the leadership, and delaying a concerted response. For Pizarro, the success of his daring act proved especially significant, for he was to gain not only the support of groups determined to overthrow Inca rule, principal among whom were the Huanca and Cañari, but also of the supporters of the recently defeated Huascar.

However crucial the seizures and subsequent deaths of Motecuhzoma and Atahualpa, these events marked only the beginning of the conquests of the Aztec and Inca empires. Both peoples had strong traditions of warfare, as well as large, well-trained, professional armies that had enabled them to control extensive territories and dominate millions of subject peoples. Both the Aztecs and Incas quickly overcame their initial hesitation, readily adapting to new circumstances, alien weapons, and forms of fighting entirely different from their own. Both fought on home ground, ensuring regular access to supplies and reinforcements. And both proved formidable and fanatical adversaries, capable of driving the Spanish to the limits of their endurance and inventiveness.

Sixteenth-century Spaniards, however, had a further, technological, advantage which, though certainly not the most decisive factor in their victories, aided their search for allies and gave them an important edge over their enemies at crucial points in their conquests. In the final battle for the Aztec capital Tenochtitlán, for example, the large vessels, equipped with artillery, that were built by the Spaniards and their Tlaxcalan allies allowed them to take control of the lake waters surrounding the city at precisely the time when its inhabitants were also suffering the effects of a devastating smallpox epidemic, rendering further resistance ineffective.

The degree of centralization that characterized the Aztec and Inca empires meant that, once the native leadership structures had collapsed, the transfer of power to the Spanish was relatively swift. The process of consolidating control over the outlying reaches of the empires, and the extension of Spanish domination beyond their perimeters, now propelled further expeditions or *entradas* into the unknown. At the same time that the Spanish Crown encouraged the ambitious and adventurous to seek new opportunities for wealth and glory, however, it sought also to limit the powers of conquerors and first settlers. In addition, though it sometimes failed in these objectives, the Spanish Crown sought to protect its native vassals from excessive exploitation and bring about their conversion to Christianity.

SEE ALSO *Christianity and Colonial Expansion in the Americas; Colonization and Companies.*

BIBLIOGRAPHY

Cieza de León, Pedro. *The Discovery and Conquest of Peru.* Translated and edited by Alexandra Parma Cook and Noble David Cook. Durham, NC: Duke University Press, 1998.

Cortés, Hernán. *Letters from Mexico.* Translated and edited by Anthony Pagden. New Haven, CT: Yale University Press, 1986.

Deagan, Kathleen, and José María Cruxent. *Columbus's Outpost Among the Taínos: Spain and America at La Isabela, 1493–1498.* New Haven, CT: Yale University Press, 2002.

Fernández-Armesto, Felipe. *Columbus.* Oxford and New York: Oxford University Press, 1991.

Góngora, Mario. *Studies in the Colonial History of Spanish America.* Translated by Richard Southern. Cambridge, U.K.: Cambridge University Press, 1975.

Hemming, John. *The Conquest of the Incas.* New York: Harcourt, 1970.

Lockhart, James, and Stuart Schwartz. *Early Latin America: A History of Colonial Spanish America and Brazil.* Cambridge, U.K.: Cambridge University Press, 1983.

Phillips, William D., Jr., and Carla Phillips. *The Worlds of Christopher Columbus.* Cambridge, U.K.: Cambridge University Press, 1992.

Thomas, Hugh. *The Conquest of Mexico.* London: Hutchinson, 1993.

Caroline A. Williams

COOK, CAPTAIN JAMES

SEE *Pacific, European presence in*

COOLIE TRADE

SEE *Chinese Diaspora*

COPPER TRADE, ASIA

Japanese copper was a significant commodity in intra-Asian trade. High-volume trade in copper began in the mid-seventeenth century. Chinese merchants and the Dutch United East India Company (VOC) exported copper from Nagasaki, and Japanese traders exported it through Tsushima. Exports rapidly increased due to the prohibition of silver exports from Japan in 1668. In the late seventeenth century the Japanese copper trade reached its peak. In the 1690s Chinese merchants on average annually exported 2,826 tons of copper, while the VOC exported 1,098 tons, and the Japanese sent 344 tons to Korea.

Japanese copper was consumed worldwide. In the seventeenth century it was imported to Europe by the VOC. However, Asia was the main consumer. Chinese junks delivered to the Chinese mainland, especially to ports in the Yangzi delta, and until the early eighteenth century to Southeast Asia, to places such as Tonkin and Ayutthaya. The VOC exported to South Asia. In terms of volume, Gujarat was the most important recipient during the seventeenth century, whereas Coromandel and Bengal were the major recipients during the eighteenth century. Copper exported via Tsushima was sold to Korea.

Japanese copper was used for artillery, household utensils, religious goods, and, most importantly, coins. In China and Korea, almost all of the Japanese copper was supplied to the mints to produce currency. A percent of the copper exported on Chinese junks was reexported by European private traders to South Asia. Competition existed for the role of deliverer to the South Asian market. In the 1710s, however, the VOC established a monopoly to deliver Japanese copper to South Asia. The Chinese government began to purchase all of its Japanese copper from the Chinese traders to Nagasaki, to meet domestic demand. European private traders were excluded from that transit trade of Japanese copper. Copper imported into South Asia was mainly smelted for minting by the VOC or by local Indian governments.

In the early eighteenth century, Japan began to restrict exports due to a decline in copper production. This created a crisis for the VOC, which had constructed its own trading network in Asia and pocketed profits from the intra-Asian trade of the seventeenth century. The VOC imported Japanese copper to South Asia and exported cotton textiles to Siam. They then delivered Siamese commodities such as deerskins and sappanwoods to Japan. Through this triangular trade, the VOC gained profits, which were used as capital for the pepper and spice trade in insular Southeast Asia. The VOC petitioned the Japanese government for the continued availability of a constant annual volume of copper allocated for export. Nonetheless, it saw a decline in its copper exports: throughout the eighteenth century the VOC exported around 500 tons per year.

From the 1730s, the English East India Company exported European copper to India. This copper was mainly produced in Britain, where volumes of production rose year by year in the early decades of the Industrial Revolution. The English trading company's annual copper imports into India reached 872 tons in the 1760s and 1,575 tons in the 1790s. Yet, this British copper trade was not as profitable as the trade in Japanese copper, because British copper was not as highly valued at Indian markets as Japanese and was only suitable for making brass and artillery.

Political instability in the Dutch homeland in the 1790s and the final loss of the Dutch establishments in South Asia in the early nineteenth century led the Dutch business in South Asia to a crisis. While the British copper industry was more expanded, Chile emerged in the nineteenth century as a copper supplier to the global market, and Japanese production fell off. It was not until the late nineteenth century that Japan recovered large-volume copper exports by introducing Western techniques for copper production.

SEE ALSO *Dutch United East India Company; Empire, Dutch.*

BIBLIOGRAPHY

Glamann, Kristof. "The Dutch East India Company's Trade in Japanese Copper, 1645–1736." *Scandinavian Economic History Review* 1 (1953): 41–79.

Shimada, Ryuto. "Dancing around the Bride: The Inter-Asian Competition for Japanese Copper, 1770–1760." *Itinerario* 27, no. 2 (2003): 37–60.

Ryuto Shimada

COROMANDEL, EUROPEANS AND MARITIME TRADE

Coromandel is the name given to the flat and agricultural southeastern stretch of India's coastline. Fragmented by numerous river deltas, Coromandel offers many suitable harbors including Pulicat, Madras (now Chennai), Pondicherry, Cuddalore, Tranquebar, Karaikal, Nagore, and Nagapattinam. Historically, the region emerged as significant through the production of textiles for export, carried by Muslim Kling and later Chulia merchants as far afield as the Burmese and Thai kingdoms, the sultanates of the Malay peninsula, north and east Sumatra, Java, the Moluccas, the Persian Gulf, and southern Arabia. It is hard to say that any one of these trading ports became preeminent in the early modern period, although with the rise of the kingdom of Golconda and its mining activities, Masulipatnam in north Coromandel became an important regional entrepôt. The scattered locations of Coromandel ports was partly a reflection of the export trade in textiles, whose production was distributed evenly across the region. Besides the oceanic trade there was considerable coastal trade northward up to Orissa and Bengal, southward to Sri Lanka, and westward to Malabar and Gujarat. In this, Muslim settlers from the Arabian Sea and local Islamic merchant communities traded side-by-side with long-standing Hindu merchant groups such as the Telugu and Tamil Chetty, though a gradual shift of Telugu interests southward suggests they may have been displaced by competition. The import trade, by contrast, was never of any great significance, except at Masulipatnam, as it consisted mainly of trade in minerals and the local movement of rice and other foodstuffs.

Europeans were attracted from the outset by the possibilities of procuring textiles for export, though the extent of sixteenth-century Portuguese involvement in the Coromandel carrying trade is questionable. In any case, the Portuguese, who were initially attracted by the legend that the apostle St. Thomas was buried at Mylapore, were never present in great numbers. Around 1540 there were perhaps six to eight hundred across Coromandel, but their settlements remained largely outside state control. According to the *Lembrança das Cousas da Índia*, written in 1525, only one state vessel was active in Coromandel.

In the seventeenth century, however, Coromandel offered crucial trading posts for the Dutch, who opened factories in Pulicat, Sadras, and Masulipatnam. As Hendrik Brouwer explained in 1612, the Coromandel Coast was "the left arm of the Moluccas, because we have noticed that without the textiles of Coromandel, commerce is dead in the Moluccas." The English by contrast were slower to patronize this coastline, and instead concentrated their trading activities in Persia and Surat in Gujarat. Only in 1644 did they build Fort St. George, around which developed the city of Madras, which prospered from its trading activities. This trade represented above all the harnessing of the European demand for

calicos, woven in Coromandel from raw cotton imported from the Deccan. The cloths produced were a variety of plain cloths (muslins and calicos) and patterned chintz. The weavers worked as household units, were organized into a number of castes under a community leader (*careedar*), and proved a mobile workforce, though they were sometimes forced to revert to agricultural livelihoods on account of competition from the emerging English machine industry and shortages in raw cotton supplies. They were paid well above a subsistence wage, though not as much as skilled laborers.

The Dutch and English were joined by the Danes, who established themselves at Tranquebar, and the French at Nizampatnam, Karaikal, and Pondicherry, which they acquired in 1674. With the arrival of Joseph Dupleix, who became governor in Pondicherry in 1742, the French Compagnie des Indes Orientales took on a martial bent. It provoked war with the English by invading Madras in September 1746, although the port was returned shortly afterward by international treaty. In 1750 Dupleix intervened in the succession dispute that followed the death of the Nawab of the Carnatic by thwarting the designs of another Muslim ruler, the Subahdar of the Deccan; shortly afterward, the French also blocked the Subahdar's attempts to control the province of Tanjore.

The English East India Company, despite its traditional aversion to warfare, could no longer afford to stay out of the conflict and intervened. Demonstrating greater skill in the field, the British army overwhelmed a French force protecting their puppet, Chanda Sahib, and further setbacks such as the failure to storm Muhammad Ali's citadel in Trichinoply undermined Dupleix's support back in France, forcing the governor's recall in 1754.

The French and the English continued to contest the region more ruthlessly than before, but a three-month French siege of Madras at the end of 1758 this time failed and the French were twice routed by local armies supported by the English in the Northern Circars. The French garrison at Pondicherry itself finally fell to the English in January 1761.

This complex of circumstances had, in the meantime, given rise to a situation in which the English could not easily extricate themselves from landholding and the development of colonial governance. Fueled by the appetite of young men bent on career and personal fortune, the Franco-British conflict in the Carnatic, together with concurrent developments in Bengal, had unwittingly set the foundations of the British Empire in India. For Coromandel, colonial rule meant the weaving industry falling under the total control of the English between 1795 and 1800, although when tensions arose the weavers still demonstrated themselves capable of collective protest.

SEE ALSO *Bengal, Maritime Trade of; Colonial Port Cities and Towns, South and Southeast Asia; English East India Company (EIC).*

BIBLIOGRAPHY

Arasaratnam, Sinnappah. *Merchants, Companies, and Commerce on the Coromandel Coast, 1650–1740.* Delhi: Oxford University Press, 1986.

Arasaratnam, Sinappah. *Maritime Commerce and English Power: Southeast India, 1750–1800.* South Asian Publications Series, no. 11. New Delhi: Stirling, 1996.

Subrahmanyam, Sanjay. *The Political Economy of Commerce: Southern India, 1500–1650.* Cambridge South Asian Studies, no. 45. New York and Cambridge, U.K.: Cambridge University Press, 1990.

Stefan Halikowski Smith

CORTÉS, HERNÁN
1484–1547

Hernán Cortés shared many of the characteristics of the sixteenth-century Spanish conquistador. Born in Medellín in the province of Extremadura in Spain, Cortés was a minor noble driven principally by the quest for wealth and glory. Ambitious for political power, he played a key role in the conquest of the Aztec Empire and the incorporation of its peoples into Spain's New World dominions.

Cortés's swift defeat of the Aztecs (1519–1521), like Francisco Pizarro's (ca. 1475–1541) victory over the Incas (1532–1533), was facilitated by the cooperation of hundreds of thousands of native allies. The sheer number of Indians fighting alongside a few hundred Spanish *conquistadores* gave the events of 1519 to 1521 the character of a great Indian uprising against Aztec domination. Though undoubtedly aided by propitious timing, Cortés's diplomatic skills were crucial in the forging of lasting alliances with the independent kingdom of Tlaxcala, which had been encircled and was vulnerable to Aztec conquest, and with the numerous subject peoples who, resentful of Aztec imperial rule, joined the fighting forces that overcame the ferocious Aztec war machine.

Cortés's audacity and determination, even when the odds were clearly stacked against him, also played a significant part in the Spaniards' success. An early decision to undertake the conquest in defiance of the governor of Cuba's strict instructions to limit his activities to exploration and trade, placed Cortés in real danger of a charge of treason should he fail to deliver to the king the largest and richest territories thus far encountered in the Americas. Only this driving need to succeed can explain the recklessness and inventiveness of his decisions: the

scuppering of his ships to prevent the followers of Cuban governor Diego Velázquez (ca. 1465–1524) from abandoning the enterprise; the return to the Aztecs' island capital, Tenochtitlán, even after an ignominious Spanish retreat during the Noche Triste (Night of Sorrow) and the loss of hundreds of his men; and the building, with Tlaxcalan assistance, of a fleet of brigantines equipped with artillery to take control of Lake Texcoco, which cut off Tenochtitlán's food supplies and weakened severely the capacity of its people, already suffering the effects of a traumatic smallpox epidemic, to further resist.

Notwithstanding the skill and tenacity with which he led the conquest of Mexico, Hernán Cortés stands apart from his fellow conquistadors in one crucial sense. Having witnessed the tragic consequences of the kind of colonization that had taken place in the Caribbean, its peoples virtually destroyed within a single generation following the Columbian voyages, he sought to ensure that no such catastrophe was repeated in New Spain. Nevertheless, as governor from 1522, he faced the unenviable task of advancing several irreconcilable aims: to secure control over the Aztecs' former dominions, redirect native tribute and labor to support a growing Spanish population, and provide his followers with the livelihoods to which they aspired and which they considered their rightful reward for participation in conquest, while at the same time protecting indigenous peoples from exploitation and abuse. Thus the *encomienda*, a modified version of the *repartimiento* first introduced in Hispaniola, was extended to the Mexican mainland, and Cortés was one of its principal beneficiaries.

Despite personal reservations, Cortés believed that the *encomienda*, with its duties towards Indians carefully defined, was necessary to encourage permanent settlement, the development of a stable society, and profitable exploitation of the colony's resources. His authority in New Spain was to be short-lived, however. To limit the powers of conquerors and *encomenderos*, officials loyal to the authority of the crown soon made their way to the new colony: It was they who were to be responsible for its government until Mexico became independent exactly three hundred years later.

SEE ALSO *Conquests and Colonization; Encomienda; New Spain, the Viceroyalty of.*

BIBLIOGRAPHY

Cortés, Hernán. *Letters from Mexico.* Translated and edited by Anthony Pagden. New Haven, CT: Yale University Press, 1986.

Hassig, Ross. *Mexico and the Spanish Conquest.* London and New York: Longman, 1994.

Thomas, Hugh. *The Conquest of Mexico.* London: Hutchinson, 1993.

Caroline A. Williams

COTTON

Cotton, a plant of the mallow family, produces fibers that can be woven into cloth. It has been valued since antiquity and its cultivation was an important factor stimulating European colonialism in regions of Asia, Africa, and the Americas; it is still a major trade commodity. Numerous species of cotton exist, but four are of commercial importance: *Gossypium arboreum* (native to Asia), *G. herbaceum* (native to Africa), and *G. hirsutum* and *G. barbadense* (both native to the Americas). Cotton plants originated in tropical regions, but are now grown worldwide in a variety of climate zones where adequate heat and water are available. The cotton plant produces capsules, called bolls, in which seeds are surrounded by a fluffy fiber, or lint. Cotton producers generally divide cotton into two types: short-staple cotton, which has shorter fibers about one inch long, and long-staple cotton, which has fibers reaching two inches in length. Long-staple cotton is more valuable, as it produces a higher quality cloth. Most cotton grown today produces white or cream-colored fibers, but many other colors, including yellow and brown, also exist. Cotton cloth is comfortable in hot climates and is insect resistant, easily washable, lightweight, and easily dyed. Cotton seeds have a variety of industrial applications, including being used in the manufacture of oils, soaps, detergents, cosmetics, fertilizers, and animal foods.

Cotton was known and used in ancient Egypt, India, China, and the Americas. Europeans probably learned about the value of cotton garments as a result of British and French commercial activities in India in the seventeenth century. Cotton fibers brought back from India led to the establishment of a cotton textile industry in Britain, especially in the city of Manchester. Cotton textile producers originally faced restrictions placed on them by the government at the behest of wool growers, who realized that cotton cloth would compete with woolens. These restrictions were largely unsuccessful, however, as the public increasingly demanded cotton cloth. Cotton in seventeenth- and early-eighteenth-century England was spun at home as a cottage industry, but with the Industrial Revolution production began to shift to large industrial mills. New spinning techniques and new mechanical looms stimulated the growth of the cotton textile industry by making cotton production easier and less expensive. The invention of the cotton gin by the American Eli Whitney in 1793 allowed cotton seeds to be easily removed mechanically, eliminating the slow and laborious process of removing the seeds by hand and lowering the cost of cotton production.

To sustain the increased levels of production made possible by industrialization, the British needed new sources of cotton. Both Egypt and the American South

Spinning Cotton, 1920s. *This elderly Egyptian man spins cotton by hand using a simple, centuries-old spinning technique.* © UNDERWOOD & UNDERWOOD/CORBIS. REPRODUCED BY PERMISSION.

emerged as important centers of cotton cultivation supplying British textile mills. India was also a producer, though its cotton was generally considered to be of lower quality, and lack of adequate infrastructure in India made export difficult. The demand for cotton and the resultant need to secure cotton supplies prompted British imperial expansion, and made Egypt and the American colonies especially important. The same applied to the French, who established cotton plantations in their own colonies in the West Indies and in West Africa.

COTTON AND THE RISE OF MODERN EGYPT

Cotton was essential in the rise of modern Egypt, which became a major cotton-producing region in the nineteenth century and continues to be a major producer today. The rise of Egypt's cotton industry was largely due to Muhammad 'Ali (there are various spellings of his name), ruler of Egypt from 1805 to 1848. Muhammad 'Ali's consolidation of Egyptian power and his early modernizing policies have earned him the name "Father of Modern Egypt."

Muhammad 'Ali (ca. 1769–1849) was born in Albania. As a soldier in the Ottoman army, he rose through the ranks, eventually becoming governor of Egypt, which was then a part of the Ottoman Empire. An autocratic, ambitious, clever, and crafty person, he quickly became the ruler of a virtually independent Egypt, after eliminating the Mamluk rulers in 1811. Muhammad 'Ali recognized that he could enhance Egypt's independence by using profits generated by cotton exports to expand the military and develop infrastructure. He used cotton profits to finance military expeditions into Syria and other Ottoman territories and to establish industry in Egypt.

Muhammad 'Ali encouraged European experts and technicians to settle in Egypt. Louis Alexis Jumel (1785–1823), a French textile engineer, came to Egypt in 1817 as the director of a spinning mill. A few years later Jumel discovered a cotton bush in a Cairo garden that was producing a superior kind of cotton, with a long staple and strong fiber. Jumel tried growing this cotton himself, and was successful in producing cotton of much greater quality than that previously grown in Egypt. Realizing that this new kind of cotton could revolutionize Egypt's cotton industry and generate large profits for the Egyptian government, Muhammad 'Ali financially supported Jumel's cotton research.

The new Jumel cotton was much in demand in Europe. Under Muhammad 'Ali's orders, Egyptian peasants, called *fellahin*, began extensively planting Jumel cotton in the delta of the Nile River. The government monopolized the cotton industry, buying raw cotton directly from the growers and selling it directly to European traders. Muhammad 'Ali also organized irrigation projects, provided credit and seed to the peasants, and brought in additional technicians from Europe. Cotton growing required a lot of labor (as did ginning), but under an authoritarian government the peasants had little choice but to accept the orders to grow cotton; the peasants, however, also realized that they too could profit from growing cotton. Muhammad 'Ali tried importing American Sea Island cotton, which was considered the world's best in quality, but this experiment was not successful, as the American plant did not grow well in Egypt (and actually caused an overall decline in cotton output as new fields were dedicated to it). Eventually, however, Sea Island cotton was successfully crossed with the Jumel variety.

By 1836 cotton accounted for 85 percent of Egypt's revenue generated from agricultural commodities, and cotton industries employed about 4 percent of the population, or about two hundred thousand people, during the 1830s. Muhammad 'Ali also constructed factories in Cairo to gin, spin, and weave cotton, bringing him into conflict with the British, who wanted Egypt to produce only raw cotton and feared that textile

manufacture would compete with their own cotton mills. Muhammad 'Ali attempted to impose an import substitution policy in Egypt, to protect Egyptian industries, to limit the importation of foreign textiles, and to achieve a favorable balance of trade, but after Egypt's unsuccessful military ventures in Syria, he was forced to agree to the Anglo-Ottoman Convention of 1838, which abolished free trade and undermined Egyptian industry. Muhammad 'Ali was successful in Syria until the Great Powers, especially Great Britain and France, decided he was becoming too powerful and set out to clip his wings by intervening militarily. Against the Ottomans he had done very well.

Egypt gradually became incorporated into the greater European economic system as a supplier of raw materials. The cotton boom of 1861 to 1866, during the American Civil War, raised prices and increased production. Cotton cultivation had four major effects on the Egyptian state. First, it changed the nature of agriculture, shifting the focus to export crops and especially cotton. Second, it changed Cairo's relationship with the rest of the country, as the capital became an industrial center and purchaser of cotton, even as governmental decentralization gave the provinces greater political autonomy. Third, it integrated the Egyptian economy into the European one. Fourth, it increased state profits and allowed Egypt to engage in industrialization and modernization. Overall, cotton production helped Egypt assume a greater level of economic independence and control than was typical for colonized states, and helped bring about its current position as a leading Arab country.

COTTON IN THE AMERICAN SOUTH

The development of English cotton mills in the seventeenth century stimulated the demand for raw cotton, and Britain attempted to ensure supplies by encouraging plantations in British colonies. The American South was highly suitable for cotton growing. Up until the invention of the cotton gin in 1793, only the long-staple, or American Sea Island, cotton (*G. barbadense*) was profitable. This cotton could only be grown in the hot and humid coastal areas of the Carolinas and Georgia. The invention of the cotton gin in 1793 allowed the short-staple cotton, *G. hirsutum*, to be easily deseeded and thus cheaply produced. This type of cotton grew well in interior regions of southeastern and western North America, and its increased production soon led to the confiscation of Native American lands and stimulated extensive settlement in such states as Alabama and Mississippi, which became centers of the cotton industry. Because cotton production required cheap labor, African slavery became the basis of the production system. The expansion of the cotton industry increased the demand for slaves.

Egyptian Cotton Ready for Transport on the Nile River. *Large bales of cotton are loaded on a barge at the banks of the Nile River in Egypt in the 1950s.* © HULTON-DEUTSCH COLLECTION/CORBIS. REPRODUCED BY PERMISSION.

Cotton was important in the development of the United States as an industrial power. In New England states such as New Hampshire and Massachusetts, entrepreneurs established their own cotton mills, producing textiles that competed with those of Britain. New England competed with Britain both for the supply of raw cotton and for markets for cotton textiles. New England cotton mills provided employment and, as output increased, European immigration was encouraged to meet the demand for new mill workers. Cotton profits were also used to stimulate other industries, helping the United States to become an industrial country not long after its independence.

Though cotton had an important role in the formation of American industries, it was also a source of conflict. Mills were located in northern states; production in the South was dependent on slave labor. The conflict over slavery in the United States was largely stimulated by cotton and was a major cause of the Civil War (1861–1865), although much cotton was also produced by those not owning slaves. The expansion of cotton production in states of the lower Mississippi Valley also stimulated conflict over the question of whether or not these new states should allow slavery, as did Northern protective tariffs on these states' textile products. During the Civil War the North blockaded Southern ports, so that cotton could not be exported to Britain. This action drove up the worldwide price of cotton, and Egypt was one of the main beneficiaries of an increased price.

After the Civil War, the cotton industry was in a difficult position, as crops had been destroyed by war, the plantation system had broken down, and slavery was abolished. In the 1880s industrial cotton mills began to relocate from New England to Southern states, taking advantage of lower wages. By 1929 over half of the country's cotton mills were in the South. In 1894 the boll weevil, a small insect that attacked cotton plants, devastated much of the Southern cotton industry, contributing to the region's increasing poverty. Cotton production began shifting to Texas and California, which today are the two leading producing states, by 1930, and was dominated increasingly by large agribusinesses, rather than family farms. Cotton's difficulties continued into the 1980s, with the development of new synthetic textiles and the relocation of many mills to Asia. Within the past few decades, however, cotton has experienced a resurgent demand: Prices have risen and production has increased as consumers return to natural fibers.

Cotton was an important crop during the colonial era and remains one today. It is used for such textiles as the denim used in jeans, important in American and global clothing fashions. It helped stimulate economic development in places such as Egypt, whereas in other areas, such as the American South, it retarded economic growth while allowing milling regions such as Britain and New England to prosper. Overall, cotton played a key role in stimulating Western imperial expansion and industrialization.

SEE ALSO *Muhammad Ali.*

BIBLIOGRAPHY

Dodge, Bertha S. *Cotton: The Plant That Would Be King.* Austin: University of Texas Press, 1984.

Fahmy, Khaled. *All the Pasha's Men: Mehmed Ali, His Army, and the Making of Modern Egypt.* Cambridge, U.K.: Cambridge University Press, 1997.

Isaacman, Allen, and Richard L. Roberts, eds. *Cotton, Colonialism, and Social History in Sub-Saharan Africa.* Portsmouth, NH: Heinemann, 1995.

Owen, E. R. J. *Cotton and the Egyptian Economy, 1820–1914.* Oxford: Clarendon, 1969.

Roberts, Richard L. *Two Worlds of Cotton: Colonialism and Regional Economy in the French Soudan, 1800–1946.* Stanford, CA: Stanford University Press, 1996.

Tignor, Robert. *Egyptian Textiles and British Capital, 1930–1956.* Cairo: American University in Cairo Press, 1989.

Yafa, Stephen. *Cotton: How a Humble Fiber Created Fortunes, Wrecked Civilizations, and Put America on the Map.* New York: Viking, 2004.

Michael Pretes

CREOLE NATIONALISM

The concept of Creole nationalism is increasingly employed in studies of nineteenth-century nationalism, most notably with reference to the independence period of Latin American history (1808–1826). The precise genealogy of the concept is unclear. While the term *nationalism* had long been employed, often loosely, to describe the creation of the Latin American republics, Creole nationalism appears to derive from the more familiar Creole patriotism. John Leddy Phelan had linked the "first glimmerings of a Mexican national consciousness" (1960, p. 760) to the late colonial Creole neo-Aztecism, but it fell to D. A. Brading to bring Creole patriotism to the forefront of Latin American historiography in his study of the emergence of Mexican nationalism, whence it found its way into the wider historiography on Latin America.

Brading locates the transformation of Creole *patriotism* into Creole *nationalism* at the Congress of Chilpancingo in 1813, at which the first Mexican Declaration of Independence was framed: "Creole patriotism, which began as the articulation of the social identity of American Spaniards, was here transmuted into the insurgent ideology of Mexican nationalism" (1991, p. 581). However, the concept's widespread presence in studies of European nationalism and of nationalism as a discrete field of study dates from the publication of Benedict Anderson's seminal *Imagined Communities: Reflections on the Origin and Spread of Nationalism* (1983).

To a degree, the emergence of Creole nationalism depended upon the enormous expansion of the public sphere after 1850, above all the increasing availability of newspapers and other printed materials. The spread of literacy was reflected in literary output. Scholars have followed Anderson in focusing on fictional literature as a site for exploring nationalism, though most would locate the beginnings of a mature nationalist sentiment only from the last decades of the nineteenth century; indeed, the best example of a Creole nationalist novel comes not from Latin America but from the Spanish

Philippines—the martyred José Rizal's (1861–1896) *Noli Me Tangere* (Touch Me Not) of 1887.

Anderson's contribution to the study of nationalism generally was to focus attention on American political projects and relate these to debates on the origins and nature of European nationalisms. His thesis had in certain measure been adumbrated in Hugh Seton-Watson's *Nations and States: An Enquiry into the Origins of Nations and the Politics of Nationalism* (1977). Historical and political science writings on nationalism had assumed that it was a European innovation—whether "primordial" or of post-1789 genesis—thereby blithely discounting the possibility that nationalism might have emerged outside of Europe.

Anderson challenged this assumption. As he put it, the "close of the era of successful national liberation movements in the Americas coincided rather closely with the onset of the age of nationalisms in Europe" (1991, p. 67). The qualifier implies that American nationalism was solely a Creole ideology and movement(s), and is commonly used with reference to elite rather than subaltern Creole groups; indigenous, *casta* (mixed-race), and "free black" and slave groups are thus excluded from nationalist projects, whether incipient or consummated. This raises the conundrum of how a valid nationalism can be said to exist when it excludes the vast majority of the putative "nation." Accordingly, historians have sought alternative neologisms to describe a relatively sophisticated, sometimes radical, elite Creole yearning for a greater measure of authority and control in the affairs of each respective viceroyalty—something akin to dominion status appears to be the ruling assumption.

Historian Eric Van Young views the Mexican insurgency of 1810 to 1821 as the "first great war of national liberation" (2001, p. 7)—albeit embracing two wars, anticolonial and internecine—while Alan Knight prefers the rubrics of "proto-patriotism" or "proto-nationalism" to describe the same events, arguing that Creole nationalism "was far from requiring the establishment of a Mexican nation: it sought, rather, a relaxation of metropolitan control, a greater measure of home rule" (2002, p. 284). It is clear that in the well-studied case of Mexico, a great popular insurgency in the countryside, studded with messianic and "naive monarchical" features, was largely independent of alternative political projects by elite Creole groups in Mexico City and other large urban centers.

That the terms *Creole patriotism* and *Creole nationalism* are so often used interchangeably reflects a very real ambivalence on the part of historians both about the inherent vagueness of the concept and its applicability to the foundational histories of the Latin American republics. Some historians interpret the palpable Creole awareness of their distinct identity, and their raft of grievances vis-à-vis American-based peninsular Spaniards, as a Creole *conciencia de sí* (awareness of self) or a maturing "American identity" that was strongly cultural in expression. This seems altogether different from Anderson's formulation of nation as "something capable of being consciously aspired to early on, rather than a slowly sharpening frame of vision," (1991, p. 67) though his definition approximates more to the concept of "amor a la patria y pasión nacional" (love of fatherland and nation and passion for one's nation) developed by the influential Spanish Benedictine Fray Benito Jerónimo Feijoo (1676–1764)—who also defended Creole talents—in his encyclopedic *Teatro Crítico Universal* (Universal Theater of Criticism, 1753–1755).

Certainly, the roots of Creole nationalism lay deep, the product of the three-century-long rivalry between Creoles and peninsulars over the latter's preferential access to jobs in the upper reaches of colonial government and the judiciary; indeed, over their arrogant bearing and dismissive view of the Creoles as feckless and morally and intellectually inferior to peninsular Spaniards (a view that implied that the Americans' very environment rendered them ipso facto decadent and unfit for high office). This pejorative view of Americans was actively countered in the public sphere, with Creole intellectuals mounting a spirited defense not only of the innate personal qualities of Creoles but also of all things American.

These Creole-peninsular tensions were especially marked in Mexico, and it was there that Creole worth found its staunchest defenders, most notably the historian and statesman Carlos María de Bustamante (1774–1848) and Fray Servando Teresa de Mier (1765–1827)—especially against radically anti-Creole Spanish publicists like Juan López de Cancelada. More impartial judges, such as Feijoo and Humboldt, buttressed Creoles' pride in their achievements, although it was Humboldt who also averred that Creole identity was predicated on Spanish foundations, because "the colonies have neither history nor national literature … [and] … have lost their national individuality" (Brading 1991, p. 519). Elsewhere, the writings of the Italian Jesuit Francisco Javier Clavigero (1731–1787) and the abbé Dominique de Pradt (1759–1837) served to combat the disparaging observations of Alexander von Humboldt (1769–1859) Georges-Louis Leclerc Buffon (1707–1788), Guillaume-Thomas Raynal (1713–1796), Corneille de Pauw 1739–1799), and William Robertson (1721–1791), who had all disseminated disdain for Creole achievements, character, and capacities.

North American independence offers a different vision of hemispheric nationalisms. It is clear that the formation of the United States represents a case of nationalism in action, but one that excluded the numerous indigenous and slave populations in a manner similar to the exclusion of indigenous, mixed-race, and African descendants from the process of Mexican independence. If the patriot movement in the thirteen American colonies may be regarded as genuinely nationalist, why then not the "war of national liberation" in Spanish America?

By the same token, if the Spanish War of Independence (the Peninsular War, 1808–1814) from French occupation is conventionally seen as a nationalist endeavor, why not the coeval, Spanish-American wars of independence from Spain itself? The United States exemplifies the way in which an imagined national community could be expansionist. The thirteen colonies at independence approximated the size of Venezuela, but burgeoned as a national bloc with the addition of French Louisiana, California, Arizona, New Mexico, Texas, Alaska, and Hawaii. Creole nationalism carried within it the seeds of expansionism.

Nevertheless, the concept of Creole nationalism contributes little to an understanding of the several transnational political projects of the Latin American independence era. Creole elites were behind both the formation and destruction of the short-lived, failed states of Greater Colombia (1819–1830) and the Central American Republic (1823–1830). Moreover, the political imaginaries of Simón Bolívar (1783–1830) and Francisco de Miranda (1750–1816) embraced a continent (South America), while a project for a New Peruvian Empire that would unite southern Peru and the regions that became Bolivia and Argentina emerged in the course of the failed Cuzco Revolution of 1814 to 1815.

Moreover, Mexican independence eventually came in the form of a short-lived empire (1822–1824), and Brazil remained an independent empire from 1822 until 1889. Indeed, some Creoles had aspirations to a constitutional monarchy, notably those of Miranda and the Argentine "liberator" José de San Martín (1778–1850). Insofar as "Creole nationalism" has any utility as an explanation of national formation in Spanish America, it surely underscores also the weakness of Creole nationalist endeavors and the innate impracticality of alternative Creole political imaginaries.

Within Spanish America, Creole patriotism seems at certain times and places to be robust, elsewhere to be paper-thin, opportunistic, and transitory. Many historians therefore would argue that, at independence, the state preceded the nation and the onset of nation, and nationalism is to be found in the late nineteenth century. Argentine nationalism seemed like an expression of the aspirations of Buenos Aires Province, as with so much of Argentine history. The sense of being Uruguayan or Paraguayan seemed hedged by localism, and nationalistic aspirations were defined more by antipathy to the Creole expansionism of Argentina and Brazil than by dissatisfaction with Spanish rule per se. In Brazil, an emerging Creole patriotism tended also to be subservient to regional identity, thereby precluding much in the way of a widespread identification with nation.

As Anderson puts it, that "well-known doubleness in early Spanish-American nationalism, its alternating grand stretch and particularistic localism" (1991, p. 62), was evident in all Latin American nationalist movements during the Atlantic revolution. Manifestly lacking in most Creole nationalist projects was a sense of social cohesion and inclusiveness, of cross-class and cross-racial horizontal solidarity. Only the failed Cuzco "Revolución de la Patria" of 1814 to 1815 witnessed an alliance that cut across all social categories, a somewhat rickety political bridge between elite and subaltern Creole, caste, and indigenous groups.

In Anderson's view, Creole nationalism provided the missing ingredient in forging an imagined community that allowed colonial subjects to defend themselves against empires and *anciens régimes*. However, in federal or poorly integrated republics or "empires," Creole nationalism was a fragile plant with shallow roots that sprouted unevenly. It flowered for a few decades and, having served its purpose, wilted with the onset of republican rule, which provided more fertile ground for Creole identity and self-interest.

SEE ALSO *Empire in the Americas, Spanish.*

BIBLIOGRAPHY

Anderson, Benedict. *Imagined Communities: Reflections on the Origin and Spread of Nationalism.* London: Verso, 1983; rev. ed., 1991.

Brading, D. A. *The Origins of Mexican Nationalism.* Cambridge, U.K.: Cambridge University Press, 1985.

Brading, D. A. *The First America: The Spanish Monarchy, Creole Patriots, and the Liberal State, 1492–1867.* Cambridge, U.K.: Cambridge University Press, 1991.

Knight, Alan. *Mexico: The Colonial Era.* Cambridge, U.K.: Cambridge University Press, 2002.

Lomnitz-Adler, Claudio. *Deep Mexico, Silent Mexico: An Anthropology of Nationalism.* Minneapolis: University of Minnesota Press, 2001.

Lynch, John. *The Spanish American Revolutions, 1808–1826,* rev. ed. New York: Norton, 1986.

Phelan, John Leddy. "Neo-Aztecism in the Eighteenth Century and the Genesis of Mexican Nationalism." In *Culture in History: Essays in Honor of Paul Radin,* edited by Stanley Diamond, 760–770. New York: Columbia University Press, 1960.

Rodríguez O., Jaime E. *The Independence of Spanish America.* Cambridge, U.K.: Cambridge University Press, 1998.

Seton-Watson, Hugh. *Nations and States: An Enquiry into the Origins of Nations and the Politics of Nationalism.* Boulder, CO: Westview, 1977.

Thurner, Mark. *From Two Republics to One Divided: Contradictions of Postcolonial Nationmaking in Andean Peru.* Durham, NC: Duke University Press, 1997.

Van Young, Eric. *The Other Rebellion: Popular Violence, Ideology, and the Mexican Struggle for Independence, 1810–1821.* Stanford, CA: Stanford University Press, 2001.

David Cahill

CROWN COLONY

A Crown Colony is a British overseas territory under the direct authority of the British Crown. As such, a Crown Colony does not possess its own representative government and is not represented in the British Parliament. The colony is administered by a governor appointed by the Crown and responsible to the colonial office (or its forerunners) and, from 1966 onward, to the Foreign and Commonwealth Office in London. The governor has wide-ranging authority and is assisted either by an appointed advisory council or by both a legislative and an executive council. Council members were usually appointed by the governor. Only at a later stage did Crown Colony government in some colonies rely on elected councils.

Crown colonies should be distinguished from other forms of colonial administration such as company rule (overseas territories administered by a private merchant company, e.g., India until 1858), dominions (self-governing territories, e.g., Canada from 1867, South Africa from 1910, protectorates (territories under the protection of the British Empire, many of which later became Crown Colonies (e.g., Aden, Nigeria, Uganda, Zanzibar), or Crown dependencies such as the Channel Islands or the Isle of Man.

Crown Colony government was devised to put the colonies under closer metropolitan control with little place for local initiative. During the eighteenth century many white settler colonies in North America had made significant advances toward representative government resulting in an increased power of the elected assemblies. After American independence in 1776 this process slowed down and the British tried to limit the power of local elected bodies. The centralized system of Crown Colony government had originally been designed for the colony of Martinique by Lord Hawkesbury (1770–1828) and was quickly introduced to the newly conquered or ceded colonies in the West Indies (Trinidad in 1802, St. Lucia in 1814), Africa (Cape Colony in 1814, Mauritius in 1814), Asia (Ceylon in 1802), and Australia (New South Wales in 1824, Van Diemen's Land in 1825, Western Australia in 1829). Most of these were non-settler colonies with a substantial indigenous population

or convict colonies that—to the central government—seemed unfit for representative government.

During the 1820s and 1830s, Crown Colony government in many of these holdings was reformed and the governor's advisory council was replaced by appointed legislative and executive councils. New South Wales, Van Diemen's Land, Western Australia, Ceylon, Mauritius, Trinidad, and Cape Colony were among the reformed colonies. For London, Crown Colony government proved to be a valuable tool of colonial administration and was applied to most of the newly acquired colonies during the nineteenth century. Until the creation of the Commonwealth of Nations in the Statute of Westminster (1931) only the most important Crown Colonies with a significant white population were granted dominion status. Between 1855 and 1890 the six Australian Crown Colonies became self-governing. The Union of South Africa received dominion status in 1910. Lesser colonies with only a small white population often received self-government relatively later on (e.g., Ceylon in 1948 and Belize in 1964). In 1997 Britain handed back its last remaining Crown Colony, Hong Kong, to China.

SEE ALSO *China, After 1945; China, First Opium War to 1945; China, to the First Opium War; Empire, British, in Asia and Pacific; Hong Kong, from World War II; Hong Kong, to World War II.*

BIBLIOGRAPHY

Anderson, David M., and David Killingray, eds. *Policing the Empire: Government, Authority, and Control, 1830–1940.* Manchester, U.K.; New York: Manchester University Press, 1991.

Burroughs, Peter. "Imperial Institutions and the Government of Empire." In *The Oxford History of the British Empire,* Vol. 3: *The Nineteenth Century,* edited by. Andrew Porter. Oxford, U.K: Oxford University Press, 1999.

Cell, John W. *British Colonial Administration in the Mid-Nineteenth Century; The Policy-Making Process.* New Haven, CT: Yale University Press, 1970.

Steele, Ian K. "The Anointed, the Appointed, and the Elected: Governance of the British Empire, 1689–1784." In *The Oxford History of the British Empire,* Vol. 2: *the Eighteenth Century,* edited by. P. J. Marshall. Oxford, U.K: Oxford University Press, 1998.

Roland Wenzlhuemer

CURZON, GEORGE NATHANIEL
1859–1925

Lord George Nathaniel Curzon was a conservative British statesman whose positions included viceroy of India and foreign secretary. Born into the aristocracy, Curzon became interested in the British territories in Asia during his years at Eton College and became acquainted with the future regent of Persia, Naser ul-Mulk, at Oxford.

After entering the British Parliament in 1886, Curzon traveled extensively in Asia throughout the next decade and expanded his perception of the empire's civilizing role. In 1889 Curzon undertook a 1,600-mile (2,575-kilometer) trek through parts of Persia by horse, after which he wrote a massive book about Persia and his travels. *Persia and the Persian Question* (1892), in its day the authoritative account of Iran during the Qajar period (1797–1925), describes the history, economy, government, geography, and the political situation in Persia at the time, emphasizing Curzon's concerns about Russia's ongoing interests in Qajar affairs. Curzon never returned to Persia, but it remained a pet concern, largely because he perceived Persia as a crucial buffer between Russia and India.

Curzon's first major post was viceroy of India (1899–1905), which was controversial since Indian nationalists perceived many of Curzon's reforms as mechanisms to strengthen imperial control. Curzon resigned from the post in 1905 after experiencing rivalry with Lord Horatio Herbert Kitchener (1850–1916), general of the Indian army.

After serving in the war cabinet during World War I (1914–1918), Curzon became British foreign secretary (1919–1924). The postwar settlements exasperated Curzon, particularly his dealings with Prime Minister David Lloyd George (1863–1945). Anticipating the force of Turkish nationalism, Curzon advised giving the Turks independence in Anatolia, but the prime minister disregarded his counsel. Rather, Turkey was hardly mentioned during the peace conference at Versailles, and the Treaty of Sèvres (1920) carved up most of the Ottoman Empire amongst the Allies, effectively denying Turkish sovereignty.

In 1923 Curzon chaired the Conference of Lausanne, at which Turkey renegotiated the terms of the Treaty of Sèvres. Ismet Inonu (1884–1973), who represented Turkey and was partially deaf, exasperated Curzon throughout the proceedings by continually asking Curzon to repeat himself and by ignoring Curzon's long lectures opposing Turkish demands. Curzon's role in the conference was successful because he was able to secure some major objectives in challenging circumstances for a diplomat; Britain was in no position to resume war, unlike the Turks, who were prepared to fight. Turkey, however, secured a far better arrangement than at Sèvres, as Turkey recovered much territory, gained full sovereignty, and paid no war reparations.

Curzon controlled British interactions with Persia following the war and shaped the Anglo-Persian Agreement of 1919, which was a policy disaster. Curzon had both imperial and paternalistic intentions as he aimed to help Iran's development, secure British influence in Iran, and eliminate Russian interference. However, Iranians perceived it as a means of making Iran a protectorate and rejected the agreement outright, largely because of the secrecy with which it was arranged.

Although Curzon was expected to become the prime minister in 1923, he was denied the position. Historians have tended to treat Curzon harshly, most likely due to his arrogant temperament as a politician and an administrator; however, he also produced impressive accomplishments as a scholar and a mixed record as a diplomat.

SEE ALSO *Empire, British.*

BIBLIOGRAPHY

Bennet, G. H. *British Foreign Policy During the Curzon Period, 1919–1924.* New York: St. Martin's Press, 1995.

Curzon, N. G. *Persia and the Persian Question.* London: Longmans, 1892.

Gilmour, David. *Curzon: Imperial Statesman.* New York : Farrar, Straus, and Giroux, 2003.

Katouzian, Homa. "The Campaign Against the Anglo-Iranian Agreement of 1919." *British Journal of Middle Eastern Studies* 25 (1) (1998): 5–46.

Nicolson, Harold George. *Curzon: The Last Phase, 1919–1925: A Study in Post-war Diplomacy.* London: Constable, 1934.

Wright, Denis. "Curzon and Persia." *The Geographic Journal* 153 (3) (1987): 343–350.

Elizabeth Brownson

D

DAUM, PAULUS ADRIANUS
1850–1898

With the exception of Multatuli (Eduard Douwes Dekker, 1820–1887) with his famous novel *Max Havelaar* (1860), Paulus Adrianus Daum is the most important author of Dutch Indies literature of the nineteenth century. The ten "Indies" novels he wrote between 1883 and 1894 appeared originally as serials in Indies newspapers.

Daum was born in The Hague. He began his journalistic career in his native town in 1876. By then he had already achieved a certain reputation as the author of (extremely romantic) novelettes. In 1878 he was appointed coeditor of the newspaper *De Locomotief* (The Locomotive) in Semarang on Java. Within a year he became its editor-in-chief. It was the start of what was to become a truly remarkable career. After *De Locomotief*, Daum managed the newspapers *Het Indisch Vaderland* (The Indies Fatherland, also published in Semarang, 1883–1885) and the *Bataviaasch Nieuwsblad* (Batavian News, 1885–1898), which under his leadership became the most widely read paper in the Indies.

Daum's appointment as a leader of *De Locomotief* offered him the freedom to display his abilities to the full. The social climate in the Indies was much more informal than in Holland, and the newspapers, too, were considerably livelier than at home. It was therefore in his Indies journalism that Daum was able to develop his stylistic skills.

It was during his first years in the East, too, that Daum became acquainted with the works of the French novelist Émile Zola (1840–1902). Zola's conception of literature brought about a complete reversal of Daum's views on literature. Like Zola, Daum began to regard observation and realistic representation as the primary goal of literature. Nevertheless Daum was also critical of Zola: unlike him, Daum did not consider the "scientific method" essential for the writing of novels. For Daum, the essence of Zola's naturalism lay in realism.

When Daum decided to write a novel himself, he knew exactly what he wanted to create: a novel that would contain an objective picture of a piece of colonial reality. He knew about the realities of the Indies as no other European: apart from the fact that he lived in the colonial society, he was, because of his journalistic observation post, shrewder than others in perceiving what went on in that society. And as a writer who had already won his spurs in journalism, he was well aware of his own ability.

In 1883 Daum published his first novel: *Uit de suiker in de tabak* (From Sugar to Tobacco). Other well-known novels are *Goena-goena* (1989), *Indische mensen in Holland* (Indies People in Holland, 1890), and *Ups en Downs in het Indische leven* (Ups and Downs of Life in the Indies, 1892). Daum's novels are set in the European society of the Indies during the last quarter of the nineteenth century. They describe the lives of planters and civil servants, of Eurasians in their marginal position, and of native Indonesians insofar as they participated in European society—as servants, for example, or as concubines of white masters. But the main subjects are the Europeans, depicted against the background of their expatriate community. Readers are told of their superficial materialism, their ambitions, and their love lives, both inside and outside marriage. Not only the "ups" of life in the Indies are described, but also the "downs"—the murder and suicide, the moral and mental decline, the despair and the loneliness of people disillusioned by the circumstances in which they find themselves.

In mid-1898 Daum's journalistic career abruptly came to an end. Because of a serious illness of the liver, he was forced to leave hurriedly for the Netherlands. It was all in vain. He died in September 1898 and found his resting place in the cemetery in Dieren (near Arnhem). He was just forty-eight years old.

SEE ALSO *Empire, Dutch; Multatuli (Eduard Douwes Dekker).*

BIBLIOGRAPHY

Beekman, E. M. "P. A. Daum (1850–1898): Dutch Colonial Society and the American South." In *Troubled Pleasures: Dutch Colonial Literature from the East Indies, 1600–1950,* 324–391. Oxford: Clarendon, 1996.

Daum, P. A. *Ups and Downs of Life in the Indies.* Translated by Elsje Qualms Sturtevant and Donald W. Sturtevant; edited by E. M. Beekman. Amherst: University of Massachusetts Press, 1987.

Daum, P. A. *Verzamelde romans.* 3 vols. Amsterdam: Nijgh and van Ditmar, 1997–1998.

Termorshuizen, Gerard. *P.A. Daum: Journalist en romancier van tempo doeloe.* Amsterdam: Nijgh and Van Ditmar, 1988.

Gerard Termorshuizen

DECOLONIZATION, EAST ASIA AND PACIFIC

In China the creation of foreign colonies and semi-colonial territories dated from 1557, when Portugal established a settlement at Macau (Aomen) in the Pearl River estuary on the South China Sea. After the Sino-British Opium War of 1839 to 1842, the first of many "unequal treaties" was imposed upon China by the victorious British government, which forced China to cede territory, allow special trade advantages, and accept foreign courts in its major cities. Britain assumed sovereign control over Hong Kong, an undeveloped island off China's southern coast near Canton (Guangzhou). Following this precedent Germany, France, Russia, the United States, and Japan all gained privileges and "extraterritorial" legal concessions in China, creating informal empires based on commercial and legal control. China even formally ceded Macao to tiny Portugal in 1887. Unable to protect itself or its former tributary states, China permitted the colonial powers to seize control of Manchuria, Indochina, and Korea. Except for Macau, all of these territories were occupied by Japan during World War II, and the informal colonial structures were abruptly replaced by Japan's military occupation government.

Japan's surrender in 1945 allowed the Nationalist (Guomindang) government to resume its authority over China. A bitter civil war ensued between the Nationalists and the Chinese Communists, and Britain quickly reoccupied the colony of Hong Kong. When the Communists assumed control of China in 1949, inaugurating a new government, the People's Republic of China (PRC), they insisted that China recover all its traditional territories, including Macau, Hong Kong Island (ceded to Britain in 1842), the nearby Kowloon Peninsula (ceded in 1860), and the adjacent "New Territories," which had been leased to Britain for ninety-nine years under an 1898 agreement. China allowed the colony to remain, but in the 1980s the British government recognized that as expiration of the lease loomed, it could not sustain Hong Kong without the New Territories, which housed the colony's electricity, water, and waste management facilities. Sino-British negotiations resulted in the return of the entire colony to Chinese sovereignty in 1997. Similar Sino-Portuguese talks led to the reversion of Macao to the PRC in 1999.

In August 1945, Japan's defeated colonial administrators in Korea transferred power to the Committee for the Preparation of Korean Independence (CPKI), which was led by the nationalist Yo Un-hyong. Relying in part on the Allies' declaration at the 1943 Cairo Conference that postwar Korea would be independent, Yo called for Korean self-determination. Hundreds of anti-Japanese nationalists imprisoned during the war were released, and within weeks helped to create CPKI cells across the country. New mass-membership organizations composed of students, women, peasants, and industrial workers were also formed. At the July 1945 Potsdam Conference the United States had agreed to allow Soviet forces to occupy Korea, but Japan's sudden surrender provoked a policy change: U.S. forces were dispatched to occupy the southern half of the Korean peninsula. With Soviet and American troops advancing, the CPKI split into distinctly pro- and anti-communist factions and began to realign into northern and southern groups. Separate regimes quickly took shape: Communist North Korea, led by anti-Japanese guerrilla fighter Kim Il-sung and supported by the Soviet Union and the new mass membership organizations, and pro-Western South Korea, led by former exile Syngman Rhee and supported by the United States.

Japan's wartime military government surrendered in August 1945. Its civil structure was reorganized during the ensuing American military occupation, which lasted until 1952. Although Japan was never formally colonized by the United States, it did accept American control over its postwar economic and military development. The United States maintained military bases in Japan and directly administered the island of Okinawa until 1972, when it was formally returned to Japan.

In the Pacific, Germany's far-flung colonial empire had collapsed with its defeat in World War I. Australia and New Zealand assumed control of German territories south of the equator, while Japan appropriated those to the north. After Japan's defeat in 1945, its Pacific possessions either reverted to their pre–World War II European administrators or fell under U.S. military occupation. The American empire in the Pacific had been growing since the 1898 Spanish-American War, after which the victorious United States had seized control of the Philippines, Guam, and American Samoa. Hawaii was also annexed in 1898. After World War II the United States granted full independence to the Philippines, but incorporated Hawaii as a state in 1959, because of its strategic location in the central Pacific. In American Samoa, self-government measures were introduced in 1948, including creation of a legislative body. In 1978 the U.S. House of Representatives accepted a delegate from Samoa, which became an unincorporated territory of the United States. Guam's relationship with the United States paralleled that of American Samoa, although it has no legislative representative in Washington. During the 1980s both Micronesia and the Marshall Islands, which had been occupied by U.S. forces during the war, asserted their independence but entered into "Compacts of Free Association" with the United States: America guaranteed the defense of the islands, and in return secured access to island-based military facilities.

The end of World War II was a watershed for many other Pacific Island territories. Under United Nations auspices, Australia and New Zealand acquired control of Western Samoa, Nauru, the Cook Islands, Niue, Papua, and New Guinea, and oversaw the pace and political design of decolonization in each. Western Samoa was the first to achieve independence, in 1962, after New Zealand supported the early introduction of self-government institutions. The Cook Islands were self-governing by 1965, although they maintained close political ties with Wellington. Australia's charge, Nauru, became independent in 1968, while the new nation of Papua New Guinea, created under Australian supervision, became fully independent in 1975 and joined the British Commonwealth. The latter nation's territory includes the island of Bougainville, where an armed struggle for independence from the government of Papua New Guinea developed during the 1990s.

Britain's Pacific possessions, like those of Australia and New Zealand, experienced accelerated progress toward decolonization during the 1960s. Fiji and Tonga achieved independence in 1970, the Solomon Islands in 1978, and the Gilbert and Ellice Islands (as Tuvalu and Kiribati) in 1978 and 1979. The unique Anglo-French condominium over the New Hebrides, established in 1906, persisted through the decolonization process. New Hebridean nationalists launched protests over colonial control of traditionally common lands, and political discontent spread during the 1960s. France reluctantly agreed to allow formation of a local assembly in 1974, and independence was granted in 1980 to the archipelago, renamed the Republic of Vanuatu, making it the last of Britain's Pacific possessions to be decolonized.

By contrast, Vanuatu was the first French Pacific possession to achieve independence. French Polynesia, a group of islands in the central South Pacific that includes Tahiti, the Austral Islands, and the Marquesas chain, came under French control in the 1840s, and most of the islands were incorporated as a single colony, Oceania, in the 1880s. Maintained by France as an overseas territory throughout the twentieth century, Polynesia has a skeleton territorial government, but most administrative decisions emanate from Paris. Isolated atolls have been used since the early 1960s for French nuclear weapons development and testing. France has been equally unwilling to decolonize New Caledonia and the Loyalty Islands, which were occupied by France in 1853 and formally became a French overseas territory in 1946. Referenda held in 1958 and 1987 demonstrated firm local approval for continuing French rule. Some limited local autonomy has been introduced in New Caledonia, and a 1999 agreement provides for gradual progress toward independence, which is slated for perhaps as early as 2013.

SEE ALSO *Anticolonialism, East Asia and the Pacific; East Asia, American Presence in; East Asia, European Presence in; Empire, British, in Asia and Pacific; Occupations, the Pacific; Pacific, American Presence in; Pacific, European Presence in; Self-Determination, East Asia and the Pacific.*

BIBLIOGRAPHY

Albertini, Rudolph von. *Decolonization: The Administration and Future of the Colonies, 1919–1960.* Translated by Francisca Garvie. Garden City, NY: Doubleday, 1971.

Cumings, Bruce. *The Origins of the Korean War*, Vol. 1: *Liberation and the Emergence of Separate Regimes, 1945–1947.* Princeton, NJ: Princeton University Press, 1981.

Keay, John. *Empire's End: A History of the Far East from High Colonialism to Hong Kong.* New York: Scribner, 1997.

MacClancy, Jeremy. "From New Hebrides to Vanuatu, 1979–1980." *Journal of Pacific History* 16, no. 2 (1981): 92–104.

Morris-Jones, W. H., and Georges Fischer, eds. *Decolonisation and After: The British and French Experience.* London: F. Cass, 1980.

Smith, Gary. *Micronesia: Decolonisation and U.S. Military Interests in the Trust Territories of the Pacific Islands*. Canberra: Peace Research Centre, Australian National University, 1991.

Van Trease, Howard. *The Politics of Land in Vanuatu: From Colony to Independence*. Suva, Fiji: Institute of Pacific Studies, University of the South Pacific, 1977.

Woolford, Don. *Papua New Guinea: Initiation and Independence*. Brisbane, Australia: University of Queensland Press, 1976.

Laura M. Calkins

DECOLONIZATION, SUB-SAHARAN AFRICA

European imperial retreat from sub-Saharan Africa, usually described as decolonization, was one of the most sudden and momentous transformations in the history of the modern world. It occurred in the aftermath of World War II. Although the granting of self-government was not entirely novel prior to the end of the war in 1945, given the independence of Liberia in 1848, South Africa in 1910, and Ethiopia in 1943, the postwar imperial transformation was nevertheless unprecedented. Between 1945 and 1965, almost all European African colonies—except the former Portuguese territories, Angola and Mozambique—regained their independence. So sudden and dramatic was the process leading to decolonization that it has since become known as "the winds of change." Some profound questions have continued to engage scholars since the demise of European colonies in Africa. For instance, to what extent was decolonization consciously planned and directed by imperial powers? Why did European withdrawal from Africa occur when it did—after the end of World War II? How did the various European powers approach the process of devolution of power? It is the purpose of this article to address these questions and to hazard a simplified analysis of this rather puzzling process.

The decolonization process in sub-Saharan Africa was quite complex, and an adequate explanation of the phenomenon must address its causes and course, including its timing, planning, and pace. The speed with which European empire crumbled following the end of World War II, and the manner in which it did so, suggest that the war was a primary cause of decolonization. It produced a chain of events globally to which imperial Europe was susceptible. Though the war was quite pivotal in the demise of European empire, several other factors—including African nationalism, the origins of which preceded World War II—cannot be ignored in any analysis. Thus, even if one may partly concur with John Flint that the decolonization process "began well

before the war started," his conclusion that the dynamic for change lay in London and not in Africa remains far-fetched (1983, pp. 389–394). This position disregards other potent forces for change such as African nationalism, Asian nationalism, U.S.-U.S.S.R. Cold War rivalry, and the United Nations. As Robert Pearce argued, decolonization was marked by "false starts, incompatible expectations, and changes of speed and direction. There was no immediate, no steady, and no straightforward crystallization of colonial policy towards Africa" (1984, p. 77). During World War II, officials of the British government, the supposed planners of the process, were confused about the method, nature, and pace of disengagement from empire; their thoughts and actions were mostly in response to both internal and external pressures.

While some European political leaders such as Oliver Stanley of Britain and Charles de Gaulle of France felt that self-government within the framework of the empire made sense, any notion of full independence belonged to the remote future. Thus, in 1943, Herbert Morrison, the British home secretary, stated, "It would be ignorant, dangerous nonsense to talk about grants of full self-government to many of the dependent territories for some time to come. In those instances it would be like giving a child of ten a latch-key, a bank account, and a shot-gun" (*Manchester Guardian*, January 11, 1943; as cited in Louis 1977, p. 14). Within a rather short period of twenty years, however, almost all European colonies in sub-Saharan Africa became completely independent. Undoubtedly, the aftermath of World War II changed everything; it strengthened African nationalist movements and consolidated global sentiments against colonial rule, thereby forcing imperial powers to begin to think about exit strategies. As Melvin Goldberg puts it, "Only after the war did the powers begin to take decolonization seriously, and even then the speed at which it proceeded was neither anticipated nor welcomed in many quarters" (1986, pp. 666–667). Clearly, control of the rate of change lay elsewhere outside the command of imperial powers; African nationalists and the global mood dictated decolonization's pace and momentum.

With its rhetoric of antiracism, antifascism, political freedom, and self-government, the World War II era marked a turning point during which African agitation for independence not only became more widespread and intense but also could no longer be silenced. The experiences of African servicemen and of those on the home front exposed European hypocrisy regarding racism, imperialism, and European claims to be the bearers of a superior civilization. Allied propaganda against Nazi Germany and the psychological effects of African participation in the war did much to develop mass consciousness of racism, oppression, and unjust colonial rule. The big lesson for Africans was that they fought and suffered to preserve for others the freedom and self-determination they did not have back home. Thus, early in 1945, a Nigerian serviceman wrote from India to the prominent Nigerian nationalist leader Herbert Macaulay: "We, overseas soldiers are coming back home with new ideas. We have been told what we fought for. That is 'freedom.' We want freedom, nothing but freedom" (Davidson 1994, p. 65). Clearly, the war demystified the long-standing claim of European racial superiority, as Africans fought alongside white soldiers and won many battles. Furthermore, African notions of "whites" as superior beings or demigods were shattered by the war. African serviceman, as Ndabaningi Sithole pointed out, "saw the so-called civilized and peaceful and orderly white people mercilessly butchering one another just as his so-called savage ancestors had done in tribal wars. He saw no difference between so-called primitive and so-called civilized man" (1959, p. 47). World War II, therefore, exposed serious contradictions in European colonial rule in Africa and helped to sharpen anticolonial sentiments and strengthen nationalist movements.

The war's social, economic, and political consequences changed the perspectives of Africans and led to heightened anticolonial militancy. As Basil Davidson has observed, the effects of the war "upset rural stability" (1994, p. 63). During the war, economic control by Europeans became more stringent than ever before. Increased production of cash crops was brutally enforced to support the war effort. In both French and British territories, forced (corvée) labor was imposed as exports continued to be hampered by inadequate transportation resulting from fear of enemy submarines. The hardships created by the war were partly responsible for the emergence of several trade (labor) unions across Africa. Increased political awareness created by wartime conditions led unions to employ strategies such as strikes and boycotts after the war. The general strike mounted by Nigerian railway, postal, and other government workers in 1945, which almost paralyzed the colonial regime, was one of the largest and most effective of such actions. The organizational efficiency and the potency of this strike constituted a serious warning sign for imperial Europe. The solidarity of the strikers, as John Hargreaves argued, "showed how wartime hardships had increased class-conscious militancy" (1996, p. 76). Unexpectedly, the strike produced positive results, as a Commission of Enquiry concurred with the workers' demand for a 50 percent cost-of-living raise. Such concessions to workers were unprecedented and nationalists were quick to fathom the larger implications, that organized protests would now elicit positive results.

International factors also hastened the course of decolonization in the postwar years. The anticolonial posture of the new superpowers—the Cold War rivals, the United States and the Soviet Union—spelled doom for European rule in Africa. The United States opposed colonialism because "it was antithetical to free trade and self-determination—both ideals that the United States had lauded in the Atlantic Charter (1941)," and the Soviet Union attacked colonialism because Marxist-Leninist philosophy described it as the "highest stage of capitalism" (Gilbert and Reynolds 2004, p. 324). Secondly, the United States, which emerged as a global power during World War II, suddenly developed an intense economic and geopolitical interest in the British Empire, including its African components. Thus, the superpowers' diplomatic support for decolonization was not necessarily a benevolent gesture aimed at benefiting Africans; indeed, the continent soon became a theater of Cold War superpower conflicts, with dire consequences. Roger Louis and Ronald Robinson argue that as the center of world power shifted from London to Washington (and later to Moscow as well), "the British felt the blow to their economy and their colonial position throughout the world." The shock emanating from this global power shift triggered "the changes of mind on the part of the British that eventually accelerated the transfer of power and the nationalization, or Africanization, of the colonial administration" (1982, p. 31).

Thirdly, the anticolonial posture of the United Nations, formed in 1945 and dedicated to world peace, was a boon to those seeking decolonization. Article 73 of the U.N. charter called on members still possessing colonies to recognize the political aspirations of their colonial subjects, to begin to develop self-government, and to assist colonial subjects in developing free political institutions appropriate to their stage of development. This article represented a moral and political statement that colonialism was no longer acceptable to the international community, and that all European colonies in Africa and Asia had the right to self-determination. In addition, the U.N. provided nationalists with a powerful forum and international moral authority with which to keep the pressure on the imperial powers; it was "a powerful instrument in the long and dangerous process of dismantling colonialism" (Sithole 1968, p. 59). Fourthly, the Atlantic Charter of 1941 adopted by U.S. president Franklin Roosevelt and British prime minister Winston Churchill proved antithetical to colonialism. Article III of the Atlantic Charter, for instance, declared that signatories must "respect the rights of all peoples to choose the form of government under which they will live" (Davidson 1994, p. 66). Although Churchill, de Gaulle, and Roosevelt later quibbled over the meaning of "all peoples," the declaration had serious implications for Afro-Asian nationalists, including Nnamdi Azikiwe of Nigeria, who claimed it should "apply to the colonies in the form of responsible self-government" (Wilson 1994, pp. 54–55). The debate about the import of this declaration ultimately aided the nationalists' cause.

Both Asian nationalism and the successful attainment of postwar independence by former British and French colonies including India, Pakistan, Burma, Vietnam, Cambodia, and Sri Lanka were quite inspirational. The Gold Coast nationalist Kwame Nkrumah even adopted Mahatma Gandhi's anticolonial strategies of positive action and passive resistance. If Africans were inspired by these changes, the colonial powers saw in them a warning that Africa might be susceptible to similar revolts. The importance of even the threat of nationalist resistance in shaping colonial policy or prompting retreat can hardly be ignored. French experiences in Madagascar, Tunisia, Algeria, and Vietnam constituted sufficient lessons that despite their relative weakness, resistance movement present in sub-Saharan Africa by 1948 might pose a serious threat to colonial rule. Arguably, then, it would be a mistake to minimize the contribution of African nationalism to the demise of European rule, even if African nationalism was not as forceful in the 1940s as it was in the late 1950s.

The stages of nationalist mobilization varied from one region to another and from one territory to another. In West Africa, nationalist movements were far more advanced than in East, Central, and Southern Africa. As far back as the late nineteenth century, a class of highly educated Africans had begun to emerge in West Africa among the Creoles of Sierra Leone (descendants of freed slaves and recaptives), which soon dispersed to other parts of the subregion. In Nigeria, the Gold Coast, and Sierra Leone, Africans educated in the languages and political ideas of their colonial masters began to formulate political objectives and new methods of attaining them. However, the mobilization of a critical mass of the African population for the anticolonial struggle required the creation of mass political parties. In West Africa, such mass parties included the National Council of Nigerians and the Cameroons (NCNC) founded in 1944 under the leadership of Nnamdi Azikiwe, the Rassemblement Democratique Africaines founded in Senegal in 1946, the United Gold Coast Convention (UGCC) formed in 1947, and the National Council of Sierra Leone founded in 1950. In East Africa, although the Kenyan African Union (KAU) was formed in 1944, it was not until 1960 that mass parties such as the Kenyan African National Union (KANU) and Kenyan African Democratic Union (KADU) emerged, in the aftermath of the Mau Mau uprising. In Tanzania the first mass party, the Tanganyikan African National Union (TANU), appeared in 1954 under the leadership of

Sékou Touré at the United Nations, October 9, 1962. *Sékou Touré, president of Guinea from 1958 to 1984, addresses the General Assembly of the United Nations in 1962. Touré was an outspoken proponent of decolonization in Africa and objected to the lack of a permanent representative from Africa in the UN Security Council.* © BETTMANN/CORBIS. REPRODUCED BY PERMISSION.

Julius Nyerere, while in Uganda the first grassroots parties emerged between 1952 and 1956. Almost everywhere in Africa, the sudden and full independence of the Gold Coast in 1957 was euphorically received and inspirational; it encouraged the formation and consolidation of mass parties and sharpened the nationalist struggle.

African nationalists were drawn from the ranks of a "modern," educated generation. First trained by mission schools within the continent, most of these elites obtained advanced training overseas in education, medicine, law, journalism, and so on. While they were overseas, many, especially those in the United States, experienced blatant racism and subsequently became intensely influenced by global political concepts of liberation, self-determination, and self-government, as well as the ideas of the Pan-Africanist movement. Upon their return to Africa, they initially sought accommodation within the colonial system only to discover that the system had no place or role for them. When their attempts to bring about reforms were likewise rebuffed, these elites began to articulate demands for self-government. World War II presented them with the opportunity to gain the masses' support for their campaign for an immediate end to colonial rule.

The Pan-Africanist movement, which was founded in 1900 by people of African descent in the diaspora, played an important and unique role in the decolonization process. Initially Pan-Africanism did not focus on a campaign to end colonial rule in Africa; however, Marcus Garvey's slogan of "Africa for Africans," and the cultural reawakening of peoples of African descent articulated by W. E. B. Du Bois and others, became very inspiring for Africans in their struggle against colonialism. The Manchester Congress of the Pan-Africanist movement held in 1945 was particularly decisive in challenging African elites to dedicate themselves to the total liberation of the continent. "All colonies," it was declared, "must be free from all foreign imperialist control whether political or economic.... We say to the peoples of the colonies that they must fight for these ends by all the means at their disposal" (Padmore 1956, pp. 171–172). African delegates to the Congress resolved to return home immediately to achieve the Manchester mandate within the shortest time possible.

By the end of 1945, Britain and France fully recognized the global anti-imperial mood that was developing in the aftermath of the war against Hitler's Germany. Additionally, dependence on their colonies during the war had exposed the need for investment in the colonies' economic and social development. As a result, Britain expanded its Colonial Development and Welfare Act of 1945 to provide more funds for the "welfare" of the colonies, while France established a similar program, Fonds d'Investment pour le Dévelopment Economique et Social (FIDES), in 1946. As it turned out, these developmental initiatives were mainly geared toward ensuring that Africa better served the needs of Europe as an exporter of raw materials and importer of manufactured goods. Nonetheless, the persistent demands of African nationalists resulted in increased government spending on social welfare. In both Britain and France, a postwar leftward shift in public opinion strengthened the position of the Labor and Socialist parties, which had campaigned for an end to old-fashioned imperialism. Imperial officials soon decided that a gentler, kinder colonialism would be necessary to calm the critics of empire at home and around the globe. The result was a rather intensive political and economic reform process. Nevertheless, even as France and Britain proposed a "new deal" for their African colonies, Portugal and Belgium continued with "business as usual" in theirs. Evidently, as lesser powers with fewer colonies and little international influence, they were less subject to the pressure to reform.

Imperial powers confronting the dual costs of repressing nationalism and modernizing colonialism soon realized they had limited options. As they recovered economically in the early 1950s and as African nationalist movements gathered momentum, they began to doubt the benefits of retaining power. Consequently, for French policy makers colonies became "a burden on the most progressive sectors of industry," while British officials concluded that "it mattered little economically whether the colonies were kept or lost" (Iliffe 1995, p. 246). For most European business ventures, the priority was maintaining good relations with whoever held power in Africa—it did not necessarily matter much if those in power were African. Besides, even if it made good business sense to hold on to colonies, nationalist pressures, which were economically and politically disruptive, would most likely sooner or later force imperial Europe toward retreat. Britain's secretary of state for the colonies, Iain Macleod, recognized this, and later commented, "We could not possibly have held by force to our territories in Africa" (Iliffe, p. 246).

Approaches to political reform and devolution of power varied from one European imperial power to another and from one sub-Saharan African region to another. Whereas Britain focused on how to effect a gradual transfer of power to friendly successor states, France (and, later, Portugal) preferred a closer integration with their colonies. Britain took the lead in acknowledging the benefits of peaceful transfer of power. Several factors accounted for this. First, the British proved more prepared than the French to deal with overseas challenges to their rule. Second, Britain's relationship to the United States was different than France's. Third, Britain's political institutions better prepared it to deal with decolonization than did France's. Finally, the character of the nationalist elites in their respective colonies was different. Britain was fortunate that it did not have to deal with Algeria and Indochina. For the British, "a negotiated transfer of power would avoid the need to defend the colonies by force of arms when frustrated nationalist claims for independence led to violent protest" (Birmingham 1995, p. 5). Economically and strategically, therefore, decolonization was beneficial, because economic exploitation—the rationale for colonization—could still be achieved without the financial and other costs of direct political control.

Yet, in the minds of many European officials, full independence still belonged to the remote future, and, ideally, progress in that direction would be very slow. Not surprisingly, only minor actions were taken to prepare Africans for their eventual independence prior to a dramatic turn of events: in 1957, the Gold Coast, regarded as Britain's model colony, blazed a trail by attaining full independence under its charismatic leader, Kwame Nkrumah. Using his newly formed Convention People's Party as a platform, Nkrumah had mobilized the masses and employed Gandhi's tactic of positive action to force Britain to concede power. In Kenya and Zimbabwe, which had sizeable populations of British settlers, the struggle for independence was quite protracted and violent. European settlers' efforts to install white minority regimes were bitterly resisted by Africans, who waged protracted and bloody guerilla warfare. In Portuguese territories, especially Angola and Mozambique, the struggle for independence was also violent, because Portugal never contemplated a retreat from Africa. It was only after a coup in Portugal in 1975, which overthrew the dictatorial regime led by Prime Minister Marcello Caetano, that Portugal decided to decolonize.

In most of the European colonies in sub-Saharan African, the transfer of power was relatively peaceful. The deciding factor was the presence or absence of European settlers. In British West Africa, with no settler colonies, decolonization was more peaceful than in East and Southern Africa, where there were European settler populations. In French territories, the devolution of power was generally peaceful, with the exception of Algeria where a bitter war ensued, largely because of the presence of a large number of French settlers. To preempt similar uprisings in French sub-Saharan Africa, the French president, Charles de Gaulle, hijacked the nationalist momentum by enforcing the referendum of 1958. This gave French colonies the choice of either accepting limited self-government while remaining within the French Community or severing ties with France to become fully independent. All French sub-Saharan territories voted to remain a part of Greater France, with the exception of Sékou Touré's Guinea, which voted in favor of complete independence. Guinea was punished severely for its unexpected choice, as France suddenly and dramatically cut all aid and support. However, the survival of Sékou Touré's proud republic coupled with the euphoria generated by the other colonies' new semi-independent status "quickly began to undermine the legitimacy of de Gaulle's new Community" (Hargreaves 1996, p. 188), and by the end of 1960, all eleven French colonies had claimed full independence.

Belgian imperialism in Africa came to a sudden end in 1960 with Belgium's hasty withdrawal from its sole, if huge, colonial possession, the Congo. According to Hargreaves, the "Belgian public's indifference to Africa was suddenly shaken by the nightmare of an Algerian-type war," and therefore "support for colonial empire evaporated quickly as African hostility, sustained by widespread international sympathy, became seriously apparent" (1996, pp. 193–194). In East and Central Africa, the transfer of power was more or less peaceful, with the exception of Kenya, where the Mau Mau uprising and the subsequent imprisonment of Jomo Kenyatta, who was accused of masterminding the rebellion, delayed

decolonization. However, following Kenyatta's release in 1963 there was a speedy transfer of power, after which Kenyatta became prime minister. In Southern Africa, Zimbabwe presented a difficult case as its white minority resisted African majority rule with the Unilateral Declaration of Independence (UDI) of 1965, which produced a protracted war that lasted until 1980, when African majority rule was achieved with Robert Mugabe as prime minister.

Clearly, the liquidation of European colonies in sub-Saharan Africa was one of the most dramatic processes of the mid-twentieth century. Even those at the center stage of imperial policy making in Europe found themselves helpless to shape the outcome. At first glance, decolonization seems consciously planned and executed, but at second look, it appears to possess a life of its own. No one was sure of what turns and twists it would take. De Gaulle confidently planned a system of limited self-government for French colonies, but Sékou Touré's Guinea surprised him by voting for full independence. Similarly, Britain was stunned by events in the Gold Coast, where a sudden and bold step toward full independence was least expected. Although the impact of World War II was crucial to the crystallization of decolonization, it would be quite misleading to ignore other related but equally significant international forces. Different powers followed different paths to decolonization, just as different African regions had different experiences shaped by a range of variables. In all cases, however, European powers were concerned with maintaining some links to their colonies even after the end of formal empire. In this concern lies the origins of the neocolonialism that has continued to define the Euro-African relationship in the postcolonial era.

SEE ALSO *Anticolonial Movements, Africa; Nationalism, Africa; Pan-Africanism; Sub-Saharan Africa, European Presence in.*

BIBLIOGRAPHY

Birmingham, David. *The Decolonization of Africa*. Athens: Ohio University Press, 1995.

Collins, Robert O., ed. *Problems in the History of Modern Africa*. Princeton, NJ: Markus Wiener, 1997.

Crook, Richard C. "Decolonization, the Colonial State, and Chieftaincy in the Gold Coast." *African Affairs* 85, no. 338 (1986): 75–106.

Davidson, Basil. *Modern Africa: A Social and Political History*. 3rd ed. London: Longman, 1994.

Flint, John. "Planned Decolonization and Its Failure in British Africa." *African Affairs* 82, no. 328 (1983): 389–411.

Fyle, C. Magbaily. *Introduction to the History of African Civilization*. Lanham, MD: University Press of America, 2001.

Gilbert, Erik, and Jonathan T. Reynolds. *Africa in World History: From Prehistory to the Present.* Upper Saddle River, NJ: Prentice Hall, 2004.

Goldberg, Melvin. "Decolonization and Political Socialization with Reference to West Africa." *Journal of Modern African Studies* 24, no. 4 (1986): 663–677.

Hargreaves, John D. *Decolonization in Africa.* 2nd ed. London: Longman, 1996.

Iliffe, John. *Africans: The History of a Continent.* Cambridge, U.K.: Cambridge University Press, 1995.

Louis, Wm. Roger, *Imperialism at Bay: The United States and the Decolonization of the British Empire, 1941–1945.* London: Oxford University Press, 1977.

Louis, Wm. Roger, and Ronald Robinson. "The United States and the Liquidation of British Empire in Tropical Africa, 1941–1951." In *The Transfer of Power in Africa: Decolonization, 1940–1960,* edited by Prosser Gifford and Wm. Roger Louis, 31–55. New Haven, CT: Yale University Press, 1982.

Padmore, George. *Pan-Africanism or Communism? The Coming Struggle for Africa.* New York: D. Dobson, 1956.

Pearce, Robert D. *The Turning Point in Africa: British Colonial Policy, 1938–48.* London: Frank Cass, 1982.

Pearce, Robert. "The Colonial Office and Planned Decolonization in Africa." *African Affairs* 83, no. 330 (1984): 77–93.

Ranger, T. O. "Connexions between 'Primary Resistance' Movements and Modern Mass Nationalism in East and Central Africa." *Journal of African History* 9, no. 3 (1968): 437–453.

Sithole, Ndabaningi. *African Nationalism.* 2nd ed. London: Oxford University Press, 1968.

Strachey, John. *The End of Empire.* London: Gollancz, 1959.

Wilson, H. S. *African Decolonization.* London: E. Arnold, 1994.

Apollos Nwauwa

DEE, JOHN
1527–1608

John Dee was an English geographer, mathematician, scientist, antiquarian scholar, and political advisor. Of Welsh ancestry, he was born in London in 1527 and was educated at St. John's College of Cambridge University, and at the University of Louvain in what is today Belgium. One of the leading scientists of his time, Dee was also a promoter of English colonial expansion and might be considered the intellectual father of the British Empire. A true Renaissance man, he was active in many fields of scholarship, including geography, mathematics, philosophy, alchemy, and astrology.

Dee had a long association with Queen Elizabeth I (1533–1603) of England, even casting the horoscope to determine the most auspicious date for her coronation in 1558. He was also a friend and associate of most of the leading figures of Elizabethan England, including such explorers as Sir Martin Frobisher (ca. 1535–1594), John Davis (1543–1605), Sir Walter Raleigh (ca. 1554–1618), Sir Francis Drake (ca. 1543–1596), and Sir Humphrey Gilbert (ca. 1539–1583), who agreed to grant Dee most of Canada if his voyage were successful, which it was not. Dee advised each of these men on their expeditions, often providing navigational information. He also advised on expeditions to find a Northeast Passage to China and was instrumental in the formation of the Muscovy Company, which opened up trade with Russia.

Dee traveled extensively on the continent of Europe and was a friend and colleague of the leading geographers and cartographers of the time, including Gerardus Mercator (1512–1594), Gemma Frisius (1508–1555), Abraham Ortelius (1527–1598), Orontius Finaeus (1494–1555), and Pedro Nuñez (1492–1577). His contacts with these scholars allowed him to assemble the largest library in England, larger even than those at Oxford and Cambridge universities. Dee was also able to invent and introduce many technical innovations, such as particular globes, compasses, and navigational charts, to English explorers, although he was unsuccessful in his attempt to introduce the Gregorian calendar into England. Later in his life, Dee also served as an advisor, mainly on alchemical topics, to the king of Poland and to Holy Roman Emperor Rudolf II (1552–1612).

Much of Dee's geographical writing was concerned with English imperial expansion. In 1570 he presented a map with accompanying text to Queen Elizabeth, outlining arguments for her title to lands in the North Atlantic and in America. He also drew up plans for the colonizing of North America. His most important geographical work, titled *General and Rare Memorials Pertayning to the Perfect Arte of Navigation,* was published in 1577. This book suggested the immediate establishment of a "Petty Navy Royal," or coast guard, to protect England's shores, as well as expansion of the "Grand Navy Royal." Dee urged England to become a maritime power and establish a "British Empire" (Dee's own phrase) that would rival Spain's and would give England commercial advantages, such as markets for its woolens.

Dee unfortunately fell out of favor after the death of Elizabeth in 1603, and he died in obscurity in 1608. Today he is often remembered for his alchemical and astrological work, though appreciation of him as a leading geographer is increasing.

SEE ALSO *Empire, British; European Explorations in North America.*

Blaise Diagne in Paris, 1922. *West African and French dignitaries place flowers on the tomb of the unknown soldier in Paris. The Senegalese statesman Blaise Diagne stands at the center with hat in hand.* **ROGER VIOLLET/GETTY IMAGES. REPRODUCED BY PERMISSION.**

BIBLIOGRAPHY

Clulee, Nicholas H. *John Dee's Natural Philosophy: Between Science and Religion.* London and New York: Routledge, 1988.

French, Peter J. *John Dee: The World of an Elizabethan Magus.* London: Routledge and Kegan Paul, 1972.

Suster, Gerald, ed. *John Dee: Essential Readings.* Berkeley, CA: North Atlantic Books, 2003.

Taylor, E. G. R. *Tudor Geography, 1485–1583.* London: Methuen, 1930.

Michael Pretes

DIAGNE, BLAISE
1872–1934

The first black African elected to the French Chamber of Deputies, Blaise Diagne transformed Senegalese politics and helped prepare the way for development of democracy in Senegal.

The Four Communes of Senegal (Saint-Louis, Dakar, Rufisque, and Gorée) had from the 1870s the right to elect a municipal council, a General Council, and a deputy to the French Parliament. Senegal was the only colony north of South Africa where ordinary Africans had the right to vote. These elections were contested largely by French commercial houses and a mulatto elite, called the *métis*, but in the first years of the twentieth century, educated Africans, organized in a group called the Young Senegalese, wanted a more important role in government.

Blaise Diagne was born on the island of Gorée, the son of a Sereer cook, but he was adopted by a member of a leading métis family and sent to a Catholic school. After secondary studies, he passed the exam for the French colonial customs service. Within the service, he was frequently transferred because of his reputation for insubordination and for encouraging local people to oppose the colonial regime.

By 1913 Diagne was dissatisfied with the constraints of the civil service and decided to contest the election for deputy from Senegal. He was not well known, but he was able to win support from different groups, of whom the most important were the Young Senegalese and the Lebu, the original inhabitants of Dakar. Diagne campaigned against the disenfranchisement of black voters and for compensation of the Lebu for their lost lands. He won a hotly contested election. The governor-general, William Ponty (1866–1915), was under pressure to annul the election, but he refused to do so.

Three months after the election, World War I broke out. This put Diagne in a strategic position because France was less populous than Germany and counted on Africa to supply some of the soldiers it needed to hold the line. Diagne used the issue to resolve problems that troubled those who voted for him. First, in 1915, he won approval of a law that allowed *originaires*, the resident of the Four Communes to serve in the better-paid regular army rather than with the colonial troops. The second problem was that it was not clear that African *originaires* were French citizens. Muslim *originaires*, the majority of the electorate, were the only voters in the French Empire who preserved Muslim personal law in matters like marriage and inheritance, rather than being subject to the Code Napoléon. In 1916 Diagne persuaded the Chamber of Deputies to pass a law recognizing *originaires* as French citizens.

After the war, Diagne organized the Republican Socialist Party. In 1919 he was reelected and his party won control of all municipal councils and the General Council. Unfortunately for Diagne, there was a sharp swing to the right in French elections, which meant less influence for Diagne in Paris. The General Council was restructured to include many appointed chiefs, who voted with the government. In 1923 Diagne forged an alliance with his former enemies, the commercial houses based in Bordeaux. He remained a deputy until his death in 1934.

SEE ALSO *Empire, French.*

BIBLIOGRAPHY

Johnson, G. Wesley. *The Emergence of Black Politics in Senegal: The Struggle for Power in the Four Communes, 1900–1920.* Stanford, CA: Stanford University Press, 1971.

Martin Klein

DIAMONDS

Diamonds are crystallized carbon compounds that are formed under extreme pressure and high temperatures deep in the earth's crust. Diamond-bearing stones are excavated by drilling holes on the side of pipes (vertical columns of rock) formed by volcanic activity in the earth crust. Africa is the richest source of diamonds, accounting for nearly half of the world's production. The major deposits are in South Africa and Botswana, with substantial deposits in the Congo Republic (Zaire), Angola, Namibia, Ghana, Central African Republic, Guinea, Sierra Leone, and Zimbabwe.

About 269,000 carats of diamonds were produced in South Africa in the 1870s, rising to approximately 505 million carats in 1906. By the early twenty-first century, South Africa was producing eight to ten million carats per year. Botswana is the world's leading producer of gem-quality diamonds, with over 30.4 million carats produced in 2003. In the Congo, diamond production jumped from 988,000 carats in 1961 to 4.6 million carats in 2003.

DISCOVERY OF DIAMONDS

In 1867 a pretty pebble found near the Orange River in South Africa was confirmed as a 21-carat diamond. Placer diamonds (stream-deposited) were found between the Vaal and Orange Rivers later in the year. Two years later an 83-carat diamond was found. The discovery of diamonds in Kimberley in 1871 showed that South Africa and other parts of Africa would be the source of an enormous quantity of high-quality diamonds. Four pipes of primary diamonds (those in which the diamonds remain inside the original host rock) were discovered at the town of Kimberley.

South Africa emerged as a major source of gem-quality diamonds and the world's leading producer in the mid-twentieth century. The diamond industry became a chief source of export earnings and the key to the economic transformation of South Africa. But the discovery of diamonds also exacerbated the colonization of the region, increased the rate of African disposition of land, and led to the political domination of black South Africans.

The British government, attracted by the prospect of mineral wealth, quickly annexed the diamond fields, repudiating the claims of the Voortrekker republics to the area. These claims, along with contestations for economic and political control of diamonds and later gold in South Africa, defined the contours of southern African colonial history. The discovery of diamonds also had a larger global implication when it led to a "diamond rush" that attracted thousands of fortune hunters from Europe, the United States, and Australia. The first rush for diamonds was followed by a gold rush to South Africa a few years later. The town of Kimberly was filled with settlers, but it was surpassed by Johannesburg when gold mining started in earnest in 1887.

Nineteenth-Century Diamond Miners in South Africa. *Laborers stand amid machinery for washing diamonds at the Bultfontein Diamond Mine near Kimberley, South Africa, in 1888.* **HULTON ARCHIVE/GETTY IMAGES. REPRODUCED BY PERMISSION.**

CONSOLIDATION, CONTROL, AND TECHNOLOGY

The development of the South African diamond industry was the work of Cecil Rhodes (1853–1902), who arrived in South Africa from England in 1870 at the age of seventeen, and founded the De Beers mining company in Kimberley in 1888. As a large number of prospectors staked out claims to various fields, two key players—Cecil Rhodes and Barney Barnato (1852–1896)—became the most successful.

Barnato arrived in South Africa from England in 1873 at the age of twenty. In 1876 he bought four claims in the Kimberley mines. He made a huge profit and later formed the Barnato Diamond Mining Company, which he merged with the Kimberley Central Mining Company in 1883. Rhodes fought intensely against competing mining interests, and by the end of 1889 he had bought off other diamond claims and was in control of the South African diamond industry in Kimberley.

After expansion of his holdings, Rhodes went on to form De Beers Consolidated Mines, which established an effective monopoly over the diamond industry in

1889. In competition, Rhodes sold one of his companies to Barnato's Kimberley Central, but Rhodes retained interests that gave him a 20 percent share in Barnato's company. Rhodes and Barnato battled viciously for the remaining stock. In 1889 Barnato sold out to Rhodes for £5,338,650. In 1896 Barnato disappeared at sea while on passage back to England, a presumed suicide. The diamond monopoly created by De Beers helped to regulate the quantity of diamonds produced in order to maintain high profits.

The discovery of new deposits near Pretoria and in South-West Africa (Namibia) in 1908 broke the De Beer monopoly. By 1909, German-controlled South-West Africa was producing about 500,000 carats of small but high-quality diamonds, and yields increased rapidly in five years. South Africa gained control of Namibia after World War I and sold the diamond deposits to Consolidated Diamond Mines, founded in 1919 by German immigrant Ernest Oppenheimer (1880–1957), who became the leader in the field. In 1929 Oppenheimer became president of the De Beers group and united both companies in a cartel. The activities of De Beers would extend to Botswana, soon to be an important producer with the discovery of three kimberlite (groups of diamond bearing rocks) deposits between 1967 and 1973.

Two important factors—legislation and technology—cemented the control of the diamond industry by the cartel. The efforts of mine owners to make a profit and eliminate pilfering in the early days led to attempts to undercut the bargaining strength of African workers. In 1872 British colonial officials were persuaded to introduce *pass laws*, which required that all "servants" be in possession of passes that stated whether the holder was legally entitled to work in the city, whether or not they had completed their contractual obligations, and whether they could leave the city. These laws, written in "color-blind" language but enforced against blacks only, limited the mobility of migrant workers, restricted their flexibility in seeking alternative employment, and limited their ability to bargain for higher wages.

De Beers and other large prospectors made a considerable effort to exclude smaller prospectors, including Africans. A special court was set up in 1880 to try cases of illicit dealings in diamonds, which was limited to licensed buyers and imposed penalties for the possession of uncut stones without a license. The Diamond Trade Act of 1872 was aimed at diamond stealing and smuggling, but it also set two dangerous social precedents. First, anyone found with an uncut diamond was required to explain how it came into his or her possession—that is, guilt was assumed, while innocence had to be proved. This is a European concept not usually found in English or American law. Second, the Diamond Trade Act allowed companies to set up "searching-houses" in a system of routine surveillance, searching, and stripping by company police. This curtailment of private rights and personal liberty became a fact of South African society.

The condition of the mines was an important factor in the consolidation of operations in a few hands. In 1872 the pipes were giant open quarries worked by 2,500 miners and 10,000 hired laborers. The technical equipment required for deep mining of diamonds excluded many companies and individuals from competition and forced many to sell off their concessions. The high cost of equipment also excluded prospective prospectors. For example, by 1875 the Kimberley mines were 58 meters (190 feet) deep, and miners were hauling material out of the hole on aerial ropeways that covered the pit like spiderwebs. Soon the hauling was driven by machinery on the edge of the pit, and in 1875 the first steam engine was installed. The cost of clearing away debris increased as the mines deepened, and slowly steam engines became necessary rather than optional. The rock became harder with depth, and by the end of the 1870s, the costs of mining had became too great

for one-man operations. The number of claim owners in the Kimberley pit dropped dramatically as people bought out their neighbors, and by 1880 new investment was pouring in. Rhodes and seven partners owned a block of ninety claims in the De Beers Mining Company Ltd., named for its landholdings on the old De Beers ranch.

DIAMONDS AND COLONIZATION

Rhodes played an immeasurable role in the colonization of southern Africa. His ambition was to extend the British imperial possession from Cape to Cairo. When Rhodes became prime minister of the Cape Colony, he dedicated his energy to the colonization of Rhodesia on behalf of the British. Rhodes, who had succeeded in monopolizing the diamond industry, sought to carve out a personal empire in present-day Zimbabwe, the original site of the fifteenth-century gold industry of Great Zimbabwe. There he ruled the Ndebele and the Shona people through his British South Africa Company.

Thus, southern Africa's history is intertwined with the mineral revolution. From this period, the region became a magnet for European investment, prospectors, and other immigrants from America and Australia. The European rush for minerals in the late nineteenth century helped shape the colonization of most of southern Africa.

The mines were a means of political, social, and economic control. The Kimberly mines attracted Africans in the early 1870s. Some sought to obtain diamond claims, but most sought jobs in the mines. An average of fifty thousand men migrated annually to the mines for a period of two to three months. Most returned home with cash and guns purchased in Kimberley. African access to guns in particular redefined African-European relations and prolonged the series of wars with restive African groups that sought to check white expansion into the interior of southern Africa.

Mining companies traditionally kept expenses to a minimum through low wages, strict control of African labor, and manipulation of the political system. Rhodes was a successful politician, and he helped draft laws that protected the mining companies. Taxation on mining profits was kept low. Segregated, controlled, fenced-off compounds housed Africans for the length of their work contracts with the company. The segregation policies that began in the mine compounds were the harbingers of the official apartheid policy that was consolidated in 1948 when the National Party won national elections.

From the late nineteenth century, Africans did not accept mining regulations and political control uncritically. African-initiated churches and African-centered political organization that emerged from the nineteenth century became the main organs of protest in a white-dominated colonial setting. The link between property ownership and suffrage guaranteed Cape blacks some level of participation in the electoral politics of the 1870s and the 1880s. The formation of the Native Educational Association in the eastern Cape in 1879 promoted "the improvement and elevation of the native races." The Imbumba Yama Nyama (literally, "hard, solid sinew"), formed in Port Elizabeth in 1882, fought for African rights. Black newspapers such as *Imvo Zabantsundu* (Native Opinion), founded by John Tengo Jabavu (1859–1921) in 1884, became a platform for expressing dissatisfaction with the injustice and inequality that blacks experienced in relation to whites in a rapidly industrializing society dominated by diamond and gold mining.

The role of diamonds in structuring African political conflicts and formations has extended beyond the colonial period. But some of the contemporary conflicts, as in Angola, have their origin in the colonial setting. In more recent times, the control of diamonds has been instrumental in fueling civil wars and crises in Liberia, Sierra Leone, the Congo, and Angola. The so-called conflict diamonds and international trade in illegal diamonds prompted the United Nations General Assembly to adopt a resolution in 2000 on the role of diamonds in fuelling conflict in Africa. The objective is to break the link between armed conflict and the illicit transaction of rough diamonds, especially in Sierra Leone and Angola, where conflict diamonds are used to fund rebel groups.

SEE ALSO *Empire, British; Germany's African Colonies; Rhodes, Cecil.*

BIBLIOGRAPHY

American Museum of Natural History. "The Nature of Diamonds." Available at http://www.amnh.org/exhibitions/diamonds/index.html.

Campbell, Greg. *Blood Diamonds: Tracing the Deadly Path of the World's Most Precious Stones.* Boulder, CO: Westview, 2004.

Duncan, Innes. *Anglo: Anglo American and the Rise of Modern South Africa.* Johannesburg, South Africa: Raven Press, 1984.

Godehard, Lenzen. *The History of Diamond Production and the Diamond Trade.* Translated by F. Bradley. London: Barrie & Jenkins, 1970.

Newbury, Colin. *The Diamond Ring: Business, Politics, and Precious Stones in South Africa, 1867–1946.* Oxford: Clarendon, 1989.

Chima J. Korieh

DINSHAWAY INCIDENT

The Dinshaway incident was a violent clash that occurred in June 1906 between Egyptian peasants in the village of Dinshaway and British soldiers who were pigeon hunting in the area. The British had occupied Egypt in 1882 at the request of the Ottoman viceroy, who used British soldiers to help to put down the Urabi Rebellion, an Egyptian constitutionalist movement. By 1906, inflation, financial corruption, and obvious contrasts between the living standards of the British and those of most native Egyptians combined to create resentment of the occupation.

On June 13, 1906, five British officers were hunting pigeons in Dinshaway, a village in the province of Minufiya in the Nile Delta. Egyptian peasants raised pigeons for eggs and considered the meat a delicacy that made men virile, so they did not approve of the British hunting the birds. For this reason, hunters had to get permission from the village headman. The five officers were granted permission by the headman and were provided with transportation. The headman, however, was not in the village upon their arrival.

The soldiers commenced hunting and, shortly thereafter, a village threshing floor caught fire. Angry peasants armed with nabouts, heavy wooden sticks tipped with lead, surrounded the officers, claiming their shots had started the fire. The officers later stated that they had willingly surrendered their weapons, but that one of the rifles had accidentally discharged twice. Curiously, the officers also claimed that these two shots were responsible for the injuries to four villagers, including the wife of the local imam. This enraged the villagers who then attacked the officers as they were trying to leave, taking the contents of their pockets and beating them with nabouts and bricks.

The beatings severely injured three officers: one had a broken arm, another a broken nose, and the other a head injury. One of the injured men attempted to run back to his camp for help, which was five miles away, but eventually collapsed. A medical exam later revealed that he had suffered a concussion during the fighting, which, in combination with sunstroke, killed him. Troops later discovered a peasant dead nearby from a blow to the head, along with another villager who had been shot in an unrelated incident. British officials believed the attack was premeditated and that the officers had been lured into a trap.

Shortly thereafter, the British had fifty-two villagers arrested for "crimes of violence against the officers and men of the army of occupation" (Parliamentary Papers 1906, pp. 1–2). Evelyn Baring (1841–1917), the first Lord Cromer and British Consul for Egypt, was in England at the time, but ordered that the villagers be tried according to an 1895 decree mandating special treatment for those who attacked British military personnel. Such crimes were to be considered by a special tribunal composed of both Egyptian and British officials that could administer swift justice and penalties of greater severity than were permitted by the Egyptian criminal code. Cromer intended the Dinshaway trial to serve as a warning to those who plotted violence against the British.

The trial was held June 27, 1906. The daughter of the villagers' attorney, Ahmed Lutfi al-Sayyid, claims that the fifty-two accused were questioned in thirty minutes by a tribunal of five men, only two of whom spoke sufficient Arabic to understand the defendants. All on the tribunal, it should be noted, knew Arabic. The officers identified twenty-one villagers as their attackers. The court was unanimous in judging these villagers guilty of premeditated murder and violent robbery. It sentenced four men to hang, nine to prison, five to public flogging, and three others to both prison and flogging. Some 500 Egyptians from the province, including the village inhabitants, watched the hangings and whippings carried out the next day.

The severity of the punishment was perhaps due to inflammatory rhetoric against the occupation in the Egyptian press that year, which had British officials anticipating resistance. Many Egyptians were intensely shocked by what they saw. The author Qasim Amin (1863–1908) reported a national sense of humiliated depression, writing that every Egyptian face evinced a "peculiar sort of sadness." He said of this sadness: "It was confused, distracted, and visibly subdued by superior force. . . . The spirits of the hanged men seemed to hover over every place in the city" (Ahmed 1960, p. 63).

Egyptian intellectuals seized upon this incident as an example of imperialist oppression. Arabic presses spread word of the trial and agony of the villagers, whom they characterized as martyrs of the occupation, and printed songs and poems of resistance. One song, reported by Afaf Lutfi al-Sayyid, said: "They fell upon Dinshwai, and spared neither man nor his brother. Slowly they hanged the one and flogged the other" (1969, p. 173). Jamal Ahmed found similar sentiments expressed in poetry: "Man's life is as cheap as a beast's, and like to wild doves are we . . . we too have chains around our necks" (1960, p. 63). Intellectuals' arguments against the occupation now found a receptive audience among the peasants, and rural violence against British soldiers increased. The incident became legendary; it came to represent, for many, the true spirit of the British occupiers, and generated widespread support for the resistance movement.

Another effect of the Dinshaway incident was a worsening in relations between Christians and Muslims. The head of the special tribunal and acting Minister of Justice was Butrus Ghali—a Coptic Christian. He was assassinated in 1911.

The British House of Commons censured Cromer for his handling of the incident. Cromer's response was a lukewarm defense of flogging, which he had previously worked to eliminate, as occasionally necessary for maintaining public order. The deputy who had been in charge during Cromer's absence, Mansfeld Findlay, wrote that Egyptians, being fatalists, did not fear death, nor did imprisonment have an effect on them; thus flogging was appropriate. Many officials involved later decided that the punishment had not fit the crime. Ultimately the uproar contributed to Cromer's resignation in 1907. His successor, Sir John Eldon Gorst (1835–1916), had the imprisoned villagers released in 1910, but the British continued to rule Egypt formally until 1922.

SEE ALSO *Baring, Evelyn.*

BIBLIOGRAPHY

Ahmed, Jamal Mohammed. *The Intellectual Origins of Egyptian Nationalism.* London, New York: Oxford University Press, 1960.

Lutfi al-Sayyid, Afaf. *Egypt and Cromer: A Study in Anglo-Egyptian Relations.* New York: Frederick A. Praeger, 1969.

Owen, Roger. "Things Fall Apart." In *Lord Cromer: Victorian Imperialist, Edwardian Proconsul.* New York: Oxford University Press, 2004.

Parliamentary Papers, Egypt no. 3. "Correspondence respecting the attack on the British officers at Denshawai." London: Harrison and Sons, 1906.

Indira Falk Gesink

DIVIDE AND RULE: THE LEGACY OF ROMAN IMPERIALISM

The ancient Romans cast a long shadow over the peoples of Europe. Even the vocabulary of modern European expansion is Roman: The words *imperialism, empire, colonialism, colony, proconsul, procurator* all come from Rome. In addition, Roman approaches towards acquisition and administration of conquered territory and individuals provided the foundation, the blueprint, for later European expansion and rule. This was true not just for the Latin-based cultures, such as France and Spain, where Roman institutions and traditions occasionally survived intact, but also for nations of Germanic ancestry, such as Britain, Holland, and Germany, where the Roman legacy was less direct but still intentional.

The study of the Romans, their literature, and institutions was an integral element in the education of the ruling classes of all European nations, from primary to university levels. This curricular focus was due in large part to the Roman Catholic Church (and its Protestant successors), which had preserved the works of master Latin stylists like Marcus Tullius Cicero (106–43 BCE), Julius Caesar (ca. 100–44 BCE), Cornelius Tacitus (ca. 55–ca. 120 CE), and Livy (Titus Livius, 59 BCE–17 CE) as teaching tools and examples of "proper" Latin. Although the focus of study was the language itself, the student could not help but absorb the detailed information offered about the experiences and institutions of the Romans. Therefore, it was because of the church's dedication to preserve "things Roman," and its universities' emphasis on the literature of antiquity, that Roman examples were well known to the educated ruling classes of any would-be imperialist nation.

Almost instinctively, it seems, the ruling elites of Europe turned to the Roman models, drummed into their heads from youth, when they began to acquire lands and subjects beyond Europe. And because of the narrow focus on a few "great" authors, these Roman models came largely from the Republican period of Roman history (509–31 BCE), especially from the Late Republic (133–31 BCE), which saw the mature articulation of Roman imperialism. During the entire Republic, but most actively during the Late Republic, Rome was at its most expansive, first overwhelming the tribes and cities of Italy and then, by 31 BCE, dominating the entire Mediterranean basin.

DIVIDE AND RULE

The Romans were unique among ancient peoples in that they willingly and freely incorporated newly conquered people into their own society, freely giving citizenship to outsiders in order to Romanize them and make them willing participants (instead of unwilling subjects or enemies) in the Roman imperial system. Romans preferred government on the cheap and as such chose to administer new lands and peoples indirectly, through indigenous collaborators, who were awarded Roman citizenship or other benefits. The Romans called this system *divide and rule* because they literally divided up conquered peoples into their component units (usually tribes and city-states), made separate alliances and treaties with each, and induced each, through a complex system of rewards, to keep an eye on the others and provide for the common defense.

All of this the later Europeans would inherit and modify, though perhaps the purest examples of the unaltered Roman system are best seen in British and French India. Although the Romans used this system, with slight modification, from their inception to destruction, the best and classic example is the Roman consolidation of the Italian peninsula south of the Rubicon and Arno rivers, described by the Late Republican historian Livy.

From its earliest days, Rome was surrounded by many powerful, independent city-states and tribes that were intent on Rome's destruction. In the rich alluvial plain of Latium alone, Rome lived among at least twelve independent Latin-speaking nations. To Rome's north was the ancient, wealthy, and highly civilized Etruscan confederation. To the south, around the Bay of Naples and beyond, were the large Greek cities of Cumae, Neapolis (modern Naples), and Posidonia. Thanks to its position on both the last available crossing of the Tiber River near the sea and the great salt trade route, Rome became a natural contact point for all of these cultures. And because of its location, and the rich trade in salt and other commodities it encouraged, Rome was coveted by all its neighbors.

To ensure its independence, Rome first needed to establish a buffer zone. The Romans did this by conquering their closest Latin neighbors, but instead of destroying them or levying taxes, as the Etruscans and Greeks did, Rome granted those closest in proximity full Roman citizenship—now these Latins would be Romans—and in return all Rome asked of its new citizen-allies was that they contribute troops to the common defense.

Of course, with these new allies, Rome inherited new enemies—that is, Rome inherited its new allies' ancestral enemies. But with a larger army Rome was able to launch many "defensive" campaigns, ostensibly to protect its new citizens, but really for the purpose of subduing the Latin nations farther away from Rome, right to the edge of Greek- and Etruscan-controlled areas.

To these newly conquered people Rome did not offer citizenship, as it had to their closer Latin brothers, but rather alliance and confederation. These allies of what the Romans would come to call *Latin-rights* status would contribute troops to the common defense, in return for which Rome would grant some of the perks of citizenship: (1) the right to do business at Rome; (2) the right to appeal the actions of Roman officials in Roman courts; and (3) the right to marry Roman citizens, the children of which unions would then be legal Roman citizens.

But the genius of this system was that Rome made a separate alliance with each Latin-rights city it conquered (the *divide* element of the equation), and each city would be offered a slightly different perk. As a result, each Latin-rights city had a separate relationship with Rome but was barred from having alliances or treaties with anyone else, including other Latin-rights peoples. Rome effectively held all of the cards, and since each city received different perks, those who espoused the Roman cause most vocally, or reported potential rebellion among the neighbors, gained the most perks.

To ensure and encourage mutual suspicion, Rome dangled the carrot of further perks, even full Roman citizenship, for those who supported Rome best, contributed the best troops, and above all kept an eye on the neighbors and alerted Rome of any disloyalty or rebellion. This was a highly competitive system and as a result, each city was intensely suspicious and jealous of the others, and thus policed the neighbors on Rome's behalf (the *rule* element).

Thus, Rome gained a group of loyal, mutually suspicious states that the Romans did not have to control by force, that would act as a buffer zone in case of invasion, and that would serve as an army for common defense and imperialist expansion. And expand Rome did, but never offensively; Rome only responded "defensively" when its friends were attacked. As had happened with the first Latin conquests, Rome continued to inherit enemies. Because of the alliance system, once Rome conquered a city-state, kingdom, or tribe, it inherited the enemies of that city-state, kingdom, or tribe. Rome thus expanded defensively into Italy, granting unequal alliances with each new ally, offering full Roman citizenship to those who had proved their loyalty, and the different perks associated with Latin rights to others—even though they were not ethnically Latin—depending on their loyalty and strategic value. *Latin rights* had become an administrative term for the Romans, and once Rome had expanded beyond Latium and the Latins, the term had come to apply to all inferior alliances in which some of the Latin perks were granted.

Rome did not rely solely on its conquered enemies to rule. In some cases, since the city of Rome itself began to grow dramatically, the Romans took land from particularly dangerous conquered people and settled colonies of Roman urban poor on it. Most often these Roman colonies were located in strategic areas. Their purpose was to control and stimulate trade, to guard against rebellion, and to protect resources and infrastructure such as roads, passes, and mines. These *coloniae* (literally, "cared-for regions") were places of opportunity, where upward mobility was possible, where people could start anew and reinvent themselves. As such, the *coloniae* were immensely popular among the masses in the city of Rome. In time, Rome eventually planted such colonies all over the Mediterranean basin, western Europe, and North Africa. These prosperous, military-economic outposts of Rome were the direct models for modern European colonies.

This system of dividing up the enemy into component units, making unequal alliances, and offering unequal perks was used quite effectively by all modern European imperialists: The British and French used the divide-and-rule system in North America, in India, in Africa, and the in Far East; the Dutch in Africa and Southeast Asia; and the Spanish in South and Central America. This Roman system of government on the cheap—using groups of the conquered, who have been selectively rewarded, to rule on behalf of the overlords—is often termed *indirect rule* by historians of modern imperialism. Indeed, many of the ethnic conflicts that plague postcolonial nations to this day have their roots in the selective rewards associated with indirect rule—the Turkish-Greek conflict over the island of Cyprus being just one of the most visible and intractable. In this case, the British empowered the Turkish minority to control the Greek majority, and the Greeks still resent it.

CLIENTAGE

So far this entry has addressed indirect rule on the national level, but the Romans employed this method even more effectively on the individual level with what they called *clientela,* or "clientage." It is clientage, even more than the group system of divide and rule, that later Europeans would use to great advantage.

The system of clientage was as old as Rome and originally applied only to Romans. Clientage bound one Roman to another through unequal ties of obligation. The Romans called the two participants the *patron* and the *client.* The patron was to care for the client—that is, the patron ensured the client had employment, food, shelter, and legal representation. In return, the client gave the patron public respect and service in the form of work or goods, and, above all, was legally bound to vote as the patron decreed.

The bonds of clientage were permanent, passed down through the generations—one had the same clients and patrons as one's father. The only way to break the bonds of clientage was to prove, in court, that the other member of the relationships had not fulfilled his obligations. Since Romans preferred personal relationships to official ones, and private, face-to-face systems to government-sponsored ones, clientage was encouraged by the ruling elite—who were, of course, Rome's patrons. The clientage system thus served as the social glue of Rome. Best of all, the system of clientage cost the Roman government nothing, but ensured that everybody had a place in Roman society, and that everybody was connected to his fellow citizens through mutual obligations.

When Rome began to expand beyond its city limits, it incorporated the newly conquered into this existing social network. Powerful Romans, especially the generals who brought new territories and peoples under Rome's protection, formed clientage relationships with these non-Romans. For example, the family of Marcus Claudius

(Claudii Marcelli, ca. 268–208 BCE) provided the general who conquered Sicily in the middle of the third century BCE, and two hundred years later, by the time of Cicero, the ruling elite of that island were still Claudian clients. In return for Roman support, Roman protection, and a local share in Roman commerce, these clients ensured their region's loyalty to Rome and paved the way for the commercial enterprises of their patron and his friends—essentially, these clients acted as Roman watchdogs. Modern parallels from every continent abound in which later Europeans, officially and unofficially, would form similar bonds of dependency with members of indigenous groups.

As Rome began to expand into the eastern edge of the Mediterranean, where kings rather than independent city-states ruled, the Roman elite included these powerful men among the lists of their clients. In fact, even before Rome had conquered an area and brought it into the Roman imperial system, the ruling elite in the Romans Senate—the body that controlled all Roman foreign policy—bound "client-kings" to Rome and used these kings to control areas of interest.

Perhaps the most famous of these client-kings was Herod the Great, king of Judea (73–4 BCE). Officially, Herod was independent from Rome and held the status of "friend and ally of the Senate and people of Rome." But he was far from autonomous as client to some of the most powerful Romans of the day—Mark Antony (ca. 83–30 BCE) and the first Roman emperor, Augustus (63 BCE–14 CE). As a loyal client, Herod had to act as his patrons wished if he was to retain their support. And Herod needed Roman support. He was a usurper to the Jewish throne, as well as a foreigner, and the Jews hated him. Only Roman support kept him on the throne, and that was the way the ruling elite in the Roman Senate wanted things.

By keeping a dependent and disliked Herod on the Jewish throne, Rome did not have to expend precious resources to conquer and administer Judea. Again and again Rome would use this inexpensive, effective method to dominate regions the Romans did not need to control directly. Yet, as the Romans discovered in the eastern Mediterranean and North Africa, and the British and French discovered in India and elsewhere, client-kings often have agendas of their own—they often intrigue secretly against their patrons, and they require a great deal of effort to put down once they turn rogue.

PSEUDOGOVERNMENTAL CORPORATIONS

Once Rome moved beyond Italy, the Romans became much more guarded in their grants of citizenship. The system of divide and rule still applied but now the Romans added a new dimension: The perks for the conquered began with tax exemption rather than citizenship. Once

Rome moved beyond Italy, it no longer rewarded former enemies quite so generously. Because of the costs incurred with overseas expansion, Rome could not afford to allow its overseas subjects to go untaxed.

Yet Rome wanted to preserve that mutual suspicion that had controlled Italy so well. The solution was selective taxation. Rome would reward especially loyal or strategic allies with tax-exempt status. This tax exemption, or partial tax forgiveness, was always held out as a reward for special clients or whole communities. Over time, many individual clients, cities, and tribes passed through tax exemption and "Latin rights" to full citizenship. By 212 CE, all areas under Roman control were given full Roman citizenship by Emperor Caracalla (188–217 CE). But as a result of this system of selective taxation, the Roman tax code was bewilderingly complex, and the Roman government, always hesitant to increase the bureaucracy, required a cost-effective, nongovernmental way to collect revenue.

In order to maximize profits and cut costs, the Romans used private corporations to collect all manner of taxes, from personal income taxes to port dues to pasture taxes. These "tax-farming" companies, as the Romans called them, would submit bids for the amount they could collect for a given region over a time period set by the government, ranging from one to ten years. The highest bidder won. Once chosen, the winning corporation would then pay the Roman government the entire sum up front—what amounted to at least one year's worth of all taxes for all inhabitants. Then, for the amount of time agreed upon in the contract, the corporation would be given government permission to collect both the original outlay and any greater amounts desired to cover expenses. Everybody won: Rome got money when it needed it without having to expend precious public resources, the tax-collecting company made a profit, and the provincials got taxed, sometimes overtaxed, although rarely dramatically and harmfully overtaxed. After all, the tax-farmers were aware of how much the taxed could pay, and they wanted to ensure that taxpayers remained healthy and taxable in the future.

In addition to tax-farming, these large corporation would also engage in other, related financial activities, such as moneylending, banking, and commodities speculation. Unfortunately, as Cicero's speeches against the Sicilian governor Gaius Verres (ca. 115–43 BCE) and private letters to his friends make clear, the tax-farmers often lent money to individuals at exorbitant rates (48 percent per annum and higher) so that the borrowers could pay taxes to those same tax-farmers. But it was not always easy to collect, and so the tax-farming corporations were permitted by the Roman government to maintain paramilitary forces in order to "shake down" local taxpayers.

The powers and authority of the tax-farmers were wide-ranging, especially in regions such as Sicily, Sardinia, and North Africa where the head tax was paid in the form of grain and other agricultural goods. Here, the tax companies would essentially control the agricultural economy. Because of their oversight of all taxes, even harbor dues and import-export fees, the tax corporations controlled trade, both in and out of the region. Cicero's speeches against Verres make clear that the tax-farmers of Sicily ran both the economy and politics of Sicily.

Because the Roman government wanted revenues without bureaucracy, and local Roman governors like Verres wanted money in the form of bribes and company shares, the tax-farming companies were allowed to grow into pseudogovernmental entities that for a short time during the Late Republic acted as if they were the Roman state. From 133 to 44 BCE, the independent, private tax companies collected taxes, lent money, fielded troops, and controlled the economies of Roman possessions outside of Italy. All of these pseudogovernmental powers were replicated by the great, modern colonial corporations—the French, Dutch, and British East India companies. The works of Cicero, especially his speeches against Gaius Verres, were perennial favorites in public school curricula. It is surely no accident that the great companies associated with European imperialism resembled their Roman predecessors so closely.

SEE ALSO *Empire, British; Empire, French; Imperialism, Cultural.*

BIBLIOGRAPHY

Badian, E. *Foreign Clientelae (264–70 B.C.).* Oxford, U.K: Clarendon Press, 1958. Corrected reprint, 1984.

Badian, E. *Publicans and Sinners: Private Enterprise in the Service of the Roman Republic.* Ithaca, NY, and London: Cornell University Press, 1972. Reprint, 1983.

Balsdon, J. P. V. D. *Romans and Aliens.* Chapel Hill: University of North Carolina Press, 1979.

Boatwright, Mary T., Daniel J. Gargola, and Richard J. A. Talbert. *The Romans: From Village to Empire.* Oxford, U.K., and New York: Oxford University Press, 2004.

Cicero, Marcus Tullius. *Selected Works: Against Verres, I, Twenty-Three Letters, the Second Philippic Against Antony, On Duties, III, On Old Age.* Translated by Michael Grant. Hammondsworth, U.K., and Baltimore, MD: Penguin, 1960.

Cicero, Marcus Tullius. *Selected Political Speeches of Cicero.* Translated by Michael Grant. Hammondsworth, U.K., and Baltimore, MD: Penguin, 1969.

Cicero, Marcus Tullius. *Murder Trials.* Translated by Michael Grant. Hammondsworth, U.K., and Baltimore, MD: Penguin, 1975.

Cicero, Marcus Tullius. *Selected Letters, Cicero.* Translated by D. R. Shackleton Bailey. Cambridge, U.K., and New York: Cambridge University Press, 1980.

Jones, Peter, and Keith Sidwell, eds. *The World of Rome: An Introduction to Roman Culture.* Cambridge, U.K., and New York: Cambridge University Press, 1997.

Laurence, Ray, and Joanne Berry, eds. *Cultural Identity in the Roman Empire.* London and New York: Routledge, 1998.

Livy, Titus. *The War with Hannibal: Books XXI–XXX of the History of Rome From its Foundation.* Translated by Betty Radice and Aubrey de Sélincourt. Hammondsworth, U.K., and Baltimore, MD: Penguin, 1965.

Livy, Titus. *Rome and the Mediterranean: Books XXXI–XLV of the History of Rome From its Foundation.* Translated by Henry Bettenson. Hammondsworth, U.K., and Baltimore, MD: Penguin, 1976.

Livy, Titus. *Rome and Italy: Books VI–X of the History of Rome From its Foundation.* Translated by Betty Radice. Hammondsworth, U.K., and Baltimore, MD: Penguin, 1982.

Livy, Titus. *The Early History of Rome: Books I–V of the History of Rome From its Foundation.* Translated by Aubrey de Sélincourt. London and New York: Penguin, 2002.

Lupher, David A. *Romans in a New World: Classical Models in Sixteenth-Century Spanish America.* Ann Arbor: University of Michigan Press, 2003.

Plutarch. *Fall of the Roman Republic: Six Lives—Marius, Sulla, Crassus, Pompey, Caesar, and Cicero.* Translated by Rex Warner. Hammondsworth, U.K., and Baltimore, MD: Penguin, 1958.

Richardson, John. *Roman Provincial Administration, 227 BC to AD 117.* Basingstoke, U.K.: Macmillan, 1976.

Sherk, Robert K., ed. and trans. *Rome and the Greek East to the Death of Augustus* (Translated documents of Greece and Rome). Cambridge, U.K., and New York: Cambridge University Press, 1984.

Sherwin-White, A. N. *The Roman Citizenship,* 2nd ed. Oxford: Clarendon Press, 1973.

Verboven, Koenraad. *The Economy of Friends: Economic Aspects of Amicitia and Patronage in the Late Republic.* Brussels: Editions Latomus, 2002.

Timothy Howe

DRAKE, SIR FRANCIS
1540–1596

Sir Francis Drake was among the more daring and famous of all the great Elizabethan seafarers. Born into a prosperous family in Devonshire, England, around 1540, Drake's life as a sailor stemmed from his family connections with William Hawkins, a Plymouth merchant who had experience of piracy against the French and Spanish, and who put Drake to sea together with his own sons. By the early 1560s Drake had joined his cousin, John Hawkins (1532–1595), to undertake slaving voyages to Africa and then to the Americas. In 1568 he was part of an English fleet that was virtually destroyed by the Spanish in the Caribbean and his anger at what he perceived to be Spanish treachery initiated a life-long struggle with Spanish interests. However, there is no evidence that Drake was driven by religious zeal, even though his father was a cleric; hope of enrichment by trade and piracy were always the main motives for Drake's activities. As an experienced seaman Drake was given a privateer's license by Queen Elizabeth (1533–1603) to plunder Spanish treasure ships returning to Europe from the Caribbean. He quickly gained a reputation as the scourge of the Spanish and Portuguese by attacking their vessels and ports as he saw fit. Between 1572 and 1573 Drake traversed Spanish Panama from the Atlantic to the Pacific Ocean with the help of local runaway slaves (*cimarrons*) who guided and supported his expedition out of resentment toward the Spanish. Drake subsequently captured the Spanish silver train at Nombre de Dios in March 1573 and returned to England with a ship full of treasure.

Drake's most famous exploit was his circumnavigation of the globe between 1577 and 1580. Initially traveling with five ships, only one, the *Pelican*, was left as Drake entered the Pacific Ocean in October 1578. Rather than heading west into the Pacific, Drake sailed north up the coast of South America attacking Spanish settlements in Peru and capturing treasure ships, eventually reaching as far north as California (or "Nova Albion" as he named it). Only now did Drake head west, eventually reaching the East Indies where he loaded up with valuable spices. His return to England in 1580, with a wealth of treasure and spices on board the renamed *Golden Hind*, caused a sensation and earned Drake a knighthood. Drake continued to hamper Spanish ambitions in the Atlantic throughout the 1580s. In 1585 he burned down the town of Santiago in the Cape Verde Islands, and a year later captured San Domingo in Hispaniola. On his way back from the Caribbean in 1586 he stopped at Roanoke Island, the new English colony in North Carolina, but instead of finding a prosperous settlement he ended up taking the half-starved settlers back to England. In 1587 he "singed the King of Spain's beard" with a daring attack at Cadiz, and played a crucial part in the defeat of the Spanish Armada in 1588, including capturing the Spanish flagship Rosario. He remained active in the Atlantic until his death from dysentery off the coast of Panama in 1596.

Drake's exploits significantly raised the profile of the English in the Atlantic basin, demonstrating to the Spanish that their monopoly could be broken and to the English that both financial and imperial gains were possible in the Americas. The contribution his voyages made to the English treasury ultimately helped to finance Elizabethan imperial expansion.

SEE ALSO *Dee, John; Empire, British; European Explorations in North America.*

BIBLIOGRAPHY

Kelsey, Harry. *Sir Francis Drake, the Queen's Pirate*. New Haven, CT: Yale University Press, 2000.

Wilson, Derek. *The World Encompassed: Drake's Great Voyage, 1577–80*. London: Hamilton, 1977.

Tim Lockley

DUAL MANDATE, AFRICA

The dual mandate is an expression of the fundamental principles of European imperialism in tropical Africa as theorized by Sir Frederick Lugard (1858–1945), the best known of the British colonial officers to serve in Africa. In his most important work on British imperialism, *The Dual Mandate in British Tropical Africa* (1922), Lugard craftily articulated the basis for European imperial design in Africa and the dynamics of the colonial administrative system of indirect rule.

In Lugard's discourse, European imperialism rested on the premise that the resources of Africa, perceived dormant, could be productively marshaled and utilized by the more technologically advanced imperial nations of Europe for the mutual benefits of the colonizer and the colonized. Lugard argued that Africa's enormous resources lay wasted not only because Africans did not recognize their uses and value, but also because they did not possess the know-how to develop and exploit them. Lugard's thesis ascribed to imperial Europe a fundamental right to Africa's "wasted bounties of nature," and also the responsibility of holding them in trust and developing them for the benefit of humankind. As custodian of Africa's resources, however, imperial Europe was committed to Africa's development and the advancement and welfare of its people. Britain as a colonizing power thus had a dual mandate: first, the exploitation of Africa's resources for imperial benefit; and second, the development of the continent.

Lugard's indirect rule became an instrument of British imperial administration in Africa. It was a concept in which existing African traditional political institutions were preserved and incorporated into the colonial administrative system for local governance. Under this system, local administrative powers resided in the native authority made up of traditional rulers or chiefs with jurisdiction over a native treasury and native courts. Lugard believed that, at the grassroots, traditional authority would constitute an effective instrument in enforcing colonial policies, administrating justice in local disputes, maintaining law and order, and collecting taxes. The efficacy of indirect rule thus necessarily rested on the existence of powerful chiefs capable of exercising political authority over their jurisdictions.

As theorized by Lugard, the native authority retained, as much as possible, its traditional powers and character. However, in practice the British turned the chiefs into agents of the colonial administration. These chiefs would lose their political autonomy and become subordinated to the authority of colonial administrative agents such as the resident or the district officer. Ostensibly, the colonial official was a sympathetic adviser and a counselor to the chiefs; in reality, though, the official would dictate colonial policies and regulations to the chiefs. The chiefs were expected to transmit these received instructions to the indigenous people and see to their implementation. Colonial policies thus reached the people through their own chiefs firsthand, giving the impression of a native rule. Colonial taxation was, for instance, in the eyes of the local taxpayer the chief's initiative. Such arrangement in which imperial orders were disguised as those of the chiefs ensured quick compliance by the people. Also, indirect rule, by utilizing the traditional elite who exercised local authority directly over the people, minimized contacts between British colonial officials and Africans, which greatly reduced friction between the two groups.

Indirect rule as a principle of colonial local government became the standard policy in most of British Africa. It was adopted by colonial officials in a number of British possessions such as Sierra Leone, the Gold Coast, and Uganda. It was in Northern Nigeria, however, that the system had its most profound expression. Following the subjugation of the Hausa-Fulani in 1903, Lugard introduced the system among the people. In practice, it proved workable largely because the existing hierarchical political order in Northern Nigeria fit perfectly with the demands of the system.

Following the Fulani jihad of 1804, the hitherto individualistic and competing Hausa states became united under a strong centralized theocratic state known as the Sokoto Caliphate. The administration of the caliphate came under the central authority of the caliph and a number of emirs who headed sub-units of the state, the emirates. The emirs were highly autocratic. In local governance, they utilized an effective system of taxation and a judicial system based on Islamic law, the Sharia. Under indirect rule, the emir's allegiance shifted from the caliph to the colonial commissioner. In Northern Nigeria, therefore, Lugard found the necessary centralized political structure and pre-exiting taxation and court systems critical for indirect rule to work.

The limitations of indirect rule were demonstrated in Southern Nigeria where Lugard extended the system after the amalgamation of northern and southern protectorates in 1914. As governor-general of a unified Nigeria, Lugard hoped that the system would work in the southern provinces. In the southwest among the Yoruba, it encountered some problems and was less successful. Although, the Yoruba possessed a centralized political system, it was less autocratic than the Sokoto Caliphate. Theoretically powerful, Yoruba traditional rulers, the *obas*, were restrained by a complex system of checks and balances. Thus, they lacked the authoritarianism of the northern emirs. Lugard aggravated many groups in Yorubaland when he ignored tradition and arbitrarily elevated the status of some rulers. The attempts of rulers to forcibly collect imposed colonial taxes bred discontentment in some parts of Yorubaland. Indirect rule was thus less successful here.

In the southeast, indirect rule proved utterly unworkable among the Igbo and other groups. Unlike northern and southwestern Nigeria, the provinces in the southeast did not possess the centralized political system required for indirect rule to work. The Igbo, for instance, lived in fragmented societies and did not develop a monarchical political institution. In the place of missing authoritarian rulers, Lugard simply manufactured his own chiefs and equipped them with political authority to rule over a people unfamiliar to a system of kingship. The created rulers, the so-called "warrant chiefs," lacked legitimacy and their attempts to exercise political authority in Igboland gave rise to deep resentment against them. In Igboland, indirect rule without legitimately constituted authority was a total failure.

SEE ALSO *Britain's African Colonies; Colonial Cities and Towns, Africa; Indirect Rule, Africa.*

BIBLIOGRAPHY

Afigbo, A. E. *The Warrant Chiefs: Indirect Rule in Southeastern Nigeria, 1891–1929.* London: Longman, 1972.

Hailey, William Malcolm. *Native Administration and Political Development in British Tropical Africa.* Nendeln, Liechtenstein: Kraus Reprint, 1979.

Ikime, Obaro and Segun Osoba, eds. *Indirect Rule in British Africa.* London: Longman, 1970.

Lugard, Frederick D. *The Dual Mandate in British Tropical Africa.* London: Blackwood and Sons, 1922.

Perham, Margery Freda. *Native Administration in Nigeria.* London: Oxford University Press, 1937.

Adebayo Oyebade

DUTCH-INDONESIAN WARS

By the spring of 1947 serious concern existed among the Dutch and the Netherlands East Indies administration over whether the Indonesian government would fully implement the Linggajati agreement of March 1947, which had ceded authority over parts of Indonesia to a Republican government—but with the understanding that Dutch commercial interests would not be harmed, and that the Republic would remain part of a loose federation under Dutch control. Black marketeering thrived, particularly the Republican rubber trade with Singapore. Anti-Dutch resistance movements were in charge of commercial crop plantations in Sumatra and Java, the prime foreign currency source. These loosely organized groups had their own agendas, often conflicting with policies of the central Republican government. As far as the Dutch were concerned, the Republic had shown itself to be incapable of controlling these resistance movements. The Dutch minister of finance expressed his fears about the deteriorating foreign currency situation of the colony, predicting bankruptcy. For the Dutch, taking quick and firm control over the plantations was considered imperative for financial and economic survival.

The Dutch planters lobby suggested military intervention, a plan welcomed by the commander of the Dutch army in the Netherlands East Indies, General H. Spoor, who predicted a military success. Other considerations also pointed toward a military option. A large number of Dutch troops (around 100,000 men) had been built up in Indonesia since 1946 without ever being deployed, as the Dutch government and army staff had found it politically difficult to decommission them. Apart from the opposition of the Dutch Communist Party, parliamentary consensus existed in the Netherlands about the necessity for military action against the Republic. A point of no return had been reached.

The Dutch ultimatum to the Republican government—which called on it to stop hostilities, to respect foreign property, and to lift a food boycott in Dutch-controlled areas—expired on July 16, 1947. On July 21, 1947, a military assault was launched under the code name *Product*, a designation indicating the assault's main objective of securing the commercial plantations and stocks (rubber, coffee, tea, etc.) on Java and Sumatra. For external political consumption the military assault was labeled a *police action*, a misleading term suggesting restricted violence and a limited scope of operation. Operations were conducted on land and from the sea, with an emphasis on East Java. Dutch marines were assigned an important role in securing economic objectives, such as plantations, and made responsible for what was generally labeled "cleansing" the area of "rebel elements." The irregular resistance movements and the still weakly organized Indonesian armed forces were taken by surprise. Armed resistance was low, and Indonesian army units were geographically dispersed or literally decimated. Seventy-six Dutch soldiers died in action, while Indonesian casualties are believed to have been much higher, though figures are impossible to verify. After the First Police Action (as the Dutch assault has come to be called), 70 percent of total rubber plantation acreage in Java and around 60 percent in Sumatra came under Dutch military control.

This military intervention created a backlash in various ways, however. While the Dutch army staff claimed military success, events soon proved them wrong. Within weeks large parts of Java's countryside were again considered unsafe for colonial administrators and those supporting them. Indonesian armed resistance actually heightened in the aftermath of the operation. The First Police Action forced the Indonesian armed forces into what proved to be a successful military strategy: guerrilla warfare.

Faith in a Dutch solution among politically moderate Indonesians broke down after the First Police Action. Leading Indonesians who had formerly supported the creation of a federal state now flocked to the Republican side, eroding further Dutch-backed political initiatives. Ten days after the launching of the operation, India and Australia called for a meeting of the United Nations Security Council to stop the Dutch violence.

Between April and June of 1948 the United Nations again urged the Dutch government to negotiate with the Republic to halt violations of the ceasefire truce by both sides, and to settle disputes over plantations and commercial crop stocks in custody of Republican and irregular resistance movements. A stalemate resulted, paving the way for a second Dutch military intervention, known as the *Second Police Action*, which was launched on December 19, 1948, and lasted until January 15, 1949.

The main objective of this military operation was to liquidate the Republic. The Republican leaders were arrested, and the city of Yogyakarta, the geographic heart and the symbol of the Republic, was occupied by Dutch troops. The number of plantations under Dutch military control was increased, particularly in Central and East Java. Dutch military observers estimated the number of Indonesian soldiers killed at 4,389, but this might be a low guess. Around 100 Dutch soldiers died. The number of civilian casualties and refugees, particularly among the Indonesian rural population, remains unknown altogether—not to mention the material damage inflicted by both armies to towns and villages in rural Java and Sumatra. Despite the apparent Dutch military success, Indonesian political and armed resistance proved by no means broken. Belying General Spoor's assertion that the elimination of the central government in Yogyakarta would leave the Indonesian army without direction, individual units remained operational. The Indonesians were prepared this time and were able to strike back successfully on occasion, applying scorched-earth tactics. Plantations, oil fields, and vital infrastructure such as roads and bridges were destroyed. Complete Dutch control over plantations in East Java was never achieved. The Second Police Action further boomeranged on another level. Due to the limited effectiveness of both police actions, Dutch planters began to lose faith in the Dutch East Indies federal government and in the Dutch army, coming instead to believe that business had to be conducted with the Republic to safeguard their interests.

Like the First Police Action, the Second Police Action became an international political issue. The U.N. Security Council demanded the release of the Republican leaders and restoration of their government. As a reward for the Republic's anticommunist position—the Indonesian government had crushed a communist uprising in Central Java in September 1948—the United States government threatened to halt its financial aid to the Dutch government, aid intended to rehabilitate the war-devastated economy of homeland and colony.

Obsessed with achieving economic recovery after World War II, yet politically paralyzed, the Dutch government gambled on a military solution in Indonesia. Yet both police actions proved counterproductive to its political objectives. The Dutch army staff underestimated the resilience of the Indonesian armed and unarmed independence movement. Violence stimulated, rather than halted, armed resistance and spurred guerrilla warfare. The two operations evoked protests from several countries in the U.N. Security Council. By the time of the Second Police Action the Dutch Government found its interests overtaken by the U.S. government's Cold War concerns. The international political tide had turned in favor of the Republic, and the Dutch hold over the colony was in collapse. The Dutch government had no other choice but to resume negotiations with the Republican government. As a result, the Van Rooijen-Rum agreement of May 1949 blocked the possibility of a third police action and paved the way for the transfer of sovereignty.

In the decades that followed Indonesian independence several Dutch veterans published their memoirs, yet overall little discussion occurred in the Netherlands about the police actions in particular or about Indonesia's decolonization in general. Considered a deeply traumatic experience, Indonesia's decolonization was a taboo subject. In the late 1960s a few Dutch military veterans testified to having witnessed or committed war crimes in Indonesia, but they were voices crying in the wilderness.

Some believe that the issue was swept under the carpet. More recently, with the "colonial generation" gradually dying out, and with memories of the colonial experience fading, sufficient "distance" has been achieved to reopen the discussion of Indonesia's decolonization. Dutch academic and nonacademic interest in the colonial period in general, and in the police actions in particular, gained momentum in the 1980s. The events meanwhile live on in the collective memory of Indonesians young and old, and in Indonesian schoolbooks, such as *Agressi militer Belanda* (Dutch military aggression). They are remembered both for the human and material losses on the Indonesian side, and for the heroic sacrifice and resistance of those who fought for independence.

SEE ALSO *Indonesian Independence, Struggle for;* *Linggadjati Agreement.*

BIBLIOGRAPHY

Cribb, R. *Gangsters and Revolutionaries. The Jakarta People's Militia and the Indonesian Revolution 1945–1949.* St. Leonards, Australia: Allen & Unwin, 1991.

Drooglever, P. J., M. J. B. Schouten & Mona Lohanda. *Guide to the Archives on Relations between the Netherlands and Indonesia 1945–1963.* The Hague, The Netherlands: ING Research Guide, 1999.

Lucas, A. *One Soul One Struggle. Region and Revolution in Indonesia.* St. Leonards, Australia: Allen & Unwin, 1991.

Taylor, A. M. *Indonesian Independence and the United Nations.* London: Stevens & Sons Ltd., 1960.

Yong Mun Cheong. *The Indonesian Revolution and the Singapore Connection, 1945–1949.* Leiden, The Netherlands: KITLV Press, 2003.

Peter Keppy

DUTCH UNITED EAST INDIA COMPANY

On March 20, 1602, the States-General (parliament) of the Dutch Republic granted the Dutch United East India Company (Verenigde Oost-Indische Compagnie, or VOC) a trade monopoly to the east of the Cape of Good Hope for a period of twenty-one years. Traders and burghers were given the opportunity to invest capital in this new trading company, and they thus become shareholders of what came to be the world's first multinational company operating in Asia.

The VOC was the outcome of a development that started with Cornelis de Houtman's (1565–1599) first Dutch voyage to Asia in 1595. His trip was followed by fifteen Dutch fleets with a total of sixty-five ships that set sail for Asia before the founding of the VOC. These fleets

VOC Insignia. *The insignia of the Dutch East India Company (VOC) adorns a building in Amsterdam.* © DAVE BARTRUFF/ CORBIS. REPRODUCED BY PERMISSION.

were financed by so-called *Voor-Compangieën,* or Early Companies, financed in turn by individual traders from the main Dutch ports of Holland and Zeeland.

During this first period, Dutch shipping surpassed the Portuguese, who were able to send a total of forty-six ships during the same years. The VOC was founded because the Early Companies began to engage in damaging mutual competition in the trade on Asian. In addition, a united company offered a more aggressive military power against the Iberian powers (Spain and Portugal), with whom the Dutch Republic was at war (the Eighty Years' War, 1568–1648).

ORGANIZATION

The port towns that were engaged in trade with the Early Companies were all represented in the new VOC. Its board of directors, called the *Gentlemen XVII,* was made up of the chambers of Amsterdam (eight directors); Zeeland (Middelburg, four directors); and Rotterdam, Delft, Hoorn, and Enkhuizen (one director each). Zeeland, or

one of the other towns, sent a seventeenth director so that Amsterdam would never have a majority vote.

The Dutch States-General gave the VOC the authority to sign contracts with sovereign powers in Asia, conclude treaties, erect fortresses, appoint governors, and maintain garrisons wherever necessary. On February 23, 1605, the Portuguese town of Ambon in the Spice Islands (in present-day Indonesia) fell into the hands of Steven van der Haghen (1563–1624), commander of a VOC fleet, and four days later a governor was appointed. This marked the beginning of the VOC's territorial expansion in Asia.

In 1609 the first governor-general (Pieter Both, 1550–1615) was appointed, and during the following years debates raged over the question of where a central overseas government could be permanently established. In 1619, with the conquest of Jaccatra (present day Jakarta), the VOC established its headquarters on Java. The new colonial city Batavia became the center of administration, trade, logistics, politics, and diplomacy. The castle of Batavia was the company's nerve center, where the governor-general and his council met and where hundreds of traders, officials, accountants, and clerks took care of a massive amount of correspondence with numerous VOC governments and factory staff throughout Southeast Asia, Formosa, Japan, China, Siam (Thailand), Burma (Myanmar), India, Ceylon (Sri Lanka), Yemen, Persia (Iran), and the Cape of Good Hope.

All the information from incoming letters and reports from those Asian factories and governments was summarized in annual general letters *(generale missiven)* to the Gentlemen XVII in the Dutch Republic. Today, the archives of the VOC administration are kept in depositories in The Hague, Jakarta, Colombo, Cape Town, and Chennai.

In 1625 the VOC employed about 4,500 Europeans in Asia. By 1700 around 18,000 personnel worked for the VOC, and in 1750 there were around 24,500 VOC employees throughout Asia. Most of the company servants worked onboard ships and in the larger territories of Batavia and Ceylon, whereas smaller factories only needed a few dozen personnel. The VOC governments in the Malay-Indonesian archipelago (Makasser, Ternate, Ambon, Banda Semarang, Malacca, etc.) needed 500 to 1,000 company servants. Most of the personnel worked as craftsmen, for the military, and in administration, trade, and justice. Some 300 to 500 men were employed as surgeons, church ministers, "visitors of the sick" *(ziekentroosters),* and schoolmasters.

The number of persons who traveled on VOC ships from Europe to Asia was much higher. From 1620 to 1630, the total number of persons on ships that left the

Dutch Republic amounted to 23,700; from 1700 to 1710, the number was 49,600. The peak was reached from 1760 to 1770, when 85,500 persons were brought to Asia by the VOC. From 1602 to 1795, almost one million Europeans reached Asia via VOC ships. Most of them were soldiers and sailors; the number of immigrants was insignificant. Forty percent of the sailors and sixty percent of the soldiers did not come from the Dutch Republic but from other European countries, particularly the German states.

The total number of ships that the VOC had in use reached one hundred around 1650. In 1725 ship numbers reached their peak of 161, with about 108 remaining by 1794. Before 1725, approximately two-thirds of the VOC's ships were traveling in Asian waters; during the rest of the eighteenth century, only one third were in Asia. However, older dilapidated ships remained in Asia, and almost a third of the Dutch ships in Asia were barely seaworthy. In Batavia, old ships were used to transport coral from the coast to the city, where it was burnt for limestone to be used in construction.

All shipbuilding occurred in the Dutch Republic, although Batavia had a large repair facility on the island of Onrust just off the coast. The VOC ordered an average of seventy to ninety ships every decade; the total number of VOC ships built from 1602 to 1795 was approximately 750.

COLONIAL EXPANSION

The relatively low number of ships and men in the enormous space of the Indian Ocean and the China Sea demanded an effective strategy to monopolize certain products, dominate some forms of long-distance trade, and make profits where the Asian and other European competitors could not. The VOC's first aim was to establish a foothold in the Moluccas.

After the conquest of Portuguese Ambon (1605), a contract was concluded with the sultan of Ternate (1607). Control of the ancient clove-producing islands of Ternate and Tidore was contested until 1663, when the Spanish withdrew to Manila. Ternate finally submitted in 1683, when the sultan was forced to sign a new contract and recognize the overlordship of the VOC. In 1621 the VOC conquered the center of nutmeg production, the small group of Banda Islands. The Dutch hastily established a Moluccan spice monopoly to prevent the English from becoming established as well. After several fleet blockades, Portuguese Malacca fell to the Dutch in 1641, but only with the support of the king of Johor. Although Aceh was invited to take part in the conquest, this Muslim kingdom rejected the proposal from Batavia.

Governor-General Jan Pietersz Coen (1587–1629) was an architect of quick colonization schemes, and securing the spice monopoly and Batavia was not enough. His broader plans included control of the China trade with Spanish Manila and Japan. After a failed attempt to settle on Chinese territory (the Pescadore Islands), the VOC built a stronghold (Fort Zeelandia) on Formosa (Taiwan) in 1624. Dutch expansion on tribal Formosa, with its numerous languages and ethnic groups, can be considered a laboratory of early European colonialism in Asia. After experiments with military action, mission posts, tax collection, sugar plantations, and a Chinese labor force, Formosa was finally taken by Koxinga (Zheng Chenggong, 1624–1662), the leader of the South Fuchien trading dynasty and defender of China's Southern Ming court, in 1662.

In South Asia, the VOC successfully undermined Portuguese positions. After settling a bargain with the king of Kandy in the interior of Ceylon in 1638, the Ceylonese (Portuguese) coastal settlements fell one by one: Batticaloa (1638), Trincomalee (1639), Negombo (1640), Galle (temporarily in 1640, finally in 1644), Colombo (1656), and Jaffna and Mannar (1658).

On India's Coromandel Coast the Dutch gained a foothold in Pulicat (Paliacatta) in 1610. From 1690 to 1781, the center of the VOC possession on the Coromandel Coast was Nagapattinam, taken from the Portuguese in 1659. Another Portuguese possession in India that was occupied by the VOC was Cochin (1663) on the Malabar Coast, plus its adjacent towns. The VOC established trading posts in the two main emporia of the Mogul Empire: Surat in the Arabian Sea and Hugli in the Bay of Bengal. One year after the closure of its factory in Aceh in 1615, the VOC opened one in Surat to buy Indian cottons from the Gujarat region. The Mughal emperor, Shah Jahan (1592–1666), forced an end to the Portuguese presence in Hugli, an important export port for silks and opium, in 1632. Four years later, the Dutch received an official *firman* (decree) from the "Great Mughal" for free passage and trade in Bengal.

In the Arabian Sea region, VOC traders (among other Europeans) were welcomed in the Persian port of Gamron and in Esfahan, Persia's center of silk trade. The most important Arabian hub was Al-Mucha (Mocha), a traditional port town with well-established connections over all of the Asian-Arabian trading network, including numerous ports across the Arabian Sea and trading centers along the shores of East Africa, including the slave entrepôt Mombasa in present-day Kenya.

The Cape of Good Hope served as a refreshing station until 1652, when Jan van Riebeeck (1619–1677) established a permanent station to arrange provisions for passing ships. Agrarian production around this station was insufficient, and during the 1670s the VOC allowed immigrants to open the immediate hinterland. The rural expansion took off at a rapid pace under Governor Simon van der Stel (1639–1712) and lasted until around 1730.

The indigenous hunter-gatherers, the Khoikhoi and the San, where not considered to be subjects of the VOC. The VOC depended on their delivery of cattle, but the expansion of VOC territories severely affected the Khoikhoi and San living space. Immigrant communities settled in Drakensteyn and Stellenbosch, where wineries produced fine wines that could be sold in VOC settlements in Asia. Numerous slaves from Asia and the East African coast made VOC society at the Cape a slave society as well.

THE VOC AS TRADER

The VOC was an organization that depended on the long-distance trade between Asia and Europe and the intra-Asian trade. The VOC's strong points were its logistics, cargo capacity, shipping technology, military power, and modern arsenal, combined with its ability to adapt to local circumstances. VOC commanders realized from the beginning that they would not be able to compete in local and regional trading networks; local trade was simply too competitive. Furthermore, trade items that could be sold over long distances could only be profitable when a monopoly was achieved.

The VOC's first monopolies were its exclusive monopolies on spices in the Moluccas and on pepper in Banten (West Java) and Sumatra (Jambi and Palembang). These spices could be sold for very high prices in Europe, and could be purchased in return for much-needed Indian textiles from Bengal and the Coromandel Coast. Textiles could be bought with precious metals from Europe (imported American silver), Japan, Persia, and Sumatra (Padang). Copper from Japan was also an essential product much in demand in India, in particular for coining. In return, raw silk from China, Bengal, or Persia was sold in Japan, along with spices from the Moluccas. The coastal control of Ceylon provided the VOC with large cinnamon growing areas. Elephants, which were transported with special ships to India, were also an important export item from Ceylon.

During the eighteenth century, in particular under growing pressure from English (country) traders and the English East India Company, the VOC gradually lost its position of preeminence. New products like coffee, Chinese tea (from Canton), and Indian textiles became popular in Europe. Maintaining the profitable spice trade, which had long been fundamental to the VOC, was not enough.

Other reasons—besides growing competition—for the decline of the VOC was a lack of good management within the Dutch Republic and the corruption of many higher officials stationed in Asia. When the Fourth Anglo-Dutch War (1780–1784) broke out, it took the directors two months to hold a meeting and discuss measures. Failing entrepreneurship and the loss of ships and capital transformed the VOC into a major debtor of the states of Holland. The enterprise did not recover during the 1780s and 1790s, and when French troops entered the Dutch Republic in 1795, the British sent naval squadrons to take over the Dutch possessions in Asia.

THE VOC AS LANDLORD

Apart from its numerous trading factories, fortresses, and outposts, the VOC also controlled extensive hinterland territories and some islands, mainly for the production of fine spices, sugar, coffee, and cinnamon. After their conquest in 1621, the five Banda Islands were transformed into a plantation economy run by slaves. More than sixty plantations were kept by private owners (*perkeniers*) who were obliged to deliver a certain amount of nutmeg and mace to the VOC at fixed prices. The government of Banda, residing in the fortress of Belgica on Banda-Neira, was responsible for the shipment of great quantities of nutmeg and mace. By 1750 most of the planters were nearly bankrupt. Low, fixed prices offered by the VOC, volcanic eruptions, bad harvests, and runaway slaves had brought them into debt.

The governor of Ambon controlled the planting and management of clove trees. As such, he acted more as a landlord than as an official of a maritime enterprise. The entire clove production of about one million pounds around 1700 was concentrated on the islands of Ambon Lease. Detailed records were kept of the number of productive and young trees in the gardens of the villagers across the islands. The original clove production areas in the north Moluccas—Ternate, Tidore, and Bacan—were subject to an eradication policy led by the governors of Ternate. The sultans of these islands were often in conflict with each other, which explains why the VOC could exercise a policy of divide-and-rule, forcing in particular the sultan of Ternate to cooperate in the campaigns to cut down clove trees in the region.

On Java, the VOC closely monitored Batavia's sugar industry, which entered a sudden boom in the 1680s. With the pacification of the neighboring sultanate of Banten, and contracts with the regencies of Cirebon on the other side of Batavia territory (1681 and 1705), a large hinterland was opened up. Sugar was mainly used as ballast in returning ships, and was sold in Surat, Persia, and Europe. A second boom occurred with coffee, which

JAN VAN RIEBEECK

Jan (Anthoniszoon) van Riebeeck (1619–1677) is credited with opening South Africa to white settlement. The son of a Dutch surgeon, he grew up in Schiedam, and married Maria de la Quellerie in 1649. Van Riebeeck joined the Dutch East India Company (Verenigde Oost-Indische Compagnie, or VOC) as an assistant surgeon and served in Batavia (now Jakarta, Indonesia) in 1639, then in Japan. In 1645 he managed a company trading-station in Indochina (in what is now Vietnam), but was dismissed for disobeying the company's strict rule against private trading.

In 1647 a VOC ship ran aground in Table Bay, a rocky area a few miles south of what is now Cape Town. Stranded on the Cape peninsula for a year, the Dutch crew built shelters, grew food, and established trade with the indigenous Khoikhoi, or Hottentots. Following this incident, the VOC voted to establish a provisioning station on the Cape to service ships undertaking the arduous voyage to the East Indies.

Van Riebeeck became commander of the Cape in June of 1651. Aboard his flagship *Drommedaris* and accompanied by four other ships, he reached Table Bay on April 6, 1652. Surviving the voyage were 90 adults, including van Riebeeck's wife; 130 persons had perished at sea.

Along with establishing a settlement, Van Riebeeck was charged with erecting a flagpole to signal ships; providing escort ships; and constructing a fort to protect settlers and warehouse food, water, and other provisions.

In addition to relying on stored foodstuffs, the group grew grain, vegetables, and fruits, and obtained cattle by trading with the Khoikhoi.

Although work on the Fort of Good Hope (Fort de Goede Hoop) began slowly, increasing numbers of ships were soon setting anchor at Cape Town (Kaapstad or De Kaap), as the settlement was called. A pier was built on the bay, and businesses and a hospital were established. Beginning in 1655 Van Riebeeck petitioned the VOC to allow Dutch citizens to farm, trade, and aid in the defense of the Cape settlement. In early 1657 the first permits were issued to allow private farms in the Cape area.

Growth brought problems, however, as the demand for laborers increased. In 1657 Van Riebeeck began importing slaves from Sumatra and Madagascar. He also encouraged exploration of the South African interior. As the Dutch settlement expanded northward, the Khoikhoi resisted forced evictions from their lands; after a failed uprising in 1659, however, they were pushed northward. When Van Riebeeck left the Cape in 1662 the settlement was home to 134 company officials, 35 "free burghers," 15 women, 22 children, and 180 slaves. Four years later the VOC decided to establish a permanent colony on the Cape.

From the Cape, Van Riebeeck moved to Malacca, in Malaysia, where his wife died in 1664. Appointed secretary to the Council of India the following year, he died in Batavia in 1677. His journal was published posthumously, appearing in both Dutch and English.

---

was introduced in the mountainous Cirebon-Priangan lands of West Java in the first decades of the eighteenth century.

Ceylon became a third major production area for the VOC. Ceylon's jungle hinterlands (later turned into gardens) of Colombo, Galle, and Negombo were exploited for cinnamon collection. The harvesting and the peeling of the bark of the cinnamon tree were done by low-caste Chalia (or Salagama) laborers. Many other castes were used for the transportation of the product to the coast.

The extensive use of certain castes and subcastes in cinnamon production resulted in changes to the social stratification of coastal Sri Lankan society during the 158 years of Dutch presence. These changes are still reflected

in the so-called *tombos*, traditional land rolls that had been used by the Portuguese and were carefully kept and revised under VOC administration in Ceylon. The kingdom of Kandy kept possession of only one port, Puttalam, although access to that port was controlled by the VOC fortress at Kalpitiya. Combined with the strict prohibitions on the export of cinnamon, VOC exploitation of coastal Ceylon also had a negative effect on society, as the monopolization of cinnamon production curtailed the activity of the rural people.

CULTURE, RELIGION, AND SCIENCE

The VOC's presence in Asia was more than a commercial, political, and military encounter. The VOC also had

Compagnie Souveraine des Indes
Orientales.

The Governor-General Meets the VOC Council in Batavia. *This early eighteenth-century engraving depicts a meeting in Batavia (now Jakarta) between the governor-general of the Dutch East India Company and members of his council.* ROGER VIOLLET/GETTY IMAGES. REPRODUCED BY PERMISSION.

a cultural, religious, and scientific impact on the region. Europeans who settled in Asia, in particular in large towns like Batavia, Colombo, and Malacca, quickly adapted to Asian lifestyles, habits, and material culture. Asian dress, the use of many servants, the consumption of betel, and the purchase of large quantities of Asian furniture, porcelain, and other household goods characterized the lives of Europeans and mestizos in VOC settlements. Thousands of testaments and household inventories kept in the national archives in Jakarta bare witness to Asian influences on European lifestyles and culture.

From the beginning, the VOC attended to the religious needs of its servants by sending Dutch Reformed ministers and "visitors of the sick," who comforted sick people and acted as catechists. In its port towns and territories, the VOC actively promoted Protestantism among the non-Muslim population. Between 1602 and 1799 the VOC employed some 650 ministers, 2,000 visitors of the sick, and even more Asian schoolmasters for the overseas churches of Ceylon, the Moluccas, the Cape of Good Hope settlements, Malacca, Batavia, Semarang, Formosa, and India.

A network of consistories (church councils) corresponded with the central church council in Batavia, which corresponded with the synods and regional classes in the Dutch Republic. Protestant mission work often required the study of several Asian languages, such as Malay, local Moluccan languages, Formosan-Sinkiang, Sinhalese, and Tamil. Noteworthy is the vocabulary, or Dutch-Malay dictionary, prepared by Caspar Wiltens and Sebastianus Danckaerts (1623); George Hendrik Werndly's Malay grammar and the first bibliography of Malay books by Europeans and indigenous authors (1736); and the translations of the Bible into Malay by Melchior Leydekker and Petrus van der Vorm (the New

Testament in 1731, the Old Testament in 1733). Johan Maurits Mohr and Herman Petrus van de Werth published this Malay Bible in Arabic script in 1758.

Natural sciences and the making of cabinets of curiosities proliferated throughout Europe in the sixteenth and seventeenth centuries to emphasize the exceptional, the rare, and the marvelous, attempting to encompass the results both of God's creation (nature) and of man's (art). These fields also received serious attention from the VOC. Already in the early seventeenth century, samples of plants and animals were sent to the University of Leiden in the Netherlands.

One of the great tropical naturalists of the seventeenth century was Georgius Everhardus Rumphius (Georg Eberhard Rumpf, 1627–1702), who is considered the founder of Indonesian botanical exploration. Rumphius was a VOC merchant who spent almost fifty years on Ambon collecting plants, precious stones, shells, sea animals, and all sorts of natural curiosities. Also known as the "Indian Pliny," after the Roman natural historian, Rumphius faced severe difficulties during his life. In 1670 he became blind; in 1674 he lost his wife and youngest daughter during an earthquake; in 1687 many of his manuscripts and drawings on natural history were lost in a fire in Ambon; and in 1692 the manuscript of his *Het Amboinse Kruid-boek* (The Ambonese Herbal) sank to the bottom of the Indian Ocean with the returning ship the *Waterland*. Thanks to the devoted support of governors-general, assistants, and his own strong will, the six volumes of his *Herbarium Amboinense,* a natural history of Ambon, were printed in Dutch and Latin in Amsterdam between 1741 and 1755.

Although Rumphius began collecting curiosities after collecting plants for his herbaria, his *D'Amboinsche Rariteitkamer* was already published in 1705. Almost three hundred years after Rumphius's death, this work was published in English by E. M. Beekman as *The Ambonese Curiosity Cabinet* (1999). Rumphius's earliest work, *De Generael Lant-Beschrijvinge van het Ambonse Gouvernement* (A General Geographical Description of the Government of Ambon), was not published until 2001. François Valentyn (1656–1727), in his *Oud en Nieuw Oost-Indiën* (1724–1726), or the Ancient and New East Indies, made extensive use of Rumphius's discoveries on flora and tropical marine life. Another important work on exotic flora in Asia is Hendrik A. van Reede tot Drakenstein's (1636/7–1691) *Hortus Indicus Malabaricus,* or Garden of India of Malabar, written between 1678 and 1693.

On April 24, 1778, a group of senior VOC officials, lay scholars, reverends, and burghers founded the *Bataviaasch Genootschap van Kunsten en Wetenschappen* (Batavian Society for Arts and Sciences). Evangelization,

geographical sketches, the study of medicine and tropical illnesses, languages, natural history, agriculture, botany, and astronomy were among the many topics discussed by its members, who published their findings in the society's *Verhandelingen* (Treatise). The society's enormous collection of books and drawings are kept in the national library in Jakarta.

SEE ALSO *Empire, Dutch.*

BIBLIOGRAPHY

Gaastra, F. S. *The Dutch East India Company: Expansion and Decline.* Zutphen, Netherlands: Walburg Pers, 2003.

Goor, Jurrien van. *De Nederlandse koloniën: Geschiedenis van de Nederlandse expansie, 1600–1975.* The Hague, Netherlands: Koninginnegracht, 1994.

Jacobs, Els M. *Koopman in Azië: De handel van de Verenigde Oost-Indische Compagnie tijdens de 18de eeuw.* Zutphen, Netherlands: Walburg Pers, 2000.

Knaap, G. J. *Kruidnagelen en christenen: De VOC en de bevolking van Ambon, 1656–1696,* 2nd ed. Leiden, Netherlands: KITLV Uitgeverij, 2004.

Landwehr, John. *VOC: A Bibliography of Publications Relating to the Dutch East India Company, 1602–1800.* Utrecht, Netherlands: HES, 1991.

Niemeijer, Hendrik E. *Batavia. Een koloniale samenleving in de zeventiende eeuw.* Amsterdam, Netherlands: Balans, 2005.

Rumphius, Georgius Everhardus. *The Ambonese Curiosity Cabinet* (1705). Translated and edited by E. M. Beekman. New Haven, CT: Yale University Press, 1999.

Schutte, G. J., ed. *De Gereformeerde kerk onder de Verenigde Oost-Indische Compagnie.* Hilversum, Netherlands: Uitgeverij Verloren, 2002.

Hendrik E. Niemeijer

DUTCH WEST INDIA COMPANY

The Dutch were late entrants in the Atlantic. Only in the late sixteenth century did Dutch merchants become involved in shipping and trade between Europe, Africa, and the Americas. Within less than two decades, however, the Dutch were important players in the Atlantic. In several towns in the provinces of Holland and Zeeland, merchants had established small companies for the gold and ivory trade with West Africa and the fur trade with North America. Private ship owners sent their vessels to the coasts of South America and the Caribbean islands in search of dyewood and salt. As the Atlantic commerce expanded, the small trading companies and private ship owners were vulnerable to the hostility of Spain and Portugal.

The West India Company's House in Amsterdam. *This illustration, published in 1693, shows the offices of the Dutch West India Company on the Cingel (or Singel) canal in Amsterdam, Netherlands.* © BETTMANN/CORBIS. REPRODUCED BY PERMISSION.

On the other hand, stiff competition between merchants was eroding profits at home. In an effort to avoid the decline of the trade, the States of Holland started negotiations designed to achieve collaboration instead of competition. At first, commercial rivalry between the provinces of Holland and Zeeland prevented plans to establish a West India Company to conduct trade with Africa and the Americas. However, during the Twelve Years' Truce (1609–1621), new plans were made, and after a long debate, the Dutch West India Company (WIC) was finally constituted by the Dutch States-General (parliament) on June 3, 1621.

ORGANIZATION

According to its charter, the Dutch West India Company held a monopoly in shipping and trade in a territory that included Africa south of the Tropic of Cancer, all of America, and the Atlantic and Pacific islands between

the two meridians drawn across the Cape of Good Hope and the eastern extremities of New Guinea. Within this territory the States-General authorized the WIC to set up colonies, to sign treaties with local rulers, to erect fortresses, and to wage war against enemies if necessary.

Like the Dutch East India Company (Verenigde Oost-Indische Compagnie, or VOC), the WIC was based on shareholders' capital, which was initially 7.1 million guilders. The company had a federal structure with five chambers: Amsterdam, Zeeland, Rotterdam, West-Friesland, and Groningen. While each chamber was run by its own directors, company policy was set by a central board of directors known as the Heeren XIX (the nineteen gentlemen). Directors of the chambers appointed representatives for each meeting of the Heeren XIX, and the composition of the board reflected the value of capital invested by the chambers. Meetings of the Heeren XIX were held two or three times per year to plan the outfitting of war fleets and merchantmen, to fix the value of cargoes, and to oversee the company's financial state, on which the payment of dividends to the shareholders was based.

ACTIVITIES

While the main objective of the WIC was to establish and defend a commercial network in the Atlantic, in practice it spent more money on privateering and war against Spain and Portugal. In 1623 the Heeren XIX developed strategies, the so-called grand design, to damage Spanish and Portuguese interests in the Atlantic and take control wherever possible. The defenses of the Spanish colonies were too strong to risk attack, but intensive privateering in the Caribbean was a good alternative. Between 1623 and 1636, the WIC captured or destroyed 547 enemy ships, including the legendary conquest of a Spanish silver fleet in 1628 by Admiral Piet Heyn (1577–1629).

Portuguese possessions in South America and West Africa, on the other hand, were less well defended, and the company's directors and the States-General agreed on a "grand design" that encompassed the conquest of Salvador, an important center of sugar cultivation in Portuguese Brazil; Luanda in Angola, the most important slave-trade station in Africa; and the Portuguese stronghold São Jorge da Mina (Elmina) on the Gold Coast. The first attempt to achieve these goals failed. From 1623 to 1625 several war fleets left the Dutch Republic to attack Portuguese colonies and settlements in the Atlantic, but none of these attacks succeeded.

In 1630 the company launched a second "grand design" that was more successful. Between 1630 and 1654, the company occupied the northern provinces of Brazil. Especially under count Johan Maurits van Nassau (1604–1679), governor of Dutch Brazil from 1636 till 1644, the export of sugar and dyewood reached a peak. During his governorship, about 28 million guilders worth of Brazilian products were shipped to the Netherlands.

The increasing demand for slaves in Brazil also spurred the Dutch to try once more to capture Luanda. In 1641 Admiral Cornelis Jol (1599–1641) left Recife with a fleet of twenty-one ships and a military force of 2,100 men for Africa. Jol captured not only Luanda but also the sugar-growing island of São Tomé. The WIC failed to take full control of these African territories, however, and lost them in 1648. In Brazil, military defeat was also at hand. After Johan Maurits left the colony, a rebellion of Portuguese planters ended the period of prosperity, finally leading to the capitulation of the Dutch in Brazil in 1654.

The WIC was more successful in capturing the Portuguese forts and factories on the Gold Coast from 1637 to 1642. These possessions, which remained Dutch until 1872, made it possible to control the Guinea trade for a long period. Between 1623 and 1674, the company shipped more than 320,000 ounces of gold and an unknown quantity of ivory, wax, and other tropical products to the Dutch Republic.

In addition to privateering, war, and commerce, the WIC colonized parts of the Guyana coast and a few Caribbean islands. The plantation colonies on the Guyana coast remained small until the end of the seventeenth century. In the Caribbean, the most important colony was Curaçao, which was occupied by the WIC in 1634. Initially the island was used as a naval base, but from the 1650s it served as an important depot for the commodity trade and the slave trade with the Spanish mainland colonies. Between 1630 and 1674, the WIC shipped approximately 84,000 slaves from Africa to Brazil, the settlements in Guyana, and Curaçao.

The drive for colonies and the long years of war against Spain and Portugal, however, had exhausted the WIC's capital and brought it close to bankruptcy. From the 1650s the WIC was haunted by financial problems that made it almost impossible to invest in a solid trading network in the Atlantic. When several plans to reform the company failed, the States-General finally decided to dissolve the WIC in September 1674.

THE SECOND WEST INDIA COMPANY

The States-General, however, were convinced that the Dutch Republic's interests in the Atlantic were best served by a chartered company, so it decided to establish a new WIC on the very day the old one disappeared. At first sight, the transformation from the old to the new company seemed little more than a debt redemption program with some minor organizational adjustments. Nevertheless, there were significant differences between the two companies. The old company was not only a trading organization and administrator of Dutch colonies, but also an instrument of war against Spain and Portugal. The second WIC, on the other hand, was primarily a commercial organization interested in the commodity trade with West Africa and the transatlantic slave trade.

Among the Dutch colonies in the company's territory, Suriname was most important, but the directors had little control over it. From 1683 the colony was owned by the Suriname Corporation (Sociëteit van Suriname), in which three parties participated: the WIC, the city of Amsterdam, and Cornelis van Aerssen van Sommelsdijck (1637–1688). Sommelsdijck was a descendant of a Dutch aristocratic family. Thanks to his share in the chartered Sociëteit van Suriname, he would be the first governor of the colony under the new arrangement. To the west of Suriname, there were three smaller Dutch plantation colonies on the banks of the rivers Berbice, Demerara, and Essequibo, of which the first mentioned was owned by a shareholders company.

The slave trade to the Guyana colonies and Caribbean islands, however, remained under company control until the 1730s. Between 1674 and 1739, the WIC shipped approximately 187,000 slaves from Africa to the colonies in the west. Not only the transatlantic slave trade, but also the commodity trade with West Africa, was an important source of income for the company. It exported more than half a million ounces of gold and approximately three million pounds of ivory from the Gold Coast between 1676 and 1731. But in 1730 the monopoly was partly lifted by the States-General and in 1734 totally abandoned. During the 1730s the company competed with private merchants. Finally, however, the directors decided to stop the transatlantic slave trade and to minimize the commodity trade with West Africa.

Even when the company withdrew from active participation in trade, it continued to play the role of intermediary and protector for private Dutch trade in the Atlantic region. The WIC was an extension of the strongly decentralized Dutch government. With its limited powers, it carried out administrative and defense functions needed to keep the colonies afloat, and many private individuals benefited in the process. In 1791, when the decentralized Dutch Republic also was at the point of disintegration, the WIC was eliminated. Soon thereafter, its "big brother" in Asia, the VOC, met the same fate. The properties of the two large trading companies became colonies of the Netherlands in the early nineteenth century.

SEE ALSO *Colonization and Companies; Mercantilism.*

BIBLIOGRAPHY

Boxer, C. R. *The Dutch in Brazil, 1624–1654.* Oxford: Clarendon, 1957.

Goslinga, Cornelis C. *The Dutch in the Caribbean and on the Wild Coast, 1580–1680.* Assen, Netherlands: Van Gorcum, 1971.

Goslinga, Cornelis C. *The Dutch in the Caribbean and in the Guianas, 1680–1791.* Assen, Netherlands: Van Gorcum, 1985.

Heijer, Henk den. *De geschiedenis van de WIC.* Zutphen, Netherlands: Walburg, 1994.

Heijer, Henk den. *Goud, ivoor, en slaven: Scheepvaart en handel van de Tweede Westindische Compagnie op Afrika, 1674–1740.* Zutphen, Netherlands: Walburg, 1997.

Jacobs, Jaap. *New Netherland: A Dutch Colony in Seventeenth-Century America.* Boston and Leiden, Netherlands: Brill, 2005.

Klooster, Wim. *Illicit Riches: Dutch Trade in the Caribbean, 1648–1795.* Leiden, Netherlands: KITLV, 1998.

Postma, Johannes Menne. *The Dutch in the Atlantic Slave Trade, 1600–1815.* Cambridge, U.K.: Cambridge University Press, 1990.

Postma, Johannes, and Victor Enthoven, eds. *Riches from Atlantic Commerce: Dutch Transatlantic Trade and Shipping, 1585–1817.* Boston and Leiden, Netherlands: Brill, 2003.

Henk den Heijer

E

EAST ASIA, AMERICAN PRESENCE IN

Having gained independence from Great Britain in 1783, the new United States looked to Asia for new markets for trade. The American merchant ship *Empress of China* left New York on February 22, 1784, carrying mostly ginseng, a root that grew wild in the Hudson River Valley and that the Chinese highly prized for medicine. Reaching Canton (Guangzhou) on August 28, 1784, the *Empress* returned to the United States with a cargo of tea, silk, and porcelain, realizing a substantial profit from the venture and contributing to the rapid growth of port cities such as Providence, Salem, Boston, New York, and Philadelphia.

Thereafter, merchant ships carrying cotton from the South and furs from the Pacific Northwest sailed to China, and by the 1840s some New England whaling ships were operating in the North Pacific. The 1844 Sino-American Treaty of Wangxia greatly expanded trade between China and the United States, and the technological superiority of American "clipper ships" led to a brief period of U.S. dominance in the China trade. Opposition at home to preferential governmental treatment of China's trade interests, combined with the greater lure of more proximate and more certain markets, meant that the United States was only a minor player in the China market until the turn of the century.

The discovery of gold at Sutter's Mill in California in 1848, combined with territorial continental conquest, led to great interest in Japan and China as ports and markets. In the mid-1850s, Commodore Matthew Perry (1794–1858) sailed to Japan with a small fleet of warships, and persuaded the Japanese to sign a treaty with the United States, ending Japan's two centuries of self-imposed isolation, and obtaining coaling and naval stations for the United States. More Americans followed—some merchants, many Protestant missionaries seeking to convert East Asians, and sailors and soldiers to protect these merchants and missionaries. For the most part, however, Americans were content to follow where Britain led. A severe economic depression in the 1890s sharpened the search for markets, and victory in the Spanish-American War (1898) brought the United States the building blocks of an empire in the Pacific—the Hawaiian Islands, the Philippines, Samoa, Midway, Guam, and Wake Island.

At the same time, the United States dealt carefully with Japan. The Meiji Restoration (1868) propelled Japan from feudalism into modernity. Japan subsequently defeated China in the first Sino-Japanese War (1894–1895), seized Taiwan and the nearby Pescadores in 1895, and then defeated Russia in the Russo-Japanese War (1904–1905), gaining control over Korea and the Liaotung Peninsula in Manchuria, a region in northeastern China. The strength of the Japanese Navy, along with the Anglo-Japanese Alliance, an agreement signed with Britain in 1902, led the United States to consider holding on to the Philippines in case a war with Japan broke out.

The Filipino Insurrection that followed the 1898 Spanish-American War proved difficult to contain, and Japan could easily interdict American communications with the distant islands. Tensions were eased by the Taft-Katsura Agreement (1905), in which the United States recognized Japan's control of Korea in return for recognition of U.S. influence in the Philippines, and the Root-Takahira Agreement (1908), in which the two countries

THE BOXERS.

UNCLE SAM (*to the obstreperous Boxer*), "I occasionally do a little boxing myself."

Uncle Sam Meets the Boxer. *This cartoon by William A. Rogers appeared in* Harper's Weekly in June 1900. *In Rogers's drawing, Uncle Sam dons boxing gloves in the form of battleships, and challenges a caricatured Chinese man to a match. The cartoon advocates a forceful military response to the Boxer Uprising.* © BETTMAN/CORBIS. REPRODUCED BY PERMISSION.

agreed to respect each other's territories in the Pacific and to honor the open-door policy toward China.

By the time of World War I (1914–1918), the United States considered itself a friend and even a protector of China. Some years earlier, during the "scramble for China," U.S. Secretary of State John Hay (1838–1905) had issued the "Open Door Notes," calling for equal access to China's markets and the preservation of China's territorial integrity and political sovereignty. In addition, the United States returned most of the onerous indemnity that China had been forced to pay the imperial powers after the antiforeigner Boxer Rebellion (1900), though the agreement stipulated the use of the money for bringing Chinese students to American colleges and universities. When Japan forced the Twenty-One Demands on China in January 1915, designed to secure Japanese control over China, the U.S. government helped China avoid acquiescing in what would have been a virtual loss of sovereignty.

The decade of the 1920s was one of lost opportunity. The United States took the lead in internationalizing the open-door system with the Washington Naval Conference (1921–1922), officially known as the Conference on the Limitation of Armaments, attended by representatives from nine countries: the United States, Japan, China, Belgium, Great Britain, France, Italy, the Netherlands, and Portugal. The conference led to the signing of three treaties in 1922. The Nine-Power Treaty guaranteed respect for China's territorial and administrative independence, the centerpiece of the Open Door Notes of 1899 and 1900. The Four-Power Treaty, signed by the United States, Japan, Great Britain, and France, helped prevent an extension of the Anglo-Japanese Alliance of 1902, and its signatories agreed to respect one another's rights regarding their holdings in the Pacific. The Five-Power Treaty, signed by the United States, Japan, Great Britain, France, and Italy, led to a ten-year moratorium on battleship and aircraft production; to further assuage Japan, the United States and Britain agreed not to fortify territory in the Pacific west of the Hawaiian Islands and north of Singapore. The Nine-Power Treaty also guaranteed China's independence, sovereignty, and territorial integrity, and it accepted the American idea of an "open door" for trade. In effect, these treaties sought to create a framework for a more peaceful and hence more profitable exploitation of China and the Chinese people.

Japanese and Chinese nationalism competed to fill the resulting vacuum. America's Republican presidents of the 1920s largely avoided foreign entanglements outside of the Caribbean region, and they certainly did not wish to take the lead in the complicated politics of East Asia. In September 1931 Japanese army officers manufactured the Mukden Incident, and within a year Japan had seized control of Manchuria. Throughout the remainder of the 1930s, Japan continued to seize more and more of China. While presidents Herbert Hoover (1874–1964) and Franklin Roosevelt (1882–1945) did not approve of such naked aggression, they felt largely powerless to intervene, given the Great Depression of the 1930s and, later, America's preoccupation with events in Europe.

World War II (1939–1945) changed America's role in East Asia. Japan, Germany, and Italy signed an alliance, and Germany plunged a wider world into war after September 1939. In the spring of 1940, as German forces seized control of Western Europe, the fate of European empires in Asia and the Pacific hung in the balance. When Japan moved to seize these resource-rich areas to help it win the long conflict in China, the United States confronted Japan, and in December 1941 entered the war after the surprise bombing of Pearl Harbor in Hawaii. For nearly six months, Japan enjoyed great success, gaining a vast empire in the southwest Pacific and Southeast Asia. However, American productivity in industries converted to military purposes, along with Japan's strategic mistakes, resulted in Japan's overwhelming defeat and surrender in August 1945.

When the war ended, the United States had defeated Japan, and U.S. armed forces accepted the Japanese surrender in the Pacific and in southern Korea. U.S. Marines helped Chinese Nationalist armies repatriate Japanese troops in northern China. And the U.S. government acquiesced in allowing Britain, France, and the Netherlands to regain colonies that had been temporarily held by Japan.

From 1945 to 1954, France engaged in a long, drawn-out, and ultimately unsuccessful colonial war in Indochina, dragging in the United States. The United States seemingly had extricated itself from the Chinese civil war when, in June 1950, the outbreak of war in Korea brought the United States and the People's Republic of China into armed conflict. Leftover issues from these long-ago conflicts, including the status of Taiwan and tense relations between the two regimes in Korea, continue to bedevil American foreign policy and America's presence in East Asia.

SEE ALSO *China, Foreign Trade; Empire, United States; Open Door Policy.*

BIBLIOGRAPHY

Dobbs, Charles M. *The United States and East Asia Since 1945.* Lewiston, NY: Mellen, 1990.

Harland, Bryce. *Collision Course: America and East Asia in the Past and the Future.* New York: St. Martin's Press, 1996.

Hunt, Michael H. *The Making of a Special Relationship: The United States and China to 1914.* New York: Columbia University Press, 1983.

Iriye, Akira. *After Imperialism: The Search for a New Order in the Far East, 1921–1931.* Cambridge, MA: Harvard University Press, 1965.

Iriye, Akira. *Across the Pacific: An Inner History of American-East Asian Relations.* New York: Harcourt, Brace, 1967.

LaFeber, Walter. *The Clash: A History of U.S.-Japan Relations.* New York: Norton, 1997.

McCormick, Thomas J. *China Market: America's Quest for Informal Empire, 1893–1901.* Chicago: Quadrangle, 1967.

Reischauer, Edwin O. *The United States and Japan,* 3rd ed. Cambridge, MA: Harvard University Press, 1965.

Charles M. Dobbs

EAST ASIA, EUROPEAN PRESENCE IN

From as far back as the first few centuries of the Christian era, a long tradition of contacts connected Europe with East Asia (the region comprised of China, Japan, Korea, and Taiwan). During the whole history of these contacts, first established by Christian emissaries from the West, the region never experienced formal incorporation into a colonial Western empire. Only two colonial port cities (Macao, 1557–1999; Hong Kong, 1841–1997), some imperial leaseholds dating to the late nineteenth century, and the south of Taiwan around the Dutch Fort Zeelandia (1624–1662) can be regarded as colonial property. Nevertheless, the impact of imperialism on East Asia should not be underestimated. In general terms, the history of the European presence in Asia can be divided into seven periods:

1. A preliminary period in the Middle Ages during which Europeans first established a toehold in Asia, only to be expelled

2. An era during which Europe reestablished their presence in Asia

3. The era of the Canton System, lasting until the First Opium War

4. The era of the Treaty System, established by the outcome of the Opium Wars

5. The first era of Western informal empire, lasting until World War I

6. A second era of informal empire between the World Wars, during which the sole dominating Western powers were Great Britain and the United States

7. And, finally, the era of emancipation following World War II

During the successive phases of increasing Western influence, a wide range of colonial presences emerged, shaped by the specific circumstances of the various Asian cultures.

THE MIDDLE AGES

European contacts with Asia during the Middle Ages were restricted to the Chinese empire; Japan, Korea, and Taiwan were only known by hearsay to European visitors and remained out of reach. The voyage of the Venetian Marco Polo (1271–1295) is the most famous due to its literary legacy, but Italian merchants frequently visited Central Asia and China and founded temporary merchant colonies. Furthermore, medieval missionaries undertook travels to the Far East, where they succeeded in producing some converts among the Mongolian population, but made hardly any headway among the Chinese. Following a dynastic change in fourteenth-century China (from the Yuan to the Ming dynasty), European foreigners were no longer welcome. In 1371 the last European merchant was expelled; at the same time, the first phase of Christian missionizing came to an end. Not until the sixteenth century did Europeans return to the Far East.

Congress of the Toilers of the Far East. *Representatives from China, Korea, Japan, and Mongolia pose for a photograph during the First Congress of the Toilers of the Far East, a meeting of Communists held in Moscow in early 1922.* © **HULTON-DEUTSCH COLLECTION/CORBIS. REPRODUCED BY PERMISSION.**

THE ERA OF EUROPEAN REESTABLISHMENT

The era during which European powers reestablished themselves in Asia was characterized by the primacy of trading interests on the European side and by a balance of power that allowed East Asian sovereigns to dictate terms. Contact with China was renewed during the sixteenth century, an era of rapid European maritime expansion. In 1513 Portuguese seafarers approached the Chinese coast. After establishing a merchant colony in India and conquering Malacca, the Portuguese reached Canton in 1517. Initial contacts failed because the Portuguese refused to accept the Ming emperor's demand that they acknowledge him as their superior and render tributes. But because trading connections were too mutually lucrative to abandon entirely, a flourishing black market developed in Southern China. In 1557 the Portuguese were officially given permission to establish a settlement on the Macao peninsula under Chinese suzerainty. In 1680 a treaty guaranteed the settlement the status of a Portuguese colony. Macao became in effect a

Portuguese-controlled city, though the territory was held under a lease arrangement; payments continued to be made to the Chinese until 1887. Macao became the launching pad for a new, largely Jesuit mission to China. It also became the center of a thriving trade with Japan, in large part because the Chinese population was prohibited from engaging in maritime trade.

In Japan, the Portuguese were able to act as the sole middlemen in the trade between Japan and other countries, due to their presence in Macao and, from 1544, the Japanese port city Nagasaki. In addition, Jesuits began entering Japan in 1549, and by 1569 were settling in Nagasaki. Temporarily, the Christian mission was quite successful; at its peak, there were around 200 churches and 150,000 baptized Japanese. In 1587, however, a wave of bloody persecutions put an end to the proselytizing. In 1609 Christianity was forbidden by Japan, and in 1613 the last missionaries dispersed. Simultaneously, the Portuguese trade with Japan came to an end, due not least to the loss of the Jesuit middlemen and their singular knowledge of the commercial and political situation.

Throughout East Asia, the initial presence of the western European chartered companies—of which the foremost were the English East India Company (EIC) and the Dutch United East India Company (the Verenigde Ostindische Compagnie, or VOC)—was limited to several restrictively defined and strongly regulated enclaves. Only on Taiwan did the Dutch succeed temporarily in establishing colonial supremacy (1624–1662) in cooperation with a local pirate prince. The VOC benefited from the demise of Ming power in areas at the periphery of the Chinese empire. The end of the dynasty in continental China and the exodus of its last vassals to Taiwan forced the company to surrender its fort, Zeelandia, and to withdraw from the island. During their short period of regional prominence, the Dutch not only held a favorable position within the Chinese-Japanese trade, they also undertook efforts in sugar cultivation, as well as in coal and sulfur mining.

Korea remained on the periphery of European attention to East Asia during this and the following era. The Western presence there consisted only of a few dispersed Dutch seafarers who ran ashore and remained for several years during the seventeenth century, becoming somewhat well integrated and respected as military and administrative specialists. With the exception of a few fleeting maritime encounters in 1604, Great Britain did not establish contact with Korea until 1797, when the first merchant ships and navy units began arriving on the Korean coast.

THE CANTON SYSTEM

During the era of the Canton System, European access to East Asian markets became both greater and more predictable, though it was nonetheless still limited and state-controlled. As a result, beginning in the eighteenth century the EIC was able to build up trading contacts, especially in the tea trade. The company's efforts focused on the port city of Canton, where the best-funded merchant partners were situated. Europeans had no possibility of direct contact with the producers of in-demand commodities. They remained restricted to Canton (and before 1757 to a few other port cities), under the control of the Chinese bureaucracy and reliant on intermediaries who served as their contacts to Chinese merchants. In 1760 a great number of older prescriptions were bundled into the Canton System, which was based on a dual monopoly. Only the chartered companies and, on the Chinese side, Hong merchants—wealthy and well-established commercial dynasties based in Canton—had permission to maintain the transcultural trade. Trading company agents were only allowed access to a restrictively

limited area outside the city walls (the "Thirteen Factories" zone), where their trading partners ran factories and shops. The system was obligatory for all European nations and, between 1757 and 1842, limited all European trading activities to Canton. Economic success made those limitations acceptable to the European merchant empires. Nonetheless, Europeans tried to ensure and improve their position by sending official delegations to petition the emperor. Numerous Portuguese, Dutch, and English delegations visited the Chinese court before the Opium Wars. The emperor regarded them as tribute missions and ignored their diplomatic concerns. Thus, they remained without real political influence until the first half of the nineteenth century; in part, they were actually counterproductive due to the contradictory understandings of their function.

After the trading companies, missionaries played the most remarkable role in building a European presence in East Asia during the early modern period—above all the Jesuits, who were able to establish themselves as advisers to the Chinese emperor and various mandarins and as scholars of the Asian sciences. Whereas in Japan proselytizing efforts fell victim to interior power struggles, in China, Christian missionaries were allowed to remain until the first half of the nineteenth century, although they were more or less isolated and developed only limited influence.

In Japan, the Dutch were the single European nation with permission to maintain commercial contacts. The Japanese imposed a more restrictive version of the Chinese Canton System on the Dutch, whose trading company was limited to a single enclave, Deshima, a man-made island located in Nagasaki's harbor. Trade with Japan was only possible via official middlemen, and access to the country was granted only during institutionalized tribute missions. The VOC was expected to send an annual delegation to the emperor's court in Edo in order to fulfill a ritualized ceremony of subjugation.

THE TREATY SYSTEM

The era of the Treaty System saw a fundamental change in the European situation. After the Chinese defeat during the first Opium War (1839–1842) and the enforced opening of port cities, the balance of power shifted in favor of the Western powers, which gained privileged access to East Asian states and markets. In China, a number of factors—the slow collapse of the Manchu dynasty in Beijing, a new phase of accelerated British expansion, the erosion of the Canton System, Britain's strong interest in the opium trade as a means to improve its balance of payment, and China's efforts to prohibit the consumption of opium—together caused a change in the British China policy from diplomacy to military intervention. Concerted naval campaigns forced the Chinese emperor to accept a number of unequal treaties, starting with the Treaty of Nanking (August 29, 1842). This treaty guaranteed British rights to the colonial property of Hong Kong (occupied by British forces since January 20, 1841), required the opening of the most important port cities (Canton, Amoy, Foochow, Ningpo, Shanghai), and granted several local privileges, such as political autonomy and tax sovereignty. The result was not territorial conquest but an extensive change in the institutional framework governing relations between China and Britain. Soon, comparable treaties with the United States (July 3, 1844), France (October 24, 1844), and Sweden (March 20, 1847) followed. During the second Opium War (1856–1860), ten further ports were opened by unequal treaties, two of them on Taiwan (Taiwanfu in the southwest, Danshui in the northeast). The treaties fixed uniform and moderate tariffs on exports and imports that were not to be increased afterward. European subjects enjoyed the status of extraterritoriality and were only responsible to the jurisdiction of their consuls. Above all, the treaty ports served as bridgeheads for the penetration of the Chinese market. The maritime customs register of 1892 lists 579 foreign enterprises in these ports, mainly based in Hong Kong and Shanghai. Within the cities, traders were able to acquire concessions giving them the right to erect commercial structures and residences. The scope of these concessions was continuously growing; in larger towns like Shanghai, multiple concessions to various nations were soon in effect.

One further consequence of the treaties was a completely new situation for the Christian missions. The mission societies, which now included Protestant organizations, were protected by several European powers and only under extraterritorial jurisdiction. Moreover, all newly baptized Chinese Christians were granted this same status.

THE FIRST ERA OF WESTERN INFORMAL EMPIRE

At the end of the nineteenth century, the European presence in East Asia entered a new phase, during which privileged market access was transformed into political, military, and economic dominance. In China, leaseholds ceded in 1898 gave European powers the right of independent territorial administration. The first leasehold of this kind was the German territory around Tsingtao (Kiaochow Bay, in the province of Shantung), which was leased for ninety-nine years (though it was captured by Japanese forces in 1914). Germany was followed by Russia (Liaotung Peninsula), Britain (the New Territories of Hong Kong and Weihaiwei Port in Shantung), and

France (Kuangchou-wan Port, opposite Hainan). More than the earlier settlements, these properties had a military character, because they served as naval bases as well as merchant centers and nuclear European settlements. But economic factors remained most important as the lure of railway and mining concessions brought new European capital to China.

The psychosocial repercussions of Chinese defeat during the Opium Wars, the newly oppressive European presence, and the often inconsiderate behavior of missionaries together caused a strengthening of xenophobic tendencies in China. The result was the development of anti-European movements, mostly drawn from the lower classes, which culminated in the Boxer Uprising of 1900. Decentralized martial arts groups connected by loose religious ties attacked Chinese Christians and their European protectors, who had ignored the disruptive effects of Christianization on traditional village social structures (the alienation of the baptized from their families, the prohibition of ancestor worship, the destruction of indigenous temples, etc.). These groups joined together in a siege of the diplomatic quarter in Beijing, which was soon broken by an allied army consisting of forces from England, France, Germany, Italy, Austria, Russia, the United States, and Japan. This allied invasion added a new dimension to the foreign military presence in China. It was not only a further step toward integrating China into Europe's informal empires, but also a major catalyst for Chinese xenophobia and feelings of inferiority—a mix that characterized Chinese attitudes toward the West throughout the twentieth century.

Notwithstanding a few violent incidents, Japan followed a very different path in its relations to the West during the second half of the nineteenth century. Since 1800, European interest in the isolated island had revived. Russian merchants were the first to try to gain access, but they met with only marginal success. In the end, it was the new Pacific power, the United States, that in 1853 used a naval squadron to enforce the opening of Japan's ports. Japan was integrated into the treaty port system, and treaties with the United States were followed by others with Russia, the Netherlands, Great Britain, France, and Prussia. As Western merchants streamed into the Japanese commercial centers, the political and military influence of the Western powers grew rapidly, particularly after the final defeat of the traditional shogunate and the beginning of the Meiji Restoration in 1868. Europe and the United States became the model for Japanese modernization; Japanese delegations visited the United States, Great Britain, and Germany. Simultaneously, a huge number of Western consultants were employed by the new Meiji government in all sectors of administration and education. The army was reorganized following the Prussian example, and a

Prussian general became the general staff's official consultant. In 1874, some 858 foreign specialists were employed by the Japanese government. Japanese private enterprises soon followed suit, so that in 1897 there were 760 foreigners employed in the construction of railways, electrical facilities, steamships, and industrial plants. The majority of them came from Great Britain (433, mostly engineers), France (145 in administration and the shipbuilding industry), America (94, mostly in the agrarian sector), and Germany (62 in medicine and the army). The first foreign communities emerged in Yokohama and Kobe, which became the bridgeheads of European cultural influence not only on intellectual matters, but also on everyday life.

Simultaneously, Korea regained European attention. Between 1885 and 1887 the British Navy ran a naval base in Korea at Port Hamilton (Komun-do). During this period, Christianity was introduced into Korea. In 1884 and 1885 American and Scottish Protestant missionaries entered the country, and in 1890 the English Church Mission established its first settlement in Seoul.

THE SECOND ERA OF WESTERN INFORMAL EMPIRE

The second era of Western informal empire was characterized by the increasing impact of the West and a shrinking number of imperial powers. The outcome of World War I limited the Western powers in East Asia to Great Britain and the United States—accompanied by an expanding Japan. The treaty system reached its apex as the economic influence of the steadily growing number of Western residents peaked during the 1920s. In China, especially during the years of the unstable republic (founded in 1911), governmental sovereignty was exceedingly restrained by the "protecting powers," which used their influence and extraterritorial status to pave the way for Western business interests. A huge number of foreign specialists were employed in leading positions in the custom service, the post office, and the salt administration. In 1915, for example, there were 152 British, 109 other European, 21 American, and 37 Japanese employees working in the revenue department together with 1,206 mostly subordinated Chinese. At the beginning of the 1920s, around 7,000 foreign enterprises were operating in the treaty ports. At the same time, 75 to 90 percent of coalmining and around 50 percent of the cotton textile industry was in foreign hands. In 1933 foreign-owned firms controlled 35 percent of the manufacturing industries' total production. Until the Japanese occupation and the Chinese revolution of 1949, the Chinese economy was completely dominated by European and American interests.

In Japan, the European presence led to rapid industrial development, based on deep ties to the world economy initially achieved through foreign influence. This industrial development offered the basis for a successful emancipation from Western dominance. As early as 1895 Japan was able to abolish the extraterritorial status of foreigners and became itself a treaty power in China. Japan's transformation into a modern nation was initiated by a "revolution from the top," which made Japan an economic power that competed with Europe and the United States and for a while made it an imperial competitor as well.

THE ERA OF EMANCIPATION

The era of emancipation saw the end of the imperial presence of Europeans in East Asia and the economic as well as political rise of the region. After the end of World War II and the defeat of Japanese imperialism, Europe played only a marginal role in East Asia. East Asia became a primary sphere of interest for the United States, which established a huge military presence, especially after the Korean War (1950–1953), and took over most of the European military bases in the region. China freed itself from Western domination through revolution, whereas Japan gained autonomy through copying and adapting modern Western institutions and practices. South Korea and Taiwan also effectively followed the latter model. Recent developments in China have brought a partial adaptation of Western models, even if the existing power structures have been maintained. In the course of those developments, the last enclaves of formal European presence disappeared when Macao and Hong Kong were returned to China.

SEE ALSO *Anticolonialism, East Asia and the Pacific; East Asia, American Presence in; Extraterritoriality; Indigenous Responses, East Asia; Missions, China; Religion, Western Presence in East Asia; Treaties, East Asia and the Pacific; Treaty Port System.*

BIBLIOGRAPHY

Boxer, Charles R. *Jan Compagnie in Japan, 1600–1817.* 2nd ed. The Hague: Nijhoff, 1950.

Ch'en, Jerome. *China and the West: Society and Culture, 1815–1937.* Bloomington: Indiana University Press, 1979.

Cheng, Shaogang. *De VOC en Formosa, 1624–1662: Een vergeten geschiedenis.* Amsterdam: Ridderprint, 1997.

Clyde, Paul Hibbert, and Burton F. Beers. *The Far East: A History of the Western Impact and the Eastern Response (1830–1970).* 5th ed. Englewood Cliffs, NJ: Prentice-Hall, 1971.

Cullen, Louis M. *A History of Japan, 1582–1941: Internal and External Worlds.* Cambridge, U.K.: Cambridge University Press, 2003.

Dermigny, Louis. *La Chine et l'Occident: Le commerce à Canton au XVIIIe siècle, 1719–1833.* Ports, Routes, Traffics, no. 18. 3 vols., plus album. Paris: S.E.V.P.E.N., 1964.

Eckert, Carter J. *Korea, Old and New: A History*. Seoul: Ilchokak, 1990.

Fairbank, John King. *Trade and Diplomacy on the China Coast: The Opening of the Treaty Ports, 1842–1854*. Cambridge, MA: Harvard University Press, 1953.

Feuerwerker, Albert. *The Foreign Establishment in China in the Early Twentieth Century*. Michigan Papers in Chinese Studies, no. 29. Ann Arbor: Center for Chinese Studies, University of Michigan, 1976.

Hoare, James. *Japan's Treaty Ports and Foreign Settlements: The Uninvited Guest, 1858–99*. Meiji Japan Series, no. 1. Folkestone, U.K.: Japan Library, 1994.

Lowe, Peter. *Britain in the Far East: A Survey from 1819 to the Present*. London: Longman, 1980.

Osterhammel, Jürgen. *China und die Weltgesellschaft: Vom 18. Jahrhundert bis in unsere Zeit*. Munich: C. H. Beck, 1989.

Tung, William L. *China and the Foreign Powers: The Impact of and Reaction to Unequal Treaties*. Dobbs Ferry, NY: Oceana, 1970.

Jürgen G. Nagel

EAST TIMOR

Situated to the southeast of Indonesia, East Timor has an area of 14,610 square kilometers (9,000 miles) and a population of approximately 840,000.

Before Europeans encountered the island of Timor it had been populated by successive waves of Malay and Melanesian migrants, who settled with the original inhabitants, the *Atoni* people of the central highlands. This ethnic mix was compounded by the arrival of Chinese, Arab, and *Gujerati* traders, who visited Timor in search of its valuable sandalwood.

The Portuguese established a colonial administration in Timor in 1702, where they fought with the Dutch for control over the island for the next three centuries. The two halves of the island finally were separated in an agreement signed by the two colonial powers in 1913: The Dutch took control of the west and the Portuguese took control of the east. The Japanese military occupied East Timor during World War II (1941–1945), and in these years 60,000 (13% of the population) died.

In 1949 West Timor became part of the Indonesian Republic. Portugal retained East Timor. On April 25, 1974, the Portuguese Armed Forces Movement overthrew the Caetano regime and began a process of decolonization in Portugal's African and Asian colonies. Faced with the possibility of an independent East Timor, the Indonesian Armed Forces invaded. The Indonesian occupation lasted from 1975 to 1999, during which approximately 200,000 of a preinvasion population

of 650,000 died at the hands of Indonesian troops or as a result of starvation after forced displacement.

In August 1999, following a referendum overseen by the United Nations (UN), the East Timorese voted overwhelmingly for independence. The Indonesian army then sponsored paramilitary groups to terrorize the population. Following international intervention to halt the carnage, Indonesian forces withdrew. After a transitional period overseen by the UN, East Timor became independent on March 20, 2002.

As of the early twenty-first century, the territory remained poor with 41 percent of its population living in poverty, although access to offshore oil and gas, combined with a development strategy based on agriculture, coffee exports, small-scale industry and tourism, gave potential for development.

SEE ALSO *Empire, Dutch; Empire, Portuguese.*

BIBLIOGRAPHY

Dunn, James. *East Timor: A People Betrayed*. Sydney: ABC Books, 1996.

Taylor, John G. *East Timor: The Price of Freedom*. Australia: Pluto Press, 1999.

John G. Taylor

ECOLOGICAL IMPACTS OF EUROPEAN COLONIZATIONS IN THE AMERICAS

The arrival of Christopher Columbus in the Americas in 1492 initiated an extensive exchange in material goods, traditions, and ideas that was to have ecological impacts not only in the Americas and Europe, but also in the wider world. These transfers are often referred to collectively as the Columbian Exchange, though the term is generally used more narrowly to describe the exchange of crops, domesticated animals, and agricultural techniques that occurred in the immediate aftermath of Columbus's arrival. Sometimes the term also includes the transfer of diseases, and may even be used more broadly to describe any form of cultural and biological exchange.

OLD WORLD CROPS AND LIVESTOCK IN THE NEW WORLD

Like most immigrants, those who went to the Americas were interested not only in improving their economic and social standing but also in replicating their culture. However, different European powers had different colonial objectives and the peoples and environments they encountered in the Americas also differed. The level of cultural exchange and its ecological impact therefore varied. The Iberians encountered dense populations particularly in the highlands and they generally sought to transform the culture of indigenous peoples. In North America, however, Northern Europeans encountered a sparsely populated land and their contacts with Native Americans were often hostile. Cultural exchange was therefore more limited and transformations often occurred indirectly through the exploitation of natural resources and the displacement of native peoples from the land. The same processes also characterized sparsely populated regions of Latin America such as Argentina and Chile.

The Spanish Crown required all ships involved in early exploratory expeditions to carry seeds, plants, and livestock for the establishment of European forms of agricultural production. Those taken by Columbus on his second voyage included wheat, chickpeas, vines, melons, onions, radishes, as well as a variety of other garden vegetables, herbs, and fruits, notably oranges and lemons.

The staple diet in the Iberian Peninsula consisted of bread, wine, and oil. The Spanish tried to encourage the production of cereals by insisting that Native Americans pay them as tribute. However, this was largely unsuccessful because wheat and barley could not be grown in tropical climates and Native Americans often lacked the ploughs and oxen necessary to cultivate them. Hence, although wheat and barley could be grown in the temperate highlands of Mexico and the Andes, there they were cultivated mainly on Spanish-owned haciendas.

For the most part, Spaniards became resigned to eating maize rather than wheat bread. Wine was not only an important beverage in the Iberian Peninsula, but was also essential for the Catholic mass. Although vines were established in the Americas in the early colonial period, and did particularly well in Chile and Peru, fear that a flourishing wine industry might compete with that in Spain led to attempts to ban further plantings. Similarly, olive trees flourished at an early date in the Peruvian coastal valleys, but they were subject to similar ineffective bans.

The Spanish and Portuguese were also interested in establishing the production of sugar, but for export to Europe rather than for local consumption. Columbus introduced sugar to Hispaniola on his second voyage. Later, the Portuguese, who had developed sugar production in Madeira, introduced it to Brazil from whence it was exported as early as the 1520s. Sugar became the mainstay of the economies of Brazil and many Caribbean islands where, because of the shortage of Native American labor, its cultivation led to the large-scale exploitation of imported African slaves.

The Iberians were not the only people to introduce new crops. Once the slave trade had begun, yams, millet, sorghum, rice, okra, aubergine, the congo bean, and ackee also arrived in the Americas. Many of these were grown on slave plantations or on small plots in the hills cultivated by free Africans. Last to arrive were plants from Arabia, Asia, and the Pacific. Some of them, such as the mango, were probably introduced from West Africa, which had received them from Arab traders. Others, such as coffee and breadfruit, did not appear until the eighteenth century when they were introduced from English, French, and Dutch colonies in the Caribbean and the Guianas.

The Iberians were more successful in establishing the raising of livestock because they faced little competition from native domesticated animals. The only animals raised in the Americas in pre-Columbian times were llama, alpaca, guinea pig, muscovy duck, and turkey. Cattle, sheep, pigs, and goats accompanied all early expeditions to the New World. Although better suited to savanna conditions, cattle raising soon became important in the Caribbean, and encouraged a good market for hides in the Iberian peninsula and by the haulage demands of sugar industry. On the mainland and in Brazil the expansion of cattle raising was linked to the development of the mining industry for which it provided hides for saddle bags and tallow for candles.

Sheep spread less widely because they were better adapted to the cooler, drier conditions. The rapid expansion of livestock was encouraged by the existence of large stretches of grassland that had not been used intensively in pre-Columbian times or else had been abandoned by declining native populations. In sparsely settled areas, such as the Pampas of Argentina and the Llanos of Venezuela, Texas, or California, feral cattle often gave rise to extensive herds.

Europeans also introduced the horse, which had been extinct in the Americas since the end of the Pleistocene. Columbus introduced horses to the Caribbean on his second voyage and a royal stud farm was established in Hispaniola in 1502 for the furtherance of Spanish military conquest. Later, horses, and more often mules, were used as a more manageable and faster means of transport than llamas. This facilitated communications between hitherto isolated societies and encouraged cultural exchange.

The nature of European contact in North America was initially significantly different. North America was relatively sparsely settled and the earliest interests of the English, Dutch, and French were in the exploitation of its natural resources rather than the establishment of agriculture. Initially they focused on Canada and the northern United States, where they exploited codfish

Sixteenth-Century Sugar Mill. *This engraving, rendered in 1590 by Theodor de Bry, depicts the activities of Indian laborers at a New World sugar mill. The workers are shown cutting and hauling sugarcane, grinding it with a millstone, cooking the mash in a cauldron, and pouring syrup.* **LIBRARY OF CONGRESS.**

and later beaver skins, which were in high demand for beaver fur hats. The latter led to the decimation of beaver stocks only saved from extinction by changing fashion and the advance of settlement with which beaver hunting was incompatible. Even in the south where the English established tobacco plantations in Virginia, the initial aim was trade rather than settlement. Only with the establishment of settler colonies in New England were Old World crops and animals introduced on a large scale. Like Iberian settlers, North American colonists introduced crops and animals with which they were familiar, but because they often settled in environments that were similar to Europe, such as the northern and middle colonies of British America or the Canadian regions colonized by the French, much northern farming focused on subsistence and local markets rather than on producing crops for export.

However, as in Latin America, the introduction of livestock had a significant impact. Sixteenth-century expeditions introduced horses to the southern United States, while northern European breeds were introduced later in the seventeenth century. Horses did not do so well in the tropics, but large herds of feral horses flourished in the more temperate grasslands of the Great Plains, as they did in the Pampas of Argentina and in Chile.

THE ADOPTION OF OLD WORLD CROPS AND LIVESTOCK

Despite pressure from Iberians, Native Americans were selective in their adoption of crops introduced from Europe. Some, such as cereals and sugar cane, necessitated fundamental changes to existing agricultural systems by requiring specially cleared fields, ploughs, and oxen, as well as specialized equipment for their cultivation or processing. Given that agriculture in most parts of Latin America was highly developed, with the crops raised providing not only a balanced and nutritious diet, but also possessing some cultural meaning, there was little incentive for Native Americans to adopt new foods introduced from Europe. Maize, beans, and squashes therefore remained the most important crops cultivated in Mexico and Central America, while in the Andes the potato and quinoa continued to dominate higher elevations, while manioc and sweet potatoes prevailed in the tropical lowlands.

Nevertheless, Native Americans did adopt those plants, such as onions and garlic, which had no equivalent in their own crop complexes or, like bananas or fruit trees, could be grown alongside indigenous plants in household gardens. They also cultivated small patches of sugar cane, which they used as a cheap and effective substitute for honey or syrup from the maguey plant. In contrast to crops, domesticated animals were widely adopted. Initially chickens and pigs were the most ubiquitous, but later native communities also raised large herds of cattle and sheep. In part of Latin America the indigenous population began to consume meat on a large scale.

Contacts between Native Americans and Northern Europeans were often hostile, reducing the opportunities for cultural exchange. However, nomadic hunter-gatherers rapidly adopted horses because it enabled them to extend their hunting and gathering grounds and to increase their mobility so that they could better defend their territories against intruders. This was also true of similar groups in southern Argentina and Chile.

CHANGES IN AGRICULTURAL IMPLEMENTS AND TECHNIQUES

Some new agricultural techniques accompanied the arrival of new plants and animals. In the Old World cereals were sown by broadcasting in specially cleared fields, whereas in the New World seeds were generally planted individually in swiddens or simple gardens. The Spanish also introduced Arabic techniques of irrigation, notably canal and reservoir irrigation, though these forms of irrigation did not differ significantly from those that existed in pre-Columbian times. Nevertheless, the extent of irrigated land, and also other intensive forms of cultivation such as terracing and raised fields, declined. This was primarily because the decline in the Native population meant that it no longer had the labor power to maintain them. In terms of agricultural implements, by far the most important introductions were iron tools,

including axes and hoes, which were not only more durable, but also made forest clearance and the cultivation of heavy soils much easier. The introduction of the plough drawn by draught animals had a more localized impact, because it required dedicated fields and an investment of capital in oxen and labor. It was therefore found primarily on European-owned haciendas.

THE DEVELOPMENT OF HACIENDAS

Given the high demand for some crops in Europe, notably sugar cane, and the growing demand for food in the cities and mining areas, that could not be supplied by declining native populations, the Iberians began to assume control of agricultural production through the acquisition of land and the development of haciendas. In pre-Columbian times a variety of types of land tenure existed: Some lands were owned by the state, communities, or private individuals, while tribal peoples and hunter-gatherers had no concept of private property. With the exception of state lands, the Iberians recognized private ownership of land, but not usufruct rights, which meant that lands that were used but not owned by indigenous communities were vulnerable to seizure by incoming settlers and their descendants. Although the Iberians attempted to replicate the large estates or *latifundia* that existed in Europe, because native rights to land were recognized in law, at the outset few large land grants were allocated. However, such land grants could be consolidated piecemeal over time and combined with lands acquired in other ways to underpin the growth of great estates held by single owners.

The Iberians disparaged manual work and looked to Native Americans, or in their absence African slaves, to provide the necessary labor. Initially this was supplied through the *encomienda*, an institution that had been used during the Reconquest of southern Spain from the Moors. An encomienda was an allocation of Indians to an individual who was given the right to exact tribute and labor from them. However, because of ill treatment, in 1549 the right of encomenderos to exact labor was withdrawn and in many regions replaced by other forced labor systems modeled on pre-Columbian forms of draft labor, such as the *repartimiento* or *mita*. Where labor was short, landowners attempted to recruit free workers by offering them incentives in the form of better wages, credit, or plots of land on their estates. Where labor demands could not be met locally, the only recourse was to import African slave labor. However, this was only an economic proposition where agricultural commodities, such as sugar, could generate sufficiently high profits to cover the high cost of importing African slaves.

These colonial labor systems, which were also used in mining, often undermined the economic and social viability of native communities. They drew labor from subsistence production, weakened kinship ties, and promoted their integration into market economies. These processes were also encouraged by population decline, migration to evade tribute and labor demands, and the alienation of native lands. At the same time Native Americans often responded positively to the new market opportunities becoming commodity producers of food, coca, alcoholic beverages, and textiles.

GOLD AND SILVER MINING

One of the prime aims of the Spanish and Portuguese in the Americas was the creation of wealth through the mining of gold and silver; initially agriculture generated lower profits and required a greater investment of time and money. Gold, silver, copper, and tin had been mined and worked by pre-Columbian peoples, notably the Incas, Aztecs, and a number of chiefdoms in Colombia and the Greater Antilles. However, Native Americans possessed no knowledge of working iron. Most of their tools and weapons were made of wood, with only some made of bronze, an alloy of copper and tin.

Mining techniques were not highly developed in the Iberian Peninsula. Initially the Spanish drew on local expertise or that of German immigrant miners, but even into the nineteenth century mining techniques were very primitive. Until the mid-sixteenth century mineral ores could only be refined by smelting, which meant that only high-grade ores could be exploited. This process depended on the production of charcoal so that vast areas around the mines were soon depleted of forest.

In about 1556 a new process of refining, called the amalgamation or patio process that used mercury and salt, was developed in Mexico by Bartolomé de Medina. This made possible the working of low-grade ores, which being associated with mountain-building processes were found mainly in highland areas. From then on mining became very much dependent on the supply of mercury from Huancavelica in Peru or Almadén in Spain.

The first gold deposits that were exploited were found in lowland riverbeds and terraces, which were excavated using simple tools, such as picks and crowbars, and panned using wooden bowls. The only difference from pre-Columbian times was the use of iron tools. This type of mining was typical of that found in the lowland gold fields of Colombia and the Greater Antilles (Hispaniola, Puerto Rico, and Cuba). Silver ores were more extensive and were found in the Andes and the highlands of Mexico. The most famous silver mine was at Potosí in Upper Peru (present-day Bolivia), but there were others at Oruro, Castrovirreina, and Cerro de Pasco in Peru, while in Mexico, the main silver belt followed the eastern flank of the Sierra Madre Occidental encompassing towns such as Guanajuato, Zacatecas, and Parral.

The impacts of these two types of mining differed. Gold panning was associated with ephemeral deposits. Here groups of itinerant workers would exploit a deposit for a short time before moving on. They often built temporary camps and brought food with them, so that their activities did not stimulate the establishment of permanent settlements or agricultural enterprises to support them. The silver mines, on the other hand, required a higher investment of capital into sinking and timbering shafts and in equipment used for keeping the mines free of water or processing the ores. Because the silver ores were extensive and could be worked for years or even decades, they also required a permanent and much larger labor force.

At the end of the sixteenth century the Andean forced labor system, the mita, was supplying more than 13,500 workers a year for the mines of Potosí. In Mexico the mines were situated in an area of sparse population, so labor had to be drawn from more distant regions in the form of free labor or African slaves. The presence of a large workforce led to the emergence of towns, whose elaborate architecture and flourishing cultural activities testified to the presence of many wealthy miner owners and merchants. Mining also acted as a major stimulus to agricultural production, first to supply food for the workers, and second to provide hides, tallow, and mules to support the mining industry. In northern Mexico large estates raising wheat, maize, and cattle were established in the hinterland of the mines. In the Andes, however, the cold climate did not favor crop production, so supplies had to be drawn from further afield, notably from northwest Argentina or central Chile.

MANUFACTURING

Native Americans produced many types of textiles. In the Andes they were often made of llama or alpaca wool, but these were not available in Mexico where indigenous textiles were made of cotton or fiber from the maguey cactus. In pre-Columbian times households undertook the production of textiles, although specialized weavers produced cloth for elites and rituals. Most of the textiles were produced on a narrow back-strap loom. In colonial times the Spanish introduced treadle looms and established larger textile mills known as *obrajes*. Although they produced some cotton cloth, most processed wool from sheep that had also been introduced in colonial times. Sheep do not fare well in hot humid climates, so that sheep raising and textile production only developed on a large scale in the cool highlands of Mexico and the Andes.

Other crafts did not see such a fusion of techniques. In pre-Columbian times Native peoples did not possess the wheel, but nevertheless produced a wide variety of pottery using the coil method. Despite the introduction of the wheel and also a simple kiln from Spain that made glazing possible, ceramic techniques remained much as they had been in pre-Columbian times. The same also appears to have been the case with basketry. Leatherworking, however, acquired new dimensions. In pre-Columbian times leather working had been confined to the use of skins obtained through hunting, but the arrival of cattle brought hides from which clothing could be manufactured. Ranching itself brought an assemblage of techniques from southern Spain, which included the rodeo, the *desgarretadero* for hocking cattle, and the lasso.

THE IMPACT OF NATIVE CROPS ON EUROPE AND THE WIDER WORLD

The impact of indigenous American crops had an equally profound effect on production and consumption patterns in Europe and the rest of the world. Attention focused initially on exotic crops, such cacao and dyes, which were produced in the Americas and exported. However, the transfer of staple food crops to the Old World brought more far-reaching effects, totally transforming basic diets in many parts of the world.

In the early colonial period the slow speed of transport and small size of ships meant that only those products that had a high value to weight ratio could be exported. One such commodity was cacao, from which the Aztec elite had made drinking chocolate, taking its name from the Nahuatl term *chocolatl*. Hernán Cortés took it to Spain in 1528, and it soon became a much-desired beverage in Europe. Meanwhile, dyestuffs, such as cochineal and indigo, produced in southern Mexico and Central America, were much sought after by textile workshops in Europe. Of more dubious value was tobacco. Columbus observed tobacco smoking in Hispaniola in 1492, and its commercial production began there on a small scale in the 1530s and in Brazil in the 1540s. Initially it was used for medicinal purposes as much as for pleasure. It did not develop into a major export crop in Latin America until the eighteenth century, though by then the British had successfully established tobacco cultivation in Virginia.

American food crops, such as potatoes, maize, and manioc, had a more extensive and persistent impact. More than two hundred varieties of potatoes were grown in the Andes in pre-Columbian times. Because the potato prefers cool, wet climates its impact in the Mediterranean was limited, but it spread to Ireland, parts of northern Europe, and Russia, where in the eighteenth century it became a major food crop that provided the basis for population growth and industrialization. Maize and manioc spread more rapidly at an earlier date. Columbus himself introduced maize to Spain and by the mid-sixteenth century it was also being cultivated in China, though there it faced competition from rice. Maize along with manioc also spread widely in West and Central Africa, encouraged by the need for provisions to support the African slave trade. Maize was more productive than African cereals, while manioc was well adapted to poor soils and drought conditions, so that they soon replaced indigenous sorghum, millet, and yams.

Diets were not only transformed by new staple foods, but also came to include a number of vegetables and fruits. Most important was the tomato. This was originally domesticated in the Andes, but its English name derives from the Aztec term *tomatl*. The early history of the tomato in Europe is obscure but it appeared in Italy in the sixteenth century where it was given the name "golden apple" or *pomi d'oro*. Other arrivals from the Americas included beans, peppers, pumpkins, pineapples, guava, papaya, avocados, and peanuts.

THE TRANSFER OF DISEASES

The transfer of diseases between the Old World and the Americas had a disproportionate impact on Native Americans. In pre-Columbian times Native Americans suffered from a range of gastrointestinal and respiratory diseases, tuberculosis, and possibly louse-borne typhus. However, the only serious infection to be carried back to Europe from the Americas was probably syphilis, though its origin continues to be debated. More devastating was the impact of crowd infections, such as smallpox, measles, plague, and influenza, which were introduced from Europe. Since Native Americans possessed no immunity to these infections because of the isolation of the continent, each epidemic caused high mortality. In addition, malaria took a heavy toll of populations in the tropical lowlands. Old World diseases were thus a major factor in the decline of the Native American population, which some researchers estimate had fallen by 90 percent by the mid-seventeenth century.

SEE ALSO *Biological Impacts of European Expansion in the Americas; Encomienda; Fur and Skin Trades in the Americas; Haciendas in Spanish America; Mining, the Americas.*

BIBLIOGRAPHY

Bauer, Arnold J. *Goods, Power, History: Latin America's Material Culture.* Cambridge, U.K.: Cambridge University Press, 2001.

Carney, Judith A. *Black Rice: The Origins of Rice Cultivation in the Americas.* Cambridge, MA: Harvard University Press, 2001.

Coe, Sophie D. *America's First Cuisines.* Austin: Texas University Press, 1994.

Cook, N. David. *Born to Die: Disease and New World Conquests, 1492–1650.* Cambridge, U.K.: Cambridge University Press, 1998.

Crosby, Alfred W. *The Columbian Exchange: Biological and Cultural Consequences of 1492.* Westport, CT: Greenwood Press, 1972.

Foster, George M. *Conquest and Culture: America's Spanish Heritage.* Chicago: Quadrangle Books, 1960.

Galloway, J. H. *The Sugar Cane Industry: A Historical Geography from its Origins to 1914.* Cambridge, U.K.: Cambridge University Press, 1989.

Kiple, Kenneth F., and Kriemhild C. Ornelas, eds. *The Cambridge World History of Food.* 2 vols. Cambridge, U.K.: Cambridge University Press, 2000.

Langer, William. "American Foods and Europe's Population Growth 1750–1850." *Journal of Social History* 8 (2) (Winter 1975): 51–66.

Melville, Elinor G. K. *A Plague of Sheep: Environmental Consequences of the Conquest of Mexico.* Cambridge, U.K.: Cambridge University Press, 1994.

Seed, Patricia. *American Pentimento: The Invention of Indians and the Pursuit of Riches.* Minneapolis: University of Minnesota Press, 2002.

Super, John C. *Food, Conquest, and the Colonization in Sixteenth-Century Spanish America.* Albuquerque: University of New Mexico Press, 1988.

Viola, Herman J., and Carolyn Margolis. *Seeds of Change.* Washington and London: Smithsonian Institution Press, 1991.

West, Robert C., and John P. Augelli. *Middle America: Its Lands and Peoples,* 3rd ed. Englewood Cliffs, NJ: Prentice-Hall, 1989.

Linda A. Newson

EDIB, HALIDE
1884–1964

Halide Edib was a Turkish nationalist, feminist, author, educator, and member of parliament who lived during one of the most turbulent times in Turkish history, experiencing and contributing to the transformation from empire into nation in the early twentieth century. As a daughter of a social secretary of Sultan Abdülhamid II (1842–1918), she grew up in elite circles around the palace, getting the most premier education available. She was educated at home and also became, in 1901, one of the earliest graduates of the American College in Istanbul. She seemed to be destined for domestic life after her marriage to one of the most important scientists of the day, mathematician and astronomer Salih Zeki (1864–1921), but the Young Turk Revolution of 1908

led to the proliferation of print media. Her writing career was launched with the columns she wrote about women and education in journals and newspapers. Her first novels, *Heyula* (*Ghost*) and *Raik'in Annesi* (*Raik's Mother*), were published in 1909, to be followed in 1910 by *Seviyye Talip*, an eponymous novel named after its murderous heroine.

She divorced her husband in 1910 when he entered a second polygamous marriage (which was allowed by law at the time) and started a new life for herself with her two sons. She made a happy match in her second marriage to Dr. Adnan Adivar (1882–1955) in 1917. Her second husband was a fellow nationalist, the head of the Red Crescent and an adviser to Atatürk (1881–1938) during the period of the formation of the Turkish Republic, and a founder of the first Turkish communist party, *Terakkiperver Cumhuriyet Firkasi*, in 1924. He wrote the first comprehensive history of science in the Ottoman Empire.

Halide Edib had a productive writing career during which she wrote twenty-one novels, many short stories (later collected in four volumes), two plays, two memoirs, and several books of historical and literary analyses. She is one of the most important authors of the Turkish republican period who contributed to the development of realistic, psychological novels. She delves into questions of identity, gender, nationalism, religion, and history in her novels. Early novels such as *Yeni Turan* (The New Turan) in 1912, *The Shirt of Flame* in 1922, and *Vurun Kahpeye* (Strike the Harlot) in 1926 depict war periods, examining the concepts of Turkishness and patriotism. She was an influential contributor to the New History thesis, which was an intellectual project of redefining a new Turkish identity out of the heritage of an imperial Ottoman past.

In all of her novels, she presented strong, passionate women who grapple not only with social limitations placed on them, but also equally with the contradictory societal expectations that burden their lives. Her most widely known novel, *Sinekli Bakkal* (1936), which was originally written in English as *The Clown and His Daughter*, attempted to create a synthesis between Western and Eastern components of Turkish identity through the love story of its protagonists. Some of her other novels are: *Kalp Agrisi* (Heartache) in 1924 and its sequel *Zeyno'nun Oglu* (Zeyno's Son) in 1927, *Yolpalas Cinayeti* (The Yolpalas Murder) in 1938, *Sonsuz Panayir* (Endless Carnival) in 1946, *Doner Ayna* (Revolving Mirror) in 1954, *Kerim Usta'nin Oglu* (Kerim Usta's Son) in 1958, and *Hayat Parcalari* (Pieces of Life) in 1963.

Halide Edib traveled the world, working on educational projects in Syria and Lebanon, collaborating on pedagogical ideals and women's issues with Isabel Fry

(1869–1958), teaching at Barnard College in New York in 1931 and lecturing in India in 1935. She presented her theoretical and historical analyses in *Turkey Faces West* (1930), *Conflict of East and West in Turkey* (1935), and *Inside India* (1937). She was a powerful public orator. Her Sultanahmet speech on June 6, 1919, following the invasions of Istanbul and Izmir by the Allied forces, became the emblem of public resistance to the occupation. She participated in the Turkish Independence War (1919–1922) as a public relations officer and nurse, earning the military ranks of corporal and sergeant. Political disagreements with Atatürk led to her half-voluntary exile with her husband Adnan Adivar from 1924 to 1939, during which time she lived in England and France, where she wrote respectively the first and second volumes of her memoirs: *Memoirs of Halide Edib* (1926) and *The Turkish Ordeal* (1928). Every aspect of her multifaceted life was extraordinary and larger than life. In the memoirs, which she originally wrote in English, she interweaves the various strands of her private and public experiences as a dual story of both her life and the birth of the Turkish nation, amply displaying her literary gifts. These memoirs not only trace the historical transition from the Ottoman Empire into Turkish nation from the pen of a witness and participant to this history, but also demonstrate a female writer's attempt to co-opt and redefine the genre of autobiography.

SEE ALSO *Atatürk, Mustafa Kemal.*

BIBLIOGRAPHY

Durakbasa, Ayse. *Halide Edib: Türk modernlesmesi ve feminizm.* Istanbul: Iletisim, 2000.

Erol, Sibel. "Introduction." In *House With Wisteria: Memoirs of Halide Edib.* Charlottesville, VA: Leopolis Press, 2003.

Kandiyoti, Deniz. "Slave Girls, Temptresses, and Comrades: Images of Women in the Turkish Novel." *Feminist Issues* 8 (1988): 33–50.

Sibel Erol

EDUCATION, MIDDLE EAST

This article presents an overview of educational developments in the Middle East from 1450 until the early twentieth century. It considers traditional Islamic education, the emergence of modern schools, the influx of missionary education, and the educational, cultural, and political impact of these developments on the Middle East. From the early modern period until World War I (1914–1918) the main sovereign states of the Middle East were the Ottoman Empire, Iran, and Morocco. In 1517 the Mamluk Empire was conquered

by the Ottomans. After 1811 Egypt became semi-independent, and in 1830 the autonomous Ottoman province of Algiers was occupied, and subsequently turned into a French colony. In 1881 the autonomous Ottoman province of Tunis became a French protectorate, and the following year Egypt was occupied by Britain. Morocco, the only independent state left in North Africa, entered French protection in 1912. By 1914 the Ottoman Empire and Iran were the only sovereign countries left in the Middle East. Thus, nineteenth-century educational modernization in the Middle East took place under varying social and political conditions. This article discusses the similar as well as differing patterns of educational reform in the above-mentioned regions. For countries such as Iran, Morocco, Tunisia, and Algeria, the period stretches to the mid-twentieth century. As in most premodern societies, traditional education in the Middle East was based mainly on religion. From the eleventh century onward Sunni Islamic orthodoxy dominated the region. It was during the period of Seljukid domination (eleventh through twelfth centuries) that religious colleges (*madrasas*) expanded in Baghdad and elsewhere in the Middle East. Following the collapse of the Shiite Fatimid caliphate, the Al-Azhar *madrasa* in Cairo, originally founded in 975 as a Shiite religious college, turned into a Sunni institution. Another intellectual impetus promoting religious instruction came from Al-Ghazali (d. 1111), who insisted on the metaphysical superiority of religious knowledge over experimental and rational sciences. When the Ottoman principality turned into a full-fledged bureaucratic empire in the early fifteenth century, the intellectual resources it could rely on for the development of cultural life were conditioned mainly by orthodox Sunni ideology and Sufism (Islamic mysticism). A consequence of the Ottoman expansion in the Middle East during the course of the sixteenth century was the transformation of the Ottoman Empire into the main Sunni Islamic power of the world. The only remaining independent Sunni state in the region was Morocco. Iran, under the Safavids, became a Shiite power. The fact that Shiism was considered by the Sunni orthodox Islamic majority as heresy affected Iran's position within the Islamic world, turning this state into an "outsider," and a religious adversary of the Ottomans. During the process of educational reform in the nineteenth and twentieth centuries, characteristics peculiar to Shiism, such as the rather independent position of the Shiite *ulama* vis-à-vis the government, would lead to developments different from those found in Sunni societies.

TRADITIONAL EDUCATION PRIOR TO THE NINETEENTH CENTURY

The Ottoman state from late fifteenth century onward acquired a Sunni Islamic identity based on the Hanafite legal school, but its population consisted of non-Muslims as well as Muslims. Though political authority was in the hands of the Muslim ruling class, cultural issues such as religion and education were left to individual religious communities. In harmony with this arrangement, school networks were maintained by communities themselves. Muslim institutional education was supported mainly by pious foundations (*vakif*). Basic education was provided by Quranic schools (*mahalle mektebi, kuttab*), often located within mosque compounds, and administered by lower Muslim clerics (*hoca, fiqî*). In North Africa, Quranic schools were mostly attached to Sufi convents. The main aim of this education was to have students memorize the Quran in classical Arabic, and to inculcate them with religious precepts. Those pupils who were able to memorize the entire Quran were considered to have succeeded in their basic education. Most graduates of Quranic schools did not acquire the basic elements of literacy as it is defined in the modern era—including proficiency in reading and writing as well as rudimentary mathematical knowledge.

Non-Muslim parochial schools serving Greek, Armenian, and Jewish communities displayed traits parallel to those of the Quranic schools. They were attached to local churches or synagogues and administered by the priest or rabbi. Reading of the Bible and other basic religious texts constituted the main part of education. The language of instruction was often the liturgical language of the church, not the vernacular of the local population.

Male graduates of Quranic schools either had to select their profession or craft themselves, or had it picked for them by parents or other relatives. Those who decided to continue institutionalized education went to *madrasas* and became member of the *ulama* stratum. The remaining ones entered professional life, and received practical education as apprentices.

Madrasas were religious colleges financially supported by pious foundations and usually located within a mosque complex. They were organized, within the Ottoman Empire, according to a hierarchical order, and in coordination with the central authority. Lower-level *madrasas* offered courses in basic subjects of Islamic scholastic knowledge such as Arabic grammar, Aristotelian logic, theology, rhetoric, geometry, and astronomy, followed by intermediate-level theology and jurisprudence. Graduates of these lower-level *madrasas* could become the *kadis* or *muftis* of small towns. Higher-level *madrasas* were located mainly in Istanbul. In these the main concentration was on Islamic jurisprudence and Quranic exegesis. At the top of this hierarchy were the Sahn-i Seman and the Süleymaniye *madrasas*. Graduates of the higher-level *madrasas* could be

appointed *kadis* or *muftis* to major Ottoman cities—that is, they became government officials. *Madrasas* in the classically Islamic lands, governed until 1516–1517 by the Mamluk regime of Egypt, suffered from Ottoman rule due to their subordination as peripheral provinces. At least in the case of Egypt, higher learning declined due to the transfer of major amounts of money to Istanbul. In peripheral Ottoman lands such as Tunis and Algiers, the curricula of *madrasas* in major centers were readjusted to conform to the religious doctrines of the official Ottoman Hanafite legal school. Outside these centers the Malikite legal school remained dominant in *madrasa* education. In southern Iraq, with its mainly Shiite population, the Shiite *madrasas* remained outside the Ottoman educational network, and in close contact with the Shiite *ulama* of neighboring Iran.

The Safavids' political takeover in Iran (1501) constitutes a turning point in that country's history. During the period of Safavid rule, the Iranian population became converted to Shiism, and education became directed toward the expansion and enforcement of Shiite religious precepts. Shiite *madrasa* education consisted of three levels: At the primary level, the Arabic language and grammar, rhetoric, logic, and basic Islamic law were taught. At the intermediate level, students encountered the philosophical texts of Avicenna, Mullah Sadra, and Hâdî-i Sebzevârî, while studying Islamic jurisprudence. At the advanced level, the main concentration was on Islamic law. Shiite *madrasas* constituted a network of their own, but without any coordinated relationship with central authority. The Shiite *ulama* exerted immense social and political authority over the government as well as over the population—far more than the *ulama* in Sunni Islamic societies, who never played the role of an alternative authority.

Under the Almohad (1147–1269) and Marinid (1269–1465) dynasties, Morocco, at the far west side of the Middle East, had enjoyed a flourishing culture. Following the reign of the Marinids, however, the country increasingly suffered from political instability and tribal revolts, which had an adverse effect on the cultural life of the country. Though the Sharifi Alawite dynasty reestablished political order (1660), an efficient central administration was not developed until the French protectorate period. Moroccan *madrasas*, not surprisingly, existed as loose bodies, without being a part of an educational network. Two major Moroccan *madrasas* were the Qarawiyin *madrasa* (in Fez) and the Yusufiya *madrasa* (in Marrakech).

As far as educational opportunities outside the *madrasa* framework were concerned, the general tendency was that boys without special aptitude for religious sciences either entered trades or crafts, or, if they had a personal connection to the bureaucracy, they might be admitted to the scribal service. A special type of educational institution in the premodern Ottoman Empire was the palace school (Enderun Mektebi), which admitted mainly promising Christian subjects from Balkan villages. Here boys were trained in the arts of war and weaponry as well as Islamic sciences, mathematics, geometry, geography, literature, and poetry. Those who reached the top educational levels acquired high administrative or military rank.

Individuals also had the opportunity to receive literary and artistic education within certain Sufi convents. In fact, members of nearly all social classes in the Ottoman lands belonged to one or another Sufi order. Religious life was no longer governed by the simple tenets of Islam but rather by the various Sufi interpretations of religious law and texts. While the details of ritual, prayer, and daily Islamic behavior were to a great extent determined by the sheikhs of Sufi orders, learned people devoted much time to the reading and writing of Sufi literature, which consisted mainly of poetry.

MODERNIZATION AND EDUCATIONAL REFORM: AN OVERVIEW

All Middle Eastern countries (the Ottoman lands, Iran, Morocco) encountered the phenomenon of a European military threat to their territorial integrity and independence, which in many cases led to colonization. The core Ottoman provinces faced this threat as early as 1683 to 1699, followed by Egypt in 1798 to 1801, and Iran in 1803 to 1815, while the social effects of the French invasion of Algiers in 1830 were felt both in Tunis and in Morocco. In the course of the nineteenth century, the Ottoman Empire, Egypt, and to some extent Tunisia, all of them equipped with central bureaucratic apparatuses, undertook comprehensive educational reforms. Iran and Morocco, on the other hand, lacked efficient bureaucracies, and thus were unable to introduce major educational modernization. In Iran, in addition, the Shiite *ulama* consistently opposed educational reforms. In Algeria and Morocco educational modernization was introduced through French colonial administration, whereas the British protectorate of Egypt and the French protectorate of Tunisia preserved to some degree their own educational institutions and traditions, created through previous internal educational reforms. Turkey and Iran survived World War I without being colonized. All these distinct developments, combined with varying internal sociopolitical conditions, led to the emergence of different patterns of educational modernization throughout the Middle East.

In most Middle Eastern countries the process of educational modernization underwent the following identical phases: At the beginning, as an outgrowth of attempts to build up military strength, some selected students were sent to Europe to study modern military technology. The next phase was the founding of a few military and naval engineering schools, to train able military officers or naval engineers. The immense cost of building a new army and navy created a need for a more efficient provincial administration and tax collection. This need led to the third stage of educational modernization: the setting up of schools that aimed to produce well-educated civil servants in order to form an efficient bureaucracy. At the same time, the expansion of basic education was understood as a necessary precondition for socioeconomic development.

At this stage of educational modernization, Middle Eastern countries encountered a crucial problem: the apparent conflict between religious values, represented by traditional education, and secular values, represented by modern schools. Or, considered at the institutional level, the issue can be framed as a conflict between two different school networks. The varying responses to this conflict also represent the different outcomes of educational modernization in Middle Eastern countries. In all Sunni Islamic societies there emerged a movement known as *Islamic Modernism*, which stressed that Islam and modernity are not mutually exclusive. This movement integrated a sizeable part of the *ulama* into the process of educational modernization. In the Ottoman Empire, Egypt, Tunisia, and Algeria the *ulama* compromised in order to retain a dominant role in the modern school network. Morocco did not experience this issue in terms of a dichotomy: traditional schools and the modern educational network were able to function together, without an apparent conflict. In Shiite Iran, however, Islamic Modernism did not influence the *ulama* establishment as happened elsewhere. The *ulama* remained outside of the process of officially directed educational modernization.

The colonization of Algeria, Tunisia, and Morocco also forced traditional and modern elites to face the conflict between Islam and modernization. In these countries, civil initiatives emerged to develop private school networks devoted to educational modernization and the promotion of Arabo-Islamic culture in the face of an ever more pervasive European colonial cultural presence. The aim was often to integrate Islamic values with the values and goals of secular education.

Another aspect of educational change was the foundation of foreign and missionary school networks. These networks were sponsored either by organizations supported or encouraged by certain European countries, or were created by purely missionary bodies driven by millenarianist or other religious motives. Whatever the motives behind them, these networks were crucial in spreading knowledge of modern foreign languages such as French and English among some urban segments of the Middle Eastern population, and they thus opened channels for the diffusion of modern ideas. At the same time, these networks also created friction and confrontation in the region, either through the breaking up of local Christian communities as a consequence of active proselytizing, or through the introduction of critical reasoning to students, who then began to evaluate their own society and political system in a critical way.

THE OTTOMAN-TURKISH EXPERIENCE

The earliest steps toward educational modernization in the Middle East occurred within the Ottoman lands. Ottoman military decline and territorial vulnerability in the face of rising powers such as Russia and Austria led the Ottoman government to promote modern education for the sake of military modernization. In 1718 through 1719 an Ottoman mission visited France with the aim of acquiring useful information in order to strengthen the empire. One result of this mission was the foundation of the first Turkish printing press in Istanbul (1729). First in 1733, then in 1773, naval engineering schools were opened. With the goal of founding a new army, Selim III (r. 1789–1807) launched the Nizam-i Cedid reforms. To supply this new corps with a body of trained military officers, another military engineering school was instituted in 1795. Following the abolition of the Janissary Corps in 1826, Mahmud II (r. 1808–1839) founded the Military Medical School (1827) and the Military Academy (1834).

Educational institutions devoted to raising competent civil administrators emerged from 1821 onward, starting with the Translation Bureau, which was founded to teach European languages to civil servants. In 1839 two primary-level specialized schools were opened with the aim of training future civil servants. These schools offered courses with a worldly perspective, including French language classes. The prevailing conception of educational reform as a tool for raising competent civil servants lasted until 1856. Between 1847 and 1856 a series of secondary-level schools, called *rüşdiyye* schools, were set up in the main provincial centers of Anatolia and the Balkans. In 1848 the first teachers, seminary was opened. These schools were supervised by the Directorate of Public Schools (1849), which was attached directly to the Sublime Porte.

Primary education, being the core part of public education, was still considered to belong to the realm of religion, and traditional Quranic schools served this purpose. However, the insufficient literacy level of Quranic school graduates became a concern, and the Sublime Porte undertook attempts to reform these institutions. Because Quranic schools were autonomous bodies attached to religious foundations, and also because of the *ulama*'s resistance, these reform attempts proved futile.

The Crimean War (1853–1856) and the admission of the Ottoman Empire into the Concert of Europe led to dramatic legal and social changes. The Reform Edict of 1856 guaranteed full equality to non-Muslim subjects of the empire. This guarantee implied that the traditional division of labor based on religious affiliation ceased to exist and non-Muslims could enter the bureaucracy and army. These developments created a qualitative shift in the prevalent notion of education, from a limited understanding of educational reform to a belief in the necessity of an all-encompassing system of modern public education. The Ministry of Public Education was founded in 1857, and in 1869 the Regulation of Public Education stipulated the setting up of government primary schools (*ibtidai* schools) and an improved type of secondary school (*idadi* schools). In 1858 first female *rüşdiyye* schools were opened in Istanbul, and the Teachers' Seminary for Girls began to function in 1870. Between 1856 and 1871, the ruling elite consisted of secular Ottomanists, who aimed to create one Ottoman nation with a supra-identity encompassing Muslims and non-Muslims. This project, foreseeing the mixed education of Muslim and non-Muslim students, required the secularization of public education. However, this goal was achieved only at the level of higher education (medical schools, engineering schools, various professional schools) and at the elite *lycée* Mekteb-i Sultânî (1868). The reasons for this limited success included the strong presence of members of the *ulama* as schoolmasters or instructors at *rüşdiyye* schools due to the scarcity of competent secular teachers to replace them, the inability to reduce the number of course subjects with an Islamic content, and the reluctance of non-Muslims to send their children to secondary-level government schools.

After 1871 a general political and economic crisis occurred, leading to internal instability as well as separatist revolts in the Balkans. The various diplomatic interventions that ensued led to the Russo-Ottoman War of 1877 to 1878, as a result of which the Ottomans lost a major part of their Balkan possessions. The autocracy of Abdülhamid II (1876–1909) emerged as a reaction against the Ottomanist policies of the past and pursued a policy of Islamicization. Religion was used as an ideological glue to keep Arabs and Albanians loyal to Istanbul. While government schools of all levels expanded throughout the empire, the curricula became a blend of Islamic and natural scientific courses. Similarly, the faculty consisted both of members of the *ulama* and secular officials. In 1900 Istanbul University was opened.

The Young Turk Revolution (1908) considered the Hamidian attempt to synthesize modernism and Islam a failure and introduced a general secularization of the curricula. The traditional *madrasas* of Istanbul were reformed into one single modern *madrasa*, with modern course subjects. In 1924, following the foundation of the Republic of Turkey, all Quranic schools and *madrasas* were closed down, in realization of the Kemalist principle of the "Unity of Instruction." After 1949 Muslim clergy began to be produced at specialized *imam-hatip* schools or theological faculties. Late Ottoman *ulama* with modernist tendencies became members of the theological faculty of Ankara. The prohibition of Sufi orders, however, led their adherents, until recent liberalization, to practice prayers and pursue education in a secret manner.

The crucial characteristics of the Ottoman-Turkish experience are the presence of a strong bureaucracy, the integration of the upper levels of the *ulama* into the process of educational reform, and the limited direct cultural impact of the West. The number of Ottomans educated in European schools was minimal, and government schools were far from being copies of European counterparts—they were redesigned according to local needs, though perceived as being "European" institutions. In fact, Ottoman elites with modern educations had their own perception of the Western world, and while they tended to consider themselves as being like Westerners, they generally had no close contact with the West. Thus, Ottoman intellectuals were probably more indigenous than they actually realized and did not conceive modernization and Westernization as a colonial experience, in contrast to Egyptian, Algerian and Moroccan elites.

EGYPTIAN, TUNISIAN, AND MOROCCAN REFORMS

In the first decades of the nineteenth century, Egypt's powerful governor, Mehmed Ali Pasha (r. 1805–1849), embarked on a vigorous program of military and economic modernization, with the aim of making his country independent. In 1809 he sent a group of young men to Europe to study the military sciences, and in 1816 a military academy was founded in Cairo. New military schools were set up in Cairo (1820) and also in Aswan and Farshut, near Qina (1822). A printing press was set up in Bulak (1822), and a medical school and hospital were founded in Cairo (1827). These were followed by other technical schools, including a School of Agriculture and Administration (1829), and a language school (1835). Medical institutions and the polytechnical school were founded by Frenchmen in Egyptian service. After 1835 primary-level military schools expanded in the provinces, in Syria in particular. These local schools aimed at producing low-level army officers with basic education to supply the army.

Civil education emerged from the 1840s onward. The first modern civil school was set up in Cairo in 1843, based on the Lancaster system. In 1847 eight new Lancasterian schools were founded in Cairo. However, the new governor, Abbas Hilmi Pasha (r. 1848–1854), closed down these government schools (1849). Following an interval of nearly fourteen years, educational reforms were resumed by Governor İsmail Pasha (r. 1863–1879). In 1863 the Ministry of Education was founded, and the Organic Law of Education (1868) provided a legal framework for the Egyptian primary school network. This law aimed at integrating Quranic schools into the state school system. In 1871 a teachers' seminary was set up to train Al-Azhar *madrasa* students as government schoolteachers. The first government girls' schools were inaugurated in 1873 and 1874.

After 1882, during the British protectorate period, the expansion of government primary schools reached the village level. Primary schools were established for both sexes. Despite these reform measures, there were only nine higher-level and three secondary government schools in Egypt around 1900; the remaining educational institutions were all either Quranic schools or *madrasas*. The Egyptian educational system, after 1882, increasingly served British colonial interests. The emerging native Arab Egyptian intelligentsia insisted on the need to found a modern university. Despite British resistance, this project was realized in 1908, in the shape of the University of Cairo.

In contrast to the Ottoman experience, Egyptian reforms are marked by discontinuities, such as the closures in 1849, and the British protectorate period. Also, early reforms were undertaken by a Turko-Circassian ruling elite, who were considered foreigners by the Arab masses. The outcome of these reforms was a division between elite and traditional education. This social cleavage lasted until the regime of Gamal Abdel Nasser (1952–1970). Comprehensive reforms covering the majority of Egyptians were only undertaken after 1952. Another contrast to the Turkish experience is the continuing importance of the Al-Azhar *madrasa*, which is now a full-fledged university. In other words, the *ulama* still continues to exert its influence in the social and political affairs of Egypt.

In Tunisia, military reforms were launched under the rule of Governor Ahmed Bey (r. 1837–1855). Previously, traditional higher education had been entrusted to the *madrasas* of Zeytouna and Kairouan. But developments such as modernization efforts in the Ottoman capital, the French threat after the invasion of neighboring Algeria (1830), and the Ottoman occupation of Tripolitania (in Libya, 1835) forced the Tunisian ruling elite to undertake efforts to modernize its army. In 1840 a military academy, the first modern school in Tunisia, was opened in Bardo. Early graduates of this school later played a considerable role in the modernization of Tunisia. In 1860 the first printing press was set up. During the government of Khaireddin Pasha (1873–1877) Quranic schools were taken under centralized government supervision with the aim of reforming them into modern primary schools (1874). In 1875 a civil high school, the Collège Sadeqi, was founded. This high school adopted the French *lycée* curriculum, and the language of instruction was French.

The French occupation of Tunisia in 1881 and the declaration of a French protectorate created a discontinuity in educational reform. Though the local government continued to exist, it was not in a position anymore to initiate reformist steps. From 1896 onward, reform initiatives emerged from civil society groups. The factors that compelled educational initiatives from below were twofold. On the one hand, the acceleration of French cultural influence among the Tunisian urban elites was reinforced through the Collège Sadeqi, the expansion of French schools, and the Jewish Alliance Israélite Universelle network. Muslim graduates of these institutions seemed increasingly to become alienated from the Arab-Islamic culture, which, under the French protectorate, appeared to face the threat of extinction. At the same time, traditional *madrasas* proved incapable of reforming their curricula and pedagogical methods.

A group of Tunisian intellectuals with modernist Islamic tendencies founded the cultural association Jâmia al-Khaldûniyya (1896). This association, in contrast to the fully-French Collège Sadeqi or the traditional Zaytuna *madrasa*, offered Arabic-language courses on natural sciences and modern subjects. This initiative was followed by other similar non-governmental ventures, which offered courses to adults on practical subjects such as mathematics or hygiene, opened special classes to expand literacy, and organized public lectures in Arabic or French on scientific topics, literature, and history. They also provided scholarships to students who aimed to further their education in France. In the 1930s the Jâmia al-Khaldûniyya already had become a full-fledged educational network of its own, reaching from primary-level schools to college-level courses and issuing graduation diplomas; it also provided industrial education and literacy classes for adults. In 1946 the Jâmia al-Khaldûniyya included institutes for Islamic studies, law, and philosophy. Following the full independence of Tunisia in 1957, this institution was replaced by the University of Tunis. The Zaytuna *madrasa* was reformed into a modern theological university.

Tunisia suffered from colonial disruption more severely than did Egypt. While previously created modern schools such as the Collège Sadeqi continued to function, French authorities did not allow local government to take further reform initiatives. As a consequence, civilian Tunisians had to launch educational initiatives, which proved to be successful. This success even overshadowed the Collège Sadeqi as well as traditional *madrasas*. Similarly to what had occurred in Turkey, it provided a basis for President Habib Bourguiba to declare an educational policy based on the "Unity of Instruction" and to institute the reformation of traditional schools. The *ulama* in modern Tunisia, as in Turkey and in contrast to Egypt, does not have any political influence.

Morocco under Sharifi rule emerged as a territorial state with relatively stable borders, but it was unable to establish a fully functioning centralized bureaucracy and impose its authority over tribes. The lack of a comprehensive countrywide civil administration prevented the development of a government-initiated school system. From the 1840s onward, European intervention in Morocco became frequent, and European educational activities in Morocco increased. The first modern schools in Morocco were foreign schools, initiated by Franciscans, Protestant missionaries, and the Alliance Israélite Universelle. As a reaction to these developments, Moroccan elites began to promote the revitalization of Islamic society by reemphasizing Islamic values, while accepting useful European innovations.

During the reign of Sidi Muhammad bin Abd ar-Rahman (r. 1859–1873) steps were taken to reform the existing *madrasas*. Subjects such as mathematics, engineering, and astronomy were introduced, even though at a basic level. In 1865 the first printing press was set up in Fez. Religious scholars were sent as students to schools in Paris, Cairo, Mecca, and Istanbul for modern education. Similar policies were continued by Moulay Hasan I (1873–1894), and those scholars who returned from abroad were offered government posts. But these measures were not accompanied by steps such as founding modern government schools.

The French protectorate over Morocco (1912–1956) did not pursue a policy of destroying traditional public institutions, but rather of developing more powerful French institutions alongside the traditional Moroccan ones. Thus, traditional Moroccan education, supported by religious foundations, and the two major *madrasas* remained intact. Traditional scholars, graduated from these *madrasas*, were indispensable as intermediaries between French officials and rural notables. Meanwhile, for the children of Moroccan elites, the colonial administration built new schools that were the exact copies of

French institutions. Graduates of these schools were offered positions in colonial administration. This development destroyed the public esteem of the *madrasas*. In the 1920s some Moroccan intellectuals set up "Free Schools." This was a significant development in terms of the emergence of a local movement pressing for educational modernization. These institutions, which were independent of French-controlled schools, applied modern pedagogical methods, included modern subjects, and taught in the Arabic language. But these schools failed to become influential within Moroccan society and could not compete with the French-controlled schools. As a consequence, a new generation of Moroccan elites arose during the French protectorate that was educated in, and experienced modernity through, the French language.

A national school system was established in Morocco only following its independence (1956). Due to the predominance of French linguistic influence, national education initially was provided mainly in the French language. On the other hand, Quranic schools and *madrasas* continued to use Arabic as the medium of instruction. From 1968 onward, Quranic schools were reformed through the inclusion of modern subjects into their curriculum. *Madrasas* have acquired the function of special religious colleges. At present, both French and Arabic are used as languages of instruction in secondary as well as higher education.

Morocco, in contrast to Egypt and Tunisia, was never an Ottoman province. However, the weakness of central authority hindered any indigenous steps toward educational modernization. Because educational modernization appeared first through foreign schools, then through French colonial institutions, modern culture in Morocco became Francophone. During the protectorate period, civil educational initiatives to promote the use of the Arabic language remained a failure. On the other hand, traditional schools and *madrasas* enjoyed continuity, despite some curricular and institutional reforms. At present, members of the *ulama* still act as *kadis* for legal issues concerning personal status. Overall, Morocco represents a model of educational reform in which revolutionary modernization has not taken place, but instead evolutionary development.

ALGERIAN MODERNIZATION

In contrast to Egypt, Tunisia, and Morocco, Algeria did not "enjoy" protectorate status but was subjected to direct colonization. The cultural agenda of France was to turn the country into a "French Algeria." The main obstacle to this agenda was the institution of Islam. Thus, the long-term French policy became to eliminate Islam, and to settle Algeria with French colons. As the traditional school system deteriorated, either due to

negligence or the hostility of the French administration, Algerians traveled to Tunisia or Morocco for their education. Tunisia's *madrasas* offered religious and other kinds of instruction to students and scholars from Algeria. Toward the end of the nineteenth century, Tunis functioned as a publishing center for Algerian scholars seeking to print religious works, which French-controlled printing presses in Algeria did not allow. The French administration founded a modern school system for French colons, the University of Algiers (1881). Muslims were initially only allowed to enter primary schools, and later secondary schools in certain specified towns.

One reaction to this cultural subjugation was a tendency among Sufis toward withdrawal from worldly life. As a consequence new Sufi orders, such as the Rahmaniyya, emerged. During the second half of the nineteenth century convents of this order (e.g., Tulqa Zawiya, Al-Hamil), located in the remote south, became important educational centers. Not only religious and mystical subjects were taught, but also courses on natural sciences. At Al-Hamil in particular, hundreds of students and scholars engaged in educational activities. Funding for these schools derived largely from the donations of the thousands of pilgrims who traveled to see the convent sheikhs each year.

Toward the end of the nineteenth century colonial rule in Algeria became more tolerant, as new francophone Muslim generations emerged. In 1894 the Association of Francophone Muslims was founded, with the aim of promoting Arabic culture. In these years Arabic works on the history of Algeria began to appear, and a bilingual newspaper was published. Thanks to these improved conditions, the reformist *ulama* of Algeria began to organize themselves. In 1931 Abdülhamid bin Badis founded the Association of the Algerian Muslim *Ulama* with the aim of reforming Islamic education in line with the principles of Islamic modernism. This association set up a network of reformed *madrasas*. Similarly, another organization, the People's Party, set up *madrasas* devoted to popular education. French colonial authorities did their best to prevent these movements, but in 1947 they were forced to acknowledge Arabic as the language of education. These *madrasas* were crucial in developing Algerian national consciousness, and the *ulama* cooperated closely with the Front de Libération Nationale (FLN) organization.

Following independence in 1962, Algeria became a socialist country. The leaders of the FLN were staunch secularists, which led to the dissolution of the Association of the Algerian Muslim *Ulama* and the prohibition of Sufi orders. In this respect Algeria followed the examples of Turkey and Tunisia, and the policy of "Unity of Instruction" was applied. The French colonial presence of more than a century left a strong linguistic imprint on Algeria. Not surprisingly, French continued to serve as a language of instruction along with Arabic. In order to overcome this colonial legacy, a policy of Arabization was applied to public education. Due to the lack of qualified Arabic-speaking teachers, instructors were imported from other Arab countries, particularly Egypt. By the year 2000, all institutions of higher learning had adopted Arabic as the language of instruction.

Among all Middle Eastern countries, it was Algeria that experienced colonialism to the most intensive degree. For Paris, Algeria was not a colony, but a core region of France. Prior to independence, numerous well-educated Algerians came to consider themselves Muslim French citizens. This phenomenon represented a crisis of identity among Algeria's urban strata. Indeed it was the traditional Sufi orders and the *ulama* who resisted French cultural domination and established alternative educational institutions. By the time Algeria became independent, the language of the urban population had become French. It is questionable to what extent the program of forced Arabization has really succeeded. Islamism rather than Arabism seems to have become the national identity of Algerians, as the developments of the last decade have shown.

IRANIAN EXPERIENCE

As with the Ottomans, modernization efforts in Iran were conditioned by military defeats at the hands of Russians (1803–1815). But in Iran these steps were taken by a provincial government and not by the central authority (the Qajar regime, 1797–1925). The governor of Azerbaijan, crown prince Abbas Mirza, launched military reforms from 1807 to 1815, with the help of French, then British experts. However, these efforts did not include the foundation of schools. This same governor sent students to Britain for technical education (in 1811 and 1815). One of these students set up a printing press in Tabriz and published the first Iranian newspaper (1837).

The first centrally initiated military reforms were undertaken during the reign of Mohammad Shah (r. 1834–1848). In 1836 British officers were engaged to form a new Iranian army. Between 1843 and 1847 new students were sent to European countries for training in a variety of technical fields. Amir Kabir, the reformist prime minister serving under Naser al-Din Shah (r. 1848–1896), hoped to establish an efficient bureaucracy, staffed by well-educated civil servants. Thus, he took the major step of setting up a modern higher educational institution. His polytechnic school (Dar al-Fonun, 1851) was the first educational institution outside Shiite *ulama* control. Instructors were brought from Austria and Italy, and

the language of instruction was French. The school offered courses ranging from military sciences to medicine. In 1860 the Ministry of Sciences—a forerunner of the Ministry of Education—was founded. Between 1851 and 1870 the number of Iranians studying abroad increased. During the period of 1870 to 1875, three specialized secondary schools were established to produce civil and military officials. But outside these ventures there was no state policy of setting up a system of modern public education, in contrast to the Ottoman Empire and Egypt.

This educational void was filled, to a very marginal extent, by foreign and missionary schools. French, American Protestant, and Jewish school networks were visited by Iranian students. Modern education for the wider Iranian public was provided for the first time by these institutions. The lack of modern public schools was strongly felt by the Iranian intelligentsia, and from 1888 onward civil initiatives emerged to found modern private schools, in Tabriz, Tehran, and Mashhad. The institutions that resulted were modeled after the Ottoman *rüşdiyye* schools, but met fierce *ulama* resistance, even to the level of physical violence. During the more liberal reign of Muzaffar al-Din Shah (r. 1896–1906), the civil organization Society for Education (1897) coordinated the increasing number of private schools. Due to the lack of a teachers' seminary and textbooks, many of the teachers and much of the teaching material was provided by the Alliance Française, and at some schools the language of instruction was French.

The Qajar period was characterized by a weak administrative infrastructure and lack of centralization. As a consequence, centrally coordinated reforms aimed at developing public education were not initiated. It was only under the authoritarian modernist regime of the Pahlavis (1925–1979) that all provinces were incorporated into an administrative network. A modern public school network was set up during the reign of Reza Shah (r. 1925–1941) and expanded under the rule of Mohammed Reza Shah (r. 1925–1979). The University of Tehran was founded in 1934.

The Shiite *ulama* was not incorporated into this process of modernization and remained as a social body apart from the officially directed developments. Though their official role within Iranian society was diminished as a consequence of administrative, legal, judicial, and educational reforms, the *ulama* stratum still continued to exist. In fact, between 1941 and 1961, Mohammed Reza Shah was anxious to keep good relations with the senior members of the clergy. During this period the city of Qum became the main center of religious education (*hawza*). Shaikh Abdülkerim Khairî in the 1920s and 1930s, and Ayatollah Burujerdî between 1946 and

1961 promoted the development and reformation of the *madrasas* of Qum. Burujerdî supported a school network, with primary and secondary levels, in which religious as well as secular subjects were taught. This network was directed by Association of Islamic Education. As a consequence, educational life in Iran remained deeply divided, as there was no meaningful relationship between the two alternative school networks.

The cordial relationship between the shah and the *ulama* broke down with the White Revolution (1963). The most important element of this series of reforms was land reform. Huge tracts of land, until then under the control of religious foundations, were taken over by the state authority. Thus *madrasas* lost their financial basis. Simultaneously, *madrasas* were put under political pressure, and many of them were closed down. The *ulama* lost its control over *madrasas*, which were handed over to the secular Organization of Endowments. These developments may seem to be similar to the closure of the *madrasas* in Turkey (1924). However, the Ottoman *madrasas* had already lost their *raison d'être* due to institutional decay throughout the previous century, and the Turkish *ulama* had, to a major extent, been incorporated into the public school system. In the Iranian case, however, the *ulama* emerged as a major source of discontent and opposition. Due to the close ties between the *ulama* and the conservative community and merchant stratum (*bazarîs*), the Shiite clergy was able to present itself as the representative of the masses, in opposition to the Shah and his administration.

SEE ALSO *Islamic Modernism.*

BIBLIOGRAPHY

Arasteh, A.Reza. *Education and Social Awakening in Iran, 1850-1968.* Leiden: E.J.Brill, 1969.

Clancy-Smith, Julia Ann. *Rebel and Saint: Muslim Notables, Populist Protest, Colonial Encounters (Algeria and Tunisia, 1800-1904).* Berkeley: University of California Press, 1994.

Heyworth-Dunne, J. *An Introduction to the History of Education in Modern Egypt.* London: Luzac & Co., 1938.

Eickelman, Dale F. *Knowledge and Power in Morocco: The Education of a Twentieth-Century Notable.* Princeton, NJ: Princeton University Press, 1985.

Fortna, Benjamin C. *Imperial Classroom. Islam, the State, and Education in the Late Ottoman Empire.* New York: Oxford University Press, 2002.

Irbouh, Hamid. *Art in the Service of Colonialism: French Art Education in Morocco, 1912-1956.* New York: Tauris, 2005.

Kazamias, Andreas M. *Education and the Quest for Modernity in Turkey.* London: George Allen and Unwin, 1966.

Léon, Antoine. *Colonisation, enseignement et éducation: étude historique et comparative.* Paris: L'Harmattan, 1991.

Mitchell, Timothy. *Colonizing Egypt.* Berkeley: University of California Press, 1991.

Nucho, Leslie S., ed. *Education in the Arab World.* Vol. 1. Washington, DC: Amideast, 1993.

Ringer, Monica M. *Education, Religion, and the Discourse of Cultural Reform in Qajar Iran.* Costa Meza, CA: Mazda Publishers, 2001.

Sayadi, Mongi. *La première association nationale moderne en Tunisie: al-Jam'iyya al-Khaldunniya (1896-1958).* Tunis: Maison Tunisienne de l'Édition, 1975.

Somel, Selçuk Akşin. *The Modernization of Public Education in the Ottoman Empire 1839-1908. Islamization, Autocracy and Discipline.* Köln: Brill, 2001.

Selçuk Akşin Somel

EDUCATION, WESTERN AFRICA

The nineteenth century constituted a momentous turning point in the history of Africa. Not only did it witness the end of the slave trade and the inauguration of legitimate commerce, the high tide of European imperial invasion, conquest, and pacification, but it also heralded the introduction of Western education. European Christian missionaries were the precursors of Western education. While Western education was a valuable instrument of effective colonization and pacification of Africa, ironically it was also very useful for the eventual decolonization of Africa. It is against this background that the history of Western education remains an overarching theme in African history. However, it is erroneous to assume that there was no system of education in Africa before the advent of the Europeans. The nature of colonialism resulted in the denigration and disruption of the African traditional cultures and systems of education to make way for Western education and European civilization. Although private schools were set up to reverse these distortions, they were too few to make any significant impact.

This article examines the central and pioneering role of the Christian missionaries in the introduction of Western education—specifically, the emergence of private and public schools—in the sub-Saharan Africa, and the place of Western education in the effective colonization and eventual decolonization of Africa. It is noteworthy that the mission school systems, modeled after European metropolitan institutions, became the cornerstone of future educational planning in postindependence Africa. At the higher education levels, European university systems were wholly adopted with little modifications in almost all of the newly independent African states. Western education became indispensable in the formation of new identities and national development.

TRADITIONAL EDUCATION

The concept of education in Africa was not a colonial invention. Prior to European colonization and subsequent introduction of Western education, traditional educational systems existed in Africa. The enduring role of education in every society is to prepare individuals to participate fully and effectively in their world; it prepares youths to be active and productive members of their societies by inculcating the skills necessary to achieve these goals. Although its functions varied, African traditional education was not compartmentalized. Fundamentally, it was targeted toward producing an individual who grew to be well grounded, skillful, cooperative, civil, and able to contribute to the development of the community. The educational structure in which well-rounded qualities were imparted was fundamentally informal; the family, kinship, village group, and the larger community participated in the educational and socialization process.

In his *Education in Africa*, Abdou Moumouni affirmed that the educational process essentially was based on a "gradual and progressive achievements, in conformity with the successive stages of physical, emotional and mental development of the child" (Moumouni 1968, p. 15). The medium of instruction was the native language or "mother tongue" through which systematic instruction was delivered by way of songs, stories, legends, and dances to stimulate children's emotions and quicken their perception as they explore and conquer their natural environment.

The African child was taught the various tribal laws and customs and wide range of skills required for success in traditional society. Traditionally, education received by Africans was oriented toward the practical. Work by Magnus Bassey (1991) indicates that those who took to fishing were taught navigational techniques like seafaring, the effects of certain stars on tide and ebb, and migrational patterns and behavior of fish. Those who took to farming had similar training. Those who learned trades and crafts, such as blacksmithing, weaving, woodwork, and bronze work, needed a high degree of specialization and were often apprenticed outside their homes for training and discipline. Those who took to the profession of traditional priesthood, village heads, kings, medicine men and women diviners, rainmakers, and rulers underwent a longer period of painstaking training and rituals to prepare them for the vital job they were to perform.

Teaching was basically by example and learning by doing. African education emphasized equal opportunity for all, social solidarity and homogeneity. It was complete and relevant to the needs and expectations of both the individuals and society. This is because it was an integral part of the social, political, and economic foundation of the African society. However, the advent of the European missionaries and the introduction of Western education through the mission schools changed, in many fundamental ways, the dynamics of African education. Western education soon took the center stage in Africa, debasing, challenging, and supplanting the traditional, informal education along with its cultural foundations.

MISSIONARIES AND WESTERN EDUCATION

The history of Western education in Africa is directly traceable to the relentless efforts of European Christian missionary bodies. Missionary activities in Africa began as early as the late fifteenth century following the successful exploratory missions sponsored by Prince Henry ("the Navigator") of Portugal. For these expeditions, Prince Henry received several letters of indulgence from the Church encouraging the propagation of the Catholic faith. Although a few Portuguese missionaries visited the courts of the *oba* (king) of Benin and Mani-Kongo for the purpose of conversion of Africans, their efforts did not translate into firm establishment of Christianity in these areas. Between the fifteenth and eighteenth centuries, Christianity made practically no headway in Africa as the Portuguese abandoned their idea of conversion. The new and lucrative trade in slaves became a European focus; missionaries now administered prayers to the slaves on the coasts before their departure to the New World.

The evangelical revival movement in Europe during late 1700s reawakened missionary zeal. Encouraged by the reports of explorers of primitive, backward, and so-called "godless" races of Africa, many evangelicals committed themselves to the task of Christianizing and "civilizing" them. The *Great Awakening* witnessed the establishment of missionary societies led by a group of influential Englishmen—the Clapham Sect—who devoted their time and energy to reviewing the problems of the moment. Two major issues of the time, the abolition of slavery and extension of Christianity outside Europe, dominated the deliberations of this group. Prominent members of the Clapham Sect, including William Wilberforce, Granville Sharp, and Zachary Macaulay, believed that the slave trade was abominable and repugnant on humanitarian ground and that abolition of the trade was a necessary precondition for the successful Christianization of Africa. Consequently, their struggles recorded a breakthrough in 1807 when the British parliament passed a bill to abolish slave trade in England. The passage of the slave bill gave stimulus to the growing number of Christian mission societies who were prepared to commence evangelical work in Africa.

Missionary concern for Africa was on two major fronts: first to help encourage Africans to abandon the inhuman trade in slaves, and secondly to teach African natives the noble ways of life. The reports of European

Missionaries in Benin. *A group of European Christian missionaries pose with students in Porto-Novo, Benin, in this illustration from the* History of the Catholic Missions *(1882).* © ARCHIVO ICONOGRAFICO, S.A./CORBIS. REPRODUCED BY PERMISSION.

travelers and their travelogues profoundly informed missionary endeavors in Africa. Their reports reinforced the myth of a Dark Continent and an uncivilized and secular people, providing the *raison d'être* for the European missionary enterprise in Africa. From the start, however, Europeans were well aware that for effective conversion and civilization of Africans to occur, the introduction of Western education through mission schools was necessary. The missionary agenda was to convert Africans to Christianity through the medium of education with the Bible as the major master text. The ability to read and understand the Bible became an overriding index of success for the missionaries.

The earliest formal, Western schools were founded in West Africa, attached to the castles in the Gold Coast, modern day Ghana. There were three of such schools; the oldest was established at Elmina by the Dutch West Indian Company in 1644 and placed under the control of the Castle Chaplain for the education of the mulatto

children for whom they felt some responsibility. These children were to be educated as Christians, speaking the Dutch language and imbibing the Dutch culture. It was hoped that the Dutch who held subordinate posts might be replaced by Africans of partly European descent who would be more accustomed to the climate than Europeans. Afflicted by fluctuating fortunes—staffing, funds, and public support—the Elmina School still lasted for more than 200 years until the Dutch departed.

A similar school was founded at Christiansborg (also in Gold Coast) by the Danes in 1722, and like Elmina, it was for mulattoes under a Danish Resident Chaplain. The teacher was a soldier. At first, this school admitted only boys who it was hoped would become soldiers who would form a mulatto guard for the Danish forts on the coast. Its curriculum was similar to Elmina's. Like the Elmina school, Christiansborg was frustrated especially by the minimal support it received from the Danish government.

The third school, which was established at Cape Coast by the English in 1752, by all accounts was the first real mission school in West Africa. Its founder, the Reverend Thomas Thompson, was sent out from England by the Society for the Propagation of the Gospel (SPG). Its curriculum was clerical. Reverend Thompson sent three Africans to England for training, two of whom died and the third, Philip Quaque, returned to Cape Coast as a missionary in 1766. He took charge of the Cape Coast School and reorganized it for instruction in "religious knowledge, reading, writing and arithmetic" (Priestley 1968, p. 112). Like the other two schools that preceded it, the Cape Coast schools suffered changes of fortune and continued in an irregular fashion until it was taken over and reorganized by the colonial government of Sierra Leone under its governor, Sir Charles McCarthy.

The advances, activities, and accomplishments of the European missionaries especially in relation to Western education before the 1800s were at best only minimal. The three schools were begun as isolated ventures rather than as coordinated beginnings of widespread educational systems. Their operations were quite irregular and their curricula were narrow as they were originally designed to serve a small percentage of the population, the mulattoes and their children. Be that as it may, there is no question that the schools influenced later education in the Gold Coast, providing an enduring educational tradition upon which others would build.

Though preceded by other groups such as the Lutheran Moravian Brethren and the London Missionary Society, the formation of the Church Missionary Society (CMS) in London in 1799 was quite auspicious for evangelism and Western education. This Society subsequently provided the leadership for the European missionary enterprise in Africa. Soon, other missionary bodies became involved; it was no longer just a matter of converting Africans to Christianity as emphasis shifted to sects and nationality. In a way, it was a scramble for the souls of Africans. These missionary groups included the Wesleyan Methodist Missionary Society (WMMS), the Presbyterian Church of Scotland, and the Baptist from the (American) Southern Baptist Convention, the Society of African Missions (the Catholic Mission) from France, the Jesuits, the Basel Missionaries, and the Lutherans.

In 1804, for instance, two German Lutheran clergy, Melchior Renner and Peter Hartwig, trained in the seminary at Berlin, sailed to Freetown for missionary work, as did the Danish Basel Mission, which sent four missionaries, Holzwarthe, Schmidt, Salbach, and Henke, to the Gold Coast in 1827. Many Sierra Leoneans, especially the recaptives, were converted to Christianity.

But the death toll among missionaries was heavy from the start, reaching a peak in the yellow fever epidemic of 1823. This frustrated European evangelical missions. Recognizing that Africans were better used to the harsh tropical West African climate, the CMS, therefore, began to support a policy of training Africans as priests for the ministry.

Thomas Fowell Buxton, a prominent member of the British parliament and vice president of the CMS had urged the cooperation of the government and the missionary societies in the "deliverance" of Africa. Joseph Shanahan, the head of the Holy Ghost Fathers in Eastern Nigeria in the early twentieth century, affirmed: "Those who hold the school holds the country, holds religion, hold its future" (Jordan 1949, p.94). Father Wauter, a Catholic missionary in Western Nigeria pointedly stated, "We knew the best way to make conversion in pagan countries was to open school. Practically all pagan boys ask to be baptized. So, when the district of Ekiti-Ondo was opened in 1916, we started schools even before there was any church or mission house" (Abernethy 1969, p.39). Clearly, education became central to the missionaries for the realization of these goals as underscored by Buxton and others. Such education, it was argued, would help reshape the African economy in favor of legitimate trade, making it possible for the emergence of a generation of educated African middle-class elite who would become leaders of the church, commerce, industry, and politics in Africa. It was, therefore, in response to the ferment of the time that the CMS founded a regular training college at Fourah Bay in Freetown, Sierra Leone, in 1827, for African clergy. Unlike the three earlier schools in the Gold Coast, the story of Western education in Sierra Leone was that of expansion, although occasionally this was frustrated by the frequent deaths of the missionaries. Fourah Bay ultimately became an important institution for Western education, where many West Africans studied for clerical or teaching profession. Perhaps the most famous of Fourah graduates was Samuel Ajayi Crowther who was ultimately ordained the first African bishop of the Anglican Church by the CMS. In 1857, following a successful private expedition up the Niger, Crowther was commissioned to establish an African mission for evangelism. He later became instrumental to the establishment of schools and missions in Eastern Nigeria. Crowther died in 1891. By 1935, however, the CMS had established schools and missions in virtually all parts of the present-day Nigeria.

In East Africa, Anglicans, Scottish Episcopalians, and Methodists had an alliance aimed at working toward a united ministry based on united training. The most enduring contribution of the alliance was in education. For instance, Alliance High School at Kikuyu in Kenya was opened in 1926, and a CMS missionary, Carey Francis, was appointed headmaster in 1940. Alexander Mackay, a teacher, evangelist, builder, and printer, was central to the educational development in Uganda. The early Christians were known as readers, and by 1880 the first translations of parts of the Bible were circulating, printed on Mackay's own press. In the 1920s through the 1930s, almost exclusively missionaries ran East African schools.

The expansion of mission schools in Africa was quite dramatic, and missionary societies were at the center stage of this development. In Nigeria, for instance, the CMS, which started with 6 schools in 1849, increased the number to 150 by 1909. Similarly, the Wesleyan Mission schools increased from 3 (with 255 pupils and 9 teachers) in 1861 to 138 schools (with 5,361 pupils and 285 teachers) in 1921, while the Roman Catholic Mission increased their schools from 2 in 1893 to about 127 in 1922. The Basel Mission Society in the Cameroon enrolled about 100 students in 1904 and 6,600 by 1914. The trend of growth was also evident in other parts of sub-Saharan Africa, especially in East Africa. For instance, in Uganda the CMS expanded the number of its schools from 72 (with 7,683 students) in 1900 to 331 schools (with 32,458 students) by 1913. In Nyasaland the Dutch Reformed Church set up 111 schools (with 10,000 students) in 1903, and by 1910 the figures went up to 865 schools with over 25,796 students.

From the start, European missionaries and their mission schools were contemptuous of African indigenous cultures. Instructions provided to Africans were designed to impart foreign (Western) cultures and values. Africans were persuaded to abandon their own culture and tradition. While the older people proved more reluctant to change, the younger ones readily succumbed to the new teachings of white missionaries, denigrating and rejecting their own cultures and tradition. Yet, the commoner and the oppressed classes were more inclined to discard the traditional ways that offered them little or no advantage. In other words, conversion depended upon the personal benefits, real or imagined, that Christianity conferred. In *Things Fall Apart* (1959), Chinua Achebe showed how the *osu* (outcasts) of Umuofia were the first to abandon their customs and tradition, seek conversion to Christianity, and receive Western education. However, in *Western Education and the Nigerian Cultural Background* (1964), Otonti Nduka noted the contradictions of missionary education for Africa: While the school taught them one set of values based on European culture and values, the home and the environment taught them African ways of life.

Soon, earlier African converts began to feel the yoke of a religion that was closely tied to European culture and

colonialism, and they challenged not only the teachings of the missionaries but mission schools' curricula and instructions. As early as the 1880s in South Africa, the African Christian clergy had rebelled against European domination of their churches. Consequently, they formed their own independent Christian churches, a movement that later spread across central Africa in the wake of European imperialism. African Church leaders saw the Bible's notion of justice and equality as applicable to all humankind; they also considered the Second Coming of Jesus Christ as signaling an end to oppression and colonialism. Similarly, the idea of private schools began to gain ground in order to check cultural alienation and to include secular education in the curricula.

In East Africa, as in other places, trouble started when the Church of Scotland missionaries (CSM) demanded that all African church elders and schoolteachers renounce female circumcision. As a result, the CSM lost 80 percent of its students as Kikuyu established independent, private (community) schools under their control. By 1933, there were 34 such schools with 5,111 students, and by 1936, the figures had increased to 50 schools. Similar private schools emerged in many parts of Africa. They include the Majola Agbebi's Agbowa Industrial Mission School in Nigeria established in 1895, John Chilembwe Providence Industrial Mission in Nyasaland established in 1910, John L. Dube's Ohlange Institute in Natal established in 1900, Eyo Ita's Independent School in Nigeria established in 1920, and Aggrey Memorial School established in Uganda in 1935. In a sense, the African independent church movement and private school initiatives were both an early expression of nationalism.

WESTERN EDUCATION AND COLONIALISM

The successful imposition of European colonial rule on Africa between 1890 and 1900 challenged and redefined the purpose of Western (commonly referred to as colonial) education in Africa. For quite some time, tensions existed between the missionaries and the new colonial governments over who should control of the schools. The missionaries jealously guarded their schools. Although they were in dire need of African auxiliaries for the colonial service, the ecclesiastical focus of instruction at the mission schools troubled the colonial administrators. In his article "Educational Policies and Reforms," Apollos Nwauwa argued that, while missionaries used education as an instrument for effective conversion of Africans to Christianity, colonial governments saw education as means of socially and politically controlling the subjects. This marked difference meant that a clash between the missionary bodies and colonial officials was inevitable. The establishment of public, government schools in many parts of Africa was a consequent of this face-off. In Nigeria, for instance, two government schools—a Muslim school and King's College both in Lagos—were opened in 1900, and by 1930, the number of government schools had increased to 51, and that of assisted schools increased to 275 while unassisted (mission) schools were 2,413. In comparison to the mission schools, government-run schools were too few. Yet, colonial governments were not prepared to commit their meager budget toward the complete takeover of education in Africa.

Thus, despite the continuing tension between them, the missionaries and the new colonial regimes recognized that they needed each other. While the various colonial governments protected the missionaries from, sometimes, hostile African groups, the missionaries were very useful agents of colonial pacification and acculturation. Since the sheer costs of running schools independent of the missionaries worried colonial administrators, some compromised solutions became necessary. Both the missionaries and colonial administrations shared similar interest in the role of education in the civilization of Africans and in creating a body of literate, obedient, organized, and productive Africans for the benefit of European imperialism. Not surprisingly, by 1925, as Roland Oliver and J.D. Fage noted, the British embarked on a far-reaching education policy "whereby colonial governments would spend their limited funds in subsidizing, inspecting, and improving the schools already operated by the Christian missions instead of founding rival and far more expensive systems of state education" (Oliver and Fage 1979, pp. 214-215). Therefore, for financial reasons as well as for a marriage of convenience, mission schools not only co-existed with government and private school, but also surpassed the latter in their rate of expansion and African patronage. As many sub-Africans became Christians, mission-run schools continued to be attractive.

Nevertheless, the nature of colonial involvement in education depended on the administrative style of each colonial power. A common feature was that in the early years of European occupation, the education of Africans was left to private, missionary initiatives, with occasion colonial government subsidies. The various colonial governments eventually became more involved through far-reaching educational policies and reforms, providing broad guidelines for the schools. The French assimilation policy dictated the nature of its education policy in Africa. Since assimilation was based on the assumption that Africans were primitive and should be transformed and absorbed into the so-called "civilized" French culture and way of life, education became a veritable instrument for accomplishing this objective. Assimilation accorded qualified Africans the rights to French citizenship with all its subordinated privileges.

To qualify for assimilation, however, the acquisition of Western education that meant the adoption of French culture was a prerequisite. Since the religious focus of the mission schools was not adequate in accomplishing the assimilation's objectives, the French colonial administration intervened to realign education accordingly. Fluency in French was a prerequisite. School administrators and teachers were directed to replace the mother tongue hitherto used by the missionaries as a medium of instruction with the French language. The use of French at all educational levels was a key element in fulfilling the policy of assimilation. It was a powerful instrument in the dissemination of French culture among the natives. The policy of association that later replaced assimilation also targeted the elite classes of Africans who met the criteria for French citizenship and who would become *assimiles* through adoption of French culture and education.

The French educational scheme for Africans was quantitatively limited and elitist. The educational focus was in the provision of primary, secondary, and vocational training meant to fit Africans to their physical environment as well as subordinate positions in the colonial service. As Ralph J. Bunche acknowledged, the French colonial educational policy was shaped by a preconceived notion of what Africa was to be, of what his status in the changing world should be, and hence the need to provide education for them "along his own lines" (Bunche 1934, p. 71). The sweeping changes of the post World War II (1941–1945) period did not result in significant shift in the French colonial educational policies. The educational system adopted by the Portuguese, Belgium, and Germany followed the French pattern very closely. Like the French, assimilation constituted the cornerstone of the Portuguese colonial policy in Africa. Believing that the African was primitive, the Portuguese designed their colonial educational system to impact Portuguese culture and values. Consequently, they regarded their colonies of Angola, Mozambique, Guinea-Bissau, and the islands of Sao Tome and Principe as overseas extension of Portugal, merely physically separated from Portugal. This notion gave a misleading signal that they were genuinely dedicated to the principle of equality with Africans. The selective and restricted educational practices of the Portuguese colonial governments contradicted their declarations on assimilation. In his article "Portuguese Africa" (1961), James Duffy observed that the Salazar's regime envisaged the formation of a devout, semi-literate, hardworking, and conservative African population.

The purpose of Portuguese education in Africa, as outlined in the Regulation of 1899, was to prepare Africans for their future roles as peasants and artisans. Thus, the type of education provided for the masses was for psychological and cultural assimilation with limited political integration. The school fees were quite high. White children were privileged over blacks. As a result, only a handful of Africans received sound primary and secondary training that prepared them for university education. This was hardly surprising because Portugal was a poor country and could not afford the educational promises based on mass education, civilization, and assimilation. Nevertheless, the limited instruction provided became a tool for the spread of Portuguese culture, language, and civilization that was essentially non-African in character.

The Belgian educational policy in Africa can be described as Platonic; it emphasized the transmission of certain unquestioned and unquestionable ethical values to Africans in relation to predetermined status and function. The policy favored primary school to the complete neglect of postprimary and university education as the case of the Congo demonstrated. For the Belgians, as George Kimble intriguingly stated, "It is better to have 90 percent of the population capable of understanding what the government is trying to do for them ... than to have 10 percent of the population so full of learning that it spends its time telling the government what to do" (Kimble 1960, p. 115).

As a result, by 1951, even though there were about 30,000 students who were enrolled in Belgian schools in the Congo, no one qualified for college entrance. At independence, there were less than twenty university graduates in the whole of Congo to run the country. No doubt, the Belgians had the worst record in the provision of education for Africans. The German educational policy was also designed to train Africans as laborers. General Von Trotha was the principal architect of the German education policy, which allowed Africans to receive practical training as laborers to ensure the regular supply of workers for the colonial system.

Under the British indirect rule system, which, in principle, preserved the African indigenous political system, basic and vocational education—and not higher education—was privileged. This was simply because there was no role for a highly educated African in a political set up that depended on the use of traditional political institutions under the kings or chiefs. The report of the Educational Committee of the Privy Council of 1867, which was quite critical of the literary education provided by the missionaries, advocated a strong vocational education for Africans. Yet, for a long time, the British left education to the discretion of the missionaries only to increasingly intervene as colonial rule became firmly established. For instance, in 1872, as work by David Abernethy (1969) notes, the government of Nigeria instituted a system of grant-in-aid, whereby mission schools meeting

certain minimal secular standards received a bursary to help defray expenses incurred in running the schools. Similar practice was also introduced in the Gold Coast, according to Foster. However, notwithstanding the increasing involvement of colonial governments in setting the policies and guidelines for education, a total take-over of mission schools did not occur before independence. The logistics for such a complete take-over proved daunting for the British colonial administrators.

On the eve of independence, therefore, government and private schools, comparatively fewer in number, co-existed with the mission schools. By 1945, there were comparatively few literate Africans who had not received all or part of their education in mission schools. Missionary control of education throughout most of the colonial era meant that the colonial rulers paid only lip service to the education of Africans. It was not until 1948 that the British established four universities in four of their African colonies after resisting the pressure by African educated elite for almost one hundred years. Inadvertently, however, the coalescence of doctrines of the Bible, the preaching of missionaries, the teachings of the mission schools, and colonial education had ingrained in the African the formidable and liberating ideas that would shake the foundations of European colonial rule.

WESTERN EDUCATION AND DECOLONIZATION

The enduring impact of Western education produced its own contradictions. Early enough, the colonial governments had recognized that their power over Africans depended not necessarily on physical but mental (psychological) control through the school system. Deficient in scope and content, colonial education promoted vocational studies and neglected technology, pure and applied sciences, and engineering. African studies were excluded from the colonial education curricula. For instance, the history syllabi emphasized the history of European activities in Africa instead of the history of Africa and Africans. It praised the Europeans who supposedly discovered Mount Kenya and Rivers Niger and Congo as if Africans who lived in the areas did not know about these rivers. In almost all instances, no mention is made of Africans who led the European explorers to their targets. Unquestionably, colonial education resulted in the erosion of African identity and imparted a limited sense of the African past.

The novelist Ngugi Wa Thiong'o (1981) noted the isolationist and alienating influences of colonial education in Africa, including contempt for their African names, languages, environment, heritage of struggle, unity, and mental abilities. Educated Africans not only became deluded hybrids alienated from their cultures and tradition, but individuals who longed for alien and "more civilized" cultures of the West. It was on this score that Walter Rodney argued that colonial education in Africa "was education for subordination, exploitation, the creation of mental confusion and the development of underdevelopment" (Rodney 1972, p. 264). By killing the communalist spirit in Africans and replacing it with a capitalistic one; by corrupting the mental sensibilities of Africans; by providing selective training to fill auxiliary positions in the colonial service, by emphasizing vocational rather than a well-rounded education; and by disregarding the peoples' cultures in the educational curriculum, colonial education, according to Rodney, fostered the underdevelopment of Africa's intellectual resources. However, despite its limited and misplaced purposes and negative effects, Western education produced some unintended positive consequences for Africans. It served as a catalyst to African nationalism.

Following the successful European invasion and imposition of colonial rule, Africans had been disconcerted by their humiliation and loss of sovereignty. European Christian missionary evangelism and religious instructions, embraced by many Africans mainly for their implicit benefits, gradually became perceived as agents of European imperialism. African suspicion increased. Revolt became imminent. From the discontent of the earlier African converts who founded their own independent Christian churches through the establishment of private schools, slowly but surely, Africans began to protest against not only European occupation but also the concomitant cultural dislocation and alienation.

Many mission-educated Africans, a number of who became teachers and members of the clergy, were not satisfied with their limited education. Consequently, they began to seek for advanced training. Because the various European colonial powers refused to establish universities in their colonies, Africans who could afford it proceeded overseas (especially the United States and United Kingdom) for further studies. Completing advanced (university) training in various fields abroad coupled with exposure to the deep cultures of the West—politics, economics, social issues—and various powerful concepts such as liberty, self-determination, equality, it was only natural for them to relate these notions to their own conditions in Africa. As the work of J. F. Ade Ajayi (1965) has affirmed, educated Africans began to use those same ideas as a standard by which to judge the intentions and actions of the European administration. Empowered and emboldened, they returned home to confront the colonial situations that would force them to question not only the very basis and justifications for European colonial rule but also other intriguing imperial notions,

including racial hierarchy, colonial differential salaries for Africans, and employment discrimination.

Unfortunately, European colonial officials were not prepared to accommodate or address the aspirations of the new but potent elite. Initially, some of these educated elite only demanded appointments and salaries in the colonial civil service commensurate with their training, with the hope of working their way up the political ladder, but European colonial officials who saw them as a threat to the status quo frustrated their hopes. This was a tactical error. African elites consequently felt marginalized. Decolonization became their ultimate goal. Implicitly, Western education had become instrumental in helping Africans in their articulation of imperialism as a global phenomenon.

By mid-1950s, graduates of African universities joined the ranks of their overseas-trained counterparts in pressing for political reforms toward the ideals of self-government. It was from the graduates of these universities that the currents of nationalism flowed across much of Africa. Yet, the effects of World War II on European powers and their colonies ultimately provided African-educated elites (nationalists) with the *raison détre* for mass mobilization against colonial rule. They readily employed political concepts, tactics, and slogans of sovereignty and self-determination, as tested in the West, not only to mobilize the masses into action but also to launch major onslaughts against European colonial rule. European retreat from the empire soon resulted in outright decolonization in Africa by the late 1950s to mid-1960s. Without a doubt, Western education remains relevant in any analysis of the rise and fall of European empires in Africa.

Without a doubt, Western education also provided the necessary tools needed by African nationalists to dislodge European colonial rule. In a sense, Western education created a kind of *Frankenstein Monster* for colonial rule. It was introduced by the Europeans to consolidate their imperial rule in Africa, but it ended up assisting Africans in the liquidation of colonial rule. However, the departure of Europeans from Africa did not result in the dumping of neither Western education nor European cultures and value systems. Rather, what followed was the wholesale adoption of European customs, political systems, and other ways of life through what has popularly become known as neo-colonialism. A contradiction remained. While empowering to Africans, Western education was also alienating.

SEE ALSO *Missionaries, Christian, Africa; Portugal's African Colonies; Religion, Western Presence in Africa; Sub-Saharan Africa, European Presence in.*

BIBLIOGRAPHY

Abernethy, David. *The Political Dilemma of Popular Education: An African Case.* Stanford, CA: Stanford University Press, 1969.

Achebe, Chinua, *Things Fall Apart.* New York: McDowell, Obolensky, 1959.

Ajayi, J. F. Ade. *Christian Missions in Nigeria 1841–1891: The Making of a New Elite.* Evanston, IL: Northwestern University Press, 1965.

Altbach, Philip G., and Gail P. Kelly, eds. *Education and the Colonial Experience.* New Brunswick, NJ: Transaction, 1984.

Ashby, Eric. *African Universities and Western Tradition.* Cambridge, MA: Harvard University Press, 1964.

Bassey, Magnus. "Missionary Rivalry and Educational Expansion in Southern Nigeria, 1885–1932." *Journal of Negro Education* 60 (1) (1991), 36-46.

Berman, Edward H., ed. *African Reactions to Missionary Education.* New York: Teachers College Press, 1975.

Bunche, Ralph J. "French Educational Policy in Togo and Dahomey." *The Journal of Negro Education,* 3 (1) (1934), 69-97.

Duffy, James. "Portuguese Africa (Angola and Mozambique): Some Crucial Problems and the Role of Education in their Resolution." *The Journal of Negro Education* 30 (1961), 294-301.

Ekechi, Felix. "Christianity." In *Africa, Vol. 2: African Cultures and Societies Before 1885*, edited by Toyin Falola. Durham, NC: Carolina Academic Press, 2000.

Foster, P. J. *Education and Social Change in Ghana.* Chicago: University of Chicago Press, 1965.

Jordan, J. P. *Bishop Shanahan of Southern Nigeria.* Dublin: Clonmore & Reynolds, 1949.

Kimble, George H. T. *Tropical Africa.* New York: The Twentieth Century Fund, 1960.

Moumouni, Abdou. *Education in Africa.* Translated by N. Phyllis. London: Deutsch, 1968.

Nwauwa, Apollos. "Educational Policies and Reforms." In *Africa Vol. 4: The End of Colonial Rule*, edited by Toyin Falola. Durham, NC: Carolina Academic Press, 2002.

Oliver, Roland, and J. D. Fage. *A Short History of Africa.* London: Penguin, 1979.

Otonti, Nduka. *Western Education and the Nigerian Cultural Background.* Ibadan, Nigeria: Oxford University Press, 1964.

Priestley, M. "Philip Quaque of Cape Coast." In *Africa Remembered: Narratives of West Africans from the Era of the Slave Trade*, edited by P. D. Curtin. Madison: University of Wisconsin Press, 1967.

Rodney, Walter. *How Europe Underdeveloped Africa.* London: Bogle-L'Ouverture Publications, 1972.

Wa Thiong'o, Ngugi. *Decolonizing the Mind: The Politics of Language in African Literature.* Portsmouth, NH: Heinemann, 1981.

White, Bob E. "Talk About School: Education and the Colonial Project in French and British Africa." *Comparative Education* 32 (1) (1996), 9-25.

Apollos O. Nwauwa

EGYPT

Egypt's first military confrontation with a modern Western power came with the arrival of the French expedition of 1798. Led personally by Napoléon Bonaparte the campaign aimed to strike at British trade and imperial interests but was also motivated by romantic notions of Egypt. French forces easily defeated the Egyptian Mamluks, first in Alexandria, then again outside Cairo at the Battle of the Pyramids. In time, however, the occupation provoked strong popular resistance that, in combination with joint action by Ottoman troops and the British fleet, forced the French to withdraw after only three years. Although militarily a failure, the French expedition had a more lasting cultural and technological impact by impressing Egyptians with the superiority of modern European warfare and science.

Following the French withdrawal, the Ottomans sought to restore order to the country. After an internal power struggle, Muhammad 'Ali, an officer of the Albanian regiment sent to Egypt by the sultan, was appointed governor of Egypt in 1805. Over the following decades he consolidated his control over the country, established a dynasty, and laid the foundations of the modern Egyptian state. Muhammad 'Ali embarked on an extensive program of modernization, the central pillar of which was military reform. Unable to recruit mercenaries from the Caucasus or transform Sudanese slaves into modern soldiers, from 1822 he began to form a new army by conscripting the native Muslim population, using Turko-Circassian officers trained by European instructors. He also developed artillery, engineering, and cavalry corps, as well as a large navy, so that by 1840 Egypt boasted the strongest military force in the region. Initially employing his forces at the behest of the sultan first in Arabia, then later in Greece during the 1820s, in 1831 he began to pursue his own imperial designs by occupying Syria and ultimately threatening Istanbul itself. Under considerable political pressure from the Europeans, particularly the British, who felt their interests threatened, Muhammad 'Ali was forced to withdraw from Syria and reduce his army to a modest eighteen thousand men under the Treaty of London signed in 1841.

Domestically, Muhammad 'Ali presided over a significant program of government reorganization establishing a series of departments that would provide the basis of the modern ministries. The country was divided into administrative districts and provincial officials were given responsibility for conscription, taxation, security, public works, agriculture, and industrial development. Turko-Circassians were favored in the higher offices, with Arabic speakers occupying the more junior positions. Due to the need for competent administrators, a series of student missions to Europe was sponsored, the first in 1826 to Paris, where future state bureaucrats received a modern education. A number of specialized local institutions were also set up to provide training in administration, accountancy, medicine, and foreign languages. Reforms were instituted in the systems of taxation and land tenure. In 1814 tax farming had been abolished and villages made responsible for taxes to be paid directly to the state. The granting of land to members of the ruling family, various military men, civil officials, notables, and tribal chiefs developed into a form of ownership dominated by large landowners. Cultivation of the land, especially of cotton, was encouraged, and the irrigation system was kept in good repair. A monopoly system forced producers to sell to the government at lower than market price and guaranteed state revenues. Assisted by improvements in communication and transport, trade with Europe increased, displacing the Ottoman Empire in economic importance. Muhammad 'Ali's industrial policy was less successful, though scholars are divided on how much this was due to local factors, such as the lack of a skilled management and workforce, investment capital, and cheap power, and how much to European competition. In 1841 the monopoly system and local industries were dismantled when Egypt was forced to accede to the Anglo-Ottoman trade agreement. Thus, while Egypt under Muhammad 'Ali was transformed into a centralized state with increased resources and power, at the same time the way was opened to greater penetration by European political and economic interests.

After the death of Muhammad 'Ali in 1848, his heirs, with the exception of 'Abbas (1848–1854), continued his policy of modernization. During the reigns of Sa'id (1854–1863) and Ismail (1863–1879), both of whom were European-educated, infrastructure projects proceeded apace. The first railway in Africa was built from Cairo to Alexandria in 1854; a telegraph system and a government postal service linked Egypt to Europe. The centerpiece of this program was the construction of the Suez Canal linking the Mediterranean and the Red Sea. Completed in 1869 and run by the privately owned Suez Canal Company (though the British government was a major shareholder), the canal enhanced Egypt's international and strategic importance. An ardent Europeanizer dedicated to the idea that Egypt was part of Europe, Ismail transformed modern Cairo into a European city, encouraged the establishment of European educational institutions, and favored the adoption of European dress among the elite.

Egypt was enjoying increasing prosperity during this period from export earnings, principally from its cotton crop, which was particularly profitable during the years of the American Civil War when Egypt was the principal source of supply for European textile manufacturers.

However, the great cost of development projects caused the Egyptian state to sink seriously into debt. Ismail's extravagant personal lifestyle added to the financial burden, as did the expense he incurred to secure the title of Khedive and the right to contract loans without authority from the sultan. In order to placate European banks and bondholders, the Egyptian government was forced to reorganize its finances and accede to various political demands. The system of Dual Control established in 1877 gave British and French representatives the authority to supervise government expenditure and revenue and in August 1878 Ismail's agreement to the formation of a "European cabinet" under Nubar Pasha that included an English finance minister and a French minister of public works extended European financial and political control. In June 1879 European pressure on the Ottoman sultan saw the dismissal of Ismail and his replacement by his more malleable son, Tawfiq. The increasing influence of European states on the governance of Egypt prompted a reaction from alienated local military officers and civil officials. In September 1881 a group of nationalist officers, led by Ahmad Urabi, surrounded the palace and insisted on the formation of a constitutional government headed by Sharif Pasha. A joint note issued by the British and French governments in the following January isolated Sharif and made European intervention against Urabi increasingly likely. When a series of riots broke out in Alexandria in June 1882, British warships anchored offshore bombarded the city and landed troops to restore order to the country. Now war minister, Urabi sought to resist British forces but his troops were defeated at Tel al-Kabir on September 13. Egypt was now under British occupation.

THE BRITISH OCCUPATION

Although the declared aim of the British government was to stay in Egypt only for as long as it took to put Egyptian finances in order, the occupation would last seventy-four years. Until 1914 it was maintained by a small army of occupation numbering twelve thousand men and by the appointment of British officers to senior positions in the Egyptian army. British advisers took up prominent positions in the civil administration. In 1905 British nationals occupied 42 percent of higher posts with only 28 percent held by Egyptians, and the remaining number by Syrians and Armenians. Political control was maintained through the Egyptian government. Lord Cromer (Evelyn Baring), the British consul-general from 1883 to 1907, exercised considerable authority in the choice of ministers who, like Mustafa Fahmi Pasha, prime minister from 1891 to 1893 and 1895 to 1908, were mostly drawn from the Turko-Circassian elite. Tawfiq proved a weak ruler and although his son 'Abbas Hilmi II tried to exercise greater independence

MEDITERRANEAN SEA

ISRAEL

GAZA STRIP

Khalîj as-Salûm
(Gulf of Salum)

Marsá Maṭrûḥ

As Sallûm

Damietta
Port Said

Alexandria

Al Maḥallah al Kubra

'Al Arîsh

JORDAN

Al Alamayn

Tantā

Al Manṣurah

Libyan Plateau

Ismailia

Suez Canal

Shibîn al Kôm

Cairo

Suez

Sinai Peninsula

Qattara Depression

Al Jizah

Helwân

Sudr

Sîwah

Pyramids of Giza

Memphis

Abu Rudeis

Mt. Catherine
8,652 ft.
2637 m.

Birkat Qārūn

Al Fayyūm

Gulf of Suez

Aṭ Ṭûr

Bani Suwayf

SAUDI ARABIA

Al Minyā

Western Desert

Arabian Desert

Al Ghurdaqah

Gulf of Aqaba

Great Sand Desert

Asyûṭ

Nile

Sûhâj

Qena

Red Sea

LIBYA

Mûṭ

Valley of the Kings

Thebes

Al Khârijah

Luxor

N
W E
S

Bârîs

Aswân

Minâ' Baranis

Aswân High Dam

Lake Nasser

SAHARA DESERT

Libyan Desert

SUDAN

EGYPT

0 50 100 150 200 Miles

0 50 100 150 200 Kilometers

Egypt

© MARYLAND CARTOGRAPHICS. REPRODUCED BY PERMISSION.

of action he was consistently outmaneuvered by Cromer. Because Egypt was still formally part of the Ottoman Empire during this period, Britain maintained a certain legal deference toward Istanbul but with the outbreak of the First World War and the Ottoman decision to join Germany, Britain formally annexed Egypt as a protectorate in 1914.

British rule emphasized economic rectitude. Financial arrangements were quickly put in place to pay off Egypt's national debt, including the costs of damage caused during Urabi's uprising. Economic policy sought to develop Egypt as a source of raw materials for British industry. To this end cotton production was intensified, effectively making Egypt a monocultural economy. An active public works program was pursued that maintained and extended irrigation works, including a system of barrages and dams (the first Aswan Dam was completed in 1902), as well as the road and rail networks. The cotton crop was largely responsible for the transformation from a subsistence to a monetary economy—by

1914 it accounted for 93 percent of Egyptian export earnings—but this led to economic growth rather than development. The industrialization of the country was neglected and low tariffs made competition with foreign imports difficult. Little investment was made in public education and literacy rates remained low. The result was the continued domination of large landholders and an increase in the number of landless peasants. The negative impact of these policies would later be central to the future economic crisis.

British colonialism also came to have a significant social influence in Egypt. Historically Egyptian society had always been ethnically and religiously pluralist, a tendency manifested by significant Christian and Jewish communities living alongside the majority Muslim population. During the nineteenth century Muhammad 'Ali had encouraged many with relevant skills to migrate to the country in order to assist in its development. Armenians, Greeks, Maltese, and Italians, many of them leaving difficult circumstances at home, arrived in large numbers to take advantage of the economic opportunities. As European influence increased, and especially after 1882, other Europeans from Britain, France, and Belgium came to form a significant part of the bourgeoisie. They benefited from the Capitulations, the system of legal and economic privileges granted by the Ottomans to those with European nationality, but also from the British policy of favoring the use of foreigners in government posts. Under the British, pluralism became increasingly identified with colonial rule, an association reinforced by the British government's arrogation to itself of the role of protector of foreign interests in the country. This policy extended to the Copts, the local Christian population, who were in government employment. Indeed, some historians regard this practice as a significant cause in the development of the religious tensions between Muslims and Copts that surfaced during the first decade of the twentieth century and reappeared at various times thereafter.

THE NATIONALIST MOVEMENT AND THE 1919 REVOLUTION

After the crushing of the Urabist movement in 1882, it took more than a decade for an Egyptian nationalist movement to stir. In the late 1890s a young lawyer, Mustafa Kamil, with support from 'Abbas Hilmi II, began to campaign for Egyptian independence and the evacuation of British forces. In December 1907 he formed the National Party as a vehicle for nationalist activity. Around the same time, the more moderate Umma Party, led by Ahmad Lutfi al-Sayyid, was also established. Unwilling to countenance a change in Egypt's status, Britain clamped down on any expressions

of nationalist agitation. After World War I (1914–1918), Egyptian leaders, expecting the loyalty of the country to be rewarded, renewed their calls for independence and sought to send an Egyptian *Wafd* (delegation) to the Paris peace conference in 1919. When the British refused to permit the presence of an Egyptian delegation, a series of uprisings, known as the 1919 or National Revolution, broke out throughout Egypt, protesting the continued British occupation. The British responded by deporting to Malta the members of the Wafd, now the de facto nationalist leadership, including its leader Sa'd Zaghlul. A commission of enquiry headed by Lord Milner, sent to Egypt in November 1919 to report on the situation, made little progress because of an Egyptian boycott. Unrest and extended negotiations continued into 1921 without resolution. Finally, to break the deadlock, the British government declared a unilateral settlement on February 22, 1922, which granted Egypt self-government with its own constitution, monarchy, and a parliamentary system, but which reserved to the British government four areas of authority: the security of imperial communications, the defense of Egypt, the protection of local foreign interests and minorities, and the status and future of Sudan.

The new constitutional arrangements inaugurated the so-called liberal period (1922–1952), but even within the terms of the settlement there were significant limitations on the Egyptian government. The constitution gave the monarchy considerable authority, regularly exercised by King Fu'ad (1922–1936), to install a series of minority governments and keep the mass-supported Wafd out of office. In addition, it was soon evident that the British continued to wield a great deal of informal influence. In November 1924, following the assassination of Sir Lee Stack, the commander of the Egyptian Army, the British high commissioner, Sir Edmund Allenby, issued a harsh ultimatum to the Egyptian government. So humiliating were its terms that Zaghlul, now prime minister, felt obliged to resign. This pattern of British interference continued, particularly during the term of Sir Miles Lampson (later Lord Killearn) as British high commissioner (1933–1946). Throughout the interwar period the question of the legal relationship between Egypt and Britain remained an active political issue. The Anglo-Egyptian Treaty, a mutual defense pact signed in 1936 and prompted by the increasing threat of war, provided the legal basis for the British use of Egypt as a base of operations during World War II (1939–1945). It also, however, included a British agreement to withdraw from Egypt in twenty years' time and pledged that Britain would support Egyptian demands to abolish the Capitulations at the Montreux Conference in 1937. Nevertheless, wartime brought confrontation. In February 1942, concerned by the pro-Axis sentiments of the Egyptian government of 'Ali Mahir, Lampson ordered British tanks to surround Abdin Palace and forced King Faruq to install a pro-Allied Wafdist government. The event vividly demonstrated the illusion of Egyptian independence and served thereafter as a source of humiliation for Egyptian nationalists.

Despite the political differences between the Wafd and the pro-palace parties the Egyptian elite was drawn from the traditional landowning class and promoted little substantial economic or social reform. The establishment of Misr Bank by Tal 'at Harb in 1920 was an attempt to nurture Egyptian-owned industry and promote a national bourgeoisie in place of the comprador bourgeoisie, but this approach had only limited success. The new political forces from both the left and right that would more effectively challenge colonialism and ultimately the legitimacy of the traditional ruling class came from other quarters. The Egyptian Communist Party, first established in 1922, was quickly suppressed by the government. The movement reemerged in the 1940s, however, and came to play an influential role after the war with its radical, secular, and anti-imperialist program. Appealing to a very different constituency, the Muslim Brotherhood had been formed by Hasan al-Banna in 1928 as a reaction to the abolition of the caliphate in 1924 and the increasing Western influence in the Islamic world. By the 1940s it had developed into a significant political force articulating a program of Islamic modernism. Another political party, Young Egypt, formed by a group of university students in the early 1930s, combined nationalist, fascist, and Islamic elements.

The period from the end of World War II until 1952 was one of increasing political instability and social tension in Egypt. Large public protests were held against the continued British occupation. In February 1946 a demonstration organized by a coalition of students and workers ended with the death of a number of protestors, caused by British action. Political violence grew with the assassination of two Egyptian prime ministers, Ahmad Mahir (d. 1945) and Mahmud Fahmi al-Nuqrashi (d. 1948), as well as Hasan al-Banna (d. 1949). The defeat of Egyptian forces by the Israelis in the Palestine War of 1948 to 1949, compounded by a scandal regarding the inferior state of Egyptian arms, added to the atmosphere of crisis. Despite the demands of a growing population, a series of governments failed to deal with Egypt's pressing economic difficulties, particularly the urgent need for land reform (2 percent of the population now owned 50 percent of the land), the lack of industrial development, and the low rates of literacy. The last Wafdist government elected at the beginning of 1950 was in many ways the last throw of the old political order. However, it proved cautious and unwilling to effectively tackle the crisis even if it finally gave way to public

pressure and abrogated the 1936 treaty in October 1951. Large demonstrations against the British occupation were held in Cairo and Alexandria during the following month. On January 25, 1952, a gun battle broke out between Egyptian police and British troops in Ismailia in which a large number of policemen died. An anti-British riot in Cairo the following day, "Black Saturday," resulted in a fire, begun by parties unknown, that burnt down much of the modern city center. King Faruq responded by dismissing the Wafdist government and a series of weak cabinets followed during the first half of 1952.

THE JULY REVOLUTION

Within the Egyptian military the continuing state of national crisis, the impotence of the political class, and the debacle in Palestine had politicized some junior officers. In late 1949 Gamal 'Abd al-Nasir formed a group called the Free Officers, many of whom were members of the first class of Egyptian graduates of the military academy; though not united in their political views, all were agreed on a broad nationalist program. On the night of July 22–23 the Free Officers seized power in a virtually bloodless coup later known as the July Revolution. The new regime was made up of a group of young officers, later formalized as the Revolutionary Command Council, fronted by a more senior officer, Brigadier General Muhammad Nagib, although Nasir was always the dominant figure. Having immediately sent the unpopular Faruq into exile, the new government embarked on a program of land reform and reconfiguration of the political order, banning all political parties in January 1953 and declaring Egypt a republic in June of the same year.

Initially, the new regime was received favorably by Western governments and particularly the United States. On October 19, 1954, after extended negotiations, Britain and Egypt reached an accord that provided for the withdrawal of British troops from Egyptian soil. (The last troops departed in June 1956.) However, Egyptian foreign policy was beginning to give Washington and London cause for concern. Early in 1955 Egypt refused to join the pro-Western Baghdad Pact and in April Nasir played a leading role in the establishment of the non-aligned movement at the Bandung Conference. More alarming for the Western alliance was Nasir's decision, after failing to purchase arms from the West, to conclude the Czech arms deal in September 1955. These concerns in part explained the American decision to withdraw its offer to finance the building of the Aswan High Dam in July 1956. Nasir's response, the announcement of the nationalization of the Suez Canal Company on July 26, prompted the Suez crisis, which ended with Egypt in control of the canal. This outcome enhanced Nasir's international status, particularly in the Arab world, and provided a clear sign of Britain's imperial decline. Suez also signaled a closer relationship between Egypt and the Soviet Union, which had agreed to fund the Aswan Dam and assist in the modernization of Egyptian military forces. However, the move toward the Soviet Union was more pragmatic than ideological in motivation. Arab nationalism was the most critical ideological element of the Nasir regime. The creation in 1958 of the United Arab Republic, the union between Egypt and Syria, seemed to embody Pan-Arab aspirations, but the merger lasted only three years partly because of Egyptian unwillingness to genuinely share power. The episode made clear that, despite all the Pan-Arab rhetoric, there were considerable political differences within the Arab world. In fact, Nasir's call to revolution would bring him into conflict with conservative Arab monarchies and other republican regimes, such as the one in Iraq, which sought to steer their own course; it would also lead to a civil war in Yemen. Nasir continued to be preeminent in the Arab world throughout the 1960s, and sponsored progressive movements throughout the Arab world, including the Palestinian Liberation Organization. In the domestic arena, Egyptian policy turned significantly to the left in the early 1960s with its espousal of Arab socialism. A series of decrees in July 1961 nationalized a wide range of banks, shipping companies, and industries and economic policy promoted industrialization and economic self-sufficiency. The following year the National Charter provided a blueprint for the government's political program and established the Arab Socialist Party as the official political party. In 1965, after a government campaign of severe repression, the Egyptian Communist Party agreed to dissolve itself in return for some of its members receiving important positions in the regime. However, the Muslim Brotherhood continued to be dealt with harshly and many of its members were imprisoned. These economic and political changes brought significant social transformations as well. In the interwar period Egypt had continued to attract foreigners, many of whom continued to occupy significant social and economic positions after 1945. In the course of the 1950s and early 1960s this population substantially departed the country. This was partly because of external events, such as the Suez crisis, which saw the expulsion of British and French nationals, many of them long-time residents. As Israel asserted itself in the region the position of the local Jewish population became increasingly precarious. Other ethnic communities, such as the Greeks and Armenians, while never expelled, found that the heightened Pan-Arab rhetoric and nationalizations made life more difficult, even as opportunities for migration to the United States, Canada, and Australia

made the idea of leaving more palatable. The result was an Egyptian postcolonial society that lost a considerable amount of human expertise and was less pluralist and more overtly Arab in character.

The spectacular defeat of Egypt by the Israelis in the 1967 War fatally wounded the pretensions of the Arab nationalist project and though Nasir remained president until his death in September 1970, he was no longer the radical force he had been. He was succeeded by Vice President Anwar Sadat, who proceeded to overturn much of the Nasserist program and move the country ideologically to the right. In 1972 Sadat expelled Soviet military advisors from Egypt. His initially successful surprise attack on the Israelis in the 1973 Yom Kippur War in the end led Egypt into a closer relationship with the United States, a fact dramatically demonstrated when he signed the Camp David peace treaty with Israel in 1979, after extended negotiations under American auspices. This treaty ended the state of belligerence between the two countries and gave Egypt back the Sinai (occupied by the Israelis since 1967), but it resulted in a decisive break with the rest of the Arab world and Egypt's expulsion from the Arab League. Domestically, Sadat pursued a policy of economic liberalization (*infitah*) that significantly opened up the economy to market forces, though popular riots in 1977 persuaded him to draw back from fuller implementation. His policy of political liberalization granted a limited right for opposition to operate. By the end of the 1970s Sadat's increasingly pro-Western policies were provoking considerable domestic opposition from leftists, Islamists, liberals, and even the Coptic Church. After a large-scale crackdown against his critics, he was assassinated in October 1981 by Islamic militants. He was succeeded by Husni Mubarak, who in less flamboyant style has maintained a close political relationship with the United States; indeed, Egypt continues to be the second most important American ally in the Middle East after Israel. It was accepted back into the Arab League in 1989. Because Egypt was directly influenced by British imperialism until 1952 and shaped by the imperatives of the Cold War thereafter, scholars remain divided over the question of whether the legacy of colonialism or indigenous factors best explain Egypt's current economic and political difficulties.

SEE ALSO *Baring, Evelyn; Cotton; Muhammad Ali; Nasir, Gamal Abd al; Suez Canal and Suez Crisis.*

BIBLIOGRAPHY

Aciman, André. *Out of Egypt: A Memoir*. New York: Farrar Strauss Giroux, 1994.

Baker, Raymond W. *Egypt's Uncertain Revolution under Nasser and Sadat*. Cambridge, MA: Harvard University Press, 1978.

Berque, Jacques. *Egypt: Imperialism and Revolution.* Translated by Jean Stewart. New York and Washington: Praeger, 1972.

Cole, Juan R. *Colonialism and Revolution in the Middle East: Social and Cultural Origins of Egypt's Urabi Movement.* Princeton, NJ: Princeton University Press, 1993.

Daly, M. W., ed. *The Cambridge History of Egypt*, Vol. 2: *Modern Egypt, from 1517 to the End of the Twentieth Century.* Cambridge, U.K.: Cambridge University Press, 1998.

Davis, Eric. *Challenging Colonialism: Bank Misr and Egyptian Industrialization, 1920–1941.* Princeton, NJ: Princeton University Press, 1983.

Fahmy, Khaled. *All the Pasha's Men: Mehmed Ali, His Army, and the Making of Modern Egypt.* New York: Cambridge University Press, 1997.

Goldschmidt, Arthur, Jr. *Modern Egypt: The Formation of a Nation-State.* Boulder, CO: Westview, 1988.

Gordon, Joel. *Nasser's Blessed Movement: Egypt's Free Officers and the July Revolution.* New York: Oxford University Press, 1991.

Kerr, Malcolm. *The Arab Cold War: Gamal 'Abd al-Nasir and His Rivals, 1958–1970.* 3d ed. London: Oxford University Press, 1971.

Louis, William Roger. *The British Empire in the Middle East, 1945–1951.* New York: Oxford University Press, 1984.

Owen, E. R. J. *Cotton and the Egyptian Economy, 1820–1914.* Oxford: Clarendon, 1969.

Sayyid-Marsot, Afaf Lutfi al-. *Egypt's Liberal Experiment, 1922–1936.* Berkeley: University of California Press, 1977.

Sayyid-Marsot, Afaf Lutfi al-. *Egypt in the Reign of Muhammad 'Ali.* Cambridge, U.K. Cambridge University Press, 1984.

Tignor, Robert L. *Modernization and British Colonial Rule in Egypt, 1882–1914.* Princeton, NJ: Princeton University Press, 1966.

Vatikiotis, P. J. *The Modern History of Egypt.* London: Weidenfeld and Nicolson, 1969.

Anthony Gorman

ELMINA

SEE *Colonial Cities and Towns, Africa*

EMPIRE, BRITISH

The term *British Empire* refers to political and geographical territories formerly under the control of the British Crown—either as colonies, dependencies, protectorates, mandates, or dominions. The coining of the term *British Empire* is mostly attributed to the Welsh astronomer, mathematician, and alchemist John Dee (1527–1608), who in a 1570 publication invoked "this Incomparable Brytish Empire." Although Great Britain came into official existence only with the Act of Union in 1707 unifying England and Scotland, the term is generally applied to the English colonial realm before that date as well. In this entry, *British Empire* will be used in this sense, referring to all English, Scottish, and British colonial territories acquired since the early seventeenth century. Until 1707, the respective protagonists are referred to as England or Scotland, from then on only as Britain or Great Britain.

It is sometimes argued that the British Empire began with King Henry II (1133–1189) declaring himself lord of Ireland in 1171, but usually the origins of empire are associated with England's expansion to overseas territories in North America in the early seventeenth century. During the eighteenth and nineteenth centuries, Britain's empire advanced to global hegemony and reached its greatest expansion shortly after World War I (1914–1918), encompassing about a quarter of the world's land area.

Decolonization after World War II (1939–1945) brought independence for most of Britain's overseas territories during the 1940s, 1950s, and 1960s. The return of Hong Kong to China in 1997 has often been described as the end of the British Empire—but even today there are a number of overseas territories remaining under British control, such as Anguilla, Bermuda, the Cayman Islands, or the Falkland Islands. British colonial engagement is often described in two phases differing in their regional focus and the underlying concept of colonialism—the First British Empire from around 1600 to American independence, and the Second British Empire from then to decolonization.

THE FIRST BRITISH EMPIRE

England—and even more so Scotland—was a latecomer in European overseas activities. During the fifteenth century it completely lacked both the economic and strategic potential to participate in early colonialist endeavors. When England finally started to develop a taste for overseas trade and settlement in the mid-sixteenth century, Portugal and Spain had both firmly established themselves as transatlantic empires and extracted substantial profits from their American holdings. Hence, early English overseas activities, such as John Hawkins's (1532–1595) three slaving expeditions to western Africa (1562–1586) or English buccaneering in the Caribbean, intruded into hitherto exclusively Portuguese and Spanish domains.

The resistance of the established colonial powers further delayed English overseas expansion. However, Sir Francis Drake's (ca. 1543–1596) circumnavigation of the globe (1577–1580) and the victory over the Spanish Armada at Gravelines (1588) established England as a major naval power and facilitated private overseas engagement on any significant scale. At the same time, economic incentives for overseas trade emerged. North America

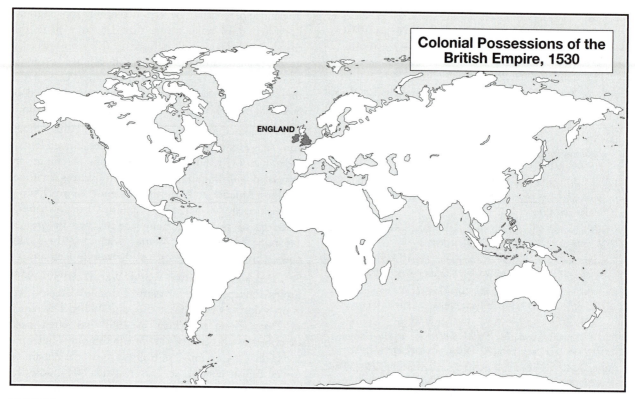

Colonial Possessions of the British Empire, 1530

ENGLAND

MAP BY XNR PRODUCTIONS. THE GALE GROUP.

offered rich fishing grounds and other resources (e.g., fur). Potential overseas markets became increasingly attractive to English producers and merchants when they lost access to Antwerp as the major cloth market during the Revolt of the Netherlands (1568–1609).

Humphrey Gilbert (ca. 1539–1583) established a settlement in Newfoundland in 1583, and Sir Walter Raleigh (ca. 1554–1618) founded a colony on Roanoke Island, Virginia, in 1585. Although both ventures had to be abandoned shortly after their founding, a first step toward English overseas expansion had been made. After peace with Spain in the Treaty of London (1604), English colonialism gained momentum. Jamestown in Virginia was founded in 1607 and became England's first permanent settlement in North America. The colony was saved from severe economic distress by the introduction in 1612 of the tobacco plant, whose cultivation immediately proved to be a highly profitable venture.

Such bright economic prospects attracted other settlers from the motherland, and numerous new settlements were founded. When the Puritan Pilgrims established Plymouth Colony in 1620, they became the first religious separatists to seek refuge in North America and thus gave an example that was later followed by many other religious groups. Salem was founded further

to the north in 1626. From the Salem settlement sprang in 1629 the Massachusetts Bay Company. The company secured itself a royal charter and was granted the administration of the colony. This practice proved successful and attracted large numbers of immigrants. By 1640, the colony boasted a total population of 11,500.

The English government saw North American colonization as a means to relieve rising population pressure in the home country, and the British encouraged emigration. Connecticut was founded in 1633, Maryland in 1634, and New Haven in 1638. The administration of the colonies rested with royally chartered joint-stock companies. In 1664 England seized New Amsterdam from the Dutch and renamed it New York. The influential Quaker William Penn (1644–1718) secured a royal charter in 1681 and established Pennsylvania as a refuge for his coreligionists. The settlement prospered and attracted a steady influx of European immigrants.

Further north, the Hudson Bay Company successfully tried to participate in the hitherto French-dominated fur trade from 1670 onwards. Territorial tensions between France and England increased and—in the course of the War of the Spanish Succession (1701–1714)—culminated in the British takeover of Acadia (a region in eastern Canada) and Newfoundland in the Treaty of Utrecht in

BRITISH EMPIRE, KEY DATES

1570: Welsh astronomer, mathematician, and alchemist John Dee coins the term British Empire

1583: English explorer and nobleman Humphrey Gilbert establishes a settlement in Newfoundland

1585: English explorer and statesman Sir Walter Raleigh, Humphrey Gilbert's step-brother, founds a colony on Roanoke Island, Virginia

1607: Jamestown, England's first permanent North American settlement, is founded in Virginia

1620: The Puritan Pilgrims establish Plymouth Colony in present day Massachusetts

1620s: English colonization of the Caribbean commences with the settlement of Saint Kitts and Barbados

1626: Salem, Massachusetts, is established

1629: The Massachusetts Bay Company—a British enterprise that establishes the Massachusetts Bay Colony at present day Boston—is formed

1655: Britain takes Jamaica from Spain

1664: England seizes New Amsterdam from the Dutch and renames it New York

1681: William Penn secures a royal charter and establishes Pennsylvania

1713: The Treaty of Utrecht results in British takeover of Acadia (a region in eastern Canada) and Newfoundland

1765: The Stamp Act prompts colonial demonstrations and an import embargo of British goods

1773: The Tea Act culminates in the so-called Boston Tea Party

1776: Thirteen American colonies declare their independence

1783: The Treaty of Paris results in Britain's acknowledgement of American independence and the end of the so-called First British Empire

1788: British colonization of Australia begins with the establishment of Sydney in New South Wales

1791: The separate provinces of Upper Canada and Lower Canada are established

1796: Britain takes Ceylon (Sri Lanka) from the Dutch

1806: British forces overtake the Dutch Cape Colony in South Africa

1840: New Zealand comes under British authority with the Treaty of Waitangi

1840: The two Canadas are reunited in the Act of Union

1842: Hong Kong falls to Britain with the Treaty of Nanjing

1858: The British Crown assumes direct control over India

1867: The British North America Act creates the Canadian Confederation

1870s: The era of "new imperialism" begins, leading to formal British control over wide parts of Africa, as well as imperial expansion in Asia and the Pacific

1876: Queen Victoria is proclaimed empress of India

1885: Britain occupies Burma

1918: Following World War I the British Empire reaches its greatest extent, but struggles to maintain control over its vast territories

1931: The Statute of Westminster and the Commonwealth of Nations give Britain's white settler dominions full sovereignty or authority over their own affairs

1945: Post-World War II decolonization begins and continues through the 1960s, bringing gradual independence for most of Britain's overseas territories

1947: India achieves independence, eventually leading to the partition of British India into Muslim Pakistan and Hindu India

1948: Ceylon and Burma achieve independence

1950s: African decolonization commences late in the decade

1961-1983: British colonies in the West Indies achieve independence

1997: Some consider the return of Hong Kong to China as the end of the British Empire

2006: A number of overseas territories remain under British control, including Anguilla, Bermuda, the Cayman Islands, and the Falkland Islands

1713. The Transportation Act of 1718 made provisions for the transportation of convicted criminals from Britain to North America. Thus emigration to the colonies further increased.

Towards the middle of the eighteenth century, tensions between New France and New England and their European motherlands mounted again and finally led to the global Seven Years' War (1754–1763 in the North American colonies, where it was called the French and Indian War; 1756–1763 in Europe). After winning the war, Britain took over the remaining French possessions in America. Only Louisiana went to Spain as compensation for the British occupation of Florida. By 1760, the British colonies in North America housed 1.6 million inhabitants—rising to 2.7 million only twenty years later. This population explosion was mainly due to the large-scale immigration of Europeans and African slaves, as well as to high natural population growth resulting from the comparatively favorable living conditions in the American colonies.

The Caribbean had been a stage for English activity since the middle of the sixteenth century. Tolerated—at times even encouraged—by the British Crown, privateers like Sir Francis Drake harassed the Spanish in the region. English colonization commenced only in the 1620s with the settlement of Saint Kitts and Barbados. Jamaica was taken from Spain in 1655. These new holdings immediately attracted European planters as the land proved well suited for the cultivation of tobacco and sugarcane.

The early tobacco plantations were mostly run as smallholdings and employed mainly convicts or "indentured" labor from Europe. Falling world-market prices for tobacco and competition from Virginia soon rendered small-scale tobacco farming unprofitable. Sugar, on the other hand, enjoyed favorable market conditions and promised quick and large profits. Although intensive in capital and labor, sugar cultivation attracted many planters and investors. The abundance of suitable land and the availability of imported slave labor led to the "sugar revolution" of 1630 to 1670, when large parts of the Caribbean were completely transformed into tropical export economies based on huge, slave-run, European-owned production units. The early years swelled the planters' coffers with immense profits and—although the profit margin had narrowed to about 5 percent by then—Caribbean sugar cultivation remained a profitable venture well into the 1820s.

Trade with Africa attracted English merchants from the early sixteenth century onwards. However, English engagement on the West African coast remained marginal at first. Mostly short-lived factories were established during the first half of the seventeenth century. These concentrated mainly on trade in redwood and gold. Only when the "sugar revolution" in the Caribbean led to

rising labor demands that could not be satisfied with European convict or indentured labor anymore did the slave trade arise as a profitable business.

The English entered the slave trade—originally dominated by Portuguese and later Dutch merchants—from the 1640s onwards and established slaving stations on the West African coast. Founded in 1672, the Royal African Company was granted the English monopoly on the slave trade and provided the North American and Caribbean plantations with African slave labor. The Treaty of Utrecht in 1713 eventually granted to the British the exclusive right to supply slaves to Spanish America—the so-called *asiento*. Hence, the British emerged as the dominant protagonists in what became known as *triangular trade*. British ships loaded slaves in Africa and sold these slaves in the Caribbean, loading sugar in exchange. They brought the sugar back to Europe, exchanging it for rum and other processed goods, which they finally sold in Africa, thus completing the triangle. Following reasonable estimates, the (triangular) slave trade brought between 9.5 and 11.5 million African slaves to American plantations from the sixteenth century until the abolition of the slave trade (1802–1833).

Since the beginning of colonization, the economic relations between the motherland and the American colonies were based on mercantilist trade doctrines. Mercantilism rested on the belief that the wealth of a country depended exclusively on the amount of gold and silver that it possessed (bullionism). Mercantilism, therefore, required a favorable balance of trade, with the home country's exports to the colonies being larger than its imports. To achieve such a favorable balance of trade, mercantilist countries restricted and protected overseas trade. The English Parliament did so by passing the first Navigation Act in 1651, reserving imports from the colonies for English merchants. Five more Navigation Acts between 1660 and 1773 extended the reach of the acts. Mercantilist trade protectionism and the seemingly arbitrary imposition of various duties and taxes during the seventeenth and eighteenth centuries continually annoyed the colonies and led to their gradual alienation from Britain.

Although Britain took over French possessions in America after the Seven Years' War, the war had been a costly enterprise. Convinced that the French and Indian War had been mostly a colonial affair benefiting the American holdings, London tried to recover its war expenses by increasing the financial burden of the colonies. In 1764 Britain halved import taxes on West Indian products and simultaneously cracked down on smuggling. A year later, the infamous Stamp Act imposed a levy on the issuing of all legal documents in the American colonies.

The colonists regarded the stamp duty as extremely unjust and staged an import embargo of British goods

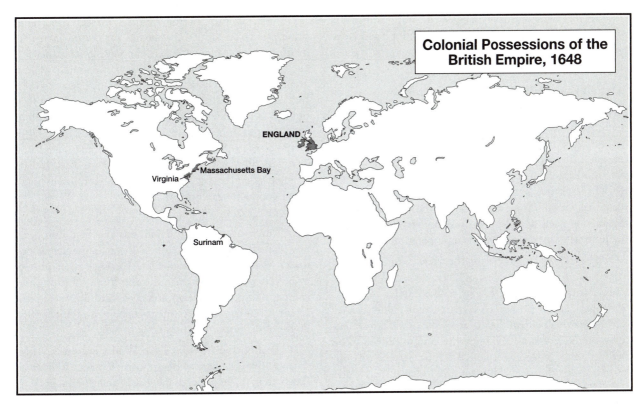

Colonial Possessions of the British Empire, 1648

ENGLAND

Massachusetts Bay

Virginia

Surinam

MAP BY XNR PRODUCTIONS. THE GALE GROUP.

and demonstrations throughout the colonies. The duty soon proved to be uncollectible and the Stamp Act had to be repealed in 1766. To compensate for this defeat, the British Parliament issued a Declaratory Act that emphasized its full legal authority in North America. However, this act remained mostly a dead letter. Duties on tea and manufactured imports introduced in 1767 had to be abolished after only two years due to the noncooperation of the colonists. Britain responded with the threat of force and stationed a garrison at Boston in 1770. Several local outbreaks of violence in the following years further alienated Britain and America.

The implementation of the detested Tea Act in 1773, cementing the English East India Company's quasimonopoly of the American tea trade, intensified the conflict and culminated in the so-called Boston Tea Party of 1773. American activists—symbolically masked as Indians—seized a shipload of tea and threw it into the sea. The conflict escalated and led to violent clashes between the "Patriots" on the American side and the "Loyalists."

However fierce, American resistance against British authority had never aimed at full independence from Great Britain until then. Only when Britain refused to enter into negotiations did thirteen American colonies declare their independence in 1776. With the help of French forces, the colonies finally managed to defeat a substantial British force sent to suppress the rebellion. The Treaty of Paris ended hostilities in 1783, and Britain had to acknowledge American independence.

Attempts of the United States to conquer the remaining British colonies in former French Canada were fended off. Although lacking representation in London and at times badly neglected, the Canadian colonies remained loyal to Britain. As stout Catholics, the Canadians feared religious discrimination at the hands of the new Americans.

By 1783, the first white decolonization of modern times had been successful, and a new state—or rather a federation of states—had arisen. As such, American independence not only inspired the French Revolution and Latin American independence movements, but it also marked the end of the so-called First British Empire. In this first phase, British colonialism focused mainly on the white settlement colonies in North America whose economic relations with the motherland were built around strict mercantilist beliefs. Although the loss of its most populous and economically important American colonies did not ultimately ruin Great Britain—as had often been predicted by contemporaries—the focus of the British

Empire had to be drastically readjusted. And readjusted it was by shifting it to the East and by heeding the louder and louder pleas for free trade.

THE SECOND BRITISH EMPIRE

When the Spanish Crown decided to fund Christopher Columbus's (1451–1506) ill-planned and little promising voyage—eventually leading to the "discovery" of the New World in 1492—it did so out of the desire to find a westward passage to Asia. Portugal's Bartholomeu Dias (ca. 1450–1500) had just recently circumnavigated the Cape of Good Hope and reached the Indian Ocean. Spain saw itself at a serious disadvantage, and funding Columbus's voyage was an act of desperation.

The colonial potential of the New World was tremendously underestimated. Hence, when Vasco da Gama (ca. 1469–1524) finally reached India in 1498, Portugal's access to the rich Indian Ocean trade seemed far more valuable than Spain's newly acquired hegemony over the New World. Although this notion proved to be wrong, and Europe's colonial focus rested on the Americas for the next 250 years, the Indian Ocean trade emerged as an extremely profitable affair for the European sea powers as well.

The Dutch entered the Indian Ocean trade, originally dominated by the Portuguese, in the late sixteenth century. When its holdings in the region began to run at a loss in the seventeenth century, Portugal refocused its attention on Brazil and left the East to the Dutch newcomers. The latter established the Verenigde Oost-Indische Compagnie (VOC, or Dutch East India Company) in 1602, granting to it a monopoly on Dutch-Asian trade. During the seventeenth century, the VOC clearly dominated European trade in the Indian Ocean.

The VOC's English counterpart, the East India Company (EIC)—although founded two years earlier in 1600—could not compete with the VOC initially. It commanded less capital and lacked the long-term perspectives and planning of the VOC. In its first years, the EIC managed to establish a small network of bases and factories on the Indian coast, including Malaya, Java, Sumatra, Sulawesi, and Japan, but it was soon expelled from the spice regions and the East Asian trade by the Dutch. The EIC had to content itself with a small number of factories on the Indian Subcontinent.

With the consent of the Mughal emperor, who controlled about 70 percent of the Indian Subcontinent, the EIC founded a factory at the port of Surat in 1613. Fort Saint George in Madras (Chennai) was built in 1641. Ten years later, the EIC established a foothold in Bengal. In 1668 it acquired Bombay (Mumbai).

With the turn of the century, market conditions started to favor the EIC. Demand for cotton increased in Europe and America, where the slave laborers needed cheap clothing. While the VOC concentrated almost exclusively on the spice trade, the EIC had access to the Indian cotton and textile market. Countering the VOC's imports of Javanese coffee, the EIC became the prime importer of Chinese tea to Europe. Thus, by the middle of the eighteenth century, the Dutch company had lost its trade supremacy in Asia. The English East Indian Company had become the single most important merchant company trading with Asia.

Although the VOC had never aimed at the creation of a Dutch overseas empire, it was the first European power in the Indian Ocean to bring larger territories under its direct domination. This practice soon proved to be economically beneficial to the VOC by giving the company direct and cheap access to local markets and a certain security of investment—albeit combined with skyrocketing administration costs.

The EIC soon followed the VOC's example. When the local ruler *(nawab)* of Bengal occupied Fort William at Calcutta in 1756 to end the EIC's trade monopoly in Bengal, the company sent an army from Madras and eventually defeated the *nawab*'s forces in the Battle of Plassey (1757). The EIC succeeded the *nawab* as direct ruler of Bengal. The Mughal emperor granted the company full rights of jurisdiction and taxation and made the EIC the legal sovereign of a vast territory on the Indian subcontinent. The company's new role was financially extremely profitable. Much of the ongoing struggle with the French Compagnie des Indes (Company of the Indies) over trade supremacy in India was funded with the new gains. The EIC conquered the French stronghold Pondicherry in 1761 and thereby marginalized the French position in India (although Pondicherry was eventually returned to France in the Treaty of Paris in 1763).

Being, after all, a private and profit-oriented enterprise, the EIC ruthlessly exploited its Indian territories. Hence, it initially extracted large profits from its holdings. Nevertheless, the company steered into financial trouble in the 1770s. Administration costs and shareholder dividends were steadily rising. In the end, the EIC had to ask the British government for help. A loan was granted on the condition of immediate administrative reforms in India. The Regulating Act was passed in 1773 and aimed at stabilizing and regulating company rule in India. The India Act of 1784 tried to intensify government control over the EIC and established the Board of Control. The act also prohibited any further expansion of the company's territory in India.

Despite such regulations, the EIC soon waged war against the French-backed sultan of Mysore and

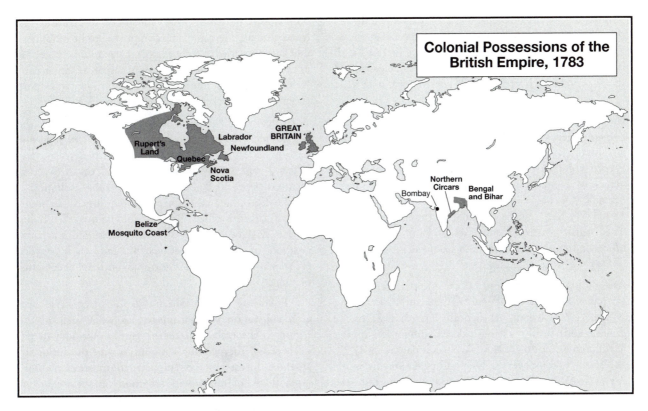

MAP BY XNR PRODUCTIONS. THE GALE GROUP.

eventually conquered Mysore in 1799. War against the Maratha Empire followed and ended with an EIC victory in 1818. Like Mysore, the Maratha territory came under direct company rule. Other princely states on the subcontinent were able to retain formal independence, but were closely bound to the company. Thus, by 1818, practically the whole Indian Subcontinent had come under formal or informal EIC control. In 1824 parts of Burma (Myanmar) were annexed. After a series of clashes with the Sikh state of the Punjab, the company defeated the Sikhs and annexed the Punjab in 1849.

Although the British military forces proved to be very effective, EIC administration in India was less so. The company's pronounced focus on economic exploitation and its total lack of intercultural competence finally led to the Indian Mutiny of 1857. Triggered by rumors that the cartridges of the new Enfield rifle were greased with pork and beef fat—an alleged practice offensive to Muslim and Hindu soldiers alike—parts of the Indian sepoy troops revolted against British domination. The rebellion took the EIC by complete surprise and proved to be a formidable challenge to British rule. Lacking unifying leadership and an overall purpose, the uprising was eventually suppressed by British forces in 1858. However, the rebellion had made obvious that the EIC could not handle the administration of India in a just and

effective manner. Thus, the British Crown took over the company's possessions in 1858 and assumed direct control over India. It reorganized the administrative structure and established a conservative administration resting largely on collaboration with traditional local elites. In 1876 Queen Victoria (1819–1901) was proclaimed empress of India.

During his famous explorations in the 1770s, Captain James Cook (1728–1779) discovered a promising replacement for the thirteen American colonies—Australia. The continent proved to be of prime strategic importance. Australia emerged as an important settlement colony—and the new destination for convict transports. Sydney in New South Wales was founded in 1788 and soon prospered. By 1810, New South Wales boasted five major settlements. The land was perfectly suited for sheep husbandry, and Australia alone satisfied 50 percent of Britain's exploding demand for raw wool by 1850. In that year, New South Wales already had 265,000 inhabitants, Tasmania had 70,000, and South Australia had 64,000. Only Western Australia lagged behind with a population of merely 4,600. Immigration to Australia was further stimulated by the discovery of rich gold deposits in 1851.

In 1855 the crown colonies New South Wales, Victoria, South Australia, and Tasmania were granted self-government within the British Empire. More sparsely populated Queensland and Western Australia followed this example in 1859 and 1890 respectively. New Zealand had come under British authority in 1840 with the Treaty of Waitangi between the British Crown and the Maori chiefs. It achieved self-government in 1852.

The remaining North American colonies were reorganized in 1791. About 50,000 loyalist refugees had swelled Quebec's population after 1783 and introduced a substantial English-speaking element in the former French colony. Acknowledging this, the separate provinces of Upper Canada (today Ontario) and Lower Canada (Quebec) were established in 1791. Only in 1840 were the Canadas reunited in the Act of Union. The British North America Act of 1867 widened the union and created the Canadian Confederation.

The British Empire further expanded in Africa and Asia during the Napoleonic Wars. Ceylon (Sri Lanka) was taken from the Dutch in 1796. At the Battle of the Nile in 1798, Britain repelled the French invasion of Egypt, and firmly established its influence in the Mediterranean. After a short-lived occupation in 1795, British forces took over the Dutch Cape Colony in South Africa in 1806. Java was occupied as well, but was eventually handed back to the Netherlands after the Congress of Vienna in 1815.

Both the South African colonies and Ceylon became strategically and economically important to the British Empire. British colonists started to arrive at Cape Colony in significant numbers from 1820 onwards. The original Boer settlers left British territory and founded the Boer colonies of Transvaal and the Orange Free State. From 1815 onwards, Ceylon's interior was systematically opened up and transformed into a plantation economy producing coffee and later tea. Elsewhere in Asia, Britain expanded its holdings as well. The Straits Settlement on the Malay Peninsula was established as a crown colony in 1826. Hong Kong fell to Britain with the Treaty of Nanjing that ended the First Opium War in 1842.

The old mercantilist practices of trade protectionism were gradually abandoned after the American Revolution and replaced by ideas of free trade. The Scottish economist Adam Smith (1723–1790) published his influential *An Inquiry into the Nature and Causes of the Wealth of Nations* in 1776 and contributed to the popularization of the laissez-faire approach. Both the character of Britain as well as that of its empire started to change in the mid-eighteenth century. On the one hand, industrialization had gripped Britain and made its economy highly flexible and dynamic. On the other hand, the nature of the British Empire had changed as a whole. Having lost the most populous of its settlement colonies, the empire rested more and more on the mainly Asian colonies of domination. These territories often boasted dense indigenous populations and were closely integrated in centuries-old trade systems. Mercantilism soon proved to be too inflexible and restrictive to fully exploit the economic potential of the new empire. From the beginning of the nineteenth century, ideas of free trade became more and more accepted and quickened the pace of empire building.

After 1858, India manifested its position as the nucleus of Britain's second empire—the "Jewel in the Crown." Ideas of "white superiority," "benevolent despotism," and the "white man's burden" began to shape relations between the "colonizers" and the "colonized." Unlike European engagement in the Americas, South Africa, or Australia, British colonialism in India, Burma, Malaya, and Ceylon lacked the significant participation of European settlers. Instead, these regions experienced an influx of European business agents and planters.

Following the Caribbean example, large-scale cash crop cultivation was introduced to wide parts of the region in the early nineteenth century. Yielding to the influence of the planting community and the European absentee investors, the colonial administration more often than not focused its attention on the welfare of the export economy and neglected the indigenous sector. British industrialization cheapened textile production and European-manufactured clothing flooded the Indian market, thereby swiftly ruining the important Indian cotton sector. This process of "deindustrialization," along with increasing population pressure, led to the emergence of widespread landlessness and the creation of an agricultural wage-labor force in (South) India. Following the abolition of slavery in the British Empire in the 1830s, South India's excess labor was exported to the plantation regions of the empire under the indenture system.

Between the late eighteenth century and the era of "new imperialism" starting in the 1870s, Britain did not experience serious competition from other European powers in its empire-building efforts. However, France started to recover from its internal problems in the middle of the nineteenth century. And the German unification of 1871 created another global player longing for colonial expansion. Italy developed similar ambitions. Internal rivalries between these powers made them over-ambitious colonizers and heralded the period of "new imperialism."

But the more accessible and economically attractive parts of the world had already been colonized (or even decolonized)—only most of Africa and large parts of the Pacific had been spared as yet. Thus began what has been aptly described as the "Scramble for Africa." The major European powers started to occupy territories in Africa. Britain secured control over the Suez Canal by occupying

Egypt in 1882. Most of southern Africa, modern Kenya, Uganda, Sudan, Nigeria, and the Gold Coast in western Africa followed.

During the partition of Africa, European rivalry manifested itself in numerous crises. French and British interests, for instance, clashed in the Fashoda Incident of 1898 when both countries strove to establish themselves in Sudan and complete their north-to-south (British) or west-to-east (French) territorial connections. Outside Africa, Britain's adoption of new imperialism led to the complete occupation of Burma in 1885 and its annexation to British India in 1886.

While the era of new imperialism saw the establishment of formal British control over wide parts of Africa and imperial expansion in Asia and the Pacific, a first devolution of power took place in the white settler colonies of North America, Australia, New Zealand, and South Africa. Self-government had already been granted to most of these colonies when the British North America Act raised Canada to dominion status in 1867. The federations of Australia and South Africa (including the self-governing territories of the Orange Free State and Transvaal) acquired dominion status in 1901 and 1910, respectively. New Zealand had chosen not to join the Australian federation and was made a dominion in 1907. However, the motherland retained legislative authority over the dominions (consolidated by the Colonial Laws Validity Act of 1865) until the creation of the Commonwealth of Nations in 1931. The dominions' foreign relations were also centrally administered through the Foreign Office in London, and the British monarch remained the head of state in the dominions.

Britain had not seriously resisted the settlement colonies' pursuit of home rule. On the contrary, in an empire of free trade it feared little economic loss and anticipated financial relief due to lower administration costs. However, in its colonies of domination the empire fiercely clung to direct control and was little willing to devolve power.

Aggressive colonial policy, combined with mounting intra-European tensions, eventually led to the outbreak of World War I in 1914. After four years of global warfare, the victors (particularly France and Britain) took over most of the colonies of the defeated. Britain inherited most of the German colonies in Africa and acquired League of Nations mandates over Palestine and Iraq, both former territories of the crumbling Ottoman Empire. The British Empire had reached its greatest extent, but found it increasingly hard to maintain control over its vast territories. Britain's economy lay in ruins and local nationalist movements demanded concessions recognizing the colonies' exhaustive financial and military support of the British war effort.

On that background, Egypt was granted quasi-independence in 1922 with British soldiers remaining solely at the Suez Canal. The Indian nationalist movement gained momentum after World War I and could not be satisfied with the half-hearted reforms of 1919 and 1935. However, as in other colonies, the Indian nationalist movement was mainly carried by local elites and thus did not initially aim at total independence but at increased political and economic autonomy within the empire. Accordingly, excluding the case of Ireland, Egypt remained the only decolonized colony of domination until the end of World War II, while the white settler dominions had achieved full sovereignty over their affairs with the Statute of Westminster and the creation of the Commonwealth of Nations in 1931.

But after World War II, the pace of decolonization quickened immediately. Facing a serious economic crisis, the government of Prime Minister Clement Attlee (1883–1967) saw no gains in keeping up colonial control over South Asia. India achieved independence in 1947; Ceylon and Burma followed a year later. Britain's sudden loss of interest in South Asia, combined with the diverse notions of local nationalist movements, rendered decolonization a thoroughly unorganized and hurried affair. Indian decolonization eventually led to the partition of British India into Muslim Pakistan and Hindu India, a development that was accompanied by a mass exodus on both sides and the death of over one million people in the resulting atrocities.

African decolonization commenced only in the late 1950s. Britain's territories in Africa had been important for the motherland's economic recovery after the war. But now Britain yielded to rising national consciousness in the colonies and released Sudan (1956), Nigeria (1960), Sierra Leone (1961), Tanganyika (1961), Uganda (1962), Kenya (1963), Zambia (1964), Malawi (1964), Gambia (1965), Botswana (1966), and Swaziland (1968). In most of these cases, the devolution of power worked comparatively smoothly. In Rhodesia, however, the presence of a substantial and influential white settler community complicated matters and eventually led to terrorism and guerrilla warfare. Rhodesia became modern Zimbabwe only in 1980.

In the West Indies, the creation of the West Indies Federation in 1958 was meant to satisfy local desire for increased autonomy. However, the largest members—Jamaica and Trinidad and Tobago—left the federation in 1961 and 1962 to become fully independent. The federation was dissolved and the remaining members became British colonies again. They achieved full independence in 1966 (Barbados), 1974 (Grenada), 1978 (Dominica), 1979 (Saint Lucia and Saint Vincent and the Grenadines), 1981 (Antigua and Barbuda), and 1983

"Highways of Empire." *This poster, showing Britain at the center of the world and its colonies and former colonies in red, was issued in 1927 by the British Empire Marketing Board to promote the purchase of goods produced in the British Empire.* **THE NATIONAL ARCHIVES OF THE UK: REF. CO956/537A. REPRODUCED BY PERMISSION.**

(Saint Kitts and Nevis). British Guyana and British Honduras on the American mainland became independent in 1966 and 1981, respectively.

With the return of Hong Kong to China in 1997, Britain handed back its last remaining crown colony. However, Great Britain today still controls strategically or financially important territories outside the British Isles, including Anguilla, Bermuda, the British Virgin Islands, the Cayman Islands, the Falkland Islands, Montserrat, Saint Helena, the Turks and Caicos islands, Gibraltar, and Pitcairn.

While British decolonization has been practically completed with the return of Hong Kong, the legacy of the British Empire still reverberates in the political, economic, social, and cultural makeup of the world today. The emergence of the English language as the international *lingua franca* and the spread of the English legal system are parts of this heritage. The dissemination of European religious and cultural ideas throughout the world needed the vehicle of European expansion in general. The British Empire, in particular, made possible the

worldwide spread of the Church of England and Puritanism.

British culture and lifestyle also influenced the emergence of national identities after decolonization. British sports, most prominently cricket, remain a favorite pastime in many former colonies. On the other hand, the hurried decolonization in large parts of Asia and Africa often left behind a geopolitical landscape full of unresolved ethnical, political, or economic issues leading to violent clashes, civil war, or international conflicts. Apartheid policy in South Africa, violence in Rhodesia/Zimbabwe, the Israel-Palestine conflict, the Sinhala-Tamil conflict in Sri Lanka, and the Kashmir conflict between India and Pakistan all have their roots in British imperial policy and decolonization.

Much of the ethnic composition of the United States, the Caribbean, parts of the Pacific, Sri Lanka, and Southeast Asia today has its origins in forced (slavery) or semiforced (the indenture system) labor migration within the British Empire. Similarly, the obvious or at times only latent racism displayed by the British colonizers towards the colonized contributed to the development of modern racist prejudice. On the other hand, the multiethnic composition of large parts of Britain today has its roots in the open British immigration policy towards former colonial subjects and commonwealth citizens.

The final question of whether the British Empire has been a boon or a bane to the colonial territories has been asked often, but cannot be answered satisfactorily. Advocates of empire—in accordance with the colonizers themselves—advance the argument that colonialism actually brought economic and political development to hitherto underdeveloped countries and regions. More critical scholars argue that colonialism in general and British imperialism in particular brought about a transfer of wealth from the periphery to the core and thus, in fact, delayed or prevented sustainable development in the colonies.

SEE ALSO *Crown Colony; Empire in the Americas, French; Empire in the Americas, Spanish; Empire, Dutch; Empire, Portuguese; Empire, United States; Indian Revolt of 1857; Scramble for Africa; Sepoy.*

BIBLIOGRAPHY

Armitage, David. *The Ideological Origins of the British Empire.* Cambridge, U.K.: Cambridge University Press, 2000.

Bayly, C. A. *Imperial Meridian: The British Empire and the World, 1780–1830.* London: Longman, 1989.

Brown, Judith, ed. *The Oxford History of the British Empire,* edited by William Roger Lewis; Vol. 4: *The Twentieth Century.* Oxford: Oxford University Press, 1999.

Cain, P. J., and A. G. Hopkins. *British Imperialism: Innovation and Expansion, 1688–1914.* Harlow, U.K.: Longman, 1993.

Cain, P. J., and A. G. Hopkins. *British Imperialism: Crisis and Deconstruction, 1914–1990.* Harlow, U.K.: Longman, 1993.

Canny, Nicholas, ed. *The Oxford History of the British Empire,* edited by William Roger Lewis; Vol. 1: *The Origins of Empire.* Oxford: Oxford University Press, 1998.

Curtin, Philip D. *The Rise and Fall of the Plantation Complex: Essays in Atlantic History,* 2nd ed. Cambridge, U.K.: Cambridge University Press, 1998.

Ferguson, Niall. *Empire: How Britain Made the Modern World.* London: Allen Lane, 2003.

James, Lawrence. *The Rise and Fall of the British Empire.* London: Little, Brown, 1994.

Lloyd, T. O. *The British Empire, 1558–1995.* Oxford: Oxford University Press, 1996.

Marshall, P. J., ed. *The Cambridge Illustrated History of the British Empire.* Cambridge, U.K.: Cambridge University Press, 1996.

Marshall, P. J., ed. *The Oxford History of the British Empire,* edited by William Roger Lewis; Vol. 2: *The Eighteenth Century.* Oxford: Oxford University Press, 1998.

Middleton, Richard. *Colonial America: A History, 1585–1776.* Oxford: Blackwell, 1996.

Porter, A. N., ed. *The Oxford History of the British Empire,* edited by William Roger Lewis; Vol. 3: *The Nineteenth Century.* Oxford: Oxford University Press, 1999.

Porter, Bernard. *The Absent-Minded Imperialists: Empire, Society, and Culture in Britain.* Oxford: Oxford University Press, 2004.

Porter, Bernard. *The Lion's Share: A Short History of British Imperialism, 1850–2004,* 4th ed. London: Longman, 2004.

Said, Edward. *Culture and Imperialism.* London: Chatto and Windus, 1992.

Said, Edward. *Orientalism.* London: Routledge, 1978.

Winks, Robin, ed. *The Oxford History of the British Empire,* edited by William Roger Lewis; Vol. 5: *Historiography.* Oxford: Oxford University Press, 1999.

Roland J. Wenzlhuemer

EMPIRE, BRITISH, IN ASIA AND PACIFIC

The British Empire in Asia and the Pacific begins with the charter awarded to the East India Company on December 31, 1600 giving the Company a monopoly of trade from the Cape of Good Hope to Magellan. The Company began trading in India in 1608. An English ambassador, Sir Thomas Roe (1581–1644), arrived in 1616 and he negotiated the establishment of a factory (trading post) at Surat. In 1639 the Company opened a factory at Madras; in 1658 it opened another on the River Hughly in Bengal; in 1668 it received the island of Bombay from the Portuguese; and in 1690 it traded from Fort William in Calcutta. It was from Calcutta, Madras, and Bombay that the East India Company began to interfere in the internal affairs of Indian rulers and to acquire territory. This process has been called the imperialism of free trade. The need to maintain highly favorable conditions for trade led to military and political control of territory.

This expansion was accomplished by taking advantage of India's political instability as the authority of the Mughal rulers was collapsing and by siding with one claimant to the throne at the time of the death of a regional ruler. The War of the Austrian Succession (1740–1748) and the Seven Years' War (1756–1763) led to English victories over the French in India, further expanding their influence. In 1748 and 1749 the rulers of Hyderabad and the Carnatic died and the English became a factor in Indian politics as local leaders sought the help of the Europeans in their struggle for power. Robert Clive (1725–1774) demonstrated how English armies with superior European weapons, training, and tactics could defeat larger Indian armies. In 1758, the English captured the Northern Sarkars. The Company was not just a trading entity, but it was becoming an increasingly powerful part of the political structure of India. Through wars, diplomacy, and indigenous collaborators, British control of territory expanded. This was a pattern that would be followed in other parts of Asia and the Pacific.

In Bengal, Clive was sent north to avenge an attack on the British at Fort William by the governor of Bengal, which had led to the deaths of 123 British in the Black Hole of Calcutta in June 1756. The Battle of Plassey followed in 1757 and is considered to be the starting date of the British Empire in India. The massive wealth aquired in Bengal led to the desire for further expansion. The Rohilla War, 1774, the wars against Mysore, ending in 1799, the war against the Pindaris (1817–1819), the three wars against the Marathas ending in 1818, the Anglo-Nepal wars (1814–1816), the invasion of Sindh (1843), the Sikh Wars (1845–1846 and 1848–1849), and the three wars against Burma (1826–1886) all expanded British authority throughout the whole of South Asia. The Company continued to administer these territories until the Mutiny of 1857 caused the British government to rule India after 1858 through a viceroy. Until independence in 1947 India was the centerpiece of Britain's empire in Asia and it was enormously profitable to businessmen, traders, soldiers, and civil servants. Its army played an important role in wars in Europe, the Middle East, Southeast Asia, and China, most notably in World Wars I (1914–1918) and II (1939–1945).

The defense of India became a paramount concern of the British. It caused them in the Great Game—a term used to describe the rivalry and strategic conflict between Britain and Russia for supremacy in Central Asia during the nineteenth century—to fight wars in Afghanistan (during 1838–1842 and 1878–1880) and to secure its northwestern frontier against Russian incursions. It incorporated Ceylon in 1815 to secure it from the French. It was in 1819 that Sir Stamford Raffles (1781–1826) established the important free port of Singapore. Singapore prospered and became the commercial and financial center of the region, even after Hong Kong became its chief rival in 1842. Half the world's tin was smelted in Singapore and rubber was also processed there. In 1826 the Straits Settlements was created to administer a number of territories in Malaya, and Singapore became the administrative capital of the Settlements, Malaya, and North Borneo. After the rise of Japan it became a fortified city, the locus of Britain's military defense strategy in the region.

There was no master plan to govern the colonies. There is some truth to the claim that the British Empire was created in a fit of absence of mind. Some colonies became directly ruled, while others were protectorates with British military and diplomatic protection but governed by chartered companies. Often, a man on the spot ruled as a potentate and acted on his own initiative. London did not interfere unless it involved the nation in costly wars or insurrections as in the Indian Mutiny of 1857. Three words have been used to describe the motives of expansion: gold, God, and glory. Gold, as in capitalism, was the driving force of colonial expansion. Trade also was important but so, too, was the gentlemanly capitalism of shipping, insurance, investment, and banking. Glory added even more incentive, especially for the colonial administrators and soldiers eager for fame and promotion by extending British authority. Missionary societies also pressured the British government to take over territory. Newly conquered lands would become part of the imperial sphere of influence, possibly colonies, if it was not too costly. Territories were also taken over to prevent other powers from doing so. The growing world of commerce required port and coaling stations for ships and secure territories for cable stations and lighthouses. The British navy was the instrument of a great deal of expansion. The colonies would be ruled as dominions, territories, federated or divided states, and other devices as well. They would be governed by a governor-general, or even a navy captain as in the Pacific. There was no uniform pattern to British rule of colonial territories.

Like Raffles, James Brooke (1803–1868) was a man on the spot who expanded British territory when he arrived in Sarawak in 1839. He helped the Sultan of Brunei suppress piracy and was rewarded by becoming a white raja, and his family ruled the state until 1946. In 1881 the British North Borneo Company received a charter from the British government and ran North Borneo for sixty years. The British government was not interested in ruling the colony but in 1888 it became a protectorate.

In the nineteenth century China became the target of the Europeans for expansion, especially the British and the French. The British hoped to reach the Chinese market from Burma, the French from Vietnam and Laos. After 1760, when Canton became an open port, the British, above all, purchased tea and silk. In exchange they illegally sold opium from India. In 1839 the Chinese destroyed 20,000 opium chests. The British retaliated and the first Opium War (1839–1842) led to the harsh Treaty of Nanking of 1842. Four more ports were opened to foreign trade. Hong Kong was ceded to the British. The Taiping Rebellion led to the second Opium War (1856–1860). French and British troops ransacked Peking and eleven more ports were opened up to the Europeans. Kowloon was given to the British. Until 1937 and the Japanese invasion, China was enormously profitable. Between 1941 and 1945 the Japanese controlled Hong Kong. In 1997 it was returned to China.

British colonization in Australia began in January 1788 with the arrival in Sydney of 1,500 people, almost half of them convicts. Captain James Cook (1728–1779) had paved the way with his three trips to the South Seas between 1768 and 1779. He mapped parts of Australia and New Zealand, and claimed the east coast for Britain. Convicts and free immigration led to the creation of the colonies of Tasmania (1825), Western Australia (1829), South Australia (1836), Victoria (1851), and Queensland (1859). On January 1, 1901, the colonies confederated and became the Commonwealth of Australia under a governor-general. Cook claimed New Zealand for Britain, but European settlement began when whaling ships arrived in the 1790s. The missionary Samuel Marsden arrived in 1814 and the systematic colonization of Edward Gibbon Wakefield's (1796–1862) New Zealand Company brought settlers to Wellington in 1840, the same year the Maoris signed away a great deal of territory, and the British established the islands as a Crown Colony. In 1907 New Zealand became a dominion, achieving full autonomy in 1947.

In the rest of the Pacific the eighteenth century saw the coming of missionaries and the nineteenth witnessed a competition for colonies and protectorates between France, Germany, the Netherlands, and the United States. Few of the islands were economically viable although some had natural resources such as Nauru (phosphate) and Fiji (sandalwood) and some, such as Fiji, served as whaling stations. The navy played a role in administering the islands and so, too, did Australia and New Zealand. New Hebrides was administered by both Britain and France. British territories included Nauru, New Hebrides, Tonga, Fiji, Gilbert, and Ellice Islands, Papua New Guinea, and the Solomon Islands. After 1960 they all became independent.

SEE ALSO *British Colonialism, Middle East; English East India Company, in China; Crown Colony; East Asia, European Presence in; Empire in the Americas, British; Hong Kong, from World War II; Hong Kong, to World War II; Open Door Policy; Opium; Opium Wars; Pacific, European Presence in; Shandong Province.*

BIBLIOGRAPHY

Cain, Peter and Tony Hopkins. *British Imperialism, 1688–2000*, 2nd ed. New York: Longman, 2001.

Louis, William Roger, editor in chief. *The Oxford History of the British Empire*, 5 vols. Oxford, U.K.: Oxford University Press, 1998–1999.

Roger D. Long

EMPIRE, DUTCH

The first phase of Dutch overseas expansion was not an imperial one in the literal sense of the word. Only in 1816, at the Convention of London, was the newly founded Kingdom of the Netherlands granted back its overseas possessions: Java, the Moluccas, some factories in India, Malacca, Suriname, and six islands in the Caribbean. These overseas territories had belonged to the former Dutch East India Company, but were taken over by the British during the French occupation of the Netherlands. Before French revolutionary troops crossed the frozen rivers of the Netherlands in 1794, and the newly founded Batavia Republic became a vassal state of France, the Dutch overseas territories belonged to trading companies. They did not belong to the Dutch Republic, or more accurately, the Seven United Provinces. Until their bankruptcies at the end of the eighteenth century, the two maritime trading companies, the United East India Company (Verenigde Oost-Indische Compagnie, or VOC) and the West India Company (WIC), administered the Dutch overseas colonies. Hence the overseas empire of the seventeenth and eighteenth centuries is called a seaborne empire, as it depended on chartered private maritime trading companies.

Dutch overseas expansion took place under unfavorable political circumstances when the Dutch Republic (founded in 1588) was at war with its overlord, Spain. In 1580, when Portugal became a subject of the Spanish crown, Dutch traders faced difficulties in purchasing fine spices in Lisbon. In 1585 and 1598 Spain confiscated all Dutch vessels visiting Iberian ports. After the Spanish conquest of the rebelling port town of Antwerp in 1585, investors moved their business to the northern Netherlands, to the port town of Amsterdam. In Amsterdam they made good profits in the sugar industry. Portuguese (Jewish) merchants, who had also fled to Amsterdam, were allowed to continue their imports from Brazil. Economically, times were favorable for overseas expansion. Dutch merchants doubled their trade with the Baltic during the last quarter of the sixteenth century. Their large fleet, ship-building facilities, and investment capital could easily be used for an expansion into the transatlantic, African, and Asian trade. In addition, strong population growth in the northern Netherlands (in particular in the provinces of Holland and Zealand) provided the expanding emporium with a sufficient labor force.

In 1602 merchants from the wealthy port towns of Holland and Zealand founded the United East India Company (the VOC). This trading organization became the most effective European trading organization in Asia, and remained so until around the middle of the eighteenth century. In 1652 the VOC established a refitting

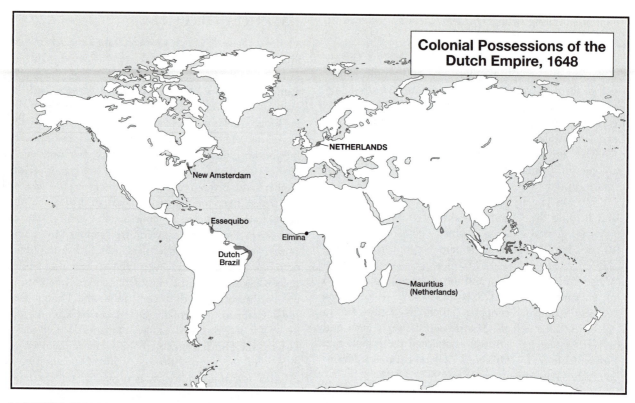

Colonial Possessions of the Dutch Empire, 1648

MAP BY XNR PRODUCTIONS. THE GALE GROUP.

station for its ships at the Cape of Good Hope. In the 1670s and 1680s this led to the first expansion into the interior, where settlers began to keep cattle and grow grapes for wine making on territory appropriated from the indigenous group, the Khoikhoi. In September of 1795, after almost 150 years of Dutch rule, the English took over the Castle of Cape Town; the Dutch permanently ceded the Cape at the London Convention of August 13, 1814.

In the waters of the West Indies and West Africa, Dutch merchants and shippers could act freely until 1607. There was no specific need for a West India Company yet. Willem Usselincx, a Calvinist merchant who had fled from Antwerp to Holland, pleaded nevertheless for the establishment of Protestant colonies in the West Indies. In due time, these colonies would be able to attack and occupy Spanish overseas possessions, he believed. The articles of the Twelve Years Truce (1609–1621) stipulated that Dutch ships were allowed to frequent the Iberian ports again, but Spanish possessions in the West Indies were now forbidden territory. Despite the truce articles, Dutch traders continued to privateer and raid in the Caribbean waters. Trade and colonization were less important, but some small colonies were founded in the Amazons and Guyana. One of the

successful tobacco and sugar plantations was Essequibo, founded by Aert Adriaenszn Groenewegen, whose daughter married a Native American chieftain.

The Dutch West Indian Company, founded immediately after the end of the Twelve Years Truce on June 3, 1621, devoted itself primarily to attacking Spanish and Portuguese possessions and privateer ships. WIC fleets captured several costly Iberian ships; for example, in Cuba's Matanzas Bay in 1628, ship commander Piet Hein captured cargo ships carrying silver valued at around 14 million Dutch guilders. The profits of privateering went partly to the stockholders who participated in the WIC, and partly toward the funding of large-scale operations aimed at conquering territory. In 1630 the WIC launched an attack on Pernambuco in Brazil, and seized Olinda and Recife. These important sugar ports were connected to a sugar-producing hinterland with many *engenhocas* (sugar factories). The Dutch conquered the great Portuguese fortress São Jorge del Mina, or Elmina, in 1637. Because the sugar industry in the Dutch Republic had grown considerably thanks to illegal trade with Portugal during the Truce, Amsterdam traders in particular were interested in investing more money in sugar plantations. In 1622 there were twenty-nine sugar refineries in Holland, twenty-five of which were owned

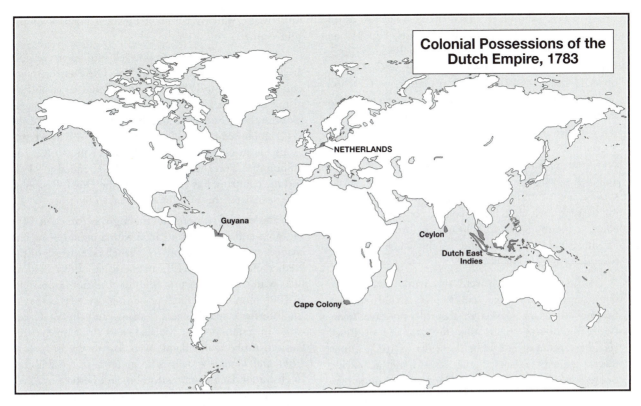

Colonial Possessions of the Dutch Empire, 1783

NETHERLANDS

Guyana

Ceylon

Dutch East Indies

Cape Colony

MAP BY XNR PRODUCTIONS. THE GALE GROUP.

by Amsterdam traders, whereas as recently as 1595 the total number of such factories totaled no more than three or four.

The sugar industry of Brazil gained new impetus under the reign of Count Johan Maurits van Nassau, governor of Dutch Brazil from 1636 to 1644. He extended Dutch territory at the expense of the Portuguese settlers, but did not succeed in winning sufficient cooperation from the Portuguese in the seven of the twelve territories (*capitanias*) the Dutch had conquered. Johan Maurits and a number of troops had to depart the colony in 1644, and the WIC board's subsequent neglect of Dutch Brazil led to an easy reconquest by combined Portuguese land and naval forces. On January 26, 1654, the Dutch signed the Capitulation of Taborda.

The loss of "neglected Brazil," as Dutch pamphleteers dubbed it, still left the Dutch with a number of other colonies. Sugar cultivation in Brazil had been a strong incentive to become engaged in the African slave trade, and after the loss of Brazil, Dutch merchants and colonists concentrated on the other possessions in the West Indies recognized by the Peace of Westphalia in 1648: Curaçao, Aruba, Bonaire, St. Maarten, Saba, and St. Eustatius. These islands were not suitable for sugar cultivation, but were nonetheless important, in particular

for the slave trade the sugar trade depended on. Suriname was seized from the English by Abraham Crijnssen in 1667, but retaken in the same year. The Peace of Breda (1667) gave Suriname to the Dutch, in return for New Netherland. Suriname first belonged to the States of Zealand, and then was given to the WIC in 1682. One year later, the WIC sold a third of Suriname to the city of Amsterdam, and another third to Cornelis van Aerssen. On May 21, 1683, the three owners formed the Geoctroyeerde Sociëteit van Suriname, which was to be under the supervision of the States General. At the time, Suriname was only a small colony with a mere twenty-five houses, fifty sugar plantations, and around 5,000 inhabitants (579 Christian colonists, 232 Jews, and 4,281 slaves) in 1683. Suriname became increasingly important for sugar growing, however. In the beginning of the eighteenth century, some 200 plantations used more than 10,000 slaves to plant, harvest, and process sugar. At the end of the same century, the colony's 533 plantations harbored around 53,000 people (including 2,000 Christians, 1,350 Jews, and 1,760 "colored"), 90 percent of whom were slaves. The 1683 charter remained valid until 1795.

With the Peace of Breda in 1667, marking the end of the second Anglo-Dutch War, the WIC lost the Cape

Coast Castle and New Netherland. The so-called Company of New Netherland had founded Fort Nassau on Manhattan Island along the Hudson River in 1615. In 1621 this fort was transferred to the WIC. On the upper Hudson, the WIC built Fort Orange in 1624, and one year later, New Amsterdam. Between seven and eight thousand people, many of them attracted by the fur trade, settled in New Netherland before the English took it over in 1664. One of the larger villages, located around Fort Orange, was the company village Beverwijck. This and other villages replicated much of Dutch village society and administration, having a burgher guard, a public Reformed church and council, orphan masters, a court, a poorhouse, a school, and so forth. It is often forgotten that New Netherland was the Dutch Republic's first successful settlement colony.

Although the Dutch were only partly successful in stabilizing colonies and cultivating territories, they became important players in the Atlantic slave trade. Beginning in the 1630s, after the conquest of Brazil and the capture of São Jorge del Mina in 1637, Dutch traders quickly expanded the slave trade in Africa. Between 1637 and 1645 the WIC transported more than 20,000 Africans to Brazil. The Dutch slave trade in Spanish America was legalized in 1662, and Curaçao became an important transit port for some 2,000 to 4,000 slaves per year. Soon the French and English became strong competitors in the slave trade, in particular after the founding of the Royal African Company of England in 1673. In 1675 the WIC had to be dissolved due to heavy losses. A second WIC quickly took over the trade of the first WIC, and the transatlantic slave trade continued to grow, reaching a peak in the 1680s, thanks to the *asiento* trade with the Spanish colonies. The second WIC's largest expansion in the slave trade came in the 1720s, thanks to the growth of Suriname's plantation economy. This growth led to an increasing export of slaves from the Gold Coast, and a decrease of exports from the Slave Coast. After 1738, with the termination of the WIC's monopoly on the slave trade and the beginning of the so-called free-trade slaving period, the numbers of Dutch free traders involved in the slave trade increased rapidly. The second WIC still exported some 6,000 slaves annually between 1744 and 1773 (reaching the peak of 9,000 annually between 1764 and 1771). Simultaneously, the Dutch free traders exported about 7,000 slaves annually from Africa. The Dutch transported approximately 550,000 slaves from the African coasts to the Americas during the seventeenth and eighteenth centuries. The other main export product from Africa was gold dust. The WIC exported an estimated 36 million Dutch guilders worth of gold between 1674 and 1740, a very important process for the city of Amsterdam, which was one of Europe's main silver and gold markets.

The Dutch seaborne empire fell into an irreversible decline during the 1780s and 1790s. The Fourth Anglo-Dutch War (1780–1784), during which a large portion of the Dutch fleet was captured, was a financial disaster for both the second WIC and the VOC. The debts of the WIC amounted to 6 million guilders in 1789, which was miniscule in comparison to the debts of the VOC: 134 million in 1796. The charter of the WIC ended in 1791, and the company was taken over by the Dutch Republic. Five years later the VOC was also taken over.

The end of two famous trading companies in both the West and the East coincided with a period of regime changes in Europe. During the French occupation of the Netherlands (1795–1813), maintaining direct trading links with the colonies proved difficult if not impossible. In 1795 most of the Dutch possessions were ceded to the English: the Cape, Malacca, Padang, and the VOC factories in Surat, Bengal, Malabar, and the Coromandel. Ceylon, Ambon, and Banda were lost to the English in 1796, and Ternate was given up in 1801. In the West the English took Demerara, Essequibo, and Berbice in 1796; Suriname fell in 1799, the islands of Curaçao, Aruba, and Bonaire in 1800, and one year later St. Eustatius, St. Maarten, and Saba. At the Peace of Amiens (March 27, 1802), brokered between England and France, the Netherlands received all these possessions back, except for Ceylon. When the war resumed one year later, almost all Dutch possessions were returned to the English again, except for Canton and Deshima. The Cape fell in 1806 and Java in 1811 (the latter after experiencing severe reforms under Governor-General Herman Willem Daendels [1807–1810]), but contact between England and its overseas territories were severely hampered by the Continental System, which Napoleon had introduced in 1806 to block all trade with England. The English capture of Curaçao in 1807 and of the Leeward Islands in 1810 was a relief for those islands' inhabitants, who had suffered severely from the prohibition of trade with England.

THE SECOND PHASE OF DUTCH COLONIAL RULE

The beginning of the nineteenth century saw a reestablishment of Dutch colonial rule in the East Indies, though this process was hampered by problems with the organization of colonial government, financial debts, political turmoil in Europe, and a weakening military presence. For many local rulers and others in Asia, a return to the old situation was unthinkable. Local sultans had shifted alliances rather quickly when the English took over the Dutch possessions, but did not readily

DUTCH EMPIRE, KEY DATES

1602: Merchants from Holland and Zealand found the United East India Company (the VOC)

1615: The Dutch Republic's first successful North American settlement, New Netherland, begins with the establishment of Fort Nassau in present day New York

1621: The end of the Twelve Years' Truce with Spain during the Dutch Revolt, or 80 Years' War, leads to the formation of The Dutch West Indian Company (WIC)

1621: Fort Nassau is transferred to the WIC

1624: The WIC builds Fort Orange in present day Albany, New York

1625: The WIC establishes New Amsterdam in what is now lower Manhattan in New York

1630: Dutch Brazil begins when the WIC launches an attack on the state of Pernambuco in eastern Brazil

1630s: The Dutch become actively involved in the slave trade

1654: Using land and naval forces, Portugal reacquires Dutch Brazil

1664: The English take over New Netherland

1667: The Dutch acquire Suriname from England

1780-1784: During the Fourth Anglo-Dutch War a large portion of the Dutch fleet is captured, negatively impacting the WIC and the VOC

1791: When its charter ends, the WIC is taken over by the Dutch Republic

1796: The Dutch Republic takes over the VOC

1814: At the Convention of London, the newly founded Kingdom of the Netherlands regains overseas possessions that were lost to Britain during the French occupation of the Netherlands

1816: Dutch colonial rule is reestablished in the East Indies

1825-1830: The Java War is the most serious challenge to newly established Dutch colonial rule

1830-1870: Dutch colonialism is characterized by exploitation and consolidation

1875-1899: A new type of colonial capitalist economy, dependent upon cheap labor, emerges as private entrepreneurs develop large tobacco plantations and pursue mining ventures in the Netherlands Indies

1900: Colonial administration introduces the so-called Ethical Policy, a largely unsuccessful program of reforms aimed at improving conditions for native Indonesians and introducing a degree of political autonomy

1927: Following uprisings by the Indonesian Communist Party, the colonial government formally discontinues the Ethical Policy

1935: The Netherlands Indies becomes a well-monitored police state

1942: After assuming control of Indonesia, the Japanese imprison resident Europeans and exploit Indonesian people, industry, and agriculture

1945: Following the capitulation of Japan, Indonesia declares its independence on August 17

1947-1948: After two Dutch-Indonesian wars, the Netherlands government finally accepts Indonesian independence

1949: On December 27, Queen Juliana transfers sovereignty to the Indonesian Republic

1975: On November 25, Suriname becomes completely independent

1988: Antillean residents indicate their desire to maintain relations with the Netherlands

2003: The Nationaal Instituut Nederlands slavernijverleden is founded

2006: Roughly 400,000 Indonesians live in the Netherlands, and approximately 3,000 Dutch citizens live in Indonesia

---

accede to the reimposition of Dutch rule in 1816 (mandated by the Convention of London of 1814). The rulers of Yogyakarta and Surakarta, however, decided to accept the return of Dutch authority. But despite attempts under governors-general Daendels and Raffles to reform colonial rule, uprisings soon occurred in the Netherlands Indies. Among these was the uprising of May 14, 1817, led by the Ambonese sergeant major Thomas Matulesia

(Pattimura) on the Ambonese island of Saparua (with the help of some tribal members from the island of Ceram). Pattimura was a Christian, and his resistance against the reintroduction of Dutch rule was strongly religiously inspired. Other conflicts occurred with the sultans of Banjarmasin, Ceribon, and Pontianak, but the most serious challenge to newly established Dutch colonial rule was the rebellion of the Javanese prince Diponegoro, which led to the Java War (1825–1830).

Dutch colonialism from 1830 to 1870 is known as a period of exploitation and consolidation. Firstly, in contrast with the British, who had abandoned slavery in 1833, the Dutch continued to permit slavery in both the Caribbean and in Indonesia. Although the Netherlands government had forbidden the slave trade in 1814, illegal shipments to Suriname continued and in Indonesia slavery and bondage were endemic in indigenous societies outside of Java and Sumatra. Slavery as such was abandoned in the Netherlands East Indies in 1858, and in the West Indies in 1863. A second exploitative feature of this period was the cultivation system on Java, which varied locally and regionally but was characterized by the drive to expropriate as many natural resources as possible, in particular coffee, indigo, and sugar.

After 1870 the colonial economy no loner depended as much on the forced delivery of sugar, coffee, indigo, and spices by the colonized. The development of railway transportation began modestly with the laying down of railway lines between Semarang-Tanggoeng (1867) and Batavia-Buitenzorg (1873). Steam shipping and the opening of the Suez Canal in 1869 helped to attract private investors. In the last quarter of the nineteenth century, several private entrepreneurs started developing large-scale plantations in the Netherlands Indies. In particular the tobacco plantations in Deli, North Sumatra, proved to be a profitable business. The cultivation of new lands for tobacco required the help of thousands of cheap laborers (mostly Chinese, Malay, and Javanese). This new type of colonial capitalist economy soon met with criticism. The harsh circumstances and unsanitary conditions in the Deli plantations, the maltreatment of coolies, and the immoral behavior of young white planters stirred the consciences of many Dutch citizens both in the colonies and in Europe. So did the attempts to subjugate the sultanate of Aceh, from 1873 onward, during the so-called Aceh War.

The modernization of the colonial economy also quickly increased the demand for minerals. Private merchants also engaged in mining of tin, for instance, after the founding of NV Billiton Maatschappij on Billiton in 1860. Coal mining on Sumatra started in the late 1880s, and in 1890 the first oil fields on that island were exploited. The Koninklijke Paketvaart Maatschappij, a shipping company founded in 1888, took over the transportation of consumer and industrial goods. The new port of Tanjung Priuk, just outside Batavia, also facilitated the flow of goods and people.

Although the Europeans in the Netherlands Indies comprised only a small minority of 60,000 in 1880, their technical skills, investments, and modernization efforts changed the archipelago for good. The introduction of urban planning, electricity, railways, and buildings done in rococo, art deco, and Jugendstil styles, and the publication of books, magazines, and newspapers—in short, the propagation of the Western bourgeois lifestyle, along with its status differences and social ranking—all had an influence on traditional Indonesian life. In particular, the colonial urban lifestyle—the splendid villas of the elite, such as Menteng in Batavia, their extravagance, their sport clubs, ballrooms, cafés, and restaurants—was increasingly attracting (but also disturbing) the educated young Indonesian elite, who found it difficult to gain access to such wealth. Europeanized Indonesians mimicked the colonial lifestyle, as did to a certain extent the locally born (*peranakan*) Chinese, but by the beginning of the twentieth century the younger Indonesian generation had come to realize that modernization and resistance were necessary.

The turn of the twentieth century saw the introduction by the colonial administration of the so-called Ethical Policy, a program of reforms aimed at improving conditions for native Indonesians and introducing a degree of political autonomy. These efforts were largely unsuccessful at improving conditions for Indonesians, however, and did not prevent the growth of anti-Dutch nationalism. The founding of Boedi Oetomo in Yogyakarta on May 20, 1908, is usually seen as the birth of the nationalist movement in Java, although this organization was still careful to formulate its ideal as: "the harmonious development of the land and people of the Netherlands Indies." This initiative was soon followed by the founding of other idealistic, often Islamic organizations such as Sarekat Islam, which organized mass congresses from its inception in 1912, and Moehammadyah, an Islamic reformist movement also founded in 1912. Simultaneously, the colonial authorities developed democratic institutions at the local and regional level. At the national level, the Volksraad (People's Council) was established in May 1918, as a first step toward autonomy within the kingdom of the Netherlands. It never developed into a parliament, however, and the government selected half of its forty-eight (in 1927, sixty) members. In the 1930s it mainly functioned as an opposition forum. The Partai Komunis Indonesia PKI (the Indonesian Communist Party), established in 1924, became the podium for the more radical protesters against Dutch colonial rule. In 1926 and 1927 the PKI organized strikes and armed resistance, which were crushed by the Royal East Indonesian Army (the KNIL). The government arrested some 13,000 people, of whom 4,500 were sentenced to prison; a great number was brought to the internment camp Boven-Digoel in New Guinea. Following these uprisings, the colonial government formally discontinued the Ethical Policy and abandoned the idea of "self-rule under Dutch control" in favor of what eventually became a police state; in response, Indonesian nationalism became stronger.

The worldwide economic crisis following the stock market crash of 1929 also had a severe impact on the Netherlands Indies. The prices of export products like rubber, sugar, and oil dropped dramatically, resulting in mass unemployment. In 1929 the Netherlands Indies exported 263,000 tons of rubber worth 232 million guilders; in 1993 the export had risen to 350,000 tons, but the value of it was only 37 million guilders. Increasing mass poverty on the one hand, and restricted government expenditures on the other, worsened the economic and political crisis. Nationalist Indonesians, since July 1929 organized in the Partai Nasional Indonesia (Indonesian National Party) under the leadership of the engineer Sukarno (1901–1970), were able to create mass movements for independence, despite persecution and imprisonment. By around 1935 most of the nationalist leaders had been imprisoned, and the Netherlands Indies had become a well-monitored police state. Against this background, Sukarno and others welcomed the Japanese in January 1942. After the loss of British Singapore, there was little to stand in the way of the Japanese advance into the archipelago and in March they controlled much of the region. Although many Indonesians welcomed the Japanese with flags and dancing, Indonesian industry and agriculture were soon exploited for the Japanese empire. Chaos and poverty were the result, and productions declined drastically, sometimes by 80 to 90 percent, as with rubber and sugar production.

The Japanese occupation was a traumatic experience for the Europeans. Within one year after the start of the occupation, 29,000 men, 25,000 women, and 29,000 children were placed in internment camps. About 18,000 Dutch men were brought to Burma to work for the Burma railroad. The Indonesian population suffered even more. The Japanese recruited some 165,000 to 200,000 "economic soldiers" or *romushas* to work in overseas projects, for instance, in Burma. Thousands of them died in forced labor projects. Millions of Indonesians suffered from malnutrition, and when the food supply collapsed in 1994 the dead bodies could be seen on the streets of Javanese cities.

The Indonesian leaders Sukarno and Mohammed Hatta were shocked by the capitulation of Japan on August 15, 1945. They had hoped for an orderly transfer of power. In May, Sukarno and his advisors had formulated a constitution and laid out the five principles (*pancasila*) of the Indonesian state: national unity, humanity, democracy, social justice, and the belief in one God. On August 17, Sukarno and Hatta declared Indonesian independence, after being pressured by nationalist youth (the *pemuda*), and after being convinced that the Japanese authorities would not intervene. The *pemuda* groups turned very violent in the months following this declaration of independence, though British troops restored order after landing in Surabaya. The new Dutch governor, Dr. H. J. van Mook, soon found that the restoration of the old order was an illusion. Negotiation with the nascent Indonesian Republic led to the Linggadjati Agreement at the end of 1946. Conservative Dutch politicians and Dutch public opinion, however, undermined this agreement, along with radical nationalists in Indonesia. After two Dutch-Indonesian wars in 1947 and 1948, the Netherlands government finally accepted Indonesian independence under international pressure. On December 27, 1949, Queen Juliana transferred sovereignty to the Indonesian Republic. To the Indonesians however, August 17, 1945, is the formal date of independence.

Dutch policies toward Suriname and the Netherlands Antilles took a different turn than in the Netherlands Indies. After the abolishment of slavery, Suriname had seen an influx of cheap laborers from India and Java, which made Suriname a multiethnic society. In 1898 the geologist G. C. Dubois found bauxite on the plantations of Rorac. A drop in European bauxite exports to the United States during World War I stimulated bauxite mining in Suriname. In 1916 the Surinaamse Bauxiet Maatschappij (Suriname Bauxite Company) was founded. During World War II, Suriname was of strategic importance because of the bauxite mines delivering aluminum for the aircraft industry in the United States. Curaçao welcomed English and French troops, as the island was a part of the Caribbean Sea Frontier guarding against German submarines.

Despite its multiethnic population of Creoles, Hindus, Javanese, and native Indians, Suriname showed enough political stability to develop democratic institutions during the 1940s and 1950s. In all of the Dutch overseas territories in the West, there was a desire for autonomy after World War II. The first Round Table Conference in 1948 resulted in a high degree of autonomy for Suriname, while the second Round Table Conference in 1952 led to a separate political status for Suriname within the kingdom. Suriname only became completely independent on November 25, 1975. By that time Suriname had already faced several political crises due to the development of political parties based on ethnic groups. Political patronage and favoritism were endemic as political leaders tried to gain the support of their own ethnic group through granting favors. By the time Suriname became independent, a large portion of the population had already settled in the Netherlands. At the end of 1975, one third of Suriname's population, around 130,000 people, lived in the Netherlands. After the military coup of February 25, 1980, led by Desi Bouterse, more people left Suriname, which sank into poverty and remained poor for the rest of the twentieth century.

The five Antillean islands remained part of the kingdom. The Round Table Conferences of 1981 and 1983 granted the right to self-determination, which provided the opportunity for Aruba to establish a "status apart" within the kingdom. Polls of all Antillean residents in 1988 showed that the majority of the island population wanted to maintain the relation with the Netherlands. Dutch politicians dropped the idea of involuntary independence, and at the end of the twentieth century the Antilles not only developed into a holiday resort for the Dutch, but also into a political burden. Many young Antilleans migrated to the Netherlands, where they faced many problems finding jobs. The growing influence of drug smugglers also contributed to repeated friction between the government in The Hague and Antillean administrators. Financially and politically, postwar involvement with the former overseas possessions in the West was a heavy burden for the Dutch government.

The legacy of the colonial past still plays an important role in internal debates in the Netherlands over topics such as Indonesian independence and slavery in the West. On July 1, 2002, a memorial to the victims of slavery was erected in Amsterdam. In particular, the descendents of slaves living in the Netherlands strive for recognition of their past, and of slavery's consequences for modern Dutch society. In 2003 the Nationaal Instituut Nederlands slavernijverleden was founded. On August 17, 2005, for the first time ever, a member of the Dutch government—the Minister of Foreign Affairs, Dr. Bernard Bot—attended the commemoration of Indonesian independence in Jakarta. Bot declared that "the Dutch government expresses its political and moral acceptance of the Proklamasi, the date the Republic of Indonesia declared independence." He also remarked, "In retrospect, it is clear that its large-scale deployment of military forces in 1947 put the Netherlands on the wrong side of history," and expressed his "profound regret for all that suffering." In 2005, some 400,000 Indonesians live in the Netherlands, and some 3,000 Dutch citizens live in Indonesia.

SEE ALSO *Aceh War; Dutch United East India Company; Dutch West India Company; Ethical Policy, Netherlands Indies; Heeren XVII; Java War; Java, Cultivation System; Netherlands Missionary Society; Royal Dutch-Indisch Army.*

BIBLIOGRAPHY

Boxer, C. R. *The Dutch in Brazil, 1624–1654.* Oxford: Clarendon, 1957.

Boxer, C. R. *The Dutch Seaborne Empire, 1600–1800.* New York: Knopf, 1965.

Doel, H. W. van den. *Het Rijk van Insulinde: Opkomst en ondergang van een Nederlandse kolonie.* Amsterdam: Prometheus, 1996.

Elphick, Richard, and Hermann Giliomee. 2d ed. *The Shaping of South African Society, 1652–1840.* Cape Town: Maskew Miller Longman, 1989.

Emmer, P. C. *De Nederlandse slavenhandel, 1500–1850.* Amsterdam: Arbeiderspers, 2003.

Gaastra, Femme S. *The Dutch East India Company.* Zutphen, Netherlands: Walburg, 2003.

Goor, J. van. *De Nederlandse koloniën: Geschiedenis van de Nederlandse expansie, 1600–1975.* The Hague: SDU Uitgeverij Koninginnegracht, 1994.

Heijer, Henk den. *Goud, ivoor, en slaven: Scheepvaart en handel van de Tweede Westindische Compagnie op Afrika, 1674–1740.* Zutphen, Netherlands: Walburg, 1997.

Jong, J. J. P. de. *De waaier van het fortuin: De Nederlanders in Azië en de Indonesische archipel, 1595–1950.* The Hague: SDU Uitgeverij Koninginnegracht, 1998.

Postma, Johannes M. *The Dutch in the Atlantic Slave Trade, 1600–1815.* Cambridge, U.K.: Cambridge University Press, 1990.

Hendrik E. Niemeijer

EMPIRE, FRENCH

The French Empire, second only to the British, was the product of France's long history of political and economic competition with other European powers, and like them, the French founded their empire on a curious mixture of exploitation, violence, and the desire to make the world a better place—that is, to remake it in their image. Unlike their contemporaries, French colonialism triggered in the seventeenth century a contradiction in French national identity that plagued France until the final collapse of its empire in the 1960s, and made its colonial policies ambiguous if not contradictory. While its Ancienne Colonies (the North American colonies founded in the sixteenth and seventeenth centuries) tipped French political philosophy in the direction of democracy and contributed to the French Revolution in

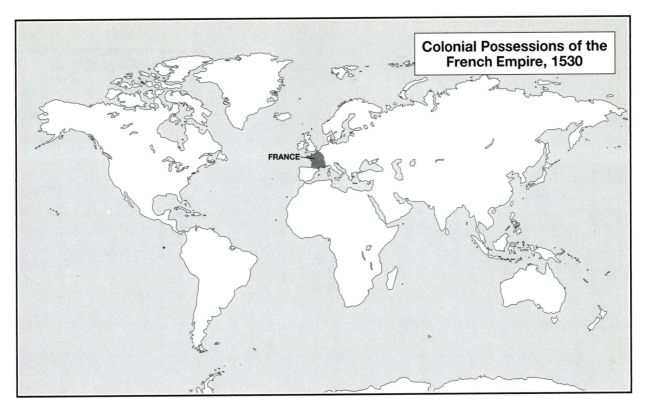

Colonial Possessions of the French Empire, 1530

FRANCE

MAP BY XNR PRODUCTIONS. THE GALE GROUP.

the late eighteenth century, French concerns about the country's prestige as a world power made the French reluctant to relinquish their later colonial empire, even when other nations did so and urged them to do likewise. Their conquest of parts of North America, the Caribbean, the Pacific Islands, Indochina, and Africa left a legacy of boundaries between colonized and colonizers made porous by commonalities of language, government, and identity.

The earliest French colonies provided the French people with examples of a free society at the same time that French presence eroded that freedom. France's earliest incursions into North America in the sixteenth and seventeenth centuries—part of the competition between France, Britain, the Netherlands, Spain, and Portugal to find new trade routes to the Far East—were simply trading posts where fishers and traders interacted relatively peacefully with the Huron, Ottawa, Ojibwa, Iroquois, Mimac, and Montagnais-Neskapi Indians, among others. But competition between the French and the Dutch started a chain reaction in Native American relationships, exacerbating old animosities between Native Americans who wanted to capture the French fur trade, as was the case with the Iroquois and the Huron, for whom European guns had turned competition into wars of extermination by 1633.

As French missionaries settled in, they upset traditional social, political, and economic relationships, drawing Native American men into Christianity with promises of land. In exchange for missionary land, they had to become cultivators of crops—women's work—for the church and whatever market was available. Their redefinitions of manhood prompted many women to resist Christianity because they did not want to lose their gender monopoly on agriculture, generating conflict within Native American communities. Other Native American women welcomed Christianity for the space it provided them as they coped with transforming communities, as did Kateri Tekakwitha (1656–1680), a Mohawk-Algonquin whom the Catholic Church beatified in 1980. By 1697 France had claimed dominion over portions of North America stretching all the way to the Caribbean, with much the same results.

The Caribbean was the site of intense competition between the Spanish, Danes, Dutch, English, and French, and their determination to extract wealth from their colonies was disastrous for the people they conquered. By the time France wrested possession of the western third of Hispaniola (Saint-Domingue, now Haiti) from Spain in 1697, most of its indigenous population had perished in the Spanish pursuit of gold. Like the other Europeans, the French turned their islands into

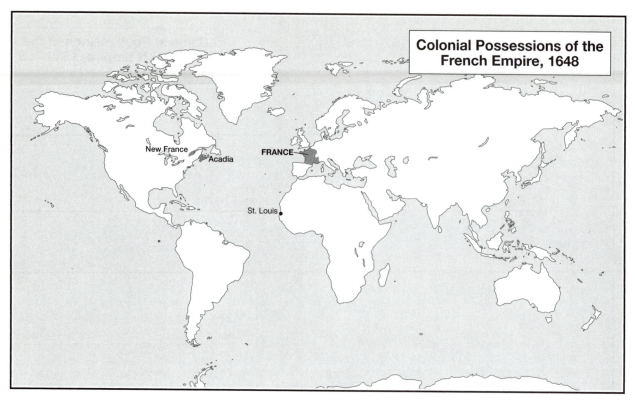

Colonial Possessions of the French Empire, 1648

New France
Acadia
FRANCE
St. Louis

MAP BY XNR PRODUCTIONS. THE GALE GROUP.

profitable sugar (and in Saint-Domingue, coffee and spice) plantations, which by the mid-eighteenth century were almost completely dependent on slave labor. By the late eighteenth century slaves greatly outnumbered European colonists (in Saint-Domingue, eight to one).

France's presence in the New World thus greatly transformed the indigenous societies with whom the French interacted—or in the Caribbean, conquered—but it also drastically reconfigured France itself. That transformation began with France's loss of its continental North American colonies to Britain after a series of wars in North America that culminated in the French and Indian War (1754–1763). That war was in fact the North American theater of the Seven Years' War (1756 to 1763) in Europe, into which France had been dragged as an ally to Austria against Prussia and its ally, Britain. That defeat compounded a growing internal crisis in France born of a burgeoning population, famine, food shortages, Louis XIV's (1638–1715) creation of a bureaucracy made of nobles who had purchased their office and were exempt from taxation, and near bankruptcy.

Such crises had existed before, but France's Ancienne Colonies added a new ingredient: the example of Native American political autonomy. Europeans were captivated

by the reports of early explorers and missionaries like Christopher Columbus (1451–1506), Amerigo Vespucci (1454–1512), and Pierre Francois Xavier de Charlevoix (1682–1761), who claimed that Native Americans lived in a state of innocence made spectacular by its lack of crime and warfare. Educated men like the philosopher and author Michel de Montaigne (1533–1592) claimed that Native American societies embodied the characteristics Plato envisioned in his *Republic*, and the French philosopher Jean-Jacques Rousseau (1712–1778) romanticized the "noble savage" into the basis for a social contract under which free citizens could live in harmony as equals. Those ideas encouraged members of the Third Estate (the group of delegates from the "common people" that constituted one of the three Estates that made up the French representative assembly, the Estates-General) to resist attempts by King Louis XVI (1754–1793) to levy new taxes by declaring themselves a National Assembly in 1789, and thus begin the French Revolution that turned France into a republic in 1792.

That transformation, built on the promise of liberty, equality, and fraternity, became the basis for a conundrum: In order to maintain that ideal, the French had to defend themselves against rulers of other nations who wanted to restore France's monarchy, neutralize opposition within

France, and maintain its position as a world power by retaining its empire, all of which required repression and violence. Democracy could not easily coexist with hierarchical empires, and terror appeared to be a necessary tool in preserving liberty. Amidst intensifying internal conflict (exemplified most horrifically by the Reign of Terror from 1793 to 1795), continued war, and a revolution in Saint-Domingue that culminated in the colony's independence as Haiti (1804), Napoléon Bonaparte (1769–1821) seized power (1799) and immediately returned France to the task of empire building.

But the seeds of democracy were now embedded in French identity, and as the mythos of the French Revolution grew, so did the ideals of liberty, equality, and fraternity that had nurtured it, requiring the French to serve two ideological masters: empire and liberty. The idea of empire did not fall with Napoléon I in 1815, and by 1830 King Charles X (1757–1836), who hoped to strengthen his own as well as reassert French national prestige, invaded northern Algeria, which marked the beginning of the scramble for empire that drove European nations in the second half of the nineteenth century. France subsequently invaded Tahiti (1843), New Caledonia (1853), Indochina (1858), Tunisia (1881), Equatorial Africa (1885), West Africa (1895), Madagascar (1896), and Morocco (1907), in general to counter other European nations' incursions into those territories, or to protect French interests, missionaries, or settlers. All of those invasions eventually led to French rule, but it was never uncontested. Conflict over French colonization arose from traditional sources—other nations opposing the French presence because they claimed a territory as their own, and colonized people struggling to resist or overthrow their conquerors—but also from the French themselves because of the contradictions embedded in their goals.

Other nations disputed French incursion continually. Both Britain and France claimed Tahiti from the late 1760s; the soldier and explorer Louis-Antoine de Bougainville's (1729–1811) praise of it as an "earthly paradise" exacerbated the problem by attracting adventurers from around the world. A large Italian settler presence in Tunisia, and repeated insurgencies in Algeria that the French believed were instigated in Tunisia, convinced the French to invade Tunisia. China and Britain challenged France's influence in Indochina. In West Africa, Britain and France competed for dominance until Britain conceded French control of a small portion of Cape Verde in 1815, but it was another eighty years before the French were able to declare their domination. France, Germany, and Spain competed for economic and political influence in Morocco until Abd al-Hafidh requested French assistance in restoring social

order in 1912 after his brother's assassination, after which France controlled Morocco. Still, the French granted Spain its previous sphere of influence, and a council of European nations made Tangier, Morocco, an "international city" in 1923.

Colonized peoples presented a more formidable obstacle. Their hostility is not difficult to understand, especially given France's espousal of liberty, equality, and fraternity. After Napoléon I revoked the Constitutional Assembly's 1794 decree emancipating all slaves in Martinique and Guadeloupe, re-enslaved people were especially unwilling to return to their former status. Slave revolts tore those colonies apart between 1816 and 1830, and in 1831 erupted in an all-out civil war. In New Caledonia, Melanesians revolted in 1878 over the fact that even in the ever-shrinking "reserves" the French had granted them they had no rights to the land, an issue that festered in sporadic rebellions until 1917.

The people of Algeria raised a sustained resistance against French invasion from 1830 until 1847 when French forces defeated the nationalist leader Abd el-Kader (1808–1883), but that was followed by uprisings in 1864, 1871, 1876, 1879, from 1881 to 1884, and in the 1890s, inspired by loss of land; demand for civil, economic, and political rights; racial tensions; and sometimes a combination of those issues. The Annamites (in central Vietnam), Thais, Laotians, and Cambodians whom the French tried to control in Indochina resisted domination until 1900 (in part supported by the Chinese), and the French were still deposing emperors until 1917.

The struggle of the colonized peoples to overthrow their French conquerors grew more focused over time because French domination, and the brutality and exploitation that often accompanied it, forced the colonized to redefine themselves in relation to the French. Although France vacillated between policies of assimilation and association, for the most part the French did not think of the people they colonized as French, nor did the colonized consider themselves French. Instead, the native peoples of French colonies first defined themselves by region or ethnicity, or sometimes by religion, and finally in terms of their colonial grouping. That process was usually wrenching because it involved fighting for independence. Most colonized people never actually stopped fighting for independence, and especially after the turn of the twentieth century they began to demand greater participation in their governance, access to education, less destructive land policies, and more equitable taxation. Only after World War II (1939–1945) did they resort to sustained violence, and between 1945 and 1960, most colonies fought for—and gained—their independence.

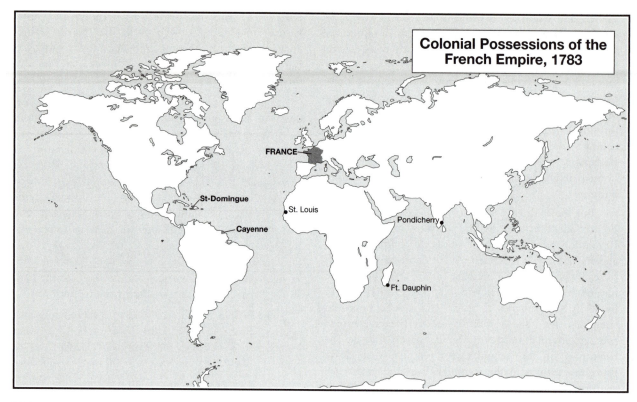

Colonial Possessions of the French Empire, 1783

FRANCE

St-Domingue

Cayenne

St. Louis

Pondicherry

Ft. Dauphin

MAP BY XNR PRODUCTIONS. THE GALE GROUP.

To some extent the decline of the French empire amounted to a series of civil wars, a struggle between settlers *(colons)* perceiving themselves to be a new breed of French person (in Algeria, for example, a "neo-French race"); indigenous people declaring an ethnic identity (as "Arabs" did in the pan-Arab movement that swept North Africa, as "Vietnamese" did in the wake of the successful nationalist coalition, Vietnam Dop Lap Dong Minh, or as the Merina did in Madagascar); and colonized individuals struggling to locate their own identity in the constructs of "otherness" that differentiated "us" from "them," compatriot from enemy. When colonized people identified themselves regionally or ethnically, their self-identity became a weapon of race politics with which the French kept them divided, as was the case in Morocco where, by 1950, Sultan Mohammed V (1909–1961), who had aligned himself with the French in return for their support, found himself trapped between the French-supported Berbers and the Istiqlal Independence Party, formed in the 1920s by mostly bourgeois radicals determined to obtain self-government.

Controlling hostile indigenous populations or slaves and managing the *colons* who were often in conflict with them was expensive. France was often obliged to import indentured labor from other colonies when indigenous people refuse to work according to market demands

or for *colons*, and most of the French colonies were a persistent economic drain. The cost in human life was greater. The French army estimated that approximately 89,000 people died in a rebellion in Madagascar (1947–1949); in the final fighting in Algeria (1959–1961), estimates of total dead—military, civilian, European, non-European, and indigenous—range around 300,000. Those external tragedies were matched by internal battles that resulted from, in Franz Fanon's words, "a double process: primarily economic; subsequently the internalization—or better, the epidermalization—of . . . inferiority" (1967, p.11).

The tragedies of colonialism were echoed—and often precipitated—by the internal struggle the French had with themselves over their colonial intentions: Did they mean to bring colonized peoples into fraternity, as full citizens with equality and liberty (a *mission civilisatrice*), or were they asserting their place as a world power with the right of conquest, subordination, and exploitation of less powerful peoples? For most of the nineteenth century, anticolonialism persisted as the dominant attitude toward what appeared to most French people as an unnecessary and almost accidental accumulation of colonies, the consequence of an ambitious military and desultory settlement. Most French people were preoccupied by the contest between

FRENCH EMPIRE, KEY DATES

1564: A French Huguenot colony is briefly established in the New World at Fort Caroline (now Jacksonville, FL)

1605: French settlement of Port Royal is established in Acacia (now Nova Scotia)

1608: Samuel de Champlain founds Quebec City, the future capital of New France

1624: French begin to settle French Guiana

1664: French East India Company is established

1697: France takes possession of Saint Domingue from Spain

1682: Explorer Robert Cavelier de La Salle names Louisiana in honor of French king

1699: Pierre Le Moyne d'Iberville establishes a permanent settlement in Louisiana

1756: France opposes Great Britain in North America's French and Indian War

1756: The Seven Years' War between France and Great Britain begins

1763: The Treaty of Paris divides France's North American holdings between Britain and Spain

1789: The French Revolution begins

1791: Toussaint l'Ouverture leads a massive slave revolt on Saint Domingue

1799: Napoleon Bonaparte comes to power

1803: Napoleon sells the colony of Louisiana to the United States

1804: Saint Domingue gains independence as Haiti

1814: Napoleon abdicates and Louis XVIII becomes king of France

1815: Great Britain concedes portions of Cape Verde to the French

1830: Charles II abdicates the French throne and Louis-Philippe becomes king

1830: France invades Algeria and begins a 17-year-long conquest

1831: Civil wars erupt in the French colonies of Martinique and Guadeloupe

1843: Tahiti becomes a French protectorate

1848: Revolution brings Napoleon III to power in Second Empire

1853: New Caledonia becomes a French protectorate

1854: France enters the two-year Crimean War as a part of the Western Alliance against Russia

1859: France enters the Austro-Italian War

1870: France's defeat in the Franco-Prussian War sparks the Paris Commune and the Third Republic

1878: Melanesians revolt in New Caledonia over land rights issues

1881: France invades Tunisia and establishes a protectorate

1884: France takes over Tonkin and Annam (now Vietnam)

1895: France invades West Africa, followed by Madagascar

1887: French Indochina is formed from Tonkin, Annam, Cambodia, Cochin-China, and Laos

1907: France invades Morocco, which becomes a protectorate in 1912

1918: France gains control of former Turkish territories following World War I

1945: French colonies overrun during World War II are restored

1946: The Union Française is established to politically unite the former French colonies

1954: France withdraws from Indochina due to strength of the native independence movement and loss at Dies Bier Phu

1958: General Charles de Gaulle becomes president of France

1958: The Union Française is replaced by the Communauté Française

1962: Algeria gains independence from France

republican government and the monarchy that generated three revolutions (1830, 1848, and 1870), as well as the three wars (the Crimean War, 1854–1856; the Austro-Italian War, 1859; and the Franco-Prussian War, 1870) and numerous skirmishes, alliances, and ententes made necessary by the empire that was supposed to secure France's place in the hierarchy of nations.

French colonial policy was dictated by French ambivalence and preoccupation. Throughout the nineteenth century, assimilation—the idea that the French could eventually make colonized peoples into French people (a policy similar to Spain's)—made empire palatable to the French. As social Darwinism, sociology, and psychology made their debut as philosophical and intellectual models for understanding human development, the idea that "primitive others" needed to evolve according to their own nature began to emerge as the policy of *association*, and by the end of the century it had replaced assimilation. Through association, a system much like Britain's approach in its colonies, France would establish economic and political administrative control over a colony, but leave civil and local affairs in the hands of local chiefs or rulers, and thereby guide French colonies to gradual democratic self-government.

Underlying both policies, however, was the contradiction that had impaled French colonialism from the seventeenth century: the French had to fight for empire to secure their position as a world power, but the quality that made them superior—their dedication to liberty, equality, and fraternity—necessitated that they make the people they colonized their equals. The irreconcilable nature of that contradiction created what Elizabeth Ezra (2000) has called a "colonial unconscious" in which the French desired to embrace their colonized peoples as equals but could not do so because they also wished to preserve the sense that they were superior, part of which was memorializing the "greater France" represented by empire. That paradox is apparent in nineteenth-century debates over imperialism, but it permeated French culture by the 1920s and continues to haunt it today. More poignant is the fact that many colonized people shared that colonial unconscious, simultaneously outraged by the degradation the French forced them to suffer, and drawn to the metropole as a site of economic and cultural empowerment.

SEE ALSO *Empire in the Americas, French; French Colonialism, Middle East; French East India Company; French Indochina; French Polynesia; Law, Colonial Systems of, French Empire.*

BIBLIOGRAPHY

Ballantyne, Tony, and Antoinette M. Burton. *Bodies in Contact: Rethinking Colonial Encounters in World History.* Durham, NC: Duke University Press, 2005.

Betts, Raymond F. *Assimilation and Association in French Colonial Theory, 1890–1914.* New York: Columbia University Press, 1961.

Betts, Raymond F. *France and Decolonisation, 1900–1960.* New York: St. Martin's, 1991.

Brunschwig, Henri. *French Colonialism, 1871–1914: Myths and Realities.* Translated by William Granville Brown. New York: Praeger, 1966.

Clayton, Anthony. *The Wars of French Decolonization.* Essex, U.K.: Longman, 1994.

Daughton, J. P. *An Empire Divided: Religion, Republicanism, and the Making of French Colonialism, 1880–1914.* New York: Oxford University Press, 2006.

Duara, Prasenjit, ed. *Decolonization: Perspectives from Then and Now.* New York: Routledge, 2004.

Ezra, Elizabeth. *The Colonial Unconscious: Race and Culture in Interwar France.* Ithaca, NY: Cornell University Press, 2000.

Fanon, Franz. *Black Skin, White Masks.* Translated by Charles Lam Markmann. New York: Grove, 1967.

Hargreaves, Alec G., ed. *Memory, Empire, and Postcolonialism: Legacies of French Colonialism.* Lanham, MD: Lexington, 2005.

Hoepli, Nancy, ed. *Aftermath of Colonialism.* New York: Wilson, 1973.

Roberts, Stephen H. *History of French Colonial Policy (1870–1925).* London: King & Son, 1929.

Watenpaugh, Keith David. *Being Modern in the Middle East: Revolution, Nationalism, Colonialism, and the Arab Middle Class.* Princeton, NJ: Princeton University Press, 2006.

Karen J. Taylor

EMPIRE IN THE AMERICAS, BRITISH

The English Empire created in the Americas can rightly be referred to as the first British empire. More than a century before British power was consolidated in India, Australasia, and Africa, colonies were settled throughout the Western hemisphere, contributing toward a mercantilist system that propelled Britain's economic status to the forefront of the world.

IMPERIAL BEGINNINGS

Though England would come to be a dominant imperial power by the mid-eighteenth century, in the sixteenth century it lagged significantly behind Spain, Portugal, and France in seeing the potential that overseas colonies offered. While Spain was building colonies in Asia and conquering the Aztecs and Incas, Portugal was settling on the coasts of Brazil and Africa and establishing trading posts in the Indian Ocean and China Sea. The French, meanwhile, were making their first attempts to settle in North America. During this period of activity, the English were nowhere to be seen.

John Cabot's (1450–1499) voyage in the service of Henry VII (1457–1509), to Labrador in 1497 was not the start of regular transatlantic ventures by the English. The failure to find the Northwest Passage and the

England's North American colonies	
1606	The London company was granted a charter for Virginia The Plymouth company was granted a charter
1624	Virginia was made a royal colony
1629	The Governor and Company of Massachusetts Bay was granted a charter
1631	The Earl of Warwick was granted a charter for the Connecticut River Valley
1632	Calvert was granted a charter for Maryland
1636	Roger Williams settled at Providence
1662	Connecticut received a charter
1663	Eight proprietors were granted a charter for Carolina
1664	The Duke of York was granted a charter to the former New Netherland, now New York
1667	The proprietors of Carolina were granted a charter for the Bahamas
1680	New Hampshire was separated from Massachusetts by a royal charter
1681	Penn was granted a charter for Pennsylvania
1691	Massachusetts Bay was granted a new charter
1702	New Jersey united as a crown colony
1733	James Oglethrope and associates granted a charter to Georgia

THE GALE GROUP.

generally inhospitable climate of the high Arctic led to a waning of interest in London. Domestic distractions such as the Reformation meant that English attention did not return to overseas exploration until the accession of Elizabeth I (1533–1603) in 1558.

From the mid-1560s onward, English sailors and adventurers rapidly improved their knowledge of the Atlantic World as they raided Spanish treasure ships that were returning from the silver and gold mines of Latin America. The first serious colonization attempt took place in 1585 at Roanoke Island in modern day North Carolina. It was conceived originally as a privateer base from which to attack Spanish ships; only secondarily was it to have an economic purpose of its own. The ultimate failure of the Roanoke colony, however, was stark evidence of England's inability to sustain an overseas venture with its mainland being under threat from the Spanish Armada.

After the accession of James I (1566–1625) in 1603 brought peace with Spain the following year, English merchants turned once again to the idea of an American colony. The Virginia Company was formed in 1606 by two groups of merchants, adventurers, and nobles based in London and Plymouth. The charter they received from James I allowed them to settle almost anywhere on the eastern seaboard of North America, though the London Company's first settlement was

directed toward the Chesapeake Bay—a safe, deep water anchorage first discovered by the English in 1586. At the same time that the English were returning to colonizing efforts in the Americas, the Dutch were also mounting a significant challenge to the Iberian monopoly in the New World. In the 1620s the Dutch occupied a large part of northeastern Brazil, and their experiments with sugar production would eventually influence the development of the English sugar islands in the Caribbean.

The first permanent English settlement at Jamestown, Virginia was plagued by weak leadership, terrible mortality rates, and poor relations with local Powhatans. It only survived by continuous migration from England of young men intent on making their fortune. The economic salvation of the colony turned out to be tobacco, not the wines, fruits, and silks fancifully imagined as being the main export commodities by initial propagandists.

The vast profits to be made from tobacco accelerated the migration of ordinary farmers, laborers, and traders from England. But the society they created was land-hungry, often violent, and temporary because many desired to return home once their fortune had been made. Even with more women migrating to the Chesapeake after 1618, Virginia remained heavily dependent on immigration for most of the seventeenth century.

New England was the site of the other major early seventeenth-century settlement on the North American mainland. English migrants came to the region to escape religious persecution in England. The Pilgrims who settled at Plymouth in 1620 had spent the previous twelve years living in Holland hoping it would prove to be the safe haven they desired. The Puritans who established Boston in 1630 also wanted to worship freely and, in addition, prove to the world that a truly religious society could be a Christian utopia.

In contrast to the young men who settled in the Chesapeake, most migrants to New England traveled in family groups and helped reestablish old-world traditional communities in America. The highly regulated and moralistic societies formed in New England did not meet with universal support. Some migrants hoped for economic opportunities in New England rather than religious ones, and Puritans often were intolerant of other religious groups such as Baptists and Quakers.

Ultimately the close-knit communities of the earliest settlers gave way to more diverse settlements because Puritan authorities were unable to prevent continued immigration from non religious people. Over time the religious utopia began to fall apart. The children of original settlers did not defend religious orthodoxy as rigorously as their parents had done, and gradually became more interested in commerce and trade.

MAP BY XNR PRODUCTIONS. THE GALE GROUP.

Away from the mainland, Bermuda had been included as part of the Virginia Company's territory in 1612. Soon after, the English became established at St. Kitts (1623), Barbados (1625), and Nevis (1628). These tiny islands attracted vast numbers of migrants. By the mid-seventeenth century they were home to more than half of the English people in the Americas. The migrants were attracted by a tropical climate that the Spanish and Dutch already demonstrated was able to support tobacco, coffee, and sugar—highly marketable commodities in

England. In terms of their contribution toward the English economy, the West Indies were far more valuable than the mainland colonies in the seventeenth century.

IMPERIAL EXPANSION, 1650–1763

By the middle of the seventeenth century the American colonies were becoming more important to the geopolitical situation as England struggled to establish itself among competing colonial powers. Oliver Cromwell (1599–1658) pursued an aggressive colonial policy between the death of Charles I in 1649 and the accession of Charles II in 1660, envisaging a Protestant alliance with the Dutch to strip Spain of its Caribbean possessions. This "Grand Design" would have weakened Spain and Catholicism, while bringing wealth, resources, and prestige to the Protestant nations. However, the only lasting success of Cromwell's "Grand Design" was the conquest of Jamaica in 1655. The restored Charles II (1630–1685) continued imperial expansion with the conquest of New York in 1664, and the granting of proprietorial charters for the settlement of the Carolinas and Pennsylvania. By the time of Charles II's death in 1685, English control extended from Maine to Charles-Town, South Carolina.

The second half of the seventeenth century was witness to the introduction of the first imperial economic policies through the Navigation Acts, which limited what, and with whom, the colonies could trade. This period of imperial consolidation came to an end with James II's (1633–1701) attempt to create the Dominion of New England in the 1680s. The Glorious Revolution (1688) that overthrew James II in England led to the reestablishment of the individual colonial governments in America, though many of these were now crown colonies and subject to a greater degree of control from London than had been the case before 1680.

The accession of William of Orange (1650–1702) as William III drew England into a succession of European wars against the French that often spilled over into the colonies. During the War of Spanish Succession (1701–1714), the British successfully attacked Acadia, renaming it Nova Scotia, and were able to fend off a Spanish attack on the new colony of Georgia in 1742 with relative ease.

The last great imperial war fought in America was the French and Indian War (1754–1763), which began in the Ohio valley and would determine whether the French settlements in Canada and Louisiana would link up to prevent the westward expansion of English colonies. Despite initial setbacks, British victories at the Plains of Abraham in 1759 and Montreal in 1760 effectively destroyed French Canada. The Treaty of Paris in 1763 saw that all of North America west of the Mississippi was ceded to Britain as well as Grenada, Tobago, and St. Vincent.

While the British were slowly consolidating control over the mainland, their colonies also had been developing and growing. Increased migration from Scotland, Ireland, and mainland Europe altered the ethnic makeup of the colonies, making them less English and more cosmopolitan. The continued development of the tobacco plantation system in Virginia, and its adoption in South Carolina for the growing of rice and indigo, encouraged a shift toward enslaved African labor.

The same type of shift toward enslaved labor occurred a century before in the West Indies, resulting in overwhelming black populations that were held in bondage by brutally repressive regimes. On the mainland, white majorities were predominant except in South Carolina, which, of all the mainland colonies, most closely resembled the Caribbean in terms of its social and economic structure. Plantation staples such as rice, sugar, indigo, and tobacco made an immense contribution toward the British economy, and made some planters fantastically rich. Non-plantation economies contributed timber, furs, and grain to a thriving imperial commerce.

CRISIS OF EMPIRE, 1763–1783

The empire reached its zenith in 1763. Britain's navy ruled the Atlantic, its colonies were contributing to national prosperity, and, with the French defeated, there was no reason to think that this could not be maintained. However, the addition of a massive area of land in Canada and Trans-Appalachia created new problems. The new land was administered in London, and had turned the Board of Trade from a body that did exactly what its name said—regulate trade—into a colonial government.

At the same time, the debts incurred fighting the French and Indian War needed to be repaid, and British ministers felt Americans should contribute toward the costs of a war that had benefited them so much. Both of these developments were regarded with suspicion by most of the mainland colonies. Attempts to tax them without their consent were seen to be absolutist measures that violated the traditional rights of Englishmen, whereas the governmental structures put in place for Quebec in 1774—with no representative assembly and safeguards for the French Catholics who remained there—were thought to be blueprints for the future government of all colonies.

The thirteen colonies that broke away in 1776 to form the United States were not always a distinct area and certainly not a united, coherent whole. While the most recent colonial additions of west and east Florida, along with Quebec, remained loyal to the British Crown, and the oldest settlements of Virginia and Massachusetts led the struggle for independence, Nova Scotia would not join in any rebellion and there was no guarantee that Georgia, for instance, would participate in one either. Loyalist sentiment in Georgia was stronger than in many other colonies. It was the only rebel colony to have British civil government restored following the British invasion in 1778.

However, Charles Cornwallis's (1738–1805) surrender at Yorktown severely weakened Britain's willingness to continue the war, and the Peace of Paris in 1783 saw the independence of the thirteen colonies recognized as the United States, with Florida returning to Spain, but Canada remaining in British hands.

BRITAIN'S AMERICAN EMPIRE AFTER 1783

The loss of the thirteen colonies wounded British imperial pride, but the consequences were not as bad as they might have been. The West Indies were economically more important to Britain than mainland America. They remained loyal largely because their white populations were small, they retained close cultural and familial ties to Britain, and because they relied on British military protection from France.

After 1783 many of the economic ties between Britain and its former colonies were re-established. American merchants and planters knew the British market was still the best one for their goods, and it was easier to trade with familiar contacts who spoke the same language than form new trading networks with Europeans.

British imperial ambitions gradually shifted east in the late eighteenth century with the consolidation of power in India through the passing of the East India Act in 1784, the settlement of Australia in 1788, and the first takeover of the Cape Colony in 1795. Lingering interest in expansion in the Americas remained also. Trinidad was added to the empire in 1793, as was Guyana in 1796, and the Falkland Islands in 1833, but following the abolition of slavery throughout the empire in the 1830s, the Caribbean islands became far less important to Britain than they had been in their eighteenth-century heyday. Canada, however, remained an important part of the empire, and it would become the first colony to be granted self-government in 1867.

SEE ALSO *African Slavery in the Americas; Colonization and Companies; Empire in the Americas, French; Empire in the Americas, Spanish.*

BIBLIOGRAPHY

Dunn, Richard S. *Sugar and Slaves: The Rise of the Planter Class in the English West Indies, 1624-1713.* New York: Norton, 1973.

Lenman, Bruce P. *Britain's Colonial Wars, 1688-1783.* London: Longman, 2001.

McFarlane, Anthony. *The British in the Americas, 1480-1815.* London: Longman, 1992.

Speck, W.A., Mary Greiter. *Colonial America: From Jamestown to Yorktown.* London: Palgrave, 2002.

Tim Lockley

EMPIRE IN THE AMERICAS, DUTCH

The overseas expansion of the Northern Netherlands began in the late sixteenth century, when Dutch ships, until then confined to European waters, embarked on explorations of the wider world. This outward thrust took place in the midst of an eighty-year war with Habsburg Spain, which would eventually give the Dutch United Provinces their independence in 1648. The Spanish monarchs unwittingly contributed to Dutch explorations outside Europe by arresting hundreds of Dutch ships in Iberian ports in the 1590s. Because the embargoes effectively ended the lively Dutch trade with the Iberian Peninsula, Dutch merchants started sending their ships on voyages outside Europe to obtain the tropical products previously obtained in Portugal and Spain: cloves, pepper, nutmeg, sugar, salt, gold, and silver. Salt and sugar initially lured the Dutch to the New World. Their search for salt took the Dutch to a natural salt lagoon off the coast of Venezuela at Punta de Araya, while sugar invited voyages to Brazil. Inheriting from Antwerp a triangular trade with Lisbon and Brazil, Amsterdam became the main outlet in northern Europe for sugar by the first years of the seventeenth century.

After a twelve-year truce (1609–1621) came to an end, the Dutch extended the war with Spain to the Americas and began planning major colonial activities there under the auspices of the newly founded West India Company (WIC). Its task was to direct and coordinate the flow of trade in the Atlantic basin, but also—even more importantly—to open new fronts against the Iberian enemies. Shipping between Portugal and Brazil suffered especially at the hands of the privateers who seized hundreds of enemy vessels. The most spectacular capture, however, occurred in 1628 in the bay of Matanzas (Cuba), when a Dutch naval force subdued the Spanish *flota* bound from Veracruz for Seville. The cargo seized was made up of prodigious quantities of precious metals, indigo, cochineal, tobacco, and dyewood.

Starting in 1624, war was also waged in mainland America. In that year, the Dutch conquered Salvador (Bahia), the capital city of Brazil, but they were ousted after only one year. In 1630 they returned to Brazil with a

Tobacco Merchants in New Amsterdam. *This etching, rendered in the 1640s by an unknown Dutch artisan, depicts the activities of a tobacco merchant in the Dutch colony of "Neiu Amsterdam" (now Manhattan). The merchant, shown at right, holds tobacco leaves in his hand, while rolled spindles of tobacco, ready for export, sit at his feet.* N. PHELPS STOKES COLLECTION, MIRIAM AND IRA D. WALLACH DIVISION OF ART, PRINTS, AND PHOTOGRAPHS, THE NEW YORK PUBLIC LIBRARY, ASTOR, LENOX, AND TILDEN FOUNDATIONS. REPRODUCED BY PERMISSION.

fleet of fifty-two ships and thirteen sloops. After a successful invasion, the territory under Dutch rule expanded before a local rebellion put them on the defensive. The Dutch finally surrendered in 1654 and eventually gave up all claims to the lands lost in exchange for the right to load salt for free in Portugal for a number of years.

Apart from an occasional windfall, the financial performance of the West India Company was miserable. Although large amounts of sugar, tobacco, and brazilwood were sent from Brazil to the Dutch Republic, the proceeds did not outweigh the very costly war in Brazil. Nor did the supply of African slaves on credit to Portuguese planters improve company finances. When it finally went bankrupt in 1674, the WIC was replaced by an organization that had little in common with its predecessor except for the name. Having already lost most of its commercial monopolies in previous decades, it was dismantled as a military machine.

In North America, Dutch settlements did not have to fear Habsburg armies. It was here that Dutch merchants had started to conduct trade soon after Henry Hudson, an Englishman in the service of the Dutch East India Company, in 1609 found the river that still bears his name. The foundation of the West India Company led to the creation of a permanent colony, New Netherland, in what is today New York State, ruled after 1626 from the town of New Amsterdam on Manhattan. In 1655 part of today's Delaware was captured from Sweden and added to New Netherland. Despite its commercial insignificance, New Netherland attracted perhaps more immigrants than all other colonies in Dutch America combined, but it fell prey to an invading English fleet in 1664.

Other colonies were founded in the Caribbean, where the Dutch conquered St. Martin (1631) and Curaçao (1634), and planted their flag on the Windward Islands of Aruba and Bonaire (1636) and the Leeward Islands of St. Eustatius (1636) and Saba (1640), as well as Tobago (off and on between 1628–1678). Finally, Guiana was a popular destination for Dutch migrants as well. Numerous small and short-lived settlements arose in this vast area between Venezuela and the Amazon delta. The most prosperous was Suriname, originally captured from England by a naval force dispatched from the province of Zeeland in 1667. Over the following one hundred years, Suriname was the Dutch plantation colony *par excellence*, producing a variety of crops including sugar, coffee, cocoa, and cotton. In the second half of the eighteenth century, its output may have equaled the combined production of the adjacent Guiana plantation colonies of Demerara, Essequibo, and Berbice.

Equally important for the Dutch economy were the Dutch entrepôts of Curaçao and St. Eustatius. Between 1660, when Curaçao became the main center of slave distribution for the Spanish colonies, and 1729, the island re-exported almost 100,000 slaves to ports in Spanish America. Merchants in Curaçao also mastered the art of contraband trade with their Spanish neighbors, gaining access to valuable cargoes of cocoa, tobacco, and precious metals. Starting in the 1730s, St. Eustatius emerged as another center of Dutch contraband trade in the Caribbean, tapping the riches from the surrounding English and French islands and from the Thirteen Colonies.

Dutch activity in the Americas was fundamentally different from that in Asia, where the Dutch East India Company (Verenigde Oostindische Compagnie or VOC) maintained a Dutch monopoly and where it established a string of factories, fortified trading posts defended by garrisons. The VOC became a highly profitable organization, as it benefited from the general commercial crisis rocking Southeast Asia in the mid-seventeenth century. The Dutch faced an entirely different situation in the Atlantic world, where the creation of an intricate network of factories did not make sense. Nor was there an Atlantic counterpart of the centuries-old inter-Asian trade in which the Europeans could participate. Whereas the VOC achieved spice monopoly, making it possible to fix prices, the WIC was unable to obtain monopoly of sugar. Not even the occupation of northeastern Brazil, the world's largest producer, helped the company achieve that goal. Another difference with the VOC was that the WIC failed to combine warfare with a vigorous commercial enterprise. In spite of the WIC's shortcomings, however, Dutch trade with the Americas grew significantly in the eighteenth century, due to the activities of hundreds of small Dutch trading firms. While historians, following contemporary observers, have traditionally considered Dutch American trade to have been relatively modest, some recent estimates put its average value near that of Dutch trade with Asia.

SEE ALSO *Colonization and Companies.*

BIBLIOGRAPHY

Boogaart, Ernst van den, Pieter Emmer, Peter Klein, and Kees Zandvliet. *La expansión holandesa en el Atlántico, 1580–1800.* Madrid: Mapfre, 1992.

Goslinga, Cornelis Ch. *The Dutch in the Caribbean and on the Wild Coast, 1580–1680.* Assen, Netherlands: Van Gorcum, 1971.

Heijer, Henk den. *De geschiedenis van de WIC.* Zutphen, Netherlands: Walburg Pers, 1994.

Jacobs, Jaap. *Een zegenrijk gewest: Nieuw-Nederland in de zeventiende eeuw.* Amsterdam: Prometheus/Bert Bakker, 1999.

Klooster, Wim. *Illicit Riches: Dutch Trade in the Caribbean, 1648–1795.* Leiden, Netherlands: KITLV Press, 1998.

Mello, José Antônio Gonsalves de. *Tempo dos flamengos: Influência da ocupação holandesa na vida e na cultura do norte do Brasil.* 2d ed. Recife, Brazil: Governo do Estado de Pernambuco, 1978.

Postma, Johannes, and Victor Enthoven, eds. *Riches from Atlantic Commerce: Dutch Trans-Atlantic Trade and Shipping, 1585–1817.* Boston: Brill, 2003.

Wim Klooster

EMPIRE IN THE AMERICAS, FRENCH

France came late to the race for the Americas. In the scramble against Spain, Portugal, and England for land, gold, and the passage to Asia, its imperial efforts were episodic, opportunistic, and not always successful. Binot Paulmier de Gonneville's voyage to the shores of Brazil in 1504 put France in the fight for the New World. Dyewoods and exotic hardwoods had attracted French merchants and, thanks to good relations with the local people, a lucrative trade between the forests of Brazil and the ports of Dieppe, St. Malo, and Le Havre was soon under way. Brazil, however, was only one small part of the New World: King Francis I wanted more. When he looked north he saw other opportunities to enhance his power and prestige, so he sent the Florentine navigator Giovanni da Verrazano to probe the coast of North America. Several encounters with local people, however, yielded neither gold, nor silver, nor even a passage to Asia. A subsequent war with Spain put a stop to Francis's ambitions and left France farther behind its rivals.

Not until 1534 did France return to the New World. Fishermen's tales and the ongoing search for the passage to Asia led Jacques Cartier into the present-day

France's North American colonies

1603	Champlain explored the St. Lawrence
1608	Champlain founded Quebec
1610	Pourtrincourt re-founded Port Royal
1634	Nicolet reached Sault Ste. Marie and Green Bay
1642	Maisonneuve founded Montreal
1665	La Point Mission established on Lake Superior
1673	Marquette descended the Mississsippi
1673	Frontenac founded Fort Frontenac on Ontario
1979–1683	La Salle founded Fort Crevecoeur Near Peoria
1683–1689	La Salle expedition to Mouth of the Mississippi
1699	Iberville established Louisiana Colony
1701	Cadillac founded Detroit
1710	Mobile founded
1718	New Orleans founded

THE GALE GROUP.

St. Lawrence River. Instead of China he found a bustling trading fair at Tadoussac and an important ally, Donacona, at a town called Stadacona. On a second voyage the following year he pushed further up the river to a series of dangerous rapids just past the town of Hochelaga, the site of present-day Montreal. He and his men wintered at Stadacona before returning to France to raise interest in founding a colony. The settlement Cartier founded near Stadacona in 1541 collapsed, however, because of cold and famine, and it would be a long time before the French returned to the shores of the St. Lawrence.

To the south, efforts to settle the shores of Brazil were only marginally more successful. In 1555, under the sponsorship of Henry IV, Nicolas Durand de Villegagnon founded Fort Coligny on Rio de Janeiro Bay and his alliance with the Tupinamba people made La France Antarctique—as the embryonic French colony was called—a promising venture. Problems developed a few years later, however, when a party of Protestants arrived in flight from the sectarian strife that was tearing France apart. If the Catholic settlers resented the newcomers, the Portuguese resented the French presence altogether, and with the destruction of Fort Coligny they drove the French inland. The small town the French survivors established, Henriville, fell to the Portuguese in 1567, ending, for the moment, the French occupation of Brazil.

The idea of planting Protestants in the New World to defuse sectarian violence between Catholics and Protestants in France was not limited to La France Antarctique. In 1562 Jean Ribault led 150 Huguenots to the northern edge of Spain's La Florida, where they founded Charlesfort at Port Royal. Two years of famine and disease were enough, however, and the handful of survivors built boats for their return voyage to France.

René de la Laudonnière led another 300 Protestants to Florida, but lack of food and poor relations with the local inhabitants inspired a mutiny. A relief expedition led by Ribault provided some small hope, but in 1565 the Spanish commander Pedro Menéndez de Avilés ordered the massacre of the colonists and the end of this French Protestant threat to Spanish Florida.

Faced with such failures, the French turned again to the St. Lawrence Valley, where a burgeoning fur trade between native people and fishermen had caught the crown's attention. In 1603 various Algonquian-speaking peoples and their Huron trading partners agreed to make a place for Samuel de Champlain and the French. Such connections introduced the French to a vast trade network that reached from the Atlantic to the Great Lakes to Hudson Bay. In 1608 Champlain founded Québec (Quebec City) where Stadacona had once stood, to give the French a permanent foothold in the trade. While the town succeeded as a trading post, it was less attractive as a destination for settlers. In an effort to share the costs and risks associated with colonization, the Crown tended to rely upon private companies to undertake the difficult work of settling the Americas. In Canada that task fell to the Company of New France, but its promoters failed to attract the numbers of immigrants who were pouring into the British colonies to the south. Between 1670 and 1730 fewer than three thousand people came to settle in New France.

The men who conducted the fur trade on behalf of France, the *coureurs de bois*, as well as the *voyageurs* who transported the furs and other goods by canoe, extended the empire's reach up the network of lakes and rivers throughout the mid-continent. The good relations they cultivated with native peoples enabled France to deploy only small garrisons and settlements, such as outposts like Detroit and Michilimackinac on the Great Lakes and Cahokia and Kaskaskia on the Mississippi River, to secure their claims to empire. The men stationed at such outposts left behind the *métis* children who were important to the society of New France. At the same time, Jesuit and Recollet missionaries followed the traders into the country to convert France's important trading partners to Catholicism. Indeed it was the fur trader Louis Jolliet and the priest Jacques Marquette who opened the Mississippi River to France in 1673. René-Robert, Cavalier de la Salle found the mouth of the Mississippi in 1682, which made the settlement of Louisiana possible in 1699. Towns sprouted at Biloxi, Mobile, and, in 1718, New Orleans. After a little more than a century of colonization, New France stretched from the Gulf of Mexico to the St. Lawrence Valley and fulfilled Louis XIV's dream of limiting the British colonies to the Atlantic seaboard.

Meanwhile France had not forgotten Brazil. The French returned to Brazil in 1612 when Henry IV granted Daniel de la Touché, Sieur de la Ravardière, permission to found the colony of Cayenne, later known as French Guiana. Malnutrition and disease thwarted early attempts, but in 1664 the Company of the West Indies put the colony on a permanent footing. Initially the colony made its money through trade with the local inhabitants, but sugar and coffee emerged as Cayenne's most important export commodities. Slaves were the colony's most important source of labor. Owing to dynastic struggles in Europe and their own military weakness, the Portuguese were unable to destroy Cayenne as they had La France Antarctique and, in the end, recognized France's claim to this portion of Guiana.

As it had done in New France and Brazil, the Crown created a company, in this case the Company of Saint Christopher, to undertake its imperial efforts in the Caribbean. In 1627 the French divided St. Christopher with the English, and then moved on to fight either the Caribs or other colonial powers for a number of other islands—including Guadeloupe, Martinique, and Saint Domingue—where enslaved people cleared the land for indigo, cotton, tobacco, cacao, and sugar plantations. Because of the importance of slavery to the empire's fortunes, in 1685 the Crown promulgated the "Black Code" to govern relations between enslaved people and free people in the colonies. While the code mandated certain requirements for food, clothing, and holidays and outlawed the torture of slaves, in practice plantation owners often departed from it to increase their yields, profits, and control. The sugar boom of the early 1700s exacerbated the situation for enslaved people, for cultivating and harvesting sugarcane was a lethal enterprise. Slave owners, however, enjoyed endless profits, and Saint Domingue emerged as the most important of France's overseas possessions.

By 1730 the French empire in the Americas counted 74,000 inhabitants of French ancestry, while nearly 150,000 enslaved people of African ancestry toiled to produce the empire's wealth. The Seven Year's War, however, ended the sugar boom and opened a long period of war and strife that imperiled the empire. With British success on the battlefield and on the high seas came the losses of Canada and Guadeloupe in 1759 and Martinique in 1762. The 1763 Peace of Paris that ended the war ceded Canada to Great Britain and the vast territory of Louisiana to Spain, while France was allowed to reclaim control of Martinique and Guadeloupe. Only two decades later the French Revolution threw the empire into further turmoil. Royalists and Republicans clashed on the islands of the Caribbean while free people of color and enslaved people sought to use the crisis to their own advantage. In 1791 rebellions broke out in Saint

Domingue. Forty thousand colonials faced half a million slaves who wanted the freedom promised by the Revolution. In 1794 the National Assembly responded by abolishing slavery in Cayenne, Saint Domingue, and Guadeloupe, but the abolition only spurred enslaved people on other French islands to press more vigorously for their own freedom.

In 1799 Napoleon Bonaparte ended the Revolution and promised to restore the empire. The Caribbean caught fire. The bloodiest fight was in Saint Domingue where a former slave named Toussaint L'Ouverture defeated French forces and proclaimed an end to Saint Domingue's colonial status. In response Napoleon dispatched a force of tough combat veterans to restore imperial control. L'Ouverture's forces eventually capitulated, and L'Ouverture was arrested and sent to France where he died in custody. Just as the French victory looked final, however, a yellow fever epidemic ravaged the French forces. And then an imperial order to reimpose slavery became public. At that moment the Franco-African commanders and soldiers who had helped defeat L'Ouverture deserted and opened combat against the French. The French forces' defeat was disastrous. In 1803 the rebel leader Jean Jacques Dessaline took the Arawak name Haiti for the republic whose independence he proclaimed. On Martinique and Guadeloupe, however, French forces prevailed, and, with the loss of Cayenne to Britain's ally Portugal, these two islands, as well as a few smaller ones, were all that remained of a once large and far-flung empire.

While war raged in the Caribbean, Napoleon set his sights on reclaiming New France. As a first step France acquired Louisiana from Spain in 1802. Renewed hostilities with England, however, made it impossible to defend the territory, so in 1803 Napoleon sold the territory to the United States and focused his efforts on the war in Europe. As in the Seven Years' War, France's defeat in the Napoleonic Wars cost the country a number of its overseas possessions. Only with the restoration of the Bourbon crown in 1815 was King Louis XVIII able to reclaim Martinique and Guadeloupe, again, from Great Britain and half of Cayenne from Portugal. The empire was on its last legs.

In some respects, the French empire in the Americas came to an end with the Revolution of 1848, which abolished slavery. Former colonies were absorbed into the French nation and granted representation in the National Assembly, while former colonists and slaves received full civic rights. In 1852, however, the president of France's Second Republic, Louis Napoleon—he was Napoleon Bonaparte's nephew—set himself up as Napoleon III, emperor of the Second French Empire. He set his sights on Mexico where squabbles over debt

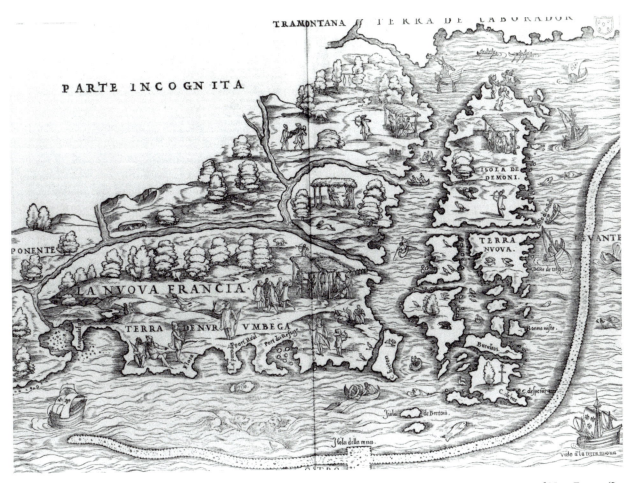

New France, 1556. *This map, attributed to Giacomo Gastaldi (ca. 1500–ca. 1565), shows the northern territory of New France (La Nuova Francia), now part of Canada. To the west is an uncharted area of the North American mainland labeled Parte Incognita.* © CORBIS. REPRODUCED BY PERMISSION.

repayments offered an opportunity for imperial adventure. After the French landed at Veracruz at the end of 1861 on the pretext of seizing customs revenues for payment of debts, the troops moved into the interior and took Mexico City in 1863. French hopes for popular Mexican support, however, were sorely disappointed. In spite of his misgivings about the invasion, Napoleon III named the Habsburg prince Ferdinand Maximilian emperor of Mexico in the hopes of salvaging something out of the situation. But when the United States demanded that France vacate Mexico, Napoleon III abandoned Maximilian. Liberal and Conservative rebel groups raised the Mexican countryside in a war of national liberation against the invaders and defeated the French in 1867. With the capture, trial, and execution of Maximilian came the final end of French imperialism in the Americas.

SEE ALSO *Cartier, Jacques; Company of New France; Haitian Revolution.*

BIBLIOGRAPHY

Boucher, Philip P. "The 'Frontier Era' of the French Caribbean, 1620s–1690s." In *Negotiated Empires: Centers and Peripheries in the Americas, 1500–1820,* edited by Christine Daniels and Michael V. Kennedy. New York: Routledge, 2002.

Fick, Carolyn. *The Making of Haiti: The Saint Domingue Revolution from Below.* Knoxville: University of Tennessee Press, 1990.

Fregosi, Paul. *Dreams of Empire: Napoleon and the First World War, 1792–1815.* London: Hutchinson, 1989.

Giraud, Marcel. *A History of French Louisiana,* Vol. 1: *The Reign of Louis XIV, 1698–1715.* Translated by Joseph C. Lambert. Baton Rouge: Louisiana State University Press, 1974.

Macdonald, N. P. *The Making of Brazil: Portuguese Roots, 1500–1822.* Sussex, U.K.: Book Guild, 1996.

Pritchard, James. *In Search of Empire: The French in the Americas, 1670–1730.* Cambridge, U.K.: Cambridge University Press, 2004.

Roberts, W. Adolphe. *The French in the West Indies.* Indianapolis, IN: Bobbs-Merrill, 1942.

Trigger, Bruce. *Natives and Newcomers: Canada's "Heroic Age" Reconsidered.* Kingston, Ontario: McGill/Queen's University Press, 1985.

James Taylor Carson

EMPIRE IN THE AMERICAS, PORTUGUESE

The Portuguese were among the first Europeans to establish colonies in the Americas. Portugal was also one of the first imperial states to grant independence to its colonies in the Western Hemisphere. A range of factors made the Portuguese Empire in the Americas unique, and these have had long-lasting implications and ramifications. Portuguese explorers played a significant role in opening areas in the region for further exploration and exploitation by other imperial states, including the introduction of the modern slave system. Furthermore, Portugal's territory was not divided into smaller colonies, which in the long term allowed the emergence of Brazil as a unified regional power. In addition, the Portuguese Empire was the only major imperial power that transferred its monarchy to the colonies.

TRADE AND COLONIALISM

Portugal attempted to establish colonies in Africa, but the defeat of a Portuguese army in Tangier, Morocco, in 1436 led the kingdom increasingly to concentrate on sea explorations in search of an alternate route to Asia that would bypass the Venetian-controlled trade routes in the Mediterranean. The Portuguese subsequently established a number of colonies and trade factories along the coast of Africa, which proved highly profitable through the export of slaves and gold.

Meanwhile, Portuguese maritime explorations continued, and in 1487 Bartholomeu Dias (ca. 1450–1500) sailed around the Cape of Good Hope. In 1498 Vasco da Gama (ca. 1469–1524) landed in India and established trading posts that were to be the building blocks of Portugal's great maritime empire in Asia. After succeeding in finding a maritime route to the East, Portugal left Spain to concentrate on the Americas, opened up by Christopher Columbus's (1451–1506) voyages in 1492. But when the Treaty of Tordesillas (1494) divided the world between Portugal and Spain along a north-south line 1,770 kilometers (1,100 miles) west of the Cape Verde Islands, Portugal unwittingly acquired the land that was to become known as Brazil.

In 1500 Pedro Álvares Cabral (ca. 1467–1520) discovered Brazil when seeking a more direct route to India.

While in the Americas, Cabral acquired brazilwood (a red wood that came to be highly sought after as a source of dye and that lent its name to the new colony in South America). A year later, Amerigo Vespucci (1454–1512) further explored the coast of modern Brazil in a series of expeditions sponsored by Portugal.

During this period, the Portuguese concentrated on exporting brazilwood from the Americas but did not seek to establish any large colonies. Instead, Lisbon devoted its attention and resources to its growing empire in Africa and Asia. The early explorers had found the coastal areas of Brazil to be sparsely populated and judged that the area's economic value was limited. Beginning in 1500, the crown offered leases to Brazilian merchant groups, but by 1506 the monarchy took direct control of the trade posts after the leases failed to attract significant interest. However, individual Portuguese merchants began to cultivate sugarcane in Pernambuco in the 1520s.

The combination of brazilwood and sugarcane made the crown reconsider the potential importance of its trade factories in Brazil, and in 1530 King João III (1502–1557) launched an initiative to create a more substantial colony. Strategic reasons also added impetus to the decision, including imperial competition in the region from France (a Portuguese expedition in 1503 discovered French incursions into Brazilian territory). The king dispatched Martín Alfonso de Sousa (d. 1564) with a fleet and instructions to rid Brazil of any French presence and to establish settlements (the French argued that Portuguese claims to territory were invalid because there were no permanent settlements in the areas claimed by Lisbon). De Sousa founded two towns, São Vicente and São Paulo.

EARLY COLONIZATION

João III ushered in the era of Portuguese colonization in Brazil in 1533 with the donatory captaincies. Under this unique system, the monarchy divided Brazil into fifteen zones, or captaincies (these were royal gifts, known as *donatarios,* granted to various courtiers and royal favorites). Each grant extended about 241 kilometers (150 miles) in length and reached into the unknown interior. These land grants were hereditary, and the monarchy hoped they would lead to a new class of colonial aristocracy. The captaincies had control over trade and taxes in their jurisdictions, except for royal monopolies.

Only two of the captaincies were economically successful, but these became enormously wealthy through sugar cultivation, and Brazil became the world's largest producer of sugar by the 1570s. The failure of the other *donatarios* led João to reassert royal control in the 1540s and to appoint a governor-general in 1549. In addition, during the 1540s the settlements faced growing attacks from the

Tupi-speaking natives. Tomé de Sousa (d. 1573) served as the first governor-general (1549–1553). His tenure was marked by significant increases in revenues and a series of military efforts against the natives and French raiders. He also founded the colonial capital, Salvador.

Relations between the natives and the Portuguese were initially cooperative. However, the donatory system displaced tribes, and the rise of sugarcane plantations led to efforts to enslave native peoples. The result was armed conflict between Portuguese settlers and natives. Accompanying de Sousa was a company of Jesuits who endeavored to convert the natives. Through their efforts, the crown created two classes of Native Americans. One category classified natives as peaceful and able to be converted (and therefore granted certain protections under the auspices of the Jesuits), while the second category was reserved for Native Americans who resisted conversion and consequently could be enslaved. Natives who converted to Christianity were resettled into Jesuit-controlled enclaves known as *aldeias*. These settlements were more successful in the southern regions. Several epidemics had devastating impacts on the indigenous population, and by 1563 some one-third to one-half of the native population had been wiped out.

Sugar cultivation required significant numbers of laborers, and the need for labor accelerated the slave trade to the Americas. In 1534 Portugal began shipping criminals to Brazil as laborers, but the relatively small numbers were not sufficient to meet demand. The Portuguese settlers were unable to enslave natives on a scale sufficient to meet their requirements. The Portuguese had started importing African slaves into Europe in 1441 and into the Spanish colonies in 1510, so that by the time of the sugar boom in Brazil, the trade had matured and was regulated through private contracts.

The crown granted official approval to import slaves into Brazil in 1559, and the slave trade dramatically increased in the 1570s. In 1570 there were about 3,000 slaves in Brazil, about 15,000 by 1600, and by 1650 more than 200,000. Brazil ultimately received 42 percent of all slaves imported into the Americas (more than any other single colony).

IMPERIAL RIVALRIES

Growing profits from sugar cultivation led to renewed interest in Brazil from the other colonial powers. In 1555 the French established a significant colony in Guanabara Bay. Known as France Antarctique, the colony was destroyed in 1567 by Mem de Sá (d. 1572), Brazil's third governor-general, who founded Rio de Janeiro on the site of the former French settlement. Subsequent French attempts to establish a new colony failed. The French did establish a major colony, France Équinoxiale, in 1611, but Portuguese troops captured the settlement in 1615 and permanently prevented any further French settlement.

There were long-running colonial conflicts between Portugal and Spain, which were exacerbated by political struggles in Europe. In 1580, however, Portugal and Spain began a period of dual monarchy under the Hapsburgs. The dual monarchy lasted until 1640, and the period was marked by a reduction of imperial tensions between the two powers. Afterwards, tensions resumed over territory around the Río de la Plata. The Portuguese built a settlement at Sacramento in 1680 on land claimed by Spain and far beyond the western boundary of the Portuguese Empire as established by the Treaty of Tordesillas. Sacramento also became a hub for smuggling goods into and out of Spanish-controlled territory.

In 1726 Spain struck back by establishing Montevideo on territory that Portugal claimed. The Treaty of Madrid (1750) fixed the borders of the Spanish and Portuguese empires in the Americas but did not completely end colonial conflict between the two powers: In 1776 the Spanish sent a large army to stem Portuguese incursions into its territory in the River Plate region.

During the 1600s, the Dutch emerged as the main rival to Portugal in the Americas. The conflict between Holland and Portugal had its roots in the period of the dual monarchy, which coincided with the Dutch struggle for independence against the Spanish. There were repeated Dutch incursions against the Brazilian colonies during the early 1600s. The Dutch captured the colonial capital Salvador in 1624 and other towns, and these areas remained under Dutch control until 1654. Intermittent conflict continued until a lasting peace agreement was signed in 1661.

THE GOLD RUSH

Gold was discovered in the interior in 1693 in the region that, because of its mining, was called *Minas Gerais*, or the General Mines. This discovery accelerated the transformation of the colony from a coastal settlement to one with significant infrastructure in the interior regions. The discovery also prompted a new wave of settlement by Portuguese and other European adventurers and put new pressures on the native population. The gold rush further accelerated the slave trade as new slaves were imported to work in the mines. The new wealth led Lisbon to concentrate more resources and attention on Brazil as the colony became the greatest source of wealth for the empire. Other precious stones, including diamonds, were also discovered, further enhancing the economic strength of the colony.

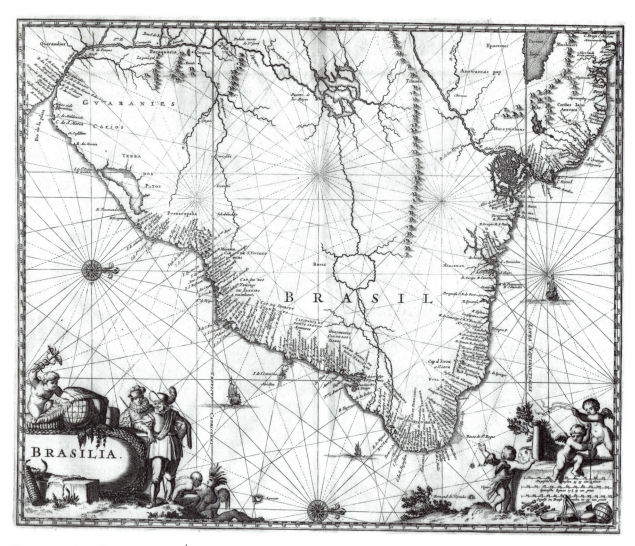

Portuguese Brazil. *In 1500 Pedro Álvares Cabral discovered a new land for Portugal when seeking a more direct route to India. While exploring the region, Cabral collected brazilwood, a useful red wood that that lent its name to the new colony in South America.* **REPRODUCED COURTESY OF MAP COLLECTION, YALE UNIVERSITY LIBRARY.**

In 1755 a severe earthquake in Lisbon led to a period of benign neglect of the colonies. The disaster enhanced the powers of the prime minister, José de Carvalho e Melo (1699–1782), the marquis de Pombal, who became a hero through his management of the disaster relief. Pombal was subsequently able to gain a great deal of influence over the monarchy. He enacted a range of reforms designed to enhance Portugal's wealth and power, known collectively as the Pombaline reforms. Pombal eliminated certain concessions enjoyed by foreign merchants, especially the British. He also reformed the economic codes that regulated the sugar and diamond trade and created chartered companies to oversee trade in northern Brazil and Portugal's fishing industry. His greatest impact on the kingdom's American colonies was the expulsion of the Jesuits, whose exile he ordered in

the belief that they held too much power and influence, especially in the remote areas of Brazil. Pombal later fell out of favor and was dismissed in 1777.

THE ANGLO-PORTUGUESE ALLIANCE AND INDEPENDENCE

The British and Portuguese were allies during wars with Holland, and a series of treaties, signed in 1642, 1654, and 1661, granted the British commercial and trade concessions in the Portuguese colonies. In addition, Portugal allied itself with Great Britain during the European dynastic wars of the early to mid 1700s.

In 1807 the French ruler Napoléon Bonaparte (1769–1821) invaded Portugal through Spain. Portugal became the center of the British land effort to defeat

Napoléon. To escape the advancing French forces, the regent, Dom João (1769–1826), the son of the mentally unbalanced Queen Maria I (1734–1816), and his court fled to Brazil (the escape was aided by the British, who ultimately moved some fifteen thousand Portuguese to Brazil and lent the government $3 million to keep it solvent). Rio de Janeiro became the new capital of the Portuguese Empire, and colonial officials in Brazil gained new power and influence. Even after Portugal was liberated from French forces, the monarchy remained in Rio.

In 1815, following the death of Maria I and the installation of João as King João VI, Brazil was elevated to the status of a kingdom with a dual monarchy. João increasingly sought to centralize power, and he launched an unpopular war to conquer Uruguay. As a result, a series of Brazilian rebellions broke out in 1817. These were known as the Pernambuco Revolution after the province where the insurrection started. The rebellion failed, but it seriously undermined the monarchy. In 1820 a military rebellion in Portugal forced the return of the king and court while republican revolts spread across Brazil.

In September 1821 the Portuguese Parliament abolished Brazil's status as a separate kingdom and sent troops to bolster the colonial government. João's son, Dom Pedro (1798–1834), who was serving as regent, led a revolt and declared Brazilian independence on September 7, 1822. He subsequently established a new imperial government with himself as Emperor Pedro I.

SEE ALSO *African Slavery in the Americas; Brazilian Independence; Henry the Navigator, Prince; Mining, the Americas; Sugar Cultivation and Trade.*

BIBLIOGRAPHY

Alden, Dauril, ed. *Colonial Roots of Modern Brazil: Papers of the Newberry Library Conference.* Berkeley: University of California Press, 1973.

Boxer, C. R. *Race Relations in the Portuguese Colonial Empire, 1415–1825.* Oxford: Clarendon Press, 1963.

Hemming, John. *Red Gold: The Conquest of the Brazilian Indians.* Cambridge, MA: Harvard University Press, 1978. Rev. ed., London: Papermac, 1995.

Kieman, Mathias C. *The Indian Policy of Portugal in the Amazon Region, 1614–1693.* Washington, D.C.: Catholic University of America Press, 1954.

Maxwell, Kenneth. *Conflicts and Conspiracies: Brazil and Portugal, 1750–1808.* Cambridge, U.K.: Cambridge University Press, 1973.

Maxwell, Kenneth. *Pombal: Paradox of the Enlightenment.* Cambridge, U.K.: Cambridge University Press, 1995.

Russell-Wood, A. J. *A World on the Move: The Portuguese in Africa, Asia, and America, 1415–1808.* New York: St. Martin's, 1992.

Schwartz, Stuart B. *Sovereignty and Society in Colonial Brazil: The High Court of Bahia and its Judges, 1609–1751.* Berkeley, University of California Press, 1973.

Sideri, Sandro. *Trade and Power: Informal Colonialism in Anglo-Portuguese Relations.* Rotterdam, Netherlands: Rotterdam University Press, 1970.

Tom Lansford

EMPIRE IN THE AMERICAS, SPANISH

The last vestiges of Spanish imperialism in the Americas disappeared in 1898 when Spain withdrew from Cuba and Puerto Rico. The mainland empire had ended seventy-four years earlier, in 1824, with the viceroy of Peru's surrender to a patriot army—a surrender that marked the end of the process of continental emancipation that had begun in Caracas and Buenos Aires in 1810. At its height, in the late eighteenth century, this imposing empire stretched from California to Chile. It incorporated not only the territories commonly referred to as "Spanish America," but also Florida (ceded to the United States in 1821), Louisiana (uncharted lands to the west of the Mississippi ceded to France in 1801 and sold to the United States in 1803), and the northern borderlands (Arizona, Texas, New Mexico, and Upper California, all of which passed to independent Mexico in 1821 and to the United States in the 1840s). Many of these territories had only a token Spanish presence, as did vast regions in South America (notably southern Chile, Patagonia, and lands east of the Andes). Nevertheless, the edifice endured for over 300 years, with only islands and isolated mainland territories in the Caribbean being lost to rival European powers during the seventeenth and eighteenth centuries.

The frontiers of empire were ill defined, despite occasional attempts to demarcate them—notably, the Treaty of Madrid (1750), which recognized that Portuguese Brazil had expanded beyond the line established at Tordesillas in 1494. However, by the mid-sixteenth century the core areas of Spanish settlement had been clearly determined by two principal factors: the availability of precious metals (initially from native treasure hoards and from the mid-1540s from silver mining) and the presence of sedentary native populations accustomed since the preconquest era to providing tribute.

The empire's initial origins are to be found, of course, in the three voyages to "the Indies" mounted by Columbus in 1492 to 1498. The first led to his landfall in the Bahamas on October 12, 1492, and took him to the

The Spanish Conquests in America

Region or People	Date
Hispaniola	1500
Puerto Rico	1507
Cuba	1511
The Mexica	1521
Guatemala	1527
The Inka	1538
Yucatan	1547
The Inka of Vilcabamba	1572
New Mexico	1696
The Itza	1697

THE GALE GROUP.

northeast coast of Cuba and the north coast of Hispaniola (modern Haiti and the Dominican Republic), where the first Spanish settlement in the Americas was founded two months later. By March 1493 Columbus was back in Spain, displaying American natives and gold to Ferdinand and Isabella. They promptly authorized his second expedition, whose seventeen ships and 1,200 men left Cadiz in September with the primary task of settling Hispaniola rather than searching for a route to Asia. His third and fourth expeditions went to Trinidad and Venezuela in 1498 to 1500 and Central America in 1502 to 1504. Although Columbus believed until his death (1506) that Asia could be reached by sailing west, his former collaborator, Amerigo Vespucci, realized during a voyage to Brazil in 1501 that the landmass he encountered was part of a hitherto-unknown continent, which he named *Mundus Novus* (New World). Increasingly, European geographers accepted his logic, and from 1507 were calling the new lands "America" in his honor.

By 1500, 6,000 men—mainly artisans, peasants, and seafarers—from southwestern Spain had migrated to Hispaniola, which gradually emerged as a base for the exploration and settlement of the other major Caribbean islands, including Puerto Rico (1508), Jamaica (1509) and Cuba (1511). Puerto Rico, in its turn, became the platform for the discovery of Florida in 1513, although the 1521 attempt by the island's governor to establish a permanent settlement there was defeated by native resistance. In Central America, too, initial attempts in 1509 to settle colonists on the isthmus of Panama were overcome by a combination of native hostility and yellow fever, with the loss of 1,000 Spaniards. However, reinforcements from Hispaniola rescued the enterprise, leading to the foundation of the city of Darien in 1510 and, three years later, the first Spanish crossing of the isthmus to the shores of the Pacific. During this period the first

contact was made with Yucatán, and further probes from Cuba in 1517 to 1518 culminated in the 1519 expedition of Hernán Cortés, which in 1521 captured the Aztec capital, Tenochtitlan, razed and rebuilt as Mexico City. This new phase of imperialism on the mainland reached even greater heights in 1533 with the capture of Cuzco, the capital of the Incas, by Francisco Pizarro. Peru, in its turn, served as the base for penetration northward into Ecuador and New Granada (modern Colombia) and southward into Upper Peru (modern Bolivia) and Chile, while new expeditions from Spain to the southern Atlantic founded Buenos Aires in 1536 and Asuncion in 1537. At both ends of this rapidly expanding empire the quest for further fabulous cities and civilizations drew intrepid Spanish explorers into increasingly remote regions, including the Amazon basin, the Guianas, and the borderlands of northern Mexico. The failure to find either treasure or easily subdued natives in these regions led to their abandonment or, at best, the establishment of isolated outposts. As a result, permanent settlement became increasingly concentrated in central and southern Mexico and the Andean region. These areas became the favored destinations for the continuous stream of new migrants—2,000 a year were sailing for America by the 1530s—as the Caribbean islands were relegated to a position of secondary importance.

An estimated 300,000 Spaniards migrated to America in 1492 to 1600. They were followed by 450,000 more in 1601 to 1700, and another 500,000 in 1701 to 1810, giving an overall total of 1,250,000. In the same period almost one million black slaves arrived from West Africa (75,000 by 1600; 292,000 in 1601–1700; 578,000 in 1701–1810). They were first shipped in significant numbers in the 1520s, as the disappearance of the native population in the Caribbean (due to ill-treatment and imported diseases such as measles and smallpox) created a demand for labor. As in British America, slaves were concentrated in areas where plantation agriculture flourished. However, blacks—slave and free—were also present in large numbers in towns and cities throughout the empire, working in Spanish households and also as artisans and shopkeepers. They had greater access to manumission (emancipation from slavery) than their counterparts in British America—a 1791 census showed, for example, that Peru had 40,000 slaves and 41,000 free blacks, while another (1797) identified 65,000 slaves and 54,000 free blacks in Cuba's total population of 272,000. This was partly because Spanish colonists were readier than the British to accept that, although all slaves were black, not all blacks had to be slaves. Most of the colonial censuses understated actual population, because of the close correlation between being counted and being registered for conscription or taxation. Moreover, categorization into ethnic groups

***Mexico or New Spaine*, 1690.** *This early map of Mexico and New Spain was prepared by the British cartographer and royal hydrographer John Seller (ca. 1630–1697).* © CORBIS. REPRODUCED BY PERMISSION.

often reflected individuals' social or economic status rather than rigid racial classification. However, it is generally accepted that by the first decade of the nineteenth century Spanish America had almost seventeen million inhabitants (peninsular Spain had ten million), of whom blacks constituted 5 percent (800,000), Spaniards (a category that included the peninsular-born minority and the more numerous American-born creoles) 18 percent (three million), "Indians"—as the Spaniards still called the native Americans—43 percent (seven million), and those of mixed descent 34 percent (5.5 million). This last group—the *castas*—was predominantly *mestizo* (Indian/Spanish) except in areas like Venezuela where blacks had been introduced from an early date, thereby encouraging the growth of the *pardo* (black/Spanish) population. In theory slaves and *castas* occupied distinctly

subordinate places in the social pyramid, while Spaniards and Indians inhabited separate "republics," each with its own hierarchical structure. The reality was that the supposedly inferior groups were often more mobile—socially and politically—than the native inhabitants. There was, however, scope for indigenous community leaders to acquire considerable wealth and prestige, in return for their crucial intermediary role in the collection of the male capitation tax known as the tribute and the delivery of quotas of community Indians for labor service in mines and other enterprises. This conscription of native labor did not constitute slavery, because workers were paid, usually in kind, and service was for fixed periods, but in reality it was a devastating scourge upon communities, causing high mortality as well as mass migration from the provinces required to provide laborers for service in the mines.

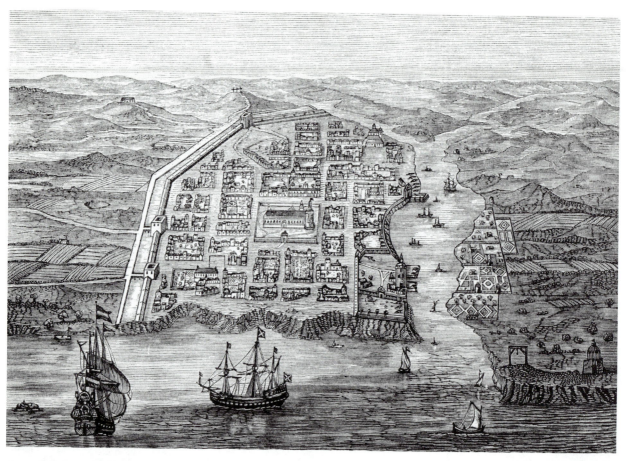

Santo Domingo at the Time of Francis Drake's Expedition. *This engraving of sixteenth-century Santo Domingo, now the capital of the Dominican Republic, appeared in Santo Domingo Past and Present (1873) by Samuel Hazard.* **BRIDGEMAN ART LIBRARY. REPRODUCED BY PERMISSION.**

Potosí alone was allocated 14,000 native conscripts a year from 1573, and thousands more voluntarily worked there and at other mining centers in order meet their fiscal obligations to Church and state. From the mid-sixteenth century the fruit of their labor—silver—was the motor driving both regional economies in America and transoceanic trade. The crown sought to protect remittances to Spain by organizing transatlantic trade into the "fleet system," whereby annual convoys sailed from Seville (later Cádiz) for Vera Cruz and the isthmus of Panama—the half-way house to Peru—to exchange Spanish products for American silver. Silver was by far the most important commodity among American exports to Spain, representing 80 percent of their value in the Habsburg period and over 50 percent in the eighteenth century, when the Bourbons successfully promoted the export of sugar, coffee, indigo, cotton, and hides from hitherto neglected regions of the empire. Two million pesos a year of taxation revenue were being remitted to Spain by the 1590s, although by the 1650s this figure had fallen to 300,000, and it would fall further during the reign of Charles II

(1665–1700) as Spain's commercial monopoly was undermined by foreign contrabandists and buccaneers. Moreover, by the seventeenth century the colonists were themselves producing and circulating many of the commodities previously imported from Spain—oil, wheat, wine, woolens—giving the empire a growing degree of economic autonomy from the metropolis, albeit within a context of continuing political subservience.

By the mid-sixteenth century the administrative parameters of Spanish America were clear. The crown established two viceroyalties—New Spain (capital Mexico City) and Peru (capital Lima); later, the latter's territory was reduced to more manageable proportions with the creation of the viceroyalties of New Granada (1739) and the Río de la Plata (1776). Each viceroyalty contained several "kingdoms," each with a crown-appointed governor (viceroy, captain-general, or president) who functioned alongside a judicial tribunal (*audiencia*) that also had administrative functions. At the subordinate level, local governors—known as *corregidores* in South America and as *alcaldes mayores* in New Spain—exercised jurisdiction over the native population and oversaw tax collection and public administration. The missionary orders—notably the Franciscans and Dominicans—were increasingly subordinated to the authority of an ever more bureaucratized church, as bishoprics were founded to both organize evangelization and cater to the religious needs of the growing Spanish population. Archbishops were appointed in Lima, Mexico City, and Santo Domingo in 1546 (and in La Plata in 1609) to oversee the activities of some forty bishops and thousands of lower clergy—who to some extent acted as general agents of the Spanish crown, alert for signs of idolatry and sedition, particularly in native communities. In remote regions the religious orders continued to exercise secular authority, notably in Paraguay where the Jesuits ran their missions until their expulsion in 1767.

This expulsion was part of a wide-ranging process of change implemented by Spain's fourth Bourbon king, Charles III (1759–1788). Building upon the piecemeal changes of the earlier Bourbons, Charles III sought systematically to restore Spain as a major international power by overhauling internal administration, tightening fiscal screws, improving defenses, and, above all, liberalizing colonial trade. "Free trade," introduced in 1778, although still prohibiting trade with foreigners, authorized the principal ports of Spanish America to trade directly with those of Spain, and reduced and simplified duties. The result was a commercial boom that made Spanish Americans richer and happier, and willing in the short term to tolerate the intensification of absolutism. It also made them increasingly confident of their ability to maintain their burgeoning prosperity without Spain, although no serious moves were made to promote that possibility until the Bourbon monarchy collapsed in 1808 and the crown of Spain passed to Joseph Bonaparte.

SEE ALSO *Government, Colonial, in Spanish America; Haciendas in Spanish America; Law, Colonial Systems of, Spanish Empire; Mexico; Mexico City; Mining, the Americas; New Spain, the Viceroyalty of; Peru under Spanish Rule; Plantations, the Americas; Spanish American Independence, 1808–1825.*

BIBLIOGRAPHY

Altman, Ida, and James Horn. *"To Make America": European Emigration in the Early Modern Period.* Berkeley: University of California Press, 1992.

Burkholder, Mark A., and Lyman L. Johnson. 2d ed. *Colonial Latin America.* Oxford: Oxford University Press, 1994.

Elliott, John H. *The Old World and the New, 1492–1650.* Cambridge, U.K.: Cambridge University Press, 1970; reprint, 1992.

Fisher, John R. *The Economic Aspects of Spanish Imperialism in America, 1492–1810.* Liverpool: Liverpool University Press, 1999.

Hennessy, Alistair. *The Frontier in Latin American History.* London: Edward Arnold, 1978.

Lynch, John. *Spain under the Hapsburgs.* 2 vols. Oxford: Blackwell, 1981.

Lynch, John. *Bourbon Spain, 1700–1808.* Oxford: Blackwell, 1989.

Parry, John H. *The Spanish Seaborne Empire.* London: Hutchinson, 1966.

John R. Fisher

EMPIRE, ITALIAN

Like Germany, Italy was a latecomer to the European scramble for African and other overseas colonial possessions. Both Germany and Italy became unified nations only in the second half of the nineteenth century, when many smaller and often fragmented states united against the longstanding hegemony of the Austro-Hungarian Empire. In Italy, however, no state with the power and influence of Prussia emerged as the focal point of the nationalist movement. Indeed, while Berlin became the capital of the new German state and in every sense a major counterpoint to Vienna, Rome remained ambiguously within the sphere of influence of the Roman Catholic papacy, which had a long history of political domination in central Italy. Likewise, while both new nations scrambled to establish colonies in areas on the fringes of established British and French colonies, there was a significant difference in their approaches. Whereas the Germans aggressively established colonies adjacent to British and French holdings in East and West Africa, the Italians seemed content to settle for "leftovers."

The initial Italian possessions in Africa were located at what were then the farthest reaches of the decrepit Ottoman Empire. The first Italian colonies were established on the Horn of Africa and in Eritrea and Somaliland in East Africa. In 1885 a Roman Catholic priest, Father Guissepe Sapeto, who was acting in effect as an agent for Italian commercial interests, purchased the port of Assab from the Afar sultanate, an Ethiopian vassal state. The area around Assab was located at the fringes of the Ethiopian Empire, the Ottoman Empire, and the Anglo-Egyptian advancements into the Sudan. In combination with the general decline of the Ottoman Empire, the Mahdist uprising in the Sudan and the confused political situation in Ethiopia following the death of the Ethiopian Emperor Johannes IV (ca. 1836–1889) enabled the Italians to expand their holdings in Eritrea well beyond Assab.

What would develop into longstanding tensions between Italy and Ethiopia had their origins in a dispute over the Ottoman port of Massawa in Eritrea, which had passed informally into the Anglo-Egyptian sphere of influence. The British ceded their own and the Egyptian claims to the port in favor of the Italians, even though the Ethiopians believed they had been promised it in return for harboring Egyptian refugees from the Mahdist massacres. Landlocked, Ethiopia naturally placed a great value on controlling a port, but the British were concerned that the French might use the Ethiopian expulsion of Roman Catholic missionaries as a pretext to oust the Ethiopians from the port in order to establish their own presence in the Horn of Africa. Tellingly, the Ottoman Turks seem to have factored very little in any of these decisions.

The Italians soon discovered, however, that Massawa was the hottest port in the world. In large part to provide a retreat from the oppressive heat, the Italians began to take possession of some of the surrounding highlands. Ras Alula (1847–1897), one of the chief lieutenants of Johannes IV, controlled the territory into which the Italians were making these incursions. Alula's forces surprised and massacred an entire Italian division near Dogaly. In fact, the Ethiopians might have driven the Italians from Massawa, and perhaps even from all of Eritrea, except that the Mahdists attacked them from the west and Johannes IV was subsequently killed in the campaign to drive the Mahdists out.

In this same regionally tumultuous period, Italy took the first steps toward establishing a fuller presence in the Horn of Africa in the Ottoman-controlled part of Somaliland, adjacent to the established colony of British Somaliland. Over three decades, from the late 1880s to the end of World War I (1914–1918), the Italians increased their holdings in Somaliland incrementally at the expense of the Turks—through purchase, seizure, and transfer by treaty. The last parcels of what would become Italian Somaliland were ceded to Italy at the end of World War I as part of its compensation for entering the war on the Allied side.

In 1896 tensions between Ethiopia and Italy escalated into the First Italo-Abyssinian War. By 1889 Menelik II (1844–1913) had defeated several rival claimants and succeeded Johannes IV as emperor of Abyssinia (Ethiopia). In return for Italian support, Menelik had agreed to recognize Italy's claim to Eritrea. To formalize this arrangement, Menelik signed the Treaty of Wichale (1889), but it turned out that there were significant variations in the Italian and Amharic (a Semitic language of Ethiopia) versions of the treaty. Most significantly, the Italian version asserted that Ethiopia should be regarded as a vassal state within the Italian Empire.

In 1893 Menelik formally renounced the Treaty of Wichale. After diplomacy and economic sanctions failed to convince him to reconsider, the Italians began to attack adjacent portions of Ethiopia from Eritrea. Menelik responded by leading a major force toward Eritrea. Because Italy's forces were outnumbered, the Italian commander, Oreste Baratieri (1841–1901), wisely retreated toward Asmara. But embarrassed by this relatively unprecedented retreat from "native" forces and grossly underestimating Menelik's leadership and the amount of Western weaponry that he had managed to acquire, the Italian government of Francesco Crispi (1819–1901) ordered Baratieri to attack the Ethiopians.

At the 1896 Battle of Adwa, an estimated 120,000 Ethiopians encircled an Italian force of fewer than 15,000. Concerned about the limited supplies and ammunition available to his forces, Baratieri tried to force a decisive battle but ordered his forces forward into an area of rugged ground almost singularly unsuited to concentrated attack. Menelik's forces won a convincing victory over the Italians. Despite the great discrepancy in the sizes of the forces, both sides suffered between 10,000 and 11,000 casualties. The remnants of Baratieri's force trickled back to Asmara, and Menelik left Eritrea convinced that the Italians would sue for peace on his terms. When the news of this humiliating defeat reached Italy, Crispi's government was forced out of office and Baratieri was recalled. The new Italian government signed the Treaty of Addis Ababa (1896) with Menelik, recognizing the full independence of Ethiopia and fixing its borders with the Italian colonies on the Horn.

Italy had more success in the Italo-Turkish War (1910–1911). Concerned that France and Great Britain would soon assume control of the entire coast of North Africa, Italy took advantage of the tensions between those rival colonial powers, and of Ottoman weakness, and seized control of the North African provinces immediately opposite its own shores, Tripolitania and Cyrenaica. Because these two provinces were not deemed economically significant and because the interior beyond the immediate coastal areas was a vast, largely uninhabitable wasteland, the French and British were willing to accept an Italian buffer between their more prosperous spheres of influence in Tunisia and Egypt. In the 1912 Treaty of Lausanne that ended the brief Italo-Turkish War, the Ottoman Turks also ceded Rhodes and the other Dodecanese Islands in the Aegean Sea to Italy, in part to stymie Greek claims to the islands.

Disturbed by extensive emigration from Italy in the late nineteenth and early twentieth century, the Italian government attempted to promote the opportunities in the new colonies as an alternative. That immigration to the colonies did occur on a fairly large scale was

---

ITALIAN EMPIRE, KEY DATES

1885: Roman Catholic priest, Farther Guissepe Sapeto, acting as an agent for Italian commercial interests, purchases the Port of Assab from the Afar Sultanate, an Ethiopian vassal state

1887: Battle of Dogali, Italians are defeated by the Ethiopian army

1889: Menelik II succeeds Johannes IV as Emperor of Abyssinia. The Italian government signs the Treaty of Wichale with Menelik II

1890: Italian Prime Minister Francesco Crispi establishes the Italian colony of Eritrea on the Red Sea

1896: Tensions between Ethiopia and Italy escalated into the First Italo-Abyssinian War

1893: Menelik II formally renounces the Treaty of Wichale

1896: Battle of Adowa, Ethiopian forces outnumber Italian forces by five to six times. The Italians suffer a resounding defeat

1911-1912: Italo-Turkish War or Turco-Italian War, Italian forces seize Ottoman provinces in Libya

1922: Benito Mussolini seizes power in Italy and declares his ambition to re-establish the glory of the Roman Empire

1934: Mussolini combines Tripolitania and Cyrenaica into a single colonial province that he calls Libya.

1935: Mussolini orders the forces he has massed in Eritrea and in Italian Somaliland to subjugate Ethiopia

1936: Italy adds Ethiopia to its East African colonies

1939: Italy annexes Albania as part of the Italian Empire

1941: Italian forces in East Africa surrender to the British

1943: All Italian soldiers have been driven out of Africa by the middle of the year

---

probably more a testament to the terrible economic conditions in southern Italy and Sicily than evidence of the actual opportunities available in the colonies. Nonetheless, the Italian government ruthlessly dispossessed the native populations from the most desirable land in the colonies, and some prosperous and attractive colonial communities were established. Most notably, despite the terrible, recurring regional conflicts of the last half of the twentieth century, Asmara, the capital of Eritrea, still retains many fine examples of Italian colonial architecture.

After his fascist regime seized power in Italy in 1923, Benito Mussolini (1883–1945) often declared his ambition to reestablish the glory of the Roman Empire. Recurringly, he would overestimate and overextend his resources in trying to realize that ambition. The two colonies in North Africa were not completely "pacified" until the late 1920s, but in 1934 Mussolini combined Tripolitania and Cyrenaica into a single colonial province that he called "Libya," resurrecting a name given to the region some 1,600 years earlier by the Roman emperor Diocletian (245–316 C.E.). Seeking to expand the colonies and to redress the humiliating defeat at Adwa, Mussolini became increasingly bellicose toward Ethiopia and escalated his demands for concessions to Italian interests in

that country. In 1935 he ordered the forces he had massed in Eritrea and in Italian Somaliland to subjugate Ethiopia.

The Italian force, which included a large contingent of Askari troops from Eritrea, numbered about 100,000. The force was supported by airplanes, tanks, and mobile artillery. In response, the Ethiopian Emperor Haile Selassie (1892–1975) was able to mobilize about 500,000 men, though many were armed with primitive firearms or even spears and shields. After several Ethiopian defeats, the League of Nations denounced the Italian aggression but then refused to impose effective economic sanctions on the Italians.

The Italian advance into Ethiopia continued steadily, but Mussolini wanted a much more dramatic victory. So he replaced the commander of the Italian forces and ordered that the full force of Italian arms be directed more ruthlessly against the remaining Ethiopian forces and against Ethiopian towns and cities that had not yet been subdued. Despite vocal international protests, Italian forces used some 300 to 500 tons of mustard gas against both combatants and civilians. Defeated and demoralized, the Ethiopian resistance collapsed, and some seven months after the Italian invasion had begun, Haile Selassie was forced into exile, where he became a gallant symbol of the growing resistance to fascism. With the Ethiopian defeat, Mussolini declared the formation of Italian East Africa, consisting of all of the Italian holdings on the Horn of Africa. Angered by the British and French opposition to his imperial ambitions, Mussolini was drawn into an increasingly friendly relationship with German dictator Adolf Hitler (1889–1945).

Although Mussolini believed that his alliance with Nazi Germany would permit him to expand his sphere of influence in the Balkans and in northern and eastern Africa, World War II (1939–1945) quickly spelled the end to Italy's short-lived colonial empire. After some initial successes against the British forces in Egypt, Italian forces were driven back and almost entirely out of Libya. Only the intervention of the Afrika Korps led by German field marshal Erwin Rommel (1891–1944) prevented the annihilation of the remaining Italian forces. As the British were subsequently trying to slow the dramatic advance of Rommel's forces, and then building up their own forces at El Alamein, Egypt, to turn the tide against him, other British and commonwealth forces undertook a much less extensive and less publicized, but nonetheless arduous and equally successful, effort to expel the Italians from the Horn of Africa. By the middle of 1943, the Italians and Germans had been driven out of Africa.

After the war, Ethiopia regained its independence. Eritrea was made an autonomous state in federation with Ethiopia. Later Ethiopian attempts to eliminate Eritrean autonomy led to a thirty-year war and ultimately complete Eritrean independence. After being administered by the United Nations, Libya became an independent kingdom in 1951 and then ostensibly a republic in 1969. In the last three decades of the twentieth century, it became a "rogue state" under the leadership of Mu'ammar Gadhafi (b. 1942). In 1949 Italian Somaliland was named a UN trust territory, but alone among Italy's colonies, it was placed again under Italian administration. In 1960 it was granted independence and almost immediately merged with the former British Somaliland to form the independent nation of Somalia.

Although Italy never established colonies in the Americas, large-scale emigration from Italy, and especially from southern Italy and Sicily, in the late nineteenth and early twentieth centuries created sizable and significant Italian populations in both North and South America, in particular within the United States and Argentina. Ironically, it has become clear that Italian cultural influences will endure in the Americas much longer than in the former colonies of the Italian Empire in Africa.

SEE ALSO *Empire, Ottoman; North Africa, European Presence in; Scramble for Africa.*

BIBLIOGRAPHY

Berkeley, George Fitz-Hardinge. *The Campaign of Adowa and the Rise of Menelik,* rev. ed. London: Constable, 1935.

Casserly, Gordon. "Tripolitania: Where Rome Resumes Sway." *National Geographic* (Aug. 1925): 131–162.

De Marco, Roland R. *The Italianization of African Natives: Government Native Education in the Italian Colonies, 1890–1937.* New York: Teachers College, Columbia University, 1943.

Labanca, Nicola. "Colonial Rule, Colonial Repression, and War Crimes in the Italian Colonies." *Journal of Modern Italian Studies* 9 (3) (2004): 301–313.

Larebo, Haile M. *The Building of an Empire: Italian Land Policy and Practice in Ethiopia, 1935–1941.* New York: Oxford University Press, 1994.

Lewis, David Levering. "Pawns of Pawns: Ethiopia and the Mahdiyya." In *The Race to Fashoda: European Colonialism and African Resistance in the Scramble for Africa.* New York: Weidenfield and Nicholson, 1987.

McCartney, Maxwell H. H., and Paul Cremona. *Italy's Foreign and Colonial Policy, 1914–1937.* New York: Oxford University Press, 1938.

Palumbo, Patrizia, ed. *A Place in the Sun: Africa in Italian Colonial Culture from Post-Unification to the Present.* Berkeley: University of California Press, 2003.

Prouty, Chris. "War with Italy: Amba Alage, Meqellle, Adwa." In *Empress Taytu and Menilek II: Ethiopia, 1883–1910.* Trenton, NJ: Red Sea Press, 1986.

Robertson, Esmonde M. *Mussolini as Empire-Builder: Europe and Africa, 1932–1936.* New York: Macmillan, 1977.

Sbacchi, Alberto. *Ethiopia Under Mussolini: Fascism and the Colonial Experience.* London: Zed, 1985.

Schanzer, Carlo. "Italian Colonial Policy in Northern Africa." *Foreign Affairs* (March 15, 1924): 446–456.

Segre, C. G. "Italo Balbo and the Colonisation of Libya." *Journal of Contemporary History* 31 (1996).

Martin Kich

EMPIRE, JAPANESE

When young radicals overthrew the Tokugawa shogun in 1868, their overriding goal was to create a strong, sovereign Japan that could overcome the unequal treaties imposed by the Western powers. Over the next seventy-seven years, until defeat in World War II (1939–1945), Japan would assemble a vast empire in east Asia and the western Pacific. Yet the course of acquiring this empire was not predetermined but buffeted with disagreement and circumstance. Indeed the new leadership split over a plan to invade Korea in 1871. That action was blocked, but in 1875 Tokyo sent a fleet to the isolated nation, forcing Korea to open up to Japanese trade and contact.

Chinese Prisoners During Sino-Japanese War. *Japanese soldiers march Chinese prisoners during the first Sino-Japanese War (1894–1895). The war marked the beginning of Japan's policy of imperial expansion.* © BETTMANN/CORBIS. REPRODUCED BY PERMISSION.

BUILDING AN EMPIRE

For the next two decades Tokyo vied with China for influence in Korea, finally clashing in the short Sino-Japanese War of 1894–95. Japan's startling victory in this conflict yielded its first major colony, the island of Taiwan (or Formosa). The Sino-Japanese War also made Japan one of the powers in China, with treaty port rights and extraterritoriality. Armed with this new status Japan participated in the suppression of the Boxer Rebellion in China in 1900. Its forces marched into Beijing with the Westerners, and Tokyo signed the Boxer Protocol, which granted it the right to station troops at various locations around northern China. Yet Japan was profoundly unhappy with moves by the Russian Empire to control both northeast China (Manchuria) and Korea, and joined with Britain in an alliance to force Russia to retreat. The two nations clashed in the Russo-Japanese War of 1904–05, and Japan's victory in this conflict left it in a much stronger position on the Asian mainland. Japan soon gained complete control over Korea, made a formal part of the empire in 1910, as well as railway concessions and

ports in southern Manchuria. Japan also gained the southern half of the Sakhalin Island off the coast of Siberia.

Tokyo never completely fixed upon a colonial policy but increasingly moved toward "assimilation" for Koreans and Chinese in Taiwan. The colonized were compelled to use Japanese surnames, to be schooled and educated in Japanese language, and to revere the Japanese emperor. When Koreans traveled to Japan, however, they discovered that few Japanese accepted them as equals; discrimination against Koreans was blatant and often deadly. World War I (1914–1918) brought Japan new opportunities; in 1915 it presented a weakened China with 21 Demands, designed to increase its power on the mainland. Japan also grabbed German territories in the area, notably the German-held islands in the southwest Pacific that Japan held until captured by the Allies in World War II. Unlike the Koreans and Chinese who could plausibly be "Japanized" few felt that the Pacific Islanders could be assimilated. Islands such as Saipan were transformed mostly by Japanese immigration.

JAPANESE EMPIRE, KEY DATES

1868: Tokugawa shogunate overthrown by radicals; Meiji period begins

1875: Japan invades Korea and establishes trade supremacy

1879: Japan annexes Ryukyu Islands

1895: Control of Formosa (Taiwan) following victory in Sino-Japanese War

1900: Japan aids China in ending Boxer Rebellion; establishes military outposts in China

1905: Japan wins Russo-Japanese War and gains more control of Asian mainland

1910: Japan annexes Korea and begins Japanese enculturation

1912: Yoshihiro succeeds to throne, Taishō period begins

1914: Japan declares war on Germany and enters World War I

1915: Japan presents China with 21 Demands

1917: Lansing-Ishi Agreement reinforces Japanese interests in China

1918: Japan launches Siberian Expedition to gain foothold in Russia; World War I ends

1919: Korean colony displays nationalism in March 1st Movement; Japan counted among "Big Five" at Treaty of Versailles

1921: Prime Minister Hara Takashi is assassinated; Japan signs disarmament agreements at Washington Conference, relinquishing claims to Chinese territory

1922: Agrees to naval limits in Pacific in Nine-Power Treaty

1923: Kantō earthquake levels Tokyo in September

1925: Japan becomes last Allied nation to withdraw from Russia

1928: Taishō dies and Hirohito becomes emperor

1929: Great Depression affects Japanese economy

1931: Japanese Prime Minister Rikken Minseitō is assassinated; Japanese Guandong Army occupies Manchuria, which is renamed Manchukuo

1933: Japan withdraws from League of Nations

1936: Japan signs Anti-Comintern Pact with Nazi Germany

1937: Italy joins Japan and Germany to form Axis Powers; Japan begins invasion of China, triggering Second Sino-Japanese War

1941: Japan bombs Pearl Harbor, Hawaii, on December 7

1943: Cairo Conference plans return of Manchuria, Taiwan, and Pescadores Islands to China

1944: Japan gains control of Dutch, French, American, and British interests in Asia

1945: U.S. drops atomic bombs on Hiroshima and Nagasaki on August 6th and 9th; Defeat in World War II leads Hirohito to surrender to Allies on August 14

1946: U.S. General Douglas MacArthur drafts model Japanese constitution

TWENTIETH-CENTURY CHANGES

In the 1920s Japan seemed to back away from expansion, becoming more democratic at home and party to naval disarmament agreements signed at Washington in 1921. The onset of the Great Depression in 1929, however, stimulated unrest in Japan and fueled the growth of an ultranationalist movement. The right wing achieved its first big success in September 1931, when Japanese army officers stationed along the railway in northeast China faked a terrorist attack and quickly seized control of northeast China. A vast territory of 30 million people most of whom were Chinese, Manchuria was organized as a puppet state, Manchukuo, by the Japanese Imperial Army, which installed the last Qing monarch as "emperor."

In July 1937 Japan began an all-out invasion of China. Within six months the Chinese had abandoned most of their coastal cities; within two years much of eastern and central China was under Japanese control, and nearly half of China's population would live, at least for a time, in occupied areas. It was by far the greatest acquisition of the Japanese Empire to date. Yet China remained an active war theater, and despite puppet governments, Japan could not create a stable political structure. In the north, where the Japanese had long planned expansion and had developed the adjacent territory in Manchukuo, Japan achieved some success in exploiting coal and iron ore. In central and south China Japanese had to rely mostly on confiscation of Chinese enterprises and extraction of agricultural products.

The final saga in Japan's empire began with the attack on Pearl Harbor in December 1941. Within six months Japan seized the colonial possessions of the Western powers in southeast Asia, including the oil-rich Dutch East Indies and British Malaya with its tin and rubber. The American Philippines was overrun and much of British Burma. The Japanese occupied French Indo-China, though nominally under Vichy control. Japan called its new empire "The Greater East-Asia Co-Prosperity Sphere."

The last gasp of the Japanese Empire was its most impressive yet but Japan failed to take advantage. Allied forces devastated Japanese commercial shipping, precluding the full use of the new colonies. Restive populations who initially welcomed Japanese "liberation" quickly became disenchanted when their ruler proved even harsher than that of the Western masters. Japan destroyed Western imperialism in southeast Asia, but it created a legacy of anti-Japanese feeling that took decades to erode.

When Emperor Hirohito announced surrender in August 1945, Japan lost all but the home islands. What had been the largest non-Western empire in the modern world was no more. And what legacy did it leave? Perhaps only in Taiwan do individuals acknowledge positive contributions of the experience. In divided Korea, few people see anything but humiliation and suffering in the colonial experience. In China, legacy over Japanese wartime atrocities still clouds relations between the two nations. As for Japan, it has found a new role as an economic giant; using trade rather than conquest to succeed.

SEE ALSO *Japan, Colonized.*

BIBLIOGRAPHY

Coble, Parks M. *Chinese Capitalists in Japan's New Order: The Occupied Lower Yangzi, 1937-1945.* Berkeley: University of California Press, 2003.

Duus, Peter. *The Abacus and the Sword: Japanese Penetration of Korea, 1895–1910.* Berkeley: University of California Press, 1995.

Duus, Peter, Ramon H. Myers, and Mark R. Peattie. *The Japanese Informal Empire in China, 1895–1937.* Princeton, NJ: Princeton University Press, 1989.

Duus, Peter, Roman H. Myers, and Mark R. Peattie. *The Japanese Wartime Empire, 1931–1945.* Princeton, NJ: Princeton University Press, 1996.

Eckert, Carter J. *Offspring of Empire: The Koch'ang Kims and the Colonial Origins of Korean Capitalism.* Seattle: University of Washington Press, 1991.

Lebra, Joyce C. *Japan's Greater East Asia Co-Prosperity Sphere in World War II.* New York: Oxford University Press, 1975.

Myers, Ramon, and Mark R. Peattie, eds. *The Japanese Colonial Empire, 1895–1945.* Princeton, NJ: Princeton University Press, 1984.

Peattie, Mark R. *Nan'yo: The Rise and Fall of the Japanese in Micronesia, 1885–1945.* Honolulu: University of Hawaii Press, 1988.

Tsurumi, E. Patricia. *Japanese Colonial Education in Taiwan, 1895–1945.* Cambridge, MA: Harvard University Press, 1977.

Young, Louise. *Japan's Total Empire: Manchuria and the Culture of Wartime Imperialism.* Berkeley: University of California Press, 1998.

Parks M. Coble

EMPIRE, OTTOMAN

The Ottoman Empire (1299–1923) was a Turkish-Muslim state that existed for more than six hundred years. It was one of the largest and longest-lived empires in history, and it represented one of the greatest civilizations of the modern period. Its territories, at its height, included Anatolia (part of present-day Turkey), the Middle East, parts of East and North Africa, and southeastern Europe, comprising a total area of more than 22 million square kilometers (about 8.5 million square miles).

The Ottoman state was established by a tribe of Oghuz Turks as one of many small Turkish principalities that emerged in Anatolia during the Mongolian breakdown of the Anatolian Seljuk State. The state was ruled by the Ottoman dynasty of the Kayi tribe. The dynasty was founded by Osman I (ca. 1258–1324; in English, *Ottoman*) in Söğüt, in the Marmara region of modern Turkey.

THE PERIOD OF ESTABLISHMENT AND EXPANSION

Situated on the borders of the tottering Byzantine Empire, Osman I quickly became a warrior of Islam, attracting the attention of wandering *ghazis*, or warriors for the faith, in Anatolia. In 1299 the Byzantine city Bilecik fell to Turks. This conquest was followed by the fall of many other Byzantine cities, villages, and forts during the early 1300s. Some of the nearby Turkish *beyliks* (principalities) and tribes were also taken over before Osman's death around 1324.

Osman's son Orhan (r. 1326–1362) conquered Bursa in 1326. Bursa became the first Ottoman capital, and facilitated the establishment of military, financial, and administrative institutions. Ottoman coins, for example, were used for the first time in Bursa. Between 1331 and 1338, the other large Byzantine cities of Iznik, Izmit, and Üsküdar fell to Turkish forces. Orhan's marriage to the daughter of the Byzantine emperor gave him a free hand in the region, and in 1354 Orhan's son Süleyman landed at Gallipoli across the Dardanelles, a

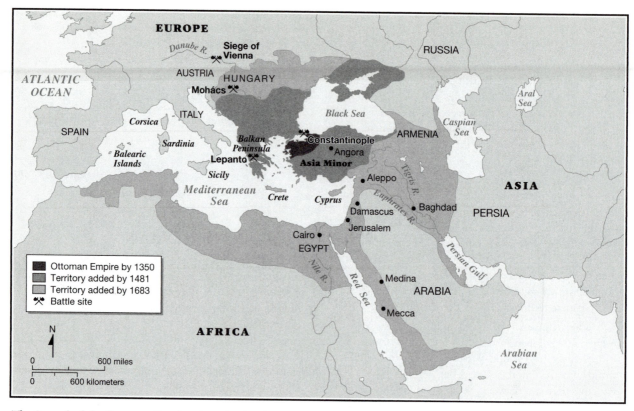

The Spread of the Ottoman Empire. *At its height, the Ottoman Empire included Anatolia, the Middle East, parts of East and North Africa, and southeastern Europe, comprising a total area of more than 22 million square kilometers (about 8.5 million square miles).* **MAP BY XNR PRODUCTIONS. THE GALE GROUP.**

strait in northwest Turkey that connects that Sea of Mamara with the Agean Sea. Süleyman died in 1360, and Orhan's son Murad I (ca. 1326–1389) became sultan. During Murad's reign, peaceful acquisition of lands in Anatolia continued, as did war against Europe.

In the early 1360s the Byzantium city of Edirne in Thrace fell to Turkish forces. Edirne was made the new Ottoman capital, and served as a base for further expansion into the Balkans. Filibe (present-day Plovdiv, Bulgaria) was captured in 1363. A combined Serbian-Bulgarian army of seventy thousand soldiers was subsequently defeated, and by 1387 large parts of the Balkan Peninsula had come under Turkish rule.

The Ottoman rulers forced the leaders of Byzantine and Serbia to pay an annual tribute. The Ottoman system of integration of local rulers and chieftains into their administrative apparatus as vassals facilitated the rapid expansion of the Ottoman Empire. Murad I further expanded his territories and influence in Anatolia through marriages and the purchase of lands

In an attempt to stop the Turkish advance, several European armies formed a union of crusaders. However, Ottoman forces inflicted a heavy defeat on the European

crusaders in the Battle of Kosovo in 1389, during which Murad I was killed by a Serbian assassin. He was succeeded by his son Bayezid I (ca. 1347–1403).

The new sultan's first move was to check the power of the Turkish Beyliks, who were challenging the Ottomans. Bayezid then turned to Europe to smash Balkan rebels. Bulgaria was put under direct Ottoman administration, and Constantinople (present-day Istanbul) was besieged for the first time. The crusaders organized by Hungary were defeated at the Battle of Nigbolu, on the Danube's shore, in 1396.

Bayezid then proceeded to Anatolia and expanded the Ottoman Empire far to the east, where it eventually came into contact with another rising Turkish dynasty, that of Timur (1336–1405), known in the West as Tamerlane. Bayezid lifted the siege of Constantinople in 1400 to meet Timur's challenge, but was defeated at the Battle of Ankara (1402) after some of his vassals deserted him. The sultan himself was captured and died in captivity in 1403. These developments led to an interregnum as Bayezid's four sons—Süleyman, İsa, Mehmed, and Musa—competed for the throne by declaring separate sultanates in Rumelia, Balıkesir, Amasya, and Bursa, respectively. Mehmed I (or

Muhammad I, ca. 1389–1421) emerged victorious in 1413, and the Ottoman state experienced a period of restoration.

Mehmed's son, Murad II (ca. 1403–1451), who succeeded him in 1421, continued the internal strengthening of the empire by taking control of further regions in the Balkans and in Anatolia, some of which had declared their independence during the period of chaos that followed the death of Bayezid. Murad also seized Selanik (Salonica or Thessaloníki, Greece) from the Venetians in 1430 and ended the Venetian blockage to the Adriatic Sea. Finally, after a victory against the combined European army at the Battle of Varna in eastern Bulgaria in 1444, Murad abdicated his throne to his twelve-year-old son, Mehmed II (ca. 1432–1481), who came to be known as "The Conqueror."

Murad took back the throne when crusaders began once again threatening the empire. The Ottomans defeated the attackers in the second Battle of Kosovo in 1448. Murad's reign saw the beginning of the *Devşirme* system of state bureaucracy. During the Devşirme period, Christian youths recruited from the Balkans were trained and organized as a new army corps called the *Janissaries*. After Murad's death in 1451, Mehmed II again succeeded him.

EMPIRE ON THE RISE

Shortly after his second ascent to the throne, Mehmed II besieged Constantinople. After fifty-three days, the Byzantine capital fell to the Ottomans in May 29, 1453, a victory that made the sultan the most prestigious ruler in the Muslim world. Even from as far away as India, letters of congratulations were sent praising him as the defender of Islam. This conquest marked an important turning point in world history.

Now, as an heir to previous civilizations, Mehmed II began to transform the Ottoman state into a worldwide empire. He kept Constantinople intact, maintained the current order, and moved the Ottoman capital there. He also renamed the city Istanbul. Mehmed invited talented artists, scholars, and craftsman from around the world, including Europe, to settle in Istanbul, thus making the city a great center of culture and civilization. Accordingly, members of different Christian and Jewish denominations were invited to set up their religious centers as *millets* (literally "nation," defined by religious affiliations) under the auspices of the sultan. This became a fundamental element in the Ottoman system of administration in which each *millet* took charge of the religious and educational needs, as well as the personal laws, of its members. Mehmed II also codified for the first time the criminal and civil laws of the Empire into a legal system known as *Kanunname*.

After the conquest of Constantinople, the expansion continued by annexing Serbia and Morea (in Greece), the city of Trabzon, the Genoese colonies on the Black Sea coast, several islands in the Aegean Sea, and Albania. Bosnia–Moldavia (a region in present-day Romania and Moldova) was forced to pay tribute, and the Khanete of the Crimea (in Ukraine) was made an Ottoman vassal state. Finally, in 1473 at the Battle of Otlukbeli, Mehmed II defeated Uzun Hasan (1453–1478) of the Akkoyunlu state, thus gaining control of all of Anatolia.

In 1480 Ottoman armies launched a campaign against Italy and captured the citadel of Otranto. Mehmed II died around the town of Gebze just outside Istanbul in 1481 on his way to another campaign against the Mamluks of Egypt. He left behind a vast empire.

Mehmed was succeeded by his son Bayezid II (1447–1512), who added Herzegovina and Moldavia (now fully) to the empire. Bayezid did not, however, push his campaign further to the west, partly because his rebellious brother Cem was being held in captivity in Rome. After fighting a year-long war for the succession, Cem had fled to Rhodes and finally ended up imprisoned in the Vatican. He died in 1495, probably as a result of poisoning. Meanwhile, in the east, the Ottomans fought against the Mamluks from 1485 to 1491. The fighting ended with no substantial Ottoman gain. Bayezid's last years saw various rebellions in eastern Anatolia instigated by Shah Ismail (r. 1501–1524) of the Safavids, who ruled parts of present-day Iran. In 1512 the sultan was obliged to hand over the throne to his son Selim I ("the Grim," ca. 1470–1520), who had taken control of the state with the support of the Janissaries.

THE AGES OF OTTOMAN SUPREMACY

Selim I greatly expanded the Ottoman Empire, virtually doubling the size of its lands. He initiated operations against Turkmen rebels who were in alliance with the Safavids, inflicting a crushing defeat on Shah Ismail at the Battle of Çaldıran in 1514. Then, Selim's forces defeated the Mamluks in 1516 at Marj Dabik and in 1517 at Ridaniye. Syria, Egypt, and the Hejaz (in present-day Saudi Arabia) were also annexed. These conquests gave the Ottomans control over the eastern coast of the Mediterranean and the shores of North Africa; they thus controlled traditional trade routes, making the Ottoman state the wealthiest in the world.

Selim also claimed the title of the "universal Muslim caliphate," which gave a great privilege as the holders of the Prophet's office and the defenders of the sacred places of Islam to the Ottomans among the Muslims of the world. These conquests opened the way to direct contact between the Ottomans and the Muslim sultanates and trading communities of the Indian Ocean. Selim I died in 1520, on his way to a military campaign in the west. He was succeeded by his son Süleyman I (ca. 1494–1566), known in the West as "the Magnificent."

Under Süleyman, Ottoman naval supremacy was assured in Mediterranean waters, and the coast up to Morocco in North Africa was annexed. In Europe, Belgrade and most of Hungary were absorbed into the Ottoman Empire after the Battle of Mohacs (1521). The Ottomans seized Vienna in 1529, but never fully conquered the city. In 1540 Hungary became an Ottoman province. The Ottoman fleet also bombarded Nice, France, in 1543.

In order to keep their east-to-west trade route open, Süleyman launched a new campaign in 1544 against the Safavids. Ottoman forces captured Azerbaijan and Tabriz (in modern Iran) in 1552, and Baghdad and Basra (in Iraq) in 1553. Süleyman died in 1566 while besieging the castle of Zigetvar in Hungary, and his son, Selim II (ca. 1524–1574), succeeded him.

In his time, Süleyman was undoubtedly the most powerful ruler in the world. During his reign, the Ottoman Empire expanded greatly, both to the east and west, and threatened to overrun the heart of Europe. Süleyman was also a major player in European politics, and he pursued an aggressive policy of destabilizing Europe. He aimed to ensure that no state became powerful enough to unify Europe. To this end, Süleyman financially supported Protestant countries when European Christianity split Europe between Catholics and Protestants. It was primarily because of this Ottoman policy that the Habsburgs were forced to offer concessions to the Protestants, and it can be argued that Protestantism would never have succeeded but for Ottoman support.

Since European expansion was detrimental to the interests of Muslims in Asia, Süleyman pursued a policy of helping Muslim countries in Asia. He thus sent naval expeditions to the Indian Ocean as far as Indonesia, claiming that this was his duty as the caliph of Islam. These expeditions brought him great popularity among world Muslims. But in the end, the Ottomans were not successful in keeping the Portuguese away from the Indian Ocean region.

Süleyman also embarked on vast cultural and architectural projects. During his reign Istanbul became the most culturally innovative city in the world, thanks mainly to the great works of the famous Turkish architect Sinan (1491–1588).

Ottoman expansion continued under Selim II. The conquest of Cyprus in 1570 led to the formation of an alliance between the Spanish, Venetian, and papal states of Europe, which defeated the Ottoman fleet at the Battle of İnebahtı (Lepanto), near Greece, in October of 1571, though this defeat inflicted no serious harm to the Ottomans.

During the reign of Murad III (1456–1595), the son of Selim II, the Ottomans engaged in wars with the Habsburgs in the west and with the Safavids in the east. Much of Hungary was lost to Austria, but the Safavids were held back. The Ottomans also began to lose their hold in the Mediterranean, and this development severed links with the empire's far-flung Egyptian and North African territories.

Murad II died in 1595 and was succeeded by his son, Mehmed III (1566–1603). Some initial gains were made on the western front when Egri and Kanije castles (in Hungary) were seized and the Austrian army was defeated at Haçova in 1596. The Romanian regions of Transylvania, Walachia, and Moldavia also became imperial Ottoman lands again. Mehmed III died in 1603 during the latter military campaigns, and his son Ahmed I (1590–1617) ascended to the throne.

Seizing this opportunity, the Safavids attacked the Ottomans, but a succession of wars ended with no gain for either side. Meanwhile, the Jelali revolts (a series of rebellions in Anatolia against the Ottoman government in reaction to various bad social and economic conditions), which were crushed by Grand Vizier (the chief minister and absolute representative of the sultan) Kuyucu Murad Paşa (d.1611) in Anatolia, signaled the advent of a period of Ottoman stagnation. Various explanations have been suggested for this decline, ranging from an internal weakening of the bureaucracy and the role of the Janissaries to the increased military efficiency of European states. Even then, however, at the beginning of the seventeenth century, the Ottoman Empire remained the most powerful single state in the world in terms of both military and economic capability.

OTTOMAN STAGNATION AND THE RISE OF EUROPE

Ahmed I was succeeded by his son Mustafa I (ca. 1592–1639) in 1617. Mustafa only ruled for a short time because of ill health and was eventually dethroned. Osman II (1604–1622) became the new sultan. When the Polish Cossacks invaded Ottoman lands, Osman, concluding that he could not meet this challenge with the undisciplined Janissaries, attempted to form a new Ottoman army. But the Janissaries rioted and killed him in 1622. After Mustafa I held the throne for a short second reign, Murad IV (ca. 1612–1640) became the sultan in 1623.

These developments led to new crises. Baghdad was lost to the Safavids and Erzurum governor Abaza Mehmed Paşa (d. 1634) rebelled in Anatolia. Murad IV reacted with ferocity, and the rebellions were suppressed. The Safavids were also pushed out again, and Revan (Erivan) and Baghdad were reconquered. Murad also

Topkapi Palace. *Built by Mehmed II in the fifteenth century and home to Ottoman sultans until the mid-nineteenth century, Topkapi Palace in Istanbul, Turkey, is now a museum.* © YANN ARTHUS-BERTRAND/CORBIS. REPRODUCED BY PERMISSION.

implemented a system of reforms, outlawing coffee and tobacco, among other things, on moral grounds. His death in 1640 marked the end of a period of reconstruction. His brother İbrahim (1615–1648) proved to be less effective.

In 1645 large portions of the island of Crete, including the city of Hania, were taken by the Venetians, who also started attacking the mainland coast. İbrahim was soon dethroned, and his son Mehmed IV (1642–1693) became sultan. New rebellions broke out in Istanbul and Anatolia. However, stability was reestablished thanks to Köprülü Mehmed Paşa (ca. 1570s–1661), who became grand vizier in 1556.

The Venetians were finally driven out of Crete in 1669. But the long period of war with the Venetians between 1645 and 1669 forced the Ottomans to acknowledge the vulnerability of their state and the need for reforms. During this period, the Ottoman state was served by the great Köprülü family, who helped halt the decline by rooting out divisive factions at the center and by closely supervising local governments.

After the death of Köprülü Fazıl Ahmed Paşa in 1676, Merzifonlu Kara Mustafa Paşa (1634–1683), became the grand vizier. Merzifonlu besieged Vienna in 1683 for a second time. After several years, the siege proved disastrous for the Ottomans; the opposite result would have had incalculably negative consequences for Europe. The European coalition finally defeated the Ottoman army, and the Treaty of Karlowitz was signed in 1699, marking the beginning of the permanent Ottoman withdrawal from Europe. The provinces of Hungary and Transylvania were handed over to Austria. During this period, recurrent internal disturbances arose in Anatolia. In the meantime, Mehmed IV had been dethroned in 1687, leaving his place to Süleyman II (ca. 1642–1691), who was in turn succeeded by Ahmed II (ca. 1643–1695) in 1691.

Although it took a coalition of European nations to bring down the Ottoman Empire, this was a period of major growth in European military technology, and the conventional Ottoman military forces could no longer stand up to the new European armies. The Ottomans also began to lose control of strategic trade routes, upon which their wealth had largely depended. Traders from the east to the west had by now changed their route, bypassing Ottoman lands by using sea-lanes around Africa. The northern trade route had to be abandoned after Russia took control of Kazan (1552) and Astrakhan (1556).

In addition, well-established European commerce began to threaten local manufacturers as mercantilist policies of selling the greatest possible quantity of goods abroad, while restricting imports, eventually left no opportunity for Ottoman exports. Ottoman lands became a vast open market for European products.

The war with Russia was the last opportunity for the Ottomans to regain lands lost at the beginning of the eighteenth century. The Treaty of Pruth (1711) was signed after a Russian defeat brought the Castle of Azak in the Black Sea region back to the Ottomans. This development kept Russia from expanding towards the Mediterranean.

After a war with Venice (1714–1718), the Ottomans recaptured several regions, including Morea, which had been ceded to the Venetians in the Treaty of Karlowitz. This advance marked the beginning of a period known as the Tulip Era, so named because of the growth in the number of gardens and lavish residences that were built in the empire to imitate European court life. The Tulip Era ended in 1730 after the Patrona Halil Riot in Istanbul, which occurred on the pretext of losses on the Iranian front. Sultan Ahmed III (1673–1736) was dethroned and his grand vizier, Nevşehirli İbrahim Paşa(1662–1730), was killed. Nevertheless, some attempts at modernization resulted in a short period of economic prosperity for the Ottoman state. The printing press, for example, was brought to the region in 1727.

OTTOMAN DECLINE AND WESTERN DOMINATION

During the reigns of Mahmud I (ca. 1696–1754) and Mustafa III (1717–1773), the Ottomans continued to experience a gradual decline in the face of growing European superiority. The Ottoman response was limited military reforms, such as establishing military colleges with the help of Claude-Alexandre, Comte de Bonneval (1675–1747), a French convert to Islam.

The Ottomans abstained from the Seven Years' War (1756–1763) in Europe and did not participate in the scheme of alliances and counter-alliances that ensued. Russia, on the other hand, continued the policy of seeking access to the Mediterranean and formed an alliance with Austria against the Ottomans. However, the Habsburgs, the most important Ottoman rival in Europe, entered into conflict with France, which kept them away from the Ottomans. Consequently, much of the remaining eighteenth century saw wars between the Russians and the Ottomans.

Wars that occurred between 1768 and 1774 and from 1787 and 1792 proved devastating for the Ottomans. The imperial Ottoman navy was wiped out at Çeşme in 1770 by the Russians, who sailed through the Baltic Sea. Crimea was first separated from the Ottoman Empire in 1774 by the Treaty of Küçük Kaynarca; the region was then annexed by the Russians in 1783. The Ottomans also had to renounce their claims to Moldavia and Walachia. Thus, Russia once again had a free hand in the Black Sea.

One important Russian gain that later had serious consequences for the Ottoman Empire was the right of protection over the orthodox Christian subjects in Ottoman territory. Sultan Mustafa III died in 1773 during the wars, and was succeeded by his brother Abdülhamid I (1725–1789), whose reign ended at his death in 1789. Selim III (1761–1808), assuming the throne in the middle of the war with Russia, quickly seized the opportunity to introduce military reforms known as *Nizam-ı Cedid*. But Selim's efforts to organize a new army in line with European military techniques were met with opposition from the Janissaries.

A new development in Europe, namely, Napoléon Bonaparte's (1769–1821) invasion of Egypt in 1798 after the French Revolution, altered the entire situation. Napoléon's advance was a major blow not only for the Ottomans but for the larger Muslim world. The invasion of Egypt was taken as an indication that after subjugating other Muslim territories in Asia, Europeans would turn their attention to Ottoman regions. As it turned out, Napoléon, under pressure from the Ottomans, Russians, and British, had to flee to France.

Although the immediate crisis was over, the Ottomans had entered a new century that was to be dominated by European wars and expansion, and by the notions of "the European balance of power" and "the Eastern question." The balance-of-power system, introduced by the 1815 Congress of Vienna, was based on the assumption that peace required setting equal powers against each other, thus limiting one country's ambitions to threaten others.

The Eastern question, however, basically, centered around one issue: If and when the Ottoman Empire disappeared, what should happen to its territories (especially the European ones)? Each power approached the matter with the aim of ensuring maximum advantage. But the general understanding was that until an acceptable solution was found, the status quo should be supported. Not surprisingly, the Ottoman Empire became a focus for European politics, and the European powers generally formulated their positions based on developments within the Ottoman Empire.

One man, Mehmed Ali (Muhammad 'Ali) Paşa (1769–1849), who was among the Ottoman soldiers sent to fight the French, was destined to become the most important figure in the political life of Egypt. The Ottoman government also had to deal with *Ayans* (local notables), who were revolting in the Balkans during the same period. This revolt facilitated the Serbian uprising of 1803, leading to a war between the Russians and Ottomans.

Selim III was imprisoned by reactionary Janissaries in 1807, and Mustafa IV (1779–1808) was put on the throne. An attempt to restore Selim to power resulted in his death, and finally his cousin Mahmud II (1785–1839), who himself had a narrow escape from death at the hands of revolting fractions, assumed the power in 1808.

Mahmud's initial step was to rid the empire of the *Ayans* who had forced him to sign an agreement called *Sened-i İttifak (Charter of Alliance),* which delegated some of Sultan's exercise of power to them and secured their position vis-à-vis the state. He did this by various means and finally took full control all over the country. But the overall Ottoman situation was deteriorating. While the war with Russia continued, Britain invaded Egypt and sent a naval force to seize the Dardanelles in 1807. Treaties were signed with the British in 1809, and with the Russians in 1812. Mahmud II then initiated a series of reforms; the most important was the abolition (*Vaka-i Hayriyye*) of the Janissary corps in 1826. Mahmud's other reforms were mainly social, economic, educational, and administrative in nature.

The 1820s were burdensome for the Ottomans. Apart from the effects of ongoing reforms, the wars with the Greeks and later the Russians were devastating. A combined British, French, and Russian force destroyed the Ottoman navy at Navarino in 1827. Although the Ottomans suppressed the Greek uprising, in the end, Greece declared its independence with the European support and the Russians gained lands in eastern Anatolia.

In 1831 France occupied Algeria and Mehmed Ali Paşa of Egypt rose in revolt, advancing as far as Kütahya in Anatolia. Mehmed Ali's advance could only be stopped by Russian intervention. The Russians required concessions in return in the 1833 Hünkar İskelesi Treaty. This treaty was followed by the Anglo-Ottoman Commercial Treaty of 1838 (*Balta Limanı*), which opened the Ottoman lands for a vast expansion of foreign trade. This gave the British the right to buy directly from the people and also intended to undermine the Russian commercial advantages, as well as to slow Mehmed Ali's financial capacity by breaking Egypt's monopoly in trade (*yed-i vahid*).

The terms of this treaty were soon replicated by treaties with other European states; the treaties abolished the use of monopolies throughout the empire and cut the level of internal duties. As a result, European merchants obtained rights to direct business, on favorable terms, with local manufacturers of various agricultural products. The Ottoman Empire thus became an open market for European goods, and a type of "free-trade imperialism" developed. This and subsequent unequal trade concessions were fundamentally different from the earlier capitulations, which had been granted from a position of strength by Süleyman the Magnificent as part of his European strategy.

THE PERIOD OF REFORMS AND MODERNIZATION

In 1839 Mehmed Ali's forces again defeated the Ottoman army at Nizip (Nezib). Mahmud II died during this time, and European powers settled the crisis by forcing Mehmed Ali to retreat to Egypt. The new sultan, Abdülmecid (1839–1861), declared a set of reform edicts called *Tanzimat.*

The Tanzimat was an attempt to transform the old Ottoman Empire into a state on the European model in almost every aspect of governance. New legal codes and administrative bodies were introduced, and the Ottoman's entire tax and conscription systems were changed. In an attempt to stop the break-up of the empire in the face of growing waves of nationalism after the French Revolution, a new concept of Ottoman citizenship was advanced as state ideology.

For a time, it looked as though the Ottoman Empire would enjoy a period of respite, but the Russians started another war, the Crimean War, in 1853. It was during this conflict that the Ottoman Empire came to be called the "sick man of Europe." Britain and France sided with the Ottomans primarily for their own purposes—namely, to check Russian ambitions. In fact, the Crimean War was a European conflict that was fought on Ottoman territory, rather than an exclusively Ottoman-motivated war. During the war, Sultan Abdülmecid was urged by his European allies to declare another set of edicts (*Islahat Fermanı* of 1856), reiterating the Tanzimat and promising further religious freedom.

The Crimean War ended in 1856 with the Treaty of Paris, which guaranteed the territorial integrity of the Ottoman Empire and recognized it as a member of the concert of Europe. But this recognition depended in part on the application of promised Ottoman reforms, which in turn gave the European powers the right to interfere in the domestic matters of the Ottoman state.

All in all the reforms had been undertaken to guarantee the survival of the country and to keep the different Ottoman nationalities together. But for a number of reasons, including European intervention, the reforms did not turn out as planned. The Ottoman's growing financial burden was aggravated by equally catastrophic uprisings in the Balkans. Heavy loans, borrowed to finance the war effort and the reform projects, finally led to the bankruptcy of the state. In addition, anti-Ottoman sentiment was also on the rise in Europe due to the assertion of British Prime Minister William Gladstone (1809–1898) that Turks were killing innocent Christians in the Balkans.

In these circumstances, intellectuals (the Young Ottomans) and opposition bureaucrats forced a change, and Sultan Abdülaziz (1830–1876) was deposed in 1876. His successor, Murad V (1840–1904), suffered a mental collapse under the pressure and was removed from the throne only three months after his accession. The reign of his brother and successor, Abdülhamid II (1842–1918), began during a desperate period for the Ottoman state. Not only was the country already at war with Serbia and Montenegro, but the impending threat from Russia resulted in a new declaration of war.

Meanwhile, elections were held, and the first Ottoman constitution was adopted. The Ottomans repeatedly asked France and Britain to keep their promise to guarantee the territorial integrity of the empire, as stipulated by the Treaty of Paris, but the Ottoman pleas were in vain. Changing political conditions in Europe, after the Italian and German unification, had long signaled a shift in the European balance of power, leaving the Ottoman Empire to its fate.

The war with Russia ended with a catastrophic defeat for the Ottomans. The Treaty of Yesilkoy, signed in 1878, made it clear that Romania and Montenegro had became independent; in addition, Bosnia was left to Austria, and Bulgaria declared its autonomy. Apart from Macedonia and some other regions, the Ottoman hold over the Balkans had ended.

However, European powers, led by Britain, opposed this Russian plan, and another conference was held in Berlin. The result of the Berlin conference, though limiting Russian gains, was even more detrimental to the Ottomans. Britain had already established effective control of the Persian Gulf, and took the island of Cyprus with the wily nily agreement of the Ottoman government on the pretext of Russian proximity to the Mediterranean Sea.

Later, in 1882, Britain occupied Egypt "in the name of the Ottoman sultan." France had done the same in Tunis in 1881. The Ottoman war with Russia also marked the end of the traditional British policy of maintaining the territorial integrity of Ottoman dominions. It was thus that Britain acquired Cyprus and Egypt, both considered important for British colonial interests.

One other outcome of the Berlin conference was the beginning of a German Ottoman rapprochement. Abdülhamid II saw Germany as a reliable ally, in contrast to France and Britain, and he hoped that with its advanced technology and strong economy Germany could help in the betterment of the Ottoman economy. This rapprochement, however, resulted in the Ottoman's increasing financial and military dependence on Germany.

The formal bankruptcy of the Ottoman state in 1875 led to the establishment of the Ottoman Public Debt Administration in 1881, which placed unconditional control of a large portion of state revenues in European hands. The Ottomans for the first time in their history had to surrender their sovereign rights over revenues to a "state within the state."

On the other hand, with the loss of the Balkan provinces, the demographic map of the Ottoman Empire dramatically changed, and the population was now predominantly Muslim. This demographic change inevitably affected state ideology. Although Ottomanism was still officially on the agenda, in reality Abdülhamid II pursued a policy of solidarity among Muslims, with an increasing emphasis on his role as head of a universal caliphate. This policy was called *pan-Islamism* by the colonizing powers, and it was interpreted as a threat to the "civilized world."

After the war, Sultan Abdülhamid II abolished the parliament and took control of all the affairs of state. He skillfully followed a deliberate policy of manipulating the rivalries of the European states. The remaining years of his reign saw a period of consolidation and stability. The Tanzimat reforms were carried out steadily, especially in the areas of education, administration, and finance; some success was achieved, particularly in finance. Unfortunately for Abdülhamid, however, the very graduates of the schools he opened initiated an opposition movement called *İttihat ve Terakki*; the supporters of the movement became known in the West as the Young Turks. The revolution forced Abdülhamid to restore the constitution in 1908; he was deposed the following year.

BEGINNING OF DISSOLUTION

The Young Turks, contrary to their expectations, found themselves in the middle of European power politics. Immediately after the revolution in 1908, Bulgaria declared its complete independence and Austria announced the annexation of Bosnia and Herzegovina. This development was followed by the Greek proclamation of their annexation of Crete. Within a short time, more territory was lost than had been lost under Abdülhamid II's entire reign.

OTTOMAN EMPIRE, KEY DATES

1299: Osman I founds Ottoman dynasty in Anatolia. The Byzantine city Bilecik, falls to the Turks, marking the first of many conquests

1326: Osman I's son, Orhan takes over the sultanate. He conquers Bursa, and Bursa becomes the first Ottoman capital

1331–1338: Large Byzantine cities of Iznik, Izmit, and Üsküdar fall to Turkish forces

1444: Murad abdicates the throne to his twelve-year-old son, Mehmed II, who came to be known as "The Conqueror"

1453: The Byzantine capital, Constantinople, falls to the Ottomans after a fifty-three day siege

1454–1455: All of Serbia and several other cities are annexed by the Ottoman Empire

1473: Mehmed II gains control of all of Anatolia during the Battle of Otlukbeli

1483: Bayezid II takes control of Herzegovina

1512–1520: Selim I greatly expands the Empire; Syria, Egypt, and the Hejaz are annexed. Ottomans now control all traditional trade routes

1540: Hungary becomes an Ottoman province

1570: Cyprus is conquered, leading to the formation of an alliance between Spanish, Venetian, and papal states of Europe

1595: Europeans form an anti-Ottoman alliance

1606: A peace treaty is signed between the Ottomans and Austria

1699: The European coalition defeats the Ottoman army; Treaty of Karlowitz is signed

1710: First Russo-Turkish War begins

1711: Treaty of Perth is signed after a Russian defeat

1768: Russo-Ottoman War begins

1774: Russians defeat the Ottomans; Treaty of Kuchuk-Kairnarji is signed

1798: Napoléon Bonaparte invades Egypt

1801: Ottoman and British forces combine to drive the French from Egypt

1805: Muhammad Ali becomes viceroy of Egypt

1838: Muhammad Ali declares Egyptian independence from Ottoman Empire

1839: Muhammad Ali defeats the Ottomans at the Battle of Nizip

1840: Britain negotiates the Treaty of London, making Muhammad Ali the ruler of Egypt and returning Syria to the Ottomans

1853: Crimean War begins

1856: Treaty of Paris is signed

1867: Bulgaria, Serbia, and Montenegro declare war on Ottoman Empire

1875: Ottoman Empire declares bankruptcy

1909: Abdülhamid II is removed from power

1911: Italy declares war against the Ottomans

1923: Treaty of Lausanne is signed, formally ending all hostilities; modern Turkey is founded

Soon Italy declared war against the Ottomans and invaded Libya in September 1911. This war resulted in the rapid decline of the Young Turk venture. Political troubles at home soon combined with a new threat from the Balkan states. Bulgaria, Serbia, and Montenegro formed an alliance and declared war against the Ottomans in early October 1912.

The Ottomans ended the hostilities with Italy on terms favorable to the Italians. Ottoman forces were thus free to deal with the Balkan threat without overstretching their limited resources. But the Balkan wars proved disastrous and virtually all the remaining Balkan territories were lost. Even Edirne, the former Ottoman capital, was

ceded to Bulgaria. However, the division of new territories that the Balkan states gained from the Ottomans led to another Balkan war, and gave the Ottomans an opportunity to recapture Eastern Thrace and Edirne.

Immediately after the first revolution in 1908, the Young Turks had desperately tried to obtain support from Britain and France, but in vain. The feeling of being let down by these powers consequently drew them to Germany. By then, Europe had split into two blocks: Germany and Austria-Hungary (the Central Powers) on one side, and Britain, France, and Russia (the Triple Entente) on the other. The Young Turks' friendship with Germany resulted in alliance with the Central Powers during World War I. Ottoman forces fought on many fronts and made a considerable contribution to the war effort.

The Ottoman success in holding back British and French forces at the Dardanelles contributed to the Russian Revolution, which led Russia to withdrawal from the war in 1917. During the war, the entente powers devised four secret agreements concerning the future of the Ottoman Empire. These were disclosed by the Russians after their withdrawal. In addition, to enlist Arab support during the war, Britain made various promises to Arab leaders, including guaranteeing Ottoman independence and recognizing the authority of the Arab caliphate. The Jewish people were also given assurances for the establishment of a national homeland in Palestine by the Balfour Declaration of 1917, an arrangement that conflicted with promises made to Arab leaders.

World War I ended with the victory of the Triple Entente powers, and the armistice was signed on November 11, 1918, with the Germans and on October 30, 1918, with the Ottomans.

THE END OF THE EMPIRE AND THE PARTITION OF ITS TERRITORIES

The aftermath of World War I fundamentally changed the political, cultural, and social order of the world. The empires of Austria-Hungary, Germany, the Ottomans, and Russia disappeared; new countries were formed and new international organizations were established.

The victorious powers saved the worst treatment for the Ottomans. Their lands were divided, with a small region in central and northern Anatolia left for the Turks. France, Italy, and Greece were given control of much of Anatolia. However, Turkish resistance led by Mustafa Kemal Paşa (Atatürk, 1881–1938) forced out the invaders. After the Turkish War of Independence, a new Treaty of Lausanne was signed in July 1923, which formally ended all hostilities and led to the foundation of modern Turkey.

Because Russian and American reluctance did not permit direct European colonial rule over the Middle East, Arab lands were parceled out as mandates under the League of Nations. Lebanon and Syria came under French mandate, while Iraq, Palestine, and Transjordan were given to the British. Egypt was left to British control, with Kuwait as a British protectorate. The North African countries of Algeria, Morocco, and Tunisia remained colonies of France, and Libya remained an Italian colony. The colonizing powers set up new boundaries, which generated territorial quarrels amongst the tribes and ethnic or religious groups. The Turks survived and managed to endure as the independent state of

Turkey, even while so many other regions became victims of European colonization.

SEE ALSO *Abdülhamid II; Mandate System; World War I, Middle East.*

BIBLIOGRAPHY

Faroqhi, Suraiya. *Approaching Ottoman History: An Introduction to the Sources.* Cambridge, U.K.: Cambridge University Press, 1999.

Fromkin, David. *A Peace to End All Peace: The Fall of the Ottoman Empire and the Creation of the Modern Middle East.* New York: Avon, 1989.

Goffman, Daniel. *The Ottoman Empire and Early Modern Europe.* Cambridge, U.K.: Cambridge University Press, 2002.

İhsanoğlu, Ekmeleddin, ed. *History of the Ottoman State, Society, & Civilisation.* Istanbul, Turkey: Ircica, 2002.

İnalcık, Halil, ed., with Donald Quataert. *An Economic and Social History of The Ottoman Empire, 1300–1914.* Cambridge, U.K.: Cambridge University Press, 1994.

Macfie, A. L. *The Eastern Question, 1774–1923.* London and New York: Longman, 1989. Rev. ed., 1996.

McCarthy, Justin. *The Ottoman Turks: An Introductory History to 1923.* London and New York: Longman, 1996.

Marriott, J.A.R. *The Eastern Question: An Historical Study of European Diplomacy.* Oxford, U.K.: The Clarendon Press, 1919.

Özcan, Azmi. *Pan-Islamism: Indian Muslims, the Ottomans, and Britain, 1877–1924.* Leiden Netherlands: Brill, 1997.

Yapp, Malcolm E. *The Making of the Modern Near East, 1792–1923.* London: Longman, 1987.

Azmi Özcan

EMPIRE, PORTUGUESE

The rise of the Portuguese empire during the sixteenth century still stands foremost in the national consciousness of today's Portuguese. The epic *The Lusíads* by Luis Vaz de Camões (1524–1580), a romanticized version of the first discoveries, is still very popular. This article discusses the political, military, and commercial driving forces behind the Portuguese expansion in the Atlantic, Africa, Asia, and Brazil, and the decline of the empire in Asia.

THE AFRICAN ADVENTURES

Portuguese expansion began in 1415 with the conquest of Ceuta (a city in Morocco) by King John I (1357–1433). His son, Prince Henry (1394–1460), sometimes erroneously called "the Navigator," inherited his father's rights to discover, privateer, and trade in the Atlantic Ocean and leased these privileges to his vassals. Some of them colonized the unpopulated islands of Madeira and the Azores

Demography of Brazil

Year	Portuguese	Indigenous slaves	African slaves
1550	2,000	4,000	Few
1583–1584	25,000	18,000	14,000
1600	30,000	60,000	60,000

Table 1 THE GALE GROUP.

in the North Atlantic. These islands became agricultural sources of sugar and wheat. Other Portuguese, driven by the desire to advance in the ranks of the nobility, as well as by their thirst for gold and the demand for slaves and pepper, accomplished the stepwise discovery of the West African coast.

After Henry's death, King Alphonso V (1432–1481) received papal confirmation of his rights of conquest and mission. He declared a royal monopoly on the trade in gold, pepper, precious stones, civet cats (for their musk), and ivory, but leased the slave trade to private contractors. Under King John II (1455–1495), Elmina (in Ghana) became a center for trade in gold and slaves. John also pushed Portuguese discoveries farther south along the African coast. In 1488 Bartolomeu Diaz (ca.

1450–1500) rounded the Cape of Good Hope and reached as far as present-day Mossel Bay, South Africa.

THE ASIAN EMPIRE

After the 1492 discovery by Christopher Columbus (1451–1506) of the West Indies, the two Iberian nations (Spain and Portugal) agreed in 1494 to divide the world in two halves. With the dividing line running through present-day Brazil (which at that time was still unknown to Europeans), the Portuguese crown would become suzerain over the waters and lands in the eastern hemisphere, the Spanish crown over the west.

King Manuel I of Portugal (1469–1521), in the belief that he was "chosen" to defeat Islam, undertook his imperialistic task with mystic zeal. In 1497 Vasco da Gama (ca. 1469–1524) was sent to discover the Indies and find spices and Christians. Setting out along a course that in the future would be followed by other European sailing traffic to India, and after various friendly and hostile encounters along the East African coast, da Gama arrived ten months later in Calicut on the southwest coast of India. His return voyage took almost a year.

The Portuguese navigator Pedro Álvarez Cabral (ca. 1467–1520), leaving Lisbon in 1500, intended to follow the same route, but when crossing the Atlantic, Cabral

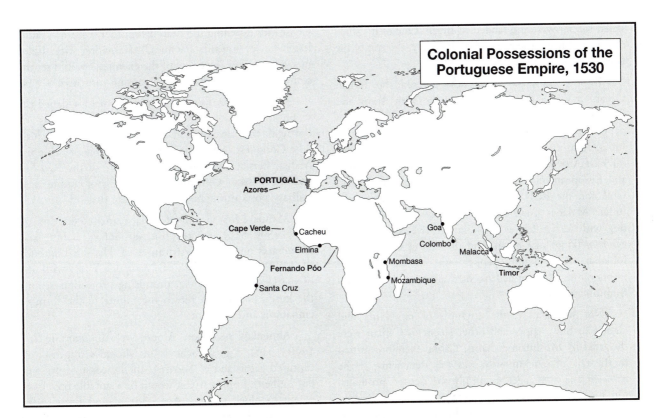

Colonial Possessions of the Portuguese Empire, 1530

MAP BY XNR PRODUCTIONS. THE GALE GROUP.

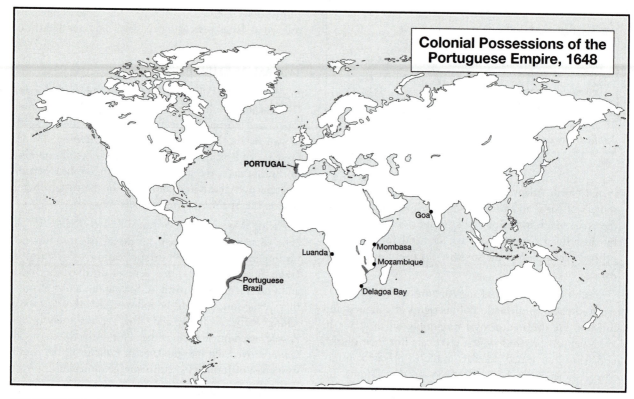

Colonial Possessions of the Portuguese Empire, 1648

MAP BY XNR PRODUCTIONS. THE GALE GROUP.

sailed too far west and landed in Brazil. One of his ships returned to bring the news of its discovery; the rest of the fleet continued to Calicut.

By the time the Portuguese entered the Indian Ocean, it was a thriving trading area, with Arabs and Gujaratis (from Northwest India) as the main carriers of pepper from the south and textiles from the north of India. Arab and Gujarati traders exchanged these goods for East African products, as well as horses, silver, gold, and European merchandise coming through the Persian Gulf and the Red Sea, or spices from Southeast Asia. India's Malabar Coast was divided into small principalities, with such rulers as the kolathiri of Cannanore, the *zamorin* (king) of Calicut, and the raja of Cochin. The Malabar trade, mainly pepper, was in the hands of immigrants: Mohammedans in Calicut and Jews and Brahmins in Cochin.

Not surprisingly, the attempts of da Gama and Cabral to buy pepper and other spices in Calicut were thwarted by Muslim merchants. Cabral therefore turned to the raja of Cochin, who was the archenemy of the *zamorin* and was eager to supply the desired products. On his second voyage, da Gama established a trading post in Cochin, but in Calicut he pursued a policy of intimidation, terrifying the other rulers of the Malabar

Coast into expelling the Arab colonists. Da Gama's ruthless behavior toward "enemies," alternating with diplomacy toward the "enemies of the enemies," would set the scene for further Portuguese expansion into Asia.

Upon da Gama's return, King Manuel I widened the scope of his policies, expanding his title—King of Portugal, the Algarve, and Lord of Guinea—to include "the Conquest, Navigation, and Commerce of Ethiopia, Arabia, Persia, and India." The closure of the Red Sea and the Persian Gulf and the opening of trading and military posts throughout Asia became first priority.

Manuel's first viceroy of India, Francisco de Almeida (ca. 1450–1510), erected forts at Sofala, Kilwa, and Mombassa on the East African coast. His son Lourenço (d. 1508) established the first Portuguese treaty with one of the kings of Sri Lanka, promising protection against the king's enemies in return for tribute in the form of cinnamon and elephants.

Almeida's successor, Afonso de Albuquerque (ca. 1460–1515), a great believer in Manuel's imperialism, captured the island of Socotra (off the coast of present-day Yemen), hoping that it would be a suitable base from which to block the Red Sea trade to and from India. However, Socotra was too far away to effectively control traffic through the Straits of Bab el Mandeb. Another

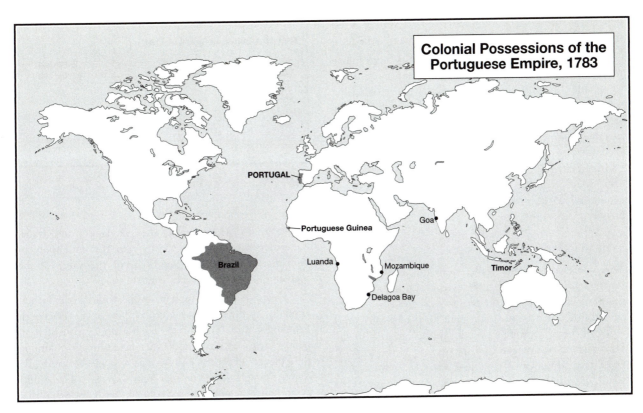

Colonial Possessions of the Portuguese Empire, 1783

MAP BY XNR PRODUCTIONS. THE GALE GROUP.

attempt in 1513 to close the Red Sea with an attack on Aden failed, and the flow of spices to Europe via this route did not stop until 1610, when the Dutch were able to undercut pepper prices in the Mediterranean.

In 1510 Afonso de Albuquerque captured Goa, a state on the west coast of India, which was to become the capital of the Portuguese State of India. In 1511 he took Malacca, the center of trade between South Asia, the Far East, and the Indonesian Archipelago. And in 1514 he managed to capture Hormuz, thereby gaining control over the traffic from the Persian Gulf. Thus, within fifteen years, a chain of military settlements was established that was expected to maintain control of sea traffic and to demand payment of license fees and excise duties.

However, after his death in 1515, Albuquerque was succeeded by Lopo Soares de Albergaria. Albergaria, who was in favor of free trade, set in motion the opening of the Asian seas to Portuguese private military and commercial initiatives, in total opposition to the centralism of Albuquerque.

The discovery in 1521 of the Philippines and the Moluccan spice islands by Ferdinand Magellan (ca 1470–1521), who sailed under the Spanish flag and made the awesome voyage through the straits that bear his name, caused the Portuguese to push further east and build a fort on Ternate, which was later relocated at Amboina

(Ambon). In 1529 the Holy Roman emperor, Charles V (1500–1558), sold his rights in the Moluccas to the Portuguese crown, and the demarcation line with the Spanish hemisphere on that side of the globe was established east of these islands. As a result, the Portuguese believed they had the right of access to the Philippines, China, and the western part of the Japanese island of Honshu. However, the Spaniards refused to leave the Philippines, and after 1571 Manila became their gateway for imports from China and Japan and for the export of South American silver to Asia.

In 1534 Diu and Bassein (both in Gujarat, northwestern India) were added to the official Portuguese Empire, and in 1543 the Indian provinces of Salcete and Bardez were added. However, Portuguese private interests went far beyond the reach of state officials. Although sea captains sometimes played the roles of diplomats and ambassadors between Goa and the indigenous rulers of the ports, they also sometimes assembled their own private armies to support their demand for trade or booty. Many Portuguese who had originally come as soldiers escaped from the control of the Portuguese state to become embedded in the local economies and trading networks of the Coromandel Coast, the Bay of Bengal, the Indonesian Archipelago, and the Far East. Futhermore, although their mission was financially dependent on Goa, Portuguese religious orders acted independently and spread their nets widely all over Asia.

In 1543 the Portuguese made their first appearance in Japan, and their Jesuit mission became particularly successful. In 1549 the Ming imperial court of China prohibited the Chinese from trading overseas and the Japanese from entering China. This gave Portuguese merchants the chance, with the Jesuits in Japan as intermediaries, to establish a monopoly in the exchange of Chinese silk, gold, and porcelain for Japanese silver. After 1557 Macao (on the southern coast of China) became a center of Portuguese private trade and missionary activity.

THE ATLANTIC BASIN

The contrast between Brazil and the countries the Portuguese encountered in Asia could not have been sharper. The land had no proprietors, money did not exist, birds' feathers were the main form of wealth, and many of the tribes were cannibals. In the early 1530s the Portuguese crown began to dispense land in the form of hereditary captaincies to people it wanted to reward. As a result, Brazil became a settlers' colony, with plenty of room for private enterprise, including the hunting of Brazilian Indians to work as slaves on the plantations. In addition, the Catholic Church found a wide-open field for missionary activities.

In 1533 large-scale sugar cultivation was introduced in Brazil. The Indian slaves who performed the heavy work were in the course of time replaced by African slaves shipped from the coasts of Guinea, Congo, and Angola. In Congo, conversion of the local king and his sons to Christianity was a convenient inroad into the slave trade. Business in Angola was contracted out to private entrepreneurs. As a result, freight traffic on the Atlantic became triangular: from Lisbon to Congo or Angola with brassware and textiles that had been bought in Antwerp, from there to Brazil with slaves, and from Brazil back to Lisbon with sugar.

Until the discovery of gold in the 1690s the further development of Brazil remained closely connected to the production of sugar, which in turn was dependent on the availability of black labor. By the end of the sixteenth century, Brazil was replacing Madeira in the sugar market. In 1600 there were about thirty thousand Portuguese living in Brazil; by 1612 this number had grown to fifty thousand. In contrast, from Hormuz to Macao, there were not more than sixteen thousand people who considered themselves Portuguese at that time.

THE ASIAN TRADE

The king of Portugal controlled the building and equipage of ships for the *Carreira da India* (the Portuguese

Growth of sugar industry in Brazil

Year	Number of mills	Production (metric tons)
1570	60	2,000
1580–1583	118	5,250
1590	N/A	7,540
1600	200	9,000
1628	235	18,000
1645	300	21,000

Table 2 THE GALE GROUP.

passage to India), as well as their navigation and trade, but others were allowed to share in this monopoly in exchange for a *quinto* (one-fifth) of the value of the merchandise brought back to Portugal.

Fleets of carracks and caravels would leave Lisbon annually by the end of March, arriving in Goa between September and November. Their cargoes consisted of people, arms, artillery, and other necessities to maintain the Portuguese presence in Asia, as well as silver and gold to buy merchandise for the return voyage. The return cargoes included pepper and other spices, cotton and silk, indigo, opium, camphor, furniture, ivory, gold jewelry, precious stones, Bahrain pearls, Persian silk and carpets, and porcelain and other Chinese products. Most of these goods were brought to Goa via established indigenous trading systems, which included the use of *cáfilas*, large fleets of small indigenous ships that had previously navigated along the west coast of India, but now sailed under the protection of the Portuguese maritime fleet after payment of a license fee (*cartaz*).

The crown organized "royal voyages" to areas where the Portuguese State of India had little or no control over local traffic. Most famous was the annual Great Voyage from Goa to Japan and back, with stops in Malacca (Melaka) and Macao. Other royal voyages traveled from Goa, Diu, and Cochin toward Coromandel, Bengal, Arakan, Pegu, the Malay Peninsula, Thailand, and the Indonesian Archipelago.

Because of the monsoon, the return vessels of the Carreira da India had to leave Goa before mid-January. The time available for carrying out repairs and loading cargoes was therefore relatively short, and late departures, bad maintenance, and overloading caused many ships to wreck during the return voyage, making the Carreira a high-risk business.

The Crown's Withdrawal. The participation of the Portuguese crown in Asian trade diminished during the 1570s. Not only were Portugal's royal voyages to Asia now leased in the form of concessions, but beginning in 1575 the Carreira da India underwent significant changes as German and Italian merchants were awarded contracts for its financing, operation, and pepper sales.

During the mid-1590s Portuguese New Christian merchants (descendants of Jews who by the end of the fifteenth century had been converted to Christianity) replaced the German and Italian merchants. Private merchandise, in particular cotton and silk, represented the major share of the value of their cargoes. In 1629 these financiers of the Carreira were allowed to leave Portugal to become moneylenders to the Spanish crown.

An attempt was made to establish a Portuguese East India company, but the project was abandoned in 1633. By that time the shipping volume leaving Lisbon was less than half of what it had been earlier.

Portuguese Decline in Asia. The decline of the Portuguese Empire in Asia is often attributed to corruption by Portuguese officials, the preference for South America within the Spanish House of Habsburg that ruled Portugal from 1580 to 1640, or simply Dutch and English aggression. However, from the early 1620s the Portuguese State of India lost control of events mainly because of major indigenous political changes in Asia, such as the expansionist wars of Shah Abbas (1571–1629) of Persia (Iran) and of the Mughals in India, as well as the formation of a centralized state in Japan, which the English and the Dutch took advantage of.

Low supplies of pepper and spices to Europe during the 1590s incited both the English and the Dutch to go and buy it for themselves. Besides trade, the Dutch United East India Company, established in 1602, aimed to thwart the Portuguese and Spanish, both of whom were under the reign of Philip II (1527–1598), the arch-enemy of the Dutch. As a result, Dutch shareholders had to wait until the early 1630s before their investments were fully honored.

In 1605 the Dutch United East India Company occupied the Portuguese fort at Amboina, and the Spanish took over the remaining Portuguese positions in the Moluccas. Portuguese merchants fled to Makassar (a port on Sulawesi in present-day Indonesia), where they continued their spice trade. Several Dutch attempts to conquer Malacca failed, and Dutch privateering in the South China Sea and blockades of Goa met with scant success.

From the beginning of the seventeenth century, political changes in India brought new rulers who abolished existing contracts with the Portuguese and were looking for trade with European newcomers. For example, in Kanara on the southwest coast of India, where political and territorial divisions had enabled the Portuguese to obtain the lowest prices for rice, wood, and pepper, the Nayaks of Ikkeri gradually expanded their territory and absorbed the smaller principalities. Their next step was to contact the English for the sale of pepper, and to play them off against the Portuguese.

The textile and indigo trade of Gujarat was the backbone of the Portuguese monopolistic *cartaz* system. In 1612, however, the Mughal emperor Jahangir (1569–1627), the successor of the conqueror Akbar (1542–1605), allowed the English to establish a trading post in Surat, and in 1620 a similar concession was made to the Dutch. Further Mughal expansion led in 1632 to the conquest of Ahmadnagar, which brought the Portuguese forts at Chaul, Bassein, and Daman under Mughal protection. In 1637 the English and the Dutch set up factories in the neighboring state of Bijapur. However, the most serious blow to the Portuguese State of India, both in terms of finances and prestige, was the conquest in 1622 of Hormuz by Shah Abbas of Persia, who thereafter allowed English and Dutch companies to establish trading posts in Bandar 'Abbas, the port of Isfahan (in present-day Iran).

During the second decade of the 1600s, the increasing number of Christians in Japan (some 222,000 in 1609) came to be seen as a political threat for the ruling class. Harsh persecution of Christians and the expulsion of Portuguese missionaries were followed by a ban on both Christianity and Portuguese ships in Japan. The Japanese authorities allowed the Dutch to stay, however. The Dutch factory on the Japanese island of Deshima remained Japan's only window to the Western world until well into the nineteenth century.

In 1636 the Dutch initiated a strategic siege of Malacca, along with seasonal blockades of Goa. Simultaneously supporting the Sri Lankan king of Kandy against the Portuguese, in 1640 the Dutch traders obtained access to the cinnamon trade in Sri Lanka. The Portuguese surrendered Malacca in 1641.

In China, the Manchu emperor's entry into the palace of Beijing in 1644 marked the beginning of the Ching dynasty. Under the Ching, Canton (now known as Guangzhou) became a free harbor for foreign trading companies, although Macao remained an important point of departure for Portuguese merchant fleets.

Another remainder of the Portuguese State of India was East Timor, which, after being ruled by a Dutch renegade and his descendants, was left in Portuguese hands in 1694.

The restoration of the Portuguese crown under the Bragança (Braganza) family in 1640 brought peace in Europe. However, the Anglo-Dutch conflicts of the 1650s and the rumor that the Portuguese might allow the English India Company free access to Portuguese possessions in Asia provoked the Dutch to capture the Portuguese settlements in southern India and Sri Lanka.

Elmina Castle. *Built in the late fifteenth century by the Portuguese, Elmina Castle in present-day Ghana was one of a string of Portuguese outposts on the west coast of Africa.* © MICHAEL DWYER/ALAMY. REPRODUCED BY PERMISSION.

Portuguese civilian communities in such places as Goa, Macao, and East Timor survived, under the Portuguese State of India, for another three hundred years.

VICTORY AROUND THE ATLANTIC

In 1621 the Dutch established the Dutch West India Company, which aimed to break the Iberian monopoly of colonization and trade in the New World and along the West African coast. In 1633 the Dutch conquered Pernambuco in northeastern Brazil, but an attempt to occupy Bahia failed. In 1637 Governor Johan Maurits van Nassau-Siegen (1604–1679) took control of the Portuguese city of Elmina in Ghana, a conquest followed in 1642 by the seizure of Luanda in Angola and the island of São Tomé.

After the Portuguese restoration of 1640, however, the Dutch became more interested in trading with Portugal than in expanding their Brazilian colony. The number of Dutch troops in Brazil was reduced, and following a revolt of the Brazilian population the Dutch were only able to maintain control over Recife and a few

other sites in Brazil. In 1648 the Portuguese recaptured São Tomé and Luanda, and in 1654 all Dutch troops in Brazil were withdrawn. In the treaty of 1661 the Dutch were indemnified for their loss of Brazil and received the same trading privileges as the English.

SEE ALSO *Empire in the Americas, Portuguese; Portugal's African Colonies.*

BIBLIOGRAPHY

Blussé, Leonard. "No Boats to China: The Dutch East India Company and the Changing Pattern of the China Sea Trade, 1635–1690." *Modern Asian Studies* 30 (1996): 51–76.

Boxer, Charles R. *The Portuguese Seaborne Empire, 1415-1825.* London: Hutchison Co., 1969.

Boyajian, James C. *Portuguese Trade in Asia Under the Habsburgs, 1580–1640.* London: John Hopkins University Press, 1993.

Camões, Luis Vaz de. *The Lusíads.* Translated by Landeg White. New York: Oxford University Press, 1997.

Chaudhuri, K. N. *Trade and Civilisation in the Indian Ocean: An Economic History from the Rise of Islam to 1750.* Cambridge, U.K.: Cambridge University Press, 1999.

Diffie, Bailey W., and George D. Winius. *Foundations of the Portuguese Empire, 1415–1580*. Minneapolis: University of Minnesota Press, 1977.

Engerman, Stanley L., and João César das Neves. "The Bricks of an Empire 1415–1999: 585 Years of Portuguese Emigration." In *The Journal of European Economic History*, Vol. 26. Rome: Banca di Roma Quadrimestrale, 1997.

Godinho, Vitórino Magalhães. "Portugal and Her Empire." In *The New Cambridge Modern History*, Vol. V. Cambridge, U.K.: Cambridge University Press, 1961.

Godinho, Vitórino Magalhães. *Os descobrimentos e a economia mundial*, Vol. IV. Lisbon: Editorial Presença, 1991.

Kato, Eiichi. "Unification and Adaptation: The Early Shogunate and Dutch Trade Policies." In *Companies and Trade: Essays on Overseas Trading Companies During the Ancien Régime*, edited by Leonard Blussé and Femme Gaastra. Leiden, Netherlands: Leiden University Press, 1981.

Mauro, Frédéric. *Le Portugal, le Brésil et l'Atlantique au XVIIe Siècle (1570-1670) Étude Économique*. Paris: Fondation Calouste Gulbenkian, 1983.

Newitt, Malyn. *A History of Portuguese Expansion 1400-1668*. Abingdon, U.K.: Routledge, 2005.

Russell-Wood, A. J. R. *The Portuguese Empire, 1415–1808: A World on the Move*. London: John Hopkins University Press, 1998.

Scammel, G. V. *The First Imperial Age: European Overseas Expansion, c. 1400–1715*. New York: Routledge, 1989.

Subrahmanyam, Sanjay. *The Portuguese Empire in Asia, 1500–1700: A Political and Economic History*. New York: Longman, 1993.

Subrahmanyam, Sanjay. *The Career and Legend of Vasco da Gama*. Cambridge, U.K.: Cambridge University Press, 1997.

Toby, Ronald P. *State and Diplomacy in Early Modern Japan: Asia in the Development of the Tokugawa Bakufu*. Princeton, NJ: Princeton University Press, 1984.

van Veen, Ernst. *Decay or Defeat? An Inquiry into the Portuguese Decline in Asia, 1580–1645*. Leiden, Netherlands: Research School of Asian, African, and Amerindian Studies, Leiden University, 2000.

Ernst van Veen

EMPIRE, RUSSIAN AND THE MIDDLE EAST

The beginning of imperialism and colonialism in western European nations has often been described as a time when rising national powers began to journey to distant lands in search of new sources of trade and capital beyond their immediate grasp. The ultimate goal, implicitly or explicitly, was to build closer ties to the Far East, with its vast markets and valuable products. This was not how Russia began its own road to empire. Russia's move in this direction began with its expansion into the steppe south of its original domains: a frontier unlike those faced by other Europeans. Given Russia's traditional lack of borders and low levels of social cohesion, the steppe presented a robust challenge to Russian sedentary cultural patterns, which developed from an economic system founded upon peasant, communal village agriculture. Because the Russians began their encounters with the Middle East in the steppe, this region linked them to the Middle East in many ways and determined how they later treated it.

Russia's expansion into the steppe occurred in two distinct phases. Its patterns of territorial expansion in an initial period between the fifteenth and seventeenth centuries more closely resembled patterns of nation building in medieval Europe than the growth of world empires during the early modern era. By the eighteenth century, Russians had shifted their approach to adopting the imperialist strategies of their European rivals to extend direct colonial control over vast areas to their south and east.

While much of the commercial, social, and political impetus of this later rise to empire on Russia's part can be observed clearly in its drive eastward across Central Asia toward the Pacific Ocean, Russian dreams of establishing a presence in the Middle East were first guided by ideological and only later by pragmatic concerns. Its desire to serve as the main guardian of Orthodox Christian tradition shaped how it became involved in the Middle East, particularly after the Ottoman conquest of Constantinople in 1453. To a greater or lesser degree, the dream of retaking Constantinople always lingered in the minds of various tsars. In a more concrete fashion, Russo-Turkish conflicts that ensued over the following four centuries continued to be motivated by Russia's attempt to protect and establish its own authority over Orthodox Christians under Ottoman rule. This took place in parallel with longstanding Russian efforts to convert Muslims and others in Central Asia to Christianity as they were brought under the tsar's authority: a project pursued for centuries with varying levels of enthusiasm by different rulers.

After the eighteenth century, the ideological and spiritual goals of protecting Orthodox Christians and their holy sites as well as attracting converts to the faith were augmented and overshadowed by Russia's growing strategic and geopolitical ambition to be recognized as a great power. To further both their strategic and ideological goals, the Russians nurtured the nationalist movements of fellow Orthodox Christians in the Balkans through Pan-Slavism. In addition, they saw the Middle East as an arena in which to assert the growing naval and military power that they had begun to develop following the reforms of Peter I ("The Great") (r. 1682–1725). The Russians' greater global focus during this period, in turn, caused western European powers to react by aiding and propping up the Ottomans, particularly during the nineteenth century, in order to prevent the Russians from acquiring too much power in Eurasia. Thus, Russian imperial agendas in the Middle East during the nineteenth century came to be defined by a complex mixture of different impulses. Russia sought to expand its commercial and geopolitical reach to equal or surpass the imperial projects of other European powers of that time, but the pursuit of this goal continued to be shaped by the enduring spiritual and ideological components of how Russia defined itself as a nation. Russia's view of its mission as a successor to the Byzantine Empire always had a profound influence on how it perceived its true role in the world, particularly in the biblical lands of the Middle East. Until the Bolshevik Revolution and the imposition of an entirely new governing paradigm, it was a thread that linked the earliest and latest involvement of Russia with the Middle East during the tsarist era.

THE BEGINNING OF RUSSIAN EXPANSION EAST AND SOUTH, 1223–1450

Russia's existence as an independent nation arose out of the confederation of various Slavic principalities dominated by merchant oligarchies that flourished in Kiev, Novgorod, and Moscow beginning in the tenth century. These trading principalities were always linked on trade routes to more powerful states farther east and south such as the Khazars in Central Asia and the Byzantine Empire with its capital in Constantinople, so the eastward focus of their merchants and traders coincided with their emergence as independent political entities. For a while, they came together into a loosely unified polity known as the *Rus*, dominated first by Kiev and later by Novgorod and Moscow, but all of these cities perceived trade east and south as an important component of their prosperity.

By the early thirteenth century, these principalities had been broken up into warring factions, which made them easy prey for the Mongol armies rapidly expanding and conquering westward from Central Asia. The Mongols exploited the Russians' internal divisions and were soon able to conquer them. Many component city-states of the *Rus* were made vassals of the Mongol khanate of the Golden Horde, and Muscovy clearly began to emerge as a leading one in the early fifteenth century with the decline of Golden Horde power. Russia fairly quickly developed as a nation from being a power subject to Muslim overlords, to being their equals, to ruling them as it grew into an empire that expanded continually eastward. Although historians have spent decades trying to get beyond the concept that Russia became a nation partly because it "threw off the Tatar yoke," this stereotypical view remained an important component of how

contemporary Russians perceived their own empire's development, regardless of how inaccurate it is.

EXPANSION TO THE SOUTH AS NATION-BUILDING: RUSSIA AND THE MIDDLE EAST, 1450–1696

The first phase of Russia's relations with the Middle East in this period began with the attempts of Ivan III ("The Great") (r. 1462–1505) to secure Russia's status as a separate, autonomous nation. Ivan engaged in complex diplomacy with various Muslim rulers in the steppe to consolidate his power, entering into alliances in the 1480s with the Crimean khan Mengli Giray, the khan of Kazan, and the Nogais against their nominal overlords: the khans of the Golden Horde. In this earliest phase, as Russia behaved like the assertive vassal of a master whose control was waning, it negotiated small-scale agreements with rivals of similar stature and military power to bolster its standing in internecine disputes, but without radically altering the status quo.

This state of affairs defined a status quo for a considerable period of time until Ivan IV ("The Terrible") (r. 1533–1584) commenced a program of extending Russian control much farther south than where it had previously reached. He conquered Kazan in 1552 and established Russian control over the Volga region, opening large parts of the steppe to Russian colonization and settlement. This influx of Russian and other settlers and colonists pushed the Crimean khans closer to the Ottomans, whose vassals they had formally become in the late fifteenth century.

After Ivan's demise, his forceful advance of Russian power in the south was undercut by a prolonged series of internal struggles and succession crises in the early seventeenth century, mitigated only partially by the establishment of the Romanov dynasty on the throne. Throughout this period, the Russians made tentative forays into the Crimea but were rebuffed by the Ottomans and did not pursue these campaigns due to an awareness of their own military weakness. Between 1637 and 1642, a group of Don Cossacks held the Ottoman fortress of Azov and only relinquished it after Tsar Mikhail Romanov persuaded them to surrender, following an Ottoman threat to kill their Orthodox subjects as retribution. At this time, in spite of such Russian advances and successes, the Ottomans still held the advantage in the evolving balance of power.

After a series of three attacks on the Crimea, in 1687, 1689, and 1695, Peter I, who took the throne in earnest in 1689, assembled a naval force that enabled him to defeat the Ottomans in 1696 fairly decisively and to secure Azov. This success helped launch Peter's modernization program and it changed how Russia viewed the Middle East.

THE MIDDLE EAST AND RUSSIAN TERRITORIAL EXPANSION, 1696–1856

Despite this first Russian success at Azov, the Ottomans succeeded in retaking it a few years later—a situation which was then reversed permanently by the Russians in the late 1730s. In 1721 Peter I had himself formally proclaimed "Emperor of All Russias." This event coincided with a new era in Russian relations with the Middle East, in which the region became an increasingly attractive imperial prize to be seized ("imperial" because an emperor now ruled Russia). The first evidence of change occurred in the early 1720s, when Russia seized control of the northern half of the west coast of the Caspian Sea down into Azerbaijan. This foray was made possible by the collapse of the ruling Safavid dynasty of Iran after their Afghan subjects invaded that country. Although the Russians were forced only a few years later to relinquish much of what they had conquered, this incursion helped set the Russian agenda for further territorial acquisition, which became more reminiscent of the way in which other European powers were acquiring colonies at this time.

In the wake of Peter's modernization and expansion programs, the idea became more widespread that Russia should extend its territorial control southward and consolidate its rule over the Black Sea to provide an appropriate outlet for its growing military power and maritime commercial needs. At a more idealized level, the pressure to establish this control caused certain Russian nobles to begin openly advocating the liberation of Constantinople from the Ottomans as well. During the 1780s, Catherine the Great's favorite courtier, Prince Grigorii Potemkin, repeatedly spoke of making it the new Russian capital.

A series of Russian-Ottoman military conflicts in the eighteenth century marked successive phases of Russia's project to secure control over the northern Black Sea region. This was reflected in documents such as the 1774 Ottoman-Russian treaty of Küçük Kaynarca, in which the Ottoman sultan was allowed to continue to claim the title of "caliph" over the Crimean Muslims only as a face-saving gesture, as he had lost political control of that region. The spiritual allegiance of the Crimeans to the sultan was decoupled from the political allegiance owed to the tsar in a way that paralleled the expansion of the tsar's rights to oversee the affairs of the sultan's Orthodox subjects. Various clauses in this treaty allowed Russia to build a church in Istanbul and have jurisdiction over it as well as the right to "make representations" to the Ottoman sultan, presumably on behalf of his Orthodox subjects, although this was not specified in the document. Regardless of the details of the

agreement, Russia used it over the next few decades to assert its right to protect all Orthodox Christians under Ottoman rule.

The end of the eighteenth century also witnessed continual Russian attempts to secure control over lands east and west of the Black Sea through the recruiting of local Orthodox Christian rulers to become either implicitly or explicitly their vassals. In Bessarabia and the Danubian Principalities in the Balkans, as well as in Georgia and Armenia in the Caucasus in the early nineteenth century, this strategy was used quite effectively to extend the range of Russian power and influence, at the same time that the Russians were achieving success more and more frequently in combat against the Ottomans.

Russia and the Ottoman Empire were also both profoundly affected by the increasingly global rivalries of the major European powers at this time. Russia suffered the great physical calamity of Napoleon's invasion, while the psychological shock of his brief but momentous occupation of Egypt (1798–1801), swiftly followed by the rising influence of European capitalism on Middle Eastern economies, had a substantial impact on the Ottoman Empire. During the rise of European manufacturing in the Industrial Revolution, the Ottomans were bound by the constraints of various capitulations agreements, which enabled an influx of European goods to dominate their markets in ways that more and more favored European economies instead of their own. Both the Russians and the Ottomans were thrust into reactive modes by the dramatic events that followed on the French Revolution during the first three decades of the nineteenth century. However, the Russians, then ruled by Tsar Nicholas I, were also able to capitalize on Ottoman insecurities, and thus to soften their previously confrontational stance toward the Ottomans. By the 1820s the Ottoman Empire appeared to Russia as preferable to many of its alternatives, despite ostensible Russian support for anti-Ottoman liberation movements led by their Orthodox brethren, such as the Greek War of Independence.

One alternative to Ottoman power that the Russians helped check, for example, was Muhammad Ali, the ostensible Ottoman governor of Egypt who by the early 1830s threatened to displace the Ottomans altogether. This prompted the Russians, in an uncommon gesture, to send troops to help the Ottomans defend themselves against him. As a result of this intervention and the preoccupation of the major European powers with the Belgian and French revolutions of 1830, the Ottomans and Russians signed the Treaty of Hünkar İskelesi in 1833 as a military alliance, to which the main contribution by the Ottomans was their agreement to keep the Bosphorus and Dardanelles demilitarized. The British and French were able to soon have this replaced by the 1841 London Straits Convention, which satisfied the Russians but brought the other Great Powers into this diplomatic process more closely.

Farther east, Russia had taken the opportunity afforded by the rise of the new Qajar dynasty in Iran (which came to power at the end of the eighteenth century) to secure control over Georgia, Armenia, and Azerbaijan. This control was formally ceded to Russia by the 1813 Gulistan Treaty with Iran, which also gave Russian merchants freer access to Iranian markets than they had ever previously enjoyed, and thus marked the beginning of the steady growth of European commercial activity in Iran throughout the nineteenth century. Although the Iranians rose up against the Russians in the 1820s under Abbas Mirza, they were again defeated and made to sign the 1828 Turkmanchai Treaty in which they were forced to offer Russia even more concessions than in the previous agreement.

Although these treaties enabled Russia to secure formal political control over the Caucasus region, this did not mean the end of local resistance to their assumption of power. For almost three decades from the 1820s until the late 1850s, Russian authority there was stymied by an extended guerilla war in Chechnya and the mountainous region of Daghestan in the northern Caucasus. It was conducted by a coalition of various mountain tribesmen united under Imam Shamil, who led them in numerous campaigns there, considered stages in a religious struggle to establish Sharia (Islamic Holy Law) in areas that had been freed from Russian control.

Through connections across the Caspian and along the major inland trade routes, though, Russia was able to establish a growing presence in Iran after 1828, in particular through its connections with Iranian Armenians: a minority community that had functioned as an important conduit of trade and influence between Russia and Iran for many centuries. In the Ottoman Empire, the role of Russia as the ultimate protector of Orthodox Christians, formally established in 1774 according to the Treaty of Küçük Kaynarca, intensified its growing rivalry with France, itself long considered the protector of all Catholics in Ottoman lands. This competition, combined with mishandled great-power diplomacy and the sudden death in 1855 of Tsar Nicholas I, who had pursued a more conciliatory policy toward the Ottomans, became a major factor in precipitating the Crimean War.

From one perspective, the Crimean War seems to have arisen due to an unfortunate coincidence of diplomatic and political miscalculations, but it was also brought on by more elemental internal conflicts in Russia itself. The nation was divided by different perceptions of the revolutions of 1830 and 1848, in France and

Europe respectively: For some, they were inspiring and exciting, for others, terrifying and chaotic. It also vacillated in its attitude toward the Ottomans; on the one hand, they were longstanding adversaries, ultimately to be removed from their illegitimate occupation of the Holy Places of Orthodox Christendom; on the other hand, they seemed far preferable to so many other possible rulers of the Middle East. From the Ottoman perspective, France's attempt to leverage its status in the Middle East as the main guardian of Catholic interests in their lands to promote its own global standing had increased suspicions, which paradoxically were not alleviated when France and Britain sided with the Ottomans in the Crimea against Russia.

In military and political terms, the British and the French made the fateful choice to come to the aid of the Ottomans at this time as their global strategy began to include the containment of Russian ambitions as an important goal. The 1856 Treaty of Paris that ended the Crimean War also formally ended the Russians' ability to claim even an implicit status as sole protectors of the Ottoman Orthodox population, because its text explicitly placed this population under the care of a consortium of European powers. The agreement also set out to ease tensions on the Black Sea, by calling for its complete demilitarization. Russian attitudes about their empire's presence and expansion in the Middle East continued to be defined by their longstanding ideological and religious views, though, as much as by commercial, geopolitical, and military considerations. As Russia's traditional role in the Ottoman Empire shifted, a new ideological force in Russia, Pan-Slavism, which became popular in the early 1870s, began to have an impact on its Ottoman policy. With regard to Russia itself, Pan-Slavism promoted a return to traditional values in contrast to the earlier modernizing reform movements of the mid-nineteenth century; at the same time, it caused the growth of popular Russian sentiment in favor of liberating "Slavic brothers" from their Ottoman rulers. This sentiment fueled a nationalist fervor that was a potent force in causing the Russo-Turkish War of 1877. This war, which had also been brought on by a constitutional crisis that had set the Ottoman sultan at odds with his newly created parliament, was only resolved at the 1878 Congress of Berlin. There, a Balkan map was drawn up that froze battle lines for a few decades, during which time tensions continuously rose behind artificially constructed barriers in Macedonia, Albania, and Bosnia-Herzegovina. From the Ottoman perspective, the losses imposed by the Congress of Berlin were devastating in terms of territory and people: Roughly a third of the Empire's territory and a fifth of its population were lost, and a terrible refugee problem ensued.

RUSSIAN AND THE MIDDLE EAST EMPIRE, KEY DATES

1200s: Mongol armies conquer the loose confederation of Slavic principalities led by the ruling-class merchants of Kiev, Novgorod, and Moscow

1480s: Ivan III brokers agreements with Muslim rulers in the steppe, hastening the decline of their common ruler, the khans of the Golden Horde

1552: Ivan IV overruns Kazan, opening the Volga region to Russian colonization

1696: Peter I defeats Ottoman forces at the fortress of Azov, expanding Russia's empire to the south

1720s: Russia continues to extend southward, gaining control of the Caspian Sea's northwest coast, though loses the territory two years later

1774: The Ottoman-Russian Treaty of Küçük Kaynarca is signed, giving Russia political control of the Crimea, and introduces Russia's claim to be the protector of all Orthodox Christians in the Ottoman Empire

Late 1700s: Russia tries to consolidate power in the Black Sea region by convincing fellow Orthodox Christian rulers to fall under the Russian Empire

1813: Iran and Russia enter the Treaty of Gulistan, giving Russia control of Georgia, Armenia, and Azerbaijan, and opening up Iran to Russian influence

1833: Russia and the Ottomans reach a military alliance by signing the Treaty of Hünkar İskelesi

1848: In Russian-controlled Azerbaijan, the first modern oil well was drilled, attracting foreign investment in the region

1853: The Crimean War begins with the Ottoman Empire declaring war on Russia. France and Great Britain side with the Ottomans, hoping to gain influence in the region and balance Russia's growing power

1856: The Treaty of Paris ends the Crimean War

1877: The Russo-Turkish War begins, inspired by Pan-Slavic ideas, with Russia looking to free fellow Slavs from Ottoman rule

1878: The Congress of Berlin settles the Russo-Turkish War, with the Ottoman Empire shrinking by one-third and new boundaries set in the Balkans, creating the states of Macedonia, Albania, and Bosnia-Herzegovina

1914: The assassination of Franz Ferdinand, Archduke of Austria, leads to the outbreak of World War I, with Russia joining sides with French and British forces against Germany, Austria-Hungary, Italy, and the Ottoman Empire

1917: The Bolshevik Revolution ends the Russian Empire

Farther east, Russia and Britain engaged in proxy struggles in Afghanistan to define the frontiers of their vast imperial projects. This finally settled down with the imposition of stable rule in Afghanistan under Amir Abd al-Rahman and the establishment in the 1890s of the Durand Line, which secured the westernmost frontiers of British India and established Afghanistan as a buffer state between Russia and the subcontinent. In the Caucasus meanwhile, the stabilization of Russian control over the region following the Crimean War also created an important conduit for modernization in the Middle East. Tiflis, the capital of Georgia and the center of Russian administration in the Caucasus, became an outpost of European culture and intellectual life there. Despite strict tsarist censorship, Persian and Turkish books and newspapers printed there became widely circulated in Iran and the Ottoman Empire.

More importantly, Azerbaijan under Russian control became one of the main sites of the birth of the modern petroleum industry. The first modern oil well was drilled near Baku in 1848 and the first refinery constructed there in 1859. When private companies were allowed to participate in its oil business in 1872, Baku rapidly grew from a provincial outpost into a wealthy and sophisticated city. European investors, including the Nobel brothers and the Rothschilds, entered the market. By the end of the nineteenth century, Azerbaijan was producing more than half of the world's oil supply. It became the site of labor troubles in December 1904, when a general strike among the oil workers there broke out, led by the young Bolshevik Georgian leader Joseph Stalin. Among Russian dissidents, this uprising helped create the revolutionary atmosphere that led to the St. Petersburg riots and massacre of "Bloody Sunday" in January 1905.

Although Russians always dominated business and government in the Caucasus during the late 1800s, some Azerbaijanis and Armenians became important leaders in various aspects of industrial production there, such as transporting oil on the Caspian Sea. Young intellectuals in the region were influenced by developments in Russia and created political parties that in turn had influence among their Iranian and Ottoman counterparts, helping to inspire the Iranian Constitutional Revolution in 1906 as well as the 1908 Young Turk Revolution in the Ottoman Empire. Following the uprisings of 1904–1905, the Russian viceroy of the Caucasus, Count Vorontsov-Dashkov, forcefully suppressed political dissent, but a small cohort of revolutionary activists continued to engage in political activity there and preserved connections with their comrades in the Middle East during the period leading up to World War I.

This era also saw the development of robust mercantile and intellectual connections between Russian-controlled Muslim areas of Central Asia and Iran and the Ottoman Empire. Because of improvements in transportation and communication, substantially larger numbers of *hajj* pilgrims from these Russian-ruled areas were traveling through the Ottoman Empire and connecting their own Muslim cultures with the larger Muslim trends in the outside world.

The tenuous peace in the Balkans that had been created by the Congress of Berlin began to unravel in the beginning of the twentieth century in various little wars. These small conflicts produced ethnic tensions that led up to Franz Ferdinand's assassination, the spark credited with setting off World War I in June 1914. This war, which caused the end of the Russian Empire following the Bolshevik Revolution of 1917, completely redefined Russia's relations with the Middle East. Communist Russia's ostensible goal now became the "liberation of the working class." After a short hiatus, however, longstanding imperial goals of consolidating and sustaining control of colonial populations reappeared. This led to the creation of a number of ethnically Muslim "Soviet Socialist Republics," which ostensibly functioned as autonomous constituent units of the larger Soviet Union, but were under the firm control of the central Soviet state and supported its political and social agendas.

CONCLUSIONS

It would be accurate to observe that Russia did finally begin to act like an imperial power to some extent in the Middle East, but only considerably after other European powers had done so and only in certain ways. Along its southern frontier, the area where its territorial expansion required the most military activity, its conquests were not regarded as colonizing enterprises until centuries after they had begun, with the result that the Russia colonial impact in places like Crimea has only been felt strongly during the past century and a half.

The Middle East proper remained only an elusive goal of conquest for Russia and served as more of an emotional rallying point in its role as the original home of

Christianity and the site of Constantinople. This emotional appeal began with Russia's attempt to assert its status as the main guardian of Eastern Orthodoxy, but evolved to include Pan-Slavism as Russians supported the nationalist dreams of Slavic populations under Ottoman rule. The Russian presence in the Middle East never developed, though, as European merchant interests had evolved there, primarily as a means to secure economic dominance. Although the Russians constantly traded with the Middle East, their relations with it were never defined by economic interests to the extent that those of other European powers were during the nineteenth and twentieth centuries.

SEE ALSO *Anglo-Russian Rivalry in the Middle East; Central Asia, European Presence in.*

BIBLIOGRAPHY

Allworth, Edward, ed. *Central Asia: 120 Years of Russian Rule.* Durham, NC: Duke University Press, 1989.

Goffman, Daniel. *The Ottoman Empire and Early Modern Europe.* Cambridge, U.K.: Cambridge University Press, 2002.

Inalcik, Halil, Suraiya Faroqhi, Bruce McGowan, Donald Quataert, and Şevket Pamuk. *An Economic and Social History of the Ottoman Empire, 1300–1914.* Cambridge, U.K.: Cambridge University Press, 1997.

Itzkowitz, Norman, and Max Mote, eds. and trans. *Mubadele: An Ottoman-Russian Exchange of Ambassadors.* Chicago: University of Chicago Press, 1970.

Khodarkovsky, Michael. *Russia's Steppe Frontier: The Making of a Colonial Empire, 1500–1800.* Bloomington: Indiana University Press, 2002.

Moss, Walter. *A History of Russia.* 2 vols. New York: McGraw-Hill, 1997.

Ernest Tucker

EMPIRE, UNITED STATES

For most of its history the United States was an expansionist power that acquired considerable territory through treaty, conquest, and annexation. However, except for one period at the end of the twentieth century, the United States did not follow the classic patterns of colonialism and imperialism. Furthermore, the nation has traditionally identified itself as an anti-imperial power that was committed to self-determination and the promotion of democracy, equality, and individual liberty.

Proponents of America's global role have often credited the United States with being the leading opponent of colonialism. Opponents of American foreign policy have argued that the United States developed a less overt form of imperialism that provides the same degree of control and reward as traditional colonialism but avoids the costs

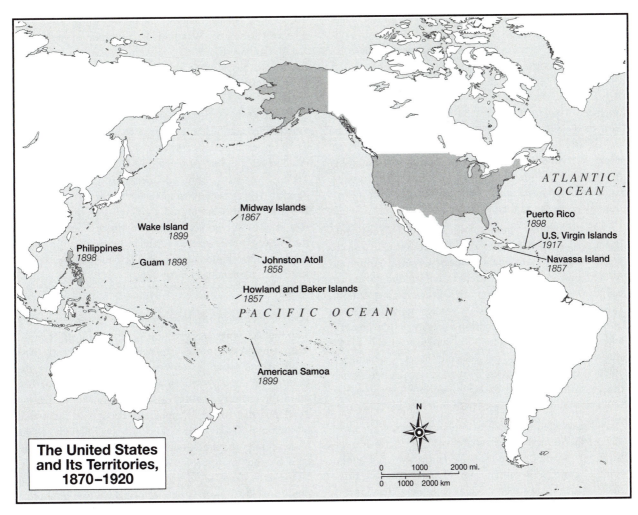

The United States and Its Territories, 1870–1920

Midway Islands
1867

Wake Island
1899

Philippines
1898

Guam *1898*

Johnston Atoll
1858

Howland and Baker Islands
1857

PACIFIC OCEAN

American Samoa
1899

Puerto Rico
1898

U.S. Virgin Islands
1917

Navassa Island
1857

ATLANTIC OCEAN

N

0   1000   2000 mi.

0   1000   2000 km

MAP BY XNR PRODUCTIONS. THE GALE GROUP.

of empire because territory is not under the formal control of the United States. In the post–World War II era there has been increased debate about the actions of the United States, even as scholars have begun to redefine the concepts of empire and colonialism in order to account for the preponderance of American power in the post–Cold War era.

AMERICAN ANTICOLONIAL TRADITIONS

The United States as a country was founded on the basis of anticolonialism and self-determination. Nonetheless, the American colonists, and later the American people, saw their western border as ill-defined, and most accepted that it was proper for the United States to expand westward. This created a dichotomy in which the nation expounded the virtues of democracy and anticolonialism yet often behaved as a colonial power as new territories were acquired. The opposing sentiments of anti-imperialism and expansionism that emerged from the American

Revolution would continue to influence American policy throughout the nation's history. In the immediate aftermath of the Revolution, U.S. anticolonialism came to be expressed on two levels: the domestic level and the level of foreign policy.

During the early period of the country, American policy was expansionistic, but not in the traditional colonial sense. Colonialism was based on the notion of foreign sovereignty: that another state had political, economic, and military control over a territory. Colonial powers sought colonies that would be economically profitable but also politically subservient to the mother country.

In contrast to traditional colonialism, successive American administrations sought to acquire territory through diplomatic means and then bind those areas to the United States by allowing them to become full political and economic participants in the nation through the process of statehood. Sovereignty, instead of being concentrated in the hands of the colonizing country, would be divided between the federal government and the state governments under the American system. American politicians, leading public figures, and newspapers asserted that the American system actually spread liberty and democracy. There was also a notion of divine right in American expansion that would later be codified in the doctrine of *manifest destiny* (the notion that the population of the United States was predestined to expand to the natural borders of the country). This represented an effort to reconcile the fact that the nation was acquiring new territories, but the peoples of these areas (usually indigenous peoples) often had little choice over incorporation into the United States.

As the United States expanded across the continent, it adopted a foreign policy that was designed to distinguish America from the European empires. American foreign policy was also crafted to bolster the American economy instead of the nation's geostrategic position. Isolationism was the core U.S. foreign policy for most of the early period of the nation's history. In his farewell address, President George Washington (1732–1799) warned his successors not to enter into "permanent" alliances with other states. However, the United States did vigorously promote its economic interests through a series of commercial treaties with other states.

One reason for American anticolonialism in the early days of the country was the inability of successive administrations to gain legal access to markets controlled by the colonial powers. Because it found itself shut off from trade with Spanish or French colonies, the United States supported a range of independence movements. Yet Washington's admonishment against formal alliances constrained the ability and willingness of American politicians to provide aid in the struggle against Spain.

In the 1820s Congressman Henry Clay (1777–1852) advocated a broad inter-American alliance against the colonial powers, but Secretary of State (and later president) John Quincy Adams (1767–1848) instead argued in favor of diplomatic support for independence movements, but not military assistance. Adams's position became the favored one and would be codified in the Monroe Doctrine (1823), in which the United States pledged to block efforts at new colonization in the Western Hemisphere in exchange for its own noninterference in European affairs. The Monroe Doctrine was one of the strongest early American expressions of anticolonialism, but it also demonstrated the dichotomous nature of U.S. policy since the United States would oppose some colonial ventures but accept others, including British efforts in Canada.

The Monroe Doctrine did acknowledge the right of existing countries in the Western Hemisphere to consolidate their regimes, and the subsequent American acquisitions of territories, including those from the Mexican-American War and the purchase of areas such as Alaska, were justified on this basis. In addition, Americans noted that their territorial gains were not overseas empires, but part of a contiguous expansion of a political union of states. This union was asserted to be different from a formal empire. Yet concurrent with anticolonial actions, the United States also engaged in quasi imperialism. For instance, the colony of Liberia was established by the American Colonization Society in 1821 as a semiprivate enterprise, and over the next twenty years various states, including Virginia and Mississippi, also attempted to develop colonies in the region. These colonies ultimately merged into a commonwealth and declared their independence in 1847 (although the United States did not formally recognize Liberian independence until 1862).

INFORMAL IMPERIALISM

The United States engaged in a variety of forms of informal imperialism in the nineteenth century, and these would lay the foundation for later U.S. actions in the twentieth century. American settlers frequently encroached upon the territory of other sovereign countries. A pattern developed that would be replicated throughout the period of manifest destiny and would also be followed as the United States acquired possessions such as Hawaii. As part of a broader pattern of westward migration, Americans would settle in areas under foreign sovereignty. These areas might include territory that was formally a part of another nation, such as Mexico or Hawaii, or that had been granted autonomy by treaty with Washington, as was the case for most of the Native American nations. As more Americans settled in these areas, they would begin to agitate for self-government or annexation to the United States.

Texas provides an example of this trend. In the 1820s large numbers of Americans began to settle in Texas. The volume of immigration was such that the Mexican government forbade additional American settlers in 1830. Within two years armed conflict broke out between the Americans and the Mexican government. This conflict culminated in a rebellion and Texan independence in 1836. After a brief period as a sovereign republic, Texas was annexed to the United States in 1845. A similar pattern occurred in Hawaii, where American missionary efforts beginning in 1820 and an American-led insurrection in 1893 led to formal annexation of the island kingdom in 1898. Native Americans also continuously found themselves forced from their territory as American settlers moved in and then demanded union with the United States.

The United States also practiced a more subtle form of colonialism: cultural imperialism. Concurrent with the settlement of Americans in continental territories was the advance of American culture, technology, and economic systems. Within the territory that became the United States, the advance of American culture eroded local societies and traditions and undermined the will and ability of people to resist U.S. expansion. American cultural imperialism would also have a profound impact on those areas that did not become part of the United States. For example, American missionaries were active throughout the Pacific region and in Africa. In addition to bringing the Christian gospel, these missionaries also brought Western ideals, cultural traditions, and language, in addition to a range of devastating diseases.

One of the most dramatic and far-reaching instances of American cultural imperialism in the nineteenth century was the dispatch of Commodore Matthew Perry's (1794–1858) two expeditions to Japan in 1853 and 1854. These two missions were sent in an effort to force the Japanese to open their country to Western trade, and Perry's missions had the impact of prompting the Japanese to launch a massive effort to industrialize and develop in order to compete with the Western powers. On one level, the missions can be viewed as anticolonial since Perry did not attempt to acquire territory, and was not authorized to do so. However, the missions had a major impact on Japanese culture in a manner that foreshadowed the globalization trends of the twentieth century (they also spurred Japan's later emergence as an imperial power). The United States would pursue a similar policy toward China by pressuring the Chinese government to open the country to American commercial interests (this open-door policy would further be applied to the imperial powers that had carved China into spheres of influence). The United States would also use military force to ensure Chinese compliance with its open-door policy during the Boxer Rebellion of 1900.

AMERICA'S IMPERIAL MOMENT

For a brief period the constraining influences of isolationism and anticolonialism were abandoned, and the United States engaged in direct imperialism and the acquisition of colonies. There was a range of motivations that propelled this short-lived effort at formal colonialism. By the 1890s the frontier in the continental United States had begun to close, and Americans began to look beyond the territorial confines of the United States for economic and other opportunities. This would include emigration to Alaska and various areas of the Pacific and Caribbean. In addition, the growing popularity of the inherently racist social Darwinism meant that many Americans accepted the notion that they were destined to rule over other peoples. Compounding these trends was a missionary impulse that convinced many in the

Woodrow Wilson, The School Teacher. This cartoon, published in the United States in 1914, comments on the role adopted by the U.S. government in the affairs of Latin American countries during the early twentieth century. In particular, the cartoonist calls attention to American efforts to promote democracy in Mexico, Venezuela, and Nicaragua. THE GRANGER COLLECTION, NEW YORK. REPRODUCED BY PERMISSION.

country of the necessity of taking a more proactive role in the world to civilize and uplift native peoples and protect them from the worst ravages of European imperialism.

In the later stages of the nineteenth century, imperialism became a domestic political issue. In 1885 President Grover Cleveland (1837–1908), a Democrat, announced that the party would oppose future expansion or the acquisition of new territory. Cleveland resisted efforts to annex Hawaii, and after he left office following his second term in 1896 his successor as leader of the party, William Jennings Bryan (1860–1925), became noted for his opposition to an expansionist foreign policy. The next Democratic president, Woodrow Wilson (1856–1924), frequently authorized military expeditions to support his foreign policies, which were paradoxically rooted in idealism, support for international law, and self-determination. Wilson's use of realist policies, including military interventions, to pursue idealistic goals foreshadowed the rise of internationalism within some circles of the Democratic Party and paralleled the internationalist wing of the Republican Party.

A growing number of elites in the United States also sought to operationalize the theories of naval officer and historian Alfred Thayer Mahan (1840–1914). Mahan argued for the need to create and maintain a powerful naval force to protect American commercial and political interests abroad. However, to maintain such a navy, the United States would need ports for refueling and repair around the globe. Mahan's arguments were diametrically opposed to traditional American isolationism, and he urged a more proactive role for the United States in the global arena. Adherents of Mahan's theories included such prominent figures as future president Theodore Roosevelt (1858–1919) and Henry Cabot Lodge (1850–1924), a powerful member of the U.S. Senate. The Pacific Ocean was of particular importance to Mahan's supporters because many perceived that the centuries-old westward movement of Americans would continue into the region. When U.S. Marines supported the American-led insurrection in Hawaii in 1893, it marked the onset of the nation's imperial moment.

Victory in the Spanish-American War (1898) allowed the United States to acquire several colonies, including Guam, the Philippines, and Puerto Rico. It also led to U.S. occupation of other areas, such as Cuba, and it ignited a vigorous debate in the United States over imperialism. While pro-imperial advocates, including Roosevelt and Indiana senator Albert Beveridge (1862–1927), extolled the virtues of American expansion and the duty of the United States to promote its values and ideals among other people, a range of opponents to American colonization also emerged. Ardent anti-imperialists, including Samuel Gompers (1850–1924), Andrew Carnegie (1835–1919), and William Graham Sumner (1840–1910), formed the Anti-Imperialist League in 1899 to oppose U.S. expansion.

Among the foremost concerns of the anti-imperialists was the incompatibility of democracy and empire. They argued that a nation that promoted self-determination and individual freedom could not also engage in imperialism. Anti-imperialists were particularly upset over the military campaign waged by the United States against Filipino insurgents who sought independence. The anti-imperialists noted that the Filipinos were fighting against a colonial power in the same fashion that Americans had once fought against the British. Many anti-imperialists also had less noble reasons for opposition to imperialism, including a fear of immigration from newly acquired territories and a belief that annexation of such territories would undercut American values and ideals because the inhabitants of these regions were perceived to be inferior to Americans.

Initially, American public and political opinion seemed to be on the side of the imperialists. In addition to the direct annexation of territory, the U.S. Congress enacted the Platt Amendment (1901), which reduced Cuba to the status of an American protectorate and gave the United States the right to intervene militarily. In their efforts to increase circulation, the leading newspapers of the day openly supported and even encouraged expansion by exaggerating stories and news items in a jingoistic style that came to be known as *yellow journalism.*

Following the assassination of President William McKinley (1843–1901), Theodore Roosevelt, an ardent imperialist, became chief executive. Roosevelt undertook a number of actions to expand American influence, particularly in the Caribbean. He envisioned the Caribbean as an "American Lake" and frequently used American power to further U.S. interests. Roosevelt's policies and style, as well as his willingness to use military force and the threat of military action, would be replicated by successive American presidents both in the Caribbean and the broader world.

A keen student of history, Roosevelt realized that the United States could avoid the costs and problems of empire by avoiding direct annexation of territory through the implementation of some of Mahan's theories. Instead of stationing large numbers of troops in economic or strategic areas, the United States could use its naval power to force regimes to comply with American demands and interests. This would allow the United States to develop spheres of influence around the world without the cost of maintaining a military garrison or a civil service. In addition, the policy meant that the United States could avoid charges from both domestic and international audiences that it was forming an empire. Roosevelt's strategy was a modification of British gunboat diplomacy, but it was based on the same premise: install a friendly regime and use a combination of naval power and rapidly deployable troops, such as the U.S. Marines, to support the local government.

This indirect form of imperialism would be repeatedly utilized throughout the twentieth century. There was a range of military interventions in the Caribbean throughout the early 1900s. In spite of pledges to formulate and implement a less intrusive foreign policy, presidents from both parties utilized military interventions in order to secure American interests. The major modification to the strategy of using military intervention to maintain spheres of influence would be the post–World War II rise of covert operations to replace overt military deployments.

THE WORLD WARS AND U.S. ANTI-IMPERIALISM

In both world wars the United States rallied public opinion against the nation's enemies by issuing appeals against imperialism. During World War I the administration of Woodrow Wilson claimed to be fighting in order to "make the world safe for democracy." The administration also contended that it was on the side of the enlightened, liberal empires (France and Great Britain) against the repressive empires of Germany and Austria-Hungary. During World War II the administration of Franklin D. Roosevelt (1882–1945) portrayed itself as fighting the fascist empires of Germany and Italy.

In the aftermath of both conflicts the United States did seek to promote self-determination and democracy. It also supported decolonization. Following World War I the Wilson administration worked to have the colonies of the former Central Powers taken over by the Allies with the expectation that these territories would be transitioned to self-rule. Instead, the Allies, including Japan, Great Britain, and France, proved unwilling to decolonize many of the areas entrusted to them. After World War II the United States would press for complete decolonization.

Many scholars contend that after World War II the American empire transitioned from a regional colonial system, based on spheres of influence and protectorates, to a quasi-imperial system with global reach. Others argue that the United States was not only not an imperial power, but that it defeated the last multistate empire, the Soviet Union, and was chiefly responsible for the rise of democracy in the post–Cold War era.

American foreign policy did radically change after World War II as the twin constraints of isolationism and the avoidance of permanent alliances both dissipated. In an effort to avoid the experiences of the post World War I era, first the Roosevelt administration and then the Harry S. Truman (1884–1972) administration embraced an internationalism that accepted a substantial role for the United States in world affairs. The result was the formation of a consensus on foreign policy that was remarkably stable throughout the Cold War, but which also laid the foundation for charges of neo-imperialism against the United States. Central to the charges of a new American imperialism was the degree of economic and military power the United States exercised during the Cold War. Even the staunchest critics of U.S. policy did not argue that the country was following the traditional paths of the empires of Europe; instead they asserted that the United States had developed a less direct but still pervasive system of control over other states.

In the aftermath of World War II the Soviet Union developed an empire that mirrored the traditional colonial entities of the nineteenth century. The Soviets directly annexed some countries, while others were treated as satellite states and were controlled from Moscow through military and political means. Most Soviet bloc states were economically dependent on Moscow, as colonies had been previously, although some strategically important allies, such as Cuba, were actually subsidized by the Soviets. Significantly, the Soviets concentrated mainly on their periphery, and it was only as the Cold War wore on that Moscow made serious bids to increase its global presence.

In contrast, the United States exerted a much more powerful influence on world affairs in the immediate post–World War II era. Unlike the Soviet empire, the United States has often been characterized as an empire of the willing or as an informal coalition. This characterization refers to the preference that many states had for American primacy as opposed to Soviet domination. This phenomenon was particularly true of Western Europe and the economically developed, established democracies of the world, including Canada, Australia, New Zealand, and others. For these countries, the United States offered military and economic assistance that was critical in efforts to rebuild after World War II. In return, the countries surrendered a degree of autonomy on security and economic issues. However, when they disagreed with the United States they often saw little in the way of sanctions or punishments from America. France's withdrawal from the North Atlantic Treaty Organization (NATO) in 1966 or disagreements over U.S. involvement in Vietnam are frequently cited as examples of the willingness of the United States to tolerate dissent within its coalition. Nonetheless, there were deep differences between how the United States treated allies that were economically and militarily developed and those states that were less developed.

Those countries that sided with the United States during the Cold War can be divided into three categories. First, there were the *allies*. Although the United States often exerted economic or diplomatic pressure on allies to develop consensus, these were states that the United States treated more or less as political equals and involved in decision-making and global strategy. Examples of allies included Great Britain, France, Germany, and Japan. Second, there were a number of states that were *associates* or partners of the United States. These countries agreed with the United States on most issues, but were more willing to oppose American policies and often used the superpower conflict to extract concessions from both the United States and the Soviet Union. Examples of associates included Brazil, Mexico, and Pakistan. Third, and finally, were the *client* states. These regimes owed their existence to U.S. support, and the United States often had to provide significant military or economic aid to ensure their survival. This dependency provided the United States with a high degree of control over these countries. States in this category included Iran, Nicaragua, and South Vietnam. These differences among countries resulted from the implementation of the core principles of American Cold War policy.

American foreign policy in the Cold War period was based on four principles: containment of the Soviet Union; the promotion of free trade; the spread of democracy; and support for multilateral international organizations. Central to post–World War II American foreign and security policy was the containment of the Soviet Union. To successive administrations of both parties, the Soviets represented a global challenge that threatened world domination. As such, all other aspects of foreign, economic, and security policy were secondary to containment. In 1945 the United States had the world's largest economy and needed export markets; therefore, polices were enacted to promote free trade, which was seen as a way to open markets. The establishment of liberal democracies was tied to the longstanding belief that democracies were less likely to go to war with each other, and democracy was seen as a bulwark against communism. Finally, multilateralism, in the form of such international institutions as the United Nations, the World Bank, or NATO, was promoted as a way to lessen the costs of global leadership and to share the burden of containment.

Each of the four goals was laudable, but their implementation was uneven and often exacerbated global inequities. For instance, National Security Council memorandum 68 (1950) enshrined the doctrine of containment in foreign policy, and it specifically repudiated colonialism. Nonetheless, the United States supported ongoing French colonialism in Indochina and British imperialism in Africa as a means to counter Soviet influence in those regions. The United States sought decolonization but was also fearful of creating vacuums that would allow for Soviet expansion. The goal of containment repeatedly led the United States to support anti-free trade and antidemocratic regimes, as long as they were anti-Soviet.

In addition, the free trade policies of the United States promoted global commerce, but they were also designed to enhance the U.S. economy. A range of economic and aid programs was implemented that mainly benefited the United States and other developed economies. One result was the continuation of unequal patterns of trade that often replicated colonial patterns. This system of trade involved the export of resources, ranging from foodstuffs to mineral resources, in exchange for the import of manufactured goods by lesser-developed states. The postwar period also witnessed the rise of multinational corporations that actively lobbied to develop policies that enhanced themselves, even at the expense of people in developing countries. Critics of the postwar global economic system argued that the unequal flow of goods and services forced lesser-developed countries into a state of dependency on the developed world (a concept known as *dependency theory*).

Successive American administrations also offered support to undemocratic regimes in return for anti-Soviet policies. Hence, American support for democracy was tempered by containment policies. The United States even undertook a number of covert operations in places such as Iran (1954), Guatemala (1954), and Chile (1973) to replace regimes that were considered antagonistic to the United States. These actions reinforced notions that the United States was acting in an imperialistic fashion and treating countries as if they were quasi colonies.

American actions toward countries during the Cold War reflected the different status of those states. America's allies and partners were far less likely to face punitive actions when they disagreed with the United States than were America's client states. Nevertheless, the United States did exercise a high degree of control and influence over all three categories of associated nations. In the end, this was because the United States was not a traditional imperial power. The United States used economic and military rewards, incentives, and punishments to exercise its power, instead of formal conquest and colonization.

Furthermore, the spread of American influence was aided by the nation's *soft power*—the attractiveness of its culture, ideals, and values. American political norms and values came to be embraced by the majority of the world's nations, even if its individual policy actions were often criticized. Colonialism, based on external sovereignty of territory, did not adequately describe the American global presence because its control and influence over other states was based less on direct sovereignty and more on indirect, subtle forms of influence. In this regard, the nation behaved more like a hegemon and less like a global empire.

A *hegemon* is a state that has the ability to set and enforce the rules of the international system. During the Cold War, the United States behaved like a hegemonic power, although its reach was rebuffed by some actors, mainly the Soviet bloc and some members of the nonaligned movement. By developing international institutions that reflected American preferences, including the World Bank, the General Agreement on Tariffs and Trade (later the World Trade Organization), and NATO, the United States was able to promote its values and interests, all the while sharing the burden of its superpower status among its allies, associates, and client states.

Because of the hegemonic potential of the United States, it did not have to formally colonize states to ensure their economic compliance or political pliancy. Furthermore, the perceived threat of Soviet expansion added incentives for many states to cooperate with the United States as members of an empire of the willing.

UNITED STATES EMPIRE, KEY DATES

1803: Thomas Jefferson negotiates the sale of the Louisiana Purchase from the French for fifteen million dollars

1821: The American Colonization Society establishes the colony of Liberia, followed by other efforts by several American states to establish colonies in West Africa

1823: The United States adopts the Monroe Doctrine, which attempts to limit new European expansion into the Americas; in return, the United States agrees not to interfere in European affairs

1836: American settlers in Texas rebel against Mexican rule and create the Republic of Texas

1845: The United States annexes Texas

1846: Disputes over the border between Mexico and Texas lead to the Mexican-American War

1848: The Treaty of Guadalupe Hidalgo ends the Mexican-American War, with Mexico agreeing to give up much of the Southwest and California for fifteen million dollars

1867: Russia sells Alaska to the United States

1893: The United States supports a rebellion in Hawaii

1898: The United States annexes Hawaii, seeing Pearl Harbor as a strategic military base

1898: The Spanish-American War begins in April, though the fighting only lasts until August when the Spanish ask for a truce. The Treaty of Paris formally ends the Spanish-American War, and the United States gains control of the former Spanish colonies of Guam, the Philippines, and Puerto Rico. Cuba is declared independent, but occupied by the United States until 1902

1899: Prominent Americans, including Andrew Carnegie, Mark Twain, and Samuel Gompers, found the Anti-Imperialist League, opposing the expansion of the United States

1901: The U.S. Congress passes the Platt Amendment, making a protectorate of Cuba and retaining the right to intervene militarily in Cuban affairs

1903: The United States supports independence for Panama in exchange for the right to build a canal through the country

1904: President Theodore Roosevelt develops the "Roosevelt Corollary," suggesting the United States has the obligation to aid smaller countries in the Western Hemisphere when threatened with economic troubles. Using this principle, the United States takes over the finances of the Dominican Republic in 1905, intervenes in Haiti in 1915, and sends the military into Nicaragua on several occasions in the early 1900s

1918: After WWI, the United States advocates decolonization, suggesting that the victorious Central Powers, including France, Great Britain, and Japan, transition their colonies to self-rule

1945: With the end of WWII, the United States looks to sustain influence by creating collations of similar-minded democracies, large and small, to balance the Soviet Union's expanding empire

1950s-1970s: To fight the perceived Soviet Communist threat, the United States covertly replaces leaders in Iran (1954), Guatemala (1954), and Chile (1973) with governments more friendly to the United States

---

During the Cold War, scholars identified the United States as a *benign hegemon*—a country that had the military and economic power to dominate the world, but whose actions benefited the majority of states in the international system.

POST–COLD WAR PRIMACY

With the end of the Cold War, the Soviet threat diminished. In addition, the economic power of the United States declined in relative terms as other economies grew faster than that of America. The result was that explicit U.S. political and economic leadership declined. Countries had less incentive to ally themselves with the United States on global issues. As a result, during the 1990s there emerged a range of issues that divided the United States from even some of its formerly close allies. Many scholars and public officials around the world began to predict that the United States was in decline and had lost any hegemonic potential it may have possessed during the Cold War.

At the beginning of the twenty-first century the United States remains the world's most powerful country in economic and military terms. Whether it can force its

The Eagle of American Imperialism. *This cartoon, drawn by Joseph Keppler Jr. in 1904, represents American imperialism as a bald eagle with its wings spread from the Caribbean to the Philippines.* **THE GRANGER COLLECTION, NEW YORK. REPRODUCED BY PERMISSION.**

will on other states is a more open question, which strikes at the heart of contemporary charges of neo-imperialism. The series of military actions at the end of the 1990s and the beginning of the 2000s demonstrated that the United States remained the world's leading military power. However, the United States found less global support for its military operations. The soft power of the United States remained considerable, although increasingly other populations were less attracted to the political and philosophical aspects of American culture, and more drawn to materialism and consumerism. In many areas of the world this trend created a backlash against what was perceived to be American cultural imperialism and the subsequent undermining of local customs, traditions, and values.

International disagreements over the "war on terror" and the 2003 invasion of Iraq also demonstrated that the United States was not able to set new rules for the international system (including the effort to promote a doctrine of preemptive military strikes—the Bush Doctrine). By 2004 the broad effort to promote multilateralism, which had been the hallmark of U.S. foreign policy since World War II, had been seriously undermined by the Bush Doctrine and the war in Iraq.

Combined with other actions, including rejection of the Kyoto Protocol on global warming and opposition to the creation of an International Criminal Court, the policies of the late 1990s and early 2000s eroded American soft power and undermined the nation's ability to exert global leadership.

Critics of the United States argue that it continues to pursue neo-imperial policies designed to bolster the nation's global power. The United States has demonstrated that it is unwilling to surrender or share any significant degree of sovereignty with international bodies. When other countries or international institutions support American policies, the United States embraces them. When there is opposition to U.S. actions, the nation ignores them. Supporters of the United States continue to assert that the nation promotes policies that uplift peoples and is willing to bare the costs necessary to provide global security. In either case, the United States clearly is the most powerful country in the contemporary world, but it is a nation that falls short of empire or hegemony.

SEE ALSO *Anti-Americanism.*

BIBLIOGRAPHY

Brown, Seyom. *Faces of Power: Constancy and Change in United States Foreign Policy from Truman to Clinton.* New York: Columbia University Press, 1994.

Burton, David H. *Theodore Roosevelt: Confident Imperialist.* Philadelphia: University of Pennsylvania Press, 1968.

Callahan, Patrick. *Logics of American Foreign Policy: Theories of America's World Role.* New York: Longman, 2004.

Daalder, Ivo H., and James M. Lindsay. *America Unbound: The Bush Revolution in Foreign Policy.* Washington, DC: Brookings Institution, 2003.

Gaddis, John Lewis. *Strategies of Containment: A Critical Appraisal of Postwar American National Security Policy.* New York: Oxford University Press, 1982; 2nd ed., 2005.

Hardt, Michael, and Antonio Negri. *Empire.* Cambridge, MA: Harvard University Press, 2000.

Huntington, Samuel P. *The Clash of Civilizations and the Remaking of World Order.* New York: Simon & Schuster, 1996.

Johnson, Chalmers. *The Sorrows of Empire: Militarism, Secrecy, and the End of the Republic.* New York: Metropolitan, 2004.

Kagan, Robert. *Of Paradise and Power: America and Europe in the New World Order.* New York: Knopf, 2003.

Kerry, Richard J. *The Star-Spangled Mirror: America's Image of Itself and the World.* Savage, MD: Rowman & Littlefield, 1990.

Lundestad, Geir. *Empire by Integration: The United States and European Integration, 1945–1997.* New York: Oxford University Press, 1998.

Meyer, William H. *Security, Economics, and Morality in American Foreign Policy: Contemporary Issues in Historical Context.* Upper Saddle River, NJ: Prentice Hall, 2004.

Nye, Joseph S., Jr. *The Paradox of American Power: Why the World's Only Superpower Can't Go It Alone.* New York: Oxford University Press, 2002.

Patrick, Stewart, and Shepard Forman, eds. *Multilateralism and U.S. Foreign Policy: Ambivalent Engagement.* Boulder, CO: Lynne Rienner, 2002.

Rapkin, David P., ed. *World Leadership and Hegemony.* Boulder, CO: Lynne Rienner, 1990.

Ruggie, John G., ed. *Multilateralism Matters: The Theory and Praxis of an Institutional Form.* New York: Columbia University Press, 1993.

Smith, Tony. *America's Mission: The United States and the Worldwide Struggle for Democracy in the Twentieth Century.* Princeton, NJ: Princeton University Press, 1994.

Tomlinson, John. *Cultural Imperialism: A Critical Introduction.* Baltimore, MD: Johns Hopkins University Press, 1991.

Tom Lansford

ENCOMIENDA

The *encomienda* was a grant of the right to use labor and exact tribute from a given group of natives conveyed to a person in return for service to the Spanish crown. The origins of the institution in the Americas dates back to 1497 when Christopher Columbus assigned native communities to Francisco Roldán and his men. Roldán and his company had risen in revolt against the Crown's authority and refused to reestablish peace except at that price. Subsequently, under Governor Frey Nicolás de Ovando (in office 1502–1509), who as Commander of the Order of Alcántara had administered *encomiendas* in Spain, the grants were institutionalized and extended to the entire Island of Hispaniola as a means to control the natives. The *encomienda* was not a land grant (*merced*). Instead, the conveyance consisted of native peoples, identified by their chiefs, put at the disposal of the *encomendero* or grantee to work in their homes or on public and private construction projects, and in their fields and mines. Initially, the natives labored without limit, benefit, or tenure. In time, royal officials made such grants with conditions: that the *encomenderos* marry, live in a nearby town, Christianize the natives, and protect and treat them benevolently. Thus began an institution that supported a class of powerful individuals, created by royal fiat, that would figure prominently in the history of the New World for the next century and into the eighteenth century on the fringes of the Spanish New World empire.

Encomenderos, addressed as *encomenderos feudatarios*, had no peers at first. They held a monopoly of local political power as the only persons able to sit on the town council. Their grants also gave them a near monopoly over native labor. Later-arriving Spanish immigrants depended on them for the help they needed to build homes and shops, tend plants and animals, or mine ore. This control and their prestige as first founders and conquerors quickly enriched the majority of *encomenderos*.

Harsh treatment of the natives and the catastrophic decline in their numbers due to disease, overwork, starvation, and flight caused the crown and Council of the Indies to reconsider the *encomienda*. Royal officials sent decrees ordering the fair treatment of the natives. These were codified in the Laws of Burgos of 1512 and again in the New Laws of 1542. One clause of the latter abolished the *encomienda* at the death of the holder. *Encomenderos* in Mexico protested this assault on their status and well-being. The *encomenderos* of Peru revolted, and eventually confronted the first viceroy, Blasco Núñez Vela. They found him unyielding in his zeal to implement the laws, so they beheaded him, setting off a civil war that was not totally quelled until 1549.

The rebellion and civil war in the Andes together with continuing news of the unchecked mistreatment of the natives and their dwindling numbers forced the crown to take steps to reconquer the Americas from an ever more powerful and semi-autonomous *encomendero* nobility. The *encomienda* was thereafter renewed (or not) on an individual basis, at the death of the previous *encomienda* holder; assigned a steep transfer tax; and gradually eliminated, except on the frontiers of the empire (e.g., Paraguay). The crown also appointed local magistrates, called *corregidores de indios*, as its representatives to mediate the relations between *encomenderos*, non-*encomendero* settlers, and the natives. In this way, the crown could more easily direct the use of indigenous labor to activities deemed worthwhile, like mining. The increasing control and eventual disappearance of these grants ended the political dominance of the *encomendero* class. Power passed to royal officials, miners, landowners, and eventually merchants. The surviving native population, under increasingly Hispanicized chiefs and overlords, then became liable for a tribute payment to a royal official and for periodic, temporary, rotating, and paid labor service to designees of the Spanish crown.

SEE ALSO *Mita; Tribute.*

BIBLIOGRAPHY

Avellaneda, Jose Ignacio. *The Conquerors of the New Kingdom of Granada.* Albuquerque: University of New Mexico Press, 1995.

Himmerich y Valencia, Robert. *The Encomenderos of New Spain, 1521–1555.* Austin: University of Texas Press, 1991.

Keith, Robert G.. "Encomienda, Hacienda, and Corregimiento in Spanish America: A Structural Analysis." *Hispanic American Historical Review* 51, no. 3 (August 1971): 431–446.

Moya Pons, Frank. *Después de Colón: Trabajo, sociedad, y política en la economía del oro.* Madrid: Alianza Editorial, 1986.

Puente Brunke, Jose de la. *Encomienda y encomenderos en el Peru: Estudio social y politico de una institucion colonial.* Seville, Spain: Diputacion Provincial de Sevilla, 1992.

Susan Elizabeth Ramírez

ENGLISH EAST INDIA COMPANY (EIC)

The English East India Company, formally known as the Governor and Company of Merchants of London Trading into the East-Indies, was first incorporated by a charter from Queen Elizabeth I (1533–1603) on December 31, 1600. The charter gave the company exclusive rights to all "Traffic and Merchandize to the *East-Indies*... beyond the *Cape of Bona Esperanza* [Good Hope], to the Streights of *Magellan.*" While this initial charter was experimental, limited to fifteen years, the East India Company was soon rechartered as a permanent body politic (1609) and over time became the most successful, most significant, and certainly the most famous of English joint-stock companies organized for overseas trade.

The English East India Company became a crucial pillar of the London financial and stock market, a key creditor to the English state, and an important player in English politics. As a joint-stock company, it, along with its rival Dutch East India Company, was the forerunner of the modern multinational corporation.

Headquartered at the India House in London's Leadenhall Street, the English East India Company was directed by twenty-four individuals known as *committees* (after 1709, *directors*), headed by a governor and deputy governor and elected by a general court of stockholders. Collectively known as the Court of Committees, these men governed an independent political system, a network of ships, soldiers, and "servants" (as its employees were known) in Europe and Asia. As a corporate body politic, the company set the institutional and ideological foundations for the British Empire in Asia.

Its beginnings, of course, were much more humble. While occasional English traders and adventurers made their way to the East Indies through the sixteenth century, no English monarch had been willing to challenge Portugal's claims to exclusive rights to the route around southern Africa. Sporadic attempts to search for a northwest or northeast passage had benefits, such as

the discovery of Newfoundland and the founding of the Russia (Muscovy) Company, but yielded no route to rival either the Portuguese or the overland caravan trade.

By the end of the century, groups of merchants, including leaders of the English Levant (Turkey) Company, began to press fervently for a chartered company to pursue the southern maritime route. Their arguments were made stronger with the capture in the West Indies of the *Madre de Dios*, a Portuguese ship laden with a vast amount of East India goods and spices, as well as the *Matricola*, a confidential Portuguese register and inventory of its Estado da India. These investors, aided by a brief that was likely authored by the geographer, explorer, and imperial theorist Richard Hakluyt (1552–1616), used this prize to demonstrate the vast fortunes to be had in East India trade. The administrative documents also seemed to prove that Portugal neither occupied nor used the hemispheric jurisdiction it claimed. Many, including Hakluyt, also interpreted the capture as a providential endorsement for an English entry into the East India trade. In 1599 Queen Elizabeth and her privy councilors relented.

The company's first voyage, four ships commanded by Captain James Lancaster (ca. 1554–1618), set sail in February 1601. These early expeditions were intended not for South Asia, but for Indonesia and its rich spice and pepper entrepôt of Banten. These English ships also sought to attack and plunder Portuguese shipping. The meteoric rise in power in Indonesia of the newly created Dutch East India Company, however, forced the British company to look for other markets.

Pepper remained the East India Company's largest import for its first several decades, but the English East India Company soon diversified into silk, indigo, saltpeter, and textiles. In addition, its servants began to develop a complex and lucrative trade to and from points within Asia, later known as the *country trade.* The company also began to turn its attention towards South Asia.

Sir Thomas Roe (1581–1644) was sent as ambassador from King James I (1566–1625) and the English East India Company to the court of the Mughal emperor Jahangir (1569–1627). In 1616 Roe secured company rights to land for its first factory, to include a trading post, warehouse, and residence, at Mughal India's busiest and most lucrative overseas commercial port, the western Gujarati town of Surat. In the following year, the company further expanded its operations in Western Asia, with a *farman* (an imperial command) from the Persian emperor permitting a factory to be established at Isfahan (a city in present-day Iran).

The English East India Company experienced great initial success. It sent twelve expeditions in its first decade and a half, and returned more than 100 percent profit over its original capital investment. By the 1630s, though, a depressed market in Europe and overextension in Asia began to take its toll on company fortunes. Meanwhile, the company faced more rivalry in England, including an antimonopoly sentiment that grew with hostility towards the king. In 1639 Charles I (1600–1649) allowed a patent for William Courteen and a consortium of traders to do business in the East Indies in places where the East India Company did not. The so-called Courteen Association did a great deal to sully the company's reputation and credit, both in London and Asia, forcing the company to spend great sums both to combat the association and to recover the company's standing in Indian markets.

Competition with European powers had also begun to intensify. By 1615, English East India Company ships had repelled two major Portuguese assaults near Surat, India, and in 1622 the Company's alliance with the Persian emperor led to the expulsion of the Portuguese from their valuable Persian Gulf outpost of Hormuz. In exchange, the company was given an outpost at Gombroon (Bandar 'Abbas) in Persia and a share of the customs receipts of the port.

Despite this success against the Portuguese, the English East India Company continued to lose ground to the Dutch in Indonesia. Perhaps most famously, in 1623 Dutch officials arrested, tortured, and executed, under the charge of treason, ten English company officials living at Amboina (present-day Ambon, Indonesia). The Amboina "massacre" became a rallying cry against the Dutch for the better part of the century. Making matters worse, in the same year company officials were also forced by the Japanese to abandon their factory at Hirado, an island near Nagasaki.

The execution of King Charles I in 1649 and the republic under Oliver Cromwell (1599–1658) in the 1650s marked the nadir of the English East India Company's fortunes in seventeenth-century England. In 1653 Cromwell declared the company's royal charter invalid, and opened the East India trade to all takers, including Courteen. Though the rival traders were never successful, their competition and sabotage of the company allowed states and merchants in Asia to drive up the expense of goods as well as diplomatic transactions. Prices of East India goods in England began to rise, while profit, customs receipts, and the financial stability of the company fell proportionally.

Eager to recover England's advantages in the East, Cromwell offered the English East India Company a new charter in October 1657, putting the company on much more solid footing than it had been on previously. Most importantly, the joint-stock, now totaling almost £750,000, was made permanent. Though technically forfeited with the restoration to the throne of King Charles II (1630–1685) in 1660, the charter was reissued with almost identical terms in 1661. Over the next several decades, Charles II and his successor, James II (1633–1701), issued further patents, expanding the company's powers to enforce law (including martial law) on English subjects in Asia, to make war and peace, to mint coins, and to "erect and build Castles, Fortifications, Forts, Garrisons, Colonies or Plantations" as the company saw fit.

Given this new financial and political foundation in Europe, the English East India Company began to enhance its network in Asia. At the core of this system were fortified sovereign cities, settlement colonies, and military outposts, as well as trading factories central to company administration. Here, company officials tended to much more than trade; they governed a growing cosmopolitan Eurasian population, which in turn demanded attention to law and justice and a civic administration requiring such infrastructure as churches, prisons, schools, hospitals, mints, courts, and, of course, systems of taxation, customs, and revenue collection.

Madras, on the southeastern Indian coast, had been in East India Company possession since 1639, when the company's representative Francis Day initially leased the land from the *nayak* (provincial governor or local sovereign) Damarla Venkatappa. At its center was Fort Saint George and the surrounding "White" or "Christian" town, but its jurisdiction also encompassed the surrounding so-called "Black" or "Gentue" town. By the 1680s, its leaders boasted (perhaps exaggeratedly) of a cosmopolitan Eurasian population of over 100,000. In 1687 the East India Company incorporated the town, giving it an urban administrative apparatus similar to English corporate cities, including a locally elected mayor, aldermen, and burgesses.

In 1668 Charles II also transferred to the English East India Company, for an annual rent of £10, the Western Indian archipelago of Bombay, given to the English Crown from Portugal seven years earlier as part of the dowry of Catherine of Braganza (1638–1705) when she married Charles. By the 1680s, Bombay had become the center of the company's commercial and political administration in India. The company also controlled the South Atlantic island of Saint Helena, where it attempted to create a plantation society, as well as a watering station for its ships. In 1696 the company was given a *zamindari* (the right to collect revenue and to administrate) over three villages in eastern India, as well

Marquis Wellesley. *The colonial administrator Richard Wellesley (1760–1842), governor-general of British India from 1797 to 1805, extended British control throughout India and expanded the territories of the British East India Company.* HULTON ARCHIVE/GETTY IMAGES. REPRODUCED BY PERMISSION.

as permission to fortify in the city that would soon be known as Calcutta, with Fort William at its center.

The English East India Company also reclaimed its position outside of India. It recovered from its expulsion by a Dutch-backed coup from Banten in 1684 with the construction of a factory and fortified city at the Sumatran port of Bengkulu in the 1690s. Additionally, its early unsuccessful factories in Siam (Thailand), Malaysia, and Japan were replaced by stations at Taiwan, Amoy (Xiamen, China), and ultimately Canton (Guangzhou, China), from which it began its large-scale eighteenth-century trade in tea and porcelain.

In this period, company leaders in London and their subordinates in Asia, particularly company committee and sometime governor Josia Child (1630–1699) and company general in Asia John Child (d. 1690, no relation), had also become much more vigilant and hawkish in the protection of the company's rights and political position in Asia. From 1686 to 1690, the company fought wars with Siam and the Mughal Empire, one in Bengal and another in Bombay. Though the latter resulted in the

occupation of the island by the Mughal Sidi tributary for two years, in the long run these experiences only reinforced the company leadership's belief in the need for military strength to defend its establishment in Asia.

The English East India Company's recovery from these wars was also hindered by events in Europe. A decade of war following England's Glorious Revolution of 1688 to 1689, which brought Mary II (1662–1694) and William III (1650–1702) to the throne, made it extremely difficult to get shipping out of the Thames, leaving the English East India Company in Asia short of money and ships. The wartime financial needs of the English state and the efforts of the House of Commons to assert its prominence also prompted the Parliament to accept the offer of a group of well-funded interlopers and disaffected former company servants for an East India charter in exchange for a loan of two million pounds. The so-called "£2 million Act" (1698) created a "new" East India Company that immediately sent ships to India, along with William Norris (ca. 1657–1702), the first ambassador from an English king since Sir Thomas Roe.

In 1695 the Scottish Parliament also chartered its own "Company of Scotland trading to Africa and the Indies," which was perhaps most infamous for its short-lived attempt to establish a colony on the isthmus of Panama. This, along with a spate of assaults on Mughal shipping in the Red Sea and Persian Gulf from English and American pirates like Henry Avery (d. 1728) and William Kidd (ca 1645–1701), greatly jeopardized the "old" company's position in Asia and Europe.

Under pressure from both English companies, the terms of the legislative union of England and Scotland of 1707 included the abolition of the Scottish company. Meanwhile, Queen Anne (1665–1714) and her lord treasurer Sidney Godolphin (1645–1712) arbitrated an agreement for a merger of the two English companies, completed in 1709. This new "United Company of Merchants of England Trading to the East Indies" inherited the old company's established commercial and political system and the new company's fiscal might. Through the early eighteenth century, it built up its western Indian naval force, the Bombay Marine, and grew in prominence in eastern India as well.

In 1717 the Mughal emperor Farrukhsiyar (d. 1719) recognized the English East India Company's growing prominence with a *farman* that granted the company customs-free trading and other privileges throughout Bengal. In Britain, the company also recovered its commercial success as Indian goods began to dominate the English market. Tea, in particular, though mostly trivial for much of the seventeenth century, became the company's most important and profitable commodity, bringing in over £12 million annually by 1770.

Anglo-French conflict, particularly the War of the Austrian Succession (1738–1742) and the Seven Years' War (1757–1765), also contributed to the buildup of British military forces in South Asia in the mid-eighteenth century. Hoping to arrest the expansion of English East India Company power, in 1756 Siraj-ud-daulah (d. 1757), *nawab* (provincial ruler) of Bengal, invaded and occupied Calcutta. In response, the company dispatched an expeditionary force, led by Captain Robert Clive (1725–1774), from Madras, which defeated the *nawab* at the Battle of Plassey in June 1757. Another company victory at Buxar in 1764 sealed its preeminence in the province, prompting the Mughal emperor to make the company *diwan*, or revenue collector and de facto administrator, in the provinces of Bengal, Bihar, and Orissa.

The *diwani* effectively gave the English East India Company sovereign power in Bengal, causing a political crisis back in Britain. In 1767 Parliament formed an ad hoc committee to hold inquiries into company actions. The House of Commons also began to pass a series of acts designed to limit company power and increase oversight of its affairs. The Regulating Act of 1773 instituted the position of governor-general to centralize company governance in India, as well as a supreme court in Calcutta to check his power.

A decade later, the India Act (1784) created a parliamentary-appointed Board of Control to supervise the company and its directors. The introduction by Edmund Burke (1729–1797), a prominent member of the British Parliament, of articles of impeachment in 1786 of the first governor-general, Warren Hastings (1732–1818), was also part of this rapid attempt by the British state to assume power over the company and thus its expanding empire in India. In its charter renewal of 1813, the company lost most of its monopoly rights, and in 1833 was shorn of its commercial functions altogether.

Despite this assault in Britain, the English East India Company continued to grow in India through the mid-nineteenth century. As its law reached further into the Bengali countryside, including the institution of a permanent settlement of revenue with *zamindars*, or landholders, in 1793 under Governor-General Charles Cornwallis (1738–1805), the company also solidified its power in southern and western India with the defeat of Tipu Sultan (1750–1799) of Mysore in 1799 and of the Maratha Confederacy in 1818. The company's bureaucracy and army, which consisted mostly of South Asian soldiers known as *sepoys*, grew proportionally. The company also expanded through the establishment of "subsidiary alliances," which though recognizing the sovereignty of South Asian princely states rendered them de facto company dependencies.

Such expansion eventually reached its limit. The mutiny of sepoys from the Third Native Cavalry at Mirath in 1857, followed by rebellion amongst soldiers, peasants, and landlords throughout northern India that lasted the better part of a year, shook the foundations of the so-called Company Raj. Parliament, the press, and the British public held the English East India Company responsible, and in 1858, after the rebellion had been suppressed, the British Crown assumed direct formal control of British India from the company, which was ultimately dissolved in 1873.

SEE ALSO *English East India Company, in China; Sepoy.*

BIBLIOGRAPHY

Andrews, Kenneth R. *Trade, Plunder, and Settlement: Maritime Enterprise and the Genesis of the British Empire, 1480–1630.* Cambridge, U.K.: Cambridge University Press, 1984.

Bowen, H. V. *Revenue and Reform: The Indian Problem in British Politics, 1757–1773.* Cambridge, U.K.: Cambridge University Press, 1991.

Bowen, H. V., Margarette Lincoln, and Nigel Rigby, eds. *The Worlds of the East India Company.* Rochester, NY: Brewer, 2002.

Brenner, Robert. *Merchants and Revolution: Commercial Change, Political Conflict, and London's Overseas Traders, 1550–1653.* Princeton, NJ: Princeton University Press, 1993.

Carruthers, Bruce G. *City of Capital: Politics and Markets in the English Financial Revolution.* Princeton, NJ: Princeton University Press, 1996.

Chaudhuri, K. N. *The English East India Company: The Study of an Early Joint-Stock Company, 1600–1640.* London: Cass, 1965.

Chaudhuri, K. N. *The Trading World of Asia and the English East India Company, 1660–1760.* Cambridge, U.K.: Cambridge University Press, 1978.

Farrington, Anthony. *Trading Places: The East India Company and Asia, 1600–1834.* London: British Library, 2002.

Furber, Holden. *Rival Empires of Trade in the Orient, 1600–1800.* Minneapolis: University of Minnesota Press, 1976.

Khan, Shafaat Ahmad. *The East India Trade in the XVIIth Century in its Political and Economic Aspects.* London: Oxford University Press, 1923.

Lawson, Philip. *The East India Company: A History.* London: Longman, 1993.

Marshall, P. J. "The English in Asia to 1700." In *The Oxford History of the British Empire*, edited by William Roger Louis; Vol. 1: *The Origins of Empire*, edited by Nicholas Canny. Oxford, U.K.: Oxford University Press, 1998.

Scott, William Robert. *The Constitution and Finance of English, Scottish, and Irish Joint-Stock Companies to 1720.* 3 vols. London: Cambridge University Press, 1910–1912. Reprint, Gloucester, MA: Peter Smith, 1968.

Sen, Sudipta. *Empire of Free Trade: The East India Company and the Making of the Colonial Marketplace.* Philadelphia: University of Pennsylvania Press, 1998.

Steensgaard, Niels. *The Asian Trade Revolution of the Seventeenth Century: The East India Companies and the Decline of the Caravan Trade.* Chicago: University of Chicago Press, 1974.

Philip J. Stern

ENGLISH EAST INDIA COMPANY, IN CHINA

In the late seventeenth century the East India Company shifted its attention in East Asia to China. Tea, silk, and porcelain were the main exports from China; silver, Bengal cotton, and, eventually, opium (traded indirectly) were the company's principal exports.

Tea had been introduced to Europe in the middle of the seventeenth century. After 1704 consumption became popular in England. To meet the public's demand the company sought regular access to China but faced resistance from the Chinese government. Disinterested in overseas trade, the government was prepared to tolerate it as long as trade was controlled and confined to the empire's periphery. By 1713 the company had secured access to Canton, although it attempted trade at other ports until 1757 when the Chinese restricted all foreign trade to Canton.

The company conducted its trade under a structure known as the Council of China. The China voyages carried five or six merchants who formed a single board or council under a chief merchant to manage all aspects of the trade during the trading season. The trading season extended from June to February, although between the 1730s and 1757 two councils existed, to foster competition. The merchants returned with the ships. In 1770 the company decided to form a permanent council. Merchants were to remain for one year in Canton, where the company had been given permission to establish a permanent factory, or trading station, in 1762.

To pay for the tea, the ships carried mainly silver. The Chinese were little interested in European manufactures. To ensure that the trade was conducted as orderly as possible, the Chinese devolved administration of all aspects of the trade to a group of merchants or Hong, organized into a guild or Co-Hong. The first Hong had been active foreign traders, but after 1730 their income depended solely on the European trade at Canton. They became brokers and bureaucrats, intermediaries between European merchants and imperial Chinese authorities. The potential for misunderstanding was great.

The company's position concerning European competitors at Canton and smugglers at home was strengthened by the Commutation Act (1784), reducing the tea duty in Britain from 125 percent to 12.5 percent. In 1757 the company imported 1.3 million kilograms (3 million pounds) of tea, in 1800, 10.5 million kilograms (23.3 million pounds), and in 1833, 15.8 million kilograms (35 million pounds). To end the drain of silver financing this boom the company responded ingeniously to two developments: British private traders' domination of the Asian country trade by the 1780s, and the company's territorial expansion in India, giving it control over the opium-producing areas of northeastern India.

Chinese imports of opium, which had been used mainly for medical purposes, were banned in 1800 as demand for the drug for recreational purposes increased. But immense profits could be made by encouraging this unlawful habit. Mutually advantageous business relationships involving the company, private British merchants (to whom the company outsourced the shipping and sales of the illicit commodity), corrupt Chinese officials, and Chinese merchants evolved. By the 1820s opium outstripped cotton as the most profitable export from India to China and became essential to the financing of the tea trade. The contraband traders exchanged their profits (bullion) for bills of exchange issued by the company in Canton (payable in London or Calcutta) enabling British traders to recycle their gains securely and the company to pay for its tea.

This virtuous circle was short lived. In 1813 the company was stripped of its trade monopoly with India and in 1833 the China trade was opened to all. Trade between Britain and China became a matter of interstate relations. These quickly soured resulting in the Opium War of 1839–42, the Treaty of Nanjing, and the forced opening of China on terms highly advantageous to Western powers and detrimental to China.

SEE ALSO *China, First Opium War to 1945; English East India Company (EIC).*

BIBLIOGRAPHY

Chaudhuri, K. N. *The Trading World of Asia and the English East India Company 1660–1760.* New York: Cambridge University Press, 1978.

Cheong, Weng Eang. *Hong Merchants of Canton: Chinese Merchants in Sino-Western Trade.* Richmond, Surrey: Curzon Press, 1997.

Fairbank, John King. *Trade and Diplomacy on the China Coast: The Opening of the Treaty Ports 1842–1854.* Cambridge, MA: Harvard University Press, 1953.

Morse, Hosea Ballou. *The Chronicles of the East India Company, Trading to China 1635–1834.* Cambridge, MA: Harvard University Press, 1926–29.

Mui, H.C. and L.H. Mui. *The Management of Monopoly: A Study of the East India Company's Conduct of its Tea Trade 1784–1833*. Vancouver: University of British Columbia Press, 1984.

Derek Massarella

ENGLISH INDENTURED SERVANTS

During the seventeenth century, emergent societies of the English Atlantic were transformed by large-scale migrations of hundreds of thousands of white settlers. Most ended up in colonies that produced the major staples of colonial trade, tobacco and sugar: approximately 180,000 went to the Caribbean, 120,000 to the Chesapeake (Virginia and Maryland), 23,000 to the Middle Colonies, and 21,000 to New England. The peak period of English emigration occurred within a single generation, from 1630 to 1660. White immigration averaged about 8,000 to 9,000 per decade during the 1630s and 1640s, then surged to 16,000 to 20,000 per decade from 1650 to 1680, before falling back to 13,000 to 14,000 in the 1680s and 1690s. Across the century, about three-quarters of immigrants arrived as indentured servants and served usually four to seven years in return for the cost of their passage, board, lodging, and various freedom dues, which were paid by the master to the servant on completion of the term of service that typically took the form of provisions, clothing, tools, rights to land, money, or a small share of the crop (tobacco or sugar). They were mostly young, male, and single and came from a broad spectrum of society, ranging from the destitute and desperate to the lower middle classes.

Sweeping changes that transformed English society during the second half of the sixteenth and early seventeenth centuries had a direct bearing on English colonizing projects and on the experience of servants before embarking for America. Of major significance, because so much stemmed from it, was the doubling of England's population from approximately 2.3 to 4.8 million in little more than a century between 1520 and 1630. This huge increase had far-reaching consequences. Rising prices and declining real wages led to a disastrous drop in the living standards of the poorer sections of society, while sporadic harvest failures and food shortages brought widespread misery throughout many parts of southern and central England. Poverty was reflected in the rapid rise in the numbers of poor in town and country alike, the spreading slums of cities, spiraling mortality rates, the massive increase in vagrancy, and the steady tramp of the young and out of work from one part of the country to another in search of subsistence. By early century, the third world of the poor had expanded dramatically in some regions, particularly in woodlands and forests, manufacturing districts, and the country's burgeoning towns, cities, and ports, where as much as half the population lived at or below the poverty line.

For the poor, taking ships to the plantations in the Chesapeake and the West Indies was a spectacular form of subsistence migration necessitated by the difficulties of earning a living and the lack of any immediate prospect of conditions getting better. These emigrants came from a wide variety of regions and communities: London and its environs, southern and central England, the West Country and, in fewer numbers, the northern counties. Many were from urban backgrounds and had lived in small market towns, manufacturing centers, provincial capitals, ports, and cities most of their lives or had moved from the countryside a few months or years before taking ship. Those leaving directly from rural communities came mainly from populous wood-pasture districts, forests and fens, and marginal areas.

Particular reasons that prompted servants to emigrate are obscure, but occasionally there are glimpses that reveal individual circumstances. Jonathan Cole, for example, "being a poor boy," contracted in 1685 to serve as servant in Barbados for seven years. Half a century before, Thomas Jarvis, from Bishopsgate, London, a tailor who had fallen on hard times, was given a £1 "towards supplying his wants" by the Drapers Company of London when he left for Virginia. James Collins from Wolvercot, Oxfordshire, moved to the capital shortly after his father died, where he was taken up from the streets as "an idle boy" in the summer of 1684. Faced with the choice of being sent to prison for vagrancy or laboring in the plantations, he opted for twelve years of service in the Chesapeake. Aboard ship, he might well have met Will Sommersett, formerly of Whitechapel, London, who had no means of supporting himself after being abandoned by his father. The length of their indentures suggests that both were no more than children when they left. Loss of one or both parents was common among poor migrants, and parishes routinely rid themselves of the expense and trouble of caring for unwanted children by indenturing them for service overseas.

The poor, orphaned, and unemployed made up the majority of servants who emigrated, but there were also skilled men like Owen Dawson of London, a joiner, and Edward Rogers of Purbury, Somerset, a carpenter, who were doubtless attracted by the likelihood of high wages in the plantations. Others—blacksmiths, glaziers, sawyers, tailors—were perhaps impressed by stories of high wages to be had in the colonies, or were persuaded to

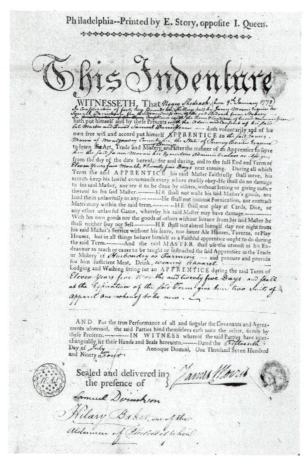

Philadelphia--Printed by E. Story, opposite I. Queen.

Certificate of Indenture. *This document, dated July 15, 1794, describes the conditions under which a former slave named Shadrach was to be apprenticed to Pennsylvania farmer James Morris. Indentured servitude was a common condition for both whites and blacks in colonial America.* HULTON ARCHIVE/GETTY IMAGES. REPRODUCED BY PERMISSION.

plantations was underpinned by African slaves, in English America the immigration of hundreds of thousands of indentured servants throughout the seventeenth century was a distinguishing feature of colonization. Indentured servants were a crucial means of building and sustaining colonial populations in English plantation societies that, owing to high mortality rates, would otherwise have collapsed. They also provided a key source of cheap labor without which the rapid growth of staple production would have been impossible. Many died young or failed to improve their economic position—exchanging one kind of poverty in England for another in America—but for a fortunate few moving to the New World opened up opportunities that would have been unthinkable at home.

SEE ALSO *Sugar Cultivation and Trade; Tobacco Cultivation and Trade.*

BIBLIOGRAPHY

Galenson, David. *White Servitude in Colonial America: An Economic Analysis.* Cambridge, U.K.: Cambridge University Press, 1981.

Games, Alison. *Migration and the Origins of the English Atlantic World.* Cambridge, MA: Harvard University Press, 1999.

Horn, James. *Adapting to a New World: English Society in the Seventeenth-Century Chesapeake.* Chapel Hill: University of North Carolina Press, 1994.

Morgan, Kenneth. *Slavery and Servitude in Colonial North America: A Short History.* New York: New York University Press, 2001.

Smith, Abbot Emerson. *Colonists in Bondage: White Servitude and Convict Labor in America, 1607–1776.* Chapel Hill: University of North Carolina Press, 1947.

James Horn

leave by the prospect of becoming independent landowners after what they construed as an apprenticeship in sugar planting or tobacco husbandry.

In terms of sheer numbers, the heyday of indentured servitude in English colonies was between 1635 and 1660. During the 1640s, West Indian sugar planters began replacing white servants with enslaved Africans, the latter being considered a more profitable long-term investment. By 1660, the enslaved population (33,000) equaled that of whites in the islands. In the Chesapeake, white servitude remained the main form of field labor for another thirty years but by the last quarter of the century wealthy tobacco planters were also switching to African slaves.

Unlike Spanish America, where Native American peoples provided a plentiful supply of labor for Spanish settlers, and Brazil, where the development of sugar

ENLIGHTENMENT AND EMPIRE

From its very beginnings in the late seventeenth century, the Enlightenment—a term used to describe a host of transformations in European cultural, social, economic, and political thought that placed a great deal of emphasis on reason and empirical knowledge—has been intimately connected to the expansion of European empire. Enlightenment thinkers valued highly and thrived on public political debate. As the modern German philosopher Jürgen Habermas (b. 1929) has described it, new social institutions like coffeehouses and the wider circulation of newspapers and political pamphlets made this kind of debate possible; it also, Habermas has argued, created a social revolution by creating a "public sphere," dominated by the urban, male middle-class and increasingly differentiated from the domestic, or the private, sphere.

Both in person and print, this newly expanding world of politics, particularly in Great Britain, was increasingly dominated by overseas affairs and imperial conflicts. Even the social spaces themselves, like the coffeehouse, had imperial roots, tying together as they did the conversations upon which the Enlightenment depended and the consumption of luxury goods, like coffee, tea, and tobacco, so deeply connected to empire.

Still, the associations between Enlightenment and empire are even deeper. The very foundation of much political theory characteristic of the Enlightenment was inspired by European expansion, and particularly by increasing contact with new peoples. It was increasingly commonplace in the Enlightenment that European explorers and colonists had found in the indigenous peoples of the Americas—and later the Pacific—human beings in their "natural state." European fascination with the extra-European world was only further nourished in the context of the expansion of the British Empire in India in the late eighteenth century and the growth of British, French, and German Orientalism, a branch of Enlightenment study concerned with cataloging and elucidating the languages, customs, and history of the East.

Meanwhile, the new languages of class and species that emerged through the efforts of natural philosophers, such as the Swedish scientist Carl von Linné (Linnaeus, 1707–1778), to sort and arrange the animal and plant world were applied equally to understanding difference and hierarchy amongst humans. As early as the late seventeenth century, the English philosopher John Locke (1632–1704) had founded his influential theory of property and his notion of an original "state of nature" on the claim in his *Second Treatise of Government* (1690) that "in the beginning all the world was America."

A century later, the notion that Europeans had discovered what the Irish statesman Edmund Burke (1729–1797) called "the great map of mankind" led *philosophes* like the Scottish Enlightenment thinkers William Robertson (1721–1793) and Adam Ferguson (1723–1816) to argue that Europe had found in its global expansion evidence of human history itself at its various stages of development. The "stadial" or "conjectural" histories that followed were even further nourished by the growth of theories that simultaneously put European civilization at the top of an evolving human history. It also provided an argument for European distinctiveness and often superiority.

While empire was the basis for some of the most fundamental intellectual assumptions of the Enlightenment, the Enlightenment in turn underpinned a great many of the ideological, political, and cultural foundations for empire. The fact that Europeans envisioned themselves as "enlightened" lent support to arguments that justified command over those who were not. More specifically, Enlightenment thought about the appropriate nature and use of law, religion, political economy, and history can be found directly influencing the thought of imperial policymakers, most notably in British India. Furthermore, the great emphasis on what contemporaries called "useful knowledge" and "improvement" demanded the discovery and exploitation of the world's resources; it also quite often justified the dispossession of those that failed themselves to do so.

In addition, the search for knowledge became an imperial imprimatur. Explorers like James Cook (1728–1779) and Louis-Antoine Bougainville (1729–1811) in the Pacific became national heroes, but their efforts at expanding Europe's imperial reach were also inseparable from scientific missions: to observe celestial phenomena; to report upon and collect exotic florae and faunae; and to gather ethnographical and geographical knowledge.

Back in Europe, this knowledge was codified by mapmakers and "armchair geographers"—figures like James Rennell (1742–1830) in Britain and J. B. B. d'Anville (1697–1782) in France. These men translated the Enlightenment emphasis on empiricism into a new cartographic rhetoric. On the one hand, they "wiped the map clean" of its assumed knowledge to demonstrate how little of the world Europeans actually knew. At the same time, surveys, cartography, and new geographical techniques, such as stood behind the Great Trigonometrical Survey in India (begun 1802), supported the demands of military expansion, revenue collection, and policing raised by these ever-growing imperial dominions.

There was also a cultural connection between Enlightenment and empire that concentrated on a fascination with collecting and consuming the "exotic" and what contemporaries referred to as "curiosity." In turn, genteel patrons of science, as well as state-supported institutions, came to serve empire. Perhaps the most vivid example of this is found in the British Royal Botanical Gardens at Kew near London. Under the stewardship of its principal patron, the naturalist Joseph Banks (1743–1820), president of Britain's Royal Society, Kew became a museum of exotic curiosities: plants from the far reaches of the world. Yet, it was also a laboratory for experimenting with their uses and possible circulation and transplantation across the empire. Similar gardens, geographical societies, scientific associations, and museums were soon found throughout Enlightenment Europe, in colonial India, and elsewhere. In the process, the rendering of much of the rest of the world as both "exotic" and "erotic," from the prelapsarian liberation of the South Seas to the hypersexualized mystique of the harem, provided another crucial ideological groundwork for the rational and reforming imperial regimes in the early nineteenth century.

This contact with new peoples, places, and political systems—and particularly the romantic idea of an uncorrupted "noble savage"—also quite frequently provided the lens through which to refract the critique of Europe that was also very much a concern of the Enlightenment. French *philosophes* like Denis Diderot (1713–1784), Jean-Jacques Rousseau (1712–1778), and Voltaire (1694–1778) capitalized on this new ethnological knowledge—and their audiences' fascination with the Americas and Asia—to put in relief the fundamental problems they saw in European politics, economy, and morality. Works like Montesquieu's (1689–1755) fictional *Persian Letters* (1721), in which two Persian travelers visit and comment both upon their own society and still Feudal France, offered both an exoticized vision of Asia and a subtle and satirical comparison between the much-maligned "Oriental despotisms" of the East and political and social behavior under the absolutist monarchies in Europe.

But the Enlightenment emphasis on the universality of human nature, reason, beauty, and natural liberty sat uncomfortably with empire's emphasis on difference, dominance, and hierarchy. This was especially stark when Enlightenment thought turned to slavery and the slave trade that underwrote European Atlantic empires. Thus, while underpinning empire, Enlightenment thought also inspired some of its most trenchant critiques. For example, Abbé Guillaume Thomas Raynal's (1713–1796) *Histoire philosophique et politique des établissements et du commerce des européens dans les deux Indes* (A Philosophical and Political History of the Establishments are commerce of Europeans in the Two Indies, 1770) popularized the idea of the noble savage and made a persuasive argument for international commerce and against much of the colonizing project, particularly Atlantic slavery.

More broadly, the rediscovery and popularization of the sixteenth-century arguments of Michel de Montaigne (1533–1592), Francisco de Vitoria (ca. 1483–1546), and in particular Bartolomé de Las Casas (1474–1566) against Spanish treatment of Amerindians, known as the *leyenda negra* or "black legend," continued to offer a powerful ideological critique of Spanish empire in the Atlantic, while also still serving as justification for the Protestant European Atlantic empires. In the late eighteenth century, Edmund Burke's calls both for conciliation with Britain's rebelling American colonies (1775) and the impeachment from 1786 to 1794 of the East India Company's governor-general, Warren Hastings (1732–1818), drew heavily upon arguments about rights, liberties, and the nature of politics at the core of the Enlightenment.

While many of these critiques criticized only the way in which European empires conducted themselves, other strands of cosmopolitan and relativist Enlightenment political theory rejected empire outright. The German philosopher Immanuel Kant (1724–1804), in his essay on "Perpetual Peace" (1795), offered a vision of an international federation of republican states that left little room for colonial empires or universal monarchies, let alone the imperial wars that underwrote them. His student, Johann Gottfried Herder (1744–1803), particularly in his *Ideas for a Philosophy of the History of Man* (1784–1791), made perhaps an even more explicit argument against colonialism. He insisted not only on the virtues of pluralism but also that the heterogeneous and hybrid nature of large empires was ultimately doomed to failure.

As the Enlightenment began to manifest itself in Europe's colonies, it also became a powerful intellectual and political challenge to those empires. Enlightenment science thrived in British America. From the well-known, like Benjamin Franklin (1706–1790) and Thomas Jefferson (1743–1826), to more anonymous and popular experimenters, the Enlightenment implicated itself quite famously in British-American culture. Moreover, from Franklin and Jefferson in the British mainland American colonies to Simón Bolívar (1783–1830) in Spanish South America to Toussaint L'Ouverture (1743–1803) in French Saint-Domingue (Haiti), the Enlightenment critique of Europe and its emphasis on republican liberty informed the wave of American revolutions against European empires in the late eighteenth and early nineteenth centuries.

The Enlightenment also influenced a host of other responses to empire in colonies, including "reform" movements such as the "Bengal Renaissance" or "Bengal Enlightenment" in early nineteenth-century India. While these movements came to have a great influence over the policy and politics of colonial rule, they also contributed its eventual rejection of colonial rule. The ideological and social revolutions of the Enlightenment became crucial to early nationalism, particularly in giving rise to an urban middle-class "public" that would in the late nineteenth and early twentieth centuries form the vanguard of anticolonial movements throughout European empires.

SEE ALSO *Anticolonialism; Empire in the Americas, Spanish; Empire, British; Empire, French.*

BIBLIOGRAPHY

Ballantyne, Tony, ed. *Science, Empire, and the European Exploration of the Pacific.* Aldershot, U.K., and Burlington, VT: Variorum, 2004.

Commager, Henry S. *The Empire of Reason: How Europe Imagined and America Realized the Enlightenment*. London: Anchor, 1977.

Drayton, Richard. *Nature's Government: Science, Imperial Britain, and the "Improvement" of the World*. New Haven, CT: Yale, 2000.

Edney, Matthew. *Mapping an Empire: The Geographical Construction of British India, 1765–1843*. Chicago: University of Chicago Press, 1997.

Habermas, Jürgen. *The Structural Transformation of the Public Sphere: An Inquiry Into a Category of Bourgeois Society*. Translated by Thomas Burger. Cambridge, MA: MIT Press, 1989.

Livingstone, David N., and Charles W. J. Withers, eds. *Geography and Enlightenment*. Chicago: University of Chicago Press, 1999.

McLaren, Martha. *British India & British Scotland, 1780–1830: Career Building, Empire Building, and a Scottish School of Thought on Indian Governance*. Akron, OH: University of Akron Press, 2001.

Marshall, P. J., and Glyndwr Williams. *The Great Map of Mankind: Perceptions of New Worlds in the Age of Enlightenment*. Cambridge, MA: Harvard, 1982.

Muthu, Sankar. *Enlightenment Against Empire*. Princeton and Oxford: Princeton University Press, 2003.

O'Brien, Karen. *Narratives of Enlightenment: Cosmopolitan History from Voltaire to Gibbon*. Cambridge, U.K., and New York: Cambridge University Press, 1997.

Outram, Dorinda. *The Enlightenment*. Cambridge, U.K.: University of Cambridge, 1995.

Pagden, Anthony. *Lords of All the World: Ideologies of Empire in Spain, Britain, and France, c. 1500–c. 1800*. New Haven, CT: Yale University Press, 1995.

Porter, Roy, and G. S. Rousseau, eds. *Exoticism in the Enlightenment*. Manchester, U.K., and New York: Manchester University Press, 1990.

Raychaudhuri, Tapan. *Europe Reconsidered: Perceptions of the West in Nineteenth-Century Bengal*, 2nd ed. Delhi and New York: Oxford University Press, 2002.

Wilson, Kathleen. *A New Imperial History: Culture, Identity, and Modernity in Britain and the Empire, 1660–1840*. Cambridge, U.K.: Cambridge University Press, 2004.

Philip J. Stern

ENLIGHTENMENT THOUGHT

A developed concept of colonialism did not exist in the eighteenth century. Enlightenment thought, therefore, did not directly address the topic of colonialism. Reference works produced in the eighteenth century, for instance, had no entries for "colonialism." But writers of the Enlightenment, in Europe and America, frequently wrote on subjects that we now recognize as falling under that topic. Eighteenth-century writers approached colonialism from widely differing perspectives and with varying goals. It is not surprising, then, that they drew diverse and even opposed conclusions about the origins, dimensions, consequences, and future of European colonialism.

EUROPEAN SUPERIORITY IN THE "AGE OF DISCOVERY"

The European "discovery" and subsequent colonization of much of North and South America from the late fifteenth through the end of the eighteenth century—as well as the exploration and colonization in Africa, Asia, and the islands of the South Pacific—informed Enlightenment thought in important ways. The "Age of Discovery" and its aftermath were interpreted by many Enlightenment thinkers as real evidence of the advances occasioned by the application of science. The Age of Discovery was also seen as an age of change leading the Western world to new stages of development.

David Hume (1711–1776), an important Scottish Enlightenment historian, philosopher, and man of letters, characterized these events as ones that led to a new epoch in the history of humankind: "America was discovered: Commerce extended: The Arts cultivated: Printing invented: Religion reform'd; And all the Governments of Europe almost chang'd" (1932). Hume considered the transformation wrought by the European discovery of America as a point from which to date "the commencement of modern History." Hume's fellow Scot, William Robertson (1721–1793), in his *History of America* (1777), argued that the Age of Discovery was the time "when Providence decreed that men were to pass the limits within which they had been so long confined, and open themselves to a more ample field wherein to display their talents, their enterprise and courage."

With the window that the Age of Discovery opened on a wider world, Enlightenment writers were led to discuss many topics related to the nature of civil society. International commerce and domestic industry, the institution of slavery and the slave trade, population growth and decline, all were debated in the "Republic of Letters." Enlightenment writers aimed to link those and similar debates to ones about human nature and also attempted to fit them into larger trends of historical development. Some Enlightenment thought on these topics was abstract and philosophical, but that was not always the case. Enlightenment thought on colonialism—as on other topics—was also often and intimately connected with the real world within which Enlightenment writers lived and wrote, as well as the historical world many aimed to recover and analyze. Enlightenment writers often filtered their ideas about colonialism through their experiences with it, past and present.

Enlightenment thinkers had a long history of earlier writings on colonialism on which they could, and did, draw. Included in that tradition were writers on ancient empires but also Spanish writers of the sixteenth and seventeenth centuries, such as Francisco de Vitoria (ca. 1483–1586); Bartolomé de Las Casas (1474–1566), who gained a reputation as the so-called Apostle of the Indies; José de Acosta (1539–1600); and Garcilaso de la Vega (1539–1616). Acosta's *Historia natural y moral de las Indias* (The Natural and Moral History of the Indies, 1590), for instance, circulated widely in the eighteenth century, not only in Spanish, but in translation throughout Europe and Britain. Like Acosta, Las Casas, in his *Apologética historia sumaria* (Brief Apologetic History), was critical of what he took to be Spain's harsh colonizing of such peoples as the Aztecs of central Mexico and the Incas of the Andes of South America. That critical edge resonated in other sixteenth-century pre-Enlightenment writers, such as Michel de Montaigne (1533–1592), for instance, whose essays, such as "On Cannibals," were skeptical about Europeans' supposed superiority over "primitive" non-European peoples.

Writers of the Enlightenment built upon those earlier and critical foundations. They also relied on travel accounts of various sorts, such as those edited by Giovanni Ramusio (1485–1557), Richard Hakluyt (c.1552–1616), and Richard Eden (ca. 1521–1576), whose *Decades of the Newe Worlde or West India* (1555, 1577) was popular in the English-speaking world, but also others that were compiled in the eighteenth century. Important here were the *Journals* of James Cook (1728–1779); the works of the Dutch naturalist Cornelius de Pauw (1739–1799), including *Recherches philosophiques sur les Américains* (Philosophical Inquiry into the Americas) (1768–1769); and Louis-Anne de Bougainville's (1729–1811) *Voyage autour du monde* (A Voyage Round the World) (1771). All of these sources, and many others, were used by Enlightenment writers as the raw materials from which to construct theories about humans, their natures, and their development.

The Enlightenment also inherited a pattern of thought that in some ways assumed European domination of the world and that was ambivalent about the implications of that domination for others. Illustrative of such ideas was the Treaty of Tordesilla (1494), which had aimed to divide the colonial world between Spain and Portugal. It was on the foundation of the Treaty of Tordesilla that Spain claimed its American empire, which, based at first on the island of Hispaniola, grew to include present-day Mexico and Peru, but also large parts of western South America, Florida, and southwestern North America. Portugal laid claim to and colonized lands to the east of the Tordesilla line, including Brazil.

This treaty and others like it gave little or no credence to the rights of the non-European peoples who happened to inhabit the lands in question. The possessions of the Iberian powers, however, faced intense rivalry from the British, French, and the Dutch, who increasingly came to want their own colonies in the sixteenth and seventeenth centuries. Taken as a whole, Europe's expansion in the early modern period acted to validate a sense of European superiority and, in the minds of many, bolstered a European right of continued expansion.

Enlightenment thought sometimes assumed this European domination of the world and also acted to buttress a European sense of superiority in other ways. The French naturalist Georges-Louis Leclerc de Buffon's (1708–1788) theory on the degeneration of animals, for instance, was a widely circulated and influential part of his *Histoire naturelle* (1749–1788) that argued for the natural inferiority of America's fauna and flora. That theory was criticized by other Enlightenment writers, including some who were colonials, such as Thomas Jefferson (1743–1826). Jefferson's *Notes on the State of Virginia* (1787) aimed to show the superior size of America's animals as well as to illustrate the natural virtues and eloquence of Native American peoples.

COLONIALISM, COMMERCE, AND POLITICS

Enlightenment thought systematized earlier writings but also took debate about colonialism into new directions. Enlightenment writers often mitigated early Spanish criticisms of colonization, for instance, especially in emphasizing what was seen to be the reciprocal advantages of commerce. That was the case in a number of important Enlightenment texts, including the monumental work of the French Enlightenment, the *Encyclopédie, ou Dictionnaire raisonné des sciences, des arts, et des métiers* (Encyclopedia, or Classified Dictionary of Sciences, Arts, and Trades; 1751–1772), edited by Denis Diderot (1713–1784) and Jean le Rond d'Alembert (1717–1783). In the *Encyclopédie*'s article for "Colonie," for instance, François Véron de Forbonnais (1722–1800) differentiated types of ancient and modern colonies, arguing that the "discovery of America towards the end of the fifteenth century has multiplied European colonies, and offers us a sixth type." Modern colonies were ones that were "either founded with an eye towards both commerce and agriculture, or have eventually moved in this direction. On this basis, these *colonies* required the conquering of territory and the driving out of existing inhabitants, in order to import new ones." But these modern colonial endeavors, and the trade associated with them, were such that by their nature they encouraged commerce to "flourish everywhere."

Important in focusing Enlightenment thought on the topic of colonialism and commerce, as he was on others, was the French social and political writer Charles-Louis de Secondat, Baron de La Brède et de Montesquieu (1689–1755). In his *Spirit of the Laws* (1748), Montesquieu gave a section to "The Discovery of two new Worlds, and in what Manner Europe is affected by it." Like Acosta and Las Casas, Montesquieu was critical of the Spanish treatment of the indigenous peoples of the Americas, writing that the Spanish "sported with the lives of the Indians." But he was also interested in tracing some of the positive consequences, for Europeans, of colonialism. When he thought about the English and French conquests in the New World, for instance, he especially was interested in delineating the commercial wealth generated by those colonial activities.

With Montesquieu, we can also see how the study of colonialism sparked interest in related topics, such as the theory of value. Montesquieu wrote that "Gold and silver are a wealth of fiction or of sign. These signs are very durable and almost indestructible by their nature. The more they increase, the more they lose of their worth, because they represent fewer things. When they conquered Mexico and Peru, the Spanish abandoned natural wealth in order to have a wealth of sign which gradually became debased" (*Spirit of the Laws*).

Like Montesquieu, writers of the Scottish Enlightenment were especially interested in discerning the economic and political consequences of colonialism. They did so in philosophical writings, but also in historical writings and popular essays.

David Hume addressed colonialism in his *Essays Moral and Political* (1741 and 1742), *Political Discourses* (1752), and at many points in the six volumes of his widely read *History of England* (1754–1762). Hume was interested, in part, in detecting the negative impacts of colonialism on the colonizer. In his essay "On the Idea of a Perfect Commonwealth" (1752), for instance, he wrote that "extensive conquests, when pursued, must be the ruin of every free government; and of the more perfect governments sooner than of the imperfect; because of the very advantages which the former possess above the latter." In his essay "Of the Balance of Power" (1752), he concluded that "The power of the house of Austria, founded on extensive but divided dominions, and their riches, derived chiefly from gold and silver, were more likely to decay, of themselves, from internal defects, than to overthrow all the bulwarks raised against them." For, he thought, "enormous monarchies are, probably, destructive to human nature; in their

progress, in their continuance, and even in their downfall, which never can be very distant from their establishment." Hume's writings were to have a particular impact in America in the eighteenth century, but other Enlightenment writers pursued similar paths.

William Robertson, a Scottish clergyman and educator, aimed in part in his historical works to turn the attention of the enlightened to the relationship between wealth and corruption. In all of his historical writings, Robertson was interested in delineating the causes of Europe's commercial expansion, a theme that is evident in his *The History of Scotland During the Reigns of Queen Mary and King James VI* (1759) and also his *The History of the Reign of the Emperor Charles V* (1769). In *The History of America* (1777), perhaps his most important book, Robertson focused his discussion of Spain's American conquests on the overriding theme that informed so much of his work, Europe's commercial expansion.

Colonialism was a central feature—even one of the guiding themes—of Adam Smith's (1723–1790) *An Inquiry into the Nature and Causes of the Wealth of Nations*, a book that included an entire chapter titled "Of Colonies." In a section called "Of the Motives for establishing new Colonies," Smith differentiated modern colonialism from that of the ancients, arguing that when Christopher Columbus (1451–1506) arrived in America in 1492 he found "nothing but a country quite covered with wood, uncultivated, and inhabited only by some tribes of naked and miserable savages." In "Causes and Prosperity of New Colonies," Smith wrote that the "colony of a civilized nation which takes possession, either of a waste country, or of one so thinly inhabited, that the natives easily give place to the new settlers, advances more rapidly to wealth and greatness than any other human society." And in "Of the Advantages which Europe has derived from the Discovery of America, and from that of a Passage to the East Indies by the Cape of Good Hope," he celebrated many of the social and political advances of England's American colonies.

The French and the Scots were not the only ones to think in these ways. English Enlightenment figures such as Edmund Burke (1729–1797) did too, as is evident from *An Account of the European Settlements in America* (1757), a book that Burke wrote with his brother, William. There, and in other writings, Burke aimed to delineate the positive effects of colonization for the commercial life of the colonizers. Similar themes may be traced in Burke's important *Annual Register*, a widely read periodical publication whose first number was printed in 1758.

COLONIALISM, UNIVERSAL HISTORY, AND RACE

Eighteenth-century writers were often drawn to sketch the history of humankind. Those histories increasingly aimed to incorporate the knowledge gained of overseas peoples. The late 1750s and early 1760s saw a number of such histories, including Antoine Yves de Goguet's *De l'origine des loix, des arts, et des sciences, et de leurs progrès chez les anciens peuples* (1759) (The Origin of Laws, Arts, and Sciences, and Their Progress among the Most Ancient Nations), Jens Kraft's *Brief History of the Various Institutions, Manners, and Opinions of Savage Peoples* (1760), and Isaak Iselin's *Philosophical Conjectures on the History of Mankind* (1764).

For other writers of the Enlightenment, such as Adam Ferguson (1723–1816), European colonialism provided evidence that was to be worked into broad understandings of humans and their developments. Widely considered to be the father of modern sociology, Ferguson in his *An Essay on the History of Civil Society* (1767) relied on travel accounts and other writings to fashion a theory of societal development that he divided into four stages—savage, barbarian, commercial, and polite.

The writings of Henry Home, Lord Kames (1696–1782), especially his *Sketches of the History of Man* (1774), helped to popularize ideas that were commonplace by the last quarter of the eighteenth century. Ideas of this sort could be used to justify colonialism as a means with which to help non-Europeans move from one stage to a higher one.

Enlightenment thought addressed, as well, the question of racial differences. A footnote to Hume's essay "Of National Characters" (1748) was important here. Hume wrote in that essay:

> I am apt to suspect the negroes, and in general all the other species of men (for there are four or five different kinds) to be naturally inferior to the whites. There never was a civilized nation of any other complexion than white, nor even any individual eminent either in action or speculation. No ingenious manufactures amongst them, no arts, no sciences. On the other hand, the most rude and barbarous of the whites, such as the ancient Germans, the present Tartans, have still something eminent about them, in their valor, form of government, or some other particular. Such a uniform and constant difference could not happen, in so many countries and ages, if nature had not made an original distinction betwixt these breeds of men.

Hume's footnote was repeated often in writings in Europe and America in the eighteenth and early nineteenth centuries. Immanuel Kant (1724–1804), an important philosopher of the German Enlightenment, for instance, cited Hume in his *Observations on the Feeling of the Beautiful and Sublime* (1764), as did Edward Long (1734–1813) in his *History of Jamaica* (1774). Other Enlightenment writers, such as Thomas Jefferson in *Notes on the State of Virginia*, struck notes not dissimilar to Hume's. However, some Enlightenment writers, including the American writer Benjamin Rush (1746–1813), satirized Hume and wrote in support of the abolition of slavery. Indeed, Enlightenment thinkers were often critical not only of slavery in particular but of colonialism in general.

ENLIGHTENED CRITICS OF COLONIALISM

Enlightenment thought was not infrequently critical of colonialism in a direct way. Louis-Armand de Lom d'Arce Lahontan (1666–1716), for instance, in his *Conversation Between the Author and a Savage of Sound Common Sense* (1702–1703) argued that "it is the so-called civilized nations that are the real barbarians, in fact: may the example set by the savage peoples teach them to recover their human dignity and their freedom." Others, such as the English writer Daniel Defoe (1660–1731), popularized similar notions. That was the case in Defoe's *Robinson Crusoe* (1719), a novel based loosely on the life of Alexander Selkirk, a real castaway, and in which Defoe's hero treated the Man Friday as a human being capable of being taught in European ways.

That critical attitude was magnified by the midpoint of the eighteenth century by writers such as Jean-Jacques Rousseau (1712–1778) in *Discours sur les sciences et les arts* (Discourse on the Sciences and the Arts) (1750) and *Discours sur l'origine et les fondements de l'inégalité parmi les hommes* (Discourse on the Origin of Inequality among Men) (1755) and François-Marie Arouet, better known by his penname, Voltaire (1694–1778). Rousseau's works and Voltaire's *Essai sur les moeurs et l'esprit des nations* (Essay on the Manner and Spirit of Nations) (1756) continue to be read today.

Not as well remembered today as an Enlightenment thinker, but illustrative of a trend that aimed to see all people as naturally equal in important respects was the Swiss physiologist and poet Albrecht von Haller (1708–1777). Von Haller wrote in 1755:

> Nothing is better calculated to dispel prejudice than an acquaintance with many different nations and their diverse manners, laws and opinions—a diversity that enables us, however, with little effort to cast aside whatever divides men and to comprehend as the voice of Nature all that they have in common. However uncouth, however primitive the inhabitants of the South Sea islands may be, however remote the Greenlander may be from Brazil or the Cape of Good Hope, the first principles of the Law of Nature are identical in

the case of all nations: to injure no man, to allow every man his due, to seek perfection in one's calling, this was the path to honour with the ancient Romans, and it is still the same for dwellers on the Davis Strait or the Hottentots.

Towards the end of the eighteenth century, Enlightenment criticisms of colonialism were heightened in a changing world in which some European colonies had fought for their independence. The thirteen colonies of British America had fought and won a war of independence from 1776 to 1783, and the French colony of Saint Domingue (present-day Haiti) claimed its independence in 1804.

Kant, in *Perpetual Peace, a Philosophical Sketch* (1785), wrote of "the *inhospitable* conduct of the civilized states of our continent, especially the commercial states" and of "the injustice which they display in *visiting* foreign countries and peoples (which in their case is the same as *conquering* them)." Diderot's later writings witness a similar tone of censure and identified the negative consequences of European colonialism, views he often put forward in works of fiction. In his *Supplément au voyage de Bougainville* (Supplement to a Voyage of Bougainville) (written in 1772, first published in 1796), for instance, Diderot had a fictitious Tahitian ask a European: "So this land is yours? Why? Because you set foot on it! If a Tahitian should one day land on your shores and engrave on one of your stones or on the bark of one of your trees, *This land belongs to the people of Tahiti*, what would you think then?"

Richard Price (1723–1791), a Welsh Enlightenment writer, assessed Britain's colonial expansion more bluntly: "Englishmen, actuated by the love of plunder and the spirit of conquest, have depopulated whole kingdoms and ruined millions of innocent peoples by the most infamous oppression and rapacity."

Perhaps the most important of the Enlightenment's anticolonialist works was produced by the Abbé Guillaume Thomas Raynal (1713–1796). The most important of Raynal's works was his multivolume *Histoire philosophique et politique des établissements et du commerce des Européens dans les deux Indes* (A Philosophical and Political History of the Establishments and Commerce of Europeans in the Two Indies). First published in an anonymous edition in 1770, the third edition of 1780 was greatly expanded and was the work not of Raynal alone but of a "*société de gens de lettres*" (society of men of letters). Raynal and his contributors, who included Diderot, offered a biting criticism of European colonialism that was widely read by contemporaries in its numerous printings and translations.

Raynal's text is perhaps best seen as an apt summation of much Enlightenment thought on colonialism.

Raynal asserted that he had "interrogated the living and the dead. I have weighed their authority. I have contrasted their testimonies. I have clarified the facts." His conclusion was that "there has never been any event which has had more impact on the human race in general and for Europeans in particular, as that of the discovery of the New World. . . . It was then that a commercial revolution began, a revolution in the balance of power, and in the customs, the industries and the government of every nation. It was through this event that men in the most distant lands were linked by new relationships and new needs." But Raynal was ambivalent when it came to assessing the implications of all of these changes. "Everything changed, and will go on changing. But will the changes of the past and those that are to come, be useful to humanity? Will they give man one day more peace, more happiness, or more pleasure? Will his condition be better, or will it be simply one of constant change?" Raynal's book was a best seller by any standard, with more than thirty editions coming out between 1770 and 1787. In 1785 Raynal's long-time interest in Europe's overseas colonies produced another work of note, his *Essai sur l'administration de St. Dominque* (Essay on the Administration of St. Domingue).

In 1791 Joseph Priestly (1733–1804), an English scientist and philosopher, was not only critical of European colonialism, he looked forward to its end, which he predicted. In his *Letters to the Right Honorable Edmund Burke, Occasioned by his Reflections on the Revolution in France*, Priestly wrote:

> The very idea of distant possessions will be even ridiculed. The East and the West Indies, and everything without ourselves will be discarded, and wholly excluded from all European systems; and only those divisions of men, and of territory, will take place which the common convenience requires, and not such as the mad and insatiable ambition or princes demands. No part of America, Africa, or Asia, will be held in subjection to any part of Europe, and all the intercourse that will be kept up among them will be for their mutual advantage.

Enlightenment writers, we see, frequently acknowledged the significance of colonialism in their thought, but they assessed its importance in disparate ways. There is no single Enlightenment understanding of European colonialism. Rather, it was judged in varying ways. Enlightenment thought provided colonialism with some of its rationale; it also provided a good deal of criticism. The consequences of Enlightenment writings for the legacy of colonialism in the nineteenth, twentieth, and twenty-first centuries continue to be debated by modern scholars.

SEE ALSO *Enlightenment and Empire.*

BIBLIOGRAPHY

Bailyn Bernard. *Atlantic History: Concept and Contours.* Cambridge, MA: Harvard University Press, 2005.

Bitterli, Urs. *Cultures in Conflict: Encounters Between European and Non-European Cultures, 1492–1800.* Translated by Ritchie Robertson. Stanford, CA: Stanford University Press, 1989.

Brown, Stewart J. "An Eighteenth-Century Historian on the Amerindians: Culture, Colonialism, and Christianity in William Robertson's *History of America.*" *Studies in World Christianity* 2 (Autumn 1996): 204–222.

Cañizares-Esguerra, Jorge. *How to Write the History of the New World: Histories, Epistemologies, and Identities in the Eighteenth-Century Atlantic World.* Stanford, CA: Stanford University Press, 2001.

Canny, Nicholas, and Anthony Pagden, eds. *Colonial Identity in the Atlantic World, 1500–1800.* Princeton, NJ: Princeton University Press, 1987.

Capaldi, Nicholas, ed. *The Enlightenment: The Proper Study of Mankind.* New York: Capricorn, 1968.

Davis, David Brion. *Slavery and Human Progress.* New York: Oxford University Press, 1984.

Dickason, Olive Patricia. *The Myth of the Savage and the Beginnings of French Colonization in the Americas.* Edmonton: University of Alberta Press, 1984.

Elliott, J. H. *The Old World and the New, 1492–1650.* Cambridge, U.K.: Cambridge University Press, 1970.

Frost, Alan. "The Pacific Ocean: The Eighteenth-Century's 'New World'." *Studies in Voltaire and the Eighteenth Century* 142 (1976): 279–322.

Gay, Peter, ed. *The Enlightenment: A Comprehensive Anthology.* New York: Simon and Schuster, 1973.

Hof, Ulrich Im. *The Enlightenment.* Translated by William E. Yuill. Oxford: Blackwell, 1994.

Honigsheim, P. "The American Indian and the Philosophy of the Enlightenment." *Osiris* 10 (1952): 91–108.

Hulme, Peter. *Colonial Encounters: Europe and the Native Caribbean, 1492–1797.* London: Methuen, 1986.

Hulme, Peter, and L. J. Jordanova, eds. *The Enlightenment and its Shadows.* London: Routledge, 1990.

Hume, David. *Essays Moral, Political, and Literary* (1777). Edited by Eugene F. Miller. Indianapolis, IN: Liberty Fund, 1987.

Hume, David. *The History of England from the Invasion of Julius Caesar to the Revolution in 1688* (1754–1762). Indianapolis, IN: Liberty Fund, 1985.

Hume, David. *The Letters of David Hume.* Edited by J.Y.T Grieg. Oxford: Clarendon Press, 1932.

Koebner, Richard. *Empire.* Cambridge, U.K.: Cambridge University Press, 1961.

Kors, Alan Charles, ed. *Encyclopedia of the Enlightenment.* New York: Oxford University Press, 2003.

Kramnick, Isaac, ed. *The Portable Enlightenment Reader.* New York: Penguin, 1995.

Marshall, P. J. "Europe and the Rest of the World." In *The Eighteenth Century,* edited by T. C. W. Blanning. Oxford: Oxford University Press, 2000.

McAlister, Lyle N. *Spain and Portugal in the New World, 1492–1700.* Minneapolis: University of Minnesota Press, 1984.

Outram, Dorinda. *The Enlightenment.* Cambridge, U.K.: Cambridge University Press, 1995.

Pagden, Anthony. *The Fall of Natural Man: The American Indian and the Origins of Comparative Ethnology.* Cambridge, U.K.: Cambridge University Press, 1982.

Pagden, Anthony. *Lords of all the World: Ideologies of Empire in Spain, Britain, and France, c. 1500–c. 1800.* London: Yale University Press, 1995.

Mark G. Spencer

ETHICAL POLICY, NETHERLANDS INDIES

In the 1901 annual speech by Queen Wilhelmina (1880–1962), the Dutch government for the first time introduced into government policy the idea of an "ethical calling" toward its main colony, the Netherlands Indies. With this statement, the ethical policy is regarded to have started. The term itself was coined by the journalist Pieter Brooshooft (1845–1921) in a pamphlet published that same year titled *De ethische koers in de koloniale politiek* (The Ethical Direction in Colonial Policy). The ethical policy was the third in a series of three policies characterizing Dutch colonial strategy between 1830 and 1942: the cultivation system, the liberal policy, and the ethical policy.

The ethical policy can be defined as a policy aiming at the submission of the complete Indonesian Archipelago under Dutch authority and the development of the country and people towards self-rule under Dutch control within a Western political framework. The first part of the definition covers the final conquest of the outer regions of the archipelago, more specifically Aceh in northern Sumatra, where the Dutch fought a protracted colonial war between 1894 and 1903. The second part refers to the importance of the role of indigenous but Western-educated elites in the administration of the Netherlands Indies and characterizes the four main areas in which the ethical policy made headway: the development of an indigenous civil administration, a social policy to combat poverty and improve welfare, support for nationalist currents, and support for agricultural development.

Three distinct periods characterized Dutch ethical policy in the Netherlands Indies: 1894 to 1905, when the emphasis was on the establishment of imperial control over the entire Indonesian Archipelago; 1905 to 1920, which saw important social and economic developments; and 1920 to 1942, which was a period of consolidation, shifting emphasis, and growing conservatism.

Ethics and an ethical approach to the Netherlands Indies first became an issue as early as the 1870s, at a time when Christian democratic parties became part of the political establishment of the Netherlands. In parliament and in the political program of his party, Christian democratic leader Abraham Kuyper (1837–1920) spoke about the "ethical calling" of the Dutch toward the East Indies. During the last decade of the century, the final colonial expansion into the outlying areas of the archipelago took place under the administration of governor-general C. H. A. van Wijck (1840–1914), in office from 1893 to 1889. On the advice of military commander and governor of Aceh J. B. van Heutsz (1851–1924) and government adviser Christiaan Snouck Hurgronje (1857–1936), the development of new ideas about pacification took root, marking the real beginning of a new colonial policy.

The idea was that the expansion of the colonial state should benefit the peoples of the Netherlands Indies, and in time lead to a multiracial independent state. The development of the country included the exploitation of natural resources, the extension of agricultural businesses, and the development of the infrastructure. The development of the indigenous population comprised education and administrative policies, including initiatives as diverse as credit for small entrepreneurs, agricultural education, poverty alleviation, irrigation, health care, the removal of tutelage from indigenous administration, tolerance for nationalism, and the development of an indigenous legal system.

The second phase of the ethical policy saw the implementation of most of the policy's aims around 1905. The civil pacification process was well under way, the economy flourished, and there was a budget for the implementation of social, health, and educational policies. Ambiguities were visible too, however. Strong expressions of nationalism were curbed, and to implement the many aspects of the ethical policy, more and more European officials were appointed. This development hampered the growth of an indigenous civil service, originally part of the ethical development agenda.

It is important for the understanding of the formulation of the ethical policy in the period between 1901 and 1920 to make a distinction between ethical policy as such and the ethical movement in Dutch colonial politics. In many cases, the ideas formulated about ethics in colonial policy were radically different from the ethical policy in action. A. W. F. Idenburg (1861–1935), a Christian democrat, was three times minister for the colonies (1901–1905, 1908–1909, 1918–1919), governor of Surinam (1905–1908), and governor-general of the Netherlands Indies (1909–1916). A sympathizer of Abraham Kuyper, Idenburg showed himself to be a socially minded colonial administrator during his terms of office in the colonies. However, as minister he was responsible for the appointment of J. B. van Heutsz to the post of governor-general in 1905, putting someone in charge who championed military and political pacification instead of the more social aspects of the ethical policy, and who was no friend of the ethical movement. With Idenburg's successors, the differences between ethical policy and ethical ideas continued to dominate the political debate. In addition, the diversity of opinions between politicians and opinion leaders in the Netherlands on the one hand, and administrators in the Netherlands Indies on the other, influenced the way ethical policy was interpreted and valued.

Between 1920 and 1942, the ethical policy took on a more conservative character, with strong shifts in emphasis during the economic crisis of the 1930s. The growing population of Java made agricultural reforms a more challenging task, and the shrinking economy pushed poverty levels up again. The development of Western-style education was halted out of fear of "half-intellectuals" entering the overstretched labor market. In addition, nationalism was increasingly regarded as a threat to Dutch authority and social order; consequently, political and administrative reforms leading to a more democratic system were halted under the administration of the conservative and autocratic governor-general B. C. de Jonge (1875–1958), in office 1931 to 1936.

Still, the final goal remained the implementation of reforms leading to a European political and societal model. The last governor-general of the Netherlands Indies, A. W. L. Tjarda van Strakenborgh Stachouwer (1888–1978), in office 1936 to 1942, undertook new initiatives in this direction. Assisted by an upward economic trend after 1935, his administration promoted the transmigration of Javanese farmers to other parts of the archipelago, as well as industrialization and the production of food crops. In education, large strides were made with the expansion of basic education, the extension of higher education to include the humanities, and the establishment of a school of governance in the administration of the colony. Additionally, the decentralization of government jurisdiction was taken up again, and the relationship between the government and the colony's representative body, the *volksraad* (peoples' council) was normalized. In the end, however, the events of World War II (1939–1945) and its immediate aftermath brought the ethical policy to an abrupt end.

SEE ALSO *Empire, Dutch; Snouck Hurgronje, Christiaan.*

BIBLIOGRAPHY
Boeke, J. H. "De ethische richting in de Nederlandsch-Indische politiek." *De Gids* 104 (1940), I, 21–35.

Creutzberg, P., ed. *Het ekonomisch beleid in Nederlandsch-Indië.* 3 vols. Groningen, Netherlands: 1972–1975.

Locher Scholten, E. B. *Ethiek in fragmenten. Vijf studies over koloniaal denken en doen van Nederlanders in de Indonesische Archipel, 1877–1942.* Utrech, Netherlands: HES Publishers, 1981.

Schmutzer, E. J. M. *Dutch Colonial Policy and the Search for Identity 1920–1931.* Leiden, Netherlands: Brill Academic Publishers, 1977.

Michel R. Doortmont

ETHIOPIA

Ethiopia is a country in eastern Africa, in the region known as the Horn of Africa; it was historically sometimes known as Abyssinia. Almost as large as Texas and California combined, the country consists of a large highland region surrounded by lowland deserts. Historically this geography isolated Ethiopia from its neighbors and from Europe, though external trade did take place. Geography was also a factor in Ethiopia remaining as one of only two African countries (the other was Liberia) that were never formally colonized by European powers.

Ethiopia is one of the likely origin places of humans and their near relatives, and anthropologists have found fossil hominids dating from about four million years ago there. Ethiopia is often thought to be the historical home of the Queen of Sheba and the biblical land of Punt, an important trading partner of ancient Egypt. The sophisticated Axum (Aksum) civilization developed in Ethiopia during the first century C.E., forming an empire that traded with India, Arabia, Egypt, and the Mediterranean world. This civilization was Christianized around 300 C.E. (or even earlier, according to some scholars); the Bible was translated into the local language of Geez, and churches and monasteries were built. Even today Ethiopia is a predominantly Christian country with over half the population belonging to the Ethiopian Orthodox Church.

The Axum empire declined around 1000 C.E. with the rise of Islam and Arab expansion. Medieval Ethiopia flourished but was isolated from the rest of Christianity. European legends of Prester John, a mythical ruler of a vast Christian empire thought to lie in Africa, stimulated European interest in the 1500s. Portugal established close relations with Ethiopia, even assisting it in its wars against Islamic invaders. After a period of instability, Ethiopia was largely unified after 1855 as a single state under the rule of Emperor Tewodros II (1818–1868). During his reign the country came into conflict with the British, who were beginning colonial expansion into East Africa.

After the power struggle following the death of Tewodros, Johannes IV (1831–1889) became emperor in 1871 and immediately found himself immersed in the colonial rivalry between British, French, Italian, and Turkish interests in the Horn of Africa. The opening of the Suez Canal in 1869 had made Ethiopia and the Red Sea strategically important, and European powers were keen on acquiring territory in the region.

After the death of Yohannes in 1889, Menelik II (1844–1913) was crowned emperor. His policy of unification, modernization, and expansion increased the territorial size of Ethiopia and brought it technological advancement. Menelik founded a new capital at Addis Ababa and introduced such innovations as electricity, telephones, railroads, and a modern military armed with European weapons. In a dispute with Italy over claims to the Red Sea coast, he granted Italy control of Eritrea in return for Italian recognition of Ethiopia's sovereignty. The Treaty of Wichale, signed in 1889, was in both the Italian and Amharic languages, and differences in these texts led to conflict between the two signatories: Italy interpreted the treaty as giving it protectorate status over Ethiopia, while Menelik did not. The Italians used their interpretation of the treaty to justify expansion into Ethiopian territory, precipitating the Battle of Adwa, fought between the Italians and Ethiopians in 1896. Italy was resoundingly defeated in the battle, an event significant in the history of African colonialism in that it was a clear victory of Africans over European colonial forces.

Menelik's grandson succeeded him as ruler but was soon deposed by the Ethiopian nobility, who substituted Menelik's daughter as empress. During this period the nobleman Ras Tafari Mekonen (1892–1975) became prince regent and the effective ruler of the country, securing its entry as a member of the League of Nations in 1923. When the empress died in 1930 Ras Tafari (whose name is the origin of the Rastafarian movement) became emperor, taking the name Haile Selassie I. Haile Selassie continued Ethiopia's modernization, attempted to form international alliances, and resisted European colonial expansion, despite British and Italian attempts to increase their neighboring colonial territories.

Italy, under its fascist ruler Benito Mussolini (1883–1945), again attempted to enlarge its African colonial empire with a second assault against Ethiopia. Mussolini also wanted to avenge Italy's humiliating loss to Ethiopia in 1896. The Italians invaded Ethiopia in 1935; other European powers failed to intervene, despite their obligations under the League of Nations, which called for sanctions to be applied against aggressor states.

Ethiopian Fighters. *A group of Ethiopian fighters assembles during the 1935 Italian invasion of the African kingdom.*
© HULTON-DEUTSCH COLLECTION/CORBIS. REPRODUCED BY PERMISSION.

The British and French were willing to appease Mussolini and refused to provide any real support for the emperor. Haile Selassie's departure from Ethiopia and his personal appeal to the League of Nations in 1936 was ineffective, and the Italians occupied Ethiopia, fusing it with their Somali and Eritrean territories to form the colony of Italian East Africa. Ethiopian popular resistance to Italian occupation was brutally suppressed; the Italians bombed hospitals and ambulances, used biological weapons, and massacred civilians.

With the beginning of World War II in 1939, Ethiopia sought help from the British and other allies against the Italians. Italy declared war against Britain in 1940, and together British and Ethiopian forces were able to defeat the Italian military in East Africa, allowing the emperor to return in 1941. After the war Ethiopia retained its independence, though the British remained influential in Ethiopian affairs until 1955, when Ethiopia sought greater contacts with the United States. In the 1960s Haile Selassie's government became increasingly corrupt and ineffectual, failing to respond effectively to famines and popular discontent. In 1974 a socialist revolution overthrew the emperor and installed a repressive Marxist regime governed by a council called the *Derg*. The Derg was itself defeated in 1991 by a popular front, and Ethiopia became a democracy. Eritrea was separated from Ethiopia and became an independent country in 1991, but border disputes and occasional warfare continue between the two countries. Agitation by other ethnic groups against central government domination and conflicts with neighboring countries continue to plague modern Ethiopia. Today one of the world's poorest countries, Ethiopia is important as a symbol of the African anticolonial struggle.

SEE ALSO *Anticolonialism; Empire, Italian.*

BIBLIOGRAPHY

Bahru Zewde. *A History of Modern Ethiopia, 1855–1974.* Athens: Ohio University Press, 1991.

Haile Selassie I. *My Life and Ethiopia's Progress: The Autobiography of Emperor Haile Selassie I.* Translated by Edward Ullendorff. Chicago: Frontline, 1999.

Henze, Paul B. *Layers of Time: A History of Ethiopia.* Basingstoke, U.K.: Palgrave Macmillan, 2000.

Marcus, Harold G. *The Life and Times of Menelik II: Ethiopia, 1844–1913.* Oxford, U.K.: Clarendon, 1975. Reprint, Trenton, NJ: Red Sea, 1995.

Marcus, Harold G. *A History of Ethiopia,* updated ed. Berkeley: University of California Press, 2002.

Mockler, Anthony. *Haile Selassie's War.* New York: Random House, 1984. Reprint, New York: Olive Branch, 2003.

Rubenson, Sven. *The Survival of Ethiopian Independence,* 4th ed. Hollywood, CA: Tsehai, 2003.

Michael Pretes

EUROCENTRISM

During most of the last two centuries, the prevailing popular view of world history held that a *mainstream* of facts could be identified in the flood of events taking place since the dawn of humanity. Essentially, this *mainstream* coincided with the history of Europe and its antecedents and successors—all the heirs and transmitters of civilization. The source of this stream of facts was located in Egypt and the Near East, and via Greece and Rome it slowly flowed westward to medieval western Europe. In the course of two colonization waves—the first starting in 1450, the second in 1870—it finally came to encompass the whole planet.

During the twentieth century, Europe's child, the United States, gradually succeeded Europe as the *mainstream*'s driving force. This *mainstream* principle divided the peoples of the earth into two categories: *active* peoples in the heart of the *mainstream* and *passive* peoples in its periphery. Non-Western cultures belonged to the passive peoples, but they could change their status and become historical agents through three forms of contact with Europe: either they had to threaten Europe (the Islamic peoples between the seventh and seventeenth centuries); be discovered, civilized, and converted by Europe (the Americas in the fifteenth and sixteenth centuries); or modernize like Europe (Russia in the eighteenth and Japan in the nineteenth century).

The *mainstream* concept of world history had at least two anomalies, the first of which was structural: The *mainstream*'s beginnings lay outside Europe—in Egypt and the Near East. This demonstrates that the *mainstream* principle has illogical characteristics. The second anomaly was teleological and related to colonialism: unlike the independence struggle of other colonies, the eighteenth-century decolonization of the United States was often portrayed (especially after 1945) as a rebellion of heroes. This anomaly can only be explained by the fact that the successors of these American heroes took the lead of *mainstream* history after 1945.

In this popular grand narrative, the era of European colonization (1450–1945) was nothing other than European history outside Europe, the European epic of discovery and incorporation of other territories. With supernatural strength, European colonizers walked around the globe, realized their plans, and met "indigenous" peoples who were inferior, deficient, and helplessly unable to resist Europe's grip.

Non-Western cultures, such as the Aztecs of Mexico or the Incas of western South America, were introduced into the narrative with brief flashbacks at the very moment of their disappearance or submission. Instances of bloody invasion, colonial mass murder, and slave trade, as well as episodes of anticolonial resistance, were explained away or minimized, and often conveniently forgotten. In the centuries of imperialism, this popular view was fed by, and penetrated into, scholarly thinking.

As late as 1965, British historian Hugh Trevor-Roper (1914–2003) could write:

> Perhaps, in the future, there will be some African history to teach. But at present there is none, or very little: there is only the history of the Europeans in Africa. The rest is largely darkness, like the history of pre-European, pre-Columbian America. And darkness is not a subject for history. Please, do not misunderstand me. I do not deny that men existed even in dark countries and dark centuries, nor that they had political life and culture, interesting to sociologists and anthropologists; but history, I believe, is essentially a form of movement, and purposive movement too. It is not a mere phantasmagoria of changing shapes and costumes, of battles and conquests, dynasties and usurpations, social forms and social disintegration. If all history is equal, as some now believe, there is no reason why we should study one section of it rather than another; for certainly we cannot study it all. Then indeed we may neglect our own history and amuse ourselves with the unrewarding gyrations of barbarous tribes in picturesque but irrelevant corners of the globe: tribes whose chief function in history, in my opinion, is to show to the present an image of the past from which, by history, it has escaped. (Trevor-Roper 1965, p. 9)

Mainstream logic perceived post-1945 decolonization as a process in which Europe withdrew—mostly voluntarily—from its colonies. Insofar as the colonized (then called "colored peoples") were able to act, they did so because Western doctrines of nationalism and human rights had "awakened" them. Most countries emerging from decolonization, however, were seen as retarded and dependent. Called *underdeveloped countries* or the *third world*, they were thought to bridge the gap only by giving up their own culture and traditions to emulate modern Europe and, by extension, the West.

FIVE LEVELS OF EUROCENTRISM

The *mainstream* principle reveals a broader tendency—namely, to perceive one's own culture as the center of everything and other cultures as its periphery. This tendency is called *ethnocentrism.*

If we exclude the seventeenth-century forerunner Francis Bacon (1561–1626)—a British historian and philosopher of science who identified four *Idols* (or fallacies), among which were Idols of the Cave (fallacies of group loyalty)—the first to describe and name this tendency was the American anthropologist William Sumner (1840–1910) in 1906. Ethnocentrism is a universal phenomenon occurring at all times and places; therefore, it is not negative but logical to give one's own culture the most attention. It exists everywhere, for example, in Europe *(Eurocentrism),* China *(Sinocentrism),* and Africa *(Afrocentrism).* The concept, however, takes a dangerous turn when, first, centrality changes into superiority, and second, this attitude of superiority is held by people who have the power to dominate others.

Eurocentrism took this double step. It became more influential than other forms of ethnocentrism because it was the cultural ideology of the European colonizers who conquered the world—first in their capacity as early modern societies; later, in the nineteenth century, in their capacity as industrial nations. The more arrogant forms of Eurocentrism had a negative impact upon non-Western cultures and their history. Depending on the non-Western cultures targeted, they manifested themselves at five levels. They are described here in order of importance.

Level 1: "Non-Western history does not exist." This *ontological Eurocentrism,* concerning the reality of non-Western history and promulgated by the German philosopher Georg Wilhelm Friedrich Hegel (1770–1831), among others, served to justify Western expansion toward those non-Western cultures that were cataloged as "primitive." "Primitive" peoples were "peoples without history" because they were deemed incapable of historical agency. Their past was seen as a succession of chaos, barbarism, poverty, and stagnation. They were thought to develop myths instead of causal logic to explain the past. They were also thought to possess a cyclical conception of time, and therefore to live in a static present, referred to as the *ethnographic present.*

Sometimes, "primitive" peoples were compared to "prehistoric" peoples (the *archaic illusion*) or to children (the *recapitulation theory*). The most radical form of ontological Eurocentrism consisted in denying that indigenous peoples had ever lived on certain territories before the arrival of the Europeans. On disembarking, the latter preferred to believe that many of these territories—especially in what are now called the Americas, South Africa and Australia—were "empty." These regions were regarded as not inhabited, not owned, and not used; this is the *terra nullius (land of no one)* doctrine.

Historiography (the writing of history) of later years has adequately and extensively refuted these misconceptions by revealing that for centuries "primitive" peoples have successfully survived, and, far from being static, they introduced important innovations (such as fire, food production, plant and animal domestication, symbols, music, language, art, etc.). Perhaps, then, negative forms of ontological Eurocentrism have disappeared today, although two of its positive forms may be said to survive. One of these positive variants maintains that the happiest peoples are those without history—a modernist variant on the centuries-old theme of the *noble savage.* Another variant, divulged by concerned anthropologists, holds that indigenous cultures are vanishing under the pressure of modernization and globalization (ironically called the *despondency theory* by American anthropologist Marshall Sahlins [b. 1930]), thereby denying any autonomy or historical agency to these cultures.

Level 2: "Non-Western history cannot be known." This *epistemological Eurocentrism* concerns the knowability of history and was the result of the primacy that for centuries had been given to written sources. Where non-Western written sources were not available, alternative sources remained unacknowledged; where alternative sources had been preserved, they were generally either ignored or destroyed by colonial authorities.

In combination with first-level Eurocentrism, two versions of epistemological Eurocentrism developed. The milder version held that "non-Western history exists but cannot be known," while the stronger version held that "non-Western history cannot be known, therefore it does not exist." Only gradually was the definition of *sources* extended to include archeological, iconographical, linguistic, and oral evidence.

Even so, it remains incontrovertible that scores of non-Western sources are lacking and that the history of certain non-Western periods, regions, and social strata cannot be reconstructed—or only with the greatest difficulty. The reasons for this shortage were climatic, political (destruction of sources by those in power), and social (in some cases, non-Western conceptions of time or history were not document- and archive-oriented). Unavoidably, this structural lack of balance between sources from different regions leads to a Eurocentric bias in the writing of world history.

Insiders and Outsiders defined

INSIDERS ACCORDING TO:

Insiders	Outsiders
We care more about our culture.	They are biased and ethnocentric.
We have superior experience, knowledge, imagination, and insight when it regards our culture.	They cannot guarantee superior or uniform insight.
Our understanding is determined by origin and identity.	Their understanding is not guaranteed by origin and identity.
	Their purist and protective cultural ownership reflex should be rejected because it leads to autobiography, not history.

OUTSIDERS ACCORDING TO:

Insiders	Outsiders
They often speak clinically about our culture.	We possess distance and detachment.
They cannot guarantee that they are impartial.	We acquire experience, knowledge, imagination, insight by disciplined training and terms of stay and study in their culture.
Their empathy with our culture is impossible.	Our empathy with their culture is possible because humans of all times and places are intellectually and psychologically comparable, and therefore knowable to a large extent.
Their version of history should be rejected for not depicting our "living" culture.	We are equipped to study cultural taboos (slavery, dictatorship, genocide) and determinants of life (demographic or ecological patterns) not immediately evident to insiders.
Their study of cultural taboos fouls our culture.	

Table 1 THE GALE GROUP.

Level 3: "Non-Western history has little value." This *ethical Eurocentrism* was the classical form of Eurocentrism. Whenever episodes of non-Western history were effectively dealt with, they were evaluated and stereotyped according to Western concepts and criteria. Typical popular prejudices heard in the post–World War II era were: "The third world is still living in the Middle Ages" or "The third world will never arrive in two generations' time at development levels that the West took two millennia to attain."

Non-Western societies ("primitive" ones and others) were thus characterized by their real or alleged deficiencies: they had no writing, no state, no unity, no prosperity, and no culture. Therefore, their history was not considered worth studying. Great achievements contradicting this view were often explained away by an assumed pristine European intervention in non-Western territory (in studies of Africa this view is known as the *Hamitic hypothesis*).

Today, non-Western history is gradually being revalorized. It has also become apparent that comparability between present-day non-Western cultures and the pre- or protoindustrial situation in Europe is very limited because the present global context is radically different from the European context in the medieval or premodern period.

Level 4: "Non-Western history is not relevant or useful." This was *utilitarian Eurocentrism*. Ignorance about non-Western history (the result of second- and third-level Eurocentrism) led to an underestimation of non-Western achievements, and particularly of numerous non-Western contributions to Western culture. It resulted in the equation of "Western culture" with "culture" as such and in the perception of seeing culture as the exclusive result of "Western genius." It was either forgotten that many contributions came from outside Europe, or it was assumed that these contributions had only been perfected by Western hands.

The combined third- and fourth-level ethnocentrism left no room for other "*mainstreams*" than the European. To be sure, European superiority at the technological level after 1500 and at the economic level between 1800 and 1945 was very real. To a large extent, post-1500 world history is effectively a story of westernization. It is not easy to reconcile dominance by one culture with the equivalence of all. However, the *mainstream* view unrealistically generalized this European superiority during a limited period of time and at one (admittedly important) level to all periods and all levels. It saw Europe, and by extension the West, as exceptions. This *exceptionalism* was often expressed in the dictum "the West and the rest."

Many explanations have been given for why and when Europe started to diverge from "the rest." These explanations may be deterministic (seeking causes in race, climate, or geography) or historical (seeking causal factors in feudalism, capitalism, the urban bourgeoisie, maritime-military superiority, etc.). Questions of European uniqueness should not obfuscate, however, that non-European territories and pre-1500 Europe cannot be lumped together in one uniform residual category.

Level 5: "Non-Western history is too difficult and too embarrassing." This *didactic Eurocentrism* concerns the ways of teaching about other cultures and naturally prevailed at schools. Undoubtedly, teaching about non-Western societies with their distinct modes of thinking entails specific didactical problems. However, these problems do not necessarily lead to confused or caricatured representations of history. When history teachers and authors of history textbooks prepare carefully, they should be able to illustrate historical mechanisms, processes, and structures with the support of non-Western examples.

Furthermore, it is certainly true that major parts of non-Western history are embarrassing stories of hunger, poverty, and injustice, and therefore painful episodes to deal with. The same can be said, however, about large portions of Western history. Besides, history should not be reduced to its embarrassing side only. History teaching is a historiographical genre reaching wide audiences; therefore, it is crucial that it presents balanced historical views.

In much of the nineteenth and first half of the twentieth centuries, the five forms of Eurocentrism described above were petrified by the doctrine of *essentialism*—the belief that cultures had a timeless kernel or essence that was more important than changing historical circumstances. Essentialism gradually evolved into *racism*—an attitude that attributed cultural differences to biological differences and transformed centrality and superiority into inherited characteristics. This led to the conviction that the European nations were elected peoples. Such was the case for large sectors of European and Western public opinion until 1945.

In the postwar decades, however, the decolonization and emergence of the third world enlarged the perception of the Western public. The popular and Eurocentric *mainstream* view of world history, although deeply engraved into mentalities, slowly disappeared—a process that is, in fact, still going on. Ethnocentrism as such, however, does not disappear—nor could it.

ORIGINS AND DOMINANCE OF THE *MAINSTREAM* VIEW OF HISTORY

Switching from future to past perspectives, it should be emphasized that the *mainstream* view of history has not always existed. At full strength, it prevailed between 1870 and 1970. It was the result of a very peculiar combination of at least three factors.

First, the Renaissance—a period in Europe (circa 1400s to 1600s) in which the roots of European tradition were relocated to antiquity—called into question medieval notions of continuity. Against this background, the newly discovered non-Western peoples in the Americas and elsewhere stimulated the evolutionary view that all peoples on earth found themselves in one of three stages of linear historical development: wild (representing "primitive" hunters living close to nature), barbarian (representing nomadic but conquering peoples), or civilized (representing sedentary civilizations). Of course, this *social evolutionism* saw Europe as the leading continent.

Second, during the Enlightenment of the eighteenth century, this view was given a peculiar dynamic when it was linked with the ideas of progress and modernization. Scholars came to think that civilized Europe had already passed through its own wild and barbarian stages. The political and industrial revolutions of the late eighteenth century encouraged this thinking in terms of progress: Such terms as *wild* and *barbarian* were replaced with "equivalents" such as *primitive, traditional, pagan,* and *premodern.*

Third, around the same time, a series of archaeological discoveries greatly improved knowledge of the early Mediterranean cultures. A few decades later—under the influence of Romantic ideas—European historians were looking for links between their national state and old and glorious civilizations in order to build their national identity on a past to be proud of (the doctrine of *historicism*).

When European countries finally started their second wave of expansion around 1870, they combined evolutionary and historicist thinking into a unique vision of world history—the vision that this entry refers to as the *mainstream* view. During this new era of imperialism, this vision was exported and forced upon colonized and other peoples in the periphery of Western expansion. It led to a slow process of historiographical acculturation and worldwide convergence of historical thinking. Even where westernized styles of historical scholarship met with resistance and had to merge with preexisting indigenous modes of historical thought (especially in non-Western countries with strong written or oral historiographical traditions), they gradually exerted dominance almost everywhere.

In the early years or the twenty-first century, if only a minority of non-Western historians seems to lament this situation, it is because the *mainstream* vision has gradually given way to more plurality and because the core of Western historical scholarship—its scientific method—developed beyond its European roots and appears to possess universal value. This is proven by the fact that non-Western historians have relentlessly criticized Eurocentric works of their Western colleagues by using the latter's own weapon: Western historical method. Indigenous historiography, where it still exists, is now seen as a valuable source of study.

In recent decades historians from all regions have exposed racist and ethnocentric features in historical writing—European and non-European. Modesty and relativism—perennial but secondary currents in the modes of thinking of European and non-European peoples—came to counterbalance earlier arrogance. Even currents that exaggerated and idealized historical achievements of non-Western peoples were observed. The circle of human beings who became included in the account of historians expanded to humanity at large. Today, many historians (though far from all) feel responsible for the whole of world history, which by definition cannot be written when non-Western history is omitted from the account.

INSIDERS AND OUTSIDERS

The next question, then, is whether people are really able to understand each other. Is there an unbridgeable gap of knowledge and understanding between cultures or can ethnocentrism be transcended, and if so, to what extent? The former view is called the *insider* perspective (members of culture *x* have monopolistic access to knowledge about *x*), whereas the latter is the *outsider* perspective (nonmembers of culture *x* have privileged access to knowledge about *x*). Table 1 gives an overview of these positions.

From Table 1, it may be concluded that both visions have advantages and disadvantages, and that, ideally, multiperspectivism is necessary for those scholars testing hypotheses and aspiring to complete knowledge. Weighing the positions of both parties, as is done in Table 1, is not enough: In addition, three facts should be pondered. The first is that radical "insiderism" leads to deadlock because all insiders are inevitably outsiders in relation to all others and therefore, on their own assumptions, are excluded from studying them.

The second fact is that outsiders *do* communicate their views about insiders and their culture, and these therefore merit study. In 1988 Mexican historian Luis González calculated that there were approximately one thousand historians writing about Mexico: About half of them were non-Mexican. If that is true for Mexico, it is even more so for numerous countries with lesser historiographical traditions. Even when outsider views are not correct or not desired, it is worth asking why they are not, especially when the holders of these views are able to exert political or other power over insiders.

The last fact is that the essence of any scholarship is its claim to universality that presupposes the possibility of knowing others. Indeed, scholars—like moderate outsiders—maintain that truth is universal, whereas insiders call it relative and experience-dependent. Without this claim to universality, the sciences of history and anthropology—with their study subjects often outside one's own time or space—would squarely come to an end, as American sociologist Robert Merton (1910–2003) clearly saw: "Taken seriously, the [Insider] doctrine puts in question the validity of just about all historical writing...If direct engagement in the life of a group is essential to understanding it, then the only authentic history is contemporary history, written in fragments by those most fully involved in making inevitably limited portions of it" (Merton 1973, p. 123).

CONCLUSION

The French anthropologist Claude Lévi-Strauss (b. 1908) has argued that a certain dose of lucid ethnocentrism is necessary to safeguard optimal cultural diversity: "Humanity...will have to learn again that each real act of creativity implies a certain deafness to the appeal of other values and that these may be refused or even disregarded. For it is not possible at the same time to lose oneself in—and identify oneself with—the other and still remain different" (Lévi-Strauss 1983, p. 47, quotation translated by Antoon De Baets).

This quotation also reveals that the key concept in any discussion about ethnocentrism is cultural diversity. This concept should be understood accurately. Overdoses of ethnocentrism and cultural relativism endanger cultural diversity. Too much ethnocentrism may lead to racism, ethnocide, or genocide; too much cultural relativism may lead to isolation or infertile uniformity.

These are all forms of exaggeration that threaten cultural diversity either by freezing or eliminating it. Historical wisdom teaches people to restrain ethnocentrism, not to eradicate it, and to encourage cultural relativism, not to exalt it. Such is the paradox: Cultures have to orient themselves toward each other, and, at the same time, stick to their own values. Both attitudes should remain in balance.

In the past, Eurocentrism, and especially its arrogant variants, was cultivated to aberrant heights, and therefore it is time to support cultural relativism today. Not to every price, however, because exchanging exalted Eurocentrism for exalted cultural relativism yields no progress. Czech author Milan Kundera (b. 1929) warned about such a risk in his *Book of Laughter and Forgetting*: "Each interpreted the other's words in his own way, and they lived in perfect harmony, the perfect solidarity of perfect mutual misunderstanding" (Kundera 1982, p. 227).

SEE ALSO *Anticolonialism; Censorship.*

BIBLIOGRAPHY

Bairoch, Paul. *Economics and World History: Myths and Paradoxes.* New York: Harvester Wheatsheaf, 1993.

Baudet, E. H. P. *Paradise on Earth: Some Thoughts on European Images of Non-European Man.* (1959). Translated by Elizabeth Wentholt. New Haven, CT: Yale University Press, 1965.

Benjamin, Thomas. "Historiography." In *Encyclopedia of Mexican History, Society and Culture*, edited by Michael S. Werner. Chicago: Fitzroy Dearborn, 1997.

Dance, E. H. *History the Betrayer: A Study in Bias.* London: Hutchinson, 1960.

De Baets, Antoon. "Der 'Hauptstrom' der Geschichte: Determinanten eines Darstellungsprinzips in Geschichtslehrbüchern." *Internationale Schulbuchforschung–International Textbook Research* 14 (4) (1992): 345–371.

De Baets, Antoon. *De figuranten van de geschiedenis: Hoe het verleden van andere culturen wordt verbeeld en in herinnering gebracht* (The Walk-Ons of History: How the Past of Other Cultures Is Represented and Remembered). Antwerp, Belgium: Epo, 1994; Hilversum, Netherlands: Verloren, 1994.

De Baets, Antoon. "Eurocentrism in the Writing and Teaching of History." In *A Global Encyclopedia of Historical Writing*, edited by D. R. Woolf. New York and London: Garland, 1998.

Evans-Pritchard, Edward E. "Anthropology and History" (1961). In *Essays in Social Anthropology*. London: Faber and Faber, 1962.

Ferro, Marc. *The Use and Abuse of History, or, How the Past Is Taught to Children.* Revised edition, translated by Norman Stone and Andrew Brown. New York: Routledge, 2003.

Fischer, David H. *Historians' Fallacies: Toward a Logic of Historical Thought.* New York: Harper, 1970.

Gordon, David C. *Self-determination and History in the Third World.* Princeton, NJ: Princeton University Press, 1971.

Hodgson, Marshall. "The Interrelations of Societies in History" (1963). In *Rethinking World History: Essays on Europe, Islam and World History.* Cambridge, U.K.: Cambridge University Press, 1993.

Hourani, Albert, Gustave von Grunebaum, and Wilfred Cantwell Smith. "General Themes." In *Historians of the Middle East*, edited by Bernard Lewis and P. M. Holt. London: Oxford University Press, 1962.

International Court of Justice. *Western Sahara: Advisory Opinion of 16 October 1975.* The Hague, Netherlands: International Court of Justice, 1975.

Kundera, Milan. *The Book of Laughter and Forgetting.* (1978). Translated by Michael Henry Heim. London: Faber and Faber, 1982.

Lefkowitz, Mary. *Not Out of Africa: How Afrocentrism Became an Excuse to Teach Myth as History.* New York: BasicBooks, 1996.

Lévi-Strauss, Claude. "Race and History" (1951). In *Race, Science, and Society*, edited by Leo Kuper. Paris: UNESCO, 1975; London: Allen & Unwin, 1975.

Lévi-Strauss, Claude. "Race et culture" (1971). In *Le Regard éloigné.* Paris: Plon, 1983.

Lewis, Bernard. *History—Remembered, Recovered, Invented.* Princeton, NJ: Princeton University Press, 1975.

Lewis, Bernard. "Other People's History." *American Scholar* 50 (1990): 397–405.

Memmi, Albert. *The Colonizer and the Colonized.* (1957). Translated by Howard Greenfeld. New York: Orion, 1965.

Merton, Robert K. "The Perspectives of Insiders and Outsiders" (1972). In *The Sociology of Science: Theoretical and Empirical Investigations.* Chicago and London: University of Chicago Press, 1973.

Moniot, Henri. "L'Histoire des peuples sans histoire." In *Faire de l'histoire*, Vol. 1: *Nouveaux problèmes*, edited by Jacques Le Goff and Pierre Nora. Paris: Gallimard, 1974.

Nandy, Ashis. "History's Forgotten Doubles." *History and Theory: Studies in the Philosophy of History.* Theme Issue 34: *World Historians and Their Critics* (1995): 44–66.

O'Brien, Patrick. "Global History: Universal and World." In *International Encyclopedia of the Social and Behavioral Sciences*, Vol. 9, edited by Neil J. Smelser and Paul B. Baltes. Oxford: Elsevier-Pergamon, 2001.

Pocock, John G. A. "The Origins of the Study of the Past: A Comparative Approach." *Comparative Studies in Society and History* 4 (2) (1962): 209–246.

Preiswerk, Roy, and Dominique Perrot. *Ethnocentrism and History: Africa, Asia, and Indian America in Western Textbooks.* (1975). New York and London: NOK, 1978.

Rorty, Richard. "Afterword." In *Historians and Social Values*, edited by Joep Leerssen and Ann Rigney. Amsterdam: Amsterdam University Press, 2000.

Rüsen, Jörn, ed. *Western Historical Thinking: An Intercultural Debate.* (1999) New York: Berghahn, 2002.

Rüsen, Jörn. "How to Overcome Ethnocentrism: Approaches to a Culture of Recognition by History in the Twenty-First Century." *History and Theory: Studies in the Philosophy of History.* Theme Issue 43: *Historians and Ethics* (2004): 118–129.

Sachs, Ignacy. *The Discovery of the Third World.* (1917). Translated by Michael Fineberg. Cambridge, MA: MIT Press, 1976.

Sahlins, Marshall. "Reports of the Death of Cultures Have Been Exaggerated." In *What Happens to History? The Renewal of Ethics in Contemporary Thought*, edited by Howard Marchitello. New York: Routledge, 2001.

Sumner, William G. *Folkways: A Study of the Sociological Importance of Usages, Manners, Customs, Mores, and Morals.* Boston: Ginn, 1906.

Trevor-Roper, Hugh. *The Rise of Christian Europe.* London: Thames and Hudson, 1965.

Vansina, Jan. *Oral Tradition as History.* London: James Currey, 1985.

Antoon De Baets

Theodor de Bry's late sixteenth-century engraving depicts coastal Indians trading with the British explorer Bartholomew Gosnold and his men. The Europeans trade knives and hats for strings of wampum. © CORBIS. REPRODUCED BY PERMISSION.

EUROPEAN EXPLORATIONS IN NORTH AMERICA

In the aftermath of Christopher Columbus's (1451–1506) voyages to the Western Hemisphere, the monarchs of western European nations sent explorers seeking a faster, more direct passage to Asia. Although these explorers failed in this mission, they helped map out a rich land for Europeans to control and colonize.

English exploration differed from that of Spain, Portugal, and France. The English monarchs did not have the wealth of their counterparts, so English merchants played a large role in English exploration and colonization. In addition, English kings for many decades were more involved in securing control over the British Isles than in seeking to expand to a New World.

Nonetheless, while beginning in more fits and starts than its neighbors, England established a strong set of colonies that in time would come to dominate North America, albeit as the independent countries of the United States and Canada.

In 1497 and 1498, an Italian explorer, Giovanni Caboto (John Cabot, ca. 1450–1499) explored North America on behalf of King Henry VII (1457–1509) of England. In this first expedition, Cabot left Bristol on May 2, 1497, with one small ship, the *Matthew*, and only eighteen men. He reached Newfoundland, which he claimed for the king, believing it to be an island off Asia. King Henry approved a second voyage and provided one ship; English merchants funded four more. The expedition set out in May 1498; one ship soon returned for repairs and the other four, as well as Cabot, disappeared, never to return.

King Henry VIII (1491–1547) followed his father, and was not as supportive of such expeditions or expenses. Sebastian Cabot (ca. 1484–1557), John's son, left in 1508 and returned to England when his crew threatened mutiny. He found that Henry VII had died and Henry VIII declined to finance a return. In time, Sebastian Cabot moved to Spain and sailed under the sponsorship of the Spanish Crown.

English exploration and adventuring in the Americas increased after Elizabeth I (1533–1603) succeeded her father, Henry VIII, in 1558. The search for a Northwest Passage to Asia continued to influence explorers: From 1576 to 1578 Martin Frobisher (ca. 1535–1594) made several transatlantic voyages in search of a Northwest Passage. After his failure, John Davis (1543–1605) made several more abortive quests for such a passage in 1585 to 1887.

During the same period, the English also became more active in intruding into Spanish domains in the Americas. Francis Drake (ca. 1543–1596) set sail in 1577 with five ships to explore the Americas and to bring home treasure and spices. He lost several ships but continued in his flagship, the *Golden Hind,* around South America. He reached California in June 1579, and thereafter sailed around Asia and Africa and returned to England, where Elizabeth knighted him on his ship.

The next year, Elizabeth authorized Sir Humphrey Gilbert (ca. 1539–1583) to "plant" an English colony in America. He envisioned a colony as a place to dispose of England's surplus population, and he aimed for what he called "Norumbega," a region later called North Virginia, and finally New England. Gilbert's first attempt, in September 1578, failed when storms forced the ships to seek refuge in Plymouth. He tried again in 1583, and he reached Newfoundland on August 3. He returned to England on one of the smaller ships in his small fleet, and as they neared the English coast that ship, the *Squirrel,* disappeared with Gilbert. But he had involved his half-brother, Sir Walter Raleigh (ca. 1554–1618), who subsequently continued to pursue schemes for English colonization in the Americas.

Raleigh received a charter similar to Gilbert's from Elizabeth I, and he sought to colonize North America to serve England and to make profit. In 1584 Raleigh sent an expedition that sailed along the Atlantic Coast of North America, and he named this area Virginia after Elizabeth, England's "Virgin queen." The expedition explored Roanoke Island, off present-day North Carolina. Three years later, Raleigh sent a colonizing expedition of men, women, and children to settle Roanoke. He intended to send more supplies the

North American discoveries	
THE FIFTEENTH AND SIXTEENTH CENTURIES	
1497	Voyage of Cabot to North America
1498	Second Voyage of Cabot to North America
1524	Verrazanno: Cape Fear to Newfoundland
1534–1541	Cartier: Gulf of St. Lawrence
1539–1543	De Soto: Mississippi River

THE GALE GROUP.

following year, but 1588 marked the appearance of the first Spanish Armada, a fleet of warships sent by Spain to invade England. For several years, England was consumed in the great effort of battling Spain, and Raleigh's supply ships could not return until 1590. When the ships arrived, the colonists had vanished, and no sign of them, save for one word, "Croatan," carved on a post, has ever been found—an enduring mystery.

This experience halted English efforts at colonization until James I (1566–1625) succeeded Elizabeth in 1603. As gold and other wealth from Spanish America flowed through Spain, sometimes to English merchants, these merchants formed early versions of limited liability corporations, so-called joint-stock companies, to explore and settle the New World and to create riches for their investors.

Equally important, one Englishman helped make a strong case for colonial settlements in North America. Richard Hakluyt (ca. 1552–1616) was an English geographer, editor, and clergyman. In 1589 he published *The Principal Navigations, Voyages, and Discoveries of the English Nation,* which consisted of eyewitness accounts and other records of more than two hundred overseas voyages. These accounts created interest in colonizing North America, and Hakluyt himself helped organize the settling of the Jamestown colony.

The idea of limited liability and Hakluyt as propagandist combined to lead to the two principal English settlements in North America, which subsequently expanded to create the thirteen colonies that existed on the eve of the American Revolution in the 1770s. Two joint-stock companies received charters in 1606. One, the Virginia Company of Plymouth, sent two ships that made landfall in August 1607 along the coast of Maine. After two months spent building a small settlement and fort and befriending local Indians for supplies, the colonists faced the harsh Maine winter; a fire destroyed the storehouse and several other buildings, and the men soon sailed for home.

The other company, the Virginia Company of London, had better luck though the venture was not

Early English Colonists Arriving at Roanoke Island, Virginia. *In 1584 Sir Walter Raleigh's expedition to North America explored Roanoke Island, off present-day North Carolina. Three years later, Raleigh sent a group of men, women, and children to settle Roanoke. By the time supply ships returned to Roanoke in 1590, all the settlers had vanished.* © BETTMANN/CORBIS. REPRODUCED BY PERMISSION.

without difficulties. In 1609 the company sent an expedition to present-day Virginia, and established Jamestown, named in honor of James I. After a rough start, John Smith (1580–1631) took control and provided needed discipline, and the settlers discovered what at the time seemed a novel crop, tobacco, which helped the colony survive and prosper. Colonies in Massachusetts, Maryland, and elsewhere followed the colony in Virginia, and eventually helped establish a line of English settlements along the Atlantic Coast.

Meanwhile, as the English struggled to establish settlements along the North American coast, French explorers fared better. The French king, François I (1494–1547), sent Jacques Cartier (1491–1557), who left Saint Malo in 1534 with two ships seeking a passage to Asia and new lands to claim for France. Cartier passed Newfoundland and found the mouth of the Saint Lawrence River. On his second voyage in 1535, he explored the Saint Lawrence and passed the sites that became the cities of Quebec and Montreal. He sailed back to France in 1536.

While French kings became caught up in warfare on the European continent, two explorers followed the path that Cartier had blazed. Samuel de Champlain (ca. 1570–1635) established France's first permanent settlement at Quebec in 1608, and further explored the upper Saint Lawrence, as well as the coasts of Nova Scotia and Maine. He found the lake reaching south of Montreal that was later named after him, and made his way along the Great Lakes to Lake Huron. In the 1680s Sieur de La Salle (1643–1687) built upon Champlain's explorations to reach the Mississippi River by portage. He claimed that great basin for the French king, Louis XIV (1638–1715), and named it Louisiana.

Missionaries, soldiers, and fur traders followed these explorers, and they interacted with American Indian tribes far better than the English colonists to the south.

In many ways, the great voyages of exploration were ending, and the era of colonial exploitation and war for territory would soon begin.

SEE ALSO *Biological Impacts of European Expansion in the Americas; Columbus, Christopher; Empire in the Americas, British; Empire in the Americas, Dutch; Empire in the Americas, French; Empire in the Americas, Portuguese; Empire in the Americas, Spanish; Hakluyt, Richard; Mission, Civilizing.*

BIBLIOGRAPHY

Bernier, Jane. *Explorers of the New World: The Earliest Voyages from Europe.* Cleveland Heights, OH: Borrower's Press, 1984.

Cumming, W. P., R. A. Skelton, and D. B. Quinn. *The Discovery of North America.* London: Elek, 1971.

Eccles, W. J. *The French in North America, 1500–1765.* East Lansing: Michigan State University Press, 1998.

Goslinga, Cornelis C. *The Dutch in the Caribbean and on the Wild Coast, 1580–1680.* Gainesville: University of Florida Press, 1971

Hamshere, Cyril. *The British in the Caribbean.* Cambridge, MA: Harvard University Press, 1972.

Horgan, Paul. *Conquistadors in North American History.* New York: Farrar, Straus, 1963.

Knight, Alan. *Mexico: From the Beginning to the Spanish Conquest.* New York: Cambridge University Press, 2002.

McFarlane, Anthony. *The British in the Americas, 1480–1815.* New York: Longman, 1994.

Morison, Samuel Eliot. *The European Discovery of America.* New York: Oxford University Press, 1971.

Newton, Arthur P. *The European Nations in the West Indies, 1493–1688.* London: A. & C. Black, 1933.

Quinn, David B. *Explorers and Colonies: America, 1500–1625.* Ronceverte, WV: Hambledon, 1990

Sokolow, Jayme A. *The Great Encounter: Native Peoples and European Settlers in the Americas, 1492–1800.* Armonk, NY: Sharpe, 2003.

Trudel, Marcel. *The Beginnings of New France, 1524–1663.* Translated by Patricia Claxton. Toronto: McClelland and Stewart, 1973.

Weddle, Robert S. *Spanish Sea: The Gulf of Mexico in North American Discovery, 1500–1685.* College Station: Texas A&M University Press, 1985.

Charles M. Dobbs

EUROPEAN EXPLORATIONS IN SOUTH AMERICA

At the end of the fifteenth century, technological developments in shipbuilding and the search for new commercial markets and spices combined with unique configurations of crusade, curiosity, and adventure to take Europeans across the Atlantic. Christopher Columbus's (1451–1506) four voyages of discovery are the most famous of these explorations, and their motivations and characteristics were continued and developed throughout the sixteenth century across the South American continent.

When Columbus caught sight of land (which he named San Salvador) in the Bahamas on October 12, 1492, he believed that he was close to Japan and a valuable westward route to the spice trade of Asia. He subsequently sailed on to Cuba and Hispaniola, naming and recording his brief encounters with native people before hurrying back to Spain to register his discoveries with the Catholic monarchs, Ferdinand II (1452–1516) and Isabella (1451–1504). By the time of the Treaty of Tordesillas (1494) with Portugal, Columbus was already on his second voyage, during which he discovered the destruction of his settlement of Navidad on Hispaniola by native people. Columbus returned to Spain in 1496 to defend himself against the complaints of bitter colonists whose dreams had yet to be realized. Columbus's third voyage (1498–1500) took him to Trinidad and the fresh water delta of the Orinoco River, which he speculated might lead to the Earthly Paradise in a vast new continent (it was Amerigo Vespucci [1454–1512], following in Columbus's wake, who received the credit for formulating this idea). In 1500 Pedro Álvars Cabral (1468–1520) landed on the Brazilian coast near Porto Seguro in Bahia on Portugal's follow-up voyage to Vasco da Gama's (1460–1524) successful sea voyage to the Indian Ocean. On his fourth voyage (1502–1504) Columbus's mystical and religious leanings thrived on his bitterness at ill-treatment by his colonists. He traced the coastline of Central America from Honduras down to Panama, on the way being captured by native people. He escaped. By now Columbus was more interested in millenarian prophecies of using New World gold to finance a crusade on Jerusalem than in augmenting his own personal fortune.

After Columbus's death in 1506, exploration of the circum-Caribbean was fuelled by two factors: the desire to capture more Indian labor to replace those native people who died of disease or abuse, and the adventurous instincts of Spanish men hoping to make their fortunes in the New World. Puerto Rico was conquered in 1508, Jamaica in 1509, and Cuba in 1511. Juan Ponce de León (1460–1521) discovered Florida in 1513. These islands provided the basis for further explorations. In 1513 an expedition was sent out from Spain under Pedrarias Dávila (1440–1531) to conquer the Isthmus of Panama. A survivor of an earlier slave-raiding expedition in 1509, Vasco Núñez de Balboa (1475–1519), crossed the isthmus first and claimed the waters of the Pacific Ocean for the Catholic monarchs in September 1513. Dávila quarrelled with Balboa and had him executed.

In this engraving (circa 1521), the Italian-born explorer, Amerigo Vespucci, (1454–1512) for whom the American continent was named, stands at the bow of his ship, surrounded by fantastic sea creatures and deities. © BETTMANN/CORBIS. REPRODUCED BY PERMISSION.

Once begun, discovery and conquest developed their own momentum. Hernán Cortés (1484–1547) came to epitomize the bold fortune hunter. Diego Velázquez (1465–1524), governor of Cuba, sent out two expeditions to explore the coast of Mexico in 1517–1518. In 1519 Cortés took advantage of the findings of these expeditions by launching the conquest of what he came to label New Spain, without authorization from Velázquez. During the next three years Cortés dedicated himself to the conquest of the empire ruled by Montezuma II (1466–1520) from the great city of Tenochtitlán. Cortés exploited, and was himself used by, pre-existing conflicts between native people. He launched major military campaigns against those who opposed him. At the same time he wrote *Cartas de relación* to Charles V (1500–1558) back in Europe, appealing over the heads of colonial officials for recognition of his extralegal conquests. Cortés's example further heightened the momentum of adventure, ambition, and exploration. Pedro de Alvarado (1485–1541), who had

served under Cortés, spent ten years in the conquest of Guatemala and El Salvador before reaching expeditions sent up from Panama by Dávila. Francisco de Montejo (1479–1553) attempted the conquest of the Yucatán in 1527, which was resisted by the Maya until their rebellion was violently suppressed in 1542.

Panama was the base for exploration of the Pacific and, eventually, the discovery and conquest of Peru. Francisco Pizarro (1475–1541) and Diego de Almagro (1475–1538) obtained permission to this end from Dávila in 1524. Returning after repeated difficulties, Pizarro was convinced that he could found a personal empire on the wealth of the rumored kingdom of the South. In 1530 he set out from Panama with about 180 men. Using Cortés's dealings with Montezuma as a model, in 1532 Pizarro captured the Inca emperor Atahualpa (1502–1533) and exploited the subsequent stumblings of the Inca empire to manipulate local factions and grievances. Atahualpa was executed in 1533.

Pizarro entrusted the exploration of the northern provinces of Quito to Sebastián de Benalcázar (1495–1551). He had to compete with a rival expedition under Pedro de Alvarado (1485–1541) who arrived from Guatemala. During the 1530s Benalcázar progressed north into the Cauca Valley. Near the capital of the Chibcha, Bogotá, he encountered two expeditions that had traveled down from the Caribbean coast, led respectively by Gonzalo Jiménez de Quesada (1495–1579) and Nikolaus Federmann (1505–1542). The groups avoided armed confrontation, and their combined findings encouraged belief in the existence of a city of gold, El Dorado, which would itself act as the spur to further explorations of New Granada and Venezuela. The consolidation of European rule in Peru foundered on rival claims to wealth and political influence. Further south, Pizarro's attempt to build a personal empire for his family and descendents was resisted by rebellions led by the Inca heir Manco Inca Yupanqui (1516–1545) during 1536–1539, and by his own bitter subordinates. Civil war between the followers of Almagro and Pizarro in 1537 and 1538 ended with Almagro's execution and a subsequent chain of bloodletting that encompassed Francisco Pizarro who was killed in 1541. In the same year his brother, Gonzalo (1502–1548), led an expedition from Quito, the consequence of which was Francisco de Orellana's (1490–1546) discovery and navigation of the river he named the Amazon because of the female warriors who attacked him during the exploration.

In addition to the Amazon, the New World provided a new lease of life for medieval legends including golden cities, fountains of youth, paradise on earth and, of course, great wealth. Alvar Núñez Cabeza de Vaca (1490–1560) survived an 1528 expedition to Florida and journeyed overland until he reached Mexico City in 1536. His stories inspired other adventurers to explore new lands; Cabeza de Vaca himself later journeyed through the Brazilian interior to Paraguay, where he was briefly governor of Asunción (1542). In 1540 Francisco Vasquez de Coronado (1510–1554) explored New Mexico and Arizona in search of the mythical Seven Cities of Cíbola, traversing through Texas, Oklahoma, and Kansas. Another of Pizarro's men, Hernando de Soto (1500–1542), sought his fortune in 1541 on an expedition through Georgia, Alabama, and Louisiana, leading to the discovery of the Mississippi River. Francisco Pizarro's advances led to many subsequent expeditions using Peru as a base. Pedro de Valdivia (1498–1553) left Cuzco in 1540 and after crossing the Andes and the Atacama Desert, founded Santiago de Chile in 1541. Valdivia was killed in battle with the Araucanians in 1553.

On the Atlantic coast, Portugal was distracted by its efforts on the route to India during the first half of the

South American discoveries	
THE FIFTEENTH AND SIXTEENTH CENTURIES	
1492–1493	First Voyage of Columbus: Caribbean
1493–1496	Second Voyage: Puerto Rico and Jamaica
1498–1500	Third Voyage of Cabot: South America
1499–1500	Ojeda and Vespucci: South America
1500	Cabral Claimed Brazil for Portugal
1502–1504	Fourth Voyage of Cabot: Central America
1513	Balboa Crossed Panama and Saw the Pacific
1517	Hernández de Córdova: Yucatan
1519–1522	Magellan Voyage Circumnavigated the Globe
1524–1528	Pizarro: The Coast of Peru
1526–1532	Sebastian Cabot: Rio de la Plata

THE GALE GROUP.

sixteenth century, but it began to explore and settle in Brazil to ward off potential French competition during mid-century, triggered by the exploratory voyages of the French Breton sailor Jacques Cartier (1491–1557). The Jesuit order was fundamental in collaborating with royal government to establish a strong central government in Brazil. The lack of immediate financial returns was a further reason delaying settlement and conquest on the Atlantic seaboard. Further south, the River Plate estuary was explored by Spanish adventurers in the hope that it might provide Columbus's long-hoped-for passage to Asia. Juan Díaz de Solis (1470–1516) explored in 1516 and Ferdinand Magellan (1480–1521) four years later. Unsuccessful, Magellan travelled south in search of such a passage and in November 1520 discovered the straits that led him into the Pacific.

While desire for gold and silver was important, explorations were also orientated by dreams of power and social advancement, shaped by encounters with indigenous people, and developed their own momentum through the influence of charismatic figures such as Columbus, Cortés, and Pizarro, whose efforts were recorded and relayed throughout the new colonial world. But if exploration had only been motivated by plunder it would not have happened at all. While Columbus may have been a self-styled discoverer, the likes of Cortés and Pizarro looked beyond the short-term in the hope of establishing permanent settlements from which they and their families could extract permanent honor, influence, and wealth. The spread of religion was also an important factor in the configuration of exploration. In difficult moments Columbus and Cortés revealed their millenarian and crusading inspirations. Chivalric tradition is particularly evident in conquistador writings, and the desire to bring Christianity to the heathen must not be discounted from the encounter between Old and New

Worlds, no matter how much it was besmirched by the often grubby and violent nature of physical conquest. Myths and legends suffused the exploration of South America by Europeans. Whether there were claims that indigenous people welcomed them as returning gods or dreams of noble savages and cities of gold, exploration was closely linked to colonization, settlement, and conversion. Indeed adventure, exploration, and quests for honor through travel remained important themes through subsequent centuries. Exploration led inextricably to empire.

SEE ALSO *European Explorations in North America.*

BIBLIOGRAPHY

Boxer, Charles. *Portuguese Seaborne Empire 1415-1825.* London: Hutchinson, 1969.

Fernández-Armesto, F. *Columbus.* Oxford: Oxford University Press, 1991.

Hemming, John. *The Search for El Dorado.* London: Joseph, 1978.

Pagden, A., ed. *Hernán Cortés Letters from Mexico.* New Haven, CT: Yale University Press, 1986.

Parry, J.H. *The Age of Reconnaissance 1450-1650.* Berkeley: University of California Press, 1963.

Sauer, Carl. *The Early Spanish Main.* Berkeley: University of California Press; London: Cambridge University Press, 1966.

Varon Gabai, R. *Francisco Pizarro and His Brothers: Illusion of Power in Sixteenth-Century Peru.* Norman: University of Oklahoma Press, 1997.

Matthew Brown

EUROPEAN MIGRATIONS TO AMERICAN COLONIES, 1492–1820

In the three centuries following the voyages of Christopher Columbus (1451–1506) to the Americas, the world was transformed by a massive transoceanic movement of peoples, the largest in human history up to that time. The migration of several million Europeans to the Americas during this period was fundamental to the formation of New World society. European settlement and diseases devastated indigenous populations and led to a scramble for lands on a continental scale that resulted in a checkerboard of Euro-American societies from the Hudson Bay in northern Canada to Tierra del Fuego, an island group off the southern tip of South America. From the Atlantic ports of Europe—principally of Britain, Spain, and Portugal—wave after wave of settlers, rich and poor, took ship seeking their fortune "beyond the seas."

MAGNITUDE AND PACE

Between 1492 and 1820, approximately 2.6 million Europeans immigrated to the Americas (compared to at least 8.8 million enslaved Africans). Across the period, slightly less than half of all migrants were British, 40 percent were Spanish and Portuguese, 6 percent were from Swiss and German states, and 5 percent were French. In terms of sheer numbers, other nationalities—Dutch, Swedish, Danish, and Finnish, for example—although contributing to the heterogeneity of Euro-American society, were negligible.

Annual rates of emigration climbed steadily across the three centuries, from 2,000 annually before 1580, to 8,000 per year in the second half of the seventeenth century, and between 13,000 and 14,000 per year in the eighteenth and early nineteenth centuries. Three principal phases of movement can be identified. The first century and a half was dominated by Spanish and Portuguese emigrants, who made up 87 percent of the 446,000 settlers leaving Europe between 1492 and 1640.

The second phase, lasting from 1640 to 1760, saw a three-fold increase in numbers of emigrants. During this period, 1.3 million settlers left Europe for the New World. Many of the British, French, Swiss, and German settlers who immigrated during this period arrived under labor contracts that typically obliged them to work between four and seven years in return for the cost of their passage, board, and lodging, and certain payments called "freedom dues." Freedom dues were made by the master to the servant on completion of the term of service, which typically took the form of provisions, clothing, tools, rights to land, money, or a small share of the crop (tobacco or sugar).

The final phase of early modern immigration, from 1760 to 1820, was once again dominated by free settlers and witnessed an enormous surge of British migrants to North America and the United States. These British migrants made up more than 70 percent of all emigrants who crossed the Atlantic in these years.

In the late fifteenth and early sixteenth centuries, the decision by Spanish and Portuguese monarchs to take possession of the New World and establish colonies governed by the crown required the transfer of large settler populations. Besides the plunder of American Indian societies, Spanish discoveries of silver mines at Potosí in Peru and Zacatecas in Mexico during the 1540s provided a significant stimulus to immigration throughout the remainder of the century. In the long run, however, the most important development that encouraged large-scale immigration of settlers from western Europe was not so much the pillage of Indian civilizations and the discovery of precious minerals as

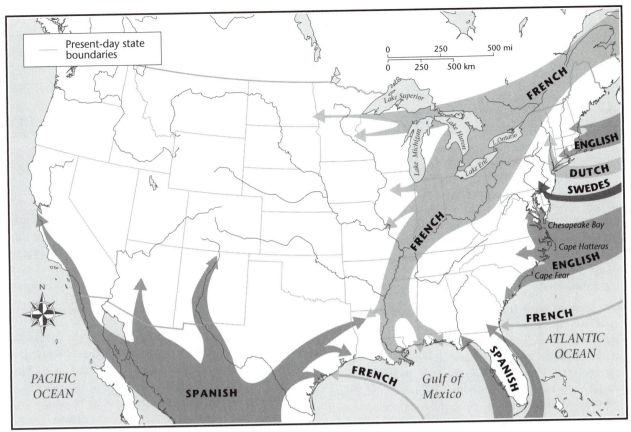

The Paths of Early European Penetration of North America. *Between 1492 and 1820, approximately 2.6 million Europeans migrated to the Americas. The Spanish moved into North America from the south; the English, Dutch and Swedes entered along the eastern seaboard; and the French mostly traveled from the northeast along the Saint Lawrence River and Great Lakes, with a few French migrants entering from the south and southeast.* **MAP BY XNR PRODUCTIONS. THE GALE GROUP.**

the production of consumables in high demand in Europe, notably sugar and to a lesser extent tobacco.

Sugar plantations had been established on the Atlantic islands of the Canaries, Madeira, and São Tomé by the Spanish and Portuguese in the second half of the fifteenth century. In the Americas, Portuguese Brazil (specifically the northeastern provinces of Pernambuco and Bahia) emerged as the epicenter of the world's sugar production by 1600, followed a half century later by a new sugar plantation complex founded by the English and French (supported by Dutch merchants and planters) on the islands of Barbados, Saint Christopher, Martinique, and Guadeloupe in the West Indies. Meanwhile in Chesapeake, the English colonies of Virginia and Maryland had begun to rapidly expand output of tobacco during the 1620s and 1630s.

In Spanish and British America alike, plantation colonies absorbed the great majority of white (and black enslaved) immigrants. Most of the 350,000 English migrants who crossed the Atlantic during the seventeenth century, for example, ended up in the West Indies

(180,000) and Chesapeake (120,000). Only about 23,000 settlers made their way to the American Middle Colonies and 21,000 to New England. English immigration represented the transfer of a massive labor force to America, which was essential for the development of staple agriculture—sugar and tobacco—in the West Indies and Chesapeake.

THE SOCIAL CHARACTER OF MIGRANTS

Gentlemen (*hildagos* in Spanish), government officials, merchants, servants, *filles du roy* (French maids), artisans, soldiers, planters, and farmers were among the tide of Europeans who embarked for the Americas in the early modern period. One vital distinction between them was whether they arrived free or were under some form of contractual labor obligation. Of the latter, the great majority were indentured servants (British), *engagés* (French), and *redemptioners* (German) who made up about half a million migrants between 1500 and 1800 and who worked under specific terms of service. Convicts and political prisoners contributed another 129,000 bound immigrants. In addition, an indeterminate number of men and women who were servants (for example, Spanish *criados*) in the service of an official, priest, or gentleman, and who might themselves be of relatively high social rank, made their way to the New World.

It is impossible to be precise about the proportion of those who arrived in America as unfree laborers. Across the entire period, certainly no less than 25 percent were servants, convicts, and prisoners. During the peak years of servant emigration in the second half of the seventeenth century, the figure was closer to 50 percent. Indentured servants made up between 70 and 85 percent of settlers who emigrated to the Chesapeake and British West Indies between 1620 and 1700. In British and French North America, cheap white labor was crucial to the early development of colonial economies and predated the adoption of enslaved African labor by several generations.

Servants came from a broad cross section of lower-class society, embracing child paupers and vagrants, unskilled laborers, those employed in low-grade service trades, domestic and agricultural servants, and poor textile workers. The great majority were young (between sixteen and twenty-five years of age), male, and single. Among sixteenth-century Spanish emigrants, women never made up more than 30 percent of the total. More than three-quarters of servants who left England in the seventeenth century were men and boys, rising to over 90 percent between 1718 and 1775. Of French *engagés* departing from Nantes and Bordeaux in the early eighteenth century, over 90 percent were male and between 67 and 70 percent were nineteen years of age or less.

Servant emigration was generally a two-stage process shaped by the same social and economic forces that influenced broader patterns of lower-class movement. Indentured servants were a subset of a much larger group of young, single, and poor men and women who moved from village to village and town to city in search of greater opportunities than were to be had at home. Cities and ports throughout Europe attracted the surplus labor of the surrounding countryside and market towns, as well as from further afield. London, for example, was a magnet for the poor, who poured into the capital and took up residence in the burgeoning slums outside the ancient city walls. According to a contemporary, they included "soldiers wanting wars to employ them, . . . serving-men whose lords and masters are dead, . . . masterless men whose masters have cast them off, [and] idle people, as lusty rogues and common beggars." They came, he observed, "hearing of the great liberality of London,"(Beier 1985, pp. 40–41).

Free emigrants—those able to fund their own transportation to America—were an equally diverse group.

Hundreds of thousands of independent farmers and tenants emigrated to set up farms and plantations. Alongside them from all parts of Europe was a steady flow of lesser gentry, professional men, and artisans—merchants, factors, teachers, doctors, priests, clergymen, accountants, ministers, weavers, smiths, carpenters, and others—in continual demand as the colonies expanded and matured. What distinguished them from servants was not only the possession of some capital to set themselves up in America but also personal or political connections.

Free migrants tended to be older than those who arrived under labor contracts, and they were more likely to arrive with their families, kin, or friends. Such family or kinship connections were of paramount importance in stimulating movement from Extremadura in Spain to the New World, for example, and also influenced (to a lesser degree) free emigration from Britain and parts of Germany.

As mentioned above, free migration was the dominant form of white movement during the sixteenth and early seventeenth centuries and in the period after 1750. A key characteristic of the second half of the eighteenth century was the increasing numbers of skilled and independent migrants opting to leave Europe against a background of growing prosperity and trade. As American commerce flourished and channels of communication were strengthened, the cost of passage fell and colonies became increasingly attractive and accessible.

Whether free or unfree, emigration from Europe to America was intensely regional. During the sixteenth and first half of the seventeenth centuries, the origins of Spanish emigrants were heavily skewed toward the southwest. Andalusia alone contributed between one-third and one-half of all migrants from Spain. In the late seventeenth and eighteenth centuries, the character of Spanish emigration changed dramatically, with far higher numbers of people moving from the poorer provinces of the north coast, the east, and from the Balearic and Canary Islands.

French migrants came chiefly from northern and western provinces and the Atlantic port towns of Rouen, Saint-Malo, Nantes, La Rochelle, and Bordeaux. Most migrants leaving England for America in the seventeenth century came from London, the Southeast, East Anglia, and the West Country. The eighteenth century, by contrast, saw large-scale movements from northern England, Ulster, southern Ireland, the western districts of the Scottish Borders and Lowlands, the Highlands, and Hebrides. German emigration embraced a wide variety of regions in the Protestant areas of the Palatinate, Nassau, Hesse,

European immigrants to America, 1500–1820

1500–1580	
Spain	100,000
Portugal	90,000
Britain	0
Total	190,000
1580–1640	
Spain	90,000
Portugal	110,000
Britain	50,000
France	4,000
Netherlands	2,000
Total	256,000
1640–1700	
Spain	70,000
Portugal	50,000
Britain	303,000
France	45,000
Netherlands	13,000
Total	481,000
1700–1760	
Spain	90,000
Portugal	250,000
Britain	289,000
France	51,000
Netherlands	5,000
Germany	97,000
Total	782,000
1760–1820	
Spain	70,000
Portugal	105,000
Britain	615,000
France	20,000
Netherlands	5,000
Germany	51,000
Other	5,000
Total	871,000
1500–1820	
Spain	420,000
Portugal	605,000
Britain	1,257,000
France	120,000
Netherlands	25,000
Germany	148,000
Other	5,000
Total	2,580,000

SOURCE: Adapted from James Horn and Philip D. Morgan (2005, 21–22).

THE GALE GROUP.

a "pity it is that thousands of my country people should stay starving att [*sic*] home when they may live here in peace and plenty, as a great many who have been transported for a punishment have found pleasure, profit and ease and would rather undergo any hardship than be forced back to their own country" (Horn 1998, p.51). America was described by one settler as a "paradise" where newcomers "had nought to do but pluck and eat," (Horn 1998, p.51). If not paradise, the New World offered the possibility of a better future for those who risked moving to America and, if they survived, a lifestyle that would have been impossible at home.

SEE ALSO *Empire in the Americas, Spanish; Empire, British; Empire, French; European Explorations in North America.*

BIBLIOGRAPHY

Altman, Ida. *Emigrants and Society: Extremadura and America in the Sixteenth Century.* Berkeley: University of California Press, 1989.

Altman, Ida, and James Horn, eds. *"To Make America": European Emigration in the Early Modern Period.* Berkeley: University of California Press, 1991.

Bailyn, Bernard. *Voyagers to the West: A Passage in the Peopling of America on the Eve of the Revolution.* New York: Knopf, 1986.

Beier, A. L. *Masterless Men: The Vagrancy Problem in England, 1560–1640.* London: Methuen, 1985.

Canny, Nicholas, ed. *Europeans on the Move: Studies on European Migration, 1500–1800.* Oxford, U.K.: Clarendon, 1994.

Choquette, Leslie. *Frenchmen into Peasants: Modernity and Tradition in the Peopling of French Canada.* Cambridge, MA: Harvard University Press, 1997.

Eltis, David, ed. *Coerced and Free Migration: Global Perspectives.* Stanford, CA: Stanford University Press, 2002.

Emmer, P. C., and M. Mörner, eds. *European Expansion and Migration: Essays on the Intercontinental Migration from Africa, Asia, and Europe.* New York: Berg, 1991.

Fogleman, Aaron Spencer. *Hopeful Journeys: German Immigration, Settlement, and Political Culture in Colonial America, 1717–1775.* Philadelphia: University of Pennsylvania Press, 1996.

Gemery, Henry. "European Emigration to North America, 1700–1820: Numbers and Quasi-Numbers." *Perspectives in American History,* New Series, 1 (1984): 283–342.

Horn, James. "British Diaspora: Emigration from Britain, 1680–1815." In *The Oxford History of the British Empire, Vol. 2: The Eighteenth Century,* edited by P. J. Marshall. Oxford, U.K.: Oxford University Press, 1998.

Horn, James, and Philip D. Morgan. "Settlers and Slaves: European and African Migrations to Early Modern British America." In *The Creation of the British Atlantic World,* edited by Elizabeth Manke and Carole Shammas. Baltimore, MD: Johns Hopkins University Press, 2005.

Baden-Durlach, and Wurttemberg, as well as the Swiss cantons of Basel, Berne, and Zurich.

Motives for leaving Europe—religious, political, or social—were as diverse as migrants' social backgrounds, but economic opportunity in the broadest sense was the single most important reason that people boarded ships for the colonies. Roderick Gordon, a Scot who immigrated to Virginia, confided to his brother in 1734,

Klooster, Wim, and Alfred Padula. *The Atlantic World: Essays on Slavery, Migration, and Imagination.* Upper Saddle River, NJ: Pearson/Prentice Hall, 2005.

Wokeck, Marianne S. *Trade in Strangers: The Beginnings of Mass Migration to North America.* University Park: Pennsylvania State University Press, 1999.

James Horn

EXPLORATION, THE PACIFIC

During the fourteenth and early fifteenth centuries, Europeans became accustomed to luxury goods, especially rare spices, imported from Asia. Islam's spread—including the 1453 fall of Constantinople (now Istanbul, Turkey) and the 1517 Ottoman invasion of Egypt—cut off this trade and lent a new urgency to Europe's quest to find a direct route to the Far East. This, in turn, resulted in an era of European exploration that eventually led to the discovery of the Pacific Ocean, the world's largest body of water extending from the western Americas to eastern Asia and Australia, and one of its most diverse cultural regions, including such civilizations as the Chinese, Aztecs, and Polynesians.

Portugal took the lead in this undertaking under Prince Henrique (1394–1460), better known as Henry the Navigator, who supported exploring parties that mapped almost the entire coastline of West Africa. In 1492 Christopher Columbus (1451–1506) attempted to circumnavigate the globe by sailing west, and mistakenly thought he had discovered a new route to Asia when he discovered the New World. In 1498 Vasco da Gama (ca. 1469–1524) rounded Africa, reached the Indian Ocean, and later arrived in India. By 1516 the Portuguese were in China, and by 1557 they had convinced the ruling Ming dynasty (1368–1644) to cede them Macao, the first European colony in Asia. In 1542 Portugal also became the first European country to trade with Japan. The Portuguese mariner Ferdinand Magellan (1480–1521) sailed around South America in 1520, landed in the Philippines in 1521, and led the expedition that became the first to circumnavigate the globe. In 1529 Spain and Portugal divided Asia between them in the Treaty of Saragossa. In 1564 a Spanish fleet conquered the Philippines, which remained a Spanish colony through 1898. Meanwhile, British influence in the Pacific region gradually grew. In 1578 Sir Francis Drake (ca. 1543–1596) transited the Strait of Magellan to the Pacific Ocean. After exploring as far north as present-day San Francisco, California, he sailed across the Pacific to the Moluccas (Spice Islands). When Drake reached Java he took on a load of spices, and returned to England in November 1580. Drake's success threatened Spain's spice monopoly, but in 1588 the British Navy destroyed the Spanish Armada, which ensured the freedom of the seas. This victory allowed another small European power—Holland—to obtain a toehold in the Pacific. The first Dutch fleet commanded by Jacob Mahu (ca. 1564–1598) reached the Pacific around 1600. Most of the ships were shipwrecked or sunk, but at least one found its way to Japan. Its pilot, William Adams (ca. 1564–1620), served the Japanese shogun until his death. After the Dutch colonized Indonesia, calling it the Dutch Indies, they moved north and landed on Formosa (Taiwan), meaning "beautiful island." In 1624 the Dutch built a fort on Formosa called Zeelandia. In February 1662 Ming loyalist Zheng Chenggong (Koxinga, 1624–1662) besieged Zeelandia and forced the Dutch to retreat. In 1683, after a fifty-nine-year absence, Taiwan returned to Chinese control.

In 1600 Queen Elizabeth I (1533–1603) of England granted a charter to the "Governor and Merchants of London Trading into the East Indies," better known as the East India Company. Beginning in 1699, the East India Company also established a trading post in the southern Chinese port of Guangzhou (Canton). Following Britain's conquest of India in 1757, King George III (1738–1820) sent Lord George Macartney (1737–1806) to open up China in 1793. Although his mission failed, British intentions to dominate trade with China eventually resulted in the first Opium War (1839–1842), which for the first time opened up other Chinese ports to foreign trade. Meanwhile, British explorers, most notably James Cook (1728–1779), continued to explore the Pacific. Based on their discoveries, the British began to colonize Australia in 1788 and New Zealand in 1790. Other European nations, like Russia, were also moving into the Pacific region. Following the fifteenth-century collapse of the Mongol Empire, Czar Ivan the Terrible (1530–1584) made Russia a Eurasian power by extending his realm from the White Sea in northwest Russia all the way to Siberia in 1584. By the late 1630s, the Russian settlement of Udsk was founded on the Sea of Okhotsk. In 1860 Russians founded the city of Vladivostok, meaning "ruler of the east," on the Pacific Ocean directly across from Japan.

Before the European advance into East Asia, Japan was isolated and its international trade was small. In 1854 U.S. Commodore Matthew Calbraith Perry (1794–1858) visited Japan and forced it to open diplomatic and trade relations with the United States. With the Meiji Restoration, which began in 1867, Japan actively adopted Western ways, including a constitutional monarchy, a modern army and navy, and international law. In May 1875 Japan annexed the southern Kuril Islands to the north of Hokkaido, and then in 1876 obtained all of the Kurils in exchange for ceding the southern half of Sakhalin Island to Russia. In 1879

CAPTAIN JAMES COOK

Born on October 27, 1728, the English explorer, navigator, and cartographer Captain James Cook is famous for his voyages in and accurate mapping of the Pacific Ocean, and for the application of scientific methods to exploration. After gaining experience with a local shipowner and undertaking several voyages to the Baltic Sea, Cook enlisted in the Royal Navy at the onset of the Anglo-French war in 1755. He was promoted to master's mate after only one month, and by the war's end in 1763 was in command of a flagship on the St. Lawrence River.

Cook's career is marked by three significant voyages. The first voyage was initiated when the Royal Society asked the British government to send a ship to the Pacific to study the transit of Venus across the sun, and to explore new lands in that area. Cook was placed in command of the vessel *Endeavour*, which set sail on August 26, 1768, with a crew that included an astronomer, two botanists, a landscape artist, and a painter of fauna.

After witnessing the transit of Venus, Cook arrived at New Zealand and made an accurate chart of the waters of the two islands, which took six months. He then sailed along the east coast of Australia. After landing at Botany Bay, near present-day Sydney, he named the region New South Wales and claimed it in the name of the king. He eventually reached England on June 12, 1771. For circumnavigating the globe, charting new waters, and discovering new land, Cook was promoted from lieutenant to commander.

Cook's second voyage began on July 13, 1772. Sailing in the *Resolution* and accompanied by the *Adventure*, he explored the New Hebrides, charted Easter Island and the Marquesas, visited Tahiti and Tonga, and discovered New Caledonia and the islands of Palmerston, Norfolk, and Niue. Cook also proved that if properly fed, a crew could make a long voyage without ill effects. From a crew of 118, he lost only one man to disease. For this feat, the Royal Society presented him with the Copley Gold Medal and elected him as a fellow.

After reaching the rank of captain in August 1775, Cook embarked upon a third and final voyage on July 12, 1776, in search of a passage around North America to the Atlantic Ocean. Sailing in the *Resolution* and accompanied by the *Discovery*, Cook was unable to find a northern passage. However, this voyage did feature the discovery of the Hawaiian Islands.

Cook's life came to a tragic and sudden end when, after returning to Hawaii for much-needed repairs, fresh supplies, and sunshine, he was clubbed and stabbed to death in a skirmish with Hawaiian natives on February 14, 1779. In 2002 *History Today* reported the possibility that Captain Cook's relatives might undergo DNA testing to determine if an arrow contained in the Australian Museum—given by Hawaii's King Kamehameha II to one of King George IV's doctors—was made from his thighbone.

Japan annexed the Ryukyu Islands, and they became the Okinawa Prefecture. After the first Sino-Japanese War (1894–1895), Japan acquired the island of Taiwan, and after World War I (1914–1918), Japan received a League of Nations mandate over the Carolines, Marianas, Marshalls, and Palau Islands.

The United States came relatively late to the Pacific, but made its mark in the early nineteenth century by dominating the whaling industry. In 1867 the United States purchased Alaska for $7,200,000. While this was jokingly called "Seward's Folly" at the time, because Secretary of State William H. Seward (1801–1872) had brokered the deal with Russia, the discovery of gold, and later petroleum, repaid this investment many times over. Thirty years later, as a result of the 1898 Spanish-American War, the United States paid Spain $20 million for the Philippines, acquired Guam as a territory, and

annexed the Hawaiian Islands, which became the fiftieth state in 1959. After World War II (1939–1945), the United States retained bases in the Philippines through 1992, on Guam, and especially on Okinawa, which still hosts many of the U.S. forces in Japan.

Most colonies in East Asia were given their independence after World War II, including the Philippines in 1946, India in 1947, Indonesia in 1949, Malaysia in 1957, and Papua New Guinea in 1975. By 1980, almost all of the Pacific Islands had achieved their political independence, with Palau becoming independent in 1994. Trade, however, remains vitally important to the world economy, and beginning in the 1990s the United States for the first time traded more with Asian nations than with Europe.

SEE ALSO *Indigenous Responses, the Pacific; Occupations, the Pacific.*

BIBLIOGRAPHY

Barratt, Glynn. *Russia in Pacific waters, 1715–1825: A Survey of the Origins of Russia's Naval Presence in the North and South Pacific.* Vancouver: University of British Columbia Press, 1981.

Dunmore, John. *Who's Who in Pacific Navigation.* Honolulu: University of Hawaii Press, 1991.

Gibson, Arrell Morgan, and John S. Whitehead. *Yankees in Paradise: The Pacific Basin Frontier.* Albuquerque: University of New Mexico Press, 1993.

McDougall, Walter A. *Let the Sea Make a Noise . . . : A History of the North Pacific from Magellan to MacArthur.* New York: Basic Books, 1993.

Bruce A. Elleman

EXPORT COMMODITIES

Debates about western European exceptionalism continue, with no agreement in sight. Why did this relatively underdeveloped area expand around the world, while China, for example, a sophisticated empire, spread abroad mainly by the informal migrations of Chinese people, and then only to the eastern Pacific Ocean, and mostly in modern times?

Economic needs clearly played a part in driving European expansion. One series of discussions points to the intensity of European exchanges, including warfare, migration, and trade, coupled with a relative lack of important raw materials (e.g., precious metals, dyes, and such "miracle" cereals as maize and paddy rice) and items of elite consumption, such as silk textiles. (The industrial uses of coal and petroleum, later plentiful in Europe, had not yet developed.)

Contacts between the medieval Italian city-states and China showed the potential for profit in trade with Asia, particularly through the export to Europe of high-value spices, such as pepper and cinnamon. These contacts were cut off in the later fourteenth century by the black death (an epidemic of bubonic plague that killed nearly a quarter of Europe's population), the breakup of the Tatar Empire, and the incursions of the Ottoman Turks. But with a demographic recovery from the plague-ridden fourteenth century and a combination of Mediterranean and Atlantic maritime and military technologies in the fifteenth century, Europeans resumed their search for valuable commercial commodities.

Portuguese sailors who traveled down the West African coast demonstrated the possibilities for obtaining sub-Saharan gold and ivory. Portuguese fishermen went even further into the ocean in search of fishing grounds to supply the salt fish trade. The kings of Portugal and Castile both sought to take control of the Atlantic islands (Madeira, the Azores, and the Canaries), and their subjects grew increasingly interested in opening maritime routes to the sources of valuable commodities in Africa and Asia.

Cultural influences and geographical location also played a part in making Portugal and Spain into the pioneers of fifteenth- and sixteenth-century European exploration and conquest. Some historians emphasize the militarism and crusading religious impulses brought on by centuries of warfare against Islam. Others have pointed out that the coastline from Lisbon to Cadiz in southern Spain is western Europe's most favored corner in an age of sailing ships, with northeasterly winds for part of the year permitting much easier and faster voyages to the south and southwest.

Moreover, Portugal and Spain controlled the clusters of "steppingstone" islands—the Cape Verdes, the Canaries, the Azores, and Madeira—which, two or three weeks out to sea, provided places to rest the crews, land the sick, and resupply with food and water. Thus Lisbon and the small Spanish ports west of Cadiz were especially favored for explorations of the West African coast and for the southern crossing to the Caribbean.

CONDITIONS INFLUENCING THE DEVELOPMENT OF LONG-DISTANCE TRADE

Europeans met very different local conditions after arriving in sub-Saharan Africa, Asia, the two Americas, and Oceania, and these influenced their ability to exploit the resources that they encountered in these lands. The influences that affected their ability to exercise power and develop long-distance trade can be roughly grouped into three categories: (1) demography and distance; (2) disease barriers; and (3) the impact of disease on native peoples.

Demography and Distance. The Portuguese, after voyages of four to six months in small ships, had the firepower and warlike temperament to bombard and destroy Indian coastal cities. But they could not dream of conquering the Indian landmass, much less that of China, because both were occupied by dense populations and strong state structures, and both shared a similar stock of diseases with the Europeans.

The Portuguese were, then, limited to establishing trading enclaves such as Goa in India and Macao in southern China, and to using warships and strategic forts to tax merchants' ships, especially when they were passing though narrow straits such as Hormuz, Palk, and Malacca. Small cargo holds, plus limits imposed by time, distance, and the cost of freight, restricted exports to Portugal to compact items of high value, such as exotic spices, precious stones, and silks. Only much later could such Europeans as the Dutch and the English occupy larger areas and export mundane commodities like jute, cotton, and tea.

Disease Barriers. Unlike the Americas, sub-Saharan Africa was fertile ground for diseases such as yellow fever, malaria, and sleeping sickness *(trypanosomiasis).* The European newcomers to Africa, lacking immunities to or treatments for such illnesses, suffered disastrous mortality when they attempted to penetrate inland. As a result, they were usually limited to offshore islands, such as Fernando Póo (now Bioko in Equatorial Guinea) and São Tomé, and breezy, cooler enclaves such as Elmina (in Ghana) and Mozambique. Even the southern tip of Africa, with its more temperate climate, saw little European expansion from the coast until the eighteenth century.

In these circumstances, Europe's largest exports were slaves, usually purchased from intermediaries. Most of them were then sold in the Americas as plantation labor. European colonization of tropical Africa had to wait for the medical revolution of the nineteenth century.

The Impact of Disease on Native Peoples. In the Americas, Hawaii, Australia, and other isolated regions, Old World diseases have been described as the "shock troops" of the conquest. No doubt such factors as weapon superiority including gunpowder, destructive and close-cropping animals such as pigs and sheep, and internecine warfare among native polities, all played major roles in the subjugation of these areas. But disease, by reducing indigenous populations so drastically, helped the invaders not only with the conquests, but also with the establishment and maintenance of social control in the new colonies.

In fact, early colonial exports and imports of this third regional category were to a large degree determined by disease and distance. Distance, time, and freight rates inhibited the development of exports from the Americas and Australia, as was the case in Asia. To give one example, the development of sugar as an export was delayed until the reduced native populations could be replaced, in part, by African slaves. Even when this happened, sugar could pay its way to European markets only from the Caribbean and northeast Brazil, which were relatively close to Europe. Distant Mexico, even more distant Peru, and the far-off Philippines could show a profit only when shipping such valuable products as bullion, precious stones, spices, and silks. These were, in fact, the major exports of the first two centuries of colonial rule.

Diseases brought by Europeans and Africans, plus colonial wars, not only aided conquest and the establishment of new regimes, but also cleared space for immigration, especially in such areas as Hawaii, New Zealand, and parts of Australia and America that because of latitude or altitude had relatively temperate climates. Thus the largest European export to these regions was people—soldiers, administrators, farmers, miners, herders, and others. Conquered territories, such as New England, present-day Argentina, Australia, and New Zealand, brutally cleared in whole or in part of their native inhabitants, soon became populated with transplanted Europeans.

COLONIAL GOVERNMENTS AND EXPORTS

The mechanisms of colonial control set up by Europeans also depended to a considerable extent on the above factors. Where the Portuguese were able to establish commercial enclaves, their control was limited to monopolizing sea lanes, manipulating local politics and trade, forming strategic alliances with native rulers, staging occasional shows of force, and incorporating marginal peoples, such as untouchables and low-caste fisherfolk. Later colonial rulers, such as the British in Hong Kong and the Dutch in Ceylon (Sri Lanka), used essentially the same tactics.

In the densely-populated regions of India, where European newcomers never numbered more than a tiny minority, the British used more elaborate methods. Local troops under British officers defeated rebellions and followed them with spectacular ceremonial punishments. Native elites were co-opted and often educated in England, new broker classes were assigned to serve as bureaucrats and minor traders, and trade and trade items were stimulated or discouraged to suit imperial needs.

In spite of enormous population losses and considerable Spanish immigration, the densely inhabited parts of America remained largely indigenous during the Spanish colonial period. There, imperial rule and the manipulation of trade, trade items, and exports had to adopt different methods.

Both the so-called Aztec and Inca empires had been based on various forms of tribute exactions from the peasantry in goods and labor. The Spanish regime, accustomed to such tributary systems, continued them with little change at first. Products such as maize, beans, and cotton cloth were collected in large quantities, then sold within the cities or redistributed via official auctions. Luxury goods such as feathers, seashells, and obsidian, culturally useless to Spaniards, were soon eliminated from the tribute system, and silver coinage and European crops and animals replaced them.

Early efforts to find American commodities suitable for export to Europe led to the development of plantation crops such as sugar and tobacco. However, it was the discovery of rich sources of precious metals that underpinned the rapid development of economic relations between Europe and the Americas. Spaniards found silver in great quantities in two major areas: in an arc of mines, including Guanajuato, Zacatecas, and San Luis Potosí, northwest of Mexico City; and in Upper Peru (now Bolivia), where the famous "rich hill" of Potosí may well be the richest silver mine ever discovered.

Here again, especially in Peru, the Spanish found a system of labor drafts, the Incan *mita*, which they expanded and used mainly as a way of supplying labor to Potosí. Thus, tribute payments and silver mines supplied Spanish America's great export—refined silver bars and silver coinage, sometimes debased. Large annual fleets, loading in Veracruz in Mexico and ports on the Isthmus of Panama, trundled slowly across the Atlantic to Seville and later Cadiz.

Conspicuous consumption of precious metals had long been a feature of European noble courts and of ecclesiastical ornamentation, but until the discovery of America, commercial Europe had been short of a high value, malleable, symbolic coinage. The influx of American silver caused what was apparently the first European general inflation, as well as a rapid monetization of even mundane transactions and a consequent speeding up of exchanges and credit understandings based on silver. Much of the imported silver soon left Spain for more advanced European economies, such as France and later the Netherlands. American silver also fuelled the development of European trade with the East.

As trade with the Pacific expanded, American silver was transferred across the Pacific via galleons traveling from Acapulco in Mexico to Manila in the Philippines; or directly to China by the age-old silk route across central Asia; or by the much longer route around the Cape of Good Hope and across the Indian Ocean. Europe's problem, until the British organized the export of opium from India to China, was that China had little need of European goods, but Europeans craved Chinese and other Asian products, especially silks, teas, and spices. The solution for Europe was to pay in silver, much of which was turned into coinage or was hoarded.

Gold exports to Europe had an older history than the Iberian conquest of America. The trans-Saharan trade from coastal West Africa, via the great warehouse cities of Gao and Timbuktu in present-day Mali, was precolonial. Forest gold was exchanged for salt and Mediterranean goods as early as the establishment of the Mali Empire of the late thirteenth and fourteenth centuries, and the trade continued into the colonial era.

After this trade declined, the hiatus in European gold imports was filled by gold panned from streams after the Spanish conquests of the major Caribbean islands. Hispaniola (the island now occupied by Haiti and the

MANILA GALLEON TRADE

After the discovery of a sea route from the Philippines to Mexico in 1565, the Spanish began employing a highly profitable, though dangerous, trade route. Ships especially outfitted to carry large cargoes set sail from Acapulco, carrying silver mined in the Americas, and headed to Manila, where the metal was exchanged for Chinese silks, porcelains, and ivory, as well as for fragrant goods from the Spice Islands and jewels from Burma, Ceylon, and Siam. The galleons then returned the much sought-after Asian goods back to Acapulco, where they were carried overland to Mexico City and then sent across the Atlantic to Spain. The first Manila galleon set sail for Acapulco in 1573.

Whereas the wind-aided passage from Acapulco to Manila took only eight to ten weeks, the return trip from Manila to Acapulco took between four and six months. Navigating the treacherous Philippine archipelago with an overloaded galleon often took over a month, and many ships that did not complete the journey before typhoon season began perished in the rough weather. Because the profits from the Manila galleon trade averaged 30 to 50 percent, adequate provisions were often rejected in favor of loading more goods on the galleons. Consequently, many ships saw 30 to 40 percent of their crews perish, with losses of 75 percent not uncommon in some years. Despite these risks, however, the Manila galleon trade continued for nearly 250 years, remaining an important source of income for Spanish merchants.

Dominican Republic) was the main source. The decline in the native population, along with shrinking yields from gold-bearing streams, put an end to this brief boom and was one reason why Spaniards left the islands to seek other sources of wealth on the American mainland. The empty Antillean landscapes became filled with semiferal cattle, and the main export became hides.

Gold from the Chocó in what is today Colombia was mined mostly by black slaves. The next boom arose in Minas Gerais in Portuguese colonial Brazil. Eighteenth-century exports were so large that some have described Portugal of that era as a gold empire in contrast to Spain's silver empire. Gold exports also arrived from convict-era Australia, from South Africa, and from elsewhere. The famous North American gold strikes in

California and the Yukon were postcolonial for the most part.

American depopulation gave rise to a transatlantic trade of its own. As populations collapsed, imported cattle and horses grazed on emptied fields and eventually swarmed everywhere. Meat consumption, much of it as jerky (dried meat strips), increased enormously in parts of the Americas. Still, the major resultant American product was hides, which were shipped to Europe in huge quantities, especially from the Caribbean islands in the sixteenth and early seventeenth centuries, when the native population had vanished and many Spaniards had moved on to mainland conquests. Lacking inexpensive glass, Europeans used hides for many kinds of containers, door and window coverings, shoes, and clothing, and, in an era of equine transportation, for saddles, tack, and wheel rims.

FOOD EXPORTS AND DIETARY CHANGES

Europe's expansion around the world changed food preferences and diet in many places. Although the American colonies did not export large quantities of foodstuffs, the Americas provided dynamic crops unknown elsewhere. Many parts of Africa subsist today on a diet of American maize, probably first brought to the west coast by Portuguese ships. American cacao in the form of chocolate occupies a special niche worldwide, although most of it today is grown in the Ivory Coast and nearby countries. Chinese, Indian, or Sri Lankan tea is the favorite beverage of many, especially in Great Britain, Ireland, Australia, and New Zealand. Coffee, imported from areas that, for the most part, were not colonized, is even more popular worldwide. The potato originated in an Andean tuber; tomatoes are another New World cultigen; and even Indian curry is based on chilies, originally found in America.

THE INDUSTRIAL AND SCIENTIFIC REVOLUTIONS

Two eighteenth-century European intensifications dramatically changed the nature and volume of colonial exports. The first was the growth of the old West African slave trade. Millions of people were brutally exported to Brazil, the Caribbean, and North America. Plantation slavery in the British, French, Dutch, Portuguese, and Spanish colonies gave rise to a sugar boom of such intensity and relative efficiency that sugar became the basis of many European fortunes and a staple of the diet there. In fact, some scholars would add sugar, a cheap and plentiful source of calories via candies, soft drinks, jams, and pastries, to coal and iron ore as essential ingredients of the Industrial Revolution in northwestern Europe.

The other relevant phenomenon of the eighteenth century was the Industrial Revolution itself. The rise of the factory and of mass production was accompanied by significant technological advances in transportation, both by land and sea, and by the beginnings of modern sanitary and epidemiological medicine. There were three main consequences for colonial exports. The first was the increased European demand for cheap, abundant raw materials such as cotton, hemp, coal, unrefined ores, and plantation foodstuffs.

In addition, the revolution in sea transportation meant that the constricting determinants of time, distance, cargo space, and freight rates were all diminished. This meant, in turn, that common mass-produced goods could now be transported for long distances and still show a profit. Australian coal could begin to supply naval stations all the way from Japan to California to central Chile. Indian and Egyptian cotton filled the needs of the mills of Lancashire in England (a role later taken by the U.S. South). The common people of Europe began to consume enormous quantities of Asian teas, Middle Eastern and Latin American coffees, and African chocolate.

The Industrial Revolution, along with lower transportation costs and an increased speed of delivery, also led to a significant rise in mass-produced, inexpensive, European exports to the colonies, where imperial preferences and monopolistic privileges were additional disadvantages for colonial producers. Examples abound. Inexpensive British textiles ruined many, although not all, local mills all the way from Mexico to Chile and throughout the Indian Subcontinent. The metallurgical revolution, with its inexpensive pots and pans, furniture, and tools undercut artisanal production throughout the colonial world. Aniline dyes from Germany ruined local and international trades in such natural colorants as indigo and cochineal. With the new availability of rapid transportation, millions of the poor left Europe for the colonies, where they expelled native peoples from their lands and purchased some of their needs from Europe.

The third consequence of the Industrial Revolution was the opening up of previously exempted areas to European colonization and exploitation. With the medical revolution, sub-Saharan Africa became less deadly for Europeans, and the race for Africa was on, bringing intense competition among the leading western European powers to establish colonies there. African colonial production of raw materials and foodstuffs, from diamonds and gold to palm oil, rubber, ivory, tin, and copper, flowed north. The Belgian Congo was perhaps the leading example of a brutal, export-oriented, colonial economy, although much of its population, as elsewhere, continued as subsistence farmers.

Other areas also became exploitable. French Indochina, Burma (Myanmar), Malaya, and even parts of Borneo and Sulawesi in present-day Indonesia witnessed the rise of plantations and mines, as well as exports of such goods as rice, copra, timber, tin, and rubber. Latecomers as colonialists were Russia, which gradually seized Siberia and much of central Asia, and the United States, which conquered Puerto Rico, Cuba, and the Philippines in 1898. These colonies quickly became tied to the U.S. market.

Many colonial exports and imports were far from tangible. Europeans took with them their cultures, ideologies, and institutions. Some of these imports, such as racism, were noxious. Others, such as the fruits of the Enlightenment, no doubt helped to weaken caste divisions in some regions, and bore within them the paradoxical seeds of the future anticolonial struggles of the subject peoples.

Western Europe also imported, acculturated, and educated many native elites, in some cases setting them further apart from their own people. Again, some of the results were contrary to the intentions of the colonial powers: Ho Chi Min (1890–1969) of Vietnam, partly educated in Paris and Moscow; Kwame Nkrumah (1909–1972) of Ghana, who studied in both the United States and Great Britain; and José Rizal (1861–1896) of the Philippines, educated in Spain, are three of the many examples of Western-educated leaders of colonial independence struggles.

The European search for resources that could be converted into commodities for long-distance trade had several important consequences. First, it helped stimulate the drive to establish overseas colonies in the Americas, Asia, and Africa. Second, colonial exports, such as maize, potatoes, cacao, and quinine, revolutionized diets and medicines around the world.

Some colonial products, such as tobacco, were noxious. Some, such as opium, were a blessing for humanity in the form of pain-relieving opiates such as morphine, but also a curse in their use as addictive drugs. Even the potato, which so vastly increased population and production on marginal lands, had disadvantages, since it also caused the development of fragile monocultures. The Great Irish Famine of the mid-1800s arose from political decisions made by the colonial power, but overdependence on the potato, struck by blight, contributed greatly to the disaster.

Sugar is a case apart. Introduced to the colonies from Europe, it was then reexported to the industrializing world in quantity, where it revolutionized diets, not always for the better. Sugar also provided the inexpensive calories needed to feed workers brought from the countryside to the factory.

Bullion's effects have been studied more than most exports. It caused inflation, but also provided a widely recognized monetary exchange, thus speeding up exchanges and the extension of credit. The hunger for precious metals, of course, led to some of the world's most dreadful injustices. Luxury products such as silk, spices, some dyestuffs, and exotic perfumes were consumed largely by elites and may have reinforced class divisions by making them more apparent.

The slave trade is yet another special case. Today, no one can reasonably defend the inhumane exploitation of so many millions, but it must be recognized that, against their will, African slaves built the economies of the Caribbean, Brazil, and North America. Slaves also contributed to the emergence of new and distinctive cultures. The role of convicts and indentured servants exported to the colonies, though less notable, also deserves mention.

In the long term, colonial exports fueled the Industrial Revolution, homogenized cultures worldwide, and helped to reduce the stock of languages and other cultural differences. In short, export commodities helped to shape many of the basic characteristics of our world today.

SEE ALSO *Cacao; Cotton; Sugar Cultivation and Trade.*

BIBLIOGRAPHY

Boahen, A. Adu. "The Coming of the Europeans (c. 1440–1700)." In *The Horizon History of Africa*, edited by Alvin M. Josephy Jr., 305–327. New Haven, CT: American Heritage, 1971.

Curtin, Philip D. "Epidemiology and the Slave Trade." *Political Science Quarterly* 83 (2) (1968): 190–216.

Curtin, Philip A. *The Atlantic Slave Trade: A Census.* Madison: University of Wisconsin Press, 1969.

Curtin, Philip D. *Cross-Cultural Trade in World History.* Cambridge, U.K.: Cambridge University Press, 1984.

Crosby, Alfred W. *The Columbian Exchange: Biological and Cultural Consequences of 1492.* Westport, CT: Greenwood, 1972.

Crosby, Alfred W. *Ecological Imperialism: The Biological Expansion of Europe, 900–1900*, 2nd ed. Cambridge, U.K.: Cambridge University Press, 2004.

MacLeod, Murdo J. "The Spanish Invasion and Its Impact on the Economic Structures of Pre-Columbian America." In *Societies Under Constraint: Economic and Social Pressures in Latin America*, edited by Robert A. McNeil. Austin, TX: SALALM, 1997.

McCormick, Michael. *Origins of the European Economy: Communications and Commerce, A.D. 300–900.* Cambridge, U.K.: Cambridge University Press, 2001.

McCusker, John J., and Kenneth Morgan, eds. *The Early Modern Atlantic Economy.* Cambridge, U.K.: Cambridge University Press, 2000.

Mintz, Sydney W. *Sweetness and Power: The Place of Sugar in Modern History.* New York: Viking Penguin, 1985.

Parry, John H. *The Establishment of the European Hegemony, 1415–1715: Trade and Exploration in the Age of the Renaissance*, 3rd ed. New York: Harper, 1966.

Rotberg, Robert I., and Theodore K. Rabb, eds. *Hunger and History: The Impact of Changing Food Production and Consumption Patterns on Society.* Cambridge, U.K.: Cambridge University Press, 1985.

Richards, W. "The Import of Firearms into West Africa in the 18th Century." *Journal of African History* 21 (1980): 43–59.

Stein, Stanley J., and Barbara H. Stein. *Silver, Trade, and War: Spain and America in the Making of Early Modern Europe.* Baltimore, MD: Johns Hopkins University Press, 2002.

Wallerstein, Immanuel. *The Modern World-System: Capitalist Agriculture and the Origins of the European World-Economy in the Sixteenth Century.* New York: Academic Press, 1974.

Wolf, Eric R. *Europe and the People Without History.* Berkeley: University of California Press, 1982.

Murdo J. MacLeod

EXTRATERRITORIALITY

Extraterritoriality is usually defined as the practice of exempting certain foreign nationals from the jurisdiction of their country of residence. The most common application of extraterritoriality is the custom of exempting foreign heads of state and diplomats from local jurisdiction. Another form of extraterritoriality is the limited immunity from local jurisdiction that U.S. servicemen on overseas duty enjoy under the Status of Force Agreements. In the nineteenth and early twentieth centuries, extraterritoriality was often used synonymously with consular jurisdiction, which was the practice of consuls exercising jurisdiction over their nationals in certain non-Western countries.

The origins of consular jurisdiction are usually traced back to medieval practices of merchant self-government in the Mediterranean region as well as to Muslim law. Proponents of the practice usually justified it by referring to the alleged incompatibility between Western and non-Western legal systems. The sultan of the Ottoman Empire gave the first formal recognition of consular jurisdiction in 1535, when he granted extraterritorial privileges to French merchants. These privileges were later extended to most European nationals in the seventeenth and eighteenth centuries in treaties collectively referred to as the Capitulations. These privileges applied mostly to civil suits and to criminal cases involving foreigners only. In East Asia, the earliest origins of consular jurisdiction are more obscure, but it is generally agreed that Chinese authorities allowed foreign merchants in the coastal ports to resolve disputes among themselves. China also has a long tradition of subjecting different ethnic and professional groups to different jurisdictions, dating back as far as to the Mongol Yuan dynasty (1279–1368).

In the eighteenth and nineteenth centuries, functionaries of the European trade companies, such as the English East India Company (EIC), often exercised limited jurisdiction over European merchants residing in Guangzhou, the only Chinese port open for overseas trade. When the monopoly of the EIC on Sino-British trade was rescinded in 1834, the British Parliament also moved to set up a consular court in China. The aim was to withdraw Britons from Chinese jurisdiction entirely, since Chinese penal practices were widely resented by British merchants. Chinese authorities did, however, resist this move and China did not formally concede extraterritorial privileges to Britons until after the Sino-British Opium War (1839–1842). These privileges were later extended to other Western countries in a number of treaties, which subsequently became known as the unequal treaties.

Western diplomats usually claimed that in contrast to the Ottoman Capitulations, the Chinese treaties granted foreigners near complete immunity from Chinese jurisdiction and they endeavored to introduce this form of extraterritoriality to other East Asian countries that were not under direct colonial control. By the 1880s, most European and North American countries had concluded extraterritorial agreements with China, Japan, Korea, Siam (Thailand), and the Ottoman Empire and its dependencies. The Treaty Powers were also able to expand the scope of extraterritoriality to include corporate entities, natives in foreign employ, and Christian converts. Consequently, extraterritoriality was increasingly resented as an instrument of indirect colonial control. In the late nineteenth century, many countries reformed their legal systems to convince the Treaty Powers to relinquish extraterritoriality.

Japan was the only country that succeeded in abolishing consular jurisdiction through legal reform prior to 1900. However, the fall of the Qing (1911) and Ottoman Empires (1923) as well as the weakening of Western imperialism following the First World War (1914–1918) increased the momentum to abolish consular jurisdiction. By the 1920s, consular jurisdiction had been eliminated in most countries except in China and Egypt, where it was not abolished until the late 1940s. Extraterritoriality has left a controversial legacy in the countries in which it was practiced and it forms an integral part in collective memories of injustices inflicted by Western imperialism.

SEE ALSO *Law, Colonial systems of.*

BIBLIOGRAPHY

Cassel, Pär. "Excavating Extraterritoriality: The 'Judicial Sub-Prefect' as a Prototype for the Mixed Court in Shanghai." *Late Imperial China* 24, (2) (2003): 156–82.

Cochran, Charles L., and Hungdah Chiu, eds. *U.S. Status of Force Agreements with Asian Countries: Selected Studies, Occasional Papers/Reprints Series in Contemporary Asian Studies* 28 (7) (1979).

Edwards, R. Randle. "Ch'ing Legal Jurisdiction over Foreigners." In *Essays on China's Legal Tradition*, edited by Jerome Alan Cohen, R. Randle Edwards, and Fu-mei Chang Chen. Princeton, NJ: Princeton University Press, 1980.

Koo, V. K. Wellington. *The Status of Aliens in China*. New York: Columbia University, 1912.

Piggott, Francis Taylor. *Exterritoriality: The Law Relating to Consular Jurisdiction and to Residence in Oriental Countries.* Hong Kong: Kelly & Walsh Ltd., 1907.

Scully, Eileen P. *Bargaining with the State from Afar: American Citizenship in Treaty Port China, 1844–1942*. New York: Columbia University Press, 2001.

Sousa, Nasim. *The Capitulatory Régime of Turkey, Its History, Origin, and Nature*. Baltimore, MD: The Johns Hopkins Press, 1933.

Pär Cassel